The Britannica

LIBRARY OF GREAT AMERICAN WRITING

VOLUME II

The Britannica
LIBRARY OF GREAT AMERICAN WRITING

VOLUME II

EDITED, WITH HISTORICAL NOTES
AND A RUNNING COMMENTARY, BY

Louis Untermeyer

Published by
BRITANNICA PRESS, *Chicago*
and distributed in association with
J. B. LIPPINCOTT COMPANY, *Philadelphia and New York*

LIBRARY OF CONGRESS CATALOG NUMBER: 60-14545
PRINTED IN THE UNITED STATES OF AMERICA

Acknowledgements for permission to reprint copyright material in this volume and pertinent copyright information about such material are listed in Volume I, beginning on the reverse of the title page.

TABLE OF CONTENTS

VOLUME II

PROMISE AND FULFILLMENT

VOICES OF OUR TIME

SAMUEL LANGHORNE CLEMENS

(*Mark Twain*)

[1835–1910]

When he died, Samuel L. Clemens had made his pseudonym, Mark Twain, not only a trademark but also a hallmark of a new kind of American writing. The classic tradition inherited from England and preserved in New England was challenged by new patterns of thought. Out of the Midwest, a raw civilization close to the wilderness, came a way of expression which was to leave a rich legacy, a brash and lusty frontier tradition. The genteel manner, which had been assailed by the high-pitched voice of New York's Walt Whitman, was even more rudely shaken and almost overwhelmed by a still stranger phenomenon, a rude humorist with the broad, vernacular-seasoned drawl of Missouri.

Samuel Langhorne Clemens, fifth child of a Virginia father and a Kentucky mother, was born November 30, 1835, in the Missouri village of Florida, a cluster of log cabins and makeshift houses with a total population of one hundred. The Clemenses did not stay there long. The impractical father, a natural prey for wildcat schemers, always hoping there would be something better somewhere else, moved the family to Hannibal, Missouri, in 1839. Here Samuel lived until he was eighteen. Though he grew up among cruelty and killings, he forgot the violence and, transforming it later in life, turned Hannibal into a happy memory, the idyllic background for Tom Sawyer.

His father died when he was twelve and, almost unschooled, the boy was taught how to set type by his oldest brother, the blundering, idealistic Orion. By the time he was twenty he had worked his way East as a journeyman printer and back again to the Middle West, where he rejoined Orion, who was publishing a newspaper in Keokuk, Iowa.

Journalism both delighted and disillusioned him. "I saw the inside of many things," he recalled many years later. "I was a reporter in a legislature. . . and thus learned to know personally three sample-bodies of the smallest minds and the selfishest souls and the coward-liest hearts that God makes." He thought of running away to South America, but he settled for what was an even more exciting prospect for a young fellow: he apprenticed himself to a Mississippi pilot.

In a series of articles which grew into Life on the Mississippi—a book which Bernard de Voto called "a study in pure ecstasy"—the reminiscent adventurer wrote: "When I was a boy there was but one permanent ambition among my comrades in our village on the west bank of the Mississippi River. That was to be a steamboatman. We had transient ambitions of other sorts, but they were only transient. When a circus came and went, it left us all burning to become clowns. The first Negro minstrel show that ever came to our section left us all suffering to try that kind of life. Now and then we hoped that, if we lived and were good, God would permit us to be pirates. Those ambitions faded out, each in turn. But the ambition to be a steamboatman always remained."

Sam Clemens was twenty-two when he began piloting. He might well have been a contented steamboatman the rest of his life, his boyhood dream fulfilled; but, after four years of pure enjoyment, the Civil War intervened, and the displaced pilot became a soldier. In "The Private History of a Campaign that Failed" he related how he happened to find himself on the Confederate side. His pilot mate was, like him, a strong Union man, but when Clemens told him that his father had once had a slave working for him, his friend was shocked. "I said in palliation of this dark fact that I had heard my father say that slavery was a great wrong, and that he would free the solitary Negro he then owned if he could think it right to give away the property of the family when he was so straitened in means. My mate retorted that a mere impulse was nothing—anybody could pretend to a good impulse. A month later the secession atmosphere had considerably thickened on the Lower Mississippi, and I became a rebel. So did he. . . He did his full share of the rebel shouting, but was bitterly opposed to letting me do mine. He said that I came of bad stock—of a father who had been willing to see slaves go free." As the article proceeded, the tone changed to horror when the writer encountered death on the battlefield. "It seemed an epitome of war, that all war must be just the killing of strangers against whom you feel no personal animosity, strangers whom, in other circumstances, you would help if you found them in trouble, and who would help you if you needed it."

Clemens was twenty-six when he was mustered out of the army and became assistant to his brother Orion, who had somehow become

Secretary of the Territory of Nevada. (Years later he tried to get William Dean Howells interested in writing a play about Orion, saying: "Do not fail to note the hopeful, glad-hearted, schoolboy cheeriness which bubbles out of every pore of this man who has been always a failure!") When he found out that there was no salary connected with his position, Clemens decided to become a prospector. Unsuccessful with a timber claim, he was no more successful with mining, and returned to his old trade of newspaperman.

It was while writing feature articles for the Territorial Enterprise in Virginia City, Nevada, that he first signed himself Mark Twain, a nom de plume which he took from the river pilot's call meaning "two fathoms deep." He remained with the Enterprise three years, struck up a friendship with Artemus Ward, and, at twenty-nine, went to San Francisco, where he worked on the Call and sent sketches to Eastern papers. One of his regional stories, "The Celebrated Jumping Frog of Calaveras County," written in the manner of the local humorists, was published in the New York Saturday Press, and so often reprinted that his pen name became an important commercial property. He was sent to Hawaii (then called the Sandwich Islands) to write travel reports; he toured Europe; he visited the Mediterranean countries, including the Holy Land; and he put together his sometimes shrewd, sometimes absurd reactions in Innocents Abroad. Circulated by subscription and agents at high prices, the book had an enormous sale. Its popularity was due to the author's odd combination of information, assumed ignorance, and frontier humor, a combination which was to be a characteristic of his work both as author and lecturer.

On the European trip, a fellow passenger had shown Clemens a picture of his sister, Olivia Langdon. Clemens fell in love with the miniature portrait. Upon his return he invaded the well-to-do Langdon home in Elmira, New York, and after an impetuous courtship which, nevertheless, lasted a year and a half, carried off the delicate daughter of the family. He never ceased to adore her. He was affected by her every gesture; he respected all her opinions—some say he was much too influenced by them. He marveled at her gentle firmness. "She merited all the worship he could give her," wrote Howells, "all the devotion, all the implicit obedience." She was twenty-five and he was ten years older when they met; forty years later he said, "From that day to this she has never been out of my mind."

It is doubtful that Olivia "reformed" or "censored" her husband, but it seems certain that she tried to "civilize" the man who had be-

come known as "the wild humorist from the Pacific slope." Before their marriage, Twain, prompted either by his mocking nature or his great love, teasingly asked her to "convert" him. His letters are full of such expressions as:

> Yes, Livy, I *do* like to have you give me synopses of Mr. Beecher's sermons—and you need not suppose that I read them over and lay them aside for good, for I do not. I read them over and over again and try to profit by them. . . I do not swear, I do not steal, I do not murder, I do not drink. My whole life is "not." I am "not" all over. . . I *can* be a Christian—I *shall* be a Christian—but when I feel as I feel today, it seems a far journey away.
>
> You know the child must crawl before it walks—and I must do right for love of you while I am in the infancy of Christianity; then I can do right for the love of the Saviour when I shall have gotten my growth. . . I ought to be ever so grateful to you, Livy, for your brave confidence in me, and for the consideration you show for me in simply *suggesting* reforms when you could be such an absolute little tyrant if you chose. I do not know of anything I could refuse to do if you wanted it done. I am reasonably afraid that you'll stop me from smoking some day; but if ever you do, you will do it with such a happy grace that I shall be swindled into the notion that I didn't *want* to smoke any more, anyhow!

Clemens had become Mark Twain to everyone by the time he moved to the East. He lived for a while in upper New York State, where he bought shares in the Buffalo Express *and, at thirty-seven, settled in Hartford, Connecticut. There he produced most of the work, sometimes sentimental, sometimes misanthropic, which was altogether his best. Whether it was buoyant or biting, whatever he wrote was honest in its own eccentric way, and native to the core.*

During the next forty years Twain produced a series of books, many of which became landmarks in American literature: Roughing It, *fascinating as autobiography and invaluable as a picture of the Far West at a particular moment of transition;* The Gilded Age, *written in collaboration with Charles Dudley Warner, a satirical novel chiefly notable for the figure of Colonel Mulberry Sellers, a windy and pathetically incurable optimist;* The Adventures of Tom Sawyer, *a half-realistic, half-romantic saga of the careless, fun-loving, and generally "normal" (as opposed to the insufferable "model") boy;* The Adventures of Huckleberry Finn, *the only sequel to surpass the original and which, according to Ernest Hemingway, was the turning point of* modern American literature—"there is nothing before; there has been nothing as good since;" Life on the Mississippi, which showed that Twain had mastered every turn and twist of the "Father of Waters;" A Connecticut Yankee at King Arthur's Court and Personal Recollections of Joan of Arc, two books which Twain considered his best, but which are among his least important—he was not at home in any country or in any other time but his own.

The last half of Twain's life was a series of triumphs followed by tragedies. One of the country's favorite citizens, he was on easy terms with the great. Everything about him was news, including the erroneous account of his demise, which led to the famous demurrer: "The report of my death has been greatly exaggerated." Crowds gathered about him in London as avidly as in New York. He profitably published not only his own volumes but also the Memoirs of U. S. Grant, the best selling book of the period. Ridiculing the "boom or bust" slogans of his day, Twain was nevertheless caught up in its money-making drive. He put all his capital, almost two hundred thousand dollars, in a typesetting machine which was to earn millions for him. When the "mechanical miracle" failed to work, he was bankrupt. He had to push himself to new projects, new books, and exhausting new lecture tours.

Financial misfortunes were accompanied by personal calamities. His oldest and most cherished daughter, Susie, died while he was lecturing in England—an only son had failed to survive infancy. He was in Vienna when he learned of the death of his brother Orion. His wife and his daughter, Jean, were crippled with hopeless invalidism. When he was sixty-nine his wife died, and Jean, a victim of epilepsy, died a few years later.

The final decade of his life marked how much the man and his writings had changed. His fiery red hair had grown into a mane of white, but the drooping moustache and the quick-darting eyes made him seem more like a wary hawk than a restless lion. The later books are not merely cynical but savage. What is Man is a diatribe on the self-seeking and self-love of humanity; The Man That Corrupted Hadleyburg suggests that not only Hadleyburg but any community can be corrupted because of an ever-lurking greed; The Mysterious Stranger, written in 1898 but withheld for eighteen years and published posthumously in 1916, is a pessimistic novelette in which Philip Traum, Satan's nephew, voices Twain's philosophy that life is nothing more than a grotesque and meaningless dream.

During his last years, Twain turned to the Autobiography which he *had begun some thirty years before. A sprawling account of his ventures, the happy days of his youth together with his dark philosophy as he faced the end, it contains passages as grim but revealing as:*

> It is my conviction that the human race is no proper target for harsh words and bitter criticisms, and that the only justifiable feeling toward it is compassion; it did not invent itself, and it had nothing to do with the planning of its weak and foolish character. . .
>
> I am saying these vain things in this frank way because I am a dead person speaking from the grave. Even I would be too modest to say them in life. I think that we never become really and genuinely our entire and honest selves until we are dead—and not then until we have been dead years and years. People ought to start dead, and then they would be honest so much earlier. . .

He even took his onetime irresponsible humor with strange seriousness. He said:

> Humor must not professedly teach, and it must not professedly preach, but it must do both if it would live forever. By forever, I mean thirty years. . . I have always preached. That is the reason that I have lasted thirty years. If the humor came of its own accord and uninvited, I have allowed it a place in my sermon, but I was not writing the sermon for the sake of the humor. I should have written the sermon just the same, whether any humor applied for admission or not.

He had built Stormfield, an imposing house in Redding, Connecticut, but he did not live long to enjoy it. He had persuaded himself that his life was somehow connected with Halley's comet, which had reappeared at his birth. When, seventy-five years later, it again appeared, he accepted the omen and, four months after Jean's burial, died of angina pectoris on April 21, 1910.

Twain's rambling Autobiography *has never been published in full. A large selection from it was published in 1924, edited by Albert Bigelow Paine, according to Paine's prim standards of propriety. Sixteen years later a more outspoken edition, including matter that Paine had omitted, was edited by Bernard DeVoto. In 1959 Charles Neider collated the best from both volumes; provided, for the first time, a chronological order; and added some forty thousand words which had not yet appeared in print. Although the picture of Twain was less confused than many had found it, it was still not clear how much (or how little) Twain had relished his role as popular entertainer, how beneficially (or adversely) he was influenced by his wife's strictures, and how deeply embedded (or how slowly acquired) was his bitterness.*

Certain things about Twain's philosophy are unquestionable. He was not only the prime jokester but also the traditional clown who laughs to hide his despair of the human condition. He hated every kind of pretension, whether it was the insipid, "sad, false delicacy" in literature or fraud and hypocrisy in public life. He never wearied exposing them; he delighted in showing up the contrast between what man preaches and what he practices, between what he murmurs on Sunday and what he actually does from Monday to Saturday. He forgot nothing, the bad as well as the beautiful. A perceptive cynic, a hilarious funmaker, he was the irrepressible boy who was, at the same time, the human sufferer, the reproachful and morally responsible man.

LEARNING THE RIVER

From *Life on the Mississippi*

WHAT WITH LYING on the rocks four days at Louisville, and some other delays, the poor old *Paul Jones* fooled away about two weeks in making the voyage from Cincinnati to New Orleans. This gave me a chance to get acquainted with one of the pilots, and he taught me how to steer the boat, and thus made the fascination of river life more potent than ever for me.

It also gave me a chance to get acquainted with a youth who had taken deck passage—more's the pity; for he easily borrowed six dollars of me on a promise to return to the boat and pay it back to me the day after we should arrive. But he probably died or forgot, for he never came. It was doubtless the former, since he had said his parents were wealthy, and he only traveled deck passage because it was cooler.

I soon discovered two things. One was that a vessel would not be likely to sail for the mouth of the Amazon under ten or twelve years; and the other was that the nine or ten dollars still left in my pocket would not suffice for so imposing an exploration as I had planned, even if I could afford to wait for a ship. Therefore it followed that I must contrive a new career. The *Paul Jones* was now bound for St. Louis. I planned a siege against my pilot, and at the end of three hard days he surrendered. He agreed to teach me the Mississippi River from New Orleans to St. Louis for five hundred dollars, payable out of the first wages I should receive after graduating. I entered upon the small enterprise of "learning" twelve or thirteen hundred miles of the great Mississippi River with the easy confidence of my time of life. If I had really known what I was about to require of my faculties, I should not have had the courage to begin. I supposed that all a pilot had to do was to keep his boat in the river, and I did not consider that that could be much of a trick, since it was so wide.

The boat backed out from New Orleans at four in the afternoon, and it was "our watch" until eight. Mr. Bixby, my chief, "straightened her up," plowed her along past the sterns of the other boats that lay at the levee, and then said, "Here, take her; shave those steamships as close as you'd peel an apple." I took the wheel, and my heart went down into my boots; for it seemed to me that we were about to scrape the side off every ship in the line, we were so close. I held my breath and began to claw the boat away from the danger; and I had my own opinion of the pilot who had known no better than to get us into such peril, but I was too wise to express it. In half a minute I had a wide margin of safety intervening between the *Paul Jones* and the ships; and within ten seconds more I was set aside in disgrace, and Mr. Bixby was going into danger again and flaying me alive with abuse of my cowardice. I was stung, but I was obliged to admire the easy confidence with which my chief loafed from side to side of his wheel, and trimmed the ships so closely that disaster seemed ceaselessly imminent. When he had cooled a little he told me that the easy water was close ashore and the current outside, and therefore we must hug the bank, upstream, to get the benefit of the former, and stay well out, downstream, to take advantage of the latter. In my own mind I resolved to be a downstream pilot and leave the upstreaming to people dead to prudence.

Now and then Mr. Bixby called my attention to certain things. Said he, "This is Six-Mile Point." I assented. It was pleasant enough information, but I could not see the bearing of it. I was not conscious that it was a matter of any interest to me. Another time he said, "This is Nine-Mile Point." Later he said, "This is Twelve-Mile Point." They were all about level with the water's edge; they all looked about alike to me; they were monotonously unpicturesque. I hoped Mr. Bixby would change the subject. But no; he would crowd up around a point, hugging the shore with affection, and then say: "The slack water ends here, abreast this bunch of China trees; now we cross over." So he crossed over. He gave me the wheel once or twice, but I had no luck. I either came near chipping off the edge of a sugar plantation, or else I yawed too far from shore, and so I dropped back into disgrace and got abused again.

The watch was ended at last, and we took supper and went to bed. At midnight the glare of a lantern shone in my eyes, and the night watchman said: "Come! Turn out!"

And then he left. I could not understand this extraordinary procedure; so I presently gave up trying to, and dozed off to sleep. Pretty soon the watchman was back again, and this time he was gruff. I was annoyed. I said: "What do you want to come bothering around here in the middle of the night for? Now as like as not I'll not get to sleep again tonight."

The watchman said: "Well, if this an't good, I'm blest."

The "off watch" was just turning in, and I heard some brutal laughter from them, and such remarks as "Hello, watchman! An't the new cub turned out yet? He's delicate, likely. Give him some sugar in a rag and send for the chambermaid to sing rock-a-by-baby to him."

About this time Mr. Bixby appeared on the scene. Something like a minute later I was climbing the pilothouse steps with some of my clothes on and the rest in my arms. Mr. Bixby was close behind commenting. Here was something fresh—this thing of getting up in the middle of the night to go to work. It was a detail in piloting that had never occurred to me at all. I knew the boats ran all night, but somehow I had never happened to reflect that somebody had to get up out of a warm bed to run them. I began to fear that piloting was not quite so romantic as I had imagined it was; there was something very real and work-like about this new phase of it.

It was a rather dingy night, although a fair number of stars were out. The big mate was at the wheel, and he had the old tub pointed at a star and was holding her straight up the middle of the river. The shores on either hand were not much more than a mile apart, but they seemed wonderfully far away and ever so vague and indistinct. The mate said: "We've got to land at Jones's plantation, sir."

The vengeful spirit in me exulted. I said to myself, I wish you joy of your job, Mr. Bixby; you'll have a good time finding Mr. Jones's plantation such a night as this, and I hope you never *will* find it as long as you live.

Mr. Bixby said to the mate: "Upper end of the plantation, or the lower?"

"Upper."

"I can't do it. The stumps there are out of water at this stage. It's no great distance to the lower, and you'll have to get along with that."

"All right, sir. If Jones don't like it he'll have to lump it, I reckon."

And then the mate left. My exultation began to cool and my wonder to come up. Here was a man who not only proposed to find this plantation on such a night, but to find either end of it you preferred. I dreadfully wanted to ask a question, but I was carrying about as many short answers as my cargo room would admit of, so I held my peace. All I desired to ask Mr.

Bixby was the simple question whether he was ass enough to really imagine he was going to find that plantation on a night when all plantations were exactly alike and all the same color. But I held in. I used to have fine inspirations of prudence in those days.

Mr Bixby made for the shore and soon was scraping it, just the same as if at had been daylight. And not only that, but singing "Father in heaven the day is declining," etc. It seemed to me that I had put my life in the keeping of a peculiarly reckless outcast. Presently he turned on me and said: "What's the name of the first point above New Orleans?"

I was gratified to be able to answer promptly, and I did. I said I didn't know.

"Don't *know?*"

This manner jolted me. I was down at the foot again, in a moment. But I had to say just what I had said before.

"Well, you're a smart one," said Mr. Bixby. "What's the name of the *next* point?"

Once more I didn't know.

"Well, this beats anything. Tell me the name of *any* point or place I told you."

I studied a while and decided that I couldn't.

"Look-a-here! What do you start out from, above Twelve-Mile point, to cross over?"

"I – I – don't know."

"You – you – don't know?" mimicking my drawling manner of speech. "What *do* you know?"

"I – I – nothing, for certain."

"By the great Caesar's ghost I believe you! You're the stupidest dunderhead I ever saw or ever heard of, so help me Moses! The idea of *you* being a pilot – *you!* Why, you don't know enough to pilot a cow down a lane."

Oh, but his wrath was up! He was a nervous man, and he shuffled from one side of his wheel to the other as if the floor was hot. He would boil a while to himself, and then overflow and scald me again.

"Look-a-here! What do you suppose I told you the names of those points for?"

I tremblingly considered a moment, and then the devil of temptation provoked me to say: "Well – to – to – be entertaining, I thought."

This was a red rag to the bull. He raged and stormed to (he was crossing the river at the time) that I judge it made him blind, because he ran over the steering oar of a trading scow. Of course the traders sent up a volley of red-hot profanity. Never was a man so grateful as Mr. Bixby was: because he was brim full, and here were subjects who would *talk back*. He threw open a window, thrust his head out, and such an eruption followed as I never had heard before. The fainter and farther away the scowmen's curses drifted, the higher Mr. Bixby lifted his voice and the weightier his adjectives grew. When he closed the window he was empty. You could have drawn a seine through his system and not caught curses enough to disturb your mother with.

Presently he said to me in the gentlest way: "My boy, you must get a little memorandum book, and every time I tell you a thing, put it down right away. There's only one way to be a pilot, and that is to get this entire river by heart. You have to know it just like A B C."

That was a dismal revelation to me; for my memory was never loaded with anything but blank cartridges. However, I did not feel discouraged long. I judged that it was best to make some allowances, for doubtless Mr. Bixby was "stretching." Presently he pulled a rope and struck a few strokes on the big bell. The stars were all gone now, and the night was as black as ink. I could hear the wheels churn along the bank, but I was not entirely certain that I could see the shore.

The voice of the invisible watchman called up from the hurricane deck: "What's this, sir?"

"Jones's plantation."

I said to myself, I wish I might venture to offer a small bet that it isn't. But I did not chirp. I only waited to see. Mr. Bixby handled the engine bells, and in due time the boat's nose came to the land, a torch glowed from the forecastle, a man skipped ashore, a darky's voice on the bank said, "Gimme de carpetbag, Mars' Jones," and the next moment we were standing up the river again, all serene. I reflected deeply a while, and then said —but not aloud: "Well, the finding of that plantation was the luckiest accident that ever happened; but it couldn't happen again in a hundred years." And I fully believed it *was* an accident, too.

By the time we had gone seven or eight hundred miles up the river, I had learned to be a tolerably plucky upstream steersman, in daylight; and before we reached St. Louis, I had made a trifle of progress in night work, but only a trifle. I had a notebook that fairly bristled with the names of towns, "points," bars, islands, reaches, etc.; but the information was to be found only in the notebook—none of it was in my head. It made my heart ache to think I had only got half of the river set down; for as our watch was four hours off and four hours on, day and night, there was a long four-hour gap in my book for every time I had slept since the voyage began.

My chief was presently hired to go on a big New Orleans boat, and I packed my satchel and went with him. She was a grand affair. When I stood in her pilothouse I was so far above the water that I seemed perched on a mountain; and her decks stretched so far away, fore and aft, below me, that I wondered how I could ever have considered the little *Paul Jones* a large craft. There were other differences, too. The *Paul Jones's* pilothouse was a cheap, dingy, battered rattletrap, cramped for room; but here was a sumptuous glass temple; room enough to have a dance in; showy red and gold window curtains; an imposing sofa; leather cushions and a back to the high bench where visiting pilots sit, to spin yarns and "look at the river"; bright, fanciful "cuspadores" instead of a broad wooden box filled with sawdust; nice new oilcloth on the floor; a hospitable big stove for winter; a wheel as high as my head, costly with inlaid work; a wire tiller-rope; bright brass knobs for the bells; and a tidy, white-aproned, black "texas-tender," to bring up tarts and ices and coffee during mid-watch day and night. Now this was "something like"; and so I began to take heart once more to believe that piloting was a romantic sort of occupation after all. The moment we were under way I began to prowl about the great steamer and fill myself with joy. She was as clean and as dainty as a drawing room; when I looked down her long, gilded saloon, it was like gazing through a splendid tunnel; she had an oil picture, by some gifted sign painter, on every stateroom door; she glittered with no end of prism-fringed chandeliers; the clerk's office was elegant, the bar was marvelous, and the barkeeper had been barbered and upholstered at incredible cost. The boiler deck (i.e., the second story of the boat, so to speak) was as spacious as a church, it seemed to me; so with the forecastle; and there was not pitiful handful of deckhands, firemen, and roustabouts down there, but a whole battalion of men. The fires were fiercely glaring from a long row of furnaces, and over them were eight huge boilers! This was unutterable pomp. The mighty engines—but enough of this. I had never felt so fine before. And when I found that the regiment of natty servants respectfully "sirred" me, my satisfaction was complete.

When I returned to the pilothouse St. Louis was gone and I was lost. Here was a piece of river which was all down in my book, but I could make neither head nor tail of it: you understand, it was turned around. I had seen it when coming upstream, but I had never faced about to see how it looked when it was behind me. My heart broke again, for it was plain that I had got to learn this troublesome river *both ways*.

The pilothouse was full of pilots, going down to "look at the river." What is called the "upper river" (the two hundred miles between St. Louis and Cairo where the Ohio comes in) was low; and the Mississippi changes its channel so constantly that the pilots used to always find it necessary to run down to Cairo to take a fresh look, when their boats were to lie in port a week—that is, when the water was at a low stage. A deal of this "looking at the river" was done by poor fellows who seldom had a berth and whose only hope of getting one lay in their being always freshly posted and therefore ready to drop into the shoes of some reputable pilot, for a single trip, on account of such pilot's sudden illness or some other necessity. And a good many of them constantly ran up and down inspecting the river, not because they ever really hoped to get a berth, but because (they being guests of the boat) it was cheaper to "look at the river" than stay ashore and pay board. In time these fellows grew dainty in their tastes, and only infested boats that had an established reputation for setting good tables. All visiting pilots were useful, for they were always ready and willing, winter or summer, night or day, to go out in the yawl and help buoy the channel or assist the boat's pilots in any way they could. They were likewise welcome because all pilots are tireless talkers, when gathered together; and as they talk only about the river they are always understood and are always interesting. Your true pilot cares nothing about anything on earth but the river, and his pride in his occupation surpasses the pride of kings.

We had a fine company of these river inspectors along, this trip. There were eight or ten; and there was abundance of room for them in our great pilothouse. Two or three of them wore polished silk hats, elaborate shirt-fronts, diamond breastpins, kid gloves, and patent leather boots. They were choice in their English, and bore themselves with a dignity proper to men of solid means and prodigious reputation as pilots. The other were more or less loosely clad, and wore upon their heads tall felt cones that were suggestive of the days of the Commonwealth.

I was a cipher in this august company, and felt subdued, not to say torpid. I was not even of sufficient consequence to assist at the wheel when it was necessary to put the tiller hard down in a hurry; the guest that stood nearest did that when occasion required—and this was pretty much all the time, because of the crookedness of the channel and the scant water. I stood in a corner; and the talk I listened to took the hope all out of me.

One visitor said to another: "Jim, how did you run Plum Point, coming up?"

"It was in the night, there, and I ran it the way one of the boys on the *Diana* told me; started out about fifty yards above the woodpile on the false point, and held on the cabin under Plum Point till I raised the reef—quarter less twain—then straightened up for the middle bar till I got well abreast the old one-limbed cottonwood in the bend, then got my stern on the cottonwood and head on the low place above the point, and came through a-booming—nine and a half."

"Pretty square crossing, an't it?"

"Yes, but the upper bar's working down fast."

Another pilot spoke up and said: "I had better water than that, and ran it lower down; started out from the false point—mark twain—raised the second reef abreast the big snag in the bend, and had quarter less twain."

One of the gorgeous ones remarked: "I don't want to find fault with your leadsmen, but that's a good deal of water for Plum Point, it seems to me."

There was an approving nod all around as this quiet snub dropped on the boaster and "settled" him. And so they went on talk-talk-talking. Meantime the thing that was running in my mind was: "Now if my ears hear aright, I have not only to get the names of all the towns and islands and bends, and so on, by heart, but I must even get up a warm personal acquaintanceship with every old snag and one-limbed cottonwood and obscure woodpile that ornaments the banks of this river for twelve hundred miles; and more than that, I must actually know where these things are in the dark, unless these guests are gifted with eyes that can pierce through two miles of solid blackness; I wish the piloting business was in Jericho and I never thought of it."

At dusk Mr. Bixby tapped the big bell three times (the signal to land), and the captain emerged from his drawing room in the forward end of the texas, and looked up inquiringly.

Mr. Bixby said: "We will lay up here all night, captain."

"Very well, sir."

That was all. The boat came to shore and was tied up for the night. It seemed to me a fine thing that the pilot could do as he pleased without asking so grand a captain's permission. I took my supper and went immediately to bed, discouraged by my day's observations and experiences. My late voyage's notebooking was but a confusion of meaningless names. It had tangled me all up in a knot every time I had looked at it in the daytime. I now hoped for respite in sleep; but no, it reveled all through my head till sunrise again, a frantic and tireless nightmare.

Next morning I felt pretty rusty and low-spirited. We went booming along, taking a good many chances, for we were anxious to "get out of the river" (as getting out to Cairo was called) before night should overtake us. But Mr. Bixby's partner, the other pilot, presently grounded the boat, and we lost so much time getting her off that it was plain the darkness would overtake us a good long way above the mouth. This was a great misfortune especially to certain of our visiting pilots, whose boats would have to wait for their return, no matter how long that might be. It sobered the pilot-house talk a good deal. Coming upstream, pilots did not mind low water or any kind of darkness; nothing stopped them but fog. But downstream work was different: a boat was too nearly helpless, with a stiff current pushing behind her; so it was not customary to run downstream at night in low water.

There seemed to be one small hope, however: if we could get through the intricate and dangerous Hat Island crossing before night, we could venture the rest, for we would have plainer sailing and better water. But it would be insanity to attempt Hat Island at night. So there was a deal of looking at watches all the rest of the day, and a constant ciphering upon the speed we were making. Hat Island was the eternal subject; sometimes hope was high and sometimes we were delayed in a bad crossing, and down it went again. For hours all hands lay under the burden of this suppressed excitement. It was even communicated to me, and I got to feeling so solicitous about Hat Island, and under such an awful pressure of responsibility, that I wished I might have five minutes on shore to draw a good, full, relieving breath and start over again. We were standing no regular watches. Each of our pilots ran such portions of the river as he had run when coming upstream, because of his greater familiarity with it; but both remained in the pilothouse constantly.

An hour before sunset, Mr. Bixby took the wheel and Mr. W. stepped aside. For the next thirty minutes every man held his watch in his hand and was restless, silent, and uneasy. At last somebody said, with a doomful sigh: "Well, yonder's Hat Island—and we can't make it."

All the watches closed with a snap; everybody sighed and muttered something about its being "too bad, too bad—ah, if we could *only* have got here half an hour sooner!" and the place was thick with the atmosphere of disappointment. Some started to go out, but loitered, hearing no bell-tap to land. The sun dipped behind the horizon, the boat went on. Inquiring looks passed from one guest to another; and one who had his hand on the doorknob, and had turned it, waited, then presently took away his hand and let the knob turn back again. We bore steadily down the bend. More looks were exchanged, and nods of surprised admiration—but no words. Insensibly the men drew together behind Mr. Bixby as the sky darkened and one or two dim stars came out. The dead silence and sense of waiting became oppressive. Mr. Bixby pulled the cord, and two deep, mellow notes from the big bell floated off on the night. Then a pause, and one more note was struck. The watchman's voice followed, from the hurricane deck: "Labboard lead, there! Stabboard lead!"

The cries of the leadsmen begun to rise out of the distance, and were gruffly repeated by the word-passers on the hurricane deck.

"M-a-r-k three! M-a-r-k three! Quarter less three! Half twain! Quarter twain! M-a-r-k twain! Quarter less—"

Mr. Bixby pulled two bell-ropes, and was answered by faint jinglings far below in the engine room, and our speed slackened. The steam began to whistle through the gauge cocks. The cries of the leadsmen went on—and it is a weird sound, always, in the night. Every pilot in the lot watching now, with fixed eyes, and talking under his breath. Nobody was calm and easy but Mr. Bixby. He would put his wheel down and stand on a spoke, and as the steamer swung into her (to me) utterly invisible marks—for we seemed to be in the midst of a wide and gloomy sea—he would meet and fasten her there.

Talk was going on, now, in low voices: "There; she's over the first reef all right!"

After a pause, another subdued voice: "Her stern's coming down just *exactly* right, by *George!* Now she's in the marks; over she goes!"

Somebody else muttered: "Oh, it was done beautiful—*beautiful!*"

Now the engines were stopped altogether, and we drifted with the current. Nor that I could see the boat drift, for I could not, the stars being all gone by this time. This drifting was the dismalest work; it held one's heart still. Presently I discovered a blacker gloom than that which surround us. It was the head of the island. We were closing right down upon it. We entered its deeper shadow, and so imminent seemed the peril that I was likely to suffocate; and I had the strongest impulse to do *something*, anything, to save the vessel. But still Mr. Bixby stood by his wheel, silent, intent as a cat, and all the pilots stood shoulder to shoulder at his back.

"She'll not make it!" somebody whispered.

The water grew shoaler and shoaler by the leadsmen's cries, till it was down to "Eight and a half! E-i-g-h-t feet! E-i-g-h-t feet! Seven and—"

Mr. Bixby said warningly through his speaking tube to the engineer: "Stand by, now!"

"Aye, aye, sir,"

"Seven and a half! Seven feet! *Six* and—"

We touch bottom! Instantly Mr. Bixby set a lot of bells ringing, shouted through the tube, "*Now* let her have it—every ounce you've got!" Then to his partner, "Put her hard down! Snatch her! Snatch her!" The boat rasped and ground her way through the sand, hung upon the apex of disaster a single tremendous instant, and then over she went! And such a shout as went up at Mr. Bixby's back never loosened the roof of a pilothouse before!

There was no more trouble after that. Mr. Bixby was a hero that night; and it was some little time, too, before his exploit ceased to be talked about by river men.

Fully to realize the marvelous precision required in laying the great steamer in her marks in that murky waste of water, one should know that not only must she pick her intricate way through snags and blind reefs, and then shave the head of the island so closely as to brush the overhanging foliage with her stern, but at one place she must pass almost within arm's reach of a sunken and invisible wreck that would snatch the hull timbers from under her if she should strike it, and destroy a quarter of a million dollars' worth of steamboat and cargo in five minutes, and maybe a hundred and fifty human lives into the bargain.

The last remark I heard that night was a compliment to Mr. Bixby, uttered in soliloquy and with unction by one of our guests. He said: "By the Shadow of Death, but he's a lightning pilot!"

THE CELEBRATED JUMPING FROG OF CALAVERAS COUNTY

IN COMPLIANCE with the request of a friend of mine, who wrote me from the East, I called on good-natured, garrulous old Simon Wheeler, and inquired after my friend's friend, Leonidas W. Smiley, as requested to do, and I hereunto append the result. I have a lurking suspicion that *Leonidas W.* Smiley is a myth; and that my friend never knew such a personage; and that he only conjectured that if I asked old Wheeler about him, it would remind him of his infamous *Jim Smiley*, and he would go to work and bore me to death with some exasperating reminiscence of him as long and as tedious as it should be useless to me. If that was the design, it succeeded.

I found Simon Wheeler dozing comfortably by the bar-room stove of the dilapidated tavern in the decayed mining camp of Angel's, and I noticed that he was fat and bald-headed, and had an expression of winning gentleness and simplicity upon his tranquil countenance. He roused up, and gave me good-day. I told him a friend had commissioned me to make some inquiries about a cherished companion of his boyhood named *Leonidas W.* Smiley—*Rev. Leonidas W.* Smiley, a young minister of the Gospel, who he had heard was at one time a resident of Angel's Camp. I added that if Mr. Wheeler could tell me anything about this Rev. Leonidas W. Smiley, I would feel under many obligations to him.

Simon Wheeler backed me into a corner and blockaded me there with his chair, and then sat down and reeled off the monotonous narrative which follows this paragraph. He never smiled, he never frowned, he never changed his voice from the gentle-flowing key to which he tuned his initial sentence, he never betrayed the slightest suspicion of enthusiasm; but all through the interminable narrative there ran a vein of impressive earnestness and sincerity, which showed me plainly that, so far from his imagining that there was anything ridiculous or funny about his story, he regarded it as a really important matter, and admired its two heroes as men of transcendent genius in *finesse*. I let him go on in his own way, and never interrupted him once.

"Rev. Leonidas W. H'm, Reverend Le—well, there was a feller here once by the name of *Jim* Smiley, in the winter of '49—or maybe it was the spring of '50—I don't recollect exactly, somehow, though what makes me think it was one or the other is because I remember the big flume warn't finished when he first came to the camp; but any way, he was the curiousest man about always betting on anything that turned up you ever see, if he could get anybody to bet on the other side; and if he couldn't he'd change sides. Any way that suited the other man would suit *him*—any way just so's he got a bet, *he* was satisfied. But still he was lucky, uncommon lucky; he most always come out winner. He was always ready and laying for a chance; there couldn't be no solit'ry thing mentioned but that feller'd offer to bet on it, and take ary side you please, as I was just telling you. If there was a horse-race, you'd find him flush or you'd find him busted at the end of it; if there was a dog-fight, he'd bet on it; if there was a cat-fight, he'd bet on it; if there was a chicken-fight, he'd bet on it; why, if there was two birds setting on a fence, he would bet you which one would fly first; or if there was a camp-meeting, he would be there reg'lar to bet on Parson Walker, which he judged to be the best exhorter about here, and he was, too, and a good man. If he even see a straddle-bug start to go anywheres, he would bet you how long it would take him to get to—to wherever he was going to, and if you took him up, he would foller that straddle-bug to Mexico but what he would find out where he was bound for and how long he was on the road. Lots of the boys here has seen that Smiley and can tell you about him. Why, it never made no difference to *him*—he'd bet on *any* thing—the dangest feller. Parson Walker's wife laid very sick once, for a good while, and it seemed as if they warn't going to save her; but one morning he come in, and Smiley up and asked him how she was, and he said she was considerable better—thank the Lord for his inf'nit' mercy—and coming on so smart that with the blessing of Prov'dence she'd get well yet; and Smiley, before he thought, says, "Well, I'll risk two-and-a-half she don't anyway."

Thish-yer Smiley had a mare—the boys called her the fifteen-minute nag, but that was only in fun, you know, because, of course, she was faster than that—and he used to win money on that horse, for all she was so slow and always had the asthma, or the distemper, or the consumption, or something of that kind. They used to give her two or three hundred yards start, and then pass her under way; but always at the fag-end of the race she'd get excited and desperate-like, and come cavorting and straddling up, and scattering her legs around limber, sometimes in the air, and sometimes out to one side amongst the fences, and kicking up m-o-r-e dust and raising m-o-r-e racket with her coughing and sneezing and blowing her nose—and *always* fetch up at the stand just about a neck ahead, as near as you could cipher it down.

And he had a little small bull-pup, that to look at him you'd think he warn't worth a cent but to set around and look ornery and lay for a chance to steal something. But as soon as money was up on him he was a different dog; his under-jaw'd begin to stick out like the fo'-castle of a steamboat, and his teeth would uncover and shine like the furnaces. And a dog might tackle him and bully-rag him, and bite him, and throw him over his shoulder two or three times, and Andrew Jackson—which was the name of the pup—Andrew Jackson would never let on but what *he* was satisfied, and hadn't expected nothing else—and the bets being doubled and doubled on the other side all the time, till the money was all up; and then all of a sudden he would grab that other dog jest by the j'int of his hind leg and freeze to it—not chaw, you understand, but only just grip and hang on till they throwed up the sponge, if it was a year. Smiley always come out winner on that pup, till he harnessed a dog once that didn't have no hind legs, because they'd been sawed off in a circular saw, and when the thing had gone along far enough, and the money was all up, and he come to make a snatch for his pet holt, he see in a minute how he'd been imposed on, and how the other dog had him in the door, so to speak, and he 'peared surprised, and then he looked sorter discouraged-like, and didn't try no more to win the fight, and so he got shucked out bad. He gave Smiley a look, as much as to say his heart was broke, and it was *his* fault, for putting up a dog that hadn't no hind legs for him to take holt of, which was his main dependence in a fight, and then he limped off a piece and laid down and died. It was a good pup, was that Andrew Jackson, and would have made a name for hisself if he'd lived, for the stuff was in him and he had genius—I know it, because he hadn't no opportunities to speak of, and it don't stand to reason that a dog could make such a fight as he could under them circumstances if he hadn't no talent. It always makes me feel sorry when I think of that last fight of his'n, and the way it turned out.

Well, thish-yer Smiley had rat-tarriers, and chicken cocks, and tom-cats and all of them kind of things, till you couldn't rest, and you couldn't fetch nothing for him to bet on but he'd match you. He ketched a frog one day, and took him home, and said he cal'klated to educate him; and so he never done nothing for three months but set in his back yard and learn that frog to jump. And you bet you he *did* learn him, too. He'd give him a little punch behind, and the next minute you'd see that frog whirling in the air like a doughnut—see him turn one summerset, or maybe a couple, if he got a start, and come down flat-footed and all right, like a cat. He got him up so in the matter of ketching flies, and kep' him in practice so constant, that he'd nail a fly every time as fur as he could see him. Smiley said all a frog wanted was education, and he could do 'most anything—and I believe him. Why, I've seen him set Dan'l Webster down here on the floor—Dan'l Webster was the name of the frog—and sing out, "Flies, Dan'l, flies!" and quicker'n you could wink he'd spring straight up and snake a fly off'n the counter there, and flop down on the floor ag'in as solid as a gob of mud, and fall to scratching the side of his head with his hind foot as indifferent as if he hadn't no idea he'd been doin' any more'n any frog might do. You never see a frog so modest and straightfor'ard as he was, for all he was so gifted. And when it come to fair and square jumping on a dead level, he could get over more ground at one straddle than any animal of his breed you ever see. Jumping on a dead level was his strong suit, you understand; and when it come to that, Smiley would ante up money on him as long as he had a red. Smiley was monstrous proud of his frog, and well he might be, for fellers that had traveled and been everywheres, all said he laid over any frog that ever *they* see.

Well, Smiley kep' the beast in a little lattice box, and he used to fetch him downtown sometimes and lay for a bet. One day a feller—a stranger in the camp, he was—come acrost him with his box, and says:

"What might be that you've got in the box?"

And Smiley says, sorter indifferent-like, "It might be a parrot, or it might be a canary, maybe, but it ain't—it's only just a frog."

And the feller took it, and looked at it careful, and turned it round this way and that, and says, "H'm—so 'tis. Well, what's *he* good for?"

"Well," Smiley says, easy and careless, "he's good enough for *one* thing, I should judge—he can outjump any frog in Calaveras County."

The feller took the box again, and took another long, particular look, and give it back to Smiley, and says, very deliberate, "Well," he says, "I don't see no p'ints about that frog that's any better'n any other frog."

"Maybe you don't," Smiley says. "Maybe you understand frogs and maybe you don't understand 'em; maybe you've had experience, and maybe you ain't only a amature, as it were. Anyways, I've got *my* opinion and

I'll risk forty dollars that he can outjump any frog in Calaveras County."

And the feller studied a minute, and then says, kinder sad like, "Well, I'm only a stranger here, and I ain't got no frog; but if I had a frog, I'd bet you."

And then Smiley says, "That's all right—that's all right—if you'll hold my box a minute, I'll go and get you a frog." And so the feller took the box, and put up his forty dollars along with Smiley's, and set down to wait.

So he set there a good while thinking and thinking to hisself, and then he got the frog out and prized his mouth open and took a teaspoon and filled him full of quail shot—filled him pretty near up to his chin—and set him on the floor. Smiley he went to the swamp and slopped around in the mud for a long time, and finally he ketched a frog, and fetched him in, and give him to this feller, and says:

"Now, if you're ready, set him alongside of Dan'l, with his forepaws just even with Dan'l's, and I'll give the word." Then he says, "One—two—three —*git!*" and him and the feller touched up the frogs from behind, and the new frog hopped off lively, but Dan'l give a heave, and hysted up his shoulders—so—like a Frenchman, but it warn't no use—he couldn't budge; he was planted as solid as a church, and he couldn't no more stir than if he was anchored out. Smiley was a good deal surprised, and he was disgusted too, but he didn't have no idea what the matter was, of course.

The feller took the money and started away; and when he was going out at the door, he sorter jerked his thumb over his shoulder—so—at Dan'l, and says again, very deliberate, "Well," he says, "*I* don't see no p'ints about that frog that's any better'n any other frog."

Smiley he stood scratching his head and looking down at Dan'l a long time, and at last says, "I do wonder what in the nation that frog throwed off for—I wonder if there ain't something the matter with him—he 'pears to look mighty baggy, somehow." And he ketched Dan'l up by the nap of the neck, and hefted him, and says, "Why blame my cats if he don't weigh five pounds!" and turned him upside down and he belched out a double handful of shot. And then he see how it was, and he was the maddest man—he set the frog down and took out after that feller, but he never ketched him. And——"

(Here Simon Wheeler heard his name called from the front yard, and got up to see what was wanted.) And turning to me as he moved away, he said: "Jest set where you are, stranger, and rest easy—I ain't going to be gone a second."

But, by your leave, I did not think that a continuation of the history of the enterprising vagabond *Jim* Smiley would be likely to afford me much information concerning the Rev. *Leonidas W*. Smiley, and so I started away.

At the door I met the sociable Wheeler returning, and he buttonholed me and recommenced:

"Well, thish-yer Smiley had a yaller, one-eyed cow that didn't have no tail, only jest a short stump like a bannanner, and—"

However, lacking both time and inclination, I did not wait to hear about the afflicted cow, but took my leave.

TOM WHITEWASHES THE FENCE

From *The Adventures of Tom Sawyer*

SATURDAY MORNING was come, and all the summer world was bright and fresh, and brimming with life. There was a song in every heart; and if the heart was young the music issued at the lips. There was cheer in every face and a spring in every step. The locust trees were in bloom and the fragrance of the blossoms filled the air. Cardiff Hill, beyond the village and above it, was green with vegetation, and it lay just far enough away to seem a Delectable Land, dreamy, reposeful, and inviting.

Tom appeared on the sidewalk with a bucket of whitewash and a long-handled brush. He surveyed the fence, and all gladness left him and a deep melancholy settled down upon his spirit. Thirty yards of board fence nine feet high. Life to him seemed hollow, and existence but a burden. Sighing he dipped his brush and passed it along the topmost plank; repeated the operation; did it again; compared the insignificant whitewashed streak with the far-reaching continent of unwhitewashed fence, and sat down on a tree-box discouraged. Jim came skipping out at the gate with a tin pail, and singing "Buffalo Gals." Bringing water from the town pump had always been hateful work in Tom's eyes, before, but now it did not strike him so. He remembered that there was company at the pump. White, mulatto, and Negro boys and girls were always there waiting their turns, resting, trading playthings, quarreling, fighting, skylarking. And he remembered that although the pump was only a hundred and fifty yards off, Jim never got back with a bucket of water under an hour—end even then somebody generally had to go after him. Tom said:

"Say, Jim, I'll fetch the water if you'll whitewash some."

Jim shook his head and said:

"Can't, Mars Tom. Ole missis, she tole me I got to go an' git dis water an' not stop foolin' roun' wid anybody. She says she spec' Mars Tom gwine to ax me to whitewash, an' she tole me go 'long an' 'tend to my own business—she 'lowed *she'd* 'tend to de whitewashin'."

"O, never you mind what she said, Jim. That's the way she always talks. Gimme the bucket—I won't be gone only a minute. *She* won't ever know."

"Oh, I dasn't, Mars Tom. Ole missis she'd take an' tar de head off'n me. Deed she would."

"*She!* She never licks anybody—whacks 'em over the head with her thimble—and who cares for that, I'd like to know. She talks awful, but talk don't hurt—anyways it don't if she don't cry. Jim, I'll give you a marvel. I'll give you a white alley!"

Jim began to waver.

"White alley, Jim! And it's a bully taw."

"My! Dat's a mighty gay marvel, I tell you! But Mars Tom I's powerful 'fraid ole missis—"

"And, besides, if you will I'll show you my sore toe."

Jim was only human—this attraction was too much for him. He put down the pail, took the white alley, and bent over the toe with absorbing interest while the bandage was being unwound. In another moment he was flying down the street with his pail and a tingling rear, Tom was whitewashing with vigor, and Aunt Polly was retiring from the field with a slipper in her hand and triumph in her eye.

But Tom's energy did not last. He began to think of the fun he had planned for this day, and his sorrows multiplied. Soon the free boys would come tripping along on all sorts of delicious expeditions, and they would make a world of fun of him for having to work—he very thought of it burnt him like a fire. He got out his worldly wealth and examined it—bits of toys, marbles, and trash; enough to buy an exchange of *work*, maybe, but not half enough to buy so much as half an hour of pure freedom. So he returned his straitened means to his pocket, and gave up the idea of trying to buy the boys. At this dark and hopeless moment an inspiration burst upon him! Nothing less than a great, magnificent inspiration.

He took up his brush and went tranquilly to work. Ben Rogers hove in sight presently—the very boy, of all boys, whose ridicule he had been dreading. Ben's gait was the hop-skip-and-jump—proof enough that his heart was light and his anticipations high. He was eating an apple, and giving a long, melodious whoop, at intervals, followed by a deep-toned ding-dong-dong, for he was personating a steamboat. As he drew near, he slackened speed, took the middle of the street, leaned far over to starboard and rounded to ponderously and with laborious pomp and circumstance—for he was personating the *Big Missouri*, and considered himself to be drawing nine feet of water. He was boat and captain and engine-bells combined, so he had to imagine himself standing on his own hurricane-deck giving the orders and executing them:

"Stop her, sir! Ting-a-ling-ling!" The headway ran almost out and he drew up slowly toward the sidewalk.

"Ship up to back! Ting-a-ling-ling!" His arms straightened and stiffened down his sides.

"Set her back on the starboard! Ting-a-ling-ling! Chow! ch-chow-wow! Chow!" His right hand, meantime, describing stately circles—for it was representing a forty-foot wheel.

"Let her go back on the labboard! Ting-a-ling-ling! Chow-ch-chow-chow!" The left hand began to describe circles.

"Stop the stabboard! Ting-a-ling-ling! Stop the labboard! Come ahead on the stabboard! Stop her! Let your outside turn over slow! Ting-a-ling-ling! Chow-ow-ow! Get out that head-line! *Lively* now! Come—out with your spring-line—what're you about there! Take a turn round that stump with the bight of it! Stand by that stage, now—let her go! Done with the engines, sir! Ting-a-ling-ling! Sh't! Sh't! (trying the gauge-cocks.)

Tom went on whitewashing—paid no attention to the steamboat. Ben stared a moment and then said:

"Hi-*yi! You're* up a stump, ain't you!"

No answer. Tom surveyed his last touch with the eye of an artist, then he gave his brush another gentle sweep and surveyed the result, as before. Ben ranged up alongside of him. Tom's mouth watered for the apple, but he stuck to his work. Ben said:

"Hello, old chap, you got to work, hey?"

Tom wheeled suddenly and said:

"Why, it's you, Ben! I warn't noticing."

"Say—I'm going in a-swimming, I am. Don't you wish you could? But of course you'd druther *work*—wouldn't you? Course you would!"

Tom contemplated the boy a bit, and said:

"What do you call work?"

"Why, ain't *that* work?"

Tom resumed his whitewashing and answered carelessly:

"Well, maybe it is, and maybe it ain't. All I know is, it suits Tom Sawyer."

"Oh come, now, you don't mean to let on that you *like* it?"

The brush continued to move.

"Like it? Well, I don't see why I oughtn't to like it. Does a boy get a chance to whitewash a fence every day?"

That put the thing in a new light. Ben stopped nibbling his apple. Tom swept his brush daintily back and forth—stepped back to note the effect—added a touch here and there—criticized the effect again—Ben watching every move and getting more and more interested, more and more absorbed. Presently he said:

"Say, Tom, let *me* whitewash a little."

Tom considered, was about to consent; but he altered his mind:

"No—no—I reckon it wouldn't hardly do, Ben. You see, Aunt Polly's awful particular about this fence—right here on the street, you know—but if it was the back fence I wouldn't mind and *she* wouldn't. Yes, she's awful particular about this fence; it's got to be done very careful; I reckon there ain't one boy in a thousand, maybe two thousand, that can do it the way it's got to be done."

"No—is that so? Oh, come, now—lemme just try. Only just a little—I'd let *you*, if you was me, Tom."

"Ben, I'd like to, honest injun; but Aunt Polly—well, Jim wanted to do it, but she wouldn't let him; Sid wanted to do it, and she wouldn't let Sid. Now don't you see how I'm fixed? If you was to tackle this fence and anything was to happen to it—"

"Oh, shucks, I'll be just as careful. Now lemme try. Say—I'll give you the core of my apple."

"Well, here—No, Ben, now don't. I'm afeard—"

"I'll give you *all* of it!"

Tom gave up the brush with reluctance in his face, but alacrity in his heart. And while the late steamer *Big Missouri* worked and sweated in the sun, the retired artist sat on a barrel in the shade close by, dangled his legs, munched his apple, and planned the slaughter of more innocents. There was no lack of material; boys happened along every little while; they came to jeer, but remained to whitewash. By the time Ben was fagged out, Tom had traded the next chance to Billy Fisher for a kite, in good repair; and when *he* played out, Johnny Miller bought in for a dead rat and a string to swing it with—and so on, and so on, hour after hour. And when the middle of the afternoon came, from being a poor poverty-stricken boy in the morning, Tom was literally rolling in wealth. He had, beside the things before mentioned, twelve marbles, part of a jew's-harp, a piece of blue bottle-glass to look through, a spool cannon, a key that wouldn't unlock anything, a fragment of chalk, a glass stopper of a decanter, a tin soldier, a couple of tadpoles, six firecrackers, a kitten with only one eye, a brass door-knob, a dog-collar—but no dog—the handle of a knife, four pieces of orange-peel, and a dilapidated old window-sash.

He had had a nice, good, idle time all the while—plenty of company—

and the fence had three coats of whitewash on it! If he hadn't run out of whitewash, he would have bankrupted every boy in the village.

Tom said to himself that it was not such a hollow world, after all. He had discovered a great law of human action, without knowing it—namely, that in order to make a man or boy covet a thing, it is only necessary to make the thing difficult to attain. If he had been a great and wise philosopher, like the writer of this book, he would now have comprehended that Work consists of whatever a body is *obliged* to do, and that Play consists of whatever a body is not obliged to do. And this would help him to understand why constructing artificial flowers or performing on a treadmill is work, while rolling tenpins or climbing Mont Blanc is only amusement. There are wealthy gentlemen in England who drive four-horse passenger-coaches twenty or thirty miles on a daily line, in the summer, because the privilege costs them considerable money; but if they are offered wages for the service, that would turn it into work and then they would resign.

The boy mused awhile over the substantial change which had taken place in his worldly circumstances, and then wended toward headquarters to report.

THE CAMEL'S APPETITE

From *Roughing It*

MULES and donkeys and camels have appetites that anything will relieve temporarily, but nothing satisfy. In Syria, once, at the headwaters of the Jordan, a camel took charge of my overcoat while the tents were being pitched, and examined it with a critical eye, all over, with as much interest as if he had the idea of getting one made like it. Then after he was done figuring on it as an article of apparel, he began to contemplate it as an article of diet. He put his foot on it, and lifted one of the sleeves out with his teeth, and chewed and chewed at it, gradually taking it in, and all the while opening and closing his eyes in a kind of religious ecstasy, as if he had never tasted anything as good as an overcoat before in his life. Then he smacked his lips once or twice, and reached after the other sleeve. Next he tried the velvet collar, and smiled a smile of such contentment that it was plain to see that he regarded that as the daintiest thing about an overcoat. The tails went next, along with some percussion-caps and cough-candy, and some fig-paste from Constantinople. And then my newspaper correspondence dropped out, and he took a chance on that—manuscript letters written for the home papers. But he was treading on dangerous ground now. He began to come across solid wisdom in those documents that was rather weighty on his stomach; and occasionally he would take a joke that would shake him up till it loosened his teeth; it was getting to be perilous times with him, but he held his grip with good courage and hopefully, till at last he began to stumble on statements that not even a camel could swallow with impunity. He began to gag and gasp, and his eyes to stand out, and his forelegs to spread, and in about a quarter of a minute he fell over as stiff as a carpenter's work-bench, and died a death of indescribable agony.

I went and pulled the manuscript out of his mouth, and found that the sensitive creature had choked to death on one of the mildest and gentlest statements of fact that I ever laid before a trusting public.

PAP STARTS IN ON A NEW LIFE

From *Huckleberry Finn*

I HAD SHUT the door to. Then I turned around, and there he was. I used to be scared of him all the time, he tanned me so much. I reckoned I was scared now, too; but in a minute I see I was mistaken—that is, after the first jolt, as you may say, when my breath sort of hitched, he being so unexpected; but right away after, I see I warn't scared of him worth bothring about.

He was most fifty, and he looked it. His hair was long and tangled and greasy and hung down, and you could see his eyes shining through like he was behind vines. It was all black, no gray; so was his long, mixed-up whiskers. There warn't no color in his face, where his face showed; it was white, not like another man's white but a white to make a body sick, a white to make a body's flesh crawl—a tree-toad white, a fish-belly white. As for his clothes—just rags, that was all. He had one ankle resting on t'other knee; the boot on that foot was busted and two of his toes stuck through, and he worked them now and then. His hat was laying on the floor—an old black slouch with the top caved in, like a lid.

I stood a-looking at him; he set there a-looking at me, with his chair tilted back a little. I set the candle down. I noticed the window was up; so he had clumb in by the shed. He kept a-looking me all over. By and by he says:

"Starchy clothes—very. You think you're a good deal of a big-bug, *don't* you?

"Maybe I am, maybe I ain't," I says.

"Don't you give me none o' your lip," says he. "You've put on considerable many frills since I been away. I'll take you down a peg before I get done with you. You're educated, too, they say—can read and write. You think you're better'n your father, now, don't you, because he can't? *I'll* take it out of you. Who told you you might meddle with such hifalut'n foolishness, hey?—who told you you could?"

"The widow. She told me."

"The widow, hey?—and who told the widow she could put in her shovel about a thing that ain't none of her business?"

"Nobody never told her."

"Well, I'll learn her how to meddle. And looky here—you drop that school, you hear? I'll learn people to bring up a boy to put on airs over his own father and let on to be better'n what *he* is. You lemme catch you fooling around that school again, you hear? Your mother couldn't read, and she couldn't write, nuther, before she died. None of the family couldn't before *they* died. *I* can't; and here you're a-swelling yourself up like this. I ain't the man to stand it—you hear? Say, lemme hear you read."

I took up a book and begun something about General Washington and the wars. When I'd read about a half a minute, he fetched the book a whack with his hand and knocked it across the house. He says:

"It's so. You can do it. I had my doubts when they told me. Now looky here; you stop that putting on frills. I won't have it. I'll lay for you, my smarty, and if I catch you about that school I'll tan you good. First you know you'll get religion, too. I never see such a son."

He took up a little blue and yaller picture of some cows and a boy, and says:

"What's this?"

"It's something they give me for learning my lessons good."

He tore it up, and says:

"I'll give you something better—I'll give you a cowhide."

He set there a-mumbling and a-growling a minute, and then he says:

"*Ain't* you a sweet-scented dandy, though? A bed, and bedclothes, and a look'n'-glass, and a piece of carpet on the floor—and your own father got to sleep with the hogs in the tanyard. I never see such a son. I bet I'll take some o' these frills out o' you before I'm done with you. Why, there ain't no end to your airs—they say you're rich. Hey?—how's that?"

"They lie—that's how."

"Looky here—mind how you talk to me; I'm a-standing about all I can stand now—so don't gimme no sass. I've been in town two days and I hain't heard nothing but about you bein' rich. I heard about it away down the river, too. That's why I come. You git me that money to-morrow—I want it."

"I hain't got no money."

"It's a lie. Judge Thatcher's got it. You git it. I want it."

"I hain't got no money, I tell you. You ask Judge Thatcher; he'll tell you the same."

"All right. I'll ask him; and I'll make him pungle, too, or I'll know the reason why. Say, how much you got in your pocket? I want it."

"I hain't got only a dollar, and I want that to—"

"It don't make no difference what you want it for—you just shell it out."

He took it and bit it to see if it was good, and then he said he was going down-town to get some whisky; said he hadn't had a drink all day. When he had got out on the shed he put his head in again and cussed me for putting on frills and trying to be better than him, and when I reckoned he was gone he come back and put his head in again and told me to mind about that school, because he was going to lay for me and lick me if I didn't drop that.

Next day he was drunk, and he went to Judge Thatcher's and bullyragged him and tried to make him give up the money, but he couldn't, and then he swore he'd make the law force him.

The judge and the widow went to law to get the court to take me away from him and let one of them be my guardian, but it was a new judge that had just come and he didn't know the old man; so he said courts mustn't interfere and separate families if they could help it, said he'd druther not take a child away from its father. So Judge Thatcher and the widow had to quit on the business.

That pleased the old man till he couldn't rest. He said he'd cowhide me till I was black and blue if I didn't raise some money for him. I borrowed three dollars from Judge Thatcher and pap took it and got drunk and went a-blowing around and cussing and whooping and carrying on, and he kept it up all over town, with a tin pan, till most midnight; then they jailed him and next day they had him before court and jailed him again for a week. But he said *he* was satisfied; said he was boss of his son and he'd make it warm for *him*.

When he got out the new judge said he was a-going to make a man of him. So he took him to his own house, and dressed him up clean and nice, and had him to breakfast and dinner and supper with the family, and was just old pie to him, so to speak. And after supper he talked to him about temperance and such things till the old man cried and said he'd been a fool and fooled away his life but now he was a-going to turn over a new leaf and be a man nobody wouldn't be ashamed of, and he hoped the judge would help him and not look down on him. The judge said he could hug him for them words; so *he* cried and his wife cried too; pap said he'd been a man that had always been misunderstood before and the judge said he believed it. The old man said that what a man wanted that was down was sympathy and the judge said it was so; so they cried again. And when it was bedtime the old man rose up and held out his hand, and says:

"Look at it, gentlemen and ladies all; take a-hold of it; shake it. There's a hand that was the hand of a hog; but it ain't so no more; it's the hand of a man that's started in on a new life and'll die before he'll go back. You mark them words—don't forget I said them. It's a clean hand now; shake it—don't be afeard."

So they shook it, one after the other, all around, and cried. The judge's wife she kissed it. Then the old man he signed a pledge—made his mark. The judge said it was the holiest time on record, or something like that. Then they tucked the old man into a beautiful room, which was the spare room, and in the night some time he got powerful thirsty and clumb out on to the porch-roof and slid down a stanchion and traded his new coat for a jug of forty-rod, and clumb back again and had a good old time; and towards daylight he crawled out again, drunk as a fiddler, and rolled off the porch and broke his left arm in two places and was most froze to death when somebody found him after sun-up. And when they come to look at that spare room they had to take soundings before they could navigate it.

The judge he felt kind of sore. He said he reckoned a body could reform the old man with a shotgun, maybe, but he didn't know no other way.

THEY'RE AFTER US

From *Huckleberry Finn*

"COME IN," says the woman, and I did. She says: "Take a cheer."

I done it. She looked me all over with her little shiny eyes, and says:

"What might your name be?"

"Sarah Williams."

"Where'bouts do you live? In this neighborhood?"

"No'm. In Hookerville, seven mile below. I've walked all the way and I'm all tired out."

"Hungry, too, I reckon. I'll find you something."

"No'm, I ain't hungry. I was so hungry I had to stop two mile below here at a farm; so I ain't hungry no more. It's what makes me so late. My mother's down sick and out of money and everything, and I come to tell my uncle Abner Moore. He lives at the upper end of the town, she says. I hain't ever been here before. Do you know him?"

"No; but I don't know everybody yet. I haven't lived here quite two weeks. It's a considerable ways to the upper end of the town. You better stay here all night. Take off your bonnet."

"No," I says; "I'll rest awhile, I reckon, and go on. I ain't afeard of the dark."

She said she wouldn't let me go by myself, but her husband would be in by and by, maybe in a hour and a half, and she'd send him along with me. Then she got to talking about her husband, and about her relations up the river, and her relations down the river, and about how much better off they used to was, and how they didn't know but they'd made a mistake coming to our town, instead of letting well alone—and so on and so on, till I was afeard *I* had made a mistake coming to her to find out what was going on in the town; but by and by she dropped on to pap and the murder and then I was pretty willing to let her clatter right along. She told about me and Tom Sawyer finding the twelve thousand dollars (only she got it twenty) and all about pap and what a hard lot he was, and what a hard lot I was, and at last she got down to where I was murdered. I says:

"Who done it? We've heard considerable about these goings-on down in Hookerville, but we don't know who 'twas that killed Huck Finn."

"Well, I reckon there's a right smart chance of people *here* that 'd like to know who killed him. Some thinks old Finn done it himself."

"No—is that so?"

"Most everybody thought it at first. He'll never know how nigh he come to getting lynched. But before night they changed around and judged it was done by a runaway nigger named Jim."

"Why *he*—"

I stopped. I reckoned I better keep still. She run on, and never noticed I had put in at all:

"The nigger run off the very night Huck Finn was killed. So there's a reward out for him—three hundred dollars. And there's a reward out for old Finn, too—two hundred dollars. You see, he come to town the morning after the murder and told about it, and was out with 'em on the ferryboat hunt, and right away after he up and left. Before night they wanted to lynch him but he was gone, you see. Well, next day they found out the nigger was gone; they found out he hadn't ben seen sence ten o'clock the night the murder was done. So then they put it on him, you see; and while they was full of it, next day, back comes old Finn, and went boo-hooing to Judge Thatcher to get money to hunt for the nigger all over Illinois with. The judge give him some, and that evening he got drunk and was around till after midnight with a couple of mighty hard-looking strangers, and then went off with them. Well, he hain't come back sence and they ain't looking for him back till this thing blows over a little, for people thinks now that he killed his boy and fixed things so folks would think robbers done it, and then he'd get Huck's money without having to bother a long time with a lawsuit. People do say he warn't any too good to do it. Oh, he's sly, I reckon. If he don't come back for a year he'll be all right. You can't prove anything on him, you know; everything will be quieted down then, and he'll walk into Huck's money as easy as nothing."

"Yes, I reckon so, 'm. I don't see nothing in the way of it. Has everybody quit thinking the nigger done it?"

"Oh, no, not everybody. A good many thinks he done it. But they'll get the nigger pretty soon now, and maybe they can scare it out of him."

"Why, are they after him yet?"

"Well, you're innocent, ain't you! Does three hundred dollars lay around every day for people to pick up? Some folks think the nigger ain't far from here. I'm one of them—but I hain't talked it around. A few days ago I was talking with an old couple that lives next door in the log shanty, and they happened to say hardly anybody ever goes to that island over yonder that they call Jackson's Island. Don't anybody live there? says I. No, nobody, says they. I didn't say any more but I done some thinking. I was pretty near certain I'd seen smoke over there, about the head of the island, a day or two before that, so I says to myself, like as not that nigger's hiding over there; anyway, says I, it's worth the trouble to give the place a hunt. I hain't seen any smoke sence, so I reckon maybe he's gone, if it was him; but husband's going over to see—him and another man. He was gone up the river; but he got back to-day, and I told him as soon as he got here two hours ago."

I had got so uneasy I couldn't set still. I had to do something with my hands; so I took up a needle off of the table and went to threading it. My hands shook and I was making a bad job of it. When the woman stopped talking I looked up, and she was looking at me pretty curious and smiling a little. I put down the needle and thread and let on to be interested—and I was, too—and says:

"Three hundred dollars is a power of money. I wish my mother could get it. Is your husband going over there to-night?"

"Oh, yes. He went up-town with the man I was telling you of, to get a boat and see if they could borrow another gun. They'll go over after midnight."

"Couldn't they see better if they was to wait till daytime?"

"Yes. And couldn't the nigger see better, too? After midnight he'll likely be asleep and they can slip around through the woods and hunt up his camp-fire all the better for the dark, if he's got one."

"I didn't think of that."

The woman kept looking at me pretty curious, and I didn't feel a bit comfortable. Pretty soon she says:

"What did you say your name was, honey?"

"M—Mary Williams."

Somehow it didn't seem to me that I said it was Mary before, so I didn't look up—seemed to me I said it was Sarah; so I felt sort of cornered and was afeard maybe I was looking it, too. I wished the woman would say something more; the longer she set still the uneasier I was. But now she says:

"Honey, I thought you said it was Sarah when you first come in?"

"Oh, yes'm, I did. Sarah Mary Williams. Sarah's my first name. Some calls me Sarah, some calls me Mary."

"Oh, that's the way of it?"

"Yes'm."

I was feeling better then but I wished I was out of there, anyway. I couldn't look up yet.

Well, the woman fell to talking about how hard times was, and how poor they had to live, and how the rats was as free as if they owned the place, and so forth and so on, then I got easy again. She was right about the rats. You'd see one stick his nose out of a hole in the corner every little while. She said she had to have things handy to throw at them when she was alone, or they wouldn't give her no peace. She showed me a bar of lead twisted up into a knot and said she was a good shot with it generly, but she'd wrenched her arm a day or two ago and didn't know whether she could throw true now. But she watched for a chance and directly banged away at a rat, but she missed him wide and said, "Ouch!" it hurt her arm so. Then she told me to try for the next one. I wanted to be getting away before the old man got back, but of course I didn't let on. I got the thing, and the first rat that showed his nose, I let drive, and if he'd 'a' stayed where he was he'd 'a' been a tolerable sick rat. She said that was first-rate and she reckoned I would hive the next one. She went and got the lump of lead and fetched it back, and brought along a hank of yarn which she wanted me to help her with. I held up my two hands and she put the hank over them, and went on talking about her and her husband's matters. But she broke off to say:

"Keep your eye on the rats. You better have the lead in your lap, handy."

So she dropped the lump into my lap just at that moment, and I clapped my legs together on it and she went on talking. But only about a minute. Then she took off the hank and looked me straight in the face, but very pleasant, and says:

"Come, now, what's your real name?"

"Wh-what, mum?"

"What's your real name? Is it Bill, or Tom, or Bob?—or what is it?"

I reckon I shook like a leaf and I didn't know hardly what to do. But I says:

"Please to don't poke fun at a poor girl like me, mum. If I'm in the way here, I'll—"

"No, you won't. Set down and stay where you are. I ain't going to hurt you and I ain't going to tell on you, nuther. You just tell me your secret, and trust me. I'll keep it; and, what's more, I'll help you. So'll my old man if you want him to. You see, your're a runaway 'prentice, that's all. It ain't anything. There ain't no harm in it. You've been treated bad and you made up your mind to cut. Bless you, child, I wouldn't tell on you. Tell me all about it now, that's a good boy."

So I said it wouldn't be no use to try to play it any longer, and I would just make a clean breast and tell her everything but she mustn't go back on her promise. Then I told her my father and mother was dead and the law had bound me out to a mean old farmer in the country thirty mile back from the river, and he treated me so bad I couldn't stand it no longer; he went away to be gone a couple of days and so I took my chance and stole some of his daughter's old clothes and cleared out, and I had been three nights coming the thirty miles. I traveled nights and hid daytimes and slept, and the bag of bread and meat I carried from home lasted me all the way, and I had a-plenty. I said I believed my uncle Abner Moore would take care of me, and so that was why I struck out for this town of Goshen.

"Goshen, child? This ain't Goshen. This is St. Petersburg. Goshen's ten mile further up the river. Who told you this was Goshen?"

"Why, a man I met at daybreak this morning, just as I was going to turn into the woods for my regular sleep. He told me when the roads forked I must take the right hand, and five mile would fetch me to Goshen."

"He was drunk, I reckon. He told you just exactly wrong."

"Well, he did act like he was drunk but it ain't no matter now. I got to be moving along. I'll fetch Goshen before daylight."

"Hold on a minute. I'll put you up a snack to eat. You might want it."

So she put me up a snack, and says:

"Say, when a cow's laying down, which end of her gets up first? Answer up prompt now–don't stop to study over it. Which end gets up first?"

"The hind end, mum."

"Well, then, a horse?"

"The for'rard end, mum."

"Which side of a tree does the moss grow on?"

"North side."

"If fifteen cows is browsing on a hillside, how many of them eats with their heads pointed the same direction?"

"The whole fifteen, mum."

"Well, I reckon you *have* lived in the country. I thought maybe you was trying to hocus me again. What's your real name, now?"

"George Peters, mum."

"Well, try to remember it, George. Don't forget and tell me it's Elexander before you go, and then get out by saying it's George Elexander when I catch you. And don't go about women in that old calico. You do a girl tolerable poor but you might fool men, maybe. Bless you, child, when you set out to thread a needle don't hold the thread still and fetch the needle up to it; hold the needle still and poke the thread at it; that's the way a woman most always does but a man always does t'other way. And when you throw at a rat or anything, hitch yourself up a-tiptoe and fetch your hand up over your head as awkward as you can and miss your rat about six or seven foot. Throw stiffarmed from the shoulder, like there was a pivot there for it to turn on, like a girl, not from the wrist and elbow, with your arm out to one side, like a boy. And, mind you, when a girl tries to catch anything in her lap she throws her knees apart; she don't clap them together, the way you did when you catched the lump of lead. Why, I spotted you for a boy when you was threading the needle and I contrived the other things just to make certain. Now trot along to your uncle, Sarah Mary Williams George Elexander Peters, and if you get into trouble you send word to Mrs. Judith Loftus, which is me, and I'll do what I can to get you out of it. Keep the river road all the way and next time you tramp take shoes and socks with you. The river road's a rocky one, and your feet'll be in a condition when you get to Goshen, I reckon."

I went up the bank about fifty yards, and then I doubled on my tracks and slipped back to where my canoe was, a good piece below the house. I jumped in and was off in a hurry. I went up-stream far enough to make the head of the island, and then started across. I took off the sun-bonnet, for I didn't want no blinders on then. When I was about the middle I heard the clock begin to strike, so I stops and listens; the sound come faint over the water but clear—eleven. When I struck the head of the island I never waited to blow, though I was most winded, but I shoved right into the timber where my old camp used to be, and started a good fire there on a high and dry spot.

Then I jumped in the canoe and dug out for our place, a mile and a half below, as hard as I could go. I landed, and slopped through the timber and up the ridge and into the cavern. There Jim laid, sound asleep on the ground. I roused him out and says:

"Git up and hump yourself, Jim! There ain't a minute to lose. They're after us!"

Jim never asked no questions, he never said a word, but the way he worked for the next half an hour showed about how he was scared. By that time everything we had in the world was on our raft and she was ready to be shoved out from the willow cove where she was hid. We put out the camp-fire at the cavern the first thing, and didn't show a candle outside after that.

I took the canoe out from the shore a little piece and took a look; but if there was a boat around I couldn't see it, for stars and shadows ain't good to see by. Then we got out the raft and slipped along down in the shade, past the foot of the island dead still—never saying a word.

THE DIARY OF ADAM AND EVE

The Diary of Adam and Eve *took twelve years to complete; Twain began it at fifty-eight and did not finish it until he had turned seventy. The change in tone as well as in spirit is immediately apparent: it starts in what promises to be the old vein of bland burlesque, but it concludes with a series of paragraphs which are as full of tenderness and wisdom, of love and beauty as anything he ever wrote.*

PART I—*Extracts from Adam's Diary*

Monday This new creature with the long hair is a good deal in the way. It is always hanging around and following me about. I don't like this; I am not used to company. I wish it would stay with the other animals. . . . Cloudy to-day, wind in the east; think we shall have rain. . . . *We?* Where did I get that word?—I remember now—the new creature uses it.

Tuesday Been examining the great waterfall. It is the finest thing on the estate, I think. The new creature calls it Niagara Falls—why, I am sure I do not know. Says it *looks* like Niagara Falls. That is not a reason, it is mere waywardness and imbecility. I get no chance to name anything myself. The new creature names everything that comes along, before I can get in a protest. And always that same pretext is offered—it *looks* like the thing. There is the dodo, for instance. Says the moment one looks at it one sees at a glance that it "looks like a dodo." It will have to keep that name, no doubt. It wearies me to fret about it, and it does no good, anyway. Dodo! It looks no more like a dodo than I do.

Wednesday Built me a shelter against the rain, but could not have it to myself in peace. The new creature intruded. When I tried to put it out it shed water out of the holes it looks with, and wiped it away with the back of its paws, and made a noise such as some of the other animals make when they are in distress. I wish it would not talk; it is always talking. That sounds like a cheap fling at the poor creature, a slur; but I do not mean it so. I have never heard the human voice before, and any new and strange sound intruding itself here upon the solemn hush of these dreaming solitudes offends my ear and seems a false note. And this new sound is so close to me; it is right at my shoulder, right at my ear, first on one side and then on the other, and I am used only to sounds that are more or less distant from me.

Friday The naming goes recklessly on, in spite of anything I can do. I had a very good name for the estate, and it was musical and pretty—GARDEN OF EDEN. Privately, I continue to call it that, but not any longer publicly. The new creature says it is all woods and rocks and scenery, and therefore has no resemblance to a garden. Says it *looks* like a park, and does not look like anything *but* a park. Consequently, without consulting me, it has been new-named—NIAGARA FALLS PARK. This is sufficiently high-handed, it seems to me. And already there is a sign up:

KEEP OFF
THE GRASS

My life is not as happy as it was.

Saturday The new creature eats too much fruit. We are going to run short, most likely. "We" again—that is *its* word; mine, too, now, from hearing it so much. Good deal of fog this morning. I do not go out in the fog myself. The new creature does. It goes out in all weathers, and stumps right in with its muddy feet. And talks. It used to be so pleasant and quiet here.

Sunday Pulled through. This day is getting to be more and more trying. It was selected and set apart last November as a day of rest. I had already six of them per week before. This morning found the new creature trying to clod apples out of that forbidden tree.

Monday The new creature says its name is Eve. That is all right, I have no objections. Says it is to call it by, when I want it to come. I said it was superfluous, then. The word evidently raised me in its respect; and indeed it is a large, good word and will bear repetition. It says it is not an It, it is a She. This is probably doubtful; yet it is all one to me; what she is were nothing to me if she would but go by herself and not talk.

Tuesday She has littered the whole estate with execrable names and offensive signs:

THIS WAY TO THE WHIRLPOOL
THIS WAY TO GOAT ISLAND
CAVE OF THE WINDS THIS WAY

She says this park would make a tidy summer resort if there was any custom for it. Summer resort—another invention of hers—just words, without any meaning. What is a summer resort? But it is best not to ask her, she has such a rage for explaining.

Friday She has taken to beseeching me to stop going over the Falls. What harm does it do? Says it makes her shudder. I wonder why; I have always done it—always liked the plunge, and coolness. I supposed it was what the Falls were for. They have no other use that I can see, and they must have been made for something. She says they were only made for scenery—like the rhinoceros and the mastodon.

I went over the Falls in a barrel—not satisfactory to her. Went over in a tub—still not satisfactory. Swam the Whirlpool and the Rapids in a fig-leaf suit. It got much damaged. Hence, tedious complaints about my extravagance. I am too much hampered here. What I need is change of scene.

Saturday I escaped last Tuesday night, and traveled two days, and built me another shelter in a secluded place, and obliterated my tracks as well as I could, but she hunted me out by means of a beast which she has tamed and calls a wolf, and came making that pitiful noise again, and shedding that water out of the places she looks with. I was obliged to return with her, but will presently emigrate again when occasion offers. She engages herself in many foolish things; among others, to study out why the animals called lions and tigers live on grass and flowers, when, as she says, the sort of teeth they wear would indicate that they were intended to eat each other. This is foolish, because to do that would be to kill each other, and that would introduce what, as I understand it, is called "death"; and death, as I have been told, has not yet entered the Park. Which is a pity, on some accounts.

Sunday Pulled through.

Monday I believe I see what the week is for: it is to give time to rest up from the weariness of Sunday. It seems a good idea. . . . She has been climbing that tree again. Clodded her out of it. She said nobody was looking. Seems to consider that a sufficient justification for chancing any dangerous thing. Told her that. The word justification moved her admiration —and envy, too, I thought. It is a good word.

Tuesday She told me she was made out of a rib taken from my body. This is at least doubtful, if not more than that. I have not missed any rib . . . She is in much trouble about the buzzard; says grass does not agree with it; is afraid she can't raise it; thinks it was intended to live on decayed flesh. The buzzard must get along the best it can with what it is provided. We cannot overturn the whole scheme to accommodate the buzzard.

Saturday She fell in the pond yesterday when she was looking at herself in it, which she is always doing. She nearly strangled, and said it was most uncomfortable. This made her sorry for the creatures which live in there, which she calls fish, for she continues to fasten names on to things that don't need them and don't come when they are called by them, which is a matter of no consequence to her, she is such a numskull, anyway; so she got a lot of them out and brought them in last night and put them in my bed to keep warm, but I have noticed them now and then all day and I don't see that they are any happier there than they were before, only quieter. When night comes I shall throw them outdoors. I will not sleep with them again, for I find them clammy and unpleasant to lie among when a person hasn't anything on.

Sunday Pulled through.

Tuesday She has taken up with a snake now. The other animals are glad, for she was always experimenting with them and bothering them; and I am glad because the snake talks, and this enables me to get a rest.

Friday She says the snake advises her to try the fruit of that tree, and says the result will be a great and fine and noble education. I told her there would be another result, too—it would introduce death into the world. That was a mistake—it had been better to keep the remark to myself; it only gave her an idea—she could save the sick buzzard, and furnish fresh meat to the despondent lions and tigers. I advised her to keep away from the tree. She said she wouldn't. I foresee trouble. Will emigrate.

Wednesday I have had a variegated time. I escaped last night, and rode a horse all night as fast as he could go, hoping to get clear out of the Park and hide in some other country before the trouble should begin; but it was not to be. About an hour after sun-up, as I was riding through a flowery plain where thousands of animals were grazing, slumbering, or playing with each other, according to their wont, all of a sudden they broke into a tempest of frightful noises, and in one moment the plain was a frantic commotion and every beast was destroying its neighbor. I knew what it meant—Eve had eaten that fruit, and death was come into the world. . . . The tigers ate my horse, paying no attention when I ordered them to desist, and they would have eaten me if I had stayed—which I didn't, but went away in much haste. . . . I found this place, outside the Park, and was fairly comfortable for a few days, but she has found me out. Found me out, and has named the place Tonawanda—says it *looks* like that. In fact I was not sorry she came, for there are but meager pickings here, and she brought some of those apples. I was obliged to eat them, I was so hungry. It was against my principles, but I find that principles have no real force except when one is well fed. . . . She came curtained in boughs and bunches of leaves, and when I asked her what she meant by such nonsense, and snatched them away and threw them down, she tittered and blushed. I had never seen a person titter and blush before, and to me it seemed unbecoming and idiotic. She said I would soon know how it was myself. This was correct. Hungry as I was, I laid down the apple half-eaten—certainly the best one I ever saw, considering the lateness of the season—and arrayed myself in the discarded boughs and branches, and then spoke to her with some severity and ordered her to go and get some more and not make such a spectacle of herself. She did it, and after this we crept down to where the wild-beast battle had been, and collected some skins, and I made her patch together a couple of suits proper for public occasions. They are uncomfortable, it is true, but stylish, and that is the main point about clothes. . . . I find she is a good deal of a companion. I see I should be lonesome and depressed without her, now that I have lost my property. Another thing, she says it is ordered that we work for our living hereafter. She will be useful. I will superintend.

Ten Days Later She accuses *me* of being the cause of our disaster! She says, with apparent sincerity and truth, that the Serpent assured her that the forbidden fruit was not apples, it was chestnuts. I said I was innocent, then, for I had not eaten any chestnuts. She said the Serpent informed her that "chestnut" was a figurative term meaning an aged and moldy joke. I turned pale at that, for I have made many jokes to pass the weary time, and some of them could have been of that sort, though I had honestly supposed that they were new when I made them. She asked me if I had made one just at the time of the catastrophe. I was obliged to admit that I had made one to myself, though not aloud. It was this. I was thinking about the Falls, and I said to myself, "How wonderful it is to see that vast body of water tumble down there!" Then in an instant a bright thought flashed into my head, and I let it fly, saying, "It would be a deal more wonderful to see it tumble *up* there!"—and I was just about to kill myself with laughing at it when all nature broke loose in war and death and I had to flee for my life. "There," she said, with triumph, "that is just it; the Serpent mentioned that very jest, and called it the First Chestnut, and said it was coeval with the creation." Alas, I am indeed to blame. Would that I were not witty; oh, that I had never had that radiant thought!

Next Year We have named it Cain. She caught it while I was up country trapping on the North Shore of the Erie; caught it in the timber a couple of miles from our dug-out—or it might have been four, she isn't certain which. It resembles us in some ways, and may be a relation. That is what she thinks, but this is an error, in my judgment. The difference in size warrants the conclusion that it is a different and new kind of animal—a fish, perhaps, though when I put it in the water to see, it sank, and she plunged in and snatched it out before there was opportunity for the experiment to determine the matter. I still think it is a fish, but she is indifferent about what it is, and will not let me have it to try. I do not understand this. The coming of the creature seems to have changed her whole nature and made her unreasonable about experiments. She thinks more of it than she does of any of the other animals, but is not able to explain why. Her mind is disordered—everything shows it. Sometimes she carries the fish in her arms half the night when it complains and wants to get to the water. At such times the water comes out of the places in her face that she looks out of, and she pats the fish on the back and makes soft sounds with her mouth to soothe it, and betrays sorrow and solicitude in a hundred ways. I have never seen her do like this with any other fish, and it troubles me greatly. She used to carry the young tigers around so, and play with them, before we lost our property, but it was only play; she never took on about them like this when their dinner disagreed with them.

Sunday She doesn't work, Sundays, but lies around all tired out, and likes to have the fish wallow over her; and she makes fool noises to amuse it, and pretends to chew its paws, and that makes it laugh. I have not seen a fish before that could laugh. This makes me doubt. . . . I have come to like Sunday myself. Superintending all the week tires a body so. There ought to be more Sundays. In the old days they were tough, but now they come handy.

Wednesday It isn't a fish. I cannot quite make out what it is. It makes curious devilish noises when not satisfied, and says "goo-goo" when it is. It is not one of us, for it doesn't walk; it is not a bird, for it doesn't fly; it is not a frog, for it doesn't hop; it is not a snake, for it doesn't crawl, I feel sure it is not a fish, though I cannot get a chance to find out whether it can swim or not. It merely lies around, and mostly on its back, with its feet up. I have not seen any other animal do that before. I said I believed it was an enigma; but she only admired the word without understanding it. In my judgment it is either an enigma or some kind of a bug. If it dies, I will take it apart and see what its arrangements are. I never had a thing perplex me so.

Three Months Later The perplexity augments instead of diminishing. I sleep but little. It has ceased from lying around, and goes about on its four legs now. Yet it differs from the other four-legged animals, in that its front legs are unusually short, consequently this causes the main part of its person to stick up uncomfortably high in the air, and this is not attractive. It is built much as we are, but its method of traveling shows that it is not of our breed. The short front legs and long hind ones indicate that it is of the kangaroo family, but it is a marked variation of the species, since the true kangaroo hops, whereas this one never does. Still it is a curious and interesting variety, and has not been catalogued before. As I discovered it, I have felt justified in securing the credit of the discovery by attaching my name to it, and hence have called it *Kangaroorum Adamiensis*. . . . It must have been a young one when it came, for it has grown exceedingly since. It must be five times as big, now, as it was then, and when discontented it is able to make from twenty-two to thirty-eight times the noise it made at first. Coercion does not modify this, but has the contrary effect. For this reason I discontinued the system. She reconciles it by persuasion, and by giving it things which she had previously told me she wouldn't give it. As already observed, I was not at home when it first came, and she told me she found it in the woods. It seems odd that it should be the only one, yet it must be so, for I have worn myself out these many weeks trying to find another one to add to my collection, and for this one to play with; for surely then it would be quieter and we could tame it more easily. But I find none, nor any vestige of any; and strangest of all, no tracks. It has to live on the ground, it cannot help itself; therefore, how does it get about without leaving a track? I have set a dozen traps, but they do no good. I catch all small animals except that one, animals that merely go into the trap out of curiosity, I think, to see what the milk is there for. They never drink it.

Three Months Later The Kangaroo still continues to grow, which is very strange and perplexing. I never knew one to be so long getting its growth. It has fur on its head now; not like kangaroo fur, but exactly like our hair except that it is much finer and softer, and instead of being black is red. I am like to lose my mind over the capricious and harassing developments of this unclassifiable zoological freak. If I could catch another one—but that is hopeless; it is a new variety, and the only sample; this is plain. But I caught a true kangaroo and brought it in, thinking that this one, being lonesome, would rather have that for company than have no kin at all, or any animal it could feel a nearness to or get sympathy from in its forlorn condition here among strangers who do not know its ways or habits, or what to do to make it feel that it is among friends; but it was a mistake—it went into such fits at the sight of the kangaroo that I was convinced it had never seen one before. I pity the poor noisy little animal, but there is nothing I can do to make it happy. If I could tame it—but that is out of the question; the more I try the worse I seem to make it. I grieves me to the heart to see it in its little storms of sorrow and passion. I wanted to let it go, but she wouldn't hear of it. That seemed cruel and not like her; and yet she may be right. It might be lonelier than ever; for since I cannot find another one, how could *it?*

Five Months Later It is not a kangaroo. No, for it supports itself by holding to her finger, and thus goes a few steps on its hind legs, and then falls down. It is probably some kind of a bear; and yet it has no tail—as yet—and no fur, except on its head. It still keeps on growing—that is a curious circumstance, for bears get their growth earlier than this. Bears are dangerous—since our catastrophe—and I shall not be satisfied to have this one prowling about the place much longer without a muzzle on. I have offered to get her a kangaroo if she would let this one go, but it did no good—she is determined to run us into all sorts of foolish risks, I think. She was not like this before she lost her mind.

A Fortnight Later I examined its mouth. There is no danger yet: it has only one tooth. It has no tail yet. It makes more noise now than it ever did before—and mainly at night. I have moved out. But I shall go over, mornings, to breakfast, and see if it has more teeth. If it gets a mouthful of teeth it will be time for it to go, tail or no tail, for a bear does not need a tail in order to be dangerous.

Four Months Later I have been off hunting and fishing a month, up in the region that she calls Buffalo; I don't know why, unless it is because there are not any buffaloes there. Meantime the bear has learned to paddle around all by itself on its hind legs, and says "poppa" and "momma." It is certainly a new species. This resemblance to words may be purely accidental, of course, and may have no purpose or meaning; but even in that case it is still extraordinary, and is a thing which no other bear can do. This imitation of speech, taken together with general absence of fur and entire absence of tail, sufficiently indicates that this is a new kind of bear. The further study of it will be exceedingly interesting. Meantime I will go off on a far expedition among the forests of the north and make an exhaustive search. There must certainly be another one somewhere, and this one will be less dangerous when it has company of its own species. I will go straightway; but I will muzzle this one first.

Three Months Later It has been a weary, weary hunt, yet I have had no success. In the mean time, without stirring from the home estate, she has caught another one! I never saw such luck. I might have hunted these woods a hundred years, I never would have run across that thing.

Next Day I have been comparing the new one with the old one, and it is perfectly plain that they are the same breed. I was going to stuff one of them for my collection, but she is prejudiced against it for some reason or other; so I have relinquished the idea, though I think it is a mistake. It would be an irreparable loss to science if they should get away. The old one is tamer than it was and can laugh and talk like the parrot, having learned this, no doubt, from being with the parrot so much, and having the imitative faculty in a highly developed degree. I shall be astonished if it turns out to be a new kind of parrot; and yet I ought not to be astonished, for it has already been everything else it could think of since those first days when it was a fish. The new one is as ugly now as the old one was at first; has the same sulphur-and-raw-meat complexion and the same singular head without any fur on it. She calls it Abel.

Ten Years Later They are *boys;* we found it out long ago. It was their coming in that small, immature shape that puzzled us; we were not used to it. There are some girls now. Abel is a good boy, but if Cain had stayed a bear it would have improved him. After all these years, I see that I was mistaken about Eve in the beginning; it is better to live outside the Garden with her than inside it without her. At first I thought she talked too much; but now I should be sorry to have that voice fall silent and pass out of my life. Blessed be the chestnut that brought us near together and taught me to know the goodness of her heart and the sweetness of her spirit!

PART II—*Eve's Diary*

(*Translated from the original*)

Saturday I am almost a whole day old, now. I arrived yesterday. That is as it seems to me. And it must be so, for if there was a day-before-yesterday I was not there when it happened, or I should remember it. It could be, of course, that it did happen, and that I was not noticing. Very well; I will be very watchful now, and if any day-before-yesterdays happen I will make a note of it. It will be best to start right and not let the record get confused, for some instinct tells me that these details are going to be important to the historian some day. For I feel like an experiment, I feel exactly like an experiment; it would be impossible for a person to feel more like an experiment than I do, and so I am coming to feel convinced that that is what I *am*—an experiment; just an experiment, and nothing more.

Then if I am an experiment, am I the whole of it? No, I think not; I think the rest of it is part of it. I am the main part of it, but I think the rest of it has its share in the matter. Is my position assured, or do I have to watch it and take care of it? The latter, perhaps. Some instinct tells me that eternal vigilance is the price of supremacy. [That is a good phrase, I think, for one so young.]

Everything looks better to-day than it did yesterday. In the rush of finishing up yesterday, the mountains were left in a ragged condition, and some of the plains were so cluttered with rubbish and remnants that the aspects were quite distressing. Noble and beautiful works of art should not be subjected to haste; and this majestic new world is indeed a most noble and beautiful work. And certainly marvelously near to being perfect, notwithstanding the shortness of the time. There are too many stars in some places and not enough in others, but that can be remedied presently, no doubt. The moon got loose last night, and slid down and fell out of the scheme—a very great loss; it breaks my heart to think of it. There isn't another thing among the ornaments and decorations that is comparable to it for beauty and finish. It should have been fastened better. If we can only get it back again—

But of course there is no telling where it went to. And besides, whoever gets it will hide it; I know it because I would do it myself. I believe I can be honest in all other matters, but I already begin to realize that the core and center of my nature is love of the beautiful, a passion for the beautiful, and that it would not be safe to trust me with a moon that belonged to another person and that person didn't know I had it. I could give up a moon that I found in the daytime, because I should be afraid some one was looking; but if I found it in the dark, I am sure I should find some kind of an excuse for not saying anything about it. For I do love moons, they are so pretty and so romantic. I wish we had five or six; I would never go to bed; I should never get tired lying on the moss-bank and looking up at them.

Stars are good, too. I wish I could get some to put in my hair. But I suppose I never can. You would be surprised to find how far off they are, for they do not look it. When they first showed, last night, I tried to knock some down with a pole, but it didn't reach, which astonished me; then I tried clods till I was all tired out, but I never got one. It was because I am left-handed and cannot throw good. Even when I aimed at the one I wasn't after I couldn't hit the other one, though I did make some close shots, for I saw the black blot of the clod sail right into the midst of the golden clusters forty or fifty times, just barely missing them, and if I could have held out a little longer maybe I could have got one.

So I cried a little, which was natural, I suppose, for one of my age, and after I was rested I got a basket and started for a place on the extreme rim of the circle, where the stars were close to the ground and I could get them with my hands, which would be better, anyway, because I could gather them tenderly then, and not break them. But it was farther than I thought, and at last I had to give it up; I was so tired I couldn't drag my feet another step; and besides, they were sore and hurt me very much.

I couldn't get back home; it was too far and turning cold; but I found some tigers and nestled in among them and was most adorably comfortable, and their breath was sweet and pleasant, because they live on strawberries. I had never seen a tiger before, but I knew them in a minute by the stripes. If I could have one of those skins, it would make a lovely gown.

To-day I am getting better ideas about distances. I was so eager to get hold of every pretty thing that I giddily grabbed for it, sometimes when it was too far off, and sometimes when it was but six inches away but seemed a foot—alas, with thorns between! I learned a lesson; also I made an axiom, all out of my own head—my very first one: *The scratched Experiment shuns the thorn.* I think it is a very good one for one so young.

I followed the other Experiment around, yesterday afternoon, at a distance, to see what it might be for, if I could. But I was not able to make out. I think it is a man. I had never seen a man, but it looked like one, and I feel sure that that is what it is. I realize that I feel more curiosity about it than about any of the other reptiles. If it is a reptile, and I suppose it is; for it has frowsy hair and blue eyes, and looks like a reptile. It has no hips; it tapers like a carrot; when it stands, it spreads itself apart like a derrick; so I think it is a reptile, though it may be architecture.

I was afraid of it at first, and started to run every time it turned around, for I thought it was going to chase me; but by and by I found it was only trying to get away, so after that I was not timid any more, but tracked it along, several hours, about twenty yards behind, which made it nervous and unhappy. At last it was a good deal worried, and climbed a tree. I waited a good while, then gave it up and went home.

To-day the same thing over. I've got it up the tree again.

Sunday It is up there yet. Resting, apparently. But that is a subterfuge: Sunday isn't the day of rest; Saturday is appointed for that. It looks to me like a creature that is more interested in resting than in anything else. It would tire me to rest so much. It tires me just to sit around and watch the tree. I do wonder what it is for; I never see it do anything.

They returned the moon last night, and I was so happy! I think it is very honest of them. It slid down and fell off again, but I was not distressed; there is no need to worry when one has that kind of neighbors; they will fetch it back. I wish I could do something to show appreciation. I would like to send them some stars, for we have more than we can use. I mean I, not we, for I can see that the reptile cares nothing for such things.

It has low tastes, and is not kind. When I went there yesterday evening in the gloaming it had crept down and was trying to catch the little speckled fishes that play in the pool, and I had to clod it to make it go up the tree again and let them alone. I wonder if *that* is what it is for? Hasn't it any heart? Hasn't it any compassion for those little creatures? Can it be that it was designed and manufactured for such ungentle work? It has the look of it. One of the clods took it back of the ear, and it used language. It gave me a thrill, for it was the first time I had ever heard speech, except my own. I did not understand the words, but they seemed expressive.

When I found it could talk I felt a new interest in it, for I love to talk; I talk, all day, and in my sleep, too, and I am very interesting, but if I had another to talk to I could be twice as interesting, and would never stop, if desired.

If this reptile is a man, it isn't an *it,* is it? That wouldn't be grammatical, would it? I think it would be *he.* I think so. In that case one would parse it thus: nominative, *he;* dative, *him;* possessive, *his'n.* Well, I will consider it a man and call it he until it turns out to be something else. This will be handier than having so many uncertainties.

Next week Sunday All the week I tagged around after him and tried to get acquainted. I had to do the talking, because he was shy, but I didn't mind it. He seemed pleased to have me around, and I used the sociable "we" a good deal, because it seemed to flatter him to be included.

Wednesday We are getting along very well indeed, now, and getting better and better acquainted. He does not try to avoid me any more, which is a good sign, and shows that he likes to have me with him. That pleases me, and I study to be useful to him in every way I can, so as to increase his regard. During the last day or two I have taken all the work of naming things off his hands, and this has been a great relief to him, for he has no gift in that line, and is evidently very grateful. He can't think of a rational name to save him, but I do not let him see that I am aware of his defect. Whenever a new creature comes along I name it before he has time to expose himself by an awkward silence. In this way I have saved him many embarrassments. I have no defect like his. The minute I set eyes on an animal I know what it is. I don't have to reflect a moment; the right name comes out instantly, just as if it were an inspiration, as no doubt it is, for I am sure it wasn't in me half a minute before. I seem to know just by the shape of the creature and the way it acts what animal it is.

When the dodo came along he thought it was a wildcat—I saw it in his eye. But I saved him. And I was careful not to do it in a way that could hurt his pride. I just spoke up in a quite natural way of pleased surprise, and not as if I was dreaming of conveying information, and said, "Well, I do declare, if there isn't the dodo!" I explained—without seeming to be explaining—how I knew it for a dodo, and although I thought maybe he was a little piqued that I knew the creature when he didn't, it was quite evident that he admired me. That was very agreeable, and I thought of it more than once with gratification before I slept. How little a thing can make us happy when we feel that we have earned it!

Thursday My first sorrow. Yesterday he avoided me and seemed to wish I would not talk to him. I could not believe it, and thought there was some mistake, for I loved to be with him, and loved to hear him talk, and so how could it be that he could feel unkind toward me when I had not done anything? But at last it seemed true, so I went away and sat lonely in the place where I first saw him the morning that we were made and I did not know what he was and was indifferent about him; but now it was a mournful place, and every little thing spoke of him, and my heart was very sore. I did not know why very clearly, for it was a new feeling; I had not experienced it before, and it was all a mystery, and I could not make it out.

But when night came I could not bear the lonesomeness, and went to the new shelter which he has built, to ask him what I had done that was wrong and how I could mend it and get back his kindness again; but he put me out in the rain, and it was my first sorrow.

Sunday It is pleasant again, now, and I am happy; but those were heavy days; I do not think of them when I can help it.

I tried to get him some of those apples, but I cannot learn to throw straight. I failed, but I think the good intention pleased him. They are forbidden, and he says I shall come to harm; but so I come to harm through pleasing him, why shall I care for that harm?

Monday This morning I told him my name, hoping it would interest him. But he did not care for it. It is strange. If he should tell me his name, I would care. I think it would be pleasanter in my ears than any other sound.

He talks very little. Perhaps it is because he is not bright, and is sensitive about it and wishes to conceal it. It is such a pity that he should feel so, for brightness is nothing; it is in the heart that the values lie. I wish I could make him understand that a loving good heart is riches, and riches enough, and that without it intellect is poverty.

Although he talks so little, he has quite a considerable vocabulary. This morning he used a surprisingly good word. He evidently recognized, himself, that it was a good one, for he worked it in twice afterward, casually. It was not good casual art, still it showed that he possesses a certain quality of perception. Without a doubt that seed can be made to grow, if cultivated.

Where did he get that word? I do not think I have ever used it.

No, he took no interest in my name. I tried to hide my disappointment, but I suppose I did not succeed. I went away and sat on the moss-bank with my feet in the water. It is where I go when I hunger for companionship, some one to look at, some one to talk to. It is not enough—that lovely white body painted there in the pool—but it is something, and something is better than utter loneliness. It talks when I talk; it is sad when I am sad; it comforts me with its sympathy; it says, "Do not be downhearted, you poor friendless girl; I will be your friend." It *is* a good friend to me, and my only one; it is my sister.

That first time that she forsook me! ah, I shall never forget that—never, never. My heart was lead in my body! I said, "She was all I had, and now she is gone!" In my despair I said, "Break, my heart; I cannot bear my life any more!" and hid my face in my hands, and there was no solace for me. And when I took them away, after a little, there she was again, white and shining and beautiful, and I sprang into her arms!

That was perfect happiness; I had known happiness before, but it was not like this, which was ecstasy. I never doubted her afterward. Sometimes she stayed away—maybe an hour, maybe almost the whole day, but I waited and did not doubt; I said, "She is busy, or she is gone a journey, but she will come." And it was so: she always did. At night she would not come if it was dark, for she was a timid little thing; but if there was a moon she would come. I am not afraid of the dark, but she is younger than I am;

she was born after I was. Many and many are the visits I have paid her; she is my comfort and my refuge when my life is hard—and it is mainly that.

Tuesday All the morning I was at work improving the estate; and I purposely kept away from him in the hope that he would get lonely and come. But he did not.

At noon I stopped for the day and took my recreation by flitting all about with the bees and the butterflies and reveling in the flowers, those beautiful creatures that catch the smile of God out of the sky and preserve it! I gathered them, and made them into wreaths and garlands and clothed myself in them while I ate my luncheon—apples, of course; then I sat in the shade and wished and waited. But he did not come.

But no matter. Nothing would have come of it, for he does not care for flowers. He calls them rubbish, and cannot tell one from another, and thinks it is superior to feel like that. He does not care for me, he does not care for flowers, he does not care for the painted sky at eventide—is there anything he does care for, except building shacks to coop himself up in from the good clean rain, and thumping the melons, and sampling the grapes, and fingering the fruit on the trees, to see how those properties are coming along?

I laid a dry stick on the ground and tried to bore a hole in it with another one, in order to carry out a scheme that I had, and soon I got an awful fright. A thin, transparent bluish film rose out of the hole, and I dropped everything and ran! I thought it was a spirit, and I *was* so frightened! But I looked back, and it was not coming; so I leaned against a rock and rested and panted, and let my limbs go on trembling until they got steady again; then I crept warily back, alert, watching, and ready to fly if there was occasion; and when I was come near, I parted the branches of a rose-bush and peeped through—wishing the man was about, I was looking so cunning and pretty—but the sprite was gone. I went there, and there was a pinch of delicate pink dust in the hole. I put my finger in, to feel it, and said *ouch!* and took it out again. It was a cruel pain. I put my finger in my mouth; and by standing first on one foot and then the other, and grunting, I presently eased my misery; then I was full of interest, and began to examine.

I was curious to know what the pink dust was. Suddenly the name of it occurred to me, though I had never heard of it before. It was *fire!* I was as certain of it as a person could be of anything in the world. So without hesitation I named it that—fire.

I had created something that didn't exist before; I had added a new thing to the world's uncountable properties; I realized this, and was proud of my achievement, and was going to run and find him and tell him about it, thinking to raise myself in his esteem—but I reflected, and did not do it. No—he would not care for it. He would ask what it was good for, and what could I answer? for if it was not *good* for something, but only beautiful, merely beautiful—

So I sighed, and did not go. For it wasn't good for anything; it could not build a shack, it could not improve melons, it could not hurry a fruit crop; it was useless, it was a foolishness and a vanity; he would despise it and say cutting words. But to me it was not despicable; I said, "Oh, you fire, I love you, you dainty pink creature, for you are *beautiful*—and that is enough!" and was going to gather it to my breast. But refrained. Then I made another maxim out of my own head, though it was so nearly like the first one that I was afraid it was only a plagiarism: "*The burnt Experiment shuns the fire.*"

I wrought again; and when I had made a good deal of fire-dust I emptied it into a handful of dry brown grass, intending to carry it home and keep it always and play with it; but the wind struck it and it sprayed up and spat out at me fiercely, and I dropped it and ran. When I looked back the blue spirit was towering up and stretching and rolling away like a cloud, and instantly I thought of the name of it—*smoke!*—though, upon my word, I had never heard of smoke before.

Soon, brilliant yellow and red flares shot up through the smoke, and I named them in an instant—*flames*—and I was right, too, though these were the very first flames that had ever been in the world. They climbed the trees, they flashed splendidly in and out of the vast and increasing volume of tumbling smoke, and I had to clap my hands and laugh and dance in my rapture, it was so new and strange and so wonderful and so beautiful!

He came running, and stopped and gazed, and said not a word for many minutes. Then he asked what it was. Ah, it was too bad that he should ask such a direct question. I had to answer it, of course, and I did. I said it was fire. If it annoyed him that I should know and he must ask; that was not my fault; I had no desire to annoy him. After a pause he asked:

"How did it come?"

Another direct question, and it also had to have a direct answer.

"I made it."

The fire was traveling farther and farther off. He went to the edge of the burned place and stood looking down, and said:

"What are these?"

"Fire-coals."

He picked up one to examine it, but changed his mind and put it down again. Then he went away. *Nothing* interests him.

But I was interested. There were ashes, gray and soft and delicate and pretty—I knew what they were at once. And the embers; I knew the embers, too. I found my apples, and raked them out, and was glad; for I am very young and my appetite is active. But I was disappointed; they were all burst open and spoiled. Spoiled apparently; but it was not so; they were better than raw ones. Fire is beautiful; some day it will be useful, I think.

Friday I saw him again, for a moment, last Monday at nightfall, but only for a moment. I was hoping he would praise me for trying to improve the estate, for I had meant well and had worked hard. But he was not pleased, and turned away and left me. He was also displeased on another account: I tried once more to persuade him to stop going over the Falls. That was because the fire had revealed to me a new passion—quite new, and distinctly different from love, grief, and those others which I had already discovered—*fear*. And it is horrible!—I wish I had never discovered it; it gives me dark moments, it spoils my happiness, it makes me shiver and tremble and shudder. But I could not persuade him, for he has not discovered fear yet, and so he could not understand me.

Extract from Adam's Diary

Perhaps I ought to remember that she is very young, a mere girl, and make allowances. She is all interest, eagerness, vivacity, the world is to her a charm, a wonder, a mystery, a joy; she can't speak for delight when she finds a new flower, she must pet it and caress it and smell it and talk to it, and pour out endearing names upon it. And she is color-mad: brown rocks, yellow sand, gray moss, green foliage, blue sky; the pearl of the dawn, the purple shadows on the mountains, the golden islands floating in crimson seas at sunset, the pallid moon sailing through the shredded cloud-rack, the star-jewels glittering in the wastes of space—none of them is of any practical value, so far as I can see, but because they have color and majesty, that is enough for her, and she loses her mind over them. If she could quiet down and keep still a couple of minutes at a time, it would be a reposeful spectacle. In that case I think I could enjoy looking at her; indeed I am sure I could, for I am coming to realize that she is a quite remarkably comely creature—lithe, slender, trim, rounded, shapely, nimble, graceful; and once when she was standing marble-white and sun-drenched on a boulder, with her young head tilted back and her hand shading her eyes, watching the flight of a bird in the sky, I recognized that she was beautiful.

Monday noon *If there is anything on the planet that she is not interested in it is not in my list. There are animals that I am indifferent to, but it is not so with her. She has no discrimination, she takes to all of them, she thinks they are all treasures, every new one is welcome.*

When the mighty brontosaurus came striding into camp, she regarded it as an acquisition, I considered it a calamity; that is a good sample of the lack of harmony that prevails in our views of things. She wanted to domesticate it, I wanted to make it a present of the homestead and move out. She believed it could be tamed by kind treatment and would be a good pet; I said a pet twenty-one feet high and eighty-four feet long would be no proper thing to have about the place, because, even with the best intentions and without meaning any harm, it could sit down on the house and mash it, for any one could see by the look of its eye that it was absent-minded.

Still, her heart was set upon having that monster, and she couldn't give it up. She thought we could start a dairy with it, and wanted me to help her milk it; but I wouldn't; it was too risky. The sex wasn't right, and we hadn't any ladder anyway. Then she wanted to ride it, and look at the scenery. Thirty or forty feet of its tail was lying on the ground, like a fallen tree, and she thought she could climb it, but she was mistaken; when she got to the steep place it was too slick and down she came, and would have hurt herself but for me.

Was she satisfied now? No. Nothing ever satisfies her but demonstration; untested theories are not in her line, and she won't have them. It is the right spirit, I concede it; it attracts me; I feel the influence of it; if I were with her more I think I should take it up myself. Well, she had one theory remaining about this colossus: she thought that if we could tame him and make him friendly we could stand him in the river and use him for a bridge. It turned out that he was already plenty tame enough—at least as far as she was concerned—so she tried her theory, but it failed: every time she got him properly placed in the river and went ashore to cross over on him, he came out and followed her around like a pet mountain. Like the other animals. They all do that.

Friday Tuesday—Wednesday—Thursday—and to-day: all without seeing him. It is a long time to be alone; still, it is better to be alone than unwelcome.

I *had* to have company—I was made for it, I think—so I made friends with the animals. They are just charming, and they have the kindest disposition and the politest ways; they never look sour, they never let you feel that you are intruding, they smile at you and wag their tail, if they've got one, and they are always ready for a romp or an excursion or anything you want to propose. I think they are perfect gentlemen. All these days we have had such good times, and it hasn't been lonesome for me, ever. Lonesome! No, I should say not. Why, there's always a swarm of them around—sometimes as much as four or five acres—you can't count them; and when you stand on a rock in the midst and look out over the furry expanse it is so mottled and splashed and gay with color and frisking sheen and sun-flash, and so rippled with stripes, that you might think it was a lake, only you know it isn't; and there's storms of sociable birds, and hurricanes of whirring wings; and when the sun strikes all that feathery commotion, you have a blazing up of all the colors you can think of, enough to put your eyes out.

We have made long excursions, and I have seen a great deal of the world; almost all of it, I think; and so I am the first traveler, and the only one. When we are on the march, it is an imposing sight—there's nothing like it anywhere. For comfort I ride a tiger or a leopard, because it is soft and has a round back that fits me, and because they are such pretty animals; but for long distance or for scenery I ride the elephant. He hoists me up with his trunk, but I can get off myself; when we are ready to camp, he sits and I slide down the back way.

The birds and animals are all friendly to each other, and there are no disputes about anything. They all talk, and they all talk to me, but it must be a foreign language, for I cannot make out a word they say; yet they often understand me when I talk back, particularly the dog and the elephant. It makes me ashamed. It shows that they are brighter than I am, and are therefore my superiors. It annoys me, for I want to be the principal Experiment myself—and I intend to be, too.

I have learned a number of things, and am educated, now, but I wasn't at first. I was ignorant at first. At first it used to vex me because, with all my watching, I was never smart enough to be around when the water was running uphill; but now I do not mind it. I have experimented and experimented until now I know it never does run uphill, except in the dark. I know it does in the dark, because the pool never goes dry, which it would, of course, if the water didn't come back in the night. It is best to prove things by actual experiment; then you *know;* whereas if you depend on guessing and supposing and conjecturing, you will never get educated.

Some things you *can't* find out; but you will never know you can't by guessing and supposing; no, you have to be patient and go on experimenting until you find out that you can't find out. And it is delightful to have it that way, it makes the world so interesting. If there wasn't anything to find out, it would be dull. Even trying to find out and not finding out is just as interesting as trying to find out and finding out, and I don't know but more so. The secret of the water was a treasure until I *got* it; then the excitement all went away, and I recognized a sense of loss.

By experiment I know that wood swims, and dry leaves, and feathers, and plenty of other things; therefore by all that cumulative evidence you know that a rock will swim; but you have to put up with simply knowing it, for there isn't any way to prove it—up to now. But I shall find a way—

then *that* excitement will go. Such things make me sad; because by and by when I have found out everything there won't be any more excitements, and I do love excitements so! The other night I couldn't sleep for thinking about it.

At first I couldn't make out what I was made for, but now I think it was to search out the secrets of this wonderful world and be happy and thank the Giver of it all for devising it. I think there are many things to learn yet—I hope so; and by economizing and not hurrying too fast I think they will last weeks and weeks. I hope so. When you cast up a feather it sails away on the air and goes out of sight; then you throw up a clod and it doesn't. It comes down, every time. I have tried it and tried it, and it is always so. I wonder why it is? Of course it *doesn't* come down, but why should it *seem* to? I suppose it is an optical illusion. I mean, one of them is. I don't know which one. It may be the feather, it may be the clod; I can't prove which it is, I can only demonstrate that one or the other is a fake, and let a person take his choice.

By watching, I know that the stars are not going to last. I have seen some of the best ones melt and run down the sky. Since one can melt, they can all melt; since they can all melt, they can all melt the same night. That sorrow will come—I know it. I mean to sit up every night and look at them as long as I can keep awake; and I will impress those sparkling fields on my memory, so that by and by when they are taken away I can by my fancy restore those lovely myriads to the black sky and make them sparkle again, and double them by the blur of my tears.

AFTER THE FALL

When I look back, the Garden is a dream to me. It was beautiful, surpassingly beautiful, enchantingly beautiful; and now it is lost, and I shall not see it any more.

The Garden is lost, but I have found *him*, and am content. He loves me as well as he can; I love him with all the strength of my passionate nature, and this, I think, is proper to my youth and sex. If I ask myself why I love him, I find I do not know, and do not really much care to know; so I suppose that this kind of love is not a product of reasoning and statistics, like one's love for other reptiles and animals. I think that this must be so. I love certain birds because of their song; but I do not love Adam on account of his singing—no, it is not that; the more he sings the more I do not get reconciled to it. Yet I ask him to sing, because I wish to learn to like everything he is interested in. I am sure I can learn, because at first I could not stand it, but now I can. It sours the milk, but it doesn't matter; I can get used to that kind of milk.

It is not on account of his brightness that I love him—no, it is not that. He is not to blame for his brightness, such as it is, for he did not make it himself; he is as God made him, and that is sufficient. There was a wise purpose in it, *that* I know. In time it will develop, though I think it will not be sudden; and besides, there is no hurry; he is well enough just as he is.

It is not on account of his gracious and considerate ways and his delicacy that I love him. No, he has lacks in these regards, but he is well enough just so, and is improving.

It is not on account of his industry that I love him—no, it is not that. I think he has it in him, and I do not know why he conceals it from me. It is my only pain. Otherwise he is frank and open with me, now. I am sure he keeps nothing from me but this. It grieves me that he should have a secret from me, and sometimes it spoils my sleep, thinking of it, but I will put it out of my mind; it shall not trouble my happiness, which is otherwise full to overflowing.

It is not on account of his education that I love him—no, it is not that. He is self-educated, and does really know a multitude of things, but they are not so.

It is not on account of his chivalry that I love him—no, it is not that. He told on me, but I do not blame him; it is a peculiarity of sex, I think, and he did not make his sex. Of course I would not have told on him, I would have perished first; but that is a peculiarity of sex, too, and I do not take credit for it, for I did not make my sex.

The why is it that I love him? *Merely because he is masculine*, I think.

At bottom he is good, and I love him for that, but I could love him without it. If he should beat me and abuse me, I should go on loving him. I know it. It is a matter of sex, I think.

He is strong and handsome, and I love him for that, and I admire him and am proud of him, but I could love him without those qualities. If he were plain, I should love him; if he were a wreck, I should love him; and I would work for him, and slave over him, and pray for him, and watch by his bedside until I died.

Yes, I think I love him merely because he is *mine* and is *masculine*. There is no other reason, I suppose. And so I think it is as I first said: that this kind of love is not a product of reasonings and statistics. It just *comes*—none knows whence—and cannot explain itself. And doesn't need to.

It is what I think. But I am only a girl, and the first that has examined this matter, and it may turn out that in my ignorance and inexperience I have not got it right.

FORTY YEARS LATER

It is my prayer, it is my longing, that we may pass from this life together—a longing which shall never perish from the earth, but shall have place in the heart of every wife that loves, until the end of time; and it shall be called by my name.

But if one of us must go first, it is my prayer that it shall be I; for he is strong, I am weak, I am not so necessary to him as he is to me—life without him would not be life; how could I endure it? This prayer is also immortal, and will not cease from being offered up while my race continues. I am the first wife; and in the last wife I shall be repeated.

AT EVE'S GRAVE

ADAM: Wheresoever she was, *there* was Eden.

A MARK TWAIN SAMPLER

Humor is the good-natured side of any truth.

*

One of the most striking differences between a cat and a lie is that a cat has only nine lives.

*

When I was a boy of fourteen, my father was so ignorant I could hardly stand to have the old man around. But when I got to be twenty-one I was astonished at how much he had learned in seven years.

*

There are three things which come to my mind which I consider excellent advice:

First, girls, don't smoke—that is, don't smoke to excess. I am seventy-three-and-a-half-years-old, and I have been smoking seventy-three of them. But I never smoke to excess—that is, I smoke in moderation, only one cigar at a time.

Second, don't drink—that is, don't drink to excess.
Third, don't marry—I mean, to excess.

*

Of all God's creatures there is only one that cannot be made subservient to the lash. That one is the cat. If man could be crossed with the cat, it would improve man. But it would deteriorate the cat.

*

There is a Moral Sense, and there is an Immoral Sense. History shows us that the Moral Sense enables us to perceive morality and how to avoid it—and the Immoral Sense enables us to perceive immorality and how to enjoy it.

*

It could probably be shown by facts and figures that there is no distinctly native American criminal class except Congress.

*

In the first place God made idiots. That was for practice. Then he made school boards.

*

Man is the only animal that blushes. Or needs to.

*

To be good is noble. But to show others how to be good is nobler—and much less trouble.

*

The holy passion of friendship is of so sweet and steady and loyal and enduring a nature that it will last through an entire lifetime—if not asked to lend money.

*

It is by the goodness of God that in our country we have those three unspeakably precious things: freedom of speech, freedom of conscience, and the prudence never to practice either of them.

*

If you pick up a starving dog and feed him and make him comfortable, he will not bite you. This is the difference between a dog and a man.

*

Be good and you will be lonesome; be virtuous and you will be eccentric.

*

Familiarity breeds contempt—also children.

*

Heaven goes by favor. If it went by merit, you would stay out and your dog would get in.

*

If you don't like the weather in New England, just wait a few minutes.

*

Put all your eggs in one basket—and watch the basket.

*

Part of the secret of success in life is to eat what you like, and let the food fight it out inside.

*

What a good time Adam had. When he said a good thing he knew nobody had said it before.

*

There are two times in a man's life when he should not speculate: when he can't afford it, and when he can.

*

We ought never to do wrong when people are looking.

*

Adam was only human. He did not want the apple for the apple's sake; he wanted it only because it was forbidden. The mistake was in not forbidding the serpent—then he would have eaten the snake.

*

Everything human is pathetic. The secret source of humor itself is not joy but sorrow—sorrow at mankind's lack of humanity. There is no humor in heaven.

SCRUPULOUS TALES BY UNSCRUPULOUS STORY-TELLERS

THE WONDERFUL ADVENTURES OF PAUL BUNYAN

No OTHER *American folk legend has grown so rapidly and so variously as that of Paul Bunyan. He exists in countless versions—a whole volume, entitled* Paul Bunyan, Last of the Frontier Demigods, *is devoted to an analysis of the books concerning this mythical hero. At first glance, he seems a combination of Ulysses, Beowulf, and Munchausen; but, unlike them, his origin was humble rather than noble, occupational rather than literary.*

His imaginary exploits were first recounted around the western lumber camps; he was the superman among the loggers long before the folklorists put him in print. The transition from the oral to the written medium vastly enlarged his audience; today the tales and characters surrounding Bunyan have grown into something like a national epic.

The following excerpts from The Wonderful Adventures of Paul Bunyan *are by Louis Untermeyer.*

Paul's Beginnings

SOME of the old people say he was born in Maine. Some say in Minnesota. Or in Michigan. There are even some who claim he came out of the pine woods of Canada. But they all agree that his name was Paul Bunyan, that he was the hero of the Northwest, and that he grew up to be the biggest thing in the whole country.

How big *was* he?

Well, the folks up in Maine say that when he was born, he outgrew his cradle before he was a week old.

"What'll we do?" said Paul's mother. "That cradle's always been big enough for the other children, and they weren't so puny either."

"Can't you starve him a little, maybe?" asked his father. "The way he goes after food he'll eat us out of house and home—and then he'll eat the house, too!"

"Don't be silly," said his mother, whose name was Jane and who prided herself on her common sense. "A growing child has got to grow. That's what he's here for."

"Well," mumbled Paul's father, who looked like his name, which was Habakkuk, "I don't see exactly what you expect me to do about it when I've got a thousand things to do and when you know—"

"I expect you to stop dragging your muddy boots all over my clean kitchen, and get out your carpenter tools and fix up a bigger cradle," said Paul's mother. And then she began to mop up the floor to show him there was no time to be wasted standing around.

So Paul's father took down his saw and chisel and plane, and made something that was a little like a box and a little like a boat. It was all of six feet long and it took him almost a week to make. But it didn't help. By the time Paul's father was finished, Paul had grown too big to fit.

"Drat the young monster," grumbled Habakkuk, forgetting he was the monster's father. "I'll have to build another cradle."

There was a fringe of woods back of the house, and Paul's father cut down a white birch twelve feet high, hollowed it out, and smoothed the sides until they shone like moonlight on silver. But by the time everything was ready, Paul was a month old and fifteen feet long.

"Well," said Habakkuk grimly, "we'll see if I can't build faster than he can grow."

This time he didn't stop to do any fine carpenterwork; he didn't smooth or polish or try anything fancy. He just took some twenty-foot boards and nailed them together. What he made was a kind of trough. And Paul fitted it to the last quarter of an inch.

But Paul's father had forgotten to put on the rockers. And how are you going to get a baby—even a twenty-foot baby—to close his eyes unless he can rock himself to sleep?

"It's something new," said Habakkuk, pretending he had made it this way on purpose. "It's a floating cradle. We'll anchor it in the Atlantic and the waves will rock him to sleep."

They anchored it in the ocean, right enough. But Paul was restless. He rocked and rocked—and the next night there was a tidal wave that wiped out half a dozen villages on the coast of Maine.

That was the beginning of the trouble. The Maine folks don't rouse easily, but when they get their dander up, they'll tear into a hurricane. But now they were helpless. They couldn't put Paul in prison for he was still an infant; besides, there was no jail big enough to hold him. They looked up the law books, but there was nothing against anyone being twenty feet tall, and there certainly was no law saying a person must stop growing.

While they were talking it over, Paul's mother rushed out of the house.

"It's gone," she cried.

"What's gone?" they echoed, irritated at being interrupted and more irritated because they couldn't come to a decision. "What's gone?"

"The box—the boat—the floating cradle—whatever you call it. And Paul with it. I looked out of the window and I couldn't believe my eyes. And what do you think I saw!"

"Stop jabbering, woman, and come to the point. What *did* you see?"

"He got out of it—don't ask me how! And then he picked it up. And then he waded to shore. And then"—she drew a dramatic breath—"then he disappeared."

"That's just like Paul," said Habakkuk, suddenly proud of the son who had caused all the excitement. "The little fellow was bound to be different. Yes sir—he was nourished on whale's milk and he cut his teeth on a saw. He's going places—going far."

Habakkuk was right. The next day they heard of Paul, he had gone far. He was away out in Minnesota.

Misadventures of Babe

THE blue snow fell—and it continued to fall for weeks without stopping. It spread over Michigan and Minnesota; it stretched across the whole Northwest.

"There must be an end to it," said Paul to Johnny Inkslinger, early one ice-blue morning. "I'm going to do some exploring. Tell the men to go on with their work—they've got plenty of food now—and I'll be back with good news, or I won't be back at all."

So Paul tramped out of the woods, cleared a few rivers, strode across a mountain or two; and there he was on the shores of Lake Superior, greatest of the Great Lakes. Ice-cakes were tossing on freezing waves, booming against each other, thudding and splintering. It sounded as if all the timber in the world were crashing upon the echoing shore.

One huge wave of white water lifted itself above the others; and there, among the grinding ice-cakes, Paul saw two ears. Nothing of the rest of the creature was visible, nothing to show if it were man or monster—just two huge ears. Then they disappeared.

Paul pulled his boots up to his hips and plunged into the icy waters. The waves roared, the ice-cakes heaved and boomed; but there was no sign of life in the vast lake. Just as he was about to turn back, the two ears appeared again. Paul threshed out and caught hold of them. He dragged them toward the shore and, as he pulled them out of the water, a head came into view, then a pair of shoulders, then two forelegs, a spindling body, rear legs, and an unhappy watersoaked tail. It was less than half alive, and all of it was sky-blue.

"Well," said Paul, carrying the little creature to his campfire on the shore, "if there can be blue snow, I suppose there can be a blue calf. Or maybe it's just blue with cold."

But when Paul worked over it and rubbed its joints and warmed it in front of the fire, the calf did not change color. If anything, the color deepened, a brighter, healthier blue. Paul had a flask of buffalo milk with him, and he poured some of this down the calf's throat. The animal didn't open its eyes, but it gave the first sign of life. It shivered a little, and, as Paul bent over, licked his face.

"What a baby," laughed Paul. "I wonder if it thinks I'm its father or its mother. Anyway, a baby it is. And, if it lives, that's what I'll call it: Babe —Babe, the Blue Ox." And he wrapped a blanket around its little frame.

In the morning Babe's eyes were open and his tongue was hanging out.

"Looks as if it might be hungry—and there's no milk left. I don't suppose it will touch my hotcakes and coffee; and now that it's living, it will be a shame if it starves to death."

But Babe ate up the hotcakes, drank the coffee, and, still hungry, took a big bite out of the coffee-pot.

"You're quite a calf!" chuckled Paul, "you'll be quite a companion when you get your strength."

As though in answer, Babe struggled to his feet, lowered his head, and butted Paul from the rear. Whether it was the blow itself or the shock of surprise, Paul was thrown ten feet and came down like a ton of rock.

"You're a little wonder," he laughed, getting to his feet and rubbing the snow out of his eyes. "You're the Babe for me. But I don't dare take you back to camp—not quite yet."

So he began feeding Babe. He tried him on every kind of food he could find—and at the end of every meal, Babe was always hungry. One day after Babe had lapped up six gallons of moose-moss soup, Paul went out to rustle up something for himself. When he returned, Babe had eaten the blankets and was chewing what was left of the pots and pans.

"Babe!" exclaimed Paul, half angry and half amused.

Babe tried to look guilty; he wanted to win Paul's sympathy with a weak and plaintive moo. But what came out of Babe was a monstrous roar, a bellow that shook the hills and knocked against the sky.

"That settles it," said Paul. "We're wasting time. If you're big enough to bellow, you're big enough to work. Now let's see if you can get to camp under your own power."

So they set out. It seemed to Paul that the further they walked, the bigger Babe grew. As he watched the young ox snort and stamp the ground, he could see the head take on weight and character, the chest grow deep and solid, the legs grow stocky, and the whole body toughen with force and energy.

When they reached camp, Babe was a match for Paul. He stood, as though sculptured out of blue stone, a giant among giants. The men were too flabbergasted to say anything. Johnny Inkslinger was the first to measure him.

"Forty-two axe-handles between the eyes—*and* a tobacco box," cried Johnny. "But there's no telling how much he weighs. There aren't scales strong enough."

"But what are you going to do with him?" asked Little Meery.

"Do? Just you wait and see," said Paul. "Just wait until he gets his growth."

Babe was full-grown by the end of the winter. The last of the blue snow melted, but Babe was bluer than ever—bluer and bigger. It was said that Babe was so long in the body you could never see all of him at one time, that Paul had to carry a pair of field glasses so he could see what the Blue Ox was doing with his hind feet. But that's probably an exaggeration. Paul knew what to do with Babe all right; and, for all his size, Babe followed Paul around like a puppy.

Even before Paul had Babe, he had his own way of logging. There never was a logger like Paul, not since acorns first learned to grow up into oaks. Squared timbers were his specialty. He'd pick out a tree. Then he'd give it four cuts—north, south, east, and west—four sharp slices from top to bottom on each side. Then, he would shout, "Timber-r-r!" so everyone would get out of the way. And when he had them all standing square and clean and shiny white, Paul would swing his axe from his waist just as if it were a scythe and he were mowing in a hayfield. Down the trees would come—Paul mowed those timbers an acre at a time—and then they were ready to be taken to market.

Getting them stacked and sorted and ready for shipment was the hardest part of the work. But now that Paul had Babe, it was easy. The Galloping Kid would swing his lasso around the trees and pile up a couple of acres of timber just like cordwood. Then Paul would hitch Babe to the load, and Babe would drag the trees down to the lake—an acre of them at a time—and tip them over into the water, a huge raft of logs.

It was a pretty sight to see. The log-raft floating away, Paul singing and Babe pawing the ground. The big blue water and the white logs flashing by in the sunshine. And there was the smell of the pine and balsam sweetening the air. And there were the sounds of the forest far off—the scolding of a squirrel, the call of a thrush, and the axes biting into the clean wood.

There was no job too hard for Babe. He could haul anything anywhere. Whenever Paul decided to move to better logging grounds, the whole camp would be hitched to Babe; and the Blue Ox would take a deep breath, heave his mighty flanks, and drag the bunkhouses, the kitchen, the dairy, and all the other houses behind him.

Perhaps Babe's hardest task was working on the narrow roads in upper Michigan. It wasn't so much the narrowness as the crookedness. Some of the roads were so crooked that they doubled back on each other, and the men would meet themselves coming back from work. But Paul fixed that. He attached one end of a cable to Babe, and the other end to the crooked road. Then he'd yell, "Pull, Babe—pul-l-l-l!"

And by the end of the winter Babe had straightened out every crooked road in northern Michigan.

But Babe had his troubles, too. He was always hungry; nothing could satisfy his appetite. Before Paul got his own hay farm, it used to take the teamsters six months to bring in one day's feed for the Blue Ox.

So Paul laid out a farm halfway between the camp and the lake—rich black loam laced by trout streams and refreshed, even on the hottest summer day, by underground springs. Since he wasn't a farmer, Paul hired a fellow from Vermont, Phil Plenty, to run the farm.

Phil Plenty was as good as his name. In Vermont they had only two seasons: winter and August. The fields were so rocky that Phil had to blast the boulders so he could plant potatoes; the cold was so intense that, six months out of twelve, the hens laid hard-boiled eggs. But now Phil had the kind of land every farmer dreams about—soil smooth as buckwheat honey, just enough clay to hold, just enough sand for drainage, warm enough for beans, cool enough for peas, not a stone in an acre, fertilized by centuries of minerals and leaf mould—a grower's paradise. Never did a farm yield so abundantly. The tomatoes grew as big as pumpkins; and the pumpkins were so big that, after he had scraped out the meat for pumpkin pies, Hot Biscuit Slim used the pumpkin shells instead of stalls for the young calves. The cabbages grew so large that two men had to saw the stalks before they could bring them in. As for the root vegetables—carrots, beets, parsnips, and turnips—the men could never get to the bottom of them; they kept on breaking them off no matter how deep they dug with their spades, until finally Paul had to invent the steam shovel to get them out of the ground. And the bees! Paul had sent east for a couple of hives so that the men could have honey with their biscuits, and the bees fattened on the giant wildflowers to such an extent that they became the size of eagles.

Babe loved the farm products and—with a few tons of hay as a snack between meals—he thrived on them all. But there was one particular vegetable he loved more than any other: parsnips—and his greed for parsnips was almost the death of him.

Phil Plenty had begun by being fond of Babe. But Babe's appetite was so enormous that Phil couldn't raise things fast enough—Babe was always a crop ahead of him. Phil and his farmers ploughed and fertilized and harrowed and cultivated and weeded and worked the fields—but Babe was always waiting to be fed. A bushel of beans topped off with a wheelbarrowload of cabbages was just a comfortable cud for the Blue Ox. When Paul's loggers complained they weren't getting enough farmstuff, Phil took it to heart. He worked his men harder; but the more things they grew, the more Babe ate. It made Phil bitter.

"That blue monster! All our work for nothing! He'll eat us out of house and home and off the earth! If there were only some way of getting rid of him!"

Phil thought of many plans. But they came to nothing. He dreamed of starving the creature, of going on strike and refusing to raise another vegetable, of an earthquake that would bury Babe or a mighty hurricane that would carry him off. But next morning Babe would be there, bellowing louder than ever for his daily rations. And back to the fields Phil would go with a heavy heart and dark thoughts.

Paul seldom visited the farm, so Phil Plenty was startled when Paul's long shadow fell across the cornfield one evening. "We're moving camp for a while," said Paul. "So you'll have to ship the crops to Wisconsin; I'll leave a few hundred horse teams to carry the stuff over. I'll want lots of fodder and all the fancy extras—especially the bee-hives with the honey. And don't forget Babe. It'll be tough work, and Babe will want plenty of his favorite parsnips."

Parsnips! That gave Phil his great idea. He knew that if he let the first growth of parsnips go to seed, the second growth would come up poison. And it was the second growth that Phil planned to ship to the Wisconsin camp.

"And that," chuckled Phil, "will be the end of that oversized bully, that blighted and bloated old Blue Ox!"

So Phil worked as he had never worked before. He lengthened the working day; he drove his men eighteen hours out of twenty-four; he enlarged the parsnip fields; he raised the greatest crop of second growth parsnips—poison parsnips—ever attempted. At last it was finished. It took two whole weeks just to load the crop, and one cool morning before dawn, horse teams brought the first of the parsnips into the Wisconsin camp.

Babe was just awake. He sniffed the air. He recognized the odor of his favorite delicacy. He pawed the ground, gave a happy snort, and started for the pile.

But Little Meery was ahead of him. Little Meery had always suspected Phil Plenty. He had heard the farmer muttering about Babe, and once he had heard him tell his men that he had a plan to make their work easier for them. Besides, Little Meery didn't like the color of these parsnips. They were a dull red instead of a healthy purple, and when he broke one open, instead of being white it was a sickly gray.

"Babe!" shouted Little Meery. "Keep away from those parsnips!"

But Babe wouldn't be stopped; he hadn't tasted a parsnip for months, and the very look of that promising pile maddened him. Little Meery tried to block him, to stand between the hungry creature and death. Babe lowered his head. He liked Little Meery, and he didn't want to trample him. Instead, Babe filled his cavernous lungs, gave one long snort, and blew Little Meery out of the way.

Little Meery was desperate. But he wasn't defeated. He knew how much Babe meant to Paul; even if it killed him, he determined to save the Blue Ox. But how?

Suddenly Little Meery thought of the bees—the bees that had grown as big as eagles! He could hear their humming, like heavy engines, in the locked hives. There was anger in that humming, for the bees had been robbed of their honey, and the wildflowers of Wisconsin had been withered by the frosts. Little Meery picked himself up and stealthily approached the hives. He lifted the hatch a few inches—a foot—three feet—until the door stood wide open.

The humming changed to a furious buzz; the buzzing became a raging roar. And the bees, thundering out of the hive, lit out for Babe. They flew straight as only a bee can fly—but it was a beeline of eagles, bees with thundering, widespread wings and beaks that tore the flesh. Babe plunged left and right to avoid them. But they came at him like bullets. A hundred at a time settled on him, zooming as they plunged. Babe shook his enormous hide, reared up on his hind legs, rolled over, But, though he crushed half a hundred giant bees, the others held fast. And another hundred flew to the attack. Babe swished his mighty tail, kicked up a cloud of solid dust, and plunged into a bed of briars. But the bees wouldn't be thrown off. They buzzed and roared; Babe blew and bellowed.

By this time the camp was boiling over. The loggers jumped into their boots; the farmers, who had unloaded the crop, picked up shovels and pitchforks. Phil Plenty, who had come along with the first wagonload, sprang at Little Meery.

"What right have you got to interfere?" shouted Phil. "Who told you to loose these bees?"

"That's my business!" Little Meery shouted back. "And your business is to feed Babe—not to poison him!"

"What!" screamed Phil, frightened and furious that his plan had been discovered. "I'll show you whose business is whose!" And he tackled Little Meery around the waist.

That was all the men needed.

"Hurrah for Little Meery!" yelled the loggers, squaring off at the farmers.

"Give it to him, Phil!" yelled the farmers, mixing it with the loggers.

Never had there been such an uproar. The crazy whoops, the battling men, the clash of poles and pitchforks, the violent buzzing of the monstrous bees, the wild bellowing of Babe—the noise was deafening. The loggers and farmers forgot they were human beings and fought like beasts; the beasts forgot they were animals and fought like men. There was blood on the ground when a fringe of pine trees was snapped apart and Paul appeared.

"What's going on here?" said Paul. He didn't have to raise his voice, for everything was suddenly quiet. The men stood ground sheepishly; Babe lowered his head and pawed the earth; the bees flew softly back to their hive.

"How did it happen? Who started it?"

For a while no one answered. Then Little Meery spoke. "It's my fault. I guess I should have waited. Or spoken more civil-like to Phil Plenty. Or something. But when I realized that he had a grudge against Babe, and that he was trying to kill the Blue Ox with poisoned parsnips——"

"Kill Babe!" shouted Paul, losing control of himself. "With poisoned parsnips! You did right, Little Meery, exactly right. I'm grateful to you—and," here he slapped his thighs and laughed, "Babe should be grateful to those bees. As for that scoundrel, Phil Plenty, we'll make him eat those poisoned vegetables, every one down to the last parsnip! And he might as well begin now. Did you hear me, Phil Plenty?"

But there was no reply. As soon as Phil caught sight of Paul's boots crashing among the trees, he disappeared, Some say he jumped into the lake and swam back to Vermont. Some say he ran west and is still running. No one expected him back, and no one ever mentioned his name again.

MORE TALL TALES

The tall tale is marked by the most scrupulous details supplied by the most unscrupulous liars. An old sea captain, quoted by Mark Twain in *Following the Equator*, swore that on one of his Arctic voyages it grew so cold that the mate's shadow froze fast to the deck and it took three men to rip it loose. "And even then," he added, with strict regard for exactness, "they could get only two-thirds of it off." Twain also related that a guide in Havana called attention to two skulls—both of Christopher Columbus: "one when he was a boy and one when he was a man."

They tell of a North Dakota farmer who started out one spring to plow the longest straight furrow in the state. He plowed all through the summer, and planted as he went. In the fall he turned around—and harvested the crop on his way back. . . The dairy farmers of Wisconsin go to even greater lengths in their boasts of the great midwestern dairyland. They say their farms are so huge that when young married couples are sent out to milk the cows, their children come back with the milk. . . But the citizens of the Far West outdo all others in their claims of vast spaces. Distances out there are so great that when the ranchers go to bed they yell "Get up! Get up!" And eight hours later they are waked by the echo.

The hottest place in the country? Southern Texas. But you get used to it—you get so that nothing nowhere else can ever be warm enough.

They tell about a man from Texas who came up to Michigan for work. It was early spring but there was still a touch of snow in the air. But the Texan couldn't stand it. He fell to the sidewalk and stiffened out.

They tried to revive him, but he didn't respond. They tried to pour whiskey down his throat, but it was no use.

"He's dead," they said. "There's nothing we can do with him. We'll have to cremate him and send the ashes home."

So they put his rigid body into a crematory oven and stoked up the fire.

Two hours later they opened the door of the furnace, and there was the man from Texas sitting bolt upright.

"For heaven's sake," he shouted. "Close that door! I'll catch my death of cold in a draft like that!" [1]

Texas—that's the place where everything grows Bigger and Better. Even the dust-storms. They say that out in the Panhandle a rancher went to town to borrow money on his ranch. "Before I can let you have anything," said the banker, shouting above the high wind, "I'll have to go out and take a look at your place." " 'Twon't be necessary," said the rancher. "Here comes the place now."

And the Texas Rangers—they grow big, too. Seems there was a riot or something in one of the towns and the mayor wired for a company of Rangers to come and disperse the mob. Pretty soon a lone Ranger showed up. "Hey," said the mayor, "it's a tough mob—I wired for a company of Rangers, not just one Ranger!"

"Well," drawled the Ranger, "you ain't got but one mob, ain't you?"

Illinois—that's where they get things done, and get them done fast! Especially in Chicago.

It seems a fellow from Chicago was visiting a friend in New York and they were walking down Fifth Avenue together.

"That building there," said the man from Chicago, pointing to one of the big hotels, "how long did it take to put that up?"

"Oh, about two years," said his New York friend.

"Not bad. But in Chicago we could have built it in half the time. And that structure—how long did *that* take?"

"That? the Public Library?" said the New Yorker, trying to outboast the Chicagoan. "Less than four months."

"Four months? We could have done it in two. And this one?" said the visitor, pointing to the hundred stories of the Empire State skyscraper.

"I can't say," replied the New Yorker cautiously. "It wasn't here last night."

[1] A variation of this tall tale was versified by Robert W. Service in "The Cremation of Sam McGee." Mark Twain used the same theme when he described Yuma, Arizona, as the hottest of all places. When a native of Yuma dies, said Twain, and goes to hell, he telegraphs back for his blankets.

Talk about fogs! In California the fogs are so thick that ships often sail right across country till they hit the Sierra Nevada mountains. Sure thing —they even tell how they shingle houses ten feet beyond the roof and nail the shingles to the fog. And it gets so cold at night your shadow freezes on the wall and they have to use blowtorches to thaw it out.

But that ain't nothing compared to Kansas, the home of the tornadoes that will pick up telephone poles and set them down—in the same order—two states away. And the telephone girls with them. Why, one morning at milking time, a Kansas tornado came along and picked up a whole town, and dropped it in Nebraska—including the wheel-tracks.

Wyoming—that's great sheep-herding country. And if you want to hold on to your sheep, you got to know how to count 'em too.

They tell about a famous sheep-counter who in a second could size up a herd, no matter how big it was. He never missed. Well, one day a wealthy rancher took him up a mountain and showed him a huge flock of sheep grazing in the valley. "About how many would you say there was?" asked the rancher.

"I wouldn't say *about* how many," said the sheep-counter. "I'd say there was exactly eight hundred and three sheep."

"That's right," said the rancher. "Now come on over to the other side of the mountain, and see if you can guess how many there is in my other herd."

"I don't guess," said the counter, and walked over to the other side of the mountain. "That's a bigger bunch—there are two thousand, five hundred and sixty-six—no, sixty-seven—sheep there."

"Gosh!" said the rancher. "That's wonderful! How do you do it?"

"It's easy," said the counter. "I just count their feet and divide by four."

"Florida's the place for snakes," said the old cracker, "rattlers, copperheads, moccasins, pretty little coral snakes that are the worst of the lot. One day I was starting to fish near the Okenfenokee when I noticed I had forgotten to bring any bait. I looked around—and there, behind a log, was a great big venomous copperhead with a fat worm in his mouth.

"I needed that worm, so just before the snake swallowed it, I reached into my back-pocket, took out my flask of whiskey, and quickly poured a few drops down the snake's throat. The whiskey was strong, and it must have burned, for the snake dropped the worm and slid off in a hurry.

"I caught my fish all right, a big fellow, too. But I was still short of bait.

"Then I heard a little slithering sound. It was the snake. He was back—with another worm in his mouth."

Talk about worms and things like that—Georgia, *that's* the state for vermin! Especially cockroaches. You never saw such roaches. Big as a man's arm. And smart! Even the small ones—the two-foot cockroaches—would eat you instead of trying to drag you off. They knew if they waited, a larger cockroach would take you away from them.

During the war the Georgia cockroaches won one battle after another. They had organization, they had! Soldiers coming back to the barracks would hear a shuffling noise in the darkness. When the light was switched on, there were the cockroaches—drilling. And they were using the company's rifles!

It's sure a tall country, said the Old Settler. And the stories have to grow to match those tall buildings and that tall timber. Why, out in the Paul Bunyan country—that's the country that runs from Michigan through Minnesota clear out to Oregon and the Pacific—they say the trees grow so high it takes a man a whole week to see the top of them.

And, speaking of Paul Bunyan, that giant lumberjack, did you ever hear of the house he built in the north woods? It was so high that he had to put the last five stories on hinges to let the moon go by.

Yes, sir—and the time Paul Bunyan went hunting. He was the surest shot and the fastest runner that ever waded across the Mississippi. They still talk of it out in the Northwest. It seems Paul sighted a big buck a mile away; it was standing on the edge of a cliff—and Paul knew if he shot him, the buck would fall off the edge and down the cliff. So Paul pulled the trigger—and as soon as the bullet left the gun, Paul ran to where the buck was standing. He ran so fast he got there ahead of the shot—he had to duck his head to let the bullet go by. Yes, sir.

And the buck? Oh, the buck was killed all right. But not by the bullet. When it saw Paul standing there, that buck was plumb scared to death. It died without waiting for the shot to reach it.

That's how things happened in the Paul Bunyan country.

Out in Iowa, where the black loam is twenty feet deep, the corn grows so high they have to climb ladders to get down the ears. Why, once out near Ames there was a boy who saw a shoot of corn coming out of the earth and when it got as high as his shoulder he started climbing it just for fun. Before he could yell "Whoa!" the cornstalk was higher than the silo, and it was still going strong. They had to shoot biscuits up to the boy to keep him from starving. Pretty soon the cornstalk got beyond rifle range and they had to drop food to the boy by airplane. Then they put an axe to the stalk, but even Paul Bunyan and all his loggers couldn't have chopped it down.

It grew all through the winter, and it lasted until the big blizzard the following year. The boy, poor kid, was never seen again. And if you don't believe the story, they'll show you the very place where the cornstalk grew.

In Ohio they still talk about Mike Fink, who was half horse and half alligator and the rest of him snapping turtle. He was the toughest fighter ever was; his fists went round like a windmill, and he never was licked in his life.

Never? Well, just once, maybe. And that was by Davy Crockett's wife—Mary Jane Whirlwind-Thunder-and-Lightning Crockett. Just to scare her, Mike dressed himself in an old alligator skin and came crawling into Mary Jane's cabin.

But Mary Jane didn't scare easy. She put her arm down the alligator's throat and turned him inside out. And there was Mike Fink. She was just about to put her arm down *his* throat when Mike gave a great whoop, dashed off and plunged into the river. He's still there.

And whenever the Ohio goes on a rampage, rising and roaring over its banks, that's Mike Fink thinking of Mary Jane Crockett and lashing his tail. Leastways, that's what they say.

YOUNG MELVIN

STRETCHING the tall tale has always been a favorite American pastime. But tales told when one liar tries to outdo the other are not confined to any one country. The Panchatantra, *a collection of Indian fables dating back to the sixth century, contains anecdotes which any professional liar might envy. For example,* "The Mice That Ate Iron" *has exactly the same twist as "Young Melvin," which was told thirteen hundred years later. The version below is from* God Bless the Devil *by James Aswell.*

AFTER HIS PAPPY passed on Young Melvin decided he wanted to travel. He'd always lived back at the forks of the creek and he hadn't ever at no time been farther from there than the crossroads.

So Young Melvin put out the fire and hid the ax and skillet and called up his hound named Bulger and he was on his way. He went over the hill and a good piece further and he come to the crossroads. He went straight to Old Man Bill Blowdy's house there. He knocked on the door.

Old Man Bill Blowdy come to the door and stuck his nose out the crack. "Who's there?" says he, not daring to come out for fear it was somebody he'd beat in some deal.

"It's me," says Young Melvin. "Just me and my hound dog Bulger."

Old man Bill Blowdy opened the door then and gave Young Melvin a sly look. "Come in and rest and eat a bite," he says, faint-like.

He was a great big fat man that was always grinning and easy talking, like butter wouldn't melt in his mouth. And he was just about the slickest, double-dealingest old cooter in the country or anywhere else at all. Nobody could beat him in a deal—never had, anyway—or when it comes to a lawsuit. Always lawing somebody, Old Man Bill Blowdy was.

"Why don't you come in, Young Melvin?" he says.

"Because I'm on my way, Mister Old Man Bill Blowdy. I'm a-going to town for sure. It's forty miles across two counties but I aim to see that town. That's why I come to see you."

Old Man Bill Blowdy started shutting the door. "Now, now, Young Melvin," he says. "I'm hard up for money right now. I couldn't loan my sweet mother, now in heaven praise be, so much as a penny."

"I don't want no money," says Young Melvin. "I ain't the borrowing kind."

So Old Man Bill Blowdy poked his head out again. "What can I do for you then?"

"Well, it's like this. You're my twenty-third cousin, my only kin in this world. I got a favor for you to do for me."

Old Man Bill Blowdy started sliding that door shut. "No, no favors. I make it a rule to do no favors and don't expect none from nobody."

"It's a favor I'm aiming to pay for," says Young Melvin.

"Oh," says Old Man Bill Blowdy, opening the door once more, "that's different now. Come right in, Young Melvin."

"No sir, no need to come in, for I'd just be coming out again. What I want you to do is keep my fox hound Bulger while I'm off on my travels. I'll pay his keep, I'll pay what's right when I come back to get him."

Old Man Bill Blowdy grinned all over his face. He thought he saw a way to make himself something extry or get him a fox hound one. Everybody knew Young Melvin was simple. Honest as the day's long but simple.

"Why yes," says Old Man Bill Blowdy. "Why yes, I'll keep Bulger for you, Young Melvin, and glad to."

So Young Melvin gave his hound dog over and bid Old Man Bill Blowdy farewell. "I'll be back next week or month or sometime. I don't know how long it'll be, for it's forty miles and across two counties to town."

Well, one day the week or month or anyhow sometime after that, here come Young Melvin down the pikeroad to the crossroads, limping and dusty and easy in mind. He went straight to Old Man Bill Blowdy's house and knocked his knuckles on the door.

Old Man Bill Blowdy stuck his nose out the crack and says, "Who's there?"

"It's me, it's Young Melvin."

"How are you, Young Melvin?"

"Fair to piddling. I walked to town and saw all the sights and then walked back here again. Forty miles and across two counties. Don't never want to roam no more. I'm satisfied now."

Old Man Bill Blowdy started shutting the door. "Glad to hear it, Young Melvin. Next time you come down to the crossroads, drop in and say hello. Any time, just any time, Young Melvin."

"Hold there! Wait a minute!" says Young Melvin.

"I'm busy," says the old man.

But Young Melvin got his foot in the door. "How about Bulger, Old Man Bill Blowdy? How about him?"

Old Man Bill Blowdy kept trying to shut the door and Young Melvin kept shoving his foot in.

"See here!" says Young Melvin. "I mean my fox hound."

"Oh him? Why, I declare to my soul I'd almost forgot that hound dog, Young Melvin. I sure almost had."

"Where is he at?" says Young Melvin, still trying to keep the old man from closing the door.

"I'll tell you," says Old Man Bill Blowdy, still trying to shut it, "I feel mighty bad about it, Young Melvin, but your Bulger is no more."

"How come? What do you mean?"

"Why, he's perished and gone, Young Melvin. The first night after you left I sort of locked him up in that little busted-down house over in the Old Ground. Well sir, Young Melvin, those last renters of mine that lived there was powerful dirty folks. They left the place just lousy with chinch bugs. Them bugs was mortal hungry by this time. So they just eat that Bulger of yours alive. Eat all but the poor thing's bones by morning—and the bones was pretty well gnawed.

"It was my fault in one way. I ought to known better than put your dog in there, Young Melvin. But I done it. So I won't charge you a penny for his keep the night I had him. I aim to do the fair thing."

Well, Old Man Bill Blowdy stuck his sly eye to the crack of the door to see how Young Melvin was taking it. He knew the boy was simple. He figured he had him. Because Old Man Bill Blowdy had Bulger hid out and he aimed to swap him for something to a man he knew in the next county.

So Young Melvin stood there looking like the good Lord had shaken him off His Christian limb. Tears come in his eyes and he sleeved his nose. "That dog was folks to me," he says. "Them chinch bugs don't know what they done to me."

He pulled his foot out of the door and he backed down the steps. He started towards home.

Old Man Bill Blowdy eased out on the porch to watch him go.

About that time Young Melvin turned around. "Mister Old Man Bill Blowdy," he says, "my place is way over the hill and a good piece further. I'm beat out and tired. Wonder if you'd loan me your mule to ride on? I'll bring it back tomorrow."

The old man knew Young Melvin was honest as the livelong day. Besides, he was so tickled with how he'd got him a good hound to swap and it not costing anything that he just called across the way to the crossroads store and got a witness to the loan and let Young Melvin take the mule. It was a fine mule, too, with the three hind ribs showing, the best sort of sign in a mule—shows he's a hard worker.

Next morning Young Melvin never showed up and Old Man Bill Blowdy got worried. He got worrieder still in the middle of the day when no sign of Young Melvin did he see.

But along about afternoon he saw Young Melvin come walking over the hill and down towards the crossroads. He run out on his porch and yelled, "Hey, Young Melvin, where's my mule?"

Young Melvin kept walking. He just shook his head. "I feel mighty bad about that mule, Mister Old Man Bill Blowdy," he called. "I sure do."

"Hey! Wait there!"

But Young Melvin went on, heading for the store at the crossroads.

So Old Man Bill Blowdy was so mad he didn't wait to get his shoes. He just jumped off the porch and run across to Square Rogers, that good old man's house up the road a ways.

"Square," he says, "I want you to handle Young Melvin. He stole my mule."

The Square waked up his deputy and the deputy went down and brought in Young Melvin. Everybody at the crossroads come tagging along behind.

Square said, "Son, they tell me you stole a mule."

"No sir, Square Rogers, I never done it," says Young Melvin.

Old Man Bill Blowdy stomped his bare feet and shook his fists. "He's a bald-faced liar!"

"Curb yourself down, Old Man Bill Blowdy," says the Square, "and let the boy tell his side. Go ahead, Young Melvin."

So Young Melvin told his side, told how he borrowed the mule and started for home. "Well," he says, "you know I live over the hill and a good piece further. I rode that mule to the top of the hill. I was minding my own business and not giving nobody any trouble. Then all on a sudden I see a turkey buzzard dropping down out of the sky. Here it come, dropping fast and crowing like a game rooster.

"First thing I knew that old buzzard just grabbed Old Man Bill Blowdy's mule by the tail and started heaving and the mule's hind legs lifted off the ground and I went flying over his head and hit a rock head-on. I failed in my senses a minute. When I could see straight I saw that buzzard sailing away with the mule, most a mile high and getting littler all the time.

"And that's how it happened. I sure am sorry, but there ain't much you can do with a thing like that, Square."

"Hold on there!" says Square Rogers, that good old man. "I've seen many a turkey buzzard in my time, Young Melvin, but never one that could crow."

"Well," says Young Melvin, "it's surprised me some too. But in a county where chinch bugs can eat up a full-grown fox hound in one night, why I just reckon a turkey buzzard has a right to crow and fly off with a mule if he wants to."

So it all come out and Square Rogers, that good old man, made Old Man

Bill Blowdy fork up Bulger and then Young Melvin gave back the mule.

Old Man Bill Blowdy was mocked down to nothing. He just grieved and pined away and it wasn't no more than ten years before he taken sick and wasted away and died.

CHANGE THE NAME OF ARKANSAS?

"Change the Name of Arkansas?" might come under the heading of Tall Boasters, Bullies, and Braggarts, but its impassioned tone places it in a class of its own. Here a native son harangues his audience with a burst of oratory and a flow of metaphors which, for wild eloquence, has seldom been surpassed on any stage or platform, or in any chamber of senators.

When an Arkansas legislator proposed that the state's name should be changed to something more "dignified," a colleague, whose name was given as Cassius M Johnson, got up and shouted:

Mr. Speaker! You yaller-bellied rascal! For the last thirty minutes I've been trying to get your attention. Every time I caught your eye, you've wormed and squirmed like a hound dog with a flea in his hide. Sir, I say damn you!

Fellow Gentlemen! You may go and tear down the honored pictures from the halls of the U.S. Senate, haul down the Stars and Stripes, desecrate the grave of George Washington and his Uncle Bushrod, curse the Goddess of Liberty, and knock down into the dust the Rights of Man—but your crimes would noway compare with what you propose to do when you change the name of Arkansas!

Change the name of Arkansas? Hell fire no!

Compare the dog fennel to the flaming sunrise—the discordant croak of an old bullfrog to the melodious tones of the nightingale—the classic strains of a Mozart to the bray of a Mexican mule—the feeble arm of a New York dude to the muscles of a Roman gladiator! But *never* change the name of Arkansas! Hell, *no!*

Hide the stars in a lard can, put out the sky to soak in a gourd, hang the Mississippi River on a clothes line, unbuckle the belly band of Time, and turn out the sun and moon to pasture. But you will never change the name of Arkansas!

The world will again pause and wonder at the audacity of the crop-eared, whomper-jawed, half-breed, mean-born, whiskey-soaked hyena who has proposed to change the name of Arkansas! He has just started to climb the political banister and wants to knock the hayseeds out of his hair, pull the splinters out of his big feet, and push on up to the governorship. He may make it, may purely blunder like a blind bull to that high office, but—

Change the name of Arkansas? Hell, Sir, *no!*

BACKWOODS WISDOM

The best barrel is only as strong as its weakest hoop.

*

An empty bag cannot support itself.

*

Ignore the bait if you don't want to struggle on the hook.

*

It takes two to make a bargain—even a bad one.

*

A poor bush is a better haven than a fine open field.

*

The back is fitted to the burden.

*

A dog, a woman, and a walnut tree,
The more you beat them, the better they be.

A crawling worm produces silk;
The blackest cow will give white milk.

*

No man is completely finished till he is dead.

*

Men's skins have many colors, but human blood is always red.

*

Don't wade if your feet can't touch the bottom.

*

Don't try to clean a blot with dirty fingers.

*

In the long run, the cheapest is the dearest.

*

The more chips, the poorer the carpenter.

*

Beware of even a little slip;
The smallest leak can sink a ship.

*

Leave the flurry
To the masses;
Take your time
And shine your glasses.

PROMISE AND FULFILLMENT

PROMISE AND FULFILLMENT

Grant's makeshift administration left a wide wake of corruption. Political leadership was at its lowest level; both parties were ethically bankrupt; the people were cynical. Since the Republicans had been discredited because of Grant's laxity and his affiliations with the rich, the Democrats had high hopes for their candidate, the upright reformer, Samuel J. Tilden, in 1876. The Republicans countered with the inoffensive Rutherford B. Hayes. Tilden was the winner by some three hundred votes, but the Republicans disputed the returns from three southern states. After shameless bargaining, a deal was made by which the three states threw their electoral votes to the Republican candidate, and Hayes was named the nineteenth president of the United States.

Hayes proved to be far more of an individual than his party had expected. He turned against the reactionaries, challenged Congress by vetoing some of its pet appropriations, and ended the pernicious Reconstruction by removing federal troops from the South. A transplanted Puritan born in Ohio, he was a severe contrast to his predecessor. Unlike Grant, Hayes was a moralizing teetotaller; his wife was nicknamed "Lemonade Lucy" because she refused to serve wine or liquor in the White House.

Success—success at any cost—was still a powerful slogan. It was the era of the "robber barons," when Jay Gould, the fraudulent stock manipulator, ran away with six million dollars, evaded the law, and said to his confederates, "Nothing is lost, boys, save honor." It was also the time of the "Horatio Alger" books, a series of more than one hundred volumes, which celebrated the theme of "rags to riches" and taught that bootblacks, newsboys, and other submerged heroes could do very well by doing good. Two hundred million copies of books with such titles as *Tattered Tom*, *Luck and Pluck*, *Brave and Bold* showed the profitable rewards of hard work, no play, and unremitting sanctimoniousness.

Swifter communications were followed by a greater sense of ease and more luxurious ways of living. Alexander Graham Bell demonstrated his invention of the telephone in 1877; a year later Thomas A. Edison exhibited the fabulous phonograph and, within another few months, the first practical electric light.

The expanding country continued to expand and the frontier continued to advance. There were the inevitable conflicts provoked by progress. Before the end of the nineteenth century the conquest of the continent was a fact, but not before clashes had ensued between the agrarians who had once composed the greater part of the population and the industrialists who were to dominate the country; between the cattlemen, who had followed the miners of the Gold Rush to the open ranges and to whom the vast grassland of the West was a limitless free pasture, and the farming homesteaders, who planned to build new commonwealths by turning the grazing land into immense corn and wheat fields. The Union Pacific railroad had spanned the country in 1869. East and West were united by bonds of iron. More than twenty thousand people strained tensely on the border of a former Indian preserve for the firing of a marshal's gun which was to declare Oklahoma open to settlers, and on April 22, 1889, feverish "boomers" in wagons, on horseback, and even on foot took possession of almost two million acres of fertile land. Great silver deposits were discovered in Nevada. Another gold rush brought more than fifty thousand prospectors to Colorado and built the cities of Boulder, Leadville, and Denver. Brigham Young and his devoutly hard-working Mormons changed the desert of Utah into flourishing farms.

Territories became states; villages turned into towns; focal centers offered the lure and challenge of the metropolis. Urbanization brought about new comforts and new problems, the mingling of many creeds and many kinds of people resulted in a melting-pot which sometimes boiled over. Millionaires' mansions existed side by side with pestilential slums and boss-driven sweatshops. Social reformers and newly-formed labor unions protested against a system which permitted such inhuman extremes, but the voices favoring the profitable *laissez faire* of the existing order prevailed.

For a while the gospel of wealth and the country's future seemed synonymous. Many statesmen urged that America's "manifest destiny" be extended not only to the so-called backward nations but to nearby neighbors. Long before the Pacific islands of Samoa and Hawaii were annexed, there was talk of an American Empire. Some saw these portents as dangerous omens, others maintained that they were natural fulfillments of the nation's golden promise. Business was booming; the land was bursting with energy; everything was moving onward and upward. Few could resist the impulse to try something new, do something spectacular, make a name and a fortune.

One of those who resisted and who, in spite of a life of studied seclusion, made a lasting name for herself was an unknown spinster, an unpublished poet, Emily Dickinson.

EMILY DICKINSON

[1830–1886]

Although the greatest of American women poets composed more than seventeen hundred poems, only seven of them appeared in print during her lifetime, and these were published without her cooperation. "Publication is the auction of the mind," declared the self-effacing recluse who considered herself a nobody, and added:

How dreary to be somebody!
How public, like a frog,
To tell your name the livelong day
To an admiring bog!

Emily Dickinson was born December 10, 1830, in Amherst, Massachusetts, at that time a community so rural that her mother's dower had been brought to the town by ox-cart. Her father, Edward Dickinson, was a lawyer, legislator, and member of the Governor's Council. There were two other children: an older sister, Lavinia, and a younger brother, Austin. All three adored their father. They also stood in awe of him: "When father is asleep on the sofa," said Emily, "the house is full." Even when he was too occupied with his work to pay attention to them, they were conscious of his omnipresence and even his omniscience. He forbade them to read "romances"—he felt that the Bible offered sufficient mental stimulus—and they tried to hide books of fiction in bushes and a hollow tree. Nevertheless, in spite of his rigorous Puritanism, Emily never heard him utter a harsh word; when he died she wrote: "His heart was pure and terrible, and I think no other like it exists. I am glad there is immortality, but would have tested it myself before entrusting him."

She attended Amherst Academy and Mount Holyoke Female Seminary; she was a model student in most ways, but she was noncomformist when it came to religious instruction. The pupils were supposed to be strictly pietistic, but Emily could not repeat the sanctimonious platitudes about sin and salvation. Words to her were not to be used lightly; they were—or should be—the considered expression of thoughts, decisions, and deeds. When Mary Lyons, first principal of the Seminary, insisted that "a young lady should be so educated that she can go as a missionary at a fortnight's notice," Emily rebelled, although she commented drily that she had "no particular objection to becoming a Christian." When Miss Lyons urged that

Christmas should not be merry but should be observed as a fast day, Emily mockingly condemned herself as "one of the bad ones," and when she returned home for the holidays persuaded her father that she need not return to Mount Holyoke.

Until her mid-twenties, she was lively, quick-witted, and playfully bantering. At eighteen she was strongly attracted to Benjamin Franklin Newton, a law student in her father's law office and, since he was nine years older and a reader of Emerson and other unorthodox writers, constituted him her "preceptor." When he died prematurely at thirty-two, she felt that an important phase of her life had ended. About a year later she fell in love precipitously and irrevocably. In Philadelphia, in the spring of 1854, on her way back from Washington, which she had visited with her father, she met the Reverend Charles Wadsworth. He was forty, married, Pastor of the Arch Street Presbyterian Church, and completely unaware of the emotion he had aroused.

Emily Dickinson realized that nothing could come of her love. She put her passion into words never shown to anyone; the unacknowledged physical longing was transcended by the metaphysical expression of her abnegation. Her poems—hundreds of them written between her twenty-seventh and thirty-fourth years—became wish-fulfillments of dreams and dramatizations of vain hopes, imagined delights, and her long frustration. In 1862 alone she wrote some three hundred and sixty poignant and often desperate poems. There may have been two or three meetings with Wadsworth after the encounter in Philadelphia—social visits rather than the clandestine trysts hinted by scandal-loving gossips—but, except for a suggested correspondence of which there is no record, there was no further contact. The Reverend Wadsworth was called to a pulpit in San Francisco, and in 1882 he died.

By this time Emily's infatuation had grown into an obsession. Wadsworth's portraits and a privately printed book of his sermons were among her most cherished possessions. She said, "I do not yet fathom that he has died, and hope I may not till he assists me in another world." Recalling her early attachment to Newton, she mourned her double loss in eight lines of pitiful resignation:

My life closed twice before its close;
   It yet remains to see
If Immortality unveil
   A third event to me,
So huge, so hopeless to conceive,
   As these that twice befell.

Parting is all we know of heaven,
And all we need of hell.

Emily Dickinson was thirty-two when she turned for counsel to Thomas Wentworth Higginson, a prominent man of letters, frequent contributor to the Atlantic Monthly, and reputed friend of young authors. With her first letter she enclosed four poems. Higginson did not quite know what to make of them or her. Years after her death he wrote: "She was much too enigmatical for me." Even when she came to consider him her friend and granted him an occasional interview, he had an instinct which told him "that the slightest attempt at direct examination would make her withdraw into her shell. . . The bee himself did not evade the schoolboy more than she evaded me; and even at this day I still stand somewhat bewildered, like the boy."

Higginson ventured to criticize her peculiar style—later, as her first editor, when her books were posthumously published, he "corrected" her poems by changing the punctuation, modifying the odd syntax, and even altering the characteristically suspended rhymes. At first, she seemed to welcome his advice. In her second letter to him she wrote:

> Thank you for the surgery; it was not so painful as I supposed. I bring you others, as you ask, though they might not differ. While my thought is undressed, I can make the distinction; but when I put them in the gown they look alike and numb.
>
> You asked how old I was? I made no verse, but one or two, until this winter, sir.
>
> I had a terror since September, I could tell to none; and so I sing, as the boy does of the burying ground, because I am afraid.
>
> You inquire about my books. For poets, I have Keats, and Mr. and Mrs. Browning. For prose, Mr. Ruskin, Sir Thomas Browne and the Revelations. I went to school, but in your manner of the phrase had no education. When a little girl, I had a friend who taught me Immortality; but venturing too near, himself, he never returned. Soon after my tutor died, and for several years my lexicon was my only companion. Then I found one more, but he was not contented I be his scholar, so he left the land.
>
> You ask of my companions. Hills, sir, and the sundown, and a dog large as myself, that my father bought me. They are better than beings because they know, but do not tell; and the noise in the pool at noon excels my piano.
>
> I have a brother and sister; my mother does not care for thought,

> and father, too busy with his briefs to notice what we do. (He buys me many books, but begs me not to read them, because he fears they joggle the mind.) They are religious, except me, and address an eclipse, every morning, whom they call their "Father."
>
> But I fear my story fatigues you. I would like to learn. Could you tell me how to grow, or is it unconveyed, like melody or witchcraft?
>
> You speak of Mr. Whitman. I never read his book, but was told that it was disgraceful...

For a while, she sent verses to Higginson, and his guarded praise pleased her; but when he found her "spasmodic" and "uncontrolled" she retreated. He failed to appreciate the poet, but she hoped he would understand the person, for she needed sympathy more than applause, and it was as a friend that she continued to correspond. When he asked for her picture, she replied:

> Could you believe me without? I had no portrait, now, but am small, like the wren; and my hair is bold, like the chestnut burr; and my eyes, like the sherry in the glass that the guest leaves. Would this do just as well?

She kept up the pretense of being Higginson's "scholar," but she went her own way in her poetic as well as her private life. She had withdrawn from all activities after Wadsworth's departure to California. She shut out the giddy world. Refusing to wear anything with color, she dressed only in vestal white. She loved music, but declined to join others in the music-room and remained seated alone outside in the hall. She immured herself in her home, saying "I do not cross my father's ground to any house or town." She made all the family bread because hers was the only bread her father liked. She cared deeply for a few friends, but was afraid of most people. Chiefly she distrusted their thinking, or lack of thinking. "How do most people live without any thoughts? There are many people in the world—you must have noticed them in the street—how do they live? How do they get strength to put on their clothes in the morning?" She abjured the usual standards in custom and criticism. In what Higginson called a "crowning extravaganza" and which has become a criterion of personal taste and emotional reaction, she remarked:

> If I read a book and it makes my whole body so cold no fire can ever warm me, I know that is poetry. If I feel physically as if the top of my head were taken off, I know that is poetry. These are the only ways I know. Is there any other way?"

As she grew older her "eccentricities" became more marked. In her forties she had a long and intimate correspondence with the venerable Judge Otis P. Lord, another platonic love-affair which was also a psychological search to recover the father she had lost and the lover she had never known. In her fifties she continually meditated on life and eternity, but she felt no need of religion and never went to church. Townspeople hinted that she was not altogether sane when she shut herself apart and sent little gifts accompanied by cryptic verses to puzzled neighbors and uncomprehending children. She became the town oddity.

At fifty-three she suffered a nervous breakdown. Recovering, she maintained that "the crisis of the sorrow of so many years is all that tires me." Two years later she contracted Bright's disease, and died May 15, 1886, in the house in which she was born.

Her poetry is distinct from any other ever composed. Emily Dickinson wrote both as a bereaved woman and a fanciful child. She could be harrowing and coy in the same poem, woefully distracted and wilfully arch. But the pertness has a way of turning into pure perception and the child suddenly becomes a seer. Her style is not a combination of styles but a contradiction of styles, reticent and irrepressible, simple and obscure, and always startling.

The forms which she preferred consisted of little stanzas, mostly short four-line verses as precise as a hymn-tune, but, small though they were, they contain immensities. They are not "orderly" or conventionally shaped; the very irregularities are evidence that she borrowed from no other poet, and her wayward diction has its own piquant charm. Her images, sometimes exact, sometimes extravagant, fuse the thing observed and the thing imagined. A dog's padding is translated into "belated feet, like intermittent plush"; a storm agitates "a strange mob of panting trees"; a train is a monstrous cat that can "lap the miles and lick the valleys up"; a snake can create horror cold as "zero at the bone"; frost is "the blond assassin"; the lightning "skips like mice"; music is "the silver strife"; tension is achieved in "the accent of a coming foot."

All her writings were collected and published posthumously. The first volume, Poems of Emily Dickinson, edited by Thomas Wentworth Higginson and a neighbor, Mabel Loomis Todd, appeared in 1890, four years after her death. Subsequent collections were issued sporadically during the next half-century. Finally the first authentic text was contained in a three-volume set edited by Thomas H. Johnson in 1955. In 1958 the Dickinson canon was completed when Johnson published three volumes of her letters.

Inimitable and unique, Emily Dickinson remains something of a mystery. The secret of her life has never been completely revealed, nor have the depths of her poetry been fully sounded. There is a greater sense of awe in her irreverence than in most religious disquisitions, more wonder in her playful perversities than in volumes of solemnities. Strangely free of the writer's hunger for publication, the natural hope of acclaim, or even the need of response, she charged the literature of her country with an intensified poetry which no woman, with the possible exception of Sappho, has surpassed.

I NEVER SAW A MOOR

I never saw a moor,
I never saw the sea;
Yet know I how the heather
  looks,
And what a wave must be.

I never spoke with God,
Nor visited in Heaven;
Yet certain am I of the spot
As if the chart were given.

ELYSIUM IS AS FAR

Elysium is as far as to
The very nearest room,
If in that room a friend await
Felicity or doom.

What fortitude the soul
  contains,
That it can so endure
The accent of a coming foot,
The opening of a door.

I NEVER LOST AS MUCH

I never lost as much but twice,
And that was in the sod;
Twice have I stood a beggar
Before the door of God!

Angels, twice descending,
Reimbursed my store.
Burglar, banker, father,
I am poor once more!

THE SOUL SELECTS

The soul selects her own society,
Then shuts the door;
On her divine majority
Obtrude no more.

Unmoved, she notes the chariots pausing
At her low gate;
Unmoved, an emperor is kneeling
Upon her mat.

I've known her from an ample nation
Choose one;
Then close the valves of her attention
Like stone.

THE HEART ASKS PLEASURE FIRST

The heart asks pleasure first;
And then, excuse from pain;
And then, those little anodynes
That deaden suffering;
And then, to go to sleep;
And then, if it should be
The will of its Inquisitor,
The liberty to die.

I CANNOT LIVE WITH YOU

I cannot live with you.
It would be life,
And life is over there
Behind the shelf

The sexton keeps the key to,
Putting up
Our life, his porcelain,
Like a cup

Discarded of the housewife,
Quaint or broken;
A newer Sèvres pleases,
Old ones crack.

I could not die with you,
For one must wait
To shut the other's gaze down,
You could not.

And I, could I stand by
And see you freeze,
Without my right of frost,
Death's privilege?

Nor could I rise with you,
Because your face
Would put out Jesus',
That new grace

Grow plain and foreign
On my homesick eye,
Except that you, than he
Shone closer by.

They'd judge us–how?
For you served Heaven, you know,
Or sought to;
I could not,

Because you saturated sight,
And I had no more eyes
For sordid excellence
As Paradise.

And were you lost, I would be,
Though my name
Rang loudest
On the heavenly fame.

And were you saved,
And I condemned to be
Where you were not,
That self were hell to me.

So we must keep apart,
You there, I here,
With just the door ajar
That oceans are,
And prayer,
And that pale sustenance,
Despair!

I HEARD A FLY BUZZ

I heard a fly buzz when I died;
  The stillness round my form
Was like the stillness in the air
  Between the heaves of storm.

The eyes beside had wrung them
    dry,
  And breaths were gathering sure
For that last onset, when the king
  Be witnessed in his power.

I willed my keepsakes, signed away
  What portion of me I
Could make assignable,–and then
  There interposed a fly,

With blue, uncertain, stumbling
    buzz,
  Between the light and me;
And then the windows failed, and
    then
  I could not see to see.

THE BRAIN IS WIDER THAN THE SKY

The brain is wider than the sky,
  For, put them side by side,
The one the other will include
  With ease, and you beside.

The brain is deeper than the sea,
  For, hold them, blue to blue,
The one the other will absorb,
  As sponges, buckets do.

The brain is just the weight of
    God,
  For, lift them, pound for
    pound,
And they will differ, if they do,
  As syllable from sound.

AUTUMN

The morns are meeker than they
  were,
The nuts are getting brown;
The berry's cheek is plumper,
The rose is out of town.

The maple wears a gayer scarf,
The field a scarlet gown.
Lest I should be old-fashioned,
I'll put a trinket on.

BECAUSE I COULD NOT STOP FOR DEATH

Because I could not stop for Death,
He kindly stopped for me;
The carriage held but just ourselves
And Immortality.

We slowly drove, he knew no haste,
And I had put away
My labor, and my leisure too,
For his civility.

We passed the school where children played,
Their lessons scarcely done;
We passed the fields of grazing grain,
We passed the setting sun.

We paused before a house that seemed
A swelling on the ground;
The roof was scarcely visible,
The cornice but a mound.

Since then 'tis centuries, but each
Feels shorter than the day
I first surmised the horses' heads
Were toward eternity.

THE MOUNTAINS GROW UNNOTICED

The mountains grow unnoticed,
Their purple figures rise
Without attempt, exhaustion,
Assistance or applause.

In their eternal faces
The sun with broad delight
Looks long—and last—and golden
For fellowship at night.

SUCCESS IS COUNTED SWEETEST

Success is counted sweetest
By those who ne'er succeed.
To comprehend a nectar
Requires sorest need.

Not one of all the purple host
Who took the flag to-day
Can tell the definition,
So clear, of victory,

As he, defeated, dying,
On whose forbidden ear
The distant strains of triumph
Break, agonized and clear.

ALTHOUGH I PUT AWAY HIS LIFE

Athough I put away his life,
An ornament too grand
For forehead low as mine to wear,
This might have been the hand

That sowed the flowers he preferred,
Or smoothed a homely pain—
Or pushed the pebble from his path,
Or played his chosen tune

On lute the least, the latest,
But just his ear could know
That what soe'er delighted it
I never would let go.

The foot to bear his errand,
A little boot I know
Would leap abroad like antelope
With just the grant to do

His weariest commandment
A sweeter to obey
Than "Hide and Seek," or skip to flutes,
Or all day chase the bee.

Your servant, Sir, will weary,
The surgeon will not come,
The world will have its own to do,
The dust will vex your fame.

The cold will force your tightest door
Some February day,
But say my apron bring the sticks
To make your cottage gay,

That I may take that promise
To Paradise with me—
To teach the angels avarice
Your kiss taught to me.

SO WELL THAT I CAN LIVE WITHOUT

So well that I can live without—
I love Thee;
Then how well is that?
As well as Jesus?
Prove it me
That He loved men
As I love Thee.

KEEPING THE SABBATH

SOME keep the Sabbath going to
church;
I keep it staying at home,
With a bobolink for a chorister,
And an orchard for a dome.

Some keep the Sabbath in
surplice;
I just wear my wings,
And instead of tolling the bell
for church,
Our little sexton sings.

God preaches,—a noted
clergyman,—
And the sermon is never long;
So instead of getting to heaven
at last,
I'm going all along!

THE FROST

APPARENTLY with no surprise
To any happy flower,
The frost beheads it at its play
In accidental power.
The blond assassin passes on,
The sun proceeds unmoved
To measure off another day
For an approving God.

INDIAN SUMMER

THESE are the days when birds come back,
A very few, a bird or two,
To take a backward look.

These are the days when skies put on
The old, old sophistries of June,
A blue and gold mistake.

Oh, fraud that cannot cheat the bee,
Almost thy plausibility
Induces my belief,

Till ranks of seeds their witness bear,
And softly through the altered air
Hurries a timid leaf!

Oh, sacrament of summer days,
Oh, last communion in the haze,
Permit a child to join,

Thy sacred emblems to partake,
Thy consecrated bread to break,
Taste thine immortal wine!

THE SKY IS LOW

The sky is low, the clouds are mean,
A travelling flake of snow
Across a barn or through a rut
Debates if it will go.

A narrow wind complains all day
How some one treated him;
Nature, like us, is sometimes caught
Without her diadem.

PUBLICATION IS THE AUCTION

Publication is the auction
Of the mind of man,
Poverty be justifying
For so foul a thing.

Possibly,—but we would rather
From our garret go
White unto the White Creator,
Than invest our snow.

Thought belongs to Him who
  gave it—
Then to him who bear
Its corporeal illustration.
Sell the royal air

In the parcel,—be the merchant
Of the Heavenly Grace,
But reduce no human spirit
To disgrace of price!

PAIN HAS AN ELEMENT OF BLANK

Pain has an element of blank;
It cannot recollect
When it began, or if there were
A day when it was not.

It has no future but itself,
Its infinite realms contain
Its past, enlightened to perceive
New periods of pain.

HOPE IS THE THING WITH FEATHERS

Hope is the thing with feathers
That perches in the soul,
And sings the tune without the words,
And never stops at all,

And sweetest in the gale is heard;
And sore must be the storm
That could abash the little bird
That kept so many warm.

I've heard it in the chillest land,
And on the strangest sea;
Yet, never, in extremity,
It asked a crumb of me.

THE WIND TAPPED LIKE A TIRED MAN

The wind tapped like a tired man,
And like a host, "Come in,"
I boldly answered; entered then
My residence within

A rapid, footless guest,
To offer whom a chair
Were as impossible as hand
A sofa to the air.

No bone had he to bind him,
His speech was like the push
Of numerous humming birds at
once
From a superior bush.

His countenance a billow,
His fingers, if he pass,
Let go a music, as of tunes
Blown tremulous in glass.

He visited, still flitting,
Then, like a timid man,
Again he tapped—'twas flurriedly—
And I became alone.

THERE CAME A WIND LIKE A BUGLE

There came a wind like a bugle;
It quivered through the grass,
And a green chill upon the heat
So ominous did pass
We barred the windows and the doors
As from an emerald ghost;
The doom's electric moccasin
That very instant passed.
On a strange mob of panting trees,
And fences fled away,
And rivers where the houses ran
The living looked that day.
The bell within the steeple wild
The flying tidings whirled.

How much can come
And much can go,
And yet abide the world!

THE SNAKE

A narrow fellow in the grass
Occasionally rides;
You may have met him,—did
  you not?
His notice sudden is.

The grass divides as with a comb,
A spotted shaft is seen;
And then it closes at your feet
And opens further on.

He likes a boggy acre,
A floor too cool for corn.
Yet when a child, and barefoot,
I more than once, at morn,

Have passed, I thought, a
  whip-lash
Unbraiding in the sun,—
When, stooping to secure it,
It wrinkled and was gone.

Several of nature's people
I know, and they know me;
I feel for them a transport
Of cordiality;

But never met this fellow,
Attended or alone,
Without a tighter breathing,
And zero at the bone.

NO RACK CAN TORTURE ME

No rack can torture me,
My soul's at liberty.
Behind this mortal bone
There knits a bolder one

You cannot prick with saw,
Nor rend with scymitar.
Two bodies therefore be;
Bind one, and one will flee.

The eagle of his nest
No easier divest
And gain the sky,
Than mayest thou,

Except thyself may be
Thine enemy.
Captivity is consciousness;
So's liberty.

HENRY ADAMS

[1838–1918]

HENRY ADAMS WAS A SCION of one of America's most distinguished families. His great-grandfather, John Adams, was the country's second president; his grandfather, John Quincy Adams, was its sixth president; his father, Charles Francis Adams, was a diplomat and foreign minister; his mother, Abigail Brooks, was the daughter of Boston's wealthiest citizen. Henry (Brooks) Adams was born in Boston, Massachusetts, February 16, 1838, and, as he wrote in his Autobiography, "Probably no child born in the year held better cards."

Nevertheless, Henry Adams did not feel that his illustrious and aristocratic antecedents were advantages. On the contrary, he believed that the traditions of the past laid a dead hand on the individual; and it was as an individual, distinct from his heritage, that Henry Adams wanted to live. A delicate child—he almost succumbed to a fever when he was three—and an indifferent student, he accepted formal education without enthusiasm. He found his courses at Harvard unsatisfactory; interested only in the teaching of Lowell and Agassiz, he graduated without honors.

In his twenty-first year he went to Germany to study civil law, but academic life bored him and he drifted to France and Italy. Within two years he returned to the United States, and, after another attempt to complete his law studies, decided against the profession and became secretary to his father, who was then a Congressman. When his father was appointed Minister to England, he went along and remained abroad seven years. He was thirty-two when he accepted an assistant-professorship at Harvard and, at the same time, the editorship of the North American Review.

His marriage to Marion Hopper at thirty-four should have made him happy; his wife was, like him, an intellectual from a prominent and wealthy family. But thirteen years later, fearing mental illness, she committed suicide; his sister, the only other woman he loved, had died of an infection two years before his marriage. Adams gave up his position at Harvard to spend his time writing in Washington and traveling about the world. When he was not globe-trotting, he was a recluse.

His writings consist of more than a dozen volumes, several of which were issued anonymously or pseudonymously. Adams went to great lengths to conceal the authorship of Democracy, a novel with a background of official Washington, and he was not known as its creator until after his death. Another novel, Esther, carried the pen-name of "Frances Snow Compton;" Adams paid for its publication and forbade the publisher to advertise the book. His two major works, Mont-Saint-Michel and Chartres and The Education of Henry Adams, were privately printed, and copies were sent to his friends, for whom, he said, he had written them. He thought that the nine-volume History of the United States During the Administrations of Jefferson and Madison was his most important accomplishment, but he maintained that few people read it and that no one liked it.

Adams lived until he was past eighty, and died in Washington, March 27, 1918. His body was buried beneath the symbolic statue St. Gaudens had designed for his wife's grave over which, according to his will, there was no name, date, or inscription of any kind. His Degradation of the Democratic Dogma was published posthumously by his brother, Brooks Adams, author of The Emancipation of Massachusetts, The Law of Civilization and Decay, and other vivid historical studies.

Beginning as an impassioned Puritan with a zeal for reform, Henry Adams became a mystic in love with the Madonna and a pessimist who despaired of everything. To a friend who inquired about his health, he replied: "I am well, as far as I know, with everything in the world except what I want; and with nothing to complain of, except the universe." He had taught medieval history at Harvard, and when, five years after the tragic death of his wife, he went to the Paris exhibition, the contrast between the medieval and the modern world convinced him there were two main forces in the world: the Virgin and the Dynamo. His adoration of the Virgin, the keynote of Mont-Saint-Michel and Chartres, was a strange departure for a descendant of the Puritans, but Adams felt that the world was lost without unity, and an infallible faith, and perhaps even with it. Everything, he came to believe, was running down, degraded and doomed, from the Adams family to the solar system. He knew that escape into the quiet and creative thinking of medievalism was impossible; order was an illusion in a world where men preferred chaos; without art and religion humanity was hopelessly bound to its inventions and its enslaving technological "progress."

Adams' sense of universal failure may have stemmed from a personal inability to live up to what a family of powerful politicians may have expected of him. He told his brother, "I never will make a speech, *never run for office, never belong to a party." The portrait of a highly fastidious soul standing against an insensitive world is so dramatically drawn in* The Education of Henry Adams *that the work reads like a piece of fiction. It is not a completely candid autobiography: it omits many things where the man's inner feelings were deeply involved, notably any allusion to his wife's suicide or even to his marriage. Nevertheless, it remains a fascinating document: a critical and dynamic examination of history as well as a challenging look at worldly philosophy, and an ironic appraisal of the ideas that make for the confusing multiplicity of the twentieth century. First and last, however, it presents the struggle of a self-probing (and sometimes self-pitying) spirit caught in the toils of a rushing and, to him, directionless civilization.*

THE BOYHOOD OF HENRY ADAMS

From *The Education of Henry Adams*

UNDER THE SHADOW of Boston State House, turning its back on the house of John Hancock, the little passage called Hancock Avenue runs, or ran, from Beacon Street, skirting the State House grounds, to Mount Vernon Street, on the summit of Beacon Hill; and there, in the third house below Mount Vernon Place, February 16, 1838, a child was born, and christened later by his uncle, the minister of the First Church after the tenets of Boston Unitarianism, as Henry Brooks Adams.

Had he been born in Jerusalem under the shadow of the Temple and circumcised in the Synagogue by his uncle the high priest, under the name of Israel Cohen, he would scarcely have been more distinctly branded, and not much more heavily handicapped in the races of the coming century, in running for such stakes as the century was to offer; but, on the other hand, the ordinary traveller, who does not enter the field of racing, finds advantage in being, so to speak, ticketed through life, with the safeguards of an old, established traffic. Safeguards are often irksome, but sometimes convenient, and if one needs them at all, one is apt to need them badly. A hundred years earlier, such safeguards as his would have secured any young man's success; and although in 1838 their value was not very great compared with what they would have had in 1738, yet the mere accident of starting a twentieth-century career from a nest of associations so colonial—

so troglodytic—as the First Church, the Boston State House, Beacon Hill, John Hancock and John Adams, Mount Vernon Street and Quincy, all crowding on ten pounds of unconscious babyhood, was so queer as to offer a subject of curious speculation to the baby long after he had witnessed the solution. What could become of such a child of the seventeenth and eighteenth centuries, when he should wake up to find himself required to play the game of the twentieth? Had he been consulted, would he have cared to play the game at all, holding such cards as he held, and suspecting that the game was to be one of which neither he nor any one else back to the beginning of time knew the rules or the risks or the stakes? He was not consulted and was not responsible, but had he been taken into the confidence of his parents, he would certainly have told them to change nothing as far as concerned him. He would have been astounded by his own luck. Probably no child, born in the year, held better cards than he. Whether life was an honest game of chance, or whether the cards were marked and forced, he could not refuse to play his excellent hand. He could never make the usual plea of irresponsibility. He accepted the situation as though he had been a party to it, and under the same circumstances would do it again, the more readily for knowing the exact values. To his life as a whole he was a consenting, contracting party and partner from the moment he was born to the moment he died. Only with that understanding—as a consciously assenting member in full partnership with the society of his age—had his education an interest to himself or to others.

As it happened, he never got to the point of playing the game at all; he lost himself in the study of it, watching the errors of the players; but this is the only interest in the story, which otherwise has no moral and little incident. A story of education—seventy years of it—the practical value remains to the end in doubt, like other values about which men have disputed since the birth of Cain and Abel; but the practical value of the universe has never been stated in dollars. Although every one cannot be a Gargantua-Napoleon-Bismarck and walk off with the great bells of Notre Dame, every one must bear his own universe, and most persons are moderately interested in learning how their neighbors have managed to carry theirs.

This problem of education, started in 1838, went on for three years, while the baby grew, like other babies, unconsciously, as a vegetable, the outside world working as it never had worked before, to get his new universe ready for him. Often in old age he puzzled over the question whether, on the doctrine of chances, he was at liberty to accept himself or his world as an accident. No such accident had ever happened before in human experience. For him, alone, the old universe was thrown into the ash-heap and a new one created. He and his eighteenth-century, troglodytic Boston were suddenly cut apart—separated forever—in act if not in sentiment, by the opening of the Boston and Albany Railroad; the appearance of the first Cunard steamers in the bay; and the telegraphic messages which carried from Baltimore to Washington the news that Henry Clay and James K. Polk were nominated for the Presidency. This was in May, 1844; he was six years old; his new world was ready for use, and only fragments of the old met his eyes.

Of all this that was being done to complicate his education, he knew only the color of yellow. He first found himself sitting on a yellow kitchen floor in strong sunlight. He was three years old when he took this earliest step in education; a lesson of color. The second followed soon; a lesson of taste. On December 3, 1841, he developed scarlet fever. For several days he was as good as dead, reviving only under the careful nursing of his family. When he began to recover strength, about January 1, 1842, his hunger must have been stronger than any other pleasure or pain, for while in after life he retained not the faintest recollection of his illness, he remembered quite clearly his aunt entering the sickroom bearing in her hand a saucer with a baked apple.

The order of impressions retained by memory might naturally be that of color and taste, although one would rather suppose that the sense of pain would be first to educate. In fact, the third recollection of the child was that of discomfort. The moment he could be removed, he was bundled up in blankets and carried from the little house in Hancock Avenue to a larger one which his parents were to occupy for the rest of their lives in the neighboring Mount Vernon Street. The season was midwinter, January 10, 1842, and he never forgot his acute distress for want of air under his blankets, or the noises of moving furniture.

As a means of variation from a normal type, sickness in childhood ought to have a certain value not to be classed under any fitness or unfitness of natural selection; and especially scarlet fever affected boys seriously, both physically and in character, though they might through life puzzle themselves to decide whether it had fitted or unfitted them for success; but this fever of Henry Adams took greater and greater importance in his eyes, from the point of view of education, the longer he lived. At first, the effect was physical. He fell behind his brothers two or three inches in height, and proportionally in bone and weight. His character and processes of mind seemed to share in this fining-down process of scale. He was not good in a fight, and his nerves were more delicate than boys' nerves ought to be. He exaggerated these weaknesses as he grew older. The habit of doubt; of distrusting his own judgment and of totally rejecting the judgment of the world; the tendency to regard every question as open; the hesitation to act except as a choice of evils; the shirking of responsibility; the love of line, form, quality; the horror of ennui; the passion for companionship and the antipathy to society—all these are well-known qualities of New England character in no way peculiar to individuals but in this instance they seemed to be stimulated by the fever, and Henry Adams could never make up his mind whether, on the whole, the change of character was morbid or healthy, good or bad for his purpose. His brothers were the type; he was the variation.

As far as the boy knew, the sickness did not affect him at all, and he grew up in excellent health, bodily and mental, taking life as it was given; accepting its local standards without a difficulty, and enjoying much of it as keenly as any other boy of his age. He seemed to himself quite normal, and his companions seemed always to think him so. Whatever was peculiar about him was education, not character, and came to him, directly and indirectly, as the result of that eighteenth-century inheritance which he took with his name.

The atmosphere of education in which he lived was colonial, revolutionary, almost Cromwellian, as though he were steeped, from his greatest grandmother's birth, in the odor of political crime. Resistance to something was the law of New England nature; the boy looked out on the world with the instinct of resistance; for numberless generations his predecessors had viewed the world chiefly as a thing to be reformed, filled with evil forces to be abolished, and they saw no reason to suppose that they had wholly succeeded in the abolition; the duty was unchanged. That duty implied not only resistance to evil, but hatred of it. Boys naturally look on all force as an enemy, and generally find it so, but the New Englander, whether boy or man, in his long struggle with a stingy or hostile universe, had learned also to love the pleasure of hating; his joys were few.

Politics, as a practice, whatever its professions, had always been the systematic organization of hatreds, and Massachusetts politics had been as harsh as the climate. The chief charm of New England was harshness of contrasts and extremes of sensibility—a cold that froze the blood, and a heat that boiled it—so that the pleasure of hating—one's self if no better victim offered—was not its rarest amusement; but the charm was a true and natural child of the soil, not a cultivated weed of the ancients. The violence of the contrast was real and made the strongest motive of education. The double exterior nature gave life its relative values. Winter and summer, cold and heat, town and country, force and freedom, marked two modes of life and thought, balanced like lobes of the brain. Town was winter confinement, school, rule, discipline; straight, gloomy streets, piled with six feet of snow in the middle; frosts that made the snow sing under wheels or runners;

thaws when the streets became dangerous to cross; society of uncles, aunts, and cousins who expected children to behave themselves, and who were not always gratified; above all else, winter represented the desire to escape and go free. Town was restraint, law, unity. Country, only seven miles away, was liberty, diversity, outlawry, the endless delight of mere sense impressions given by nature for nothing, and breathed by boys without knowing it.

Boys are wild animals, rich in the treasures of sense, but the New England boy had a wider range of emotions than boys of more equable climates. He felt his nature crudely, as it was meant. To the boy Henry Adams, summer was drunken. Among senses, smell was the strongest—smell of hot pine-woods and sweet-fern in the scorching summer noon; of new-mown hay; of ploughed earth; of box hedges; of peaches, lilacs, syringas; of stables, barns, cow-yards; of salt water and low tide on the marshes; nothing came amiss. Next to smell came taste, and the children knew the taste of everything they saw or touched, from pennyroyal and flagroot to the shell of a pignut and the letters of a spelling-book—the taste of A-B, AB, suddenly revived on the boy's tongue sixty years afterwards. Light, line, and color as sensual pleasures, came later and were as crude as the rest. The New England light is glare, and the atmosphere harshens color. The boy was a full man before he ever knew what was meant by atmosphere; his idea of pleasure in light was the blaze of a New England sun. His idea of color was a peony, with the dew of early morning on its petals. The intense blue of the sea, as he saw it a mile or two away, from the Quincy hills; the cumuli in a June afternoon sky; the strong reds and greens and purples of colored prints and children's picture-books, as the American colors then ran; these were ideals. The opposites or antipathies, were the cold grays of November evenings, and the thick, muddy thaws of Boston winter. With such standards, the Bostonian could not but develop a double nature. Life was a double thing. After a January blizzard, the boy who could look with pleasure into the violent snow-glare of the cold white sunshine, with its intense light and shade, scarcely knew what was meant by tone. He could reach it only by education.

Winter and summer, then, were two hostile lives, and bred two separate natures. Winter was always the effort to live; summer was tropical license. Whether the children rolled in the grass, or waded in the brook, or swam in the salt ocean, or sailed in the bay, or fished for smelts in the creeks, or netted minnows in the salt-marshes, or took to the pine-woods and the granite quarries, or chased muskrats and hunted snapping-turtles in the swamps, or mushrooms or nuts on the autumn hills, summer and country were always sensual living, while winter was always compulsory learning.

Summer was the multiplicity of nature; winter was school.

The bearing of the two seasons on the education of Henry Adams was no fancy; it was the most decisive force he ever knew; it ran through life, and made the division between its perplexing, warring, irreconcilable problems, irreducible opposites, with growing emphasis to the last year of study. From earliest childhood the boy was accustomed to feel that, for him, life was double. Winter and summer, town and country, law and liberty, were hostile, and the man who pretended they were not, was in his eyes a schoolmaster—that is, a man employed to tell lies to little boys. Though Quincy was but two hours' walk from Beacon Hill, it belonged in a different world. For two hundred years, every Adams, from father to son, had lived within sight of State Street, and sometimes had lived in it, yet none had ever taken kindly to the town, or been taken kindly by it. The boy inherited his double nature. He knew as yet nothing about his great-grandfather, who had died a dozen years before his own birth: he took for granted that any great-grandfather of his must have always been good, and his enemies wicked; but he divined his great-grandfather's character from his own. Never for a moment did he connect the two ideas of Boston and John Adams; they were separate and antagonistic; the idea of John Adams went with Quincy. He knew his grandfather John Quincy Adams only as an old man of seventy-five or eighty who was friendly and gentle with him, but except that he heard his grandfather always called "the President," and his grandmother "the Madam," he had no reason to suppose that his Adams grandfather differed in character from his Brooks grandfather who was equally kind and benevolent. He liked the Adams side best, but for no other reason than that it reminded him of the country, the summer, and the absence of restraint. Yet he felt also that Quincy was in a way inferior to Boston, and that socially Boston looked down on Quincy. The reason was clear enough even to a five-year old child. Quincy had no Boston style. Little enough style had either; a simpler manner of life and thought could hardly exist, short of cave-dwelling. The flint-and-steel with which his grandfather Adams used to light his own fires in the early morning was still on the mantelpiece of his study. The idea of a livery or even a dress for servants, or of an evening toilette, was next to blasphemy. Bathrooms, water-supplies, lighting, heating, and the whole array of domestic comforts, were unknown at Quincy. Boston had already a bathroom, a water-supply, a furnace, and gas. The superiority of Boston was evident, but a child liked it no better for that.

JOHN HAY

[1838–1905]

A POLITICIAN WHO WAS also a poet, John Hay pursued two different careers simultaneously and successfully. He was born October 8, 1838, at Salem, Indiana; was graduated at the age of twenty from Brown University; and, after studying law in the office of Abraham Lincoln, was admitted to the bar, in 1861. Lincoln liked him so well that he made Hay his assistant private secretary, a post which he filled until Lincoln's death.

After the end of the Civil War, Hay served his country as Secretary of the United States Legations at Paris, Vienna, and Madrid. At thirty-two, when he returned from Spain, he brought with him a volume of sketches, Castilian Days, which he hoped would win the regard of the public. However, he found everyone reading Bret Harte's stories of the rude and rowdy West, so he speculated on the possibility of doing something similar for a region closer to his own territory. The result was Pike County Ballads, six racy pieces of dialect verse in a vein different from anything Hay wrote before or after. He did not take them seriously—he referred to them as his "doggerel diversions"—yet these rhymed narratives have outlasted all his most serious works.

In his late thirties Hay became an editorial writer for the New York Tribune; in his early forties he was Assistant Secretary of State; nearing sixty he was appointed Ambassador to Great Britain by President McKinley and, subsequently, Secretary of State. In the last capacity he directed the peace negotiations with Spain after the Spanish-American war and conducted important negotiations with Germany, England, Russia, and China. He died in the town of Newburg, New Hampshire, July 1, 1905.

Besides his poetry, Hay wrote a brilliant novel, The Breadwinners, but, since it dealt with labor unrest, Hay was fearful of its possible effect on his political life, and it was issued anonymously. When challenged as to his part in it, Hay refused to acknowledge the authorship. He collaborated with John G. Nicolay on the minutely detailed Abraham Lincoln: A History, an authorized biography which ran to ten volumes. A collection of his Addresses appeared a year after his death.

In spite of all his creative labors, Hay's fame rests on the swinging rhymes of Pike County Ballads, especially "Banty Tim"—a forerunner of Kipling's "Gunga Din"—and the continually reprinted "Little Breeches" and "Jim Bludso."

LITTLE BREECHES

I DON'T go much on religion,
  I never ain't had no show;
But I've got a middlin' tight grip, sir,
  On the handful o' things I know.
I don't pan out on the prophets
  And free-will, and that sort of thing,–
But I b'lieve in God and the angels,
  Ever sence one night last spring.

I come into town with some turnips,
  And my little Gabe come along,–
No four-year-old in the county
  Could beat him for pretty and strong,
Peart and chipper and sassy,
  Always ready to swear and fight,–
And I'd larnt him to chaw terbacker
  Jest to keep his milk-teeth white.

The snow come down like a blanket
  As I passed by Taggart's store;
I went in for a jug of molasses
  And left the team at the door.
They scared at something and started,–
  I heard one little squall,
And hell-to-split over the prairie
  Went team, Little Breeches, and all.

Hell-to-split over the prairie!
  I was almost froze with skeer;
But we rousted up some torches,
  and sarched for 'em far and near.
At last we struck hosses and wagon,
  Snowed under a soft white mound,
Upsot, dead beat,–but of little Gabe
  No hide nor hair was found.

And here all hope soured on me,
  Of my fellow-critter's aid,–
I jest flopped down on my marrow-bones,
  Crotch-deep in the snow, and prayed.
. . . .
By this, the torches was played out,
  And me, and Isrul Parr

Went off for some wood to a sheepfold
  That he said was somewhar thar.

We found it at last, and a little shed
  Where they shut up the lambs at night.
We looked in and seen them huddled thar,
  So warm and sleepy and white;
And thar sot Little Breeches and chirped,
  As peart as ever you see,
"I want a chaw of terbacker,
  And that's what's the matter of me."

How did he git thar? Angels.
  He could never have walked in that storm;
They jest scooped down and toted him
  To whar it was safe and warm.
And I think that saving a little child,
  And fotching him to his own,
Is a derned sight better business
  Than loafing around the Throne.

JIM BLUDSO

OF THE PRAIRIE BELLE

WALL, no! I can't tell whar he lives,
  Becase he don't live, you see;
Leastways, he's got out of the habit
  Of livin' like you and me.
Whar have you been for the last three years
  That you haven't heard folks tell
How Jimmy Bludso passed in his checks
  The night of the Prairie Belle?

He weren't no saint,—them engineers
  Is all pretty much alike,—
One wife in Natchez-under-the-Hill
  And another one here, in Pike;
A keerless man in his talk was Jim,
  And an awkward hand in a row,
But he never flunked, and he never lied,—
  I reckon he never knowed how.

And this was all the religion he had,—
  To treat his engine well;
Never be passed on the river;
  To mind the pilot's bell;
And if ever the Prairie Belle took fire,—
  A thousand times he swore,
He'd hold her nozzle agin the bank
  Till the last soul got ashore.

All boats has their day on the Mississip,
  And her day come at last,—
The Movastar was a better boat,
  But the Belle she *wouldn't* be passed.
And so she come tearin' along that night—
  The oldest craft on the line—
With a nigger squat on her safety-valve,
  And her furnace crammed, rosin and pine.

The fire bust out as she clared the bar,
  And burnt a hole in the night,
And quick as a flash she turned, and made
  For the willer-bank on the right.
There was runnin' and cursin', but Jim yelled
    out,
  Over all the infernal roar,
"I'll hold her nozzle agin the bank
  Till the last galoot's ashore."

Through the hot, black breath of the burnin'
    boat
  Jim Bludso's voice was heard,
And they all had trust in his cussedness,
  And knowed he would keep his word.
And, sure's you're born, they all got off
  Afore the smokestacks fell,—
And Bludso's ghost went up alone
  In the smoke of the Prairie Belle.

He weren't no saint,—but at jedgment
  I'd run my chance with Jim,
'Longside of some pious gentlemen
  That wouldn't shook hands with him.
He seen his duty, a dead-sure thing,—
  And went for it thar and then;
And Christ ain't a-going to be too hard
  On a man that died for men.

BANTY TIM

I reckon I git your drift, gents—
You 'low the boy shan't stay;
This is a white man's country;
You're dimocrats, you say;
And whereas, and seein', and wherefore
The times bein' all out o' j'int,
The nigger has got to mosey
From the limits o' Spunky P'int.

Let's reason the thing a minut.
I'm an old-fashioned dimocrat, too.
Though I laid my politics out o' the way
For to keep till the war was through.
But I come back here, allowin'
To vote as I used to do,
Though it gravels me like the devil to train
Along o' sich fools as you.

Now, dog my cats if I kin see
In all the light of day,
What you've got to do with the question
Ef Tim shall go or stay.
And furder than that I give notice,
Ef one of you tetches the boy,
He kin check his trunks to a warmer clime
Than he'll find in Illanoy.

Why, blame your hearts, jest hear me.
You know that ungodly day
When our left struck Vicksburg Heights,
How ripped and torn and tattered we lay.
When the rest retreated I stayed behind,
Fur reasons sufficient to me—
With a rib caved in and a leg on a strike,
I sprawled on that cursed glacee.

Lord! how the hot sun went for us,
And br'iled and blistered and burned!
How the rebel bullets whizzed round us
When a cuss in his death grip turned!
Till long toward dusk I seen a thing
I couldn't believe for a spell;

That nigger—that Tim—was a crawlin' to me
  Through that fireproof, gilt-edged hell!

The rebels seen him as quick as me,
  And the bullets buzzed like bees;
But he jumped for me and shouldered me,
  Though a shot brought him once to his knees.
But he staggered up and packed me off,
  With a dozen stumbles and falls,
Till safe in our line he drapped us both,
  His black hide riddled with balls.

So, my gentle gazelles, thar's my answer,
  And here stands Banty Tim;
He trumped death's ace for me that day,
  And I'm not going back on him!
You may rezoloot till the cows come home
  But ef one of you tetches the boy,
He'll wrastle his hash tonight in hell,
  Or my name's not Tilmon Joy!

EDWARD ROWLAND SILL

[1841–1887]

FRAIL AND OVERSENSITIVE, *Edward Rowland Sill fell short of the goals he had assigned himself. He was born April 29, 1841, in Windsor, Connecticut. Both his parents died before he was twelve, and he was brought up by an uncle in Ohio. Graduated at twenty from Yale, where he was editor of the Yale Literary Magazine, Sill tried to harden himself with work and travel. Following the example of Richard Henry Dana, Jr., he sailed around the Horn, after which he attempted to support himself by clerking in a California bank, handling mail in a Post office, and working on a ranch. The rough life was too much for him and at twenty-five he returned East. He was scarcely more successful there. He studied at the Harvard Divinity School, and found he was at heart a skeptic. He tried newspaper work, and learned to hate* journalism. He wrote poems, but was so timid that he submitted them under the pen-name of "Andrew Hedbrooke." Unable to ally himself either with the conservatives, whom he despised, or with the radicals, whom he distrusted, Sill became an uncomfortable solitary.

It was as a teacher that he finally achieved something like security. At one time he was professor of English at the University of California and, at another, superintendent of schools at Cuyahoga Falls, Ohio. He remained in Ohio during his last years and contributed essays and poems to various magazines under his pseudonym. He died, after an operation, February 28, 1887, when he was not yet forty-six.

Only one volume, The Hermitage and Other Poems, was published during his lifetime. Another, The Venus of Milo and Other Poems, was privately printed in his forty-third year. There were two other posthumous collections.

A stoic who, in spite of religious skepticism, was an idealist, Sill combined a bravery of spirit and severity of style. "Opportunity" and "The Fool's Prayer" are his most characteristic as well as his most quoted poems.

OPPORTUNITY

This I beheld, or dreamed it in a dream:—
There spread a cloud of dust along a plain;
And underneath the cloud, or in it, raged
A furious battle, and men yelled, and swords
Shocked upon swords and shields. A prince's banner
Wavered, then staggered backward, hemmed by foes.
A craven hung along the battle's edge,
And thought, "Had I a sword of keener steel—
That blue blade that the king's son bears,—but this
Blunt thing—!" he snapped and flung it from his hand,
And lowering crept away, and left the field.
Then came the king's son, wounded, sore bestead,
And weaponless, and saw the broken sword,
Hilt-buried in the dry and trodden sand,
And ran and snatched it, and with battle-shout
Lifted afresh he hewed his enemy down,
And saved a great cause that heroic day.

THE FOOL'S PRAYER

The royal feast was done; the King
  Sought some new sport to banish care,
And to his jester cried: "Sir Fool,
  Kneel now, and make for us a prayer!"

The jester doffed his cap and bells,
  And stood the mocking court before;
They could not see the bitter smile
  Behind the painted grin he wore.

He bowed his head, and bent his knee
  Upon the monarch's silken stool;
His pleading voice arose: "O Lord,
  Be merciful to me, a fool!

"No pity, Lord, could change the heart
  From red with wrong to white as wool;
The rod must heal the sin: but, Lord,
  Be merciful to me, a fool!

" 'Tis not by guilt the onward sweep
  Of truth and right, O Lord, we stay;
'Tis by our follies that so long
  We hold the earth from heaven away.

"These clumsy feet, still in the mire,
  Go crushing blossoms without end;
These hard, well-meaning hands we thrust
  Among the heart-strings of a friend.

"The ill-timed truth we might have kept—
  Who knows how sharp it pierced and stung?
The word we had not sense to say—
  Who knows how grandly it had rung?

"Our faults no tenderness should ask,
  The chastening stripes must cleanse them all;
But for our blunders—oh, in shame
  Before the eyes of heaven we fall.

"Earth bears no balsam for mistakes;
  Men crown the knave, and scourge the tool

That did his will. But Thou, O Lord,
  Be merciful to me, a fool!"

The room was hushed; in silence rose
  The King and sought his gardens cool,
And walked apart, and murmured low,
  "Be merciful to me, a fool!"

SIDNEY LANIER

[1842–1881]

ONE OF THE MOST variously gifted of Southern writers, Sidney Lanier died before he was forty. He was born February 3, 1842, in Macon, Georgia. He was a musician by inheritance—the Laniers had been among the founders of the Society of Music under Charles II—and, although he was at his most proficient on the flute, there was no instrument the boy could not play before he was twelve. He was only eighteen when he was graduated from Oglethorpe University. A year later, in 1861, he volunteered as a private in the Confederate Army. While serving as a scout and blockade-runner he was captured and imprisoned at Point Lookout. When he was released, his health was broken. Infected with the germs of tuberculosis, a disease fatal to most members of his family, he spent the rest of his life in a losing struggle against it, as he said, "merely not dying."

Desperately poor as well as ill at twenty-three, he became a hotel clerk, wrote his first book—a novel entitled Tiger Lilies—taught school, assisted in his father's law office, and, although he never took a bar examination, practiced law intermittently. At twenty-five he married Mary Day and, in spite of adversity, achieved great happiness with his wife and their four sons. A few years later he was fortunate in obtaining the position of first flutist with the Peabody Symphony Orchestra in Baltimore, where he had free access to the music and literature which he not only craved but needed. Baltimore became his haven. At thirty-seven he was appointed lecturer in English literature at Johns Hopkins University, and it was for his course there that he wrote the brilliant if inconclusive The Science of English Verse.

Poems, *published when he was thirty-five, was followed by several storybooks for boys, the posthumously-published* Shakespeare and His Forerunners, The English Novel and the Principle of its Development, *and* Music and Poetry. *In his late thirties it became evident that he could not go on teaching or even writing, and, suddenly enfeebled, Lanier was brought to the mountains of North Carolina. There, at Lynn, he died on September 7, 1881.*

Much of Lanier's poetry suffers from its very lushness and his conscious effort to bring versification over into the province of music. His theory that English verse has for its basis not accent but a strict musical quantity, *and that, therefore,* time *is the true element of rhythm, is a false conclusion, the contention of one who wrote, "Whatever turn I have for art is purely musical—poetry being with me merely a tangent into which I shoot." Nevertheless, some of his ballads rise above his theorizing, while the ingeniously alliterative "Song of the Chattahoochee" and the longer "The Marshes of Glynn" come close to proving his contention.*

SONG OF THE CHATTAHOOCHEE

Out of the hills of Habersham,
Down the valleys of Hall,
I hurry amain to reach the plain,
Run the rapid and leap the fall,
Split at the rock and together again,
Accept my bed, or narrow or wide,
And flee from folly on every side
With a lover's pain to attain the plain
Far from the hills of Habersham,
Far from the valleys of Hall.

All down the hills of Habersham,
All through the valleys of Hall,
The rushes cried *Abide, abide,*
The wilful water weeds held me thrall,
The laving laurel turned my tide,
The ferns and the fondling grass said *Stay,*
The dewberry dipped for to work delay,
And the little reeds sighed *Abide, abide,*

Here in the hills of Habersham,
Here in the valleys of Hall.

High o'er the hills of Habersham,
Veiling the valleys of Hall,
The hickory told me manifold
Fair tales of shade, the poplar tall
Wrought me her shadowy self to hold,
The chestnut, the oak, the walnut, the pine,
Overleaning, with flickering meaning and
sign,
Said, *Pass not, so cold, these manifold*
Deep shades of the hills of Habersham,
These glades in the valleys of Hall.

And oft in the hills of Habersham,
And oft in the valleys of Hall,
The white quartz shone, and the smooth
brook-stone
Did bar me of passage with friendly brawl,
And many a luminous jewel lone
—Crystals clear or a-cloud with mist,
Ruby, garnet, and amethyst—
Made lures with the lights of streaming stone
In the clefts of the hills of Habersham,
In the beds of the valleys of Hall.

But oh, not the hills of Habersham,
And oh, not the valleys of Hall
Avail: I am fain for to water the plain.
Downward the voices of Duty call—
Downward, to toil and be mixed with the
main,
The dry fields burn, and the mills are to turn,
And a myriad flowers mortally yearn,
And the lordly main from beyond the plain
Calls o'er the hills of Habersham,
Calls through the valleys of Hall.

AMBROSE BIERCE

[1842–1916?]

The life of Ambrose Bierce was begun in obscurity and ended in mystery. He was born June 24, 1842, on an impoverished farm in Meigs County, Ohio. Youngest of nine children, he suffered through childhood and enlisted as a drummer in the Union Army at the outset of the Civil War. Twice wounded, he was advanced to lieutenant and then, with a citation for bravery, to major. Uncertain what to do after the war, Bierce decided on journalism as the least arduous pursuit, went to California, and edited the San Francisco News Letter.

Married in his late twenties, he left America for England, where he published three volumes of grim humor whose character was indicated by the titles: The Fiend's Delight, Nuggets and Dust, Cobwebs from an Empty Skull. After four years abroad, Bierce returned to San Francisco and remained there twenty-five years, writing brisk causeries, fantastic fiction, newspaper columns, and miscellaneous hackwork to support his wife and three children. His serious short stories were rejected by one editor after another.

His life grew increasingly difficult; misfortune was followed by tragedy. His wife left him; one son was fatally shot in a sordid affair; another son died an alcoholic. At seventy-one Bierce headed for Mexico. His purpose was vague: it was not clear whether he went there to join the revolutionists or merely to report their activities. He became a legend. Tales of his recklessness percolated through the press. It was rumored that in 1916 he was killed in battle under the banner of the rebel Villa. It was also said that he was seen alive ten years later, living under an assumed name. The actual facts have never been established.

It was not only because of the tempting alliteration that he was known as "Bitter Bierce." He regarded humanity with suspicion and its vaunted virtues with skepticism. The short stories, finally collected in Tales of Soldiers and Civilians, range from the ironic to the supernatural. Macabre humor is evident throughout, not only in his narratives but also in his odd fables, his handbook of literary misdemeanors (Write It Right), the caustic epigrams in The Devil's Dictionary, and his essays which, he said, covered everything, including "government, dreams, writers of dialect, and dogs." In common with his stories, Bierce's witticisms are always pointed, and the point is usually tipped with poison.

AN OCCURRENCE AT OWL CREEK BRIDGE

I

A man stood upon a railroad bridge in northern Alabama, looking down into the swift water twenty feet below. The man's hands were behind his back, the wrists bound with a cord. A rope closely encircled his neck. It was attached to a stout cross-timber above his head and the slack fell to the level of his knees. Some loose boards laid upon the sleepers supporting the metals of the railway supplied a footing for him and his executioners—two private soldiers of the Federal army, directed by a sergeant who in civil life may have been a deputy sheriff. At a short remove upon the same temporary platform was an officer in the uniform of his rank, armed. He was a captain. A sentinel at each end of the bridge stood with his rifle in the position known as "support," that is to say, vertical in front of the left shoulder, the hammer resting on the forearm thrown straight across the chest—a formal and unnatural position, enforcing an erect carriage of the body. It did not appear to be the duty of these two men to know what was occurring at the centre of the bridge; they merely blockaded the two ends of the foot planking that traversed it.

Beyond one of the sentinels nobody was in sight; the railroad ran straight away into a forest for a hundred yards, then, curving, was lost to view. Doubtless there was an outpost farther along. The other bank of the stream was open ground—a gentle acclivity topped with a stockade of vertical tree trunks, loop-holed for rifles, with a single embrasure through which protruded the muzzle of a brass cannon commanding the bridge. Midway of the slope between bridge and fort were the spectators—a single company of infantry in line, at "parade rest," the butts of the rifles on the ground, the barrels inclining slightly backward against the right shoulder, the hands crossed upon the stock. A lieutenant stood at the right of the line, the point of his sword upon the ground, his left hand resting upon his right. Excepting the group of four at the centre of the bridge, not a man moved. The company faced the bridge, staring stonily, motionless. The sentinels, facing the banks of the stream, might have been statues to adorn the bridge. The captain stood with folded arms, silent, observing the work of his subordinates, but making no sign. Death is a dignitary who when he comes announced is to be received with formal manifestations of respect, even by those most familiar with him. In the code of military etiquette silence and fixity are forms of deference.

The man who was engaged in being hanged was apparently about thirty-five years of age. He was a civilian, if one might judge from his habit, which was that of a planter. His features were good—a straight nose, firm mouth, broad forehead, from which his long, dark hair was combed straight back, falling behind his ears to the collar of his well-fitting frock-coat. He wore a mustache and pointed beard, but no whiskers; his eyes were large and dark gray, and had a kindly expression which one would hardly have expected in one whose neck was in the hemp. Evidently this was no vulgar assassin. The liberal military code makes provision for hanging many kinds of persons, and gentlemen are not excluded.

The preparations being complete, the two private soldiers stepped aside and each drew away the plank upon which he had been standing. The sergeant turned to the captain, saluted and placed himself immediately behind that officer, who in turn moved apart one pace. These movements left the condemned man and the sergeant standing on the two ends of the same plank, which spanned three of the cross-ties of the bridge. The end upon which the civilian stood almost, but not quite, reached a fourth. This plank had been held in place by the weight of the captain; it was now held by that of the sergeant. At a signal from the former the latter would step aside, the plank would tilt and the condemned man go down between two ties. The arrangement commended itself to his judgment as simple and effective. His face had not been covered nor his eyes bandaged. He looked a moment at his "unsteadfast footing," then let his gaze wander to the swirling water of the stream racing madly beneath his feet. A piece of dancing driftwood caught his attention and his eyes followed it down the current. How slowly it appeared to move! What a sluggish stream!

He closed his eyes in order to fix his last thoughts upon his wife and children. The water, touched to gold by the early sun, the brooding mists under the banks at some distance down the stream, the fort, the soldiers, the piece of drift—all had distracted him. And now he became conscious of a new disturbance. Striking through the thought of his dear ones was a sound which he could neither ignore nor understand, a sharp, distinct, metallic percussion like the stroke of a blacksmith's hammer upon the anvil; it had the same ringing quality. He wondered what it was, and whether immeasurably distant or near by—it seemed both. Its recurrence was regular, but as slow as the tolling of a death knell. He awaited each stroke with impatience and—he knew not why—apprehension. The intervals of silence grew progressively longer; the delays became maddening. With their greater infrequency the sounds increased in strength and sharpness. They hurt his ear like the thrust of a knife; he feared he would shriek. What he heard was the ticking of his watch.

He unclosed his eyes and saw again the water below him. "If I could free my hands," he thought, "I might throw off the noose and spring into the stream. By diving I could evade the bullets and, swimming vigorously, reach the bank, take to the woods and get away home. My home, thank God, is as yet outside their lines; my wife and little ones are still beyond the invader's farthest advance."

As these thoughts, which have here to be set down in words, were flashed into the doomed man's brain rather than evolved from it the captain nodded to the sergeant. The sergeant stepped aside.

II

Peyton Farquhar was a well-to-do planter, of an old and highly respected Alabama family. Being a slave owner and like other slave owners a politician he was naturally an original secessionist and ardently devoted to the Southern cause. Circumstances of an imperious nature, which it is unnecessary to relate here, had prevented him from taking service with the gallant army that had fought the disastrous campaigns ending with the fall of Corinth, and he chafed under the inglorious restraint, longing for the release of his energies, the larger life of the soldier, the opportunity for distinction. That opportunity, he felt, would come, as it comes to all in war time. Meanwhile he did what he could. No service was too humble for him to perform in aid of the South, no adventure too perilous for him to undertake if consistent with the character of a civilian who was at heart a soldier, and who in good faith and without too much qualification assented to at least a part of the frankly villainous dictum that all is fair in love and war.

One evening while Farquhar and his wife were sitting on a rustic bench near the entrance to his grounds, a gray-clad soldier rode up to the gate and asked for a drink of water. Mrs. Farquhar was only too happy to serve him with her own white hands. While she was fetching the water her husband approached the dusty horseman and inquired eagerly for news from the front.

"The Yanks are repairing the railroads," said the man, "and are getting ready for another advance. They have reached the Owl Creek bridge, put it in order and built a blockade on the north bank. The commandant has issued an order, which is posted everywhere, declaring that any civilian caught interfering with the railroad, its bridges, tunnels or trains will be summarily hanged. I saw the order."

"How far is it to the Owl Creek bridge?" Farquhar asked.

"About thirty miles."

"Is there no force on this side the creek?"

"Only a picket post half a mile out, on the railroad, and a single sentinel at this end of the bridge."

"Suppose a man—a civilian and student of hanging—should elude the picket post and perhaps get the better of the sentinel," said Farquhar, smiling, "what could he accomplish?"

The soldier reflected. "I was there a month ago," he replied. "I observed that the flood of last winter had lodged a great quantity of driftwood against the wooden pier at this end of the bridge. It is now dry and would burn like tow."

The lady had now brought the water, which the soldier drank. He thanked her ceremoniously, bowed to her husband and rode away. An hour later, after nightfall, he repassed the plantation, going northward in the direction from which he had come. He was a Federal scout.

III

As Peyton Farquhar fell straight downward through the bridge he lost consciousness and was as one already dead. From this state he was awakened—ages later, it seemed to him—by the pain of a sharp pressure upon his throat, followed by a sense of suffocation. Keen, poignant agonies seemed to shoot from his neck downward through every fibre of his body and limbs. These pains appeared to flash along well-defined lines of ramification and to beat with an inconceivably rapid periodicity. They seemed like streams of pulsating fire heating him to an intolerable temperature. As to his head, he was conscious of nothing but a feeling of fulness—of congestion. These sensations were unaccompanied by thought. The intellectual part of his nature was already effaced; he had power only to feel, and feeling was torment. He was conscious of motion. Encompassed in a luminous cloud, of which he was now merely the fiery heart, without material substance, he swung through unthinkable arcs of oscillation, like a vast pendulum. Then all at once, with terrible suddenness, the light about him shot upward with the noise of a loud plash; a frightful roaring was in his ears, and all was cold and dark. The power of thought was restored; he knew that the rope had broken and he had fallen into the stream. There was no additional strangulation; the noose about his neck was already suffocating him and kept the water from his lungs. To die of hanging at the bottom of a river!—the idea seemed to him ludicrous. He opened his eyes in the darkness and saw above him a gleam of light, but how distant, how inaccessible! He was still sinking, for the light became fainter and fainter until it was a mere glimmer. Then it began to grow and brighten, and he knew that he was rising toward the surface—knew it with reluctance, for he was now very comfortable. "To be hanged and drowned," he thought, "that is not so bad; but I do not wish to be shot. No; I will not be shot; that is not fair."

He was not conscious of an effort, but a sharp pain in his wrist apprised him that he was trying to free his hands. He gave the struggle his attention, as an idler might observe the feat of a juggler, without interest in the outcome. What splendid effort!—what magnificent, what superhuman strength! Ah, that was a fine endeavor! Bravo! The cord fell away; his arms parted and floated upward, the hands dimly seen on each side in the growing light. He watched them with a new interest as first one and then the other pounced upon the noose at his neck. They tore it away and thrust it fiercely aside, its undulations resembling those of a water-snake. "Put it back, put it back!" He thought he shouted these words to his hands, for the undoing of the noose had been succeeded by the direst pang that he had yet experienced. His neck ached horribly; his brain was on fire; his heart, which had been fluttering faintly, gave a great leap, trying to force itself out at his mouth. His whole body was racked and wrenched with an insupportable anguish! But his disobedient hands gave no heed to the command. They beat the water vigorously with quick, downward strokes, forcing him to the surface. He felt his head emerge; his eyes were blinded by the sunlight; his chest expanded convulsively, and with a supreme and crowning agony his lungs engulfed a great draught of air, which instantly he expelled in a shriek!

He was now in full possession of his physical senses. They were, indeed, preternaturally keen and alert. Something in the awful disturbance of his organic system had so exalted and refined them that they made record of things never before perceived. He felt the ripples upon his face and heard their separate sounds as they struck. He looked at the forest on the bank of the stream, saw the individual trees, the leaves and the veining of each leaf—saw the very insects upon them: the locusts, the brilliant-bodied flies, the gray spiders stretching their webs from twig to twig. He noted the prismatic colors in all the dewdrops upon a million blades of grass. The humming of the gnats that danced above the eddies of the stream, the beating of the dragon-flies' wings, the strokes of the water-spiders' legs, like oars which had lifted their boat—all these made audible music. A fish slid along beneath his eyes and he heard the rush of its body parting the water.

He had come to the surface facing down the stream; in a moment the visible world seemed to wheel slowly round, himself the pivotal point, and he saw the bridge, the fort, the soldiers upon the bridge, the captain, the sergeant, the two privates, his executioners. They were in silhouette against the blue sky. They shouted and gesticulated, pointing at him. The captain had drawn his pistol, but did not fire; the others were unarmed. Their movements were grotesque and horrible, their forms gigantic.

Suddenly he heard a sharp report and something struck the water smartly within a few inches of his head, spattering his face with spray. He heard a second report, and saw one of the sentinels with his rifle at his shoulder, a light cloud of blue smoke rising from the muzzle. The man in the water saw the eye of the man on the bridge gazing into his own through the sights of the rifle. He observed that it was a gray eye and remembered having read that gray eyes were keenest, and that all famous markmen had them. Nevertheless, this one had missed.

A counter-swirl had caught Farquhar and turned him half round; he was again looking into the forest on the bank opposite the fort. The sound of a clear, high voice in a monotonous singsong now rang out behind him and came across the water with a distinctness that pierced and subdued all other sounds, even the beating of the ripples in his ears. Although no soldier, he had frequented camps enough to know the dread significance of that deliberate, drawling, aspirated chant; the lieutenant on shore was taking a part in the morning's work. How coldly and pitilessly—with what an even, calm intonation, presaging, and enforcing tranquillity in the men—with what accurately measured intervals fell those cruel words:

"Attention, company! . . . Shoulder arms! . . . Ready! . . . Aim! . . . Fire!"

Farquhar dived—dived as deeply as he could. The water roared in his ears like the voice of Niagara, yet he heard the dulled thunder of the volley and, rising again toward the surface, met shining bits of metal, singularly flattened, oscillating slowly downward. Some of them touched him on the face and hands, then fell away, continuing their descent. One lodged between his collar and neck; it was uncomfortably warm and he snatched it out.

As he rose to the surface, gasping for breath, he saw that he had been a long time under water; he was perceptibly farther down stream—nearer to safety. The soldiers had almost finished reloading; the metal ramrods flashed all at once in the sunshine as they were drawn from the barrels, turned in the air, and thrust into their sockets. The two sentinels fired again, independently and ineffectually.

The hunted man saw all this over his shoulder; he was now swimming vigorously with the current. His brain was as energetic as his arms and legs; he thought with the rapidity of lightning.

"The officer," he reasoned, "will not make that martinet's error a second time. It is as easy to dodge a volley as a single shot. He has probably already given the command to fire at will. God help me, I cannot dodge them all!"

An appalling splash within two yards of him was followed by a loud, rushing sound, *diminuendo*, which seemed to travel back through the air to the fort and died in an explosion which stirred the very river to its deeps! A rising sheet of water curved over him, fell down upon him, blinded him, strangled him! The cannon had taken a hand in the game. As he shook his head free from the commotion of the smitten water he heard the deflected shot humming through the air ahead, and in an instant it was cracking and smashing the branches in the forest beyond.

"They will not do that again," he thought; "the next time they will use a charge of grape. I must keep my eye upon the gun; the smoke will apprise me—the report arrives too late; it lags behind the missile. That is a good gun."

Suddenly he felt himself whirled round and round—spinning like a top. The water, the banks, the forests, the now distant bridge, fort and men—all were commingled and blurred. Objects were represented by their colors only; circular horizontal streaks of color—that was all he saw. He had been caught in a vortex and was being whirled on with a velocity of advance and gyration that made him giddy and sick. In a few moments he was flung upon the gravel at the foot of the left bank of the stream—the southern bank—and behind a projecting point which concealed him from his enemies. The sudden arrest of his motion, the abrasion of one of his hands on the gravel, restored him, and he wept with delight. He dug his fingers into the sand, threw it over himself in handfuls and audibly blessed it. It looked like diamonds, rubies, emeralds; he could think of nothing beautiful which it did not resemble. The trees upon the bank were giant garden plants; he noted a definite order in their arrangement, inhaled the fragrance of their blooms. A strange, roseate light shone through the spaces among their trunks and the wind made in their branches the music of æolian harps. He had no wish to perfect his escape—was content to remain in that enchanting spot until retaken.

A whiz and rattle of grapeshot among the branches high above his head roused him from his dream. The baffled cannoneer had fired him a random farewell. He sprang to his feet, rushed up the sloping bank, and plunged into the forest.

All that day he traveled, laying his course by the rounding sun. The forest seemed interminable; nowhere did he discover a break in it, not even a woodman's road. He had not known that he lived in so wild a region. There was something uncanny in the revelation.

By nightfall he was fatigued, footsore, famishing. The thought of his wife and children urged him on. At last he found a road which led him in what he knew to be the right direction. It was as wide and straight as a city street, yet it seemed untraveled. No fields bordered it, no dwelling anywhere. Not so much as the barking of a dog suggested human habitation.

The black bodies of the trees formed a straight wall on both sides, terminating on the horizon in a point, like a diagram in a lesson in perspective. Overhead, as he looked up through this rift in the wood, shone great golden stars looking unfamiliar and grouped in strange constellations. He was sure they were arranged in some order which had a secret and malign significance. The wood on either side was full of singular noises, among which—once, twice, and again—he distinctly heard whispers in an unknown tongue.

His neck was in pain and lifting his hand to it he found it horribly swollen. He knew that it had a circle of black where the rope had bruised it. His eyes felt congested; he could no longer close them. His tongue was swollen with thirst; he relieved its fever by thrusting it forward from between his teeth into the cold air. How softly the turf had carpeted the untraveled avenue—he could no longer feel the roadway beneath his feet!

Doubtless, despite his suffering, he had fallen asleep while walking, for now he sees another scene—perhaps he has merely recovered from a delirium. He stands at the gate of his own home. All is as he left it, and all bright and beautiful in the morning sunshine. He must have traveled the entire night. As he pushes open the gate and passes up the wide white walk, he sees a flutter of female garments; his wife, looking fresh and cool and sweet, steps down from the veranda to meet him. At the bottom of the steps she stands waiting, with a smile of ineffable joy, an attitude of matchless grace and dignity. Ah, how beautiful she is! He springs forward with extended arms. As he is about to clasp her he feels a stunning blow upon the back of the neck; a blinding white light blazes all about him with a sound like the shock of a cannon—then all is darkness and silence!

Peyton Farquhar was dead; his body, with a broken neck, swung gently from side to side beneath the timbers of the Owl Creek bridge.

THE DEVIL'S DICTIONARY

Selected Definitions

ABSTAINER: a weak person who yields to the temptation of denying himself a pleasure.

ACQUAINTANCE: a degree of friendship called slight when its object is poor or obscure, and intimate when he is rich or famous.

Admiration: our polite recognition of another's resemblance to ourselves.

Alliance: in international politics, the union of two thieves who have their hand so deeply inserted in each other's pockets that they cannot separately plunder a third.

Bait: a preparation that renders the hook more palatable. The best kind is beauty.

Belladonna: in Italian a beautiful lady; in English a deadly poison. A striking example of the essential identity of the two tongues.

Bigot: One who is obstinately and zealously attached to an opinion that you do not entertain.

Bore: a person who talks when you wish him to listen.

Brain: the apparatus with which we think we think.

Bride: a woman with a fine prospect of happiness behind her.

Cabbage: a familiar kitchen-garden vegetable about as large and wise as a man's head.

Connoisseur: a specialist who knows everything about something and nothing about anything else. An old wine-bibber having been smashed in a railway collision, some wine was poured upon his lips to revive him. "Pauillac, 1873," he murmured and died.

Conservative: a statesman who is enamored of existing evils, as distinguished from the Liberal, who wishes to replace them with others.

Coward: one who in a perilous emergency thinks with his legs.

Cynic: a blackguard whose faulty vision sees things as they are, not as they ought to be.

Daring: a conspicuous quality of a man in security.

Diaphragm: a muscular partition separating disorders of the chest from disorders of the bowels.

Discussion: a method of confirming others in their errors.

Education: that which discloses to the wise and disguises from the foolish their lack of understanding.

Egotist: a person of low taste, more interested in himself than in me.

Faith: belief without evidence in what is told by one who speaks without knowledge, of things without parallel.

Fashion: a despot whom the wise ridicule and obey.

Genealogy: an account of one's descent from an ancestor who did not care to trace his own.

Helpmate: a wife, or bitter half.

History: an account, mostly false, of events unimportant, which are brought about by rulers mostly knaves, and soldiers mostly fools.

HOSPITALITY: the virtue which induces us to feed and lodge certain persons who are not in need of food and lodging.
LECTURER: one with his hand in your pocket, his tongue in your ear, and his faith in your patience.
MARRIAGE: the state or condition of a community consisting of a master, a mistress, and two slaves, making, in all, two.
PEACE: in international affairs, a period of cheating between two periods of fighting.
POSITIVE: being mistaken at the top of one's voice.

HENRY JAMES

[1843–1916]

THE JAMES FAMILY WAS SO WELL ENDOWED *with the things of this world that its members could wholeheartedly devote themselves to things of the spirit. Henry James, Sr., who had inherited an estate valued at three million dollars, turned away from commercialism, became a follower of Swedenborg, and spent his life studying the metaphysics of creation; he was a wise and gentle soul whom Emerson considered "a true comfort, with heroic manners, and a serenity like the sun." William James, his oldest son, was a philosopher whose first book,* Principles of Psychology, *is still a central work in its field. His* Pragmatism *led readers away from abstractions and closed systems of thought toward concreteness, facts, and the power of action; while* The Varieties of Religious Experience *explored man's secret power of vision. It was said that William James wrote philosophy as though it were fiction, while his brother Henry wrote fiction as though it were philosophy.*

Henry, William's junior by fifteen months, was born April 15, 1843, in New York City. He was barely a year old when he was taken on the first of many trips abroad; he was educated—his detractors say over-educated—by private tutors in Paris, Boulogne, Geneva, and London. He was fourteen when he began to write.

At nineteen Henry James entered Harvard Law School. He remained less than a year, for he soon found out that he wanted to be a man of letters, not a man of law. James Russell Lowell, Charles Eliot

Norton, and other members of the Boston literati were his mentors, and at twenty-one James appeared in print in the North American Review. Although the family had made their home in Cambridge, James had fallen in love with Europe. In his mid-twenties he toured extensively, lived for a while in Italy, studied the French theatre in Paris, and met Zola, Flaubert, and Turgenev. England became his home.

In England he began to write novels of "the international situation" which were to act as literary liaison between the Old and the New World. James was acutely conscious of his role. Ten years after Roderick Hudson, his first work of any importance, he wrote to his brother William: "I aspire to write in such a way that it would be impossible for an outsider to say whether I am at a given moment an American writing about England or an Englishman writing about America. . . So far from being ashamed of such an ambiguity, I would be exceedingly proud of it."

Critics have been pleased to divide James's work into three historical periods: the writings of James the First, James the Second, and The Old Pretender. The classification seems flippant but it is not altogether unjust. The early work presents uncertainties in technique, weaknesses in plot, development, and relations between characters. The middle period, which includes Daily Miller, Washington Square, and The Portrait of a Lady, is marked by an intricacy of delineation and stylistic subtleties utterly unlike anything previously attempted in American fiction. The later novels and short stories (What Maisie Knew, The Turn of the Screw, The Awkward Age, The Sacred Fount, The Ambassadors, The Golden Bowl) grow increasingly more complicated, indirect in manner, packed and impeded with parenthetical statements, restatements, and reservations. It sometimes seems that James not only wrote in but also thought in parentheses.

At forty, following the death of his mother, James returned to the United States for a short visit, but he was no longer at home in the country of his birth; he went back to England and did not revisit America for another twenty-one years. He hoped for a career as a dramatist, but the plays which he wrote in his forties and fifties were failures and, rebuffed, James left London and the world of the theatre for a country house in Rye, Sussex. There he lived in comfort and "impenetrable respectability." He grew more corpulent and more conservative; he was glad to attend "functions;" he dressed like a bank president and ceremoniously wore dark suits with silk lapels, stiff collars with wide wings, and a formal top hat. He never married.

As James advanced into his sixties his plots became more implausible, his style more involuted, and his sentences more tortuous and tortured. He became a specialist in craftsmanship; he grew so preoccupied with method that he neglected ordinary human values. He lost contact with what was normal but, to him, obvious and inane. He considered Mark Twain not only commonplace but unspeakably vulgar.

In his sixty-third year James made one more effort to understand the country of his origin. He spent a season with his brother William and traveled in the South and West, lecturing as he went. He did not like what he experienced. "I found my native land, after so many years, interesting, formidable, fearsome, and fatiguing. . . It is an extraordinary world—but almost cruelly charmless." He was intimidated by the powerful masculinity of the country, its gigantic strength, and the "aggressive gregariousness" which he felt bred crudity and corruption. He congratulated himself on having escaped all this and, after a year, was glad to return to the seclusion of Rye.

Back in England, James continued his elaborately involved fiction. He also resumed playwriting, but he could not stand the strain of working in two opposed media. At sixty-six there was a breakdown, brought on by the death of his brother and the shock of the First World War. His dislike of Germany and his ever-deepening attachment to England made him give up his American citizenship; in June, 1915, he became a naturalized British subject. Six months later he was given the Order of Merit, but he did not live long to enjoy the honor. A few weeks after the presentation of the award he had a heart attack. Pneumonia followed, and he died, February 8, 1916, at the age of seventy-three.

Readers of Henry James are divided into two opposing camps. There is no middle ground between those who regard him as a creative ironist who transformed the European novel by giving it an American perspective, and those who consider him a victim of his own oversubtle technique. The chief charge against him is that he lacked passion and disdained the raw material of life; that, alternately fascinated and repelled by High Society, his constant concern with the leisure class is snobbish, rootless, exhaustive and, in the end, exhausting. If, according to Van Wyck Brooks, his work was the outcome of "a deranged set of values, of a mind working in the void, uncorrected by any clear consciousness of human cause and effect," it was also a record of the corrupt life of the middle class, a corruption which, said Newton Arvin, he saw with "deadly lucidity . . . as few of his contemporaries saw it."

It was the death of the genteel tradition that James was portraying in both England and America. William James pointed out that, although his brother severed his ties with America, he never really became an Englishman: he was, William remarked, a citizen of the James country, a country of the mind. In that country he addressed a special audience, an audience of agile intelligence willing to follow him through endless tangles of infinitesimal details, to be rewarded by the accurate precisions of a mind at once fastidious and analytical.

James employed a knife-edged sensibility against the dulling insensibilities of his age; his favorite theme was the artist in search of himself, the individual in conflict with society. "The Real Thing," one of his most characteristic short stories, centers about the conflict between art and life, an opposition which James examined with probing delicacy and revealed with esthetic delight.

THE REAL THING

I

WHEN THE PORTER'S WIFE, who used to answer the housebell, announced "A gentleman and a lady, sir," I had, as I often had in those days—the wish being father to the thought—an immediate vision of sitters. Sitters my visitors in this case proved to be; but not in the sense I should have preferred. There was nothing at first however to indicate that they mightn't have come for a portrait. The gentleman, a man of fifty, very high and very straight, with a moustache slightly grizzled and a dark grey walking-coat admirably fitted, both of which I noted professionally—I don't mean as a barber or yet as a tailor—would have struck me as a celebrity if celebrities often were striking. It was a truth of which I had for some time been conscious that a figure with a good deal of frontage was, as one might say, almost never a public institution. A glance at the lady helped to remind me of this paradoxical law: she also looked too distinguished to be a "personality." Moreover one would scarcely come across two variations together.

Neither of the pair immediately spoke—they only prolonged the preliminary gaze suggesting that each wished to give the other a chance. They were visibly shy; they stood there letting me take them in—which, as I afterwards perceived, was the most practical thing they could have done.

In this way their embarrassment served their cause. I had seen people painfully reluctant to mention that they desired anything so gross as to be represented on canvas; but the scruples of my new friends appeared almost insurmountable. Yet the gentleman might have said "I should like a portrait of my wife, and the lady might have said "I should like a portrait of my husband." Perhaps they weren't husband and wife—this naturally would make the matter more delicate. Perhaps they wished to be done together—in which case they ought to have brought a third person to break the news.

"We come from Mr. Rivet," the lady finally said with a dim smile that had the effect of a moist sponge passed over a "sunk" piece of painting, as well as of a vague allusion to vanished beauty. She was as tall and straight, in her degree, as her companion, and with ten years less to carry. She looked as sad as a woman could look whose face was not charged with expression; that is her tinted oval mask showed waste as an exposed surface shows friction. The hand of time had played over her freely, but to an effect of elimination. She was slim and stiff, and so well-dressed, in dark blue cloth, with lappets and pockets and buttons, that it was clear she employed the same tailor as her husband. The couple had an indefinable air of prosperous thrift—they evidently got a good deal of luxury for their money. If I was to be one of their luxuries it would behoove me to consider my terms.

"Ah Claude Rivet recommended me?" I echoed; and I added that it was very kind of him, though I could reflect that, as he only painted landscape, this wasn't a sacrifice.

The lady looked very hard at the gentleman, and the gentleman looked round the room. Then staring at the floor a moment and stroking his moustache, he rested his pleasant eyes on me with the remark: "He said you were the right one."

"I try to be, when people want to sit."

"Yes, we should like to," said the lady anxiously.

"Do you mean together?"

My visitors exchanged a glance. "If you could do anything with *me* I suppose it would be double," the gentleman stammered.

"Oh yes, there's naturally a higher charge for two figures than for one."

"We should like to make it pay," the husband confessed.

"That's very good of you," I returned, appreciating so unwonted a sympathy—for I suppose he meant pay the artist.

A sense of strangeness seemed to dawn on the lady. "We mean for the illustrations—Mr. Rivet said you might put one in."

"Put in—an illustration?" I was equally confused.

"Sketch her off, you know," said the gentleman, colouring.

It was only then that I understood the service Claude Rivet had rendered me; he had told them how I worked in black-and-white, for magazines, for story-books, for sketches of contemporary life, and consequently had copious employment for models. These things were true, but it was not less true—I may confess it now; whether because the aspiration was to lead to everything or to nothing I leave the reader to guess—that I couldn't get the honours, to say nothing of the emoluments, of a great painter of portraits out of my head. My "illustrations" were my pot-boilers; I looked to a different branch of art—far and away the most interesting it had always seemed to me—to perpetuate my fame. There was no shame in looking to it also to make my fortune; but that fortune was by so much further from being made from the moment my visitors wished to be "done" for nothing. I was disappointed; for in the pictorial sense I had immediately *seen* them. I had seized their type—I had already settled what I would do with it. Something that wouldn't absolutely have pleased them, I afterwards reflected.

"Ah you're—you're—a?" I began as soon as I had mastered my surprise. I couldn't bring out the dingy word "models": it seemed so little to fit the case.

"We haven't had much practice," said the lady.

"We've got to *do* something, and we've thought that an artist in your line might perhaps make something of us," her husband threw off. He further mentioned that they didn't know many artists and that they had gone first, on the off-chance—he painted views of course, but sometimes put in figures; perhaps I remembered—to Mr. Rivet, whom they had met a few years before at a place in Norfolk where he was sketching.

"We used to sketch a little ourselves," the lady hinted.

"It's very awkward, but we absolutely *must* do something," her husband went on.

"Of course we're not so *very* young," she admitted with a wan smile.

With the remark that I might as well know something more about them the husband had handed me a card extracted from a neat new pocket-book—their appurtenances were all of the freshest—and inscribed with the words "Major Monarch." Impressive as these words were they didn't carry my knowledge much further; but my visitor presently added: "I've left the army and we've had the misfortune to lose our money. In fact our means are dreadfully small."

"It's awfully trying—a regular strain," said Mrs. Monarch.

They evidently wished to be discreet—to take care not to swagger because they were gentlefolk. I felt them willing to recognise this as something of a drawback at the same time that I guessed at an underlying sense—their consolation in adversity—that they *had* their points. They certainly had; but these advantages struck me as preponderantly social; such for instance as would help to make a drawing-room look well. However, a drawing-room was always, or ought to be, a picture.

In consequence of his wife's allusion to their age Major Monarch observed: "Naturally it's more for the figure that we thought of going in. We can still hold ourselves up." On the instant I saw that the figure was indeed their strong point. His "naturally" didn't sound vain, but it lighted up the question. "*She* has the best one," he continued, nodding at his wife with a pleasant after-dinner absence of circumlocution. I could only reply, as if we were in fact sitting over our wine, that this didn't prevent his own from being very good; which led him in turn to make answer: "We thought that if you ever have to do people like us we might be something like it. *She* particularly—for a lady in a book, you know."

I was so amused by them that, to get more of it, I did my best to take their point of view; and though it was an embarrassment to find myself appraising physically, as if they were animals on hire or useful blacks, a pair whom I should have expected to meet only in one of the relations in which criticism is tacit, I looked at Mrs. Monarch judicially enough to be able to exclaim after a moment with conviction: "Oh yes, a lady in a book!" She was singularly like a bad illustration.

"We'll stand up, if you like," said the Major; and he raised himself before me with a really grand air.

I could take his measure at a glance—he was six feet two and a perfect gentleman. It would have paid any club in process of formation and in want of a stamp to engage him at a salary to stand in the principal window. What struck me at once was that in coming to me they had rather missed their vocation; they could surely have been turned to better account for advertising purposes. I couldn't of course see the thing in detail, but I could see them make somebody's fortune—I don't mean their own. There was something in them for a waistcoat-maker, an hotel-keeper or a soap-vendor. I could imagine "We always use it" pinned on their bosoms with the greatest effect; I had a vision of the brilliancy with which they would launch a table d'hôte.

Mrs. Monarch sat still, not from pride but from shyness, and presently her husband said to her: "Get up, my dear, and show how smart you are." She obeyed, but she had no need to get up to show it. She walked to the end of the studio and then came back blushing, her fluttered eyes on the partner of her appeal. I was reminded of an incident I had accidentally had a glimpse of in Paris—being with a friend there, a dramatist about to produce a play, when an actress came to him to ask to be entrusted with a part. She went through her paces before him, walked up and down as Mrs. Monarch was doing. Mrs. Monarch did it quite as well, but I abstained from applauding. It was very odd to see such people apply for such poor pay. She looked as if she had ten thousand a year. Her husband had used the word that described her: she was in the London current jargon essentially and typically "smart." Her figure was, in the same order of ideas, conspicuously and irreproachably "good." For a woman of her age her waist was surprisingly small; her elbow moreover had the orthodox crook. She held her head at the conventional angle, but why did she come to *me?* She ought to have tried on jackets at a big shop. I feared my visitors were not only destitute but "artistic"—which would be a great complication. When she sat down again I thanked her, observing that what a draughtsman most valued in his models was the faculty of keeping quiet.

"Oh *she* can keep quiet," said Major Monarch. Then he added jocosely: "I've always kept her quiet."

"I'm not a nasty fidget, am I?" It was going to wring tears from me, I felt, the way she hid her head, ostrich-like, in the other broad bosom.

The owner of this expanse addressed his answer to me. "Perhaps it isn't out of place to mention—because we ought to be quite business-like, oughtn't we?—that when I married her she was known as the Beautiful Statue."

"Oh dear!" said Mrs. Monarch ruefully.

"Of course I should want a certain amount of expression," I rejoined.

"Of *course!*"—and I had never heard such unanimity.

"And then I suppose you know that you'll get awfully tired."

"Oh we *never* get tired!" they eagerly cried.

"Have you had any kind of practice?"

They hesitated—they looked at each other. "We've been photographed—*immensely*," said Mrs. Monarch.

"She means the fellows have asked us themselves," added the Major.

"I see—because you're so good-looking."

"I don't know what they thought, but they were always after us."

"We always get our photographs for nothing," smiled Mrs. Monarch.

"We might have brought some, my dear," her husband remarked.

"I'm not sure we have any left. We've given quantities away," she explained to me.

"With our autographs and that sort of thing," said the Major.

"Are they to be got in the shops?" I enquired as a harmless pleasantry.

"Oh yes, *hers*—they used to be."

"Not now," said Mrs. Monarch with her eyes on the floor.

II

I could fancy the "sort of thing" they put on the presentation copies of their photographs, and I was sure they wrote a beautiful hand. It was odd how quickly I was sure of everything that concerned them. If they were now so poor as to have to earn shillings and pence they could never have had much of a margin. Their good looks had been their capital, and they had good-humouredly made the most of the career that this resource marked out for them. It was in their faces, the blankness, the deep intellectual repose of the twenty years of country-house visiting that had given them pleasant intonations. I could see the sunny drawing-rooms, sprinkled with periodicals she didn't read, in which Mrs. Monarch had continuously sat; I could see the wet shrubberies in which she had walked, equipped to admiration for either exercise. I could see the rich covers the Major had helped to shoot and the wonderful garments in which, late at night, he repaired to the smoking-room to talk about them. I could imagine their leggings and waterproofs, their knowing tweeds and rugs, their rolls of sticks and cases of tackle and neat umbrellas; and I could evoke the exact appearance of their servants and the compact variety of their luggage on the platforms of country stations.

They gave small tips, but they were liked; they didn't do anything themselves, but they were wlecome. The looked so well everywhere; they gratified the general relish for stature, complexion, and "form." They knew it without fatuity or vulgarity, and they respected themselves in consequence. They weren't superficial; they were thorough and kept themselves up—it had been their line. People with such a taste for activity had to have some line. I could feel how even in a dull house they could have been counted on for the joy of life. At present something had happened—it didn't matter what, their little income had grown less, it had grown least—and they had to do something for pocket-money. Their friends could like them, I made out, without liking to support them. There was something about them that represented credit—their clothes, their manners, their type; but if credit is a large empty pocket in which an occasional chink reverberates, the chink at least must be audible. What they wanted of me was to help to make it so. Fortunately they had no children—I soon divined that. They would also perhaps wish our relations to be kept secret: this was why it was "for the figure"—the reproduction of the face would betray them.

I liked them—I felt, quite as their friends must have done—they were so simple; and I had no objection to them if they would suit. But somehow with all their perfections I didn't easily believe in them. After all they were amateurs, and the ruling passion of my life was the detestation of the amateur. Combined with this was another perversity—an innate preference for the represented subject over the real one: the defect of the real one was so apt to be a lack of representation. I like things that appeared; then one was sure. Whether they *were* or not was a subordinate and almost always a profitless question. There were other considerations, the first of which was that I already had two or three recruits in use, notably a young person with big feet, in alpaca, from Kilburn, who for a couple of years had come to me regularly for my illustrations and with whom I was still—perhaps ignobly—satisfied. I frankly explained to my visitors how the case stood, but they had taken more precautions than I supposed. They had reasoned out their opportunity, for Claude Rivet had told them of the projected *édition de luxe* of one of the writers of our day—the rarest of the novelists—who, long neglected by the multitudinous vulgar and dearly prized by the attentive (need I mention Philip Vincent?) had had the happy fortune of seeing, late in life, the dawn and then the full light of a higher criticism; an estimate in which on the part of the public there was something really of expiation. The edition preparing, planned by a publisher of taste, was practically an act of high reparation; the wood-cuts with which it was to be enriched were the homage of English art to one of the most independent representatives of English letters. Major and Mrs. Monarch confessed to me they had hoped I might be able to work *them* into my branch of the enterprise. They knew I was to do the first of the books, "Rutland Ramsay," but I had to make clear to them that my participation in the rest of the affair—this first book was to be a test—must depend on the satisfaction I should give. If this should be limited my employers would drop me with scarce common forms. It was therefore a crisis for me, and naturally I was making special preparations, looking about for new people, should they be necessary, and securing the best types. I admitted however that I should like to settle down to two or three good models who would do for everything.

"Should we have often to—a—put on special clothes?" Mrs. Monarch timidly demanded.

"Dear yes—that's half the business."

"And should we be expected to supply our own costumes?"

"Oh no; I've got a lot of things. A painter's models put on—or put off—anything he likes."

"And you mean—a—the same?"

"The same?"

Mrs. Monarch looked at her husband again.

"Oh she was just wondering," he explained, "if the costumes are in *general* use." I had to confess that they were, and I mentioned further that some of them—I had a lot of genuine greasy last-century things—had served their time, a hundred years ago, on living world-stained men and women; on figures not perhaps so far removed, in that vanished world, from *their* type, the Monarchs', *quoi!* of a breeched and bewigged age. "We'll put on anything that *fits,*" said the Major.

"Oh I arrange that—they fit in the pictures."

"I'm afraid I should do better for the modern books. I'd come as you like," said Mrs. Monarch.

"She has got a lot of clothes at home: they might do for contemporary life," her husband continued.

"Oh I can fancy scenes in which you'd be quite natural." And indeed I could see the slipshod rearrangements of stale properties—the stories I tried to produce pictures for without the exasperation of reading them—whose sandy tracts the good lady might help to people. But I had to return to the fact that for this sort of work—the daily mechanical grind—I was already equipped: the people I was working with were fully adequate.

"We only thought we might be more like *some* characters," said Mrs. Monarch mildly, getting up.

Her husband also rose; he stood looking at me with a dim wistfulness that was touching in so fine a man. "Wouldn't it be rather a pull sometimes to have—a—to have—?" He hung fire; he wanted me to help him by phrasing what he meant. But I couldn't—I didn't know. So he brought it out awkwardly: "The *real* thing; a gentleman, you know, or a lady." I was quite ready to give a general assent—I admitted that there was a great deal in that. This encouraged Major Monarch to say, following up his appeal with an unacted gulp: "It's awfully hard—we've tried everything." The gulp was communicative; it proved too much for his wife. Before I knew it Mrs. Monarch had dropped again upon a divan and burst into tears. Her husband sat down beside her, holding one of her hands; whereupon she quickly dried her eyes with the other, while I felt embarrassed as she looked up at me. "There isn't a confounded job I haven't applied for—waited for—prayed for. You can fancy we'd be pretty bad first. Secretaryships and that sort of thing? You might as well ask for a peerage. I'd be *anything*—I'm strong; a messenger or a coalheaver. I'd put on a gold-laced cap and open carriage-doors in front of the haberdasher's; I'd hang about a station to carry potmanteaux; I'd be a postman. But they won't *look* at you; there are thousands as good as yourself already on the ground. *Gentlemen,* poor beggars, who've drunk their wine, who've kept their hunters!"

I was as reassuring as I knew how to be, and my visitors were presently on their feet again while, for the experiment, we agreed on an hour. We were discussing it when the door opened and Miss Churm came in with a wet umbrella. Miss Churm had to take the omnibus to Maida Vale and then walk half a mile. She looked a trifle blowsy and slightly splashed. I scarcely ever saw her come in without thinking afresh how odd it was that, being so little in herself, she should yet be so much in others. She was a meagre little Miss Churm, but was such an ample heroine of romance. She was only a freckled cockney, but she could represent everything, from a fine lady to a shepherdess; she had the faculty as she might have had a fine voice or long hair. She couldn't spell and she loved beer, but she had two or three "points," and practice, and a knack, and mother-wit, and a whimsical sensibility, and a love of the theatre, and seven sisters, and not an ounce of respect, especially for the *h*. The first thing my visitors saw was that her umbrella was wet, and in their spotless perfection they visibly winced at it. The rain had come on since their arrival.

"I'm all in a soak; there *was* a mess of people in the 'bus. I wish you lived near a stytion," said Miss Churm. I requested her to get ready as quickly as possible, and she passed into the room in which she always changed her dress. But before going out she asked me what she was to get into this time.

"It's the Russian princess, don't you know?" I answered; "the one with the 'golden eyes,' in black velvet, for the long thing in the *Cheapside*."

"Golden eyes? I *say!*" cried Miss Churm, while my companions watched her with intensity as she withdrew. She always arranged herself, when she was late, before I could turn round; and I kept my visitors a little on purpose, so that they might get an idea, from seeing her, what would be expected of themselves. I mentiond that she was quite my notion of an excellent model—she was really very clever.

"Do you think she looks like a Russian princess?" Major Monarch asked with lurking alarm.

"When I make her, yes."

"Oh if you have to *make* her—!" he reasoned, not without point.

"That's the most you can ask. There are so many who are not makeable."

"Well now, *here's* a lady"—and with a persuasive smile he passed his arm into his wife's—"who's already made!"

"Oh I'm not a Russian princess," Mrs. Monarch protested a little coldly. I could see she had known some and didn't like them. There at once was a complication of a kind I never had to fear with Miss Churm.

This young lady came back in black velvet—the gown was rather rusty and very low on her lean shoulders—and with a Japanese fan in her red hands. I reminded her that in the scene I was doing she had to look over someone's head. "I forget whose it is; but it doesn't matter. Just look over a head."

"I'd rather look over a stove," said Miss Churm; and she took her station near the fire. She fell into position, settled herself into a tall attitude, gave a certain backward inclination to her head and a certain forward droop to her fan, and looked, at least to my prejudiced sense, distinguished and charming, foreign and dangerous. We left her looking so while I went downstairs with Major and Mrs. Monarch.

"I believe I could come about as near it as that," said Mrs. Monarch.

"Oh you think she's shabby, but you must allow for the alchemy of art."

However, they went off with an evident increase of comfort founded on their demonstrable advantage in being the real thing. I could fancy them shuddering over Miss Churm. She was very droll about them when I went back, for I told her what they wanted.

"Well, if *she* can sit I'll tyke to book-keeping," said my model.

"She's very ladylike," I replied as an innocent form of aggravation.

"So much the worse for *you.* That means she can't turn round."

"She'll do for the fashionable novels."

"Oh yes, she'll *do* for them!" my model humorously declared. "Ain't they bad enough without her?" I had often sociably denounced them to Miss Churm.

III

It was for the elucidation of a mystery in one of these works that I first tried Mrs. Monarch. Her husband came with her, to be useful if necessary—it was sufficiently clear that as a general thing he would prefer to come with her. At first I wondered if this were for "propriety's" sake—if he were going to be jealous and meddling. The idea was too tiresome, and if it had been confirmed it would speedily have brought our acquaintance to a close. But I soon saw there was nothing in it and that if he accompanied Mrs. Monarch it was—in addition to the chance of being wanted—simply because he had nothing else to do. When they were separate his occupation was gone and they never *had* been separate. I judged rightly that in their awkward situation their close union was their main comfort and that this union had no weak spot. It was a real marriage, an encouragement to the hesitating, a nut for pessimists to crack. Their address was humble—I remember afterwards thinking it had been the only thing about them that was really professional—and I could fancy the lamentable lodgings in which the Major would have been left alone. He could sit there more or less grimly with his wife—he couldn't sit there anyhow without her.

He had too much tact to try and make himself agreeable when he couldn't be useful; so when I was too absorbed in my work to talk he simply sat and waited. But I liked to hear him talk—it made my work, when not interrupting it, less mechanical, less special. To listen to him was to combine the excitement of going out with the economy of staying at home. There was only one hindrance—that I seemed not to know any of the people this brilliant couple had known. I think he wondered extremely, during the term of our intercourse, whom the deuce I *did* know. He hadn't a stray sixpence of an idea to fumble for, so we didn't spin it very fine; we confined ourselves to questions of leather and even of liquor—saddlers and breeches-makers and how to get excellent claret cheap—and matters like "good trains" and the habits of small game. His lore on these last subjects was astonishing—he managed to interweave the station-master with the ornithologist. When he couldn't talk about greater things he could talk cheerfully about smaller, and since I couldn't accompany him into reminiscences of the fashionable world he could lower the conversation without a visible effort to my level.

So earnest a desire to please was touching in a man who could so easily have knocked one down. He looked after the fire and had an opinion on the draught of the stove without my asking him, and I could see that he thought many of my arrangements not half knowing. I remember telling him that if I were only rich I'd offer him a salary to come and teach me how to live. Sometimes he gave a random sigh of which the essence might have been: "Give me even such a bare old barrack as *this*, and I'd do something with it!" When I wanted to use him he came alone; which was an illustration of the superior courage of women. His wife could bear her solitary second floor, and she was in general more discreet; showing by various small reserves that she was alive to the propriety of keeping our relations markedly professional—not letting them slide into sociability. She wished it to remain clear that she and the Major were employed, not cultivated, and if she approved of me as a superior, who could be kept in his place, she never thought me quite good enough for an equal.

She sat with great intensity, giving the whole of her mind to it, and was capable of remaining for an hour almost as motionless as before a photographer's lens. I could see she had been photographed often, but somehow the very habit that made her good for that purpose unfitted her for mine. At first I was extremely pleased with her ladylike air, and it was a satisfaction, on coming to follow her lines, to see how good they were and how far they could lead the pencil. But after a little skirmishing I began to find her too insurmountably stiff; do what I would with it my drawing looked like a photograph or a copy of a photograph. Her figure had no variety of expression—she herself had no sense of variety. You may say that this was my business and was only a question of placing her. Yet I placed her in every conceivable position and she managed to obliterate their differences. She was always a lady certainly, and into the bargain was always the same lady. She was the real thing, but always the same thing. There were moments when I rather writhed under the serenity of her confidence that she *was* the real thing. All her dealings with me and all her husband's were an implication that this was lucky for *me*. Meanwhile I found myself trying to invent types that approached her own, instead of making her own transform itself—in the clever way that was not impossible for instance to poor Miss Churm. Arrange as I would and take the precautions I would, she always came out, in my pictures, too tall—landing me in the dilemma of having represented a fascinating woman as seven feet high, which (out of respect perhaps to my own very much scantier inches) was far from my idea of such a personage.

The case was worse with the Major—nothing I could do would keep *him* down, so that he became useful only for the representation of brawny giants. I adored variety and range, I cherished human accidents, the illustrative note; I wanted to characterise closely, and the thing in the world I most hated was the danger of being ridden by a type. I had quarrelled with some of my friends about it; I had parted company with them for maintaining that one *had* to be, and that if the type was beautiful—witness Raphael and Leonardo—the servitude was only a gain. I was neither Leonardo nor Raphael—I might only be a presumptuous young modern searcher; but I held that everything was to be sacrificed sooner than character. When they claimed that the obsessional form could easily *be* character I retorted, perhaps superficially, "Whose?" It couldn't be everybody's—it might end in being nobody's.

After I had drawn Mrs. Monarch a dozen times I felt surer even than before that the value of such a model as Miss Churm resided precisely in the fact that she had no positive stamp, combined of course with the other fact that what she did have was a curious and inexplicable talent for imitation. Her usual appearance was like a curtain which she could draw up at request for a capital performance. This performance was simply suggestive; but it was a word to the wise—it was vivid and pretty. Sometimes even I thought it, though she was plain herself, too insipidly pretty; I made it a reproach to her that the figures drawn from her were monotonously (*bêtement*, as we used to say) graceful. Nothing made her more angry; it was so much her pride to feel she could sit for characters that had nothing in common with each other. She would accuse me at such moments of taking away her "reputytion."

It suffered a certain shrinkage, this queer quantity, from the repeated visits of my new friends. Miss Churm was greatly in demand, never in want of employment, so I had no scruple in putting her off occasionally, to try them more at my ease. It was certainly amusing at first to do the real thing—it was amusing to do Major Monarch's trousers. They *were* the real thing, even if he did come out colossal. It was amusing to do his wife's back hair—it was so mathematically neat—and the particular "smart" tension of her tight stays. She lent herself especially to positions in which the face was somewhat averted or blurred; she abounded in ladylike back views and *profils perdus*. When she stood erect she took naturally one of the attitudes in which court-painters represent queens and princesses; so that I found myself wondering whether, to draw out this accomplishment, I couldn't get the editor of the *Cheapside* to publish a really royal romance, "A Tale of Buckingham Palace." Sometimes however the real thing and the make-believe came into contact; by which I mean that Miss Churm, keeping an appointment or coming to make one on days when I had much work in hand, encountered her invidious rivals. The encounter was not on their part, for they noticed her no more than if she had been the housemaid; not from intentional loftiness, but simply because as yet, professionally, they didn't know how to fraternise, as I could imagine they would have liked—or at least that the Major would. They couldn't talk about the omnibus—they always walked; and they didn't know what else to try—she wasn't interested in good trains or cheap claret. Besides, they must have felt—in the air—that she was amused at them, secretly derisive of their ever knowing how. She wasn't a person to conceal the limits of her faith if she had had a chance to show them. On the other hand Mrs. Monarch didn't think her tidy; for why else did she takes pains to say to me—it was going out of the way, for Mrs. Monarch—that she didn't like dirty women?

One day when my young lady happened to be present with my other sitters—she even dropped in, when it was convenient, for a chat—I asked her to be so good as to lend a hand in getting tea, a service with which she was familiar and which was one of a class that, living as I did in a small way, with slender domestic resources, I often appealed to my models to render. They liked to lay hands on my property, to break the sitting, and sometimes the china—it made them feel Bohemian. The next time I saw Miss Churm after this incident she surprised me greatly by making a scene about it—she accused me of having wished to humiliate her. She hadn't resented the outrage at the time, but had seemed obliging and amused, enjoying the comedy of asking Mrs. Monarch, who sat vague and silent, whether she would have cream and sugar, and putting an exaggerated simper into the question. She had tried intonations—as if she too wished to pass for the real thing—till I was afraid my other visitors would take offence.

Oh they were determined not to do this, and their touching patience was the measure of their great need. They would sit by the hour, uncomplaining, till I was ready to use them; they would come back on the chance of being wanted and would walk away cheerfully if it failed. I used to go the door with them to see in what magnificent order they retreated. I tried to find other employment for them—I introduced them to several artists. But they didn't "take," for reasons I could appreciate, and I became rather anxiously aware that after such disappointments they fell back upon me with a heavier weight. They did me the honour to think me most *their* form. They weren't romantic enough for the painters, and in those days there were few serious workers in black-and-white. Besides, they had an eye to the great job I had mentioned to them—they had secretly set their hearts on supplying the right essence for my pictorial vindication of our fine novelist. They knew that for this undertaking I should want no costume-effects, none of the frippery of past ages—that it was a case in which everything would be contemporary and satirical and presumably genteel. If I could work them into it their future would be assured, for the labour would of course be long and the occupation steady.

One day Mrs. Monarch came without her husband—she explained his absence by his having had to go to the City. While she sat there in her usual relaxed majesty there came at the door a knock which I immediately recognised as the subdued appeal of a model out of work. It was followed by the entrance of a young man whom I at once saw to be a foreigner and who proved in fact an Italian acquainted with no English word but my name, which he uttered in a way that made it seem to include all others. I hadn't then visited his country, nor was I proficient in his tongue; but as he was not so meanly constituted—what Italian is?—as to depend only on that member for expression he conveyed to me, in familiar but graceful mimicry, that he was in search of exactly the employment in which the lady before me was engaged. I was not struck with him at first, and while I continued to draw I dropped few signs of interest or encouragement. He stood his ground however—not importunately, but with a dumb dog-like fidelity in his eyes that amounted to innocent impudence, the manner of a devoted servant—he might have been in the house for years—unjustly suspected. Suddenly it struck me that this very attitude and expression made a picture; whereupon I told him to sit down and wait till I should be free. There was another picture in the way he obeyed me, and I observed as I worked that there were others still in the way he looked wonderingly, with his head thrown back, about the high studio. He might have been crossing himself in Saint Peter's. Before I finished I said to myself "The fellow's a bankrupt orange-monger, but a treasure."

When Mrs. Monarch withdrew he passed across the room like a flash to open the door for her, standing there with the rapt pure gaze of the young Dante spellbound by the young Beatrice. As I never insisted, in such situations, on the blankness of the British domestic, I reflected that he had the making of a servant—and I needed one, but couldn't pay him to be only that—as well as of a model; in short I resolved to adopt my bright adventurer if he would agree to officiate in the double capacity. He jumped at my offer, and in the event my rashness—for I had really known nothing about him—wasn't brought home to me. He proved a sympathetic though a desultory ministrant, and had in a wonderful degree the *sentiment de la pose*. It was uncultivated, instinctive, a part of the happy instinct that had guided him to my door and helped him to spell out my name on the card nailed to it. He had had no other introduction to me than a guess, from the shape of my high north window, seen outside, that my place was a studio and that as a studio it would contain an artist. He had wandered to England in search of fortune, like other itinerants, and had embarked, with a partner and a small green hand-cart, on the sale of penny ices. The ices had melted away and the partner had dissolved in their train. My young man wore tight yellow trousers with reddish stripes and his name was Oronte. He was sallow but fair, and when I put him into some old clothes of my own he looked like an Englishman. He was as good as Miss Churm, who could look, when requested, like an Italian.

IV

I thought Mrs. Monarch's face slightly convulsed when, on her coming back with her husband, she found Oronte installed. It was strange to have to recognise in a scrap of a lazzarone a competitor to her magnificent Major. It was she who scented danger first, for the Major was anecdotically unconscious. But Oronte gave us tea, with a hundred eager confusions—he had never been concerned in so queer a process—and I think she thought better of me for having at last an "establishment." They saw a couple of drawings that I had made of the establishment, and Mrs. Monarch hinted that it never would have struck her he had sat for them. "Now the drawings you make from *us*, they look exactly like us," she reminded me, smiling in triumph; and I recognised that this was indeed just their defect. When I drew the Monarchs I couldn't anyhow get away from them—get into the character I wanted to represent; and I hadn't the least desire my model should be discoverable in my picture. Miss Churm never was, and Mrs. Monarch thought I hid her, very properly, because she was vulgar; whereas if she was lost it was only as the dead who go to heaven are lost—in the gain of an angel the more.

By this time I had got a certain start with "Rutland Ramsay," the first novel in the great projected series; that is I had produced a dozen drawings, several with the help of the Major and his wife, and I had sent them in for approval. My understanding with the publishers, as I have already hinted, had been that I was to be left to do my work, in this particular case, as I liked, with the whole book committed to me; but my connexion with the rest of the series was only contingent. There were moments when, frankly, it *was* a comfort to have the real thing under one's hand; for there were characters in "Rutland Ramsay" that were very much like it. There were people presumably as erect as the Major and women of as good a fashion as Mrs. Monarch. There was a great deal of country-house life—treated, it is true, in a fine fanciful ironical generalised way—and there was a considerable implication of knickerbockers and kilts. There were certain things I had to settle at the outset; such things for instance as the exact appearance of the hero and the particular bloom and figure of the heroine. The author of course gave me a lead, but there was a margin for interpretation. I took the Monarchs into my confidence, I told them frankly what I was about, I mentioned my embarrassments and alternatives. "Oh take *him!*" Mrs. Monarch murmured sweetly, looking at her husband; and "What could you want better than my wife?" the Major enquired with the comfortable candour that now prevailed between us.

I wasn't obliged to answer these remarks—I was only obliged to place my sitters. I wasn't easy in mind, and I postponed a little timidly perhaps the solving of my question. The book was a large canvas, the other figures were numerous, and I worked off at first some of the episodes in which the hero and the heroine were not concerned. When once I had set *them* up I should have to stick to them—I couldn't make my young man seven feet high in one place and five feet nine in another. I inclined on the whole to the latter measurement, though the Major more than once reminded me that *he* looked about as young as any one. It was indeed quite possible to arrange him, for the figure, so that it would have been difficult to detect his age. After the spontaneous Oronte had been with me a month, and after I had given him to understand several times over that his native exuberance would presently constitute an insurmountable barrier to our further intercourse, I waked to a sense of his heroic capacity. He was only five feet seven, but the remaining inches were latent. I tried him almost secretly at first, for I was really rather afraid of the judgement my other models would pass on such a choice. If they regarded Miss Churm as little better than a snare what would they think of the representation by a person so little the real thing as an Italian street-vendor of a protagonist formed by a public school?

If I went a little in fear of them it wasn't because they bullied me, because they had got an oppressive foothold, but because in their really pathetic decorum and mysteriously permanent newness they counted on me so intensely. I was therefore very glad when Jack Hawley came home: he was always of such good counsel. He painted badly himself, but there was no one like him for putting his finger on the place. He had been absent from England for a year; he had been somewhere—I don't remember where—to get a fresh eye. I was in a good deal of dread of any such organ, but we were old friends; he had been away for months and a sense of emptiness was creeping into my life. I hadn't dodged a missile for a year.

He came back with a fresh eye, but with the same old black velvet blouse, and the first evening he spent in my studio we smoked cigarettes till the small hours. He had done no work himself, he had only got the eye; so the field was clear for the production of my little things. He wanted to see what I had produced for the *Cheapside*, but he was disappointed in the exhibition. That at least seemed the meaning of two or three comprehensive groans which, as he lounged on my big divan, his leg folded under him, looking at my latest drawings, issued from his lips with the smoke of the cigarette.

"What's the matter with you?" I asked.

"What's the matter with *you?*"

"Nothing save that I'm mystified."

"You are indeed. You're quite off the hinge. What's the meaning of this new fad?" And he tossed me, with visible irreverence, a drawing in which I happened to have depicted both my elegant models. I asked if he didn't think it good, and he replied that it struck him as execrable, given the sort of thing I had always represented myself to him as wishing to arrive at; but I let that pass—I was so anxious to see exactly what he meant. The two figures in the picture looked colossal, but I supposed this was *not* what he meant, inasmuch as, for aught he knew to the contrary, I might have been trying for some such effect. I maintained that I was working exactly in the same way as when he last had done me the honour to tell me I might do something some day. "Well, there's a screw loose somewhere," he answered; "wait a bit and I'll discover it." I depended upon him to do so: where else was the fresh eye? But he produced at last nothing more luminous than "I don't know—I don't like your types." This was lame for a critic who had never consented to discuss with me anything but the question of execution, the direction of strokes and the mystery of values.

"In the drawings you've been looking at I think my types are very handsome."

"Oh they won't do!"

"I've been working with new models."

"I see you have. *They* won't do."

"Are you very sure of that?"

"Absolutely—they're stupid."

"You mean *I* am—for I ought to get round that."

"You *can't*—with such people. Who are they?"

I told him, so far as was necessary, and he concluded heartlessly: "Ce sont des gens qu'il faut mettre à la porte."

"You've never seen them; they're awfully good"—I flew to their defence.

"Not seen them? Why all this recent work of yours drops to pieces with them. It's all I want to see of them."

"No one else has said anything against it—the *Cheapside* people are pleased."

"Every one else is an ass, and the *Cheapside* people the biggest asses of all. Come, don't pretend at this time of day to have pretty illusions about the public, especially about publishers and editors. It's not for *such* animals you work—it's for those who know, *coloro che sanno;* so keep straight for *me* if you can't keep straight for yourself. There was a certain sort of thing you used to try for—and a very good thing it was. But this twaddle isn't *in* it." When I talked with Hawley later about "Rutland Ramsay" and its possible successors he declared that I must get back into my boat again or I should go to the bottom. His voice in short was the voice of warning.

I noted the warning, but I didn't turn my friends out of doors. They bored me a good deal; but the very fact that they bored me admonished me not to sacrifice them—if there was anything to be done with them—simply to irritation. As I look back at this phase they seem to me to have pervaded my life not a little. I have a vision of them as most of the time in my studio, seated against the wall on an old velvet bench to be out of the way, and resembling the while a pair of patient courtiers in a royal ante-chamber. I'm convinced that during the coldest weeks of the winter they held their ground because it saved them fire. Their newness was losing its gloss, and it was impossible not to feel them objects of charity. Whenever Miss Churm arrived they went away, and after I was fairly launched in "Rutland Ramsay" Miss Churm arrived pretty often. They managed to express to me tacitly that they supposed I wanted her for the low life of the book, and I let them suppose it, since they had attempted to study the work—it was lying about the studio—without discovering that it dealt only with the highest circles. They had dipped into the most brilliant of our novelists without deciphering many passages. I still took an hour from them, now and again, in spite of Jack Hawley's warning: it would be time enough to dismiss them, if dismissal should be necessary, when the rigour of the season was over. Hawley had made their acquaintance—he had met them at my fireside—and thought them a ridiculous pair. Learning that he was a painter they tried to approach him, to show him too that they were the real thing; but he looked at them, across the big room, as if they were miles away: they were a compendium of everything he most objected to in the social system of his country. Such people as that, all convention and patent-leather, with ejaculations that stopped conversation, had no business in a studio. A studio was a place to learn to see, and how could you see through a pair of feather-beds?

The main inconvenience I suffered at their hands was that at first I was shy of letting it break upon them that my artful little servant had begun to sit to me for "Rutland Ramsay." They knew I had been odd enough—they were prepared by this time to allow oddity to artists—to pick a foreign vagabond out of the streets when I might have had a person with whiskers and credentials; but it was some time before they learned how high I rated his accomplishments. They found him in an attitude more than once, but they never doubted I was doing him as an organ-grinder. There were several things they never guessed, and one of them was that for a striking scene in the novel, in which a footman briefly figured, it occurred to me to make use of Major Monarch as the menial. I kept putting this off, I didn't like to ask him to don the livery—besides the difficulty of finding a livery to fit him. At last, one day late in the winter, when I was at work on the despised Oronte, who caught one's idea on the wing, and was in the glow of feeling myself go very straight, they came in, the Major and his wife, with their society laugh about nothing (there was less and less to laugh at); came in like country-callers—they always reminded me of that—who have walked across the park after church and are presently persuaded to stay to luncheon. Luncheon was over, but they could stay to tea—I knew they wanted it. The fit was on me, however, and I couldn't let my ardour cool and my work wait, with the fading daylight, while my model prepared it. So I asked Mrs. Monarch if she would mind laying it out—a request which for an instant brought all the blood to her face. Her eyes were on her husband's for a second, and some mute telegraphy passed between them. Their folly was over the next instant; his cheerful shrewdness put an end to it. So far from pitying their wounded pride, I must add, I was moved to give it as complete a lesson as I could. They bustled about together and got out the cups and saucers and made the kettle boil. I know they felt as if they were waiting on my servant, and when the tea was prepared I said: "He'll have a cup, please—he's tired." Mrs. Monarch brought him one where he stood, and he took it from her as if he had been a gentleman at a party squeezing a crush-hat with an elbow.

Then it came over me that she had made a great effort for me—made it with a kind of nobleness—and that I owed her a compensation. Each time I saw her after this I wondered what the compensation could be. I couldn't go on doing the wrong thing to oblige them. Oh it *was* the wrong thing, the stamp of the work for which they sat—Hawley was not the only person to say it now. I sent in a large number of the drawings I had made for "Rutland Ramsay," and I received a warning that was more to the point than Hawley's. The artistic adviser of the house for which I was working was of opinion that many of my illustrations were not what had been looked for. Most of these illustrations were the subjects in which the Monarchs had figured. Without going into the question of what *had* been looked for, I had to face the fact that at this rate I shouldn't get the other books to do. I hurled myself in despair on Miss Churm—I put her through all her paces. I not only adopted Oronte publicly as my hero, but one morning when the Major looked in to see if I didn't require him to finish a *Cheapside* figure for which he had begun to sit the week before, I told him I had changed my mind—I'd do the drawing from my man. At this my visitor turned pale and stood looking at me. "Is *he* your idea of an English gentleman?" he asked.

I was disappointed, I was nervous, I wanted to get on with my work; so I replied with irritation: "Oh my dear Major—I can't be ruined for *you!*"

It was a horrid speech, but he stood another moment—after which, without a word, he quitted the studio. I drew a long breath, for I said to myself that I shouldn't see him again. I hadn't told him definitely that I was in danger of having my work rejected, but I was vexed at his not having felt the catastrophe in the air, read with me the moral of our fruitless collaboration, the lesson that in the deceptive atmosphere of art even the highest respectability may fail of being plastic.

I didn't owe my friends money, but I did see them again. They reappeared together three days later, and, given all the other facts, there was something tragic in that one. It was a clear proof they could find nothing else in life to do. They had threshed the matter out in a dismal conference—they had digested the bad news that they were not in for the series. If they weren't useful to me even for the *Cheapside* their function seemed difficult to determine, and I could only judge at first that they had come, forgivingly, decorously, to take a last leave. This made me rejoice in secret that I had little leisure for a scene; for I had placed both my other models in position together and I was pegging away at a drawing from which I hoped to derive glory. It had been suggested by the passage in which Rutland Ramsay, drawing up a chair to Artemisia's piano-stool, says extraordinary things to her while she ostensibly fingers out a difficult piece of music. I had done Miss Churm at the piano before—it was an attitude in which she knew how to take on an absolutely poetic grace. I wished the two figures to "compose" together with intensity, and my little Italian had entered perfectly into my conception. The pair were vividly before me, the piano had been pulled out; it was a charming show of blended youth and murmured love, which I had only to catch and keep. My visitors stood and looked at it, and I was friendly to them over my shoulder.

They made no response, but I was used to silent company and went on with my work, only a little disconcerted—even though exhilarated by the sense that *this* was at least the ideal thing—at not having got rid of them after all. Presently I heard Mrs. Monarch's sweet voice beside or rather above me: "I wish her hair were a little better done." I looked up and she was staring with a strange fixedness at Miss Churm, whose back was turned to her. "Do you mind my just touching it?" she went on—a question which made me spring up for an instant as with the instinctive fear that she might do the young lady a harm. But she quieted me with a glance I shall never forget—I confess I should like to have been able to paint *that*—and went for a moment to my model. She spoke to her softly, laying a hand on her shoulder and bending over her; and as the girl, understanding, gratefully assented, she disposed her rough curls, with a few quick passes, in such a way as to make Miss Churm's head twice as charming. It was one of the most heroic personal services I've ever seen rendered. Then Mrs. Monarch turned away with a low sigh and, looking about her as if for something to do, stooped to the floor with a noble humility and picked up a dirty rag that had dropped out of my paint-box.

The Major meanwhile had also been looking for something to do, and, wandering to the other end of the studio, saw before him my breakfast-things neglected, unremoved. "I say, can't I be useful *here?*" he called out to me with an irrepressible quaver. I assented with a laugh that I fear was awkward, and for the next ten minutes, while I worked, I heard the light clatter of china and the tinkle of spoons and glass. Mrs. Monarch assisted her husband—they washed up my crockery, they put it away. They wandered off into my little scullery, and I afterwards found that they had cleaned my knives and that my slender stock of plate had an unprecedented surface. When it came over me, the latent eloquence of what they were doing, I confess that my drawing was blurred for a moment—the picture swam. They had accepted their failure, but they couldn't accept their fate. They had bowed their heads in bewilderment to the perverse and cruel law in virtue of which the real thing could be so much less precious than the unreal; but they didn't want to starve. If my servants were my models, then my models might be my servants. They would reverse the parts—the others would sit for the ladies and gentlemen and *they* would do the work. They would still be in the studio—it was an intense dumb appeal to me not to turn them out. "Take us on," they wanted to say—"we'll do *anything*."

My pencil dropped from my hand; my sitting was spoiled and I got rid of my sitters, who were also evidently rather mystified and awestruck. Then, alone with the Major and his wife I had a most uncomfortable moment. He put their prayer into a single sentence: "I say, you know—just let *us* do for you, can't you?" I couldn't—it was dreadful to see them emptying my slops; but I pretended I could, to oblige them, for about a week. Then I gave them a sum of money to go away, and I never saw them again. I obtained the remaining books, but my friend Hawley repeats that Major and Mrs. Monarch did me a permanent harm, got me into false ways. If it be true I'm content to have paid the price—for the memory.

SARAH ORNE JEWETT

[1849–1909]

Sarah Orne Jewett's adoration of her father shaped both her life and her work: it prevented her from marrying any of the men drawn to her dark beauty, and it determined her reserved manner of writing. "Great writers do not try to write about people and things," she remembered him saying, "they tell them just as they are." She had reason enough to follow his precepts. A beloved country doctor, he was also a scholar; he had taught at Bowdoin College and was President of the Medical Society of Maine. She was born September 3, 1849, in South Berwick, Maine. Her birthplace became the "Deephaven" of her fiction, and her countless drives with her father as he made the rounds of his patients taught her more than she ever learned from the local Academy and private tutors.

It was from these rides and visits in the outlying districts that she established an intimacy with the northern New England countryside. Tentatively she began to record aspects of the life and landscape which most observers found unalluring, to uncover the beauty beneath the bleakness. "By the Morning Boat" begins:

> On the coast of Maine, where many green islands and salt inlets fringe the deep-cut shore line; where balsam firs and bayberry bushes send their fragrance far seaward, and song-sparrows sing all day, and the tide runs plashing in and out among the weedy ledges; where cowbells tinkle on the hills and herons stand in the shady coves—on the lonely coast of Maine stood a small gray house facing the morning light. All the weather-beaten houses of that region face the sea apprehensively, like the women who live in them.

It was some time before she was sufficiently sure of herself to submit work over her own name—for a while she used the pseudonym of "Alice C. Eliot"—but her first collection of regional studies entitled Deephaven appeared when she was in her late twenties. Her reputation grew rapidly; she was accepted by the powerful Boston group which included Lowell, Howells, and Aldrich; she was praised by Tennyson and Henry James. She traveled abroad, but she was only at home in her own country and particularly her own corner of Maine. She was the first woman to receive an honorary Litt. D., an award conferred upon her by Bowdoin College, her father's alma mater. Before she died, June 24, 1909, fourteen volumes of her stories had been published, besides a collection of verse and a number of books for children.

Sarah Orne Jewett realized her limitations, but within her narrow range she was a finished and almost flawless artist. She depicted better than anyone of her day the communities built around the farms which were being abandoned and the clipper-proud seaports which, because of the steamships, were losing their character as well as their prestige. "She early learned to love her country for what it was," wrote Willa Cather, who was strongly influenced by her delicate precisions. "She had not only the eye, she had the ear . . . The language her people speak to each other is a native tongue. No writer can invent it. It is made in the hard school of experience, in communities where language has been undisturbed long enough to take on color and character from the nature and experiences of the people . . . If I were asked to name three American books which have the possibility of a long, long life I would say at once, The Scarlet Letter, Huckleberry Finn, and The Country of the Pointed Firs."

It is from The Country of the Pointed Firs that "The Hiltons' Holiday" has been taken. The author's own favorite, it is a small but unmistakable masterpiece.

THE HILTON'S HOLIDAY

I

THERE WAS A BRIGHT, FULL MOON in the clear sky, and the sunset was still shining faintly in the west. Dark woods stood all about the old Hilton farmhouse, save down the hill, westward, where lay the shadowy fields which John Hilton, and his father before him, had cleared and tilled with much toil,—the small fields to which they had given the industry and even affection of their honest lives.

John Hilton was sitting on the doorstep of his house as he moved his head in and out of the shadows, turning now and then to speak to his wife, who sat just within the doorway; one could see his good face, rough and somewhat unkempt, as if he were indeed a creature of the shady woods and brown earth, instead of the noisy town. It was late in the long spring evening, and he had just come from the lower field as cheerful as a boy, proud of having finished the planting of his potatoes.

"I had to do my last row mostly by feelin'," he said to his wife. "I'm proper glad I pushed through, an' went back an' ended off after supper. 'T would have taken me a good part o' to-morrow mornin', an' broke my day."

" 'T ain't no use for ye to work yourself all to pieces John," answered the woman quickly. "I declare it does seem harder than ever that we couldn't have kep' our boy; he'd been comin' fourteen years old this fall, most a grown man and he'd work right 'longside of ye now the whole time."

" 'T was hard to lose him; I do seem to miss little John," said the father sadly. "I expect there was reasons why 't was best. I feel able an' smart to work; my father was a girt strong man, an' a monstrous worker afore me. 'T ain't that; but I was thinkin' by myself to-day what a sight o' company the boy would ha' been. You know, small's he was, how I could trust to leave him anywheres with the team, and how he'd beseech to go with me wherever I was goin'; always right in my tracks I used to tell 'em. Poor little John, for all he was so young he had a great deal o' judgment; he'd ha' made a likely man."

The mother sighed heavily as she sat within the shadow.

"But then there's the little girls, a sight o' help an' company," urged the father eagerly, as if it were wrong to dwell upon sorrow and loss. "Katy, she's most as good as a boy, except that she ain't very rugged. She's a real little farmer, she's helped me a sight this spring; an' you've got Susan Ellen, that makes a complete little housekeeper for ye as far as she's learnt. I don't see but we're better off than most folks, each on us having a work-mate."

"That's so, John," acknowledged Mrs. Hilton wistfully, beginning to rock steadily in her straight, splint-bottomed chair. It was always a good sign when she rocked.

"Where be the little girls so late?" asked their father. " 'T is gettin' long past eight o'clock. I don't know when we've all set up so late, but it's so kind o' summer-like an' pleasant. Why, where be they gone?"

"I've told ye; only over to Becker's folks," answered the mother. "I don't see myself what keeps 'em so late; they beseeched me after supper till I let 'em go. They're all in a dazzle with the new teacher; she asked 'em to come over. They say she's unusual smart with 'rethmetic, but she has a kind of a gorpen look to me. She's goin' to give Katy some pieces for her doll, but I told Katy she ought to be ashamed wantin' dolls' pieces, big as she's gettin' to be. I don't know's she ought, though; she ain't but nine this summer."

"Let her take her comfort," said the kind-hearted man. "Them things draws her to the teacher, an' makes them acquainted. Katy's shy with new folks, more so 'n Susan Ellen, who's of the business kind. Katy's shy-feelin' and wishful."

"I don't know but she is," agreed the mother slowly. "Ain't it sing'lar how well acquainted you be with that one, an' I with Susan Ellen? 'T was always so from the first. I'm doubtful sometimes our Katy ain't one that'll be like to get married—anyways not about here. She lives right with herself, but Susan Ellen ain't nothin' when she's alone, she's always after company; all the boys is waitin' on her a'ready. I ain't afraid but she'll take her pick when the time comes. I expect to see Susan Ellen well settled,—she feels grown up now,—but Katy don't care one mite 'bout none o' them things. She wants to be rovin' out o' doors. I do believe she'd stand an' hark to a bird the whole forenoon."

"Perhaps she'll grow up to be a teacher," suggested John Hilton. "She takes to her book more 'n the other one. I should like one on 'em to be a teacher same's my mother was. They're good girls as anybody's got."

"So they be," said the mother, with unusual gentleness and the creak of her rocking-chair was heard, regular as the ticking of a clock. The night breeze stirred in the great woods, and the sound of a brook that went falling down the hillside grew louder and louder. Now and then one could hear the plaintive chirp of a bird. The moon glittered with whiteness like a winter moon, and shone upon the low-roofed house until its small window-panes gleamed like silver, and one could almost see the colors of a blooming bush of lilac that grew in a sheltered angle by the kitchen door. There was an incessant sound of frogs in the lowlands.

"Be you sound asleep, John?" asked the wife presently.

"I don't know but what I was a'most," said the tired man, starting a little. "I should laugh if I was to fall sound asleep right here on the step; 't is the bright night, I expect, makes my eyes feel heavy, an' 't is so peaceful. I was up an' dressed a little past four an' out to work. Well, well!" and he laughed sleepily and rubbed his eyes. "Where's the little girls? I'd better step along an' meet 'em."

"I wouldn't just yet; they'll get home all right, but 't is late for 'em certain. I don't want 'em keepin' Mis' Becker's folks up neither. There, le' 's wait a few minutes," urged Mrs. Hilton.

"I've be'n a-thinkin' all day I'd like to give the child'n some kind of a treat," said the father, wide awake now. "I hurried up my work 'cause I had it so in mind. They don't have the opportunities some do, an' I want 'em to know the world, an' not stay right here on the farm like a couple o' bushes."

"They're a sight better off not to be so full o' notions as some is," protested the mother suspiciously.

"Certain," answered the farmer; "but they're good, bright child'n, an' commencin' to take a sight o' notice. I want 'em to have all we can give 'em. I want 'em to see how other folks does things."

"Why, so do I,"—here the rocking-chair stopped ominously,—"but so long 's they're contented"—

"Contented ain't all in this world; hopper-toads may have that quality an' spend all their time a-blinkin'. I don't know's bein' contented is all there is to look for in a child. Ambition 's somethin' to me."

"Now you've got your mind on to some plot or other." (The rocking-chair began to move again.) "Why can't you talk right out?"

" 'T ain't nothin' special," answered the good man, a little ruffled; he was never prepared for his wife's mysterious powers of divination. "Well there, you do find things out the faster! I only thought perhaps I'd take 'em to-morrow, an' go off somewhere if 't was a good day. I've been promisin' for a good while I'd take 'em to Topham Corners; they've never been there since they was very small."

"I believe you want a good time yourself. You ain't never got over bein' a boy." Mrs. Hilton seemed much amused. "There, go if you want to an' take 'em; they've got their summer hats an' new dresses. I don't know o' nothin' that stands in the way. I should sense it better if there was a circus or anythin' to go to. Why don't you wait an' let the girls pick 'em some strawberries or nice ros'berries, and then they could take an' sell 'em to the stores?"

John Hilton reflected deeply. "I should like to get me some good yellow-turnip seed to plant late. I ain't more 'n satisfied with what I've been gettin' o' late years o' Ira Speed. An' I'm goin' to provide me with a good hoe; mine's gettin' wore out an' all shackly. I can't seem to fix it good."

"Them's excuses," observed Mrs. Hilton, with friendly tolerance. "You just cover up the hoe with somethin', if you get it—I would. Ira Speed's so jealous he'll remember it of you this twenty year, your goin' an' buyin' a new hoe o' anybody but him."

"I've always thought 't was a free country," said John Hilton soberly. "I don't want to vex Ira neither; he favors us all he can in trade .'T is difficult for him to spare a cent, but he's as honest as daylight."

At this moment there was a sudden sound of young voices, and a pair of young figures came out from the shadow of the woods into the moon-lighted open space. An old cock crowed loudly from his perch in the shed, as if he were a herald of royalty. The little girls were hand in hand, and a brisk young dog capered about them as they came.

"Wa'n't it dark gittin' home through the woods this time o' night?" asked the mother hastily, and not without reproach.

"I don't love to have you gone so late; mother an' me was timid about ye, and you've kep' Mis' Becker's folks up, I expect," said their father regretfully. "I don't want to have it said that my little girls ain't got good manners."

"The teacher had a party," chirped Susan Ellen, the elder of the two children. "Goin' home from school she asked the Grover boys, an' Mary an' Sarah Speed. An' Mis' Becker was real pleasant to us: she passed round some cake, an' handed us sap sugar on one of her best plates, an' we played games an' sung some pieces too. Mis' Becker thought we did real well. I can pick out most of a tune on the cabinet organ; teacher says she'll give me lessons."

"I want to know, dear!" exclaimed John Hilton.

"Yes, an' we played Copenhagen, an' took sides spellin', an' Katy beat everybody spellin' there was there."

Katy had not spoken; she was not so strong as her sister, and while Susan Ellen stood a step or two away addressing her eager little audience, Katy had seated herself close to her father on the doorstep. He put his arm around her shoulders, and drew her close to his side, where she stayed.

"Ain't you got nothin' to tell, daughter?" he asked, looking down fondly; and Katy gave a pleased little sigh for answer.

"Tell 'em what's goin' to be the last day o' school, and about our trimmin' the schoolhouse," she said; and Susan Ellen gave the programme in most spirited fashion.

" 'T will be a great time," said the mother, when she had finished. "I don't see why folks wants to go trapesin' off to strange places when such things is happenin' right about 'em." But the children did not observe her mysterious air. "Come, you must step yourselves right to bed!"

They all went into the dark, warm house; the bright moon shone upon it steadily all night, and the lilac flowers were shaken by no breath of wind until the early dawn.

II

The Hiltons always waked early. So did their neighbors, the crows and song-sparrows and robins, the light-footed foxes and squirrels in the woods. When John Hilton waked, before five o'clock, an hour later than usual because he had sat up so late, he opened the house door and came out into the yard, crossing the short green turf hurriedly as if the day were too far spent for any loitering. The magnitude of the plan for taking a whole day of pleasure confronted him seriously, but the weather was fair, and his wife, whose disapproval could not have been set aside, had accepted and even smiled upon the great project. It was inevitable now, that he and the children should go to Topham Corners. Mrs. Hilton had the pleasure of waking them, and telling the news.

In a few minutes they came frisking out to talk over the great plans. The cattle were already fed, and their father was milking. The only sign of high festivity was the wagon pulled out into the yard, with both seats put in as if it were Sunday; but Mr. Hilton still wore his every-day clothes, and Susan Ellen suffered instantly from disappointment.

"Ain't we goin', father?" she asked complainingly; but he nodded and smiled at her, even though the cow, impatient to get to pasture, kept whisking her rough tail across his face. He held his head down and spoke cheerfully, in spite of this vexation.

"Yes, sister, we're goin' certain', an' goin' to have a great time too." Susan Ellen thought that he seemed like a boy at that delightful moment, and felt new sympathy and pleasure at once. "You go an' help mother about breakfast an' them things; we want to get off quick 's we can. You coax mother now, both on ye, an' see if she won't go with us."

"She said she wouldn't be hired to," responded Susan Ellen. "She says it's goin' to be hot, an' she's laid out to go over an' see how her aunt Tamsen Brooks is this afternoon."

The father gave a little sigh; then he took heart again. The truth was that his wife made light of the contemplated pleasure, and, much as he usually valued her companionship and approval, he was sure that they should have a better time without her. It was impossible, however, not to feel guilty of disloyalty at the thought. Even though she might be completely unconscious of his best ideals, he only loved her and the ideals the more, and bent his energies to satisfying her indefinite expectations. His wife still kept much of that youthful beauty which Susan Ellen seemed likely to reproduce.

An hour later the best wagon was ready, and the great expedition set forth. The little dog sat apart, and barked as if it fell entirely upon him to voice the general excitement. Both seats were in the wagon, but the empty place testified to Mrs. Hilton's unyielding disposition. She had wondered why one broad seat would not do, but John Hilton meekly suggested that the wagon looked better with both. The little girls sat on the back seat dressed alike in their Sunday hats of straw with blue ribbons, and their little plaid shawls pinned neatly about their small shoulders. They wore gray thread gloves, and sat very straight. Susan Ellen was half a head the taller, but otherwise, from behind, they looked much alike. As for their father, he was in his Sunday best,—a plain black coat, and a winter hat of felt, which was heavy and rusty-looking for that warm early summer day. He had it in mind to buy a new straw hat at Topham, so that this with the turnip seed and the hoe made three important reasons for going.

"Remember an' lay off your shawls when you get there, an' carry them over your arms," said the mother, clucking like an excited hen to her chickens. "They'll do to keep the dust off your new dresses goin' an' comin.' An' when you eat your dinners don't get spots on you, an' don't point at folks as you ride by, an' stare, or they'll know you come from the country. An' John, you call into Cousin Ad'line Marlow's an' see how they all be, an' tell her I expect her over certain to stop awhile before hayin'. It always eases her phthisic to git up here on the highland, an' I've got a new notion about doin' over her best-room carpet sence I see her that'll save rippin' one breadth. An' don't come home all wore out; an', John, don't you go an' buy me no kickshaws to fetch home. I ain't a child, an' you ain't got no money to waste. I expect you'll go, like 's not, an' buy you some kind of foolish boy's hat; do look an' see if it's reasonable good straw, an' won't splinter all off round the edge. An' you mind, John"—

"Yes, yes, hold on!" cried John impatiently; then he cast a last affectionate, reassuring look at her face, flushed with the hurry and responsibility of starting them off in proper shape. "I wish you was goin' too," he said, smiling. "I do so!" Then the old horse started, and they went out at the bars, and began the careful long descent of the hill. The young dog, tethered to the lilac-bush, was frantic with piteous appeals; the little girls piped their eager good-bys again and again, and their father turned many times to look back and wave his hand. As for their mother, she stood alone and watched them out of sight.

There was one place far out on the high-road where she could catch a last glimpse of the wagon, and she waited what seemed a very long time until it appeared and then was lost to sight again behind a low hill. "They're nothin' but a pack o' child'n together," she said aloud; and then felt lonelier than she expected. She even stooped and patted the unresigned little dog as she passed him, going into the house.

The occasion was so much more important than any one had foreseen that both the little girls were speechless. It seemed at first like going to church in new clothes, or to a funeral; they hardly knew how to behave at the beginning of a whole day of pleasure. They made grave bows at such persons of their acquaintance as happened to be straying in the road. Once or twice they stopped before a farmhouse, while their father talked an inconsiderately long time with some one about the crops and the weather, and even dwelt upon town business and the doings of the selectmen, which might be talked of at any time. The explanations that he gave of their excursion seemed quite unnecessary. It was made entirely clear that he had a little business to do at Topham Corners, and thought he had better give the little girls a ride; they had been very steady at school, and he had finished planting, and could take the day as well as not. Soon, however, they all felt as if such an excursion were an every-day affair, and Susan Ellen began to ask eager questions, while Katy silently sat apart enjoying herself as she never had done before. She liked to see the strange houses, and the children who belonged to them; it was delightful to find flowers that she knew growing all along the road, no matter how far she went from home. Each small homestead looked its best and pleasantest, and shared the exquisite beauty that early summer made,—shared the luxury of greenness and floweriness that decked the rural world. There was an early peony or a late lilac in almost every dooryard.

It was seventeen miles to Topham. After a while they seemed very far from home, having left the hills far behind, and descended to a great level country with fewer tracts of woodland, and wider fields where the crops were much more forward. The houses were all painted, and the roads were smoother and wider. It had been so pleasant driving along that Katy dreaded going into the strange town when she first caught sight of it, though Susan Ellen kept asking with bold fretfulness if they were not almost there. They counted the steeples of four churches, and their father presently showed them the Topham Academy, where their grandmother once went to school, and told them that perhaps some day they would go there too. Katy's heart gave a strange leap; it was such a tremendous thing to think of, but instantly the suggestion was transformed for her into one of the certainties of life. She looked with solemn awe at the tall belfry, and the long rows of windows in the front of the academy, there where it stood high and white among the clustering trees. She hoped that they were going to drive by, but something forbade her taking the responsibility of saying so.

Soon the children found themselves among the crowded village houses. Their father turned to look at them with affectionate solicitude.

"Now sit up straight and appear pretty," he whispered to them. "We're among the best people now, an' I want folks to think well of you."

"I guess we're as good as they be," remarked Susan Ellen, looking at some innocent passers-by with dark suspicion, but Katy tried indeed to sit straight, and folded her hands prettily in her lap, and wished with all her heart to be pleasing for her father's sake. Just then an elderly woman saw the wagon and the sedate party it carried, and smiled so kindly that it seemed to Katy as if Topham Corners had welcomed and received them. She smiled back again as if this hospitable person were an old friend, and entirely forgot that the eyes of all Topham had been upon her.

"There, now we're coming to an elegant house that I want you to see; you'll never forget it," said John Hilton. "It's where Judge Masterson lives, the great lawyer; the handsomest house in the county, everybody says."

"Do you know him, father?" asked Susan Ellen.

"I do," answered John Hilton proudly. "Him and my mother went to school together in their young days, and were always called the two best scholars of their time. The judge called to see her once; he stopped to our house to see her when I was a boy. An' then, some years ago—you've heard me tell how I was on the jury, an' when he heard my name spoken he looked at me sharp, and asked if I wa'n't the son of Catharine Winn, an' spoke most beautiful of your grandmother, an' how well he remembered their young days together."

"I like to hear about that," said Katy.

"She had it pretty hard, I'm afraid, up on the old farm. She was keepin' school in our district when father married her—that's the main reason I backed 'em down when they wanted to tear the old schoolhouse all to pieces," confided John Hilton, turning eagerly. "They all say she lived longer up here on the hill than she could anywhere, but she never had her health. I wa'n't but a boy when she died. Father an' me lived alone afterward till the time your mother come; 't was a good while, too; I wa'n't married so young as some. 'T was lonesome, I tell you; father was plumb discouraged losin' of his wife, an' her long sickness an' all set him back, an' we'd work all day on the land an' never say a word. I s'pose 't is bein' so lonesome early in life that makes me so pleased to have some nice girls growin' up round me now."

There was a tone in her father's voice that drew Katy's heart toward him with new affection. She dimly understood, but Susan Ellen was less interested. They had often heard this story before, but to one child it was always new and to the other old. Susan Ellen was apt to think it tiresome to hear about her grandmother, who, being dead, was hardly worth talking about.

"There's Judge Masterson's place," said their father in an every-day manner, as they turned a corner, and came into full view of the beautiful old white house standing behind its green trees and terraces and lawns. The children had never imagined anything so stately and fine, and even Susan Ellen exclaimed with pleasure. At that moment they saw an old gentleman, who carried himself with great dignity, coming slowly down the wide box-bordered path toward the gate.

"There he is now, there's the judge!" whispered John Hilton excitedly, reining his horse quickly to the green roadside. "He's goin' down-town to his office; we can wait right here an' see him. I can't expect him to remember me; its been a good many years. Now you are goin' to see the great Judge Masterson!"

There was a quiver of expectation in their hearts. The judge stopped at his gate, hesitating a moment before he lifted the latch, and glanced up the street at the country wagon with its two prim little girls on the back seat, and the eager man who drove. They seemed to be waiting for something; the old horse was nibbling at the fresh roadside grass. The judge was used to being looked at with interest, and responded now with a smile as he came out to the sidewalk, and unexpectedly turned their way. Then he suddenly lifted his hat with grave politeness, and came directly toward them.

"Good-morning, Mr. Hilton," he said. "I am very glad to see you, sir"; and Mr. Hilton, the little girls' own father, took off his hat with equal courtesy, and bent forward to shake hands.

Susan Ellen cowered and wished herself away, but little Katy sat straighter than ever, with joy in her father's pride and pleasure shining in her pale, flower-like little face.

"These are your daughters, I am sure," said the old gentleman kindly, taking Susan Ellen's limp and reluctant hand; but when he looked at Katy, his face brightened. "How she recalls your mother!" he said with great feeling. "I am glad to see this dear child. You must come to see me with your father, my dear," he added, still looking at her. "Bring both the little girls, and let them run about the old garden; the cherries are just getting ripe," said Judge Masterson hospitably. "Perhaps you will have time to stop this afternoon as you go home?"

"I should call it a great pleasure if you would come and see us again some time. You may be driving our way, sir," said John Hilton.

"Not very often in these days," answered the old judge. "I thank you for the kind invitation. I should like to see the fine view again from your hill westward. Can I serve you in any way while you are in town? Good-by, my little friends!"

Then they parted, but not before Katy, the shy Katy, whose hand the judge still held unconsciously while he spoke, had reached forward as he said good-by, and lifted her face to kiss him. She could not have told why, except that she felt drawn to something in the serious, worn face. For the first time in her life the child had felt the charm of manners; perhaps she owned a kinship between that which made him what he was, and the spark of nobleness and purity in her own simple soul. She turned again and again to look back at him as they drove away.

"Now you have seen one of the first gentlemen in the country," said their father. "It was worth comin' twice as far"—but he did not say any more, nor turn as usual to look in the children's faces.

III

In the chief business street of Topham a great many country wagons like the Hiltons' were fastened to the posts, and there seemed to our holiday-makers to be a great deal of noise and excitement.

"Now I've got to do my errands, and we can let the horse rest and feed," said John Hilton. "I'll slip his headstall right off, an' put on his halter. I'm goin' to buy him a real good treat o' oats. First we'll go an' buy me my straw hat; I feel as if this one looked a little past to wear in Topham. We'll buy the things we want, an' then we'll walk all along the street, so you can look in the windows an' see the han'some things, same's your mother likes to. What was it mother told you about your shawls?"

"To take 'em off an' carry 'em over our arms," piped Susan Ellen, without comment, but in the interest of alighting and finding themselves afoot upon the pavement the shawls were forgotten. The children stood at the doorway of a shop while their father went inside, and they tried to see what the Topham shapes of bonnets were like, as their mother had advised them; but everything was exciting and confusing, and they could arrive at no decision. When Mr. Hilton came out with a hat in his hand to be seen in a better light, Katy whispered that she wished he would buy a shiny one like

Judge Masterson's; but her father only smiled and shook his head, and said that they were plain folks, he and Katy. There were dry-goods for sale in the same shop, and a young clerk who was measuring linen kindly pulled off some pretty labels with gilded edges and gay pictures, and gave them to the little girls, to their exceeding joy. He may have had small sisters at home, this friendly lad, for he took pains to find two pretty blue boxes besides, and was rewarded by their beaming gratitude.

It was a famous day; they even became used to seeing so many people pass. The village was full of its morning activity, and Susan Ellen gained a new respect for her father, and an increased sense of her own consequence, because even in Topham several persons knew him and called him familiarly by name. The meeting with an old man who had once been a neighbor seemed to give Mr. Hilton the greatest pleasure. The old man called to them from a house doorway as they were passing, and they all went in. The children seated themselves wearily on the wooden step, but their father shook his old friend eagerly by the hand, and declared that he was delighted to see him so well and enjoying the fine weather.

"Oh, yes," said the old man, in a feeble, quavering voice, "I'm astonishin' well for my age. I don't complain, John, I don't complain."

They talked long together of people whom they had known in the past, and Katy, being a little tired, was glad to rest, and sat still with her hands folded, looking about the front yard. There were some kinds of flowers that she never had seen before.

"This is the one that looks like my mother," her father said, and touched Katy's shoulder to remind her to stand up and let herself be seen. "Judge Masterson saw the resemblance; we met him at his gate this morning."

"Yes, she certain does look like your mother, John," said the old man, looking pleasantly at Katy, who found that she liked him better than at first. "She does, certain; the best of young folks is, they remind us of the old ones. 'T is nateral to cling to life, folks say, but for me, I git impatient at times. Most everybody's gone now, an' I want to be goin'. 'T is somethin' before me, an' I want to have it over with. I want to be there 'long o' the rest o' the folks. I expect to last quite a while though; I may see ye couple o' times more, John."

John Hilton responded cheerfully, and the children were urged to pick some flowers. The old man awed them with his impatience to be gone. There was such a townful of people about him, and he seemed as lonely as if he were the last survivor of a former world. Until that moment they had felt as if everything were just beginning.

"Now I want to buy somethin' pretty for your mother," said Mr. Hilton, as they went soberly away down the street, the children keeping fast hold of his hands. "By now the old horse will have eat his dinner and had a good rest, so pretty soon we can jog along home. I'm goin' to take you round by the academy, and the old North Meetinghouse where Dr. Barstow used to preach. Can't you think o' somethin' that your mother'd want?" he asked suddenly, confronted by a man's difficulty of choice.

"She was talkin' about wantin' a new pepper-box, one day; the top o' the old one won't stay on," suggested Susan Ellen, with delightful readiness. "Can't we have some candy, father?"

"Yes, ma'am," said John Hilton, smiling and swinging her hand to and fro as they walked. "I feel as if some would be good myself. What's all this?" They were passing a photographer's doorway with its enticing array of portraits. "I do declare!" he exclaimed excitedly, "I'm goin' to have our pictures taken; 't will please your mother more 'n a little."

This was, perhaps, the greatest triumph of the day, except the delightful meeting with the judge; they sat in a row, with the father in the middle, and there was no doubt as to the excellence of the likeness. The best hats had to be taken off because they cast a shadow, but they were not missed, as their owners had feared. Both Susan Ellen and Katy looked their brightest and best; their eager young faces would forever shine there; the joy of the holiday was mirrored in the little picture. They did not know why their father was so pleased with it; they would not know until age had dowered them with the riches of association and remembrance.

Just at nightfall the Hiltons reached home again, tired out and happy. Katy had climbed over into the front seat beside her father, because that was always her place when they went to church on Sundays. It was a cool evening, there was a fresh sea wind that brought a light mist with it, and the sky was fast growing cloudy. Somehow the children looked different; it seemed to their mother as if they had grown older and taller since they went away in the morning, and as if they belonged to the town now as much as to the country. The greatness of their day's experience had left her far behind; the day had been silent and lonely without them, and she had had their supper ready, and been watching anxiously, ever since five o'clock. As for the children themselves they had little to say at first—they had eaten their luncheon early on the way to Topham. Susan Ellen was childishly cross, but Katy was pathetic and wan. They could hardly wait to show the picture, and their mother was as much pleased as everybody had expected.

"There, what did make you wear your shawls?" she exclaimed a moment afterward, reproachfully. "You ain't been an' wore 'em all day long? I wanted folks to see how pretty your new dresses was, if I did make 'em. Well, well! I wish more'n ever now I'd gone an' seen to ye!"

"An' here's the pepper-box!" said Katy, in a pleased, unconscious tone.

"That really is what I call beautiful," said Mrs. Hilton, after a long and doubtful look. "Our other one was only tin. I never did look so high as a chiny one with flowers, but I can get us another any time for every day. That's a proper hat, as good as you could have got, John. Where's your new hoe?" she asked as he came toward her from the barn, smiling with satisfaction.

"I declare to Moses if I didn't forget all about it," meekly acknowledged the leader of the great excursion. "That an' my yellow-turnip seed, too; they went clean out o' my head, there was so many other things to think of. But 't ain't no sort o' matter; I can get a hoe just as well to Ira Speed's."

His wife could not help laughing. "You an' the little girls have had a great time. They was full o' wonder to me about everything, and I expect they'll talk about it for a week. I guess we was right about havin' 'em see somethin' more o' the world."

"Yes," answered John Hilton, with humility, "yes, we did have a beautiful day. I didn't expect so much. They looked as nice as anybody, and appeared so modest an' pretty. The little girls will remember it perhaps by an' by. I guess they won't never forget this day they had 'long o' father."

It was evening again, the frogs were piping in the lower meadows, and in the woods, higher up the great hill, a little owl began to hoot. The sea air, salt and heavy, was blowing in over the country at the end of the hot bright day. A lamp was lighted in the house, the happy children were talking together, and supper was waiting. The father and mother lingered for a moment outside and looked down over the shadowy fields; then they went in, without speaking. The great day was over, and they shut the door.

JAMES WHITCOMB RILEY

[1849–1916]

James Whitcomb Riley derived his nickname, *"The Hoosier Poet," from the fact that his native state claimed him as its unofficial laureate. He was born October 7, 1849, in the little Indiana town of Greenfield, twenty miles from Indianapolis. His father was a lawyer of Pennsylvania Dutch ancestry; in spite of popular belief, Riley was not,* as his bucolic verses suggest, a struggling son of the soil. On the contrary, he was educated for the law. His temperament, however, was ill suited to the study and citation of obscure legal decisions, and at eighteen he abandoned Blackstone for adventures with a group of traveling mountebanks. During the intermissions, Riley beat the bass-drum, made a "pitch," and sold patent medicines. When the routines grew stale, Riley wrote new ones, made local versions of popular songs, and, when needed, took part in the performances.

Riley had been improvising rhymes since childhood. In his late twenties he sent some verses to the Indianapolis Journal. They were in dialect, ostensibly the work of an unlettered farmer, "Benj. F. Johnson, of Boone." The verses grew into a series, and when they were published under the title The Old Swimmin' Hole Riley leaped into popularity. Such subsequent collections as Afterwhiles, Pipes o' Pan at Zekesbury, and Rhymes of Childhood won readers through their homely idiom, broad simplicity, and unashamed sentimentality. The poet's popularity increased when he appeared on the lecture platform with Bill Nye, balancing Nye's zany humor with appealing warmth and whimsicality. A national celebrity, Riley died July 22, 1916.

At his worst, Riley was the forerunner of a school of "cheerful philosophy" poetasters who offer glib truisms rather than truth, and the precursor of versifying columnists who turn out an artificial smile a day for newspaper syndicates. At his best his direct speech and quiet conviction make such a poem as "When the Frost is on the Punkin" a part of American folk-stuff.

WHEN THE FROST IS ON THE PUNKIN

WHEN the frost is on the punkin and the fodder's in the shock
And you hear the kyouck and gobble of the struttin' turkey-cock,
And the clackin' of the guineys, and the cluckin' of the hens,
And the rooster's hallylooyer as he tiptoes on the fence;
O, it's then's the times a feller is a-feelin' at his best,
With the risin' sun to greet him from a night of peaceful rest,
As he leaves the house, bare-headed, and goes out to feed the stock,
When the frost is on the punkin and the fodder's in the shock.

They's something kindo' harty-like about the atmusfere
When the heat of summer's over and the coolin' fall is here—
Of course we miss the flowers, and the blossums on the trees,
And the mumble of the hummin'-birds and buzzin' of the bees;
But the air's so appetizin'; and the landscape through the haze
Of a crisp and sunny morning of the early autumn days
Is a pictur' that no painter has the colorin' to mock—
When the frost is on the punkin and the fodder's in the shock.

The husky, rusty, russel of the tossels of the corn,
And the raspin' of the tangled leaves, as golden as the morn;
The stubble in the furries—kindo' lonesomelike, but still
A-preachin' sermuns to us of the barns they growed to fill;
The strawstack in the medder, and the reaper in the shed;
The hosses in theyr stalls below—the clover overhead!—
O, it sets my hart a-clickin' like the tickin' of a clock,
When the frost is on the punkin and the fodder's in the shock!

Then your apples all is gethered, and the ones a feller keeps
Is poured around the celler-floor in red and yeller heaps;
And your cider-makin' 's over, and your wimmern-folks is through
With their mince and apple-butter, and theyr souse and saussage, too! . . .
I don't know how to tell it—but ef sich a thing could be
As the Angels wantin' boardin', and they'd call around on *me*—
I'd want to 'commodate 'em—all the whole-indurin' flock—
When the frost is on the punkin and the fodder's in the shock!

LAFCADIO HEARN

[1850–1904]

LAFCADIO HEARN'S EXISTENCE was a triumph over misfortunes that would have wrecked any other man's career. He was born in 1850—a family Bible indicates the month as August although Hearn always gave the date as June 27—on the Ionian island of Santa Maura. His father was an Irish surgeon-major stationed in Greece; his mother was a Greek beauty; he was named Lafcadio after Leucadia, the ancient name of Santa Maura, one of the islands supposedly frequented by Sappho.

He was six years old when his parents' marriage was dissolved and he was placed in the care of his father's widowed aunt, an ardent Catholic who sent him to a parochial school. During a game at St. Cuthbert's College, in Yorkshire, England, he lost the sight of his left eye. Subsequent strain on the right eye was so severe that it protruded to an extent that disfigured his face. Already abnormally sensitive, he grew increasingly recessive and, as an overcompensation, rebellious. He informed the Jesuit fathers that he had decided to become a Pantheist, and, when he was dismissed, went to Paris.

Before he was twenty Hearn had been schooled at another Catholic institution—one near Rouen, France—had shipped to America, had starved in New York, where he peddled odds and ends, and had learned to set type. Traveling west, he became a reporter on the Cincinnati Enquirer. His flair for handling such grotesque stories as that of a charred body found in a furnace gave him a reputation for sensationalism. When it was discovered that he was living with a mulatto woman and, worse, claimed he had married her, his employer felt he had carried his love of sensation too far and discharged him.

Another publisher hired him to send reports of the Hayes-Tilden presidential campaign from New Orleans; instead Hearn wrote a series of sketches of life among the Creoles. He invested his savings, about one hundred dollars, in a restaurant where nothing cost more than five cents; it lasted three weeks. Undeterred by failure, he studied Creole folklore, was helped by the notable student and writer of Louisiana folklore George Washington Cable, and supported himself by finding and translating foreign novelties, which were published later as Stray Leaves from Strange Literatures.

In his late thirties Hearn came to New York, where, for a while, everything went well. He contributed to Harper's Weekly and Harper's Bazaar, wrote a novel, Chita, and cemented a friendship with Henry E. Krehbiel, music critic of the New York Tribune. The bright prospect darkened. Hearn was quick to take umbrage over trifles; he quarreled with his publishers; he made himself obnoxious to his friends, especially to the Krehbiels. He grew to hate New York and extended his revulsion to the entire American scene. He contracted to write a series of stories about the Orient and, at forty, went to Japan.

It was not long before he was thoroughly Orientalized. He taught at the Imperial University of Tokyo; he contributed to Japanese newspapers; he married Setsu Koizumi, a twenty-two-year old girl of high Samurai heritage; he became a Japanese subject and gave himself a

Japanese name, Koizumi Yakumo. His lectures were collected in several volumes, some of which were published after his death of heart failure, September 26, 1904. He had told the oldest of his three sons to put his bones in a cheap jar and bury it on some hill, but he was given a formal funeral according to Buddhist ritual.

Hearn was one of the first to bring the exotic and Oriental into American literature. Not as bizarre or as powerful as Poe, he perfected an almost translucent prose when dealing with the literature of the East and a vivid straightforward style when depicting the stories and superstitions of the West. The twelve volumes which comprise his work, ranging from critical essays to poetical fairy tales, are mainly of interest to students; but Hearn's interpretations of the factual oddities as well as the imaginative fictions of life have an undimmed color and an unfailing appeal.

NEW ORLEANS SUPERSTITIONS

I

THE QUESTION "WHAT IS VOUDOOISM?" could scarcely be answered to-day by any resident of New Orleans unfamiliar with the life of the African west coast, or the superstitions of Hayti, either through study or personal observation. The old generation of planters in whose day Voudooism had a recognized existence—so dangerous as a motive power for black insurrection that severe measures were adopted against it—has passed away; and the only person I ever met who had, as a child in his colored nurse's care, the rare experience of witnessing a Voudoo ceremonial, died some three years ago, at the advanced age of seventy-six. As a religion—an imported faith—Voudooism in Louisiana is really dead; the rites of its serpent worship are forgotten; the meaning of its strange and frenzied chants, whereof some fragments linger as refrains in Negro song, is not now known even to those who remember the words; and the story of its former existence is only revealed to the folklorists by the multitudinous débris of African superstition which it has left behind it. These only I propose to consider now; for what is to-day called Voudooism in New Orleans means, not an African cultus, but a curious class of Negro practices, some possibly derived from it, and others which bear resemblance to the magic of the Middle Ages. What could be more mediæval, for instance, than molding a waxen heart, and sticking pins in it, or melting it slowly before a fire, while charms are being repeated with the hope that as the waxen heart melts or breaks, the life of some enemy will depart? What, again, could remind us more of thirteenth-century superstition than the burning of a certain number of tapers to compel some absent person's return, with the idea that before the last taper is consumed a mysterious mesmerism will force the wanderer to cross rivers and mountains if necessary on his or her way back?

The fear of what are styled "Voudoo charms" is much more widely spread in Louisiana than any one who had conversed only with educated residents might suppose; and the most familiar superstition of this class is the belief in what I might call *pillow magic*, which is the supposed art of causing wasting sicknesses or even death by putting certain objects into the pillow of the bed in which the hated person sleeps. Feather pillows are supposed to be particularly well adapted to this kind of witchcraft. It is believed that by secret spells a "Voudoo" can cause some monstrous kind of bird or nondescript animal to shape itself into being out of the pillow feathers—like the *tupilek* of the Esquimau *iliseenek* (witchcraft). It grows very slowly, and by night only; but when completely formed, the person who has been using the pillow dies. Another practice of pillow witchcraft consists in tearing a living bird asunder—usually a cock—and putting portions of the wings into the pillow. A third form of the black-art is confined to putting certain charms or fetiches—consisting of bones, hair, feathers, rags, strings, or some fantastic combination of these and other trifling objects—into any sort of a pillow used by the party whom it is desired to injure. . .

Some say that putting grains of corn into a child's pillow "prevents it from growing any more"; others declare that a bit of cloth in a grown person's pillow will cause wasting sickness; but different parties questioned by me gave each a different signification to the use of similar charms. Putting an open pair of scissors under the pillow before going to bed is supposed to insure a pleasant sleep in spite of fetiches; but the surest way to provide against being "hoodooed," as American residents call it, is to open one's pillow from time to time. . .

Pillow magic alone, however, is far from being the only recognized form of maleficent Negro witchcraft. Placing charms before the entrance of a house or room, or throwing them over a wall into a yard, is believed to be a deadly practice. When a charm is laid before a room door or hall door, oil is often poured on the floor or pavement in front of the threshold. It is supposed that whoever *crosses an oil line* falls into the power of the Voudoos. To break the oil charm, sand or salt should be strewn upon it. Only a few days before writing this article a very intelligent Spaniard told me that shortly after having discharged a dishonest colored servant he found before his bedroom door one evening a pool of oil with a charm lying in the middle of it, and a candle burning near it. The charm contained some bones, feathers, hairs, and rags—all wrapped together with a string—and a dime. No superstitious person would have dared to use that dime; but my friend, not being superstitious, forthwith put it into his pocket.

The presence of that coin I can only attempt to explain by calling attention to another very interesting superstition connected with New Orleans fetichism. The Negroes believe that in order to make an evil charm operate it is necessary *to sacrifice something.* Wine and cake are left occasionally in dark rooms, or candies are scattered over the sidewalk, by those who want to make their fetich hurt somebody. If food or sweetmeats are thus thrown away, they must be abandoned without a parting glance; the witch or wizard must not look back while engaged in the sacrifice.

Scattering dirt before a door, or making certain figures on the wall of a house with chalk, or crumbling dry leaves with the fingers and scattering the fragments before a residence, are also forms of a maleficent conjuring which sometimes cause serious annoyance. Happily the conjurers are almost as afraid of the counter-charms as the most superstitious persons are of the conjuring. An incident which occurred recently in one of the streets of the old quarter known as "Spanish Town" afforded me ocular proof of the fact. Through malice or thoughtlessness, or possibly in obedience to secret orders, a young Negro girl had been tearing up some leaves and scattering them on the sidewalk in front of a cottage occupied by a French family. Just as she had dropped the last leaf the irate French woman rushed out with a broom and a handful of salt, and began to sweep away the leaves, after having flung salt both upon them and upon the little Negress. The latter actually screamed with fright, and cried out, "*Oh, pas jeté plis disel après moin, madame! pas bisoin jeté disel après moin; mo pas pé vini icite encore.*" (Oh, madam, don't throw any more salt after me; you needn't throw any more salt after me; I won't come here any more.)

The naughty little Negress at whom the salt was thrown seemed to fear the salt more than the broom pointed at her. But she was not yet fully educated, I suspect, in regard to superstitions. The Negro's terror of a broom is of very ancient date—it may have an African origin. It was commented upon by Moreau de Saint-Méry in his work on San Domingo, published in 1796. "What especially irritates the Negro," he wrote, "is to have a broom passed over any part of his body. He asks at once whether the person imagined that he was dead, and remains convinced that the act shortens his life." Very similar ideas concerning the broom linger in New Orleans. To point either end of a broom at a person is deemed bad luck; and many an ignorant man would instantly knock down or violently abuse the party who should point a broom at him. Moreover, the broom is supposed to have mysterious power as a means of getting rid of people. "If you are pestered by visitors whom you would wish never to see again, sprinkle salt on the floor after they go, and sweep it out by the same door through which they have gone, and they will never come back." To use a broom in the evening is bad luck: *balayer le soir, on balaye sa fortune* (to sweep in the evening is to sweep your good luck away), remains a well-quoted proverb.

I do not know of a more mysterious disease than muscular atrophy in certain forms, yet it is by no means uncommon either in New Orleans or in the other leading cities of the United States. But in New Orleans, among the colored people, and among many of the uneducated of other races, the victim of muscular atrophy is believed to be the victim of Voudooism. A notion is prevalent that Negro witches possess knowledge of a secret poison which may terminate life instantly or cause a slow "withering away," according as the dose is administered. A Frenchman under treatment for paralysis informed me that his misfortune was certainly the work of Voudoos, and that his wife and child had died through the secret agency of Negro wizards. Mental aberration is also said to be caused by the administration of poisons whereof some few Negroes are alleged to possess the secret. In short, some very superstitious persons of both races live in perpetual dread of imaginary Voudoos, and fancy that the least ailment from which they suffer is the work of sorcery. It is very doubtful whether any knowledge of those animal or vegetable poisons which leave no trace of their presence in the blood, and which may have been known to some slaves of African birth, still lingers in Louisiana, wide-spread as is the belief to the contrary. During the last decade there have been a few convictions of blacks for the crime of poisoning, but there was nothing at all mysterious or peculiar about these cases, and the toxic agent was invariably the most vulgar of all—arsenic, or some arsenious preparation in the shape of rat poison.

II

A Negro charm to retain the affections of a lover consists in tying up the legs of a rooster to the head, and plunging the creature alive into a vessel of gin or other spirits. Tearing the live bird asunder is another cruel charm, by which some Negroes believe that a sweetheart may become magically fettered to the man who performs the quartering. Here, as in other parts of the world, the crowing hen is killed, the hooting of the owl presages death or bad luck, and the crowing of the cock by day presages the arrival of company. The wren (*roitelet*) must not be killed: *c'est zozeau bon Dié* (it is the good God's bird)—a belief, I think, of European origin.

It is dangerous to throw hair-combings away instead of burning them, because birds may weave them into their nests, and while the nest remains, the person to whom the hair belonged will have a continual headache. It is bad luck to move a cat from one house to another; seven years' bad luck to kill a cat; and the girl who steps, accidentally or otherwise, on a cat's tail need not expect to be married the same year. The apparition of a white butterfly means good news. The neighing of a horse before one's door is bad luck. When a fly bothers one very persistently, one may expect to meet an acquaintance who has been absent many years.

There are many superstitions about marriage, which seem to have a European origin, but are not less interesting on that account. "Twice a bridesmaid, never a bride," is a proverb which needs no comment. The bride must not keep the pins which fastened her wedding dress. The husband must never take off his wedding ring: to take it off will insure him bad luck of some kind. If a girl who is engaged accidentally lets a knife fall, it is a sign that her lover is coming. Fair or foul weather upon her marriage day augurs a happy or unhappy married life.

The superstitions connected with death may be all imported, but I have never been able to find a foreign origin for some of them. It is bad luck to whistle or hum the air that a band plays at a funeral. If a funeral stops before your house, it means that the dead wants company. It is bad luck to cross a funeral procession, or to count the number of carriages in it; if you do count them, you may expect to die after the expiration of as many weeks as there were carriages at the funeral. If at the cemetery there be any unusual delay in burying the dead, caused by any unlooked-for circumstances, such as the tomb proving too small to admit the coffin, it is a sign that the deceased is selecting a companion from among those present, and one of the mourners must soon die. It is bad luck to carry a spade through a house. A bed should never be placed with its foot pointing toward the street door, for corpses leave the house feet foremost. It is bad luck to travel with a priest; this idea seems to me of Spanish importation; and I am inclined to attribute a similar origin to the strange tropical superstition about the banana, which I obtained, nevertheless, from an Italian. You must not *cut* a banana, but simply break it with the fingers, because in cutting it you *cut the cross*. It does not require a very powerful imagination to discern in a severed section of the fruit the ghostly suggestion of a crucifixion.

Some other Creole superstitions are equally characterized by naïve beauty. Never put out with your finger the little red spark that tries to linger on the wick of a blown-out candle: just so long as it burns, some soul in purgatory enjoys rest from torment. Shooting-stars are souls escaping from purgatory: if you can make a good wish three times before the star disappears, the wish will be granted. . .

I will conclude with selections from a list of superstitions which I find widely spread, not citing them as of indubitable Creole origin, but simply calling attention to their prevalence in New Orleans, and leaving the comparative study of them to folklorists.

Turning the foot suddenly in walking means bad or good luck. If the right foot turns, it is bad luck; if the left, good. Some reverse the conditions, making the turning of the left foot bad luck. . .

Never leave a house by a different door from that by which you entered it; it is "carrying away the good luck of the place." Never live in a house you build before it has been rented for at least a year. When an aged person repairs his or her house, he or she is soon to die. Never pass a child through a window; it stops his growth. Stepping over a child does the same; therefore, whoever takes such a step inadvertently must step back again to break the evil spell. Never tilt a rocking-chair when it is empty. Never tell a bad dream before breakfast, unless you want it "to come true"; and never pare the nails on Monday morning before taking a cup of coffee.

SUPERSTITIONS RHYMED AND UNRHYMED

SIGNS AND PORTENTS *are not restricted to the New Orleans of Lafcadio Hearn. In his perennial anxiety to find out what will happen next before it happens (and to prevent it, if possible, since he usually suspects the worst), man has developed some rules of thumb—habits and incantations designed to ward off the expected misfortune and bring about the unlikely good fortune. No mere star-gazing astrology, this household necromancy involves days of the week, kitchen objects, and other people's pets. It's called superstition; hardly anyone believes in it and almost everyone practices it. Below are a number of these superstitious beliefs, some set out in verse, by which Americans have at-*

tempted (and continue to attempt) to bring a little order to planting crops, falling in love, bringing up children, and deciding when to cross the street.

See a pin and pick it up
All the day you'll have good luck.
See a pin and let it lay,
Bad luck you will have all day.

The same holds true for pennies which, when found, should be slipped into your shoe for best effect. Which shoe is a matter of personal intuition since arguments have been put forward on both sides.

Friday night's dream on a Saturday told
Is sure to come true be it never so old.

Saturday is special in this respect, for during the rest of the week dreams only come true if recounted before breakfast.

The maid who, on the first of May,
Goes to the fields at break of day,
And washes in dew from the hawthorn tree,
Will ever after handsome be.

The maid who lacks a hawthorn tree or the inclination to greet the dawn is not altogether lost for she can, at least, rid herself of freckles by washing in watermelon juice.

Wedding Day

Marry on Monday, marry for wealth;
Marry on Tuesday, marry for health;
Marry on Wednesday, the best day of all;
Marry on Thursday, marry for crosses;
Marry on Friday, marry for losses;
Marry on Saturday, no luck at all.

Whatever day she chooses, the bride must have

Something old,
Something new,
Something borrowed,
Something blue.

And on the day of the wedding she must never be seen by her bridegroom until the ceremony.

Birthday

Monday's child is fair of face;
Tuesday's child is full of grace;
Wednesday's child is full of woe;
Thursday's child has far to go;
Friday's child is loving and giving;
Saturday's child works hard for its living;
And a child that is born on the Sabbath day,
Is fair and wise and good and gay.

To make certain of the good luck (or to counteract the bad), pass the baby three times around the leg of a table.

Animals, Stray and Otherwise

There's nothing good about a black cat, particularly if he crosses your path (there are, of course, some who believe that there's everything good about a black cat, but they're in the minority and it seems wiser to play safe). The dog is man's friend, but if he crosses the hunter's path the hunter will find no game; on the other hand, if the dog follows him the hunting will be fine. A dog howling at night is a sure sign of a death. A child breathed on by a horse will have whooping cough. If the horse stumbles three times, his rider is going to die.

Crops and the Moon

For best results, potatoes and other root vegetables must be planted in the dark of the moon. Plants which bear their fruit above the ground must be put out in the light of the moon.

Around the House

Spilled salt means a quarrel; to ward it off, throw a few grains over your left shoulder. If, by accident, you put any of your clothes on inside out, you'll have good luck if you leave them that way. Break a mirror, seven years' bad luck. And *never* open an umbrella indoors.

They that wash on Monday
Have all the week to dry;
They that wash on Tuesday
Are not so much awry;

They that wash on Wednesday
Are not so much to blame;
They that wash on Thursday
Wash for shame;
They that wash on Friday
Wash for need;
And they that wash on Saturday
Are slovenly indeed!

On the Street

Step on a crack, break your mother's back;
Step on a line, break your mother's spine.

Other dire consequences may result from walking on the cracks (or sometimes from *not* walking on them—the rules vary with the age and consequent length of leg of the participant). In any case, when walking with a friend be sure you both go around obstacles, such as telephone poles and other people, on the same side; should one of you go to the right and the other to the left, the friendship will be broken (antidote: say, "Bread and butter").

Among Actors

Don't put a hat on a bed. Don't whistle in dressing rooms. Never recite *Macbeth* backstage. Have someone kick you before you go on, and don't say, "Good luck," say, "Break a leg!"

Among Sailors

Seafaring men seem to have been especially prone to superstition. In the days of sail gales were often murderous and winds always unpredictable. Ships were either lucky or jinxed, and an experienced sailor kept a sharp eye out for the Jonah who might easily ruin a voyage. There were hundreds of signs and portents, scores of things to do or to avoid doing.

Sunday sail, never fail,
Friday sail, ill luck and gale.

Red sky at night, sailors' delight;
Red in the morning, sailors take warning.

When he was becalmed, the sailor whistled for a breeze. If he wanted a good fair wind, he stuck a knife in the after side of the mast.

A small bird or a bee that dropped on deck brought good luck; but a crow or a hawk or an owl in the rigging was a sure sign of impending misfortune.

The prudent sailor nailed a horseshoe to the mast to keep witches away; avoided anyone who came on board with a black valise; refrained from driving nails on Sunday; saw to it that nobody came aboard with an umbrella; never let a hatch be turned upside down when it was taken off.

The Weather

The weather has always been a matter of concern not only to sailors but to all people—farmers, travelers, merchants, lovers, and children planning picnics. Here prognostication reached its height and the person who, by observation of the signs of nature or by interpretation of his rheumatic twinges, could forecast a few days or weeks ahead was a respected sage in the community. Every locality boasted its own meteorological expert, but the one authority that was generally respected throughout the country was The Old Farmer's Almanac (Calculated on a New and Improved Plan)*. Its forecasts for the year were scanned and compared with the competing predictions offered by the calendars supplied by the local dry goods merchants. The predicted storms and cold spells that materialized were remembered as proof of the* Almanac's *infallibility; its mistakes were set down as near-misses and soon forgotten. Here is a sampling of an alphabetical listing of* Prognostics of the Weather *published in the* Almanac *in 1855 and carried on for a number of years thereafter:*

BATS flitting about late in the evening, in spring and autumn, foretell a fine day on the morrow.

BEES, when they remain in their hives, or fly but a short distance from them, foretell showers and rainy weather.

BEETLES flying about late at evening foretell a fine day on the morrow.

BIRDS are particularly sensitive as to changes of the weather. The gull, seemingly one of the most stupid of birds, will fly inland, on the approach of a storm, long before it appears, and will fly out to sea again when fair weather is coming. Swallows fly low before the approach of a storm, and high when fair weather is upon us. When the blue jay comes near the houses and screams, foul weather is at hand. The peacock will squall, the guinea-hen call "come back," the cock crow upon the fence less than usual, the quail call out "more wet," and be more noisy than he is wont. The crow will "caw," the owl screech, the water-fowl scream and plunge into the water, the thrush will sing loud and long, and most of the bird tribe will pick their feathers, plume themselves, and fly to their nests, before stormy weather, seeming anxious to avoid trouble.

BLUE SKY.—When there is a piece of blue sky seen on a rainy morning, big enough, as the proverb says, "to make a Dutchman a pair of breeches," we shall probably have a fine afternoon.

CANDLEMAS DAY.—(Feb. 2d.)

If Candlemas Day be fair and bright,
Winter will have another flight;
But if Candlemas Day be cloudy and rain,
Winter has gone, not to come again.

CHICKENS, when they are more noisy than usual, are said by some to prognosticate rain.

CHICKWEED.—When open in the morning, fair weather may be expected; when closed, rain. It is called, like the pimpernel, the poor man's weather-glass, or barometer. As long as they continue to unfold and display themselves, the whole day may be depended on. If, however, the flowers withdraw into their green envelope, the pedestrian need wish no better hint to take his umbrella in his walk.

CHRISTMAS.—The clemency of the season at Christmas is a blessing to the poor, whatever it be to the coal-merchants. We may fear, however, for its effects on health, if there be truth in the old adage:

When Christmas is white
The graveyard is lean;
But fat is the graveyard
When Christmas is green.

COBWEBS.—If on the grass early in the morning, they indicate fair weather that day.

COLORS of various shades in the sky and clouds are tokens of different phenomena, or changes. Much red . . . always forebodes wind or rain. . . Sometimes, however, much red indicates a fine day, if the morning be gray. The following lines of the poet are familiar to most of our readers.

An evening red and a morning gray,
Will set the traveller on his way;
But an evening gray and a morning red,
Will pour down rain on the pilgrim's head.

A greenish color of the sky near the horizon often shows that we may expect more wet weather. The most beautiful greenish tints are seen in autumn, and in that season the purple of the falling haze is often a sign of a continuation of fine weather.

CORN HUSKS.—If these adhere closely and are more difficult to pull apart than usual, it is a sign of hard winter.

FISH.—When fish bite readily, and gambol near the surface of streams or ponds, it is an indication that foul or wet weather is near.

FLIES.—These and various sorts of volatile insects, become more troublesome, and sting and bite more than usual, before, as well as in the intervals of, rainy weather, particularly in autumn. This remark applies to several kinds of flies. Horse-flies are more troublesome before the fall of rain.

FROGS, by their clamorous croaking, indicate rainy weather; as does, likewise, their coming abroad in great numbers of an evening; but this sign applies more obviously to toads.

GEESE are not such "geese" as we think them; their movements are impelled and controlled by strong and almost unerring instincts. When washing, or taking wing with a clamorous noise and flying to water, they portend rain. Geese are excellent guards against fire or thieves, always watchful, and giving notice by their noise of any unusual movements about them. When wild geese are observed to migrate southward or westward in greater numbers than usual in autumn and winter, they are said to indicate hard weather; when to the northward, warmer weather. In general, the early appearance of flocks of geese or other wild fowls in the south foreshows a severe winter. A curious illustration of their instinct is seen in their flight, which is wedge-shaped, the leader cleaving the air for those who follow, and at stated intervals falling in the rear, and his place being supplied by another, who pursues the same course; which proceeding will at once be seen to facilitate as much as possible the flight and preserve the strength of the flock.

GNATS.—When these bite keenly and fly near the ground, we look for wind or rain; when they fly in a vortex in the beams of the setting sun, they forebode fair weather; when they frisk about more widely in the open air at eve, they foreshow heat; and when they assemble under trees and bite more than usual, they indicate rain.

GOATS-BEARD.—This plant, called also salsify and oyster-plant, will not unclose its flowers in cloudy weather. From its habit of closing its flowers at noon it has received the common name of "Go-to-bed-at-noon," and in many districts of England the farmers' boys are said to regulate their dinner-hour by the closing of the goats-beard.

Gossamer, as it is called, being the fine web of a certain species of spider, floating in the air in abundance and lodging on the trees or rigging of vessels, and on other objects, affords a sign of fine settled weather in autumn, as does the much covering of the ground and herbage by the woof of the spiders in general.

Portents in General

Sneeze on a Monday, you sneeze for danger;
Sneeze on a Tuesday, you sneeze for a stranger;
Sneeze on a Wednesday, you sneeze for a letter;
Sneeze on a Thursday, for something better;
Sneeze on a Friday, you sneeze for sorrow;
Sneeze on a Saturday, your sweetheart tomorrow;
Sneeze on a Sunday, your safety seek,
For you will have trouble the whole of the week.

Never begin anything on a Friday.
Keep your fingers crossed,
a horseshoe over the door,
and touch wood.

EDWIN MARKHAM

[1852–1940]

Most of the poetry *written by Edwin Markham during his long life was either lightly melodious or heavily declamatory. But two blank verse monologues, "The Man with the Hoe" and "Lincoln, the Man of the People," achieved a towering if somewhat tumid eloquence. Their author was born April 23, 1852, in Oregon City, Oregon, but spent his youth on a ranch in a wild valley of the Suisin Hills in central California. At eighteen he gave up bronco riding to become a teacher; during the next thirty years he was an educator, principal of a high school, headmaster, and superintendent.*

Markham had always composed verse, but it was little noticed until, in his forty-eighth year, "The Man with the Hoe" appeared in the San Francisco Examiner. It was a time of social and economic stress, and the poem, suggested by Millet's painting of the same name, was reprinted throughout the country. Markham took Millet's bowed peasant and made him the dumb expression of protest, a symbol of the poverty-stricken, exploited laborer in every nation, "the landless workman of the world." Two years later his almost equally popular poem, "Lincoln, the Man of the People," voiced something in a similar strain, although on a vastly different subject. The same passion that led the poet to champion the common worker made him extol the great commoner in the martyred president. Many other poems followed—there were eight volumes—and Markham continued to write until his death on Staten Island in his eighty-eighth year. However, although some of his lyrics and epigrammatic quatrains are frequently quoted, he never again achieved the height of his two peak poems.

THE MAN WITH THE HOE

Bowed by the weight of centuries he leans
Upon his hoe and gazes on the ground,
The emptiness of ages in his face,
And on his back the burden of the world.
Who made him dead to rapture and despair,
A thing that grieves not and that never hopes,
Stolid and stunned, a brother to the ox?
Who loosened and let down this brutal jaw?
Whose was the hand that slanted back his brow?
Whose breath blew out the light within this brain?

Is this the Thing the Lord God made and gave
To have dominion over sea and land;
To trace the stars and search the heavens for power;
To feel the passion of Eternity?

Is this the dream He dreamed who shaped the suns
And marked their ways upon the ancient deep?
Down all the caverns of Hell to their last gulf
There is no shape more terrible than this—
More tongued with censure of the world's blind greed—
More filled with signs and portents for the soul—
More packt with danger to the universe.

What gulfs between him and the seraphim!
Slave of the wheel of labor, what to him
Are Plato and the swing of Pleiades?
What the long reaches of the peaks of song,
The rift of dawn, the reddening of the rose?
Through this dread shape the suffering ages look;
Time's tragedy is in that aching stoop;
Through this dread shape humanity betrayed,
Plundered, profaned, and disinherited,
Cries protest to the Judges of the World,
A protest that is also prophecy.

O masters, lords and rulers in all lands,
Is this the handiwork you give to God,
This monstrous thing distorted and soul-quenched?
How will you ever straighten up this shape;
Touch it again with immortality;
Give back the upward looking and the light;
Rebuild in it the music and the dream;
Make right the immemorial infamies,
Perfidious wrongs, immedicable woes?

O masters, lords and rulers in all lands,
How will the Future reckon with this man?
How answer his brute question in that hour
When whirlwinds of rebellion shake all shores?
How will it be with kingdoms and with kings—
With those who shaped him to the thing he is—
When this dumb terror shall rise to judge the world,
After the silence of the centuries?

LINCOLN, THE MAN OF THE PEOPLE

When the Norn Mother saw the Whirlwind Hour
Greatening and darkening as it hurried on,
She left the Heaven of Heroes and came down

To make a man to meet the mortal need.
She took the tried clay of the common road—
Clay warm yet with the ancient heat of Earth,
Dashed through it all a strain of prophecy;
Tempered the heap with thrill of human tears;
Then mixed a laughter with the serious stuff.
Into the shape she breathed a flame to light
That tender, tragic, ever-changing face.
Here was a man to hold against the world,
A man to match the mountains and the sea.

The color of the ground was in him, the red earth;
The smell and smack of elemental things:
The rectitude and patience of the cliff;
The good-will of the rain that loves all leaves;
The friendly welcome of the wayside well;
The courage of the bird that dares the sea;
The gladness of the wind that shakes the corn;
The mercy of the snow that hides all scars;
The secrecy of streams that make their way
Beneath the mountain to the rifted rock;
The undelaying justice of the light
That gives as freely to the shrinking flower
As to the great oak flaring to the wind—
To the grave's low hill as to the Matterhorn
That shoulders out the sky.

Sprung from the West,
The strength of virgin forests braced his mind,
The hush of spacious prairies stilled his soul.
Up from log cabin to the Capitol,
One fire was on his spirit, one resolve—
To send the keen ax to the root of wrong,
Clearing a free way for the feet of God.
And evermore he burned to do his deed
With the fine stroke and gesture of a king:
He built the rail-pile as he built the State,
Pouring his splendid strength through every blow,
The conscience of him testing every stroke,
To make his deed the measure of a man.

So came the Captain with the thinking heart;
And when the judgment thunders split the house,
Wrenching the rafters from their ancient rest,

He held the ridgepole up, and spiked again
The rafters of the Home. He held his place—
Held the long purpose like a growing tree—
Held on through blame and faltered not at praise.
And when he fell in whirlwind, he went down
As when a lordly cedar, green with boughs,
Goes down with a great shout upon the hills,
And leaves a lonesome place against the sky.

WILLIAM SYDNEY PORTER

(*O. Henry*)

[1862–1910]

Before he became O. Henry, *the chronicler of the millions who crowd Bagdad-on-the-Subway, as he liked to call New York, was called William Sydney Porter. Born at Greensboro, North Carolina, September 11, 1862, the son of an improvident physician, he had little schooling. At fifteen he clerked in his uncle's drugstore and, after five years, left to work on a ranch in Texas. From ranching he turned to bookkeeping, went to the state capital, became a draftsman in a land office, and then a bank-teller.*

At twenty-five he married—it was a runaway romance—and divided his time between a desk at the bank and his writing desk at home. Some of his sketches appeared in the papers; a few years later he brought out a humorous weekly, The Rolling Stone, *and moved to Houston. He was thirty-four when he was indicted for alleged embezzlement of funds.*

Porter was scarcely a criminal. He seems to have been guilty of carelessness and irregularity—the bank management was extremely slipshod—and he might never have been sentenced for the technical manipulation, except that before his trial he did a foolish thing. He ran away, headed for New Orleans, and took a banana boat to Honduras. There he consorted with various refugees, including the outlaw Al Jennings. He traveled to Mexico and South America, and might have safely remained there had not his wife's deathbed illness brought him back to Texas. Arrested, he was tried and sentenced to prison for five years and, because of good behavior, served a little more than three years of his term.

Like John Bunyan, who wrote nine of his books in prison, and Richard Lovelace, who declared that "stone walls do not a prison make," Porter turned incarceration into a creative escape. The man who had hitherto penned nothing more weighty than comic skits developed into a serious and mature writer. Drawing his material from his own experiences south of the border and those of his fellow-inmates—one of them was the "Jimmy Valentine" of "A Retrieved Reformation"—he sent out stories to magazines which were glad to accept them. He chose a pseudonym which, it is said, was derived from a prison guard, Orrin Henry.

In his fortieth year he was invited to New York by the editor of a magazine, and there he remained the rest of his life. He wrote, consuming a couple of quarts of whiskey a day, spasmodically and reluctantly; he had to be hounded, cajoled, goaded, and continually bombarded to finish his manuscripts in time for promised deadlines. Nevertheless, for a considerable time he did fulfill his contract with the New York World to produce a tale a week at the rate of $100 a story. Before he died of tuberculosis at forty-eight, June 5, 1910, he had spun some six hundred tales, vignettes, dramatic episodes, and trenchant pieces of pure fiction.

Collected under such titles as The Four Million, The Trimmed Lamp, The Voice of the City, Roads of Destiny, and Rolling Stones, many of O. Henry's plots are contrived, marred by coincidence, and weakened by sentimentality. He delighted in swift characterizations; he liked surprise so much that he made almost a formula of the trick ending. On the other hand, he had a deft way of exposing pretension, and his quick eye caught countless facets of life's incalculable whirligig. In common with Maupassant and Maugham, he was essentially a teller of tales, and he continues to hold large audiences as a narrator who is only occasionally a critical commentator, and as a craftsman who is alternately realistic, romantic, and ironic, but always undeniably readable.

A MUNICIPAL REPORT

The cities are full of pride,
Challenging each to each—
This from her mountainside,
That from her burthened beach.
RUDYARD KIPLING

Fancy a novel about Chicago or Buffalo, let us say, or Nashville, Tennessee! There are just three big cities in the United States that are "story cities"—New York, of course, New Orleans, and, best of the lot, San Francisco.—FRANK NORRIS

EAST IS EAST, and West is San Francisco, according to Californians. Californians are a race of people; they are not merely inhabitants of a state. They are the Southerners of the West. Now, Chicagoans are no less loyal to their city; but when you ask them why, they stammer and speak of lake fish and the new Odd Fellows' Building. But Californians go into detail.

Of course they have, in the climate, an argument that is good for half an hour while you are thinking of your coal bills and heavy underwear. But as soon as they come to mistake your silence for conviction, madness comes upon them, and they picture the city of the Golden Gate as the Bagdad of the New World. So far, as a matter of opinion, no refutation is necessary. But, dear cousins all (from Adam and Eve descended), it is a rash one who will lay his finger on the map and say: "In this town there can be no romance—what could happen here?" Yes, it is a bold and a rash deed to challenge in one sentence history, romance, and Rand and McNally.

NASHVILLE.—A city, port of delivery, and the capital of the State of Tennessee, is on the Cumberland River and on the N. C. & St. L. and the L. & N. railroads. This city is regarded as the most important educational center in the South.

I stepped off the train at 8 P.M. Having searched the thesaurus in vain for adjectives, I must, as a substitution, hie me to comparison in the form of a recipe.

Take of London fog 30 parts; malaria 10 parts; gas leaks 20 parts; dewdrops gathered in a brickyard at sunrise 25 parts; odor of honeysuckle 15 parts. Mix.

The mixture will give you an approximate conception of a Nashville drizzle. It is not so fragrant as a moth ball nor as thick as pea soup; but 'tis enough—'twill serve.

I went to a hotel in a tumbril. It required strong self-suppression for me to keep from climbing to the top of it and giving an imitation of Sidney Carton. The vehicle was drawn by beasts of a bygone era and driven by something dark and emancipated.

I was sleepy and tired; so when I got to the hotel I hurriedly paid it the fifty cents it demanded (with approximate lagniappe, I assure you). I knew its habits; and I did not want to hear it prate about its old "marster" or anything that happened "befo' de wah."

The hotel was one of the kind described as "renovated." That means twenty thousand dollars' worth of new marble pillars, tiling, electric lights and brass cuspidors in the lobby, and a new L. & N. timetable and a lithograph of Lookout Mountain in each one of the great rooms above. The management was without reproach, the attention full of exquisite Southern courtesy, the service as slow as the progress of a snail and as good-humored as Rip Van Winkle. The food was worth traveling a thousand miles for. There is no other hotel in the world where you can get such chicken livers *en brochette*.

At dinner I asked a Negro waiter if there was anything doing in town. He pondered gravely for a minute and then replied: "Well, boss, I don't really reckon there's anything at all doin' after sundown."

Sundown had been accomplished; it had been drowned in the drizzle long before. So that spectacle was denied me. But I went forth upon the streets in the drizzle to see what might be there.

> It is built on undulating grounds; and the streets are lighted by electricity at a cost of $32,470 per annum.

As I left the hotel there was a race riot. Down upon me charged a company of freedmen, or Arabs, or Zulus, armed with—no, I saw with relief that they were not rifles, but whips. And I saw dimly a caravan of black, clumsy vehicles; and at the reassuring shouts, "Kyar you anywhere in the town, boss, fuh fifty cents," I reasoned that I was merely a "fare" instead of a victim.

I walked through long streets, all leading uphill. I wondered how those streets ever came down again. Perhaps they didn't until they were "graded." On a few of the "main streets" I saw lights in stores here and there; saw streetcars go by, conveying worthy burghers hither and yon; saw people pass engaged in the art of conversation; and heard a burst of semi-lively laughter issuing from a soda-water and ice-cream parlor. The streets other than "main" seemed to have enticed upon their borders houses consecrated to peace and domesticity. In many of them lights shone behind discreetly drawn window shades; in a few, pianos tinkled orderly and irreproachable music. There was, indeed, little "doing." I wished I had come before sundown. So I returned to my hotel.

In November, 1864, the Confederate General Hood advanced against Nashville, where he shut up a National force under General Thomas. The latter then sallied forth and defeated the Confederates in a terrible conflict.

All my life I have heard of, admired, and witnessed the fine marksmanship of the South in its peaceful conflicts in the tobacco-chewing regions. But in my hotel a surprise awaited me. There were twelve bright, new, imposing, capacious brass cuspidors in the great lobby, tall enough to be called urns and so wide-mouthed that the crack pitcher of a lady baseball team should have been able to throw a ball into each one of them at five paces distant. But, although a terrible battle had raged and was still raging, the enemy had not suffered. Bright, new, imposing, capacious, untouched, they stood. But, shades of Jefferson Brick! the tile floor—the beautiful tile floor! I could not avoid thinking of the battle of Nashville, and trying to draw, as is my foolish habit, some deductions about hereditary marksmanship.

Here I first saw Major (by misplaced courtesy) Wentworth Caswell. I knew him for a type the moment my eyes suffered from the sight of him. A rat has no geographical habitat. My old friend, A. Tennyson, said, as he so well said almost everything:

> Prophet, curse me the blabbing lip,
> And curse me the British vermin, the rat.

Let us regard the word "British" as interchangeable *ad lib.* A rat is a rat.

This man was hunting about the hotel lobby like a starved dog that had forgotten where he had buried a bone. He had a face of great acreage, red, pulpy, and with a kind of sleepy massiveness like that of Buddha. He possessed one single virtue—he was smoothly shaven. The mark of the beast is not indelible upon a man until he goes about with a stubble. I think that if he had not used his razor that day I would have repulsed his advances, and the criminal calendar of the world would have been spared the addition of one murder.

I happened to be standing within five feet of a cuspidor when Major Caswell opened fire upon it. I had been observant enough to perceive that the attacking force was using Gatlings instead of squirrel rifles; so I sidestepped so promptly that the Major seized the opportunity to apologize to a noncombatant. He had the blabbing lip. In four minutes he had become my friend and had dragged me to the bar.

I desire to interpolate here that I am a Southerner. But I am not one by profession or trade. I eschew the string tie, the slouch hat, the Prince Albert, the number of bales of cotton destroyed by Sherman, and plug chewing. When the orchestra plays "Dixie" I do not cheer. I slide a little lower on the leather-cornered seat and—well—order another Würzburger and wish that Longstreet had—but what's the use?

Major Caswell banged the bar with his fist, and the first gun at Fort Sumter reëchoed. When he fired the last one at Appomattox I began to hope. But then he began on family trees, and demonstrated that Adam was only a third cousin of a collateral branch of the Caswell family. Genealogy disposed of, he took up, to my distaste, his private family matters. He spoke of his wife, traced her descent back to Eve, and profanely denied any possible rumor that she may have had relations in the land of Nod.

By this time I began to suspect that he was trying to obscure by the noise the fact that he had ordered the drinks, on the chance that I would be bewildered into paying for them. But when they were down he crashed a silver dollar loudly upon the bar. Then, of course, another serving was obligatory. And when I had paid for that I took leave of him brusquely; for I wanted no more of him. But before I had obtained my release he had prated loudly of an income that his wife received, and showed a handful of silver money.

When I got my key at the desk the clerk said to me courteously: "If that man Caswell has annoyed you, and if you would like to make a complaint, we will have him ejected. He is a nuisance, a loafer, and without any known means of support, although he seems to have money most of the time. But we don't seem to be able to hit upon any means of throwing him out legally."

"Why, no," said I, after some reflection; "I don't see my way clear to make a complaint. But I would like to place myself on record as asserting that I do not care for his company. Your town," I continued, "seems to be a quiet one. What manner of entertainment, adventure, or excitement have you to offer to the stranger within your gates?"

"Well, sir," said the clerk, "there will be a show here next Thursday. It is—I'll look it up and have the announcement sent up to your room with the ice water. Good night."

After I went up to my room I looked out of the window. It was only about ten o'clock, but I looked upon a silent town. The drizzle continued, spangled with dim lights, as far apart as currants in a cake sold at the Ladies' Exchange.

"A quiet place," I said to myself, as my first shoe struck the ceiling of the occupant of the room beneath mine. "Nothing of the life here that gives color and variety to the cities in the East and West. Just a good, ordinary, humdrum, business town."

> Nashville occupies a foremost place among the manufacturing centers of the country. It is the fifth boot and shoe market in the United States, the largest candy and cracker manufacturing city in the South, and does an enormous wholesale drygoods, grocery, and drug business.

I must tell you how I came to be in Nashville, and I assure you the digression brings as much tedium to me as it does to you. I was traveling elsewhere on my own business, but I had a commission from a Northern literary magazine to stop over there and establish a connection between the publication and one of its personal contributors, Azalea Adair.

Adair (there was no clue to the personality except the handwriting) had sent in some essays (lost art!) and poems that had made the editors swear approvingly over their one o'clock luncheon. So they had commissioned me to round up said Adair and corner by contract his or her output at two cents a word before some other publisher offered her ten or twenty.

At nine o'clock the next morning, after my chicken livers *en brochette* (try them if you find that hotel), I strayed out into the drizzle, which was still on for an unlimited run. At the first corner, I came upon Uncle Caesar. He was a stalwart Negro older than the pyramids, with gray wool and a face that reminded me of Brutus, and a second afterwards of the late King Cetewayo. He wore the most remarkable coat that I ever had seen or expect to see. It reached to his ankles and had once been a Confederate gray in color. But rain and sun and age had so variegated it that Joseph's coat, beside it, would have faded to a pale monochrome. I must linger with that coat, for it has to do with the story—the story that is so long in coming, because you can hardly expect anything to happen in Nashville.

Once it must have been the military coat of an officer. The cape of it had vanished, but all adown its front it had been frogged and tasseled magnificently. But now the frogs and tassels were gone. In their stead had been patiently stitched (I surmise by some surviving "black mammy") new frogs made of cunningly twisted common hempen twine. This twine was frayed and disheveled. It must have been added to the coat as a substitute for vanished splendors, with tasteless but painstaking devotion, for it followed faithfully the curves of the long-missing frogs. And, to complete the comedy and pathos of the garment, all its buttons were gone save one. The second button from the top alone remained. The coat was fastened by other twine strings tied through the buttonholes and other holes rudely pierced on the opposite side. There was never such a weird garment so fantastically bedecked and of so many mottled hues. The lone button was the size of a half dollar, made of yellow horn and sewed on with coarse twine.

This Negro stood by a carriage so old that Ham himself might have started a hack line after he left the ark with the two animals hitched to it. As I approached he threw open the door, drew out a feather duster, waved it without using it, and said in deep, rumbling tones:

"Step right in, suh; ain't a speck of dust in it—jus' got back from a funeral, suh."

I inferred that on such gala occasions carriages were given an extra cleaning. I looked up and down the street and perceived that there was little choice among the vehicles for hire that lined the curb. I looked in my memorandum book for the address of Azalea Adair.

"I want to go to 861 Jessamine Street," I said, and was about to step into the hack.

But for an instant the thick, gorilla-like arm of the old Negro barred me. On his massive and saturnine face a look of sudden suspicion and enmity flashed for a moment. Then, with quickly returning conviction, he asked blandishingly: "What are you gwine there for, boss?"

"What is that to you?" I asked a little sharply.

"Nothin', suh, jus' nothin'. Only it's a lonesome kind of part of town and few folks ever has business there. Step right in. The seats is clean—jes' got back from a funeral, suh."

A mile and a half it must have been to our journey's end. I could hear nothing but the fearful rattle of the ancient hack over the uneven brick paving; I could smell nothing but the drizzle, now further flavored with coal smoke and something like a mixture of tar and oleander blossoms. All I could see through the streaming windows were two rows of dim houses.

> The city has an area of 10 square miles; 181 miles of streets of which 137 miles are paved; a system of waterworks that cost $2,000,000, with 77 miles of mains.

Eight-sixty-one Jessamine Street was a decayed mansion. Thirty yards back from the street it stood, outmerged in a splendid grove of trees and untrimmed shrubbery. A row of box bushes overflowed and almost hid the paling fence from sight; the gate was kept closed by a rope noose that encircled the gatepost and the first paling of the gate. But when you got inside you saw that Eight-sixty-one was a shell, a shadow, a ghost of former grandeur and excellence. But in the story, I have not yet got inside.

When the hack had ceased from rattling and the weary quadrupeds came to a rest, I handed my Jehu his fifty cents with an additional quarter, feeling a glow of conscious generosity as I did so. He refused it.

"It's two dollars, suh," he said.

"How's that?" I asked. "I plainly heard you call out at the hotel: 'Fifty cents to any part of the town.'"

"It's two dollars, suh," he repeated obstinately. "It's a long ways from the hotel."

"It is within the city limits and well within them," I argued. "Don't think that you have picked up a greenhorn Yankee. Do you see those hills over there?" I went on, pointing toward the east (I could not see them, myself, for the drizzle); "well, I was born and raised on their other side. You old fool nigger, can't you tell people from other people when you see 'em?"

The grim face of King Cetewayo softened. "Is you from the South, suh? I reckon it was them shoes of yourn fooled me. They is somethin' sharp in the toes for a Southern gen'l'man to wear."

"Then the charge is fifty cents, I suppose?" said I inexorably.

His former expression, a mingling of cupidity and hostility, returned, remained ten seconds, and vanished.

"Boss," he said, "fifty cents is right; but I *needs* two dollars, suh; I'm *obleeged* to have two dollars. I ain't *demandin'* it now, suh, after I knows whar you's from; I'm jus' sayin' that I *has* to have two dollars tonight, and business is mighty po'."

Peace and confidence settled upon his heavy features. He had been luckier than he had hoped. Instead of having picked up a greenhorn, ignorant of rates, he had come upon an inheritance.

"You confounded old rascal," I said, reaching down to my pocket, "you ought to be turned over to the police."

For the first time I saw him smile. He knew; he *knew;* HE KNEW.

I gave him two one-dollar bills. As I handed them over I noticed that one of them had seen parlous times. Its upper right-hand corner was missing, and it had been torn through the middle, but joined again. A strip of blue tissue paper, pasted over the split, preserved its negotiability.

Enough of the African bandit for the present: I left him happy, lifted the rope, and opened the creaky gate.

The house, as I said, was a shell. A paint brush had not touched it in twenty years. I could not see why a strong wind should not have bowled it over like a house of cards until I looked again at the trees that hugged it close—the trees that saw the battle of Nashville and still drew their protecting branches around it against storm and enemy and cold.

Azalea Adair, fifty years old, white-haired, a descendant of the cavaliers, as thin and frail as the house she lived in, robed in the cheapest and cleanest dress I ever saw, with an air as simple as a queen's, received me.

The reception room seemed a mile square, because there was nothing in it except some rows of books, on unpainted white-pine bookshelves, a cracked marble-top table, a rag rug, a hairless horsehair sofa, and two or three chairs. Yes, there was a picture on the wall, a colored crayon drawing of a cluster of pansies. I looked around for the portrait of Andrew Jackson and the pinecone hanging basket, but they were not there.

Azalea Adair and I had conversation, a little of which will be repeated to you. She was a product of the old South, gently nurtured in the sheltered life. Her learning was not broad, but was deep and of splendid originality in its somewhat narrow scope. She had been educated at home, and her knowledge of the world was derived from inference and by inspiration. Of such is the precious, small group of essayists made. While she talked to me I kept brushing my fingers, trying, unconsciously, to rid them guiltily of the absent dust from the half-calf backs of Lamb, Chaucer, Hazlitt, Marcus Aurelius, Montaigne, and Hood. She was exquisite, she was a valuable discovery; nearly everybody nowadays knows too much—oh, so much too much—of real life.

I could perceive clearly that Azalea Adair was very poor. A house and a dress she had—not much else, I fancied. So, divided between my duty to the magazine and my loyalty to the poets and essayists, who fought Thomas in the valley of the Cumberland, I listened to her voice, which was like a harpsichord's, and found that I could not speak of contracts. In the presence of the nine Muses and the three Graces one hesitated to lower the topic to two cents. There would have to be another colloquy after I had regained my commercialism. But I spoke of my mission, and three o'clock of the next afternoon was set for the discussion of the business proposition.

"Your town," I said, as I began to make ready to depart (which is the time for smooth generalities), "seems to be a quiet, sedate place. A home town, I should say, where few things out of the ordinary ever happen."

> It carries on extensive trade in stoves and hollow ware with the West and South, and its flouring mills have a daily capacity of more than two thousand barrels.

Azalea Adair seemed to reflect.

"I have never thought of it that way," she said, with a kind of sincere intensity that seemed to belong to her. "Isn't it in the still, quiet places that things do happen? I fancy that when God began to create the earth on the first Monday morning one could have leaned out one's window and heard the drops of mud splashing from His trowel as He built up the everlasting hills. What did the noisiest project in the world—I mean the building of the tower of Babel—result in finally? A page and a half of Esperanto in the *North American Review.*"

"Of course," I said platitudinously, "human nature is the same everywhere; but there is more color—er—more drama and movement and—er—romance in some cities than in others."

"On the surface," said Azalea Adair. "I have traveled many times round the world in a golden airship wafted on two wings—print and dreams. I have seen (on one of my imaginary tours) the Sultan of Turkey bowstring with his own hands one of his wives who had uncovered her face in public. I have seen a man in Nashville tear up his theater tickets because his wife was going out with her face covered—with rice powder. In San Francisco's Chinatown I saw the slave girl Sing Yee dipped slowly, inch by inch, in boiling almond oil to make her swear she would never see her American lover again. She gave in when the boiling oil had reached three inches above her knee. At a euchre party in East Nashville the other night, I saw Kitty Morgan cut dead by seven of her schoolmates and lifelong friends because she had married a house painter. The boiling oil was sizzling as high as her heart; but I wish you could have seen the fine little smile that she carried from table to table. Oh, yes, it is a humdrum town. Just a few miles of red brick houses and mud stores and lumber yards."

Someone knocked hollowly at the back of the house. Azalea Adair breathed a soft apology and went to investigate the sound. She came back in three minutes with brightened eyes, a faint flush on her cheeks, and ten years lifted from her shoulders.

"You must have a cup of tea before you go," she said, "and a sugar cake."

She reached and shook a little iron bell. In shuffled a small Negro girl about twelve, barefoot, not very tidy, glowering at me with thumb in mouth and bulging eyes.

Azalea Adair opened a tiny, worn purse and drew out a dollar bill, with the upper right-hand corner missing, torn in two pieces and pasted together again with a strip of blue tissue paper. It was one of the bills I had given the piratical Negro—there was no doubt of it.

"Go up to Mr. Baker's store on the corner, Impy," she said, handing the girl the dollar bill, "and get me a quarter of a pound of tea—the kind he always sends me—and ten cents' worth of sugar cakes. Now, hurry. The supply of tea in the house happens to be exhausted," she explained to me.

Impy left by the back way. Before the scrape of her hard, bare feet had died away on the back porch, a wild shriek—I was sure it was hers—filled the hollow house. Then the deep, gruff tones of an angry man's voice mingled with the girl's further squeals and unintelligible words.

Azalea Adair rose without surprise or emotion and disappeared. For two minutes I heard the hoarse rumble of the man's voice; then something like an oath and a slight scuffle, and she returned calmly to her chair.

"This is a roomy house," she said, "and I have a tenant for part of it. I am sorry to have to rescind my invitation to tea. It was impossible to get the kind I always use at the store. Perhaps tomorrow Mr. Baker will be able to supply me."

I was sure that Impy had not had time to leave the house. I inquired concerning streetcar lines and took my leave. After I was well on my way I remembered that I had not learned Azalea Adair's name. But tomorrow would do.

That same day I started in on the course of iniquity that this uneventful city forced upon me. I was in the town only two days, but in that time I managed to lie shamelessly by telegraph, and to be an accomplice—after the fact, if that is the correct legal term—to a murder.

As I rounded the corner nearest my hotel the Afrite coachman of the polychromatic, nonpareil coat seized me, swung open the dungeony door of his peripatetic sarcophagus, flirted his feather duster, and began his ritual: "Step right in, boss. Carriage is clean—jus' got back from a funeral. Fifty cents to any—"

And then he knew me and grinned broadly. " 'Scuse me, boss; you is de gen'l'man what rid out with me dis mawnin'. Thank you kindly, suh."

"I am going out to Eight-sixty-one again tomorrow afternoon at three," said I, "and if you will be here, I'll let you drive me. So you know Miss Adair?" I concluded, thinking of my dollar bill.

"I belonged to her father, Judge Adair, suh," he replied.

"I judge that she is pretty poor," I said. "She hasn't much money to speak of, has she?"

For an instant I looked again at the fierce countenance of King Cetewayo, and then he changed back to an extortionate old Negro hack-driver.

"She ain't gwine to starve, suh," he said slowly. "She has reso'ces, suh; she has reso'ces."

"I shall pay you fifty cents for the trip," said I.

"Dat is puffeckly correct, suh," he answered humbly. "I jus' *had* to have dat two dollars dis mawnin', boss."

I went to the hotel and lied by electricity. I wired the magazine: "A. Adair holds out for eight cents a word."

The answer that came back was: "Give it to her quick, you duffer."

Just before dinner "Major" Wentworth Caswell bore down upon me with the greetings of a long-lost friend. I have seen few men whom I have so instantaneously hated, and of whom it was so difficult to be rid. I was standing at the bar when he invaded me; therefore I could not wave the white ribbon in his face. I would have paid gladly for the drinks, hoping, thereby, to escape another; but he was one of those despicable, roaring, advertising bibbers who must have brass bands and fireworks attend upon every cent that they waste in their follies.

With an air of producing millions he drew two one-dollar bills from a pocket and dashed one of them upon the bar. I looked once more at the dollar bill with the upper right-hand corner missing, torn through the middle, and patched with a strip of blue tissue paper. It was my dollar bill again. It could have been no other.

I went up to my room. The drizzle and the monotony of a dreary, eventless Southern town had made me tired and listless. I remember that just before I went to bed I mentally disposed of the mysterious dollar bill (which might have formed the clue to a tremendously fine detective story of San Francisco) by saying to myself sleepily: "Seems as if a lot of people here own stock in the Hack-Driver's Trust. Pays dividends promptly, too. Wonder if—" Then I fell asleep.

King Cetewayo was at his post the next day, and rattled my bones over the stones out to Eight-sixty-one. He was to wait and rattle me back again when I was ready.

Azalea Adair looked paler and cleaner and frailer than she had looked on the day before. After she had signed the contract at eight cents per word, she grew still paler and began to slip out of her chair. Without much trouble I managed to get her up on the antediluvian horsehair sofa and then I ran out to the sidewalk and yelled to the coffee-colored pirate to bring a doctor. With a wisdom that I had not suspected in him, he abandoned his team and struck off up the street afoot, realizing the value of speed. In ten minutes he returned with a grave, gray-haired, and capable man of medicine. In a few words (worth much less than eight cents each) I explained to him my presence in the hollow house of mystery. He bowed with stately understanding and turned to the old Negro.

"Uncle Caesar," he said calmly, "run up to my house and ask Miss Lucy to give you a cream pitcher full of fresh milk and half a tumbler of port wine. And hurry back. Don't drive—run. I want you to get back sometime this week."

It occurred to me that Dr. Merriman also felt a distrust as to the speeding powers of the land pirate's steeds. After Uncle Caesar was gone, lumberingly but swiftly, up the street, the doctor looked me over with great politeness and as much careful calculation until he had decided that I might do.

"It is only a case of insufficient nutrition," he said. "In other words, the result of poverty, pride, and starvation. Mrs. Caswell has many devoted friends who would be glad to aid her, but she will accept nothing except from that old Negro, Uncle Caesar, who was once owned by her family."

"Mrs. Caswell!" said I, in surprise. And then I looked at the contract and saw that she had signed it "Azalea Adair Caswell."

"I thought she was Miss Adair," said I.

"Married to a drunken, worthless loafer, sir," said the doctor. "It is said that he robs her even of the small sums that her old servant contributes toward her support."

When the milk and wine had been brought, the doctor soon revived Azalea Adair. She sat up and talked of the beauty of the autumn leaves that were then in season, and their height of color. She referred lightly to her fainting seizure as the outcome of an old palpitation of the heart. Impy fanned her as she lay on the sofa. The doctor was due elsewhere, and I followed him to the door. I told him that it was within my power and intentions to make a reasonable advance of money to Azalea Adair on future contributions to the magazine, and he seemed pleased.

"By the way," he said, "perhaps you would like to know that you have had royalty for a coachman. Old Caesar's grandfather was a king in Congo. Caesar himself has royal ways, as you may have observed."

As the doctor was moving off I heard Uncle Caesar's voice inside: "Did he git bofe of dem two dollars from you, Mis' Zalea?"

"Yes, Caesar," I heard Azalea Adair answer weakly.

And then I went in and concluded business negotiations with our contributor. I assumed the responsibility of advancing fifty dollars, putting it as a necessary formality in binding our bargain. And then Uncle Caesar drove me back to the hotel.

Here ends all of the story as far as I can testify as a witness. The rest must be only bare statements of facts.

At about six o'clock I went out for a stroll. Uncle Caesar was at his corner. He threw open the door of his carriage, flourished his duster, and began his depressing formula: "Step right in, suh. Fifty cents to anywhere in the city—hack's pufficky clean, suh—jus' back from a funeral—"

And then he recognized me. I think his eyesight was getting bad. His coat had taken on a few more faded shades of color, the twine strings were more frayed and ragged, the last remaining button—the button of yellow horn—was gone. A motley descendant of kings was Uncle Caesar!

About two hours later I saw an excited crowd besieging the front door of the drugstore. In a desert where nothing happens this was manna; so I edged my way inside. On an extemporized couch of empty boxes and chairs was stretched the mortal corporeality of Major Wentworth Caswell. A doctor was testing him for the immortal ingredient. His decision was that it was conspicuous by its absence.

The erstwhile Major had been found dead on a dark street and brought by curious and ennuied citizens to the drugstore. The late human being had been engaged in terrific battle—the details showed that. Loafer and reprobate though he had been, he had been also a warrior. But he had lost. His hands were yet clinched so tightly that his fingers would not be opened. The gentle citizens who had known him stood about and searched their vocabularies to find some good words, if it were possible, to speak of him. One kind-looking man said, after much thought: "When 'Cas' was about fo'teen he was one of the best spellers in school."

While I stood there the fingers of the right hand of "the man that was," which hung down the side of a white-pine box, relaxed and dropped something at my feet. I covered it with one foot quickly, and a little later on I picked it up and pocketed it. I reasoned that in his last struggle his hand must have seized that object unwittingly and held it in a death grip.

At the hotel that night the main topic of conversation, with the possible exceptions of politics and prohibition, was the demise of Major Caswell. I heard one man say to a group of listeners:

"In my opinion, gentlemen, Caswell was murdered by some of those no-account niggers for his money. He had fifty dollars this afternoon which he showed to several gentlemen in the hotel. When he was found the money was not on his person."

I left the city the next morning at nine, and as the train was crossing the bridge over the Cumberland River, I took out of my pocket a yellow horn overcoat button the size of a fifty-cent piece, with frayed ends of coarse twine hanging from it, and cast it out of the window into the slow, muddy waters below.

I wonder what's doing in Buffalo!

FINLEY PETER DUNNE

[1867–1936]

ONE OF THE MOST SKEPTICAL *as well as one of the most serious critics of the period, Finley Peter Dunne, won wide audiences because of his deceptively affable humor. He was born June 10, 1867, in Chicago,*

Illinois. His parents exactly fitted the neighborhood, which was middle-class Irish-American Catholic, and it was the Irish cadences sharpened by American turns of speech that he reproduced with such charm and fidelity. Dunne had little more than an elementary education when he was given a job as reporter on the Chicago Herald. From the age of seventeen until his death in his seventieth year he was in journalism; he rose from copy boy to city editor, leaving Chicago for New York, where he became editor of Collier's Weekly and part owner of the American Magazine.

In his late twenties Dunne invented Mr. Dooley, a highly articulate bartender who opened his mind to his wondering friend Mr. Hennessy as liberally as Sherlock Holmes confided to the admiring Watson. The first volume of the pseudo-dialogues—actually Dooley's soliloquies interrupted now and then by Hennessy—was published when Dunn was thirty-one; it was called Mr. Dooley in Peace and War and was followed by ten more collections of pithy and almost perfect little essays.

Current events were Dunne's (and Dooley's) field, politics was the favorite target. Dunne hated pretense, particularly the hypocrisy which disguised aggrandizement as "manifest destiny"; he never tired of satirizing the claims of the expansionists which he felt dragged democracy into imperialism and which (abetted by an inflammatory "yellow press") would lead—and did lead—to war, a forced war with Spain. Savage and subtle at the same time, Dunne both amused and aroused his readers. He was always a surprise, pungent, penetrating, and even (as in "On the Popularity of Firemen") quietly pathetic.

ON WAR PREPARATIONS

"WELL," MR. HENNESSY ASKED, "how goes th' war?"

"Splendid, thank ye," said Mr. Dooley. "Fine, fine. It makes me hear-rt throb with pride that I'm a citizen iv th' Sixth Wa-ard."

"Has th' ar-rmy started f'r Cuba yet?"

"Wan ar-rmy, says ye? Twinty! Las' Choosdah an advance ar-rmy iv wan hundherd an' twinty thousand men landed fr'm th' Gussie, with tin thousand cannons hurlin' projick-tyles weighin' eight hundherd pounds sivinteen miles. Winsdah night a second ar-rmy iv injineers, miners, plumbers, an' lawn tinnis experts, numberin' in all four hundherd an' eighty thousan' men, ar-rmed with death-dealin' canned goods, was hurried to Havana to storm th' city.

"Thursdah mornin' three thousand full rigimints acrost to Matoonzas, an' afther a spirited battle captured th' Rainy Christiny golf links, two up an' hell to play, an' will hold thim again all comers. Th' same afthernoon th' reg'lar cavalry, consistin' iv four hundherd an' eight thousan' well-mounted men, was loaded aboord th' tug *Lucy J.*, and departed on their earend iv death amidst th' cheers iv eight millyon sojers left behind at Chickamaha. These cav'lry'll co-operate with Commodore Schlow; an' whin he desthroys th' Spanish fleet, as he does ivry Sundah an' holy day except in Lent, an' finds out where they ar-re an' desthroys thim, afther batterin' down th' forts where they ar-re con-cealed so that he can't see thim, but thinks they ar-re on their way f'r to fight Cousin George Dooley, th' cav'lry will make a dash back to Tampa, where Gin'ral Miles is preparin' to desthroy th' Spanish at wan blow,—an' he's th' boy to blow.

"The gin'ral arrived th' other day, fully prepared f'r th' bloody wurruk iv war. He had his intire fam'ly with him. He r-rode recklessly into camp, mounted on a superb specyal ca-ar. As himsilf an' Uncle Mike Miles, an' Cousin Hennery Miles, an' Master Miles, aged eight years, dismounted fr'm th' specyal train, they were received with wild cheers be eight millyon iv th' bravest sojers that iver give up their lives f'r their counthry. Th' press cinchorship is so pow'rful that no news is allowed to go out; but I have it fr'm th' specyal corryspondint iv Mesilf, Clancy th' Butcher, Mike Casey, an' th' City Direchtry that Gin'ral Miles instantly repaired himsilf to th' hotel, where he made his plans f'r cr-rushin' th' Spanyards at wan blow. He will equip th' ar-rmy with blow-guns at wanst. His uniforms ar-re comin' down in specyal steel protected bullyon trains fr'm th' mint, where they've been kept f'r a year. He has ordhered out th' gold resarve f'r to equip his staff, numberin' eight thousan' men, manny iv whom ar-re clubmen; an' as soon as he can have his pitchers took, he will cr-rush th' Spanish with wan blow. Th' pur-pose iv th' gin'ral is to permit no delay. Decisive action is demanded be th' people. An', whin th' hot air masheens has been sint to th' front, Gin'ral Miles will strike wan blow that'll be th' damdest blow since th' year iv th' big wind in Ireland.

"Iv coorse, they'se dissinsions in th' cabinet; but they don't amount to nawthin'. Th' Sicrety iv War is in favor iv sawin' th' Spanish ar-rmy into two-be-four joists. Th' Sicrety iv th' Threeasury has a scheme f'r roonin' thim be lindin' thim money. Th' Sicrety iv th' Navy wants to sue thim befure th' Mattsachusetts Supreme Coort. I've heerd that th' Prisident is arrangin' a knee dhrill, with th' idee iv prayin' th' villyans to th' divvil. But these diff'rences don't count. We're all wan people, an' we look to Gin'ral Miles to desthroy th' Spanish with wan blow. Whin it comes, trees will be lifted out be th' roots. Morro Castle'll cave in, an' th' air'll be full iv Spanish whiskers. A long blow, a sthrong blow, an' a blow all together."

"We're a gr-reat people," said Mr. Hennessy, earnestly.

"We ar-re," said Mr. Dooley. "We ar-re that. An' th' best iv it is, we know we ar-re."

EXPANSION

"WHIN WE PLANT what Hogan calls th' starry banner iv Freedom in th' Ph'lippeens," said Mr. Dooley, "an' give th' sacred blessin' iv liberty to the poor, downtrodden people iv thim unfortunate isles,—dam thim!—we'll larn thim a lesson."

"Sure," said Mr. Hennessy, sadly, "we have a thing or two to larn oursilves."

"But it isn't f'r thim to larn us," said Mr. Dooley. "'Tis not f'r thim wretched an' degraded crathers, without a mind or a shirt iv their own, f'r to give lessons in politeness an' liberty to a nation that manny-facthers more dhressed beef than anny other imperyal nation in th' wurruld. We say to thim: 'Naygurs,' we say, 'poor, dissolute, uncovered wretches,' says we, 'whin th' crool hand iv Spain forged man'cles f'r ye'er limbs, as Hogan says, who was it crossed th' say an' sthruck off th' comealongs? We did,—by dad, we did. An' now, ye mis'rable childish-minded apes, we propose f'r to larn ye th' uses iv liberty. In ivry city in this unfair land we will erect school-houses an' packin' houses an' houses iv correction; an' we'll larn ye our language, because 'tis aisier to larn ye ours than to larn oursilves yours. An' we'll give ye clothes, if ye pay f'r thim; an', if ye don't, ye can go without. An', whin ye're hungry, ye can go to th' morgue—we mane th' resth'rant—an' ate a good square meal iv ar-rmy beef. An' we'll sind th' gr-reat Gin'ral Eagan over f'r to larn ye etiquette, an' Andrew Carnegie to larn ye pathriteism with blow-holes into it, an' Gin'ral Alger to larn ye to hould onto a job; an', whin ye've become edycated an' have all th' blessin's iv civilization that we don't want, that'll count ye one. We can't give ye anny votes, because we haven't more thin enough to go round now; but we'll threat ye th' way a father shud threat his childher if we have to break ivry bone in ye'er bodies. So come to our ar-rms,' says we.

"But glory be, 'tis more like a rasslin' match than a father's embrace. Up gets this little monkey iv an' Aggynaldoo, an' says he, 'Not for us,' he says. 'We thank ye kindly; but we believe,' he says, 'in pathronizin' home industhries,' he says. 'An',' he says, 'I have on hand,' he says, 'an' f'r sale,' he says, 'a very superyor brand iv home-made liberty, like ye'er mother used to make,' he says. ' 'Tis a long way fr'm ye'er plant to here,' he says, 'an' be th' time a cargo iv liberty,' he says, 'got out here an' was handled be th' middlemen,' he says, 'it might spoil,' he says. 'We don't want anny col' storage or embalmed liberty,' he says. 'What we want an' what th' ol' reliable house iv Aggynaldoo,' he says, 'supplies to th' thrade,' he says, 'is fr-esh liberty r-right off th' far-rm,' he says. 'I can't do annything with ye'er proposition,' he says. 'I can't give up,' he says, 'th' rights f'r which f'r five years I've fought an' bled ivry wan I cud reach,' he says. 'Onless,' he says, 'ye'd feel like buyin' out th' whole business,' he says. 'I'm a pathrite,' he says; 'but I'm no bigot,' he says.

"An' there it stands, Hinnissy, with th' indulgent parent kneelin' on th' stomach iv his adopted child, while a dilygation fr'm Boston bastes him with an umbrella. There it stands, an' how will it come out I dinnaw. I'm not much iv an expansionist mesilf. F'r th' las' tin years I've been thryin' to decide whether 'twud be good policy an' thrue to me thraditions to make this here bar two or three feet longer, an manny's th' night I've laid awake tryin' to puzzle it out. But I don't know what to do with th' Ph'lippeens anny more thin I did las' summer, befure I heerd tell iv thim. We can't give thim to anny wan without makin' th' wan that gets thim feel th' way Doherty felt to Clancy whin Clancy med a frindly call an' give Doherty's childher th' measles. We can't sell thim, we can't ate thim, an' we can't throw thim into th' alley whin no wan is lookin'. An' 'twud be a disgrace f'r to lave befure we've pounded these frindless an' ongrateful people into insinsibility. So I suppose, Hinnissy, we'll have to stay an' do th' best we can, an' lave Andhrew Carnegie secede fr'm th' Union. They'se wan consolation; an' that is, if th' American people can govern thimsilves, they can govern annything that walks."

"An' what 'd ye do with Aggy—wah-d'ye-call-him?" asked Mr. Hennessy.

"Well," Mr. Dooley replied, with brightening eyes, "I know what they'd do with him in this ward. They'd give that pathrite what he asks, an' thin they'd throw him down an' take it away fr'm him."

ON THE POPULARITY OF FIREMEN

I KNOWED a man be th' name iv Clancy wanst, Jawn. He was fr'm th' County May-o, but a good man f'r all that; an', whin he'd growed to be a big, sthrappin' fellow, he wint on to th' fire departmint. They'se an Irishman 'r two on th' fire departmint an' in th' army, too, Jawn, though ye'd think be hearin' some talk they was all runnin' prim'ries an' thryin' to be cinthral comitymen. So ye wud. Ye niver hear iv thim on'y whin they die; an' thin, murther, what funerals they have!

"Well, this Clancy wint on th' fire departmint, an' they give him a place in thruck twinty-three. All th' r-road was proud iv him, an' faith he was proud iv himsilf. He r-rode free on th' sthreet ca-ars, an' was th' champeen hand-ball player f'r miles around. Ye shud see him goin' down th' sthreet, with his blue shirt an' his blue coat with th' buttons on it, an' his cap on his ear. But ne'er a cap or coat'd he wear whin they was a fire. He might be shiv'rin' be th' stove in th' ingine house with a buffalo robe over his head; but, whin th' gong sthruck, 'twas off with coat an' cap an' buffalo robe, an' out come me brave Clancy, bare-headed an' bare hand, dhrivin' with wan line an' spillin' th' hose cart on wan wheel at ivry jump iv th' horse. Did anny wan iver see a fireman with his coat on or a polisman with his off? Why, wanst, whin Clancy was standin' up f'r Grogan's eighth, his son come runnin' in to tell him they was a fire in Vogel's packin' house. He dhropped th' kid at Father Kelly's feet, an' whipped off his long coat an' wint tearin' f'r th' dure, kickin' over th' poorbox an' buttin' ol' Mis' O'Neill that'd come in to say th' stations. 'Twas lucky 'twas wan iv th' Grogans. They're a fine family f'r falls. Jawn Grogan was wurrukin' on th' top iv Metzri an' O'Connell's brewery wanst, with a man be th' name iv Dorsey. He slipped an' fell wan hundherd feet. Whin they come to see if he was dead, he got up, an' says he: 'Lave me at him.' 'At who?' says they. 'He's deliryous,' they says. 'At Dorsey,' says Grogan. 'He thripped me.' So it didn't hurt Grogan's eighth to fall four 'r five feet.

"Well, Clancy wint to fires an' fires. Whin th' big organ facthry burnt, he carried th' hose up to th' fourth story an' was squirtin' whin th' walls fell. They dug him out with pick an' shovel, an' he come up fr'm th' brick an' boards an' saluted th' chief. 'Clancy,' says th' chief, 'ye betther go over an' get a dhrink.' He did so, Jawn. I heerd it. An' Clancy was that proud!

"Whin th' Hogan flats on Halsted Sthreet took fire, they got all th' people out but wan; an' she was a woman asleep on th' fourth flure. 'Who'll go up?' says Bill Musham. 'Sure, sir,' says Clancy, 'I'll go'; an' up he wint. His captain was a man be th' name iv O'Connell, fr'm th' County Kerry; an' he had his fut on th' ladder whin Clancy started. Well, th' good man wint into th' smoke, with his wife faintin' down below. 'He'll be kilt,' says his brother. 'Ye don't know him,' says Bill Musham. An' sure enough, whin ivry wan'd give him up, out comes me brave Clancy, as black as a Turk, with th' girl in his arms. Th' others wint up like monkeys, but he shtud wavin' thim off, an' come down th' ladder face forward. 'Where'd ye larn that?' says Bill Musham. 'I seen a man do it at th' Lyceem whin I was a kid,' says Clancy. 'Was it all right?' 'I'll have ye up before th' ol' man,' says Bill Musham. 'I'll teach ye to come down a laddher as if ye was in a quadhrille, ye horse-stealin', ham-sthringin' May-o man,' he says. But he didn't. Clancy wint over to see his wife. 'O Mike,' says she, ' 'twas fine,' she says. 'But why d'ye take th' risk?' she says. 'Did ye see th' captain?' he says with a scowl. 'He wanted to go. Did ye think I'd follow a Kerry man with all th' ward lukkin' on?' he says.

"Well, so he wint dhrivin' th' hose-cart on wan wheel, an' jumpin' whin he heerd a man so much as hit a glass to make it ring. All th' people looked up to him, an' th' kids followed him down th' sthreet; an' 'twas th' gr-reatest priv'lige f'r anny wan f'r to play dominos with him near th' joker. But about a year ago he come in to see me, an' says he, 'Well, I'm goin' to quit.' 'Why,' says I, 'ye'er a young man yet,' I says. 'Faith,' he says, 'look at me hair,' he says,—'young heart, ol' head. I've been at it these twinty year, an' th' good woman's wantin' to see more iv me thin blowin' into a saucer iv coffee,' he says. 'I'm goin' to quit,' he says, 'on'y I want to see wan more good fire,' he says. 'A rale good ol' hot wan,' he says, 'with th' win' blowin' f'r it an' a good dhraft in th' ilivator-shaft, an' about two stories, with pitcher-frames an' gasoline an' excelsior, an' to hear th' chief yellin': "Play 'way, sivinteen. What th' hell an' damnation are ye standin' aroun' with that pipe f'r? Is this a fire 'r a dam livin' pitcher? I'll break ivry man iv eighteen, four, six, an' chem'cal five to-morrah mornin' befure breakfast." Oh,' he says, bringin' his fit down, 'wan more, an' I'll quit.'

"An' he did, Jawn. Th' day th' Carpenter Brothers' box factory burnt. 'Twas wan iv thim big, fine-lookin' buildings that pious men built out iv celluloid an' plasther iv Paris. An' Clancy was wan iv th' men undher whin th' wall fell. I seen thim bringin' him home; an' th' little woman met him at th' dure, rumplin' her apron in her hands."

WILLIAM ALLEN WHITE

[1868–1944]

Born February 10, 1868, *in Emporia, Kansas, William Allen White became known as "the sage of Emporia," the quiet but convincing voice of middle-class, middle-western America. He grew up sixty miles south of his birthplace, in the pioneer town of Eldorado, where gospel hymns were sung every morning, where the railroad was just coming in, and where the boy's playground was the prairie, which came within a hundred yards of the schoolhouse. He learned the printer's trade and, while attending Kansas State University, became a newspaper reporter, then business manager, then editorial writer. At twenty-seven he bought the Emporia Gazette, which he continued to own and edit until his death on January 29 1944, two weeks before his seventy-sixth birthday.*

A Republican and a liberal, White endeared himself to everyone because of his geniality as well as his tolerance and warm human understanding. His paper was read throughout the nation by people who differed with him on many issues but who admired the straightforwardness of his manner and the calm confidence with which he maintained his principles. Nevertheless, the piece of White's writing which will probably live longest is not a political document or a philosophic editorial but a simple obituary. A father's heartbroken tribute to his seventeen-year-old daughter, it is a homespun elegy, more tender and more touching than many a classic memorial essay.

MARY WHITE

The Associated Press reports carrying the news of Mary White's death declared that it came as the result of a fall from a horse. How she would have hooted at that! She never fell from a horse in her life. Horses have fallen on her and with her—"I'm always trying to hold 'em in my lap," she used to say. But she was proud of few things, and one was that she could ride anything that had four legs and hair. Her death resulted not from a fall, but from a blow on the head which fractured her skull, and the blow came from the limb of an overhanging tree on the parking.

The last hour of her life was typical of its happiness. She came home from a day's work at school, topped off by a hard grind with the copy on the High School Annual, and felt that a ride would refresh her. She climbed into her khakis, chattering to her mother about the work she was doing, and hurried to get her horse and be out on the dirt roads for the country air and the radiant green fields of the spring. As she rode through the town on an easy gallop she kept waving at passers-by. She knew everyone in town. For a decade the little figure with the long pigtail and the red hair ribbon has been familiar on the streets of Emporia, and she got in the way of speaking to those who nodded at her. She passed the Kerrs, walking the horse, in front of the Normal Library, and waved at them; passed another friend a few hundred feet farther on, and waved to her. The horse was walking and as she turned into North Merchant Street she took off her cowboy hat, and the horse swung into a lope. She passed the Tripletts and waved her cowboy hat at them, still moving gayly north on Merchant Street. A *Gazette* carrier passed—a high-school boy friend—and she waved at him, but with her bridle hand; the horse veered quickly, plunged into the parking where the low-hanging limb faced her, and while she still looked back, waving, the blow came. But she did not fall from the horse; she slipped off, dazed a bit, staggered, and fell in a faint. She never quite recovered consciousness.

But she did not fall from the horse, neither was she riding fast. A year or so ago she used to go like the wind. But the habit was broken, and she used the horse to get into the open to get fresh, hard exercise, and to work off a certain surplus energy that welled up in her and needed a physical outlet. That need has been in her heart for years. It was back of the impulse that kept the dauntless, little brown-clad figure on the streets and country roads of this community and built into a strong, muscular body what had been a frail and sickly frame during the first years of her life. But the riding gave her more than a body. It released a gay and hardy soul. She was the happiest thing in the world. And she was happy because she was enlarging her horizon. She came to know all sorts and conditions of men. Charley O'Brien, the traffic cop, was one of her best friends. W. L. Holtz, the Latin teacher, was another. Tom O'Connor, farmer-politician, and Rev. J. H. J. Rice, preacher and police judge, and Frank Beach, music master, were her special friends, and all the girls, black and white, above the track and below the track, in Pepville and Stringtown, were among her acquaintances. And she brought home riotous stories of her adventures. She loved to rollick; persiflage was her natural expression at home. Her humor was a continual bubble of joy. She seemed to think in hyperbole and metaphor. She was mischievous without malice, as full of faults as an old shoe. No angel was Mary White, but an easy girl to live with, for she never nursed a grouch five minutes in her life.

With all her eagerness for the out-of-doors, she loved books. On her table when she left her room were a book by Conrad, one by Galsworthy, *Creative Chemistry* by E. E. Slosson, and a Kipling book. She read Mark Twain, Dickens, and Kipling before she was ten—all of their writings. Wells and Arnold Bennett particularly amused and diverted her. She was entered as a student in Wellesley in 1922; was assistant editor of the High School Annual this year, and in line for election to the editorship of the Annual next year. She was a member of the executive committee of the High School Y.W.C.A.

Within the last two years she had begun to be moved by an ambition to draw. She began as most children do by scribbling in her school books, funny pictures. She bought cartoon magazines and took a course—rather casually, naturally, for she was, after all, a child, with no strong purposes—and this year she tasted the first fruits of success by having her pictures accepted by the High School Annual. But the thrill of delight she got when Mr. Ecord, of the Normal Annual, asked her to do the cartooning for that book this spring was too beautiful for words. She fell to her work with all her enthusiastic heart. Her drawings were accepted, and her pride—always repressed by a lively sense of the ridiculousness of the figure she was cutting—was a really gorgeous thing to see. No successful artist ever drank a deeper draft of satisfaction than she took from the little fame her work was getting among her school fellows. In her glory, she almost forgot her horse—but never her car.

For she used the car as a jitney bus. It was her social life. She never had a "party" in all her nearly seventeen years—wouldn't have one; but she never drove a block in the car in her life that she didn't begin to fill the car with pick-ups! Everybody rode with Mary White—white and black, old and young, rich and poor, men and women. She liked nothing better than to fill the car full of long-legged high-school boys and an occasional girl, and parade the town. She never had a "date" nor went to a dance, except once with her brother Bill, and the "boy proposition" didn't interest her—yet. But young people—great, spring-breaking, varnish-cracking, fender-bending, door-sagging carloads of "kids"—gave her great pleasure. Her zests were keen. But the most fun she ever had in her life was acting as chairman of the committee that got up the big turkey dinner for the poor folks at the county home; scores of pies, gallons of slaw, jam, cakes, preserves, oranges, and a wilderness of turkey were loaded in the car and taken to the county home. And, being of a practical turn of mind, she risked her own Christmas dinner by staying to see that the poor folks actually got it all. Not that she was a cynic; she just disliked to tempt folks. While there she found a blind colored uncle, very old, who could do nothing but make rag rugs, and she rustled up from her school friends rags enough to keep him busy for a season. The last engagement she tried to make was to take the guests at the county home out for a car ride. And the last endeavor of her life was to try to get a rest room for colored girls in the high school. She found one girl reading in the toilet, because there was no better place for a colored girl to loaf, and it inflamed her sense of injustice and she became a nagging harpy to those who, she thought, could remedy the evil.

The poor she had always with her, and was glad of it. She hungered and thirsted for righteousness; and was the most impious creature in the world. She joined the Congregational Church without consulting her parents; not particularly for her soul's good. She never had a thrill of piety in her life, and would have hooted at a "testimony." But even as a little child she felt the church was an agency for helping people to more of life's abundance, and she wanted to help. She never wanted help for herself. Clothes meant little to her. It was a fight to get a new rig on her; but eventually a harder fight to get it off. She never wore a jewel and had no ring but her high-school class ring, and never asked for anything but a wrist watch. She refused to have her hair up, though she was nearly seventeen. "Mother," she protested, "you don't know how much I get by with, in my braided pigtails, that I could not with my hair up." Above every other passion of her life was her passion not to grow up, to be a child. The tomboy in her, which was big, seemed to loathe to be put away forever in skirts. She was a Peter Pan, who refused to grow up.

Her funeral yesterday at the Congregational Church was as she would have wished it; no singing, no flowers save the big bunch of red roses from her Brother Bill's Harvard classmen—Heavens, how proud that would have made her! and the red roses from the *Gazette* force—in vases at her head and feet. A short prayer, Paul's beautiful essay on "Love," from the thirteenth chapter of First Corinthians, some remarks about her democratic spirit by her friend, John H. J. Rice, pastor and police judge, which she would have deprecated if she could, a prayer sent down for her by her friend, Carl Nau, and opening the service the slow, poignant movement from Beethoven's "Moonlight Sonata," which she loved, and closing the service a cutting from the joyously melancholy first movement of Tchaikovsky's *Symphonie Pathétique*, which she liked to hear in certain moods on the phonograph; then the Lord's Prayer by her friends in the high school.

That was all.

For her pall bearers, only her friends were chosen: her Latin teacher, W. L. Holtz; her high-school principal, Rice Brown; her doctor, Frank Foncannon; her friend, W. W. Finney; her pal at the *Gazette* office, Walter Hughes; and her brother Bill. It would have made her smile to know that her friend, Charley O'Brien, the traffic cop, had been transferred from Sixth and Commercial to the corner near the church to direct her friends who came to bid her good-by.

A rift in the clouds in a gray day threw a shaft of sunlight upon her coffin as her nervous, energetic little body sank to its last sleep. But the soul in her, the glowing, gorgeous, fervent soul of her, surely was flaming in eager joy upon some other dawn.

BOOTH TARKINGTON

[1869–1946]

BOOTH TARKINGTON IS A PRIME EXAMPLE of a writer who forsook the financial rewards of spurious romances in favor of unflinching realism, and found that the truth was not only stranger but more profitable than fiction. He was born July 29, 1869, in Indianapolis, Indiana, and, although he was educated in the East and lived in many foreign places (Paris, Rome, Capri, among others) and for a long time in Kennebunkport, Maine, he always spoke and thought of Indianapolis as home. "Almost all Hoosiers are that way about where they grew up," he said.

In his youth he hoped to be a painter. "But," he recalled, "at last I found out that my hand would never do what my mind wanted it to do; and so, since my hand could make nothing better than symbols (written words, that is), I discovered I was a writer." As a writer Tarkington proclaimed himself a loyal Hoosier with his first book, appropriately named The Gentleman from Indiana.

After that debut Tarkington produced more than half a hundred works, which ran the gamut from headlong escapism to accurately detailed analyses of the contemporary scene. For a while it seemed that he would continue to invent smoothly fashioned entertainments like Monsieur Beaucaire, *one of the most popular "costume stories" of the period, but he surprised his readers by turning to a shrewd contempla-*

tion of everyday realities. He so delighted millions with the adolescent exploits of Penrod *that a series of sequels resulted:* Penrod and Sam, Penrod Jashber, *and* Seventeen. *His interpretations of "the truth and mystery of human nature" made the critics re-evaluate him; the frank and sometimes bitterly mature chronicle of* The Magnificent Ambersons *and* Alice Adams, *studies in disillusion, won Pulitzer Prizes in 1919 and 1922. He was seventy-six when he died in Indianapolis, May 19, 1946.*

Admired for his versatility and respected for his integrity, Tarkington wrote too much and too easily to satisfy most critics. None, however, disputed his rank as one of boyhood's favorite laureates. If not as glorious as their famous predecessors, Penrod and Sam belong in the company of Tom Sawyer and Huck Finn.

THE QUIET AFTERNOON

From *Penrod*

PERHAPS MIDDLE-AGED people might discern Nature's real intentions in the matter of pain if they would examine a boy's punishments and sorrows, for he prolongs neither beyond their actual duration. With a boy, trouble must be of Homeric dimensions to last overnight. To him, every next day is really a new day. Thus, Penrod woke, next morning, with neither the unspared rod, nor Mr. Kinosling in his mind. Tar, itself, so far as his consideration of it went, might have been an undiscovered substance. His mood was cheerful and mercantile; some process having worked mysteriously within him, during the night, to the result that his first waking thought was of profits connected with the sale of old iron—or perhaps a ragman had passed the house, just before he woke.

By ten o'clock he had formed a partnership with the indeed amiable Sam, and the firm of the Schofield and Williams plunged headlong into commerce. Heavy dealings in rags, paper, old iron and lead gave the firm a balance of twenty-two cents on the evening of the third day; but a venture in glassware, following, proved disappointing on account of the scepticism of all the durggists in that part of town, even after seven laborious hours had been spent in cleansing a wheelbarrow-load of old medicine bottles with hydrant water and ashes. Likewise, the partners were disheartened by their failure to dispose of a crop of "greens," although they had uprooted specimens of that decorative unappreciated flower, the dandelion, with such persistence and energy that the Schofields' and Williams' lawns looked curiously haggard for the rest of that summer.

The fit passed: business languished; became extinct. The dog-days had set in.

One August afternoon was so hot that even boys sought indoor shade. In the dimness of the vacant carriage-house of the stable, lounged Masters Penrod Schofield, Samuel Williams, Maurice Levy, Georgie Bassett, and Herman. They sat still and talked. It is a hot day, in rare truth, when boys devote themselves principally to conversation, and this day was that hot.

Their elders should beware such days. Peril hovers near when the fierceness of weather forces inaction and boys in groups are quiet. The more closely volcanoes, Western rivers, nitroglycerin, and boys are pent, the deadlier is their action at the point of outbreak. Thus, parents and guardians should look for outrages of the most singular violence and of the most peculiar nature during the confining weather of February and August.

The thing which befell upon this broiling afternoon began to brew and stew peacefully enough. All was innocence and languor; no one could have foretold the eruption.

They were upon their great theme: "When I get to be a man!" Being human, though boys, they considered their present estate too commonplace to be dwelt upon. So, when the old men gather, they say: "When I was a boy!" It really is the land of nowadays that we never discover.

"When I'm a man," said Sam Williams, "I'm goin' to hire me a couple of coloured waiters to swing me in a hammock and keep pourin' ice-water on me all day out o' those waterin'-cans they sprinkle flowers from. I'll hire you for one of 'em, Herman."

"No; you ain' goin' to," said Herman promptly. "You ain' no flowuh. But nev' min' nat, anyway. Ain' nobody goin' hiah me whens *I*'m a man. Goin' be my own boss. *I*'m go' be a rai'road man!"

"You mean like a superintendent, or sumpthing like that, and sell tickets?" asked Penrod.

"Sup'in–nev' min' nat! Sell ticket? *No* suh! Go' be a *po*'tuh! My uncle a po'tuh right now. Solid gole buttons–oh, oh!"

"Generals get a lot more buttons than porters," said Penrod. "Generals——"

"Po'tuhs make the bes' livin'," Herman interrupted. "My uncle spen' mo' money 'n any white man n'is town."

"Well, I rather be a general," said Penrod, "or a senator, or sumpthing like that."

"Senators live in Warshington," Maurice Levy contributed the information. "I been there. Warshington ain't so much; Niag'ra Falls is a hundred times as good as Warshington. So's 'Tlantic City, I was there, too. I been everywhere there is. I——"

"Well, anyway," said Sam Williams, raising his voice in order to obtain the floor, "anyway, I'm goin' to lay in a hammock all day, and have ice-water sprinkled on top o' me, and I'm goin' to lay there all night, too, and the next day. I'm goin' to lay there a couple o' years, maybe."

"I bet you don't!" exclaimed Maurice. "What'd you do in winter?"

"What?"

"What you goin' to do when it's winter, out in a hammock with water sprinkled on top o' you all day? I bet you——"

"I'd stay right there," Sam declared, with strong conviction, blinking as he looked out through the open doors at the dazzling lawn and trees, trembling in the heat. "They couldn't sprinkle too much for *me!*"

"It'd make icicles all over you, and——"

"I wish it would," said Sam. "I'd eat 'em up."

"And it'd snow on you——"

"Yay! I'd swaller it as fast as it'd come down. I wish I had a *barrel* o' snow right now. I wish this whole barn was full of it. I wish they wasn't anything in the whole world except just good ole snow."

Penrod and Herman rose and went out to the hydrant, where they drank long and ardently. Sam was still talking about snow when they returned.

"No, I wouldn't just roll in it. I'd stick it all round inside my clo'es, and fill my hat. No, I'd freeze a big pile of it all hard, and I'd roll her out flat and then I'd carry her down to some ole tailor's and have him make me a *suit* out of her, and——"

"Can't you keep still about your ole snow?" demanded Penrod petulantly. "Makes me so thirsty I can't keep still, and I've drunk so much now I bet I bust. That ole hydrant water's mighty near hot anyway."

"I'm goin' to have a big store, when I grow up," volunteered Maurice.

"Candy store?" asked Penrod.

"*No*, sir! I'll have candy in it, but not to eat, so much. It's goin' to be a deportment store: ladies' clothes, gentlemen's clothes, neckties, china goods, leather goods, nice lines in woollings and lace goods——"

"Yay! I wouldn't give a five-for-a-cent marble for your whole store," said Sam. "Would you, Penrod?"

"Not for ten of 'em; not for a million of 'em! *I'm* goin' to have——"

"Wait!" clamoured Maurice. "You'd be foolish, because they'd be a toy deportment in my store where they'd be a hundred marbles! So, how much would you think your five-for-a-cent marble counts for? And when

I'm keepin' my store I'm goin' to get married."

"Yay!" shrieked Sam derisively. "*Married!* Listen!" Penrod and Herman joined in the howl of contempt.

"Certumly I'll get married," asserted Maurice stoutly. "I'll get married to Marjorie Jones. She likes me awful good, and I'm her beau."

"What makes you think so?" inquired Penrod in a cryptic voice.

"Because she's my beau, too," came the prompt answer. "I'm her beau because she's my beau; I guess that's plenty reason! I'll get married to her as soon as I get my store running nice."

Penrod looked upon him darkly, but, for the moment, held his peace.

"Married!" jeered Sam Williams. "Married to Marjorie Jones! You're the only boy I ever heard say he was going to get married. I wouldn't get married for–why, I wouldn't for–for——" Unable to think of any inducement the mere mention of which would not be ridiculously incommensurate, he proceeded: "I wouldn't do it! What you want to get married for? What do married people do, except just come home tired, and worry around and kind of scold? You better not do it, M'rice; you'll be mighty sorry."

"Everybody gets married," stated Maurice, holding his ground. "They gotta."

"I'll bet *I* don't!" Sam returned hotly. "They better catch me before they tell *me* I have to. Anyway, I bet nobody has to get married unless they want to."

"They do, too," insisted Maurice. "They *gotta!*"

"Who told you?"

"Look at what my own papa told me!" cried Maurice, heated with argument. "Didn't he tell me your papa had to marry your mamma, or else he never'd got to handle a cent of her money? Certumly, people gotta marry. Everybody. You don't know anybody over twenty years old that isn't married–except maybe teachers."

"Look at policemen!" shouted Sam triumphantly. "You don't s'pose anybody can make policemen get married, I reckon, do you?"

"Well, policemen, maybe," Maurice was forced to admit. "Policemen and teachers don't, but everybody else gotta."

"Well, I'll be a policeman," said Sam. "*Then* I guess they won't come around tellin' me I have to get married. What you goin' to be, Penrod?"

"Chief police," said the laconic Penrod.

"What you?" Sam inquired of quiet Georgie Bassett.

"I am going to be," said Georgie, consciously, "a minister."

This announcement created a sensation so profound that it was followed by silence. Herman was the first to speak.

"You mean preachuh?" he asked incredulously. "You goin' *preach?*"

"Yes," answered Georgie, looking like Saint Cecilia at the organ.

Herman was impressed. "You know all 'at preachuh talk?"

"I'm going to learn it," said Georgie simply.

"How loud kin you holler?" asked Herman doubtfully.

"He can't holler at all," Penrod interposed with scorn. "He hollers like a girl. He's the poorest hollerer in town!"

Herman shook his head. Evidently he thought Georgie's chance of being ordained very slender. Nevertheless, a final question put to the candidate by the coloured expert seemed to admit one ray of hope.

"How good kin you clim a pole?"

"He can't climb one at all," Penrod answered for Georgie. "Over at Sam's turning-pole you ought to see him try to——"

"Preachers don't have to climb poles," Georgie said with dignity.

"*Good* ones do," declared Herman. "Bes' one ev' *I* hear, he clim up an' down same as a circus man. One n'em big 'vivals outen whens we livin' on a fahm, preachuh clim big pole right in a middle o' the church, what was to hol' roof up. He clim way high up, an' holler: 'Goin' to heavum, goin' to heavum, goin' to heavum *now*. Hallelujah, praise my Lawd!' An' he slide down little, an' holler: 'Devil's got a hol' o' my coat-tails; devil tryin' to drag me down! Sinnuhs, take wawnun! Devil got a hol' o' my coat-tails; I'm a-goin' to hell, oh Lawd!' Nex', he clim up little mo', an' yell an' holler: 'Done shuck ole devil loose; goin' straight to heavum again! Goin' to heavum, goin' to heavum, my Lawd!' Nex', he slide down some mo' an' holler, 'Leggo my coat-tails, ole devil! Goin' to hell agin, sinnuhs! Goin' straight to hell, my Lawd!' An' he clim an' he slide, an' he slide, an' he clim, an' all time holler: 'Now 'm a-goin' to heavum; now 'm a-goin' to hell! Goin' to heavum, heavum, heavum, my Lawd!' Las' he slide all a-way down, jes' a-squallin' an' a-kickin' an' a-rarin' up an' squealin', 'Goin' to hell. Goin' to hell! Ole Satum got my soul! Goin' to hell! Goin' to hell! Goin' to hell, hell, hell!' "

Herman possessed that extraordinary facility for vivid acting which is the great native gift of his race, and he enchained his listeners. They sat fascinated and spellbound.

"Herman, tell that again!" said Penrod, breathlessly.

Herman, nothing loath, accepted the encore and repeated the Miltonic episode, expanding it somewhat, and dwelling with a fine art upon those portions of the narrative which he perceived to be most exciting to his audience. Plainly, they thrilled less to Paradise gained than to its losing, and the dreadful climax of the descent into the Pit was the greatest treat of all.

The effect was immense and instant. Penrod sprang to his feet.

"Georgie Bassett couldn't do that to save his life," he declared. "*I'm* goin' to be a preacher! *I'd* be all right for one, wouldn't I, Herman?"

"So am I!" Sam Williams echoed loudly. "I guess I can do it if *you* can. I'd be better'n Penrod, wouldn't I, Herman?"

"I am, too!" Maurice shouted. "I got a stronger voice than anybody here, and I'd like to know what——"

The three clamoured together indistinguishably, each asserting his qualifications for the ministry according to Herman's theory, which had been accepted by these sudden converts without question.

"Listen to *me!*" Maurice bellowed, proving his claim to at least the voice by drowning the others. "Maybe I can't climb a pole so good, but who can holler louder'n this? Listen to *me-e-e!*"

"Shut up!" cried Penrod, irritated. "Go to heaven; go to hell!"

"Oo-o-oh!" exclaimed Georgie Bassett, profoundly shocked.

Sam and Maurice, awed by Penrod's daring, ceased from turmoil, staring wide-eyed.

"You cursed and swore!" said Georgie.

"I did not!" cried Penrod, hotly. "That isn't swearing."

"You said, 'Go to a big H'!" said Georgie.

"I did not! I said, 'Go to heaven,' before I said a big H. That isn't swearing, is it, Herman? It's almost what the preacher said, ain't it, Herman? It ain't swearing now, any more—not if you put 'go to heaven' with it, is it, Herman? You can say it all you want to, long as you say 'go to heaven' first, *can't* you, Herman? Anybody can say it if the preacher says it, can't they, Herman? I guess I know when I ain't swearing, don't I, Herman?"

Judge Herman ruled for the defendant, and Penrod was considered to have carried his point. With fine consistency, the conclave established that it was proper for the general public to "say it," provided "go to heaven" should in all cases precede it. This prefix was pronounced a perfect disinfectant, removing all odour of impiety or insult; and, with the exception of Georgie Bassett (who maintained that the minister's words were "going" and "gone," not "go"), all the boys proceeded to exercise their new privilege so lavishly that they tired of it.

But there was no diminution of evangelical ardour; again were heard the clamours of dispute as to which was the best qualified for the ministry, each of the claimants appealing passionately to Herman, who, pleased but confused, appeared to be incapable of arriving at a decision.

During a pause, Georgie Bassett asserted his prior rights. "Who said it first, I'd like to know?" he demanded. "I was going to be a minister from long back of to-day, I guess. And I guess I said I was going to be a minister right to-day before any of you said anything at all. *Didn't* I, Herman?

You heard me, didn't you, Herman? That's the very thing started you talking about it, wasn't it, Herman?"

"You' right," said Herman. "You the firs' one to say it."

Penrod, Sam, and Maurice immediately lost faith in Herman. They turned from him and fell hotly upon Georgie.

"What if you did say it first?" Penrod shouted. "You couldn't *be* a minister if you were a hundred years old!"

"I bet his mother wouldn't let him be one," said Sam. "She never lets him do anything."

"She would, too," retorted Georgie. "Ever since I was little, she——"

"He's too sissy to be a preacher!" cried Maurice. "Listen at his squeaky voice!"

"I'm going to be a better minister," shouted Georgie, "than all three of you put together. I could do it with my left hand!"

The three laughed bitingly in chorus. They jeered, derided, scoffed, and raised an uproar which would have had its effect upon much stronger nerves than Georgie's. For a time he contained his rising choler and chanted monotonously, over and over: "*I could! I could, too! I could! I could, too!*" But their tumult wore upon him, and he decided to avail himself of the recent decision whereby a big H was rendered innocuous and unprofane. Having used the expression once, he found it comforting, and substituted it for: "I could! I could, too!"

But it relieved him only temporarily. His tormentors were unaffected by it and increased their howlings, until at last Georgie lost his head altogether. Badgered beyond bearing, his eyes shining with a wild light, he broke through the besieging trio, hurling little Maurice from his path with a frantic hand.

"I'll show you!" he cried, in this sudden frenzy. "You give me a chance, and I'll prove it right *now!*"

"That's talkin' business!" shouted Penrod. "Everybody keep still a minute. Everybody!"

He took command of the situation at once, displaying a fine capacity for organization and system. It needed only a few minutes to set order in the place of confusion and to determine, with the full concurrence of all parties, the conditions under which Georgie Bassett was to defend his claim by undergoing what may be perhaps intelligibly defined as the Herman test. Georgie declared he could do it easily. He was in a state of great excitement and in no condition to think calmly or, probably, he would not have made the attempt at all. Certainly he was overconfident.

It was during the discussion of the details of this enterprise that Georgie's mother, a short distance down the street, received a few female callers, who came by appointment to drink a glass of iced tea with her, and to meet the Rev. Mr. Kinosling. Mr. Kinosling was proving almost formidably interesting to the women and girls of his own and other flocks. What favour of his fellow clergymen a slight precociousness of manner and pronunciation cost him was more than balanced by the visible ecstasies of ladies. They blossomed at his touch.

He had just entered Mrs. Bassett's front door, when the son of the house, followed by an intent and earnest company of four, opened the alley gate and came into the yard. The unconscious Mrs. Bassett was about to have her first experience of a fatal coincidence. It was her first, because she was the mother of a boy so well behaved that he had become a proverb of transcendency. Fatal coincidences were plentiful in the Schofield and Williams families, and would have been familiar to Mrs. Bassett had Georgie been permitted greater intimacy with Penrod and Sam.

Mr. Kinosling sipped his iced tea and looked about him approvingly. Seven ladies leaned forward, for it was to be seen that he meant to speak.

"This cool room is a relief," he said, waving a graceful hand in a neatly limited gesture, which everybody's eyes followed, his own included. "It is a relief and a retreat. The windows open, the blinds closed—that is as it should be. It is a retreat, a fastness, a bastion against the heat's assault. For me, a quiet room—a quiet room and a book, a volume in the hand, held lightly between the fingers. A volume of poems, lines metrical and cadenced; something by a sound Victorian. We have no later poets."

"Swinburne?" suggested Miss Beam, an eager spinster. "Swinburne, Mr. Kinosling? Ah, *Swinburne!*"

"Not Swinburne," said Mr. Kinosling chastely. "No."

That concluded all the remarks about Swinburne.

Miss Beam retired in confusion behind another lady; and somehow there became diffused an impression that Miss Beam was erotic.

"I do not observe your manly little son," Mr. Kinosling addressed his hostess.

"He's out playing in the yard," Mrs. Bassett returned. "I heard his voice just now, I think."

"Everywhere I hear wonderful report of him," said Mr. Kinosling. "I may say that I understand boys, and I feel that he is a rare, a fine, a pure, a lofty spirit. I say spirit, for spirit is the word I hear spoken of him."

A chorus of enthusiastic approbation affirmed the accuracy of this proclamation, and Mrs. Bassett flushed with pleasure. Georgie's spiritual perfection was demonstrated by instances of it, related by the visitors; his piety was cited, and wonderful things he had said were quoted.

"Not all boys are pure, of fine spirit, of high mind," said Mr. Kinosling, and continued with true feeling: "You have a neighbour, dear Mrs. Bassett, whose household I indeed really feel it quite impossible to visit until such time when better, firmer, stronger handed, more determined discipline shall prevail. I find Mr. and Mrs. Schofield and their daughter charming——"

Three or four ladies said "Oh!" and spoke a name simultaneously. It was as if they had said, "Oh, the bubonic plague!"

"Oh! Penrod Schofield!"

"Georgie does not play with him," said Mrs. Bassett quickly—"that is, he avoids him as much as he can without hurting Penrod's feelings. Georgie is very sensitive to giving pain. I suppose a mother should not tell these things, and I know people who talk about their own children are dreadful bores, but it was only last Thursday night that Georgie looked up in my face so sweetly, after he had said his prayers and his little cheeks flushed, as he said: "Mamma, I think it would be right for me to go more with Penrod. I think it would make him a better boy."

A sibilance went about the room. "Sweet! How sweet! The sweet little soul! Ah, *sweet!*"

"And that very afternoon," continued Mrs. Bassett, "he had come home in a dreadful state. Penrod had thrown tar all over him."

"Your son has a forgiving spirit!" said Mr. Kinosling with vehemence. "A too forgiving spirit, perhaps." He set down his glass. "No more, I thank you. No more cake, I thank you. Was it not Cardinal Newman who said——"

He was interrupted by the sounds of an altercation just outside the closed blinds of the window nearest him.

"Let him pick his tree!" It was the voice of Samuel Williams. "Didn't we come over here to give him one of his own trees? Give him a fair show, can't you?"

"The little lads!" Mr. Kinosling smiled. "They have their games, their outdoor sports, their pastimes. The young muscles are toughening. The sun will not harm them. They grow; they expand; they learn. They learn fair play, honour, courtesy, from one another, as pebbles grow round in the brook. They learn more from themselves than from us. They take shape, form, outline. Let them."

"Mr. Kinosling!" Another spinster—undeterred by what had happened to Miss Beam—leaned far forward, her face shining and ardent. "Mr. Kinosling, there's a question I *do* wish to ask you."

"My dear Miss Cosslit," Mr. Kinosling responded, again waving his hand and watching it, "I am entirely at your disposal."

"*Was* Joan of Arc," she asked fervently, "inspired by spirits?"

He smiled indulgently. "Yes—and no," he said. "One must give both answers. One must give the answer, yes; one must give the answer, no."

"Oh, *thank* you!" said Miss Cosslit, blushing. "She's one of my great enthusiasms, you know."

"And I have a question, too," urged Mrs. Lora Rewbush, after a moment's hasty concentration. "I've never been able to settle it for myself, but *now*——"

"Yes?" said Mr. Kinosling encouragingly.

"Is—ah—is—oh, yes: Is Sanskrit a more difficult language than Spanish, Mr. Kinosling?"

"It depends upon the student," replied the oracle, smiling. "One must not look for linguists everywhere. In my own especial case—if one may cite one's self as an example—I found no great, no insurmountable difficulty in mastering, in conquering either."

"And may *I* ask one?" ventured Mrs. Bassett. "Do you think it is right to wear egrets?"

"There are marks of quality, of caste, of social distinction," Mr. Kinosling began, "which must be permitted, allowed, though perhaps regulated. Social distinction, one observes, almost invariably implies spiritual distinction as well. Distinction of circumstances is accompanied by mental distinction. Distinction is hereditary; it descends from father to son, and if there is one thing more true than 'Like father, like son,' it is—" he bowed gallantly to Mrs. Bassett—"it is, 'Like mother, like son.' What these good ladies have said this afternoon of *your*——"

This was the fatal instant. There smote upon all ears the voice of Georgie, painfully shrill and penetrating—fraught with protest and protracted strain. His plain words consisted of the newly sanctioned and disinfected curse with a big H.

With an ejaculation of horror, Mrs. Bassett sprang to the window and threw open the blinds.

Georgie's back was disclosed to the view of the tea-party. He was endeavouring to ascend a maple tree about twelve feet from the window. Embracing the trunk with arms and legs, he had managed to squirm to a point above the heads of Penrod and Herman, who stood close by, watching him earnestly—Penrod being obviously in charge of the performance. Across the yard were Sam Williams and Maurice Levy, acting as a jury on the question of voice-power, and it was to a complaint of theirs that Georgie had just replied.

"That's right, Georgie," said Penrod encouragingly. "They can, too, hear you. Let her go!"

"Going to heaven!" shrieked Georgie, squirming up another inch. "Going to heaven, heaven, heaven!"

His mother's frenzied attempts to attract his attention failed utterly. Georgie was using the full power of his lungs, deafening his own ears to all other sounds. Mrs. Bassett called in vain; while the tea-party stood petrified in a cluster about the window.

"Going to heaven!" Georgie bellowed. "Going to heaven! Going to heaven, my Lord! Going to heaven, heaven, heaven!"

He tried to climb higher, but began to slip downward, his exertions causing damage to his apparel. A button flew into the air, and his knickerbockers and his waistband severed relations.

"Devil's got my coat-tails, sinners! Old devil's got my coat-tails!" he announced appropriately. The he began to slide. He relaxed his clasp of the tree and slid to the ground.

"Going to hell!" shrieked Georgie, reaching a high pitch of enthusiasm in this great climax. "Going to hell! Going to hell! I'm gone to hell, hell, hell!"

With a loud scream, Mrs. Bassett threw herself out of the window, alighting by some miracle upon her feet with ankles unsprained.

Mr. Kinosling, feeling that his presence as spiritual adviser was demanded in the yard, followed with greater dignity through the front door. At the corner of the house a small departing figure collided with him violently. It was Penrod, tactfully withdrawing from what promised to be a family scene of unusual painfulness.

Mr. Kinosling seized him by the shoulders and, giving way to emotion, shook him viciously.

"You horrible boy!" exclaimed Mr. Kinosling. "You ruffianly creature! Do you know what's going to happen to you when you grow up? Do you realize what you're going to *be!*"

With flashing eyes, the indignant boy made known his unshaken purpose. He shouted the reply:

"A minister!"

EDWIN ARLINGTON ROBINSON

[1869–1935]

A New Englander who managed to be both traditional and original, Edwin Arlington Robinson was born December 22, 1869, in Head Tide, Maine. His father was a grain merchant, owner of the town's general store, and bank director. While Edwin was still in his infancy, the family moved to nearby Gardiner, a manufacturing town of a few thousand people. The times were hard; nothing went well. There were two older brothers: one of them was an unsuccessful businessman and the other, schooled to be a doctor, became a drug addict. The youngest of the Robinsons was a lonely boy who grew up to be an even more lonely man. He identified himself with everyone and everything that was solitary, fearful, and frustrated. Shortly after attaining his majority, he wrote, "The truth is I have lived in Gardiner for nearly twenty years and, metaphorically speaking, have hardly been out of the yard . . . Solitude tends to magnify one's ideas of individuality; it sharpens one's sympathy with failure. It renders a man suspicious of the whole natural plan and leads him to wonder whether the invisible powers are a fortuitous issue of unguided cosmos or the cosmos itself."

Robinson's life was an uncertain progress of ideas and a few fortuitous events. He entered Harvard but, after two years, had to leave college because the family could no longer afford to keep him there. He wrote a few prose sketches which were summarily returned; a poem (the now-famous "The House on the Hill") was accepted by a quarterly without payment. He was twenty-six years old when a magazine published his sonnet about Poe; the fee was seven dollars. His first book, The Torrent and the Night Before, was twice rejected. Robinson finally scraped up fifty-two dollars to have it privately printed.

Nearly thirty, Robinson collected another few dollars and went to New York. Hoping somehow to live by poetry, he tried to dispose of his wares in the literary market place, but at thirty-three all that he had earned from writing was the seven dollars paid for the Poe sonnet. He moved from one rooming house to another, each one dingier than the last. He lived on the free lunches which went with glasses of cheap whiskey. He got a job as checker at twenty cents an hour in the subway which was then being built.

He was ill and almost starving when he was saved by a curious circumstance. One of President Theodore Roosevelt's sons called his father's attention to Robinson's second book, Captain Craig, which, published in 1902, had been completely ignored. Roosevelt found him a position in the New York Custom House, and Robinson (so he wrote to a friend) could now not only afford to write poetry but to own two pairs of shoes at the same time. By the time Roosevelt left the White House and Robinson lost his post, he had attracted a small circle of admirers who took care of him.

Relieved of financial pressures, Robinson was free to compose longer works as well as the epigrammatic lyrics which were his specialty. In a dozen years there were a dozen books; three of them were awarded the Pulitzer Prize. At sixty he was physically tired but he kept on writing. In his sixty-sixth year he was disabled because of a growth in the pancreas. When he was brought to the New York Hospital, it was found inadvisable to operate; he died there, April 6, 1935.

It is for Robinson's incisive short poems, rather than for his prolix narratives, that he will be remembered. With the strictest economy of line, he drew portraits of untypical but memorable native figures, mediocrities and misfits who were failures in the eyes of the successful world: Richard Cory, who "glittered when he walked" but who, one calm summer night "went home and put a bullet through his head"; Miniver Cheevy sighing for "what was not," unfitted for the present and unable to live in the past; the ruined, once-rich Bewick Finzer, coming for his pension, "familiar as an old mistake and futile as regret"; Mr. Flood, the battered but ingratiating dipsomaniac, lifting his jug above the town

> Where strangers would have shut the many doors
> That many friends had opened long ago.

Although he was not an innovator, Robinson put new power into old forms. He sharpened the outlines of his quatrains and added poignancy to the rhythms of light verse. He gave the discarded and the dispossessed nobility and made a kind of triumph of defeat.

RICHARD CORY

Whenever Richard Cory went down town,
  We people on the pavement looked at him:
He was a gentleman from sole to crown,
  Clean favored, and imperially slim.

And he was always quietly arrayed,
  And he was always human when he talked;
But still he fluttered pulses when he said,
  "Good-morning," and he glittered when he walked.

And he was rich—yes, richer than a king—
  And admirably schooled in every grace:
In fine, we thought that he was everything
  To make us wish that we were in his place.

So on we worked, and waited for the light,
  And went without the meat, and cursed the bread;
And Richard Cory, one calm summer night,
  Went home and put a bullet through his head.

CLIFF KLINGENHAGEN

Cliff Klingenhagen had me in to dine
With him one day; and after soup and meat,
And all the other things there were to eat,
Cliff took two glasses and filled one with wine
And one with wormwood. Then, without a sign
For me to choose at all, he took the draught
Of bitterness himself, and lightly quaffed
It off, and said the other one was mine.

And when I asked him what the deuce he meant
By doing that, he only looked at me
And grinned, and said it was a way of his.
And though I know the fellow, I have spent
Long time a-wondering when I shall be
As happy as Cliff Klingenhagen is.

BEWICK FINZER

Time was when his half million drew
  The breath of six per cent;
But soon the worm of what-was-not
  Fed hard on his content;
And something crumbled in his brain
  When his half million went.

Time passed, and filled along with his
  The place of many more;
Time came, and hardly one of us
  Had credence to restore,
From what appeared one day, the man
  Whom we had known before.

The broken voice, the withered neck,
  The coat worn out with care,
The cleanliness of indigence,
  The brilliance of despair,
The fond imponderable dreams
  Of affluence,—all were there.

Poor Finzer, with his dreams and schemes,
  Fares hard now in the race,
With heart and eye that have a task
  When he looks in the face
Of one who might so easily
  Have been in Finzer's place.

He comes unfailing for the loan
  We give and then forget;
He comes, and probably for years
  Will he be coming yet,—
Familiar as an old mistake,
  And futile as regret.

MR. FLOOD'S PARTY

Old Eben Flood, climbing alone one night
Over the hill between the town below
And the forsaken upland hermitage
That held as much as he should ever know
On earth again of home, paused warily.
The road was his with not a native near;
And Eben, having leisure, said aloud,
For no man else in Tilbury Town to hear:

"Well, Mr. Flood, we have the harvest moon
Again, and we may not have many more;
The bird is on the wing, the poet says,
And you and I have said it here before.

Drink to the bird." He raised up to the light
The jug that he had gone so far to fill,
And answered huskily: "Well, Mr. Flood,
Since you propose it, I believe I will."

Alone, as if enduring to the end
A valiant armor of scarred hopes outworn,
He stood there in the middle of the road
Like Roland's ghost winding a silent horn.
Below him, in the town among the trees,
Where friends of other days had honored him,
A phantom salutation of the dead
Rang thinly till old Eben's eyes were dim.

Then, as a mother lays her sleeping child
Down tenderly, fearing it may awake,
He set the jug down slowly at his feet
With trembling care, knowing that most things break;
And only when assured that on firm earth
It stood, as the uncertain lives of men
Assuredly did not, he paced away,
And with his hand extended paused again:

"Well, Mr. Flood, we have not met like this
In a long time; and many a change has come
To both of us, I fear, since last it was
We had a drop together. Welcome home!"
Convivially returning with himself,
Again he raised the jug up to the light;
And with an acquiescent quaver said:
"Well, Mr. Flood, if you insist, I might.

"Only a very little, Mr. Flood—
For auld lang syne. No more, sir; that will do."
So, for the time, apparently it did,
And Eben evidently thought so too;
For soon amid the silver loneliness
Of night he lifted up his voice and sang,
Secure, with only two moons listening,
Until the whole harmonious landscape rang—

"For auld lang syne." The weary throat gave out,
The last word wavered; and the song being done,
He raised again the jug regretfully
And shook his head, and was again alone.

There was not much that was ahead of him,
And there was nothing in the town below—
Where strangers would have shut the many doors
That many friends had opened long ago.

LUKE HAVERGAL

Go to the western gate, Luke Havergal,
There where the vines cling crimson on the wall,
And in the twilight wait for what will come.
The leaves will whisper there of her, and some,
Like flying words, will strike you as they fall;
But go, and if you listen, she will call.
Go to the western gate, Luke Havergal—
Luke Havergal.

No, there is not a dawn in eastern skies
To rift the fiery night that's in your eyes;
But there, where western glooms are gathering,
The dark will end the dark, if anything:
God slays himself with every leaf that flies,
And hell is more than half of paradise.
No, there is not a dawn in eastern skies—
In eastern skies.

Out of a grave I come to tell you this,
Out of a grave I come to quench the kiss
That flames upon your forehead with a glow
That blinds you to the way that you must go.
Yes, there is yet one way to where she is,
Bitter, but one that faith may never miss.
Out of a grave I come to tell you this—
To tell you this.

There is the western gate, Luke Havergal,
There are the crimson leaves upon the wall.
Go, for the winds are tearing them away,—
Nor think to riddle the dead words they say,
Nor any more to feel them as they fall;
But go, and if you trust her she will call.
There is the western gate, Luke Havergal—
Luke Havergal.

THE HOUSE ON THE HILL

They are all gone away,
  The House is shut and still,
There is nothing more to say.

Through broken walls and gray
  The winds blow bleak and shrill;
They are all gone away.

Nor is there only one today
  To speak them good or ill:
There is nothing more to say.

Why is it then we stray
  Around that sunken sill?
They are all gone away,

And our poor fancy-play
  For them is wasted skill:
There is nothing more to say.

There is ruin and decay
  In the House on the Hill:
They are all gone away,
There is nothing more to say.

AN OLD STORY

Strange that I did not know him then,
  That friend of mine.
I did not even show him then
  One friendly sign;

But cursed him for the ways he had
  To make me see
My envy of the praise he had
  For praising me.

I would have rid the earth of him
  Once, in my pride.
I never knew the worth of him
  Until he died.

WALT WHITMAN

The master-songs are ended, and the man
That sang them is a name. And so is God
A name. And so is love, and life, and death,
And everything. But we, who are too blind
To read what we have written, or what faith
Has written for us, do not understand:
We only blink, and wonder.

Last night it was the song that was the man,
And now it is the man that is the song.
We do not hear him very much today:
His piercing and eternal cadence rings
Too pure for us—too powerfully pure,

Too lovingly triumphant and too large.
But there are some that hear him, and they know
That he shall sing tomorrow for all men,
And that all time shall listen.

The master-songs are ended? Rather say
No songs are ended that are ever sung,
And that no names are dead names. When we write
Men's letters on proud marble or on sand,
We write them there forever.

CREDO

I cannot find my way; there is no star
In all the shrouded heavens anywhere;
And there is not a whisper in the air
Of any living voice but one so far
That I can hear it only as a bar
Of lost, imperial music, played when fair
And angel fingers wove, and unaware,
Dead leaves to garlands where no roses are.

No, there is not a glimmer, nor a call,
For one that welcomes, welcomes when he fears,
The black and awful chaos of the night;
For through it all—above, beyond it all—
I know the far-sent message of the years,
I feel the coming glory of the light!

THEODORE DREISER

[1871–1945]

No one who knew the Dreisers could have imagined that the son who was christened Theodore Herman Albert would become one of the country's most candid and most uncompromising realistic writers. His mother was a superstitious Mennonite who ran a cheap boarding house and took in washing. Behind her husband's back she summoned a neighbor to "save" the sickly Theodore by spells and witchcraft. His father, a fanatically religious day laborer, was an intolerant Catholic who believed that mortal thought was debased and human pleasure despicable. There were thirteen children—Theodore was the twelfth—and their poverty was such that they lived chiefly on cornmeal mush and fried potatoes; they went without shoes and brought home coal which they stole from railroad yards. All of them felt they must escape in any possible way the rigors of poverty and their father's inhuman demands. One of Theodore's sisters lived illicitly with an architect, and left him to run away with a married man, a restaurant manager who had stolen some fifteen thousand dollars; another sister bore a child to a man too well connected to think of marrying her. But one brother, Paul, who changed his name to Dresser, became a successful writer of popular songs. Theodore himself supplied the first verse and chorus for Paul's best known song, "On the Banks of the Wabash."

Theodore Dreiser was born August 27, 1871, in Terre Haute, Indiana. The family was always on the move; young Dreiser got a little education in Warsaw, Indiana, the rest (one year) at Indiana University. By the time he was seventeen he had worked as a dishwasher in a dingy cafe, car-checker in the train yards, and clerk in a hardware store. His mother died when he was nineteen, and when the priest withheld his blessing Dreiser turned against the Church. At twenty he went to St. Louis as a reporter, became engaged to a schoolteacher, moved on to Toledo, Cleveland, Pittsburgh, and eventually New York. Reading such novelists of actual life as Balzac and Dickens, and such philosopher-scientists as Huxley, Tyndall, and Spencer, he resolved that, since life seemed to have no ideal meaning, to examine the sources of worldly success and failure.

Theodore would have starved in New York had he not been rescued by his easy-living, playboy brother Paul. Paul persuaded a publisher friend to give him a job, and Theodore was allowed to do free-lance work in between his editorial chores. He supported himself in this way, got married, and, tired of hack writing, wrote his first book, Sister Carrie. His most popular novel, it was also his most roundly condemned. The plot of seduction and adultery (suggested by his sisters' experiences) was not new; what was new was the frank and completely amoral tone in which the story was told. One major publisher refused to have anything to do with it. Another volunteered to publish it, but when Mrs. Doubleday, the publisher's wife, read the proofs she was so shocked that, although the firm was legally bound to issue the volume, the publishers kept most of the edition at the printer's and virtually suppressed the book. Only a few hundred copies found their way into the bookstores. Dreiser felt that he was as much a failure as his father.

At thirty he was not only depressed but destitute. He sent his wife back to her family in Missouri and moved from one rundown room to another. Once more his brother Paul came to his assistance: he sent him to a health farm in the country, saw to it that his energy and spirits were restored, and watched over him until he was hired as fiction editor of a chain of magazines that specialized in trashy romances. Successful at last, he was now leading a cultural double life. As a creative writer he was continuing to study the unglamorized facts ot life and the sordid situations which existed wherever he looked; as the editor of a group of "pulp" magazines he had to announce: "We cannot admit stories which deal with immoral relations, or which are disgusting in their realism and fidelity to life." Somehow, he was able to produce his second novel, Jennie Gerhardt.

As in Sister Carrie, Dreiser again presented a woman seduced by one man and the mistress of another, but who, in spite of her amorality, wins the reader's sympathy by her natural goodness. Dreiser now had not only developed his pattern of thought but his plan of action as well. Everything he wrote thereafter conformed—or attempted to conform—to his central thesis: "For myself I accept no creed. I do not know what truth is, what beauty is, what love is, and what hope is. I do not believe any one absolutely, and I do not doubt any one absolutely. I think that people are both evil and well-intentioned." Nevertheless, although he was distrustful of black-and-white thinking and self-divided about the ultimate aim of everything, he never ceased to probe for the truth beneath the superficial veneer of human conduct. Using the millionaire manipulator and embezzler Charles T. Yerkes as his model, he wrote a "trilogy of desire," a richly documented saga of a ruthless industrialist's dramatic rise and fall: The Financier, The Titan, The Stoic.

The "Genius," written when he was forty-four, transfers the theme of ruthlessness from industry to art. Although it showed the destructive force of passion instead of the corruptive power of money and was something of a moral preachment, strait-laced readers were aroused. Ministers denounced it; Societies for the Prevention of Vice, fulminating against its "obscenity and blasphemy," managed to have it suppressed; libraries not only took it off their shelves but banned Dreiser's other works.

For a while, Dreiser was too discouraged to try anything on a similarly large scale. He occupied himself with plays, melodramatic fables, a travel book, a collection of essays, short stories. He was in his mid-fifties when he took the newspaper report of a crime and turned it into the two-volume An American Tragedy, which many consider his major accomplishment. Once more, money and the standards of social success were his interrelated themes. But this time the hero-victim was not a captain of industry or a tycoon but a weakling, an upstart opportunist caught between his mean backgrounds and the glittering heights to which he not only aspired but committed murder to reach—a case history that was a nightmare version of a typical Horatio Alger story with a tragic instead of a traditionally happy ending.

After Dreiser entered his sixties, his self-division became increasingly apparent. Not content to be a writer, he wanted to be an oracle. He dabbled in politics and philosophy; he indulged in clumsy metaphysics and muddled ideologies. He supported the Spanish Loyalists in their fight against dictatorship, but equivocated about Hitler; he alternately championed and repudiated Communism, and finally confessed that the contradictions of the twentieth century were too much for him. His imaginary malaises—he had been a hypochondriac for years—developed into a definite illness, and after a kidney attack he died December 28, 1945.

Any reader of Dreiser must be prepared for long, dull passages and heavy disquisitions unrelieved by any glint of grace or humor; he must be willing to make his way through morasses of stereotypes and mountains of exasperating trivialities. But he will be rewarded by a sense of magnitude, by a rough-hewn honesty, an essential integrity of purpose, and, in such a moving story as "The Lost Phoebe," great tenderness. Many of Dreiser's followers have written more subtly, but it was Dreiser who made it easier for them to write so fearlessly and sensitively about what it had been forbidden to write about at all.

THE LOST PHOEBE

THEY LIVED TOGETHER in a part of the country which was not so prosperous as it had once been, about three miles from one of those towns that, instead of increasing in population, is steadily decreasing. The territory was not very thickly settled; perhaps a house every other mile or so, with large areas of corn- and wheat-land and fallow fields that at odd seasons had been sown to timothy and clover. Their particular house was part log and part frame, the log portion being the old original home of Henry's grandfather. The new portion, of now rain-beaten, time-worn slabs, through which the wind squeaked in the chinks at times, and which several overshadowing elms and a butternut tree made picturesque and reminiscently pathetic, but a little damp, was erected by Henry when he was twenty-one and just married.

That was forty-eight years before. The furniture inside, like the house outside, was old and mildewy and reminiscent of an earlier day. You have seen the what-not of cherry wood, perhaps, with spiral legs and fluted top. It was there. The old-fashioned four-poster bed, with its ball-like protuberances and deep curving incisions, was there also, a sadly alienated descendant of an early Jacobean ancestor. The bureau of cherry was also high and wide and solidly built, but faded-looking, and with a musty odor. The rag carpet that underlay all these sturdy examples of enduring furniture was a weak, faded, lead and pink colored affair woven by Phoebe Ann's own hands, when she was fifteen years younger than she was when she died. The creaky wooden loom on which it had been done now stood like a dusty, bony skeleton, along with a broken rocking-chair, a worm-eaten clothes press—Heavens knows how old—a lime-stained bench that had once been used to keep flowers on outside the door, and other decrepit factors of household utility, in an east room that was a lean-to against this so-called main portion. All sorts of other broken-down furniture were about this place; an antiquated clothes-horse, cracked in two of its ribs; a broken mirror in an old cherry frame, which had fallen from a nail and cracked itself three days before their youngest son, Jerry, died; an extension hat-rack, which once had had porcelain knobs on the ends of its pegs; and a sewing machine, long since outdone in its clumsy mechanism by rivals of a newer generation.

The orchard to the east of the house was full of gnarled old apple trees, worm eaten as to trunks and branches, and fully ornamented with green and white lichens, so that it had a sad, greenish-white, silvery effect in moonlight. The low outhouses, which had once housed chickens, a horse or two, a cow, and several pigs, were covered with patches of moss as to their roof, and the sides had been free of paint for so long that they were blackish-gray as to color, and a little spongy. The picket fence in front, with its gate squeaky and askew, and the side fences of the stake-and-rider type were in an equally run-down condition. As a matter of fact, they had aged synchronously with the persons who lived here, old Henry Reifsneider and his wife Phoebe Ann.

They had lived here, these two, ever since their marriage, forty-eight years before, and Henry had lived here before that from his childhood up. His father and mother, well along in years when he was a boy, had invited him to bring his wife here when he had first fallen in love and decided to marry; and he had done so. His father and mother were the companions of himself and his wife for ten years after they were married, when both died; and then Henry and Phoebe were left with their five children growing lustily apace. But all sorts of things had happened since then. Of the seven children, all told, that had been born to them, three had died; one girl had gone to Kansas; one boy had gone to Sioux Falls, never even to be heard of after; another boy had gone to Washington; and the last girl lived five counties away in the same State, but was so burdened with cares of her own that she rarely gave them a thought. Time and a commonplace home life that had never been attractive had weaned them thoroughly, so that, wherever they were, they gave little thought as to how it might be with their father and mother.

Old Henry Reifsneider and his wife Phoebe were a loving couple. You perhaps know how it is with simple natures that fasten themselves like lichens on the stones of circumstance and weather their days to a crumbling conclusion. The great world sounds widely, but it has no call for them. They have no soaring intellect. The orchard, the meadow, the cornfield, the pig-pen, and the chicken-lot measure the range of their human activities. When the wheat is headed it is reaped and threshed; when the corn is browned and frosted it is cut and shocked; when the timothy is in full head it is cut, and the hay-cock erected. After that comes winter, with the hauling of grain to market, the sawing and splitting of wood, the simple chores of fire-building, meal-getting, occasional repairing, and visiting. Beyond these and the changes of weather—the snows, the rains, and the fair days—there are no immediate, significant things. All the rest of life is a far-off, clamorous phantasmagoria, flickering like Northern lights in the night, and sounding as faintly as cow-bells tinkling in the distance.

Old Henry and his wife Phoebe were as fond of each other as it is possible for two old people be who have nothing else in this life to be fond of. He was a thin old man, seventy when she died, a queer, crotchety person with coarse gray-black hair and beard, quite straggly and unkempt. He looked at you out of dull, fishy, watery eyes that had deep-brown crow's-feet at the sides. His clothes, like the clothes of many farmers, were aged and angular and baggy, standing out at the pockets, not fitting about the neck, protuberant and worn at elbow and knee. Phoebe Ann was thin and shapeless, a very umbrella of a woman, clad in shabby black, and with a black bonnet for her best wear. As time had passed, and they had only themselves to look after, their movements had become slower and slower, their activities fewer and fewer. The annual keep of pigs had been reduced from five to one grunting porker, and the single horse which Henry now retained was a sleepy animal, not over-nourished and not very clean. The chickens, of which formerly there was a large flock, had almost disappeared, owing to ferrets, foxes, and the lack of proper care, which produces disease. The former healthy garden was now a straggling memory of itself, and the vines and flower-beds that formerly ornamented the windows and dooryard had now become choking thickets. A will had been made which divided the small tax-eaten property equally among the remaining four, so that it was really of no interest to any of them. Yet these two lived together in peace and sympathy, only that now and then old Henry would become unduly cranky, complaining almost invariably that something had been neglected or mislaid which was of no importance at all.

"Phoebe, where's my corn knife? You ain't never minded to let my things alone no more."

"Now you hush, Henry," his wife would caution him in a cracked and squeaky voice. "If you don't, I'll leave yuh. I'll git up and walk out of here some day, and then where would y' be? Y' ain't got anybody but me to look after yuh, so yuh just behave yourself. Your corn knife's on the mantel where it's allus been unless you've gone an' put it summers else."

Old Henry, who knew his wife would never leave him under any circumstances, used to speculate at times as to what he would do if she were to die. That was the one leaving that he really feared. As he climbed on the chair at night to wind the old, long-pendulumed, double-weighted clock, or went finally to the front and the back door to see that they were safely shut in, it was a comfort to know that Phoebe was there, properly ensconced on her side of the bed, and that if he stirred restlessly in the night, she would be there to ask what he wanted.

"Now, Henry, do lie still! You're as restless as a chicken."

"Well, I can't sleep, Phoebe."

"Well, yuh needn't roll so, anyhow. Yuh kin let me sleep."

This usually reduced him to a state of somnolent ease. If she wanted a pail of water, it was a grumbling pleasure for him to get it; and if she did rise first to build the fires, he saw that the wood was cut and placed within easy reach. They divided this simple world nicely between them.

As the years had gone on, however, fewer and fewer people had called. They were well-known for a distance of as much as ten square miles as old Mr. and Mrs. Reifsneider, honest, moderately Christian, but too old to be really interesting any longer. The writing of letters had become an almost impossible burden too difficult to continue or even negotiate via others, although an occasional letter still did arrive from the daughter in Pemberton County. Now and then some old friend stopped with a pie or cake or a roasted chicken or duck, or merely to see that they were well; but even these kindly minded visits were no longer frequent.

One day in the early spring of her sixty-fourth year Mrs. Reifsneider took sick, and from a low fever passed into some indefinable ailment which, because of her age, was no longer curable. Old Henry drove to Swinnerton, the neighboring town, and procured a doctor. Some friends called, and the immediate care of her was taken off his hands. Then one chill spring night she died, and old Henry, in a fog of sorrow and uncertainty, followed her body to the nearest graveyard, an unattractive space with a few pines growing in it. Although he might have gone to the daughter in Pemberton or sent for her, it was really too much trouble and he was too weary and fixed. It was suggested to him at once by one friend and another that he come to stay with them awhile, but he did not see fit. He was so old and so fixed in his notions and so accustomed to the exact surroundings he had known all his days, that he could not think of leaving. He wanted to remain near where they had put his Phoebe; and the fact that he would have to live alone did not trouble him in the least. The living children were notified and the care of him offered if he would leave, but he would not.

"I kin make a shift for myself," he continually announced to old Dr. Morrow, who had attended his wife in this case. "I kin cook a little, and, besides, it don't take much more'n coffee an' bread in the mornin's to satisfy me. I'll get along now well enough. Yuh just let me be." And after many pleadings and proffers of advice, with supplies of coffee and bacon and baked bread duly offered and accepted, he was left to himself. For a while he sat idly outside his door brooding in the spring sun. He tried to revive his interest in farming, and to keep himself busy and free from thought by looking after the fields, which of late had been much neglected. It was a gloomy thing to come in of an evening, however, or in the afternoon, and find no shadow of Phoebe where everything suggested her. By degrees he put a few of her things away. At night he sat beside his lamp and read in the papers that were left him occasionally or in a Bible that he had neglected for years, but he could get little solace from these things. Mostly he held his hand over his mouth and looked at the floor as he sat and thought of what had become of her, and how soon he himself would die. He made a great business of making his coffee in the morning and frying himself a little bacon at night; but his appetite was gone. The shell in which he had been housed so long seemed vacant, and its shadows were suggestive of immedicable griefs. So he lived quite dolefully for five long months, and then a change began.

It was one night, after he had looked after the front and the back door, wound the clock, blown out the light, and gone through all the selfsame motions that he had indulged in for years, that he went to bed not so much to sleep as to think. It was a moonlight night. The green-lichen-covered orchard just outside and to be seen from his bed where he now lay was a silvery affair, sweetly spectral. The moon shone through the east windows, throwing the pattern of the panes on the wooden floor, and making the old furniture, to which he was accustomed, stand out dimly in the room. As usual he had been thinking of Phoebe and the years when they had been young together, and of the children who had gone, and the poor shift he was making of his present days. The house was coming to be in a very bad state indeed. The bed-clothes were in disorder and not clean, for he made a wretched shift of washing. It was a terror to him. The roof leaked, causing things, some of them, to remain damp for weeks at a time, but he was getting into that brooding state where he would accept anything rather than exert himself. He preferred to pace slowly to and fro or to sit and think.

By twelve o'clock of this particular night he was asleep, however, and by two had waked again. The moon by this time had shifted to a position on the western side of the house, and it now shone in through the windows of the living-room and those of the kitchen beyond. A certain combination of furniture—a chair near a table with his coat on it, the half-open kitchen door casting a shadow, and the position of a lamp near a paper—gave him an exact representation of Phoebe leaning over the table as he had often seen her do in life. It gave him a great start. Could it be she—or her ghost? He had scarcely ever believed in spirits; and still—. He looked at her fixedly in the feeble half-light, his old hair tingling oddly at the roots, and then sat up. The figure did not move. He put his thin legs out of the bed and sat looking at her, wondering if this could really be Phoebe. They had talked of ghosts often in their lifetime, of apparitions and omens; but they had never agreed that such things could be. It had never been a part of his wife's creed that she could have a spirit that could return to walk the earth. Her after-world was quite a different affair, a vague heaven, no less, from which the righteous did not trouble to return. Yet here she was now, bending over the table in her black skirt and gray shawl, her pale profile outlined against the moonlight.

"Phoebe," he called, thrilling from head to toe, and putting out one bony hand, "have yuh come back?"

The figure did not stir, and he arose and walked uncertainly to the door, looking at it fixedly the while. As he drew near, however, the apparition resolved itself into its primal content—his old coat over the high backed chair, the lamp by the paper, the half-open door.

"Well," he said to himself, his mouth open, "I thought shore I saw her." And he ran his hand strangely and vaguely through his hair, the while his nervous tension relaxed. Vanished as it had, it gave him the idea that she might return.

Another night, because of this first illusion, and because his mind was now constantly on her and he was old, he looked out of the window that was nearest his bed and commanded a hen-coop and pig-pen and a part of the wagon-shed, and there, a faint mist exuding from the damp of the ground, he thought he saw her again. It was one of those little wisps of mist, one of those faint exhalations of the earth that rise in a cool night after a warm day, and flicker like small white cypresses of fog before they disappear. In life it had been a custom of hers to cross this lot from her kitchen door to the pig-pen to throw in any scrap that was left from her cooking, and here she was again. He sat up and watched it strangely, doubtfully, because of his previous experience, but inclined, because of the nervous titillation that passed over his body, to believe that spirits really were, and that Phoebe, who would be concerned because of his lonely state, must be thinking about him, and hence returning. What other way would she have? How otherwise could she express herself? It would be within the province of her charity so to do, and like her loving interest in him. He quivered and watched it eagerly; but, a faint breath of air stirring, it wound away toward the fence and disappeared.

A third night, as he was actually dreaming, some ten days later, she came to his bedside and put her hand on his head.

"Poor Henry!" she said. "It's too bad."

He roused out of his sleep, actually to see her, he thought, moving from his bedroom into the one living room, her figure a shadowy mass of black. The weak straining of his eyes caused little points of light to flicker about the outlines of her form. He arose, greatly astonished, walked the floor in the cool room, convinced that Phoebe was coming back to him. If he only thought sufficiently, if he made it perfectly clear by his feeling that he needed her greatly, she would come back, this kindly wife, and tell him what to do. She would perhaps be with him much of the time, in the night, anyhow; and that would make him less lonely, his state more endurable.

In age and with the feeble it is not such a far cry from the subtleties of illusion to actual hallucination, and in due time this transition was made for Henry. Night after night he waited, expecting her return. Once in his weird mood he thought he saw a pale light moving about the room, and another time he thought he saw her walking in the orchard after dark. It was one morning when the details of his lonely state were virtually unendurable that he woke with the thought that she was not dead. How he had arrived at this conclusion it is hard to say. His mind had gone. In its place was a fixed illusion. He and Phoebe had had a senseless quarrel. He had reproached her for not leaving his pipe where he was accustomed to find it, and she had left. It was an aberrated fulfillment of her old jesting threat that if he did not behave himself she would leave him.

"I guess I could find yuh ag'in," he had always said. But her cackling threat had always been:

"Yuh'll not find me if I ever leave yuh. I guess I kin git some place where yuh can't find me."

This morning when he arose he did not think to build the fire in the customary way or to grind his coffee and cut his bread, as was his wont, but solely to meditate as to where he should search for her and how he should induce her to come back. Recently the one horse had been dispensed with because he found it cumbersome and beyond his needs. He took down his soft crush hat after he had dressed himself, a new glint of interest and determination in his eye, and taking his black crook cane from behind the door, where he had always placed it, started out briskly to look for her among the nearest neighbors. His old shoes clumped soundly in the dust as he walked, and his gray-black locks, now grown rather long, straggled out in a dramatic fringe or halo from under his hat. His short coat stirred busily as he walked, and his hands and face were peaked and pale.

"Why, hello, Henry! Where're yuh goin' this mornin'?" inquired Farmer Dodge, who, hauling a load of wheat to market, encountered him on the public road. He had not seen the aged farmer in months, not since his wife's death, and he wondered now, seeing him looking so spry.

"Yuh ain't seen Phoebe, have yuh?" inquired the old man, looking up quizzically.

"Phoebe who?" inquired Farmer Dodge, not for the moment connecting the name with Henry's dead wife.

"Why, my wife Phoebe, o' course. Who do yuh s'pose I mean?" He stared up with a pathetic sharpness of glance from under his shaggy, gray eyebrows.

"Wall, I'll swan, Henry, yuh ain't jokin', are yuh?" said the solid Dodge, a pursy man, with a smooth, hard, red face. "It can't be your wife yuh're talkin' about. She's dead."

"Dead! Shucks!" retorted the demented Reifsneider. "She left me early this mornin', while I was sleepin'. She allus got up to build the fire, but she's gone now. We had a little spat last night, an' I guess that's the reason. But I guess I kin find her. She's gone over to Matilda Race's, that's where she's gone."

He started briskly up the road, leaving the amazed Dodge to stare in wonder after him.

"Well, I'll be switched!" he said aloud to himself. "He's clean out'n his head. That poor old feller's been livin' down there till he's gone outen his mind. I'll have to notify the authorities." And he flicked his whip with great enthusiasm. "Geddap!" he said, and was off.

Reifsneider met no one else in this poorly populated region until he reached the whitewashed fence of Matilda Race and her husband three miles away. He had passed several other houses en route, but these not being within the range of his illusion were not considered. His wife, who had known Matilda well, must be here. He opened the picket-gate which guarded the walk, and stamped briskly up to the door.

"Why, Mr. Reifsneider," exclaimed old Matilda herself, a stout woman, looking out of the door in answer to his knock, "what brings yuh here this morning'?"

"Is Phoebe here?" he demanded eagerly.

"Phoebe who? What Phoebe?" replied Mrs. Race, curious as to this sudden development of energy on his part.

"Why, my Phoebe, o' course. My wife Phoebe. Who do yuh s'pose? Ain't she here now?"

"Lawsy me!" exclaimed Mrs. Race, opening her mouth. "Yuh pore man! So you're clean out'n your mind now. Yuh come right in and sit down. I'll git yuh a cup o' coffee. O' course your wife ain't here; but yuh come in an' sit down. I'll find her fer yuh after a while. I know where she is."

The old farmer's eyes softened, and he entered. He was so thin and pale a specimen, pantalooned and patriarchal, that he aroused Mrs. Race's extremest sympathy as he took off his hat and laid it on his knees quite softly and mildly.

"We had a quarrel last night, an' she left me," he volunteered.

"Laws! laws!" sighed Mrs. Race, there being no one present with whom to share her astonishment as she went to her kitchen. "The pore man! Now somebody's just got to look after him. He can't be allowed to run around the country this way lookin' for his dead wife. It's turrible."

She boiled him a pot of coffee and brought in some of her new-baked bread and fresh butter. She set out some of her best jam and put a couple of eggs to boil, lying whole-heartedly the while.

"Now yuh stay right there, Uncle Henry, till Jake comes in, an' I'll send him to look for Phoebe. I think it's more'n likely she's over to Swinnerton with some o' her friends. Anyhow, we'll find out. Now yuh just drink this coffee an' eat this bread. Yuh must be tired. Yuh've had a long walk this mornin'." Her idea was to take counsel with Jake, "her man," and perhaps have him notify the authorities.

She bustled about, meditating on the uncertainties of life, while old

Reifsneider thrummed on the rim of his hat with his pale fingers and later ate abstractedly of what she offered. His mind was on his wife, however, and since she was not here, or did not appear, it wandered vaguely away to a family by the name of Murray, miles away in another direction. He decided after a time that he would not wait for Jack Race to hunt his wife but would seek her for himself. He must be on, and urge her to come back.

"Well, I'll be goin'," he said, getting up and looking strangely about him. "I guess she didn't come here after all. She went over to the Murrays, I guess. I'll not wait any longer, Mis' Race. There's a lot to do over to the house today." And out he marched in the face of her protests taking to the dusty road again in the warm spring sun, his cane striking the earth as he went.

It was two hours later that this pale figure of a man appeared in the Murrays' doorway, dusty, perspiring, eager. He had tramped all of five miles, and it was noon. An amazed husband and wife of sixty heard his strange query, and realized also that he was mad. They begged him to stay to dinner, intending to notify the authorities later and see what could be done; but though he stayed to partake of a little something, he did not stay long, and was off again to another distant farmhouse, his idea of many things to do and his need of Phoebe impelling him. So it went for that day and the next and the next, the circle of his inquiry ever widening.

The process by which a character assumes the significance of being peculiar, his antics weird, yet harmless, in such a community is often involute and pathetic. This day, as has been said, saw Reifsneider at other doors, eagerly asking his unnatural question, and leaving a trail of amazement, sympathy, and pity in his wake. Although the authorities were informed—the county sheriff, no less—it was not deemed advisable to take him into custody; for when those who knew old Henry, and had for so long, reflected on the condition of the county insane asylum, a place which, because of the poverty of the district, was of staggering aberration and sickening environment, it was decided to let him remain at large; for, strange to relate, it was found on investigation that at night he returned peaceably enough to his lonesome domicile there to discover whether his wife had returned, and to brood in loneliness until the morning. Who would lock up a thin, eager, seeking old man with iron-gray hair and an attitude of kindly, innocent inquiry, particularly when he was well known for a past of only kindly servitude and reliability? Those who had known him best rather agreed that he should be allowed to roam at large. He could do no harm. There were many who were willing to help him as to food, old clothes, the odds and ends of his daily life—at least at first. His figure after a time became not so much a commonplace as an accepted curiosity, and the replies, "Why, no, Henry; I ain't see her," or "No, Henry; she ain't been here today," more customary.

For several years thereafter then he was an odd figure in the sun and rain, on dusty roads and muddy ones, encountered occasionally in strange and unexpected places, pursuing his endless search. Undernourishment, after a time, although the neighbors and those who knew his history gladly contributed from their store, affected his body; for he walked much and ate little. The longer he roamed the public highway in this manner, the deeper became his strange hallucination; and finding it harder and harder to return from his more and more distant pilgrimages, he finally began taking a few utensils with him from his home, making a small package of them, in order that he might not be compelled to return. In an old tin coffee-pot of large size he placed a small tin cup, a knife, fork, and spoon, some salt and pepper, and to the outside of it, by a string forced through a pierced hole, he fastened a plate, which could be released, and which was his woodland table. It was no trouble for him to secure the little food that he needed, and with a strange, almost religious dignity, he had no hesitation in asking for that much. By degrees his hair became longer and longer, his once black hat became an earthen brown, and his clothes threadbare and dusty.

For all of three years he walked, and none knew how wide were his perambulations, nor how he survived the storms and cold. They could not see him, with homely rural understanding and forethought, sheltering himself in haycocks, or by the sides of cattle, whose warm bodies protected him from the cold, and whose dull understandings were not opposed to his harmless presence. Overhanging rocks and trees kept him at times from the rain, and a friendly hay-loft or corn-crib was not above his humble consideration.

The involute progression of hallucination is strange. From asking at doors and being constantly rebuffed or denied, he finally came to the conclusion that although his Phoebe might not be in any of the houses at the doors of which he inquired, she might nevertheless be within the sound of his voice. And so, from patient inquiry, he began to call sad, occasional cries, that ever and anon waked the quiet landscapes and ragged hill regions, and set to echoing his thin "O-o-o Phoebe! O-o-o Phoebe!" It had a pathetic, albeit insane, ring, and many a farmer or plowboy came to know it even from afar and say, "There goes old Reifsneider."

Another thing that puzzled him greatly after a time and after many hundreds of inquiries was, when he no longer had any particular dooryard in view and no special inquiry to make, which way to go. These crossroads, which occasionally led in four or even six directions, came after a time to puzzle him. But to solve this knotty problem, which became more and more of a puzzle, there came to his aid another hallucination. Phoebe's spirit or some power of the air or wind or nature would tell him. If he stood at the center of the parting of the ways, closed his eyes, turned thrice about, and called "O-o-o Phoebe!" twice, and then threw his cane straight before him, that would surely indicate which way to go, for Phoebe, or one of these mystic powers would surely govern its direction and fall! In whichever direction it went, even though, as was not infrequently the case, it took him back along the path he had already come, or across fields, he was not so far gone in his mind but that he gave himself ample time to search before he called again. Also the hallucination seemed to persist that at some time he would surely find her. There were hours when his feet were sore, and his limbs weary, when he would stop in the heat to wipe his seamed brow, or in the cold to beat his arms. Sometimes, after throwing away his cane, and finding it indicating the direction from which he had just come, he would shake his head wearily and philosophically, as if contemplating the unbelievable or an untoward fate, and then start briskly off. His strange figure came finally to be known in the farthest reaches of three or four counties. Old Reifsneider was a pathetic character. His fame was wide.

Near a little town called Watersville, in Green County, perhaps four miles from that minor center of human activity, there was a place or precipice locally known as the Red Cliff, a sheer wall of red sandstone, perhaps a hundred feet high, which raised its sharp face for half a mile or more above the fruitful cornfields and orchards that lay beneath, and which was surmounted by a thick grove of trees. The slope that slowly led up to it from the opposite side was covered by a rank growth of beech, hickory, and ash, through which threaded a number of wagon-tracks crossing at various angles. In fair weather it had become old Reifsneider's habit, so inured was he by now to the open, to make his bed in some such patch of trees as this, to fry his bacon or boil his eggs at the foot of some tree, before laying himself down for the night. Occasionally, so light and inconsequential was his sleep, he would walk at night. More often, the moonlight or some sudden wind stirring in the trees or a reconnoitering animal arousing him, he would sit up and think, or pursue his quest in the moonlight or the dark, a strange, unnatural, half wild, half savage-looking but utterly harmless creature, calling at lonely road crossings, staring at dark and shuttered houses, and wondering where, where Phoebe could really be.

That particular lull that comes in the systole-diastole of this earthly ball at two o'clock in the morning invariably aroused him, and though he might not go any farther he would sit up and contemplate the darkness or the stars, wondering. Sometimes in the strange processes of his mind he would fancy that he saw moving among the trees the figure of his lost wife, and then he would get up to follow, taking his utensils, always on a string, and his cane. If she seemed to evade him too easily he would run, or plead, or, suddenly losing track of the fancied figure, stand awed or disappointed, grieving for the moment over the almost insurmountable difficulties of his search.

It was in the seventh year of these hopeless peregrinations, in the dawn of a similar springtime to that in which his wife had died, that he came at last one night to the vicinity of this selfsame patch that crowned the rise to the Red Cliff. His far-flung cane, used as a divining-rod at the last cross-roads, had brought him hither. He had walked many, many miles. It was after ten o'clock at night, and he was very weary. Long wandering and little eating had left him but a shadow of his former self. It was a question now not so much of physical strength but of spiritual endurance which kept him up. He had scarcely eaten this day, and now, exhausted, he set himself down in the dark to rest and possibly to sleep.

Curiously on this occasion a strange suggestion of the presence of his wife surrounded him. It would not be long now, he counseled with himself, although the long months had brought him nothing, until he should see her, talk to her. He fell asleep after a time, his head on his knees. At midnight the moon began to rise, and at two in the morning, his wakeful hour, was a large silver disk shining through the trees to the east. He opened his eyes when the radiance became strong, making a silver pattern at his feet and lighting the woods with strange lusters and silvery, shadowy forms. As usual, his old notion that his wife must be near occurred to him on this occasion, and he looked about him with a speculative, anticipatory eye. What was it that moved in the distant shadows along the path by which he had entered—a pale, flickering will-o'-the-wisp that bobbed gracefully among the trees and riveted his expectant gaze? Moonlight and shadows combined to give it a strange form and a stranger reality, this fluttering of bog-fire or dancing of wandering fireflies. Was it truly his lost Phoebe? By a circuitous route it passed about him, and in his fevered state he fancied that he could see the very eyes of her, not as she was when he last saw her in the black dress and shawl, but now a strangely younger Phoebe, gayer, sweeter, the one whom he had known years before as a girl. Old Reifsneider got up. He had been expecting and dreaming of this hour all these years, and now as he saw the feeble light dancing lightly before him he peered at it questioningly, one thin hand in his gray hair.

Of a sudden there came to him now for the first time in many years the full charm of her girlish figure as he had known it in boyhood, the pleasing, sympathetic smile, the brown hair, the blue sash she had once worn about her waist at a picnic, her gay, graceful movements. He walked around the base of the tree, straining with his eyes, forgetting for once his cane and utensils, and following eagerly after. On she moved before him, a will-o'-the-wisp of the spring, a little flame above her head, and it seemed as though among the small saplings of ash and beech and the thick trunks of hickory and elm that she signaled with a young, a lightsome hand.

"Oh, Phoebe! Phoebe!" he called. "Have yuh really come? Have yuh really answered me?" And hurrying faster, he fell once, scrambling lamely to his feet, only to see the light in the distance dancing illusively on. On and on he hurried until he was fairly running, brushing his ragged arms against the trees striking his hands and face against impeding twigs. His hat was gone, his lungs were breathless, his reason quite astray, when coming to the edge of the cliff he saw her below among a silvery bed of apple trees now blooming in the spring.

"Oh, Phoebe!" he called. "Oh, Phoebe! Oh, no, don't leave me!" And feeling the lure of a world where love was young and Phoebe, as this vision presented her, a delightful epitome of their quondam youth, he gave a gay cry of "Oh, wait, Phoebe!" and leaped.

Some farmer-boys, reconnoitering this region of bounty and prospect some few days afterward, found first the tin utensils tied together under the tree where he had left them, and then later at the foot of the cliff, pale, broken, but elate, a molded smile of peace and delight upon his lips, his body. His old hat was discovered lying under some low-growing saplings, the twigs of which had held it back. No one of all the simple population knew how eagerly and joyously he had found his lost mate.

STEPHEN CRANE

[1871–1900]

The Red Badge of Courage, *the story of an army at war written by a youth who had never even visited a battlefield, is a seminal piece of American writing. A masterpiece of understatement and honesty, it set, according to the* Atlantic Monthly, *"a new fashion in literature;" H. G. Wells hailed it as "the first expression of the opening mind of a new period, a record of intensity beyond all precedent." The intensity* was both the author's distinction and his undoing. He spent himself in a brief fury of creative energy and died before he was thirty.

Youngest of a family of fourteen children, Stephen Crane was born November 1, 1871, in Newark, New Jersey. His father was a devout but dull Methodist minister; his mother, from whom he inherited his creative gift, helped support the household by writing religious stories. By the time the boy was eight, the family had lived in several New Jersey towns, the background for Crane's juvenile tales, Whilomville Stories. When he was nine his father died; the family moved again and finally settled in Asbury Park, New Jersey, where one of Stephen's brothers ran a news reporting agency and where Stephen attended school. After more schooling at a military institute in New York, one term at Lafayette College, Easton, Pennsylvania, and another at Syracuse University, where he made a name for himself as captain of the baseball team, Stephen became a reporter.

He was eighteen when his mother died and, leaving home, he joined a mixed group of artists and writers on New York's lower East Side. For five years he kept himself from starvation by turning out small sketches and odd bits of journalism. He had been at work on a novel—it is said that he wrote it in two days when he was twenty—but no publisher bothered to look at it. Finally he borrowed $869 to have one thousand copies of Maggie: A Girl of the Streets printed in paper wrappers and, persuaded that publication of the book might hurt his career as journalist, signed it with a pseudonym: "Johnston Smith." The printer, who made about five hundred dollars on the deal, refused to put his name on the title page.

Maggie was a strange book for anyone to have written in the early Eighteen Nineties, especially for the son of two pious parents. It concerned a prostitute and detailed the sordidness and violence of the slums in a language that was loose, tough, and arresting. An unreservedly realistic novel—it anticipated Dreiser's Sister Carrie by seven years—it was perfunctorily noticed. A few copies were sold, but most of the edition was turned over to Crane who kept himself warm by burning copies in the fireplace. Nevertheless, the book was read and praised by such writers as Hamlin Garland and William Dean Howells, who said that the integrity and purpose of the book was "as present in the working out of this poor girl's squalid romance as in any classic fable."

Crane turned to a much larger canvas for his next work: a microcosm of the Civil War. He was neither a historian nor a researcher, but he lived over the whole struggle through what he learned by eye and by ear: tales told by old veterans, the spate of records and reminiscences which were coming from the press, and, perhaps most of all, the graphic photographs taken on the battlefields. Again Crane had trouble getting his book published. He could not afford to pay for more than half the typing; Hamlin Garland paid for the other half. Crane was not quite twenty-four when The Red Badge of Courage was published and became the great success of 1895. Crane was compared to Zola and Tolstoy; the book went through thirteen editions in less than a year. The enthusiastic reception led to a reissue of Maggie (this time with Crane's name on the cover) and the publication of a volume of remarkable free verse, The Black Riders and Other Lines.

The background of The Red Badge of Courage is the Civil War, but it could be any war fought by bewildered soldiers—farmers, blacksmiths, clerks, and mule-drivers who know nothing about the politics, technique, or even the reasons for the conflict. There are no romantic heroes or dastardly villains. The youth, Henry Fleming, who is the central figure of the story, is undergoing his first experience in combat at the battle of Chancellorsville. Crane uncovers every nuance of his confused emotions: boyish ardor, excessive bravado, deep cowardice, guilt, and without heroics, final courage. The English critics were even more enthusiastic than the American reviewers. The Daily Chronicle told its readers that "in the whole range of literature we can call to mind nothing so searching in its analysis."

Writer, reporter, and famous novelist in his mid-twenties, Crane was considered such an authority on war that the next move was obvious. Newspapers bid for his services, and he was sent as war correspondent to cover the Greco-Turkish campaign and, later, the insurrection in Cuba. Meanwhile, he had become involved in several scandals. One of the girls with whom he associated had been arrested as a street-walker and when Crane, who had always been interested in prostitutes, came to her defense the policeman claimed (falsely) that Crane was a drug addict and kept narcotics in his room. Another girl blackmailed him and sued for support; but the court refused to issue a warrant for Crane's arrest. A third woman, considerably older than himself—some critics have made much of the fact that Crane, seeking a mother, gravitated to older women—claimed that she had given him money, only part of which had been returned, and continued to harass the young author.

Crane was twenty-seven when he went to England with Cora Taylor, who was also known as Lady Stewart and Imogene Carter. She had been married to an English captain who was heir to a title, had been several men's mistress, and was running a brothel in Florida when he met her. Handsome, blonde and full-blooded, quite a few years his senior, she fell completely in love with him. They lived together as man and wife—there may even have been a bigamous marriage, for the captain refused to divorce her—and she devoted herself to taking care of her sick lover. Crane's experiences in Cuba had ruined his never-robust health. The ship that carried him had been wrecked, and he and three other men were tossed about in a heavy sea for three days—Crane turned the disaster into "The Open Boat," which Howells called "the finest short story in English." When Crane was sent to Greece Cora went along, assuming the role of war correspondent to be near him. After the armistice, she took him back to England, where he seemed at ease with Joseph Conrad, Henry James, and other literati, but when the Spanish-American War broke out he signed as war correspondent for the New York World and also sent dispatches to the Journal. He exposed himself conspicuously in battle—he was not only sick but suicidal.

When he returned once more to England Cora tried desperately to divert him. She took over a huge house in Brede in Sussex and entertained extravagantly. As a result, Crane went deeply into debt and, no matter how frenetically he drove himself to write, felt himself sinking in a quicksand of obligations. He wrote panoramic descriptions of the world's great battles, more short stories, and even juvenile tales. Hemorrhages stopped all work; it was hoped that he could be saved if he were out of England. Cora took him to Badenweiler in the German Black Forest. But it was too late: he died there, June 5, 1900. His body was brought back to the United States and buried in the Crane plot in Elizabeth, New Jersey.

Besides his novels Crane wrote about seventy short stories—his Collected Works, published twenty-five years after his death, occupy twelve volumes. His small books of poems are only now beginning to be properly appreciated. Crane never labelled The Black Riders and War Is Kind "poetry." He felt such a designation too pretentious and spoke of them only as "lines." The tone is usually bitter; they are expressions of protest, the cries of a discouraged spirit. But the "lines" are never negligible. Crane was twenty years ahead of the Imagists, that school of poets which concentrated on a poetry which is hard and clear and often acrid. In his verse as well as his prose he made an image of a grim but sharp-cut world beyond Howell's simple "realism" and Garland's conscious "veritism." The world in which Crane lived so short a time was not only too much with him but too much for him.

From THE RED BADGE OF COURAGE

CHAPTER I

THE COLD PASSED RELUCTANTLY from the earth, and the retiring fogs revealed an army stretched out on the hills, resting. As the landscape changed from brown to green, the army awakened, and began to tremble with eagerness at the noise of rumors. It cast its eyes upon the roads, which were growing from long troughs of liquid mud to proper thoroughfares. A river, amber-tinted in the shadow of its banks, purled at the army's feet; and at night, when the stream had become of a sorrowful blackness, one could see across it the red, eyelike gleam of hostile camp-fires set in the low brows of distant hills.

Once a certain tall soldier developed virtues and went resolutely to wash a shirt. He came flying back from a brook waving his garment bannerlike. He was swelled with a tale he had heard from a reliable friend, who had heard it from a truthful cavalryman, who had heard it from his trustworthy brother, one of the orderlies at division headquarters. He adopted the important air of a herald in red and gold.

"We're goin' t' move t' morrah–sure," he said pompously to a group in the company street. "We're goin' 'way up the river, cut across, an' come around in behint 'em."

To his attentive audience he drew a loud and elaborate plan of a very brilliant campaign. When he had finished, the blue-clothed men scattered into small arguing groups between the rows of squat brown huts. A negro teamster who had been dancing upon a cracker box with the hilarious encouragement of twoscore soldiers was deserted. He sat mournfully down. Smoke drifted lazily from a multitude of quaint chimneys.

"It's a lie! that's all it is–a thunderin' lie!" said another private loudly. His smooth face was flushed, and his hands were thrust sulkily into his trousers' pockets. He took the matter as an affront to him. "I don't believe the derned old army's ever going to move. We're set. I've got ready to move eight times in the last two weeks, and we ain't moved yet."

The tall soldier felt called upon to defend the truth of a rumor he himself had introduced. He and the loud one came near to fighting over it.

A corporal began to swear before the assemblage. He had just put a costly board floor in his house, he said. During the early spring he had refrained from adding extensively to the comfort of his environment because he had felt that the army might start on the march at any moment.

Of late, however, he had been impressed that they were in a sort of eternal camp.

Many of the men engaged in a spirited debate. One outlined in a peculiarly lucid manner all the plans of the commanding general. He was opposed by men who advocated that there were other plans of campaign. They clamored at each other, numbers making futile bids for the popular attention. Meanwhile, the soldier who had fetched the rumor bustled about with much importance. He was continually assailed by questions.

"What's up, Jim?"

"Th' army's goin' t' move."

"Ah, what yeh talkin' about? How yeh know it is?"

"Well, yeh kin b'lieve me er not, jest as yeh like. I don't care a hang."

There was much food for thought in the manner in which he replied. He came near to convincing them by disdaining to produce proofs. They grew much excited over it.

There was a youthful private who listened with eager ears to the words of the tall soldier and to the varied comments of his comrades. After receiving a fill of discussions concerning marches and attacks, he went to his hut and crawled through an intricate hole that served it as a door. He wished to be alone with some new thoughts that had lately come to him.

He lay down on a wide bunk that stretched across the end of the room. In the other end, cracker boxes were made to serve as furniture. They were grouped about the fireplace. A picture from an illustrated weekly was upon the log walls, and three rifles were paralleled on pegs. Equipments hung on handy projections, and some tin dishes lay upon a small pile of firewood. A folded tent was serving as a roof. The sunlight, without, beating upon it, made it glow a light yellow shade. A small window shot an oblique square of whiter light upon the cluttered floor. The smoke from the fire at times neglected the clay chimney and wreathed into the room, and this flimsy chimney of clay and sticks made endless threats to set ablaze the whole establishment.

The youth was in a little trance of astonishment. So they were at last going to fight. On the morrow, perhaps, there would be a battle, and he would be in it. For a time he was obliged to labor to make himself believe. He could not accept with assurance an omen that he was about to mingle in one of those great affairs of the earth.

He had, of course, dreamed of battles all his life—of vague and bloody conflicts that had thrilled him with their sweep and fire. In visions he had seen himself in many struggles. He had imagined peoples secure in the shadow of his eagle-eyed prowess. But awake he had regarded battles as crimson blotches on the pages of the past. He had put them as things of the bygone with his thought-images of heavy crowns and high castles. There was a portion of the world's history which he had regarded as the time of wars, but it, he thought, had been long gone over the horizon and had disappeared forever.

From his home his youthful eyes had looked upon the war in his own country with distrust. It must be some sort of a play affair. He had long despaired of witnessing a Greeklike struggle. Such would be no more, he had said. Men were better, or more timid. Secular and religious education had effaced the throat-grappling instinct, or else firm finance held in check the passions.

He had burned several times to enlist. Tales of great movements shook the land. They might not be distinctly Homeric, but there seemed to be much glory in them. He had read of marches, sieges, conflicts, and he had longed to see it all. His busy mind had drawn for him large pictures extravagant in color, lurid with breathless deeds.

But his mother had discouraged him. She had affected to look with some contempt upon the quality of his war ardor and patriotism. She could calmly seat herself and with no apparent difficulty give him many hundreds of reasons why he was of vastly more importance on the farm than on the field of battle. She had had certain ways of expression that told him that her statements on the subject came from a deep conviction. Moreover, on her side, was his belief that her ethical motive in the argument was impregnable.

At last, however, he had made firm rebellion against this yellow light thrown upon the color of his ambitions. The newspapers, the gossip of the village, his own picturings, had aroused him to an uncheckable degree. They were in truth fighting finely down there. Almost every day the newspapers printed accounts of a decisive victory.

One night, as he lay in bed, the winds had carried to him the clangoring of the church bell as some enthusiast jerked the rope frantically to tell the twisted news of a great battle. This voice of the people rejoicing in the night had made him shiver in a prolonged ecstasy of excitement. Later, he had gone down to his mother's room and had spoken thus: "Ma, I'm going to enlist."

"Henry, don't be a fool," his mother had replied. She had then covered her face with the quilt. There was an end to the matter for that night.

Nevertheless, the next morning he had gone to a town that was near his mother's farm and had enlisted in a company that was forming there. When he had returned home his mother was milking the brindle cow. Four others stood waiting. "Ma, I've enlisted," he had said to her diffidently. There was a short silence. "The Lord's will be done, Henry," she had finally replied, and had then continued to milk the brindle cow.

When he had stood in the doorway with his soldier's clothes on his back, and with the light of excitement and expectancy in his eyes almost defeating the glow of regret for the home bonds, he had seen two tears leaving their trails on his mother's scarred cheeks.

Still, she had disappointed him by saying nothing whatever about returning with his shield or on it. He had privately primed himself for a beautiful scene. He had prepared certain sentences which he thought could be used with touching effect. But her words destroyed his plans. She had doggedly peeled potatoes and addressed him as follows: "You watch out, Henry, an' take good care of yerself in this here fighting business—you watch out, an' take good care of yerself. Don't go a-thinkin' you can lick the hull rebel army at the start, because yeh can't. Yer jest one little feller amongst a hull lot of others, and yeh've got to keep quiet an' do what they tell yeh. I know how you are, Henry.

"I've knet yeh eight pair of socks, Henry, and I've put in all yer best shirts, because I want my boy to be jest as warm and comf'able as anybody in the army. Whenever they get holes in 'em, I want yeh to send 'em right-away back to me, so's I kin dern 'em.

"An' allus be careful an' choose yer comp'ny. There's lots of bad men in the army, Henry. The army makes 'em wild, and they like nothing better than the job of leading off a young feller like you, as ain't never been away from home much and has allus had a mother, an' a-learning 'em to drink and swear. Keep clear of them folks, Henry. I don't want yeh to ever do anything, Henry, that yeh would be 'shamed to let me know about. Jest think as if I was a-watchin' yeh. If yeh keep that in yer mind allus, I guess yeh'll come out about right.

"Yeh must allus remember yer father, too, child, an' remember he never drunk a drop of licker in his life, and seldom swore a cross oath.

"I don't know what else to tell yeh, Henry, excepting that yeh must never do no shirking, child, on my account. If so be a time comes when yeh have to be kilt or do a mean thing, why, Henry, don't think of anything 'cept what's right, because there's many a woman has to bear up 'ginst sech things these times, and the Lord'll take keer of us all.

"Don't forgit about the socks and the shirts, child; and I've put a cup of blackberry jam with yer bundle, because I know yeh like it above all things. Good-by, Henry. Watch out, and be a good boy."

He had, of course, been impatient under the ordeal of this speech. It had not been quite what he expected, and he had borne it with an air of irritation. He departed feeling vague relief.

Still, when he had looked back from the gate, he had seen his mother kneeling among the potato parings. Her brown face, upraised, was stained with tears, and her spare form was quivering. He bowed his head and went on, feeling suddenly ashamed of his purposes.

From his home he had gone to the seminary to bid adieu to many schoolmates. They had thronged about him with wonder and admiration. He had felt the gulf now between them and had swelled with calm pride. He and some of his fellows who had donned blue were quite overwhelmed with privileges for all of one afternoon, and it had been a very delicious thing. They had strutted.

A certain light-haired girl had made vivacious fun at his martial spirit, but there was another and darker girl whom he had gazed at steadfastly, and he thought she grew demure and sad at sight of his blue and brass. As he had walked down the path between the rows of oaks, he had turned his head and detected her at a window watching his departure. As he perceived her, she had immediately begun to stare up through the high tree branches at the sky. He had seen a good deal of flurry and haste in her movement as she changed her attitude. He often thought of it.

On the way to Washington his spirit had soared. The regiment was fed and caressed at station after station until the youth had believed that he must be a hero. There was a lavish expenditure of bread and cold meats, coffee, and pickles and cheese. As he basked in the smiles of the girls and was patted and complimented by the old men, he had felt growing within him the strength to do mighty deeds of arms.

After complicated journeyings with many pauses, there had come months of monotonous life in a camp. He had had the belief that real war was a series of death struggles with small time in between for sleep and meals; but since his regiment had come to the field the army had done little but sit still and try to keep warm.

He was brought then gradually back to his old ideas. Greeklike struggles would be no more. Men were better, or more timid. Secular and religious education had effaced the throat-grappling instinct, or else firm finance held in check the passions.

He had grown to regard himself merely as a part of a vast blue demonstration. His province was to look out, as far as he could, for his personal comfort. For recreation he could twiddle his thumbs and speculate on the thoughts which must agitate the minds of the generals. Also, he was drilled and drilled and reviewed, and drilled and drilled and reviewed.

The only foes he had seen were some pickets along the river bank. They were a sun-tanned, philosophical lot, who sometimes shot reflectively at the blue pickets. When reproached for this afterward, they usually expressed sorrow, and swore by their gods that the guns had exploded without their permission. The youth, on guard duty one night, conversed across the stream with one of them. He was a slightly ragged man, who spat skillfully between his shoes and possessed a great fund of bland and infantile assurance. The youth liked him personally.

"Yank," the other had informed him, "yer a right dum good feller." This sentiment, floating to him upon the still air, had made him temporarily regret war.

Various veterans had told him tales. Some talked of gray, bewhiskered hordes who were advancing with relentless curses and chewing tobacco with unspeakable valor; tremendous bodies of fierce soldiery who were sweeping along like the Huns. Others spoke of tattered and eternally hungry men who fired despondent powders. "They'll charge through hell's fire an' brimstone t' git a holt on a haversack, an' sech stomachs ain't a-lastin' long," he was told. From the stories, the youth imagined the red, live bones sticking out through slits in the faded uniforms.

Still, he could not put a whole faith in veterans' tales, for recruits were their prey. They talked much of smoke, fire, and blood, but he could not tell how much might be lies. They persistently yelled, "Fresh fish!" at him, and were in no wise to be trusted.

However, he perceived now that it did not greatly matter what kind of soldiers he was going to fight, so long as they fought, which fact no one disputed. There was a more serious problem. He lay in his bunk pondering upon it. He tried to mathematically prove to himself that he would not run from a battle.

Previously he had never felt obliged to wrestle too seriously with this question. In his life he had taken certain things for granted, never challenging his belief in ultimate success, and bothering little about means and roads. But here he was confronted with a thing of moment. It had suddenly appeared to him that perhaps in a battle he might run. He was forced to admit that as far as war was concerned he knew nothing of himself.

A sufficient time before he would have allowed the problem to kick its heels at the outer portals of his mind, but now he felt compelled to give serious attention to it.

A little panic-fear grew in his mind. As his imagination went forward to a fight, he saw hideous possibilities. He contemplated the lurking menaces of the future, and failed in an effort to see himself standing stoutly in the midst of them. He recalled his visions of broken-bladed glory, but in the shadow of the impending tumult he suspected them to be impossible pictures.

He sprang from the bunk and began to pace nervously to and fro. "Good Lord, what's th' matter with me?" he said aloud.

He felt that in this crisis his laws of life were useless. Whatever he had learned of himself was here of no avail. He was an unknown quantity. He saw that he would again be obliged to experiment as he had in early youth. He must accumulate information of himself, and meanwhile he resolved to remain close upon his guard lest those qualities of which he knew nothing should everlastingly disgrace him. "Good Lord!" he repeated in dismay.

After a time the tall soldier slid dexterously through the hole. The loud private followed. They were wrangling.

"That's all right," said the tall soldier as he entered. He waved his hand expressively. "You can believe me or not, jest as you like. All you got to do is to sit down and wait as quiet as you can. Then pretty soon you'll find out I was right."

His comrade grunted stubbornly. For a moment he seemed to be searching for a formidable reply. Finally he said: "Well, you don't know everything in the world, do you?"

"Didn't say I knew everything in the world," retorted the other sharply. He began to stow various articles snugly into his knapsack.

The youth, pausing in his nervous walk, looked down at the busy figure. "Going to be a battle, sure, is there, Jim?" he asked.

"Of course there is," replied the tall soldier. "Of course there is. You jest wait 'til to-morrow, and you'll see one of the biggest battles ever was. You jest wait."

"Thunder!" said the youth.

"Oh, you'll see fighting this time, my boy, what'll be regular out-and-out fighting," added the tall soldier, with the air of a man who is about to exhibit a battle for the benefit of his friends.

"Huh!" said the loud one from a corner.

"Well," remarked the youth, "like as not this story'll turn out jest like them others did."

"Not much it won't," replied the tall soldier, exasperated. "Not much it won't. Didn't the cavalry all start this morning?" He glared about him. No one denied his statement. "The cavalry started this morning," he continued. "They say there ain't hardly any cavalry left in camp. They're going to Richmond, or some place, while we fight all the Johnnies. It's some dodge like that. The regiment's got orders, too. A feller what seen 'em go to headquarters told me a little while ago. And they're raising blazes all over camp—anybody can see that."

"Shucks!" said the loud one.

The youth remained silent for a time. At last he spoke to the tall soldier. "Jim!"

"What?"

"How do you think the reg'ment 'll do?"

"Oh, they'll fight all right, I guess, after they once get into it," said the other with cold judgment. He made a fine use of the third person. "There's been heaps of fun poked at 'em because they're new, of course, and all that; but they'll fight all right, I guess."

"Think any of the boys 'll run?" persisted the youth.

"Oh, there may be a few of 'em run, but there's them kind in every regiment, 'specially when they first goes under fire," said the other in a tolerant way. "Of course it might happen that the hull kit-and-boodle might start and run, if some big fighting came first-off, and then again they might stay and fight like fun. But you can't bet on nothing. Of course they ain't never been under fire yet, and it ain't likely they'll lick the hull rebel army all-to-oncet the first time; but I think they'll fight better than some, if worse than others. That's the way I figger. They call the reg'ment 'Fresh fish' and everything; but the boys come of good stock, and most of 'em 'll fight like sin after they oncet git shootin'," he added, with a mighty emphasis on the last four words.

"Oh, you think you know—" began the loud soldier with scorn.

The other turned savagely upon him. They had a rapid altercation, in which they fastened upon each other various strange epithets.

The youth at last interrupted them. "Did you ever think you might run yourself, Jim?" he asked. On concluding the sentence he laughed as if he had meant to aim a joke. The loud soldier also giggled.

The tall private waved his hand. "Well," said he profoundly, "I've thought it might get too hot for Jim Conklin in some of them scrimmages, and if a whole lot of boys started and run, why, I s'pose I'd start and run. And if I once started to run, I'd run like the devil, and no mistake. But if everybody was a-standing and a-fighting, why, I'd stand and fight. Be jiminey, I would. I'll bet on it."

"Huh!" said the loud one.

The youth of this tale felt gratitude for these words of his comrade. He had feared that all of the untried men possessed a great and correct confidence. He now was in a measure reassured.

II

The next morning the youth discovered that his tall comrade had been the fast-flying messenger of a mistake. There was much scoffing at the latter by those who had yesterday been firm adherents of his views, and there was even a little sneering by men who had never believed the rumor.

The tall one fought with a man from Chatfield Corners and beat him severely.

The youth felt, however, that his problem was in no wise lifted from him. There was, on the contrary, an irritating prolongation. The tale had created in him a great concern for himself. Now, with the newborn question in his mind, he was compelled to sink back into his old place as part of a blue demonstration.

For days he made ceaseless calculations, but they were all wondrously unsatisfactory. He found that he could establish nothing. He finally concluded that the only way to prove himself was to go into the blaze, and then figuratively to watch his legs to discover their merits and faults. He reluctantly admitted that he could not sit still and with a mental slate and pencil derive an answer. To gain it, he must have blaze, blood, and danger, even as a chemist requires this, that, and the other. So he fretted for an opportunity.

Meanwhile he continually tried to measure himself by his comrades. The tall soldier, for one, gave him some assurance. This man's serene unconcern dealt him a measure of confidence, for he had known him since childhood, and from his intimate knowledge he did not see how he could be capable of anything that was beyond him, the youth. Still, he thought that his comrade might be mistaken about himself. Or, on the other hand, he might be a man heretofore doomed to peace and obscurity, but, in reality, made to shine in war.

The youth would have liked to have discovered another who suspected himself. A sympathetic comparison of mental notes would have been a joy to him.

He occasionally tried to fathom a comrade with seductive sentences. He looked about to find men in the proper mood. All attempts failed to bring forth any statement which looked in any way like a confession to those doubts which he privately acknowledged in himself. He was afraid to make an open declaration of his concern, because he dreaded to place some unscrupulous confidant upon the high plane of the unconfessed from which elevation he could be derided.

In regard to his companions his mind wavered between two opinions, according to his mood. Sometimes he inclined to believing them all heroes. In fact, he usually admitted in secret the superior development of the higher qualities in others. He could conceive of men going very insignificantly about the world bearing a load of courage unseen, and, although he had known many of his comrades through boyhood, he began to fear that his judgment of them had been blind. Then, in other moments, he flouted these theories, and assured himself that his fellows were all privately wondering and quaking.

His emotions made him feel strange in the presence of men who talked excitedly of a prospective battle as of a drama they were about to witness, with nothing but eagerness and curiosity apparent in their faces. It was often that he suspected them to be liars.

He did not pass such thoughts without severe condemnation of himself. He dinned reproaches at times. He was convicted by himself of many shameful crimes against the gods of traditions.

In his great anxiety his heart was continually clamoring at what he considered the intolerable slowness of the generals. They seemed content to perch tranquilly on the river bank, and leave him bowed down by the weight of a great problem. He wanted it settled forthwith. He could not long bear such a load, he said. Sometimes his anger at the commanders reached an acute stage, and he grumbled about the camp like a veteran.

One morning, however, he found himself in the ranks of his prepared regiment. The men were whispering speculations and recounting the old rumors. In the gloom before the break of the day their uniforms glowed a deep purple hue. From across the river the red eyes were still peering. In the eastern sky there was a yellow patch like a rug laid for the feet of the coming sun; and against it, black and patternlike, loomed the gigantic figure of the colonel on a gigantic horse.

From off in the darkness came the trampling of feet. The youth could occasionally see dark shadows that moved like monsters. The regiment stood at rest for what seemed a long time. The youth grew impatient. It was unendurable the way these affairs were managed. He wondered how long they were to be kept waiting.

As he looked all about him and pondered upon the mystic gloom, he began to believe that at any moment the ominous distance might be aflare, and the rolling crashes of an engagement come to his ears. Staring once at the red eyes across the river, he conceived them to be growing larger, as the orbs of a row of dragons advancing. He turned toward the colonel and saw him lift his gigantic arm and calmly stroke his mustache.

At last he heard from along the road at the foot of the hill the clatter of a horse's galloping hoofs. It must be the coming of orders. He bent forward, scarce breathing. The exciting clickety-click, as it grew louder and louder, seemed to be beating upon his soul. Presently a horseman with jangling equipment drew rein before the colonel of the regiment. The two held a short, sharp-worded conversation. The men in the foremost ranks craned their necks.

As the horseman wheeled his animal and galloped away he turned to shout over his shoulder, "Don't forget that box of cigars!" The colonel mumbled in reply. The youth wondered what a box of cigars had to do with war.

A moment later the regiment went swinging off into the darkness. It was now like one of those moving monsters wending with many feet. The air was heavy, and cold with dew. A mass of wet grass, marched upon, rustled like silk.

There was an occasional flash and glimmer of steel from the backs of all these huge crawling reptiles. From the road came creakings and grumblings as some surly guns were dragged away.

The men stumbled along still muttering speculations. There was a subdued debate. Once a man fell down, and as he reached for his rifle a comrade, unseeing, trod upon his hand. He of the injured fingers swore bitterly and aloud. A low, low, tittering laugh went among his fellows.

Presently they passed into a roadway and marched forward with easy strides. A dark regiment moved before them, and from behind also came the tinkle of equipments on the bodies of marching men.

The rushing yellow of the developing day went on behind their backs. When the sunrays at last struck full and mellowingly upon the earth, the youth saw that the landscape was streaked with two long, thin, black columns which disappeared on the brow of a hill in front and rearward vanished in a wood. They were like two serpents crawling from the cavern of the night.

The river was not in view. The tall soldier burst into praises of what he thought to be his powers of perception.

Some of the tall one's companions cried with emphasis that they, too, had evolved the same thing, and they congratulated themselves upon it. But there were others who said that the tall one's plan was not the true one at all. They persisted with other theories. There was a vigorous discussion.

The youth took no part in them. As he walked along in careless line he was engaged with his own eternal debate. He could not hinder himself from dwelling upon it. He was despondent and sullen, and threw shifting glances about him. He looked ahead, often expecting to hear from the advance the rattle of firing.

But the long serpents crawled slowly from hill to hill without bluster of smoke. A dun-colored cloud of dust floated away to the right. The sky overhead was of a fairy blue.

The youth studied the faces of his companions, ever on the watch to detect kindred emotions. He suffered disappointment. Some ardor of the air which was causing the veteran commands to move with glee—almost with song—had infected the new regiment. The men began to speak of victory as of a thing they knew. Also, the tall soldier received his vindication. They were certainly going to come around in behind the enemy.

They expressed commiseration for that part of the army which had been left upon the river bank, felicitating themselves upon being a part of a blasting host.

The youth, considering himself as separated from the others, was saddened by the blithe and merry speeches that went from rank to rank. The company wags all made their best endeavors. The regiment tramped to the tune of laughter.

The blatant soldier often convulsed whole files by his biting sarcasms aimed at the tall one.

And it was not long before all the men seemed to forget their mission. Whole brigades grinned in unison, and regiments laughed.

A rather fat soldier attempted to pilfer a horse from a dooryard. He planned to load his knapsack upon it. He was escaping with his prize when a young girl rushed from the house and grabbed the animal's mane. There followed a wrangle. The young girl, with pink cheeks and shining eyes, stood like a dauntless statue.

The observant regiment, standing at rest in the roadway, whooped at once, and entered whole-souled upon the side of the maiden. The men became so engrossed in this affair that they entirely ceased to remember their own large war. They jeered the piratical private, and called attention to various defects in his personal appearance; and they were wildly enthusiastic in support of the young girl.

To her, from some distance, came bold advice. "Hit him with a stick."

There were crows and catcalls showered upon him when he retreated without the horse. The regiment rejoiced at his downfall. Loud and vociferous congratulations were showered upon the maiden, who stood panting and regarding the troops with defiance.

At nightfall the column broke into regimental pieces, and the fragments went into the fields to camp. Tents sprang up like strange plants. Camp fires, like red, peculiar blossoms, dotted the night.

The youth kept from intercourse with his companions as much as circumstances would allow him. In the evening he wandered a few paces into the gloom. From this little distance the many fires, with the black forms of men passing to and fro before the crimson rays, made weird and satanic effects.

He lay down in the grass. The blades pressed tenderly against his cheek. The moon had been lighted and was hung in a treetop. The liquid stillness of the night enveloping him made him feel vast pity for himself. There was a caress in the soft winds; and the whole mood of the darkness, he thought, was one of sympathy for himself in his distress.

He wished, without reserve, that he was at home again making the endless rounds from the house to the barn, from the barn to the fields, from the fields to the barn, from the barn to the house. He remembered he had often cursed the brindle cow and her mates, and had sometimes flung milking stools. But, from his present point of view, there was a halo of happiness about each of their heads, and he would have sacrificed all the brass buttons on the continent to have been enabled to return to them. He told himself that he was not formed for a soldier. And he mused seriously upon the radical differences between himself and those men who were dodging implike around the fires.

As he mused thus he heard the rustle of grass, and, upon turning his head, discovered the loud soldier. He called out, "Oh, Wilson!"

The latter approached and looked down. "Why, hello, Henry; is it you? What you doing here?"

"Oh, thinking," said the youth.

The other sat down and carefully lighted his pipe. "You're getting blue, my boy. You're looking thundering peeked. What the dickens is wrong with you?"

"Oh, nothing," said the youth.

The loud soldier launched then into the subject of the anticipated fight. "Oh, we've got 'em now!" As he spoke his boyish face was wreathed in a gleeful smile, and his voice had an exultant ring. "We've got 'em now. At last, by the eternal thunders, we'll lick 'em good!"

"If the truth was known," he added, more soberly, "*they've* licked *us* about every clip up to now; but this time—this time—we'll lick 'em good!"

"I thought you was objecting to this march a little while ago," said the youth coldly.

"Oh, it wasn't that," explained the other. "I don't mind marching, if there's going to be fighting at the end of it. What I hate is this getting moved here and moved there, with no good coming of it, as far as I can see, excepting sore feet and damned short rations."

"Well, Jim Conklin says we'll get a plenty of fighting this time."

"He's right for once, I guess, though I can't see how it come. This time we're in for a big battle, and we've got the best end of it, certain sure. Gee rod! how we will thump 'em!"

He arose and began to pace to and fro excitedly. The thrill of his enthusiasm made him walk with an elastic step. He was sprightly, vigorous, fiery in his belief in success. He looked into the future with clear, proud eye, and he swore with the air of an old soldier.

The youth watched him for a moment in silence. When he finally spoke his voice was as bitter as dregs. "Oh, you're going to do great things, I s'pose!"

The loud soldier blew a thoughtful cloud of smoke from his pipe. "Oh, I don't know," he remarked with dignity; "I don't know. I s'pose I'll do as well as the rest. I'm going to try like thunder." He evidently complimented himself upon the modesty of this statement.

"How do you know you won't run when the time comes?" asked the youth.

"Run?" said the loud one; "run?—of course not!" He laughed.

"Well," continued the youth, "lots of good-a-'nough men have thought they was going to do great things before the fight, but when the time come they skedaddled."

"Oh, that's all true, I s'pose," replied the other; "but I'm not going to skedaddle. The man that bets on my running will lose his money, that's all." He nodded confidently.

"Oh, shucks!" said the youth. "You ain't the bravest man in the world, are you?"

"No, I ain't," exclaimed the loud soldier indignantly; "and I didn't say I was the bravest man in the world, neither. I said I was going to do my share of fighting—that's what I said. And I am, too. Who are you, anyhow? You talk as if you thought you was Napoleon Bonaparte." He glared at the youth for a moment, and then strode away.

The youth called in a savage voice after his comrade: "Well, you needn't git mad about it!" But the other continued on his way and made no reply.

He felt alone in space when his injured comrade had disappeared. His failure to discover any mite of resemblance in their view points made him more miserable than before. No one seemed to be wrestling with such a terrific personal problem. He was a mental outcast.

He went slowly to his tent and stretched himself on a blanket by the side of the snoring tall soldier. In the darkness he saw visions of a thousand-tongued fear that would babble at his back and cause him to flee, while others were going coolly about their country's business. He admitted that he would not be able to cope with this monster. He felt that every nerve in his body would be an ear to hear the voices, while other men would remain stolid and deaf.

And as he sweated with the pain of these thoughts, he could hear low, serene sentences. "I'll bid five." "Make it six." "Seven." "Seven goes."

He stared at the red, shivering reflection of a fire on the white wall of his tent until, exhausted and ill from the monotony of his suffering, he fell asleep.

I SAW A MAN

I saw a man pursuing the horizon;
Round and round they sped.
I was disturbed at this;
I accosted the man.
"It is futile," I said,
"You can never—"
"You lie," he cried,
And ran on.

THE WAYFARER

The wayfarer,
Perceiving the pathway to truth,
Was struck with astonishment.
It was thickly grown with weeds.
"Ha," he said,
"I see that no one has passed here
In a long time."
Later he saw that each weed
Was a singular knife.
"Well," he mumbled at last,
"Doubtless there are other roads."

THE BLADES OF GRASS

In Heaven,
Some little blades of grass
Stood before God.
"What did you do?"
Then all save one of the little blades
Began eagerly to relate
The merits of their lives.

This one stayed a small way behind,
Ashamed.
Presently, God said,
"And what did you do?"
The little blade answered, "Oh, my Lord,
Memory is bitter to me;
For, if I did good deeds,
I know not of them."
Then God, in all his splendor,
Arose from his throne.
"Oh, best little blade of grass!" he said.

THE CANDID MAN

Forth went the candid man
And spoke freely to the wind—
When he looked about him he was in a far strange country.

Forth went the candid man
And spoke freely to the stars—
Yellow light tore sight from his eyes.
"My good fool," said a learned bystander,
"Your operations are mad."

"You are too candid," cried the candid man.
And when his stick left the head of the learned bystander
It was two sticks.

JAMES WELDON JOHNSON

[1871–1938]

Poet, essayist and teacher, James Weldon Johnson was also a lawyer, song-writer, novelist, and diplomat. Born June 17, 1871, in Jacksonville, Florida, he attended Columbia University where he received his A. M. After becoming principal of a high school in Jacksonville, he studied law and was admitted to the Florida bar in his twenty-sixth year, the first Negro attorney allowed to practice since the Civil War. A few years later he came to New York, where, collaborating with his brother, he wrote sketches for vaudeville and light opera. He served as United States Consul in Puerto Cabello, Venezuela, and later in Corinto, Nicaragua, became secretary of the National Association for Advancement of Colored People, and occupied the chair of Creative Literature at Fisk University. At the height of his career he was killed when the automobile in which he and his wife were driving was struck by a railroad train near Wiscasset, Maine. His wife was seriously injured, and Johnson was killed instantly, June 26, 1938.

The Autobiography of An Ex-Colored Man was Johnson's first and most important prose work. Published anonymously when he had turned forty, it was followed by the still more personal Along This Way. But it is as a poet that Johnson claims the reader's attention with God's Trombones. The volume consists of seven Negro sermons in free verse in the manner of old Negro plantation sermons. "The Creation" is particularly large in conception. It reflects the sonorous language and uninhibited imagery of old time Negro preachers—a mixture of Biblical and tropical figures held together with dignity and discipline.

THE CREATION

(A Negro Sermon)

And God stepped out on space,
And He looked around and said,
"*I'm lonely—*
I'll make me a world."

And far as the eye of God could see
Darkness covered everything,
Blacker than a hundred midnights
Down in a cypress swamp.

Then God smiled,
And the light broke,
And the darkness rolled up on one side,
And the light stood shining on the other,
And God said, "*That's good!*"

Then God reached out and took the light in His hands,
And God rolled the light around in His hands,
Until He made the sun;
And He set that sun a-blazing in the heavens.
And the light that was left from making the sun
God gathered up in a shining ball
And flung against the darkness,
Spangling the night with the moon and stars.
Then down between
The darkness and the light
He hurled the world;
And God said, "*That's good!*"

Then God himself stepped down–
And the sun was on His right hand,
And the moon was on His left;
The stars were clustered about His head,
And the earth was under His feet.
And God walked, and where He trod
His footsteps hollowed the valleys out
And bulged the mountains up.

Then He stopped and looked and saw
That the earth was hot and barren.
So God stepped over to the edge of the world
And He spat out the seven seas;
He batted His eyes, and the lightnings flashed;
He clapped His hands, and the thunders rolled;
And the waters above the earth came down,
The cooling waters came down.

Then the green grass sprouted,
And the little red flowers blossomed,

The pine-tree pointed his finger to the sky,
And the oak spread out his arms;
The lakes cuddled down in the hollows of the ground,
And the rivers ran down to the sea;
And God smiled again,
And the rainbow appeared,
And curled itself around His shoulder.

Then God raised His arm and He waved His hand
Over the sea and over the land,
And He said, "*Bring forth! Bring forth!*"
And quicker than God could drop His hand,
Fishes and fowls
And beasts and birds
Swam the rivers and the seas,
Roamed the forests and the woods,
And split the air with their wings,
And God said, "*That's good!*"

Then God walked around
And God looked around
On all that He had made.
He looked at His sun,
And He looked at His moon,
And He looked at His little stars;
He looked on His world
With all its living things,
And God said, "*I'm lonely still.*"

Then God sat down
On the side of a hill where He could think;
By a deep, wide river He sat down;
With His head in His hands,
God thought and thought,
Till He thought, "*I'll make me a man!*"

Up from the bed of the river
God scooped the clay;
And by the bank of the river
He kneeled Him down;
And there the great God Almighty,
Who lit the sun and fixed it in the sky,
Who flung the stars to the most far corner of the night,
Who rounded the earth in the middle of His hand—

This Great God,
Like a mammy bending over her baby,
Kneeled down in the dust
Toiling over a lump of clay
Till He shaped it in His own image;
Then into it He blew the breath of life,
And man became a living soul.
Amen. Amen.

WILLA CATHER

[1873–1947]

Although she later became famous *for the quality of her prose, it was with a book of poems, April Twilights, that Willa Seibert Cather made her debut. She was born December 7, 1873—the year is sometimes given as 1875—at Winchester, Virginia, of Anglo-Irish antecedents. In her ninth year the family moved to a pioneer ranch in Nebraska, where she was brought up among the immigrants and second-generation Americans to whom most of her novels were devoted. She hated the clatter and confusion of industrialism and refused to come to terms with it. Physically, as well as creatively, Willa Cather was at home only in the long and quiet stretches of open country. The best of her writing evokes the calm of prairies, the majesty of mountain peaks, the naturalness of such a village as Sante Fé before it became the Greenwich Village of the West and when it reflected the composure of Indian craftsmen, rug weavers, and pottery makers.*

In her twenties she came east and supported herself first by newspaper work, then by teaching in Pennsylvania. She never married. From her thirty-first to her thirty-seventh year she was managing editor of McClure's Magazine. She left that periodical to travel for she had a romantic dream of living in France. But, unlike Edith Wharton, she could not be happy anywhere except in her own land, especially in its vast prairies and deserts. Her life was free of drama. She published some fifteen volumes before her death at seventy-three in New York City, April 24, 1947.

Willa Cather wrote with great insight and with even greater restraint. Her work is warmer and more tender than Edith Wharton's; she pre-

ferred the manner of Sarah Orne Jewett, "The look—shy, kind, and a little wistful—that shines out at one from good country faces on remote farms." The look, the understatement, the fleeting suggestion seemed to her far more effective than any array of factual information. She preferred the Impressionists to the Realists. Realism to her was a mere cataloguing of a great number of material objects and mechanical processes.

The implied significance, "the inexplicable presence of the thing not named," supports and strengthens Willa Cather's spare and almost plotless volumes, from the early O Pioneers, The Song of the Lark, and My Antonia through A Lost Lady, The Professor's House, and Death Comes for the Archbishop. *Her main theme was struggle—the struggle of the transplanted European with the soil, of the sensitive creator with his environment—and she developed it with clarity in what Katherine Anne Porter called her "calm, well-tempered voice, talking wonderful good sense without much emphasis on the points."*

Besides her preoccupation with the foreign-born, Willa Cather was most concerned with the problems of the artist in modern society. "Paul's Case," one of her most sensitive stories, is the outstanding feature of her collection, Youth and the Bright Medusa.

PAUL'S CASE

IT WAS PAUL'S AFTERNOON TO APPEAR before the faculty of the Pittsburgh High School to account for his various misdemeanors. He had been suspended a week ago, and his father had called at the Principal's office and confessed his perplexity about his son. Paul entered the faculty room suave and smiling. His clothes were a trifle outgrown, and the tan velvet on the collar of his open overcoat was frayed and worn; but for all that there was something of the dandy about him, and he wore an opal pin in his neatly knotted black four-in-hand, and a red carnation in his buttonhole. This latter adornment the faculty somehow felt was not properly significant of the contrite spirit befitting a boy under the ban of suspension.

Paul was tall for his age and very thin, with high, cramped shoulders and a narrow chest. His eyes were remarkable for a certain hysterical brilliancy, and he continually used them in a conscious, theatrical sort of way, peculiarly offensive in a boy. The pupils were abnormally large, as though he were addicted to belladonna, but there was a glassy glitter about them which that drug does not produce.

When questioned by the Principal as to why he was there, Paul stated, politely enough, that he wanted to come back to school. This was a lie, but Paul was quite accustomed to lying; found it, indeed, indispensable for overcoming friction. His teachers were asked to state their respective charges against him, which they did with such a rancor and aggrievedness as evinced that this was not a usual case. Disorder and impertinence were among the offenses named, yet each of his instructors felt that it was scarcely possible to put into words the real cause of the trouble, which lay in a sort of hysterically defiant manner of the boy's; in the contempt which they all knew he felt for them, and which he seemingly made not the least effort to conceal. Once, when he had been making a synopsis of a paragraph at the blackboard, his English teacher had stepped to his side and attempted to guide his hand. Paul had started back with a shudder and thrust his hands violently behind him. The astonished woman could scarcely have been more hurt and embarrassed had he struck at her. The insult was so involuntary and definitely personal as to be unforgettable. In one way and another, he had made all his teachers, men and women alike, conscious of the same feeling of physical aversion. In one class he habitually sat with his hand shading his eyes; in another he always looked out of the window during the recitation; in another he made a running commentary on the lecture, with humorous intent.

His teachers felt this afternoon that his whole attitude was symbolized by his shrug and his flippantly red carnation flower, and they fell upon him without mercy, his English teacher leading the pack. He stood through it smiling, his pale lips parted over his white teeth. (His lips were continually twitching, and he had a habit of raising his eyebrows that was contemptuous and irritating to the last degree.) Older boys than Paul had broken down and shed tears under that ordeal, but his set smile did not once desert him, and his only sign of discomfort was the nervous trembling of the fingers that toyed with the buttons of his overcoat, and an occasional jerking of the other hand which held his hat. Paul was always smiling, always glancing about him, seeming to feel that people might be watching him and trying to detect something. This conscious expression, since it was as far as possible from boyish mirthfulness, was usually attributed to insolence or "smartness."

As the inquisition proceeded, one of his instructors repeated an impertinent remark of the boy's, and the Principal asked whether he thought that a courteous speech to make to a woman. Paul shrugged his shoulders slightly and his eyebrows twitched.

"I don't know," he replied. "I didn't mean to be polite or impolite, either. I guess it's a sort of way I have, of saying things regardless."

The Principal asked him whether he didn't think that a way it would be well to get rid of. Paul grinned and said he guessed so. When he was told that he could go, he bowed gracefully and went out. His bow was like a repetition of the scandalous red carnation.

His teachers were in despair, and his drawing master voiced the feeling of them all when he declared there was something about the boy which none of them understood. He added: "I don't really believe that smile of his comes altogether from insolence; there's something sort of haunted about it. The boy is not strong, for one thing. There is something wrong about the fellow."

The drawing master had come to realize that, in looking at Paul, one saw only his white teeth and the forced animation of his eyes. One warm afternoon the boy had gone to sleep at his drawing board, and his master had noted with amazement what a white, blue-veined face it was; drawn and wrinkled like an old man's about the eyes, the lips twitching even in his sleep.

His teachers left the building dissatisfied and unhappy; humiliated to have felt so vindictive toward a mere boy, to have uttered this feeling in cutting terms, and to have set each other on, as it were, in the gruesome game of intemperate reproach. One of them remembered having seen a miserable street cat set at bay by a ring of tormentors.

As for Paul, he ran down the hill whistling the Soldiers' Chorus from *Faust*, looking wildly behind him now and then to see whether some of his teachers were not there to witness his light-heartedness. As it was now late in the afternoon and Paul was on duty that evening as usher at Carnegie Hall, he decided that he would not go home to supper.

When he reached the concert hall the doors were not yet open. It was chilly outside, and he decided to go up into the picture gallery—always deserted at this hour—where there were some of Raffelli's gay studies of Paris streets and an airy blue Venetian scene or two that always exhilarated him. He was delighted to find no one in the gallery but the old guard, who sat in the corner, a newspaper on his knee, a black patch over one eye and the other closed. Paul possessed himself of the place and walked confidently up and down, whistling under his breath. After a while he sat down before a blue Rico and lost himself. When he bethought him to look at his watch, it was after seven o'clock, and he rose with a start and ran downstairs, making a face at Augustus Caesar, peering out from the cast-room, and an evil gesture at the Venus of Milo as he passed her on the stairway.

When Paul reached the ushers' dressing-room half a dozen boys were there already, and he began excitedly to tumble into his uniform. It was one of the few that at all approached fitting, and Paul thought it very becoming—though he knew the tight, straight coat accentuated his narrow chest, about which he was exceedingly sensitive. He was always excited while he dressed, twanging all over to the tuning of the strings and the preliminary flourishes of the horns in the music-room; but tonight he seemed quite beside himself, and he teased and plagued the boys until, telling him that he was crazy, they put him down on the floor and sat on him.

Somewhat calmed by his suppression, Paul dashed out to the front of the house to seat the early comers. He was a model usher. Gracious and smiling he ran up and down the aisles. Nothing was too much trouble for him; he carried messages and brought programs as though it were his greatest pleasure in life, and all the people in his section thought him a charming boy, feeling that he remembered and admired them. As the house filled, he grew more and more vivacious and animated, and the color came to his cheeks and lips. It was very much as though this were a great reception and Paul were the host. Just as the musicians came out to take their places, his English teacher arrived with checks for the seats which a prominent manufacturer had taken for the season. She betrayed some embarrassment when she handed Paul the tickets, and a *hauteur* which subsequently made her feel very foolish. Paul was startled for a moment, and had the feeling of wanting to put her out; what business had she here among all these fine people and gay colors? He looked her over and decided that she was not appropriately dressed and must be a fool to sit downstairs in such togs. The tickets had probably been sent her out of kindness, he reflected, as he put down a seat for her, and she had about as much right to sit there as he had.

When the symphony began Paul sank into one of the rear seats with a long sigh of relief, and lost himself as he had done before the Rico. It was not that symphonies, as such, meant anything in particular to Paul, but the first sigh of the instruments seemed to free some hilarious spirit within him; something that struggled there like the Genius in the bottle found by the Arab fisherman. He felt a sudden zest of life; the lights danced before his eyes and the concert hall blazed into unimaginable splendor. When the soprano soloist came on, Paul forgot even the nastiness of his teacher's being there, and gave himself up to the peculiar intoxication such personages always had for him. The soloist chanced to be a German woman, by no means in her first youth, and the mother of many children; but she wore a satin gown and a tiara, and she had that indefinable air of achievement, that world-shine upon her, which always blinded Paul to any possible defects.

After a concert was over, Paul was often irritable and wretched until he got to sleep,—and tonight he was even more than usually restless. He had the feeling of not being able to let down; of its being impossible to give up this delicious excitement which was the only thing that could be called living at all. During the last number he withdrew and, after hastily changing his clothes in the dressing-room, slipped out to the side door where the singer's carriage stood. Here he began pacing rapidly up and down the walk, waiting to see her come out.

Over yonder the Schenley, in its vacant stretch, loomed big and square through the fine rain, the windows of its twelve stories glowing like those of a lighted cardboard house under a Christmas tree. All the actors and singers of any importance stayed there when they were in the city, and a number of the big manufacturers of the place lived there in the winter. Paul had often hung about the hotel, watching the people go in and out, longing to enter and leave schoolmasters and dull care behind him forever.

At last the singer came out, accompanied by the conductor, who helped her into her carriage and closed the door with a cordial *auf wiedersehen*,—which set Paul to wondering whether she were not an old sweetheart of his. Paul followed the carriage over to the hotel, walking so rapidly as not to be far from the entrance when the singer alighted and disappeared behind the swinging glass doors which were opened by a Negro in a tall hat and a long coat. In the moment that the door was ajar, it seemed to Paul that he, too, entered. He seemed to feel himself go after her up the steps, into the warm, lighted building, into an exotic, a tropical world of shiny, glistening surfaces and basking ease. He reflected upon the mysterious dishes that were brought into the dining-room, the green bottles in buckets of ice, as he had seen them in the supper party pictures of the Sunday supplement. A quick gust of wind brought the rain down with sudden vehemence, and Paul was startled to find that he was still outside in the slush of the gravel driveway; that his boots were letting in the water and his scanty overcoat was clinging wet about him; that the lights in front of the concert hall were out, and that the rain was driving in sheets between him and the orange glow of the windows above him. There it was, what he wanted—tangibly before him, like the fairy world of a Christmas pantomime; as the rain beat in his face, Paul wondered whether he were destined always to shiver in the black night outside, looking up at it.

He turned and walked reluctantly toward the car tracks. The end had to come some time; his father in his night-clothes at the top of the stairs, explanations that did not explain, hastily improvised fictions that were forever tripping him up, his upstairs room and its horrible yellow wall paper, the creaking bureau with the greasy plush collar-box, and over his painted wooden bed the pictures of George Washington and John Calvin, and the framed motto, "Feed my Lambs," which had been worked in red worsted by his mother, whom Paul could not remember.

Half an hour later, Paul alighted from the Negley Avenue car and went slowly down one of the side streets off the main thoroughfare. It was a highly respectable street, where all the houses were exactly alike, and where business men of moderate means begot and reared large families of children, all of whom went to Sabbath-school and learned the shorter catechism, and were interested in arithmetic; all of whom were as exactly alike as their homes, and of a piece with the monotony in which they lived. Paul never went up Cordelia Street without a shudder of loathing. His home was next to the house of the Cumberland minister. He approached it tonight with the nerveless sense of defeat, the hopeless feeling of sinking back forever into ugliness and commonness that he had always had when he came home. The moment he turned into Cordelia Street he felt the waters close above his head. After each of these orgies of living, he experienced all the physical depression which follows a debauch; the loathing of respectable beds, of common food, of a house permeated by kitchen odors; a shuddering repulsion for the flavorless, colorless mass of everyday existence; a morbid desire for cool things and soft lights and fresh flowers.

The nearer he approached the house, the more absolutely unequal Paul felt to the sight of it all; his ugly sleeping chamber; the cold bathroom with the grimy zinc tub, the cracked mirror, the dripping spiggots; his father, at the top of the stairs, his hairy legs sticking out from his nightshirt, his feet thrust into carpet slippers. He was so much later than usual that there would certainly be inquiries and reproaches. Paul stopped short before the door. He felt that he could not be accosted by his father tonight; that he could not toss again on that miserable bed. He would not go in. He would tell his father that he had no car fare, and it was raining so hard he had gone home with one of the boys and stayed all night.

Meanwhile, he was wet and cold. He went around to the back of the house and tried one of the basement windows, found it open, raised it cautiously, and scrambled down the cellar wall to the floor. There he stood, holding his breath, terrified by the noise he had made; but the floor above him was silent, and there was no creak on the stairs. He found a soap-box, and carried it over to the soft ring of light that streamed from the furnace door, and sat down. He was horribly afraid of rats, so he did not try to sleep, but sat looking distrustfully at the dark, still terrified lest he might have awakened his father. In such reactions, after one of the experiences which made days and nights out of the dreary blanks of the calendar, when his senses were deadened, Paul's head was always singularly clear. Suppose his father had heard him getting in at the window and had come down and shot him for a burglar? Then, again, suppose his father had come down, pistol in hand, and he had cried out in time to save himself, and his father had been horrified to think now nearly he had killed him? Then, again, suppose a day should come when his father would remember that night, and wish there had been no warning cry to stay his hand? With this last supposition Paul entertained himself until daybreak.

The following Sunday was fine; the sodden November chill was broken by the last flash of autumnal summer. In the morning Paul had to go to church and Sabbath-school, as always. On seasonable Sunday afternoons the burghers of Cordelia Street usually sat out on their front "stoops," and talked to their neighbors on the next stoop, or called to those across the street in neighborly fashion. The men sat placidly on gay cushions placed upon the steps that led down to the sidewalk, while the women, in their Sunday "waists," sat in rockers on the cramped porches, pretending to be greatly at their ease. The children played in the streets; there were so many of them that the place resembled the recreation grounds of a kindergarten. The men on the steps—all in their shirt sleeves, their vests unbuttoned—sat with their legs well apart, their stomachs comfortably protruding, and talked of the prices of things, or told anecdotes of the sagacity of their various chiefs and overlords. They occasionally looked over the multitude of squabbling children, listened affectionately to their high-pitched, nasal voices, smiling to see their own proclivities reproduced in their offspring, and interspersed their legends of the iron kings with remarks about their sons' progress at school, their grades in arithmetic, and the amounts they had saved in their toy banks. On this last Sunday of November, Paul sat all the afternoon on the lowest step of his stoop, staring into the street, while his sisters, in their rockers, were talking to the minister's daughters next door about how many shirtwaists they had made in the last week, and how many waffles someone had eaten at the last church supper. When the weather was warm, and his father was in a particularly jovial frame of mind, the girls made lemonade, which was always brought out in a red-glass pitcher, ornamented with forget-me-nots in blue enamel. This the girls thought very fine, and the neighbors joked about the suspicious color of the pitcher.

Today Paul's father, on the top step, was talking to a young man who shifted a restless baby from knee to knee. He happened to be the young man who was daily held up to Paul as a model, and after whom it was his father's dearest hope that he would pattern. This young man was of a ruddy complexion, with a compressed, red mouth, and faded, near-sighted eyes, over which he wore thick spectacles, with gold bows that curved about his ears. He was clerk to one of the magnates of a great steel corporation, and was looked upon in Cordelia Street as a young man with a future. There was a story that, some five years ago—he was now barely twenty-six—he had been a trifle "dissipated," but in order to curb his appetites and save the loss of time and strength that a sowing of wild oats might have entailed, he had taken his chief's advice, oft reiterated to his employees, and at twenty-one had married the first woman whom he could persuade to share his fortunes. She happened to be an angular school mistress, much older than he, who also wore thick glasses, and who had now borne him four children, all near-sighted, like herself.

The young man was relating how his chief, now cruising in the Mediterranean, kept in touch with all the details of the business, arranging his office hours on his yacht just as though he were at home, and "knocking off work enough to keep two stenographers busy." His father told, in turn, the plan his corporation was considering, of putting in an electric railway plant at Cairo. Paul snapped his teeth; he had an awful apprehension that they might spoil it all before he got there. Yet he rather liked to hear these legends of the iron kings, that were told and retold on Sundays and holidays; these stories of palaces in Venice, yachts on the Mediterranean, and high play at Monte Carlo appealed to his fancy, and he was interested in the triumphs of cash boys who had become famous, though he had no mind for the cash-boy stage.

After supper was over, and he had helped to dry the dishes, Paul nervously asked his father whether he could go to George's to get some help in geometry, and still more nervously asked for car fare. This latter request he had to repeat, as his father, on principle, did not like to hear requests for money, whether much or little. He asked Paul whether he could not go to some boy who lived nearer, and told him that he ought not to leave his school work until Sunday; but he gave him the dime. He was not a poor man, but he had a worthy ambition to come up in the world. His only reason for allowing Paul to usher was that he thought a boy ought to be earning a little.

Paul bounded upstairs, scrubbed the greasy odor of the dishwater from his hands with the ill-smelling soap he hated, and then shook over his fingers a few drops of violet water from the bottle he kept hidden in his drawer. He left the house with his geometry conspicuously under his arm, and the moment he got out of Cordelia Street and boarded a downtown car, he shook off the lethargy of two deadening days, and began to live again.

The leading juvenile of the permanent stock company which played at one of the downtown theaters was an acquaintance of Paul's, and the boy had been invited to drop in at the Sunday night rehearsals whenever he could. For more than a year Paul had spent every available moment loitering about Charley Edwards's dressing-room. He had won a place among Edwards's following not only because the young actor, who could not afford to employ a dresser, often found him useful, but because he recognized in Paul something akin to what churchmen term "vocation."

It was at the theater and at Carnegie Hall that Paul really lived; the rest was but a sleep and a forgetting. This was Paul's fairy tale, and it had for him all the allurement of a secret love. The moment he inhaled the gassy, painty, dusty odor behind the scenes, he breathed like a prisoner set free, and felt within him the possibility of doing or saying splendid, brilliant things. The moment the cracked orchestra beat out the overture from *Martha*, or jerked at the serenade from *Rigoletto*, all stupid and ugly things slid from him, and his senses were deliciously, yet delicately fired.

Perhaps it was because, in Paul's world, the natural nearly always wore the guise of ugliness, that a certain element of artificiality seemed to him necessary in beauty. Perhaps it was because his experience of life elsewhere was so full of Sabbath-school picnics, petty economies, wholesome advice as to how to succeed in life, and the unescapable odors of cooking that he found this existence so alluring, these smartly-clad men and women so attractive, that he was so moved by these starry apple orchards that bloomed perennially under the limelight.

It would be difficult to put it strongly enough how convincingly the stage entrance of that theater was for Paul the actual portal of Romance. Certainly none of the company ever suspected it, least of all Charley Edwards. It was very like the old stories that used to float about London of fabulously rich Jews, who had subterranean halls, with palms, and fountains, and soft lamps and richly apparelled women who never saw the disenchanting light of London day. So, in the midst of that smoke-palled city, enamored of figures and grimy toil, Paul had his secret temple, his wishing-carpet, his bit of blue-and-white Mediterranean shore bathed in perpetual sunshine.

Several of Paul's teachers had a theory that his imagination had been perverted by garish fiction; but the truth was, he scarcely ever read at all. The books at home were not such as would either tempt or corrupt a youthful mind, and as for reading the novels that some of his friends urged upon him—well, he got what he wanted much more quickly from music;

any sort of music, from an orchestra to a barrel organ. He needed only the spark, the indescribable thrill that made his imagination master of his senses, and he could make plots and pictures enough of his own. It was equally true that he was not stage-struck—not, at any rate, in the usual acceptation of that expression. He had no desire to become an actor, any more than he had to become a musician. He felt no necessity to do any of these things; what he wanted was to see, to be in the atmosphere, float on the wave of it, to be carried out, blue league after blue league, away from everything.

After a night behind the scenes, Paul found the school-room more than ever repulsive; the bare floors and naked walls; the prosy men who never wore frock coats, or violets in their buttonholes; the women with their dull gowns, shrill voices, and pitiful seriousness about prepositions that govern the dative. He could not bear to have the other pupils think, for a moment, that he took these people seriously; he must convey to them that he considered it all trivial, and was there only by way of a joke, anyway. He had autograph pictures of all the members of the stock company which he showed his classmates, telling them the most incredible stories of his familiarity with these people, of his acquaintance with the soloists who came to Carnegie Hall, his suppers with them and the flowers he sent them. When these stories lost their effect, and his audience grew listless, he would bid all the boys good-by, announcing that he was going to travel for a while; going to Naples, to California, to Egypt. Then, next Monday, he would slip back, conscious and nervously smiling; his sister was ill, and he would have to defer his voyage until spring.

Matters went steadily worse with Paul at school. In the itch to let his instructors know how heartily he despised them, and how thoroughly he was appreciated elsewhere, he mentioned once or twice that he had no time to fool with theorems; adding—with a twitch of the eyebrows and a touch of that nervous bravado which so perplexed them—that he was helping the people down at the stock company; they were old friends of his.

The upshot of the matter was, that the Principal went to Paul's father, and Paul was taken out of school and put to work. The manager at Carnegie Hall was told to get another usher in his stead; the doorkeeper at the theater was warned not to admit him to the house; and Charley Edwards remorsefully promised the boy's father not to see him again.

The members of the stock company were vastly amused when some of Paul's stories reached them—especially the women. They were hard-working women, most of them supporting indolent husbands or brothers, and they laughed rather bitterly at having stirred the boy to such fervid and florid inventions. They agreed with the faculty and with his father, that Paul's was a bad case.

The east-bound train was plowing through a January snowstorm; the dull dawn was beginning to show gray when the engine whistled a mile out of Newark. Paul started up from the seat where he had lain curled in uneasy slumber, rubbed the breath-misted window glass with his hand, and peered out. The snow was whirling in curling eddies above the white bottom lands, and the drifts lay already deep in the fields and along the fences, while here and there the long dead grass and dried weed stalks protruded black above it. Lights shone from the scattered houses, and a gang of laborers who stood beside the track waved their lanterns.

Paul had slept very little, and he felt grimy and uncomfortable. He had made the all-night journey in a day coach because he was afraid if he took a Pullman he might be seen by some Pittsburgh business man who had noticed him in Denny & Carson's office. When the whistle woke him, he clutched quickly at his breast pocket, glancing about him with an uncertain smile. But the little, clay-bespattered Italians were still sleeping, the slatternly women across the aisle were in open-mouthed oblivion, and even the crumby, crying babies were for the nonce stilled. Paul settled back to struggle with his impatience as best he could.

When he arrived at the Jersey City station, he hurried through his breakfast, manifestly ill at ease and keeping a sharp eye about him. After he reached the Twenty-third Street station, he consulted a cabman, and had himself driven to a men's furnishing establishment which was just opening for the day. He spent upward of two hours there, buying with endless reconsidering and great care. His new street suit he put on in the fitting-room; the frock coat and dress clothes he had bundled into the cab with his new shirts. Then he drove to a hatter's and a shoe house. His next errand was at Tiffany's, where he selected silver-mounted brushes and a scarf-pin. He would not wait to have his silver marked, he said. Lastly, he stopped at a trunk shop on Broadway, and had his purchases packed into various traveling bags.

It was a little after one o'clock when he drove up to the Waldorf, and, after settling with the cabman, went into the office. He registered from Washington; said his mother and father had been abroad, and that he had come down to await the arrival of their steamer. He told his story plausibly and had no trouble, since he offered to pay for them in advance, in engaging his rooms; a sleeping-room, sitting room and bath.

Not once, but a hundred times Paul had planned his entry into New York. He had gone over every detail of it with Charley Edwards, and in his scrap book at home there were pages of description about New York hotels, cut from the Sunday papers.

When he was shown to his sitting room on the eighth floor, he saw at a glance that everything was as it should be; there was but one detail in his mental picture that the place did not realize, so he rang for the bell boy and sent him down for flowers. He moved about nervously until the boy returned, putting away his new linen and fingering it delightedly as he did so. When the flowers came, he put them hastily into water, and then tumbled into a hot bath. Presently he came out of his white bathroom, resplendent in his new silk underwear, and playing with the tassels of his red robe. The snow was whirling so fiercely outside his windows that he could scarcely see across the street; but within, the air was deliciously soft and fragrant. He put the violets and jonquils on the tabouret beside the couch, and threw himself down with a long sigh, covering himself with a Roman blanket. He was thoroughly tired; he had been in such haste, he had stood up to such a strain, covered so much ground in the last twenty-four hours, that he wanted to think how it had all come about. Lulled by the sound of the wind, the warm air, and the cool fragrance of the flowers, he sank into deep, drowsy retrospection.

It had been wonderfully simple; when they had shut him out of the theater and concert hall, when they had taken away his bone, the whole thing was virtually determined. The rest was a mere matter of opportunity. The only thing that at all surprised him was his own courage—for he realized well enough that he had always been tormented by fear, a sort of apprehensive dread that, of late years, as the meshes of the lies he had told closed about him, had been pulling the muscles of his body tighter and tighter. Until now, he could not remember a time when he had not been dreading something. Even when he was a little boy, it was always there—behind him, or before, or on either side. There had always been the shadowed corner, the dark place into which he dared not look, but from which something seemed always to be watching him—and Paul had done things that were not pretty to watch, he knew.

But now he had a curious sense of relief, as though he had at last thrown down the gauntlet to the thing in the corner.

Yet it was but a day since he had been sulking in the traces; but yesterday afternoon that he had been sent to the bank with Denny & Carson's deposit, as usual—but this time he was instructed to leave the book to be balanced. There was above two thousand dollars in checks, and nearly a thousand in the bank notes which he had taken from the book and quietly transferred to his pocket. At the bank he had made out a new deposit slip. His nerves had been steady enough to permit of his returning to the office, where he had finished his work and asked for a full day's holiday tomorrow, Saturday, giving a perfectly reasonable pretext. The bank book, he knew, would not be returned before Monday or Tuesday, and his father would be out of town for the next week. From the time he slipped the bank notes into his pocket until he boarded the night train for New York, he had not known a moment's hesitation.

How astonishingly easy it had all been; here he was, the thing done; and this time there would be no awakening, no figure at the top of the stairs. He watched the snowflakes whirling by his window until he fell asleep.

When he awoke, it was four o'clock in the afternoon. He bounded up with a start; one of his precious days gone already! He spent nearly an hour in dressing, watching every stage of his toilet carefully in the mirror. Everything was quite perfect; he was exactly the kind of boy he had always wanted to be.

When he went downstairs, Paul took a carriage and drove up Fifth Avenue toward the Park. The snow had somewhat abated; carriages and tradesmen's wagons were hurrying soundlessly to and fro in the winter twilight; boys in woolen mufflers were shoveling off the doorsteps; the avenue stages made fine spots of color against the white street. Here and there on the corners whole flower gardens blooming behind glass windows, against which the snow flakes stuck and melted; violets, roses, carnations, lilies of the valley–somehow vastly more lovely and alluring that they blossomed thus unnaturally in the snow. The Park itself was a wonderful stage winter-piece.

When he returned, the pause of the twilight had ceased, and the tune of the streets had changed. The snow was falling faster, lights streamed from the hotels that reared their many stories fearlessly up into the storm, defying the raging Atlantic winds. A long, black stream of carriages poured down the avenue, intersected here and there by other streams, tending horizontally. There were a score of cabs about the entrance of his hotel, and his driver had to wait. Boys in livery were running in and out of the awning stretched across the sidewalk, up and down the red velvet carpet laid from the door to the street. Above, about, within it all, was the rumble and roar, the hurry and toss of thousands of human beings as hot for pleasure as himself, and on every side of him towered the glaring affirmation of the omnipotence of wealth.

The boy set his teeth and drew his shoulders together in a spasm of realization; the plot of all dramas, the text of all romances, the nerve-stuff of all sensations was whirling about him like the snowflakes. He burnt like a faggot in a tempest.

When Paul came down to dinner, the music of the orchestra floated up the elevator shaft to greet him. As he stepped into the thronged corridor, he sank back into one of the chairs against the wall to get his breath. The lights, the chatter, the perfumes, the bewildering medley of color—he had, for a moment, the feeling of not being able to stand it. But only for a moment; these were his own people, he told himself. He went slowly about the corridors, through the writing-rooms, smoking-rooms, reception-rooms, as though he were exploring the chambers of an enchanted palace, built and peopled for him alone.

When he reached the dining room he sat down at a table near a window. The flowers, the white linen, the many-colored wine glasses, the gay toilettes of the women, the low popping of corks, the undulating repetitions of the *Blue Danube* from the orchestra, all flooded Paul's dream with bewildering radiance. When the roseate tinge of his champagne was added —that cold, precious, bubbling stuff that creamed and foamed in his glass— Paul wondered that there were honest men in the world at all. This was what all the world was fighting for, he reflected; this was what all the struggle was about. He doubted the reality of his past. Had he ever known a place called Cordelia Street, a place where fagged-looking business men boarded the early car? Mere rivets in a machine they seemed to Paul,— sickening men, with combings of children's hair always hanging to their coats, and the smell of cooking in their clothes. Cordelia Street—Ah, that belonged to another time and country! Had he not always been thus, had he not sat here night after night, from as far back as he could remember, looking pensively over just such shimmering textures, and slowly twirling the stem of a glass like this one between his thumb and middle finger? He rather thought he had.

He was not in the least abashed or lonely. He had no especial desire to meet or to know any of these people; all he demanded was the right to look on and conjecture, to watch the pageant. The mere stage properties were all he contended for. Nor was he lonely later in the evening, in his loge at the Opera. He was entirely rid of his nervous misgivings, of his forced aggressiveness, of the imperative desire to show himself different from his surroundings. He felt now that his surroundings explained him. Nobody questioned the purple; he had only to wear it passively. He had only to glance down at his dress coat to reassure himself that here it would be impossible for anyone to humiliate him.

He found it hard to leave his beautiful sitting room to go to bed that night, and sat long watching the raging storm from his turret window. When he went to sleep, it was with the lights turned on in his bedroom; partly because of his old timidity, and partly so that, if he should wake in the night, there would be no wretched moment of doubt, no horrible suspicion of yellow wall paper, or of Washington and Calvin above his bed.

On Sunday morning the city was practically snow-bound. Paul breakfasted late, and in the afternoon he fell in with a wild San Francisco boy, a freshman at Yale, who said he had run down for a "little flyer" over Sunday. The young man offered to show Paul the night side of the town, and the two boys went off together after dinner, not returning to the hotel until seven o'clock the next morning. They had started out in the confiding warmth of a champagne friendship, but their parting in the elevator was singularly cool. The freshman pulled himself together to make his train, and Paul went to bed. He awoke at two o'clock in the afternoon, very thirsty and dizzy, and rang for ice water, coffee, and the Pittsburgh papers.

On the part of the hotel management, Paul excited no suspicion. There was this to be said for him, that he wore his spoils with dignity and in no way made himself conspicuous. His chief greediness lay in his ears and eyes, and his excesses were not offensive ones. His dearest pleasures were the gray winter twilights in his sitting room; his quiet enjoyment of his flowers, his clothes, his wide divan, his cigarette and his sense of power. He could not remember a time when he had felt so at peace with himself. The mere release from the necessity of petty lying, lying every day and every day, restored his self-respect. He had never lied for pleasure, even at school; but to make himself noticed and admired, to assert his difference from other Cordelia Street boys; and he felt a good deal more manly, more honest, even, now that he had no need for boastful pretensions, now that he could, as his actor friends used to say, "dress the part." It was characteristic that remorse did not occur to him. His golden days went by without a shadow, and he made each as perfect as he could.

On the eighth day after his arrival in New York, he found the whole affair exploited in the Pittsburgh papers, exploited with a wealth of detail which indicated that local news of a sensational nature was at a low ebb. The firm of Denny & Carson announced that the boy's father had refunded the full amount of his theft, and that they had no intention of prosecuting. The Cumberland minister had been interviewed, and expressed his hope of yet reclaiming the motherless lad, and Paul's Sabbath-school teacher declared that she would spare no effort to that end. The rumor had reached Pittsburgh that the boy had been seen in a New York hotel, and his father had gone East to find him and bring him home.

Paul had just come in to dress for dinner; he sank into a chair, weak in the knees, and clasped his head in his hands. It was to be worse than jail, even; the tepid waters of Cordelia Street were to close over him finally and forever. The gray monotony stretched before him in hopeless, unrelieved years; Sabbath-school, Young People's Meeting, the yellow-papered room, the damp dish-towels; it all rushed back upon him with sickening vividness. He had the old feeling that the orchestra had suddenly stopped, the sinking sensation that the play was over. The sweat broke out on his face, and he sprang to his feet, looked about him with his white, conscious smile, and winked at himself in the mirror. With something of the childish belief in miracles with which he had so often gone to class, all his lessons unlearned, Paul dressed and dashed whistling down the corridor to the elevator.

He had no sooner entered the dining room and caught the measure of the music, than his remembrance was lightened by his old elastic power of claiming the moment, mounting with it, and finding it all sufficient. The glare and glitter about him, the mere scenic accessories had again, and for the last time, their old potency. He would show himself that he was game, he would finish the thing splendidly. He doubted, more than ever, the existence of Cordelia Street, and for the first time he drank his wine recklessly. Was he not after all, one of these fortunate beings? Was he not still himself, and in his own place? He drummed a nervous accompaniment to the music and looked about him, telling himself over and over that it had paid.

He reflected drowsily, to the swell of the violin and the chill sweetness of his wine, that he might have done it more wisely. He might have caught an outbound steamer and been well out of their clutches before now. But the other side of the world had seemed too far away and too uncertain then; he could not have waited for it; his need had been too sharp. If he had to choose over again, he would do the same thing tomorrow. He looked affectionately about the dining room, now gilded with a soft mist. Ah, it had paid indeed!

Paul was awakened next morning by a painful throbbing in his head and feet. He had thrown himself across the bed without undressing, and had slept with his shoes on. His limbs and hands were lead heavy, and his tongue and throat were parched. There came upon him one of those fateful attacks of clear-headedness that never occurred except when he was physically exhausted and his nerves hung loose. He lay still and closed his eyes and let the tide of realities wash over him.

His father was in New York; "stopping at some joint or other," he told himself. The memory of successive summers on the front stoop fell upon him like a weight of black water. He had not a hundred dollars left; and he knew now, more than ever, that money was everything, the wall that stood between all he loathed and all he wanted. The thing was winding itself up; he had thought of that on his first glorious day in New York, and had even provided a way to snap the thread. It lay on his dressing-table now; he had got it out last night when he came blindly up from dinner,—but the shiny metal hurt his eyes, and he disliked the look of it, anyway.

He rose and moved about with a painful effort, succumbing now and again to attacks of nausea. It was the old depression exaggerated; all the world had become Cordelia Street. Yet somehow he was not afraid of anything, was absolutely calm; perhaps because he had looked into the dark corner at last, and knew. It was bad enough, what he saw there; but somehow not so bad as his long fear of it had been. He saw everything clearly now. He had a feeling that he had made the best of it, that he had lived the sort of life he was meant to live, and for half an hour he sat staring at the revolver. But he told himself that was not the way, so he went downstairs and took a cab to the ferry.

When Paul arrived at Newark, he got off the train and took another cab, directing the driver to follow the Pennsylvania tracks out of the town. The snow lay heavy on the roadways and had drifted deep in the open fields. Only here and there the dead grass or dried weed stalks projected, singularly black, above it. Once well into the country, Paul dismissed the carriage and walked, floundering along the tracks, his mind a medley of irrelevant things. He seemed to hold in his brain an actual picture of everything he had seen that morning. He remembered every feature of both his drivers, the toothless old woman from whom he had bought the red flowers in his coat, the agent from whom he had got his ticket, and all of his fellow-passengers on the ferry. His mind, unable to cope with vital matters near at hand, worked feverishly and deftly at sorting and grouping these images. They made for him a part of the ugliness of the world, of the ache in his head, and the bitter burning on his tongue. He stooped and put a handful of snow into his mouth as he walked, but that, too, seemed hot. When he reached a little hillside, where the tracks ran through a cut some twenty feel below him, he stopped and sat down.

The carnations in his coat were drooping with the cold, he noticed; all their red glory over. It occurred to him that all the flowers he had seen in the show windows that first night must have gone the same way, long before this. It was only one splendid breath they had, in spite of their brave mockery at the winter outside the glass. It was a losing game in the end, it seemed, this revolt against the homilies by which the world is run. Paul took one of the blossoms carefully from his coat and scooped a little hole in the snow, where he covered it up. Then he dozed a while, from his weak condition, seeming insensible to the cold.

The sound of an approaching train woke him, and he started to his feet, remembering only his resolution, and afraid lest he should be too late. He stood watching the approaching locomotive, his teeth chattering, his lips drawn away from them in a frightened smile; once or twice he glanced nervously sidewise, as though he were being watched. When the right moment came, he jumped. As he fell, the folly of his haste occurred to him with merciless clearness, the vastness of what he had left undone. There flashed through his brain, clearer than ever before, the blue of Adriatic water, the yellow of Algerian sands.

He felt something strike his chest,—his body was being thrown swiftly through the air, on and on, immeasurably far and fast, while his limbs gently relaxed. Then, because the picture-making mechanism was crushed, the disturbing visions flashed into black, and Paul dropped back into the immense design of things.

CLARENCE DAY

[1874–1935]

THE SMALL BUT BRILLIANTLY *satirical section of Clarence (Shepard) Day's writings was swamped by the success of his autobiographical series:* Life With Father, Life With Mother, God and My Father, Father and I. *An unforgettable group portrait of upper-class life in New York's late nineteenth century,* Life With Father *was equally successful when dramatized: the play ran for eight consecutive years.*

Born in New York City in 1874, Clarence Day immortalized a family tradition that was already well established when he inherited it. His grandfather was the founder of the New York Sun; his uncle, Ben Day, invented the engraving process which still bears his name; his father was a governor of the Stock Exchange. Educated at St. Paul's school and Yale, Clarence Day became the junior partner of his colorful and choleric father but, at the outbreak of the Spanish-American War, quit Wall Street and enlisted in the Navy.

Day was a sick youth when he returned to America; in Cuba he had contracted the arthritis that made him an invalid the rest of his life.

He was crippled so badly that he could not leave his bed; he could barely hold a pencil, and most of his lines had to be dictated. Nevertheless, he was able to direct a glove business, attend to his affairs as a stock broker, and somehow to illustrate a series of remarkably whimsical books. His work continued to be both serene and satirical; there was never a trace of bitterness or self-pity in any of it. A forerunner of James Thurber, Day combined sympathy with mockery in such illustrated essays and humorous philosophies as This Simian World, Scenes from the Mesozoic, *and* After All.

A bedridden invalid to the end, he died of pneumonia, December 28, 1935.

FATHER HIRES A COOK

ONE LATE AFTERNOON when Father came up from downtown, he found his home much upset. Our cook had walked out and left us. I was a child of four, George was two, and there was a new baby besides. Mother was ill. She hadn't been able to leave us to go to an agency. And as she was no hand at cooking herself, the outlook for dinner was poor.

This state of affairs was unprecedented in all Father's experience. In his father's home, they never changed their servants suddenly; they seldom changed them at all; and as his mother was a past mistress of cooking, he had always been doubly protected. Since his marriage, he had had to live a much bumpier life. But this was the worst yet.

He asked Mother, who was lying in bed, what she was going to do about it. There were no telephones then, and she couldn't do anything at all, at the moment; but she said she would try to go to an agency in the morning and see what she could find. "In the morning? Good God!" Father said. "Where is the place, anyhow?" And he clapped on his hat and strode out again, over toward Sixth Avenue.

As I heard the story years afterward, it was late when he got there, and he bounded up the front stoop two or three steps at a time, and went quickly into the little office, where the gaslights were burning. He had never been in such a place before, and to his surprise it was empty, except for a severe-looking woman who sat at a desk at one side. "Where do you keep 'em?" he urgently demanded, his mind on the question of dinner.

She looked at him, got out her pen, and opened a large book deliberately. "I will take your name and address," she informed him, "and then, if you please, you may give me the details as to what kind of person you require and when you would wish her to call."

But Father had no time, he told her, for any damned fol-de-rol. "Where do you keep 'em?" he said again. She was standing in the way of his dinner. I can imagine how his face must have reddened and how his eyes must have blazed at her. "I am asking you where you keep them!" he roared.

"Why, the girls are in there," the lady explained, to calm him, "but clients are not allowed in that room. If you will tell me the kind of position you wish me to fill for you, I will have one come out."

Before she'd half finished, Father had thrown open the door and gone in. There sat a crowd of the girls, young and old, sickly and brawny, of all shapes and sizes; some ugly, some pretty and trim and stylish, some awkward; nurses, ladies' maids, waitresses, washerwomen, and cooks.

The manager was by now at Father's elbow, trying to make him get out, and insisting that he tell her the position he wished her to fill. But Father was swiftly glancing around at the crowd, and he paid no attention. He noticed a little woman in the corner, with honest gray eyes, who sat there, shrewd-looking and quiet. He pointed his cane over at her and said, "I'll take that one."

The manager was flustered, but still she kept trying to enforce her authority. She protested she didn't yet know the position. . . .

"Cook," Father said, "cook."

"But Margaret doesn't wish to be a cook, she wants—"

"You can cook, can't you?" Father demanded.

Margaret's plain little face was still pink with excitement and pleasure at being chosen above all that roomful by such a masterful gentleman. Father had probably smiled at her, too, for they liked each other at once. Well, she said, she had cooked for one family.

"Of course she can cook," Father said.

He said afterward, when describing the incident, "I knew at once she could cook."

The manager didn't like this at all. The discipline of the office was spoiled. "If you are going to take her anyhow," she said acidly, "what day would you wish her to come, and will you please give me your name?"

"Yes, yes," Father said, without giving it. "Come on, Margaret." And he planked down the fee and walked out.

Margaret followed him through the door and trotted over to our home at his heels. He sent her down to the kitchen immediately, while he went upstairs to dress.

"I don't know why you make such a fuss about engaging new servants. It's simple enough," he said comfortably to Mother that evening, after Margaret's first dinner.

It was the first of a long series, for she stayed with us twenty-six years.

FATHER FEELS STARVED

In the summers, when we went to the country, our usual plan was to hire a temporary cook to go with us, so that Margaret could stay in town. We hated to leave her, but the idea was that somebody must stay to take care of the house. There were no electric burglar alarms in those days, and few special watchmen. Little Margaret made a pretty small watchman, for she was no size at all, but she had an indomitable spirit. So we'd leave her on guard while we went up to our summer home in Harrison with a substitute cook.

But this didn't work well. No matter how few the substitute's faults were, Father had no patience with them. One summer, I remember, there was a nice woman, Delia, who got on well with Mother because she was so obliging and pleasant, but who didn't suit Father at all. "I don't give a damn how obliging she is," he kept saying. "If she won't oblige me by cooking something fit to eat, she can go."

This didn't sound unreasonable, but Delia cooked well enough for the rest of us, and Mother hated to risk getting someone else who'd be temperamental. Our dining-room consequently became a battleground morning and night. At breakfast, Father would put down his coffee cup in disgust and roar: "Slops! Damn it, slops! Does she call this confounded mess coffee? Isn't there a damned soul in Westchester County who knows how to make coffee but me? I swear to God I can't even imagine how she concocts such atrocities. I come down to this room hungry every morning, and she tries to fill me with slops! Take it away, I tell you!" he would bellow to the waitress. "Take this accursed mess away!" And while she and Delia were frantically hurrying to make a fresh pot, he would savagely devour his omelet and bacon, and declare that his breakfast was ruined.

The longer Delia stayed with us, the more alarmed Father became. He ate heartily, as Mother kept pointing out to him, but he said he didn't feel nourished. He said it was no use to argue about it; he felt all gone inside. One night after he had had a four-course dinner, he fretfully got up from the table, went into the library with his cigar, and moaned that he was starved. His moans were, as always, full-throated, and they came from the heart. Every now and then, when his miserable condition seemed to strike him afresh, he laid down his book and shouted "Starved! Starved!" in a grief-stricken roar.

When Mother went in the library to quiet him, he told her he'd be damned if he'd stand it. "I refuse to be sent to my grave, do you hear me, by that infernal bog-trotting imbecile you keep in my kitchen."

"Now Clare, a Japanese is coming tomorrow, I told you. This is Delia's last night. I do hope you'll like Tobo. He won't know our ways right at the start, of course, but he is a very good cook."

Father was appeased for the moment by the dismissal of Delia. But the next night, when he found that the first dish was too Oriental, he said in an annoyed tone to Mother, "Will you kindly explain to your man Tobo that I am not a coolie?" And after eating the rest of his dinner, he pushed his plate away and went up to his bedroom, declaring vehemently that he was poisoned. He undressed, lay down on his sofa, and filled the air with deep groans.

From time to time he stopped and dozed a little, or listened to what he could hear of our talk. His feeling was that we shouldn't be talking at all. We ought to be sitting with bowed heads in silence until he recovered. "Poisoned!" he suddenly boomed, to remind us. "Oh, God! I am poisoned!"

At this point, Mother, who was down in the library, laughed. Father heard her. He jumped up from his sofa and marched from his bedroom indignantly into the hall. "I'm a sick man!" he thundered robustly. "And nobody in this house gives a damn!"

Mother hurried upstairs to see what he wanted. He insisted on her rubbing his back. Sick or well, that always soothed him, and he would have liked her to do it for hours. He loved to close his eyes, with someone's hand moving quietly on him, while a feeling of comfort flowed into his thoughts and his nerves.

Mother didn't think much of rubbing, however. She didn't like it herself. When anyone rubbed her, she stiffened and resisted at once. Consequently she had no idea of the right way to do it. When she had to rub Father, she always got tired of it in a very few minutes.

She gave him some hasty little rubs and digs as well as she could, but just as he was beginning to relax, she said, "There now, Clare, that's enough."

Father was so disappointed by this that it reminded him that he was poisoned, and the only cure he could think of was the dismissal of Tobo.

The next day old Margaret was sent for to come at once to the country, and the house in town was locked up and left to take care of itself.

She came in a hack from the Harrison station. She was an odd sight. Her face looked familiar in her little black bonnet, tied under her chin, but she seemed strangely swollen and bulky; she stuck out in queer places; and as she crowded through the back door, she bruised me with her hard, bony hip. Only it wasn't her hip, it turned out; it was her favorite saucepan, which was tied to her waist under her skirt. Several large spoons, a dipper, a skillet, and two pair of shoes were made fast under it elsewhere. In her arms she had some bundles wrapped in newspapers, which Mother thought at first held her clothes, but when Margaret opened them we found they contained cheeses, melons, fresh coffee, a leg of lamb, some sweet potatoes, and other provisions. Margaret had no faith at all in being able to buy any supplies in the country. She had brought as complete a larder to Harrison as though we were at the North Pole.

"But didn't you bring any clothes with you, Margaret? Not even an apron?" asked Mother.

Little Margaret pursed her lips closely together and didn't answer at first. Then, as Mother stood waiting, she said unwillingly, "I have me other clothes on me."

She had wanted to have her hands free, it seemed, to bring us something good to eat. So under her street dress she was wearing two other dresses on that hot summer day, a collection of stiffly starched petticoats, three aprons, two night-gowns, and pretty much all the rest of her wardrobe.

As she was climbing upstairs to unpeel and unpack herself, Father saw her. "Is that you, Margaret?" he called, suddenly feeling much better. "Thank God!"

FATHER THUMPS ON THE FLOOR

OLD MARGARET WAS JUST THE KIND of cook that we wanted. Lots of cooks can do rich dishes well. Margaret couldn't. But she cooked simple, everyday dishes in a way that made our mouths water. Her apple pies were the most satisfying pies I've ever tasted. Her warmed-up potatoes were so delicious I could have made my whole dinner of them.

Yet even Margaret sometimes miscalculated. A large, royal-looking steak would be set before Father, which, upon being cut into, would turn out to be too underdone. Father's face would darken with disappointment. If the earth had begun to wobble and reel in its orbit he could scarcely have been more disapproving. He would raise his foot, under the table, and stamp slowly and heavily three times on the rug. Thud; thud; thud.

At this solemn signal, we would hear Margaret leave the kitchen below us and come clumping step by step up the stairs to the dining-room door.

"Margaret, look at that steak."

Margaret would step nearer and peer with a shocked look at the platter. "The Lord bless us and save us," she would say to herself in a low voice. She would then seize the platter and make off with it, to better it the best way she could, and Father would gloomily wait and eat a few vegetables and pour out a fresh glass of claret.

Father and Margaret were united by the intense interest they both took in cooking. Each understood the other instinctively. They had a complete fellow-feeling. Mother's great interest was in babies—she had never been taught how to cook. All she wanted was to keep Father pleased somehow; and if it was too difficult she didn't always care about even that.

At table it was Father who carved the fowl, or sliced the roast lamb or beef. I liked to watch him whet the knife and go at it. He had such a fine, easy hand. To a hungry boy, he seemed over-deliberate and exact in his strokes, yet in a moment or two he had done. And usually the cooking had been as superb as the carving. Sometimes it was so perfect that Father's face would crinkle with pleasure, and with a wink at us he'd summon Margaret with his usual three measured thumps. She would appear, clutching her skirts with both hands, and looking worried. "What's wanting?" she'd ask.

"Margaret," Father would tell her affectionately, "that fricasseed chicken is *good*."

Margaret would turn her wrinkled face aside, and look down, and push the flat of her hand out toward Father. It was the same gesture she used when she said "Get along with you" to flatterers. She couldn't say that to Father, but she would beam at him, and turn and go out, and stump back down the dark little stairs without ever a word.

Every once in a while, when the household bills were getting too high, a platter with three tiny French chops on it would be placed before Father, and a larger dish full of cold corned beef or Irish stew before Mother. At this sight we boys would stop talking and become round-eyed and still.

Father would look over at Mother's dish to see if it seemed appetizing, for he often said there was nothing better than one of Margaret's stews.

The stew usually seemed possible enough to him, yet not quite what he wanted. He would then ask Mother if she'd have a chop.

Mother always said, "No."

"They look nice and juicy," Father would urge her, but she would say again she didn't want any, and turn her eyes away from the platter.

Father would then look around at the rest of us, doubtfully. He had four sons, all with appetites. He would clear his throat as though getting ready to offer a chop to each boy in turn; but he usually compromised by saying, "Will anyone else have a chop?"

"No, Clare," Mother would quickly and impatiently reply, "they're for you. The rest of us are going to have stew tonight." And she'd smile brightly but a little watchfully around at us boys, to be sure that we were making no fuss about it, while she hurried to get the thing settled.

We boys would then earnestly watch Father while he ate the three chops.

Not that we didn't like Margaret's stew, which was the best in the world, but we regarded dinner as a special occasion, and we often had stew for lunch.

If some of us had taken up Father's offer, and left him with only one chop or none, I suppose that he would have asked Mother, "Where are the rest of the chops?" and been very cross about it when she told him there weren't any more. But his offer of them to us was sincere, though it cost him a struggle. He wanted plenty of food bought for everyone. His instincts were generous. Only, it made him cross if he suffered for those generous instincts.

Long after Margaret died, Father was speaking one night of how good her things always had tasted.

"I wish she could hear you," said Mother. She smiled tenderly at the thought of that gallant and dear little figure. "If anybody ever was sure of going to Heaven," she added, "I know it was Margaret."

This struck Father as a recommendation of the place. He took a sip of cognac and said casually, "I'll look her up when I get there. I'll have her take care of me."

Mother started to say something but checked herself.

"What's the matter?" he asked.

"Well, Clare dear," said Mother, "Margaret must be in some special part of Heaven, she was so good. You'd be very fortunate, Clare, to get to the same part as Margaret."

"Hah!" Father said, suddenly scowling. "I'll make a devil of a row if I don't."

STORY OF A FARMER

THERE ONCE WAS a tall husky fellow, with big hands and feet, and not much education (though he came of a fairly good family). He had very bad teeth. His father had left him a farm, and that was his great interest—farming. He had the kind of feeling about farming that a good shoemaker has about shoes. Of course, he complained more or less, and felt dissatisfied and discouraged, and threatened to give up his farm when things went badly. But there was nothing else he could have willingly turned to; and he was never weary of experimenting with different ways of planting his crops.

He was a sound-thinking man, and men trusted him. He grew prominent. He held some offices. As a result, when he was forty-three he had to go away from home for some years. This was while he was managing an army. And I ought to explain that it was a hard army to manage. It was not only badly equipped and poorly trained, but sometimes the men would run away in the midst of a battle. That made this man angry. He was ordinarily composed and benign in his manner, but when he saw the soldiers showing fear, he used to become violently aroused, and would swear at them and strike them. His nature loathed cowardice. He cared nothing for danger himself, perhaps because of his teeth, and he couldn't understand why these other men dreaded to die.

All his life, when he was at table with others, he used to sit there in silence, drumming on the cloth with his fork. He seldom joked. He was hardly ever playful. People said he was too dignified, too solemn. Well! one isn't apt to be a comedian, precisely, with toothache. He was only twenty-two when he began having his teeth pulled, they tortured him so; and he kept on losing them, painfully, year after year.

About this army again—he didn't want to manage it. He had had quite a liking for military work, as a youth, and had even gone on a small expedition to see active service, though his mother had interfered all she could, and tried hard to prevent him. But as this was all the experience he ever had had, and as he had never studied warfare, he didn't know anything about handling large bodies of troops.

However, he had a clear mind and a good natural insight; and in spite of his ignorance, of which he was painfully conscious, he managed to win the war, and then thankfully returned to his farm. He went back with enthusiasm. He had been away for eight years altogether, and for six of those years he did not once set foot on his fields. He had found time, however, in between whiles, to talk with the farmers in the northerly parts of his country, and collect new ideas. He now began to experiment with plaster of Paris and powdered stone as fertilizers. He tried clover, rye, peas, oats, and carrots to strengthen his land. He tried mud. He planted potatoes with manure, and potatoes without, and noted exactly what the difference was in the yield. His diary speaks of the chinch bugs attacking his corn, and of the mean way the rain had of passing by on the other side of the river, falling generously there, while "not enough fell here to wet a handkerchief." He laboriously calculated the number of seed in a pound (this retired Commander!) and found that red clover had 71,000, timothy 298,000, and barley 8,925.

He also began at this time to use false teeth, which fitted him badly. And he was laid up occasionally with malaria, and fever, and ague. And he was called upon to help frame a constitution for his little nation—a busy period. He had an attack of rheumatism, too, which lasted over six months, and it was sometimes so bad he could hardly raise his hand to his head or turn over in bed. And when the national constitution had been adopted, they elected him president. That meant a lot of outside work for another eight years.

Some of this work he hated. He hated speech-making, for instance. At his inauguration he was so agitated and embarrassed that men saw he trembled, and when he read his speech, his voice was almost too low to be heard. He was always very conscious of having a poor education, and being a bad speller, and so forth. But the people didn't care about that, much: they trusted his judgment, and admired the man's goodness and spirit.

A sculptor was sent to make a statue of him, late in his life. He couldn't get him to pose satisfactorily—no noble attitudes. In vain did the sculptor talk about state affairs and that war. Such things did not stir him. He remained either stiff or relaxed. But one day when they were out on the farm together; and as this man watched his live-stock, he unconsciously took a fine, alive attitude. So the sculptor made a statue of him that way; and that statue is famous.

In spite of his usual benignity, this man had a temper. He used to get very angry and warm at times, when unfairly criticized. At one of his cabinet meetings, for instance, says a contemporary, he became "much inflamed, got into one of those passions when he cannot command himself, ran on much on the personal abuse which had been bestowed on him [and said] that, by God, he had rather be in his grave than in his present situation; that he had rather be on his farm than to be made emperor of the world, and yet that they were charging him with wanting to be a king; that that rascal Freneau sent him three of his papers every day, as if he thought he would become the distributor of his papers; that he could see nothing in this but an impudent design to insult him," etc., etc. Poor, stung human being; with all his serenity gone!

A great portrait painter said of him that his features were indicative of the strongest and most ungovernable passions; and had he been born in the forests, it was his opinion that he would have been the fiercest man among the savage tribes.

This was the temperament that smoldered in him: the lurking flame that he had to live with daily. But by reflection and resolution he obtained a firm ascendancy over it.

One night when he was sixty-seven years old he woke up at about two in the morning feeling very unwell. He had had a sore throat, and now he couldn't swallow; he felt suffocated—a miserable feeling. His wife would have got up to call a servant; but he wouldn't allow her to do it lest she should catch cold. He lay there for four hours in the cold bedroom, his body in a chill, before receiving any attention or before even a fire was lighted. Then they sent for the doctors. They bled the old hero three times, taking the last time a quart. He was physically a vigorous man, but this weakened him greatly. "I find I am going," he said. He was in great pain, and said, "Doctor, I die hard." A little later he added: "I feel I am going. I thank you for your attention; you had better not take any more trouble about me, but let me go off quietly." His breathing became much easier just at the end.

Did he look back over his life as he lay there, waiting, and what did he think of it? That his farming had been interesting though difficult, and much interrupted? That his fellow-men had really asked a good many sacrifices of him, and not left him nearly as much time as he wished for his fields? Or did he think that in death he would at least have no more trouble with teeth? A set of dental instruments was found in one of his drawers after the funeral. In others were memoranda about affairs of state he had worked at, and various kinds of plows he had tried, and his farming accounts.

His name was George Washington.

JACK LONDON

[1876–1916]

Dead at forty, Jack London lived more lives than all the writers who outlived him. Born January 12, 1876, the illegitimate son of a romantic, reckless mother and a roaming astrologer-spiritualist who never saw his child, the boy grew up to be a tramp, a sailor, a day laborer, an adventurer in the Klondike, a war correspondent in Japan, and a writer whose enormously popular books were translated into every living language. He had little schooling. Between the ages of ten and eighteen he peddled newspapers, cleaned barrooms, delivered ice, became a longshoreman, an oyster pirate, joined Coxey's resentful army of the unemployed, and was sent to prison for thirty days as a vagrant. He became a socialist. When at twenty he went looking for gold in Alaska, he carried with him as strange a trio of books as ever accompanied a traveler: Marx's Das Kapital, Darwin's Origin of Species, and Milton's Paradise Lost.

London's writing, like his life, was a mixed longing for vagabondage and respectability, for the lawlessness of "the great open spaces" and the luxuries of civilization. Less than a year after his birth, his mother married John London, a farmer, and her son having been given his foster-father's cognomen, concealed his actual parentage so well that it was not discovered until after his death. The conflict of law and lawlessness runs through everything he wrote. It begins with his first volume, The Son of the Wolf, published when London was twenty-four, a collection of tales of the Far North commemorating the frontiersmen "who sought their heritage and left their bones among the shadows of the circle." Raw though the work was, it achieved a kind of Arctic splendor in which, true to the principles of Darwin, "the hoary game of natural selection was played out with all the ruthlessness of its primeval environment." Two other volumes followed immediately, but it was not until The Call of the Wild, written when London was twenty-seven, that he became famous. The book sold well over a million copies. Publishers sought and subsidized him. The Century Magazine paid him $4,000 for The Sea Wolf. The Hearst newspapers sent him to the Orient to report the Russo-Japanese War. Money continued to roll in from lecture tours, short stories, and the autobiographical novel, Martin Eden. London built a boat, "The Snark," which cost $30,000, and a castle in California, "The Wolf House," where he entertained prodigiously.

Although he wrote fifty books, which earned him more than a million dollars, he was always insecure. The stigma of his birth and fear of the future drove him to overproduction, to overwork, and to alcohol. As he sank deeper into debt, he drank more heavily. He was only forty when he died. Uremic poisoning was said to have been the cause of his death, but it was evident that he had committed suicide by means of a well-calculated overdose of morphine.

London's work centers about the law of Eat or Be Eaten. "Life itself is meat. Life lives on life," he said. To London the world was a reeking arena of supermen and superbeasts, a place of warring appetites, "pursuing and being pursued, hunting and being hunted . . . in blindness and confusion, with violence and disorder, a chaos of gluttony and slaughter, ruled over by chance, merciless, planless, endless." Such a concept called for an almost barbaric emotionalism, and London had neither the time nor the taste for subtleties of any kind. It is in the depiction of animal instincts that London excells—and it is most compact in the powerful short story "To Build a Fire."

TO BUILD A FIRE

DAY HAD BROKEN COLD AND GREY, exceedingly cold and grey, when the man turned aside from the main Yukon trail and climbed the high earth-bank, where a dim and little-travelled trail led eastward through the fat spruce timberland. It was a steep bank, and he paused for breath at the top, excusing the act to himself by looking at his watch. It was nine o'clock. There was no sun nor hint of sun, though there was not a cloud in the sky. It was a clear day, and yet there seemed an intangible pall over the face of things, a subtle gloom that made the day dark, and that was due to the absence of sun. This fact did not worry the man. He was used to the lack of sun. It had been days since he had seen the sun, and he knew that a few more days must pass before that cheerful orb, due south, would just peep above the sky-line and dip immediately from view.

The man flung a look back along the way he had come. The Yukon lay a mile wide and hidden under three feet of ice. On top of this ice were as many feet of snow. It was all pure white, rolling in gentle undulations where the ice-jams of the freeze-up had formed. North and south, as far as his eye could see, it was unbroken white, save for a dark hair-line that curved and twisted from around the spruce-covered island to the south, and that curved and twisted away into the north, where it disappeared behind another spruce-covered island. This dark hair-line was the trail—the main trail—that led south five hundred miles to the Chilkoot Pass, Dyea, and salt water; and that led north seventy miles to Dawson, and still on to the north a thousand miles to Nulato, and finally to St. Michael on Bering Sea, a thousand miles and half a thousand more.

But all this—the mysterious, far-reaching hair-line trail, the absence of sun from the sky, the tremendous cold, and the strangeness and weirdness of it all—made no impression on the man. It was not because he was long used to it. He was a newcomer in the land, a *chechaquo*, and this was his first winter. The trouble with him was that he was without imagination. He was quick and alert in the things of life, but only in the things, and not in the significances. Fifty degrees below zero meant eighty-odd degrees of frost. Such fact impressed him as being cold and uncomfortable, and that was all. It did not lead him to meditate upon his frailty as a creature of temperature, and upon man's frailty in general, able only to live within certain narrow limits of heat and cold; and from there on it did not lead him to the conjectural field of immortality and man's place in the universe. Fifty degrees below zero stood for a bite of frost that hurt and that must be guarded against by the use of mittens, ear-flaps, warm moccasins, and thick socks. Fifty degrees below zero was to him just precisely fifty degrees below zero. That there should be anything more to it than that was a thought that never entered his head.

As he turned to go on, he spat speculatively. There was a sharp, explosive crackle that startled him. He spat again. And again, in the air, before it could fall to the snow, the spittle crackled. He knew that at fifty below spittle crackled on the snow, but this spittle had crackled in the air. Undoubtedly it was colder than fifty below—how much colder he did not know. But the temperature did not matter. He was bound for the old claim on the left fork of Henderson Creek, where the boys were already. They had come over across the divide from the Indian Creek country, while he had come the roundabout way to take a look at the possibilities of getting out logs in the spring from the islands in the Yukon. He would be in to camp by six o'clock; a bit after dark, it was true, but the boys would be there, a fire would be going, and a hot supper would be ready. As for lunch, he pressed his hand against the protruding bundle under his jacket. It was also under his shirt, wrapped up in a handkerchief and lying against the naked skin. It was the only way to keep the biscuits from freezing. He smiled agreeably to himself as he thought of those biscuits, each cut open and sopped in bacon grease, and each enclosing a generous slice of fried bacon.

He plunged in among the big spruce trees. The trail was faint. A foot of snow had fallen since the last sled had passed over, and he was glad he was without a sled, travelling light. In fact, he carried nothing but the lunch wrapped in the handkerchief. He was surprised, however, at the cold. It certainly was cold, he concluded, as he rubbed his numb nose and cheek-bones with his mittened hand. He was a warm-whiskered man, but the hair on his face did not protect the high cheek-bones and the eager nose that thrust itself aggressively into the frosty air.

At the man's heels trotted a dog, a big native husky, the proper wolf-dog, grey-coated and without any visible or temperamental difference from its brother, the wild wolf. The animal was depressed by the tremendous cold. It knew that it was no time for travelling. Its instinct told it a truer tale than was told to the man by the man's judgment. In reality, it was not merely colder than fifty below zero; it was colder than sixty below, than seventy below. It was seventy-five below zero. Since the freezing-point is thirty-two above zero, it meant that one hundred and seven degrees of frost obtained. The dog did not know anything about thermometers. Possibly in its brain there was no sharp consciousness of a condition of very cold such as was in the man's brain. But the brute had its instinct. It experienced a vague but menacing apprehension that subdued it and made it slink along at the man's heels, and that made it question eagerly every unwonted movement of the man as if expecting him to go into camp or to seek shelter somewhere and build a fire. The dog had learned fire, and it wanted fire, or else to burrow under the snow and cuddle its warmth away from the air.

The frozen moisture of its breathing had settled on its fur in a fine powder of frost, and especially were its jowls, muzzle, and eyelashes whitened by its crystalled breath. The man's red beard and mustache were likewise frosted, but more solidly, the deposit taking the form of ice and increasing with every warm, moist breath he exhaled. Also, the man was chewing tobacco, and the muzzle of ice held his lips so rigidly that he was unable to clear his chin when he expelled the juice. The result was that a crystal beard of the color and solidity of amber was increasing its length on his chin. If he fell down it would shatter itself, like glass, into brittle fragments. But he did not mind the appendage. It was the penalty all tobacco-chewers paid in that country, and he had been out before in two cold snaps. They had not been so cold as this, he knew, but by the spirit thermometer at Sixty Mile he knew they had been registered at fifty below and at fifty-five.

He held on through the level stretch of woods for several miles, crossed a wide flat of nigger-heads, and dropped down a bank to the frozen bed of a small stream. This was Henderson Creek, and he knew he was ten miles from the forks. He looked at his watch. It was ten o'clock. He was making four miles an hour, and he calculated that he would arrive at the forks at half-past twelve. He decided to celebrate that event by eating his lunch there.

The dog dropped in again at his heels, with a tail drooping discouragement, as the man swung along the creek-bed. The furrow of the old sled-trail was plainly visible, but a dozen inches of snow covered the marks of the last runners. In a month no man had come up or down that silent creek. The man held steadily on. He was not much given to thinking, and just then particularly he had nothing to think about save that he would eat lunch at the forks and that at six o'clock he would be in camp with the boys. There was nobody to talk to; and, had there been, speech would have been impossible because of the ice-muzzle on his mouth. So he continued monotonously to chew tobacco and to increase the length of his amber beard.

Once in a while the thought reiterated itself that it was very cold and that he had never experienced such cold. As he walked along he rubbed his cheek-bones and nose with the back of his mittened hand. He did this automatically, now and again changing hands. But rub as he would, the instant he stopped his cheek-bones went numb, and the following instant the end of his nose went numb. He was sure to frost his cheeks; he knew that, and experienced a pang of regret that he had not devised a nose-strap of the sort Bud wore in cold snaps. Such a strap passed across the cheeks, as well, and saved them. But it didn't matter much, after all. What were frosted cheeks? A bit painful, that was all; they were never serious.

Empty as the man's mind was of thoughts, he was keenly observant, and he noticed the changes in the creek, the curves and bends and timber-jams, and always he sharply noted where he placed his feet. Once, coming around a bend, he shied abruptly, like a startled horse, curved away from the place where he had been walking, and retreated several paces back along the trail. The creek he knew was frozen clear to the bottom,—no creek could contain water in that arctic winter,—but he knew also that there were springs that bubbled out from the hillsides and ran along under the snow and on top the ice of the creek. He knew that the coldest snaps never froze these springs, and he knew likewise their danger. They were traps. They hid pools of water under the snow that might be three inches deep, or three feet. Sometimes a skin of ice half an inch thick covered them, and in turn was covered by the snow. Sometimes there were alternate layers of water and ice-skin, so that when one broke through he kept on breaking through for a while, sometimes wetting himself to the waist.

That was why he had shied in such panic. He had felt the give under his feet and heard the crackle of a snow-hidden ice-skin. And to get his feet wet in such a temperature meant trouble and danger. At the very least it meant delay, for he would be forced to stop and build a fire, and under its protection to bare his feet while he dried his socks and moccasins. He stood and studied the creek-bed and its banks, and decided that the flow of water came from the right. He reflected awhile, rubbing his nose and cheeks, then skirted to the left, stepping gingerly and testing the footing for each step. Once clear of the danger, he took a fresh chew of tobacco and swung along at his four-mile gait.

In the course of the next two hours he came upon several similar traps. Usually the snow above the hidden pools had a sunken, candied appearance that advertised the danger. Once again, however, he had a close call; and once, suspecting danger, he compelled the dog to go on in front. The dog did not want to go. It hung back until the man shoved it forward, and then it went quickly across the white, unbroken surface. Suddenly it broke through, floundered to one side, and got away to firmer footing. It had wet its forefeet and legs, and almost immediately the water that clung to it turned to ice. It made quick efforts to lick the ice off its legs, then dropped down in the snow and began to bite out the ice that had formed between the toes. This was a matter of instinct. To permit the ice to remain would mean sore feet. It did not know this. It merely obeyed the mysterious prompting that arose from the deep crypts of its being. But the man knew, having achieved a judgment on the subject, and he removed the mitten from his right hand and helped tear out the ice-particles. He did not expose his fingers more than a minute, and was astonished at the swift numbness that smote them. It certainly was cold. He pulled on the mitten hastily, and beat the hand savagely across his chest.

At twelve o'clock the day was at its brightest. Yet the sun was too far south on its winter journey to clear the horizon. The bulge of the earth intervened between it and Henderson Creek, where the man walked under a clear sky at noon and cast no shadow. At half-past twelve, to the minute, he arrived at the forks of the creek. He was pleased at the speed he had made. If he kept it up, he would certainly be with the boys by six. He unbuttoned his jacket and shirt and drew forth his lunch. The action consumed no more than a quarter of a minute, yet in that brief moment the numbness laid hold of the exposed fingers. He did not put the mitten on, but, instead, struck the fingers a dozen sharp smashes against his leg. Then he sat down on a snow-covered log to eat. The sting that followed upon the striking of his fingers against his leg ceased so quickly that he was startled. He had had no chance to take a bite of biscuit. He struck the fingers repeatedly and returned them to the mitten, baring the other hand for the purpose of eating. He tried to take a mouthful, but the ice-muzzle prevented. He had forgotten to build a fire and thaw out. He chuckled at his foolishness, and as he chuckled he noted the numbness creeping into the exposed fingers. Also, he noted that the stinging which had first come to his toes when he sat down was already passing away. He wondered whether the toes were warm or numb. He moved them inside the moccasins and decided that they were numb.

He pulled the mitten on hurriedly and stood up. He was a bit frightened. He stamped up and down until the stinging returned into the feet. It certainly was cold, was his thought. That man from Sulphur Creek had spoken the truth when telling how cold it sometimes got in the country. And he had laughed at him at the time! That showed one must not be too sure of things. There was no mistake about it, it *was* cold. He strode up and down, stamping his feet and threshing his arms, until reassured by the returning warmth. Then he got out matches and proceeded to make a fire. From the undergrowth, where high water of the previous spring had lodged a supply of seasoned twigs, he got his fire-wood. Working carefully from a small beginning, he soon had a roaring fire, over which he thawed the ice from his face and in the protection of which he ate his biscuits. For the moment the cold of space was outwitted. The dog took satisfaction in the fire, stretching out close enough for warmth and far enough away to escape being singed.

When the man had finished, he filled his pipe and took his comfortable time over a smoke. Then he pulled on his mittens, settled the earflaps of his cap firmly about his ears, and took the creek trail up the left fork. The dog was disappointed and yearned back toward the fire. This man did not know cold. Possibly all the generations of his ancestry had been ignorant of cold, of real cold, of cold one hundred and seven degrees below freezing-point. But the dog knew; all its ancestry knew, and it had inherited the knowledge. And it knew that it was not good to walk abroad in such fearful cold. It was the time to lie snug in a hole in the snow and wait for a curtain of cloud to be drawn across the face of outer space whence this cold came. On the other hand, there was no keen intimacy between the dog and the man. The one was the toil-slave of the other, and the only caresses it had ever received were the caresses of the whiplash and of harsh and menacing throat-sounds that threatened the whiplash. So the dog made no effort to communicate its apprehension to the man. It was not concerned in the welfare of the man; it was for its own sake that it yearned back toward the fire. But the man whistled, and spoke to it with the sound of whip-lashes, and the dog swung in at the man's heels and followed after.

The man took a chew of tobacco and proceeded to start a new amber beard. Also, his moist breath quickly powdered with white his mustache, eyebrows, and lashes. There did not seem to be so many springs on the left fork of the Henderson, and for half an hour the man saw no signs of any. And then it happened. At a place where there were no signs, where the soft, unbroken snow seemed to advertise solidity beneath, the man broke through. It was not deep. He wet himself halfway to the knees before he floundered out to the firm crust.

He was angry, and cursed his luck aloud. He had hoped to get into camp with the boys at six o'clock, and this would delay him an hour, for he would have to build a fire and dry out his foot-gear. This was imperative at that low temperature—he knew that much; and he turned aside to the bank, which he climbed. On top, tangled in the underbrush about the trunks of several small spruce trees, was a high-water deposit of dry fire-wood—sticks and twigs, principally, but also larger portions of seasoned branches and fine, dry, last-year's grasses. He threw down several large pieces on top of the snow. This served for a foundation and prevented the young flame from drowning itself in the snow it otherwise would melt. The flame he got by touching a match to a small shred of birch-bark that he took from his pocket. This burned even more readily than paper. Placing it on the foundation, he fed the young flame with wisps of dry grass and with the tiniest dry twigs.

He worked slowly and carefully, keenly aware of his danger. Gradually, as the flame grew stronger, he increased the size of the twigs with which he fed it. He squatted in the snow, pulling the twigs out from their entanglement in the brush and feeding directly to the flame. He knew there must be no failure. When it is seventy-five below zero, a man must not fail in his first attempt to build a fire—that is, if his feet are wet. If his feet are dry, and he fails, he can run along the trail for half a mile and restore his circulation. But the circulation of wet and freezing feet cannot be restored by running when it is seventy-five below. No matter how fast he runs, the wet feet will freeze the harder.

All this the man knew. The old-timer on Sulphur Creek had told him about it the previous fall, and now he was appreciating the advice. Already all sensation had gone out of his feet. To build the fire he had been forced to remove his mittens, and the fingers had quickly gone numb. His pace of four miles an hour had kept his heart pumping blood to the surface of his body and to all the extremities. But the instant he stopped, the action of the pump eased down. The cold of space smote the unprotected tip of the planet, and he, being on that unprotected tip, received the full force of the blow. The blood of his body recoiled before it. The blood was alive, like the dog, and like the dog it wanted to hide away and cover itself up from the fearful cold. So long as he walked four miles an hour, he pumped that blood, willy-nilly, to the surface; but now it ebbed away and sank down into the recesses of his body. The extremities were the first to feel its absence. His wet feet froze the faster, and his exposed fingers numbed the faster, though they had not yet begun to freeze. Nose and cheeks were already freezing, while the skin of his body chilled as it lost its blood.

But he was safe. Toes and nose and cheeks would be only touched by the frost, for the fire was beginning to burn with strength. He was feeding it with twigs the size of his finger. In another minute he would be able to feed it with branches the size of his wrist, and then he could remove his wet foot-gear, and, while it dried, he could keep his naked feet warm by the fire, rubbing them at first, of course, with snow. The fire was a success. He was safe. He remembered the advice of the old-timer on Sulphur Creek, and smiled. The old-timer had been very serious in laying down the law that no man must travel alone in the Klondike after fifty below. Well, here he was; he had had the accident; he was alone; and he had saved himself. Those old-timers were rather womanish, some of them, he thought. All a man had to do was to keep his head, and he was all right. Any man who was a man could travel alone. But it was surprising, the rapidity with which his cheeks and nose were freezing. And he had not thought his fingers could go lifeless in so short a time. Lifeless they were, for he could scarcely make them move together to grip a twig, and they seemed remote from his body and from him. When he touched a twig, he had to look and see whether or not he had hold of it. The wires were pretty well down between him and his finger-ends.

All of which counted for little. There was the fire, snapping and crackling and promising life with every dancing flame. He started to untie his moccasins. They were coated with ice; the thick German socks were like sheaths of iron halfway to the knees; and the moccasin strings were like rods of steel all twisted and knotted as by some conflagration. For a moment he tugged with his numb fingers, then, realizing the folly of it, he drew his sheath-knife.

But before he could cut the strings, it happened. It was his own fault or, rather, his mistake. He should not have built the fire under the spruce tree. He should have built it in the open. But it had been easier to pull the twigs from the brush and drop them directly on the fire. Now the tree under which he had done this carried a weight of snow on its boughs. No wind had blown for weeks, and each bough was fully freighted. Each time he had pulled a twig he had communicated a slight agitation to the tree—an imperceptible agitation, so far as he was concerned, but an agitation sufficient to bring about the disaster. High up in the tree one bough capsized its load of snow. This fell on the boughs beneath, capsizing them. This process continued, spreading out and involving the whole tree. It grew like an avalanche, and it descended without warning upon the man and the fire, and the fire was blotted out! Where it had burned was a mantle of fresh and disordered snow.

The man was shocked. It was as though he had just heard his own sentence of death. For a moment he sat and stared at the spot where the fire had been. Then he grew very calm. Perhaps the old-timer on Sulphur Creek was right. If he had only had a trail-mate he would have been in no danger now. The trail-mate could have built the fire. Well, it was up to him to build the fire over again, and this second time there must be no failure. Even if he succeeded, he would most likely lose some toes. His feet must be badly frozen by now, and there would be some time before the second fire was ready.

Such were his thoughts, but he did not sit and think them. He was busy all the time they were passing through his mind. He made a new foundation for a fire, this time in the open, where no treacherous tree could blot it out. Next, he gathered dry grasses and tiny twigs from the high-water flotsam. He could not bring his fingers together to pull them out, but he was able to gather them by the handful. In this way he got many rotten twigs and bits of green moss that were undesirable, but it was the best he could do. He worked methodically, even collecting an armful of the larger branches to be used later when the fire gathered strength. And all the while the dog sat and watched him, a certain yearning wistfulness in its eyes, for it looked upon him as the fire-provider, and the fire was slow in coming.

When all was ready, the man reached in his pocket for a second piece of birch-bark. He knew the bark was there, and, though he could not feel it with his fingers, he could hear its crisp rustling as he fumbled for it. Try as he would, he could not clutch hold of it. And all the time, in his consciousness, was the knowledge that each instant his feet were freezing. This thought tended to put him in a panic, but he fought against it and kept calm. He pulled on his mittens with his teeth, and threshed his arms back and forth, beating his hands with all his might against his sides. He did this sitting down, and he stood up to do it; and all the while the dog sat in the snow, its wolf-brush of a tail curled around warmly over its forefeet, its sharp wolf-ears pricked forward intently as it watched the man.

And the man, as he beat and threshed with his arms and hands, felt a great surge of envy as he regarded the creature that was warm and secure in its natural covering.

After a time he was aware of the first far-away signals of sensation in his beaten fingers. The faint tingling grew stronger till it evolved into a stinging ache that was excruciating, but which the man hailed with satisfaction. He stripped the mitten from his right hand and fetched forth the birch-bark. The exposed fingers were quickly going numb again. Next he brought out his bunch of sulphur matches. But the tremendous cold had already driven the life out of his fingers. In his effort to separate one match from the others, the whole bunch fell in the snow. He tried to pick it out of the snow, but failed. The dead fingers could neither touch nor clutch. He was very careful. He drove the thought of his freezing feet, and nose, and cheeks, out of his mind, devoting his whole soul to the matches. He watched, using the sense of vision in place of that of touch, and when he saw his fingers on each side the bunch, he closed them—that is, he willed to close them, for the wires were down, and the fingers did not obey. He pulled the mitten on the right hand, and beat it fiercely against his knee. Then, with both mittened hands, he scooped the bunch of matches, along with much snow, into his lap. Yet he was no better off.

After some manipulation he managed to get the bunch between the heels of his mittened hands. In this fashion he carried it to his mouth. The ice crackled and snapped when by a violent effort he opened his mouth. He drew the lower jaw in, curled the upper lip out of the way, and scraped the bunch with his upper teeth in order to separate a match. He succeeded in getting one, which he dropped on his lap. He was no better off. He could not pick it up. Then he devised a way. He picked it up in his teeth and scratched it on his leg. Twenty times he scratched before he succeeded in lighting it. As it flamed he held it with his teeth to the birch-bark. But the burning brimstone went up his nostrils and into his lungs, causing him to cough spasmodically. The match fell into the snow and went out.

The old-timer on Sulphur Creek was right, he thought in the moment of controlled despair that ensued: after fifty below, a man should travel with a partner. He beat his hands, but failed in exciting any sensation. Suddenly he bared both hands, removing the mittens with his teeth. He caught the whole bunch between the heels of his hands. His arm-muscles not being frozen enabled him to press the hand-heels tightly against the matches. Then he scratched the bunch along his leg. It flared into flame, seventy sulphur matches at once! There was no wind to blow them out. He kept his head to one side to escape the strangling fumes, and held the blazing bunch to the birch-bark. As he so held it, he became aware of sensation in his hand. His flesh was burning. He could smell it. Deep down below the surface he could feel it. The sensation developed into pain that grew acute. And still he endured it, holding the flame of the matches clumsily to the bark that would not light readily because his own burning hands were in the way, absorbing most of the flame.

At last, when he could endure no more, he jerked his hands apart. The blazing matches fell sizzling into the snow, but the birch-bark was alight. He began laying dry grasses and the tiniest twigs on the flame. He could not pick and choose, for he had to lift the fuel between the heels of his hands. Small pieces of rotten wood and green moss clung to the twigs, and he bit them off as well as he could with his teeth. He cherished the flame carefully and awkwardly. It meant life, and it must not perish. The withdrawal of blood from the surface of his body now made him begin to shiver, and he grew more awkward. A large piece of green moss fell squarely on the little fire. He tried to poke it out with his fingers, but his shivering frame made him poke too far, and he disrupted the nucleus of the little fire, the burning grasses and tiny twigs separating and scattering. He tried to poke them together again, but in spite of the tenseness of the effort, his shivering got away with him, and the twigs were hopelessly scattered. Each twig gushed a puff of smoke and went out. The fire-provider had failed. As he looked apathetically about him, his eyes chanced on the dog, sitting across the ruins of the fire from him, in the snow, making restless, hunching movements, slightly lifting one forefoot and then the other, shifting its weight back and forth on them with wistful eagerness.

The sight of the dog put a wild idea into his head. He remembered the tale of the man, caught in a blizzard, who killed a steer and crawled inside the carcass, and so was saved. He would kill the dog and bury his hands in the warm body until the numbness went out of them. Then he could build another fire. He spoke to the dog, calling it to him; but in his voice was a strange note of fear that frightened the animal, who had never known the man to speak in such way before. Something was the matter, and its suspicious nature sensed danger—it knew not what danger, but somewhere, somehow, in its brain arose an apprehension of the man. It flattened its ears down at the sound of the man's voice, and its restless, hunching movements and the liftings and shiftings of its forefeet became more pronounced; but it would not come to the man. He got on his hands and knees and crawled toward the dog. This unusual posture again excited suspicion, and the animal sidled mincingly away.

The man sat up in the snow for a moment and struggled for calmness. Then he pulled on his mittens, by means of his teeth, and got upon his feet. He glanced down at first in order to assure himself that he was really standing up, for the absence of sensation in his feet left him unrelated to the earth. His erect position in itself started to drive the webs of suspicion from the dog's mind; and when he spoke peremptorily, with the sound of whip-lashes in his voice, the dog rendered its customary allegiance and came to him. As it came within reaching distance, the man lost his control. His arms flashed out to the dog, and he experienced genuine surprise when he discovered that his hands could not clutch, that there was neither bend nor feeling in the fingers. He had forgotten for the moment that they were frozen and that they were freezing more and more. All this happened quickly, and before the animal could get away, he encircled its body with his arms. He sat down in the snow, and in this fashion held the dog, while it snarled and whined and struggled.

But it was all he could do, hold its body encircled in his arms and sit there. He realized that he could not kill the dog. There was no way to do it. With his helpless hands he could neither draw nor hold his sheath-knife nor throttle the animal. He released it, and it plunged wildly away, with tail between its legs, and still snarling. It halted forty feet away and surveyed him curiously, with ears sharply pricked forward. The man looked down at his hands in order to locate them, and found them hanging on the ends of his arms. It struck him as curious that one should have to use his eyes in order to find out where his hands were. He began threshing his arms back and forth, beating the mittened hands against his sides. He did this for five minutes, violently, and his heart pumped enough blood up to the surface to put a stop to his shivering. But no sensation was aroused in the hands. He had an impression that they hung like weights on the ends of his arms, but when he tried to run the impression down, he could not find it.

A certain fear of death, dull and oppressive, came to him. This fear quickly became poignant as he realized that it was no longer a mere matter of freezing his fingers and toes, or of losing his hands and feet, but that it was a matter of life and death with the chances against him. This threw him into a panic, and he turned and ran up the creek-bed along the old, dim trail. The dog joined in behind and kept up with him. He ran blindly, without intention, in fear such as he had never known in his life. Slowly, as he ploughed and floundered through the snow, he began to see things again,—the banks of the creek, the old timber-jams, the leafless aspens, and the sky. The running made him feel better. He did not shiver. Maybe, if he ran on, his feet would thaw out; and, anyway, if he ran far enough, he would reach camp and the boys. Without doubt he would lose some fingers and toes and some of his face; but the boys would take care of him, and save the rest of him when he got there. And at the same time there was another thought in his mind that said he would never get to the camp and the boys; that it was too many miles away, that the freezing had too great a start on him, and that he would soon be stiff and dead. This thought he kept in the background and refused to consider. Sometimes it pushed itself forward and demanded to be heard, but he thrust it back and strove to think of other things.

It struck him as curious that he could run at all on feet so frozen that he could not feel them when they struck the earth and took the weight of his body. He seemed to himself to skim along above the surface, and to have no connection with the earth. Somewhere he had once seen a winged Mercury, and he wondered if Mercury felt as he felt when skimming over the earth.

His theory of running until he reached camp and the boys had one flaw in it: he lacked the endurance. Several times he stumbled, and finally he tottered, crumpled up, and fell. When he tried to rise, he failed. He must sit and rest, he decided, and next time he would merely walk and keep on going. As he sat and regained his breath, he noted that he was feeling quite warm and comfortable. He was not shivering, and it even seemed that a warm glow had come to his chest and trunk. And yet, when he touched his nose or cheeks, there was no sensation. Running would not thaw them out. Nor would it thaw out his hands and feet. Then the thought came to him that the frozen portions of his body must be extending. He tried to keep this thought down, to forget it, to think of something else; he was aware of the panicky feeling that it caused, and he was afraid of the panic. But the thought asserted itself, and persisted, until it produced a vision of his body totally frozen. This was too much, and he made another wild run along the trail. Once he slowed down to a walk, but the thought of the freezing extending itself made him run again.

And all the time the dog ran with him, at his heels. When he fell down a second time, it curled its tail over its forefeet and sat in front of him, facing him, curiously eager and intent. The warmth and security of the animal angered him, and he cursed it till it flattened down its ears appeasingly. This time the shivering came more quickly upon the man. He was losing in his battle with the frost. It was creeping into his body from all sides. The thought of it drove him on, but he ran no more than a hundred feet, when he staggered and pitched headlong. It was his last panic. When he had recovered his breath and control, he sat up and entertained in his mind the conception of meeting death with dignity. However, the conception did not come to him in such terms. His idea of it was that he had been making a fool of himself, running around like a chicken with its head cut off—such was the simile that occurred to him. Well, he was bound to freeze anyway, and he might as well take it decently. With this new-found peace of mind came the first glimmerings of drowsiness. A good idea, he thought, to sleep off to death. It was like taking an anæsthetic. Freezing was not so bad as people thought. There were lots worse ways to die.

He pictured the boys finding his body next day. Suddenly he found himself with them, coming along the trail and looking for himself. And, still with them, he came around a turn in the trail and found himself lying in the snow. He did not belong with himself any more, for even then he was out of himself, standing with the boys and looking at himself in the snow. It certainly was cold, was his thought. When he got back to the States he could tell the folks what real cold was. He drifted on from this to a vision of the old-timer on Sulphur Creek. He could see him quite clearly, warm and comfortable, and smoking a pipe.

"You were right, old hoss; you were right," the man mumbled to the old-timer of Sulphur Creek.

Then the man drowsed off into what seemed to him the most comfortable and satisfying sleep he had ever known. The dog sat facing him and waiting. The brief day drew to a close in a long, slow twilight. There were no signs of a fire to be made, and, besides, never in the dog's experience had it known a man to sit like that in the snow and make no fire. As the twilight drew on, its eager yearning for the fire mastered it, and with a great lifting and shifting of forefeet, it whined softly, then flattened its ears down in anticipation of being chidden by the man. But the man remained silent. Later, the dog whined loudly. And still later it crept close to the man and caught the scent of death. This made the animal bristle and back away. A little longer it delayed, howling under the stars that leaped and danced and shone brightly in the cold sky. Then it turned and trotted up the trail in the direction of the camp it knew, where were the other food-providers and fire-providers.

SHERWOOD ANDERSON

[1876–1941]

THE ANDERSONS WERE ROVERS. The father, Irwin Anderson, whom his son fictionalized as "Windy McPherson," roamed restlessly through the Middle West—seven children were born in seven different towns. Sherwood Anderson was born September 13, 1876, in Camden, one of the smaller Ohio cities. He grew up in several other Ohio towns, with little schooling except for a brief term at Wittenberg College. He started to work before he was fourteen, drifted from one job to another, went to Cuba, where he served during the Spanish-American War, and returned to his native state. He married, became manager of a paint factory in Elyria, and seemed to settle down to comfortable middle-class existence.

Nearing forty, however, the family restlessness reasserted itself, and Anderson made a complete break with his past. It is said that, in the middle of writing a business letter, he had a sudden revulsion against the whole routine of life. He walked out of the room, slammed the door, and never returned to the office. Sympathetic friends claimed that it was a nervous breakdown; others, remembering Gauguin's abandonment of his family ties, considered it a typical artist's way of escaping responsibility.

Determined to be a writer, Anderson went to Chicago, where he was both influenced and encouraged by Theodore Dreiser and Carl Sandburg. His first semi-autobiographical book, Windy McPherson's Son, was followed by Marching Men and Winesburg, Ohio. With Winesburg, Ohio Anderson caught the attention of America by expressing its youth and uncertainties, its energy and lack of both vision and direction. Like D. H. Lawrence, he gave sex an almost mystical power and, also like Lawrence, he considered man's instinct a greater force than reason. However, his treatment of human behavior was generally naturalistic. The books written after his late forties—Poor White, The Triumph of the Egg, Many Marriages (Anderson was married four times), Horses and Men, Dark Laughter—are mainly about psychologically displaced people groping toward some sort of freedom.

Anderson's habit of wandering led him from the Middle West to New York, to Europe, to New Orleans, and to Virginia, where he spent the last seventeen years of his life writing and editing. He had so little passion for politics that he simultaneously edited two newspapers in

Marion, Virginia, one of them Republican and one Democratic. He was on his way to South America when, eating hors d'oeuvres, he swallowed part of a toothpick, which pierced the lining of his intestine. He was rushed to a hospital at Colon, Panama, where he died of peritonitis, March 8, 1941.

A naturalist who was also a mystic, Anderson asks questions about the way in which instinctual longings affect men and women perplexed by life and usually thwarted by it. During his lifetime his novels created something of a sensation; today it is conceded that his short stories are more characteristic of the man. Many of these stories are about his own boyhood; his confusion and timidity are touchingly portrayed in "I'm a Fool," perhaps his best known story.

I'M A FOOL

IT WAS A HARD JOLT for me, one of the most bitterest I ever had to face. And it all came about through my own foolishness, too. Even yet sometimes, when I think of it, I want to cry or swear or kick myself. Perhaps, even now, after all this time, there will be a kind of satisfaction in making myself look cheap by telling of it.

It began at three o'clock one October afternoon as I sat in the grandstand at the fall trotting and pacing meet a Sandusky, Ohio.

To tell the truth, I felt a little foolish that I should be sitting in the grandstand at all. During the summer before, I had left my home town with Harry Whitehead and, with a nigger named Burt, had taken a job as swipe with one of the two horses Harry was campaigning through the fall race meets that year. Mother cried and my sister Mildred, who wanted to get a job as a schoolteacher in our town that fall, stormed and scolded about the house all during the week before I left. They both thought it something disgraceful that one of our family should take a place as a swipe with race horses. I've an idea Mildred thought my taking the place would stand in the way of her getting the job she'd been working so long for.

But after all I had to work, and there was no other work to be got. A big lumbering fellow of nineteen couldn't just hang around the house, and I had got too big to mow people's lawns and sell newspapers. Little chaps who could get next to people's sympathies by their sizes were always getting jobs away from me. There was one fellow who kept saying to everyone who wanted a lawn mowed or a cistern cleaned, that he was saving money to work his way through college, and I used to lay awake nights thinking up ways to injure him without being found out. I kept thinking of wagons running over him and bricks falling on his head as he walked along the street. But never mind him.

I got the place with Harry and I liked Burt fine. We got along splendid together. He was a big nigger with a lazy sprawling body and soft, kind eyes, and when it came to a fight he could hit like Jack Johnson. He had Bucephalus, a big black pacing stallion that could do 2.09 or 2.10, if he had to, and I had a little gelding named Doctor Fritz that never lost a race all fall when Harry wanted him to win.

We set out from home late in July in a boxcar with the two horses; and after that, until late November, we kept moving along to the race meets and the fairs. It was a peachy time for me, I'll say that. Sometimes now I think that boys who are raised regular in houses, and never have a fine nigger like Burt for best friend, and go to high schools and college, and never steal anything, or get drunk a little, or learn to swear from fellows who know how, or come walking up in front of a grandstand in their shirt sleeves and with dirty horsey pants on when the races are going on and the grandstand is full of people all dressed up—What's the use of talking about it? Such fellows don't know nothing at all. They've never had no opportunity.

But I did. Burt taught me how to rub down a horse and put the bandages on after a race and steam a horse out and a lot of valuable things for any man to know. He could wrap a bandage on a horse's leg so smooth that if it had been the same color you would think it was his skin, and I guess he'd have been a big driver, too, and got to the top like Murphy and Walter Cox and the others if he hadn't been black.

Gee whizz, it was fun. You got to a county seat town, maybe say on a Saturday or Sunday, and the fair began the next Tuesday and lasted until Friday afternoon. Doctor Fritz would be, say, in the 2.25 trot on Tuesday afternoon, and on Thursday afternoon Bucephalus would knock 'em cold in the "free for all" pace. It left you a lot of time to hang around and listen to horse talk, and see Burt knock some yap cold that got too gay, and you'd find out about horses and men and pick up a lot of stuff you could use all the rest of your life, if you had some sense and salted down what you heard and felt and saw.

And then at the end of the week when the race meet was over, and Harry had run home to tend to his livery stable business, you and Burt hitched the two horses to carts and drove slow and steady across the country to the place for the next meeting, so as to not overheat the horses, etc., you know.

Gee whizz, Gosh amighty, the nice hickory nut and beechnut and oaks and other kinds of trees along the roads, all brown and red, and the good smells, and Burt singing a song that was called "Deep River," and the country girls at the windows of houses and everything. You can stick your colleges up your nose for all me. I guess I know where I got my education.

Why, one of those little burgs of towns you come to on the way, say now on a Saturday afternoon, and Burt says, "Let's lay up here." And you did.

And you took the horses to a livery stable and fed them, and you got your good clothes out of a box and put them on.

And the town was full of farmers gaping, because they could see you were race horse people, and the kids maybe never see a nigger before and was afraid and run away when the two of us walked down their main street.

And that was before prohibition and all that foolishness, and so you went into a saloon, the two of you, and all the yaps come and stood around, and there was always someone pretended he was horsey and knew things and spoke up and began asking questions, and all you did was to lie and lie all you could about what horses you had, and I said I owned them, and then some fellow said "Will you have a drink of whisky?" and Burt knocked his eye out the way he could say, offhand like, "Oh, well, all right, I'm agreeable to a little nip. I'll split a quart with you." Gee whizz.

But that isn't what I want to tell my story about. We got home late in November and I promised mother I'd quit the race horses for good. There's a lot of things you've got to promise a mother because she don't know any better.

And so, there not being any work in our town any more than when I left there to go to the races, I went off to Sandusky and got a pretty good place taking care of horses for a man who owned a teaming and delivery and storage and coal and real estate business there. It was a pretty good place with good eats, and a day off each week, and sleeping on a cot in a big barn, and mostly just shoveling in hay and oats to a lot of big good-enough skates of horses that couldn't have trotted a race with a toad. I wasn't dissatisfied and I could send money home.

And then, as I started to tell you, the fall races come to Sandusky and I got the day off and I went. I left the job at noon and had on my good clothes and my new brown derby hat, I'd just bought the Saturday before, and a stand-up collar.

First of all I went downtown and walked about with the dudes. I've always thought to myself, "Put up a good front," and so I did it. I had forty dollars in my pocket and so I went into the West House, a big hotel, and walked up to the cigar stand. "Give me three twenty-five cent cigars," I said. There was a lot of horsemen and strangers and dressed-up people from other towns standing around in the lobby and in the bar, and I mingled amongst them. In the bar there was a fellow with a cane and a Windsor tie on, that it made me sick to look at him. I like a man to be a man and dress up, but not to go put on that kind of airs. So I pushed him aside, kind of rough, and had me a drink of whisky. And then he looked at me, as though he thought maybe he'd get gay, but he changed his mind and didn't say anything. And then I had another drink of whisky, just to show him something, and went out and had a hack out to the races, all to myself, and when I got there I bought myself the best seat I could get, up in the grandstand, but didn't go in for any of those boxes. That's putting on too many airs.

And so there I was, sitting up in the grandstand as gay as you please and looking down on the swipes coming out with their horses, and with their dirty horsey pants on and the horse blankets swung over their shoulders, same as I had been doing all the year before. I liked one thing about the same as the other, sitting up there and feeling grand and being down there and looking up at the yaps and feeling grander and more important, too. One thing's about as good as another, if you take it just right. I've often said that.

Well, right in front of me, in the grandstand that day, there was a fellow with a couple of girls and they was about my age. The young fellow was a nice guy all right. He was the kind maybe that goes to college and then comes to be a lawyer or maybe a newspaper editor or something like that, but he wasn't stuck on himself. There are some of that kind are all right and he was one of the ones.

He had his sister with him and another girl, and the sister looked around over his shoulder, accidental at first, not intending to start anything—she wasn't that kind—and her eyes and mine happened to meet.

You know how it is. Gee, she was a peach! She had on a soft dress, kind of a blue stuff and it looked carelessly made, but was well sewed and made and everything. I knew that much. I blushed when she looked right at me and so did she. She was the nicest girl I've ever seen in my life. She wasn't stuck on herself and she could talk proper grammar without being like a schoolteacher or something like that. What I mean is, she was O.K. I think maybe her father was well-to-do, but not rich to make her chesty because she was his daughter, as some are. Maybe he owned a drugstore or a dry-goods store in their home town, or something like that. She never told me and I never asked.

My own people are all O.K. too, when you come to that. My grandfather was Welsh and over in the old country, in Wales he was—But never mind that.

The first heat of the first race come off and the young fellow setting there with the two girls left them and went down to make a bet. I knew what he was up to, but he didn't talk big and noisy and let everyone around know he was a sport, as some do. He wasn't that kind. Well, he came back and I heard him tell the two girls what horse he'd bet on, and when the heat was trotted they all half got to their feet and acted in the excited, sweaty way people do when they've got money down on a race, and the horse they bet on is up there pretty close at the end, and they think maybe he'll come on with a rush, but he never does because he hasn't got the old juice in him, come right down to it.

And then, pretty soon, the horses came out for the 2.18 pace and there was a horse in it I knew. He was a horse Bob French had in his string but Bob didn't own him. He was a horse owned by a Mr. Mathers down at Marietta, Ohio.

This Mr. Mathers had a lot of money and owned some coal mines or something, and he had a swell place out in the country, and he was stuck on race horses, but was a Presbyterian or something, and I think more than likely his wife was one, too, maybe a stiffer one than himself. So he never raced his horses hisself, and the story round the Ohio race tracks was that when one of his horses got ready to go to the races he turned him over to Bob French and pretended to his wife he was sold.

So Bob had the horses and he did pretty much as he pleased and you can't blame Bob—at least, I never did. Sometimes he was out to win and sometimes he wasn't. I never cared much about that when I was swiping a horse. What I did want to know was that my horse had the speed and could go out in front, if you wanted him to.

And, as I'm telling you, there was Bob in this race with one of Mr. Mathers' horses, was named "About Ben Ahem" or something like that, and was fast as a streak. He was a gelding and had a mark of 2.21, but could step in 0.8 or 0.9.

Because when Burt and I were out, as I've told you, the year before, there was a nigger Burt knew, worked for Mr. Mathers and we went out there one day when we didn't have no race on at the Marietta Fair and our boss Harry was gone home.

And so everyone was gone to the fair but just this one nigger and he took us all through Mr. Mathers' swell house and he and Burt tapped a bottle of wine Mr. Mathers had hid in his bedroom, back in a closet, without his wife knowing, and he showed us this Ahem horse. Burt was always stuck on being a driver but didn't have much chance to get to the top, being a nigger, and he and the other nigger gulped that whole bottle of wine and Burt got a little lit up.

So the nigger let Burt take this About Ben Ahem and step him a mile in a track Mr. Mathers had all to himself, right there on the farm. And Mr. Mathers had one child, a daughter, kinda sick and not very good-looking, and she came home and we had to hustle and get About Ben Ahem stuck back in the barn.

I'm only telling you to get everything straight. At Sandusky, that afternoon I was at the fair, this young fellow with the two girls was fussed, being with the girls and losing his bet. You know how a fellow is that way. One of them was his girl and the other his sister. I had figured that out.

"Gee whizz," I says to myself, "I'm going to give him the dope."

He was mighty nice when I touched him on the shoulder. He and the girls were nice to me right from the start and clear to the end. I'm not blaming them.

And so he leaned back and I give him the dope on About Ben Ahem. "Don't bet a cent on this first heat because he'll go like an oxen hitched to a plow, but when the first heat is over go right down and lay on your pile." That's what I told him.

Well, I never saw a fellow treat anyone sweller. There was a fat man sitting beside the little girl, that had looked at me twice by this time, and I at her, and both blushing, and what did he do but have the nerve to turn and ask the fat man to get up and change places with me so I could set with his crowd.

Gee whizz, craps amighty. There I was. What a chump I was to go and get gay up there in the West House bar, and just because that dude was standing there with a cane and that kind of a necktie on, to go and get all balled up and drink that whisky, just to show off.

Of course she would know, me setting right beside her and letting her smell of my breath. I could have kicked myself right down out of that grandstand and all around that race track and made a faster record than most of the skates of horses they had there that year.

Because that girl wasn't any mutt of a girl. What wouldn't I have give right then for a stick of chewing gum to chew, or a lozenger, or some licorice, or most anything. I was glad I had those twenty-five cent cigars in my pocket and right away I give that fellow one and lit one myself.

Then that fat man got up and we changed places and there I was, plunked right down beside her.

They introduced themselves and the fellow's best girl, he had with him, was named Miss Elinor Woodbury, and her father was a manufacturer of barrels from a place called Tiffin, Ohio. And the fellow himself was named Wilbur Wessen and his sister was Miss Lucy Wessen.

I suppose it was their having such swell names got me off my trolley. A fellow, just because he has been a swipe with a race horse, and works taking care of horses for a man in the teaming, delivery, and storage business, isn't any better or worse than anyone else. I've often thought that, and said it too.

But you know how a fellow is. There's something in that kind of nice clothes, and the kind of nice eyes she had, and the way she had looked at me, awhile before, over her brother's shoulder, and me looking back at her, and both of us blushing.

I couldn't show her up for a boob, could I?

I made a fool of myself, that's what I did. I said my name was Walter Mathers from Marietta, Ohio, and then I told all three of them the smashingest lie you ever heard. What I said was that my father owned the horse About Ben Ahem and that he had let him out to this Bob French for racing purposes, because our family was proud and had never gone into racing that way, in our own name, I mean. Then I had got started and they were all leaning over and listening, and Miss Lucy Wessen's eyes were shining, and I went the whole hog.

I told about our place down at Marietta, and about the big stables and the grand brick house we had on a hill, up above the Ohio River, but I knew enough not to do it in no bragging way. What I did was to start things and then let them drag the rest out of me. I acted just as reluctant to tell as I could. Our family hasn't got any barrel factory, and, since I've known us, we've always been pretty poor, but not asking anything of anyone at that, and my grandfather, over in Wales—but never mind that.

We set there talking like we had known each other for years and years, and I went and told them that my father had been expecting maybe this Bob French wasn't on the square, and had sent me up to Sandusky on the sly to find out what I could.

And I bluffed it through I had found out all about the 2.18 pace, in which About Ben Ahem was to start.

I said he would lose the first heat by pacing like a lame cow and then he would come back and skin 'em alive after that. And to back up what I said I took thirty dollars out of my pocket and handed it to Mr. Wilbur Wessen and asked him, would he mind, after the first heat, to go down and place it on About Ben Ahem for whatever odds he could get. What I said was that I didn't want Bob French to see me and none of the swipes.

Sure enough the first heat come off and About Ben Ahem went off his stride, up the back stretch, and looked like a wooden horse or a sick one, and come in to be last. Then this Wilbur Wessen went down to the betting place under the grandstand and there I was with the two girls, and when that Miss Woodbury was looking the other way once, Lucy Wessen kinda, with her shoulder you know, kinda touched me. Not just tucking down, I don't mean. You know how a woman can do. They get close, but not getting gay either. You know what they do. Gee whizz.

And then they give me a jolt. What they had done, when I didn't know, was to get together, and they had decided Wilbur Wessen would bet fifty dollars, and the two girls had gone and put in ten dollars each, of their own money, too. I was sick then, but I was sicker later.

About the gelding, About Ben Ahem, and their winning their money, I wasn't worried a lot about that. It come out O.K. Ahem stepped the next three heats like a bushel of spoiled eggs going to market before they could be found out, and Wilber Wessen had got nine to two for the money. There was something else eating at me.

Because Wilbur came back, after he had bet the money, and after that he spent most of his time talking to that Miss Woodbury, and Lucy Wessen and I was left alone together like on a desert island. Gee, if I'd only been on the square or if there had been any way of getting myself on the square. There ain't any Walter Mathers, like I said to her and them, and there hasn't ever been one, but if there was, I bet I'd go to Marietta, Ohio, and shoot him tomorrow.

There I was, big boob that I am. Pretty soon the race was over, and Wilbur had gone down and collected our money, and we had a hack downtown, and he stood us a swell supper at the West House, and a bottle of champagne beside.

And I was with that girl and she wasn't saying much, and I wasn't saying much either. One thing I know. She wasn't stuck on me because of the lie about my father being rich and all that. There's a way you know. . . . Craps amighty. There's a kind of girl, you see just once in your life, and if you don't get busy and make hay, then you're gone for good and all, and might as well go jump off a bridge. They give you a look from inside of them somewhere, and it ain't no vamping, and what it means is—you want that girl to be your wife, and you want nice things around her like flowers and swell clothes, and you want her to have the kids you're going to have, and you want good music played and no ragtime. Gee whizz.

There's a place over near Sandusky, across a kind of bay, and it's called Cedar Point. And after we had supper we went over to it in a launch, all by ourselves. Wilbur and Miss Lucy and that Miss Woodbury had to catch a ten o'clock train back to Tiffin, Ohio, because, when you're out with girls like that you can't get careless and miss any trains and stay out all night, like you can with some kinds of Janes.

And Wilbur blowed himself to the launch and it cost him fifteen cold punks, but I wouldn't never have knew if I hadn't listened. He wasn't no tin horn kind of a sport.

Over at the Cedar Point place, we didn't stay around where there was a gang of common kind of cattle at all.

There was big dance halls and dining places for yaps, and there was a beach you could walk along and get where it was dark, and we went there.

She didn't talk hardly at all and neither did I, and I was thinking how glad I was my mother was all right, and always made us kids learn to eat with a fork at table, and not swill soup, and not be noisy and rough like a gang you see around a race track that way.

Then Wilbur and his girl went away up the beach and Lucy and I sat down in a dark place, where there was some roots of old trees, the water had washed up, and after that the time, till we had to go back in the launch and they had to catch their trains, wasn't nothing at all. It went like winking your eye.

Here's how it was. The place we were setting in was dark, like I said, and there was the roots from that old stump sticking up like arms, and there was a watery smell, and the night was like—as if you could put your hand out and feel it—so warm and soft and dark and sweet like an orange.

I most cried and I most swore and I most jumped up and danced, I was so mad and happy and sad.

When Wilbur come back from being alone with his girl, and she saw him coming, Lucy she says, "We got to go to the train now," and she was most crying too, but she never knew nothing I knew, and she couldn't be so all busted up. And then, before Wilbur and Miss Woodbury got up to where we was, she put her face up and kissed me quick and put her head up against me and she was all quivering and—Gee whizz.

Sometimes I hope I have cancer and die. I guess you know what I mean. We went in the launch across the bay to the train like that, and it was dark, too. She whispered and said it was like she and I could get out of the boat and walk on the water, and it sounded foolish, but I knew what she meant.

And then quick we were right at the depot, and there was a big gang of yaps, the kind that goes to the fairs, and crowded and milling around like cattle, and how could I tell her? "It won't be long because you'll write and I'll write to you." That's all she said.

I got a chance like a hay barn afire. A swell chance I got.

And maybe she would write me, down at Marietta that way, and the letter would come back, and stamped on the front of it by the U.S.A. "There ain't any such guy," or something like that, whatever they stamp on a letter that way.

And me trying to pass myself off for a big bug and a swell—to her, as decent a little body as God ever made. Craps amighty—a swell chance I got!

And then the train come in, and she got on it, and Wilbur Wessen he come and shook hands with me, and that Miss Woodbury was nice too and bowed to me, and I at her, and the train went and I busted out and cried like a kid.

Gee, I could have run after that train and made Dan Patch look like a freight train after a wreck but, socks amighty, what was the use? Did you ever see such a fool?

I'll bet you what—if I had an arm broke right now or a train had run over my foot—I wouldn't go to no doctor at all. I'd go set down and let her hurt and hurt—that's what I'd do.

I'll bet you what—if I hadn't a drunk that booze I'd a never been such a boob as to go tell such a lie—that couldn't never be made straight to a lady like her.

I wish I had that fellow right here that had on a Windsor tie and carried a cane. I'd smash him for fair. Gosh darn his eyes. He's a big fool—that's what he is.

And if I'm not another you just go find me one and I'll quit working and be a bum and give him my job. I don't care nothing for working, and earning money, and saving it for no such boob as myself.

NATIVES AND NEWCOMERS

FROM THE BEGINNING *of history there have been records of conflicts between Town and Country, Native and Newcomer, Villager and Visitor. The traditional feud has been shortened and reduced to the absurd in little dialogs, which, usually, are little more than two-line jokes. In the brief exchange of hostilities the countryman always has the last—and winning—word.*

The following examples, said to have originated Down East, have been adopted as local retorts all over America.

"Hey, old settler, where does this darn road go?"
"It don't go nowhere. Stays right here."

*

"Have you really lived in this tumble-down shack all your life?"
"Nope. Not yet."

*

"That Boston politician has been orating for half an hour. What's he talking about?"
"He ain't said."

*

"How far is it to the next town?"
"Don't know. Never measured it."
"How long will it take me to get there?"
"Don't know. How fast do you walk?"
"You don't know much, do you?"
"No. But I know I ain't lost."

*

"Can I take this road back to New York?"
"Why not? You city-folks have taken everything else."

*

"How many miles is it to Manchester?"
"In the direction you're goin', about fifty thousand."

*

"How much money did old man Williams leave?"
"All of it."

*

"When's the next train to town?"
"It left an hour ago."

"What's the best way out of this godforsaken hole to get me to Boston?"
"Mister, if I was you, I wouldn't start from here."

*

"You farmers certainly could use some rain, couldn't you?"
"Yup."
"It hasn't rained for a long time, has it?"
"Nope."
"Do you think it's ever going to rain?"
"Be an awful dry spell if it don't."

REGIONAL MAXIMS

There's no cure for the disease known as old age.

*

If you jump at the moon you may fall in the mud.

*

The higher they fly, the lower they fall.

*

When angry count ten; when furious count a hundred.

*

The best answer to a fool is silence.

*

Man is the one animal that can be skinned more than once.

*

The sweetest apples are on the top of the tree or on the other side of the wall.

*

Anger is a stone thrown into a hornet's nest.

You never miss the water till the well runs dry.

*

When you argue with a fool make sure that he is not doing the same.

*

Too smart for his age, too big for his britches.

*

Ask me no questions, I'll tell you no lies.

*

Go to bed with a dog, you'll wake up with fleas.

*

A person with butter-fingers should not climb ropes.

*

Spare the rod and spoil the child.

*

In every land, in every weather,
Birds of a feather flock together.

THE LAST LAUGH

MANY PEOPLE THINK OF DEATH *with anguish, fear and terror, but almost as many look on man's final catastrophe with equanimity. Some even regard the grave with levity—there are thousands of tombstones whose carved inscriptions attest that men enjoy having not only the last word but also the last laugh. Most epitaphs are merely factual; others are pious; but a study of American cemeteries reveals an unsuspected range of fancy, from light whimsicality to broad and sometimes bitter humor.*

Perhaps the most profound and playful as well as the most whimsical of epitaphs is the one that Benjamin Franklin (who was as proud of being a printer as he was of being a statesman) wrote for himself:

The Body of Benjamin Franklin,
Printer,
Like the Covering of an old Book,
Its Contents torn out,
And stript of its Lettering and Gilding,
Lies here, Food for Worms;
But the Work shall not be lost,
It will (as he believes) appear once more,
In a new and more beautiful Edition,
Corrected and Amended
By the Author.

A later American personality caused even more comment in his day than did Benjamin Franklin. His body was brought back East, and the inscription on a tablet outside of Whittingham, Vermont, has made many a tourist lift a critical or at least a quizzical eyebrow.

Brigham Young
Born in this spot in 1801
A man of much courage and superb equipment

The man who was the most prominent if not the most reputable of bad men, Jesse James, was glorified as the "American Robin Hood," who also supposedly "robbed the rich and gave to the poor." Ballads were sung in Jesse James' honor, and his mother memorialized the scornful lines about his betrayal by a member of his band:

Murdered by a Traitor and a Coward
Whose Name is not Worthy to Appear Here

Brevity is proverbially the soul of wit, especially on a gravestone. Probably the shortest epitaph is the one about a workhouse pauper. It contains just two grim syllables:

Thorpe's
Corpse

Although not quite as terse, many inscriptions are both concise and irreverent. In the days of the California Gold Rush an unfortunate and unknown gambler received this brusque adieu:

He called Ed Smith a liar.

Another shooting affair is commemorated in a sentence which, because of a misplaced phrase, twists a tribute into absurdity:

To the Memory
of
Abraham Beaulieu
Born 15 September 1822
Accidentally shot 4th April 1844
As a mark of affection
from his brother

There seems to be an entire school of Graveyard Poets. The love of rhyme has occasioned many sentiments which started out to be heart-rending but ended in unintentional humor. For example:

Under this sod lies Johnny Round
Who was lost at sea and was never found.

*

To all my friends I bid adieu;
A more sudden death you never knew.
As I was leading the old mare to drink,
She kicked and killed me quicker'n a wink.

The obituary poet seems to have been particularly pleased with himself when he combined poetry with plays on words. Names of the deceased offered a special opportunity for puns. Among the hundreds of punning epitaphs the following are memorable:

Here lies a certain Elizabeth Mann
Who lived an old maid and died an old Mann.

Under this sod and under these trees
Is buried the body of Solomon Pease.
But here in his hole lies only his pod;
His soul is shelled out and gone up to God.

Here lies, free from blood and slaughter,
Once Underwood—now under water.

The epitaph to Captain Underwood who, like Johnny Round, met his death by drowning, is a kind of Irish bull. Another absurdity was engraved on the tombstone of another soldier. A tragic event was made ridiculous when the stonecutter took a phrase from the Bible and put it in the wrong place:

Sacred to the memory of Major Bush,
Killed by the chance Discharge of a Pistol
By his Orderly.
Well done, Good and Faithful Servant.

It is said that Strange Creek, West Virginia, got its name from a surveyor, William Strange, who, separated from his companions, was found dead near a tree on which he had carved this couplet:

Strange is my name and I'm on strange ground;
Strange it is I can't be found.

According to Charles L. Wallis, who compiled a book of American Epitaphs, Stories on Stone, *this incredible epitaph was found in a cemetery in Girard, Pennsylvania:*

In memory of
Ellen Shannon
Aged 26 Years
Who was fatally burned
March 21st 1870
by the explosion of a lamp
filled with "R. E. Danforth's
Non Explosive
Burning Fluid"

Wallis also quotes two epitaphs in which the stonecutter made a typographical error. Wallis implies that the first, a variation on the much-used phrase "My glass is run," may have been a purposeful joke.

My glass is Rum

*

Lord, she is Thin

Puns seem to prevail when verse is employed. It is not known whether dentists' patients and landlords' victims had anything to do with the following curt disposals; but there can be no doubt that they would have relished them.

Stranger, approach this spot with gravity;
John Brown is filling his last cavity.

*

Here lies Richard Dent
In his cheapest tenement.

Many twentieth-century authors have facetiously suggested epitaphs for themselves. Dorothy Parker recommended this modest line for her remains: "Excuse my dust." Pearl Buck's publisher suggested that the Nobel Prize winner might have over her turf a line which incorporates the title of her most outstanding book: "Here lies Pearl Buck's Good Earth." A fellow-poet supplied Ogden Nash with a not inappropriate epitaph:

Nash's
Ashes

The stony jests are not subtle and the chuckle is brief, but it is unquestionably the last laugh that lasts.

VOICES OF OUR TIME

VOICES OF OUR TIME

The first half of the twentieth century saw more changes, more violent upheavals, and more technological progress than any previous thousand years. A new awareness of man's unknown potentialities and nature's untapped forces upset all earlier knowledge of the natural world. A stone was just a stone, a lifeless bit of matter, until modern science discovered the energy within the atom and found a way of releasing its stupendous power. Man's ageless dream of flying finally was fulfilled. Today jet liners streak across continents and oceans—yet the era of controlled flight dates only from 1903 when the Wrights at Kitty Hawk managed to get their heavier-than-air machine into the air and kept it there for three and a half seconds.

However, from their inception the benefits of an age of automation were offset by a distrust of those mechanical marvels which had in them the power either to make over or to destroy the world. New concepts of the organization (and disorganization) of matter, the use of electronics in commerce and communication, the possibility of living in outer space, the significance of man's role in an expanding universe—all these were scarcely less revolutionary and unsettling than man's new image of himself and his efforts to explain his deeds and desires in terms of a continual struggle between his disciplined conduct as a member of the community and his hidden, usually lawless, impulses. He had gradually to accept the fact that his reasoning self is not the master but merely guardian of his instinctive drives.

This was the background for twentieth-century thought. If it was not expressed directly, it was reflected in the tense and searching writing of the period. Two major wars and a subsequent "cold war," which was no substitute for a genuine peace, brought about universal bewilderment and anxiety. The loss of old faiths, the unhappy adjustment to a lack of ideals, and a groping toward new values characterized literature as well as life in the troubled twentieth century. Nevertheless, there were hopeful portents. There was among the artists as great a passion to experiment and to probe new methods of communication as among the scientists. Never before had there been a more determined or desperate search for essential truth behind superficial "reality," for the power to see, as Blake said, not merely with but through the eye.

With the beginning of the twentieth century the arts in America took on fresh vitality. Moreover, they became pronouncedly and definitely American. American architecture, thanks to the pioneering work of Louis Sullivan and Frank Lloyd Wright, not only stressed strength and simplification by eliminating foreign irrelevances, but also emphasized form and function through a style shaped in native earth, stone, and steel. American music, variously expressed by the neoromanticism of Aaron Copland and the dynamic use of "blues," dance tunes, and other surprises by George Gershwin, quickened pulses with rhythms which never before had been taken seriously. American painting ranged from the realistic transcriptions of John Sloan, Robert Henri, George Bellows, and other members of the "Ashcan School" through the stylized regionalism of Grant Wood and Thomas Hart Benton to the stark abstractions of Jackson Pollock and Stuart Davis. American literature came of age and covered an incredible panorama. It ranged from the extreme of convention to the limit of revolt; expressing every variety of experimentation, it kept pace with the ever-increasing speed of change.

Europe, which had always regarded the arts in America with their polite condescension, suddenly recognized their vigor and viability. In a special number in November, 1959, the London Times Literary Supplement wrote, "It is true to say that the flowering of the American imagination has been the chief event in the sphere of living art since the end of the First World War . . . It has become the most powerful stream of Western thought and culture . . . We in Europe today take the vitality of the arts in America so much for granted that we seldom pause to assess it for the remarkable phenomenon that it is."

Illustrated by the poems and the short stories that some have considered our major literary achievement, it is this phenomenon which is exemplified in the pages that follow.

ROBERT FROST

[1875–]

THE LIFE AND WORK of Robert Frost present a peculiar study in opposites. Frost is the most profound as well as the most playful of modern poets. He uses a colloquial language with straightforward speech rhythms and turns it not only into dramatic monologues but also into eloquent little lyrics. He is a so called "nature poet" but, instead of offering pretty pastorals, he examines nature with a careful scrutiny that is not without skepticism. Simple on the surface, his poetry has a way of suggesting subtle and even metaphysical depths. The voice so seemingly regional in style and accent is full of universal meanings. Frost's very origin is a kind of paradox. Acclaimed as "the poet of contemporary New England," he was born in San Francisco, California, March 26, 1875.

Frost's father had been a "copperhead," sympathetic to the South, and young Frost inherited his father's nonconformist traits. He resisted a formal education; although he entered Dartmouth at seventeen, he remained there only three months. Four years later he tried college again, this time at Harvard, but after two years he quit again. He had been working since he was twelve. His father had died of tuberculosis when his son was ten, and, before he was twenty, Robert had been a piece-worker in a shoe shop, bobbin boy in a textile mill, reporter and column writer for a local newspaper. At twenty-one he married his high-school sweetheart, who had also been his co-valedictorian. They had six children, only two of whom were living when Eleanor Frost died in 1938.

Frost was nineteen when a poem of his was published in The Independent but, though this magazine printed six more of Frost's poems during the next fourteen years, no other periodical or publisher showed any interest in his kind of poetry. Frost was almost forty when his first book, A Boy's Will, was printed. It is part of the paradox that the book was published in England rather than in America.

Frost had gone to England for various reasons. He had tried teaching but feared being committed to it; he had tried farming but had been defeated by a stubborn soil that yielded little. The English critics were kind to A Boy's Will: it was praised by such poets as Rupert Brooke, Lascelles Abercrombie, and Edward Thomas, who dedicated his first book of poems to Frost. The general response was cordial but not considerable.

It was his second book, North of Boston*—also published in England —which made Frost a celebrity. America suddenly discovered him; critics who had barely noticed his first book outdid each other in enthusiasm; college after college bid to have him on its campus. After his return to America he became "poet in residence" at the University of Michigan and, later, was on the staffs of Dartmouth and Amherst Colleges. By the time he was seventy he had published a dozen volumes, including two plays, had received honorary degrees from about thirty universities, had won the Gold Medal of the National Institute of Arts and Letters, and had been the only poet to be awarded the Pulitzer Prize four times.*

At eighty-five Frost still continued to write homespun monologues and lyrics of everyday life, causing critics to compare him again and again with Wordsworth. The later poems speculated on the immediate and ultimate destiny of man, sounding the heights of quiet rapture and the depths of isolation. Employing for the most part the vocabulary of the average man, Frost made poetry talk as well as sing, and struck a balance between pathos and shrewdness. Nowhere in previous American poetry had there been so curious a combination of wisdom and whimsicality, of—as Frost himself wrote of E. A. Robinson—"outer seriousness and inner humor." The beginnings of many of his poems have the charm of being both alluring and provocative. For example:

Something there is that doesn't love a wall . . .

My long two-pointed ladder's sticking through a tree
Toward heaven still . . .

The city had withdraw into itself
And left at last the country to the country . . .

There was never a sound beside the wood but one,
And that was my long scythe whispering to the ground . . .

Having a wheel and four legs of its own
Has never availed the cumbersome grindstone
To get it anywhere that I can see . . .

When I see birches bend to left and right
Across the line of straighter darker trees,
I like to think some boy's been swinging them . . .

I have been one acquainted with the night . . .

Blood has been harder to dam back than water.
Just when we think we have it impounded safe

Behind new barrier walls (and let it chafe!)
It breaks away in some new kind of slaughter . . .

Although Frost resents being thought of as an academician, he is a born teacher. He has compared the way in which scholars and poets come by their knowledge: "Scholars get theirs with conscientious thoroughness along projected lines of logic; poets get theirs cavalierly . . . They stick to nothing deliberately, but let what will stick to them like burrs when they walk in the field." Speaking of the poetic process he wrote to a friend: "A poem is never a put-up job so to speak. It begins as a lump in the throat, a sense of wrong, a homesickness, a lovesickness. It is never a thought to begin with . . . It finds its thought, or makes its thought . . . It finds the thought, and then the thought finds the words." Frost's poems are a fulfillment of this process. They are the essence of living poetry, "words that have become deeds."

THE PASTURE

I'm going out to clean the pasture spring;
I'll only stop to rake the leaves away
(And wait to watch the water clear, I may):
I shan't be gone long.—You come too.

I'm going out to fetch the little calf
That's standing by the mother. It's so young,
It totters when she licks it with her tongue.
I shan't be gone long.—You come too.

MENDING WALL

Something there is that doesn't love a wall,
That sends the frozen-ground-swell under it,
And spills the upper bowlders in the sun;
And makes gaps even two can pass abreast.
The work of hunters is another thing:
I have come after them and made repair
Where they have left not one stone on a stone,
But they would have the rabbit out of hiding,

To please the yelping dogs. The gaps I mean,
No one has seen them made or heard them made,
But at spring mending-time we find them there.
I let my neighbor know beyond the hill;
And on a day we meet to walk the line
And set the wall between us once again.
We keep the wall between us as we go.
To each the bowlders that have fallen to each.
And some are loaves and some so nearly balls
We have to use a spell to make them balance:
"Stay where you are until our backs are turned!"
We wear our fingers rough with handling them.
Oh, just another kind of outdoor game,
One on a side. It comes to little more:
There where it is we do not need the wall:
He is all pine and I am apple-orchard.
My apple trees will never get across
And eat the cones under his pines, I tell him.
He only says, "Good fences make good neighbors."
Spring is the mischief in me, and I wonder
If I could put a notion in his head:
"*Why* do they make good neighbors? Isn't it
Where there are cows? But here there are no cows.
Before I built a wall I'd ask to know
What I was walling in or walling out,
And to whom I was like to give offense.
Something there is that doesn't love a wall,
That wants it down!" I could say "elves" to him,
But it's not elves exactly, and I'd rather
He said it for himself. I see him there,
Bringing a stone grasped firmly by the top
In each hand, like an old-stone savage armed.
He moves in darkness, as it seems to me,
Not of woods only and the shade of trees.
He will not go behind his father's saying,
And he likes having thought of it so well
He says again, "Good fences make good neighbors."

THE DEATH OF THE HIRED MAN

Mary sat musing on the lamp-flame at the table
Waiting for Warren. When she heard his step,
She ran on tip-toe down the darkened passage

To meet him in the doorway with the news
And put him on his guard. "Silas is back."
She pushed him outward with her through the door
And shut it after her. "Be kind," she said.

She took the market things from Warren's arms
And set them on the porch, then drew him down
To sit beside her on the wooden steps.
"When was I ever anything but kind to him?
But I'll not have the fellow back," he said.
"I told him so last haying, didn't I?
'If he left then,' I said, 'that ended it.'
What good is he? Who else will harbor him
At his age for the little he can do?
What help he is there's no depending on.
Off he goes always when I need him most.
'He thinks he ought to earn a little pay,
Enough at least to buy tobacco with,
So he won't have to beg and be beholden.'
'All right,' I say, 'I can't afford to pay
Any fixed wages, though I wish I could.'
'Someone else can.' 'Then someone else will have to.'
I shouldn't mind his bettering himself
If that was what it was. You can be certain,
When he begins like that, there's someone at him
Trying to coax him off with pocket-money,—
In haying time, when any help is scarce.
In winter he comes back to us. I'm done."

"Sh! not so loud: he'll hear you," Mary said.

"I want him to: he'll have to soon or late."

"He's worn out. He's asleep beside the stove.
When I came up from Rowe's I found him here,
Huddled against the barn-door fast asleep,
A miserable sight, and frightening, too—
You needn't smile—I didn't recognize him—
I wasn't looking for him—and he's changed.
Wait till you see."

"Where did you say he'd been?"

"He didn't say, I dragged him to the house,
And gave him tea and tried to make him smoke.

I tried to make him talk about his travels,
Nothing would do: he just kept nodding off."

"What did he say? Did he say anything?"

"But little."

"Anything? Mary, confess
He said he'd come to ditch the meadow for me."

"Warren!"

"But did he? I just want to know."

"Of course he did. What would you have him say?
Surely you wouldn't grudge the poor old man
Some humble way to save his self-respect.
He added, if you really care to know,
He meant to clear the upper pasture, too.
That sounds like something you have heard before?
Warren, I wish you could have heard the way
He jumbled everything. I stopped to look
Two or three times—he made me feel so queer—
To see if he was talking in his sleep.
He ran on Harold Wilson—you remember—
The boy you had in haying four years since.
He's finished school, and teaching in his college.
Silas declares you'll have to get him back.
He says they two will make a team for work:
Between them they will lay this farm as smooth!
The way he mixed that in with other things.
He thinks young Wilson a likely lad, though daft
On education—you know how they fought
All through July under the blazing sun,
Silas up on the cart to build the load,
Harold along beside to pitch it on."

"Yes, I took care to keep well out of earshot."

"Well, those days trouble Silas like a dream.
You wouldn't think they would. How some things linger!
Harold's young college boy's assurance piqued him.
After so many years he still keeps finding
Good arguments he sees he might have used.

I sympathize. I know just how it feels
To think of the right thing to say too late.
Harold's associated in his mind with Latin.
He asked me what I thought of Harold's saying
He studied Latin like the violin
Because he liked it—that an argument!
He said he couldn't make the boy believe
He could find water with a hazel prong—
Which showed how much good school had ever done him.
He wanted to go over that. But most of all
He thinks if he could have another chance
To teach him how to build a load of hay—"

"I know, that's Silas' one accomplishment.
He bundles every forkful in its place,
And tags and numbers it for future reference,
So he can find and easily dislodge it
In the unloading. Silas does that well.
He takes it out in bunches like birds' nests.
You never see him standing on the hay
He's trying to lift, straining to lift himself."

"He thinks if he could teach him that, he'd be
Some good perhaps to someone in the world.
He hates to see a boy the fool of books.
Poor Silas, so concerned for other folk,
And nothing to look backward to with pride,
And nothing to look forward to with hope,
So now and never any different."

Part of a moon was falling down the west,
Dragging the whole sky with it to the hills.
Its light poured softly in her lap. She saw
And spread her apron to it. She put out her hand
Among the harp-like morning-glory strings,
Taut with the dew from garden bed to eaves,
As if she played unheard some tenderness
That wrought on him beside her in the night.
"Warren," she said, "he has come home to die:
You needn't be afraid he'll leave you this time."

"Home," he mocked gently.

"Yes, what else but home?

It all depends on what you mean by home.
Of course he's nothing to us, any more
Than was the hound that came a stranger to us
Out of the woods, worn out upon the trail."

"Home is the place where, when you have to go there,
They have to take you in."

"I should have called it
Something you somehow haven't to deserve."

Warren leaned out and took a step or two,
Picked up a little stick, and brought it back
And broke it in his hand and tossed it by.
"Silas has better claim on us, you think,
Than on his brother? Thirteen little miles
As the road winds would bring him to his door.
Silas has walked that far no doubt today.
Why didn't he go there? His brother's rich,
A somebody—director in the bank."

"He never told us that."

"We know it though."

"I think his brother ought to help, of course.
I'll see to that if there is need. He ought of right
To take him in, and might be willing to—
He may be better than appearances.
But have some pity on Silas. Do you think
If he'd had any pride in claiming kin
Or anything he looked for from his brother,
He'd keep so still about him all this time?"

"I wonder what's between them."

"I can tell you.
Silas is what he is—we wouldn't mind him—
But just the kind that kinsfolk can't abide.
He never did a thing so very bad.
He don't know why he isn't quite as good
As anyone. He won't be made ashamed
To please his brother, worthless though he is."

"I can't think Si ever hurt anyone."

"No, but he hurt my heart the way he lay
And rolled his old head on that sharp-edged chair-back.
He wouldn't let me put him on the lounge.
You must go in and see what you can do.
I made the bed up for him there tonight.
You'll be surprised at him—how much he's broken.
His working days are done; I'm sure of it."

"I'd not be in a hurry to say that."

"I haven't been. Go, look, see for yourself.
But, Warren, please remember how it is:
He's come to help you ditch the meadow.
He has a plan. You mustn't laugh at him.
He may not speak of it, and then he may.
I'll sit and see if that small sailing cloud
Will hit or miss the moon."

It hit the moon.
Then there were three there, making a dim row,
The moon, the little silver cloud, and she.

Warren returned—too soon, it seemed to her,
Slipped to her side, caught up her hand and waited.

"Warren?" she questioned.

"Dead," was all he answered.

THE ROAD NOT TAKEN

Two roads diverged in a yellow wood,
And sorry I could not travel both
And be one traveler, long I stood
And looked down one as far as I could
To where it bent in the undergrowth;

Then took the other, as just as fair,
And having perhaps the better claim,
Because it was grassy and wanted wear;
Though as for that the passing there
Had worn them really about the same,

And both that morning equally lay
In leaves no step had trodden black.
Oh, I kept the first for another day!
Yet knowing how way leads on to way,
I doubted if I should ever come back.

I shall be telling this with a sigh
Somewhere ages and ages hence:
Two roads diverged in a wood, and I—
I took the one less traveled by,
And that has made all the difference.

BIRCHES

When I see birches bend to left and right
Across the line of straighter darker trees,
I like to think some boy's been swinging them.
But swinging doesn't bend them down to stay.
Ice-storms do that. Often you must have seen them
Loaded with ice a sunny winter morning
After a rain. They click upon themselves
As the breeze rises, and turn many-colored
As the stir cracks and crazes their enamel.
Soon the sun's warmth makes them shed crystal shells
Shattering and avalanching on the snow-crust—
Such heaps of broken glass to sweep away
You'd think the inner dome of heaven had fallen.
They are dragged to the withered bracken by the load,
And they seem not to break; though once they are bowed
So low for long, they never right themselves:
You may see their trunks arching in the woods
Years afterwards, trailing their leaves on the ground
Like girls on hands and knees that throw their hair
Before them over their heads to dry in the sun.
But I was going to say when Truth broke in
With all her matter-of-fact about the ice-storm
I should prefer to have some boy bend them
As he went out and in to fetch the cows—
Some boy too far from town to learn baseball,
Whose only play was what he found himself,
Summer or winter, and could play alone.
One by one he subdued his father's trees
By riding them down over and over again

Until he took the stiffness out of them,
And not one but hung limp, not one was left
For him to conquer. He learned all there was
To learn about not launching out too soon
And so not carrying the tree away
Clear to the ground. He always kept his poise
To the top branches, climbing carefully
With the same pains you use to fill a cup
Up to the brim, and even above the brim.
Then he flung outward, feet first, with a swish,
Kicking his way down through the air to the ground.

So was I once myself a swinger of birches;
And so I dream of going back to be.
It's when I'm weary of considerations,
And life is too much like a pathless wood
Where your face burns and tickles with the cobwebs
Broken across it, and one eye is weeping
From a twig's having lashed across it open.
I'd like to get away from earth awhile
And then come back to it and begin over.
May no fate willfully misunderstand me
And half grant what I wish and snatch me away
Not to return. Earth's the right place for love:
I don't know where it's likely to go better.
I'd like to go by climbing a birch tree,
And climb black branches up a snow-white trunk
Toward heaven, till the tree could bear no more,
But dipped its top and set me down again.
That would be good both going and coming back.
One could do worse than be a swinger of birches.

THE RUNAWAY

Once when the snow of the year was beginning to fall,
We stopped by a mountain pasture to say, "Whose colt?"
A little Morgan had one forefoot on the wall,
The other curled at his breast. He dipped his head
And snorted to us. And then he had to bolt.
We heard the miniature thunder where he fled,
And we saw him, or thought we saw him, dim and gray,
Like a shadow against the curtain of falling flakes.
"I think the little fellow's afraid of the snow.

He isn't winter-broken. It isn't play
With the little fellow at all. He's running away.
I doubt if even his mother could tell him, 'Sakes,
It's only weather.' He'd think she didn't know!
Where is his mother? He can't be out alone."
And now he comes again with a clatter of stone
And mounts the wall again with whited eyes
And all his tail that isn't hair up straight.
He shudders his coat as if to throw off flies.
"Whoever it is that leaves him out so late,
When other creatures have gone to stall and bin,
Ought to be told to come and take him in."

THE WITCH OF COÖS

I stayed the night for shelter at a farm
Behind the mountain, with a mother and son,
Two old-believers. They did all the talking.

MOTHER. Folks think a witch who has familiar spirits
She could call up to pass a winter evening,
But won't, should be burned at the stake or something.
Summoning spirits isn't "Button, button,
Who's got the button," I would have them know.

SON. Mother can make a common table rear
And kick with two legs like an army mule.

MOTHER. And when I've done it, what good have I done?
Rather than tip a table for you, let me
Tell you what Ralle the Sioux Control once told me.
He said the dead had souls, but when I asked him
How could that be—I thought the dead were souls,
He broke my trance. Don't that make you suspicious
That there's something the dead are keeping back?
Yes, there's something the dead are keeping back.

SON. You wouldn't want to tell him what we have
Up attic, mother?

MOTHER. Bones—a skeleton.

SON. But the headboard of mother's bed is pushed
Against the attic door: the door is nailed.

It's harmless. Mother hears it in the night
Halting perplexed behind the barrier
Of door and headboard. Where it wants to get
Is back into the cellar where it came from.

MOTHER. We'll never let them, will we, son! We'll never!

SON. It left the cellar forty years ago
And carried itself like a pile of dishes
Up one flight from the cellar to the kitchen,
Another from the kitchen to the bedroom,
Another from the bedroom to the attic,
Right past both father and mother, and neither stopped it.
Father had gone upstairs; mother was downstairs.
I was a baby: I don't know where I was.

MOTHER. The only fault my husband found with me—
I went to sleep before I went to bed,
Especially in winter when the bed
Might just as well be ice and the clothes snow.
The night the bones came up the cellar-stairs
Toffile had gone to bed alone and left me,
But left an open door to cool the room off
So as to sort of turn me out of it.
I was just coming to myself enough
To wonder where the cold was coming from,
When I heard Toffile upstairs in the bedroom
And thought I heard him downstairs in the cellar.
The board we had laid down to walk dry-shod on
When there was water in the cellar in spring
Struck the hard cellar bottom. And then someone
Began the stairs, two footsteps for each step,
The way a man with one leg and a crutch,
Or a little child, comes up. It wasn't Toffile:
It wasn't anyone who could be there.
The bulkhead double-doors were double-locked
And swollen tight and buried under snow.
The cellar windows were banked up with sawdust
And swollen tight and buried under snow.
It was the bones. I knew them—and good reason.
My first impulse was to get to the knob
And hold the door. But the bones didn't try
The door; they halted helpless on the landing,
Waiting for things to happen in their favor.

The faintest restless rustling ran all through them.
I never could have done the thing I did
If the wish hadn't been too strong in me
To see how they were mounted for this walk.
I had a vision of them put together
Not like a man, but like a chandelier.
So suddenly I flung the door wide on him.
A moment he stood balancing with emotion,
And all but lost himself. (A tongue of fire
Flashed out and licked along his upper teeth.
Smoke rolled inside the sockets of his eyes.)
Then he came at me with one hand outstretched,
The way he did in life once; but this time
I struck the hand off brittle on the floor,
And fell back from him on the floor myself.
The finger-pieces slid in all directions.
(Where did I see one of those pieces lately?
Hand me my button-box–it must be there.)
I sat up on the floor and shouted, "Toffile,
It's coming up to you." It had its choice
Of the door to the cellar or the hall.
It took the hall door for the novelty,
And set off briskly for so slow a thing,
Still going every which way in the joints, though,
So that it looked like lightning or a scribble,
From the slap I had just now given its hand.
I listened till it almost climbed the stairs
From the hall to the only finished bedroom,
Before I got up to do anything;
Then ran and shouted, "Shut the bedroom door,
Toffile, for my sake!" "Company?" he said,
"Don't make me get up; I'm too warm in bed."
So lying forward weakly on the handrail
I pushed myself upstairs, and in the light
(The kitchen had been dark) I had to own
I could see nothing. "Toffile, I don't see it.
It's with us in the room though. It's the bones."
"What bones?" "The cellar bones–out of the grave."
That made him throw his bare legs out of bed
And sit up by me and take hold of me.
I wanted to put out the light and see
If I could see it, or else mow the room,
With our arms at the level of our knees,
And bring the chalk-pile down. "I'll tell you what–
It's looking for another door to try.

The uncommonly deep snow has made him think
Of his old song, *The Wild Colonial Boy*,
He always used to sing along the tote road.
He's after an open door to get outdoors.
Let's trap him with an open door up attic."
Toffile agreed to that, and sure enough,
Almost the moment he was given an opening,
The steps began to climb the attic stairs.
I heard them. Toffile didn't seem to hear them.
"Quick!" I slammed to the door and held the knob.
"Toffile, get nails." I made him nail the door shut
And push the headboard of the bed against it.
Then we asked was there anything
Up attic that we'd ever want again.
The attic was less to us than the cellar.
If the bones liked the attic, let them have it.
Let them stay in the attic. When they sometimes
Come down the stairs at night and stand perplexed
Behind the door and headboard of the bed,
Brushing their chalky skull with chalky fingers,
With sounds like the dry rattling of a shutter,
That's what I sit up in the dark to say—
To no one any more since Toffile died.
Let them stay in the attic since they went there.
I promised Toffile to be cruel to them
For helping them be cruel once to him.

SON. We think they had a grave down in the cellar.

MOTHER. We know they had a grave down in the cellar.

SON. We never could find out whose bones they were.

MOTHER. Yes, we could too, son. Tell the truth for once.
They were a man's his father killed for me.
I mean a man he killed instead of me.
The least I could do was to help dig their grave.
We were about it one night in the cellar.
Son knows the story: but 'twas not for him
To tell the truth, suppose the time had come.
Son looks surprised to see me end a lie
We'd kept all these years between ourselves
So as to have it ready for outsiders.
But tonight I don't care enough to lie—
I don't remember why I ever cared.

Toffile, if he were here, I don't believe
Could tell you why he ever cared himself....

She hadn't found the finger bone she wanted
Among the buttons poured out in her lap.
I verified the name next morning: Toffile.
The rural letter box said Toffile Lajway.

STOPPING BY WOODS ON A SNOWY EVENING

Whose woods these are I think I know.
His house is in the village though;
He will not see me stopping here
To watch his woods fill up with snow.

My little horse must think it queer
To stop without a farmhouse near
Between the woods and frozen lake
The darkest evening of the year.

He gives his harness bells a shake
To ask if there is some mistake.
The only other sound's the sweep
Of easy wind and downy flake.

The woods are lovely, dark and deep,
But I have promises to keep,
And miles to go before I sleep,
And miles to go before I sleep.

TWO TRAMPS IN MUD-TIME

Out of the mud two strangers came
And caught me splitting wood in the yard.
And one of them put me off my aim
By hailing cheerily "Hit them hard!"
I knew pretty well why he dropped behind
And let the other go on a way.
I knew pretty well what he had in mind:
He wanted to take my job for pay.

Good blocks of beech it was I split,
As large around as the chopping-block;
And every piece I squarely hit
Fell splinterless as a cloven rock.
The blows that a life of self-control
Spares to strike for the common good
That day, giving a loose to my soul,
I spent on the unimportant wood.

The sun was warm but the wind was chill.
You know how it is with an April day:
When the sun is out and the wind is still,
You're one month on in the middle of May.
But if you so much as dare to speak,
A cloud comes over the sunlit arch,
A wind comes off a frozen peak,
And you're two months back in the middle of March.

A bluebird comes tenderly up to alight
And fronts the wind to unruffle a plume,
His song so pitched as not to excite
A single flower as yet to bloom.
It is snowing a flake: and he half knew
Winter was only playing possum.
Except in color he isn't blue,
But he wouldn't advise a thing to blossom.

The water for which we may have to look
In summertime with a witching-wand,
In every wheelrut's now a brook,
In every print of a hoof a pond.
Be glad of water, but don't forget
The lurking frost in the earth beneath
That will steal forth after the sun is set
And show on the water its crystal teeth.

The time when most I loved my task
These two must make me love it more
By coming with what they came to ask.
You'd think I never had felt before
The weight of an ax head poised aloft,
The grip on earth of outspread feet,
The life of muscles rocking soft
And smooth and moist in vernal heat.

Out of the woods two hulking tramps
(From sleeping God knows where last night
But not long since in the lumber camps).
They thought all chopping was theirs of right.
Men of the woods and lumber-jacks,
They judged me by their appropriate tool.
Except as a fellow handled an ax,
They had no way of knowing a fool.

Nothing on either side was said.
They knew they had but to stay their stay
And all their logic would fill my head:
As that I had no right to play
With what was another man's work for gain.
My right might be love but theirs was need.
And where the two exist in twain
Theirs was the better right—agreed.

But yield who will to their separation,
My object in life is to unite
My avocation and my vocation
As my two eyes make one in sight.
Only where love and need are one,
And the work is play for mortal stakes,
Is the deed ever really done
For Heaven and the future's sakes.

THE GIFT OUTRIGHT

The land was ours before we were the land's.
She was our land more than a hundred years
Before we were her people. She was ours
In Massachusetts, in Virginia;
But we were England's, still colonials,
Possessing what we still were unpossessed by,
Possessed by what we now no more possessed.
Something we were withholding made us weak
Until we found out that it was ourselves
We were withholding from our land of living,
And forthwith found salvation in surrender.
Such as we were we gave ourselves outright
(The deed of gift was many deeds of war)
To the land vaguely realizing westward,
But still unstoried, artless, unenhanced,
Such as she was, such as she would become.

CHOOSE SOMETHING LIKE A STAR

O Star (the fairest one in sight),
We grant your loftiness the right
To some obscurity of cloud—
It will not do to say of night,
Since dark is what brings out your light.
Some mystery becomes the proud.
But to be wholly taciturn
In your reserve is not allowed.
Say something to us we can learn
By heart and when alone repeat.
Say something! And it says "I burn."
But say with what degree of heat.
Talk Fahrenheit, talk Centigrade.
Use language we can comprehend.
Tell us what elements you blend.
It gives us strangely little aid,
But does tell something in the end.
And steadfast as Keats' Eremite,
Not even stooping from its sphere,
It asks a little of us here.
It asks of us a certain height,
So when at times the mob is swayed
To carry praise or blame too far,
We may choose something like a star
To stay our minds on and be staid.

CARL SANDBURG

[1878–]

Carl Sandburg's reputation as a poet has been somewhat overshadowed if not dimmed by his renown as Lincoln's most important biographer. He was born January 6, 1878, in Galesburg, Illinois, a son of Swedish immigrants who changed their name from Johnson to Sandburg to distinguish themselves from the many other Johnsons in the community. There was little time or money for the boy's schooling; he went to work on a milk wagon when he was thirteen. By the time he was twenty he had learned to support himself in a dozen different ways: porter in a barber shop, scene-shifter in a run-down theatre, laborer in a brick yard, dishwasher in a Denver hotel, harvest-hand in Kansas wheat fields, house-painter in his home town. At twenty he enlisted in the Sixth Illinois Infantry as a volunteer in the Spanish-American War and saw service in Puerto Rico. Returning to Galesburg, he entered Lombard College, where he became janitor of the gymnasium, captain of the basketball team, and editor of the college paper. Between his twenty-fourth and thirty-second years he traveled across the country and settled for awhile in Wisconsin as an organizer of the Socialist Democratic Party.

Sandburg had found poetry as a child: he began to write poetry almost as soon as he could read. At twenty-six he scraped together a few dollars and published a booklet which he called In Reckless Ecstasy. The title indicated both the kind and quality of the twenty-two page pamphlet, which contained free-verse poems in the manner of Whitman. They echoed Whitman's rhetorical phrases as well as his belief in the brotherhood of man. Later Sandburg was to make the comparison with Whitman still more striking. In common with "the poet of democracy," he liked to use the free and gusty talk of the American people; he put the clamor of the city streets as well as the deep silences of the prairies into poetry; and he, too, exalted the spirit as well as the memory of Lincoln.

By the time he had reached his eighties, Sandburg had written a great variety of volumes. He was the author of some eight books of poetry, a novel (Remembrance Rock) and an autobiography (Always the Young Strangers). He was also a compiler of folk songs (The American Songbag) and writer of stories for children (Rootabaga Stories and Early Moon). His six-volume biography of Abraham Lincoln was a poet's interpretation as well as a scholar's monumental study —the last four volumes (Abraham Lincoln: The War Years) were awarded the Pulitzer Prize for the best historical work of 1939, and Sandburg was given the Gold Medal for History and Biography by the American Academy of Arts and Letters.

In words that are muscular yet somehow mystical, Sandburg rhapsodizes over the native scene. His is an authentic expression of a new and native culture and its special application to the sprawling Midwest. His style, his subject matter, and his credo are all synthesized in his most affirmative book of poetry: The People, Yes. "Above all," wrote Henry Steele Commager, "Sandburg is the poet of the plain people, of farmers and steel workers and coal miners, of the housewife and stenographer, and the streetwalker, too; of children at play and at work; of hoboes *and bums . . . of immigrants and natives." He lives up to the estimate of poetry given by the Irish playwright J. M. Synge: "The poetry of exaltation will be always the highest; but when men lose their poetic feeling for ordinary life, their exalted poetry is likely to lose its strength of exaltation in the way men cease to build beautiful churches when they have lost happiness in building shops." Sandburg has never lost either his poetic feeling for ordinary life or his strength of exaltation.*

CHICAGO

Hog Butcher for the World,
Tool Maker, Stacker of Wheat,
Player with Railroads and the Nation's Freight Handler;
Stormy, husky, brawling,
City of the Big Shoulders:
They tell me you are wicked and I believe them, for I have seen your painted women under the gas lamps luring the farm boys.
And they tell me you are crooked and I answer: Yes, it is true I have seen the gunman kill and go free to kill again.
And they tell me you are brutal and my reply is: On the faces of women and children I have seen the marks of wanton hunger.
And having answered so I turn once more to those who sneer at this my city, and I give them back the sneer and say to them:
Come and show me another city with lifted head singing so proud to be alive and coarse and strong and cunning.
Flinging magnetic curses amid the toil of piling job on job, here is a tall bold slugger set vivid against the little soft cities;
Fierce as a dog with tongue lapping for action, cunning as a savage pitted against the wilderness,
Bareheaded,
Shoveling,
Wrecking,
Planning,
Building, breaking, rebuilding.
Under the smoke, dust all over his mouth, laughing with white teeth,
Under the terrible burden of destiny laughing as a young man laughs,
Laughing even as an ignorant fighter laughs who has never lost a battle,
Bragging and laughing that under his wrist is the pulse, and under his ribs the heart of the people,
Laughing!

Laughing the stormy, husky, brawling laughter of Youth, half-naked, sweating, proud to be Hog Butcher, Tool Maker, Stacker of Wheat, Player with Railroads and Freight Handler to the Nation.

FOG

The fog comes
on little cat feet.
It sits looking
over harbor and city
on silent haunches
and then moves on.

GRASS

Pile the bodies high at Austerlitz and Waterloo.
Shovel them under and let me work—
I am the grass; I cover all.

And pile them high at Gettysburg
And pile them high at Ypres and Verdun.
Shovel them under and let me work.
Two years, ten years, and passengers ask the conductor:
What place is this?
Where are we now?

I am the grass.
Let me work.

COOL TOMBS

When Abraham Lincoln was shoveled into the tombs, he forgot the copperheads and the assassin . . . in the dust, in the cool tombs.

And Ulysses Grant lost all thought of con men and Wall Street, cash and collateral turned ashes . . . in the dust, in the cool tombs.

Pocahontas' body, lovely as a poplar, sweet as a red haw in November or a pawpaw in May, did she wonder? does she remember? . . . in the dust, in the cool tombs?

Take any streetful of people buying clothes and groceries, cheering a hero or throwing confetti and blowing tin horns . . . tell me if the lovers are losers . . . tell me if any get more than the lovers . . . in the dust . . . in the cool tombs.

LIMITED

I am riding on a limited express, one of the crack trains of the nation.
Hurtling across the prairie into blue haze and dark air go fifteen all-steel coaches holding a thousand people.
(All the coaches shall be scrap and rust and all the men and women laughing in the diners and sleepers shall pass to ashes.)
I ask a man in the smoker where he is going and he answers: "Omaha."

THEY HAVE YARNS

From "*The People, Yes*"

They have yarns
Of a skyscraper so tall they had to put hinges
On the two top stories so to let the moon go by,
Of one corn crop in Missouri when the roots
Went so deep and drew off so much water
The Mississippi riverbed that year was dry,
Of pancakes so thin they had only one side,
Of "a fog so thick we shingled the barn and six feet out on the fog,"
Of Pecos Pete straddling a cyclone in Texas and riding it to the west coast where "it rained out under him,"
Of the man who drove a swarm of bees across the Rocky Mountains and the Desert "and didn't lose a bee,"
Of a mountain railroad curve where the engineer in his cab can touch the caboose and spit in the conductor's eye,
Of the boy who climbed a cornstalk growing so fast he would have starved to death if they hadn't shot biscuits up to him,
Of the old man's whiskers: "When the wind was with him his whiskers arrived a day before he did,"
Of the hen laying a square egg and cackling, "Ouch!" and of hens laying eggs with the dates printed on them,
Of the ship captain's shadow: it froze to the deck one cold winter night,
Of mutineers on that same ship put to chipping rust with rubber hammers,
Of the sheep counter who was fast and accurate: "I just count their feet and divide by four,"

Of the man so tall he must climb a ladder to shave himself,
Of the runt so teeny-weeny it takes two men and a boy to see him,
Of mosquitoes: one can kill a dog, two of them a man,
Of a cyclone that sucked cookstoves out of the kitchen, up the chimney flue, and on to the next town,
Of the same cyclone picking up wagon-tracks in Nebraska and dropping them over in the Dakotas,
Of the hook-and-eye snake unlocking itself into forty pieces, each piece two inches long, then in nine seconds flat snapping itself together again,
Of the watch swallowed by the cow—when they butchered her a year later the watch was running and had the correct time,
Of horned snakes, hoop snakes that roll themselves where they want to go, and rattlesnakes carrying bells instead of rattles on their tails,
Of the herd of cattle in California getting lost in a giant redwood tree that had hollowed out,
Of the man who killed a snake by putting its tail in its mouth so it swallowed itself,
Of railroad trains whizzing along so fast they reach the station before the whistle,
Of pigs so thin the farmer had to tie knots in their tails to keep them from crawling through the cracks in their pens,
Of Paul Bunyan's big blue ox, Babe, measuring between the eyes forty-two ax-handles and a plug of Star tobacco exactly,
Of John Henry's hammer and the curve of its swing and his singing of it as "a rainbow round my shoulder."

"Do tell!"
"I want to know!"
"You don't say so!"
"For the land's sake!"
"Gosh all fish-hooks!"
"Tell me some more.
I don't believe a word you say
but I love to listen
to your sweet harmonica
to your chin-music.
Your fish stories hang together
when they're just a pack of lies:
you ought to have a leather medal:
you ought to have a statue
carved of butter: you deserve
a large bouquet of turnips."

"Yessir," the traveler drawled,
"Away out there in the petrified forest

everything goes on the same as usual.
The petrified birds sit in their petrified nests
and hatch their petrified young from petrified eggs."

A high pressure salesman jumped off the Brooklyn Bridge and was saved by a policeman. But it didn't take him long to sell the idea to the policeman. So together they jumped off the bridge.

One of the oil men in heaven started a rumor of a gusher down in hell. All the other oil men left in a hurry for hell. As he gets to thinking about the rumor he had started he says to himself there might be something in it after all. So he leaves for hell in a hurry.

"The number 42 will win this raffle, that's my number." And when he won they asked him whether he guessed the number or had a system. He said he had a system, "I took up the old family album and there on page 7 was my grandfather and grandmother both on page 7. I said to myself this is easy for 7 times 7 is the number that will win and 7 times 7 is 42."

Once a shipwrecked sailor caught hold of a stateroom door and floated for hours till friendly hands from out of the darkness threw him a rope. And he called across the night, "What country is this?" and hearing voices answer, "New Jersey," he took a fresh hold on the floating stateroom door and called back half-wearily, "I guess I'll float a little farther."

An Ohio man bundled up the tin roof of a summer kitchen and sent it to a motor car maker with a complaint of his car not giving service. In three weeks a new car arrived for him and a letter: "We regret delay in shipment but your car was received in a very bad order."

A Dakota cousin of this Ohio man sent six years of tin can accumulations to the same works, asking them to overhaul his car. Two weeks later came a rebuilt car, five old tin cans, and a letter: "We are also forwarding you five parts not necessary in our new model."

Thus fantasies heard at filling stations in the midwest. Another relates to a Missouri mule who took aim with his heels at an automobile rattling by. The car turned a somersault, lit next a fence, ran right along through a cornfield till it came to a gate, moved onto the road and went on its way as though nothing had happened. The mule heehawed with desolation, "What's the use?"

Another tells of a farmer and his family stalled on a railroad crossing, how they jumped out in time to see a limited express knock it into flinders, the farmer calling, "Well, I always did say that car was no shucks in a real pinch."

When the Masonic Temple in Chicago was the tallest building in the United States west of New York, two men who would cheat the eyes out of you if you gave 'em a chance, took an Iowa farmer to the top of the building and asked him, "How is this for high?" They told him that for $25 they would go down in the basement and turn the building around on its turn-table for him while he stood on the roof and saw how this seventh wonder of the world worked. He handed them $25. They went. He waited. They never came back.

This is told in Chicago as a folk tale, the same as the legend of Mrs. O'Leary's cow kicking over the barn lamp that started the Chicago fire, when the Georgia visitor, Robert Toombs, telegraphed an Atlanta crony, "Chicago is on fire, the whole city burning down, God be praised!"

Nor is the prize sleeper Rip Van Winkle and his scolding wife forgotten, nor the headless horseman scooting through Sleepy Hollow

Nor the sunken treasure-ships in coves and harbors, the hideouts of gold and silver sought by Coronado, nor the Flying Dutchman rounding the Cape doomed to nevermore pound his ear nor ever again take a snooze for himself

Nor the sailor's caretaker Mother Carey seeing to it that every seafaring man in the afterworld has a seabird to bring him news of ships and women, an albatross for the admiral, a gull for the deckhand

Nor the sailor with a sweetheart in every port of the world, nor the ships that set out with flying colors and all the promises you could ask, the ships never heard of again

Nor Jim Liverpool, the riverman who could jump across any river and back without touching land he was that quick on his feet

Nor Mike Fink along the Ohio and the Mississippi, half wild horse and half cock-eyed alligator, the rest of him snags and snapping turtle. "I can out-run, out-jump, out-shoot, out-brag, out-drink, and out-fight, rough and tumble, no holts barred, any man on both sides of the river from Pittsburgh to New Orleans and back again to St. Louis. My trigger finger itches and I want to go redhot. War, famine and bloodshed puts flesh on my bones, and hardship's my daily bread."

VACHEL LINDSAY

[1879–1931]

A TRAGIC INNOCENT, *part missionary and part minstrel, Vachel Lindsay broke his heart because he could not keep on exchanging his rhymes for bread. He was born November 10, 1879, in Springfield, Illinois, the second of six children. His father was an evangelist, his mother was* an artist. Lindsay tried to be both. He not only idolized but idealized the city of his birth. He saw it as a symbol of a transfigured America, the cultural capital of the United States. Lincoln had lived there, and it had been the home of another martyr, John P. Altgeld, memorialized by Lindsay in a noble poem, "The Eagle that is Forgotten."

Although he had begun to write poetry before he attended Hiram College, it was as an artist that he hoped to glorify Springfield. He attended the Art Institute of Chicago and the New York School of Art, where he studied under Robert Henri. He had, however, none of the traditional carefree artistic temperament. He was a crusader rather than a bohemian. He lectured for the Y.M.C.A., became a fanatical prohibitionist, and barnstormed for the Anti-Saloon League. He printed a little magazine and gave away copies wherever he went. He undertook extensive walking tours and, combining the roles of missionary and troubadour, wandered through the South and Middle West, offering his Rhymes to Be Traded for Bread in exchange for a night's lodging.

His first book, General William Booth Enters into Heaven, proclaimed his dual allegiance to preaching and poetry. Published when he was thirty-four, it combines religion, ragtime verse, and what he called "the higher vaudeville." This was followed by several volumes which accentuated Lindsay's manner. Strident but determinedly serious, he roused the reader with a percussive power rare to poetry; his lines vibrated with the blare of military bands, the syncopated beat of jazz, the crude din of dance halls, the roars of fast automobiles and torch-light parades. The poems were most effective when heard in public recitals: Lindsay had a rolling baritone voice and he used it with hypnotic effect. He became not only a national phenomenon but also a favorite platform personality.

In spite of his popularity or, perhaps, because of it, Lindsay grew fearful of the future. He suspected he was being listened to not as a poet or a reformer, but an entertainer. He grew creatively insecure and emotionally maladjusted. He fell in love frequently and unsuccessfully, most ardently with Sara Teasdale, who was frightened by his vehemence. He was forty-six when he married Elizabeth Conner, the twenty-three-year-old daughter of a Presbyterian clergyman. There were two children. For a while all went well. Lindsay was both adoring and adored, but gradually the old nagging fears and doubts assailed him. He had overextended himself. Audiences no longer cared to hear the rhyming revivalist; the most sought-after poet-performer of his day ceased to be in demand. His fears of poverty were justified when he fell into debt. He began to hear voices; he imagined himself persecuted.

He saw enemies everywhere, even in his own home. He turned upon his wife, railed against her for having robbed him of his virginity, and fell into fits of insanity. On December 5, 1931, he drank a bottle of disinfectant and killed himself.

Lindsay wrote energetically but carelessly, and much of his work is merely noisy, while some of it is maudlin. However, at his best, in such poems as "General William Booth Enters into Heaven," "The Eagle that is Forgotten," "Abraham Lincoln Walks at Midnight," and "The Congo," he put a new vigor into modern poetry; he gave it the vocal resonance which had been sounded by the ancient chanters and ballad-singers. A poet who tried (and sometimes failed) to reach people on every level, Lindsay's very zeal was a rebuff to apathy and disillusion. His raucous rhymes and pounding rhythms caught (and still catch) the ear and quickened the pulse of any listener.

THE CONGO

I. Their Basic Savagery

Fat black bucks in a wine-barrel room,
Barrel-house kings, with feet unstable,
Sagged and reeled and pounded on the table, *A deep rolling bass.*
Pounded on the table,
Beat an empty barrel with the handle of a broom,
Hard as they were able,
Boom, boom, Boom,
With a silk umbrella and the handle of a broom,
Boomlay, boomlay, boomlay, Boom.

Then I had religion, Then I had a vision.
I could not turn from their revel in derision.
Then I saw the Congo, creeping through the black, *More deliberate. Solemnly chanted.*
Cutting through the jungle with a golden track.

Then along that riverbank
A thousand miles
Tattooed cannibals danced in files;
Then I heard the boom of the blood-lust song *A rapidly piling climax of speed and racket.*
And a thigh-bone beating on a tin-pan gong.

And "BLOOD" screamed the whistles and the fifes of the warriors,
"BLOOD" screamed the skull-faced, lean witch-doctors,
"Whirl ye the deadly voo-doo rattle,
Harry the uplands,
Steal all the cattle,
Rattle-rattle, rattle-rattle,
Bing!
Boomlay, boomlay, boomlay, BOOM,"
A roaring, epic, rag-time tune
From the mouth of the Congo
To the Mountains of the Moon.

With a philosophic pause.

Death is an Elephant,
Torch-eyed and horrible,
Foam-flanked and terrible.
BOOM, steal the pygmies,
BOOM, kill the Arabs,
BOOM, kill the white men,
Hoo, Hoo, Hoo.
Listen to the yell of Leopold's ghost
Burning in Hell for his hand-maimed host.
Hear how the demons chuckle and yell
Cutting his hands off, down in Hell.
Listen to the creepy proclamation,
Blown through the lairs of the forest-nation,
Blown past the white-ants' hill of clay,
Blown past the marsh where the butterflies play:—
"Be careful what you do,
Or Mumbo-Jumbo, God of the Congo,
And all of the other
Gods of the Congo,
Mumbo-Jumbo will hoo-doo you,
Mumbo-Jumbo will hoo-doo you,
Mumbo-Jumbo will hoo-doo you."

Shrilly and with a heavily accented meter.

Like the wind in the chimney.

All the o sounds very golden. Heavy accents very heavy. Light accents very light. Last line whispered.

II. THEIR IRREPRESSIBLE HIGH SPIRITS

Wild crap-shooters with a whoop and a call
Danced the juba in their gambling-hall
And laughed fit to kill, and shook the town,
And guyed the policemen and laughed them down
With a boomlay, boomlay, boomlay, BOOM. . . .

Rather shrill and high.

THEN I SAW THE CONGO, CREEPING THROUGH THE BLACK,
CUTTING THROUGH THE JUNGLE WITH A GOLDEN TRACK.
A negro fairyland swung into view,
A minstrel river
Where dreams come true.
The ebony palace soared on high
Through the blossoming trees to the evening sky,
The inlaid porches and casements shone
With gold and ivory and elephant-bone.
And the black crowd laughed till their sides were sore
At the baboon butler in the agate door,
And the well-known tunes of the parrot band
That thrilled on the bushes of that magic land.
A troupe of skull-faced witch-men came
Through the agate doorway in suits of flame,
Yes, long-tailed coats with a gold-leaf crust
And hats that were covered with diamond-dust.
And the crowd in the court gave a whoop and a call
And danced the juba from wall to wall.
But the witch-men suddenly stilled the throng.
With a stern cold glare, and a stern old song:—
"Mumbo-Jumbo will hoo-doo you." . . .

Read exactly as in first section.

Lay emphasis on the delicate ideas. Keep as light-footed as possible.

With pomposity.

With a great deliberation and ghostliness.

Just then from the doorway, as fat as shotes,
Came the cake-walk princes in their long red coats,
Shoes with a patent leather shine,
And tall silk hats that were red as wine.
And they pranced with their butterfly partners there,
Coal-black maidens with pearls in their hair,
Knee-skirts trimmed with the jessamine sweet,
And bells on their ankles and little black feet.
And the couples railed at the chant and the frown
Of the witch-men lean, and laughed them down.
(O rare was the revel, and well worth while
That made those glowering witch-men smile).

With overwhelming assurance, good cheer, and pomp.

With growing speed and sharply marked dance-rhythm.

The cake-walk royalty then began
To walk for a cake that was tall as a man
To the tune of "Boomlay, boomlay, BOOM,"
While the witch-men laughed, with a sinister air,
And sang with the scalawags prancing there:—
"Walk with care, walk with care,
Or Mumbo-Jumbo, God of the Congo,
And all of the other
Gods of the Congo,

With a touch of negro dialect, and as rapidly as possible toward the end.

Mumbo-Jumbo will hoo-doo you.
Beware, beware, walk with care,
Boomlay, boomlay, boomlay, boom.
Boomlay, boomlay, boomlay, boom,
Boomlay, boomlay, boomlay, boom,
Boomlay, boomlay, boomlay,
BOOM."
O rare was the revel, and well worth while
That made those glowering witch-men smile.

Slow philosophic calm.

III. THE HOPE OF THEIR RELIGION

Heavy bass. With a literal imitation of camp-meeting racket, and trance.

A good old negro in the slums of the town
Preached at a sister for her velvet gown.
Howled at a brother for his low-down ways,
His prowling, guzzling, sneak-thief days.
Beat on the Bible till he wore it out,
Starting the jubilee revival shout.
And some had visions, as they stood on chairs,
And sang of Jacob, and the golden stairs.
And they all repented, a thousand strong,
From their stupor and savagery and sin and wrong
And slammed their hymn books till they shook the room
With "Glory, glory, glory,"
And "Boom, boom, BOOM."

Exactly as in the first section.

THEN I SAW THE CONGO, CREEPING THROUGH THE BLACK,
CUTTING THROUGH THE JUNGLE WITH A GOLDEN TRACK.
And the gray sky opened like a new-rent veil
And showed the Apostles with their coats of mail.
In bright white steel they were seated round
And their fire-eyes watched where the Congo wound.
And the twelve Apostles, from their thrones on high,
Thrilled all the forest with their heavenly cry:—

Sung to the tune of "Hark, ten thousand harps and voices"

"Mumbo-Jumbo will die in the jungle;
Never again will he hoo-doo you,
Never again will he hoo-doo you."

With growing deliberation and joy.

Then along that river, a thousand miles
The vine-snared trees fell down in files.
Pioneer angels cleared the way
For a Congo paradise, for babes at play,
For sacred capitals, for temples clean.
Gone were the skull-faced witch-men lean.

There, where the wild ghost-gods had wailed
A million boats of the angels sailed
With oars of silver, and prows of blue
And silken pennants that the sun shone through.
'Twas a land transfigured, 'twas a new creation.
Oh, a singing wind swept the negro nation
And on through the backwoods clearing flew:—
"Mumbo-Jumbo is dead in the jungle.
Never again will he hoo-doo you.
Never again will he hoo-doo you."

In a rather high key—as delicately as possible.

To the tune of "Hark, ten thousand harps and voices."

Redeemed were the forests, the beasts and the men,
And only the vulture dared again
By the far, lone mountains of the moon
To cry, in the silence, the Congo tune:—
"Mumbo-Jumbo will hoo-doo you,
Mumbo . . . Jumbo . . . will . . . hoo-doo . . . you."

Dying off into a penetrating, terrified whisper.

GENERAL WILLIAM BOOTH ENTERS INTO HEAVEN

(*To be sung to the tune of "The Blood of the Lamb" with indicated instruments*)

I

(*Bass drum beaten loudly.*)
Booth led boldly with his big bass drum—
(Are you washed in the blood of the Lamb?)
The Saints smiled gravely and they said: "He's come."
(Are you washed in the blood of the Lamb?)
Walking lepers followed, rank on rank,
Lurching bravos from the ditches dank,
Drabs from the alleyways and drug fiends pale—
Minds still passion-ridden, soul-powers frail:—
Vermin-eaten saints with moldy breath,
Unwashed legions with the ways of Death—
(Are you washed in the blood of the Lamb?)

(*Banjos.*)
Every slum had sent its half-a-score
The round world over. (Booth had groaned for more.)
Every banner that the wide world flies
Bloomed with glory and transcendent dyes.
Big-voiced lasses made their banjos bang,

Tranced, fanatical they shrieked and sang:—
"Are you washed in the blood of the Lamb?"
Hallelujah! It was queer to see
Bull-necked convicts with that land make free.
Loons with trumpets blowed a blare, blare, blare
On, on upward thro' the golden air!
(Are you washed in the blood of the Lamb?)

II

(Bass drum slower and softer.)
Booth died blind and still by faith he trod,
Eyes still dazzled by the ways of God.
Booth led boldly, and he looked the chief,
Eagle countenance in sharp relief,
Beard a-flying, air of high command
Unabated in that holy land.

(Sweet flute music.)
Jesus came from out the court-house door,
Stretched his hands above the passing poor.
Booth saw not, but led his queer ones there
Round and round the mighty court-house square.
Yet in an instant all that blear review
Marched on spotless, clad in raiment new.
The lame were straightened, withered limbs uncurled
And blind eyes opened on a new, sweet world.

(Bass drum louder.)
Drabs and vixens in a flash made whole!
Gone was the weasel-head, the snout, the jowl!
Sages and sibyls now, and athletes clean,
Rulers of empires, and of forests green!

(Grand chorus of all instruments. Tambourines to the foreground.)
The hosts were sandaled, and their wings were fire!
(Are you washed in the blood of the Lamb?)
But their noise played havoc with the angel-choir.
(Are you washed in the blood of the Lamb?)
Oh, shout Salvation! It was good to see
Kings and Princes by the Lamb set free.
The banjos rattled and the tambourines
Jing-jing-jingled in the hands of Queens.

(*Reverently sung, no instruments.*)
And when Booth halted by the curb for prayer
He saw his Master thro' the flag-filled air.
Christ came gently with a robe and crown
For Booth the soldier, while the throng knelt down.
He saw King Jesus. They were face to face,
And he knelt a-weeping in that holy place.
Are you washed in the blood of the Lamb?

THE EAGLE THAT IS FORGOTTEN

(*John P. Altgeld. Born December 30, 1847; died March 12, 1902*)

Sleep softly . . . eagle forgotten . . . under the stone.
Time has its way with you there, and the clay has its own.
"We have buried him now," thought your foes, and in secret rejoiced.
They made a brave show of their mourning, their hatred unvoiced,
They had snarled at you, barked at you, foamed at you, day after day,
Now you were ended. They praised you, . . . and laid you away.

The others that mourned you in silence and terror and truth,
The widow bereft of her pittance, the boy without youth,
The mocked and the scorned and the wounded, the lame and the poor
That should have remembered forever, . . . remember no more.

Where are those lovers of yours, on what name do they call
The lost, that in armies wept over your funeral pall?
They call on the names of a hundred high-valiant ones,
A hundred white eagles have risen, the sons of your sons,
The zeal in their wings is a zeal that your dreaming began
The valor that wore out your soul in the service of man.

Sleep softly, . . . eagle forgotten, . . . under the stone,
Time has its way with you there, and the clay has its own.
Sleep on, O brave-hearted, O wise man, that kindled the flame—
To live in mankind is far more than to live in a name,
To live in mankind, far, far more . . . than to live in a name.

ABRAHAM LINCOLN WALKS AT MIDNIGHT

(In Springfield, Illinois)

It is portentous, and a thing of state
That here at midnight, in our little town
A mourning figure walks, and will not rest,
Near the old court-house pacing up and down,

Or by his homestead, or in shadowed yards
He lingers where his children used to play,
Or through the market, on the well-worn stones
He stalks until the dawn-stars burn away.

A bronzed, lank man! His suit of ancient black,
A famous high top-hat and plain worn shawl
Make him the quaint great figure that men love,
The prairie-lawyer, master of us all.

He cannot sleep upon his hillside now.
He is among us:—as in times before!
And we who toss and lie awake for long,
Breathe deep, and start, to see him pass the door.

His head is bowed. He thinks of men and kings.
Yea, when the sick world cries, how can he sleep?
Too many peasants fight, they know not why;
Too many homesteads in black terror weep.

The sins of all the war-lords burn his heart.
He sees the dreadnaughts scouring every main.
He carries on his shawl-wrapped shoulders now
The bitterness, the folly and the pain.

He cannot rest until a spirit-dawn
Shall come;—the shining hope of Europe free:
A league of sober folk, the workers' earth,
Bringing long peace to Cornland, Alp and Sea.

It breaks his heart that kings must murder still,
That all his hours of travail here for men
Seem yet in vain. And who will bring white peace
That he may sleep upon his hill again?

WALLACE STEVENS

[1879–1955]

WALLACE STEVENS WAS A DOUBLE PERSONALITY *with two distinct functions: he was the vice president of the Hartford Accident and Indemnity Company, and a poet whose highly personal idiom kept him apart from the mainstream of modern poetry. He was born October 2, 1879, in Reading, Pennsylvania, of Dutch and German ancestry. He attended Harvard University, studied law at New York Law School and, after practicing in New York, moved to Connecticut. He married, and divided his time between being a business man and a special kind of creator until he died in his seventy-sixth year, August 2, 1955. His* Collected Poems *received the National Book Award as well as the Pulitzer Prize in the year of his death.*

Shunning publicity, Stevens waited until he was in his mid-forties before he published his first book, Harmonium. *Most critics agreed that he was "a poet's poet" whose lines did not make the usual adjustment to meaning but had a kind of logic of their own. Little concerned with human beings and their emotions, Stevens was preoccupied with poetic ambiguities, balancing opposites in what he called a "fictive music." Although the verses often lack an easily recognizable sequence, the phrasing is always precise and makes a fine concordance of sound. Such poems as "Sunday Morning" and "Peter Quince at the Clavier" have a teasing philosophy, but it is Stevens' gift of metaphor which leaps*

In the high imagination, triumphantly.

The quality of Stevens' mind is implicit in the very titles with which he disturbs casual readers and delights those who take the time and trouble to understand him. "The Paltry Nude Starts on a Spring Voyage," "On the Manner of Addressing Clouds," "The Emperor of Ice Cream," "Hymn from a Watermelon Pavilion," "The Revolutionists Stop for Orangeade," "Dance of the Macabre Mice," "The Sense of the Sleight-of-hand Man," "So-And-So Reclining on Her Couch," "The Ultimate Poem is Abstract"—such titles furnish a key to Stevens' fascination with metaphors as well as his concept of poetry. Since everything Stevens says is said obliquely, aloofly, and non-sequentially, for him the "ultimate poem" is abstract. His poetry is not essentially in the translation of words into ordinary meanings, but in the allusiveness of the words themselves.

SUNDAY MORNING

I

Complacencies of the peignoir, and late
Coffee and oranges in a sunny chair,
And the green freedom of a cockatoo
Upon a rug, mingle to dissipate
The holy hush of ancient sacrifice.
She dreams a little, and she feels the dark
Encroachment of that old catastrophe,
As a calm darkens among water-lights.
The pungent oranges and bright green wings
Seem things in some procession of the dead,
Winding across wide water, without sound.
The day is like wide water, without sound,
Stilled for the passing of her dreaming feet
Over the seas, to silent Palestine,
Dominion of the blood and sepulcher.

II

She hears, upon that water without sound,
A voice that cries: "The tomb in Palestine
Is not the porch of spirits lingering;
It is the grave of Jesus, where He lay."
We live in an old chaos of the sun,
Or old dependency of day and night,
Or island solitude, unsponsored, free,
Of that wide water, inescapable.
Deer walk upon our mountains, and the quail
Whistle about us their spontaneous cries:
Sweet berries ripen in the wilderness;
And in the isolation of the sky,
At evening, casual flocks of pigeons make
Ambiguous undulations as they sink,
Downward to darkness, on extended wings.

III

She says: "I am content when wakened birds,
Before they fly, test the reality
Of misty fields, by their sweet questionings;
But when the birds are gone, and their warm fields

Return no more, where, then, is paradise?"
There is not any haunt of prophecy,
Nor any old chimera of the grave,
Neither the golden underground, nor isle
Melodious, where spirits gat them home,
Nor visionary South, nor cloudy palm
Remote on heaven's hill, that has endured
As April's green endures; or will endure
Like her remembrance of awakened birds,
Or her desire for June and evening, tipped
By consummation of the swallow's wings.

IV

She says, "But in contentment I still feel
The need of some imperishable bliss."
Death is the mother of beauty; hence from her,
Alone, shall come fulfillment to our dreams
And our desires. Although she strews the leaves
Of sure obliteration on our paths—
The path sick sorrow took, the many paths
Where triumph rang its brassy phrase, or love
Whispered a little out of tenderness—
She makes the willow shiver in the sun
For maidens who were wont to sit and gaze
Upon the grass, relinquished to their feet.
She causes boys to bring sweet-smelling pears
And plums in ponderous piles. The maidens taste
And stray impassioned in the littering leaves.

V

Supple and turbulent, a ring of men
Shall chant in orgy on a summer morn
Their boisterous devotion to the sun—
Not as a god, but as a god might be,
Naked among them, like a savage source.
Their chant shall be a chant of paradise,
Out of their blood, returning to the sky;
And in their chant shall enter, voice by voice,
The windy lake wherein their lord delights,
The trees, like seraphim, and echoing hills,
That choir among themselves long afterward.

They shall know well the heavenly fellowship
Of men that perish and of summer morn—
And whence they came and whither they shall go,
The dew upon their feet shall manifest.

PETER QUINCE AT THE CLAVIER

I

Just as my fingers on these keys
Make music, so the self-same sounds
On my spirit make a music, too.

Music is feeling, then, not sound;
And thus it is that what I feel,
Here in this room, desiring you,

Thinking of your blue-shadowed silk,
Is music. It is like the strain
Waked in the elders by Susanna:

Of a green evening, clear and warm,
She bathed in her still garden, while
The red-eyed elders, watching, felt

The basses of their beings throb
In witching chords, and their thin blood
Pulse pizzicati of Hosanna.

II

In the green water, clear and warm,
Susanna lay,
She searched
The touch of springs,
And found
Concealed imaginings.
She sighed,
For so much melody.

Upon the bank, she stood
In the cool
Of spent emotions.

She felt, among the leaves,
The dew
Of old devotions.

She walked upon the grass,
Still quavering.
The winds were like her maids
On timid feet,
Fetching her woven scarves,
Yet wavering.

A breath upon her hand
Muted the night.
She turned—
A cymbal crashed,
And roaring horns.

III

Soon, with a noise like tambourines,
Came her attendant Byzantines.

They wondered why Susanna cried
Against the elders by her side;

And as they whispered, the refrain
Was like a willow swept by rain.

Anon, their lamps' uplifted flame
Revealed Susanna and her shame.

And then, the simpering Byzantines
Fled, with a noise like tambourines.

IV

Beauty is momentary in the mind—
The fitful tracing of a portal;
But in the flesh it is immortal.

The body dies; the body's beauty lives.
So evenings die, in their green going,
A wave, interminably flowing.

So gardens die, their meek breath scenting
The cowl of Winter, done repenting.
So maidens die, to the auroral
Celebration of a maiden's choral.

Susanna's music touched the bawdy strings
Of those white elders; but, escaping,
Left only Death's ironic scraping.
Now, in its immortality, it plays
On the clear viol of her memory,
And makes a constant sacrament of praise.

WILLIAM CARLOS WILLIAMS

[1 8 8 3 –]

An admirer of Wallace Stevens' poetry, *but opposed to his central theory, William Carlos Williams is as straightforward as Stevens is indirect: his poems are built on solid blocks of statements rather than on a series of suggestions. He was born September 17, 1883, in Rutherford, New Jersey, of mixed West Indian and Dutch, Jewish and Episcopalian ancestry. He studied medicine in Switzerland, received his M.D. at the University of Pennsylvania, did graduate work in Leipzig, and published his first volume of poetry at twenty-three.*

It was some time before Williams freed himself from his influences, chiefly Ezra Pound and the Imagists, and began to use his own distinctive language. By the time he was seventy-six he had published thirty-eight books of prose and poetry, including Patterson, *a five-volume combination of both. The speech in all but the first few is foursquare, matter-of-fact.*

In common with Whitman, Williams believes that everything has intrinsic beauty and is dignified by use. "No ideas but in things" he declares. He has, as Wallace Stevens wrote, "a passion for the anti-poetic," and he avoids conventional form as well as the traditional poetic idiom. If Williams lacks discrimination, he is faithful to his subjects: everything he touches is revealed in sharp focus and clear detail. He brings significance to what is too often considered insignificant.

A GOODNIGHT

Go to sleep—though of course you will not—
to tideless waves thundering slantwise against
strong embankments, rattle and swish of spray
dashed thirty feet high, caught by the lake wind,
scattered and strewn broadcast in over the steady
car rails! Sleep, sleep! Gulls' cries in a wind-gust
broken by the wind; calculating wings set above
the field of waves breaking.
Go to sleep to the lunge between foam-crests,
refuse churned in the recoil. Food! Food!
Offal! Offal! that holds them in the air, wave-white
for the one purpose, feather upon feather, the wild
chill in their eyes, the hoarseness in their voices—
sleep, sleep . . .

Gentlefooted crowds are treading out your lullaby.
Their arms nudge, they brush shoulders,
hitch this way, then that, mass and surge at the crossings—
lullaby, lullaby! The wild-fowl police whistles,
the enraged roar of the traffic, machine shrieks:
it is all to put you to sleep,
to soften your limbs in relaxed postures,
and that your head slip sidewise, and your hair loosen
and fall over your eyes and over your mouth,
brushing your lips wistfully that you may dream,
sleep and dream—

A black fungus springs out about lonely church doors—
sleep, sleep. The Night, coming down upon
the wet boulevard, would start you awake with his
message, to have in at your window. Pay no
heed to him. He storms at your sill with
cooings, with gesticulations, curses!
You will not let him in. He would keep you from sleeping.
He would have you sit under your desk lamp
brooding, pondering; he would have you
slide out the drawer, take up the ornamented dagger
and handle it. It is late, it is nineteen-nineteen—
go to sleep, his cries are a lullaby;
his jabbering is a sleep-well-my-baby; he is
a crackbrained messenger.

The maid waking you in the morning
when you are up and dressing,
the rustle of your clothes as you raise them—
it is the same tune.
At table the cold, greenish, split grapefruit, its juice
on the tongue, the clink of the spoon in
your coffee, the toast odors say it over and over.

The open street-door lets in the breath of
the morning wind from over the lake.
The bus coming to a halt grinds from its sullen brakes—
lullaby, lullaby. The crackle of a newspaper,
the movement of the troubled coat beside you—
sleep, sleep, sleep, sleep . . .
It is the sting of snow, the burning liquor of
the moonlight, the rush of rain in the gutters packed
with dead leaves: go to sleep, go to sleep.
And the night passes—and never passes—

TO A DOG INJURED IN THE STREET

IT IS MYSELF,
        not the poor beast lying there
                yelping with pain
that brings me to myself with a start—
        as at the explosion
                of a bomb, a bomb that has laid
all the world waste.
        I can do nothing
                but sing about it
and so I am assuaged
        from my pain.

A DROWSY NUMBNESS drowns my sense
        as if of hemlock
                I had drunk. I think
of the poetry
        of René Char
                and all he must have seen
and suffered
        that has brought him
                to speak only of
sedgy rivers,

of daffodils and tulips
whose roots they water,
even to the freeflowing river
that laves the rootlets
of those sweet scented flowers
that people the
milky
way.

I REMEMBER *Norma*
our English setter of my childhood
her silky ears
and expressive eyes.
She had a litter
of pups one night
in our pantry and I kicked
one of them
thinking, in my alarm,
that they
were biting her breasts
to destroy her.

I REMEMBER also
a dead rabbit
lying harmlessly
on the outspread palm
of a hunter's hand.
As I stood by
watching
he took a hunting knife
and with a laugh
thrust it
up into the animal's private parts.
I almost fainted.

WHY SHOULD I think of that now?
the cries of a dying dog
are to be blotted out
as best I can.
René Char,
you are a poet who believes
in the power of beauty
to right all wrongs.
I believe it also.

With invention and courage
we shall surpass
the pitiful dumb beasts,
let all men believe it,
as you have taught me also
to believe it.

H. L. MENCKEN

[1880–1956]

Anathema to political reactionaries and academic Philistines because of his diabolical cleverness and his continual attacks on conventional respectability, Henry Louis Mencken was one of America's great satirists. When he raged—and he assailed everything from religious reformers and "smut-hounds" to pompous senators—it was because of man's failure to live up to the dignity of inherent human values.

He was born September 12, 1880, in Baltimore, Maryland. His forebears were German, and he was the son, he wrote, "of parents who were both American born. . . On my graduation (from Baltimore Polytechnic) my father took me into his tobacco business, but I did not like it, and when he died in 1899, I got a job on the Baltimore Herald." He remained a journalist all his life—a journalist who, as editor of The Smart Set and The American Mercury, became one of the country's most controversial essayists.

Mencken's critical offensive against all buncombe brought him a host of followers. His style was widely (though never successfully) imitated; sophisticated undergraduates quoted from The American Mercury as though it were a campus Bible. On the other hand, Mencken's admirers were outnumbered by his antagonists. One of the latter challenged him: "If you find this country so full of queer and unlovely things, why do you live here?" Unabashed, Mencken replied: "Why do people go to the zoo?" He liked oddities and strange phenomena, and he liked even more to arouse his wrathful opponents, to (as he put it) "stir up the animals."

Mencken was at his most provocative, challenging every platitude and pretension, ridiculing the puritanical shibboleths when, in his late sixties, he suffered a stroke that affected all his faculties except the power to think. He sank into a long aphasia, was totally inactive —a tragic end for one of the liveliest mentalities of his times—and died in his seventy-sixth year, January 29, 1956.

Everything that Mencken wrote disclosed an irreverent spirit, a purposeful mischief-maker who fought anything that had the least taint of sanctimonious cant. He was, in a literal sense, a "disturber of the peace," but the ideas which disturbed his enemies amused even when they irritated. He loved to confound the sententious with such unruly "maxims" as: "Love is the delusion that one woman differs from another." "Bachelors know more about women than married men; if they didn't, they'd be married too." "It's hard to believe that a man is telling the truth when you know that you would lie if you were in his place." "On one issue, at least, men and women agree: both distrust women." "Conscience is the inner voice that warns us that someone may be looking." "Clergyman: a ticket-speculator outside the gate of heaven." "A truth is something somehow discreditable to someone." "Say what you will about the Ten Commandments, you must always come back to the pleasant fact that there are only ten of them."

Mencken is most quotable in the biographical Heathen Days, the critical Prejudices, and In Defence of Women (a defence for which no woman would give thanks). It is, however, as a scholar that he is most respected. The monumental, much-revised The American Language is his major work and will probably outlast his punishing invectives and his most ingenious epigrams.

DOWNFALL OF A REVOLUTIONARY

From *Heathen Days*

OF ALL THE EMINENT CHARACTERS who flourished in the West Baltimore of my infancy, the one most venerated by the boys of my generation was Hoggie Unglebower, an uncouth youth whose empire and influence, radiating out from an humble stable in the alley which ran behind our house in Hollins street, covered altogether an area of at least half a square mile. No storekeeper of that time and place was better known, whether for good or for evil, nor any cop, however heinous, nor any ma'am in the public school up Hollins street hill, nor bad nigger in Vincent alley, nor blind man in practice at Hollins market. Between the longitude of the market and the wilderness of Steuart's Hill, all through a chunk of territory four or five blocks thick, he was a hero to every boy above the age of seven.

The reader of today, soaked in the Freudian sewage for so many years, will assume at once, I suppose, that Hoggie must have been a Lothario, and his headquarters a seraglio. Nothing could have been further from the truth. He was actually almost a Trappist in his glandular life, and his hormones never gave him any visible trouble until much later on, as I shall show in due course. In the days of his greatest glory his view of all human females was predominantly disdainful, but it never led him to use them wickedly, or even impolitely. When a hired girl issued into the alley to flag a rag-and-bone man or hunt for a lost garbage box he would whistle at her satirically and shout "Ah, there!" but at the same time he always took off his hat. To women of greater age and station he was courteous to an extreme degree, and when he visited a neighboring dwelling with his terriers to purge it of rats he always wiped his feet at the back door, and never failed to address the lady of the house as Ma'am.

No, Hoggie was not carnal in the Catechism sense, and I incline to think that that was one of the reasons all the boys so greatly respected him. The male infantry of today, debauched by Progressive Education and the sex hygiene quackery, are said to be adepts at the arts of love before they are more than half house-broken, but that was certainly not true in my time. The boys of that Mousterian generation, until adolescence came down upon them, regarded girls with frank aversion, and had as little truck with them as with cats or cops. It is, of course, a fact that the probable delights of amour were occasionally discussed, but it was always vaguely and with a considerable uneasiness, for any move to put a concrete project into effect would have involved a close approach to females, and that was never done if it could be helped. What made Hoggie a personage was nothing in that line; it was mainly, and perhaps even only, his successful and notorious resistance to the doctrine that cleanliness is next to godliness.

In his father's stable he led the life dreamed of as ideal by all normal boys, then, now, and forever. No one, it appeared, had any authority (at all events any authority that he recognized) to make him comb his hair, or brush his clothes, or shine his shoes, or wash behind the ears. He wallowed there day in and day out, including especially Sundays, in such slops as every normal boy longs to own, but is seldom permitted to have. Preferring the society of horses and dogs to that of men, he lived among them freely and unashamedly, sleeping with them, eating with them, and sharing his confidences with them. He got his hair cut when he damned well pleased, and it wasn't often. Hating neckties, he never wore them. When he thirsted, he drank from the end of the stable hose, and if anyone stopped to gape at him he squeezed the hose (which was old, soft and full of holes) and sent a fine stream into the gaper's eye.

In brief, a magnificent specimen of Natural Man, somehow surviving unscathed every corruption of an effete and pusillanimous civilization. He came of a bourgeois family and had been to school, but had fought off successfully every effort to denaturize him. His days were busy, and full of enterprises that, to us boys, were important, difficult and romantic. He was the architect, builder and navigator of the largest and fastest double-decker sleds known in West Baltimore, and probably the best repairer of boys' wagons ever seen in Christendom. He knew how to knock a barrel to pieces without splitting any of the staves, and how to put it together again. He could teach tricks to horses, and had so far mastered their vocabulary of whinnies and pawings that he carried on long conversations with them, often laughing at their pawky humor. He was a dog doctor of great gifts, and kept a large stock of medicines for his patients on a shelf in the stable. To cops, despite all their clubs, handcuffs and sidearms, he presented a calm and unflickering eye, and they had a high respect for him, for when he went to the aid of one who was overwhelmed by a passel of bad niggers, the bad niggers lost consciousness almost instantly, and awoke in the watch-house with huge bumps on their heads. Hoggie, disdaining firearms, did his fighting with clubs, and had an arsenal of them ready to hand—little ones for light jobs, and thick, warty shillalahs for really earnest work. When he came down upon a skull something gave way, and it was never Hoggie or his weapon.

He was the best dog-trainer for miles around, and could transfer even the sorriest mutt into a competent ratter. For this purpose he liked to have them young; indeed, he preferred to begin on them as soon as their eyes were open. At that age, of course, they were no match for actual rats, and even the more active sort of mice had the edge on them. To equalize the odds, Hoggie would catch infant rats in a trap, pull their teeth with a pair of pliers, and then throw them into a barrel with a couple of his pupils. As the latter gained in strength and technique, he would test them with rats of gradually larger growth, retaining at first one tooth each, and then two, and then four or five, and finally a whole set, upper and lower. Now and then a freshman was badly mauled in these exercises, but Hoggie did not despair, for he knew that any sort of educational process was bound to be painful, and he preferred the hard way for dogs as for men. His graduates were all recognized virtuosi. One day he let me go along as he took one to a hay-and-feed warehouse for a final examination. The candidate was only a spindly black-and-tan, but within three minutes by the watch he had unearthed, run down and killed a whole bucket of rats, some of them of the fearsome sewer variety, with fangs two inches long.

Hoggie admired dogs, and was admired by them in turn, though his medicating of them ran to heroic measures. His usual prescription for the common run of canine malaises was the better part of half a pound of Glauber's salts. The colored quacks who practised a Dahomeyan farriery in Reveille's livery stable down the street hesitated to give so large a dose to anything short of a cart horse, but Hoggie believed that it was foolish to temporize with disease, and proved it by curing most of his patients. He was also adept at surgery, and could point to at least a dozen dogs that he had treated successfully for broken bones. He sutured the lacerations that followed dog-fights with the thick, black thread used by shoemakers, and always waxed it carefully before setting to work. He was, I believe, the first canine dentist ever in practice in Baltimore; to this day, in fact, they are rare. He pulled the damaged teeth of his patients with the same pair of pliers that he employed to prepare rats for his academy, and sometimes he had to pull very hard. I heard him say once that most dogs, like most human beings, were born with too many teeth, and that getting rid of half a dozen or so toned up their systems and improved their dispositions.

No one that I ever heard of approached him in the delicate art of trimming puppies' tails. His technique was of the whirlwind variety: the tail was off before the puppy had a chance to be alarmed. In my earliest days he had a formidable rival in old Julius, an Aframerican with headquarters in Reveille's stable, but as the years passed he gobbled all of Julius's practice, and in the end his mastery was admitted by everyone. In that era the different breeds of dogs in vogue nearly all wore their tails clipped, so Hoggie was kept busy. I have seen him knock off six or eight of an afternoon, with the whole Hollins-street gang for a gallery. Our own dogs, from the early eighties onward to the middle nineties, all passed through his hands, and every one of them was friendly to him afterward, and wagged its stump whenever it encountered him. He also treated dogs when they took to nibbling grass in the yard or showed other signs of indisposition—always with that massive dose of Glauber's salts as a starter. He had plenty of other medicines, and used them freely on occasion, but he depended mainly on the Glauber's salts, just as Dr. Wiley, our family doctor, depended on castor oil.

Hoggie's incurable boyishness was shown by the fact that, for all his fondness for horses and dogs, he hated cats with a blind and implacable hatred, and spent a great deal of his time tracking them down and executing them. There was a time, indeed, when his chronic war upon them aroused some ill-will in the neighborhood—but not, of course, among the boys. What was done about it I forget, but for a while he locked himself in his stable, and refused to have any truck with human society. Even the cops were given to understand that their room was preferred to their company. But then a stray cat scratched a baby down the block, and under cover of the ensuing uproar Hoggie emerged from his solitude, and resumed his crusade. I well recall the day when, as a gesture of triumph, he threw eight dead cats into the alley in one lot, and got into a row with the street cleaner who had to haul them away. The street cleaner, it appeared, held that a person engaged in such wholesale slaughters should dispose of his own dead, and not dump them on public officials. He cited the example of the hotels which carted off their own garbage, and that of the candy factory down the alley which kept a wagon to handle its own boiler ashes, but Hoggie refused to allow any weight to the argument. So far as he was concerned, he said, the cats could lie in the alley until the Judgment Day, along with the rats that he heaved out almost daily—the melancholy refuse of his college for puppies. The street cleaner muttered a while longer and threatened several times to submit the whole matter to Murphy the cop, but in the end he loaded the cats upon his cart, and during the weeks that followed he loaded many others. Until a fresh generation of kittens worked its way in from Hollins market, the Union Square neighborhood was almost as bare of *Felidae* as Greenland. A few, of course, survived in houses, but they were kept as closely penned as canary birds.

The boys of the Hollins-street gang believed, like well-educated American boys everywhere else, that cats had nine lives, but Hoggie dissented. He admitted freely that no cat within his experience ever had so little as one life, but he insisted that his researches indicated that five was the limit. Indeed, it was only battle-scarred old Toms who went even that far: the average free-lance cat, depleted by its wandering, precarious life, was disposed of finally after being killed three or four times. One day the alley metaphysician, Old Wesley, undertook to point out a possible statistical fallacy in this doctrine. What evidence was there, he demanded, that the Toms which Hoggie killed five times had not been killed four times before by other executioners, thus making up the classical nine? This argument, rather to the astonishment of his listening admirers, floored Hoggie completely. The louder he howled against it, the more he became confused and out of temper, and in the end he was reduced to the sorry expedient of denouncing Wesley as a sassy nigger, and threatening to set the medical students on him. His failure in the debate, and above all his resort to what amounted to forensic blackmail, lowered his stock with the boys of Hollins street, but not for long. In a little while he recovered face gloriously by staging, in the privacy of his stable, a dog-fight that went down into history as the most gory ever seen in West Baltimore.

Despite his unhappy encounter with Old Wesley, he was commonly on good terms with the colored people who lived in the alley, and exercised a general jurisdiction over them, milder and more understanding than that of the cops. They had a high respect for him, and went to him in their troubles, though in his practice as dog-doctor and cat-and-rat exterminator he was uncomfortably close to a medical student. He did not hold himself out as skilled at human medicine, but the bottles he kept for dosing dogs were at the disposal of any blackamoor who wanted to try them, and many professed to be benefited. In particular, the liniment he used on dogs run over by carts was said to be very efficacious against rheumatoid afflictions in *Anthropoidea.* Once he scared off all his Aframerican patients by stuffing a dead cat with oats, and using black shoe-buttons for its eyes. This gruesome object, while it remained on exhibition, kept all the colored people out of his stable, though we white boys thought it was very nobby. It didn't last long, for the huge, ferocious rats of Hollins market quickly heard of it, and one night they rushed the stable and devoured it, eyes and all. All that remained of it the next morning was a carriage-bolt that Hoggie had employed to counteract the flaccidity of the oats.

His downfall I can place with reasonable accuracy in the year 1890, when I was ten years old and he must have been about twenty-two or three. One afternoon in Summer, on my way to Reveille's livery stable to visit my father's horse, John, who was laid up with epizootic, I encountered Hoggie at the corner of Baltimore street in such vestments that I stopped dead in my tracks, and gaped at him as if he had been a cop in motley or a two-headed boy. He had on a brand-new suit of store clothes, golden brown in color, and wore a pair of the immense yellow shoes then in fashion—as wide, almost, as a street-car at the ball of the foot, but stretched out to a long point at the toe. On his head was a cartwheel straw hat with a brim at least six inches deep, and a gorgeous red-and-white ribbon. His collar, which was of fresh celluloid, rose above a boiled shirt that gleamed like snow on the Alps, and around it he wore a bright green four-in-hand tie, with the ends tucked over to expose a stud that glittered like a diamond, but was no doubt something else. He was shaved so closely that his neck and chin were criss-crossed with red gashes, and the rest of his face was a brilliant vermilion. Finally, and most amazing of all, his hair—at least such of it as I could see below his hat—was cropped to its roots according to the best technique of Barber Lehnert. As I passed him, I caught a gust of Jockey Club scent, familiar to me as the special favorite of our current hired girl. I was so astonished that I passed him without greeting him, staring foolishly. He paid no attention to me, but stalked along painfully, like a man in a barrel. I spread the news over the neighborhood, and Hoggie's secret quickly leaked out.

He had succumbed at last, after all his years of outlawry, to one of the most conventional of human weaknesses: he had fallen in love. The ancient psychosis that had floored and made a mock of Marc Antony, Dante and Goethe—but *not* Shakespeare, Napoleon Bonaparte or George Washington—had now fetched him too. Some inconsiderable and probably pie-faced slip of a girl, name unknown, had collared him, tamed him, and made of him the dreadful popinjay that I had seen. The rest of the pathetic story follows classical lines, and is soon told. Hoggie disappeared from his stable, and was reported to be occupying a bedroom in the Unglebower family home, and actually eating at table. In a little while he vanished altogether, and reports came in that he was married to the lady, living in far Northwest Baltimore, and at work as a horse-car driver. That was the last I ever heard of him.

THE HILLS OF ZION

From *Prejudices: Fifth Series*

IT WAS HOT WEATHER when they tried the infidel Scopes at Dayton, Tenn., but I went down there very willingly, for I was eager to see something of evangelical Christianity as a going concern. In the big cities of the Republic, despite the endless efforts of consecrated men, it is laid up with a wasting disease. The very Sunday-school superintendents, taking jazz from the stealthy radio, shake their fire-proof legs; their pupils, moving into adolescence, no longer respond to the proliferating hormones by enlisting for missionary service in Africa, but resort to necking instead. Even in Dayton, I found, though the mob was up to do execution upon Scopes, there was a strong smell of antinomianism. The nine churches of the village were all half empty on Sunday, and weeds choked their yards. Only two or three of the resident pastors managed to sustain themselves by their ghostly science; the rest had to take orders for mail-order pantaloons or work in the adjacent strawberry fields; one, I heard, was a barber. On the courthouse green a score of sweating theologians debated the darker passages of Holy Writ day and night, but I soon found that they were all volunteers, and that the local faithful, while interested in their exegesis as an intellectual exercise, did not permit it to impede the indigenous debaucheries. Exactly twelve minutes after I reached the village I was taken in tow by a Christian man and introduced to the favorite tipple of the Cumberland Range: half corn liquor and half Coca-Cola. It seemed a dreadful dose to me, but I found that the Dayton illuminati got it down with gusto, rubbing their tummies and rolling their eyes. I include among them the chief local proponents of the Mosaic cosmogony. They were all hot for Genesis, but their faces were far too florid to belong to teetotalers, and when a pretty girl came tripping down the main street, which was very often, they reached for the places where their neckties should have been with all the amorous enterprise of movie actors. It seemed somehow strange.

An amiable newspaper woman of Chattanooga, familiar with those uplands, presently enlightened me. Dayton, she explained, was simply a great capital like any other. That is to say, it was to Rhea county what Atlanta was to Georgia or Paris to France. That is to say, it was predominantly epicurean and sinful. A country girl from some remote valley of the county, coming into town for her semi-annual bottle of Lydia Pinkham's Vegetable Compound, shivered on approaching Robinson's drugstore quite as a country girl from up-State New York might shiver on approaching the Metropolitan Opera House. In every village lout she saw a potential white-slaver. The hard sidewalks hurt her feet. Temptations of the flesh bristled to all sides of her, luring her to Hell. This newspaper woman told me of a session with just such a visitor, holden a few days before. The latter waited outside one of the town hot-dog and Coca-Cola shops while her husband negotiated with a hardware merchant across the street. The newspaper woman, idling along and observing that the stranger was badly used by the heat, invited her to step into the shop for a glass of Coca-Cola. The invitation brought forth only a gurgle of terror. Coca-Cola, it quickly appeared, was prohibited by the country lady's pastor, as a levantine and Hell-sent narcotic. He also prohibited coffee and tea—and pies! He had his doubts about white bread and boughten meat. The newspaper woman, interested, inquired about ice-cream. It was, she found, not specifically prohibited, but going into a Coca-Cola shop to get it would be clearly sinful. So she offered to get a saucer of it, and bring it out to the sidewalk. The visitor vacillated—and came near being lost. But God saved her in the nick of time. When the newspaper woman emerged from the place she was in full flight up the street. Later on her husband, mounted on a mule, overtook her four miles out the mountain pike.

This newspaper woman, whose kindness covered city infidels as well as Alpine Christians, offered to take me back in the hills to a place where the old-time religion was genuinely on tap. The Scopes jury, she explained, was composed mainly of its customers, with a few Dayton sophisticates added to leaven the mass. It would thus be instructive to climb the heights and observe the former at their ceremonies. The trip, fortunately, might be made by automobile. There was a road running out of Dayton to Morgantown, in the mountains to the westward, and thence beyond. But foreigners, it appeared, would have to approach the sacred grove cautiously, for the upland worshipers were very shy, and at the first sight of a strange face they would adjourn their orgy and slink into the forest. They were not to be feared, for God had long since forbidden them to practise assassination, or even assault, but if they were alarmed a rough trip would go for naught. So, after dreadful bumpings up a long and narrow road, we parked our car in a little woodpath a mile or two beyond the tiny village of Morgantown, and made the rest of the approach on foot, deployed like skirmishers. Far off in a dark, romantic glade a flickering light was visible, and out of the silence came the rumble of exhortation. We could distinguish the figure of the preacher only as a moving mote in the light: it was like looking down the tube of a dark-field microscope. Slowly and cautiously we crossed what seemed to be a pasture, and then we stealthily edged further and further. The light now grew larger and we could begin to make out what was going on. We went ahead on all fours, like snakes in the grass.

From the great limb of a mighty oak hung a couple of crude torches of the sort that car inspectors thrust under Pullman cars when a train pulls in at night. In the guttering glare was the preacher, and for a while we could see no one else. He was an immensely tall and thin mountaineer in blue jeans, his collarless shirt open at the neck and his hair a tousled mop. As he preached he paced up and down under the smoking flambeaux, and at each turn he thrust his arms into the air and yelled "Glory to God!" We crept nearer in the shadow of the cornfield, and began to hear more of his discourse. He was preaching on the Day of Judgment. The high kings of the earth, he roared, would all fall down and die; only the sanctified would stand up to receive the Lord God of Hosts. One of these kings he mentioned by name, the king of what he called Greece-y. The king of Greece-y, he said, was doomed to Hell. We crawled forward a few more yards and began to see the audience. It was seated on benches ranged round the preacher in a circle. Behind him sat a row of elders, men and women. In front were the younger folk. We crept on cautiously, and individuals rose out of the ghostly gloom. A young mother sat suckling her baby, rocking as the preacher paced up and down. Two scared little girls hugged each other, their pigtails down their backs. An immensely huge mountain woman, in a gingham dress, cut in one piece, rolled on her heels at every "Glory to God!" To one side, and but half visible, was what appeared to be a bed. We found afterward that half a dozen babies were asleep upon it.

The preacher stopped at last, and there arose out of the darkness a woman with her hair pulled back into a little tight knot. She began so quietly that we couldn't hear what she said, but soon her voice rose resonantly and we could follow her. She was denouncing the reading of books. Some wandering book agent, it appeared, had come to her cabin and tried to sell her a specimen of his wares. She refused to touch it. Why, indeed, read a book? If what was in it was true, then everything in it was already in the Bible. If it was false, then reading it would imperil the soul. This syllogism from the Caliph Omar complete, she sat down. There followed a hymn, led by a somewhat fat brother wearing silver-rimmed country spectacles. It droned on for half a dozen stanzas, and then the first speaker resumed the floor. He argued that the gift of tongues was real and that education was a snare. Once his children could read the Bible, he said, they had enough. Beyond lay only infidelity and damnation. Sin stalked the cities. Dayton itself was a Sodom. Even Morgantown had begun to forget God. He sat down, and a female aurochs in gingham got up. She began quietly, but was soon leaping and roaring, and it was hard to follow her. Under cover of the turmoil we sneaked a bit closer.

A couple of other discourses followed, and there were two or three hymns. Suddenly a change of mood began to make itself felt. The last hymn ran longer than the others, and dropped gradually into a monotonous, unintelligible chant. The leader beat time with his book. The faithful broke out with exultations. When the singing ended there was a brief palaver that we could not hear, and two of the men moved a bench into the circle of light directly under the flambeaux. Then a half-grown girl emerged from the darkness and threw herself upon it. We noticed with astonishment that she had bobbed hair. "This sister," said the leader, "has asked for prayers." We moved a bit closer. We could now see faces plainly, and hear every word. At a signal all the faithful crowded up to the bench and began to pray—not in unison, but each for himself. At another they all fell on their knees, their arms over the penitent. The leader kneeled facing us, his head alternately thrown back dramatically or buried in his hands. Words spouted from his lips like bullets from a machine-gun—appeals to God to pull the penitent back out of Hell, defiances of the demons of the air, a vast impassioned jargon of apocalyptic texts. Suddenly he rose to his feet, threw back his head and began to speak in the tongues—blub-blub-blub, gurgle-gurgle-gurgle. His voice rose to a higher register. The climax was a shrill, inarticulate squawk, like that of a man throttled. He fell headlong across the pyramid of supplicants.

From the squirming and jabbering mass a young woman gradually detached herself—a woman not uncomely, with a pathetic homemade cap on her head. Her head jerked back, the veins of her neck swelled, and her fists went to her throat as if she were fighting for breath. She bent backward until she was like half a hoop. Then she suddenly snapped forward. We caught a flash of the whites of her eyes. Presently her whole body began to be convulsed—great throes that began at the shoulders and ended at the hips. She would leap to her feet, thrust her arms in air, and then hurl herself upon the heap. Her praying flattened out into a mere delirious caterwauling. I describe the thing discreetly, and as a strict behaviorist. The lady's subjective sensations I leave to infidel pathologists, privy to the works of Ellis, Freud and Moll. Whatever they were, they were obviously not painful, for they were accompanied by vast heavings and gurglings of a joyful and even ecstatic nature. And they seemed to be contagious, too, for soon a second penitent, also female, joined the first, and then came a third, and a fourth, and a fifth. The last one had an extraordinary violent attack. She began with mild enough jerks of the head, but in a moment she was bounding all over the place, like a chicken with its head cut off. Every time her head came up a stream of hosannas would issue out of it. Once she collided with a dark, undersized brother, hitherto silent and stolid. Contact with her set him off as if he had been kicked by a mule. He leaped into the air, threw back his head, and began to gargle as if with a mouthful of BB shot. Then he loosed one tremendous, stentorian sentence in the tongues, and collapsed.

By this time the performers were quite oblivious to the profane universe and so it was safe to go still closer. We left our hiding and came up to the little circle of light. We slipped into the vacant seats on one of the rickety benches. The heap of mourners was directly before us. They bounced into us as they cavorted. The smell that they radiated, sweating there in that obscene heap, half suffocated us. Not all of them, of course, did the thing in the grand manner. Some merely moaned and rolled their eyes. The female ox in gingham flung her great bulk on the ground and jabbered an unintelligible prayer. One of the men, in the intervals between fits, put on his spectacles and read his Bible. Beside me on the bench sat the young mother and her baby. She suckled it through the whole orgy, obviously fascinated by what was going on, but never venturing to take any hand in it. On the bed just outside the light the half a dozen other babies slept peacefully. In the shadows, suddenly appearing and as suddenly going away, were vague figures, whether of believers or of scoffers I do not know. They seemed to come and go in couples. Now and then a couple at the ringside would step out and vanish into the black night. After a while some came back, the males looking somewhat sheepish. There was whispering outside the circle of vision. A couple of Model T Fords lurched up the road, cutting holes in the darkness with their lights. Once someone out of sight loosed a bray of laughter.

All this went on for an hour or so. The original penitent, by this time, was buried three deep beneath the heap. One caught a glimpse, now and then, of her yellow bobbed hair, but then she would vanish again. How she breathed down there I don't know; it was hard enough six feet away, with a strong five-cent cigar to help. When the praying brothers would rise up for a bout with the tongues their faces were streaming with perspiration. The fat harridan in gingham sweated like a longshoreman. Her hair got loose and fell down over her face. She fanned herself with her skirt. A powerful old gal she was, plainly equal in her day to a bout with obstetrics and a week's washing on the same morning, but this was worse than a week's washing. Finally, she fell into a heap, breathing in great, convulsive gasps.

Finally, we got tired of the show and returned to Dayton. It was nearly eleven o'clock—an immensely late hour for those latitudes—but the whole town was still gathered in the courthouse yard, listening to the disputes of theologians. The Scopes trial had brought them in from all directions. There was a friar wearing a sandwich sign announcing that he was the Bible champion of the world. There was a Seventh Day Adventist arguing that Clarence Darrow was the beast with seven heads and ten horns described in Revelation xiii, and that the end of the world was at hand. There was an evangelist made up like Andy Gump, with the news that atheists in Cincinnati were preparing to descend upon Dayton, hang the eminent Judge Raulston, and burn the town. There was an ancient who maintained that no Catholic could be a Christian. There was the eloquent Dr. T. T. Martin, of Blue Mountain, Miss., come to town with a truck-load of torches and hymn-books to put Darwin in his place. There was a singing brother bellowing apocalyptic hymns. There was William Jennings Bryan, followed everywhere by a gaping crowd. Dayton was having a roaring time. It was better than the circus. But the note of devotion was simply not there; the Daytonians, after listening a while, would slip away to

Robinson's drug-store to regale themselves with Coca-Cola, or to the lobby of the Aqua Hotel, where the learned Raulston sat in state, judicially picking his teeth. The real religion was not present. It began at the bridge over the town creek, where the road makes off for the hills.

THE AMERICAN LANGUAGE

In 1936, Mencken published a new, revised edition of his massive The American Language. *In the same year he wrote for the* Yale Review *this essay, summing up his personal and thoroughly American approach to his subject.*

THE FIRST ENGLISHMAN to notice an Americanism sneered at it aloofly, thus setting a fashion that many of his countrymen have been following ever since. He was one Francis Moore, a ruffian who came out to Georgia with Oglethorpe in 1735, and the word that upset him was *bluff*, in the sense of "a cliff or headland with a broad precipitous face." He did not deign to argue against it; he simply dismissed it as "barbarous," apparently assuming that all Englishmen of decent instincts would agree with him. For nearly a century they seem to have done so, and *bluff* lingered sadly below the salt. When it was printed at all in Great Britain it was set off by sanitary quotation marks, or accompanied by other hints of deprecation, as *rubberneck*, *hot spot*, and *nerts* are accompanied today. But then, in 1830, the eminent Sir Charles Lyell used it shamelessly in the first volume of his monumental *Principles of Geology*, and from that day to this it has been a perfectly respectable if somewhat unfamiliar word in England, with a place in every dictionary.

Its history is the history of almost countless other Americanisms. They have been edging their way into English since early colonial times, and, for more than a century past, in constantly increasing volume; but I can't recall one that didn't have to run a gantlet of opposition in the motherland, at times verging upon the frantic. After the Revolution, that opposition took on the proportions of a holy war. Never an American book came out that the English reviewers did not belabor its vocabulary violently. The brunt of the attack, of course, had to be borne by the poetasters of the era—for example, Joel Barlow, whose *Columbiad* (1807) loosed a really terrifying geyser of abuse. But even the most serious writers got their share—among them, Jefferson, John Marshall, Noah Webster, and John Quincy Adams. Jefferson's crime was that he had invented the verb *to belittle*. It was, one may argue plausibly, a very logical, useful, and perhaps even nifty word, and seventy-five years later the prissy Anthony Trollope was employing it without apology. But when Jefferson ventured to use it in his *Notes on Virginia* (1787) the *London Review* tossed and raged in a manner befitting the discovery of a brace of dueling pistols beneath the cope of the Archbishop of Canterbury; and for several years following, its dudgeon was supported virtuously by most of the other reviews. "What an expression!" roared the *London*. "It may be an elegant one in Virginia, but for our part, all we can do is to *guess* at its meaning. For shame, Mr. Jefferson! Freely, good sir, will we forgive all your attacks, impotent as they are illiberal, upon our national character; but for the future spare—O spare, we beseech you, our mother tongue!"

The underscoring of *guess* was a fling in passing at another foul Americanism. It was the belief of most Englishmen then, as it is today, that the use of the verb in the sense of *to suppose* or *assume* originated in this country. It is actually to be found, in that meaning precisely, in *Measure for Measure* and *Henry VI;* nay, in Chaucer, Wycliffe, and Gower. But such historical considerations have never daunted the more ardent preservers of the King's English. When a word acquires an American flavor it becomes anathema to them, even though it may go back to Boadicea. *To advocate* offers an instructive example. It appeared in English in the dark backward and abysm of time, but during the eighteenth century it seems to have dropped out of general use, though Burke used it. Towards the end of the century it came into vogue in this country, and soon it made its way back to the land of its birth. It was received with all the honors proper to an invasion of Asiatic cholera. The reviews denounced it as loutish, "Gothic," and against God, and lumped it with *to compromit* and *to happify* as proof that civilization was impossible in America, and would be so forevermore. Even Benjamin Franklin, returning from England in 1789, was alarmed into begging Noah Webster to "reprobate" it, along with *to notice*, *to progress*, and *to oppose*. There is no record of Noah's reply, but it is most unlikely that he did any reprobating, for when he began to make dictionaries he included all four verbs, and they have been listed in every considerable dictionary published since, whether in this country or in England.

The leader of the heroic struggle to keep Americanisms out of Britain, in its early stages, was the celebrated William Gifford, editor of the *Quarterly Review*. Gifford was a killer in general practice, and his savage assaults on

Wordsworth, Shelley, and Keats are still unpleasantly remembered. He was the first magazine editor in history to make the trade pay, and when he died in 1828 he left £25,000 and was buried in Westminster Abbey. One of his major specialties was the villainousness of everything American, from politics to table manners and from theology to speechways. Among the allegations that he either made himself or permitted his contributors to make were these: (*a*) that the Americans employed naked colored women to wait upon them at table, (*b*) that they kidnapped Scotsmen, Irishmen, Hollanders, and Welshmen and sold them into slavery, and (*c*) that they were planning to repudiate the English language altogether, and adopt Hebrew in its place. This last charge, as it flew from tongue to tongue, acquired variorum readings. One of them made the new American language an Indian dialect, another made it Greek, and a third was to the effect that the people of Britain would be forced to acquire Greek, thus leaving English to the wicked will of the barbaric Yankees. It all sounds idiotic today, but in 1814 it was taken quite seriously by many Englishmen. Gifford was a tyrannical editor and so vastly enjoyed slashing his contributors' copy that Southey once denounced him as "a butcherly review-gelder." But anything that was against the damyankee passed his eye unscathed, and he piled up accusations in a manner so shameless that the *North American Review* was moved to protest that if the tirade went on it would "turn into bitterness the last drops of good will towards England that exist in the United States."

In the early twenties of that century there was some amelioration, and when Gifford retired from the *Quarterly* in 1824, voices that were almost conciliatory began to be heard. They heaped praises on Niagara Falls, found something to commend in Cooper's *Spy*, and even had kind words for the speed and luxuriousness of American canalboats. But my most diligent researches have failed to unearth anything complimentary to the American language. It continued to be treated as a grotesque and immoral gibberish, full of uncouth terms and at war with all the canons of English. Every British traveler who came to these shores between the War of 1812 and the Civil War had something to say about the neologisms his ears and eyes encountered on his tour, and nearly all were constrained to deplore them. Captain Basil Hall, who was here in 1827 and 1828, went about in a palpitating daze, confounded and outraged by the signs on American places of business. *Clothing Store* he interpreted after long thought, and *Flour and Feed Store* after prayer and soul-searching, but what on earth was a *Leather and Finding Store?* Captain Thomas Hamilton, who followed five years later, found it impossible to penetrate to "the precise import" of *Dry-Goods Store*, and when he encountered an establishment offering *Hollow Ware, Spiders, and Fire-Dogs* he gave up in despair.

Hall was not one to take it lying down. He decided to call upon Noah Webster, whose American Dictionary of the English Language had just come out, to find out what the Yankees meant by using the mother tongue so cruelly. Webster shocked him by arguing stoutly that "his countrymen had not only a right to adopt new words, but were obliged to modify the language to suit the novelty of the circumstances, geographical and political, in which they were placed." The great lexicographer "who taught millions to spell but not one to sin" went on to observe judicially that it was "quite impossible to stop the progress of language—it is like the course of the Mississippi, the motion of which, at times, is scarcely perceptible; yet even then it possesses a momentum quite irresistible. Words and expressions will be forced into use in spite of all the exertions of all the writers in the world."

"But surely," persisted Hall, "such innovations are to be deprecated?"

"I don't think that," replied old Noah. "If a word becomes universally current in America, where English is spoken, why should it not take its station in the language?"

"Because," declared Hall with magnificent pertinacity, "there are words enough already."

This heroic dogma is still heard in England, where even native novelties are commonly opposed violently, and not infrequently strangled at birth. There seems to be, in the modern Englishman, very little of that ecstasy in wordmaking which so prodigiously engrossed his Elizabethan forebears. Shakespeare alone probably put more new words into circulation than all the English writers since Carlyle, and they were much better ones. The ideal over there today is not picturesque and exhilarating utterance, but correct and reassuring utterance, and one of its inevitable fruits is that bowwow jargon which Sir Arthur Quiller-Couch describes in *On the Art of Writing* as "the medium through which boards of government, county councils, syndicates, committees, commercial firms, express the processes as well as the conclusions of their thought, and so voice the reason of their being." It is, at its worst, at least in accord with what are taken to be the principles of English grammar, and at its best it shows excellent manners and even a kind of mellifluous elegance; indeed, the English, taking one with another, may be said to write much better than we do—at all events by the standards of the schoolmaster. But what they write is seldom animated by anything properly describable as bounce. It lacks novelty, variety, audacity. There is little juice in it. The reader confronted by it is treated politely and lulled pleasantly, but he seldom enjoys the enchantment of surprise. That diligent search for new and racy locutions which occupied so much of the workday of Walt Whitman and William Dean Howells alike, and is practiced so assiduously by scores of saucy Andersons and Hemingways, Sandburgs and Saroyans today, is carried on across the ocean by only a few extravagant eccentrics, virtually all of whom—for example, James Joyce and Ezra Pound—are non- and even anti-Englishmen. The hundred-per-cent English writers, save when they stoop to conscious wickedness, seldom depart very far from the jargon of Quiller-Couch. It is by no means a monopoly of the classes he named, nor is it reserved for solemn occasions. I find it also in my favorite English weekly, the *News of the World*, which is devoted principally to sports, the theaters, and the more scabrous varieties of crime, and is probably a far better mirror of England than the *Times*. When the *News of the World* reports the downfall of a rural dean or a raid on a Mayfair night club, the thing is done in a style so tight and brittle that nothing to match it is discoverable in this country, at least outside the pages of the *Homiletic Review*. "When we want to freshen our speech," Mrs. Virginia Woolf was lately saying, "we borrow from American—*poppycock, rambunctious, flip-flop, booster, good mixer*. All the expressive, ugly, vigorous slang which creeps into use among us, first in talk, later in writing, comes from across the Atlantic."

But whether slang or something better, it always encounters opposition—sometimes merely sullen, but at other times extremely violent. At more or less regular intervals, war upon the invasion is declared formally, and there ensues a long uproar, with the papers full of choleric letters to the editor. One such sharpening of activity was loosed early in 1933, when the chief constable of Wallasey, a suburb of Liverpool, reported in alarm that his policemen were being called *cops* by the tougher youngsters of the place, and otherwise insulted with blasphemies picked up from American movies. "*Oh-yeahs*," he said, "are frequent in answer to charges, and we are promised *shoots-up in the burg* [*sic*] and threatened to be *bumped-off*." Half the amateur publicists who took a hand in the discussion which followed, advocated using the cat on the offenders, and the other half demanded that American movies be barred from England as intolerable public menaces, like cattle infected with foot-and-mouth disease. As usual, the debate ended in philological futilities. Was *oh yeah* actually English, even bad English, insane English? Or was it only an American borrowing from one of the dialects of the savage Red Indians, or maybe from Polish, Pennsylvania Dutch, Gullah, Yiddish, or some other such godless and anti-British lingo? No matter! *Oh yeah* continues to flourish from the Lizard to Unst, and with it *cop* flourishes too. The latter, in fact, has swept upward from the level of bad boys baiting constables to that of bishops following their transcendental occasions. Even before the chief constable of Wallasey sounded his cry of "Wolf!" a right reverend father in God had been charged before the Farnham (Surrey) magistrates with applying *speed-cop* on a public road to a member of the *mobile police*. Overhauled in his car, so the testimony went, he had demanded, "Are you a *speed-cop?*" His Lordship denied with some heat that he had used the term, or anything else so unseemly, but the magistrates apparently concluded that he must have let it slip, for they took a serious view of his very modest adventure in speeding, fined him £10, and suspended his driving license for three months. I give his name and dignities as a warning to lesser evil-doers. He was the Right Reverend Cyril Henry Gelding-Bird, D.D. (Oxon.), Assistant Bishop of Guildford and Archdeacon of Dorking, and a man previously unknown to the police.

Whenever an Americanism comes publicly into question in England, there are efforts to track down its etymology, and sometimes the theories offered are extremely bizarre. In January, 1935, for example, the London *Morning Post* opened its columns to a furious and fantastic discussion of the verb-phrase, *to get his goat*. I content myself with one of the explanations: "Among the Negroes in Harlem it is the custom for each household to keep a goat to act as general scavenger. Occasionally one man will steal another's goat, and the household débris then accumulates to the general annoyance." The truth is that *to get his goat* seems to be of French origin; and in the form of *prendre sa chèvre*, philological genealogists have traced it back to the year 1585. But whatever is strange and upsetting is put down, in England, to the hellish ingenuity of Americans—save, of course, when genuine Americanisms are claimed as really English. This last happens often enough to give what may be called a cockeyed aspect to the perennial pother. In 1934 even the learned Dr. C. T. Onions, one of the editors of the great Oxford Dictionary, succumbed to the madness by offering to find in the dictionary any alleged Americanism that a reporter for the London *Evening News* could name. The reporter began discreetly with *fresh* (in the sense of *saucy*), *to figure* (in the sense of *to believe* or *conclude*), and *to grill* (in the sense of *to question*), and Dr. Onions duly found them all. But when the reporter proceeded to *bunkum*, the learned editor had to forget conveniently that its progenitor was the thoroughly American *buncombe*, when *rake-off* followed he had to admit that the earliest example in the dictionary was from an American work, and when *boloney* and *nerts* were hurled at him he blew up with a bang.

Here, of course, Dr. Onions and his interlocutor ended on the level of slang, but there is no telling where they would be if they could be translated to the year 2036. *Boloney*, like *to belittle*, has the imprimatur of an eminent tribune of the people, and is quite as respectable, philologically speaking, as *buncombe*, *gerrymander*, *pork barrel*, *filibuster*, *carpetbagger*, *gag rule*, or *on the fence*. All these came into American from the argot of politics, and got only frowns from the schoolmarm, but they are all quite sound American today, and most of them have gone into English. As for *nerts*, it seems to be but one more member of an endless dynasty of euphemisms, beginning with *zounds* and coming down to *son-of-a-gun*, *gee*, and *darn*. *Darn*, like *nerts*, is an Americanism, and Dr. Louise Pound has demonstrated that it descends from *eternal*, which first turned into *tarnal* and then lost its tail and borrowed the head of *damn*. I have heard a bishop use it freely in private discourse, with a waggish sprinkling of actual *damns*. *Son-of-a-gun* is now so feeble and harmless that the Italians in America use it as a satirical designation for native Americans, who seem to them to fall far behind the Italian talent for profanity and objurgation. It is, I believe, a just criticism. Some time ago I was engaged by a magazine to do an article on American and English swearwords. After two or three attempts I had to give it up, for I found that neither branch of our ancient Frisian tongue could show anything worthy of serious consideration. The antinomians of England stick to two or three banal obscenities, one of which, *bloody*, is obscene only formally, and we Americans seldom get beyond variations of *hell* and *damn*. A single Neapolitan boatman could swear down the whole population of Anglo-Saxondom.

Bloody is perfectly innocuous in the United States, and it may be innocuous in England also on some near tomorrow—or even more disreputable than it is today. There is no predicting the social career of words. Dr. Leonard Bloomfield says that even "our word *whore*, cognate with the Latin *carus* (dear), must have been at one time a polite substitute for some term now lost." Prophecy fails just as dismally when propriety does not come into question. Shakespeare's numerous attempts to introduce new words, some of them his own inventions and others borrowed from the slang of the Bankside, failed almost as often as they succeeded. He found ready takers for *courtship*, *lonely*, *sportive*, *multitudinous*, *hubbub* and *bump*, but his audiences would have none of *definement*, in the sense of description, or of *citizen* as an adjective, and both seem strange and uncouth to us today, though all the others are as familiar and as decorous as *cat* or *rat*. When John Marston used *strenuous* in 1599 it was attacked by Ben Jonson as barbarous, but a dozen years later it had got into Chapman's Homer, and by 1670 it was being used by Milton. It remained perfectly respectable until 1900, when Theodore Roosevelt announced the Strenuous Life. Both the idea and the term struck the American fancy, and in a little while the latter passed into slang and was worn so threadbare that all persons of careful speech sickened of it. To this day it carries a faintly ridiculous connotation, and is seldom used seriously. But by 1975 it may be restored to the dignity of *psychopath* or *homoousian.* No one can say yes with any confidence, and no one can say no. "Even the greatest purist," observes Robert Lynd, "does not object to the inclusion of *bogus* in a literary English vocabulary, though a hundred years ago it was an American slang word meaning an apparatus for coining false money. *Carpetbagger* and *bunkum* are other American slang words that have naturalized themselves in English speech, and *mob* is an example of English slang that was once as vulgar as *photo.*"

Three Americanisms borrowed by English to one Briticism come into American! The true score, I suspect, is even more favorable to the Yankee as wordmaker. Down to 1820, according to Sir William Craigie, the trans-Atlantic trade in neologisms ran mainly westward, but then it began to shift, and today it is very heavily eastward. It would be difficult to recall a dozen British inventions that have entered the common American vocabulary since the World War, but the number of Americanisms taken into English must run to hundreds, and perhaps even to thousands. The American movie and talkie, of course, have been responsible for the introduction of many of them, but there is something beyond that, and something more fundamental. They are adopted in England simply because England has nothing to offer in competition with them—that is, nothing so apt or pungent, nothing so good. His Lordship of Guildford did not apply *speed-cop* to that *mobile policeman* as a voluntary act of subversion, born of a desire to shock and insult the realm; he let it slip for the single reason that it was an irresistibly apposite and satisfying term. And so with all the other Americanisms that challenge and consume their British congeners. They win fairly on palpable points and by every rule of the game. Confronted by the same novelty, whether in object or in situation, the Americans always manage to fetch up a name for it that not only describes it but also illuminates it, whereas the English, since the Elizabethan stimulant oozed out of them, have been content merely to catalogue it. There was a brilliant exemplification of the two approaches in the early days of railways. The English, having to name the wedge-shaped fender that was put in front of the first locomotives, called it a *plow,* which was almost exactly what it was, but the Americans gave it the bold and racy appellation of *cowcatcher.* For the casting which guides the wheels from one rail to another the English coined the depressingly obvious name of *crossing-plate;* the Americans, setting their imaginations free, called it a *frog.* The same sharp contrast appears every time there is a call for a new word today. The American *movie* is obviously much better than the English *cinema;* it is even better English. So is *radio* better than *wireless,* though it may be

Latin, and *job-holder* better than *public servant*, though it is surely literal enough, and *shock absorber* vastly better than *anti-bounce clip*, and *highball* than *whisky and soda*, and *bouncer* than *chucker-out*, and *chain store* than *multiple shop*, and *string bean* than *French bean*, and *union suit* than *combination*. Confronting the immensely American *rubberneck*, Dr. J. Y. T. Greig of Newcastle could only exclaim, "One of the best words ever coined!" And in the face of *lounge lizard*, Horace Annesley Vachell fell silent like Sir Isaac Newton on the seashore, overwhelmed by the solemn grandeur of the linguistic universe.

One finds in current American all the characters and tendencies that marked the rich English of Shakespeare's time—an eager borrowing of neologisms from other languages, a bold and often very ingenious use of metaphor, and a fine disdain of the barricades separating the parts of speech. The making of new words is not carried on only, or even principally, to fill gaps in the vocabulary; indeed, one may well agree with Captain Hall that "there are words enough already." It is carried on because there survives in the American something that seems to have faded out of the Englishman: an innocent joy in wordmaking for its own sake, a voluptuous delight in the vigor and elasticity of the language. The search for the *mot juste* is an enterprise that is altogether too pedantic for him; he much prefers to solve his problem by non-Euclidian devices. *Hoosegow* was certainly not necessary when it appeared, for we already had a large repertory of synonyms of *jail*. But when the word precipitated itself from the Spanish *juzgado* somewhere along the Rio Grande it won quick currency, and in a little while it was on the march through the country, and soon or late, I suppose, it will produce its inevitable clipped forms, *hoose* and *gow*, and its attendant adjective and verb. *Corral*, which entered by the same route in the forties of the last century, had hatched a verb before the Civil War, and that verb, according to Webster's New International (1934) now has four separate and distinct meanings. *Bummer*, coming in from the German, is now clipped to *bum*, and is not only noun, verb, and adjective but also adverb. *Buncombe*, borrowed by the English as *bunkum*, has bred *bunco* and *bunk* at home, both of which rove the parts of speech in a loose and easy way, and the last of which has issue in the harsh verb *to debunk*, still under heavy fire in England.

The impact of such lawless novelties upon the more staid English of the motherland is terrific. The more they are denounced as heathen and outlandish, the quicker they get into circulation. Nor do they prosper only on the level of the vulgate, and among careless speakers. There are constant complaints in the English newspapers about their appearance in the parliamentary debates, and even in discourses from the sacred desk, and they begin to show themselves also in belles-lettres, despite the English dislike of new ways of writing. Their progress, in fact, is so widespread and so insidious that they often pop up in the diatribes that revile them; the Englishman, conquered at last, can no longer protest against Americanisms without using them. Moreover, they are now supported actively by a definitely pro-American party of writers and scholars, and though it is still small in numbers, at least compared to the patriot band, it shows some distinguished names. The later Robert Bridges, Poet Laureate, was an active member of it, and among its other adherents are Wyndham Lewis, Edward Shanks, Richard Aldington, and Sir John Foster Fraser. Sir William Craigie, perhaps the first of living lexicographers, is so greatly interested in the American form of English that he has spent the years since 1925 in a scientific examination of it, and will presently begin the publication of an elaborate dictionary. If only because of the greater weight of the population behind it, it seems destined to usurp the natural leadership of British English and to determine the general course of the language hereafter. But its chief advantage in this struggle is really not the numerical one, but the fact that its daring experiments and iconoclasms lie in the grand tradition of English and are signs of its incurable normalcy and abounding vigor.

How far it will move away from the theorizing of grammarians and the policing of schoolmarms remains to be seen. They still make valiant efforts to curb its wayward spirit, but with gradually diminishing success. When, a few years ago, the late Sterling A. Leonard of the University of Wisconsin submitted a long series of their admonitions to a committee of educated Americans, including many philologians, he found that opinion was against them on that high level almost as decidedly as it was on lower ones. His judges favored scores of forms that the school grammars and popular handbooks of usage still condemn. Since then a more direct attack upon the conservative position has been made by Dr. Robert C. Pooley of the same university. He shows that some of the rules laid down with most assurance by pedants have no support in either history or logic, and are constantly violated by writers of unquestionable authority. There have even been rumblings of revolt in the conservative camp. The late George Philip Krapp of Columbia, who was surely anything but a radical, was of the opinion that English would undergo profound changes in the United States, and that many of them would be of such a character that its very grammatical structure would be shaken. Dr. George O. Curme of Northwestern University is another eminent grammarian who warns his colleagues that the rules they cherish have no genuine authority, and must be overhauled from time to time. Once they steel themselves to that sacrifice of their professional dignity, he says, "it will give a thrill to English-speaking students to discover that the English language does not belong to the schoolteacher but belongs to them, and that its future destiny will soon rest entirely in their hands."

Dr. Curme is always careful to think and speak of American as no more than a variation of English. But it must be obvious that, in late years, the tail has begun a vigorous wagging of the dog. "The facts that we ought to realize," says Edward Shanks to his fellow Britons, "and that we ignore when we talk loftily about Americanisms, are that America is making a formidable contribution to the development of our language, and that all our attempts to reject that contribution will in the long run be vain."

SARA TEASDALE

[1884–1933]

Few people reading the quiet lyrics of Sara Teasdale would suspect that she lived a life of quiet desperation and that her end was tragic. She was born August 8, 1884, in St. Louis, Missouri, and educated there. In youth she was fond of travel but, as she matured, she disliked moving about, and finally made her home in New York City.

She was both fascinated and frightened by what she called "the beautiful exuberance" of Vachel Lindsay, who courted her anxiously and vehemently. She tried to persuade herself that there could be something more than friendship between them—she told a mutual friend she admired "the fresh humanity of the man—full of eccentricities—aggressively himself—but a real lover of mankind, with a humorous tenderness for its weakness." Lindsay, however, was too much for her. At the time of the courtship she was nearing thirty, a woman who regarded herself as a semi-invalid, who wanted security rather than passion. She, who had been in love with poetry all her life, began to suspect that a poet might not make the best life-companion. After a long period of indecision, she married Ernst Filsinger, a merchant from St. Louis.

It was an unsuccessful marriage. She retreated into a psychological as well as a physical privacy. She did not resent her husband: she resented marriage. Although her poetry grew warmer, her life grew more spinsterlike. Twelve years passed before she made up her mind to leave her patient husband, but the separation was inevitable.

After the divorce, she lived in seclusion, her ill health aggravated by her unhappiness. Vachel Lindsay's death increased her sense of loneliness. She put her affairs in the precise order characteristic of her, and felt she had earned her right to stop living.

The gods have given life; I gave them song.
The debt is paid, and now I turn to go.

A year and a month after Lindsay's suicide, on January 28, 1933, she swallowed an overdose of sleeping tablets. Her body was found submerged in the bathtub of her New York apartment.

Sara Teasdale's poetry was consciously and unaffectedly feminine. "I have a theory," she wrote, "that the only way women can hope to make their work compare with men's work, is not by trying to rival what men say or do, but by trying to supplement it." Her note may be small but it is undeniably pure. The early lyrics are light, but the melodic movement runs slower and deeper in such volumes as Flame and Shadow, Dark of the Moon, *and* Strange Victory. *The emotion is intense without being whipped up; the beauty is in the restraint, the delicate selectiveness, and the final serenity.*

I SHALL NOT CARE

When I am dead and over me bright April
  Shakes out her rain-drenched hair,
Though you should lean above me broken-hearted,
  I shall not care.

I shall have peace, as leafy trees are peaceful
  When rain bends down the bough;
And I shall be more silent and cold-hearted
  Than you are now.

THE LONG HILL

I must have passed the crest a while ago
  And now I am going down—

Strange to have crossed the crest and not to know,
  But the brambles were always catching the hem of my gown.

All the morning I thought how proud I should be
  To stand there straight as a queen,
Wrapped in the wind and the sun with the world under me—
  But the air was dull, there was little I could have seen.

It was nearly level along the beaten track
  And the brambles caught in my gown—
But it's no use now to think of turning back,
  The rest of the way will be only going down.

LET IT BE FORGOTTEN

Let it be forgotten, as a flower is forgotten,
  Forgotten as a fire that once was singing gold,
Let it be forgotten for ever and ever,
  Time is a kind friend, he will make us old.

If anyone asks, say it was forgotten
  Long and long ago,
As a flower, as a fire, as a hushed footfall
  In a long-forgotten snow.

WISDOM

It was a night of early spring,
  The winter-sleep was scarcely broken;
Around us shadows and the wind
  Listened for what was never spoken.

Though half a score of years are gone,
  Spring comes as sharply now as then—
But if we had it all to do
  It would be done the same again.

It was a spring that never came;
  But we have lived enough to know
That what we never have, remains;
  It is the things we have that go.

NIGHT SONG AT AMALFI

I asked the heaven of stars
  What I should give my love—
It answered me with silence,
  Silence above.

I asked the darkened sea,
  Down where the fishermen go—
It answered me with silence—
  Silence below.

Oh, I could give him weeping,
  Or I could give him song—
But how can I give silence
  My whole life long?

DAMON RUNYON

[1884–1946]

HAD THE CITY OF NEW YORK decided to appoint a historian for Broadway, the likeliest candidate would have been a hard-working newspaperman who, like Charles Dickens and Mark Twain before him, turned to writing stories. Not receiving an official appointment, Damon Runyon elected himself the chronicler of the bookies, babes, crapshooters, horse-players, and gangsters whose world centers about Times Square. Guys and dolls, whose ear-splitting, grammar-bending language is as evocative of New York as Cockney is of London, they answer to such weird names as Harry the Horse, Nicely-Nicely Jones, Madame La Gimp, Izzy Cheesecake, Hymie Banjo Eyes, and the Lemon Drop Kid—tough birds, with gaudy plumage and hearts as soft as delicatessen cream cheese.

Alfred Damon Runyon was born in Manhattan—Manhattan, Kansas—on October 4, 1884, and he grew up far from the neon glow of Broadway. His first pieces appeared in the Pueblo (Colorado) Chieftain, where his father was chief printer. Damon Runyon was then thirteen. At fourteen, convincing a recruiting officer he was eighteen, he enlisted in the Army and went to the Philippines. Later, roving reporting took him to the West again, to Pueblo, Denver, and San Francisco. He had already an ear for men's speech and an eye which spotted unerringly the ironic humor in a situation. His earlier stories echo the twang and wheeze of railroad bullies, bums who hitched freights, and that floating society which crowded the jails of lonely desert towns.

A job as sportswriter for the New York American brought Runyon east in 1911 and dropped him among promoters, city bums, and glassy-eyed dames whose inflections rang in his ears and became the trademark of his stories. He went abroad as a war correspondent, but New York was his beat and he always returned to the big town whose laureate he became. He wore O. Henry's mantle with ease, and his profound understanding of New York and New Yorkese was praised by the most critical. Though his stories appeared often in magazines and he did a series of film scripts (among them "Little Miss Marker," which began the career of Shirley Temple), he always called himself a sportswriter. The voice of his stories—usually told in the first person—does stand off, like a reporter, from the people whose lives he describes. "My father's whole approach to life," his son wrote, "was the same as the fictional counterpart in his stories, the anonymous narrator 'I,' who attempted to remain the detached observer of the passing crowd." Detached he may have been, but not uncaring, for he was a humanist as well as a humorist, fond of his Manhattan characters, catching and eternally preserving their swagger, their pride, and their hard-boiled humor. When he died, December 10, 1946, of cancer, his body was cremated and, by his own request, his ashes were scattered from a plane over Manhattan.

We think of folk tales as being set in the country in old times. Runyon's stories are modern, set in the city. However their people are real, not fiction's stock characters, and their Broadway is genuine—for the reader who has never been east of the Rockies, for the Englishman whose edition has a glossary to make its idiom comprehensible, or for the theater-goer watching Guys and Dolls. Tough, sharp-humored, and pushovers for a pretty dame or a teary stumblebum, Harry the Horse and his friends have their place in the folklore of America along with Paul Bunyan and Pecos Bill.

SENSE OF HUMOR

One night I am standing in front of Mindy's restaurant on Broadway, thinking of practically nothing whatever, when all of a sudden I feel a very terrible pain in my left foot. In fact, this pain is so very terrible that it causes me to leap up and down like a bullfrog, and to let out loud cries of agony, and to speak some very profane language, which is by no means my custom, although of course I recognize the pain as coming from a hot foot, because I often experience this pain before.

Furthermore, I know Joe the Joker must be in the neighborhood, as Joe the Joker has the most wonderful sense of humor of anybody in this town, and is always around giving people the hot foot, and gives it to me more times than I can remember. In fact, I hear Joe the Joker invents the hot foot, and it finally becomes a very popular idea all over the country. The way you give a hot foot is to sneak up behind some guy who is standing around thinking of not much, and stick a paper match in his shoe between the sole and the upper along about where his little toe ought to be, and then light the match. By and by the guy will feel a terrible pain in his foot, and will start stamping around, and hollering, and carrying on generally, and it is always a most comical sight and a wonderful laugh to one and all to see him suffer.

No one in the world can give a hot foot as good as Joe the Joker, because it takes a guy who can sneak up very quiet on the guy who is to get the hot foot, and Joe can sneak up so quiet many guys on Broadway are willing to lay odds that he can give a mouse a hot foot if you can find a mouse that wears shoes. Furthermore, Joe the Joker can take plenty of care of himself in case the guy who gets the hot foot feels like taking the matter up, which sometimes happens, especially with guys who get their shoes made to order at forty bucks per copy and do not care to have holes burned in these shoes.

But Joe does not care what kind of shoes the guys are wearing when he feels like giving out hot foots, and furthermore, he does not care who the guys are, although many citizens think he makes a mistake the time he gives a hot foot to Frankie Ferocious. In fact, many citizens are greatly horrified by this action, and go around saying no good will come of it.

This Frankie Ferocious comes from over in Brooklyn, where he is considered a rising citizen in many respects, and by no means a guy to give hot foots to, especially as Frankie Ferocious has no sense of humor whatever. In fact, he is always very solemn, and nobody ever sees him laugh, and he certainly does not laugh when Joe the Joker gives him a hot foot one day on Broadway when Frankie Ferocious is standing talking over a business matter with some guys from the Bronx.

He only scowls at Joe, and says something in Italian, and while I do not understand Italian, it sounds so unpleasant that I guarantee I will leave town inside of the next two hours if he says it to me.

Of course Frankie Ferocious' name is not really Ferocious, but something in Italian like Feroccio, and I hear he originally comes from Sicily, although he lives in Brooklyn for quite some years, and from a modest beginning he builds himself up until he is a very large operator in merchandise of one kind and another, especially alcohol. He is a big guy of maybe thirty-odd, and he has hair blacker than a yard up a chimney, and black eyes, and black eyebrows, and a slow way of looking at people.

Nobody knows a whole lot about Frankie Ferocious, because he never has much to say, and he takes his time saying it, but everybody gives him plenty of room when he comes around, as there are rumors that Frankie never likes to be crowded. As far as I am concerned, I do not care for any part of Frankie Ferocious, because his slow way of looking at people always makes me nervous, and I am always sorry Joe the Joker gives him a hot foot, because I figure Frankie Ferocious is bound to consider it a most disrespectful action, and hold it against everybody that lives on the island of Manhattan.

But Joe the Joker only laughs when anybody tells him he is out of line in giving Frankie the hot foot, and says it is not his fault if Frankie has no sense of humor. Furthermore, Joe says he will not only give Frankie another hot foot if he gets a chance, but that he will give hot foots to the Prince of Wales or Mussolini, if he catches them in the right spot, although Regret, the horse player, states that Joe can have twenty to one any time that he will not give Mussolini any hot foots and get away with it.

Anyway, just as I suspect, there is Joe the Joker watching me when I feel the hot foot, and he is laughing very heartily, and furthermore, a large number of other citizens are also laughing heartily, because Joe the Joker never sees any fun in giving people the hot foot unless others are present to enjoy the joke. Well, naturally when I see who it is gives me the hot foot I join in the laughter, and go over and shake hands with Joe, and when I shake hands with him there is more laughter, because it seems Joe has a hunk of Limburger cheese in his duke, and what I shake hands with is this Limburger. Furthermore, it is some of Mindy's Limburger cheese, and everybody knows Mindy's Limburger is very squashy, and also very loud.

Of course I laugh at this, too, although to tell the truth I will laugh much more heartily if Joe the Joker drops dead in front of me, because I do not like to be made the subject of laughter on Broadway. But my laugh is really quite hearty when Joe takes the rest of the cheese that is not on my fingers and smears it on the steering wheels of some automobiles parked in front of Mindy's, because I get to thinking of what the drivers will say when they start steering their cars.

Then I get to talking to Joe the Joker, and I ask him how things are up in Harlem, where Joe and his younger brother, Freddy, and several other guys have a small organization operating in beer, and Joe says things are as good as can be expected considering business conditions. Then I ask him how Rosa is getting along, this Rosa being Joe the Joker's ever-loving wife, and a personal friend of mine, as I know her when she is Rosa Midnight and is singing in the old Hot Box before Joe hauls off and marries her.

Well, at this question Joe the Joker starts laughing, and I can see that something appeals to his sense of humor, and finally he speaks as follows:

"Why," he says, "do you not hear the news about Rosa? She takes the wind on me a couple months ago for my friend Frankie Ferocious, and is living in an apartment over in Brooklyn, right near his house, although," Joe says, "of course you understand I am telling you this only to answer your question, and not to holler copper on Rosa."

Then he lets out another large ha-ha, and in fact Joe the Joker keeps laughing until I am afraid he will injure himself internally. Personally, I do not see anything comical in a guy's ever-loving wife taking the wind on him for a guy like Frankie Ferocious, so when Joe the Joker quiets down a bit I ask him what is funny about the proposition.

"Why," Joe says, "I have to laugh every time I think of how the big greaseball is going to feel when he finds out how expensive Rosa is. I do not know how many things Frankie Ferocious has running for him in Brooklyn," Joe says, "but he better try to move himself in on the mint if he wishes to keep Rosa going." Then he laughs again, and I consider it wonderful the way Joe is able to keep his sense of humor even in such a situation as this, although up to this time I always think Joe is very daffy indeed about Rosa, who is a little doll, weighing maybe ninety pounds with her hat on and quite cute.

Now I judge from what Joe the Joker tells me that Frankie Ferocious knows Rosa before Joe marries her and is always pitching to her when she is singing in the Hot Box, and even after she is Joe's ever-loving wife, Frankie occasionally calls her up, especially when he commences to be a rising citizen of Brooklyn, although of course Joe does not learn about these calls until later. And about the time Frankie Ferocious commences to be a rising citizen of Brooklyn, things begin breaking a little tough for Joe the Joker, what with the depression and all, and he has to economize on Rosa in spots, and if there is one thing Rosa cannot stand it is being economized on.

Along about now, Joe the Joker gives Frankie Ferocious the hot foot, and just as many citizens state at the time, it is a mistake, for Frankie starts calling Rosa up more than somewhat, and speaking of what a nice place Brooklyn is to live in—which it is, at that—and between these boosts for Brooklyn and Joe the Joker's economy, Rosa hauls off and takes the subway to Borough Hall, leaving Joe a note telling him that if he does not like it he knows what he can do.

"Well, Joe," I say, after listening to his story, "I always hate to hear of these little domestic difficulties among my friends, but maybe this is all for the best. Still, I feel sorry for you, if it will do you any good," I say.

"Do not feel sorry for me," Joe says. "If you wish to feel sorry for anybody, feel sorry for Frankie Ferocious, and," he says, "if you can spare a little more sorrow, give it to Rosa."

And Joe the Joker laughs very hearty again and starts telling me about a little scatter that he has up in Harlem where he keeps a chair fixed up with electric wires so he can give anybody that sits down in it a nice jolt, which sounds very humorous to me, at that, especially when Joe tells me how they turn on too much juice one night and almost kill Commodore Jake.

Finally Joe says he has to get back to Harlem, but first he goes to the telephone in the corner cigar stores and calls up Mindy's and imitates a doll's voice, and tells Mindy he is Peggy Joyce, or somebody, and orders fifty dozen sandwiches sent up at once to an apartment in West Seventy-second Street for a birthday party, although of course there is no such number as he gives, and nobody there will wish fifty dozen sandwiches if there is such a number.

Then Joe gets in his car and starts off, and while he is waiting for the traffic lights at Fiftieth Street, I see citizens on the sidewalks making sudden leaps, and looking around very fierce, and I know Joe the Joker is plugging them with pellets made out of tin foil, which he fires from a rubber band hooked between his thumb and forefinger.

Joe the Joker is very expert with this proposition, and it is very funny to see the citizens jump, although once or twice in his life Joe makes a miscue and knocks out somebody's eye. But it is all in fun, and shows you what a wonderful sense of humor Joe has.

Well, a few days later I see by the papers where a couple of Harlem guys Joe the Joker is mobbed up with are found done up in sacks over in Brooklyn, very dead indeed, and the coppers say it is because they are trying to move in on certain business enterprises that belong to nobody but Frankie Ferocious. But of course the coppers do not say Frankie Ferocious puts these guys in the sacks, because in the first place Frankie will report them to Headquarters if the coppers say such a thing about him, and in the second place putting guys in sacks is strictly a St. Louis idea and to have a guy put in a sack properly you have to send to St. Louis for experts in this matter.

Now, putting a guy in a sack is not as easy as it sounds, and in fact it takes quite a lot of practice and experience. To put a guy in a sack properly, you first have to put him to sleep, because naturally no guy is going to walk into a sack wide awake unless he is a plumb sucker. Some people claim the best way to put a guy to sleep is to give him a sleeping powder of some kind in a drink but the real experts just tap the guy on the noggin with a blackjack, which saves the expense of buying the drink. Anyway, after the guy is asleep, you double him up like a pocketknife, and tie a cord or a wire around his neck and under his knees. Then you put him in a gunny sack, and leave him some place, and by and by when the guy wakes up and finds himself in the sack, naturally he wants to get out and the first thing he does is to try to straighten out his knees. This pulls the cord around his neck up so tight that after a while the guy is all out of breath. So then when somebody comes along and opens the sack they find the guy dead, and nobody is responsible for this unfortunate situation, because after all the guy really commits suicide, because if he does not try to straighten out his knees he may live to a ripe old age, if he recovers from the tap on the noggin.

Well, a couple of days later I see by the papers where three Brooklyn citizens are scragged as they are walking peaceably along Clinton Street, the scragging being done by some parties in an automobile who seem to have a machine gun, and the papers state that the citizens are friends of Frankie Ferocious, and that it is rumored the parties with the machine gun are from Harlem.

I judge by this that there is some trouble in Brooklyn, especially as about a week after the citizens are scragged in Clinton Street, another Harlem guy is found done up in a sack like a Virginia ham near Prospect Park, and now who is it but Joe the Joker's brother, Freddy, and I know Joe is going to be greatly displeased by this.

By and by it gets so nobody in Brooklyn will open as much as a sack of potatoes without first calling in the gendarmes, for fear a pair of No. 8 shoes will jump out at them.

Now one night I see Joe the Joker, and this time he is all alone, and I wish to say I am willing to leave him all alone, because something tells me he is hotter than a stove. But he grabs me as I am going past, so naturally I stop to talk to him, and the first thing I say is how sorry I am about his brother.

"Well," Joe the Joker says, "Freddy is always a kind of sap. Rosa calls him up and asks him to come over to Brooklyn to see her. She wishes to talk to Freddy about getting me to give her a divorce," Joe says, "so she can marry Frankie Ferocious, I suppose. Anyway," he says, "Freddy tells Commodore Jake why he is going to see her. Freddy always likes Rosa, and thinks maybe he can patch it up between us. So," Joe says, "he winds up in a sack. They get him after he leaves her apartment. I do not claim Rosa will ask him to come over if she has any idea he will be sacked," Joe says, "but," he says, "she is responsible. She is a bad-luck doll."

Then he starts to laugh, and at first I am greatly horrified, thinking it is because something about Freddy being sacked strikes his sense of humor, when he says to me like this:

"Say," he says, "I am going to play a wonderful joke on Frankie Ferocious."

"Well, Joe," I say, "you are not asking me for advice, but I am going to give you some free gratis, and for nothing. Do not play any jokes on Frankie Ferocious, as I hear he has no more sense of humor than a nanny goat. I hear Frankie Ferocious will not laugh if you have Al Jolson, Eddie Cantor, Ed Wynn, and Joe Cook telling him jokes all at once. In fact," I say, "I hear he is a tough audience."

"Oh," Joe the Joker says, "he must have some sense of humor somewhere to stand for Rosa. I hear he is daffy about her. In fact, I understand she is the only person in the world he really likes, and trusts. But I must play a joke on him. I am going to have myself delivered to Frankie Ferocious in a sack."

Well, of course I have to laugh at this myself, and Joe the Joker laughs with me. Personally, I am laughing just at the idea of anybody having themselves delivered to Frankie Ferocious in a sack, and especially Joe the Joker, but of course I have no idea Joe really means what he says.

"Listen," Joe says, finally. "A guy from St. Louis who is a friend of mine is doing most of the sacking for Frankie Ferocious. His name is Ropes McGonnigle. In fact," Joe says, "he is a very dear old pal of mine, and he has a wonderful sense of humor like me. Ropes McGonnigle has nothing whatever to do with sacking Freddy," Joe says, "and he is very indignant about it since he finds out Freddy is my brother, so he is anxious to help me play a joke on Frankie. Only last night," Joe says, "Frankie Ferocious sends for Ropes and tells him he will appreciate it as a special favor if Ropes will bring me to him in a sack. I suppose," Joe says, "that

Frankie Ferocious hears from Rosa what Freddy is bound to tell her about my ideas on divorce. I have very strict ideas on divorce," Joe says, "especially where Rosa is concerned. I will see her in what's-this before I ever do her and Frankie Ferocious such a favor as giving her a divorce.

"Anyway," Joe the Joker says, "Ropes tells me about Frankie Ferocious propositioning him, so I send Ropes back to Frankie Ferocious to tell him he knows I am to be in Brooklyn tomorrow night, and furthermore, Ropes tells Frankie that he will have me in a sack in no time. And so he will," Joe says.

"Well," I say, "personally, I see no percentage in being delivered to Frankie Ferocious in a sack, because as near as I can make out from what I read in the papers, there is no future for a guy in a sack that goes to Frankie Ferocious. What I cannot figure out," I say, "is where the joke on Frankie comes in."

"Why," Joe the Joker says, "the joke is, I will not be asleep in the sack, and my hands will not be tied, and in each of my hands I will have a John Roscoe, so when the sack is delivered to Frankie Ferocious and I pop out blasting away, can you not imagine his astonishment?"

Well, I can imagine this, all right. In fact, when I get to thinking of the look of surprise that is bound to come to Frankie Ferocious' face when Joe the Joker comes out of the sack I have to laugh, and Joe the Joker laughs right along with me.

"Of course," Joe says, "Ropes McGonnigle will be there to start blasting with me, in case Frankie Ferocious happens to have any company."

Then Joe the Joker goes on up the street, leaving me still laughing from thinking of how amazed Frankie Ferocious will be when Joe bounces out of the sack and starts throwing slugs around and about. I do not hear of Joe from that time to this, but I hear the rest of the story from very reliable parties.

It seems that Ropes McGonnigle does not deliver the sack himself, after all, but sends it by an expressman to Frankie Ferocious' home. Frankie Ferocious receives many sacks such as this in his time, because it seems that it is a sort of passion with him to personally view the contents of the sacks and check up on them before they are distributed about the city, and of course Ropes McGonnigle knows about this passion from doing so much sacking for Frankie.

When the expressman takes the sack into Frankie's house, Frankie personally lugs it down into his basement, and there he outs with a big John Roscoe and fires six shots into the sack, because it seems Ropes McGonnigle tips him off to Joe the Joker's plan to pop out of the sack and start blasting.

I hear Frankie Ferocious has a very strange expression on his pan and is laughing the only laugh anybody ever hears from him when the gendarmes break in and put the arm on him for murder, because it seems that when Ropes McGonnigle tells Frankie of Joe the Joker's plan, Frankie tells Ropes what he is going to do with his own hands before opening the sack. Naturally, Ropes speaks to Joe the Joker of Frankie's idea about filling the sack full of slugs, and Joe's sense of humor comes right out again.

So, bound and gagged, but otherwise as right as rain in the sack that is delivered to Frankie Ferocious, is by no means Joe the Joker, but Rosa.

RING LARDNER

[1885–1933]

America's colloquial writers owe more than they have acknowledged, or perhaps realized, to a humorist whose ear was as accurate as a tape recorder, whose outlook was at once somber and wild, and whose reputation was built not on his stories but on his fame as a sportswriter. It will always be a question whether the "real" Ring Lardner was an explorer of the American dialect, a sentimental reporter, a melancholy analyst, or a mad wag. Much has been said about his ability as a reporter of the contemporary scene, especially in the field of sports, in which he was widely imitated but inimitable. But few commentators have paid tribute to his remarkable range, from knockabout farce to murderous realism, from surrealistic plays to clinical dissections of current society, high and low.

He was born Ringgold Wilmer Lardner, on March 6, 1885. He shortened it to Ring W. Lardner, and then dropped the middle initial for fear people might say it stood for Worm. Graduating from high school in his native Niles, Michigan, he wanted to attend the University of Michigan to study, he said, "football and dentistry," but went, instead, to Armour Institute in Chicago, as a student of mechanical engineering. After a semester he "passed in rhetoric and out of Armour." A missing consignment of cream cheese ended his employment as a local freight agent. When his brother was unable to accept a position offered him on the South Bend (Indiana) Times, *Lardner grabbed the opening and so began, at twenty-one, his years with the newspapers. For a year he covered police stations, courts, ball games, and movies in*

South Bend. Then he moved on to newspapers in Chicago, a St. Louis baseball weekly, more Chicago papers, and finally turned up as a columnist on the Chicago Tribune.

In 1914 the first of his series of baseball stories, "You Know Me, Al," appeared, creating a new genre: stories that were broadly comic and unexpectedly caustic. The speech was a queer composite of American and English—a blend that has been referred to as "Ringlish." His ear was tuned to the accuracies—and inaccuracies—of the spoken word, making his language exact and excruciating. His eye was equally quick, catching the smallest gesture and most furtive flicker.

At forty, with the collection How to Write Short Stories, *the satirist supplanted the humorist. Here was a Swiftian annoyance with and loathing of mankind's boors and braggarts, a striking-out at the popular contemporary fable that everything was lovely, a flaying expressed in strictly American terms and thinly covered by the layer of nonsense which made people laugh. He brought out a wild autobiography,* The Story of a Wonder Man. *He collaborated with George M. Cohan and George S. Kaufman on successful Broadway plays and appeared regularly as the radio reviewer in the elegant* New Yorker. *Yet his friend, F. Scott Fitzgerald, said that he "stopped finding fun in his work ten years before he died." He lived only to forty-eight.*

Some of his unhappiness was the result of never being able to escape identification as a sportswriter. More of it came from the twinging melancholy of the ultimate satirist, the man whom William Bolitho called "the greatest and most sincere pessimist America has produced."

Lardner's humor is as original as Mark Twain's. Native to the core, its laughs are as full-throated as they are unforced; its accents, coming from the baseball field and the barber-shop, as well as the metropolitan pent-house and the country club, are real. They bring the breath—and breadth—of America.

ALIBI IKE

I

HIS RIGHT NAME was Frank X. Farrell, and I guess the X stood for "Excuse me." Because he never pulled a play, good or bad, on or off the field, without apologizin' for it.

"Alibi Ike" was the name Carey wished on him the first day he reported down South. O' course we all cut out the "Alibi" part of it right away for the fear he would overhear it and bust somebody. But we called him "Ike" right to his face and the rest of it was understood by everybody on the club except Ike himself.

He ast me one time, he says:

"What do you all call me Ike for? I ain't no Yid."

"Carey give you the name," I says. "It's his nickname for everybody he takes a likin' to."

"He mustn't have only a few friends then," says Ike. "I never heard him say 'Ike' to nobody else."

But I was goin' to tell you about Carey namin' him. We'd been workin' out two weeks and the pitchers was showin' somethin' when this bird joined us. His first day out he stood up there so good and took such a reef at the old pill that he had everyone lookin'. Then him and Carey was together in left field, catchin' fungoes, and it was after we was through for the day that Carey told me about him.

"What do you think of Alibi Ike?" ast Carey.

"Who's that?" I says.

"This here Farrell in the outfield," says Carey.

"He looks like he could hit," I says.

"Yes," says Carey, "but he can't hit near as good as he can apologize."

Then Carey went on to tell me what Ike had been pullin' out there. He'd dropped the first fly ball that was hit to him and told Carey his glove wasn't broke in good yet, and Carey says the glove could easy of been Kid Gleason's gran'father. He made a whale of a catch out o' the next one and Carey says "Nice work!" or somethin' like that, but Ike says he could of caught the ball with his back turned only he slipped when he started after it and, besides that, the air currents fooled him.

"I thought you done well to get to the ball," says Carey.

"I ought to been settin' under it," says Ike.

"What did you hit last year?" Carey ast him.

"I had malaria most o' the season," says Ike. "I wound up with .356."

"Where would I have to go to get malaria?" says Carey, but Ike didn't wise up.

I and Carey and him set at the same table together for supper. It took him half an hour longer'n us to eat because he had to excuse himself every time he lifted his fork.

"Doctor told me I needed starch," he'd say, and then toss a shoveful o' potatoes into him. Or, "They ain't much meat on one o' these chops," he'd tell us, and grab another one. Or he'd say: "Nothin' like onions for a cold," and then he'd dip into the perfumery.

"Better try that apple sauce," says Carey. "It'll help your malaria."

"Whose malaria?" says Ike. He'd forgot already why he didn't only hit .356 last year.

I and Carey begin to lead him on.

"Whereabouts did you say your home was?" I ast him.

"I live with my folks," he says. "We live in Kansas City—not right down in the business part—outside a ways."

"How's that come?" says Carey. "I should think you'd get rooms in the post office."

But Ike was too busy curin' his cold to get that one.

"Are you married?" I ast him.

"No," he says. "I never run round much with girls, except to shows onct in a wile and parties and dances and roller skatin'."

"Never take 'em to the prize fights, eh?" says Carey.

"We don't have no real good bouts," says Ike. "Just bush stuff. And I never figured a boxin' match was a place for the ladies."

Well, after supper he pulled a cigar out and lit it. I was just goin' to ask him what he done it for, but he beat me to it.

"Kind o' rests a man to smoke after a good work-out," he says. "Kind o' settles a man's supper, too."

"Looks like a pretty good cigar," says Carey.

"Yes," says Ike. "A friend o' mine give it to me—a fella in Kansas City that runs a billiard room."

"Do you play billiards?" I ast him.

"I used to play a fair game," he says. "I'm all out o' practice now—can't hardly make a shot."

We coaxed him into a four-handed battle, him and Carey against Jack Mack and I. Say, he couldn't play billiards as good as Willie Hoppe; not quite. But to hear him tell it, he didn't make a good shot all evenin'. I'd leave him an awful-lookin' layout and he'd gather 'em up in one try and then run a couple o' hundred, and between every carom he'd say he'd put too much stuff on the ball, or the English didn't take, or the table wasn't true, or his stick was crooked, or somethin'. And all the time he had the balls actin' like they was Dutch soldiers and him Kaiser William. We started out to play fifty points, but we had to make it a thousand so as I and Jack and Carey could try the table.

The four of us set round the lobby a wile after we was through playin', and when it got along toward bedtime Carey whispered to me and says:

"Ike'd like to go to bed, but he can't think up no excuse."

Carey hadn't hardly finished whisperin' when Ike got up and pulled it:

"Well, good night, boys," he says. "I ain't sleepy, but I got some gravel in my shoes and it's killin' my feet."

We knowed he hadn't never left the hotel since we'd came in from the grounds and changed our clo'es. So Carey says:

"I should think they'd take them gravel pits out o' the billiard room."

But Ike was already on his way to the elevator, limpin'.

"He's got the world beat," says Carey to Jack and I. "I've knew lots o' guys that had an alibi for every mistake they made; I've heard pitchers say that the ball slipped when somebody cracked one off'n em; I've heard infielders complain of a sore arm after heavin' one into the stand, and I've saw outfielders tooken sick with a dizzy spell when they've misjudged a fly ball. But this baby can't even go to bed without apologizin', and I bet he excuses himself to the razor when he gets ready to shave."

"And at that," says Jack, "he's goin' to make us a good man."

"Yes," says Carey, "unless rheumatism keeps his battin' average down to .400."

Well, sir, Ike kept whalin' away at the ball all through the trip till everybody knowed he'd won a job. Cap had him in there regular the last few exhibition games and told the newspaper boys a week before the season opened that he was goin' to start him in Kane's place.

"You're there, kid," says Carey to Ike, the night Cap made the 'nnouncement. "They ain't many boys that wins a big league berth their third year out."

"I'd of been up here a year ago," says Ike, "only I was bent over all season with lumbago."

II

It rained down in Cincinnati one day and somebody organized a little game o' cards. They was shy two men to make six and ast I and Carey to play.

"I'm with you if you get Ike and make it seven-handed," says Carey.

So they got a hold of Ike and we went up to Smitty's room.

"I pretty near forgot how many you deal," says Ike. "It's been a long wile since I played."

I and Carey give each other the wink, and sure enough, he was just as ig'orant about poker as billiards. About the second hand, the pot was opened two or three ahead of him, and they was three in when it come his turn. It cost a buck and he throwed in two.

"It's raised, boys," somebody says.

"Gosh, that's right, I did raise it," says Ike.

"Take out a buck if you didn't mean to tilt her," says Carey.

"No," says Ike, "I'll leave it go."

Well, it was raised back at him and then he made another mistake and raised again. They was only three left in when the draw come. Smitty'd opened with a pair o' kings and he didn't help 'em. Ike stood pat. The guy that'd raised him back was flushin' and he didn't fill. So Smitty checked and Ike bet and didn't get no call. He tossed his hand away, but I grabbed it and give it a look. He had king, queen, jack and two tens. Alibi Ike he must have seen me peekin', for he leaned over and whispered to me.

"I overlooked my hand," he says. "I thought all the wile it was a straight."

"Yes," I says, "that's why you raised twice by mistake."

They was another pot that he come into with tens and fours. It was tilted a couple o' times and two o' the strong fellas drawed ahead of Ike. They each drawed one. So Ike throwed away his little pair and come with four tens. And they was four treys against him. Carey'd looked at Ike's discards and then he says:

"This lucky bum busted two pair."

"No, no, I didn't," says Ike.

"Yes, yes, you did," says Carey, and showed us the two fours.

"What do you know about that?" says Ike. "I'd of swore one was a five spot."

Well, we hadn't had no pay day yet, and after a wile everybody except Ike was goin' shy. I could see him gettin' restless and I was wonderin' how he'd make the get-away. He tried two or three times. "I got to buy some collars before supper," he says.

"No hurry," says Smitty. "The stores here keeps open all night in April."

After a minute he opened up again.

"My uncle out in Nebraska ain't expected to live," he says. "I ought to send a telegram."

"Would that save him?" says Carey.

"No, it sure wouldn't," says Ike, "but I ought to leave my old man know where I'm at."

"When did you hear about your uncle?" says Carey.

"Just this mornin'," says Ike.

"Who told you?" ast Carey.

"I got a wire from my old man," says Ike.

"Well," says Carey, "your old man knows you're still here yet this afternoon if you was here this mornin'. Trains leavin' Cincinnati in the middle o' the day don't carry no ball clubs."

"Yes," says Ike, "that's true. But he don't know where I'm goin' to be next week."

"Ain't he got no schedule?" ast Carey.

"I sent him one openin' day," says Ike, "but it takes mail a long time to get to Idaho."

"I thought your old man lived in Kansas City," says Carey.

"He does when he's home," says Ike.

"But now," says Carey, "I s'pose he's went to Idaho so as he can be near your sick uncle in Nebraska."

"He's visitin' my other uncle in Idaho."

"Then how does he keep posted about your sick uncle?" ast Carey.

"He don't," says Ike. "He don't even know my other uncle's sick. That's why I ought to wire and tell him."

"Good night!" says Carey.

"What town in Idaho is your old man at?" I says.

Ike thought it over.

"No town at all," he says. "But he's near a town."

"Near what town?" I says.

"Yuma," says Ike.

Well, by this time he'd lost two or three pots and he was desperate. We was playin' just as fast as we could, because we seen we couldn't hold him much longer. But he was tryin' so hard to frame an escape that he couldn't pay no attention to the cards, and it looked like we'd get his whole pile away from him if we could make him stick.

The telephone saved him. The minute it begun to ring, five of us jumped for it. But Ike was there first.

"Yes," he says, answerin' it. "This is him. I'll come right down."

And he slammed up the receiver and beat it out o' the door without even sayin' good-by.

"Smitty'd ought to locked the door," says Carey.

"What did he win?" ast Carey.

We figured it up—sixty-odd bucks.

"And the next time we ask him to play," says Carey, "his fingers will be so stiff he can't hold the cards."

Well, we set round a wile talkin' it over, and pretty soon the telephone rung again. Smitty answered it. It was a friend of his'n from Hamilton and he wanted to know why Smitty didn't hurry down. He was the one that had called before and Ike had told him he was Smitty.

"Ike'd ought to split with Smitty's friend," says Carey.

"No," I says, "he'll need all he won. It costs money to buy collars and to send telegrams from Cincinnati to your old man in Texas and keep him posted on the health o' your uncle in Cedar Rapids, D.C."

III

And you ought to heard him out there on that field! They wasn't a day when he didn't pull six or seven, and it didn't make no difference whether he was goin' good or bad. If he popped up in the pinch he should of made a base hit and the reason he didn't was so-and-so. And if he cracked one for three bases he ought to had a home run, only the ball wasn't lively, or the wind brought it back, or he tripped on a lump o' dirt, roundin' first base.

They was one afternoon in New York when he beat all records. Big Marquard was workin' against us and he was good.

In the first innin' Ike hit one clear over that right field stand, but it was a few feet foul. Then he got another foul and then the count come to two and two. Then Rube slipped one acrost on him and he was called out.

"What do you know about that!" he says afterward on the bench. "I lost count. I thought it was three and one, and I took a strike."

"You took a strike all right," says Carey. "Even the umps knowed it was a strike."

"Yes," says Ike, "but you can bet I wouldn't of took it if I'd knew it was the third one. The score board had it wrong."

"That score board ain't for you to look at," says Cap. "It's for you to hit that old pill against."

"Well," says Ike, "I could of hit that one over the score board if I'd knew it was the third."

"Was it a good ball?" I says.

"Well, no, it wasn't," says Ike. "It was inside."

"How far inside?" says Carey.

"Oh, two or three inches or half a foot," says Ike.

"I guess you wouldn't of threatened the score board with it then," says Cap.

"I'd of pulled it down the right foul line if I hadn't thought he'd call it a ball," says Ike.

Well, in New York's part o' the innin' Doyle cracked one and Ike run back a mile and a half and caught it with one hand. We was all sayin' what a whale of a play it was, but he had to apologize just the same as for gettin' struck out.

"That stand's so high," he says, "that a man don't never see a ball till it's right on top o' you."

"Didn't you see that one?" ast Cap.

"Not at first," says Ike; "not till it raised up above the roof o' the stand."

"Then why did you start back as soon as the ball was hit?" says Cap.

"I knowed by the sound that he'd got a good hold of it," says Ike.

"Yes," says Cap, "but how'd you know what direction to run in?"

"Doyle usually hits 'em that way, the way I run," says Ike.

"Why don't you play blindfolded?" says Carey.

"Might as well, with that big high stand to bother a man," says Ike. "If I could of saw the ball all the time I'd of got it in my hip pocket."

Along in the fifth we was one run to the bad and Ike got on with one out. On the first ball throwed to Smitty, Ike went down. The ball was outside and Meyers throwed Ike out by ten feet.

You could see Ike's lips movin' all the way to the bench and when he got there he had his piece learned.

"Why didn't he swing?" he says.

"Why didn't you wait for his sign?" says Cap.

"He give me his sign," says Ike.

"What is his sign with you?" says Cap.

"Pickin' up some dirt with his right hand," says Ike.

"Well, I didn't see him do it," Cap says.

"He done it all right," says Ike.

Well, Smitty went out and they wasn't no more argument till they come in for the next innin'. Then Cap opened it up.

"You fellas better get your signs straight," he says.

"Do you mean me?" says Smitty.

"Yes," Cap says. "What's your sign with Ike?"

"Slidin' my left hand up to the end o' the bat and back," says Smitty.

"Do you hear that, Ike?" ast Cap.

"What of it?" says Ike.

"You says his sign was pickin' up dirt and he says it's slidin' his hand. Which is right?"

"I'm right," says Smitty. "But if you're arguin' about him goin' last innin', I didn't give him no sign."

"You pulled your cap down with your right hand, didn't you?" ast Ike.

"Well, s'pose I did," says Smitty. "That don't mean nothin'. I never told you to take that for a sign, did I?"

"I thought maybe you meant to tell me and forgot," says Ike.

They couldn't none of us answer that and they wouldn't of been no more said if Ike had of shut up. But wile we was settin' there Carey got on with two out and stole second clean.

"There!" says Ike. "That's what I was tryin' to do and I'd of got away with it if Smitty'd swang and bothered the Indian."

"Oh!" says Smitty. "You was tryin' to steal then, was you? I thought you claimed I give you the hit and run."

"I didn't claim no such a thing," says Ike. "I thought maybe you might of gave me a sign, but I was goin' anyway because I thought I had a good start."

Cap prob'ly would of hit him with a bat, only just about that time Doyle booted one on Hayes and Carey come acrost with the run that tied.

Well, we go into the ninth finally, one and one, and Marquard walks McDonald with nobody out.

"Lay it down," says Cap to Ike.

And Ike goes up there with orders to bunt and cracks the first ball into that right-field stand! It was fair this time, and we're two ahead, but I didn't think about that at the time. I was too busy watchin' Cap's face. First he turned pale and then he got red as fire and then he got blue and purple, and finally he just laid back and busted out laughin'. So we wasn't afraid to laugh ourselfs when we seen him doin' it, and when Ike come in everybody on the bench was in hysterics.

But instead o' takin' advantage, Ike had to try and excuse himself. His play was to shut up and he didn't know how to make it.

"Well," he says, "if I hadn't hit quite so quick at that one I bet it'd of cleared the center-field fence."

Cap stopped laughin'.

"It'll cost you plain fifty," he says.

"What for?" says Ike.

"When I say 'bunt' I mean 'bunt,'" says Cap.

"You didn't say 'bunt,'" says Ike.

"I says 'Lay it down,'" says Cap. "If that don't mean 'bunt,' what does it mean?"

"'Lay it down' means 'bunt' all right," says Ike, "but I understood you to say 'Lay on it.'"

"All right," says Cap, "and the little misunderstandin' will cost you fifty."

Ike didn't say nothin' for a few minutes. Then he had another bright idear.

"I was just kiddin' about misunderstandin' you," he says. "I knowed you wanted me to bunt."

"Well, then, why didn't you bunt?" ast Cap.

"I was goin' to on the next ball," says Ike. "But I thought if I took a good wallop I'd have 'em all fooled. So I walloped at the first one to fool 'em, and I didn't have no intention o' hittin' it."

"You tried to miss it, did you?" says Cap.

"Yes," says Ike.

"How'd you happen to hit it?" ast Cap.

"Well," Ike says, "I was lookin' for him to throw me a fast one and I was goin' to swing under it. But he come with a hook and I met it right square where I was swingin' to go under the fast one."

"Great!" says Cap. "Boys," he says, "Ike's learned how to hit Marquard's curve. Pretend a fast one's comin' and then try to miss it. It's a good thing to know and Ike'd ought to be willin' to pay for the lesson. So I'm goin' to make it a hundred instead o' fifty."

The game wound up 3 to 1. The fine didn't go, because Ike hit like a wild man all through that trip and we made pretty near a clean-up. The night we went to Philly I got him cornered in the car and I says to him:

"Forget them alibis for a wile and tell me somethin'. What'd you do that for, swing that time against Marquard when you was told to bunt?"

"I'll tell you," he says. "That ball he throwed me looked just like the one I struck out on in the first innin' and I wanted to show Cap what I could of done to that other one if I'd knew it was the third strike."

"But," I says, "the one you struck out on in the first innin' was a fast ball."

"So was the one I cracked in the ninth," says Ike.

IV

You've saw Cap's wife, o' course. Well, her sister's about twict as good-lookin' as her, and that's goin' some.

Cap took his missus down to St. Louis the second trip and the other one come down from St. Joe to visit her. Her name is Dolly, and some doll is right.

Well, Cap was goin' to take the two sisters to a show and he wanted a beau for Dolly. He left it to her and she picked Ike. He'd hit three on the nose that afternoon—off'n Sallee, too.

They fell for each other that first evenin'. Cap told us how it come off. She begin flatterin' Ike for the star game he'd played and o' course he begin excusin' himself for not doin' better. So she thought he was modest and it went strong with her. And she believed everything he said and that made her solid with him—that and her make-up. They was together every mornin' and evenin' for the five days we was there. In the afternoons Ike played the grandest ball you ever see, hittin' and runnin' the bases like a fool and catchin' everything that stayed in the park.

I told Cap, I says: "You'd ought to keep the doll with us and he'd make Cobb's figures look sick."

But Dolly had to go back to St. Joe and we come home for a long serious.

Well, for the next three weeks Ike had a letter to read every day and he'd set in the clubhouse readin' it till mornin' practice was half over. Cap didn't say nothin' to him, because he was goin' so good. But I and Carey wasted a lot of our time tryin' to get him to own up who the letters was from. Fine chanct!

"What are you readin'?" Carey'd say. "A bill?"

"No," Ike'd say, "not exactly a bill. It's a letter from a fella I used to go to school with."

"High school or college?" I'd ask him.

"College," he'd say.

"What college?" I'd say.

Then he'd stall a wile and then he'd say:

"I didn't go to the college myself, but my friend went there."

"How did it happen you didn't go?" Carey'd ask him.

"Well," he'd say, "they wasn't no colleges near where I lived."

"Didn't you live in Kansas City?" I'd say to him.

One time he'd say he did and another time he didn't. One time he says he lived in Michigan.

"Where at?" says Carey.

"Near Detroit," he says.

"Well," I says, "Detroit's near Ann Arbor and that's where they got the university."

"Yes," says Ike, "they got it there now, but they didn't have it there then."

"I come pretty near goin' to Syracuse," I says, "only they wasn't no railroads runnin' through there in them days."

"Where'd this friend o' yours go to college?" says Carey.

"I forget now," says Ike.

"Was it Carlisle?" ast Carey.

"No," says Ike, "his folks wasn't very well off."

"That's what barred me from Smith," I says.

"I was goin' to tackle Cornell's," says Carey, "but the doctor told me I'd have hay fever if I didn't stay up North."

"Your friend writes long letters," I says.

"Yes," says Ike; "he's tellin' me about a ball player."

"Where does he play?" ast Carey.

"Down in the Texas League—Fort Wayne," says Ike.

"It looks like a girl's writin'," Carey says.

"A girl wrote it," says Ike. "That's my friend's sister, writin' for him."

"Didn't they teach writin' at this here college where he went?" says Carey.

"Sure," Ike says, "they taught writin', but he got his hand cut off in a railroad wreck."

"How long ago?" I says.

"Right after he got out o' college," says Ike.

"Well," I says, "I should think he'd of learned to write with his left hand by this time."

"It's his left hand that was cut off," says Ike; "and he was left-handed."

"You get a letter every day," says Carey. "They're all the same writin'. Is he tellin' you about a different ball player every time he writes?"

"No," Ike says. "It's the same ball player. He just tells me what he does every day."

"From the size o' the letters, they don't play nothin' but double-headers down there," says Carey.

We figured that Ike spent most of his evenin's answerin' the letters from his "friend's sister," so we kept tryin' to date him up for shows and parties to see how he'd duck out of 'em. He was bugs over spaghetti, so we told him one day that they was goin' to be a big feed of it over to Joe's that night and he was invited.

"How long'll it last?" he says.

"Well," we says, "we goin' right over there after the game and stay till they close up."

"I can't go," he says, "unless they leave me come home at eight bells."

"Nothin' doin'," says Carey. "Joe'd get sore."

"I can't go then," says Ike.

"Why not?" I ast him.

"Well," he says, "my landlady locks up the house at eight and I left my key home."

"You can come and stay with me," says Carey.

"No," he says, "I can't sleep in a strange bed."

"How do you get along when we're on the road?" says I.

"I don't never sleep the first night anywheres," he says. "After that I'm all right."

"You'll have time to chase home and get your key right after the game," I told him.

"The key ain't home," says Ike. "I lent it to one o' the other fellas and he's went out o' town and took it with him."

"Couldn't you borry another key off'n the landlady?" Carey ast him.

"No," he says, "that's the only one they is."

Well, the day before we started East again, Ike come into the clubhouse all smiles.

"Your birthday?" I ast him.

"No," he says.

"What do you feel so good about?" I says.

"Got a letter from my old man," he says. "My uncle's goin' to get well."

"Is that the one in Nebraska?" says I.

"Not right in Nebraska," says Ike. "Near there."

But afterwards we got the right dope from Cap. Dolly'd blew in from Missouri and was goin' to make the trip with her sister.

V

Well, I want to alibi Carey and I for what come off in Boston. If we'd of had any idear what we was doin', we'd never did it. They wasn't nobody outside o' maybe Ike and the dame that felt worse over it than I and Carey.

The first two days we didn't see nothin' of Ike and her except out to the park. The rest o' the time they was sight-seein' over to Cambridge and down to Revere and out to Brook-a-line and all the other places where the rubes go.

But when we come into the beanery after the third game Cap's wife called us over.

"If you want to see somethin' pretty," she says, "look at the third finger on Sis's left hand."

Well, o' course we knowed before we looked that it wasn't goin' to be no hangnail. Nobody was su'prised when Dolly blew into the din' room with it—a rock that Ike'd bought off'n Diamond Joe the first trip to New York. Only o' course it'd been set into a lady's-size ring instead o' the automobile tire he'd been wearin'.

Cap and his missus and Ike and Dolly ett supper together, only Ike didn't eat nothin', but just set there blushin' and spillin' things on the table-cloth. I heard him excusin' himself for not havin' no appetite. He says he couldn't never eat when he was clost to the ocean. He'd forgot about them sixty-five oysters he destroyed the first night o' the trip before.

He was goin' to take her to a show, so after supper he went upstairs to change his collar. She had to doll up, too, and o' course Ike was through long before her.

If you remember the hotel in Boston, they's a little parlor where the piano's at and then they's another little parlor openin' off o' that. Well, when Ike come down Smitty was playin' a few chords and I and Carey was harmonizin'. We seen Ike go up to the desk to leave his key and we called him in. He tried to duck away, but we wouldn't stand for it.

We ast him what he was all duded up for and he says he was goin' to the theayter.

"Goin' alone?" says Carey.

"No," he says, "a friend o' mine's goin' with me."

"What do you say if we go along?" says Carey.

"I ain't only got two tickets," he says.

"Well," says Carey, "we can go down there with you and buy our own seats; maybe we can all get together."

"No," says Ike. "They ain't no more seats. They're all sold out."

"We can buy some off'n the scalpers," says Carey.

"I wouldn't if I was you," says Ike. "They say the show's rotten."

"What are you goin' for, then?" I ast.

"I didn't hear about it bein' rotten till I got the tickets," he says.

"Well," I says, "if you don't want to go I'll buy the tickets from you."

"No," says Ike, "I wouldn't want to cheat you. I'm stung and I'll just have to stand for it."

"What are you goin' to do with the girl, leave her here at the hotel?" I says.

"What girl?" says Ike.

"The girl you ett supper with," I says.

"Oh," he says, "we just happened to go into the dinin' room together, that's all. Cap wanted I should set down with 'em."

"I noticed," says Carey, "that she happened to be wearin' that rock you bought off'n Diamond Joe."

"Yes," says Ike. "I lent it to her for a wile."

"Did you lend her the new ring that goes with it?" I says.

"She had that already," says Ike. "She lost the set out of it."

"I wouldn't trust no strange girl with a rock o' mine," says Carey.

"Oh, I guess she's all right," Ike says. "Besides, I was tired o' the stone. When a girl asks you for somethin', what are you goin' to do?"

He started out toward the desk, but we flagged him.

"Wait a minute!" Carey says. "I got a bet with Sam here, and it's up to you to settle it."

"Well," says Ike, "make it snappy. My friend'll be here any minute."

"I bet," says Carey, "that you and that girl was engaged to be married."

"Nothin' to it," says Ike.

"Now look here," says Carey, "this is goin' to cost me real money if I lose. Cut out the alibi stuff and give it to us straight. Cap's wife just as good as told us you was roped."

Ike blushed like a kid.

"Well, boys," he says, "I may as well own up. You win, Carey."

"Yatta boy!" says Carey. "Congratulations!"

"You got a swell girl, Ike," I says.

"She's a peach," says Smitty.

"Well, I guess she's O. K.," says Ike. "I don't know much about girls."

"Didn't you never run round with 'em?" I says.

"Oh, yes, plenty of 'em," says Ike. "But I never seen none I'd fall for."

"That is, till you seen this one," says Carey.

"Well," says Ike, "this one's O. K., but I wasn't thinkin' about gettin' married yet a wile."

"Who done the askin'—her?" says Carey.

"Oh, no," says Ike, "but sometimes a man don't know what he's gettin' into. Take a good-lookin' girl, and a man gen'ally almost always does about what she wants him to."

"They couldn't no girl lasso me unless I wanted to be lassoed," says Smitty.

"Oh, I don't know," says Ike. "When a fella gets to feelin' sorry for one of 'em it's all off."

Well, we left him go after shakin' hands all round. But he didn't take Dolly to no show that night. Some time wile we was talkin' she'd came into that other parlor and she'd stood there and heard us. I don't know how much she heard. But it was enough. Dolly and Cap's missus took the midnight train for New York. And from there Cap's wife sent her on her way back to Missouri.

She'd left the ring and a note for Ike with the clerk. But we didn't ask Ike if the note was from his friend in Fort Wayne, Texas.

VI

When we'd came to Boston Ike was hittin' plain .397. When we got back home he'd fell off to pretty near nothin'. He hadn't drove one out o' the infield in any o' them other Eastern parks, and he didn't even give no excuse for it.

To show you how bad he was, he struck out three times in Brooklyn one day and never opened his trap when Cap ast him what was the matter. Before, if he'd whiffed oncet in a game he'd of wrote a book tellin' why.

Well, we dropped from first place to fifth in four weeks and we was still goin' down. I and Carey was about the only ones in the club that spoke to each other, and all as we did was remind ourself o' what a boner we'd pulled.

"It's goin' to beat us out o' the big money," says Carey.

"Yes," I says. "I don't want to knock my own ball club, but it looks like a one-man team, and when that one man's dauber's down we couldn't trim our whiskers."

"We ought to knew better," says Carey.

"Yes," I says, "but why should a man pull an alibi for bein' engaged to such a bearcat as she was?"

"He shouldn't," says Carey. "But I and you knowed he would or we'd never start talkin' to him about it. He wasn't no more ashamed o' the girl than I am of a regular base hit. But he just can't come clean on no subjec'."

Cap had the whole story, and I and Carey was as pop'lar with him as an umpire.

"What do you want me to do, Cap?" Carey'd say to him before goin' up to hit.

"Use your own judgment," Cap'd tell him. "We want to lose another game."

But finally, one night in Pittsburgh, Cap had a letter from his missus and he come to us with it.

"You fellas," he says, "is the ones that put us on the bum, and if you're sorry I think they's a chancet for you to make good. The old lady's out to St. Joe and she's been tryin' her hardest to fix things up. She's explained that Ike don't mean nothin' with his talk; I've wrote and explained that to Dolly, too. But the old lady says that Dolly says that she can't believe it. But Dolly's still stuck on this baby, and she's pinin' away just the same as Ike. And the old lady says she thinks if you two fellas would write to the girl and explain how you was always kiddin' with Ike and leadin' him on, and how the ball club was all shot to pieces since Ike quit hittin', and how he acted like he was goin' to kill himself, and this and that, she'd fall for it and maybe soften down. Dolly, the old lady says, would believe you before she'd believe I and the old lady, because she thinks it's her we're sorry for, and not him."

Well, I and Carey was only too glad to try and see what we could do. But it wasn't no snap. We wrote about eight letters before we got one that looked good. Then we give it to the stenographer and had it wrote out on a typewriter and both of us signed it.

It was Carey's idear that made the letter good. He stuck in somethin' about the world's serious money that our wives wasn't goin' to spend unless she took pity on a "boy who was so shy and modest that he was afraid to come right out and say that he had asked such a beautiful and handsome girl to become his bride."

That's prob'ly what got her, or maybe she couldn't of held out much longer anyway. It was four days after we sent the letter that Cap heard from his Missus again. We was in Cincinnati.

"We've won," he says to us. "The old lady says that Dolly says she'll give him another chance. But the old lady says it won't do no good for Ike to write a letter. He'll have to go out there."

"Send him to-night," says Carey.

"I'll pay half his fare," I says.

"I'll pay the other half," says Carey.

"No," says Cap, "the club'll pay his expenses. I'll send him scoutin'."

"Are you goin' to send him to-night?"

"Sure," says Cap. "But I'm goin' to break the news to him right now. It's time we win a ball game."

So in the clubhouse, just before the game, Cap told him. And I certainly felt sorry for Rube Benton and Red Ames that afternoon! I and Carey was standin' in front o' the hotel that night when Ike come out with his suitcase.

"Sent home?" I says to him.

"No," he says, "I'm goin' scoutin'."

"Where to?" I says. "Fort Wayne?"

"No, not exactly," he says.

"Well," says Carey, "have a good time."

"I ain't lookin' for no good time," says Ike. "I says I was goin' scoutin'."

"Well, then," says Carey, "I hope you see somebody you like."

"And you better have a drink before you go," I says.

"Well," says Ike, "they claim it helps a cold."

SINCLAIR LEWIS

[1885–1951]

THE FIRST AMERICAN to win the Nobel Prize for literature received the award for books which were scathing disclosures of life in his country. During the 1920's, Sinclair Lewis had become a dominating figure in American letters, exploring and laying bare the cheap quality of provincial thinking, the shabby pretensions, false social standards, and the hypocritical camaraderie of American business life. His Main Street *became a national symbol, his* Babbitt *a catchword for the kind of businessman to whom money is the gauge of success, and merchandise a measure of the Good Life.*

Sinclair Lewis was born on February 7, 1885, the son of a country doctor whom he idolized and who became an idealized character in his novels. Lewis' affection did not extend to a fondness for his birthplace, Sauk Center, Minnesota, a typical small town of the Middle West; he wrote of it as "Gopher Prairie," thickly homespun, anticultural, and esthetically depressing. From Sauk Center the sophisticated East seemed fascinating; when he graduated from the local schools, Lewis went to Yale. He became the editor of the literary magazine and he wrote unceasingly—purple poetry and prose on the most romantic subjects. "It may be interesting to note," he said, looking back at forty-five, "that one who was later to try to present ordinary pavements trod by real boots should have written nearly always of Guinevere and Lancelot, of weary bitterns among sad Irish reeds, of story-book castles with troubadours vastly indulging in wine, a commodity of which the author was singularly ignorant." "In regions where castles and the memory of troubadours really did exist," he added later, "—in Kent and Cornwall, Fontainebleau and London and Rome—he sat writing of Minnesota prairie villages."

Graduated from Yale in 1908, Lewis followed lost causes and developed an interest in socialism. He worked as a volunteer janitor and laundryman in Upton Sinclair's cooperative colony at Englewood, New Jersey, until it burned down. He drifted to Panama and California, then gradually found his way back East. At twenty-five he settled in New York. He wrote, but no one published what he had written, so he earned a living from a series of jobs for publishers—as a sub-editor for fifteen dollars a week; as office boy; as manuscript reader; as assistant editor of Adventure; as editor of a newspaper syndicate; as advertising writer, cataloguer, and book reviewer; and as the author of Hike and the Aeroplane, a boys' story published when he was twenty-seven under the pseudonym of "Tom Graham."

When he was twenty-nine a novel was finally published, signed with his own name. Our Mr. Wrenn, the story of a New York clerk who frees himself from Philistine respectability, showed the influence, diluted but definite, of H. G. Wells. Lewis greatly admired Wells for "his casual humanism more even than his indignation at cruelty—a discoverer of the importance of the pettiest and drabbest character."

In the series of novels written before Lewis was thirty-five—The Trail of the Hawk, The Job, and Free Air—he manipulated the plots to project a collision between the elements of convention and revolt, between the established upholders of the status quo and the essential iconoclast; but the struggle was only faintly indicated. The books were easy-reading compromises which their author later dismissed as manufactured products, "dead before the ink was dry."

Then came Main Street, a literary explosion which shook the nation and shocked a great part of it. At thirty-five Lewis had begun to write to tell the truth, no matter how much displeasure he might cause or how few readers would buy his books. To his surprise the book caused controversy and sold a million copies; it was translated into all the European and several Asiatic languages, and shot its author into international prominence. It attacked the narrow mentality which governs small towns and was, as Lewis himself noted, his first novel "to rouse the embattled peasantry. . . One of the most treasured American myths had been that all American villages were peculiarly noble and happy, and here an American attacked that myth. Hundreds of thousands read the book with the same masochistic pleasure that one has in sucking an aching tooth."

Between the early and late novels Lewis supported himself by turning out and peddling short stories, most of which he considered inconsequential potboilers though he allowed the best to be published in a volume of Selected Short Stories. At twenty-nine he had married Grace Hegger, from whom he was divorced eleven years later. In 1928 he married the journalist and columnist, Dorothy Thompson, a marriage which lasted fourteen years.

Lewis' head was full of novels, penetrating and provocative. Two years after Main Street had jolted the country, Babbitt created an equally great stir. Lewis spoke of it as "the story of the Tired Business Man, the Man in the Pullman smoker, our American ruler." "Zenith," the setting of Babbitt, is the urban version of "Gopher Prairie," with the same little cheats and big hypocrisies, the gimcrack values and charlatan virtues, where "the standard advertised wares—toothpastes, socks, tires, cameras, instantaneous hot water-heaters—were at first the signs, then the substitutes for joy and passion and wisdom."

Lewis continued to assail the complacency of material progress in Arrowsmith, perhaps his most controlled and most fully realized novel, a fighting defense of the doctor-scientist; in Elmer Gantry, an exposure of those who make religion a racket; and in The Man Who Knew Coolidge, a large-scale cartoon baring the stupidity of the self-righteous know-nothings who run business and shape the mind of the community. The leading figure of Dodsworth was more complex than Lewis' other merchants, battling personal as well as economic pressures, "a part of a crowd vigorously pushing one another toward nowhere."

Despite his successes in his chosen idiom, there was critical disap-

probation of the lack of subtlety, the black-and-white exaggerations, the characters who could be called caricatures. However, Lewis built his books with solidity and enriched them with the most delicately revealing inflections of ordinary speech. A craftsman with a reformer's spirit, one of the sharpest delineators of his country's bad manners, he was also the most accurate reporter of its colloquial speech.

His passion for literary freedom made him conclude that prizes, like titles, were dangerous. When he was awarded the Pulitzer Prize in 1926 for Arrowsmith, *he stirred up a storm of adverse comment by refusing to accept the honor. Four years later he almost apologized for accepting the Nobel Prize.*

Lewis continued diagnosing and dissecting. Powerful works alternated with weakly-conceived novels. It Can't Happen Here, *a frightening forecast of a possible fascist dictatorship in America, and an honest appraisal of racial problems,* Kingsblood Royal, *are the most notable of the books produced after his fiftieth birthday.*

After being accepted as a reformer, Lewis grew increasingly conservative. In The Prodigal Parents, *the worst of his twenty-two novels, he inveighs against the radicalism of American youth, and the scorner of Babbitt seems to become Babbitt's defender. An unflagging but naïve nonconformist, he became uncertain of his aim, unsure of his "place."*

His second marriage ended in another divorce. Miss Thompson was granted the custody of their son—the son of his first marriage had been killed in World War II. Lewis moved to New York, then Minnesota, then Massachusetts. He fought with and lost many of his friends. He became ill. Still he read, researched, and wrote. At sixty-four he published an unrewarding historical novel, The God-Seeker. *Sick, but determinedly working on, he went to Italy where, briefly, he grew better, then collapsed after an attack of pneumonia and died, far from everything that was familiar, in Rome, January 10, 1951.*

An ambivalent critic, Lewis was a Utopian who made fun of Utopias, an anti-sentimentalist whose heart was full of folksy sentiment. Irony and idealism somehow are mingled in all his work. There are many inconsistencies, for Lewis, sure enough about his direction, was never positive about the goal. The central figure of the saga is Babbitt, a symbol who bears various names. He is the prefabricated bourgeois, the standardized middle-class citizen for whom Sinclair Lewis had as much love as loathing. As with Babbitt, so with the country; of the nation which elicited all of his scorn and all of his devotion, Lewis is reported to have said, during that last Italian journey, "I love America. I love it, but I don't like it."

The excerpts which follow are among Lewis's most characteristic writings. "The Towers of Zenith," the first chapter of Babbitt, *not only establishes the character of the story's central figure, a prospering, self-satisfied businessman, but also sets the scene: a busy city of some three hundred thousand somewhere in the Middle West. "First and Last," literally the first and last chapters of* Dodsworth, *presents a double picture of Samuel Dodsworth, a wealthy automobile manufacturer who retires, goes to Europe with his light-minded wife, Fran, and falls in love with an American widow, Edith Cortright. Dodsworth, who had appeared briefly in* Babbitt, *is described in a few lines: "To define what Sam Dodsworth was at fifty, it is easiest to state what he was not. He was none of the things which most Europeans and many Americans expect in a leader of industry. . . He rarely shouted, never slapped people on the back, and he had attended only six baseball games since 1900. He knew, and thoroughly, the Babbitts and baseball fans, but only in business. . . He was common sense apotheosized; he had the energy and reliability of a dynamo. . . And all the while he dreamed of motors like thunderbolts, as poets less modern than himself might dream of stars and roses and nymphs by a pool."*

THE TOWERS OF ZENITH

From *Babbitt*

I

THE TOWERS OF ZENITH aspired above the morning mist; austere towers of steel and cement and limestone, sturdy as cliffs and delicate as silver rods. They were neither citadels nor churches, but frankly and beautifully office-buildings.

The mist took pity on the fretted structures of earlier generations: the Post Office with its shingle-tortured mansard, the red brick minarets of hulking old houses, factories with stingy and sooted windows, wooden tenements colored like mud. The city was full of such grotesqueries, but the clean towers were thrusting them from the business center, and on the farther hills were shining new houses, homes—they seemed—for laughter and tranquillity.

Over a concrete bridge fled a limousine of long sleek hood and noiseless engine. These people in evening clothes were returning from an all-night rehearsal of a Little Theater play, an artistic adventure considerably illuminated by champagne. Below the bridge curved a railroad, a maze of green and crimson lights. The New York Flyer boomed past, and twenty lines of polished steel leaped into the glare.

In one of the skyscrapers the wires of the Associated Press were closing down. The telegraph operators wearily raised their celluloid eye-shades after a night of talking with Paris and Peking. Through the building crawled the scrubwomen, yawning, their old shoes slapping. The dawn mist spun away. Cues of men with lunch-boxes clumped toward the immensity of new factories, sheets of glass and hollow tile, glittering shops where five thousand men worked beneath one roof, pouring out the honest wares that would be sold up the Euphrates and across the veldt. The whistles rolled out in greeting a chorus cheerful as the April dawn; the song of labor in a city built—it seemed—for giants.

II

There was nothing of the giant in the aspect of the man who was beginning to awaken on the sleeping-porch of a Dutch Colonial house in that residential district of Zenith known as Floral Heights.

His name was George F. Babbitt. He was forty-six years old now, in April, 1920, and he made nothing in particular, neither butter nor shoes nor poetry, but he was nimble in the calling of selling houses for more than people could afford to pay.

His large head was pink, his brown hair thin and dry. His face was babyish in slumber, despite his wrinkles and the red spectacle-dents on the slopes of his nose. He was not fat but he was exceedingly well fed; his cheeks were pads, and the unroughened hand which lay helpless upon the khaki-colored blanket was slightly puffy. He seemed prosperous, extremely married and unromantic; and altogether unromantic appeared this sleeping-porch, which looked on one sizable elm, two respectable grass-plots, a cement driveway, and a corrugated iron garage. Yet Babbitt was again dreaming of the fairy child, a dream more romantic than scarlet pagodas by a silver sea.

For years the fairy child had come to him. Where others saw but Georgie Babbitt, she discerned gallant youth. She waited for him, in the darkness beyond mysterious groves. When at last he could slip away from the crowded house he darted to her. His wife, his clamoring friends, sought to follow, but he escaped, the girl fleet beside him, and they crouched together on a shadowy hillside. She was so slim, so white, so eager! She cried that he was gay and valiant, that she would wait for him, that they would sail—

Rumble and bang of the milk-truck.

Babbitt moaned, turned over, struggled back toward his dream. He could see only her face now, beyond misty waters. The furnace-man slammed the basement door. A dog barked in the next yard. As Babbitt sank blissfully into a dim warm tide, the paper-carrier went by whistling, and the rolled-up *Advocate* thumped the front door. Babbitt roused, his stomach constricted with alarm. As he relaxed, he was pierced by the familiar and irritating rattle of someone cranking a Ford: snap-ah-ah, snap-ah-ah, snap-ah-ah. Himself a pious motorist, Babbitt cranked with the unseen driver, with him waited through taut hours for the roar of the starting engine, with him agonized as the roar ceased and again began the infernal patient snap-ah-ah—a round, flat sound, a shivering cold-morning sound, a sound infuriating and inescapable. Not till the rising voice of the motor told him that the Ford was moving was he released from the panting tension. He glanced once at his favorite tree, elm twigs against the gold patina of sky, and fumbled for sleep as for a drug. He who had been a boy very credulous of life was no longer greatly interested in the possible and improbable adventures of each new day.

He escaped from reality till the alarm-clock rang, at seven-twenty.

III

It was the best of nationally advertised and quantitatively produced alarm clocks, with all modern attachments, including cathedral chime, intermittent alarm, and a phosphorescent dial. Babbitt was proud of being awakened by such a rich device. Socially it was almost as creditable as buying expensive cord tires.

He sulkily admitted now that there was no more escape, but he lay and detested the grind of the real-estate business, and disliked his family, and disliked himself for disliking them. The evening before, he had played poker at Vergil Gunch's till midnight, and after such holidays he was irritable before breakfast. It may have been the tremendous home-brewed beer of the prohibition-era and the cigars to which that beer enticed him; it may have been resentment of return from this fine, bold man-world to a restricted region of wives and stenographers, and of suggestions not to smoke so much.

From the bedroom beside the sleeping-porch, his wife's detestably cheerful "Time to get up, Georgie boy," and the itchy sound, the brisk and scratchy sound, of combing hairs out of a stiff brush.

He grunted; he dragged his thick legs, in faded baby-blue pajamas, from under the khaki blanket; he sat on the edge of the cot, running his fingers through his wild hair, while his plump feet mechanically felt for his slippers. He looked regretfully at the blanket—forever a suggestion to him of freedom and heroism. He had bought it for a camping trip which had never come off. It symbolized gorgeous loafing, gorgeous cursing, virile flannel shirts.

He creaked to his feet, groaning at the waves of pain which passed behind his eyeballs. Though he waited for their scorching recurrence, he looked blurrily out at the yard. It delighted him, as always; it was the neat yard of a successful business man of Zenith, that is, it was perfection, and made him also perfect. He regarded the corrugated iron garage. For the three-hundred-and-sixty-fifth time in a year he reflected, "No class to that tin shack. Have to build me a frame garage. But by golly it's the only thing on the place that isn't up-to-date!" While he stared he thought of a community garage for his acreage development, Glen Oriole. He stopped puffing and jiggling. His arms were akimbo. His petulant, sleep-swollen face was set in harder lines. He suddenly seemed capable, an official, a man to contrive, to direct, to get things done.

On the vigor of his idea he was carried down the hard, clean, unused-looking hall into the bathroom.

Though the house was not large it had, like all houses on Floral Heights, an altogether royal bathroom of porcelain and glazed tile and metal sleek as silver. The towel-rack was a rod of clear glass set in nickel. The tub was long enough for a Prussian Guard, and above the set bowl was a sensational exhibit of tooth-brush holder, shaving-brush holder, soap-dish, sponge-dish, and medicine-cabinet, so glittering and so ingenious that they resembled an electrical instrument-board. But the Babbitt whose god was Modern Appliances was not pleased. The air of the bathroom was thick with the smell of a heathen toothpaste. "Verona been at it again! 'Stead of sticking to Lilidol, like I've re-peat-ed-ly asked her, she's gone and gotten some confounded stinkum stuff that makes you sick!"

The bath-mat was wrinkled and the floor was wet. (His daughter Verona eccentrically took baths in the morning, now and then.) He slipped on the mat, and slid against the tub. He said "Damn!" Furiously he snatched up his tube of shaving-cream, furiously he lathered, with a belligerent slapping of the unctuous brush, furiously he raked his plump cheeks with a safety-razor. It pulled. The blade was dull. He said, "Damn—oh—oh—damn it!"

He hunted through the medicine-cabinet for a packet of new razor-blades (reflecting, as invariably, "Be cheaper to buy one of these dinguses and strop your own blades,") and when he discovered the packet, behind the round box of bicarbonate of soda, he thought ill of his wife for putting it there and very well of himself for not saying "Damn." But he did say it, immediately afterward, when with wet and soap-slippery fingers he tried to remove the horrible little envelope and crisp clinging oiled paper from the new blade.

Then there was the problem, oft-pondered, never solved, of what to do with the old blade, which might imperil the fingers of his young. As usual, he tossed it on top of the medicine-cabinet, with a mental note that some day he must remove the fifty or sixty other blades that were also, temporarily, piled up there. He finished his shaving in a growing testiness increased by his spinning headache and by the emptiness in his stomach. When he was done, his round face smooth and streamy and his eyes stinging from soapy water, he reached for a towel. The family towels were wet, wet and clammy and vile, all of them wet, he found, as he blindly snatched them—his own face-towel, his wife's, Verona's, Ted's, Tinka's, and the lone bath-towel with the huge welt of initial. Then George F. Babbitt did a dismaying thing. He wiped his face on the guest-towel! It was a pansy-embroidered trifle which always hung there to indicate that the Babbitts were in the best Floral Heights society. No one had ever used it. No guest had ever dared to. Guests secretively took a corner of the nearest regular towel.

He was raging, "By golly, here they go and use up all the towels, every doggone one of 'em, and they use 'em and get 'em all wet and sopping, and never put out a dry one for me—of course, I'm the goat!—and then I want one and— I'm the only person in the doggone house that's got the slightest doggone bit of consideration for other people and thoughtfulness and consider there may be others that may want to use the doggone bathroom after me and consider—"

He was pitching the chill abominations into the bath-tub, pleased by the vindictiveness of that desolate flapping sound; and in the midst his wife serenely trotted in, observed serenely, "Why Georgie dear, what are you doing? Are you going to wash out the towels? Why, you needn't wash out the towels. Oh, Georgie, you didn't go and use the guest-towel, did you?"

It is not recorded that he was able to answer.

For the first time in weeks he was sufficiently roused by his wife to look at her.

IV

Myra Babbitt—Mrs. George F. Babbitt—was definitely mature. She had creases from the corners of her mouth to the bottom of her chin, and her plump neck bagged. But the thing that marked her as having passed the line was that she no longer had reticences before her husband, and no longer worried about not having reticences. She was in a petticoat now, and corsets which bulged, and unaware of being seen in bulgy corsets. She had become so dully habituated to married life that in her full matronliness she was as sexless as an anemic nun. She was a good woman, a kind woman, a diligent woman, but no one, save perhaps Tinka her ten-year-old, was at all interested in her or entirely aware that she was alive.

After a rather thorough discussion of all the domestic and social aspects of towels she apologized to Babbitt for his having an alcoholic headache; and he recovered enough to endure the search for a B.V.D. undershirt which had, he pointed out, malevolently been concealed among his clean pajamas.

He was fairly amiable in the conference on the brown suit.

"What do you think, Myra?" He pawed at the clothes hunched on a chair in their bedroom, while she moved about mysteriously adjusting and patting her petticoat and, to his jaundiced eye, never seeming to get on with her dressing. "How about it? Shall I wear the brown suit another day?"

"Well, it looks awfully nice on you."

"I know, but gosh, it needs pressing."

"That's so. Perhaps it does."

"It certainly could stand being pressed, all right."

"Yes, perhaps it wouldn't hurt it to be pressed."

"But gee, the coat doesn't need pressing. No sense in having the whole darn suit pressed, when the coat doesn't need it."

"That's so."

"But the pants certainly need it, all right. Look at them—look at those wrinkles—the pants certainly do need pressing."

"That's so. Oh, Georgie, why couldn't you wear the brown coat with the blue trousers we were wondering what we'd do with them?"

"Good Lord! Did you ever in all my life know me to wear the coat of one suit and the pants of another? What do you think I am? A busted bookkeeper?"

"Well, why don't you put on the dark gray suit today, and stop in at the tailor and leave the brown trousers?"

"Well, they certainly need— Now where the devil is that gray suit? Oh, yes, here we are."

He was able to get through the other crises of dressing with comparative resoluteness and calm.

His first adornment was the sleeveless dimity B.V.D. undershirt, in which he resembled a small boy humorlessly wearing a cheesecloth tabard at a civic pageant. He never put on B.V.D.'s without thanking the God of Progress that he didn't wear tight, long, old-fashioned undergarments, like his father-in-law and partner, Henry Thompson. His second embellishment was combing and slicking back his hair. It gave him a tremendous forehead, arching up two inches beyond the former hair-line. But most wonder-working of all was the donning of his spectacles.

There is character in spectacles—the pretentious tortoise-shell, the meek pince-nez of the school teacher, the twisted silver-framed glasses of the old villager. Babbitt's spectacles had huge, circular, frameless lenses of the very best glass; the ear-pieces were thin bars of gold. In them he was the modern business man; one who gave orders to clerks and drove a car and played occasional golf and was scholarly in regard to Salesmanship. His head suddenly appeared not babyish but weighty, and you noted his heavy, blunt nose, his straight mouth and thick, long upper lip, his chin overfleshy but strong; with respect you beheld him put on the rest of his uniform as a Solid Citizen.

The gray suit was well cut, well made, and completely undistinguished. It was a standard suit. White piping on the V of the vest added a flavor of law and learning. His shoes were black laced boots, good boots, honest boots, standard boots, extraordinarily uninteresting boots. The only frivolity was in his purple knitted scarf. With considerable comment on the matter to Mrs. Babbitt (who, acrobatically fastening the back of her blouse to her skirt with a safety-pin, did not hear a word he said), he chose between the purple scarf and a tapestry effect with stringless brown harps among blown palms, and into it he thrust a snake-head pin with opal eyes.

A sensational event was changing from the brown suit to the gray the contents of his pockets. He was earnest about these objects. They were of eternal importance, like baseball or the Republican Party. They included a fountain pen and a silver pencil (always lacking a supply of new leads) which belonged in the righthand upper vest pocket. Without them he would have felt naked. On his watch-chain were a gold penknife, silver cigar-cutter, seven keys (the use of two of which he had forgotten), and incidentally a good watch. Depending from the chain was a large, yellowish elk's-tooth—proclamation of his membership in the Brotherly and Protective Order of Elks. Most significant of all was his loose-leaf pocket note-book, that modern and efficient note-book which contained the addresses of people whom he had forgotten, prudent memoranda of postal money-orders which had reached their destinations months ago, stamps which had lost their mucilage, clippings of verses by T. Cholmondeley Frink and of the newspaper editorials from which Babbitt got his opinions and his polysyllables, notes to be sure and do things which he did not intend to do, and one curious inscription—D.S.S. D.M.Y.P.D.F.

But he had no cigarette-case. No one had ever happened to give him one, so he hadn't the habit, and people who carried cigarette-cases he regarded as effeminate.

Last, he stuck in his lapel the Boosters' Club button. With the conciseness of great art the button displayed two words: "Boosters—Pep!" It made Babbitt feel loyal and important. It associated him with Good Fellows, with men who were nice and human, and important in business circles. It was his V.C., his Legion of Honor ribbon, his Phi Beta Kappa key.

With the subtleties of dressing ran other complex worries. "I feel kind of punk this morning," he said. "I think I had too much dinner last evening. You oughtn't to serve those heavy banana fritters."

"But you asked me to have some."

"I know, but— I tell you, when a fellow gets past forty he has to look after his digestion. There's a lot of fellows that don't take proper care of themselves. I tell you at forty a man's a fool or his doctor—I mean, his own doctor. Folks don't give enough attention to this matter of dieting. Now I think—Course a man ought to have a good meal after the day's work, but it would be a good thing for both of us if we took lighter lunches."

"But Georgie, here at home I always do have a light lunch."

"Mean to imply I make a hog of myself, eating down-town? Yes, sure! You'd have a swell time if you had to eat the truck that new steward hands out to us at the Athletic Club! But I certainly do feel out of sorts, this morning. Funny, got a pain down here on the left side—but no, that wouldn't be appendicitis, would it? Last night, when I was driving over to Verg Gunch's, I felt a pain in my stomach, too. Right here it was—kind of a sharp shooting pain. I— Where'd that dime go to? Why don't you serve more prunes at breakfast? Of course I eat an apple every evening—an apple a day keeps the doctor away—but still, you ought to have more prunes, and not all these fancy doodads."

"The last time I had prunes you didn't eat them."

"Well, I didn't feel like eating 'em, I suppose. Matter of fact, I think I did eat some of 'em. Anyway— I tell you it's mighty important to— I was saying to Verg Gunch, just last evening, most people don't take sufficient care of their diges—"

"Shall we have the Gunches for our dinner, next week?"

"Why sure; you bet."

"Now see here, George: I want you to put on your nice dinner-jacket that evening."

"Rats! The rest of 'em won't want to dress."

"Of course they will. You remember when you didn't dress for the Littlefields' supper-party, and all the rest did, and how embarrassed you were."

"Embarrassed, hell! I wasn't embarrassed. Everybody knows I can put on as expensive a Tux. as anybody else, and I should worry if I don't happen to have it on sometimes. All a darn nuisance, anyway. All right for a woman, that stays around the house all the time, but when a fellow's worked like the dickens all day, he doesn't want to go and hustle his head off getting into the soup-and-fish for a lot of folks that he's seen in just reg'lar ordinary clothes that same day."

"You know you enjoy being seen in one. The other evening you admitted you were glad I'd insisted on your dressing. You said you felt a lot better for it. And oh, Georgie, I do wish you wouldn't say 'Tux.' It's 'dinner-jacket.'"

"Rats, what's the odds?"

"Well, it's what all the nice folks say. Suppose Lucile McKelvey heard you calling it a 'Tux.'"

"Well, that's all right now! Lucile McKelvey can't pull anything on me! Her folks are common as mud, even if her husband and her dad are millionaires! I suppose you're trying to rub in *your* exalted social position! Well, let me tell you that your revered paternal ancestor, Henry T., doesn't even call it a 'Tux.'! He calls it a 'bobtail jacket for a ringtail monkey,' and you couldn't get him into one unless you chloroformed him!"

"Now don't be horrid, George."

"Well, I don't want to be horrid, but Lord! you're getting as fussy as Verona. Ever since she got out of college she's been too rambunctious to live with—doesn't know what she wants—well, I know what she wants!—all she wants is to marry a millionaire, and live in Europe, and hold some preacher's hand, and simultaneously at the same time stay right here in Zenith and be some blooming kind of a socialist agitator or boss charity-worker or some damn thing! Lord, and Ted is just as bad! He wants to go to college, and he doesn't want to go to college. Only one of the three that knows her own mind is Tinka. Simply can't understand how I ever came to have a pair of shillyshallying children like Rone and Ted. I may not be any Rockefeller or James J. Shakespeare, but I certainly do know my own mind, and I do keep right on plugging along in the office and— Do you know the latest? Far as I can figure out, Ted's new bee is he'd like to be a movie actor and— And here I've told him a hundred times, if he'll go to college and law-school and make good, I'll set him up in business and—Verona just exactly as bad. Doesn't know what she wants. Well, well, come on! Aren't you ready yet? The girl rang the bell three minutes ago."

V

Before he followed his wife, Babbitt stood at the westernmost window of their room. This residential settlement, Floral Heights, was on a rise; and though the center of the city was three miles away—Zenith had between three and four hundred thousand inhabitants now—he could see the top of the Second National Tower, an Indiana limestone building of thirty-five stories.

Its shining walls rose against April sky to a simple cornice like a streak of white fire. Integrity was in the tower, and decision. It bore its strength lightly as a tall soldier. As Babbitt stared, the nervousness was soothed from his face, his slack chin lifted in reverence. All he articulated was "That's one lovely sight!" but he was inspired by the rhythm of the city; his love of it renewed. He beheld the tower as a temple-spire of the religion of business, a faith passionate, exalted, surpassing common men; and as he clumped down to breakfast he whistled the ballad "Oh, by gee, by gosh, by jingo" as though it were a hymn melancholy and noble.

FIRST AND LAST

From *Dodsworth*

I

THE ARISTOCRACY OF ZENITH were dancing at the Kennepoose Canoe Club. They two-stepped on the wide porch, with its pillars of pine trunks, its bobbing Japanese lanterns; and never were there dance-frocks with wider sleeves nor hair more sensuously piled on little smiling heads, never an August evening more moon-washed and spacious and proper for respectable romance.

Three guests had come in these new-fangled automobiles, for it was now 1903, the climax of civilization. A fourth automobile was approaching, driven by Samuel Dodsworth.

The scene was a sentimental chromo—crisping lake, lovers in canoes singing "Nelly Was a Lady," all very lugubrious and happy; and Sam Dodsworth enjoyed it. He was a large and formidable young man, with a healthy brown mustache and a chaos of brown hair on a massive head. He was, at twenty-eight, assistant superintendent of that most noisy and unsentimental institution, the Zenith Locomotive Works, and in Yale (class of 1896) he had played better than average football, but he thought well of the most sentimental sorts of moonlight.

Tonight he was particularly uplifted because he was driving his first car. And it was none of your old-fashioned "gasoline buggies," with the engine under the seat. The engine bulked in front, under a proud hood over two feet long, and the steering column was not straight but rakishly tilted. The car was sporting and rather dangerous, and the lights were powerful affairs fed by acetylene gas. Sam sped on, with a feeling of power, of dominating the universe, at twelve dizzy miles an hour.

At the Canoe Club he was greeted by Tub Pearson, admirable in white kid gloves. Tub—Thomas J. Pearson—round and short and jolly, class-jester and class-dandy at Yale, had been Sam Dodsworth's roommate and chief admirer throughout college, but now Tub had begun to take on an irritable dignity as teller and future president of his father's bank in Zenith.

"It runs!" Tub marveled, as Sam stepped in triumph from the car. "I've got a horse all ready to tow you back!"

Tub had to be witty, whatever happened.

"Certainly it runs! I'll bet I was up to eighteen miles an hour!"

"Yeh! I'll bet that some day automobiles'll run forty!" Tub jeered. "Sure! Why, they'll just about drive the poor old horse right off the highway!"

"They will! And I'm thinking of tying up with this new Revelation Company to manufacture 'em."

"Not seriously, you poor chump?"

"Yes."

"Oh, my Lord!" Tub wailed affectionately. "Don't be crazy, Sambo! My dad says automobiles are nothing but a fad. Cost too much to run. In five years, he says, they'll disappear."

Sam's answer was not very logical:

"Who's the young angel on the porch?"

If she was an angel, the girl at whom Sam was pointing, she was an angel of ice; slim, shining, ash-blonde, her self-possessed voice very cool as she parried the complimentary teasing of half a dozen admirers; a crystal candle-stick of a girl among black-and-white lumps of males.

"You remember her—Frances Voelker—Fran Voelker—old Herman's

kid. She's been abroad for a year, and she was East, in finishing-school, before that. Just a brat—isn't over nineteen or twenty, I guess. Golly, they say she speaks German and French and Italian and Woof-woof and all known languages."

Herman Voelker had brewed his way into millions and respectability. His house was almost the largest in Zenith—certainly it had the greatest amount of turrets, colored glass windows, and lace curtains—and he was leader among the German-Americans who were supplanting the New Englanders throughout the state as controllers of finance and merchandising. He entertained German professors when they came lecturing and looking, and it was asserted that one of the genuine hand-painted pictures which he had recently brought back from Nuremberg was worth nearly ten thousand dollars. A worthy citizen, Herman, and his tart beer was admirable, but that this beef-colored burgher should have fathered anything so poised and luminous as Fran was a miracle.

The sight of her made Sam Dodsworth feel clumsy as a St. Bernard looking at a white kitten. While he prophesied triumphs for the motor car, while he danced with other girls, he observed her airy dancing and her laughter. Normally, he was not particularly afraid of young women, but Fran Voelker seemed too fragile for his thick hands. Not till ten did he speak to her, when a partner left her, a flushed Corybant, in a chair near Sam's.

"Do you remember me—Dodsworth? Years since I've seen you."

"Remember! Heavens! I wondered if you were going to notice me. I used to steal the newspaper from Dad to get the news of your football heroisms. And when I was a nice young devil of eight, you once chased me out of your orchard for stealing apples."

"Did I? Wouldn't dare to now! Mavenex' dance?"

"Well— Let me see. Oh. The next is with Levering Mott, and he's already ruined three of my two slippers. Yes."

If he did not dance with any particular neatness, a girl knew where she was, with Sam Dodsworth. He had enough strength and decision to let a young woman understand who was doing the piloting. With Fran Voelker, he was inspired; he waltzed as though he was proud of his shining burden. He held her lightly enough and, after the chaste custom of the era, his hands were gloved. But his finger-tips felt a current from her body. He knew that she was the most exquisite child in the world; he knew that he was going to marry her and keep her forever in a shrine; he knew that after years of puzzled wonder about the purpose of life, he had found it.

"She's like a lily—no, she's too lively. She's like a humming bird—no, too kind of dignified. She's—oh, she's a flame!"

They sat talking by the lake at midnight. Out on the dappled water, seen through a cloud of willow leaves, the youngsters in canoes were now singing "My Old Kentucky Home." Zenith was still in the halcyon William Dean Howells days; not yet had it become the duty of young people to be hard and brisk, and knowing about radios, jazz, and gin.

Fran was a white shadow, in a lace shawl over her thin yellow dancing frock, as she drooped down on a newspaper which he had solemnly spread for her on the long grass. Sam trembled a little, and sounded very pompous, rather boyish:

"I suppose you went everywhere in Europe."

"More or less. France and Spain and Austria and Switzerland and— Oh, I've seen the Matterhorn by moonlight, and Santa Maria della Salute at dawn. And I've been almost frozen to death in a mistral at Avignon!"

"I suppose you'll be bored in Zenith."

She laughed, in a small competent way. "I know *so* much about Europe—I'm no Cook's tripper!—that I know I don't know anything! All I can do in French is to order breakfast. Six months from now, all I'll remember of Germany is the names of nineteen towns, and how the Potsdamer Platz looks when you're waiting for a droschke. But you've *done* things. What are you doing now, by the way?"

"Assistant supe at the Locomotive Works. But I'm going to take a big gamble and— Ever ride in an automobile?"

"Oh yes, several times, in Paris and New York."

"Well, I believe that in twenty years, say by 1923 or '4, they'll be as common as buggies are now! I'm going in on a new company here—Revelation Automobile Company. I'll get less salary, but it's a swell gamble. Wonderful future. I've been working on my mechanical drawing lately, and I've got the idea that they ought to get away from imitating carriages. Make a—it sounds highbrow, but I mean what you might call a new kind of beauty for autos. Kind of long straight lines. The Revelation boss thinks I'm crazy. What do you think?"

"Oh, splendid!"

"And I've bought me an automobile of my own."

"Oh, really?"

"Let me drive you home tonight!"

"No, sorry; Mama is coming for me."

"You've got to let me take you for a ride. Soon!"

"Perhaps next Sunday. . . . We must go back to the clubhouse, don't you think?"

He sprang up, meekly. As he lifted her to her feet, as he felt her slim hands, he murmured, "Certainly like to see Europe some day. When I graduated, I thought I'd be a civil engineer and see the Brazil jungle and China and all over. Reg'lar Richard Harding Davis stuff! But— Certainly going to see Europe, anyway. Maybe I might run into you over there, and you might show me some of it."

"I'd love to!"

Ah, if she desired Europe, he would master it, and give it to her on a platter of polished gold!

There was the telephone call to her when he should have been installing machinery at the Revelation Automobile Company. There was the drive with her in his new car, very careful, though once he ventured on seventeen miles an hour. There was the dinner at the Voelkers', in the room with carved beams like a Hofbräuhaus, and Sam's fear that if Fran was kept on food like this, roast goose and stuffed cabbage and soup with Leberknödel, she would lose her race-horse slimness.

And there was even a moment when, recalling his vow made in Massachusetts Tech after graduating from Yale that he would cut loose from America and see the great world, he warned himself that between Fran and tying himself to the urgent new motor industry, he would be caught for life. The vision of himself as a Richard Harding Davis hero returned wistfully. . . Riding a mountain trail, two thousand sheer feet above a steaming valley; sun-helmet and whipcord breeches; tropical rain on a tin-roofed shack; a shot in the darkness as he sat over a square-face of gin with a ragged tramp of Noble Ancestry. But his mind fled back to the excitement of Fran's image: her spun-glass hair, her tingling hands, her lips that were forever pursing in fantastic pouts, her chatter that fell suddenly into inexplicable silence, her cool sureness that made him feel foggy and lumbering.

In a slaty November drizzle, they were tramping the cliffs along the Chaloosa River. Fran's cheeks were alight and she was humming, but when they stopped to look at the wash of torn branches in the flooded river Sam felt that he must be protective. She was too slight and precious for such hardship as an autumnal rain. He drew the edge of his mackintosh over her woolly English topcoat.

"You must be soaked! I'm a brute to let you stay out!"

She smiled at him, very close. "I like it!"

It seemed to him that she had snuggled closer. He kissed her—for the first time, and very badly indeed.

"Oh, please don't!" she begged, a little shocked, her lively self-possession gone.

"Fran, you've got to marry me!"

She slipped from the shelter of his raincoat and, arms akimbo, said impishly, "Oh, really? Is that a new law?"

"It is!"

"The great Yale athlete speaks! The automobile magnate!"

Very gravely: "No, just a scared lump of meat that's telling you he worships you!"

Still she stared at him, among the autumn-bedraggled weeds on the river bank; she stared impudently, but quite suddenly she broke, covered her eyes with her hands, and while he clumsily dabbled at her cheeks with a huge handkerchief, she sobbed:

"Oh, Sam, my dear, but I'm so grasping! I want the whole world, not just Zenith! I *don't* want to be a good wife and mother and play cribbage prettily! I want splendor! Great horizons! Can we look for them together?"

"We will!" said Sam.

It was not till 1908, when he had been married for five years to Fran Voelker and they had had two babies, Emily and Brent, that Samuel Dodsworth came on his real struggle at the Revelation Automobile Company.

His superiors in the company had equally prized him for his steadiness and industry and fretted at him for being a dreamer. He was crazy as a poet, they said. Not only did he venture to blaspheme against the great Renault-Darracq dogmas of car-designing, not only did he keep on raving about long "stream-lines," but he insisted that the largest profits would lie in selling automobiles as cheaply as possible to as many customers as possible. He was only assistant manager of production in 1908, but he owned a little stock, and his father-in-law, portly old Herman Voelker, owned more. It was hard to discharge Sam, even when he growled at the president of the company, "If you keep the Rev looking like the one-horse-shay, we'll go bankrupt."

They tried to buy him out, and Sam, who had been absorbed in blue prints and steel castings, had to learn something about the tricks of financing: about bonds, transfer of stock, call loans, discounts to dealers. With Voelker's money behind him, he secured twenty-three per cent. of the stock, he was made vice president and manager of production, he brought out the first four-door model, and he saw the Revelation become the sensation of America for a season and one of its best-selling cars for a score of years.

And never, these twenty years, did he come nearer to the Brazilian jungle than Wall Street, nearer to the tinkling pagodas than the Revelation agency in Kansas City.

But he was too busy to be discontented; and he managed to believe that Fran loved him. . . .

XXXV

For days they drifted in perfect calm, and he was proud that the enervating thought of Fran was gone from him.

All one morning they explored the ridge above Posilipo, found fragments of a Roman emperor's villa and the carp-pond in which he used to drown his slaves as the best fishfood, and discovered the mausoleum which, history asserts, was the tomb of Vergil, or of some one else. They straggled home, up the long street which was a wilderness of children and carts, and sank down sighing in the cool drawing-room.

"*Colazione*, *Teresa*," he ordered, then: "Curious, Edith, but this house that you've rented, and that belongs to an Italian I never saw till the other day, is the first that I ever felt was really mine. I actually dare give an order!"

"But I'm sure your Fran never *meant* to be a domestic dictator. . . ."

The gardener had left the mail on the table, but Sam did not pick it up till after lunch, and then but carelessly. On top was a letter from Fran. He pretended, not very skillfully, that he had to go to his room, and he read Fran's letter alone:

I haven't much excuse, probably I've been a fool and not appreciated you but anyway, maybe with no right to, I am turning to you rather desperately. Kurt's mother finally came up from Austria. She was pretty rude to me. She indicated, oh quite clearly that for the Catholic and Highly Noble Kurtrl to marry a female who was (or soon would be) heinously divorced, who was an American, and who was too old to bear him heirs, would be disastrous. And she didn't spare me very much in putting it that way, either. Not a pretty scene—me sitting there smoking in Kurt's flat and trying to look agreeable while she wailed at Kurt and ignored me. And Kurt stood by her. Oh, his nice little sentimental heart bled for me, and since then he's had such a good time being devastated and trying to take both sides at once. But he "thought ve had better put off the marriage for maybe a couple of years till ve von her over." God! Is he a man or a son? There ain't going to be no vinning over, and no marriage! I'm sick of his cowardice, when I risked so much, but why go into that.

If you still care to bend your Olympian head and forgive the probably wicked and unforgivable Magdalene or however it's spelled, I should be glad to join you again, anyway I've stopped divorce proceedings. Of course I realize that in saying this so honestly, without efforts to protect myself as most women would, I risk another humiliation at your hands such as I had from Kurt. Of course I don't know how far you have committed yourself in the rather strange relations with this Mrs. Cortwright in which you have apparently had so much pleasure and relief from my aggravating self, though how you could be willing to take snubs from the highly proper Italians by thus living with her openly instead of concealing things is beyond—

Oh forgive me, forgive me, dear Sambo darling, forgive me, your bad child Fran! I sound so beastly and snotty when in my heart I'm desolated and scared and lost and I turn to you as the Rock of Ages! I wrote so abominably and unjustly because I'm so wretched, so desperate, and I won't even tear it up—I want you to know that if you do let your bad Fran come back, she probably hasn't learned as much as she should in her mediocre little tragedy, she'll probably be just as snobbish and demanding as ever, though God knows I don't want to be, I am so tired of thread-bare grandeurs now and want so much to be simple and honest.

I think you will credit me with not trying to come back just because you are rich and strong, and Kurt poor and honest. It's just— Oh, you know what it is! I venture to turn to you because I do know that once, anyway, you loved me a great deal. And if we could manage to stick together, it will be so much better for Brent and Emily—oh, I know, probably its shameless of me to speak of that so late, but it is true.

I find there is a boat leaving Hamburg September 19, Cherbourg the next day, the *Deutschland* and if you *care* to join me on it, or meet me in Paris, I should be—Oh Sam, if you still do love me, you mustn't be proud, you mustn't take this chance to punish me, but come, because otherwise—Oh, I don't know what I *will* do! I've been so proud! Now I feel the world is jeering at me! I don't dare leave my flat, don't dare answer the phone and hear their pitying laughter, I have my maid answer it for me, and usually it is still Kurt, but I'll never see him again, never, he talks of killing himself but he won't—his Mamma wouldn't let him!

As soon as you get this, won't you please telephone me here, from Naples.

If you feel like coming, I hope this will not inconvenience your hostess, Mrs. Cortright, whom I remember so agreeably in Venice, kindly give her my regards. But I hope that my appeal may be somewhat more important to you than even your social duty to that doubtless most charming lady who is I am sure much less irritating than I.

Her whole handwriting changed then; he felt that the rest of the letter had been written hours later:

Oh, Sam, I do need you so, did I ever tell you that I adore you?

Your shamed and wretched little Fran.

He blundered down to the drawing-room, snorting, "Got to run into Naples. May be late for tea. Don't wait."

"What is it?"

"Oh, it's nothing."

He fled from her.

All the way down, on the tram, he asked himself whether he wanted to have Fran again, and whether he was really going to join her, and to both he answered with perfect blankness. But when he asked whether he wanted to leave Edith, he denied it, sharply, with fury, reflecting wretchedly how good she had been, how honest, how understanding, and perceiving there was rising in him a passion for her greater than the mystic vexation with which Fran had fascinated him.

And he was going to desert Edith, going to be weak enough to betray her?

"Oh, probably," he sighed, when for an hour, at the American Express Company, he had been waiting for the telephone call to Berlin.

He seemed to wait forever.

He was as conscious of the scene in the express office as though he had sat there for years. A picture of a big New York Central locomotive. Racks of pamphlets about spicy places—Burma and Bangkok and São Paulo—he would never see them now, because Fran would find them crude and unfashionable. A tourist lady writing letters and between sentences boasting to her mother of the *won-derful* corals she had found on the Piazza dei Martiri—

Then startlingly, "Your Berlin call!"

He heard Fran's voice, quicksilver voice, eagerness of the wildly playing child in its lifting mutations:

"Oh, Sam, it really is you? You really are coming, dearest? You do forgive poor Fran?"

"Sure. Be on the boat. *On the boat.* Yes, the nineteenth, yes, sure, we'll talk over everything, good-bye, honey, you better get the tickets as you're there in Germany. *Get the steamer tickets*, good-bye, honey, I'll wire you a confirmation."

He walked back most of the way, looking old and slow and sweaty, laboring over the coming scene with Edith. She would be very polite but surprised, contemptuous of him for returning to the servitude of Fran's witchery.

He slunk in a few minutes after six.

She was reading by the great window in the drawing-room. She glanced up, then, wondering, "What is it? What's happened?"

"Well—"

He stood by the window, making much of clipping and lighting a cigar, and he did not look at her as he grumbled, "Fran's lover, this Count Obersdorf, has turned her down. His mother thought she was kind of déclassé—divorce and all that. Poor kid, that must've been hard on her. She's given up the idea of divorce, and she's sailing for home. She'll be kind of— Oh, people'll talk a lot, I guess. I'm afraid I'll have to go with her. Fact, I'll have to catch the midnight for Rome, tonight. . . . I wish there were some way of telling you all that you've—"

"Sam!"

She had sprung up. He was astonished by the fury in her quiet eyes.

"I won't let you go back to that woman! And I won't see you killed—yes, killed!—by her sweet, gay, well-mannered, utter damned selfishness! Her only thought about anybody is what they give her! The world offers you sun and wind, and Fran offers you death, fear and death! Oh, I'd seen how you've aged five years in five minutes, after one of her complaining letters! And you won't be helping her—you'll just make her feel all the more that she can do any selfish, cruel thing she wants to and come out of it unscathed! Think of Peking and Cairo! No! Think of the farm you could have in Michigan, among the pines! Think of how natural and contented you'd be—yes, *we'd* be—back there—"

"I know, Edith; I know every bit of it. I just can't help it. She's my child. I've got to take care of her."

"Yes. Well." The passion did not fade from her eyes, but snapped out, as though one should turn off a light, and she said dully, "Sorry. I was impertinent. At least let me help you pack."

Throughout the packing, dinner, and the rather dreadful waiting afterward, when he could not find two civil words to put together, she was a little abrupt of speech, very courteous. She asked questions about Zenith. She politely hoped that she might see him "and Mrs. Dodsworth" some distant day. Only once was she near to intimacy, when, after a torturing pause, she blurted, "There really isn't much to say, is there! But I do want you to know that because you've seemed to like me, you've given me a new assurance."

When he tried to counter with florid compliments, she bustled out to the kitchen.

The sound of the coming taxicab released him from the eternity of sitting dead in a tomb. While the servants straggled out with his luggage, he held her hand, patting it.

"It is all ready, Signore," said the maid. She received the highly expected tip, and with a "Com' beck soon!" which sounded sincere, she vanished.

In the twilight outside the tree-shadowed door, he awkwardly shook hands with Edith, but while he was trying to say something agreeable, she cried:

"It's too late now. But I thought that some day—I thought it would be easy for me to talk, and I would tell you all sorts of things about how I feel and think. That it's been pleasant to be with you. That you're bigger than you know, not smaller, like celebrities. That you've made me willing to stop being afraid of the world, and to attack it again. I've felt—" She seized his rough sleeve. "That curious feeling, always a surprise every time I was with you, of 'Why, it's *you!*' That feeling that you were different from any other living person—not necessarily one bit finer but—oh, different! I shouldn't say any of this, but before it's quite too late—too late!—I want to try to be reckless. But I can't say any of the things I thought. Bless you, my dear! And God keep you through the wickedness of this Happy Ending!"

He kissed her, a terrible clinging kiss, and lumbered over to the roadway and his taxicab. He looked back. She seemed to start toward him, then closed the door quickly. Through a window he heard her voice, weary and spiritless: "Only one for breakfast, Teresa."

He was alone with a yawning taxi-driver, as a breeze came up from the bay in the Southern darkness.

XXXVI

Fran was lovely, very young, in a gray-squirrel mantle.

"I got it for almost *nothing*, at the summer sales in Berlin," she said. "Why is it most women never can seem to economize? I'll bet your wonderful flame, Mrs. Cost—Cortright? funny, I never *can* seem to remember her name—she's frightfully clever, I'm sure, but I'll bet she'd have paid twice as much for it."

The late September was cold even for mid-Atlantic. Fran smoothed the fur, draped it closer in her steamer-chair. She seemed to him like a leopard with its taut limbs hidden by a robe.

Now, after tea hour on the S.S. *Deutschland*, a raging sunset smeared the waves with a frightening crimson. They smelled a storm. The ship ducked before the attacking waves. But Fran was full of liveliness and well-being. As she talked, she nodded every instant to people they had met aboard, the men who were always in a knot about her at the dances, the matrons who talked of "that charming Mrs. Dodsworth—she told me she was much younger than her husband—he's a little slow, don't you think—but she's so fond of him—looks after him like a daughter."

Fran cuddled down in her richness of fur.

"Oh, it's nice to be *going* somewhere!" she said. "I bet we'll both be crazy to start off somewhere, maybe back to Paris, when we've been home a few months. (What an *atrocious* hat that woman has on and my *dear*, will you regard her shoes! Why they *allow* people like that in the first cabin?) And you can't know how tired I got of sticking around Berlin forever 'n' ever! Oh, you were so right about Kurt, Sam dear. I don't know how you guessed it! You'd be the first to admit you aren't usually so *awfully* good at judging character, except in the case of business men, but you were right with—Oh, he was so *bossy!* He was furious if I so much as suggested I'd like to run down to Baden-Baden by myself. And where he got the idea that he was so important—Oh, his family may be as old as the Coliseum—the Coliseo—but when I saw his mother, my *dear*, the most awful old country frump—"

"Don't!" said Sam. "Don't know why, but I kind of hate to hear you riding Kurt and his mother that way. They were probably hurt, too."

Most graciously, quite forgivingly, "Yes, you're right. Sorry, M'sieu! I'll be a good girl. And of course everything is all right now. After all, it's such a wonderful Happy Ending to our wild little escapades! We've both learned lots, don't you think? and now I won't be so flighty and you won't be so irritable, I'm sure you won't."

There was dancing in the verandah café. Young Tom Allen, the polo player—young Tom, all black and ivory and grin—came to ask her to dance. She smiled up at him, airily patted Sam's arm, and scampered away, while Tom seemed to be holding her hand under shelter of her squirrel robe,

The sunset was angry now, the color of port wine.

Sam staggered around and around the slanting deck, alone, and alone he stood aft, looking back in the direction of Europe. But there was only foggy gray.

He awoke, bewildered, at two in the morning. The storm had come; the steamer was pitching abominably. In his half sleep he heard Edith whimpering in her sleep in the twin bed beside him. Smiling, glad to comfort her who had been all comfort to him here in sun-bright Naples, he stretched out his arm, sleepily stroked her thin wrist.

He startled, he sat up and gasped, at the astonishment of hearing the voice of Fran.

"Oh, thank you! Nice of you to wake me up. Having a kind of nightmare. My, it's rough!"

In his agitation he tightened his fingers on her wrist.

"Oh, Sam, *don't*—Oh, don't be *ardent!* Not yet. I must get used—And I'm so sleepy!" Very brightly: "You don't mind, do you? Nighty-night!"

He lay awake. In the watery light from the transom he saw the sheen of her silver toilet things on the dresser. He thought of this tremendous steamer, pounding the waves. He thought of the modern miracle of the radio, up above, of the automatic electric steering apparatus. Yet on the bridge were sailors, unautomatic, human, eternal. The ship, too, was eternal, as a vehicle of man's old voyaging. Its creaking seemed to him like the creaking of an ancient Greek trireme.

But while his thoughts reached out thus for things heroic, he heard her placid breathing and he smelled not the sea gale but perfume that came from little crystal vials among her silver toilet-things that were vaster than the hull of the steamer, stronger than the storm.

He felt that he would never sleep again.

He closed his great fist, tight. Then it relaxed, and he was asleep.

He roused to hear her bubbling, in a stormy dawn:

"Are you awake? Don't let me disturb you. Horrid morning! Let's get up some bridge. We'll get Mr. Ballard and Tom Allen. He's a dear boy, isn't he! Though I feel like a mother toward him. Oh, Sam, if you aren't too sleepy—Oh. While we're in New York, I think I'll see if I can't pick up a really nice Chinese evening wrap. Tom told me about a shop. Of course I have those others, but they're getting so shabby, and after all, you don't expect me to look a fright, like Matey Pearson, do you! I'll make her eyes start out of her head with the Marcel Rochas frock I got in Paris, and think, I only had two days to get it in! Zenith will simply foam at the mouth! Oh, after all, it *is* kind of nice to be going home—for a while—after all we've gone through—and Sam, I wonder if you understand that *I* understand probably you were just as brave and honest as I was, even with the hideous suffering I had to face in Berlin! And—Oh, I don't know what reminded me of it, but you must be careful with the Ballards. I'm afraid you bored them last evening, talking about Italian motors. You must remember that they have a villa in Florence, and they're used to the real Italy, and artists and the nobility and so on. But of course it doesn't matter. And–Do you mind ringing for coffee? That's an old dear!"

The scent of her perfumes seemed stronger than by night, in the sleep-thickened air of the stateroom.

He slowly raised himself to ring for the steward. He had said nothing whatever.

She blissfully dropped off to sleep again, and he bathed, dressed, swayed out on deck. The open portion of the promenade deck was protected by canvas against which the water crashed, sending streams between the lashings to trickle along the deck. He labored forward, stood solemnly at a window looking ahead at the bow plunging into the waves, at the foam hurled over the forepeak, at a desolate immigrant in a tattered old raincoat trying to keep a footing on the forward deck.

It was black ahead. To a landsman it was menacing. Yet there was strength in the stormy air and, after a long breath, stretching out his great arms, Sam began to plow around the deck.

His eyes seemed turned inward; his lips moved a little in his meditation.

After half an hour, breakfastless, he suddenly climbed the stairs from A Deck to the Boat Deck and, down a narrow corridor, past the tiny florist-shop, came to the wireless bureau–a narrow desk across a small room, like a telegraph office in a minor hotel.

Emotionlessly, he wrote and handed in a message to Edith Cortright: "Will you be naples three weeks from now?"

He went down to breakfast. All morning and half the afternoon he played bridge, watching Fran flirt with the ebullient Tom Allen.

The answer to his radio came just before tea-time: "No but shall be venice for couple months bless you edith."

For an hour, while Fran made much of tea with half a dozen men, Sam sat alone in the smoking-room, pretending to read whenever any lone and necessitous drinker came in to look for a drinking companion.

At the dressing-hour, he said mildly to Fran, "I wonder if we mightn't have dinner here in our stateroom tonight? I want to talk about things. We've sort of avoided it."

"Good Heavens, Sambo, what's come over you? Do you regard it as particularly cheerful to dine in this beastly little hole of a room on a rough night like this? Besides! I promised the Ballards we'd join them in the grill for dinner–such a common, stupid commercial crowd in the salon."

"But we must talk."

"My dear man, I think we'll manage it, with four full days ahead of us on this steamer! I'm really not going off to the Riviera or any place, you know!"

It was not till late in the evening that he had his chance. As they came down to the stateroom at bedtime, Fran very lively after a session in the smoking-room, he said, without prelude:

"Not much use trying to do it tactfully. Wanted to, but—Fran, we can't make a go of it, and I'm going back and join Edith Cortright."

"I don't quite understand. What have I done now? Oh, my God, if you haven't learned—You haven't learned anything, not one single thing, out of all our sorrows! Still criticizing me, and such a kind sweet way of springing something beastly cruel on me just when I've been happy, as I have tonight!" She faced him, hands clenched. "Will you *kindly*, Mr. Dodsworth, be a little less mysterious and tell me just what it is I've done to hurt your tender little feelings *this* time?"

"Nothing. We just can't make a go of it. You don't get me. I'm not making a scene. I'm not trying to bully you. I meant just what I said. I'm going back to Italy, from New York, on the first ship. I'm not blaming or criticizing—"

She sat abruptly on the chair before her dressing-table. She said quietly, with fear edging her voice, "And what is to become of me?"

"I don't know. If I did, I wouldn't have met you on the ship."

She moaned. "Oh! You do manage to hurt! I congratulate you! You see, I've been flattering myself you really wanted to come back to me!"

He started to say something comforting, then held it back in panic, as if in danger. "I'm not going to be polite, Fran. You know how awfully I've loved you, a good many years. You tampered with it. . . . What's going to become of you? I don't know. But I guess it'll be just the same thing that's been becoming of you this past couple of years. You haven't needed me. You've found people to play with, and plenty of beaux. I suppose you'll go on finding them—"

"And this is the man that 'loved me awfully'—"

"Wait! For the first time in all our arguments, I'm going to think of what would become of *me!* I can't help you. I'm just your attendant. But me—you can kill me. I didn't used to mind your embarrassing me and continually putting me in my place. Didn't even know you were doing it. But I do now, and I won't stand it!"

"Was it your dear Mrs. Cortright who taught you that lovely theory? about embarrassing you? After the years when I've never allowed one single soul to criticize you—"

"Understand? I'm *finished!*"

He did not, unfortunately, leave her in any heroic and dignified way. He flounced out of the stateroom like a child in a tantrum. And that was because he knew that only by childish violence could he escape from her logic, and because he knew that he must escape, even over the side of the lurching ship. For she was indeed perfectly logical and sound. She knew what she wanted!

It was misery for him to look out at her from the taxicab which he was taking to the Italian Line dock, after three days in New York; to see her standing in front of the hotel, alone, deserted, her eyes pitiful, and to realize that he might never see her again. The look in her eyes had been the meaning of life for him, and he was deserting it.

They were dining at the Ritz in Paris, Edith and Sam, feeling superior to its pretentiousness, because that evening they had determined to return to America, when his divorce should be complete, and to experiment with caravans. They were gay, well dined and well content.

But after his second cognac the orchestra played selections from Viennese operettas, and he remembered how happy Fran and he had been in Berlin. He remembered the wretchedness of the letter he had received from her that day. She was staying with Emily in Zenith; she said that she was seeing no one; that his "*dear* friends Tub and Matey" were a little too polite; and that she was thinking of going, in a few days, to Italy—

Through the darkness beyond the music, he saw her fleeing, a desolate wraith, and his heart was heavy with pity for the frightened and bewildered child who once had laughed so eagerly with him.

He came out of his silence with a consciousness that Edith was watching him. She said lightly, "You enjoy being sad about her! But hereafter, every time there is a music, I shall also think of Cecil Cortright. How handsome he was! He spoke five languages! How impatient I was with him! How I failed him! How virtuous it makes me feel to flay myself! What a splendid, uncommon grief I have! Dear Sam! . . . What a job it is to give up the superiority of being miserable and self-sacrificing!"

He stared, he pondered, he suddenly laughed, and in that laughter found a youthfulness he had never known in his solemn youth.

He was, indeed, so confidently happy that he completely forgot Fran and he did not again yearn over her, for almost two days.

EZRA POUND

[1885–]

UNINTELLIGIBLE TO MANY READERS, scorned because of his racist theories and his mad alliance with fascism, Ezra Pound was, nevertheless, one of the dominant influences on modern poetry and prose. James Joyce wrote: "Nothing could be more true than to say we all owe a great deal to him—I, most of all." He was born October 30, 1885, in Hailey, Idaho. His forebears were New Englanders; his mother was related to the Longfellows. He attended the University of Pennsylvania and Hamilton College, specialized in languages and comparative literature and, after being graduated, taught at Wabash College in Indiana. He was an "instructor with professorial functions" for only four months before he was dismissed because of "bohemianism."

Pound struck out for Europe still "an instructor with professorial functions," determined to instruct Europeans as well as expatriated Americans. His arrogance as well as his erudition became a legend. He married, had a son and, by the time he was thirty, was the author of five volumes which showed him to be equally the master of such archaic structures as the sestina and the most modern experiments in free form. In protest against the stereotypes of contemporary writing, he organized a small band of poets and gave them a characterizing name. He called them Imagists, partly to stress the importance of the image itself and partly to emphasize the use of the exact word in rhythms based on cadence rather than on a strict metrical beat. He not only influenced disciples and imitators but some of the most important writers of the day, including William Butler Yeats and T. S. Eliot, with his acrid and conversational style.

The Cantos, of which there are more than a hundred and which began appearing when Pound was forty, are often considered his chief work. They are also his most puzzling production. A series of interrupted and seemingly inchoate monologues, they were acclaimed by his admirers as an epic, a grand design of "ideas in action," the ideas of the past continually colliding with the ideas of the present. On the other hand, there were many who believed that the Cantos marked the descent of a real but eccentric talent into an abyss of incomprehensibility. Even Yeats concluded that Pound's "deliberate nobility" was constantly "interrupted, broken, twisted into nothing by its direct opposite, nervous obsession, nightmare, stammering confusion."

In his forties Pound settled in Rapallo on the Italian Riveria. When the Second World War broke out, he sided with the Fascists and broadcast anti-American propaganda by short wave from Rome. In May, 1945, he was taken prisoner, indicted for treason, and flown to Washington to stand trial. However, a board of psychiatrists declared him insane. He was committed to St. Elizabeth's Hospital. He remained there twelve years. When he was released in July, 1958, he returned to Italy.

The fact that Pound was misguided in politics and unbalanced as a person should not blind the reader to his importance as a poet. An expert technician and cultural pioneer, he had a genius not only for controversy but also for creation. Modern poetry would not be nearly as modern without him.

A VIRGINAL

No, no! Go from me. I have left her lately.
I will not spoil my sheath with lesser brightness,
For my surrounding air has a new lightness;
Slight are her arms, yet they have bound me straitly
And left me cloaked as with a gauze of ether;
As with sweet leaves; as with a subtle clearness.
Oh, I have picked up magic in her nearness
To sheathe me half in half the things that sheathe her.

No, no! Go from me. I have still the flavor,
Soft as spring wind that's come from birchen bowers.
Green come the shoots, aye April in the branches,
As winter's wound with her sleight hand she staunches,
Hath of the trees a likeness of the savor:
As white their bark, so white this lady's hours.

BALLAD OF THE GOODLY FERE

(*Simon Zelotes speaketh it somewhile after the Crucifixion*)

Ha' we lost the goodliest fere o' all
For the priests and the gallows tree?

Aye, lover he was of brawny men,
O' ships and the open sea.

When they came wi' a host to take Our Man
His smile was good to see,
"First let these go!" quo' our Goodly Fere,
"Or I'll see ye damned," says he.

Aye, he sent us out through the crossed high spears,
And the scorn of his laugh rang free,
"Why took ye not me when I walked about
Alone in the town?" says he.

Oh we drank his "Hale" in the good red wine
When we last made company,
No capon priest was the Goodly Fere
But a man o' men was he.

I ha' seen him drive a hundred men
Wi' a bundle o' cords swung free,
When they took the high and holy house
For their pawn and treasury.

They'll no get him a' in a book I think
Though they write it cunningly;
No mouse of the scrolls was the Goodly Fere
But aye loved the open sea.

If they think they ha' snared our Goodly Fere
They are fools to the last degree.
"I'll go to the feast," quo' our Goodly Fere,
"Though I go to the gallows tree."

"Ye ha' seen me heal the lame and the blind,
And wake the dead," says he,
"Ye shall see one thing to master all:
'Tis how a brave man dies on the tree."

A son of God was the Goodly Fere
That bade us his brothers be.
I ha' seen him cow a thousand men.
I ha' seen him upon the tree.

He cried no cry when they drave the nails
And the blood gushed hot and free,

The hounds of the crimson sky gave tongue
But never a cry cried he.

I ha' seen him cow a thousand men
On the hills o' Galilee,
They whined as he walked out calm between,
Wi' his eyes like the gray o' the sea.

Like the sea that brooks no voyaging
With the winds unleashed and free,
Like the sea that he cowed at Gennesaret
Wi' twey words spoke' suddenly.

A master of men was the Goodly Fere,
A mate of the wind and sea,
If they think they ha' slain our Goodly Fere
They are fools eternally.
I ha' seen him eat o' the honey-comb
Sin' they nailed him to the tree.

PORTRAIT D'UNE FEMME

Your mind and you are our Sargasso Sea,
London has swept about you this score years
And bright ships left you this or that in fee:
Ideas, old gossip, oddments of all things,
Strange spars of knowledge and dimmed wares of price.
Great minds have sought you—lacking someone else.
You have been second always. Tragical?
No. You preferred it to the usual thing:
One dull man, dulling and uxorious,
One average mind—with one thought less, each year.
Oh, you are patient. I have seen you sit
Hours, where something might have floated up.
And now you pay one. Yes, you richly pay.
You are a person of some interest, one comes to you
And takes strange gain away:
Trophies fished up; some curious suggestion;
Fact that leads nowhere; and a tale for two,
Pregnant with mandrakes, or with something else
That might prove useful and yet never proves,
That never fits a corner or shows use,
Or finds its hour upon the loom of days:

The tarnished, gaudy, wonderful old work;
Idols, and ambergris and rare inlays.
These are your riches, your great store; and yet
For all this sea-hoard of deciduous things,
Strange woods half sodden, and new brighter stuff:
In the slow float of differing light and deep,
No! there is nothing! In the whole and all,
Nothing that's quite your own.
Yet this is you.

ELINOR WYLIE

[1885–1928]

Unaffected and seemingly unconscious of the changing poetic trends of her time, Elinor Wylie set a fashion of her own: the creation of a glistening prose and verse which did not try to conceal its craftsmanship. She was born Elinor Hoyt, September 7, 1885, in Somerville, New Jersey. Her grandfather had been Governor of Pennsylvania; her father was Assistant Attorney-General under McKinley and Solicitor-General under Theodore Roosevelt. Educated at private schools, she was brought up in Washington society and shortly after her "coming out" married Philip Hichborn, son of an admiral. A son was born of the union, but the marriage was short-lived. In her twenty-fourth year, she eloped with Horace Wylie and lived abroad. After a divorce had been obtained, Elinor Hoyt Hichborn married Wylie and lived in England, where her first small book of verses, Incidental Numbers, *was published anonymously when she was twenty-seven.*

The First World War brought the Wylies back to America and, through her brother, she met the poet and editor, William Rose Benét. By this time she was a celebrity—she had written two volumes of poems and a much-discussed novel, Jennifer Lorn*—and in her mid-thirties, the center of a distinguished literary circle, she married Benét.*

An extraordinarily beautiful woman, she attracted everyone and was fully conscious of her ability to attract. She had the look of the Egyptian Queen Nefertiti, the delicate features, the exquisitely carved neck, the small, proud mouth. She mirrored herself in her verse:

The limbs fine, narrow and strong,
Like the wind they walk along,
Like the whirlwind, bad to follow,
The cheekbones high, the cheeks hollow. . .

At forty she went to England alone. Gossip was busy again. There was a story that, dressed as a Druid priestess, she had recited poetry among the prehistoric megaliths of Stonehenge, and an even wilder tale that she had spent the night weeping over an obscure grave because she had been told that a lock of Shelley's hair was buried there. Shelley had become an obsession with her: she had written a sonnet sequence entitled "A Red Carpet for Shelley," and a novel, The Orphan Angel, *which placed a resuscitated Shelley in America. When she returned to the United States she was unhappy and ill. She had an almost fatal accident, and feared she would never walk again. However, she recovered sufficiently to revisit England and brought back with her the manuscript of her finest volume,* Angels and Earthly Creatures. *She made the final corrections on the manuscript when, still suffering from the results of her fall, she was struck with paralysis and died December 15, 1928.*

Although her poetry is not as mannered as her prose, it is definitely stylized. It is, for the most part, lyrical and, at the same time, intellectual. Extremely discriminating, everything Elinor Wylie wrote was trimmed and refined. The emotion is severely controlled, but there is brilliance as well as beauty in its very discipline.

VELVET SHOES

Let us walk in the white snow
  In a soundless space;
With footsteps quiet and slow,
  At a tranquil pace,
  Under veils of white lace.

I shall go shod in silk,
  And you in wool,
White as a white cow's milk,
  More beautiful
  Than the breast of a gull.

We shall walk through the still town
  In a windless peace;
We shall step upon white down,
  Upon silver fleece,
  Upon softer than these.

We shall walk in velvet shoes:
  Wherever we go
Silence will fall like dews
  On white silence below.
  We shall walk in the snow.

PURITAN SONNET

Down to the Puritan marrow of my bones
There's something in this richness that I hate.
I love the look, austere, immaculate,
Of landscapes drawn in pearly monotones.
There's something in my very blood that owns
Bare hills, cold silver on a sky of slate,
A thread of water, churned to milky spate
Streaming through slanted pastures fenced with stones.

I love those skies, thin blue or snowy gray,
Those fields sparse-planted, rendering meager sheaves;
That spring, briefer than apple-blossom's breath,
Summer, so much too beautiful to stay,
Swift autumn, like a bonfire of leaves,
And sleepy winter, like the sleep of death.

THE EAGLE AND THE MOLE

Avoid the reeking herd,
Shun the polluted flock,
Live like that stoic bird,
The eagle of the rock.

The huddled warmth of crowds
Begets and fosters hate;
He keeps, above the clouds,
His cliff inviolate.

When flocks are folded warm,
And herds to shelter run,
He sails above the storm,
He stares into the sun.

If in the eagle's track
Your sinews cannot leap,
Avoid the lathered pack,
Turn from the steaming sheep.

If you would keep your soul
From spotted sight or sound,
Live like the velvet mole;
Go burrow underground.

And there hold intercourse
With roots of trees and stones,
With rivers at their source,
And disembodied bones.

THE PEBBLE

If any have a stone to shy,
Let him be David and not I;
The lovely shepherd, brave and vain,
Who has a maggot in the brain,
Which, since the brain is bold and pliant,
Takes the proportions of a giant.
Alas, my legendary fate!
Who sometimes rage, but never hate.
Long, long before the pebble flieth
I see a virtue in Goliath;
Yea, in the Philistine his face,
A touching majesty and grace;
Then like the lights of evening shine
The features of the Philistine
Until my spirit faints to see
The beauty of my enemy.
If any have a stone to fling
Let him be a shepherd-king,
Who is himself so beautiful
He may detest the gross and dull
With holy rage and heavenly pride

To make a pebble sanctified
And feather its course with wings of scorn.
But, from the day that I was born
Until like corn I bow to the sickle,
I am in hatred false and fickle.
I am most cruel to anyone
Who hates me with devotion;
I will not freeze, I will not burn;
I make his heart a poor return
For all the passion that he spends
In swearing we shall never be friends;
For all the pains his passion spent
In hatred I am impotent;
The sad perversity of my mind
Sees in him my kin and kind.
Alas, my shameful heritage,
False in hate and fickle in rage!
Alas, to lack the power to loathe!
I like them each; I love them both;
Philistine and shepherd-king
They strike the pebble from my sling;
My heart grows cold, my spirit grows faint;
Behold, a hero and a saint
Where appeared, a moment since,
A giant and a heathen prince;
And I am bound and given over
To be no better than a lover,
Alas, who strove as a holy rebel!
They have broke my sling and stole my pebble:
If any have a stone to throw
It is not I, ever or now.

THE LION AND THE LAMB

I SAW a Tiger's golden flank,
I saw what food he ate,
By a desert spring he drank;
The Tiger's name was Hate.

Then I saw a placid Lamb
Lying fast asleep;
Like a river from its dam
Flashed the Tiger's leap.

I saw a Lion tawny-red,
Terrible and brave;
The Tiger's leap overhead
Broke like a wave.

In sand below or sun above
He faded like a flame.
The Lamb said, "I am Love;
Lion, tell your name."

The Lion's voice thundering
Shook his vaulted breast,
"I am Love. By this spring,
Brother, let us rest."

VAN WYCK BROOKS

[1886–]

More renowned as a literary historian than as a critic, Van Wyck Brooks outlined the cultural course of his country in a series of volumes collectively entitled Makers and Finders: A History of the Writer in America, 1800–1915. *He was born February 16, 1886, son of a stockbroker, in Plainfield, New Jersey. Graduated from Harvard in 1908, having been one of the editors of the* Harvard Advocate, *he turned to journalism. He lived abroad for some years and published his first book,* The Wine of the Puritans, *in London in his twenty-third year.*

After his return to America he lived in various parts of the United States: in California, where he married his first wife, in New York, in Westport, Connecticut, and, after an illness which lasted about five years, settled in the town of Bridgewater, Connecticut, with his second wife, Gladys Rice Billings.

Besides having edited a half dozen works by other authors, Brooks was literary editor of the Freeman *from 1920 to 1924, wrote articles for the* Encyclopædia Britannica *and, in 1937, received the Pulitzer Prize in history for* The Flowering of New England. *The volume also received the National Book Award and was given the Limited Edition Club's Gold Medal for "the book most likely to attain the stature of a classic."*

Brooks has been commended and criticized for his method. His books—there are some twenty of them—illuminated his subjects' writings through their lives. He found new values in old works, and rediscovered authors who had been too long obscured. In a review of The Confident Years *(1952), Malcolm Cowley declared that Brooks' importance lay in "his proof that in literature this country has long possessed a usable past," an estimate fully justified by the volumes which furnished backgrounds more illuminating than most critical analyses.*

The World of Washington Irving, *published when Brooks was in his late fifties, is one of his most intimate books. Especially fascinating is a chapter devoted to John James Audubon, the great naturalist and animal portraitist who, born in Haiti, made the wild life of America known to the entire world.*

AUDUBON

From *The World of Washington Irving*

MEANWHILE, NEAR PHILADELPHIA, where Alexander Wilson was toiling over his drawings of American birds, another naturalist appeared, a rival ornithologist who was less heroic than Wilson perhaps but a man of much more splendid gifts. John James Audubon was nineteen years younger than Wilson,—he was born in 1785,—and his life was hard enough; but the poor, pinched, moody Scotchman was all but unbefriended on his dolorous way, while the great romantic Audubon was to charm the world.[1]

Audubon, a Frenchman, the son of a rich West Indian merchant, had arrived in the United States in 1803; and he lived on a farm that his father had bought, Mill Grove, on the Perkioming, which had once belonged to William Penn. As a boy of eighteen, with money to waste, he had been the gayest of the gay, at balls, at skating-matches and riding-parties; and he had gone out shooting in silk stockings and satin breeches, pumps and the finest ruffled shirts. His guns and his fishing-tackle were the most expensive and most ornate, he had ridden the finest of horses; and, during the years

[1] Alexander Wilson died in 1813, as a result of a cold caught in a reckless adventure. He had finished seven volumes of the *American Ornithology*. Two further volumes were edited by his friend George Ord, and four subsequent volumes were added by Prince Charles Lucien Bonaparte, Napoleon's nephew.

when poor Wilson was working with Bartram, only a few miles away, Audubon spent his days dancing and fencing. So it seemed to those who knew nothing of the "frenzy" which the sight of birds already stirred in his blood. Tall, with a rapid springing step, with long hair and an eagle's beak, with deep grey eyes as restless as the glance of an eagle, he loved colour and brilliant effects and he liked to masquerade; he sometimes dressed as a French sailor, in a short jacket and dungarees, with a red handkerchief round his head, rings in his ears and long moustaches. Dramatic, expansive and vivacious, he suggested the old French voyageurs in his daring and dash, with a touch of the troubadour also.

It was during this time on the Perkioming that Audubon met Lucy Bakewell, the daughter of an English merchant who lived near by, the Lucy who was to share with him many years of poverty, for the days of his prosperity were brief. His father had been for a while an officer in the French navy and had been at Yorktown with De Grasse at the time of the surrender of Cornwallis, and he had lived in Haiti, where Audubon was probably born, on land that was still a part of Santo Domingo. Presumably illegitimate, Audubon had been taken to France, where the family had a country-house near Nantes, and he had developed as a boy a passion for natural history: he loved La Fontaine's fables of animals and birds. His room was full of eggs, shells, nests and mosses. At seventeen he went to Paris, where he studied drawing under David. This was only for a few months,—he drew in coloured chalks, and also from casts of ancient horses, whose vast eyes and noses he never forgot,—and he had no further formal instruction until years later the painter Sully gave him a few lessons in the use of oils. But he made drawings of French birds, and he brought these drawings with him when his father decided to place him on the American farm. He began to observe the birds on the Perkioming, and he found a cave that was a haunt of phœbes. He was making a study of this cave when Humboldt came to Philadelphia and a great dinner was given for him at Peale's Museum, at which Bartram and Wilson were present. Audubon, watching the birds closely, observed that every family had its own characteristic attitudes, its way of standing, flying and pursuing its prey, and he longed to represent them as alive and moving. He was disgusted with the stiff little profiles that he had brought with him from France, and, remembering David's manikins, he tried a manikin of a bird, a contrivance of wood, cork and wires. Throwing this away, he galloped off to Norristown and bought some other wires of various sizes, and then he shot a kingfisher at a neighbouring creek. He fastened the body to a board, with wires attached to the head and feet, and, behold, he had a real kingfisher to examine at his leisure, bill, nostrils, eyes, legs and tongue. By means of threads he could lower the wings and the tail. He was soon picturing birds on the wing or on sprays of leaves, with fruit or berries, painting them against their native background, not knowing perhaps that he was the first to do so; and he used crayons to soften his water-colours. He had broken with the tradition of museum-painting. At the same time he stuffed and mounted squirrels, opossums and snakes in such a way that they too seemed alive. Moreover, he banded a young phœbe to see if it would come back in the spring,—this was another of Audubon's original notions. Meanwhile, Lucy taught him English, which he was always to speak with an accent, and Audubon gave her lessons in drawing and French.

He returned to France for about a year, and there for the first time he read Buffon and learned to classify the birds. Reappearing at Mill Grove with a bundle of new drawings, he cast about for a way of earning a living; for Audubon's early good fortune had ended in smoke. He heard of the French colony at Louisville, where Lewis and Clark had met for their expedition, and he thought of setting up there as a frontier trader. He tried it, the prospects appeared to be good, and he went back for Lucy; and they set out together for the Ohio. They followed the Conestoga wagons over the Reading road, through the country where Daniel Boone was born, to Lancaster, Harrisburg, Carlisle,—the home of the novelist Brackenridge now,—then over the "Blue Juniata" and so to Pittsburgh. Thence on a flat-boat they floated down the river, sleeping in buffalo robes and in tents on the shore. These flat-boats were sometimes forty feet long, and their decks were travelling farm-yards, covered with hay, ploughs, wagons, cattle and horses, and the pigs and the children scampered about, while the women worked at their washtubs or knitted at the end of the day by the cabin door. They passed pirogues, keel-boats and barges, laden with furs, lead, flour and pork, or coming up from New Orleans with coffee and sugar, and there were often boats as well that were floating tinshops or country stores, with paint, boots, crockery and hardware for the settlers on the river. Often, in fear of the Indians and the still more dreadful river pirates, the boats travelled only at night, moving along through the darkness without lights or fire. But they were lively enough by day, when the boatmen danced and sang on the decks. Audubon danced with them and played his flute. On shore, around the campfire, they all told stories. Some of the boatmen were Spanish hunters, others were French Canadian trappers who had seen the northern lakes and the prairies of the West, and their boats were already the "floating enchantments" that Mark Twain knew in later years along the lower stretches of the Mississippi. They charmed the young people who were growing up in solitude and silence away from the dull routine of the river farms.[1] Audubon, both then and later, knew the life of the river-boats well, and once he agreed to pay for his passage by keeping the party in game. He would leave the boat at a bend of the river and walk for miles across the country, shooting, while he explored the woods for birds. Then he rejoined the boat around the bend.

Thus began the twenty years that Audubon passed on the frontier before he set out for England to publish his work. He felt at home in Kentucky at once, the land of the great horn spoon, an ornithological paradise, with its winding rivers and soft mild air, that lay in the path of migration from the North to the Gulf. The woods were aflutter with unknown birds, egrets, herons, bitterns and warblers, and in Louisville, in the big stone houses, with their long galleries and massive walls, Audubon found friends who shared his interests. Wherever he travelled, in later years, in woodland cabins, in Labrador, up the Missouri river, on Florida wreckers, he was to fall in with men who knew their forest-world, for the pioneers were a race of naturalists.[2] At Louisville, some of the French refugees were observant and serious students, men like the Corsican Colonel Landi, who had fought at Waterloo, in Mayne Reid's novel *The Boy Hunters*. This former colonel of chasseurs, who had served in Napoleon's army, had settled in a French village on the Mississippi, and there he lived with his three sons, "drawing his lessons from nature herself" in a valley teeming with objects of interest to the naturalist and the hunter. For Landi was a naturalist, and "not a closet-naturalist either." [3] Like Audubon he was fond of the outside world, and he liked to set out on forest excursions whence he returned laden with spoils, the skins of birds and animals, plants and rocks. He brought up his three sons to swim, dive and paddle and bring down birds on the wing and beasts on the run, and meanwhile he corresponded with Charles Lucien Bonaparte, the naturalist who befriended

[1] "The boats float by their dwellings, on beautiful spring mornings, when the verdant forest, the mild and delicious temperature of the air, the delightful azure of the sky of this country, the fine bottom on the one hand, and the romantic bluff on the other, the broad and smooth stream rolling calmly down the forest, and floating the boat gently forward,—all these circumstances harmonize in the excited youthful imagination. The boatmen are dancing to the violin on the deck of their boat. They scatter their wit among the girls on the shore who come down to the water's edge to see the pageant pass. The boat glides on until it disappears behind a point of wood."—Timothy Flint, *Recollections of the Valley of the Mississippi*.

[2] This was the case in every region and in all social classes. Farmers, ministers, statesmen and woodsmen shared this interest in natural history. See, for two of a hundred examples, William Byrd's diary and the journal of Latrobe, the architect. Jonathan Edwards, aged twelve, wrote an elaborate description of "the wondrous way of the working of the forest spider."

[3] Reading Mayne Reid in his boyhood years later, William James became convinced that a "closet-naturalist" must be the "vilest kind of wretch."

Audubon later. In response to a request of this nephew of Napoleon he sent his "young Nimrods" out on their great expedition. They were to produce the skin of a white buffalo, as rare as the white whale that Ahab sought. The gallant Captain Mayne Reid knew the Mississippi valley, where he spent many months a few years later, and he heard of émigrés there,—perhaps he even found a few,—who resembled and suggested his Colonel Landi. Audubon had known them at Louisville, and he found planters from Virginia who were sympathetic also. Mulberry Hill, across the river, was the home of George Rogers Clark, a student of natural history from his early childhood, as William Clark, his brother, was, the companion of Meriwether Lewis on the great expedition to the Columbia river. It was William Clark who had made the maps on the expedition and drawn the birds, animals and fishes they had found on the way. Audubon knew both the Clarks, and, when he was off on trading trips, Lucy stayed with the family at Mulberry Hill.

Audubon kept a pioneer store. He sold shotguns, shotbags and powder-horns, calicoes and axes, and one day, in 1810, Alexander Wilson, hoping to find a subscriber, appeared at the door. He showed his drawings to the young man behind the counter, who studied them one by one with a knowing eye, and presently, lifting a bolt of cloth on a shelf behind him, produced some drawings of his own. He was glad to share his discoveries with the grim wan Wilson, and together they went on a hunt in the forest near by; and a year or two later, in Philadelphia, whither he went to replenish his stock, Audubon looked Wilson up again. He was at work on a drawing of a bald-headed eagle, and the two set out for a visit to Peale's Museum, where they found Rembrandt Peale also at work, completing a picture of Napoleon crossing the Alps. But Wilson had scented a dangerous rival in this young man who had been roving the woods, exploring and looking at birds with the glance of a lover, and he never forgave the gay adventurer who failed to subscribe to his book and who had a guitar and a fiddle as well as a flute.

Up at four or five in the morning, before it was time to open the store, Audubon was out with his dog and gun, following the buffalo paths and the Indian trails; and he learned to thread the woods like an Indian, living for days on parched corn, as if he had been born a wilderness hunter. In his deerskin shirt and leggings, with his tomahawk and flowing locks, he might have been a younger Daniel Boone, and more than once he met Boone, who had come back to Kentucky, to pay a debt at Frankfort on one occasion. They took to each other at sight and went hunting together. Boone was a very old man but still hale and athletic, bare-legged and moccasined, with his long Kentucky rifle; and when they spent the night in a cabin, Boone, stoical as ever, arranged a few folds of blankets and slept on the floor. He preferred to leave the bed to the soft young Frenchman. In the morning they found a grove of walnuts, oaks and hickories, and Boone gave Audubon a lesson in barking off squirrels. He shot the bark on which the squirrel sat, and the little creature whirled off, killed by the concussion. Snuffing the candle and hitting the nail on the head were other feats of Boone's Kentucky rifle, and the old man related some of his adventures. He had marked a spot with three gashes in an ash-tree, and he had found the spot thirty years later when the bark had grown over the gashes. Taking an axe, he cut away a few chips, and there were the marks of the tomahawk under the wood. Once, to save some whites from a massacre, he had walked a hundred and sixty miles, stopping only once for a meal, and he described to Audubon his hair-breadth escape from the Indians and spoke of his fur-trapping days on the Missouri. These tales were famous along the frontier, but they always seemed new when the old man told them. Audubon later painted a portrait of Boone.

The Louisville store was not a success,—perhaps there were too many rival traders,—and Audubon pushed further West on the Ohio. With his young French partner he settled at Henderson, a village half lost in the canebrake, and there with Lucy he lived for several years. Meanwhile, he set off on journeys to dispose of his goods, sometimes in his own skiff, sometimes joining a party of hunters on their way to the French settlements on the Missouri. He had his first glimpse of the Mississippi, and he visited Ste. Geneviève, the old lead-shipping port on the west bank of the river. He made many trips to Shawneetown. Now and then, to procure new goods, he rode back to Philadelphia, once following a roundabout route by Nashville and Knoxville, through the Cumberland Gap, through Virginia, past the Natural Bridge, and Lucy rode with him once, mounted on Barro. This was the little wild bay horse that waded swamps and swam rivers and cleared logs and fences like an elk. Lucy thought little of riding fifteen hundred miles through the forest, and Audubon could shoot from the saddle as well as on foot; but he often walked on these trading trips, spending his nights in squatters' cabins or, if need were, in his blanket on the ground. With his knapsack and his dog Zephyr, he followed old trails through the woods and usually found a good supper at the end of the day. Tired, wet and hungry, he would stumble into a log-hut and feel the sudden warmth of the "Welcome, stranger!" The wife would take his deerskin coat and hang it by the fire, while the husband wiped his gun and cleaned the lock. The children roused by the stranger's arrival peeped from under the buffalo-robe and then turned over on the bearskin to resume their slumber, while the eggs were murmuring and spluttering in the frying-pan and the chickens were puffing and swelling over the embers. He could always count on some sparkling cider or a jug of monongahela. The squatters told their story and Audubon listened. Their Virginia land was worn out and they had pushed on with their wagons and horses, driving their cattle before them; or perhaps they had come from the Carolinas through Georgia and Alabama, cutting their way with axes in the tangled forest, building rafts to cross the streams and clearing their small patch with fire. They depended on the trading-boats for their fish-hooks, flour and ammunition. The ever-companionable Audubon was at home with them. He found hospitality everywhere, and, as he wrote later, there was only one occasion in twenty-five years when his life had been in danger from his fellow-creatures. That was the time when he stumbled into the wrong cabin and saw the old woman grinding her carving-knife. Once he joined a party of Osages and hunted with them through the swamps and canebrake. He watched their sugar-making, with their sap-bowls swung by grapevines, and gathered their lore on the use of herbs and roots. Audubon, who despised all medicine, was willing to hear of Indian remedies, and, while he scorned all other meat, he was always ready for game. He went off on another hunt with some friendly Shawnees. They were shooting swans to sell the skins, while their squaws made soup of nuts and bear-fat. Eager to find every bird, he sometimes vanished for days at a time, returning heaven knew whence with some new trophy, and once, observing a strange flock that was flying southeast over the river he jumped into the saddle and sped off in pursuit. He rode across Kentucky and Tennessee and into North Carolina, following the flock. Many a night he spent by great Kentucky campfires, with four or five big ash-trees, sixty feet long, cut and piled up with leaves and brush. He learned to call wild turkeys with a piece of bone through which he was able to mimic the notes of the bird, and he could hear their soft tread over the twigs and the dry leaves and the rustle of their wings in a far-away thicket.

For several years the Audubons prospered. Their two Kentucky boys were born, and Audubon bought land and sold it at a profit. He was immensely active and superlatively happy. Meanwhile, he continued to work at his drawings,—for he always called these pictures drawings,—and he struggled with problems of design. He liked bold outlines of birds in flight, sometimes without any background, arranging the figures alone in a decorative pattern, but he placed his orioles in a flowering tulip-tree and his grackles were stripping stalks of Indian corn. He made graceful arrangements of grass, water and trees, and he loved the wild grape with its fruit and the mallow in bloom. He painted a great wild turkey and the blue-winged teal and some barn-owls on a branch with the Ohio and the hills behind them; and he represented the snowbirds in winter on twigs with hanging oval berries. At the same time he kept a voluminous journal, noting all he had learned of the habits of the birds, and he carried this journal with him on all his travels, carefully writing down the events of the day. Never trusting to memory, he recorded every incident of which he had been the eye-witness on the spot, and all manner of observations went into the journal. He described scenes, characters and adventures as well as the birds,—the coon-hunter loading his rifle, corn-shucking, wolf-pitting, the hurricane, the bear-hunt and the barbecue. He noted the brilliant grasses and flowers of the prairie, the sound of the boatman's horn winding from afar, the hooting of the great owl and the muffled murmur of its wings as it sailed smoothly over the river. He pictured the skiff on the stream, the trees with their flowing festoons of vines, the fruits and the foliage, yellow, bronze and carmine, the raccoon, the opossum, the rabbit, the wolf and the bear; and he wrote little character-sketches of the queer folk who came his way or whom he was always encountering in the villages and the woods. For one, there was Rafinesque, the naturalist from Constantinople, who suddenly appeared at Henderson, eager to see him. This was the small bent bearded man in the coat of yellow nankeen who bore the big bundle of clover over his back. He was collecting plants, shells and fishes and had heard of Audubon's drawings of flowers and birds; and when he wrecked Audubon's violin, using it to smash the bats, how could one resist pulling his leg? Audubon told Rafinesque about the devil-jack diamond fish whose bullet-proof scales would strike fire with flint. Rafinesque went into the journal, with other sketches of trappers and foresters, Indians, voyageurs, squatters and their toils and sports, pictures of the frontier, the notes of an artist that were written with all the freshness of morning in the woods. Audubon was a story-teller in a world of story-tellers, and these notes were campfire talk, and the best of their kind. Later, to relieve the tedium of his purely ornithological writing, he shaped them into the *Episodes* that garnished his books.

It was not perhaps before 1820 that Audubon made up his mind to complete the *Birds of America* and publish his work. All of his projects had failed for making a living, the store, the mill that he built at Henderson, the steamboat that he built and sold only to find that the purchaser had swindled him. He was imprisoned for debt, then, drifting to Shippingport, he played his violin at plantation dances. He was a dancing-master and a fencing-master. He opened a drawing-class at Louisville, and he decorated the cabin of a river steamboat with a painting of the falls of the Ohio. He took up portrait-painting and moved to Cincinnati, where he stuffed fishes for the new Western Museum. He was put to almost as many shifts as the

King and the Duke in *Huckleberry Finn* along the river towns of the Mississippi, where they had a go at elocution, dancing, doctoring, mesmerizing, lecturing, telling fortunes and floating on a raft. At last he had nothing left but his drawings and his gun, and it was then that he resolved to finish his work at any cost, while Lucy stayed with friends at Shippingport. There were hundreds of birds that he had not yet seen, and he had not explored Louisiana. So he sailed down the river, without a penny in his pocket. At Natchez he paid for some shoes by painting the shoemaker's portrait, and he passed Bayou Sara and Baton Rouge, skirting the great plantations that increased on every hand, while the perfume of the orange-blossoms drifted over the stream. He could see over the levee the upper windows of the houses and the long streamers of moss on the cypress-trees; and then he saw the tall spars and the flags of all the nations, and he was in New Orleans at last.

Still living on the keelboat, shooting his game in the neighbouring bayous, he walked the streets in search of commissions for portraits, and he found numbers of sitters, though the town was full of portrait-painters, attracted by the rich planters and traders of the port. Thomas Sully soon arrived, and Vanderlyn was there, the friend of Washington Irving's boyhood in Paris, for whom Audubon himself sat, a few years later in New York, posing for a figure of Andrew Jackson.[1] Audubon had some success, though he took small pride in his portraits, and he painted, among others, the famous Père Antoine, the old priest who had ruled New Orleans since the American occupation from his little cabin cell in Bourbon Street. With his coarse brown cassock and his sandalled feet and long white beard, Père Antoine was the spiritual director of the city, the theme of many a later story and legend. There were people who took Audubon also for a missionary priest, with the hair flowing loose over his shoulders. New Orleans swarmed with Negroes, mulattoes and Spaniards, Yankee traders, Frenchmen, Indians and trappers, and sometimes one saw a black vulture walking in the street; and the legendary grave of Manon Lescaut was a resort of strangers outside the town. In the market one found heaps of purple finches, and bobolinks and bluebirds were sold for food, and Audubon bought many of these to draw from; but he worked best from living birds, usually setting them free when he finished the drawing. He spent most of a month on a great white heron, making hundreds of small sketches and using the quills of a trumpeter swan for the beaks and eyes of the smaller birds. He drew the Louisiana insects, wonderful butterflies, dragonflies, bees, and he made lovely patterns of fruits, the papaw and the muscadine

[1] As Gouverneur Morris posed for the figure of George Washington that Houdon made in Paris. This is the statue that is now in the capitol at Richmond.

and the berries that he found in the deep green bayous. He paddled through the cypress swamps and the salt marshes of the Delta, a watery region teeming with herons and terns. With his notebook and pencil always at hand, he followed the trappers' water-trails, pushing his pirogue through the long grasses where the pink water-hyacinths and the irises grew; and here, among the forest swamps, as everywhere he went, his ears were alert for all that was human also. He heard from the Negroes tales of talking animals, raccoons, opossums and rabbits whose stratagems and wiles enabled them to survive in a world that was hostile, the "humour of the underman" that was to find its ultimate form in Joel Chandler Harris's *Uncle Remus*. Once he met a tall Negro in a miry bayou and stumbled into a camp of runaway slaves. The children had been sold and scattered and the Negro had reassembled his family after unheard-of adventures and escapes through the woods. It happened that Audubon knew their master, and, struck by their goodness of heart, he spent the night with the family by their fire in the canebrake. Then he persuaded the master to buy them back.

Six years passed before Audubon set out for England, with more than four hundred drawings ready for the engraver. He had gone back to Philadelphia to show his work to the men of science, but the partisans of Alexander Wilson would have none of this rival. They were publishing the last volumes of Wilson's work, and there was no chance for Audubon in his own country. But Thomas Sully praised and helped him, and Charles Lucien Bonaparte was his friend and well-wisher. Bonaparte was continuing the work of Wilson in further volumes, with drawings done by Titian Peale, while he lived at Bordentown with his uncle Joseph. Audubon had travelled on foot part of the way to Philadelphia, and he left for home as penniless as ever, often sleeping in the woods, with his big knife at his side and the rusty tin box that contained his drawings and colours. But he had made an excursion to Niagara, where he used the last of his linen to clean his gun, and at Pittsburgh he found several subscribers; and there he met Lafayette, who had come back for a visit, and made a portrait-drawing of this friend of his father. He arrived at Bayou Sara ragged, with a pirate's beard, but with a bulging notebook and dozens of drawings. Luckily, he had many friends in the liberal plantation-houses, with their libraries and music-rooms and fine old gardens, at Baton Rouge, Feliciana, Natchez, and Lucy had found work as a governess at one of these plantations, where Audubon also taught dancing, drawing and French. Some of the planters themselves were Frenchmen, others Virginians and Carolinians, easy-going, kind and cultivated, and Audubon's talent flowered in this friendly air. He was soon able to pay his expenses to England.

There Audubon spent three years. He was forty-one years old, and in England the "American woodsman" became a lion. There he found many subscribers and the fine engraver whose work he could scarcely distinguish from the original drawings. Later he returned with Lucy to supervise this work, and he wrote most of his *Episodes* at Edinburgh, selecting passages from his journals, which he combined and edited, in a series of separate volumes describing the birds. The Scottish naturalist William MacGillivray helped him in this labour of writing, for he was not quite at home in the English language, and he needed assistance not only with his grammar but in more technical ornithological matters. Perhaps Lucy also washed and ironed his text a little, and yet the style was undoubtedly Audubon's own: it reflected his cheerful personality, winning, gay and bland, eager to please and interest the companionable reader.

By turns despondent and happy in England, as everywhere throughout his life, he was anxious above all to return to the woods, to redraw many of his earlier birds in the fine free style of his later work and especially to find new specimens. He wished to represent, on a continental scale, all the birds of all the American regions, and he needed more water-birds, the birds that were hardest to track as they swept over the ocean and sought refuge among rocks that were inaccessible on the shore. After his first visit to England, he explored the New Jersey harbours and beaches, and he set out at last for Florida, the abode of the frigate pelican and the sandhill crane, the egret, the brown gannet, the flamingo and the rose-coloured curlew. Audubon was famous now; he was finding subscribers at home, and everyone was ready to assist him. He dined at the White House with President Jackson, and arrangements were made for him to skirt the southern coast on a revenue-cutter. He stopped for a while at St. Augustine first and sailed up the St. John's river, following in the wake of the Bartrams years before; and meandering along the creeks and pursuing old Seminole trails he watched the live-oakers in the forest felling their trees. Once the mosquitoes extinguished his candles, and, closing his journal in despair, he crushed more than a hundred at a single blow. Then, joining the crew of the "Marion," he swept down to the Florida keys and went on a little excursion to the Dry Tortugas. The "Marion" was a wrecker, but there were wreckers and wreckers, and this was not one of the blackguard pirate-vessels that set false lights on the reefs to plunder ships. It was a fine big government sloop whose crew were jovial sons of Neptune, licensed to hunt out the stealthy pirates; and the officers, moreover, had collected eggs, shells, corals and mosses which they were delighted to share with Audubon. They were searching the keys and the shoals where the pirates lurked, the great coral reefs where parrot-fish and angel-fish swam through a magical sea of purple and gold. Audubon pushed his little barque for miles over the soapy flats and crouched in the long grasses of the blue lagoons, seeking the distrustful birds in their hidden breeding-places in the jungles of bamboo and tamarind. He scoured the small wild islets, the haunts of egrets and pelicans, and slept through many a night on the burning sand, and then what a pleasure it was to relate his adventures to the friendly and interested audience in the cabin of the ship. He had observed the huge sea-turtles, laying their eggs by moonlight in the well-known sands. Slowly they moved landward, with their heads alone above the water, then laboriously dragged their bodies up the slope. Audubon had been close enough to hear their hurried breathing, expressing suspicion and fear. He could have spent a year studying these turtles.

After this survey of Florida, he had to see the top of the continent. He wished to find the northern nesting-places of many of the birds he had known so well in the South. At Savannah, he found six subscribers,—at a thousand dollars, no small triumph,—and he visited the sea islands and pushed on to Charleston, to which he often returned in later years. Charleston was the home of the naturalist John Bachman, whose daughters married Audubon's two sons, and the conchologist Edmund Ravenel. Then all the Audubons met in Boston and went together to Maine and New Brunswick, the land of the Canada jay and the great grey owl. They formed a family partnership, and John Audubon worked with his father while Victor ran over to England to assist him there. John was one of the young students who joined in the voyage to Labrador, in the summer of 1833, when Audubon chartered a schooner and they sailed from Eastport, in fisherman's togs, with legs like the leg of the bear. They were heading for a world of rain and fog, and Audubon, up at three in the morning, could scarcely keep the paper dry on his big drawing-table under the hatch. The fog collected and fell from the rigging and he had to close the hatch and work by the light of a candle in the middle of the day. He sometimes drew for seventeen hours at a stretch. But he was used to wet clothes, and this wild and dreary Labrador thrilled his imagination as it chilled his heart. It was dark and cold in June, a land of barren rocks and silence, save for the roar of the surf on the granite ledges and the croaking of the ravens in the fog, and there were bays without end and rocky islands of all shapes where the guillemots and the cormorants nested in the fissures. On shore one sank to the knees in the spongy moss. When the water was too rough, Audubon worked on board the ship while the young men scattered to the islands and the harbours, collecting birds, plants and flowers for him to draw, assembling for a dinner of hashed eider-ducks and an evening of natural history, music and stories. Audubon's flute was always ready, and they journalized, comparing notes, exploring the gullet of a diver or skinning a grouse, or they examined the leaves of the plants and weighed and dissected the birds in the steady light of candles that were thrust into bottles. They made pets of puffins, gulls and hawks, and the hold was full of birdskins and flowers in press and jars containing reptiles and fishes. In these wonderful summer months, Audubon made many drawings, the grouse with the wild peas and the Labrador tea-plant, the red-throated loon and twenty-one others, and he found the nest of the horned lark and several new species, the Lincoln's sparrow, for one, and the Labrador falcon. Meanwhile, he talked with Canadian sealers and visited their huts and observed the brutal work of the pirate eggers. He gathered more notes for his *Episodes*, and, as always, in this lonely region he found fellow-naturalists in fishermen, traders and doctors of passing ships.

This was in the far future, and even the journey to Labrador was not the last of Audubon's peregrinations. He was still to visit the Yellowstone river, following the route of Lewis and Clark, and he never lost his hope of a glimpse of the Rockies. Nor did he ever lose the ardour with which, as a writer and painter, he surveyed and reported the primal American world, observing, while he drew the birds, the human *dramatis personae* of a rising civilization in its elemental phases. He saw, with an eye as genial as Whitman's, with a simple heart and a spacious mind, the frontiersman, the hunter, the trapper, the whaler and the sailor, the farmer and the fisherman, the lumberer and the pioneer who were building a world for Americans to find a home in. Through the opening years of the nineteenth century, and even as late as the forties, while literature in America dawned and spread, he was the voice and the mirror of all the frontiers that encircled the centres of culture and their men of thought.

JOHN HALL WHEELOCK

[1886–]

An encourager of experimental young poets, John Hall Wheelock remained a traditional lyricist all his life. He was born September 9, 1886, at Far Rockaway, New York and began writing in his boyhood. He attended Harvard, where he began a long friendship with Van Wyck Brooks; the young collegians made their first appearance in print with Verses By Two Undergraduates. *Wheelock completed his education in Germany and, while preparing for his Ph.D.,* composed most of The Human Fantasy, *which was published in 1911,* a year after his return to America. *He was twenty-five when he became affiliated with the publishing house of Charles Scribner's Sons. He remained with the firm as director and senior editor until 1957, when he retired to devote himself entirely to poetry.*

Wheelock's early verse is chiefly nostalgic; a prevailing sense of loss is relieved by short bursts of ecstasy and exultation. Ten volumes appeared before Poems Old and New *was published in 1956. He continued working, on* The Gardener and other Poems *and on a collection of essays,* Prefaces to Poetry. *His later work is more metaphysical, concerned, as one critic said "with the mystery, the beauty, and the unity of life." "Evening Contemplation," written at the age of seventy-two, is one of Wheelock's richest and most distinguished contributions.*

EVENING CONTEMPLATION

Over the meadow-land
Where I so often have watched them,
To an ancient sound of the sea
Heavy upon this coast,
The summer stars look down—
A part of them, yet separate,
Singled by consciousness,
I stand and survey them here.
Deneb, Vega, Altair
Hang high in the pure vault,
Trembling, and far below them
Venus, a fiery bloom
Fallen from the bough of heaven,
The great galactic vine,
Is glowing deep in the west.
Now from the fields unnumbered
Small creatures lift their hymn,
Cricket and grasshopper
Welcome with shrill noise
The illustrious presences,
They are here, they are here, they are here
The glory that dwells in darkness
Has visited earth once more.

The heavens preserve their secret,
From the rim of the huge vault
To the high sidereal arches
No sound. Perpetual silence!
Infinite peace! But oh,
Universe of hushed light,
That peace will not deceive me;
Horrible process, divine
Agony and splendor,
Too well I know your ways,
Their grandeur and their vileness:
The tenderness, the brute
Bestiality, the bloody
Pattern of things on earth,
The fangs that rend the living
Body, the cruel delight,
The terror and the torment,
I know them—and in the heavens
Your dread and violent way
From nebula to system,
The throes of your vast elation,
Convulsions, whirlwinds of stars,
Fierce galaxies without number,
Staining the virgin darkness.
Also, the high sublime
Way of your lonely dreaming
In arches of ordered color
Where the rainbow curves the light
Over a trailing cloud,
The sorrow of void sea-spaces,
And the bolt of bright flame,
And the listening heart of a mother—
I know them, O divine truth,
Who stand here, for a moment
Permitted while the red blood
In leaping faithfulness flushes
Body and brain with the old
Incomparable elixir—
Permitted so, for a time,
To be aware of you now,
To worship and to adore you,
Holy substance of things,
From which the body of love
Is fashioned, the oceanic

Rhythm, the wild Spring rain,
And the music of a Beethoven,
And of which I too am part
Forever. Oh, consoling
Thought, forever, forever
One with your timeless being,
More fully even than now,
When the temporal separation
Through consciousness shall be ended,
That consciousness in which
So briefly you were mirrored,
O sole and perfect truth,
When I lie down to mix
With your beauty in the darkness,
When I drag your glory down
With me, into the grave.

MARIANNE MOORE

[1887–]

To MARIANNE MOORE *poetry was the accumulation and illumination of odd appearances, stray quotations, queer animals and curious objects: a jerboa, nine nectarines, a carriage from Sweden, a sojourn in a whale, a monkey puzzle, a steam roller, an Egyptian glass bottle in the shape of a fish, a pangolin, four quartz crystal clocks, the staff of Aesculapius, a wood-weasel, "imaginary gardens with real toads in them."*

She was born November 15, 1887, in St. Louis, Missouri, and educated at Bryn Mawr; she taught stenography, bookkeeping, and commercial law, as well as English at the Carlisle Indian School in Pennsylvania. In her mid-thirties she was a librarian; nearing forty she was on the staff of The Dial as acting editor until the magazine ceased publication in 1929. Although her output was small, all of her books received wide critical notice as well as awards. She had already received several honors when, in 1951, she won all three of the most coveted: the Bollingen Prize, the National Book Award, and the Pulitzer Prize. Two years later she was given the Gold Medal for Poetry by the National Institute of Arts and Letters.

Marianne Moore's poetry is more thoughtful than musical; quotations are fitted into a precise pattern the way little stones are transformed by a mosaic-maker into a unifying design. To an almost microscopic observation Miss Moore adds a whimsical imagination. The lion is a fearful monster with a "ferocious chrysanthemum head"; oar-blades move together "like the feet of water-spiders"; elephants have "fogcolored skin and strictly practical appendages"; the lizard is a "nervous naked sword on little feet"; the butterfly, "trampling the air as it trampled the flowers," paws like an incredibly small and weightless Pegasus. Hers is a poetry of details, of scissorlike effects, and multiple associations; it demands several readings before one can fully delight in its intellectual play. Once the reader has given himself to her clipped essays in verse, he will agree that, as she phrases it in the title of one of her poems, "the mind is an enchanting thing."

NEVERTHELESS

you've seen a strawberry
  that's had a struggle; yet
  was, where the fragments met,

a hedgehog or a star-
  fish for the multitude
  of seeds. What better food

than apple-seeds—the fruit
  within the fruit—locked in
  like counter-curved twin

hazel-nuts? Frost that kills
  the little rubber-plant-leaves
  of *kok-saghyz*-stalks, can't

harm the roots; they still grow
  in frozen ground. Once where
  there was a prickly-pear-

leaf clinging to barbed wire,
  a root shot down to grow
  in earth two feet below;

as carrots form mandrakes
  or a ram's-horn root some-
  times. Victory won't come

to me unless I go
  to it; a grape-tendril
  ties a knot in knots till

knotted thirty times,—so
  the bound twig that's under-
  gone and over-gone, can't stir.

The weak overcomes its
  menace, the strong over-
  comes itself. What is there

like fortitude! What sap
  went through that little thread
  to make the cherry red!

WHAT ARE YEARS?

What is our innocence,
what is our guilt? All are
naked, none is safe. And whence
is courage: the unanswered question,
the resolute doubt—
dumbly calling, deafly listening—that
in misfortune, even death,
encourages others
and in its defeat, stirs

the soul to be strong? He
sees deep and is glad, who
accedes to mortality
and in his imprisonment, rises
upon himself as
the sea in a chasm, struggling to be
free and unable to be,
in its surrendering
finds its continuing.

So he who strongly feels,
behaves. The very bird,
grown taller as he sings, steels
his form straight up. Though he is captive,
his mighty singing
says, satisfaction is a lowly
thing, how pure a thing is joy.
This is mortality,
this is eternity.

IN DISTRUST OF MERITS

Strengthened to live, strengthened to die for
medals and positioned victories?
They're fighting, fighting, fighting the blind
man who thinks he sees,—
who cannot see that the enslaver is
enslaved; the hater, harmed. O shining O
firm star, O tumultuous
ocean lashed till small things go
as they will, the mountainous
wave makes us who look, know

depth. Lost at sea before they fought! O
star of David, star of Bethlehem,
O black imperial lion
of the Lord—emblem
of a risen world—be joined at last, be
joined. There is hate's crown beneath which all is
death; there's love without which none
is king; the blessed deeds bless
the halo. As contagion
of sickness makes sickness,

contagion of trust can make trust. They're
fighting in deserts and caves, one by
one, in battalions and squadrons;
they're fighting that I
may yet recover from the disease, *my*
self; some have it lightly, some will die. "Man's
wolf to man?" And we devour
ourselves? The enemy could not
have made a greater breach in our
defenses. One pilot-

ing a blind man can escape him, but
Job disheartened by false comfort knew,
that nothing is so defeating
as a blind man who
can see. O alive who are dead, who are
proud not to see, O small dust of the earth
that walks so arrogantly,
trust begets power and faith is
an affectionate thing. We
vow, we make this promise

to the fighting—it's a promise—"We'll
never hate black, white, red, yellow, Jew,
Gentile, Untouchable." We are
not competent to
make our vows. With set jaw they are fighting,
fighting, fighting,—some we love whom we know,
some we love but know not—that
hearts may feel and not be numb.
It cures me; or am I what
I can't believe in? Some

in snow, some on crags, some in quicksands,
little by little, much by much, they
are fighting fighting fighting that where
there was death there may
be life. "When a man is prey to anger,
he is moved by outside things; when he holds
his ground in patience patience
patience, that is action or
beauty," the soldier's defense
and hardest armor for

the fight. The world's an orphan's home. Shall
we never have peace without sorrow?
without pleas of the dying for
help that won't come? O
quiet form upon the dust, I cannot
look and yet I must. If these great patient
dyings—all these agonies
and woundbearings and blood shed—
can teach us how to live, these
dyings were not wasted.

Hate-hardened heart, O heart of iron,
iron is iron till it is rust.
There never was a war that was
not inward; I must
fight till I have conquered in myself what
causes war, but I would not believe it.
I inwardly did nothing.
O Iscariotlike crime!
Beauty is everlasting
and dust is for a time.

ROBINSON JEFFERS

[1887–]

ROBINSON JEFFERS ACTS AS A SHARP *and often shocking counter-irritant to complacency. Explaining one of his poems, he himself admitted, "I was irritated into extravagance by the excessive value that people* seemed to attribute to human consciousness." In "Margrave" he points at the degradation of humanity and speaks of the stars as

> fleeing the contagion
> of consciousness that infects this corner of space.

He was born John Robinson Jeffers in Allegheny, Pennsylvania, January 10, 1887, the first child of a forty-nine-year-old father who taught Old Testament literature in Western Theological Seminary. The boy read Greek when he was five; before he was fourteen he had been educated in France, Switzerland, and Germany. At fifteen he discovered Nietzsche. Returning to America, he entered Occidental College and, after being graduated, attended the University of Southern California. When his parents moved to Seattle he entered the School of Forestry at the University of Washington.

In his twenty-seventh year he married Una Call Kuster and published his first volume of poems, Flagons and Apples. The couple were planning to go to Europe when the First World War broke out. Instead, as Jeffers wrote, "the August news turned us to the village of Carmel. When the stage-coach topped the hill from Monterey and we looked down through pines and sea-fogs on Carmel Bay, it was evident that we had come without knowing it to our inevitable place." There, on the wild California coast, Jeffers became a stonemason and, with his own hands, built a house which was both a habitation and an ivory tower made of granite boulders.

During the next forty years Jeffers published seventeen volumes of poetry which, for the most part, pronounced an uncompromising negation. If man has any nobility, he implies, it is in his stoical acceptance of suffering and continual defeat. Jeffers has an especial sympathy for the rebel who is doomed to failure—"wherever there has been rebellion against any of the tyrannies of darkness, there is a touch of his spirit." He scorns the easy-going, pleasure-seeking America which, beginning as a democracy, threatens to be "thickening to empire." "The love of freedom has been the quality of Western man," says Jeffers, but he fears that freedom may soon be lost.

> We are easy to manage, a gregarious people,
> Full of sentiment, clever at mechanics,
> And we love our luxuries.

Jeffers foresees a race so equipped with "unmeasured power, incredible passion, enormous craft" that it will not only debauch itself but sink in its own defilement. Nevertheless, his very intimations of *futility make the reader reappraise his sense of values. Moreover, there is a huge difference between Jeffers the philosopher and Jeffers the poet. Even at its bitterest the poetry, as opposed to the negative philosophy, is positive. It is full of a harsh beauty, packed with "unmeasured power, incredible passion, enormous craft."*

AGE IN PROSPECT

Praise youth's hot blood if you will, I think that happiness
Rather consists in having lived clear through
Youth and hot blood, on to the wintrier hemisphere
Where one has time to wait and to remember.

Youth and hot blood are beautiful, so is peacefulness.
Youth had some islands in it, but age is indeed
An island and a peak; age has infirmities,
Not few, but youth is all one fever.

To look around and to love in his appearances,
Though a little calmly, the universal God's
Beauty is better I think than to lip eagerly
The mother's breast or another woman's.

And there is no possession more sure than memory's;
But if I reach that gray island, that peak,
My hope is still to possess with eyes the homeliness
Of ancient loves, ocean and mountains,

And meditate the sea-mouth of mortality
And the fountain six feet down with a quieter thirst
Than now I feel for old age; a creature progressively
Thirsty for life will be for death too.

TO THE STONE-CUTTERS

Stone-cutters fighting time with marble, you foredefeated
Challengers of oblivion,
Eat cynical earnings, knowing rock splits, records fall down,
The square-limbed Roman letters

Scale in the thaws, wear in the rain. The poet as well
Builds his monument mockingly;
For man will be blotted out, the blithe earth die, the brave sun
Die blind, his heart blackening:
Yet stones have stood for a thousand years, and pained thoughts found
The honey of peace in old poems.

PROMISE OF PEACE

The heads of strong old age are beautiful
Beyond all grace of youth. They have strange quiet,
Integrity, health, soundness, to the full
They've dealt with life and been attempered by it.
A young man must not sleep; his years are war
Civil and foreign but the former's worse;
But the old can breathe in safety now that they are
Forgetting what youth meant, the being perverse,
Running the fool's gauntlet and being cut
By the whips of the five senses. As for me,
If I should wish to live long it were but
To trade those fevers for tranquillity,
Thinking though that's entire and sweet in the grave
How shall the dead taste the deep treasure they have?

HURT HAWKS

The broken pillar of the wing jags from the clotted shoulder,
The wing trails like a banner in defeat,
No more to use the sky forever but live with famine
And pain a few days: cat nor coyote
Will shorten the week of waiting for death, there is game without talons.

He stands under the oak-bush and waits
The lame feet of salvation; at night he remembers freedom
And flies in a dream, the dawns ruin it.
He is strong and pain is worse to the strong, incapacity is worse.

The curs of the day come and torment him
At distance, no one but death the redeemer will humble that head,
The intrepid readiness, the terrible eyes.
The wild God of the world is sometimes merciful to those
That ask mercy, not often to the arrogant.

You do not know him, you communal people, or you have forgotten him;
Intemperate and savage, the hawk remembers him;
Beautiful and wild, the hawks, and men that are dying remember him.

I'd sooner, except the penalties, kill a man than a hawk; but the great redtail
Had nothing left but unable misery
From the bone too shattered for mending, the wing that trailed under his talons when he moved.
We had fed him six weeks, I gave him freedom,
He wandered over the foreland hill and returned in the evening, asking for death,
Not like a beggar, still eyed with the old
Implacable arrogance. I gave him the lead gift in the twilight.
What fell was relaxed,
Owl-downy, soft feminine feathers; but what
Soared: the fierce rush: the night-herons by the flooded river cried fear at its rising
Before it was quite unsheathed from reality.

T. S. ELIOT

[1888–]

ONE OF THE MOST INFLUENTIAL literary figures of his day, an essayist and playwright whom many have rated the greatest contemporary English poet, Thomas Stearns Eliot was, at least by birth, breeding, and background, American. Born September 26, 1888, the youngest of six children, he was descended on both sides from New England stock. An ancestor, Thomas Stearns, had emigrated from East Coker (celebrated by the poet in Four Quartets) to Massachusetts in 1670; one of his forebears on his mother's side was Isaac Stearns, one of the original members of the Massachusetts Bay Colony. His Boston grandfather founded Washington University and the first Unitarian Church in St. Louis.

His Puritan ancestry brought him to Harvard, where he specialized in literature and philosophy. He continued these studies in France, when he went to the Sorbonne, and in Germany. During the First World War he was a schoolmaster, found that he disliked teaching, took a job as a banker, and finally became an editor and publisher. He rose to full partnership in the firm of Faber & Faber, became a British subject and, at forty, announced that he was now "a royalist in politics, a classicist in literature, and Anglo-Catholic in religion." Eliot had married at twenty-seven and, after his wife died in 1947, he remained a widower for more than ten years until, at sixty, he married his secretary, Valerie Fletcher.

Eliot's early Prufrock and Other Observations, published during the First World War, in his thirtieth year, was unlike anything previously written in English. Its abrupt contrasts of preciosity and vulgarity, of charm and horror, owed something to the French symbolists, but its combination of wit and weariness was his own. Eliot voiced the creeping disillusion of his time in a manner that many found difficult because of its subtleties, but which was recognizably tense and ironic. Eliot exposed the hollowness of a society composed of pompous industrialists, corrupt politicians, frayed aristocrats, middle-aged, neurotic women, and sexless dilettanti whose lives are "measured out with coffee spoons."

The ironies were further defined and the cynicism underlined in the Sweeney poems, which shocked many readers with their juxtaposition of sensuousness and ugliness, of lovely songs and birds' droppings. Later, in The Sacred Wood, Eliot declared: "The contemplation of the horrid or sordid or disgusting is the necessary and negative aspect of the impulse toward the pursuit of beauty." This statement became something of a crédo when, in The Use of Poetry, he wrote: "The essential advantage for a poet is not to have a beautiful world with which to deal; it is to be able to see beneath both beauty and ugliness—to see the boredom, and the horror, and the glory."

After Prufrock Eliot's poems grew darker in tone and deeper in intent. "The boredom, and the horror, and the glory" were spread out on the large canvas of The Wasteland. An unusually difficult poem, it is divided into five movements which some have considered a verbal symphony; composed around a series of literary echoes and private allusions, it succeeds in spite of its intricate dissonances, chiefly because of the power of its music, its forceful images and its haunting implications. The world of The Wasteland is a world of disorder and desolation but not wholly of despair. In it there is a suggestion of hope, a spiritual yearning emphasized in the later poems.

Before a degree of tranquility had been attained Eliot had to make a break with everything written before The Wasteland. The Hollow Men was that break. Turning from the outer to the inner world, Eliot depicted a state of hopeless destitution. Men who are not human beings but figures stuffed with straw gather on stony soil in a valley of dying stars. These scarecrows are without vision; they lean together without thought; their dry voices whisper meaninglessly. The poem proceeds through a land of stone images in "death's dream kingdom." Here humanity approaches a shabby end by way of a distorted nursery rhyme ("Here we go around the prickly pear") as the poem turns a child's bit of doggerel into a litany of final frustration:

> This is the way the world ends
> This is the way the world ends
> This is the way the world ends
> Not with a bang but a whimper.

All his foregoing works seem to have been a preparation for Eliot's later plays and poems. "Journey of the Magi," "A Song for Simeon," "Marina," and "Ash Wednesday," trace the progress of the intellect toward the spirit. They represent a turning away from the barren landscape of The Wasteland and The Hollow Men toward a world of wonder and unearthly peace.

The feeling of such a world was achieved in Four Quartets, perhaps the most perceptive and deeply philosophical poem of the century. In it Eliot examines the elements of time and timelessness, the sense of a shifting present and the permanent sense of poetry.

> Every phrase and every sentence is an end and a beginning;
> Every poem is an epitaph.

In his mid-forties Eliot had begun to write plays. The Rock, a pageant play, was followed by Murder in the Cathedral and The Family Reunion, plays dealing with the basic problems of good and evil. Ten years after The Family Reunion, Eliot showed that he could handle the problem with a lighter as well as a defter touch. The Cocktail Party, The Confidential Clerk, and The Elder Statesman, written between Eliot's sixty-second and seventieth years, are pointed, realistic, and penetrating comedies. They were as successful on Broadway as they were in London's West End, a complete surprise to those who had dismissed Eliot as another precious poet whom it was impossible to enjoy. At sixty Eliot was awarded the Nobel Prize for "work as a trail-blazing pioneer of modern poetry." In the same year he was also honored by King George VI with the Order of Merit. The events brought forth a salvo of tributes. Eliot was acclaimed as a man who had thought his way from wit to wisdom and felt his way from a scoffing skepticism *into a religious serenity. He was hailed as a resuscitator of poetry and a deliverer from intellectual despondency. W. H. Auden spoke for his fellows when, commemorating Eliot's sixtieth birthday, he praised the prophetic poet*

> ... who, not speechless with shock but finding the right
> Language for thirst and fear, did most to
> Prevent a panic.

THE LOVE SONG OF J. ALFRED PRUFROCK

> *S'io credesse che mia risposta fosse*
> *A persona che mai tornasse al mondo,*
> *Questa fiamma staria senza piu scosse.*
> *Ma perciocche giammai di questo fondo*
> *Non torno vivo alcun, s'i'odo il vero,*
> *Senza tema d'infamia ti rispondo.*[1]

Let us go then, you and I,
When the evening is spread out against the sky
Like a patient etherized upon a table;
Let us go, through certain half-deserted streets,
The muttering retreats
Of restless nights in one-night cheap hotels
And sawdust restaurants with oyster-shells:
Streets that follow like a tedious argument
Of insidious intent
To lead you to an overwhelming question . . .
Oh, do not ask, "What is it?"
Let us go and make our visit.

In the room the women come and go
Talking of Michelangelo.

The yellow fog that rubs its back upon the window-panes,
The yellow smoke that rubs its muzzle on the window-panes
Licked its tongue into the corners of the evening,

---

[1] The quotation is from Dante's *The Divine Comedy* and might be translated as: "If I thought my story would get back to the world, then this flame would shake no more. But since, if what I hear is true, that none did ever return alive from these depths, I answer you without fear of misrepresentation." The speaker in the poem is not actually in hell, but Eliot suggests that he is lost in the depths of indecision and disillusion. Thus Prufrock is a symbol of the tired, inactive, and resigned souls in the tumultuous hell of the modern world.

Lingered upon the pools that stand in drains,
Let fall upon its back the soot that falls from chimneys,
Slipped by the terrace, made a sudden leap,
And seeing that it was a soft October night,
Curled once about the house, and fell asleep.

And indeed there will be time
For the yellow smoke that slides along the street,
Rubbing its back upon the window-panes;
There will be time, there will be time
To prepare a face to meet the faces that you meet;
There will be time to murder and create,
And time for all the works and days of hands
That lift and drop a question on your plate;
Time for you and time for me,
And time yet for a hundred indecisions,
And for a hundred visions and revisions,
Before the taking of a toast and tea.

In the room the women come and go
Talking of Michelangelo.

And indeed there will be time
To wonder, "Do I dare?" and, "Do I dare?"
Time to turn back and descend the stair,
With a bald spot in the middle of my hair—
[They will say: "How his hair is growing thin!"]
My morning coat, my collar mounting firmly to the chin,
My necktie rich and modest, but asserted by a simple pin—
[They will say: "But how his arms and legs are thin!"]
Do I dare
Disturb the universe?
In a minute there is time
For decisions and revisions which a minute will reverse.

For I have known them all already, known them all:—
Have known the evenings, mornings, afternoons,
I have measured out my life with coffee spoons;
I know the voices dying with a dying fall
Beneath the music from a farther room.
So how should I presume?

And I have known the eyes already, known them all—
The eyes that fix you in a formulated phrase,

And when I am formulated, sprawling on a pin,
When I am pinned and wiggling on the wall,
Then how should I begin
To spit out all the butt-ends of my days and ways?
    And how should I presume?

And I have known the arms already, known them all—
Arms that are braceleted and white and bare
[But in the lamplight, downed with light brown hair!]
Is it perfume from a dress
That makes me so digress?
Arms that lie along a table, or wrap about a shawl.
    And should I then presume?
    And how should I begin?

Shall I say, I have gone at dusk through narrow streets
And watched the smoke that rises from the pipes
Of lonely men in shirt-sleeves, leaning out of windows? . . .

I should have been a pair of ragged claws
Scuttling across the floors of silent seas.

And the afternoon, the evening, sleeps so peacefully!
Smoothed by long fingers,
Asleep . . . tired . . . or it malingers,
Stretched on the floor, here beside you and me.
Should I, after tea and cakes and ices,
Have the strength to force the moment to its crisis?
But though I have wept and fasted, wept and prayed,
Though I have seen my head [grown slightly bald] brought in upon a platter,
I am no prophet—and here's no great matter;
I have seen the moment of my greatness flicker,
And I have seen the eternal Footman hold my coat, and snicker,
And in short, I was afraid.

And would it have been worth it, after all,
After the cups, the marmalade, the tea,
Among the porcelain, among some talk of you and me,
Would it have been worth while,
To have bitten off the matter with a smile,
To have squeezed the universe into a ball
To roll it toward some overwhelming question,

To say: "I am Lazarus, come from the dead,
Come back to tell you all, I shall tell you all"—
If one, settling a pillow by her head,
    Should say: "That is not what I meant at all.
    That is not it, at all."

And would it have been worth it, after all,
Would it have been worth while,
After the sunsets and the dooryards and the sprinkled streets,
After the novels, after the teacups, after the skirts that trail along the floor—
And this, and so much more?—
It is impossible to say just what I mean!
But as if a magic lantern threw the nerves in patterns on a screen:
Would it have been worth while
If one, settling a pillow or throwing off a shawl,
And turning toward the window, should say:
    "That is not it at all,
    That is not what I meant, at all."

No! I am not Prince Hamlet, nor was meant to be;
Am an attendant lord, one that will do
To swell a progress, start a scene or two,
Advise the prince; no doubt, an easy tool,
Deferential, glad to be of use,
Politic, cautious, and meticulous;
Full of high sentence, but a bit obtuse;
At times, indeed, almost ridiculous—
Almost, at times, the Fool.

I grow old. . . . I grow old. . . .
I shall wear the bottoms of my trousers rolled.

Shall I part my hair behind? Do I dare to eat a peach?
I shall wear white flannel trousers, and walk upon the beach.
I have heard the mermaids singing, each to each.

I do not think that they will sing to me.
I have seen them riding seaward on the waves
Combing the white hair of the waves blown back
When the wind blows the water white and black.

We have lingered in the chambers of the sea
By sea-girls wreathed with seaweed red and brown
Till human voices wake us, and we drown.

THE HOLLOW MEN

Mistah Kurtz—he dead.

A penny for the Old Guy.

I

We are the hollow men
We are the stuffed men
Leaning together
Headpiece filled with straw. Alas!
Our dried voices, when
We whisper together
Are quiet and meaningless
As wind in dry grass
Or rats' feet over broken glass
In our dry cellar

Shape without form, shade without colour,
Paralyzed force, gesture without motion;

Those who have crossed
With direct eyes, to death's other Kingdom
Remember us—if at all—not as lost
Violent souls, but only
As the hollow men
The stuffed men.

II

Eyes I dare not meet in dreams
In death's dream kingdom
These do not appear:
There, the eyes are
Sunlight on a broken column
There, is a tree swinging
And voices are
In the wind's singing
More distant and more solemn
Than a fading star.

Let me be no nearer
In death's dream kingdom
Let me also wear
Such deliberate disguises

Rat's coat, crowskin, crossed staves
In a field
Behaving as the wind behaves
No nearer–

Not that final meeting
In the twilight kingdom

III

This is the dead land
This is cactus land
Here the stone images
Are raised, here they receive
The supplication of a dead man's hand
Under the twinkle of a fading star.

Is it like this
In death's other kingdom
Waking alone
At the hour when we are
Trembling with tenderness
Lips that would kiss
Form prayers to broken stone.

IV

The eyes are not here
There are no eyes here
In this valley of dying stars
In this hollow valley
This broken jaw of our lost kingdoms

In this last of meeting places
We grope together
And avoid speech
Gathered on this beach of the tumid river

Sightless, unless
The eyes reappear
As the perpetual star
Multifoliate rose
Of death's twilight kingdom
The hope only
Of empty men.

V

Here we go round the prickly pear
Prickly pear prickly pear
Here we go round the prickly pear
At five o'clock in the morning.

Between the idea
And the reality
Between the motion
And the act
Falls the Shadow
For Thine is the Kingdom

Between the conception
And the creation
Between the emotion
And the response
Falls the Shadow
Life is very long

Between the desire
And the spasm
Between the potency
And the existence
Between the essence
And the descent
Falls the Shadow
For Thine is the Kingdom

For Thine is
Life is
For Thine is the

This is the way the world ends
This is the way the world ends
This is the way the world ends
Not with a bang but a whimper.

JOURNEY OF THE MAGI

"A cold coming we had of it,
Just the worst time of the year
For a journey, and such a long journey:

The ways deep and the weather sharp,
The very dead of winter."
And the camels galled, sore-footed, refractory,
Lying down in the melting snow.
There were times we regretted
The summer palaces on slopes, the terraces,
And the silken girls bringing sherbet.
Then the camel men cursing and grumbling
And running away, and wanting their liquor and women,
And the night-fires going out, and the lack of shelters,
And the cities hostile and the towns unfriendly
And the villages dirty and charging high prices:
A hard time we had of it.
At the end we preferred to travel all night,
Sleeping in snatches,
With the voices singing in our ears, saying
That this was all folly.

Then at dawn we came down to a temperate valley,
Wet, below the snow line, smelling of vegetation;
With a running stream and a water-mill beating the darkness,
And three trees on the low sky,
And an old white horse galloped away in the meadow.
Then we came to a tavern with vine-leaves over the lintel,
Six hands at an open door dicing for pieces of silver,
And feet kicking the empty wine-skins.
But there was no information, and so we continued
And arriving at evening, not a moment too soon
Finding the place; it was (you may say) satisfactory.

All this was a long time ago, I remember,
And I would do it again, but set down
This set down
This: were we led all that way for
Birth or Death? There was a Birth, certainly,
We had evidence and no doubt. I had seen birth and death,
But had thought they were different; this Birth was
Hard and bitter agony for us, like Death, our death.
We returned to our places, these Kingdoms,
But no longer at ease here, in the old dispensation,
With an alien people clutching their gods.
I should be glad of another death.

EUGENE O'NEILL

[1888–1953]

When Sinclair Lewis accepted the Nobel Prize in 1930 with a half-modest, half-satirical speech, he startled his hearers by saying, "Had you chosen Eugene O'Neill, who had done nothing much in American drama save to transform it utterly in ten or twelve years, from a false world of neat and competent trickery to a world of splendor and fear and greatness, you would have been reminded that he has done something far worse than scoffing—he has seen life as not to be neatly arranged in the study of a scholar, but as a terrifying, magnificent, and often quite horrible thing, akin to the tornado, the earthquake, the devastating fire."

It was to "the devastating fire" that O'Neill devoted himself, breaking every law of dramaturgy in an effort to project his own passionate intensity across the footlights, to find a theatrical image of man as he knew him to be, frantically seeking an outlet for that tragic energy which, inevitably, consumed him.

In a third-floor backroom of a family hotel in New York, on October 16, 1888, Eugene Gladstone O'Neill was born, the second son of James O'Neill, a matinée idol, the perennial star of The Count of Monte Cristo, and Ella Quinlan O'Neill. With his father's touring troupe, O'Neill traveled up and down the country until he was eight years old, when he was sent to a Roman Catholic boarding school. Betts Academy in Stamford, Connecticut, was followed by Princeton, where his formal education ended, after less than a year in the college, when he tossed a beer bottle through an instructor's window.

He began a long series of erratic wanderings. He went to Honduras, but returned home when he contracted a tropical fever. He married Kathleen Jenkins, by whom he had a son, Eugene Jr., and became the assistant stage manager for his father's company, but neither the work nor domesticity suited him. He then shipped as an ordinary seaman on a freighter bound for Buenos Aires. After a year of sailing he came home to New York and went on a prolonged carouse which ended in New Orleans, where his father was playing. For four months he was an actor; for another four months, a newspaper reporter. It was discovered he had a light case of tuberculosis and he went to a sanatorium in Connecticut.

For five months he was forced to be inactive, and only his mind could move. Then the disorganized fragments of his life came into focus. He began reading, chiefly plays, and especially Strindberg, who, he said, "first gave me the vision of what modern drama could be, and inspired me with the urge to write for the theater." As soon as he was pronounced well he went to work, turning out eleven violent, Strindberg-like one-act plays and two long ones. He reread and destroyed most of them. However, his father had six of the survivors printed in a volume called Thirst and Other Plays. His father also made it possible for him to enter the drama workshop at Harvard where he studied with George Pierce Baker, who became his friend and most influential critic.

O'Neill was then twenty-six. At twenty-eight, with a satchel full of scripts, he went to Provincetown and saw his first play produced. Successful in their Wharf Theater, O'Neill and the Provincetown Players moved to New York's Greenwich Village. The players staged ten of O'Neill's one-acts between 1917 and 1920, when his first full-length play, Beyond the Horizon, was produced. It ran for more than a hundred performances and was awarded the Pulitzer Prize, an honor the playwright was to receive twice again—for Anna Christie in 1922 and, in 1928, for Strange Interlude.

The plays, particularly the earlier ones, are crude; but they are not patterned on tailor-made entertainment, competently contrived, pretty and comforting. They thrash about in darkness to find a wild beauty in things that are violent or ugly; they seek to find form and significance in a world which is formless except in the repeated pattern of men's self-destruction. O'Neill's heroes are doomed—one commentator speaks of his "haunted heroes"—not by gods but by the lack of them, and are no less tragic for being helpless.

Finding the popular theatrical formulas ineffective, O'Neill looked back to ancient, classical forms, devised new ones, forgot the rules, and rushed from realism to fantasy to expressionism in an effort to catch the essence of human suffering. The Emperor Jones violated the rule against long speeches by being practically a monologue and broke the edict about changing an established mood by shifting the line of the play from modern realism to expressionistic fantasy. The Hairy Ape alternated scenes of pure realism with fantasy turned into symbolism. Masks became the symbols of men's "public faces," contrasted to the real selves they dared not show the world, in The Great God Brown. Strange Interlude used the old theatrical "aside" to expose the characters' inmost thoughts. With Mourning Becomes Electra O'Neill stretched the resources of the theater to the uttermost. Using the form of a classical trilogy, he created a modern, psychological study of a family destroyed by hate and passion. The play ran for five hours, with an intermission for dinner.

The character of O'Neill's life changed almost as rapidly as the shapes of his plays. He moved from New England to Bermuda, to France, to San Francisco, New York, and Cape Cod. His first marriage had lasted only three years. At thirty he married Agnes Boulton, by whom he had two children, a son, Shane, and a daughter, Oona; they were divorced in 1929. At forty-two O'Neill was married again, to Carlotta Monterey, a beautiful actress. He began planning A Tale of Possessors Self-Dispossessed, a cycle of nine plays which was to form a saga of the rise and fall of an American family from 1775 to 1932. A Touch of the Poet, not seen until 1959, six years after the playwright's death, was to have been among the first plays of the cycle.

If O'Neill's forms sometimes were shocking to theatrical traditionalists, the impact of what he said within the forms was, for some audiences, horrific. Although the surprisingly gentle comedy, Ah, Wilderness, was an immediate, long-running success, it was difficult to get the controversial All God's Chillun Got Wings on the stage at all because the authorities feared it might lead to race riots. Desire Under the Elms was violently attacked for its "undisguised immorality." When the Nobel Prize was awarded to O'Neill in 1936, it came as a rebuke to the Philistines and an unexpected tribute to the playwright whose works were more often performed than those of any contemporary dramatist except Shaw.

Suddenly O'Neill seemed to lose his "luck of time" and his power. At fifty he was sick and unhappy. His family was disintegrating. He had never forgiven his daughter for marrying the comedian, Charlie Chaplin. His son, Shane, had been in a federal hospital for narcotics addicts. In 1950, Eugene Jr., a teacher and a brilliant Greek scholar, committed suicide. O'Neill himself had been struck, at fifty-six, with a muscular ailment which made writing difficult; worse, he found he could not write by dictating. He destroyed many pages of his great, unfinished cycle. In 1953, completely incapacitated by illness, he contracted bronchial pneumonia and, on November 27, he died. By his own wish he was buried without ceremony, and only his wife, his doctor, and a nurse stood beside the grave as his casket was lowered into it.

In a not-too-laudatory obituary, the Times conceded that "before O'Neill, the United States had theater; after O'Neill it had drama." At the time O'Neill's plays seemed to have lost their appeal and were not often performed. The Iceman Cometh, presented in 1946 (his first new play in twelve years), had been an enigmatic failure. A Moon for the Misbegotten had closed during its out-of-town tryout. The critical mood of the time was indicated by the critic Eric Bentley's tellingly-titled article, "Trying to Like O'Neill."

Less than five years after the playwright's death, an off-Broadway production of The Iceman Cometh was a striking success. Peter Wood's London production of the play, a few years later, was equally well received. Interest developed in O'Neill plays as yet unread and unproduced. The Swedish theater, perhaps because it, too, had been raised on Strindberg, had never lost its interest in O'Neill, and it was to a theater in Stockholm that Carlotta O'Neill gave permission for the first performances of A Long Day's Journey into Night. O'Neill himself had said that the autobiographical play should not be presented until twenty-five years after his death, but Mrs. O'Neill, knowing that all those who could have been hurt by the play's revelations were dead, allowed the Swedish performances, which were immediately acclaimed. There soon followed much-applauded New York and London productions of the fascinating, tortured study of a family—recognizably O'Neill's family—whose members, seeking to find each other and themselves, rushed to destruction. Ah, Wilderness, the playwright's one warm, unashamedly sentimental play of family life, and A Long Day's Journey into Night represent the opposite poles of O'Neill's world—the one a wistful idealization of a young man's approaching adult life; the other, the tragic reality O'Neill faced himself, a horror which sent him roaming the earth, experimenting with forms of expression, questioning everything and crying to the heavens for an answer.

It is too early to determine O'Neill's final status as a dramatist. It is obvious that he was a provocative innovator, a breaker of established forms and a builder of new ones. When he failed, he failed abysmally; but his failures were due to an excess of purpose, never to an impoverishment of the imagination. Sometimes unable to set the overwhelming concepts into effective speech, he, like his characters, rushed ahead, hauled along by the intensity of the idea he had to express, the problem he felt he must solve. He had seen "the death of the old God and the failure of science and materialism to give any satisfactory new one for the surviving primitive religious instinct to find a meaning for life in, and to comfort its fears of death with." In The Emperor Jones, one of O'Neill's most interesting experiments and most successful one-acts, the drum-beats of the primitive, old world overcome the modern, civilized man, reawakening in him the instincts his scientific society could never destroy.

Of O'Neill's Mourning Becomes Electra, Joseph Wood Krutch remarked: "Once more we have a great play which . . . means the same thing that Oedipus and Hamlet and Macbeth mean—namely, that human beings are great and terrible creatures when they are in the grip of great passions, and that the spectacle of them is not only absorbing but also and at once horrible and cleansing." When such a play as A Long Day's Journey into Night is put on the stage, it becomes evident that O'Neill spent his career in the theater searching for that cathartic purification which would make meaningful—and bearable—the horrors through which he saw men put themselves.

THE EMPEROR JONES

SCENE ONE

THE AUDIENCE CHAMBER *in the palace of the Emperor—a spacious, high-ceilinged room with bare, white-washed walls. The floor is of white tiles. In the rear, to the left of center, a wide archway giving out on a portico with white pillars. The palace is evidently situated on high ground for beyond the portico nothing can be seen but a vista of distant hills, their summits crowned with thick groves of palm trees. In the right wall, center, a smaller arched doorway leading to the living quarters of the palace. The room is bare of furniture with the exception of one huge chair made of uncut wood which stands at center, its back to rear. This is very apparently the Emperor's throne. It is painted a dazzling, eye-smiting scarlet. There is a brilliant orange cushion on the seat and another smaller one is placed on the floor to serve as a footstool. Strips of matting, dyed scarlet, lead from the foot of the throne to the two entrances.*

It is late afternoon but the sunlight still blazes yellowly beyond the portico and there is an oppressive burden of exhausting heat in the air.

As the curtain rises, a native negro woman sneaks in cautiously from the entrance on the right. She is very old, dressed in cheap calico, bare-footed, a red bandana handkerchief covering all but a few stray wisps of white hair. A bundle bound in colored cloth is carried over her shoulder on the end of a stick. She hesitates beside the doorway, peering back as if in extreme dread of being discovered. Then she begins to glide noiselessly, a step at a time, toward the doorway in the rear. At this moment, SMITHERS *appears beneath the portico.*

SMITHERS *is a tall, stoop-shouldered man about forty. His bald head, perched on a long neck with an enormous Adam's apple, looks like an egg. The tropics have tanned his naturally pasty face with its small, sharp features to a sickly yellow, and native rum has painted his pointed nose to a startling red. His little, washy-blue eyes are red-rimmed and dart about him like a ferret's. His expression is one of unscrupulous meanness, cowardly and dangerous. He is dressed in a worn riding suit of dirty white drill, puttees, spurs, and wears a white cork helmet. A cartridge belt with an automatic revolver is around his waist. He carries a riding whip in his hand. He sees the woman and stops to watch her suspiciously. Then, making up his mind, he steps quickly on tiptoe into the room. The woman, looking back over her shoulder continually, does not see him until it is too late. When she does* SMITHERS *springs forward and grabs her firmly by the shoulder. She struggles to get away, fiercely but silently.*

SMITHERS. (*tightening his grasp—roughly*) Easy! None o' that, me birdie. You can't wiggle out, now I got me 'ooks on yer.

WOMAN. (*seeing the uselessness of struggling, gives way to frantic terror, and sinks to the ground, embracing his knees supplicatingly*) No tell him! No tell him, Mister!

SMITHERS. (*with great curiosity*) Tell 'im? (*Then scornfully*) Oh, you mean 'is bloomin' Majesty. What's the gaime, any'ow? What are you sneakin' away for? Been stealin' a bit, I s'pose. (*He taps her bundle with his riding whip significantly*).

WOMAN. (*shaking her head vehemently*) No, me no steal.

SMITHERS. Bloody liar! But tell me what's up. There's somethin' funny goin' on. I smelled it in the air first thing I got up this mornin'. You blacks are up to some devilment. This palace of 'is is like a bleedin' tomb. Where's all the 'ands? (*The woman keeps sullenly silent.* SMITHERS *raises his whip threateningly*) Ow, yer won't, won't yer? I'll show yer what's what.

WOMAN. (*coweringly*) I tell, Mister. You no hit. They go—all go. (*She makes a sweeping gesture toward the hills in the distance*).

SMITHERS. Run away—to the 'ills?

WOMAN. Yes, Mister. Him Emperor—Great Father (*She touches her forehead to the floor with a quick mechanical jerk*) Him sleep after eat. Then they go—all go. Me old woman. Me left only. Now me go too.

SMITHERS. (*his astonishment giving way to an immense, mean satisfaction*) Ow! So that's the ticket! Well, I know bloody well wot's in the air—when they runs orf to the 'ills. The tom-tom 'll be thumping out there bloomin' soon. (*With extreme vindictiveness*) And I'm bloody glad of it, for one! Serve 'im right! Puttin' on airs, the stinkin' nigger! 'Is Majesty! Gawd blimey! I only 'opes I'm there when they takes 'im out to shoot 'im. (*Suddenly*) 'E's still 'ere all right, ain't 'e?

WOMAN. Him sleep.

SMITHERS. 'E's bound to find out soon as 'e wakes up. 'E's cunnin' enough to know when 'is time's come. (*He goes to the doorway on right and whistles shrilly with his fingers in his mouth. The old woman springs to her feet and runs out of the doorway, rear.* SMITHERS *goes after her, reaching for his revolver*) Stop or I'll shoot! (*Then stopping—indifferently*) Pop orf then, if yer like, yer black cow. (*He stands in the doorway, looking after her*).

(JONES *enters from the right. He is a tall, powerfully-built, full-blooded negro of middle age. His features are typically negroid, yet there is something decidedly distinctive about his face—an underlying strength of will, a hardy, self-reliant confidence in himself that inspires respect. His eyes are alive with a keen, cunning intelligence. In manner he is shrewd, suspicious, evasive. He wears a light blue uniform coat, sprayed with brass buttons, heavy gold chevrons on his shoulders, gold braid on the collar, cuffs, etc. His pants are bright red with a light blue stripe down the side. Patent leather laced boots with brass spurs, and a belt with a long-barrelled, pearl-handled revolver in a holster complete his make up. Yet there is something not altogether ridiculous about his grandeur. He has a way of carrying it off*).

JONES. (*not seeing anyone—greatly irritated and blinking sleepily—shouts*) Who dare whistle dat way in my palace? Who dare wake up de Emperor? I'll git de hide frayled off some o' you niggers sho'!

SMITHERS. (*showing himself—in a manner half-afraid and half-defiant*) It was me whistled to yer. (*As* JONES *frowns angrily*) I got news for yer.

JONES. (*putting on his suavest manner, which fails to cover up his contempt for the white man*) Oh, it's you, Mister Smithers. (*He sits down on his throne with easy dignity*) What news you got to tell me?

SMITHERS. (*coming close to enjoy his discomfiture*) Don't yer notice nothin' funny today?

JONES. (*coldly*) Funny? No. I ain't perceived nothin' of de kind!

SMITHERS. Then yer ain't so foxy as I thought yer was. Where's all your court? (*sarcastically*) the Generals and the Cabinet Ministers and all?

JONES. (*imperturbably*) Where dey mostly runs to minute I closes my eyes—drinkin' rum and talkin' big down in de town. (*Sarcastically*) How come you don't know dat? Ain't you sousin' with 'em most every day?

SMITHERS. (*stung but pretending indifference—with a wink*) That's part of the day's work. I got ter—ain't I—in my business?

JONES. (*contemptuously*) Yo' business!

SMITHERS. (*imprudently enraged*) Gawd blimey, you was glad enough for me ter take yer in on it when you landed here first. You didn' 'ave no 'igh and mighty airs in them days!

JONES. (*his hand going to his revolver like a flash—menacingly*) Talk polite, white man! Talk polite, you heah me! I'm boss heah now, is you fergettin'? (*The Cockney seems about to challenge this last statement with the facts but something in the other's eyes holds and cows him*).

SMITHERS. (*in a cowardly whine*) No 'arm meant, old top.

JONES. (*condescendingly*) I accepts yo' apology. (*Lets his hand fall from his revolver*) No use'n you rakin' up ole times. What I was den is one thing. What I is now 's another. You didn't let me in on yo' crooked work out o' no kind feelin's dat time. I done de dirty work fo' you—and most o' de brain work, too, fo' dat matter—and I was wu'th money to you, dat's de reason.

SMITHERS. Well, blimey, I give yer a start, didn't I?—when no one else would. I wasn't afraid to 'ire you like the rest was—'count of the story about your breakin' jail back in the States.

JONES. No, you didn't have no s'cuse to look down on me fo' dat. You been in jail you'self more'n once.

SMITHERS. (*furiously*) It's a lie! (*Then trying to pass it off by an attempt at scorn*) Garn! Who told yer that fairy tale?

JONES. Dey's some tings I ain't got to be tole. I kin see 'em in folk's eyes. (*Then after a pause—meditatively*) Yes, you sho' give me a start. And it didn't take long from dat time to git dese fool, woods' niggers right where I wanted dem. (*With pride*) From stowaway to Emperor in two years! Dat's goin' some!

SMITHERS. (*with curiosity*) And I bet you got yer pile o' money 'id safe some place.

JONES. (*with satisfaction*) I sho' has! And it's in a foreign bank where no pusson don't ever git it out but me no matter what come. You didn't s'pose I was holdin' down dis Emperor job for de glory in it, did you? Sho'! De fuss and glory part of it, dat's only to turn de heads o' de low-flung, bush niggers dat's here. Dey wants de big circus show for deir money. I gives it to 'em an' I gits de money. (*With a grin*) De long green, dat's me every time! (*Then rebukingly*) But you ain't got no kick agin me, Smithers. I'se paid you back all you done for me many times. Ain't I pertected you and winked at all de crooked tradin' you been doin' right out in de broad day? Sho' I has—and me makin' laws to stop it at de same time! (*He chuckles*).

SMITHERS. (*grinning*) But, meanin' no 'arm, you been grabbin' right and left yourself, ain't yer? Look at the taxes you've put on 'em! Blimey! You've squeezed 'em dry!

JONES. (*chuckling*) No, dey ain't *all* dry yet. I'se still heah, ain't I?

SMITHERS. (*smiling at his secret thought*) They're dry right now, you'll find out. (*Changing the subject abruptly*) And as for me breakin' laws, you've broke 'em all yerself just as fast as yer made 'em.

JONES. Ain't I de Emperor? De laws don't go for him. (*Judicially*) You heah what I tells you, Smithers. Dere's little stealin' like you does, and dere's big stealin' like I does. For de little stealin' dey gits you in jail soon or late. For de big stealin' dey makes you Emperor and puts you in de Hall o' Fame when you croaks. (*Reminiscently*) If dey's one thing I learns in ten years on de Pullman ca's listenin' to de white quality talk, it's dat same fact. And when I gits a chance to use it I winds up Emperor in two years.

SMITHERS. (*unable to repress the genuine admiration of the small fry for the large*) Yes, yer turned the bleedin' trick, all right. Blimey, I never seen a bloke 'as 'ad the bloomin' luck you 'as.

JONES. (*severely*) Luck? What you mean—luck?

SMITHERS. I suppose you'll say as that swank about the silver bullet ain't luck—and that was what first got the fool blacks on yer side the time of the revolution, wasn't it?

JONES. (*with a laugh*) Oh, dat silver bullet! Sho' was luck. But I makes dat luck, you heah? I loads de dice! Yessuh! When dat murderin' nigger ole Lem hired to kill me takes aim ten feet away and his gun misses fire and I shoots him dead, what you heah me say?

SMITHERS. You said yer'd got a charm so's no lead bullet'd kill yer. You was so strong only a silver bullet could kill yer, you told 'em. Blimey, wasn't that swank for yer—and plain, fat-'eaded luck?

JONES. (*proudly*) I got brains and I uses 'em quick. Dat ain't luck.

SMITHERS. Yer know they wasn't 'ardly liable to get no silver bullets. And it was luck 'e didn't 'it you that time.

JONES. (*laughing*) And dere all dem fool bush niggers was kneelin' down and bumpin' deir heads on de ground like I was a miracle out o' de Bible. Oh, Lawd, from dat time on I has dem all eatin' out of my hand. I cracks de whip and dey jumps through.

SMITHERS. (*with a sniff*) Yankee bluff done it.

JONES. Ain't a man's talkin' big what makes him big—long as he makes folks believe it? Sho', I talks large when I ain't got nothin' to back it up, but I ain't talkin' wild just de same. I knows I kin fool 'em—I *knows* it—and dat's backin' enough fo' my game. And ain't I got to learn deir lingo and teach some of dem English befo' I kin talk to 'em? Ain't dat wuk? You ain't never learned ary word er it, Smithers, in de ten years you been heah, dough you knows it's money in yo' pocket tradin' wid 'em if you does. But you'se too shiftless to take de trouble.

SMITHERS. (*flushing*) Never mind about me. What's this I've 'eard about yer really 'avin' a silver bullet moulded for yourself?

JONES. It's playin' out my bluff. I has de silver bullet moulded and I tells 'em when de time comes I kills myself wid it. I tells 'em dat's 'cause I'm de on'y man in de world big enuff to git me. No use'n deir tryin'. And dey falls down and bumps deir heads. (*He laughs*) I does dat so's I kin take a walk in peace widout no jealous nigger gunnin' at me from behind de trees.

SMITHERS. (*astonished*) Then you 'ad it made—'onest?

JONES. Sho' did. Heah she be. (*He takes out his revolver, breaks it, and takes the silver bullet out of one chamber*) Five lead an' dis silver baby at de last. Don't she shine pretty? (*He holds it in his hand, looking at it admiringly, as if strangely fascinated*).

SMITHERS. Let me see. (*Reaches out his hand for it*).

JONES. (*harshly*) Keep yo' hands whar dey b'long, white man (*He replaces it in the chamber and puts the revolver back on his hip*).

SMITHERS. (*snarling*) Gawd blimey! Think I'm a bleedin' thief, you would.

JONES. No, 'tain't dat. I knows you'se scared to steal from me. On'y I ain't 'lowin' nary body to touch dis baby. She's my rabbit's foot.

SMITHERS. (*sneering*) A bloomin' charm, wot? (*Venomously*) Well, you'll need all the bloody charms you 'as before long, s' 'elp me!

JONES. (*judicially*) Oh, I'se good for six months yit 'fore dey gits sick o' my game. Den, when I sees trouble comin', I makes my get-away.

SMITHERS. Ho! You got it all planned, ain't yer?

JONES. I ain't no fool. I knows dis Emperor's time is sho't. Dat why I make hay when de sun shine. Was you thinkin' I'se aimin' to hold down dis job for life? No, suh! What good is gittin' money if you stays back in dis raggedy country? I wants action when I spends. And when I sees dese niggers gittin' up deir nerve to tu'n me out, and I'se got all de money in sight, I resigns on de spot and beats it quick.

SMITHERS. Where to?

JONES. None o' yo' business.

SMITHERS. Not back to the bloody States, I'll lay my oath.

JONES. (*suspiciously*) Why don't I? (*Then with an easy laugh*) You mean 'count of dat story 'bout me breakin' from jail back dere? Dat's all talk.

SMITHERS. (*skeptically*) Ho, yes!

JONES. (*sharply*) You ain't 'sinuatin' I'se a liar, is you?

SMITHERS. (*hastily*) No, Gawd strike me! I was only thinkin' o' the bloody lies you told the blacks 'ere about killin' white men in the States.

JONES. (*angered*) How come dey're lies?

SMITHERS. You'd 'ave been in jail if you 'ad, wouldn't yer then? (*With venom*) And from what I've 'eard, it ain't 'ealthy for a black to kill a white man in the States. They burns 'em in oil, don't they?

JONES. (*with cool deadliness*) You mean lynchin' 'd scare me? Well, I tells you, Smithers, maybe I does kill one white man back dere. Maybe I does. And maybe I kills another right heah 'fore long if he don't look out.

SMITHERS. (*trying to force a laugh*) I was on'y spoofin' yer. Can't yer take a joke? And you was just sayin' you'd never been in jail.

JONES. (*in the same tone—slightly boastful*) Maybe I goes to jail dere for gettin' in an argument wid razors ovah a crap game. Maybe I gits twenty years when dat colored man die. Maybe I gits in 'nother argument wid de prison guard was overseer ovah us when we're wukin' de road. Maybe he hits me wid a whip and I splits his head wid a shovel and runs away and files de chain off my leg and gits away safe. Maybe I does all dat an' maybe I don't. It's a story I tells you so's you knows I'se de kind of man dat if you evah repeats one word of it, I ends yo' stealin' on dis yearth mighty damn quick!

SMITHERS. (*terrified*) Think I'd peach on yer? Not me! Ain't I always been yer friend?

JONES. (*suddenly relaxing*) Sho' you has—and you better be.

SMITHERS. (*recovering his composure—and with it his malice*) And just to show yer I'm yer friend, I'll tell yer that bit o' news I was goin' to.

JONES. Go ahead! Shoot de piece. Must be bad news from de happy way you look.

SMITHERS. (*warningly*) Maybe it's gettin' time for you to resign—with that bloomin' silver bullet, wot? (*He finishes with a mocking grin*).

JONES. (*puzzled*) What's dat you say? Talk plain.

SMITHERS. Ain't noticed any of the guards or servants about the place today, I 'aven't.

JONES. (*carelessly*) Dey're all out in de garden sleepin' under de trees. When I sleeps, dey sneaks a sleep, too, and I pretends I never suspicions it. All I got to do is to ring de bell and dey come flyin', makin' a bluff dey was wukin' all de time.

SMITHERS. (*in the same mocking tone*) Ring the bell now an' you'll bloody well see what I means.

JONES. (*startled to alertness, but preserving the same careless tone*) Sho' I rings. (*He reaches below the throne and pulls out a big, common dinner bell which is painted the same vivid scarlet as the throne. He rings this vigorously—then stops to listen. Then he goes to both doors, rings again, and looks out*).

SMITHERS. (*watching him with malicious satisfaction, after a pause—mockingly*) The bloody ship is sinkin' an' the bleedin' rats 'as slung their 'ooks.

JONES. (*in a sudden fit of anger flings the bell clattering into a corner*) Low-flung, woods' niggers! (*Then catching* SMITHERS' *eye on him, he controls himself and suddenly bursts into a low chuckling laugh*) Reckon I overplays my hand dis once! A man can't take de pot on a bob-tailed flush all de time. Was I sayin' I'd sit in six months mo'? Well, I'se changed my mind den. I cashes in and resigns de job of Emperor right dis minute.

SMITHERS. (*with real admiration*) Blimey, but you're a cool bird, and no mistake.

JONES. No use'n fussin'. When I knows de game's up I kisses it good-by widout no long waits. Dey've all run off to de hills, ain't dey?

SMITHERS. Yes—every bleedin' man jack of 'em.

JONES. Den de revolution is at de post. And de Emperor better git his feet smokin' up de trail. (*He starts for the door in rear*).

SMITHERS. Goin' out to look for your 'orse? Yer won't find any. They steals the 'orses first thing. Mine was gone when I went for 'im this mornin'. That's wot first give me a suspicion of wot was up.

JONES. (*alarmed for a second, scratches his head, then philosophically*) Well, den I hoofs it. Feet, do yo' duty! (*He pulls out a gold watch and looks at it*) Three-thuty. Sundown's at six-thuty or dereabouts. (*Puts his watch back—with cool confidence*) I got plenty o' time to make it easy.

SMITHERS. Don't be so bloomin' sure of it. They'll be after you 'ot and 'eavy. Ole Lem is at the bottom o' this business an' 'e 'ates you like 'ell. 'E'd rather do for you than eat 'is dinner, 'e would!

JONES. (*scornfully*) Dat fool no-count nigger! Does you think I'se scared o' him? I stands him on his thick head more'n once befo' dis, and I does it again if he comes in my way—(*Fiercely*) And dis time I leave him a dead nigger fo' sho'!

SMITHERS. You'll 'ave to cut through the big forest—an' these blacks 'ere can sniff and follow a trail in the dark like 'ounds. You'd 'ave to 'ustle to get through that forest in twelve hours even if you knew all the bloomin' trails like a native.

JONES. (*with indignant scorn*) Look-a-heah, white man! Does you think I'se a natural bo'n fool? Give me credit fo' havin' some sense, fo' Lawd's sake! Don't you s'pose I'se looked ahead and made sho' of all de chances? I'se gone out in dat big forest, pretendin' to hunt, so many times dat I knows it high an' low like a book. I could go through on dem trails wid my eyes shut. (*With great contempt*) Think dese ign'rent bush niggers dat ain't got brains enuff to know deir own names even can catch Brutus Jones? Huh, I s'pects not! Not on yo' life! Why, man, de white men went after me wid bloodhounds where I come from an' I jes' laughs at 'em. It's a shame to fool dese black trash around heah, dey're so easy. You watch me, man. I'll make dem look sick, I will. I'll be 'cross de plain to de edge of de forest by time dark comes. Once in de woods in de night dey got a swell chance o' findin' dis baby! Dawn tomorrow I'll be out at de oder side and on de coast whar dat French gunboat is stayin'. She picks me up, takes me to Martinique when she go dar, and dere I is safe wid a mighty big bankroll in my jeans. It's easy as rollin' off a log.

SMITHERS. (*maliciously*) But s'posin' somethin' 'appens wrong an' they do nab yer?

JONES. (*decisively*) Dey don't—dat's de answer.

SMITHERS. But, just for argyment's sake—what'd you do?

JONES. (*frowning*) I'se got five lead bullets in dis gun good enuff fo' common bush niggers—and after dat I got de silver bullet left to cheat 'em out o' gittin' me.

SMITHERS. (*jeeringly*) Ho, I was fergettin' that silver bullet. You'll bump yourself orf in style, won't yer? Blimey!

JONES. (*gloomily*) You kin bet yo' whole roll on one thing, white man. Dis baby plays out his string to de end and when he quits, he quits wid a bang de way he ought. Silver bullet ain't none too good for him when he go, dat's a fac'! (*Then shaking off his nervousness—with a confident laugh*) Sho'! What is I talkin' about? Ain't come to dat yit and I never will—not wid trash niggers like dese yere. (*Boastfully*) Silver bullet bring me luck anyway. I kin outguess, outrun, outfight, an' outplay de whole lot o' dem all ovah de board any time o' de day er night! You watch me! (*From the distant hills comes the faint, steady thump of a tom-tom, low and vibrating. It starts at a rate exactly corresponding to normal pulse beat—72 to the minute—and continues at a gradually accelerating rate from this point uninterruptedly to the very end of the play*).

(JONES *starts at the sound. A strange look of apprehension creeps into his face for a moment as he listens. Then he asks, with an attempt to regain his most casual manner*) What's dat drum beatin' fo'?

SMITHERS. (*with a mean grin*) For you. That means the bleedin' ceremony 'as started. I've 'eard it before and I knows.

JONES. Cer'mony? What cer'mony?

SMITHERS. The blacks is 'oldin' a bloody meetin', 'avin' a war dance, gettin' their courage worked up b'fore they starts after you.

JONES. Let dem! Dey'll sho' need it!

SMITHERS. And they're there 'oldin' their 'eathen religious service—makin' no end of devil spells and charms to 'elp 'em against your silver bullet. (*He guffaws loudly*) Blimey, but they're balmy as 'ell!

JONES. (*a tiny bit awed and shaken in spite of himself*) Huh! Takes more'n dat to scare dis chicken!

SMITHERS. (*scenting the other's feeling—maliciously*) Ternight when it's pitch black in the forest, they'll 'ave their pet devils and ghosts 'oundin' after you. You'll find yer bloody 'air 'll be standin' on end before termorrow mornin'. (*Seriously*) It's a bleedin' queer place, that stinkin' forest, even in daylight. Yer don't know what might 'appen in there, it's that rotten still. Always sends the cold shivers down my back minute I gets in it.

JONES. (*with a contemptuous sniff*) I ain't no chicken-liver like you is. Trees an' me, we'se friends, and dar's a full moon comin' bring me light. And let dem po' niggers make all de fool spells dey'se a min' to. Does yo' s'pect I'se silly enuff to b'lieve in ghosts an' ha'nts an' all dat ole woman's talk? G'long, white man! You ain't talkin' to me. (*With a chuckle*) Doesn't you know dey's got to do wid a man was member in good standin' o' de Baptist Church? Sho' I was dat when I was porter on de Pullmans, befo' I gits into my little trouble. Let dem try deir heathen tricks. De Baptist Church done pertect me and land dem all in hell. (*Then with more confident satisfaction*) And I'se got little silver bullet o' my own, don't forgit!

SMITHERS. Ho! You 'aven't give much 'eed to your Baptist Church since you been down 'ere. I've 'eard myself you 'ad turned yer coat an' was takin' up with their blarsted witch-doctors, or whatever the 'ell yer calls the swine.

JONES. (*vehemently*) I pretends to! Sho' I pretends! Dat's part o' my game from de fust. If I finds out dem niggers believes dat black is white, den I yells it out louder 'n deir loudest. It don't git me nothin' to do missionary work for de Baptist Church. I'se after de coin, an' I lays my Jesus on de shelf for de time bein'. (*Stops abruptly to look at his watch—alertly*) But I ain't got de time to waste on no more fool talk wid you. I'se gwine away from heah dis secon'. (*He reaches in under the throne and pulls out an expensive Panama hat with a bright multi-colored band and sets it jauntily on his head*) So long, white man! (*With a grin*) See you in jail sometime, maybe!

SMITHERS. Not me, you won't. Well, I wouldn't be in yer bloody boots for no bloomin' money, but 'ere's wishin' yer luck just the same.

JONES. (*contemptuously*) You're de frightenedest man evah I see! I tells you I'se safe's 'f I was in New York City. It takes dem niggers from now to dark to git up de nerve to start somethin'. By dat time, I'se got a head start dey never kotch up wid.

SMITHERS. (*maliciously*) Give my regards to any ghosts yer meets up with.

JONES. (*grinning*) If dat ghost got money, I'll tell him never ha'nt you less'n he wants to lose it.

SMITHERS. (*flattered*) Garn! (*Then curiously*) Ain't yer takin' no luggage with yer?

JONES. I travels light when I wants to move fast. And I got tinned grub buried on de edge o' de forest. (*Boastfully*) Now say dat I don't look ahead an' use my brains! (*With a wide, liberal gesture*) I will all dat's left in de palace to you–and you better grab all you kin sneak away wid befo' dey gits here.

SMITHERS. (*gratefully*) Righto–and thanks ter yer. (*As* JONES *walks toward the door in rear–cautioningly*) Say! Look 'ere, you ain't goin' out that way, are yer?

JONES. Does you think I'd slink out de back door like a common nigger? I'se Emperor yit, ain't I? And de Emperor Jones leaves de way he comes, and dat black trash don't dare stop him–not yit, leastways (*He stops for a moment in the doorway, listening to the far-off but insistent beat of the tom-tom*) Listen to dat roll-call, will you? Must be mighty big drum carry dat far. (*Then with a laugh*) Well, if dey ain't no whole brass band to see me off, I sho' got de drum part of it. So long, white man. (*He puts his hands in his pockets and with studied carelessness, whistling a tune, he saunters out of the doorway and off to the left*).

SMITHERS. (*looks after him with a puzzled admiration*) 'E's got 'is bloomin' nerve with 'im, s'elp me! (*Then angrily*) Ho–the bleedin' nigger –puttin' on 'is bloody airs! I 'opes they nabs 'im an' gives 'im what's what!

CURTAIN

SCENE TWO

THE END OF THE PLAIN *where the Great Forest begins. The foreground is sandy, level ground dotted by a few stones and clumps of stunted bushes cowering close against the earth to escape the buffeting of the trade wind. In the rear the forest is a wall of darkness dividing the world. Only when the eye becomes accustomed to the gloom can the outlines of separate trunks of the nearest trees be made out, enormous pillars of deeper blackness. A somber monotone of wind lost in the leaves moans in the air. Yet this sound serves but to intensify the impression of the forest's relentless immobility, to form a background throwing into relief its brooding, implacable silence.*

(JONES *enters from the left, walking rapidly. He stops as he nears the edge of the forest, looks around him quickly, peering into the dark as if searching for some familiar landmark. Then, apparently satisfied that he is where he ought to be, he throws himself on the ground, dog-tired*).

Well, heah I is. In de nick o' time, too! Little mo' an' it'd be blacker'n de ace of spades heahabouts. (*He pulls a bandana handkerchief from his hip pocket and mops off his perspiring face*) Sho'! Gimme air! I'se tuckered out sho' 'nuff. Dat soft Emperor job ain't no trainin' fo' a long hike ovah dat plain in de brilin' sun. (*Then with a chuckle*) Cheer up, nigger, de worst is yet to come. (*He lifts his head and stares at the forest. His chuckle peters out abruptly. In a tone of awe*) My goodness, look at dem woods, will you? Dat no-count Smithers said dey'd be black an' he sho' called de turn. (*Turning away from them quickly and looking down at his feet, he snatches at a chance to change the subject—solicitously*) Feet, you is holdin' up yo' end fine an' I sutinly hopes you ain't blisterin' none. It's time you git a rest. (*He takes off his shoes, his eyes studiously avoiding the forest. He feels of the soles of his feet gingerly*) You is still in de pink—on'y a little mite feverish. Cool yo'selfs. Remember you done got a long journey yit befo' you. (*He sits in a weary attitude, listening to the rhythmic beating of the tom-tom. He grumbles in a loud tone to cover up a growing uneasiness*) Bush niggers! Wonder dey wouldn't git sick o' beatin' dat drum. Sound louder, seem like. I wonder if dey's startin' after me? (*He scrambles to his feet, looking back across the plain*) Couldn't see dem now, nohow, if dey was hundred feet away. (*Then shaking himself like a wet dog to get rid of these depressing thoughts*) Sho', dey's miles an' miles behind. What you gittin' fidgety about? (*But he sits down and begins to lace up his shoes in great haste, all the time muttering reassuringly*) You know what? Yo' belly is empty, dat's what's de matter wid you. Come time to eat! Wid nothin' but wind on yo' stumach, o' course you feels jiggedy. Well, we eats right heah an' now soon's I gits dese pesky shoes laced up. (*He finishes lacing up his shoes*) Dere! Now le's see! (*Gets on his hands and knees and searches the ground around him with his eyes*) White stone, white stone, where is you? (*He sees the first white stone and crawls to it—with satisfaction*) Heah you is! I knowed dis was de right place. Box of grub, come to me. (*He turns over the stone and feels in under it—in a tone of dismay*) Ain't heah! Gorry, is I in de right place or isn't I? Dere's 'nother stone. Guess dat's it. (*He scrambles to the next stone and turns it over*) Ain't heah, neither! Grub, whar is you? Ain't heah. Gorry, has I got to go hungry into dem woods—all de night? (*While he is talking he scrambles from one stone to another, turning them over in frantic haste. Finally, he jumps to his feet excitedly*) Is I lost de place? Must have! But how dat happen when I was followin' de trail across de plain in broad daylight? (*Almost plaintively*) I'se hungry, I is! I gotta git my feed. Whar's my strength gonna come from if I doesn't? Gorry, I gotta find dat grub high an' low somehow! Why it come dark so quick like dat? Can't see nothin'. (*He scratches a match on his trousers and peers about him. The rate of the beat of the far-off tom-tom increases perceptibly as he does so. He mutters in a bewildered voice*) How come all dese white stones come heah when I only remembers one? (*Suddenly, with a frightened gasp, he flings the match on the ground and stamps on it*) Nigger, is you gone crazy mad? Is you lightin' matches to show dem whar you is? Fo' Lawd's sake, use yo' haid. Gorry, I'se got to be careful! (*He stares at the plain behind him apprehensively, his hand on his revolver*) But how come all dese white stones? And whar's dat tin box o' grub I hid all wrapped up in oilcloth?

(*While his back is turned, the* LITTLE FORMLESS FEARS *creep out from the deeper blackness of the forest. They are black, shapeless, only their glittering little eyes can be seen. If they have any describable form at all it is that of a grubworm about the size of a creeping child. They move noiselessly, but with deliberate, painful effort, striving to raise themselves on end, failing and sinking prone again.* JONES *turns about to face the forest. He stares up at the tops of the trees, seeking vainly to discover his whereabouts by their conformation*).

Can't tell nothin' from dem trees! Gorry, nothin' 'round heah looks like I evah seed it befo'. I'se done lost de place sho' 'nuff! (*With mournful foreboding*) It's mighty queer! It's mighty queer! (*With sudden forced defiance—in an angry tone*) Woods, is you tryin' to put somethin' ovah on me?

(*From the formless creatures on the ground in front of him comes a tiny gale of low mocking laughter like a rustling of leaves. They squirm upward toward him in twisted attitudes.* JONES *looks down, leaps backward with a yell of terror, yanking out his revolver as he does so—in a quavering voice*) What's dat? Who's dar? What is you? Git away from me befo' I shoots you up! You don't?—

(*He fires. There is a flash, a loud report, then silence broken only by the far-off, quickened throb of the tom-tom. The formless creatures have scurried back into the forest.* JONES *remains fixed in his position, listening intently. The sound of the shot, the reassuring feel of the revolver in his hand, have somewhat restored his shaken nerve. He addresses himself with renewed confidence*).

Dey're gone. Dat shot fix 'em. Dey was only little animals—little wild pigs, I recken. Dey've maybe rooted out yo' grub an' eat it. Sho', you fool nigger, what you think dey is—ha'nts? (*Excitedly*) Gorry, you give de game away when you fire dat shot. Dem niggers heah dat fo' su'tin! Time you beat it in de woods widout no long waits. (*He starts for the forest—hesitates before the plunge—then urging himself in with manful resolution*) Git in, nigger! What you skeered at? Ain't nothin' dere but de trees! Git in! (*He plunges boldly into the forest*).

SCENE THREE

IN THE FOREST. *The moon has just risen. Its beams, drifting through the canopy of leaves, make a barely perceptible, suffused, eerie glow. A dense low wall of underbrush and creepers is in the nearer foreground, fencing in a small triangular clearing. Beyond this is the massed blackness of the forest like an encompassing barrier. A path is dimly discerned leading down to the clearing from left, rear, and winding away from it again toward the right. As the scene opens nothing can be distinctly made out. Except for the beating of the tom-tom, which is a trifle louder and quicker than at the close of the previous scene, there is silence, broken every few seconds by a queer, clicking sound. Then gradually the figure of the negro,* JEFF, *can be discerned crouching on his haunches at the rear of the triangle. He is middle-aged, thin, brown in color, is dressed in a Pullman porter's uniform and cap. He is throwing a pair of dice on the ground before him, picking them up, shaking them, casting them out with the regular, rigid, mechanical movements of an automaton. The heavy, plodding footsteps of someone approaching along the trail from the left are heard and* JONES' *voice, pitched on a slightly higher key and strained in a cheery effort to overcome its own tremors.*

De moon's rizen. Does you heah dat, nigger? You gits more light from dis out. No mo' buttin' yo' fool head agin' de trunks an' scratchin' de hide off yo' legs in de bushes. Now you sees whar yo'se gwine. So cheer up! From now on you has a snap. (*He steps just to the rear of the triangular clearing and mops off his face on his sleeve. He has lost his Panama hat. His face is scratched, his brilliant uniform shows several large rents*) What time's it gittin' to be, I wonder? I dassent light no match to find out. Phoo'. It's wa'm an' dat's a fac'! (*Wearily*) How long I been makin' tracks in dese woods? Must be hours an' hours. Seems like fo'evah! Yit can't be, when de moon's jes' riz. Dis am a long night fo' yo', yo' Majesty! (*With a mournful chuckle*) Majesty! Der ain't much majesty 'bout dis baby now. (*With attempted cheerfulness*) Never min'. It's all part o' de game. Dis night come to an end like everything else. And when you gits dar safe and has dat bankroll in yo' hands you laughs at all dis (*He starts to whistle but checks himself abruptly*) What yo' whistlin' for, you po' dope! Want all de worl' to heah you? (*He stops talking to listen*) Heah dat ole drum! Sho' gits nearer from de sound. Dey's packin' it along wid 'em. Time fo' me to move. (*He takes a step forward, then stops—worriedly*) What's dat odder queer clickety sound I heah? Dere it is! Sound close! Sound like—sound like— Fo' God sake, sound like some nigger was shootin' crap! (*Frightenedly*) I better beat it quick when I gits dem notions. (*He walks quickly into the clear space—then stands transfixed as he sees* JEFF*—in a terrified gasp*) Who dar? Who dat? Is dat you, Jeff? (*Starting toward the other, forgetful for a moment of his surroundings and really believing it is a living man that he sees—in a tone of happy relief*) Jeff! I'se sho' mighty glad to see you! Dey tol' me you done died from dat razor cut I gives you. (*Stopping suddenly, bewilderedly*) But how you come to be heah, nigger? (*He stares fascinatedly at the other who continues his mechanical play with the dice.* JONES' *eyes begin to roll wildly. He stutters*) Ain't you gwine—look up—can't you speak to me? Is you—is you—a ha'nt? (*He jerks out his revolver in a frenzy of terrified rage*) Nigger, I kills you dead once. Has I got to kill you ag'in? You take it den. (*He fires. When the smoke clears away* JEFF *has disappeared.* JONES *stands trembling—then with a certain reassurance*) He's gone, anyway. Ha'nt or not ha'nt, dat shot fix him. (*The beat of the far-off tom-tom is perceptibly louder and more rapid.* JONES *becomes conscious of it—with a start, looking back over his shoulder*) Dey's gittin' near! Dey's comin' fast! And heah I is shootin' shots to let 'em know jes' whar I is! Oh, Gorry, I'se got to run. (*Forgetting the path he plunges wildly into the underbrush in the rear and disappears in the shadow*).

SCENE FOUR

IN THE FOREST. *A wide dirt road runs diagonally from right, front, to left, rear. Rising sheer on both sides the forest walls it in. The moon is now up. Under its light the road glimmers ghastly and unreal. It is as if the forest had stood aside momentarily to let the road pass through and accomplish its veiled purpose. This done, the forest will fold in upon itself again and the road will be no more.* JONES *stumbles in from the forest on the right. His uniform is ragged and torn. He looks about him with numbed surprise when he sees the road, his eyes blinking in the bright moonlight. He flops down exhaustedly and pants heavily for a while. Then with sudden anger.*

I'm meltin' wid heat! Runnin' an' runnin' an' runnin'! Damn dis heah coat! Like a straitjacket! (*He tears off his coat and flings it away from him, revealing himself stripped to the waist*) Dere! Dat's better! Now I kin breathe! (*Looking down at his feet, the spurs catch his eye*) And to hell wid dese high-fangled spurs. Dey're what's been a-trippin' me up an' breakin' my neck. (*He unstraps them and flings them away disgustedly*) Dere! I gits rid o' dem frippety Emperor trappin's an' I travels lighter. Lawd! I'se tired! (*After a pause, listening to the insistent beat of the tom-tom in the distance*) I must 'a' put some distance between myself an' dem—runnin' like dat—and yit—dat damn drum sounds jes' de same—nearer, even. Well, I guess I a'most holds my lead anyhow. Dey won't never catch up. (*With a sigh*) If on'y my fool legs stands up. Oh, I'se sorry I evah went in for dis. Dat Emperor job is sho' hard to shake. (*He looks around him suspiciously*) How'd dis road evah git heah? Good level road, too. I never remembers seein' it befo'. (*Shaking his head apprehensively*) Dese woods is sho' full o' de queerest things at night. (*With a sudden terror*) Lawd God, don't let me see no more o' dem ha'nts! Dey gits my goat! (*Then trying to talk himself into confidence*) Ha'nts! You fool nigger, dey ain't no such things! Don't de Baptist parson tell you dat many time? Is you civilized, or is you like dese ign'rent black niggers heah? Sho'! Dat was all in yo' own head. Wasn't nothin' dere. Wasn't no Jeff! Know what? You jus' get seein' dem things 'cause yo' belly's empty and you's sick wid hunger inside. Hunger 'fects yo' head and yo' eyes. Any fool know dat. (*Then pleading fervently*) But bless God, I don't come across no more o' dem, whatever dey is! (*Then cautiously*) Rest! Don't talk! Rest! You needs it. Den you gits on yo' way again. (*Looking at the moon*) Night's half gone a'most. You hits de coast in de mawning! Den you's all safe.

(*From the right forward a small gang of negroes enter. They are dressed in striped convict suits, their heads are shaven, one leg drags limpingly, shackled to a heavy ball and chain. Some carry picks, the others shovels. They are followed by a white man dressed in the uniform of a prison guard. A Winchester rifle is slung across his shoulders and he carries a heavy whip. At a signal from the* GUARD *they stop on the road opposite where* JONES *is sitting.* JONES, *who has been staring up at the sky, unmindful of their noiseless approach, suddenly looks down and sees them. His eyes pop out, he tries to get to his feet and fly, but sinks back, too numbed by fright to move. His voice catches in a choking prayer*).

Lawd Jesus!

(*The* PRISON GUARD *cracks his whip—noiselessly—and at that signal all the convicts start to work on the road. They swing their picks, they shovel, but not a sound comes from their labor. Their movements, like those of* JEFF *in the preceding scene, are those of automatons,—rigid, slow, and mechanical. The* PRISON GUARD *points sternly at* JONES *with his whip, motions him to take his place among the other shovelers.* JONES *gets to his feet in a hypnotized stupor. He mumbles subserviently*).

Yes, suh! Yes, suh! I'se comin'.

(*As he shuffles, dragging one foot, over to his place, he curses under his breath with rage and hatred*).

God damn yo' soul, I gits even wid you yit, sometime.

(*As if there were a shovel in his hands he goes through weary, mechanical gestures of digging up dirt, and throwing it to the roadside. Suddenly the* GUARD *approaches him angrily, threateningly. He raises his whip and lashes* JONES *viciously across the shoulders with it.* JONES *winces with pain and cowers abjectly. The* GUARD *turns his back on him and walks away contemptuously. Instantly* JONES *straightens up. With arms upraised as if his shovel were a club in his hands he springs murderously at the unsuspecting* GUARD. *In the act of crashing down his shovel on the white man's skull,* JONES *suddenly becomes aware that his hands are empty. He cries despairingly*).

Whar's my shovel? Gimme my shovel 'til I splits his damn head! (*Appealing to his fellow convicts*) Gimme a shovel, one o' you, fo' God's sake!

(*They stand fixed in motionless attitudes, their eyes on the ground. The* GUARD *seems to wait expectantly, his back turned to the attacker.* JONES *bellows with baffled, terrified rage, tugging frantically at his revolver*).

I kills you, you white debil, if it's de last thing I evah does! Ghost or debil, I kill you agin!

(*He frees the revolver and fires point blank at the* GUARD'*s back. Instantly the walls of the forest close in from both sides, the road and the figures of the convict gang are blotted out in an enshrouding darkness. The only sounds are a crashing in the underbrush as* JONES *leaps away in mad flight and the throbbing of the tom-tom, still far distant, but increased in volume of sound and rapidity of beat*).

SCENE FIVE

A LARGE CIRCULAR CLEARING, *enclosed by the serried ranks of gigantic trunks of tall trees whose tops are lost to view. In the center is a big dead stump worn by time into a curious resemblance to an auction block. The moon floods the clearing with a clear light.* JONES *forces his way in through the forest on the left. He looks wildly about the clearing with hunted, fearful glances. His pants are in tatters, his shoes cut and misshapen, flapping about his feet. He slinks cautiously to the stump in the center and sits down in a tense position, ready for instant flight. Then he holds his head in his hands and rocks back and forth, moaning to himself miserably.*

Oh, Lawd, Lawd! Oh, Lawd, Lawd! (*Suddenly he throws himself on his knees and raises his clasped hands to the sky—in a voice of agonized pleading*) Lawd Jesus, heah my prayer! I'se a po' sinner, a po' sinner! I knows I done wrong, I knows it! When I cotches Jeff cheatin' wid loaded dice my anger overcomes me and I kills him dead! Lawd, I done wrong! When dat guard hits me wid de whip, my anger overcomes me, and I kills him dead. Lawd, I done wrong! And down heah whar dese fool bush niggers raises me up to the seat o' de mighty, I steals all I could grab. Lawd, I done wrong! I knows it! I'se sorry! Forgive me, Lawd! Forgive dis po' sinner! (*Then beseeching terrifiedly*) And keep dem away, Lawd! Keep dem away from me! And stop dat drum soundin' in my ears! Dat begin to sound ha'nted, too. (*He gets to his feet, evidently slightly reassured by his prayer—with attempted confidence*) De Lawd'll preserve me from dem ha'nts after dis. (*Sits down on the stump again*) I ain't skeered o' real men. Let dem come. But dem odders—(*He shudders—then looks down at his feet, working his toes inside the shoes—with a groan*) Oh, my po' feet! Dem shoes ain't no use no more 'ceptin' to hurt. I'se better off widout dem. (*He unlaces them and pulls them off—holds the wrecks of the shoes in his hands and regards them mournfully*) You was real, A-one patin' leather, too. Look at you now. Emperor, you'se gittin' mighty low!

(*He sighs dejectedly and remains with bowed shoulders, staring down at the shoes in his hands as if reluctant to throw them away. While his attention is thus occupied, a crowd of figures silently enter the clearing from all sides. All are dressed in Southern costumes of the period of the fifties of the last century. There are middle-aged men who are evidently well-to-do planters. There is one spruce, authoritative individual—the* AUCTIONEER. *There is a crowd of curious spectators, chiefly young belles and dandies who have come to the slave-market for diversion. All exchange courtly greetings in dumb show and chat silently together. There is something stiff, rigid, unreal, marionettish about their movements. They group themselves about the stump. Finally a batch of slaves is led in from the left by an attendant—three men of different ages, two women, one with a baby in her arms, nursing. They are placed to the left of the stump, beside* JONES.

The white planters look them over appraisingly as if they were cattle, and exchange judgments on each. The dandies point with their fingers and make witty remarks. The belles titter bewitchingly. All this in silence save for the ominous throb of the tom-tom. The AUCTIONEER *holds up his hand, taking his place at the stump. The groups strain forward attentively. He touches* JONES *on the shoulder peremptorily, motioning for him to stand on the stump—the auction block.*

JONES *looks up, sees the figures on all sides, looks wildly for some opening to escape, sees none, screams and leaps madly to the top of the stump to get as far away from them as possible. He stands there, cowering, paralyzed with horror. The* AUCTIONEER *begins his silent spiel. He points to* JONES, *appeals to the planters to see for themselves. Here is a good field hand, sound in wind and limb as they can see. Very strong still in spite of his being middle-aged. Look at that back. Look at those shoulders. Look at the muscles in his arms and his sturdy legs. Capable of any amount of hard labor. Moreover, of a good disposition, intelligent and tractable. Will any gentleman start the bidding? The* PLANTERS *raise their fingers, make their bids. They are apparently all eager to possess* JONES. *The bidding is lively, the crowd interested. While this has been going on,* JONES *has been seized by the courage of desperation. He dares to look down and around him. Over his face abject terror gives way to mystification, to gradual realization—stutteringly*).

What you all doin', white folks? What's all dis? What you all lookin' at me fo'? What you doin' wid me, anyhow? (*Suddenly convulsed with raging hatred and fear*) Is dis a auction? Is you sellin' me like dey uster befo' de war? (*Jerking out his revolver just as the* AUCTIONEER *knocks him down to one of the planters—glaring from him to the purchaser*) And *you* sells me? And *you* buys me? I shows you I'se a free nigger, damn yo' souls! (*He fires at the* AUCTIONEER *and at the* PLANTER *with such rapidity that the two shots are almost simultaneous. As if this were a signal the walls of the forest fold in. Only blackness remains and silence broken by* JONES *as he rushes off, crying with fear—and by the quickened, ever louder beat of the tom-tom*)

SCENE SIX

A CLEARED SPACE *in the forest. The limbs of the trees meet over it forming a low ceiling about five feet from the ground. The interlocked ropes of creepers reaching upward to entwine the tree trunks give an arched appearance to the sides. The space thus enclosed is like the dark, noisome hold of some ancient vessel. The moonlight is almost completely shut out and only a vague wan light filters through. There is the noise of someone approaching from the left, stumbling and crawling through the undergrowth.* JONES' *voice is heard between chattering moans.*

Oh, Lawd, what I gwine do now? Ain't got no bullet left on'y de silver one. If mo' o' dem ha'nts come after me, how I gwine skeer dem away? Oh, Lawd, on'y de silver one left—an' I gotta save dat fo' luck. If I shoots dat one I'm a goner sho'! Lawd, it's black heah! Whar's de moon? Oh, Lawd, don't dis night evah come to an end! (*By the sounds, he is feeling his way cautiously forward*) Dere! Dis feels like a clear space. I gotta lie down an' rest. I don't care if dem niggers does cotch me. I gotta rest.

(*He is well forward now where his figure can be dimly made out. His pants have been so torn away that what is left of them is no better than a breech cloth. He flings himself full length, face downward on the ground, panting with exhaustion. Gradually it seems to grow lighter in the enclosed space and two rows of seated figures can be seen behind* JONES. *They are sitting in crumpled, despairing attitudes, hunched, facing one another with their backs touching the forest walls as if they were shackled to them. All are negroes, naked save for loin cloths. At first they are silent and motionless. Then they begin to sway slowly forward toward each and back again in unison, as if they were laxly letting themselves follow the long roll of a ship at sea. At the same time, a low, melancholy murmur rises among them, increasing gradually by ryhthmic degrees which seem to be directed and controlled by the throb of the tom-tom in the distance, to a long, tremulous wail of despair that reaches a certain pitch, unbearably acute, then falls by slow gradations of tone into silence and is taken up again.* JONES *starts, looks up, sees the figures, and throws himself down again to shut out the sight. A shudder of terror shakes his whole body as the wail rises up about him again. But the next time, his voice, as if under some uncanny compulsion, starts with the others. As their chorus lifts he rises to a sitting posture similar to the others, swaying back and forth. His voice reaches the highest pitch of sorrow, of desolation. The light fades out, the other voices cease, and only darkness is left.* JONES *can be heard scrambling to his feet and running off, his voice sinking down the scale and receding as he moves farther and father away in the forest. The tom-tom beats louder, quicker, with a more insistent, triumphant pulsation*).

SCENE SEVEN

THE FOOT OF A GIGANTIC TREE *by the edge of a great river. A rough structure of boulders, like an altar, is by the tree. The raised river bank is in the nearer background. Beyond this the surface of the river spreads out, brilliant and unruffled in the moonlight, blotted out and merged into a veil of bluish mist in the distance.* JONES' *voice is heard from the left rising and falling in the long, despairing wail of the chained slaves, to the rhythmic beat of the tom-tom. As his voice sinks into silence, he enters the open space. The expression of his face is fixed and stony, his eyes have an obsessed glare, he moves with a strange deliberation like a sleep-walker or one in a trance. He looks around at the tree, the rough stone altar, the moonlit surface of the river beyond, and passes his hand over his head with a vague gesture of puzzled bewilderment. Then, as if in obedience to some obscure impulse, he sinks into a kneeling, devotional posture before the altar. Then he seems to come to himself partly, to have an uncertain realization of what he is doing, for he straightens up and stares about him horrifiedly—in an incoherent mumble.*

What—what is I doin'? What is—dis place? Seems like I know dat tree—an' dem stones—an' de river. I remember—seems like I been heah befo'. (*Tremblingly*) Oh, Gorry, I'se skeered in dis place! I'se skeered. Oh, Lawd, pertect dis sinner!

(*Crawling away from the altar, he cowers close to the ground, his face hidden, his shoulders heaving with sobs of hysterical fright. From behind the trunk of the tree, as if he had sprung out of it, the figure of the* CONGO WITCH-DOCTOR *appears. He is wizened and old, naked except for the fur of some small animal tied about his waist, its bushy tail hanging down in front. His body is stained all over a bright red. Antelope horns are on each side of his head, branching upward. In one hand he carries a bone rattle, in the other a charm stick with a bunch of white cockatoo feathers tied to the end. A great number of glass beads and bone ornaments are about his neck, ears, wrist, and ankles. He struts noiselessly with a queer prancing step to a position in the clear ground between* JONES *and the altar. Then with a preliminary, summoning stamp of his foot on the earth, he begins to dance and to chant. As if in response to his summons the beating of the tom-tom grows to a fierce, exultant boom whose throbs seem to fill the air with vibrating rhythm.* JONES *looks up, starts to spring to his feet, reaches a half-kneeling, half-squatting position and remains rigidly fixed there, paralyzed with awed fascination by this new apparition. The* WITCH-DOCTOR *sways, stamping with his foot, his bone rattle clicking the time. His voice rises and falls in a weird, monotonous croon, without articulate word divisions. Gradually his dance becomes clearly one of a narrative in pantomime, his croon is an incantation, a charm to allay the fierceness of some implacable deity demanding sacrifice. He flees, he is pursued by devils, he hides, he flees again. Ever wilder and wilder becomes his flight, nearer and nearer draws the pursuing evil, more and more the spirit of terror gains possession of him. His croon, rising to intensity, is punctuated by shrill cries.* JONES *has become completely hypnotized. His voice joins in the incantation, in the cries, he beats time with his hands and sways his body to and fro from the waist. The whole spirit and meaning of the dance has entered into him, has become his spirit. Finally the theme of the pantomime halts on a howl of despair, and is taken up again in a note of savage hope. There is a salvation. The forces of evil demand sacrifice. They must be appeased. The* WITCH-DOCTOR *points with his wand to the sacred tree, to the river beyond, to the altar, and finally to* JONES *with a ferocious command.* JONES *seems to sense the meaning of this. It is he who must offer himself for sacrifice. He beats his forehead abjectly to the ground, moaning hysterically*).

Mercy, Oh, Lawd! Mercy! Mercy on dis po' sinner.

(*The* WITCH-DOCTOR *springs to the river bank. He stretches out his arms and calls to some God within its depths. Then he starts backward slowly, his arms remaining out. A huge head of a crocodile appears over the bank and its eyes, glittering greenly, fasten upon* JONES. *He stares into them fascinatedly. The* WITCH-DOCTOR *prances up to him, touches him with his wand, motions with hideous command toward the waiting monster.* JONES *squirms on his belly nearer and nearer, moaning continually*).

Mercy, Lawd! Mercy!

(*The crocodile heaves more of his enormous hulk onto the land.* JONES *squirms toward him. The* WITCH-DOCTOR'S *voice shrills out in furious exultation, the tom-tom beats madly.* JONES *cries out in a fierce, exhausted spasm of anguished pleading*).

Lawd, save me! Lawd Jesus, heah my prayer!

(*Immediately, in answer to his prayer, comes the thought of the one bullet left him. He snatches at his hip, shouting defiantly*).

De silver bullet! You don't git me yit!

(*He fires at the green eyes in front of him. The head of the crocodile sinks back behind the river bank, the* WITCH-DOCTOR *springs behind the sacred tree and disappears.* JONES *lies with his face to the ground, his arms outstretched, whimpering with fear as the throb of the tom-tom fills the silence about him with a somber pulsation, a baffled but revengeful power*).

SCENE EIGHT

DAWN. *Same as Scene Two, the dividing line of forest and plain. The nearest tree trunks are dimly revealed but the forest behind them is still a mass of glooming shadow. The tom-tom seems on the very spot, so loud and continuously vibrating are its beats.* LEM *enters from the left, followed by a small squad of his soldiers, and by the Cockney trader,* SMITHERS. LEM *is a heavy-set, ape-faced old savage of the extreme African type, dressed only in a loin cloth. A revolver and cartridge belt are about his waist. His soldiers are in different degrees of rag-concealed nakedness. All wear broad palmleaf hats. Each one carries a rifle.* SMITHERS *is the same as in Scene One. One of the soldiers, evidently a tracker, is peering about keenly on the ground. He points to the spot where* JONES *entered the forest.* LEM *and* SMITHERS *come to look.*

SMITHERS. (*after a glance, turns away in disgust*) That's where 'e went in right enough. Much good it'll do yer. 'E's miles orf by this an' safe to the Coast, damn 's 'ide! I tole yer yer'd lose im, didn't I?—wastin' the 'ole bloomin' night beatin' yer bloody drum and castin' yer silly spells! Gawd blimey, wot a pack!

LEM. (*gutturally*) We cotch him. (*He makes a motion to his soldiers who squat down on their haunches in a semi-circle*).

SMITHERS. (*exasperatedly*) Well, ain't yer goin' in an' 'unt 'im in the woods? What the 'ell's the good of waitin'?

LEM. (*imperturbably—squatting down himself*) We cotch him.

SMITHERS. (*turning away from him contemptuously*) Aw! Garn! 'E's a better man than the lot o' you put together. I 'ates the sight o' 'im but I'll say that for 'im. (*A sound comes from the forest. The soldiers jump to their feet, cocking their rifles alertly.* LEM *remains sitting with an imperturbable expression, but listening intently. He makes a quick signal with his hand. His followers creep quickly into the forest, scattering so that each enters at a different spot*).

SMITHERS. You ain't thinkin' that would be 'im, I 'ope?

LEM. (*calmly*) We cotch him.

SMITHERS. Blarsted fat 'eads! (*Then after a second's thought—wonder-*

ingly) Still an' all, it might 'appen. If 'e lost 'is bloody way in these stinkin' woods 'e'd likely turn in a circle without 'is knowin' it.

LEM. (*peremptorily*) *Sssh!* (*The reports of several rifles sound from the forest, followed a second later by savage, exultant yells. The beating of the tom-tom abruptly ceases.* LEM *looks up at the white man with a grin of satisfaction*) We cotch him. Him dead.

SMITHERS. (*with a snarl*) 'Ow d'yer know it's 'im an' 'ow d'yer know 'e's dead?

LEM. My mens dey got um silver bullets. Lead bullet no kill him. He got um strong charm. I cook um money, make um silver bullet, make um strong charm, too.

SMITHERS. (*astonished*) So that's wot you was up to all night, wot? You was scared to put after 'im till you'd moulded silver bullets, eh?

LEM (*simply stating a fact*) Yes. Him got strong charm. Lead no good.

SMITHERS. (*slapping his thigh and guffawing*) Haw-haw! If yer don't beat all 'ell! (*Then recovering himself—scornfully*) I'll bet yer it ain't 'im they shot at all, yer bleedin' looney!

LEM. (*calmly*) Dey come bring him now. (*The soldiers come out of the forest, carrying* JONES' *limp body. He is dead. They carry him to* LEM, *who examines his body with great satisfaction.* SMITHERS *leans over his shoulder—in a tone of frightened awe*) Well, they did for yer right enough, Jonesey, me lad! Dead as a 'erring! (*Mockingly*) Where's yer 'igh an' mighty airs now, yer bloomin' Majesty? (*Then with a grin*) Silver bullets! Gawd blimey, but yer died in the 'eighth o' style, any'ow!

CURTAIN

JOHN CROWE RANSOM

[1888–   ]

ORGANIZER OF THE GROUP known as the Fugitives, editor of the Kenyon Review, and founder of the American school of critics which championed the New Criticism, John Crowe Ransom was born April 30, 1888, in Pulaski, Tennessee, a place distinguished, according to Ransom, as the deathplace of Sam Davis, the Confederate martyr, and as the birthplace of the Klu Klux Klan. After receiving his B.A. at Vanderbilt University in Nashville, Ransom was a Rhodes scholar who *completed his formal education at Christ Church College in Oxford. He taught at Vanderbilt from his twenty-sixth to his forty-ninth year, at which time he left the South for the North and moved to Kenyon College in Gambier, Ohio, where he kept on teaching for another twenty years.*

As an essayist John Crowe Ransom is sometimes abstruse and discursive but more often sharply revealing. It is as a poet, however, that he makes the deepest impression. Whether he writes soliloquies or narratives, Ransom employs understatement and a kind of teasing evasiveness with fine effect, and even his lyrics flicker with bland mockery. He is fond of using assonances and "slant rhymes"—such as "body-study," "little-scuttle," "thunder-tinder," "feature-nature," "window-shadow," "gentle-lintel"—which give his lines a kind of acrid music.

Apart from his unusual technique Ransom's vocabulary is piquant; he says surprising and sometimes savage things with great delicacy. It is a scholar's voice which pronounces the most elegant and macabre fancies with cavalier grace.

HERE LIES A LADY

Here lies a lady of beauty and high degree.
Of chills and fever she died, of fever and chills,
The delight of her husband, her aunts, an infant of three,
And of medicos marveling sweetly on her ills.

For either she burned, and her confident eyes would blaze,
And her fingers fly in a manner to puzzle their heads—
What was she making? Why, nothing; she sat in a maze
Of old scraps of laces, snipped into curious shreds—

Or this would pass, and the light of her fire decline
Till she lay discouraged and cold as a thin stalk white and blown,
And would not open her eyes, to kisses, to wine.
The sixth of these states was her last; the cold settled down.

Sweet ladies, long may ye bloom, and toughly I hope ye may thole,
But was she not lucky? In flowers and lace and mourning,
In love and great honor we bade God rest her soul
After six little spaces of chill, and six of burning.

JANET WALKING

Beautifully Janet slept
Till it was deeply morning. She woke then
And thought about her dainty-feathered hen,
To see how it had kept.

One kiss she gave her mother,
Only a small one gave she to her daddy
Who would have kissed each curl of his shining baby;
No kiss at all for her brother.

"Old Chucky, Old Chucky!" she cried,
Running on little pink feet upon the grass
To Chucky's house, and listening. But alas,
Her Chucky had died.

It was a transmogrifying bee
Came droning down on Chucky's old bald head
And sat and put the poison. It scarcely bled,
But how exceedingly

And purply did the knot
Swell with the venom and communicate
Its rigor! Now the poor comb stood up straight
But Chucky did not.

So there was Janet
Kneeling on the wet grass, crying her brown hen
(Translated far beyond the daughters of men)
To rise and walk upon it.

And weeping fast as she had breath
Janet implored us, "Wake her from her sleep!"
And would not be instructed in how deep
Was the forgetful kingdom of death.

BELLS FOR JOHN WHITESIDE'S DAUGHTER

There was such speed in her little body,
And such lightness in her footfall,
It is no wonder that her brown study
Astonishes us all.

Her wars were bruited in our high window.
We looked among orchard trees and beyond,
Where she took arms against her shadow,
Or harried unto the pond

The lazy geese, like a snow cloud
Dripping their snow on the green grass,
Tricking and stopping, sleepy and proud,
Who cried in goose, Alas,

For the tireless heart within the little
Lady with rod that made them rise
From their noon apple-dreams, and scuttle
Goose-fashion under the skies!

But now go the bells, and we are ready;
In one house we are sternly stopped
To say we are vexed at her brown study,
Lying so primly propped.

LADY LOST

This morning, there flew up the lane
A timid lady-bird to our bird-bath
And eyed her image dolefully as death;
This afternoon, knocked on our windowpane
To be let in from the rain.

And when I caught her eye
She looked aside, but at the clapping thunder
And sight of the whole earth blazing up like tinder
Looked in on us again most miserably,
Indeed as if she would cry.

So I will go out into the park and say,
"Who has lost a delicate brown-eyed lady
In the West End Section? Or has anybody
Injured some fine woman in some dark way,
Last night or yesterday?

"Let the owner come and claim possession,
No questions will be asked. But stroke her gently
With loving words, and she will evidently

Resume her full soft-haired white-breasted fashion,
And her right home and her right passion."

PARTING, WITHOUT A SEQUEL

She has finished and sealed the letter
At last, which he so richly has deserved,
With characters venomous and hatefully curved,
And nothing could be better.

But even as she gave it,
Saying to the blue-capped functioner of doom,
"Into his hands," she hoped the leering groom
Might somewhere lose and leave it.

Then all the blood
Forsook the face. She was too pale for tears,
Observing the ruin of her younger years.
She went and stood

Under her father's vaunting oak
Who kept his peace in wind and sun, and glistened
Stoical in the rain; to whom she listened
If he spoke.

And now the agitation of the rain
Rasped his sere leaves, and he talked low and gentle,
Reproaching the wan daughter by the lintel;
Ceasing, and beginning again.

Away went the messenger's bicycle,
His serpent's track went up the hill forever.
And all the time she stood there hot as fever
And cold as any icicle.

CONRAD AIKEN

[1889–   ]

ALTHOUGH AN ASTUTE and unusually sensitive critic as well as a creator of eerie and probing tales, Conrad (Potter) Aiken was, first and last, a poet. He was born August 5, 1889, in Savannah, Georgia. Some critics maintain that his subjective psychological prose and his introspective verse are the unconscious results of an early shock—he was ten years old when, in a fit of insanity, his father killed his mother and committed suicide.

After the tragedy, Aiken was brought to Massachusetts. Here, with the exception of residences abroad, he lived most of his life. When he entered Harvard at seventeen, T. S. Eliot, Van Wyck Brooks, and John Hall Wheelock were among his classmates. After his marriage to Jessie MacDonald, by whom he had three children alliteratively named John, Jane, and Joan, he lived on the west coast of England for some years. He was London correspondent for The New Yorker in his mid-forties; remarried, he returned to Massachusetts and settled in a rambling house accurately called "Forty-one Doors" on Cape Cod.

It was some time before Aiken struck his own recognizable note. Such early volumes as Earth Triumphant and Turns and Movies show a dependence on the fashion of the moment mixed with traditions of the past. In his late twenties Aiken began to produce a series of volumes notable for their subtle inflections and weaving, wavering music. His Selected Poems won the Pulitzer Prize in 1930. Twenty-three years later his Collected Poems, comprising some eighteen previously published books, received the National Book Award. He was appointed to the Library of Congress' Chair in Poetry and, approaching seventy, was given the Gold Medal for Poetry by the Institute of Arts and Letters.

Aiken's prose is less nebulous than his verse, but it is equally resonant and much of it conveys, like his poetry, the sense of incantation. His fiction, frequently employing the "stream-of-consciousness" method of narration, is never without distinction. It includes his slightly disguised autobiography, Ushant; a strange novel, Blue Voyage; and two short stories, "Silent Snow, Secret Snow" and "Mr. Arcularis," which, widely anthologized, are among the minor classics of the period.

MR. ARCULARIS

Mr. Arcularis stood at the window of his room in the hospital and looked down at the street. There had been a light shower, which had patterned the sidewalks with large drops, but now again the sun was out, blue sky was showing here and there between the swift white clouds, a cold wind was blowing the poplar trees. An itinerant band had stopped before the building and was playing, with violin, harp, and flute, the finale of "Cavalleria Rusticana." Leaning against the window-sill—for he felt extraordinarily weak after his operation—Mr. Arcularis suddenly, listening to the wretched music, felt like crying. He rested the palm of one hand against a cold window-pane and stared down at the old man who was blowing the flute, and blinked his eyes. It seemed absurd that he should be so weak, so emotional, so like a child—and especially now that everything was over at last. In spite of all their predictions, in spite, too, of his own dreadful certainty that he was going to die, here he was, as fit as a fiddle—but what a fiddle it was, so out of tune!—with a long life before him. And to begin with, a voyage to England ordered by the doctor. What could be more delightful? Why should he feel sad about it and want to cry like a baby? In a few minutes Harry would arrive with his car to take him to the wharf; in an hour he would be on the sea, in two hours he would see the sunset behind him, where Boston had been, and his new life would be opening before him. It was many years since he had been abroad. June, the best of the year to come—England, France, the Rhine—how ridiculous that he should already be homesick!

There was a light footstep outside the door, a knock, the door opened, and Harry came in.

"Well, old man, I've come to get you. The old bus actually got here. Are you ready? Here, let me take your arm. You're tottering like an octogenarian!"

Mr. Arcularis submitted gratefully, laughing, and they made the journey slowly along the bleak corridor and down the stairs to the entrance hall. Miss Hoyle, his nurse, was there, and the Matron, and the charming little assistant with freckles who had helped to prepare him for the operation. Miss Hoyle put out her hand.

"Goodbye, Mr. Arcularis," she said, "and *bon voyage*."

"Goodbye, Miss Hoyle, and thank you for everything. You were very kind to me. And I fear I was a nuisance."

The girl with the freckles, too, gave him her hand, smiling. She was very pretty, and it would have been easy to fall in love with her. She reminded him of someone. Who was it? He tried in vain to remember while he said goodbye to her and turned to the Matron.

"And not too many latitudes with the young ladies, Mr. Arcularis!" she was saying.

Mr. Arcularis was pleased, flattered, by all this attention to a middle-aged invalid, and felt a joke taking shape in his mind, and no sooner in his mind than on his tongue.

"Oh, no latitudes," he said, laughing. "I'll leave the latitudes to the ship!"

"Oh, come now," said the Matron, "we don't seem to have hurt him much, do we?"

"I think we'll have to operate on him again and *really* cure him," said Miss Hoyle.

He was going down the front steps, between the potted palmettos, and they all laughed and waved. The wind was cold, very cold for June, and he was glad he had put on his coat. He shivered.

"Damned cold for June!" he said. "Why should it be so cold?"

"East wind," Harry said, arranging the rug over his knees. "Sorry it's an open car, but I believe in fresh air and all that sort of thing. I'll drive slowly. We've got plenty of time."

They coasted gently down the long hill toward Beacon Street, but the road was badly surfaced, and despite Harry's care Mr. Arcularis felt his pain again. He found that he could alleviate it a little by leaning to the right, against the arm-rest, and not breathing too deeply. But how glorious to be out again! How strange and vivid the world looked! The trees had innumerable green fresh leaves—they were all blowing and shifting and turning and flashing in the wind; drops of rainwater fell downward sparkling; the robins were singing their absurd, delicious little four-noted songs; even the street cars looked unusually bright and beautiful, just as they used to look when he was a child and had wanted above all things to be a motorman. He found himself smiling foolishly at everything, foolishly and weakly, and wanted to say something about it to Harry. It was no use, though—he had no strength, and the mere finding of words would be almost more than he could manage. And even if he should succeed in saying it, he would then most likely burst into tears. He shook his head slowly from side to side.

"Ain't it grand?" he said.

"I'll bet it looks good," said Harry.

"Words fail me."

"You wait till you get out to sea. You'll have a swell time."

"Oh, swell! . . . I hope not. I hope it'll be calm."

"Tut tut."

When they passed the Harvard Club Mr. Arcularis made a slow and somewhat painful effort to turn in his seat and look at it. It might be the last chance to see it for a long time. Why this sentimental longing to stare at it, though? There it was, with the great flag blowing in the wind, the Harvard seal now concealed by the swift folds and now revealed, and there were the windows in the library, where he had spent so many delightful hours reading—Plato, and Kipling, and the Lord knows what—and the balconies from which for so many years he had watched the Marathon. Old Talbot might be in there now, sleeping with a book on his knee, hoping forlornly to be interrupted by anyone, for anything.

"Goodbye to the old club," he said.

"The bar will miss you," said Harry, smiling with friendly irony and looking straight ahead.

"But let there be no moaning," said Mr. Arcularis.

"What's *that* a quotation from?"

" 'The Odyssey.' "

In spite of the cold, he was glad of the wind on his face, for it helped to dissipate the feeling of vagueness and dizziness that came over him in a sickening wave from time to time. All of a sudden everything would begin to swim and dissolve, the houses would lean their heads together, he had to close his eyes, and there would be a curious and dreadful humming noise, which at regular intervals rose to a crescendo and then drawlingly subsided again. It was disconcerting. Perhaps he still had a trace of fever. When he got on the ship he would have a glass of whisky. . . . From one of these spells he opened his eyes and found that they were on the ferry, crossing to East Boston. It must have been the ferry's engines that he had heard. From another spell he woke to find himself on the wharf, the car at a standstill beside a pile of yellow packing cases.

"We're here because we're here because we're here," said Harry.

"Because we're here," added Mr. Arcularis.

He dozed in the car while Harry—and what a good friend Harry was!—attended to all the details. He went and came with tickets and passports and baggage checks and porters. And at last he unwrapped Mr. Arcularis from the rugs and led him up the steep gangplank to the deck, and thence by devious windings to a small cold stateroom with a solitary porthole like the eye of a cyclops.

"Here you are," he said, "and now I've got to go. Did you hear the whistle?"

"No."

"Well, you're half asleep. It's sounded the all-ashore. Goodbye, old fellow, and take care of yourself. Bring me back a spray of edelweiss. And send me a picture postcard from the Absolute."

"Will you have it finite or infinite?"

"Oh, infinite. But with your signature on it. Now you'd better turn in for a while and have a nap. Cheerio!"

Mr. Arcularis took his hand and pressed it hard, and once more felt like crying. Absurd! Had he become a child again?

"Goodbye," he said.

He sat down in the little wicker chair, with his overcoat still on, closed his eyes, and listened to the humming of the air in the ventilator. Hurried footsteps ran up and down the corridor. The chair was not too comfortable, and his pain began to bother him again, so he moved, with his coat still on, to the narrow berth and fell asleep. When he woke up, it was dark, and the porthole had been partly opened. He groped for the switch and turned on the light. Then he rang for the steward.

"It's cold in here," he said. "Would you mind closing the port?"

The girl who sat opposite him at dinner was charming. Who was it she reminded him of? Why, of course, the girl at the hospital, the girl with the freckles. Her hair was beautiful, not quite red, not quite gold, nor had it been bobbed; arranged with a sort of graceful untidiness, it made him think of a Melozzo da Forli angel. Her face was freckled, she had a mouth which was both humorous and voluptuous. And she seemed to be alone.

He frowned at the bill of fare and ordered the thick soup.

"No hors d'oeuvres?" asked the steward.

"I think not," said Mr. Arcularis. "They might kill me."

The steward permitted himself to be amused and deposited the menu card on the table against the water bottle. His eyebrows were lifted. As he moved away, the girl followed him with her eyes and smiled.

"I'm afraid you shocked him," she said.

"Impossible," said Mr. Arcularis. "These stewards, they're dead souls. How could they be stewards otherwise? And they think they've seen and known everything. They suffer terribly from the *déjà vu*. Personally, I don't blame them."

"It must be a dreadful sort of life."

"It's because they're dead that they accept it."

"Do you think so?"

"I'm sure of it. I'm enough of a dead soul myself to know the signs!"

"Well, I don't know what you mean by that!"

"But nothing mysterious! I'm just out of hospital, after an operation. I was given up for dead. For six months I had given *myself* up for dead. If you've ever been seriously ill you know the feeling. You have a posthumous feeling—a mild, cynical tolerance for everything and everyone. What is there you haven't seen or done or understood? Nothing."

Mr. Arcularis waved his hands and smiled.

"I wish I could understand you," said the girl, "but I've never been ill in my life."

"Never?"

"Never."

"Good God!"

The torrent of the unexpressed and inexpressible paralyzed him and rendered him speechless. He stared at the girl, wondering who she was and then, realizing that he had perhaps stared too fixedly, averted his gaze, gave a little laugh, rolled a pill of bread between his fingers. After a second or two he allowed himself to look at her again and found her smiling.

"Never pay any attention to invalids," he said, "or they'll drag you to the hospital."

She examined him critically, with her head tilted a little to one side, but with friendliness.

"You don't *look* like an invalid," she said.

Mr. Arcularis thought her charming. His pain ceased to bother him, the disagreeable humming disappeared, or rather, it was dissociated from himself and became merely, as it should be, the sound of the ship's engines, and he began to think the voyage was going to be really delightful. The parson on his right passed him the salt.

"I fear you will need this in your soup," he said.

"Thank you. Is it as bad as that?"

The steward, overhearing, was immediately apologetic and solicitous. He explained that on the first day everything was at sixes and sevens. The girl looked up at him and asked him a question.

"Do you think we'll have a good voyage?" she said.

He was passing the hot rolls to the parson, removing the napkins from them with a deprecatory finger.

"Well, madam, I don't like to be a Jeremiah, but——"

"Oh, come," said the parson, "I hope we have no Jeremiahs."

"What do you mean?" said the girl.

Mr. Arcularis ate his soup with gusto—it was nice and hot.

"Well, maybe I shouldn't say it, but there's a corpse on board, going to Ireland; and I never yet knew a voyage with a corpse on board that we didn't have bad weather."

"Why, steward, you're just superstitious! What nonsense!"

"That's a very ancient superstition," said Mr. Arcularis. "I've heard it many times. Maybe it's true. Maybe we'll be wrecked. And what does it matter, after all?" He was very bland.

"Then let's be wrecked," said the parson coldly.

Nevertheless, Mr. Arcularis felt a shudder go through him on hearing the steward's remark. A corpse in the hold—a coffin? Perhaps it was true. Perhaps some disaster would befall them. There might be fogs. There might be icebergs. He thought of all the wrecks of which he had read. There was the *Titanic*, which he had read about in the warm newspaper room at the Harvard Club—it had seemed dreadfully real, even there. That band, playing "Nearer My God to Thee" on the after-deck while the ship sank! It was one of the darkest of his memories. And the *Empress of Ireland*—all those poor people trapped in the smoking room, with only one door between them and life, and that door locked for the night by the deck steward, and the deck steward nowhere to be found! He shivered, feeling a draft, and turned to the parson.

"How do these strange delusions arise?" he said.

The parson looked at him searchingly, appraisingly—from chin to forehead, from forehead to chin—and Mr. Arcularis, feeling uncomfortable, straightened his tie.

"From nothing but fear," said the parson. "Nothing on earth but fear."

"How strange!" said the girl.

Mr. Arcularis again looked at her—she had lowered her face—and again tried to think of whom she reminded him. It wasn't only the little freckle-faced girl at the hospital—both of them had reminded him of someone else. Someone far back in his life: remote, beautiful, lovely. But he couldn't think. The meal came to an end, they all rose, the ship's orchestra played a feeble foxtrot, and Mr. Arcularis, once more alone, went to the bar to have his whisky. The room was stuffy, and the ship's engines were both audible and palpable. The humming and throbbing oppressed him, the rhythm seemed to be the rhythm of his own pain, and after a short time he found his way, with slow steps, holding on to the walls in his moments of weakness and dizziness, to his forlorn and white little room. The port had been—thank God!—closed for the night; it was cold enough anyway. The white and blue ribbons fluttered from the ventilator, the bottle and glasses clicked and clucked as the ship swayed gently to the long, slow motion of the sea. It was all very peculiar—it was all like something he had experienced somewhere before. What was it? Where was it? . . . He untied his tie, looking at his face in the glass, and wondered, and from time to time put his hand to his side to hold in the pain. It wasn't at Portsmouth, in his childhood, nor at Salem, nor in the rose garden at his Aunt Julia's, nor in the schoolroom at Cambridge. It was something very queer, very intimate, very precious. The jackstones, the Sunday-school cards which he had loved when he was a child. . . . He fell asleep.

The sense of time was already hopelessly confused. One hour was like another, the sea looked always the same, morning was indistinguishable from afternoon—and was it Tuesday or Wednesday? Mr. Arcularis was sitting in the smoking room, in his favorite corner, watching the parson teach Miss Dean to play chess. On the deck outside he could see the people passing and repassing in their restless round of the ship. The red jacket went by, then the black hat with the white feather, then the purple scarf, the brown tweed coat, the Bulgarian mustache, the monocle, the Scotch cap with fluttering ribbons, and in no time at all the red jacket again, dipping past the windows with its own peculiar rhythm, followed once more by the black hat and the purple scarf. How odd to reflect on the fixed little orbits of these things—as definite and profound, perhaps, as the orbits of the stars, and as important to God or the Absolute. There was a kind of tyranny in this fixedness, too—to think of it too much made one uncomfortable. He closed his eyes for a moment, to avoid seeing for the fortieth time the Bulgarian mustache and the pursuing monocle. The parson was explaining the movements of knights. Two forward and one to the side. Eight possible moves, always to the opposite color from that on which the piece stands. Two forward and one to the side: Miss Dean repeated the words several times with reflective emphasis. Here, too, was the terrifying fixed curve of the infinite, the creeping curve of logic which at last must become the final signpost at the edge of nothing. After that—the deluge. The great white light of annihilation. The bright flash of death. . . . Was it merely the sea which made these abstractions so insistent, so intrusive? The mere notion of *orbit* had somehow become extraordinarily naked; and to rid himself of the discomfort and also to forget a little the pain which bothered his side whenever he sat down, he walked slowly and carefully into the writing room, and examined a pile of superannuated magazines and catalogues of travel. The bright colors amused him, the photographs of remote islands and mountains, savages in sampans or sarongs or both—it was all very far off and delightful, like something in a dream or a fever. But he found that he was too tired to read and was incapable of concentration. Dreams! Yes, that reminded him. That rather alarming business—sleep-walking!

Later in the evening—at what hour he didn't know—he was telling Miss Dean about it, as he had intended to do. They were sitting in deck chairs on the sheltered side. The sea was black, and there was a cold wind. He wished they had chosen to sit in the lounge.

Miss Dean was extremely pretty—no, beautiful. She looked at him, too, in a very strange and lovely way, with something of inquiry, something of sympathy, something of affection. It seemed as if, between the question and the answer, they had sat thus for a very long time, exchanging an unspoken secret, simply looking at each other quietly and kindly. Had an hour or two passed? And was it at all necessary to speak?

"No," she said, "I never have."

She breathed into the low words a note of interrogation and gave him a slow smile.

"That's the funny part of it. I never had either until last night. Never in my life. I hardly ever even dream. And it really rather frightens me."

"Tell me about it, Mr. Arcularis."

"I dreamed at first that I was walking, alone, in a wide plain covered with snow. It was growing dark, I was very cold, my feet were frozen and numb, and I was lost. I came then to a signpost—at first it seemed to me there was nothing on it. Nothing but ice. Just before it grew finally dark, however, I made out on it the one word 'Polaris.'"

"The Pole Star."

"Yes—and you see, I didn't myself know that. I looked it up only this morning. I suppose I must have seen it somewhere? And of course it rhymes with my name."

"Why, so it does!"

"Anyway, it gave me—in the dream—an awful feeling of despair, and the dream changed. This time, I dreamed I was standing *outside* my stateroom in the little dark corridor, or *cul-de-sac*, and trying to find the door-handle to let myself in. I was in my pajamas, and again I was very cold. And at this point I woke up. . . . The extraordinary thing is that's exactly where I was!"

"Good heavens. How strange!"

"Yes. And now the question is, *Where had I been?* I was frightened, when I came to—not unnaturally. For among other things I *did* have, quite definitely, the feeling that I *had been* somewhere. Somewhere where it was very cold. It doesn't sound very proper. Suppose I had been seen!"

"That might have been awkward," said Miss Dean.

"Awkward! It might indeed. It's very singular. I've never done such a thing before. It's this sort of thing that reminds one—rather wholesomely, perhaps, don't you think?"—and Mr. Arcularis gave a nervous little laugh—"how extraordinarily little we know about the workings of our own minds or souls. After all, what *do* we know?"

"Nothing—nothing—nothing—nothing," said Miss Dean slowly.

"*Absolutely* nothing."

Their voices had dropped, and again they were silent; and again they looked at each other gently and sympathetically, as if for the exchange of something unspoken and perhaps unspeakable. Time ceased. The orbit—so it seemed to Mr. Arcularis—once more became pure, became absolute. And once more he found himself wondering who it was that Miss Dean—Clarice Dean—reminded him of. Long ago and far away. Like those pictures of the islands and mountains. The little freckle-faced girl at the hospital was merely, as it were, the stepping stone, the signpost, or, as in algebra, the "equals" sign. But what was it they both "equaled"? The jackstones came again into his mind and his Aunt Julia's rose garden—at sunset; but this was ridiculous. It couldn't be simply that they reminded him of his childhood! And yet why not?

They went into the lounge. The ship's orchestra, in the oval-shaped balcony among faded palms, was playing the finale of "Cavalleria Rusticana," playing it badly.

"Good God!" said Mr. Arcularis, "can't I ever escape from that damned sentimental tune? It's the last thing I heard in America, and the last thing I *want* to hear."

"But don't you like it?"

"As music? No! It moves me too much, but in the wrong way."

"What, exactly, do you mean?"

"Exactly? Nothing. When I heard it at the hospital—when was it?—it made me feel like crying. Three old Italians tootling it in the rain. I suppose, like most people, I'm afraid of my feelings."

"Are they so dangerous?"

"Now then, young woman! Are you pulling my leg?"

The stewards had rolled away the carpets, and the passengers were beginning to dance. Miss Dean accepted the invitation of a young officer, and Mr. Arcularis watched them with envy. Odd, that last exchange of remarks—very odd; in fact, everything was odd. Was it possible that they were falling in love? Was that what it was all about—all these concealed references and recollections? He had read of such things. But at his age! And with girl of twenty-one! It was ridiculous.

After an amused look at his old friend Polaris from the open door on the sheltered side, he went to bed.

The rhythm of the ship's engines was positively a persecution. It gave one no rest, it followed one like the Hound of Heaven, it drove on, out into space and across the Milky Way and then back home by way of Betelgeuse. It was cold there, too. Mr. Arcularis, making the round trip by way of

Betelgeuse and Polaris, sparkled with frost. He felt like a Christmas tree. Icicles on his fingers and icicles on his toes. He tinkled and spangled in the void, hallooed to the waste echoes, rounded the buoy on the verge of the Unknown, and tacked glitteringly homeward. The wind whistled. He was barefooted. Snowflakes and tinsel blew past him. Next time, by George, he would go farther still—for altogether it was rather a lark. Forward into the untrodden! as somebody said. Some intrepid explorer of his own backyard, probably, some middle-aged professor with an umbrella: those were the fellows for courage! But give us time, thought Mr. Arcularis, give us time, and we will bring back with us the night-rime of the Obsolute. Or was it Absolete? If only there weren't this perpetual throbbing, this iteration of sound, like a pain, these circles and repetitions of light—the feeling as of everything coiling inward to a center of misery. . . .

Suddenly it was dark, and he was lost. He was groping, he touched the cold, white, slippery woodwork with his fingernails, looking for an electric switch. The throbbing, of course, was the throbbing of the ship. But he was almost home—almost home. Another corner to round, a door to be opened, and there he would be. Safe and sound. Safe in his father's home.

It was at this point that he woke up: in the corridor that led to the dining saloon. Such pure terror, such horror, seized him as he had never known. His heart felt as if it would stop beating. His back was toward the dining saloon; apparently he had just come from it. He was in his pajamas. The corridor was dim, all but two lights having been turned out for the night, and—thank God!—deserted. Not a soul, not a sound. He was perhaps fifty yards from his room. With luck he could get to it unseen. Holding tremulously to the rail that ran along the wall, a brown, greasy rail, he began to creep his way forward. He felt very weak, very dizzy, and his thoughts refused to concentrate. Vaguely he remembered Miss Dean—Clarice—and the freckled girl, as if they were one and the same person. But he wasn't in the hospital, he was on the ship. Of course. How absurd. The Great Circle. Here we are, old fellow . . . steady round the corner . . . hold hard to your umbella. . . .

In his room, with the door safely shut behind him, Mr. Arcularis broke into a cold sweat. He had no sooner got into his bunk, shivering, than he heard the night watchman pass.

"But where"—he thought, closing his eyes in agony—"have I been? . . ."

A dreadful idea had occurred to him.

"It's nothing serious—how could it be anything serious? Of course, it's nothing serious," said Mr. Arcularis.

"No, it's nothing serious," said the ship's doctor urbanely.

"I knew you'd think so. But just the same—"

"Such a condition is the result of worry," said the doctor. "Are you worried—do you mind telling me—about something? Just try to think."

"Worried?"

Mr. Arcularis knitted his brows. *Was* there something? Some little mosquito of a cloud disappearing into the southwest, the northeast? Some little gnat-song of despair? But no, that was all over. All over.

"Nothing," he said, "nothing whatever."

"It's very strange," said the doctor.

"Strange! I should say so. I've come to sea for a rest, not for a nightmare! What about a bromide?"

"Well, I can give you a bromide, Mr. Arcularis—"

"Then, please, if you don't mind, give me a bromide."

He carried the little phial hopefully to his stateroom, and took a dose at once. He could see the sun through his porthole. It looked northern and pale and small, like a little peppermint, which was only normal enough, for the latitude was changing with every hour. But why was it that doctors were all alike? And all, for that matter, like his father, or that other fellow at the hospital? Smythe, his name was. Doctor Smythe. A nice, dry little fellow, and they said he was a writer. Wrote poetry, or something like that. Poor fellow—disappointed. Like everybody else. Crouched in there, in his cabin, night after night, writing blank verse or something—all about the stars and flowers and love and death; ice and the sea and the infinite; time and tide—well, every man to his own taste.

"But it's nothing serious," said Mr. Arcularis, later, to the parson. "How could it be?"

"Why, of course not, my dear fellow," said the parson, patting his back. "How could it be?"

"I know it isn't and yet I worry about it."

"It would be ridiculous to think it serious," said the parson. Mr. Arcularis shivered; it was colder than ever. It was said that they were near icebergs. For a few hours in the morning there had been a fog, and the siren had blown—devastatingly—at three-minute intervals. Icebergs caused fog—he knew that.

"These things always come," said the parson, "from a sense of guilt. You feel guilty about something. I won't be so rude as to inquire what it is. But if you could rid yourself of the sense of guilt—"

And later still, when the sky was pink:

"But is it anything to worry about?" said Miss Dean. "Really?"

"No. I suppose not."

"Then don't worry. We aren't children any longer!"

"Aren't we? I wonder!"

They leaned, shoulders touching, on the deck-rail, and looked at the sea, which was multitudinously incarnadined. Mr. Arcularis scanned the horizon in vain for an iceberg.

"Anyway," he said, "the colder we are the less we feel!"

"I hope that's no reflection on *you*," said Miss Dean.

"Here . . . feel my hand," said Mr. Arcularis.

"Heaven knows, it's cold!"

"It's been to Polaris and back! No wonder."

"Poor thing, poor thing!"

"Warm it."

"May I?"

"You can."

"I'll try."

Laughing, she took his hand between both of hers, one palm under and one palm over, and began rubbing it briskly. The decks were deserted, no one was near them, everyone was dressing for dinner. The sea grew darker, the wind blew colder.

"I wish I could remember who you are," he said.

"And you—who are you?"

"Myself."

"Then perhaps *I* am yourself."

"Don't be metaphysical!"

"But I *am* metaphysical!"

She laughed, withdrew, pulled the light coat about her shoulders.

The bugle blew the summons for dinner—"The Roast Beef of Old England"—and they walked together along the darkening deck toward the door, from which a shaft of soft light fell across the deck rail. As they stepped over the brass door sill Mr. Arcularis felt the throb of the engines again; he put his hand quickly to his side.

"*Auf wiedersehen,*" he said. "*Tomorrow and tomorrow and tomorrow.*"

Mr. Arcularis was finding it impossible, absolutely impossible, to keep warm. A cold fog surrounded the ship, had done so, it seemed, for days. The sun had all but disappeared, the transition from day to night was almost unnoticeable. The ship, too, seemed scarcely to be moving—it was as if anchored among walls of ice and rime. Monstrous that, merely because it was June, and supposed, therefore, to be warm, the ship's authorities should consider it unnecessary to turn on the heat! By day, he wore his heavy coat and sat shivering in the corner of the smoking room. His teeth chattered, his hands were blue. By night, he heaped blankets on his bed, closed the porthole's black eye against the sea, and drew the yellow curtains across it, but in vain. Somehow, despite everything, the fog crept in, and the icy fingers touched his throat. The steward, questioned about it, merely said, "Icebergs." Of course—any fool knew that. But how long, in God's name, was it going to last? They surely ought to be past the Grand Banks by this time! And surely it wasn't necessary to sail to England by way of Greenland and Iceland!

Miss Dean—Clarice—was sympathetic.

"It's simply because," she said, "your vitality has been lowered by your illness. You can't expect to be your normal self so soon after an operation! When *was* your operation, by the way?"

Mr. Arcularis considered. Strange—he couldn't be quite sure. It was all a little vague—his sense of time had disappeared.

"Heaven knows!" he said. "Centuries ago. When I was a tadpole and you were a fish. I should think it must have been at about the time of the Battle of Teutoburg Forest. Or perhaps when I was a Neanderthal man with a club!"

"Are you sure it wasn't farther back still?"

What did she mean by that?

"Not at all. Obviously, we've been on this damned ship for ages—for eras—for æons. And even on this ship, you must remember, I've had plenty of time, in my nocturnal wanderings, to go several times to Orion and back. I'm thinking, by the way, of going farther still. There's a nice little star off to the left, as you round Betelgeuse, which looks as if it might be right at the edge. The last outpost of the finite. I think I'll have a look at it and bring you back a frozen rime-feather."

"It would melt when you got it back."

"Oh, no, it wouldn't—not on *this* ship!"

Clarice laughed.

"I wish I could go with you," she said.

"If only you would! If only—"

He broke off his sentence and looked hard at her—how lovely she was, and how desirable! No such woman had ever before come into his life; there had been no one with whom he had at once felt so profound a sympathy and understanding. It was a miracle, simply—a miracle. No need to put his arm around her or to kiss her—delightful as such small vulgarities would be. He had only to look at her, and to feel, gazing into those extraordinary eyes, that she knew him, had always known him. It was as if, indeed, she might be his own soul.

But as he looked thus at her, reflecting, he noticed that she was frowning.

"What is it?" he said.

She shook her head, slowly.

"I don't know."

"Tell me."

"Nothing. It just occurred to me that perhaps you weren't looking quite so well."

Mr. Arcularis was startled. He straightened himself up.

"What nonsense! Of course, this pain bothers me—and I feel astonishingly weak—"

"It's more than that—much more than that. Something is worrying you horribly." She paused, and then with an air of challenging him, added, "Tell me, did you—"

Her eyes were suddenly asking him blazingly the question he had been afraid of. He flinched, caught his breath, looked away. But it was no use, as he knew; he would have to tell her. He had known all along that he would have to tell her.

"Clarice," he said—and his voice broke in spite of his effort to control it—"it's killing me, it's ghastly! Yes, I did."

His eyes filled with tears, he saw that her own had done so also. She put her hand on his arm.

"I knew," she said. "I knew. But tell me."

"It's happened twice again—*twice*—and each time I was farther away. The same dream of going round a star, the same terrible coldness and helplessness. That awful whistling curve. . . ." He shuddered.

"And when you woke up"—she spoke quietly—"where were you when you woke up? Don't be afraid!"

"The first time I was at the farther end of the dining saloon. I had my hand on the door that leads into the pantry."

"I see. Yes. And the next time?"

Mr. Arcularis wanted to close his eyes in terror—he felt as if he were going mad. His lips moved before he could speak, and when at last he did speak it was in a voice so low as to be almost a whisper.

"I was at the bottom of the stairway that leads down from the pantry to the hold, past the refrigerating plant. It was dark, and I was crawling on my hands and knees . . . *crawling on my hands and knees!* . . ."

"Oh!" she said, and again, "Oh!"

He began to tremble violently; he felt the hand on his arm trembling also. And then he watched a look of unmistakable horror come slowly into

Clarice's eyes, and a look of understanding, as if she saw. . . . She tightened her hold on his arm.

"Do you think. . . ." she whispered.

They stared at each other.

"I know," he said. "And so do you. . . . Twice more—three times—and I'll be looking down into an empty. . . ."

It was then that they first embraced—then, at the edge of the infinite, at the last signpost of the finite. They clung together desperately, forlornly, weeping as they kissed each other, staring hard one moment and closing their eyes the next. Passionately, passionately, she kissed him, as if she were indeed trying to give him her warmth, her life.

"But what nonsense!" she cried, leaning back, and holding his face between her hands, her hands which were wet with his tears. "What nonsense! It can't be!"

"It is," said Mr. Arcularis slowly.

"But how do you know? . . . How do you know where the—"

For the first time Mr. Arcularis smiled.

"Don't be afraid, darling—you mean the coffin?"

"How could you know where it is?"

"I don't need to," said Mr. Arcularis. . . . "I'm already almost there."

Before they separated for the night, in the smoking room, they had several whisky cocktails.

"We must make it gay!" Mr. Arcularis said. "Above all, we must make it gay. Perhaps even now it will turn out to be nothing but a nightmare from which both of us will wake! And even at the worst, at my present rate of travel, I ought to need two more nights! It's a long way, still, to that little star."

The parson passed them at the door.

"What! turning in so soon?" he said. "I was hoping for a game of chess."

"Yes, both turning in. But tomorrow?"

"Tomorrow, then, Miss Dean! And good night!"

"Good night."

They walked once round the deck, then leaned on the railing and stared into the fog. It was thicker and whiter than ever. The ship was moving barely perceptibly, the rhythm of the engines was slower, more subdued and remote, and at regular intervals, mournfully, came the long reverberating cry of the foghorn. The sea was calm, and lapped only very tenderly against the side of the ship, the sound coming up to them clearly, however, because of the profound stillness.

" 'On such a night as this—' " quoted Mr. Arcularis grimly.

"'On such a night as this–'"

Their voices hung suspended in the night, time ceased for them, for an eternal instant they were happy. When at last they parted it was by tacit agreement on a note of the ridiculous.

"Be a good boy and take your bromide!" she said.

"Yes, mother, I'll take my medicine!"

In his stateroom, he mixed himself a strong potion of bromide, a very strong one, and got into bed. He would have no trouble in falling asleep; he felt more tired, more supremely exhausted, than he had ever been in his life; nor had bed ever seemed so delicious. And that long, magnificent, delirious swoop of dizziness . . . the Great Circle . . . the swift pathway to Arcturus. . .

It was all as before, but infinitely more rapid. Never had Mr. Arcularis achieved such phenomenal, such supernatural, speed. In no time at all he was beyond the moon, shot past the North Star as if it were standing still (which perhaps it was?), swooped in a long, bright curve round the Pleiades, shouted his frosty greetings to Betelgeuse, and was off to the little blue star which pointed the way to the Unknown. Forward into the untrodden! Courage, old man, and hold on to your umbrella! Have you got your garters on? Mind your hat! In no time at all we'll be back to Clarice with the frozen rime-feather, the time-feather, the snowflake of the Absolute, the Obsolete. If only we don't wake . . . if only we needn't wake . . . if only we don't wake in that–in that–time and space . . . somewhere or nowhere . . . cold and dark . . . "Cavalleria Rusticana" sobbing among the palms; if a lonely . . . if only . . . the coffers of the poor–not coffers, not coffers, not coffers, Oh, God, not coffers, but light, delight, supreme white and brightness, whirling lightness above all–and freezing–freezing–freezing. . . .

At this point in the void the surgeon's last effort to save Mr. Arcularis's life had failed. He stood back from the operating table and made a tired gesture with a rubber-gloved hand.

"It's all over," he said. "As I expected."

He looked at Miss Hoyle, whose gaze was downward, at the basin she held. There was a moment's stillness, a pause, a brief flight of unexchanged comment, and then the ordered life of the hospital was resumed.

MORNING SONG FROM "SENLIN"

It is morning, Senlin says, and in the morning
When the light drips through the shutters like the dew,
I arise, I face the sunrise,
And do the things my fathers learned to do.
Stars in the purple dusk above the rooftops
Pale in a saffron mist and seem to die,
And I myself on a swiftly tilting planet
Stand before a glass and tie my tie.

Vine-leaves tap my window,
Dew-drops sing to the garden stones,
The robin chirps in the chinaberry tree
Repeating three clear tones.

It is morning. I stand by the mirror
And tie my tie once more.
While waves far off in a pale rose twilight
Crash on a white sand shore.
I stand by a mirror and comb my hair:
How small and white my face!—
The green earth tilts through a sphere of air
And bathes in a flame of space.
There are houses hanging above the stars
And stars hung under a sea . . .
And a sun far off in a shell of silence
Dapples my walls for me. . . .

It is morning, Senlin says, and in the morning
Should I not pause in the light to remember God?
Upright and firm I stand on a star unstable,
He is immense and lonely as a cloud.
I will dedicate this moment before my mirror
To him alone, for him I will comb my hair.
Accept these humble offerings, clouds of silence!
I will think of you as I descend the stair.

Vine-leaves tap my window,
The snail-track shines on the stones;
Dew-drops flash from the chinaberry tree
Repeating two clear tones.

It is morning, I awake from a bed of silence,
Shining I rise from the starless waters of sleep.
The walls are about me still as in the evening,
I am the same, and the same name still I keep.
The earth revolves with me, yet makes no motion,
The stars pale silently in a coral sky.
In a whistling void I stand before my mirror,
Unconcerned, and tie my tie.

There are horses neighing on far-off hills
Tossing their long white manes,
And mountains flash in the rose-white dusk,
Their shoulders black with rains. . . .

It is morning, I stand by the mirror
And surprise my soul once more;
The blue air rushes above my ceiling,
There are suns beneath my floor. . . .

. . . It is morning, Senlin says, I ascend from darkness
And depart on the winds of space for I know not where;
My watch is wound, a key is in my pocket,
And the sky is darkened as I descend the stair.
There are shadows across the windows, clouds in heaven,
And a god among the stars; and I will go
Thinking of him as I might think of daybreak
And humming a tune I know. . . .

Vine-leaves tap at the window,
Dew-drops sing to the garden stones,
The robin chirps in the chinaberry tree
Repeating three clear tones.

PORTRAIT OF A GIRL

This is the shape of the leaf, and this of the flower,
And this the pale bole of the tree
Which watches its bough in a pool of unwavering water
In a land we never shall see.

The thrush on the bough is silent, the dew falls softly,
In the evening is hardly a sound. . . .
And the three beautiful pilgrims who come here together
Touch lightly the dust of the ground.

Touch it with feet that trouble the dust but as wings do,
Come shyly together, are still,
Like dancers who wait in a pause of the music, for music
The exquisite silence to fill . . .

This is the thought of the first, and this of the second,
And this the grave thought of the third:
"Linger we thus for a moment, palely expectant,
And silence will end, and the bird

"Sing the pure phrase, sweet phrase, clear phrase in the twilight
To fill the blue bell of the world;
And we, who on music so leaflike have drifted together,
Leaflike apart shall be whirled

"Into what but the beauty of silence, silence forever? . . ."
. . . This is the shape of the tree,
And the flower and the leaf, and the three pale beautiful pilgrims:
This is what you are to me.

ROBERT BENCHLEY

[1889–1945]

Though he began as a drama critic, Robert Charles Benchley found the human drama so curious and incalculable that he became a humorist, a wry recorder of the troubles of the average man beset by everyday problems. Benchley was well fitted to do this because he himself suffered from a curious sense of inadequacy—someone said he was misfortune's fool, a fool who, somehow, made a fortune out of his mishaps.

Benchley was born September 15, 1889, in Worcester, Massachusetts. He never intended to be a humorist. After receiving his B.A. from Harvard in his twenty-third year he wanted to write a life of Queen Anne and become a social service worker. Instead, he translated French catalogues, was personnel manager for a paper company, was given a job in the advertising department of a magazine and, in his late twenties, became a journalist. With Dorothy Parker as his coworker, he edited Vanity Fair*, became a critic of the drama and a contributor of* The New Yorker*. In his thirties he discovered that he was* *not only an actor but also a born master of ceremonies. He had his own droll motion picture series and a radio program, and in 1936 he won a film award for a memorable piece of mock-research, "How to Sleep." Many of his later years were spent in Hollywood. He died suddenly of a cerebral hemorrhage November 21, 1945.*

Benchley's gift for parody and absurd non sequiturs is illustrated by the titles of such books as My Ten Years in a Quandary and How They Grew, 20,000 Leagues Under the Sea, or David Copperfield, *and* Inside Benchley. *His ability to communicate utter bewilderment is at its best in* The Treasurer's Report, *which began as a parlor trick played by Benchley and became a favorite selection in anthologies devoted to sheer humor.*

THE TREASURER'S REPORT

The report is delivered by an Assistant Treasurer who has been called in to pinch-hit for the regular Treasurer who is ill. He is not a very good public-speaker, this assistant, but after a few minutes of confusion is caught up by the spell of his own oratory and is hard to stop.

I SHALL TAKE but a very few moments of your time this evening, for I realize that you would much rather be listening to this interesting entertainment than to a dry financial statement . . . but I *am* reminded of a story—which you have probably all of you heard.

It seems that there were these two Irishmen walking down the street when they came to a—oh, I should have said in the first place that the parrot which was hanging out in *front* of the store—or rather belonging to one of these two fellows—the *first* Irishman, that is—was—well, *anyway*, this parrot—

(*After a slight cogitation, he realizes that, for all practical purposes, the story is as good as lost; so he abandons it entirely and, stepping forward, drops his facile, story-telling manner and assumes a quite spurious business-like air.*)

Now, in connection with reading this report, there are one or two points which Dr. Murnie wanted brought up in connection with it, and he has asked me to bring them up in connec—to bring them up.

In the first place, there is the question of the work which we are trying to do up there at our little place at Silver Lake, a work which we feel not only fills a very definite need in the community but also fills a very definite need—er—in the community. I don't think that many members of the Society realize just how big the work is that we are trying to do up there. For instance, I don't think that it is generally known that most of our boys are between the age of fourteen. We feel that, by taking the boy at this age, we can get closer to his real nature—for a boy *has* a very real nature, you may be sure—and bring him into closer touch not only with the school, the parents, and with each other, but also with the town in which they live, the country to whose flag they pay allegiance, and to the—ah—(*trailing off*) town in which they live.

Now the fourth point which Dr. Murnie wanted brought up was that in connection with the installation of the new furnace last Fall. There seems to have been considerable talk going around about this not having been done quite as economically as it might—have—been—done, when, as a matter of fact, the whole thing *was* done just as economically as possible —in fact, even *more* so. I have here a report of the Furnace Committee, showing just how the whole thing was handled from start to finish.

(*Reads from report, with considerable initial difficulty with the stiff covers.*)

Bids were submitted by the following firms of furnace contractors, with a clause stating that if we did not engage a firm to do the work for us we should pay them nothing for submitting the bids. This clause alone saved us a great deal of money.

The following firms, then, submitted bids:

Merkle, Wybigant Co., the Eureka Dust Bin and Shaker Co., The Elite Furnace Shop, and Harris, Birnbauer and Harris. The bid of Merkle, Wybigant being the lowest, Harris Birnbauer were selected to do the job.

(*Here a page is evidently missing from the report, and a hurried search is carried on through all the pages, without result.*)

Well, that pretty well clears up that end of the work.

Those of you who contributed so generously last year to the floating hospital have probably wondered what became of the money. I was speaking on this subject only last week at our up-town branch, and, after the meeting, a dear little old lady, dressed all in lavender, came up on the platform, and, laying her hand on my arm, said: 'Mr. So-and-so (calling me by name), Mr. So-and-so, what the hell did you do with all the money we gave you last year?' Well, I just laughed and pushed her off the platform, but it has occurred to the committee that perhaps some of you, like that little old lady, would be interested in knowing the disposition of the funds.

Now, Mr. Rossiter, unfortunately our treasurer—or rather Mr. Rossiter our *treasurer, unfortunately* is confined at his home tonight with a bad head-cold and I have been asked (*he hears someone whispering at him from the wings, but decides to ignore it*) and I have been asked if I would (*the whisperer will not be denied, so he goes over to the entrance and receives a brief message, returning beaming and laughing to himself*). Well, the joke seems to be on *me!* Mr. Rossiter has *pneumonia!*

Following, then, is a summary of the Treasurer's Report:

(*Reads, in a very businesslike manner.*)

During the year 1929—and by that is meant 1928—the Choral Society received the following in donations:

B. L. G.	$500
G. K. M.	500
Lottie and Nellie W.	500
In memory of a happy summer at Rye Beach	10
Proceeds of a sale of coats and hats left in the boat-house	14.55
And then the Junior League gave a performance of 'Pinafore' for the benefit of the Fund which, unfortunately, resulted in a deficit of	300
Then, from dues and charges	2,354.75
And, following the installation of the new furnace, a saving in coal amounting to $374.75—which made Dr. Murnie very happy, you may be sure.	
Making a total of receipts amounting to	$3,645.75

This is all, of course, reckoned as of June.

In the matter of expenditures, the Club has not been so fortunate. There was the unsettled condition of business, and the late Spring, to contend with, resulting in the following—er—rather discouraging figures, I am afraid.

Expenditures	$23,574.85
Then there was a loss, owing to—several things—of	3,326.70
Car-fare	4,452.25
And then, Mrs. Rawlins' expense account, when she went down to see the work they are doing in Baltimore, came to $256.50, but I am sure that you will all agree that it was worth it to find out—er—what they are doing in Baltimore.	

And then, under the general head of Odds and Ends....... 2,537.50
Making a total disbursement of.........................
(*hurriedly*) $416,546.75

or a net deficit of—ah—several thousand dollars.

Now, these figures bring us down only to October. In October my sister was married, and the house was all torn up, and in the general confusion we lost track of the figures of May and August. All those wishing the *approximate* figures for May and August, however, may obtain them from me in the vestry after the dinner, where I will be with pledge cards for those of you who wish to subscribe over and above your annual dues, and I hope that each and every one of you here tonight will look deep into his heart and (*archly*) into his pocketbook, and see if he cannot find it there to help us to put this thing over with a bang (*accompanied by a wholly ineffectual gesture representing a bang*) and to help and make this just the biggest and best year the Armenians have ever had. . . . I thank you.

(*Exits, bumping into proscenium.*)

THE TOOTH, THE WHOLE TOOTH, AND NOTHING BUT THE TOOTH

SOME WELL-KNOWN SAYING (it doesn't make much difference what) is proved by the fact that everyone likes to talk about his experiences at the dentist's. For years and years little articles like this have been written on the subject, little jokes like some that I shall presently make have been made, and people in general have been telling other people just what emotions they experience when they crawl into the old red plush guillotine.

They like to explain to each other how they feel when the dentist puts "that buzzer thing" against their bicuspids, and, if sufficiently pressed, they will describe their sensations on mouthing a rubber dam.

"I'll tell you what I hate," they will say with great relish, "when he takes that little nut-pick and begins to scrape. Ugh!"

"Oh, I'll tell you what's worse than that," says the friend, not to be outdone, "when he is poking around careless-like, and strikes a nerve. Wow!"

And if there are more than two people at the experience-meeting, everyone will chip in and tell what he or she considers to be the worst phase of the dentist's work, all present enjoying the narration hugely and none so much as the narrator who has suffered so.

This sort of thing has been going on ever since the first mammoth gold tooth was hung out as a bait to folks in search of a good time. (By the way, when *did* the present obnoxious system of dentistry begin? It can't be so very long ago that the electric auger was invented, and where would a dentist be without an electric auger? Yet you never hear of Amalgam Filling Day, or any other anniversary in the dental year. There must be a conspiracy of silence on the part of the trade to keep hidden the names of the men who are responsible for all this.)

However many years it may be that dentists have been plying their trade, in all that time people have never tired of talking about their teeth. This is probably due to the inscrutable workings of Nature who is always supplying new teeth to talk about.

As a matter of fact, the actual time and suffering in the chair is only a fraction of the gross expenditure connected with the affair. The preliminary period, about which nobody talks, is much the worse. This dates from the discovery of the wayward tooth and extends to the moment when the dentist places his foot on the automatic hoist which jacks you up into range. Giving gas for tooth-extraction is all very humane in its way, but the time for anaesthetics is when the patient first decides that he must go to the dentist. From then on, until the first excavation is started, should be shrouded in oblivion.

There is probably no moment more appalling than that in which the tongue, running idly over the teeth in a moment of care-free play, comes suddenly upon the ragged edge of a space from which the old familiar filling has disappeared. The world stops and you look meditatively up to the corner of the ceiling. Then quickly you draw your tongue away, and try to laugh the affair off, saying to yourself:

"Stuff and nonsense, my good fellow! There is nothing the matter with your tooth. Your nerves are upset after a hard day's work, that's all."

Having decided this to your satisfaction, you slyly, and with a poor attempt at being casual, slide the tongue back along the line of adjacent teeth, hoping against hope that it will reach the end without mishap.

But there it is! There can be no doubt about it this time. The tooth simply has got to be filled by someone, and the only person who can fill it with anything permanent is a dentist. You wonder if you might not be able to patch it up yourself for the time being,—a year or so—perhaps with a little spruce-gum and a coating of new-skin. It is fairly far back, and wouldn't have to be a very sightly job.

But this has an impracticable sound, even to you. You might want to eat some peanut-brittle (you never can tell when someone might offer you peanut-brittle these days), and the new-skin, while serviceable enough in the case of cream soups and custards, couldn't be expected to stand up under heavy crunching.

So you admit that, since the thing has got to be filled, it might as well be a dentist who does the job.

This much decided, all that is necessary is to call him up and make an appointment.

Let us say that this resolve is made on Tuesday. That afternoon you start to look up the dentist's number in the telephone-book. A great wave of relief sweeps over you when you discover that it isn't there. How can you be expected to make an appointment with a man who hasn't got a telephone? And how can you have a tooth filled without making an appointment? The whole thing is impossible, and that's all there is to it. God knows you did your best.

On Wednesday there is a slightly more insistent twinge, owing to bad management of a sip of ice-water. You decide that you simply must get in touch with that dentist when you get back from lunch. But you know how those things are. First one thing and then another came up, and a man came in from Providence who had to be shown around the office, and by the time you had a minute to yourself it was five o'clock. And, anyway, the tooth didn't bother you again. You wouldn't be surprised if, by being careful, you could get along with it as it is until the end of the week when you will have more time. A man has to think of his business, after all, and what is a little personal discomfort in the shape of an unfilled tooth to the satisfaction of work well done in the office?

By Saturday morning you are fairly reconciled to going ahead, but it is only a half day and probably he has no appointments left, anyway. Monday is really the time. You can begin the week afresh. After all, Monday is really the logical day to start in going to the dentist.

Bright and early Monday morning you make another try at the telephone-book, and find, to your horror, that some time between now and last Tuesday the dentist's name and number have been inserted into the directory. There it is. There is no getting around it: "Burgess, Jas. Kendal, DDS. . . . Courtland—2654." There is really nothing left to do but to call him up. Fortunately the line is busy, which gives you a perfectly good excuse for putting it over until Tuesday. But on Tuesday luck is against you and you get a clear connection with the doctor himself. An appointment is arranged for Thursday afternoon at 3:30.

Thursday afternoon, and here it is only Tuesday morning! Almost anything may happen between now and then. We might declare war on

Mexico, and off you'd have to go, dentist appointment or no dentist appointment. Surely a man couldn't let a date to have a tooth filled stand in the way of his doing his duty to his country. Or the social revolution might start on Wednesday, and by Thursday the whole town might be in ashes. You can picture yourself standing, Thursday afternoon at 3:30 on the ruins of the City Hall, fighting off marauding bands of reds, and saying to yourself, with a sigh of relief: "Only to think! At this time I was to have been climbing into the dentist's chair!" You never can tell when your luck will turn in a thing like that.

But Wednesday goes by and nothing happens. And Thursday morning dawns without even a word from the dentist saying that he has been called suddenly out of town to lecture before the Incisor Club. Apparently, everything is working against you.

By this time, your tongue has taken up a permanent resting-place in the vacant tooth, and is causing you to talk indistinctly and incoherently. Somehow you feel that if the dentist opens your mouth and finds the tip of your tongue in the tooth, he will be deceived and go away without doing anything.

The only thing left is for you to call him up and say that you have just killed a man and are being arrested and can't possibly keep your appointment. But any dentist would see through that. He would laugh right into his transmitter at you. There is probably no excuse which it would be possible to invent which a dentist has not already heard eighty or ninety times. No, you might as well see the thing through now.

Luncheon is a ghastly rite. The whole left side of your jaw has suddenly developed an acute sensitiveness and the disaffection has spread to the four teeth on either side of the original one. You doubt if it will be possible for him to touch it at all. Perhaps all he intends to do this time is to look at it anyway. You might even suggest that to him. You could very easily come in again soon and have him do the actual work.

Three-thirty draws near. A horrible time of day at best. Just when a man's vitality is lowest. Before stepping in out of the sunlight into the building in which the dental parlor is, you take one look about you at the happy people scurrying by in the street. Carefree children that they are! What do they know of Life? Probably that man in the silly-looking hat never had trouble with so much as his baby-teeth. There they go, pushing and jostling each other, just as if within ten feet of them there was not a man who stands on the brink of the Great Misadventure. Ah well! Life is like that!

Into the elevator. The last hope is gone. The door clangs and you look hopelessly about you at the stupid faces of your fellow passengers. How can people be so clownish? Of course, there is always the chance that the elevator will fall and that you will all be terribly hurt. But that is too much to expect. You dismiss it from your thoughts as too impractical, too visionary. Things don't work out as happily as that in real life.

You feel a certain glow of heroic pride when you tell the operator the right floor number. You might just as easily have told him a floor too high or too low, and that would, at least, have caused delay. But after all, a man must prove himself a man and the least you can do is to meet Fate with an unflinching eye and give the right floor number.

Too often has the scene in the dentist's waiting-room been described for me to try to do it again here. They are all alike. The antiseptic smell, the ominous hum from the operating-rooms, the 1921 "Literary Digests," and the silent, sullen, group of waiting patients, each trying to look unconcerned and cordially disliking everyone else in the room,—all these have been sung by poets of far greater lyric powers than mine. (Not that I really think that they *are* greater than mine, but that's the customary form of excuse for not writing something you haven't got time or space to do. As a matter of fact, I think I could do it much better than it has ever been done before.)

I can only say that, as you sit looking, with unseeing eyes, through a large book entitled, "The Great War in Pictures," you would gladly change places with the most lowly of God's creatures. It is inconceivable that there should be anyone worse off than you, unless perhaps it is some of the poor wretches who are waiting with you.

That one over in the arm-chair, nervously tearing to shreds a copy of "The Dental Review and Practical Inlay Worker." She may have something frightful the trouble with her. She couldn't possibly look more worried. Perhaps it is very, very painful. This thought cheers you up considerably. What cowards women are in times like these!

And then there comes the sound of voices from the next room.

"All right, Doctor, and if it gives me any more pain shall I call you up? . . . Do you think that it will bleed much more? . . . Saturday morning, then, at eleven. . . . Good bye, Doctor."

And a middle-aged woman emerges (all women are middle-aged when emerging from the dentist's office) looking as if she were playing the big emotional scene in "John Ferguson." A wisp of hair waves dissolutely across her forehead between her eyes. Her face is pale, except for a slight inflammation at the corners of her mouth, and in her eyes is that far-away look of one who has been face to face with Life. But she is through. She should care how she looks.

The nurse appears, and looks inquiringly at each one in the room. Each one in the room evades the nurse's glance in one last, futile attempt to fool someone and get away without seeing the dentist. But she spots you and nods pleasantly. God, how pleasantly she nods! There ought to be a law against people being as pleasant as that.

"The doctor will see you now," she says.

The English language may hold a more disagreeable combination of words than "The doctor will see you now." I am willing to concede something to the phrase "Have you anything to say before the current is turned on." That may be worse for the moment, but it doesn't last so long. For continued, unmitigating depression, I know nothing to equal "The doctor will see you now." But I'm not narrow-minded about it. I'm willing to consider other possibilities.

Smiling feebly, you trip over the extended feet of the man next to you, and stagger into the delivery-room, where, amid a ghastly array of death-masks of teeth, blue flames waving eerily from Bunsen burners, and the drowning sound of perpetually running water which chokes and gurgles at intervals, you sink into the chair and close your eyes.

. . . . . .

But now let us consider the spiritual exaltation that comes when you are at last let down and turned loose. It is all over, and what did it amount to? Why, nothing at all. A-ha-ha-ha-ha-ha! Nothing at all.

You suddenly develop a particular friendship for the dentist. A splendid fellow, really. You ask him questions about his instruments. What does he use this thing for, for instance? Well, well, to think of a little thing like that making all that trouble. A-ha-ha-ha-ha-ha! . . . And the dentist's family, how are they? Isn't that fine!

Gaily you shake hands with him and straighten your tie. Forgotten is the fact that you have another appointment with him for Monday. There is no such thing as Monday. You are through for today, and all's right with the world.

As you pass out through the waiting-room, you leer at the others unpleasantly. The poor fishes! Why can't they take their medicine like grown people and not sit there moping as if they were going to be shot?

Heigh-ho! Here's the elevator-man! A charming fellow! You wonder if he knows that you have just had a tooth filled. You feel tempted to tell him and slap him on the back. You feel tempted to tell everyone out in the bright, cheery street. And what a wonderful street it is too! All full of nice, black snow and water. After all, Life is sweet!

And then you go and find the first person whom you can accost without being arrested and explain to him just what it was that the dentist did to you, and how you felt, and what you have got to have done next time.

Which brings us right back to where we were in the beginning, and perhaps accounts for everyone's liking to divulge their dental secrets to others. It may be a sort of hysterical relief that, for the time being, it is all over with.

EDNA ST. VINCENT MILLAY

[1892–1950]

A SYMBOL OF HER DAY not only in her way of life but also in her poetry, Edna St. Vincent Millay was born February 12, 1892, in Rockland, Maine. When she was nineteen she submitted a poem of some two hundred lines, "Renascence," to an anthology contest and, although it failed to win a prize, it attracted so much attention that, almost overnight, she became famous. The poem began as simply as a child's rhyme but it ascended into ecstasy and ended in a flash of revelation.

O God, I cried, no dark disguise
Can e'er hereafter hide from me
Thy radiant identity! . . .
God, I can push the grass apart
And lay my finger on Thy heart!

After she had been "discovered," a sponsor sent her to Vassar College, from which she was graduated in 1917. Established in Greenwich Village, she supported herself by writing anything that might find a market. She wrote light verse and serious poems, as well as prose sketches under the pseudonym of "Nancy Boyd"; she composed skits and plays for the Provincetown Players and joined the group as an actress.

Her elfin beauty—she had copper-colored hair and green eyes—her poetry, and her rebelliousness combined to make her a legend. She was both the emancipated woman and the clever little girl who was always shocking her elders, especially by insisting on a woman's right to be as promiscuous as any man. She had just turned thirty when she was awarded the Pulitzer Prize for The Harp-Weaver and Other Poems, *in which the ballad-like title poem was surpassed by the distinction and sonority of the sonnets. In the same year she married*

Eugen Boissevain, a Dutch-American business man and, tired of metropolitan life and the rounds of lecturing which had occupied her, moved to a secluded home at Austerlitz, New York, in the southern Berkshires. She feared growing old and, never in robust health, did not live to face what to her was the tragedy of age. Her husband died in 1949 and she survived him by only a year. She was not yet fifty-nine when a neighbor found her dead in her large and lonely house, October 19, 1950. It was assumed that she had died of heart failure.

Edna St. Vincent Millay's reputation waned considerably after her death. Critics pointed to the limitations of her personality which were reflected in her poetry, the coddled archaisms, the simpering flippancies and self-pity; they diagnosed her preoccupation with youth and her reluctance to accept maturity as an adolescent emotionalism which displayed self-dramatization instead of self-discovery. Nevertheless, the pendulum has begun to swing back in her favor. She is as popular as she once was—in the 1920s she seemed to be America's woman poet laureate—but critics now see in her poems a grandeur beyond their rhetoric. The early petulance and "cuteness" is succeeded by deep personal feeling. "Renascence" remains the astonishing work of a prodigy, but such sonnets as "What Lips My Lips Have Kissed," "Pity Me Not," and "Euclid Alone Has Looked on Beauty Bare" are dignified as well as passionate. They have the shape and solidity of permanence.

RENASCENCE

All I could see from where I stood
Was three long mountains and a wood;
I turned and looked another way,
And saw three islands in a bay.
So with my eyes I traced the line
Of the horizon, thin and fine,
Straight around till I was come
Back to where I'd started from;
And all I saw from where I stood
Was three long mountains and a wood.
Over these things I could not see;
These were the things that bounded me;
And I could touch them with my hand,
Almost, I thought, from where I stand.

And all at once things seemed so small
My breath came short, and scarce at all.
But, sure, the sky is big, I said;
Miles and miles above my head;
So here upon my back I'll lie
And look my fill into the sky.
And so I looked, and, after all,
The sky was not so very tall.
The sky, I said, must somewhere stop,
And—sure enough!—I see the top!
The sky, I thought, is not so grand;
I 'most could touch it with my hand!
And, reaching up my hand to try,
I screamed to feel it touch the sky.

I screamed, and—lo!—Infinity
Came down and settled over me;
Forced back my scream into my chest,
Bent back my arm upon my breast,
And, pressing of the Undefined
The definition on my mind,
Held up before my eyes a glass
Through which my shrinking sight did pass
Until it seemed I must behold
Immensity made manifold;
Whispered to me a word whose sound
Deafened the air for worlds around,
And brought unmuffled to my ears
The gossiping of friendly spheres,
The creaking of the tented sky,
The ticking of Eternity.

I saw and heard, and knew at last
The How and Why of all things, past,
And present, and forevermore.
The universe, cleft to the core,
Lay open to my probing sense
That, sickening, I would fain pluck thence
But could not,—nay! But needs must suck
At the great wound, and could not pluck
My lips away till I had drawn
All venom out.—Ah, fearful pawn!
For my omniscience I paid toll
In infinite remorse of soul.

All sin was of my sinning, all
Atoning mine, and mine the gall
Of all regret. Mine was the weight
Of every brooded wrong, the hate
That stood behind each envious thrust,
Mine every greed, mine every lust.
And all the while for every grief,
Each suffering, I craved relief
With individual desire,—
Craved all in vain! And felt fierce fire
About a thousand people crawl;
Perished with each,—then mourned for all!
A man was starving in Capri;
He moved his eyes and looked at me;
I felt his gaze, I heard his moan,
And knew his hunger as my own.
I saw at sea a great fog-bank
Between two ships that struck and sank;
A thousand screams the heavens smote;
And every scream tore through my throat;
No hurt I did not feel, no death
That was not mine; mine each last breath
That, crying, met an answering cry
From the compassion that was I.
All suffering mine, and mine its rod;
Mine, pity like the pity of God.
Ah, awful weight! Infinity
Pressed down upon the finite me!
My anguished spirit, like a bird,
Beating against my lips I heard;
Yet lay the weight so close about
There was no room for it without.
And so beneath the weight lay I
And suffered death, but could not die.

Long had I lain thus, craving death,
When quietly the earth beneath
Gave way, and inch by inch, so great
At last had grown the crushing weight,
Into the earth I sank till I
Full six feet under ground did lie,
And sank no more,—there is no weight
Can follow here, however great.
From off my breast I felt it roll,

And as it went my tortured soul
Burst forth and fled in such a gust
That all about me swirled the dust.

Deep in the earth I rested now;
Cool is its hand upon the brow
And soft its breast beneath the head
Of one who is so gladly dead.
And all at once, and over all,
The pitying rain began to fall.
I lay and heard each pattering hoof
Upon my lowly, thatched roof.
And seemed to love the sound far more
Than ever I had done before.
For rain it hath a friendly sound
To one who's six feet underground;
And scarce the friendly voice or face:
A grave is such a quiet place.

The rain, I said, is kind to come
And speak to me in my new home.
I would I were alive again
To kiss the fingers of the rain,
To drink into my eyes the shine
Of every slanting silver line,
To catch the freshened, fragrant breeze
From drenched and dripping apple-trees.
For soon the shower will be done,
And then the broad face of the sun
Will laugh above the rain-soaked earth
Until the world with answering mirth
Shakes joyously, and each round drop
Rolls, twinkling, from its grass-blade top.
How can I bear it; buried here,
While overhead the sky grows clear
And blue again after the storm?
O, multi-colored, multiform,
Beloved beauty over me,
That I shall never, never see
Again! Spring-silver, autumn-gold,
That I shall never more behold!
Sleeping your myriad magics through,
Close-sepulchered away from you!
O God, I cried, give me new birth,

And put me back upon the earth!
Upset each cloud's gigantic gourd
And let the heavy rain, down-poured
In one big torrent, set me free,
Washing my grave away from me!

I ceased; and, through the breathless hush
That answered me, the far-off rush
Of herald wings came whispering
Like music down the vibrant string
Of my ascending prayer, and—crash!
Before the wild wind's whistling lash
The startled storm-clouds reared on high
And plunged in terror down the sky,
And the big rain in one black wave
Fell from the sky and struck my grave.

I know not how such things can be,
I only know there came to me
A fragrance such as never clings
To aught save happy living things;
A sound as of some joyous elf
Singing sweet songs to please himself,
And, through and over everything,
A sense of glad awakening.
The grass, a tip-toe at my ear,
Whispering to me I could hear;
I felt the rain's cool finger-tips
Brushed tenderly across my lips,
Laid gently on my sealèd sight,
And all at once the heavy night
Fell from my eyes and I could see,—
A drenched and dripping apple-tree,
A last long line of silver rain,
A sky grown clear and blue again.

And as I looked a quickening gust
Of wind blew up to me and thrust
Into my face a miracle
Of orchard-breath, and with the smell,—
I know not how such things can be!—
I breathed my soul back into me.

Ah! Up then from the ground sprang I
And hailed the earth with such a cry

As is not heard save from a man
Who has been dead and lives again.
About the trees my arms I wound;
Like one gone mad I hugged the ground;
I raised my quivering arms on high;
I laughed and laughed into the sky,
Till at my throat a strangling sob
Caught fiercely, and a great heart-throb
Sent instant tears into my eyes;
O God, I cried, no dark disguise
Can e'er hereafter hide from me
Thy radiant identity!
Thou canst not move across the grass
But my quick eyes will see Thee pass,
Nor speak, however silently,
But my hushed voice will answer Thee.
I know the path that tells Thy way
Through the cool eve of every day;
God, I can push the grass apart
And lay my finger on Thy heart!

The world stands out on either side
No wider than the heart is wide;
Above the world is stretched the sky,—
No higher than the soul is high.
The heart can push the sea and land
Farther away on either hand;
The soul can split the sky in two,
And let the face of God shine through.
But East and West will pinch the heart
That cannot keep them pushed apart;
And he whose soul is flat—the sky
Will cave in on him by and by.

SPRING

To what purpose, April, do you return again?
Beauty is not enough.
You can no longer quiet me with the redness
Of little leaves opening stickily.
I know what I know.
The sun is hot on my neck as I observe
The spikes of the crocus.

The smell of the earth is good.
It is apparent that there is no death.
But what does that signify?
Not only under ground are the brains of men
Eaten by maggots.
Life in itself
Is nothing,
An empty cup, a flight of uncarpeted stairs.
It is not enough that yearly, down this hill,
April
Comes like an idiot, babbling and strewing flowers.

WHAT LIPS MY LIPS HAVE KISSED

What lips my lips have kissed, and where, and why,
I have forgotten, and what arms have lain
Under my head till morning; but the rain
Is full of ghosts tonight, that tap and sigh
Upon the glass and listen for reply;
And in my heart there stirs a quiet pain
For unremembered lads that not again
Will turn to me at midnight with a cry.

Thus in the winter stands the lonely tree,
Nor knows what birds have vanished one by one,
Yet knows its boughs more silent than before:
I cannot say what loves have come and gone;
I only know that summer sang in me
A little while, that in me sings no more.

PITY ME NOT

Pity me not because the light of day
At close of day no longer walks the sky;
Pity me not for beauties passed away
From field and thicket as the year goes by;
Pity me not the waning of the moon,
Nor that the ebbing tide goes out to sea,
Nor that a man's desire is hushed so soon,
And you no longer look with love on me.

This have I known always: love is no more
Than the wide blossom which the wind assails;
Than the great tide that treads the shifting shore,
Strewing fresh wreckage gathered in the gales.
Pity me that the heart is slow to learn
What the swift mind beholds at every turn.

EUCLID ALONE HAS LOOKED ON BEAUTY BARE

Euclid alone has looked on Beauty bare.
Let all who prate of Beauty hold their peace,
And lay them prone upon the earth and cease
To ponder on themselves, the while they stare
At nothing, intricately drawn nowhere
In shapes of shifting lineage; let geese
Gabble and hiss, but heroes seek release
From dusty bondage into luminous air.

O blinding hour, O holy, terrible day,
When first the shaft into his vision shone
Of light anatomized! Euclid alone
Has looked on Beauty bare. Fortunate they
Who, though once only and then but far away,
Have heard her massive sandal set on stone.

ARCHIBALD MACLEISH

[1892–]

One of the most versatile talents of his times—lawyer, editor, teacher, diplomat, politician, and polemist—Archibald MacLeish was particularly successful as a poet. He was born May 7, 1892, in Glencoe, Illinois. Son of an affluent merchant, he was sent East and educated at the Hotchkiss School, Yale, and Harvard. He received his L.L.B. from Harvard in 1919, taught there briefly, and for the next three years practiced law in Boston. He had married a singer, Ada Hitchcock, while he was still in college, and at thirty-one he went abroad with his family and lived in France. There he was exposed to the French sym-

bolist poets, as well as to Pound and Eliot, all of whom were reflected in his work.

Between his twenty-fifth and fortieth years MacLeish published eight volumes of poetry. Conquistador was awarded the Pulitzer Prize in 1932. In his forties he played many different roles. He joined the staff of the magazine Fortune, became curator of the Nieman Collection of Contemporary Journalism at Harvard, and was made Librarian of Congress by President Franklin D. Roosevelt. He held the position for five years, during which time he directed the Office of Facts and Figures, was assistant director to the Office of War Information, and, at the outbreak of the Second World War, became Roosevelt's Assistant Secretary of State—it was an open secret that MacLeish helped prepare many of the President's speeches and "fireside chats." After the armistice he was instrumental in the organization of UNESCO and was the chairman of the American delegation at its first general conference. At fifty-seven he returned to teaching as Boylston Professor of Oratory and Rhetoric at Harvard.

At sixty-two MacLeish was the author of eighteen volumes of poetry as well as several collections of essays, plays, and political addresses. Four years later he published his largest and most successful work: J. B., a dramatic reworking of the Book of Job, a theatricalized debate centering about the paradox of God's seeming cruelties and the persistence of love in spite of horrifying injustice. Although its theological theme and its intellectual idiom might have been thought to limit its appeal, it was a popular as well as a critical success wherever it was performed.

MacLeish had already been rewarded as well as honored by receiving the Pulitzer Prize for the second time for his Collected Poems: 1917–1952, a retrospective volume which also won the Bollingen Prize and the National Book Award. Although some commentators were critical of MacLeish's ambiguities and claimed that his style and attitude fluctuated to fit the taste and temper of the moment, none could dispute his craftsmanship. "The End of the World" contains such a packed dramatic vision that the reader is scarcely aware he is being confronted with a formal sonnet, while "Memorial Rain" and "Epistle to be Left in the Earth" are as clear and passionate, as vivid and moving as they are rich in music and meaning.

MEMORIAL RAIN

Ambassador Puser the ambassador
Reminds himself in French, felicitous tongue,
What these (young men no longer) lie here for
In rows that once, and somewhere else, were young—

All night in Brussels the wind had tugged at my door:
I had heard the wind at my door and the trees strung
Taut, and to me who had never been before
In that country it was a strange wind blowing
Steadily, stiffening the walls, the floor,
The roof of my room. I had not slept for knowing
He too, dead, was a stranger in that land
And felt beneath the earth in the wind's flowing
A tightening of roots and would not understand,
Remembering lake winds in Illinois,
That strange wind. I had felt his bones in the sand
Listening.

—Reflects that these enjoy
Their country's gratitude, that deep repose,
That peace no pain can break, no hurt destroy,
That rest, that sleep—

At Ghent the wind rose.
There was a smell of rain and a heavy drag
Of wind in the hedges but not as the wind blows
Over fresh water when the waves lag
Foaming and the willows huddle and it will rain:
I felt him waiting.

—Indicates the flag
Which (may he say) enisles in Flanders' plain
This little field these happy, happy dead
Have made America—

In the ripe grain
The wind coiled glistening, darted, fled,
Dragging its heavy body: at Waereghem
The wind coiled in the grass above his head:
Waiting—listening—

—Dedicates to them
This earth their bones have hallowed, this last gift
A grateful country—

Under the dry grass stem
The words are blurred, are thickened, the words sift
Confused by the rasp of the wind, by the thin grating
Of ants under the grass, the minute shift
And tumble of dusty sand separating
From dusty sand. The roots of the grass strain,
Tighten, the earth is rigid, waits—he is waiting—

And suddenly, and all at once, the rain!

The people scatter, they run into houses, the wind
Is trampled under the rain, shakes free, is again
Trampled. The rain gathers, running in thinned
Spurts of water that ravel in the dry sand
Seeping into the sand under the grass roots, seeping
Between cracked boards to the bones of a clenched hand:
The earth relaxes, loosens, he is sleeping,
He rests, he is quiet, he sleeps in a strange land.

IMMORTAL AUTUMN

I speak this poem now with grave and level voice
In praise of autumn of the far-horn-winding fall
I praise the flower-barren fields the clouds the tall
Unanswering branches where the wind makes sullen noise

I praise the fall it is the human season now
No more the foreign sun does meddle at our earth
Enforce the green and thaw the frozen soil to birth
Nor winter yet weigh all with silence the pine bough

But now in autumn with the black and outcast crows
Share we the spacious world the whispering year is gone
There is more room to live now the once secret dawn
Comes late by daylight and the dark unguarded goes

Between the mutinous brave burning of the leaves
And winter's covering of our hearts with his deep snow
We are alone there are no evening birds we know
The naked moon the tame stars circle at our eaves

It is the human season on this sterile air
Do words outcarry breath the sound goes on and on
I hear a dead man's cry from autumn long since gone

I cry to you beyond this bitter air.

THE END OF THE WORLD

Quite unexpectedly as Vasserot
The armless ambidextrian was lighting
A match between his great and second toe
And Ralph the lion was engaged in biting
The neck of Madame Sossman while the drum
Pointed, and Teeny was about to cough
In waltz-time swinging Jocko by the thumb—
Quite unexpectedly the top blew off:

And there, there overhead, there, there, hung over
Those thousands of white faces, those dazed eyes,
There in the starless dark, the poise, the hover,
There with vast wings across the canceled skies,
There in the sudden blackness, the black pall
Of nothing, nothing, nothing—nothing at all.

EPISTLE TO BE LEFT IN THE EARTH

. . . It is colder now
there are many stars
we are drifting
North by the Great Bear
the leaves are falling
The water is stone in the scooped rocks
to southward
Red sun gray air
the crows are
Slow on their crooked wings
the jays have left us
Long since we passed the flares of Orion
Each man believes in his heart he will die
Many have written last thoughts and last letters
None know if our deaths are now or forever
None know if this wandering earth will be found

We lie down and the snow covers our garments
I pray you
you (if any open this writing)
Make in your mouths the words that were our names
I will tell you all we have learned
I will tell you everything

The earth is round
there are springs under the orchards
The loam cuts with a blunt knife
beware of
Elms in thunder
the lights in the sky are stars
We think they do not see
we think also
The trees do not know nor the leaves of the grasses
hear us
The birds too are ignorant
Do not listen
Do not stand at dark in the open windows
We before you have heard this
they are voices
They are not words at all but the wind rising
Also none among us has seen God
(. . . We have thought often
The flaws of sun in the late and driving weather
Pointed to one tree but it was not so)
As for the nights I warn you the nights are dangerous
The wind changes at night and the dreams come

It is very cold
there are strange stars near Arcturus

Voices are crying an unknown name in the sky

DOROTHY PARKER

[1893–]

The girl whom Alexander Woolcott was to call "so odd a blend of Little Nell and Lady Macbeth" was born Dorothy Rothschild on August 22, 1893, in West End, New Jersey. Educated at Miss Dana's School in Morristown, New Jersey, and the Blessed Sacrament Convent in New York City, she found her first literary job at Vogue. The salary was ten dollars a week; to supplement it she began to write occasional verse. She moved to Vanity Fair and wrote dramatic criticism. In

1917 she married Edwin Parker and, as Dorothy Parker, became a frequent contributor of poetry to magazines, especially that new, sophisticated weekly which seemed particularly designed for her own talent for sharpness and irony, The New Yorker. Here began the reputation for witticisms, wise-cracks, and epigrams—real and apocryphal—from which she has never escaped. She became a member of The New Yorker staff, a book reviewer, in 1927. She also occasionally acted as drama critic, and her whiplash disposals were much feared. She once dismissed an actress' pretentious performance by saying that "she ran the gamut of emotions from A to B."

Her first collection of verse, Enough Rope, appeared in her thirty-fourth year. It was a best-seller. Dorothy Parker was now a national name and her barbed words were constantly quoted. She retired from The New Yorker to free-lance. Sunset Gun, another collection of caustic verse, was published in 1928, the year her marriage ended in a divorce.

Dorothy Parker's first short stories appeared in 1930. The title of the volume, Laments for the Living, was an indication of that bitter tang which, always characteristic of her verse, was more and more to flavor her prose. Famous for her wit, she was a desperately serious person, a satirist, as she said herself, not a humorist. She was gifted with the "light touch" and the ability to turn a phrase or tune a rhyme; but she had, too, a sardonic understanding of people which inevitably emerged through the surface of her writing. "The humorist isn't happy anyway," she said. "Today he's whistling past worse graveyards to worse tunes."

More stories appeared, and more verse. In 1933 she married the actor Alan Campbell, went to Hollywood, and worked on a series of film scripts. Here Lies, another collection of stories, was published in 1939. Almost two decades later she resumed book-reviewing and appeared on radio and television programs.

Never shallow in her writing, or in her other interests, Dorothy Parker turned more often to serious matters. War developed in Europe; an intense liberal, she devoted herself to the battle against fascism.

In 1924 she had worked on the script of a play with Elmer Rice, and she turned to the theater again in 1949, collaborating with Ross Evans on a play, The Coast of Illyria. Ladies of the Corridor, which she wrote with Armand d'Usseau, had a moderately successful run in New York in 1953. The story of a group of aged and aging women in a New York residential hotel, it displays Miss Parker's unique ability to portray, sympathetically but without compromise, aimless, empty lives in a bus-

tling modern world. It was a theme she had handled before, most notably in "Big Blonde," a story which, coming in the midst of other, lighter fiction, stood out as a sharp, serious study of quiet, unrelenting desperation.

W. Somerset Maugham said of Dorothy Parker as a story-builder that she "knows exactly where to begin and where to end." Her ear is tuned to the sound of human speech and her eye is on the lookout for the unguarded moment when a person reveals himself. In her serious stories, as in her most quick-witted verse, her aim at man's dimwittedness is accurate and deadly.

BIG BLONDE

I

HAZEL MORSE WAS A LARGE, FAIR WOMAN of the type that incites some men when they use the word "blonde" to click their tongues and wag their heads roguishly. She prided herself upon her small feet and suffered for her vanity, boxing them in snub-toed, high-heeled slippers of the shortest bearable size. The curious things about her were her hands, strange terminations to the flabby white arms splattered with pale tan spots—long, quivering hands with deep and convex nails. She should not have disfigured them with little jewels.

She was not a woman given to recollections. At her middle thirties, her old days were a blurred and flickering sequence, an imperfect film, dealing with the actions of strangers.

In her twenties, after the deferred death of a hazy widowed mother, she had been employed as a model in a wholesale dress establishment—it was still the day of the big woman, and she was then prettily colored and erect and high-breasted. Her job was not onerous, and she met numbers of men and spent numbers of evenings with them, laughing at their jokes and telling them she loved their neckties. Men liked her, and she took it for granted that the liking of many men was a desirable thing. Popularity seemed to her to be worth all the work that had to be put into its achievement. Men liked you because you were fun, and when they liked you they took you out, and there you were. So, and successfully, she was fun. She was a good sport. Men like a good sport.

No other form of diversion, simpler or more complicated, drew her attention. She never pondered if she might not be better occupied doing something else. Her ideas, or, better, her acceptances, ran right along with those of the other substantially built blondes in whom she found her friends.

When she had been working in the dress establishment some years she met Herbie Morse. He was thin, quick, attractive, with shifting lines about his shiny, brown eyes and a habit of fiercely biting at the skin around his finger nails. He drank largely; she found that entertaining. Her habitual greeting to him was an allusion to his state of the previous night.

"Oh, what a peach you had," she used to say, through her easy laugh. "I thought I'd die, the way you kept asking the waiter to dance with you."

She liked him immediately upon their meeting. She was enormously amused at his fast, slurred sentences, his interpolations of apt phrases from vaudeville acts and comic strips; she thrilled at the feel of his lean arm tucked firm beneath the sleeve of her coat; she wanted to touch the wet, flat surface of his hair. He was as promptly drawn to her. They were married six weeks after they had met.

She was delighted at the idea of being a bride; coquetted with it, played upon it. Other offers of marriage she had had, and not a few of them, but it happened that they were all from stout, serious men who had visited the dress establishment as buyers; men from Des Moines and Houston and Chicago and, in her phrase, even funnier places. There was always something immensely comic to her in the thought of living elsewhere than New York. She could not regard as serious proposals that she share a Western residence.

She wanted to be married. She was nearing thirty now, and she did not take the years well. She spread and softened, and her darkening hair turned her to inexpert dabblings with peroxide. There were times when she had little flashes of fear about her job. And she had had a couple of thousand evenings of being a good sport among her male acquaintances. She had come to be more conscientious than spontaneous about it.

Herbie earned enough, and they took a little apartment far uptown. There was a Mission-furnished dining room with a hanging central light globed in liver-colored glass; in the living room were an "overstuffed suite," a Boston fern, and a reproduction of the Henner *Magdalene* with the red hair and the blue draperies; the bedroom was in gray enamel and old rose, with Herbie's photograph on Hazel's dressing table and Hazel's likeness on Herbie's chest of drawers.

She cooked—and she was a good cook—and marketed and chatted with the delivery boys and the colored laundress. She loved the flat, she loved her life, she loved Herbie. In the first months of their marriage she gave him all the passion she was ever to know.

She had not realized how tired she was. It was a delight, a new game, a holiday, to give up being a good sport. If her head ached or her arches throbbed, she complained piteously, babyishly. If her mood was quiet, she did not talk. If tears came to her eyes, she let them fall.

She fell readily into the habit of tears during the first year of her marriage. Even in her good sport days she had been known to weep lavishly and disinterestedly on occasion. Her behavior at the theater was a standing joke. She could weep at anything in a play—tiny garments, love both unrequited and mutual, seduction, purity, faithful servitors, wedlock, the triangle.

"There goes Haze," her friends would say, watching her. "She's off again."

Wedded and relaxed, she poured her tears freely. To her who had laughed so much, crying was delicious. All sorrows became her sorrows; she was Tenderness. She would cry long and softly over newspaper accounts of kidnaped babies, deserted wives, unemployed men, strayed cats, heroic dogs. Even when the paper was no longer before her, her mind revolved upon these things and the drops slipped rhythmically over her plump cheeks.

"Honestly," she would say to Herbie, "all the sadness there is in the world when you stop to think about it!"

"Yeah," Herbie would say.

She missed nobody. The old crowd, the people who had brought her and Herbie together, dropped from their lives, lingeringly at first. When she thought of this at all it was only to consider it fitting. This was marriage. This was peace.

But the thing was that Herbie was not amused.

For a time he had enjoyed being alone with her. He found the voluntary isolation novel and sweet. Then it palled with a ferocious suddenness. It was as if one night, sitting with her in the steam-heated living room, he would ask no more; and the next night he was through and done with the whole thing.

He became annoyed by her misty melancholies. At first, when he came home to find her softly tired and moody, he kissed her neck and patted her shoulder and begged her to tell her Herbie what was wrong. She loved that. But time slid by, and he found that there was never anything really, personally, the matter.

"Ah, for God's sake," he would say. "Crabbing again. All right, sit here and crab your head off. I'm going out."

And he would slam out of the flat and come back late and drunk.

She was completely bewildered by what happened to their Marriage. First they were lovers; and then, it seemed without transition, they were enemies. She never understood it.

There were longer and longer intervals between his leaving his office and his arrival at the apartment. She went through agonies of picturing him run over and bleeding, dead and covered with a sheet. Then she lost her fears for his safety and grew sullen and wounded. When a person wanted to be with a person he came as soon as possible. She desperately wanted him to want to be with her; her own hours only marked the time till he would come. It was often nearly nine o'clock before he came home to dinner. Always he had had many drinks, and their effect would die in him, leaving him loud and querulous and bristling for affronts.

He was too nervous, he said, to sit and do nothing for an evening. He boasted, probably not in all truth, that he had never read a book in his life.

"What am I expected to do—sit around this dump on my tail all night?" he would ask rhetorically. And again he would slam out.

She did not know what to do. She could not manage him. She could not meet him.

She fought him furiously. A terrific domesticity had come upon her, and she would bite and scratch to guard it. She wanted what she called "a nice home." She wanted a sober, tender husband, prompt at dinner, punctual at work. She wanted sweet, comforting evenings. The idea of intimacy with other men was terrible to her; the thought that Herbie might be seeking entertainment in other women set her frantic.

It seemed to her that almost everything she read—novels from the drugstore lending library, magazine stories, women's pages in the papers—dealt with wives who lost their husbands' love. She could bear those, at that, better than accounts of neat, companionable marriage and living happily ever after.

She was frightened. Several times when Herbie came home in the evening he found her determinedly dressed—she had had to alter those of her clothes that were not new, to make them fasten—and rouged.

"Let's go wild to-night, what do you say?" she would hail him. "A person's got lots of time to hang around and do nothing when they're dead."

So they would go out, to chop houses and the less expensive cabarets. But it turned out badly. She could no longer find amusement in watching Herbie drink. She could not laugh at his whimsicalities, she was so tensely counting his indulgences. And she was unable to keep back her remonstrances—"Ah, come on, Herb, you've had enough, haven't you? You'll feel something terrible in the morning."

He would be immediately enraged. All right, crab; crab, crab, crab, that was all she ever did. What a lousy sport *she* was! There would be scenes, and one or the other of them would rise and stalk out in fury.

She could not recall the definite day that she started drinking, herself. There was nothing separate about her days. Like drops upon a window-pane, they ran together and trickled away. She had been married six months; then a year; then three years.

She had never needed to drink, formerly. She could sit for most of a night at a table where the others were imbibing earnestly and never droop in looks or spirits, nor be bored by the doings of those about her. If she took a cocktail, it was so unusual as to cause twenty minutes or so of jocular comment. But now anguish was in her. Frequently, after a quarrel, Herbie would stay out for the night, and she could not learn from him where the time had been spent. Her heart felt tight and sore in her breast, and her mind turned like an electric fan.

She hated the taste of liquor. Gin, plain or in mixtures, made her promptly sick. After experiment, she found that Scotch whisky was best for her. She took it without water, because that was the quickest way to its effect.

Herbie pressed it on her. He was glad to see her drink. They both felt it might restore her high spirits, and their good times together might again be possible.

" 'Atta girl," he would approve her. "Let's see you get boiled, baby."

But it brought them no nearer. When she drank with him there would be a little while of gayety and then, strangely without beginning, they would be in a wild quarrel. They would wake in the morning not sure what it had all been about, foggy as to what had been said and done, but each deeply injured and bitterly resentful. There would be days of vengeful silence.

There had been a time when they had made up their quarrels, usually in bed. There would be kisses and little names and assurances of fresh starts . . . "Oh, it's going to be great now, Herb. We'll have swell times. I was a crab. I guess I might have been tired. But everything's going to be swell. You'll see."

Now there were no gentle reconciliations. They resumed friendly relations only in the brief magnanimity caused by liquor, before more liquor drew them into new battles. The scenes became more violent. There were shouted invectives and pushes, and sometimes sharp slaps. Once she had a black eye. Herbie was horrified next day at sight of it. He did not go to work; he followed her about, suggesting remedies and heaping dark blame on himself. But after they had had a few drinks—"to pull themselves together"—she made so many wistful references to her bruise that he shouted at her, and rushed out, and was gone for two days.

Each time he left the place in rage he threatened never to come back. She did not believe him, nor did she consider separation. Somewhere in her head or her heart was the lazy, nebulous hope that things would change and she and Herbie settle suddenly into soothing married life. Here were her home, her furniture, her husband, her station. She summoned no alternatives.

She could no longer bustle and potter. She had no more vicarious tears; the hot drops she shed were for herself. She walked ceaselessly about the rooms, her thoughts running mechanically round and round Herbie. In those days began the hatred of being alone that she was never to overcome. You could be by yourself when things were all right, but when you were blue you got the howling horrors.

She commenced drinking alone, little, short drinks all through the day. It was only with Herbie that alcohol made her nervous and quick in offense. Alone, it blurred sharp things for her. She lived in a haze of it. Her life took on a dream-like quality. Nothing was astonishing.

A Mrs. Martin moved into the flat across the hall. She was a great blonde woman of forty, a promise in looks of what Mrs. Morse was to be. They made acquaintance, quickly became inseparable. Mrs. Morse spent her days in the opposite apartment. They drank together, to brace themselves after the drinks of the nights before.

She never confided her troubles about Herbie to Mrs. Martin. The subject was too bewildering to her to find comfort in talk. She let it be assumed that her husband's business kept him much away. It was not regarded as important; husbands, as such, played but shadowy parts in Mrs. Martin's circle.

Mrs. Martin had no visible spouse; you were left to decide for yourself whether he was or was not dead. She had an admirer, Joe, who came to see her almost nightly. Often he brought several friends with him—"The Boys," they were called. The Boys were big, red, good-humored men, perhaps forty-five, perhaps fifty. Mrs. Morse was glad of invitations to join the parties—Herbie was scarcely ever at home at night now. If he did come home, she did not visit Mrs. Martin. An evening alone with Herbie meant inevitably a quarrel, yet she would stay with him. There was always her thin and wordless idea that, maybe, this night, things would begin to be all right.

The boys brought plenty of liquor along with them whenever they came to Mrs. Martin's. Drinking with them, Mrs. Morse became lively and good-natured and audacious. She was quickly popular. When she had drunk enough to cloud her most recent battle with Herbie, she was excited by their approbation. Crab, was she? Rotten sport, was she? Well, there were some that thought different.

Ed was one of The Boys. He lived in Utica—had "his own business" there, was the awed report—but he came to New York almost every week. He was married. He showed Mrs. Morse the then current photographs of Junior and Sister, and she praised them abundantly and sincerely. Soon it was accepted by the others that Ed was her particular friend.

He staked her when they all played poker; sat next her and occasionally rubbed his knee against hers during the game. She was rather lucky. Frequently she went home with a twenty-dollar bill or a ten-dollar bill or a handful of crumpled dollars. She was glad of them. Herbie was getting, in her words, something awful about money. To ask him for it brought an instant row.

"What the hell do you do with it?" he would say. "Shoot it all on Scotch?"

"I try to run this house halfway decent," she would retort. "Never thought of that, did you? Oh, no, his lordship couldn't be bothered with that."

Again, she could not find a definite day to fix the beginning of Ed's proprietorship. It became his custom to kiss her on the mouth when he came in, as well as for farewell, and he gave her little quick kisses of approval all through the evening. She liked this rather more than she disliked it. She never thought of his kisses when she was not with him.

He would run his hand lingeringly over her back and shoulders.

"Some dizzy blonde, eh?" he would say. "Some doll."

One afternoon she came home from Mrs. Martin's to find Herbie in the bedroom. He had been away for several nights, evidently on a prolonged drinking bout. His face was gray, his hands jerked as if they were on wires. On the bed were two old suitcases, packed high. Only her photograph remained on his bureau, and the wide doors of his closet disclosed nothing but coat hangers.

"I'm blowing," he said. "I'm through with the whole works. I got a job in Detroit."

She sat down on the edge of the bed. She had drunk much the night before, and the four Scotches she had had with Mrs. Martin had only increased her fogginess.

"Good job?" she said.

"Oh, yeah," he said. "Looks all right."

He closed a suitcase with difficulty, swearing at it in whispers.

"There's some dough in the bank," he said. "The bank book's in your top drawer. You can have the furniture and stuff."

He looked at her, and his forehead twitched.

"God damn it, I'm through, I'm telling you," he cried. "I'm through."

"All right, all right," she said. "I heard you, didn't I?"

She saw him as if he were at one end of a cañon and she at the other. Her head was beginning to ache bumpingly, and her voice had a dreary, tiresome tone. She could not have raised it.

"Like a drink before you go?" she asked.

Again he looked at her, and a corner of his mouth jerked up.

"Cockeyed again for a change, aren't you?" he said. "That's nice. Sure, get a couple of shots, will you?"

She went to the pantry, mixed him a stiff highball, poured herself a couple of inches of whisky, and drank it. Then she gave herself another portion and brought the glasses into the bedroom. He had strapped both suitcases and had put on his hat and overcoat.

He took his highball.

"Well," he said, and he gave a sudden, uncertain laugh. "Here's mud in your eye."

"Mud in your eye," she said.

They drank. He put down his glass and took up the heavy suitcase.

"Got to get a train around six," he said.

She followed him down the hall. There was a song, a song that Mrs. Martin played doggedly on the phonograph, running loudly through her mind. She had never liked the thing.

Night and daytime,
Always playtime.
Ain't we got fun?

At the door he put down the bags and faced her.

"Well," he said. "Well, take care of yourself. You'll be all right, will you?"

"Oh, sure," she said.

He opened the door, then came back to her, holding out his hand.

" 'Bye, Haze," he said. "Good luck to you."

She took his hand and shook it.

"Pardon my wet glove," she said.

When the door had closed behind him she went back to the pantry.

She was flushed and lively when she went in to Mrs. Martin's that evening. The Boys were there, Ed among them. He was glad to be in town, frisky and loud and full of jokes. But she spoke quietly to him for a minute.

"Herbie blew to-day," she said. "Going to live out West."

"That so?" he said. He looked at her and played with the fountain pen clipped to his waistcoat pocket.

"Think he's gone for good, do you?" he asked.

"Yeah," she said. "I know he is. I know. Yeah."

"You going to live on across the hall just the same?" he said. "Know what you're going to do?"

"Gee, I don't know," she said. "I don't give much of a damn."

"Oh, come on, that's no way to talk," he told her. "What you need—you need a little snifter. How about it?"

"Yeah," she said. "Just straight."

She won forty-three dollars at poker. When the game broke up Ed took her back to her apartment.

"Got a little kiss for me?" he asked.

He wrapped her in his big arms and kissed her violently. She was entirely passive. He held her away and looked at her.

"Little tight, honey?" he asked anxiously. "Not going to be sick, are you?"

"Me?" she said. "I'm swell."

II

When Ed left in the morning he took her photograph with him. He said he wanted her picture to look at, up in Utica. "You can have that one on the bureau," she said.

She put Herbie's picture in a drawer, out of her sight. When she could look at it she meant to tear it up. She was fairly successful in keeping her mind from racing around him. Whisky slowed it for her. She was almost peaceful, in her mist.

She accepted her relationship with Ed without question or enthusiasm. When he was away she seldom thought definitely of him. He was good to her; he gave her frequent presents and a regular allowance. She was even able to save. She did not plan ahead of any day, but her wants were few, and you might as well put money in the bank as have it lying around.

When the lease of her apartment neared its end it was Ed who suggested moving. His friendship with Mrs. Martin and Joe had become strained over a dispute at poker; a feud was impending.

"Let's get the hell out of here," Ed said. "What I want you to have is a place near the Grand Central. Make it easier for me."

So she took a little flat in the Forties. A colored maid came in every day to clean and to make coffee for her—she was "through with that housekeeping stuff," she said, and Ed, twenty years married to a passionately domestic woman, admired this romantic uselessness and felt doubly a man of the world in abetting it.

The coffee was all she had until she went out to dinner, but alcohol kept her fat. Prohibition she regarded only as a basis for jokes. You could always get all you wanted. She was never noticeably drunk and seldom nearly sober. It required a larger daily allowance to keep her misty-minded. Too little, and she was achingly melancholy.

Ed brought her to Jimmy's. He was proud, with the pride of the transient who would be mistaken for a native, in his knowledge of small, recent restaurants occupying the lower floors of shabby brownstone houses; places where, upon mentioning the name of an habitué friend, might be obtained strange whisky and fresh gin in many of their ramifications. Jimmy's place was the favorite of his acquaintances.

There, through Ed, Mrs. Morse met many men and women, formed quick friendships. The men often took her out when Ed was in Utica. He was proud of her popularity.

She fell into the habit of going to Jimmy's alone when she had no engagement. She was certain to meet some people she knew, and join them. It was a club for her friends, both men and women.

The women at Jimmy's looked remarkably alike, and this was curious, for, through feuds, removals and opportunities of more profitable contacts, the personnel of the group changed constantly. Yet always the newcomers resembled those whom they replaced. They were all big women and stout, broad of shoulder and abundantly breasted, with faces thickly clothed in soft, high-colored flesh. They laughed loud and often, showing opaque and lusterless teeth like squares of crockery. There was about them the health of the big, yet a slight, unwholesome suggestion of stubborn preservation. They might have been thirty-six or forty-five or anywhere between.

They composed their titles of their own first names with their husband's surnames—Mrs. Florence Miller, Mrs. Vera Riley, Mrs. Lilian Block. This gave at the same time the solidity of marriage and the glamour of freedom. Yet only one or two were actually divorced. Most of them never referred to their dimmed spouses; some, a shorter time separate, described them in terms of great biological interest. Several were mothers, each of an only child—a boy at school somewhere, or a girl being cared for by a grandmother. Often, well on toward morning, there would be displays of kodak portraits and of tears.

They were comfortable women, cordial and friendly and irrepressibly matronly. Theirs was the quality of ease. Become fatalistic, especially about money matters, they were unworried. Whenever their funds dropped alarmingly, a new donor appeared; this had always happened. The aim of each was to have one man, permanently, to pay all her bills, in return for which she would have immediately given up other admirers and probably would have become exceedingly fond of him; for the affections of all of them were, by now, unexacting, tranquil, and easily arranged. This end, however, grew increasingly difficult yearly. Mrs. Morse was regarded as fortunate.

Ed had a good year, increased her allowance and gave her a sealskin coat. But she had to be careful of her moods with him. He insisted upon gayety. He would not listen to admissions of aches or weariness.

"Hey, listen," he would say, "I got worries of my own, and plenty. Nobody wants to hear other people's troubles, sweetie. What you got to do, you got to be a sport and forget it. See? Well, slip us a little smile, then. That's my girl."

She never had enough interest to quarrel with him as she had with Herbie, but she wanted the privilege of occasional admitted sadness. It was strange. The other women she saw did not have to fight their moods. There was Mrs. Florence Miller who got regular crying jags, and the men sought only to cheer and comfort her. The others spent whole evenings in grieved recitals of worries and ills; their escorts paid them deep sympathy. But she was instantly undesirable when she was low in spirits. Once, at Jimmy's, when she could not make herself lively, Ed had walked out and left her.

"Why the hell don't you stay home and not go spoiling everybody's evening?" he had roared.

Even her slightest acquaintance seemed irritated if she were not conspicuously light-hearted.

"What's the matter with you, anyway?" they would say. "Be your age, why don't you? Have a little drink and snap out of it."

When her relationship with Ed had continued nearly three years he moved to Florida to live. He hated leaving her; he gave her a large check and some shares of a sound stock, and his pale eyes were wet when he said good-bye. She did not miss him. He came to New York infrequently, perhaps two or three times a year, and hurried directly from the train to see her. She was always pleased to have him come and never sorry to see him go.

Charley, an acquaintance of Ed's that she had met at Jimmy's, had long admired her. He had always made opportunities of touching her and leaning close to talk to her. He asked repeatedly of all their friends if they had ever heard such a fine laugh as she had. After Ed left Charley became the main figure in her life. She classified him and spoke of him as "not so bad." There was nearly a year of Charley; then she divided her time between him and Sydney, another frequenter of Jimmy's; then Charley slipped away altogether.

Sydney was a little, brightly dressed, clever Jew. She was perhaps nearest contentment with him. He amused her always; her laughter was not forced.

He admired her completely. Her softness and size delighted him. And he thought she was great, he often told her, because she kept gay and lively when she was drunk.

"Once I had a gal," he said, "used to try to throw herself out of the window every time she got a can on, Jee-*zuss*," he added feelingly.

Then Sydney married a rich and watchful bride, and then there was Billy. No—after Sydney came Fred, then Billy. In her haze she never recalled how men entered her life and left it. There were no surprises. She had no thrill at their advent nor woe at their departure. She seemed to be always able to attract men. There was never another as rich as Ed, but they were all generous to her, in their means.

Once she had news of Herbie. She met Mrs. Martin dining at Jimmy's, and the old friendship was vigorously renewed. The still admiring Joe, while on a business trip, had seen Herbie. He had settled in Chicago, he looked fine, he was living with some woman—seemed to be crazy about her. Mrs. Morse had been drinking vastly that day. She took the news with mild interest, as one hearing of the sex peccadilloes of somebody whose name is, after a moment's groping, familiar.

"Must be damn near seven years since I saw him," she commented. "Gee, seven years."

More and more her days lost their individuality. She never knew dates, nor was sure of the day of the week.

"My God, was that a year ago!" she would exclaim, when an event was recalled in conversation.

She was tired so much of the time. Tired and blue. Almost everything could give her the blues. Those old horses she saw on Sixth Avenue—struggling and slipping along the car tracks, or standing at the curb, their heads dropped level with their worn knees. The tightly stored tears would squeeze from her eyes as she teetered past on her aching feet in the stubby, champagne-colored slippers.

The thought of death came and stayed with her and lent her a sort of drowsy cheer. It would be nice, nice and restful, to be dead.

There was no settled, shocked moment when she first thought of killing herself; it seemed to her as if the idea had always been with her. She pounced upon all the accounts of suicides in the newspapers. There was an epidemic of self-killings—or maybe it was just that she searched for the stories of them so eagerly that she found many. To read of them roused reassurance in her; she felt a cozy solidarity with the big company of the voluntary dead.

She slept, aided by whisky, till deep into the afternoons, then lay abed, a bottle and glass at her hand, until it was time to dress to go out for dinner. She was beginning to feel toward alcohol a little puzzled distrust, as toward an old friend who has refused a simple favor. Whisky could still soothe her for most of the time, but there were sudden, inexplicable moments when the cloud fell treacherously away from her, and she was sawn by the sorrow and bewilderment and nuisance of all living. She played voluptuously with the thought of cool, sleepy retreat. She had never been troubled by religious belief, and no vision of an after-life intimidated her. She dreamed by day of never again putting on tight shoes, of never having to laugh and listen and admire, of never more being a good sport. Never.

But how would you do it? It made her sick to think of jumping from heights. She could not stand a gun. At the theater, if one of the actors drew a revolver, she crammed her fingers into her ears and could not even look at the stage until after the shot had been fired. There was no gas in her flat. She looked long at the bright blue veins in her slim wrists—a cut with a razor blade, and there you'd be. But it would hurt, hurt like hell, and there would be blood to see. Poison—something tasteless and quick and painless—was the thing. But they wouldn't sell it to you in the drug stores, because of the law.

She had few other thoughts.

There was a new man now—Art. He was short and fat and exacting and hard on her patience when he was drunk. But there had been only occasionals for some time before him, and she was glad of a little stability. Too, Art must be away for weeks at a stretch, selling silks, and that was restful. She was convincingly gay with him, though the effort shook her viciously.

"The best sport in the world," he would murmur, deep in her neck. "The best sport in the world."

One night, when he had taken her to Jimmy's, she went into the dressing room with Mrs. Florence Miller. There, while designing curly mouths on their faces with lip rouge, they compared experiences of insomnia.

"Honestly," Mrs. Morse said, "I wouldn't close an eye if I didn't go to bed full of Scotch. I lie there and toss and turn and toss and turn. Blue! Does a person get blue lying awake that way!"

"Say, listen, Hazel," Mrs. Miller said impressively, "I'm telling you I'd be awake for a year if I didn't take veronal. That stuff makes you sleep like a fool."

"Isn't it poison or something?" Mrs. Morse asked.

"Oh, you take too much and you're out for the count," said Mrs. Miller. "I just take five grains—they come in tablets. I'd be scared to fool around with it. But five grains and you cork off pretty."

"Can you get it anywhere?" Mrs. Morse felt superbly Machiavellian.

"Get all you want in Jersey," said Mrs. Miller. "They won't give it to you here without you have a doctor's prescription. Finished? We'd better go back and see what the boys are doing."

That night Art left Mrs. Morse at the door of her apartment; his mother was in town. Mrs. Morse was still sober, and it happened that there was no whisky left in her cupboard. She lay in bed, looking up at the black ceiling.

She rose early, for her, and went to New Jersey. She had never taken the tube, and did not understand it. So she went to the Pennsylvania Station and bought a railroad ticket to Newark. She thought of nothing in particular on the trip out. She looked at the uninspired hats of the women about her and gazed through the smeared window at the flat, gritty scene.

In Newark, in the first drug store she came to, she asked for a tin of talcum powder, a nail brush, and a box of veronal tablets. The powder and the brush were to make the hypnotic seem also a casual need. The clerk was entirely unconcerned. "We only keep them in bottles," he said, and wrapped up for her a little glass vial containing ten white tablets, stacked one on another.

She went to another drug store and bought a face cloth, an orangewood stick, and a bottle of veronal tablets. The clerk was also uninterested.

"Well, I guess I got enough to kill an ox," she thought, and went back to the station.

At home, she put the little vials in the drawer of her dressing table and stood looking at them with a dreamy tenderness.

"There they are, God bless them," she said, and she kissed her finger tip and touched each bottle.

The colored maid was busy in the living room.

"Hey, Nettie," Mrs. Morse called. "Be an angel, will you? Run around to Jimmy's and get me a quart of Scotch."

She hummed while she awaited the girl's return.

During the next few days, whisky ministered to her as tenderly as it had done when she first turned to its aid. Alone, she was soothed and vague, at Jimmy's she was the gayest of the groups. Art was delighted with her.

Then, one night, she had an appointment to meet Art at Jimmy's for an early dinner. He was to leave afterward on a business excursion, to be away for a week. Mrs. Morse had been drinking all the afternoon; while she dressed to go out she felt herself rising pleasurably from drowsiness to high spirits. But as she came out into the street the effects of the whisky deserted her completely, and she was filled with a slow, grinding wretchedness so horrible that she stood swaying on the pavement, unable for a moment to move forward. It was a gray night with spurts of mean, thin snow, and the streets shone with dark ice. As she slowly crossed Sixth Avenue consciously dragging one foot past the other, a big, scarred horse pulling a rickety express wagon crashed to his knees before her. The driver swore and screamed and lashed the beast insanely, bringing the whip back over his shoulder for every blow, while the horse struggled to get a footing on the slippery asphalt. A group gathered and watched with interest.

Art was waiting, when Mrs. Morse reached Jimmy's.

"What's the matter with you, for God's sake?" was his greeting to her.

"I saw a horse," she said. "Gee, I—a person feels sorry for horses. I—it isn't just horses. Everything's kind of terrible, isn't it? I can't help getting sunk."

"Ah, sunk, me eye," he said. "What's the idea of all the bellyaching? What have you got to be sunk about?"

"I can't help it," she said.

"Ah, help it, me eye," he said. "Pull yourself together, will you? Come on and sit down, and take that face off you."

She drank industriously and she tried hard, but she could not overcome her melancholy. Others joined them and commented on her gloom, and she could do no more for them than smile weakly. She made little dabs at her eyes with her handkerchief, trying to time her movements so they would be unnoticed, but several times Art caught her and scowled and shifted impatiently in his chair.

When it was time for him to go to his train she said she would leave, too, and go home.

"And not a bad idea, either," he said. "See if you can't sleep yourself out of it. I'll see you Thursday. For God's sake, try and cheer up by then, will you?"

"Yeah," she said. "I will."

In her bedroom she undressed with a tense speed wholly unlike her usual slow uncertainty. She put on her nightgown, took off her hair net, and passed the comb quickly through her dry, varicolored hair. Then she took the two little vials from the drawer and carried them into the bathroom. The splintering misery had gone from her, and she felt the quick excitement of one who is about to receive an anticipated gift.

She uncorked the vials, filled a glass with water, and stood before the mirror, a tablet between her fingers. Suddenly she bowed graciously to her reflection and raised the glass to it.

"Well, here's mud in your eye," she said.

The tablets were unpleasant to take, dry and powdery and sticking obstinately halfway down her throat. It took her a long time to swallow all twenty of them. She stood watching her reflection with deep, impersonal interest, studying the movements of the gulping throat. Once more she spoke aloud to it.

"For God's sake, try and cheer up by Thursday, will you?" she said. "Well, you know what he can do. He and the whole lot of them."

She had no idea how quickly to expect effect from the veronal. When she had taken the last tablet she stood uncertainly, wondering, still with a courteous, vicarious interest, if death would strike her down then and there. She felt in no way strange, save for a slight stirring of sickness from the effort of swallowing the tablets, nor did her reflected face look at all different. It would not be immediate, then; it might even take an hour or so.

She stretched her arms high and gave a vast yawn.

"Guess I'll go to bed," she said. "Gee, I'm nearly dead."

That struck her as comic, and she turned out the bathroom light and went in and laid herself down in her bed, chuckling softly all the time.

"Gee, I'm nearly dead," she quoted. "That's a hot one!"

III

Nettie, the colored maid, came in late the next afternoon to clean the apartment and found Mrs. Morse in her bed. But then, that was not unusual. Usually, though, the sounds of cleaning waked her, and she did not like to wake up. Nettie, an agreeable girl, had learned to move softly about her work.

But when she had done the living room and stolen in to tidy the little square bedroom, she could not avoid a tiny clatter as she arranged the objects on the dressing table. Instinctively she glanced over her shoulder at the sleeper, and without warning a sickly uneasiness crept over her. She came to the bed and stared down at the woman lying there.

Mrs. Morse lay on her back, one flabby white arm flung up, the wrist against her forehead. Her stiff hair hung untenderly along her face. The bed covers were pushed down, exposing a deep square of soft neck and a pink nightgown, its fabric worn uneven by many launderings; her great breasts, freed from their tight confiner, sagged beneath her armpits. Now and then she made knotted, snoring sounds, and from the corner of her opened mouth to the blurred turn of her jaw ran a lane of crusted spittle.

"Mis' Morse," Nettie called. "Oh, Mis' Morse! It's terrible late."

Mrs. Morse made no move.

"Mis' Morse," said Nettie. "Look, Mis' Morse. How'm I goin' get this bed made?"

Panic sprang upon the girl. She shook the woman's hot shoulder.

"Ah, wake up, will yuh?" she whined. "Ah, please wake up."

Suddenly the girl turned and ran out in the hall to the elevator door, keeping her thumb firm on the black, shiny button until the elderly car and its Negro attendant stood before her. She poured a jumble of words over the boy and led him back to the apartment. He tiptoed creakingly in to the bedside; first gingerly, then so lustily that he left marks in the soft flesh, he prodded the unconscious woman.

"Hey, there!" he cried, and listened intently, as for an echo.

"Jeez. Out like a light," he commented.

At his interest in the spectacle, Nettie's panic left her. Importance was big in both of them. They talked in quick, unfinished whispers, and it was the boy's suggestion that he fetch the young doctor who lived on the ground floor. Nettie hurried along with him. They looked forward to the limelit moment of breaking their news of something untoward, something pleasurably unpleasant. Mrs. Morse had become the medium of drama. With no ill wish to her, they hoped that her state was serious, that she would not let them down by being awake and normal on their return. A little fear of this determined them to make the most, to the doctor, of her present condition. "Matter of life and death" returned to Nettie from her thin store of reading. She considered startling the doctor with the phrase.

The doctor was in and none too pleased at interruption. He wore a yellow and blue striped dressing gown, and he was lying on his sofa, laughing, with a dark girl, her face scaly with inexpensive powder, who perched on the arm. Half-emptied highball glasses stood beside them, and her coat and hat were neatly hung up with the comfortable implication of a long stay.

Always something, the doctor grumbled. Couldn't let anybody alone after a hard day. But he put some bottles and instruments into a case, changed his dressing gown for his coat, and started out with the Negroes.

"Snap it up there, big boy," the girl called after him. "Don't be all night."

The doctor strode loudly into Mrs. Morses' flat and on to the bedroom, Nettie and the boy right behind him. Mrs. Morse had not moved; her sleep was as deep, but soundless, now. The doctor looked sharply at her, then plunged his thumbs into the lidded pits above her eyeballs and threw his weight upon them. A high, sickened cry broke from Nettie.

"Look like he tryin' to push her right on th'ough the bed," said the boy. He chuckled.

Mrs. Morse gave no sign under the pressure. Abruptly the doctor abandoned it, and with one quick movement swept the covers down to the foot of the bed. With another he flung her nightgown back and lifted the thick, white legs, cross-hatched with blocks of tiny, iris-colored veins. He pinched them repeatedly, with long, cruel nips, back of the knees. She did not awaken.

"What's she been drinking?" he asked Nettie, over his shoulder.

With the certain celerity of one who knows just where to lay hands on a thing, Nettie went into the bathroom, bound for the cupboard where Mrs. Morse kept her whisky. But she stopped at the sight of the two vials, with their red and white labels, lying before the mirror. She brought them to the doctor.

"Oh, for the Lord Almighty's sweet sake!" he said. He dropped Mrs. Morse's limp legs and pushed them impatiently across the bed. "What did she want to go taking that tripe for? Rotten yellow trick, that's what a thing like that is. Now we'll have to pump her out, and all that stuff. Nuisance, a thing like that is; that's what it amounts to. Here, George, take me down in the elevator. You wait here, maid. She won't do anything."

"She won't die on me, will she?" cried Nettie.

"No," said the doctor. "God, no. You couldn't kill her with an ax."

IV

After two days Mrs. Morse came back to consciousness, dazed at first, then with a comprehension that brought with it the slow, saturating wretchedness.

"Oh, Lord, oh, Lord," she moaned, and tears for herself and for life striped her cheeks.

Nettie came in at the sound. For two days she had done the ugly, incessant tasks in the nursing of the unconscious, for two nights she had caught broken bits of sleep on the living room couch. She looked coldly at the big, blown woman in the bed.

"What you been tryin' to do, Mis' Morse?" she said. "What kine o' work is that, takin' all that stuff?"

"Oh, Lord," moaned Mrs. Morse again, and she tried to cover her eyes with her arms. But the joints felt stiff and brittle, and she cried out at their ache.

"That's no way to ack, takin' them pills," said Nettie. "You can thank you' stars you heah at all. How you feel now?"

"Oh, I feel great," said Mrs. Morse. "Swell, I feel."

Her hot, painful tears fell as if they would never stop.

"Tha's no way to take on, cryin' like that," Nettie said. "After what you done. The doctor, he says he could have you arrested, doin' a thing like that. He was fit to be tied, here."

"Why couldn't he let me alone?" wailed Mrs. Morse. "Why the hell couldn't he have?"

"That's terr'ble, Mis' Morse, swearin' an' talkin' like that," said Nettie, "after what people done for you. Here I ain' had no sleep at all, an' I had to give up goin' out to my other ladies!"

"Oh, I'm sorry, Nettie," she said. "You're a peach. I'm sorry I've given you so much trouble. I couldn't help it. I just got sunk. Didn't you ever feel like doing it? When everything looks just lousy to you?"

"I wouldn't think o' no such thing," declared Nettie. "You got to cheer up. Tha's what you got to do. Everybody's got their troubles."

"Yeah," said Mrs. Morse. "I know."

"Come a pretty picture card for you," Nettie said. "Maybe that will cheer you up."

She handed Mrs. Morse a post card. Mrs. Morse had to cover one eye with her hand, in order to read the message; her eyes were not yet focusing correctly.

It was from Art. On the back of a view of the Detroit Athletic Club he had written:

Greeting and salutations. Hope you have lost that gloom. Cheer up and don't take any rubber nickels. See you on Thursday.

She dropped the card to the floor. Misery crushed her as if she were between great smooth stones. There passed before her a slow, slow pageant of days spent lying in her flat, of evenings at Jimmy's being a good sport, making herself laugh and coo at Art and other Arts; she saw a long parade of weary horses and shivering beggars and all beaten, driven, stumbling things. Her feet throbbed as if she had crammed them into the stubby champagne-colored slippers. Her heart seemed to swell and fester.

"Nettie," she cried, "for heaven's sake, pour me a drink, will you?"

The maid looked doubtful.

"Now you know, Mis' Morse," she said, "you been near daid. I don' know if the doctor he let you drink nothin' yet."

"Oh, never mind him," she said. "You get me one and bring in the bottle. Take one yourself."

"Well," said Nettie.

She poured them each a drink, deferentially leaving hers in the bathroom to be taken in solitude, and brought Mrs. Morse's glass in to her.

Mrs. Morse looked into the liquor and shuddered back from its odor. Maybe it would help. Maybe, when you had been knocked cold for a few days, your very first drink would give you a lift. Maybe whisky would be her friend again. She prayed without addressing a God, without knowing a God. Oh, please, please, let her be able to get drunk, please keep her always drunk.

She lifted the glass.

"Thanks, Nettie," she said. "Here's mud in your eye."

The maid giggled. "Tha's the way, Mis' Morse," she said. "You cheer up, now."

"Yeah," said Mrs. Morse. "Sure."

BARTOLOMEO VANZETTI

[1888–1927]

ONE OF THE MOST bitterly prolonged and fiercely controversial cases in legal history was the trial of two men for murder in Dedham, Massachusetts. On April 15, 1920, a paymaster and his guard had been killed, a payroll of about $16,000 had been seized, and the killers had escaped. Two immigrants, Bartolomeo Vanzetti and Nicola Sacco, a fish peddler and a cobbler, were picked up and charged with the crime. They were tried and found guilty of murder, with no recommendation for mercy. Their case was appealed; it went on for six years.

During those six years thousands of people came to doubt the justice of the verdict. It was a time of a "red scare" and witch hunts, when feelings against all foreigners and nonconformists ran high. Sacco and Vanzetti were philosophical anarchists whose creed included political violence but not commercial crime, and many believed that the two men were convicted not because they had committed murder but because they had committed themselves to a dangerous philosophy. Protests poured in from all over the world; pickets paraded around the courthouse carrying placards saying: "Sacco and Vanzetti Must Not Die." Nevertheless, the two were executed in 1927.

The echoes of what began as a small-town prosecution and developed into a cause célèbre continued to agitate for more than thirty years. In 1959 a bill was introduced in Massachusetts asking posthumous pardons for Sacco and Vanzetti on the ground that they had been "victims of the anti-foreigner hysteria of the times." The bill was sidetracked and no pardons were issued.

Two documents follow. The first is Vanzetti's misspelled, dignified, and even noble statement to the court. The second is a letter to the son of his friend and companion, Nicola Sacco. The letter has been compared to William Lloyd Garrison's "I am in earnest; I will not equivocate; I will not excuse; I will not retreat a single inch; and I will be heard."

VANZETTI TO JUDGE THAYER

IF IT HAD NOT BEEN for these things, I might have live out my life talking at street corners to scorning men. I might have die, unmarked, unknown, a failure. Now we are not a failure. This is our career and our triumph. Never in our full life could we hope to do such work for tolerance, for joostice, for man's onderstanding of man as now we do by accident. Our words—our lives—our pains—nothing! The taking of our lives—lives of a good shoemaker and a poor fish peddler—all! That last moment belongs to us—that agony is our triumph.

VANZETTI TO SACCO'S SON

August 21, 1927. From the Death House
of Massachusetts State Prison

MY DEAR DANTE:

I still hope, and we will fight until the last moment, to revindicate our right to live and to be free, but all the forces of the State and of the money and reaction are deadly against us because we are libertarians or anarchists.

I write little of this because you are now and yet too young to understand these things and other things of which I would like to reason with you.

But, if you do well, you will grow and understand your father's and my case and your father's and my principles, for which we will soon be put to death.

I tell you now that all that I know of your father, he is not a criminal, but one of the bravest men I ever knew. Some day you will understand what I am about to tell you. That your father has sacrificed everything dear and sacred to the human heart and soul for his fate in liberty and justice for all. That day you will be proud of your father, and if you come brave enough, you will take his place in the struggle between tyranny and liberty and you will vindicate his (our) names and our blood.

If we have to die now, you shall know, when you will be able to understand this tragedy in its fullest, how good and brave your father has been with you, your father and I, during these eight years of struggle, sorrow, passion, anguish and agony.

Even from now you shall be good, brave with your mother, with Ines, and with Susie—brave, good Susie—and do all you can to console and help them.

I would like you to also remember me as a comrade and friend to your father, your mother and Ines, Susie and you, and I assure you that neither have I been a criminal, that I have committed no robbery and no murder, but only fought modestily to abolish crimes from among mankind and for the liberty of all.

Remember Dante, each one who will say otherwise of your father and I, is a liar, insulting innocent dead men who have been brave in their life. Remember and know also, Dante, that if your father and I would have been cowards and hypocrits and rinnegetors of our faith, we would not have been put to death. They would not even have convicted a lebbrous dog; not even executed a deadly poisoned scorpion on such evidence as that they framed against us. They would have given a new trial to a matricide and abitual felon on the evidence we presented for a new trial.

Remember, Dante, remember always these things; we are not criminals; they convicted us on a frame-up; they denied us a new trial; and if we will be executed after seven years, four months and seventeen days of unspeakable tortures and wrong, it is for what I have already told you; because we were for the poor and against the exploitation and oppression of the man by the man.

The documents of our case, which you and other ones will collect and preserve, will prove to you that your father, your mother, Ines, my family and I have sacrificed by and to a State Reason of the American Plutocratic reaction.

The day will come when you will understand the atrocious cause of the above written words, in all its fullness. Then you will honor us.

Now Dante, be brave and good always. I embrace you.

P.S. I left the copy of *An American Bible* to your mother now, for she will like to read it, and she will give it to you when you will be bigger and able to understand it. Keep it for remembrance. It will also testify to you how good and generous Mrs. Gertrude Winslow has been with us all. Good-bye Dante.

Bartolomeo

JAMES THURBER

[1894–]

A WRY AND FANTASTIC HUMORIST whose "little wheels of invention are set in motion by the damp hand of melancholy," James Thurber was born December 8, 1894, in Columbus, Ohio. He attended Ohio State University, where he edited the undergraduate humor magazine, and left college to be a code clerk in the State Department. After the First

World War he became a reporter and worked on several newspapers. In his thirty-third year he joined the staff of The New Yorker and, after seven crowded years, left the staff in order to have more time for his own work. He moved to Cornwall, Connecticut, but continued to be one of the most valued contributors to the metropolitan magazine.

Thurber had lost an eye because of a bow-and-arrow accident in childhood, and the strain on his other eye was so great that by the time he was fifty he was almost blind. Nevertheless, he was able to continue writing and drawing—his portrayals of cowed men, aggressive women, and doleful dogs became famous—by painstakingly inscribing large letters and designs on huge sheets of paper. He said philosophically, "My one-eighth vision happily obscures sad and ungainly sights, leaving only the vivid and the radiant." In spite of his handicap, by the time he was sixty he had produced twenty volumes which included straight-faced nonsense, burlesques of current literary fashions, distorted murder mysteries, moral fairytales for children, morally dubious fables for adults, a play—The Male Animal, and stories which were described as "a mixture of laughing gas and deadly nightshade." "The Secret Life of Walter Mitty," a half-comic, half-pitiful revelation of the typical housebroken husband, is his most reprinted piece of fiction; it has been transmogrified for radio, television, and a Hollywood vehicle for Danny Kaye.

One of Thurber's most characteristic pieces is a hilarious whimsicality. Scribner's Magazine had published a series of three "if" articles: "If Booth Had Missed Lincoln," "If Napoleon Had Escaped to America," and "If Lee Had Not Won the Battle of Gettysburg." When Thurber was asked to contribute something to the series, he took his cue from the last title and wrote "If Grant Had Been Drinking at Appomattox."

In his mid-sixties Thurber spent almost two years writing The Years With Ross, an account of his association with the unaccountable editor and founder of The New Yorker. Ross often declared that writers were a dime a dozen and had put Thurber to work as an executive editor, a role which Thurber did not relish. However, before he was able to free himself of the responsibility, Thurber's association with Ross had sharpened his own talent for clarity and precision.

Thurber considers humanity with a tartness that is not without tenderness but also includes a liberal dash of criticism. He is a jester who is part Jeremiah. The Thurber Carnival and Thurber Country contain many of his most bewildering yet logical pieces of madness. "Humor," said Thurber, "is a kind of emotional chaos told about calmly and *quietly in retrospect." This may not be a satisfying definition for all humor, but it completely defines the kind of humor with which Thurber regards the unpredictable acts and accidents of a wayward and usually perverse fate.*

THE NIGHT THE BED FELL

I SUPPOSE THAT THE HIGH-WATER MARK of my youth in Columbus, Ohio, was the night the bed fell on my father. It makes a better recitation (unless, as some friends of mine have said, one has heard it five or six times) than it does a piece of writing, for it is almost necessary to throw furniture around, shake doors, and bark like a dog, to lend the proper atmosphere and verisimilitude to what is admittedly a somewhat incredible tale. Still, it did take place.

It happened, then, that my father had decided to sleep in the attic one night, to be away where he could think. My mother opposed the notion strongly because, she said, the old wooden bed up there was unsafe: it was wobbly and the heavy headboard would crash down on my father's head in case the bed fell, and kill him. There was no dissuading him, however, and at a quarter past ten he closed the attic door behind him and went up the narrow twisting stairs. We later heard ominous creakings as he crawled into bed. Grandfather, who usually slept in the attic bed when he was with us, had disappeared some days before. (On these occasions he was usually gone six or eight days and returned growling and out of temper, with the news that the federal Union was run by a passel of blockheads and that the Army of the Potomac didn't have any more chance than a fiddler's bitch.)

We had visiting us at this time a nervous first cousin of mine named Briggs Beall, who believed that he was likely to cease breathing when he was asleep. It was his feeling that if he were not awakened every hour during the night, he might die of suffocation. He had been accustomed to setting an alarm clock to ring at intervals until morning, but I persuaded him to abandon this. He slept in my room and I told him that I was such a light sleeper that if anybody quit breathing in the same room with me, I would wake instantly. He tested me the first night—which I had suspected he would—by holding his breath after my regular breathing had convinced him I was asleep. I was not asleep, however, and called to him. This seemed to allay his fears a little, but he took the precaution of putting a glass of spirits of camphor on a little table at the head of his bed. In case I didn't arouse him until he was almost gone, he said, he would sniff the camphor, a powerful reviver. Briggs was not the only member of his family who had his crotchets. Old Aunt Melissa Beall (who could whistle like a man, with two fingers in her mouth) suffered under the premonition that she was destined to die on South High Street, because she had been born on South High Street and married on South High Street. Then there was Aunt Sarah Shoaf, who never went to bed at night without the fear that a burglar was going to get in and blow chloroform under her door through a tube. To avert this calamity—for she was in greater dread of anesthetics than of losing her household goods—she always piled her money, silverware, and other valuables in a neat stack just outside her bedroom, with a note reading: "This is all I have. Please take it and do not use your chloroform, as this is all I have." Aunt Gracie Shoaf also had a burglar phobia, but she met it with more fortitude. She was confident that burglars had been getting into her house every night for forty years. The fact that she never missed anything was to her no proof to the contrary. She always claimed that she scared them off before they could take anything, by throwing shoes down the hallway. When she went to bed she piled, where she could get at them handily, all the shoes there were about her house. Five minutes after she had turned off the light, she would sit up in bed and say "Hark!" Her husband, who had learned to ignore the whole situation as long ago as 1903, would either be sound asleep or pretend to be sound asleep. In either case he would not respond to her tugging and pulling, so that presently she would arise, tiptoe to the door, open it slightly and heave a shoe down the hall in one direction, and its mate down the hall in the other direction. Some nights she threw them all, some nights only a couple of pair.

But I am straying from the remarkable incidents that took place during the night that the bed fell on father. By midnight we were all in bed. The layout of the rooms and the disposition of their occupants is important to an understanding of what later occurred. In the front room upstairs (just under father's attic bedroom) were my mother and my brother Herman, who sometimes sang in his sleep, usually "Marching Through Georgia" or "Onward Christian Soldiers." Briggs Beall and myself were in a room adjoining this one. My brother Roy was in a room across the hall from ours. Our bull terrier, Rex, slept in the hall.

My bed was an army cot, one of those affairs which are made wide enough to sleep on comfortably only by putting up, flat with the middle section, the two sides which ordinarily hang down like the sideboards of a dropleaf table. When these sides are up, it is perilous to roll too far toward the edge, for then the cot is likely to tip completely over, bringing the whole bed down on top of one, with a tremendous banging crash. This, in fact, is precisely what happened, about two o'clock in the morning. (It was my mother who, in recalling the scene later, first referred to it as "the night the bed fell on your father.")

Always a deep sleeper, slow to arouse (I had lied to Briggs), I was at first unconscious of what had happened when the iron cot rolled me onto the floor and toppled over on me. It left me still warmly bundled up and unhurt, for the bed rested above me like a canopy. Hence I did not wake up, only reached the edge of consciousness and went back. The racket, however, instantly awakened my mother, in the next room, who came to the immediate conclusion that her worst dread was realized: the big wooden bed upstairs had fallen on father. She therefore screamed, "Let's go to your poor father!" It was this shout, rather than the noise of my cot falling, that awakened Herman, in the same room with her. He thought that mother had become, for no apparent reason, hysterical. "You're all right, Mamma!" he shouted, trying to calm her. They exchanged shout for shout for perhaps ten seconds: "Let's go to your poor father!" and "You're all right!" That woke up Briggs. By this time I was conscious of what was going on, in a vague way, but did not yet realize that I was under my bed instead of on it. Briggs, awakening in the midst of loud shouts of fear and apprehension, came to the quick conclusion that he was suffocating and that we were all trying to "bring him out." With a low moan, he grasped the glass of camphor at the head of his bed and instead of sniffing it poured it over himself. The room reeked of camphor. "Ugf, ahfg," choked Briggs, like a drowning man, for he had almost succeeded in stopping his breath under the deluge of pungent spirits. He leaped out of bed and groped toward the open window, but he came up against one that was closed. With his hand, he beat out the glass, and I could hear it crash and tinkle on the alleyway below. It was at this juncture that I, in trying to get up, had the uncanny sensation of feeling my bed above me! Foggy with sleep, I now suspected, in my turn, that the whole uproar was being made in a frantic endeavor to extricate me from what must be an unheard-of and perilous situation. "Get me out of this!" I bawled. "Get me out!" I think I had the nightmarish belief that I was entombed in a mine. "Gugh," gasped Briggs, floundering in his camphor.

By this time my mother, still shouting, pursued by Herman, still shouting, was trying to open the door to the attic, in order to go up and get my father's body out of the wreckage. The door was stuck, however, and wouldn't yield. Her frantic pulls on it only added to the general banging and confusion. Roy and the dog were now up, the one shouting questions, the other barking.

Father, farthest away and soundest sleeper of all, had by this time been awakened by the battering on the attic door. He decided that the house was on fire. "I'm coming, I'm coming!" he wailed in a slow, sleepy voice—it took him many minutes to regain full consciousness. My mother, still believing he was caught under the bed, detected in his "I'm coming!" the mournful, resigned note of one who is preparing to meet his Maker. "He's dying!" she shouted.

"I'm all right!" Briggs yelled to reassure her. "I'm all right!" He still believed that it was his own closeness to death that was worrying mother. I found at last the light switch in my room, unlocked the door, and Briggs and I joined the others at the attic door. The dog, who never did like Briggs, jumped for him—assuming that he was the culprit in whatever was going on—and Roy had to throw Rex and hold him. We could hear father crawling out of bed upstairs. Roy pulled the attic door open, with a mighty jerk and father came down the stairs, sleepy and irritable but safe and sound. My mother began to weep when she saw him. Rex began to howl. "What in the name of God is going on here?" asked father.

The situation was finally put together like a gigantic jigsaw puzzle. Father caught a cold from prowling around in his bare feet but there were no other bad results. "I'm glad," said mother, who always looked on the bright side of things, "that your grandfather wasn't here."

THE SECRET LIFE OF WALTER MITTY

WE'RE GOING THROUGH!" The Commander's voice was like thin ice breaking. He wore his full-dress uniform, with the heavily braided white cap pulled down rakishly over one cold gray eye. "We can't make it, sir. It's spoiling for a hurricane, if you ask me." "I'm not asking you, Lieutenant Berg," said the Commander. "Throw on the power lights! Rev her up to 8,500! We're going through!" The pounding of the cylinders increased: ta-pocketa-pocketa-pocketa-*pocketa-pocketa*. The Commander stared at the ice forming on the pilot window. He walked over and twisted a row of complicated dials. "Switch on No. 8 auxiliary!" he shouted. "Switch on

No. 8 auxiliary!" repeated Lieutenant Berg. "Full strength in No. 3 turret!" shouted the Commander. "Full strength in No. 3 turret!" The crew, bending to their various tasks in the huge, hurtling eight-engined Navy hydroplane, looked at each other and grinned. "The Old Man'll get us through," they said to one another. "The Old Man ain't afraid of Hell!" . . .

"Not so fast! You're driving too fast!" said Mrs. Mitty. "What are you driving so fast for?"

"Hmm?" said Walter Mitty. He looked at his wife, in the seat beside him, with shocked astonishment. She seemed grossly unfamiliar, like a strange woman who had yelled at him in a crowd. "You were up to fifty-five," she said. "You know I don't like to go more than forty. You were up to fifty-five." Walter Mitty drove on toward Waterbury in silence, the roaring of the SN202 through the worst storm in twenty years of Navy flying fading in the remote, intimate airways of his mind. "You're tensed up again," said Mrs. Mitty. "It's one of your days. I wish you'd let Dr. Renshaw look you over."

Walter Mitty stopped the car in front of the building where his wife went to have her hair done. "Remember to get those overshoes while I'm having my hair done," she said. "I don't need overshoes," said Mitty. She put her mirror back into her bag. "We've been all through that," she said, getting out of the car. "You're not a young man any longer." He raced the engine a little. "Why don't you wear your gloves? Have you lost your gloves?" Walter Mitty reached in a pocket and brought out the gloves. He put them on, but after she had turned and gone into the building and he had driven on to a red light, he took them off again. "Pick it up, brother!" snapped a cop as the light changed, and Mitty hastily pulled on his gloves and lurched ahead. He drove around the streets aimlessly for a time, and then he drove past the hospital on his way to the parking lot.

. . . "It's the millionaire banker, Wellington McMillan," said the pretty nurse. "Yes?" said Walter Mitty, removing his gloves slowly. "Who has the case?" "Dr. Renshaw and Dr. Benbow, but there are two specialists here, Dr. Remington from New York and Mr. Pritchard-Mitford from London. He flew over." A door opened down a long, cool corridor and Dr. Renshaw came out. He looked distraught and haggard. "Hello, Mitty," he said. "We're having the devil's own time with McMillan, the millionaire banker and close personal friend of Roosevelt. Obstreosis of the ductal tract. Tertiary. Wish you'd take a look at him." "Glad to," said Mitty.

In the operating room there were whispered introductions: "Dr. Remington, Dr. Mitty, Mr. Pritchard-Mitford, Dr. Mitty." "I've read your book on streptothricosis," said Pritchard-Mitford, shaking hands. "A brilliant performance, sir." "Thank you," said Walter Mitty. "Didn't know you were in the States, Mitty," grumbled Remington. "Coals to Newcastle, bringing Mitford and me up here for a tertiary." "You are very kind," said Mitty. A huge, complicated machine, connected to the operating table, with many tubes and wires, began at this moment to go pocketa-pocketa-pocketa. "The new anesthetizer is giving way!" shouted an interne. "There is no one in the East who knows how to fix it!" "Quiet, man!" said Mitty, in a low, cool voice. He sprang to the machine, which was now going pocketa-pocketa-queep-pocketa-queep. He began fingering delicately a row of glistening dials. "Give me a fountain pen!" he snapped. Someone handed him a fountain pen. He pulled a faulty piston out of the machine and inserted the pen in its place. "That will hold for ten minutes," he said. "Get on with the operation." A nurse hurried over and whispered to Renshaw, and Mitty saw the man turn pale. "Coreopsis has set in," said Renshaw nervously. "If you would take over, Mitty?" Mitty looked at him and at the craven figure of Benbow, who drank, and at the grave, uncertain faces of the two great specialists. "If you wish," he said. They slipped a white gown on him; he adjusted a mask and drew on thin gloves; nurses handed him shining . . .

"Back it up, Mac! Look out for that Buick!" Walter Mitty jammed on the brakes. "Wrong lane, Mac," said the parking-lot attendant, looking at Mitty closely. "Gee. Yeh," muttered Mitty. He began cautiously to back out of the lane marked "Exit Only." "Leave her sit there," said the attendant. "I'll put her away." Mitty got out of the car. "Hey, better leave the key." "Oh," said Mitty, handing the man the ignition key. The attendant vaulted into the car, backed it up with insolent skill, and put it where it belonged.

They're so damn cocky, thought Walter Mitty, walking along Main Street; they think they know everything. Once he had tried to take his chains off, outside New Milford, and he had got them wound around the axles. A man had had to come out in a wrecking car and unwind them, a young, grinning garageman. Since then Mrs. Mitty always made him drive to a garage to have the chains taken off. The next time, he thought, I'll wear my right arm in a sling; they won't grin at me then. I'll have my right arm in a sling and they'll see I couldn't possibly take the chains off myself. He kicked at the slush on the sidewalk. "Overshoes," he said to himself, and he began looking for a shoe store.

When he came out into the street again, with the overshoes in a box under his arm, Walter Mitty began to wonder what the other thing was his wife had told him to get. She had told him twice, before they set out from their house for Waterbury. In a way he hated these weekly trips to town—he was always getting something wrong. Kleenex, he thought, Squibb's, razor blades? No. Toothpaste, toothbrush, bicarbonate, carborundum, initiative and referendum? He gave it up. But she would remember it. "Where's the what's-its-name?" she would ask. "Don't tell me you forgot the what's-its-name." A newsboy went by shouting something about the Waterbury trial.

. . . "Perhaps this will refresh your memory." The District Attorney suddenly thrust a heavy automatic at the quiet figure on the witness stand. "Have you ever seen this before?" Walter Mitty took the gun and examined it expertly. "This is my Webley-Vickers 50.80," he said calmly. An excited buzz ran around the courtroom. The judge rapped for order. "You are a crack shot with any sort of firearms, I believe?" said the District Attorney, insinuatingly. "Objection!" shouted Mitty's attorney, "We have shown that the defendant could not have fired the shot. We have shown that he wore his right arm in a sling on the night of the fourteenth of July." Walter Mitty raised his hand briefly and the bickering attorneys were stilled. "With any known make of gun," he said evenly, "I could have killed Gregory Fitzhurst at three hundred feet *with my left hand*." Pandemonium broke loose in the courtroom. A woman's scream rose above the bedlam and suddenly a lovely, dark-haired girl was in Walter Mitty's arms. The District Attorney struck at her savagely. Without rising from his chair. Mitty let the man have it on the point of the chin. "You miserable cur!" . . .

"Puppy biscuit," said Walter Mitty. He stopped walking and the buildings of Waterbury rose up out of the misty courtroom and surrounded him again. A woman who was passing laughed. "He said 'Puppy biscuit,'" she said to her companion. "That man said 'Puppy biscuit' to himself." Walter Mitty hurried on. He went into an A. & P., not the first one he came to but a smaller one farther up the street. "I want some biscuit for small, young dogs," he said to the clerk. "Any special brand, sir?" The greatest pistol shot in the world thought a moment. "It says 'Puppies Bark for It' on the box," said Walter Mitty.

His wife would be through at the hairdresser's in fifteen minutes, Mitty saw in looking at his watch, unless they had trouble drying it; sometimes they had trouble drying it. She didn't like to get to the hotel first; she would want him to be there waiting for her as usual. He found a big leather chair in the lobby, facing a window, and he put the overshoes and the puppy biscuit on the floor beside it. He picked up an old copy of *Liberty* and sank down into the chair. "Can Germany Conquer the World Through the Air?" Walter Mitty looked at the pictures of bombing planes and of ruined streets.

. . . "The cannonading has got the wind up in young Raleigh, sir," said the sergeant. Captain Mitty looked up at him through tousled hair. "Get him to bed," he said wearily. "With the others. I'll fly alone." "But you can't sir," said the sergeant anxiously. "It takes two men to handle that bomber and the Archies are pounding hell out of the air. Von Richtman's circus is between here and Saulier." "Somebody's got to get that ammunition dump," said Mitty. "I'm going over. Spot of brandy?" He poured a drink for the sergeant and one for himself. War thundered and whined around the dugout and battered at the door. There was a rending of wood and splinters flew through the room. "A bit of a near thing," said Captain Mitty carelessly. "The box barrage is closing in," said the sergeant. "We only live once, Sergeant," said Mitty, with his faint, fleeting smile. "Or do we?" He poured another brandy and tossed it off. "I never see a man could hold his brandy like you, sir," said the sergeant. "Begging your pardon, sir." Captain Mitty stood up and strapped on his huge Webley-Vickers automatic. "It's forty kilometers through hell, sir," said the sergeant. Mitty finished one last brandy. "After all," he said softly, "what isn't?" The pounding of the cannon increased; there was the rat-tat-tatting of machine guns, and from somewhere came the menacing pocketa-pocketa-pocketa of the new flame-throwers. Walter Mitty walked to the door of the dugout humming "Auprès de Ma Blonde." He turned and waved to the sergeant. "Cheerio!" he said. . . .

Something struck his shoulder. "I've been looking all over this hotel for you," said Mrs. Mitty. "Why do you have to hide in this old chair? How did you expect me to find you?" "Things close in," said Walter Mitty vaguely. "What?" Mrs. Mitty said. "Did you get the what's-its-name? The puppy biscuit? What's in that box?" "Overshoes," said Mitty. "Couldn't you have put them on in the store?" "I was thinking," said Walter Mitty. "Does it ever occur to you that I am sometimes thinking?" She looked at him. "I'm going to take your temperature when I get you home," she said.

They went out through the revolving doors that made a faintly derisive whistling sound when you pushed them. It was two blocks to the parking lot. At the drugstore on the corner she said, "Wait here for me. I forgot something. I won't be a minute." She was more than a minute. Walter Mitty lighted a cigarette. It began to rain, rain with sleet in it. He stood up against the wall of the drugstore, smoking. . . . He put his shoulders back and his heels together. "To hell with the handkerchief," said Walter Mitty scornfully. He took one last drag on his cigarette and snapped it away. Then, with that faint, fleeting smile playing about his lips, he faced the firing squad; erect and motionless, proud and disdainful, Walter Mitty the Undefeated, inscrutable to the last.

IF GRANT HAD BEEN DRINKING AT APPOMATTOX

THE MORNING OF THE NINTH of April 1865, dawned beautifully. General Meade was up with the first streaks of crimson in the eastern sky. General Hooker and General Burnside were up, and had breakfasted, by a quarter after eight. The day continued beautiful. It drew on toward eleven o'clock. General Ulysses S. Grant was still not up. He was asleep in his famous old navy hammock, swung high above the floor of his headquarters' bedroom. Headquarters was distressingly disarranged: papers were strewn on the floor; confidential notes from spies scurried here and there in the breeze from an open window; the dregs of an overturned bottle of wine flowed pinkly across an important military map.

Corporal Shultz, of the Sixty-fifth Ohio Volunteer Infantry, aide to General Grant, came into the outer room, looked around him, and sighed. He entered the bedroom and shook the General's hammock roughly. General Ulysses S. Grant opened one eye.

"Pardon, sir," said Corporal Shultz, "but this is the day of surrender. You ought to be up, sir."

"Don't swing me," said Grant, sharply, for his aide was making the hammock sway gently. "I feel terrible," he added, and he turned over and closed his eye again.

"General Lee will be here any minute now," said the Corporal firmly, swinging the hammock again.

"Will you cut that out?" roared Grant. "D'ya want to make me sick, or what?" Shultz clicked his heels and saluted. "What's he coming here for?" asked the General.

"This is the day of surrender, sir," said Shultz. Grant grunted bitterly.

"Three hundred and fifty generals in the Northern armies," said Grant, "and he has to come to *me* about this. What time is it?"

"You're the Commander-in-Chief, that's why," said Corporal Shultz. "It's eleven twenty-five, sir."

"Don't be crazy," said Grant. "Lincoln is the Commander-in-Chief. Nobody in the history of the world ever surrendered before lunch. Doesn't he know that any army surrenders on its stomach?" He pulled a blanket up over his head and settled himself again.

"The generals of the Confederacy will be here any minute now," said the Corporal. "You really ought to be up, sir."

Grant stretched his arms above his head and yawned.

"All right, all right," he said. He rose to a sitting position and stared about the room. "This place looks awful," he growled.

"You must have had quite a time of it last night, sir," ventured Shultz.

"Yeh," said General Grant, looking around for his clothes. "I was wrassling some general. Some general with a beard."

Schultz helped the commander of the Northern armies in the field to find his clothes.

"Where's my other sock?" demanded Grant. Schultz began to look around for it. The General walked uncertainly to a table and poured a drink from a bottle.

"I don't think it wise to drink, sir," said Shultz.

"Nev' mind about me," said Grant, helping himself to a second, "I can take it or let it alone. Didn' ya ever hear the story about the fella went to Lincoln to complain about me drinking to much? 'So-and-So says Grant drinks too much,' this fella said. 'So-and-So is a fool,' said Lincoln. So this fella went to What's-His-Name and told him what Lincoln said and he came roarin' to Lincoln about it. 'Did you tell So-and-So I was a fool?' he said. 'No,' said Lincoln, 'I thought he knew it.'" The General smiled, reminiscently, and had another drink. "*That's* how I stand with Lincoln," he said, proudly.

The soft thudding sound of horses' hooves came through the open window. Shultz hurriedly walked over and looked out.

"Hoof steps," said Grant, with a curious chortle.

"It is General Lee and his staff," said Shultz.

"Show him in," said the General, taking another drink. "And see what the boys in the back room will have."

Shultz walked smartly over to the door, opened it, saluted, and stood aside. General Lee, dignified against the blue of the April sky, magnificent in his dress uniform, stood for a moment framed in the doorway. He walked in, followed by his staff. They bowed, and stood silent. General Grant stared at them. He only had one boot on and his jacket was unbuttoned.

"I know who you are," said Grant. "You're Robert Browning, the poet."

"This is General Robert E. Lee," said one of his staff, coldly.

"Oh," said Grant. "I thought he was Robert Browning. He certainly looks like Robert Browning. There was a poet for you, Lee: Browning. Did ja ever read 'How They Brought the Good News from Ghent to Aix'? 'Up Derek, to saddle, up Derek, away; up Dunder, up Blitzen, up Prancer, up Dancer, up Bouncer, up Vixen, up ——"

"Shall we proceed at once to the matter in hand?" asked General Lee, his eyes disdainfully taking in the disordered room.

"Some of the boys was wrassling here last night," explained Grant. "I threw Sherman, or some general a whole lot like Sherman. It was pretty dark." He handed a bottle of Scotch to the commanding officer of the Southern armies, who stood holding it, in amazement and discomfiture. "Get a glass, somebody," said Grant, looking straight at General Longstreet. "Didn't I meet you at Cold Harbor?" he asked. General Longstreet did not answer.

"I should like to have this over with as soon as possible," said Lee. Grant looked vaguely at Shultz, who walked up close to him, frowning.

"The surrender, sir, the surrender," said Corporal Shultz in a whisper.

"Oh sure, sure," said Grant. He took another drink. "All right," he said. "Here we go." Slowly, sadly, he unbuckled his sword. Then he handed it to the astonished Lee. "There you are, General," said Grant. "We dam' near licked you. If I'd been feeling better we *would* of licked you."

THE TRUTH ABOUT TOADS

A Fable

ONE MIDSUMMER NIGHT at the Fauna Club, some of the members fell to boasting, each of his own unique distinction or achievement.

"I am the real Macaw," squawked the Macaw proudly.

"O.K.., Mac, take it easy," said the Raven, who was tending bar.

"You should have seen the one I got away from," said the Marlin. "He must have weighed a good two hundred and thirty-five pounds."

"If it weren't for me, the sun would never rise," bragged the Rooster, "and the desire of the night for the morrow would never be gratified." He wiped a tear away. "If it weren't for me, nobody would get up."

"If it weren't for me, there wouldn't *be* anybody," the Stork reminded him proudly.

"I tell them when spring is coming," the Robin chirped.

"I tell them when winter will end," the Groundhog said.

"I tell them how deep the winter will be," said the Woolly Bear.

"I swing low when a storm is coming," said the Spider. "Otherwise it wouldn't come, and the people would die of a drought."

The Mouse got into the act. "You know where it says, 'Not a creature was stirring, not even a mouse'?" he hiccuped. "Well, gentlemen, that little old mouse was little old me."

"Quiet!" said the Raven, who had been lettering a sign and now hung it prominently above the bar: "Open most hearts and you will see graven upon them Vanity."

The members of the Fauna Club stared at the sign. "Probably means the Wolf, who thinks he founded Rome," said the Cat.

"Or the great Bear, who thinks he is made of stars," said the Mouse.

"Or the golden Eagle, who thinks he's made of gold," said the Rooster.

"Or the Sheep, who thinks men couldn't sleep unless they counted sheep," said the Marlin.

The Toad came up to the bar and ordered a green mint frappé with a firefly in it.

"Fireflies will make you lightheaded," warned the bartender.

"Not me," said the Toad. "Nothing can make me lightheaded. I have a precious jewel in my head." The other members of the club looked at him with mingled disbelief.

"Sure, sure," grinned the bartender, "It's a toadpaz, ain't it, Hoppy?"

"It is an extremely beautiful emerald," said the Toad coldly, removing the firefly from his frappé and swallowing it. "Absolutely priceless emerald. *More* than priceless. Keep 'em comin'."

The bartender mixed another green mint frappé, but he put a slug in it this time instead of a firefly.

"I don't think the Toad has a precious jewel in his head," said the Macaw.

"I do," said the Cat. "Nobody could be that ugly and live unless he had an emerald in his head."

"I'll bet you a hundred fish he hasn't," said the Pelican.

"I'll bet you a hundred clams he has," said the Sandpiper.

The Toad, who was pretty well frappéd by this time, fell asleep, and the members of the club debated how to find out whether his head held an emerald, or some other precious stone. They summoned the Woodpecker from the back room and explained what was up. "If he hasn't got a hole in his head, I'll make one," said the Woodpecker.

There wasn't anything there, gleaming or lovely or precious. The bartender turned out the lights, the Rooster crowed, the sun came up, and the members of the Fauna Club went silently home to bed.

MORAL: *Open most heads and you will find nothing shining, not even a mind.*

DONALD OGDEN STEWART

[1894–]

A SATIRIST SO KEEN *that he has been appreciated only by an enthusiastic few rather than by the many, Donald Ogden Stewart was born in the same year and the same city as Thurber: Columbus, Ohio, November 30, 1894. He evinced early a sense of fun and his remarks were, he remembered, "recounted by his proud mother upon the slightest provocation. . . But he bears a long red scar on his head—such as might be made by a brick or other missile—as evidence of one little red-headed girl's lack of appreciation of his humorous efforts."*

After being graduated from Yale, unsure of his ability to earn a living as a writer, Stewart tried various jobs. Groomed (but not too well-groomed) for a business career, he worked for a public service corporation, taught navigation and, at the end of the First World War, began to write—or, rather, to re-write—literature with his tongue in both cheeks. The titles of his volumes indicate their character as well as their contents: A Parody Outline of History; Perfect Behavior, *a bland burlesque of a dozen handbooks of etiquette;* Mr. and Mrs. Haddock Abroad, *a take-off on the journals kept by travelers on the Grand Tour; and* Aunt Polly's Story of Mankind, *a parody of simplified "outlines" of man's knowledge.*

After writing comedies for the stage, Stewart had a highly successful career in Hollywood as the author of screen plays, a career that was cut short in the late 1940s when his antipathy to fascism and his sympathy with the Spanish loyalists and other liberal causes made him suspect as a radical. With his second wife, Ella Winters, widow of Lincoln Steffens, he left America and bought a house in the once-rural Hampstead section of London, not far from Keat's house.

The mellow air of England entered into Stewart's work. Although its edge was not dulled, his satire grew less sardonic. Without sacrificing any of the fun, his humor became not only more probing but also more penetrating.

THE BEGINNINGS

From *Aunt Polly's Story of Mankind*

"CHILDREN," SAID AUNT POLLY, feeling that the time had now come to begin her little plan, "how would you like to hear Aunt Polly tell you the Story of Mankind?"

"Of who?" asked Samuel.

"Of 'whom', dear, would be better," corrected Aunt Polly.

"Of whom?" repeated Samuel.

"Of mankind, dear," said Aunt Polly.

"Is it interesting?" asked Mary.

"Very interesting, dear," replied Aunt Polly. "It is the true story of how man began and how he has been getting steadily better and better."

"That doesn't sound interesting," said Mary, somewhat impolitely.

"A true story?" asked Samuel.

"Yes, dear," replied Aunt Polly, for Aunt Polly, although religious, was not "narrow" and she believed—and rightly, too—that it was a mistake to try to conceal from children after a certain age the true facts about the history of the world. "You must put out of your heads for a while all you have learned about Adam and Eve and the garden of Eden, for, children, all of that is only a beautiful, beautiful legend and if you will listen to Aunt Polly she will tell you the truth," and so, in order that the children might come to appreciate the wonderful world in which they lived and therefore become truly reverent and respectful to their elders who had created this wonderful world for them, she began to tell the children the true wonderful story of the progress of mankind. And that was Aunt Polly's clever little plan.

"Before people began living on the earth," commenced Aunt Polly, "it was not a place where one would particularly care to live. In the beginning, if the truth were told, it was just a flaming ball whirling uselessly around another flaming ball which we to-day know to be the sun. And this had to continue for a long, long time until the surface of the earth could be cooled off sufficiently to allow life to take place so that the progress of mankind could commence."

"Is it still cooling off, Aunt Polly?" asked Samuel.

"What, dear?" said Aunt Polly.

"The earth," said Samuel.

"Why, yes, I suppose so," replied Aunt Polly.

"Won't it get cold some day?" asked Samuel.

"Not with the sun to give us his nice warmth," replied patient Aunt Polly.

"And the sun isn't cooling off?" asked the boy.

"Why, no," replied Aunt Polly. "At least—Samuel dear, you must remember that all this took a very long time—oh, millions of years—and is all part of a great plan. Now, after the earth had been cooled off—"

"What plan, Aunt Polly?" asked the irritatingly persistent boy.

"Samuel—please, dear," said Aunt Polly, giving him a kindly look of rebuke. "Now, after the earth had been cooled sufficiently, which took, as I have said, many, many years, a wonderful thing happened—something without which we would none of us be here to-day. Can you guess?"

"The discovery of aeroplanes," said David.

"No, dear," replied his mother. "Something more important than that."

"The invention of smokeless powder," said David.

"No, dear," said she, "it was something which took place long before that. It was the invention of life. Yes—long, long ago, when the earth had been cooled off, life began—"

"How, Aunt Polly?" asked Mary.

"What do you mean, dear?" said she.

"How did life begin?" asked the girl.

"I am coming to that, dear," responded the patient lady. "At first it was just a little cell floating on the water like—"

"Ivory soap," suggested Mary.

"No, dear," replied Aunt Polly. "That is not a very dignified thought for a little girl to have, and life is very dignified indeed—human life, that is. Now, this little cell floating on the water—"

"Who put it there, Aunt Polly?" asked Samuel.

"Perhaps you can tell him, David," suggested Aunt Polly.

"God put it there," said David, promptly.

"Why?" asked Mary.

"Why?" responded Aunt Polly, smiling at the unconscious blasphemy of the child. "Why—so that you and your brother and your sister could be born into this wonderful world."

"Cousin David, too?" asked Mary.

"Yes, dear," said Aunt Polly. "Cousin David and your Aunt Polly and your Uncle Frederick."

"Oh, Gosh," exclaimed Mary.

"Mary," said Aunt Polly severely, "ladies do not use such words, do they?"

"No, Aunt Polly," replied Mary.

"And we all came from that first cell, Aunt Polly?" asked Samuel.

"Yes, dear," replied Aunt Polly.

"Appleby too?" asked Mary, indicating Aunt Polly's chauffeur.

"Why, yes, dear," said Aunt Polly.

"Then we are all related to Appleby," said Mary.

"We aren't either," exclaimed David.

"Hush, dear," said Aunt Polly, putting a reproving finger to her lips, and smiling understandingly at Appleby.

"Now, those early forms of life," went on Aunt Polly, "were not particularly interesting and, if the truth were told, many of them were quite disagreeable looking objects. The world at that time was a great deal like a —well, like a large bath tub full of horrid floating things, although of course they did not have bath tubs at that time. But after a while these wretched floating objects decided to spread out over the land and some of them gradually took curious shapes and grew to be perfectly enormous things and they were called mammoths and mastodons and other big names."

"Where are they now, Aunt Polly?" asked Mary, curiously.

"Oh, they all disappeared long ago," replied Aunt Polly.

"Why?" asked Samuel.

"Well, because they were all more or less absurd and quite useless," explained Aunt Polly, "and so they died away in order that man could begin life properly."

"But, Aunt Polly," said Samuel, "wasn't that a waste?"

"A waste of what, dear?" questioned Aunt Polly.

"Why, I mean, if they were going to die out what was the use of starting them?"

"Well, dear," replied Aunt Polly, "they may have been an experiment."

"Oh," said Samuel. "And man is another experiment?"

"Of course not, dear," replied Aunt Polly. "Man is man—and animals are animals. Don't you see? Man has a soul, and animals haven't."

"What's a soul, Aunt Polly?" asked little Mary.

"A soul is what distinguishes man from the animals," explained the patient Aunt Polly.

"Oh," said Mary.

"But it all started from that same cell, Aunt Polly," said Samuel.

"Yes," said Aunt Polly. "Well, no—not exactly. You see, it was all part of a great plan."

"What plan, Aunt Polly?" asked Samuel for the second time.

"Now, Samuel dear," said Aunt Polly forcefully and yet kindly, "you are not to ask Aunt Polly questions unless they have some meaning. A little boy who asks questions just for the sake of asking is apt to be considered a nuisance, isn't he, dear?"

"Yes, Aunt Polly," replied Samuel, but I am afraid that Aunt Polly's rebuke had no real effect on the irritating boy.

"Well, now," continued Aunt Polly, "the earth gradually became more and more a place where man would want to exist and so after a great many years your great great great great *great* ancestors began to live in the forests and caves. But those first men were not much like the men you see to-day and if the truth were told they were very, very uncouth. But you must remember, children, that the right kind of people could not come into the world and begin to progress until the world was ready for them, and in those early days when everything was quite primitive and uncivilized it is hardly fair to expect that men could have nice comfortable homes like we have or look or act like your Uncle Frederick, for example.

"Didn't they have any manners at all?" asked David earnestly.

"No, dear," replied his mother.

"No table manners?" asked David.

"Unfortunately not, dear," replied Aunt Polly.

"And no tooth brushes?"

"No tooth brushes," was Aunt Polly's answer.

"Well, then, they every one of them had pyorrhea, didn't they," said David proudly.

"Why, perhaps, dear—but you see they lived differently," said Aunt Polly.

"But it says in the advertisements—" insisted David.

"I know, dear," said Aunt Polly, "but you must remember that they didn't know about pyorrhea in those days."

"Oh," said David. "And didn't they have dentists?"

"No, dear—the poor creatures had no dentists," said Aunt Polly.

"Or doctors?" asked David.

"No, David," said Aunt Polly, "they had no doctors, either."

"Well, then," asked David in a puzzled tone, "who took out their tonsils and adenoids?"

"They couldn't have them taken out, dear," replied Aunt Polly. "You see, all those things are the result of centuries of progress. We must learn, children, to take the right attitude toward everything in history, even the unpleasant things, and when I tell you, for example, that those early men did not wear any clothes but were covered with long disagreeable hair you must remember that great oaks from little acorns grow and those ancestors of ours, rough as they were, might be called the acorns from which have sprung the nice big oaks of our own civilization, as I shall show you."

"They didn't wear any clothes at all?" asked Mary.

"No, dear," replied Aunt Polly. "At what are you laughing, dear? Tell Aunt Polly"; for Aunt Polly loved a good joke and always joined in when merriment was about.

"Nothing, Aunt Polly," replied Mary. "I was just thinking if you and Uncle Frederick and Appleby—"

Aunt Polly blushed. "Mary dear," she said firmly.

"Yes, Aunt Polly," said Mary. "But wouldn't—"

"Mary!" and this time Aunt Polly was quite firm.

"Yes, Aunt Polly," replied Mary and the silly girl stopped her giggling.

"What did they do all day, Aunt Polly?" asked Samuel.

"Who, dear?" asked Aunt Polly.

"Those naked men," replied Samuel.

"Samuel dear," said Aunt Polly, "I wouldn't call them that."

"But they *were* naked," insisted the thoughtless boy.

"Yes, dear," replied Aunt Polly, "but we don't talk about those things, do we? No. Why, dear, their daily life was quite uninteresting and consisted largely in a search for food and shelter which seems to us a horrible waste of time and a most unidealistic sort of existence, doesn't it? And, children, much as I dislike to say it, I am afraid that there were very few ideals among those early men, for they had no churches, no schools, no laws, no policemen, no soldiers—"

"No policemen?" asked David.

"Now, David, think," replied his mother. "I just said that there were no laws, didn't I, dear? And what are policemen for?"

"To arrest people," replied David.

"Why, dear?" asked his mother.

"Because they have been bad," answered David.

"Yes, dear," replied Aunt Polly, "that is to say, because they have not obeyed the laws. And in those days they had no laws."

"Then everybody was bad," said David.

"No, dear," replied Aunt Polly. "Why do you say that?"

"Well," explained David, "if you don't have any laws how can people obey them?"

"David dear," replied the patient lady, "you must remember the law is something which only civilized people have."

"Like pyorrhea, Aunt Polly?" ask Mary.

"Children," said Aunt Polly, somewhat vexed, "if you want Aunt Polly to go on, you must not make such thoughtless remarks."

"Yes, Aunt Polly," replied the children, with the exception of Genevieve, who was dreamily watching the trees and houses spin by as the car rolled quietly over the paved streets.

"Well, then," said Aunt Polly, "I shall be very patient this time and tell you the exact difference between those early men and the men of to-day and if you will just put on your little thinking caps you will see how foolish many of your questions are. Now in those early days every man was what we call a 'law unto himself' which means that instead of obeying his government, each man made his own laws and, of course, under such conditions, people could not live peaceably and there was always constant fighting going on. And it was not the right kind of fighting at all, because instead of making war for some ideal, each man fought only for himself and it was therefore a very unidealistic kind of warfare, I assure you. And the result of all this was that only the strongest and most intelligent—of course, intelligent for those times—were able to survive and if it had not been that man was destined to something higher, as I shall show you, this might have gone on and on until—well, I don't know what might have happened. Certainly there would have been no progress and you and I would not be able to-day to ride around in your Uncle Frederick's nice comfortable limousine, children, and we owe a great deal to the men who thought of making the first laws."

"Who started the laws, Aunt Polly?" asked Samuel.

"Well," replied Aunt Polly, "laws came naturally, of course, as men began to become civilized. At first there were only a few laws, but as humanity progressed they made more and more laws because, don't you see, they discovered so many unlawful things of which their ancestors had been ignorant, and so to-day we have a great many laws and a great many men called congressmen who devote their whole lives to the discovery of unlawful things and the making of new laws, and a great many more men called lawyers who devote their lives to the study of all these laws and we have policemen to keep us from breaking the laws and prisons in which to put the people who do break them. Do you see, children?"

"Yes, Aunt Polly," replied the children.

"And so," continued Aunt Polly, looking out of the window of the automobile to see what Genevieve was gazing at, "those early men did not have lawyers or policemen or prisons and they lived miserable, unhealthy lives, always fighting or quarreling, because their civilization was based on selfishness instead of on law or order. Drive a little more slowly here, Appleby," added Aunt Polly, giving her chauffeur a pleasant smile, "for I thought I saw a motor cycle policeman at that last cross street."

"What did they fight *about*, Aunt Polly?" asked Samuel.

"Oh, about the most trifling things," replied she. "They were always fighting each other whenever one group managed to find a place where something they all wanted could be found more plentifully than in another. You see they had no idea of property, and so instead of settling such questions by law every tribe had to fight for what they had in order that some stronger tribe would not take it away. And those fights must have been unspeakably brutal because there was, of course, no Christianity and no laws regarding civilized warfare."

"How many were killed?" asked David.

"I don't know, dear," replied Aunt Polly.

"I bet they didn't kill as many as in the Great War," said David. "Did they?"

"I don't think so, dear," replied Aunt Polly.

"Why, I bet they killed a million in the Great War," said David, somewhat boastfully.

"A million nothing," exclaimed Samuel. "It was three million."

"Ho, ho—three million!" said David. "I bet it wasn't."

"Well, I bet they killed two million then," said Samuel, "because I saw it in the paper and that ain't—"

"That *isn't*, dear," corrected Aunt Polly.

"That *isn't* counting the wounded."

"Oh, I bet you it is," said David. "They only killed a million."

"Didn't."

"Did."

"Children," remonstrated Aunt Polly, "if you want Aunt Polly to go on—"

"Yes, Aunt Polly—please," said the children, instantly ceasing their childish bickering.

"You must remember," she said, "that the Great War was a very different thing from those early fights which were the result of the ignorant and unchristian and unidealistic sort of lives the people were living at that time, and now please let us not talk any more about the subject."

"It *was* two million, wasn't it?" asked Samuel.

"I said," replied Aunt Polly, severely, "that we would not talk any more about it, Samuel."

"Yes, Aunt Polly," said the boy.

"Now, the thing I want to impress upon you about those early men," went on Aunt Polly, "is the fact that they lived very primitively, which affected their lives so that we must not really blame them for many of the disgusting things they did. They dwelt in caves, almost like animals, and the caves themselves were often unspeakably filthy places, miserably lighted, with no heat. In fact, children, it is only when you consider the handicaps under which the cave men lived that you can take anything like the right attitude toward those people. I have always said that if you give a person a bright, comfortable home and insist that he keep it clean you may expect that he will act like a decent civilized being, but if you let him live in a cave, with no sanitary regulations and no incentive to personal cleanliness, you can only expect the worst. And so, children, let us pass quickly over this primitive period of our history, remembering only that it teaches above everything else the value of cleanliness and sanitation in our daily lives.

"Now," concluded Aunt Polly, cheerfully, "that will be all I shall put into your little heads to-day, and next time, if you want me to, I shall tell about the beginning of progress and the early civilizations in Egypt and other places. Would you like that?"

"Oh, yes, Aunt Polly—please, Aunt Polly," cried the delighted children, which pleased her very much, and so came to an end the first chapter of Aunt Polly's true story of the glorious progress of mankind.

KATHERINE ANNE PORTER

[1894–]

KATHERINE ANNE PORTER CREATED A PROSE STYLE *so distilled that it seemed refined of every crude or base element. She was born May 15, 1894, in Indian Creek, Texas—one of her ancestors was Daniel Boone —and was educated in small schools in her native state and Louisiana. She traveled considerably, and was twice married and twice divorced.*

Although she supported herself by many kinds of writing for hire— book reviews, political pieces, translations, editing other writers' manuscripts—she refused to publish any of her own work until she was thirty. "I have written and destroyed manuscripts quite literally by the trunkful," she declared. "I spent fifteen years wandering about, weighted horribly with masses of paper and little else. Yet for this vocation I was and am willing to live and die, and I consider very few other things of the slightest importance."

She is an extremely slow and unusually careful craftsman, and her first full-length novel, No Safe Harbor, *was announced for publication as early as 1942 but, after eighteen years, was still unpublished. She had, however, won an enthusiastic, highly-discriminating audience and an enviable place in contemporary American literature with the novelette*

Noon Wine *and her volumes of short stories,* Flowering Judas, Pale Horse, Pale Rider, *and* The Leaning Tower. *It is from the last volume that "The Old Order," a beautifully-realized evocation of the old South, is taken.*

THE OLD ORDER

IN THEIR LATER YEARS, the Grandmother and old Nannie used to sit together for some hours every day over their sewing. They shared a passion for cutting scraps of the family finery, hoarded for fifty years, into strips and triangles, and fitting them together again in a carefully disordered patchwork, outlining each bit of velvet or satin or taffeta with a running briar stitch in clear lemon-colored silk floss. They had contrived enough bed and couch covers, tablespreads, dressing-table scarfs, to have furnished forth several households. Each piece as it was finished was lined with yellow silk, folded, and laid away in a chest, never again to see the light of day. The Grandmother was the great-granddaughter of Kentucky's most famous pioneer: he had, while he was surveying Kentucky, hewed out rather competently a rolling pin for his wife. This rolling pin was the Grandmother's irreplaceable treasure. She covered it with an extraordinarily complicated bit of patchwork, added golden tassels to the handles, and hung it in a conspicuous place in her room. She was the daughter of a notably heroic captain in the War of 1812. She had his razors in a shagreen case and a particularly severe-looking daguerreotype taken in his old age, with his chin in a tall stock and his black satin waistcoat smoothed over a still-handsome military chest. So she fitted a patchwork case over the shagreen and made a sort of envelope of cut velvet and violet satin, held together with briar stitching, to contain the portrait. The rest of her handiwork she put away, to the relief of her grandchildren, who had arrived at the awkward age when Grandmother's quaint old-fashioned ways caused them acute discomfort.

In the summer the women sat under the mingled trees of the side garden, which commanded a view of the east wing, the front and back porches, a good part of the front garden and a corner of the small fig grove. Their choice of this location was a part of their domestic strategy. Very little escaped them: a glance now and then would serve to keep them fairly well informed as to what was going on in the whole place. It is true they had not seen Miranda the day she pulled up the whole mint bed to give to a pleasant strange young woman who stopped and asked her for a sprig of fresh mint. They had never found out who stole the giant pomegranates growing too near the fence: they had not been in time to stop Paul from setting himself on fire while experimenting with a miniature blowtorch, but they had been on the scene to extinguish him with rugs, to pour oil on him, and lecture him. They never saw Maria climbing trees, a mania she had to indulge or pine away, for she chose tall ones on the opposite side of the house. But such casualties were so minor a part of the perpetual round of events that they did not feel defeated nor that their strategy was a failure. Summer, in many ways so desirable a season, had its drawbacks. The children were everywhere at once and the Negroes loved lying under the hackberry grove back of the barns playing seven-up, and eating watermelons. The summer house was in a small town a few miles from the farm, a compromise between the rigorously ordered house in the city and the sprawling old farmhouse which Grandmother had built with such pride and pains. It had, she often said, none of the advantages of either country, or city, and all the discomforts of both. But the children loved it.

During the winters in the city, they sat in Grandmother's room, a large squarish place with a small coal grate. All the sounds of life in the household seemed to converge there, echo, retreat, and return. Grandmother and Aunt Nannie knew the whole complicated code of sounds, could interpret and comment on them by an exchange of glances, a lifted eyebrow, or a tiny pause in their talk.

They talked about the past, really—always about the past. Even the future seemed like something gone and done with when they spoke of it. It did not seem an extension of their past, but a repetition of it. They would agree that nothing remained of life as they had known it, the world was changing swiftly, but by the mysterious logic of hope they insisted that each change was probably the last; or if not, a series of changes might bring them, blessedly, back full circle to the old days they had known. Who knows why they loved their past? It had been bitter for them both, they had questioned the burdensome rule they lived by every day of their lives, but without rebellion and without expecting an answer. This unbroken thread of inquiry in their minds contained no doubt as to the utter rightness and justice of the basic laws of human existence, founded as they were on God's plan; but they wondered perpetually, with only a hint now and then to each other of the uneasiness of their hearts, how so much suffering and confusion could have been built up and maintained on such a foundation. The Grandmother's role was authority, she knew that; it was her duty to portion out activities, to urge or restrain where necessary, to teach morals, manners, and religion, to punish and reward her own household according to a fixed code. Her own doubts and hesitations she concealed, also, she reminded herself, as a matter of duty. Old Nannie had no ideas at all as to her place in the world. It had been assigned to her before birth, and for her daily rule she had all her life obeyed the authority nearest to her.

So they talked about God, about heaven, about planting a new hedge of rosebushes, about the new ways of preserving fruit and vegetables, about eternity and their mutual hope that they might pass it happily together, and often a scrap of silk under their hands would start them on long trains of family reminiscences. They were always amused to notice again how the working of their memories differed in such important ways. Nannie could recall names to perfection; she could always say what the weather had been like on all important occasions, what certain ladies had worn, how handsome certain gentlemen had been, what there had been to eat and drink. Grandmother had masses of dates in her mind, and no memories attached to them: her memories of events seemed detached and floating beyond time. For example, the 26th of August, 1871, had been some sort of red-letter day for her. She had said to herself then that never would she forget that date; and indeed, she remembered it well, but she no longer had the faintest notion what had happened to stamp it on her memory. Nannie was no help in the matter; she had nothing to do with dates. She did not know the year of her birth, and would never have had a birthday to celebrate if Grandmother had not, when she was still Miss Sophia Jane, aged ten, opened a calendar at random, closed her eyes, and marked a date unseen with a pen. So it turned out that Nannie's birthday thereafter fell on June 11, and the year, Miss Sophia Jane decided, should be 1827, her own birth year, making Nannie just three months younger than her mistress. Sophia Jane then made an entry of Nannie's birth date in the family Bible, inserting it just below her own. "Nannie Gay," she wrote, in stiff careful letters, "(black)," and though there was some uproar when this was discovered, the ink was long since sunk deeply into the paper, and besides no one was really upset enough to have it scratched out. There it remained, one of their pleasantest points of reference.

They talked about religion, and the slack way the world was going nowadays, the decay of behavior, and about the younger children, whom these topics always brought at once to mind. On these subjects they were firm, critical, and unbewildered. They had received educations which furnished them an assured habit of mind about all the important appearances of life, and especially about the rearing of young. They relied with perfect acquiescence on the dogma that children were conceived in sin and brought forth in iniquity. Childhood was a long state of instruction and probation for adult life, which was in turn a long, severe, undeviating devotion to duty, the largest part of which consisted in bringing up children. The young were difficult, disobedient, and tireless in wrongdoing, apt to turn unkind and undutiful when they grew up, in spite of all one had done for them, or had tried to do: for small painful doubts rose in them now and again when they looked at their completed works. Nannie couldn't abide her newfangled grandchildren. "Wuthless, shiftless lot, jes plain scum, Miss Sophia Jane; I cain't undahstand it aftah all the raisin' dey had."

The Grandmother defended them, and dispraised her own second generation—heartily, too, for she sincerely found grave faults in them—which Nannie defended in turn. "When they are little, they trample on your feet, and when they grow up they trample on your heart." This was about all there was to say about children in any generation, but the fascination of the theme was endless. They said it thoroughly over and over with thousands of small variations, with always an example among their own friends or family connections to prove it. They had enough material of their own. Grandmother had borne eleven children, Nannie thirteen. They boasted of it. Grandmother would say, "I am the mother of eleven children," in a faintly amazed tone, as if she hardly expected to be believed, or could even quite believe it herself. But she could still point to nine of them. Nannie had lost ten of hers. They were all buried in Kentucky. Nannie never doubted or expected anyone else to doubt she had children. Her boasting was of another order. "Thirteen of 'em," she would say, in an appalled voice, "yas, my Lawd and my Redeemah, thirteen!"

The friendship between the two old women had begun in early childhood, and was based on what seemed even to them almost mythical events. Miss Sophia Jane, a prissy, spoiled five-year-old, with tight black ringlets which were curled every day on a stick, with her stiffly pleated lawn pantalettes and tight bodice, had run to meet her returning father, who had been away buying horses and Negroes. Sitting on his arm, clasping him around the neck, she had watched the wagons filing past on the way to the barns and quarters. On the floor of the first wagon sat two blacks, male and female, holding between them a scrawny, half-naked black child, with a round nubbly head and fixed bright monkey eyes. The baby Negro had a potbelly and her arms were like sticks from wrist to shoulder. She clung with narrow, withered, black-leather fingers to her parents, a hand on each.

"I want the little monkey," said Sophia Jane to her father, nuzzling his cheek and pointing. "I want that one to play with."

Behind each wagon came two horses in lead, but in the second wagon there was a small shaggy pony with a thatch of mane over his eyes, a long tail like a brush, a round, hard barrel of a body. He was standing in straw to the knees, braced firmly in a padded stall with a Negro holding his bridle. "Do you see that?" asked her father. "That's for you. High time you learned to ride."

Sophia Jane almost leaped from his arm for joy. She hardly recognized her pony or her monkey the next day, the one clipped and sleek, the other clean in new blue cotton. For a while she could not decide which she loved more, Nannie or Fiddler. But Fiddler did not wear well. She outgrew him in a year, saw him pass without regret to a small brother, though she refused to allow him to be called Fiddler any longer. The name she reserved for a long series of saddle horses. She had named the first in honor of Fiddler Gay, an old Negro who made the music for dances and parties. There was only one Nannie and she outwore Sophia Jane. During all their lives together it was not so much a question of affection between them as a simple matter of being unable to imagine getting on without each other.

Nannie remembered well being on a shallow platform out in front of a great building in a large busy place, the first town she had ever seen. Her father and mother were with her, and there was a thick crowd around them. There were several other small groups of Negroes huddled together with white men bustling them about now and then. She had never seen any of these faces before, and she never saw but one of them again. She remembered it must have been summer, because she was not shivering with cold in her cotton shift. For one thing, her bottom was still burning from a spanking someone (it might have been her mother) had given her just before they got on the platform, to remind her to keep still. Her mother and father were field hands, and had never lived in white folks' houses. A tall gentleman with a long narrow face and very high curved nose, wearing a great-collared blue coat and immensely long light-colored trousers (Nannie could close her eyes and see him again, clearly, as he looked that day) stepped up near them suddenly, while a great hubbub rose. The red-faced man standing on a stump beside them shouted and droned, waving his arms and pointing at Nannie's father and mother. Now and then the tall gentleman raised a finger, without looking at the black people on the platform. Suddenly the shouting died down, the tall gentleman walked over and said to Nannie's father and mother, "Well, Eph! Well, Steeny! Mister Jimmerson comin' to get you in a minute." He poked Nannie in the stomach with a thickly gloved forefinger. "Regular crowbait," he said to the auctioneer. "I should have had lagniappe with this one."

"A pretty worthless article right now, sir, I agree with you," said the auctioneer, "but it'll grow out of it. As for the team, you won't find a better, I swear."

"I've had an eye on 'em for years," said the tall gentleman, and walked away, motioning as he went to a fat man sitting on a wagon tongue, spitting quantities of tobacco juice. The fat man rose and came over to Nannie and her parents.

Nannie had been sold for twenty dollars: a gift, you might say, hardly sold at all. She learned that a really choice slave sometimes cost more than a thousand dollars. She lived to hear slaves brag about how much they had cost. She had not known how little she fetched on the block until her own mother taunted her with it. This was after Nannie had gone to live for good at the big house, and her mother and father were still in the fields. They lived and worked and died there. A good worming had cured Nannie's potbelly, she thrived on plentiful food and a species of kindness not so indulgent, maybe, as that given to the puppies; still it more than fulfilled her notions of good fortune.

The old women often talked about how strangely things come out in this life. The first owner of Nannie and her parents had gone, Sophia Jane's father said, hog-wild about Texas. It was a new Land of Promise, in 1832. He had sold out his farm and four slaves in Kentucky to raise the money to take a great twenty-mile stretch of land in southwest Texas. He had taken his wife and two young children and set out, and there had been no more news of him for many years. When Grandmother arrived in Texas forty years later, she found him a prosperous ranchman and district judge. Much later, her youngest son met his granddaughter, fell in love with her, and married her—all in three months.

The judge, by then eighty-five years old, was uproarious and festive at the wedding. He reeked of corn liquor, swore by God every other breath, and was raring to talk about the good old times in Kentucky. The Grandmother showed Nannie to him. "Would you recognize her?" "For God Almighty's sake!" bawled the judge, "is that the strip of crowbait I sold to your father for twenty dollars? Twenty dollars seemed like a fortune to me in those days!"

While they were jolting home down the steep rocky road on the long journey from San Marcos to Austin, Nannie finally spoke out about her grievance. "Look lak a jedge might had better raisin'," she said, gloomily, "look lak he didn't keer how much he hurt a body's feelin's."

The Grandmother, muffled down in the back seat in the corner of the old carryall, in her worn sealskin pelisse, showing coffee brown at the edges, her eyes closed, her hands wrung together, had been occupied once more in reconciling herself to losing a son, and, as ever, to a girl and a family of which she could not altogether approve. It was not that there was anything seriously damaging to be said against any of them; only—well, she wondered at her sons' tastes. What had each of them in turn found in the wife he had chosen? The Grandmother had always had in mind the kind of wife each of her sons needed; she had tried to bring about better marriages for them than they had made for themselves. They had merely resented her interferences in what they considered strictly their personal affairs. She did not realize that she had spoiled and pampered her youngest son until he was in all probability unfit to be any kind of a husband, much less a good one. And there was something about her new daughter-in-law, a tall, handsome, firm-looking young woman, with a direct way of speaking, walking, talking, that seemed to promise that the spoiled Baby's days of clover were ended. The Grandmother was annoyed deeply at seeing how self-possessed the bride had been, how she had had her way about the wedding arrangements down to the last detail, how she glanced now and then at her new husband with calm, humorous, level eyes, as if she had already got him sized up. She had even suggested at the wedding dinner that her idea of a honeymoon would be to follow the chuck wagon on the round-up, and help in the cattle-branding on her father's ranch. Of course she may have been joking. But she was altogether too Western, too modern, something like the "new" woman who was beginning to run wild, asking for the vote, leaving her home and going out in the world to earn her own living . . .

The Grandmother's narrow body shuddered to the bone at the thought of women so unsexing themselves; she emerged with a start from the dark reverie of foreboding thoughts which left a bitter taste in her throat. "Never mind, Nannie. The judge just wasn't thinking. He's very fond of his good cheer."

Nannie had slept in a bed and had been playmate and workfellow with her mistress; they fought on almost equal terms, Sophia Jane defending Nannie fiercely against any discipline but her own. When they were both seventeen years old, Miss Sophia Jane was married off in a very gay wedding. The house was jammed to the roof and everybody present was at least fourth cousin to everybody else. There were forty carriages and more than two hundred horses to look after for two days. When the last wheel disappeared down the lane (a number of the guests lingered on for two weeks), the larders and bins were half empty and the place looked as if a troop of cavalry had been over it. A few days later Nannie was married off to a boy she had known ever since she came to the family, and they were given as a wedding present to Miss Sophia Jane.

Miss Sophia Jane and Nannie had then started their grim and terrible race of procreation, a child every sixteen months or so, with Nannie nursing both, and Sophia Jane, in dreadful discomfort, suppressing her milk with bandages and spirits of wine. When they each had produced their fourth child, Nannie almost died of puerperal fever. Sophia Jane nursed both children. She named the black baby Charlie, and her own child Stephen, and she fed them justly turn about, not favoring the white over the black, as Nannie felt obliged to do. Her husband was shocked, tried to forbid her; her mother came to see her and reasoned with her. They found her very difficult and quite stubborn. She had already begun to develop her implicit character, which was altogether just, humane, proud, and simple. She had many small vanities and weaknesses on the surface: a love of luxury and a tendency to resent criticism. This tendency was based on her feeling of superiority in judgment and sensibility to almost everyone around her. It made her very hard to manage. She had a quiet way of holding her ground which convinced her antagonist that she would really die, not just threaten to, rather than give way. She had learned now that she was badly cheated in giving her children to another woman to feed; she resolved never again to be cheated in just that way. She sat nursing her child and her foster child, with a sensual warm pleasure she had not dreamed of, translating her natural physical relief into something holy, God-sent, amends from heaven for what she had suffered in childbed. Yes, and for what she missed in the marriage bed, for there also something had failed. She said to Nannie quite calmly, "From now on, you will nurse your children and I will nurse mine," and it was so. Charlie remained her special favorite among the Negro children. "I understand now," she said to her older sister Keziah, "why the black mammies love their foster children. I love mine." So Charlie was brought up in the house as playmate for her son Stephen, and exempted from hard work all his life.

Sophia Jane had been wooed at arm's length by a mysteriously attractive young man whom she remembered well as rather a snubby little boy with curls like her own, but shorter, a frilled white blouse and kilts of the Macdonald tartan. He was her second cousin and resembled her so closely they had been mistaken for brother and sister. Their grandparents had been first cousins, and sometimes Sophia Jane saw in him, years after they were married, all the faults she had most abhorred in her elder brother: lack of aim, failure to act at crises, a philosophic detachment from practical affairs, a tendency to set projects on foot and then leave them to perish or to be finished by someone else; and a profound conviction that everyone around him should be happy to wait upon him hand and foot. She had fought these fatal tendencies in her brother, within the bounds of wifely prudence she fought them in her husband, she was long after to fight them again in two of her sons and in several of her grandchildren. She gained no victory in any case, the selfish, careless, unloving creatures lived and ended as they had begun. But the Grandmother developed a character truly portentous under the discipline of trying to change the characters of others. Her husband shared with her the family sharpness of eye. He disliked and feared her deadly willfullness, her certainty that her ways were not only right but beyond criticism, that her feelings were important, even in the lightest matter, and must not be tampered with or treated casually. He had disappeared at the critical moment when they were growing up, had gone to college and then for travel; she forgot him for a long time, and when she saw him again forgot him as he had been once for all. She was gay and sweet and decorous, full of vanity and incredibly exalted daydreams which threatened now and again to cast her over the edge of some mysterious forbidden frenzy. She dreamed recurrently that she had lost her virginity (her virtue, she called it), her sole claim to regard, consideration, even to existence, and after frightful moral suffering which masked altogether her physical experience she would wake in a cold sweat, disordered and terrified. She had heard that her cousin Stephen was a little "wild," but that was to be expected. He was leading, no doubt, a dashing life full of manly indulgences, the sweet dark life of the knowledge of evil which caused her hair to crinkle on her scalp when she thought of it. Ah, the delicious, the free, the wonderful, the mysterious and terrible life of men! She thought about it a great deal. "Little daydreamer," her mother or father would say to her, surprising her in a brown study, eyes moist, lips smiling vaguely over her embroidery or her book, or with hands fallen on her lap, her face turned away to a blank wall. She memorized and saved for these moments scraps of high-minded poetry, which she instantly quoted at them when they offered her a penny for her thoughts; or she broke into a melancholy little song of some kind, a song she knew they liked. She would run to the piano and tinkle the tune out with one hand, saying, "I love this part best," leaving no doubt in their minds as to what her own had been occupied with. She lived her whole youth so, without once giving herself away; not until she was in middle age, her husband dead, her property dispersed, and she found herself with a houseful of children, making a new life for them in another place, with all the responsibilities of a man but with none of the privileges, did she finally emerge into something like an honest life: and yet, she was passionately honest. She had never been anything else.

Sitting under the trees with Nannie, both of them old and their long battle with life almost finished, she said, fingering a scrap of satin, "It was not fair that Sister Keziah should have had this ivory brocade for her wedding dress, and I had only dotted swiss . . ."

"Times was harder when you got married, Missy," said Nannie. "Dat was de yeah all de crops failed."

"And they failed ever afterward, it seems to me," said Grandmother.

"Seems to me like," said Nannie, "dotted swiss was all the style when you got married."

"I never cared for it," said Grandmother.

Nannie, born in slavery, was pleased to think she would not die in it. She was wounded not so much by her state of being as by the word describing it. Emancipation was a sweet word to her. It had not changed her way of living in a single particular, but she was proud of having been able to say to her mistress, "I aim to stay wid you as long as you'll have me." Still, Emancipation had seemed to set right a wrong that stuck in her heart like a thorn. She could not understand why God, Whom she loved, had seen fit to be so hard on a whole race because they had got a certain kind of skin. She talked it over with Miss Sophia Jane. Many times. Miss Sophia Jane was always brisk and opinionated about it: "Nonsense! I tell you, God does not know whether a skin is black or white. He sees only souls. Don't be getting notions, Nannie—of course you're going to heaven."

Nannie showed the rudiments of logic in a mind altogether untutored. She wondered, simply and without resentment, whether God, who had been so cruel to black people on earth, might not continue His severity in the next world. Miss Sophia Jane took pleasure in reassuring her; as if she, who had been responsible for Nannie, body and soul in this life, might also be her sponsor before the judgment seat.

Miss Sophia Jane had taken upon herself all the responsibilities of her tangled world, half white, half black, mingling steadily and the confusion growing ever deeper. There were so many young men about the place, always, younger brothers-in-law, first cousins, second cousins, nephews. They came visiting and they stayed, and there was no accounting for them nor any way of controlling their quietly headstrong habits. She learned early to keep silent and give no sign of uneasiness, but whenever a child was born in the Negro quarters, pink, wormlike, she held her breath for three days, she told her eldest granddaughter, years later, to see whether the newly born would turn black after the proper interval . . . It was a strain that told on her, and ended by giving her a deeply grounded contempt for men. She could not help it, she despised men. She despised them and was ruled by them. Her husband threw away her dowry and her property in wild investments in strange territories: Louisiana, Texas; and without protest she watched him play away her substance like a gambler. She felt that she could have managed her affairs profitably. But her natural activities lay elsewhere, it was the business of a man to make all decisions and dispose of all financial matters. Yet when she got the reins in her hands, her sons could persuade her to this and that enterprise or investment; against her will and judgment she accepted their advice, and among them they managed to break up once more the stronghold she had built for the future of her family. They got from her their own start in life, came back for fresh help when they needed it, and were divided against each other. She saw it as her natural duty to provide for her household, after her husband had fought stubbornly through the War, along with every other man of military age in the connection; had been wounded, had lingered helpless, and had died of his wound long after the great fervor and excitement had faded in hopeless defeat, when to be a man wounded and ruined in the War was merely to have proved oneself, perhaps, more heroic than wise. Left so, she drew her family together and set out for Louisiana, where her husband, with her money, had bought a sugar refinery. There was going to be a fortune in sugar, he said; not in raising the raw material, but in manufacturing it. He had schemes in his head for operating cotton gins, flour mills, refineries. Had he lived . . . but he did not live, and Sophia Jane had hardly repaired the house she bought and got the orchard planted when she saw that, in her hands, the sugar refinery was going to be a failure.

She sold out at a loss, and went on to Texas, where her husband had bought cheaply, some years before, a large tract of fertile black land in an almost unsettled part of the country. She had with her nine children, the youngest about two, the eldest about seventeen years old; Nannie and her three sons, Uncle Jimbilly, and two other Negroes, all in good health, full of hope and greatly desiring to live. Her husband's ghost persisted in her, she was bitterly outraged by his death almost as if he had willfully deserted her. She mourned for him at first with dry eyes, angrily. Twenty years later, seeing after a long absence the eldest son of her favorite daughter, who had died early, she recognized the very features and look of the husband of her youth, and she wept.

During the terrible second year in Texas, two of her younger sons, Harry and Robert, suddenly ran away. They chose good weather for it, in mid-May, and they were almost seven miles from home when a neighboring farmer saw them, wondered and asked questions, and ended by persuading them into his gig, and so brought them back.

Miss Sophia Jane went through the dreary ritual of discipline she thought appropriate to the occasion. She whipped them with her riding whip. Then she made them kneel down with her while she prayed for them, asking God to help them mend their ways and not be undutiful to their mother; her duty performed, she broke down and wept with her arms around them. They had endured their punishment stoically, because it would have been disgraceful to cry when a woman hit them, and besides, she did not hit very hard; they had knelt with her in a shamefaced gloom, because religious feeling was a female mystery which embarrassed them, but when they saw her tears they burst into loud bellows of repentance. They were only nine and eleven years old. She said in a voice of mourning, so despairing it frightened them: "Why did you run away from me? What do you think I brought you here for?" as if they were grown men who could realize how terrible the situation was. All the answer they could make, as they wept too, was that they had wanted to go back to Louisiana to eat sugar cane. They had been thinking about sugar cane all winter . . . Their mother was stunned. She had built a house large enough to shelter them all, of hand-sawed lumber dragged by oxcart for forty miles, she had got the fields fenced in and the crops planted, she had, she believed, fed and clothed her children; and now she realized they were hungry. These two had worked like men; she felt their growing bones through their thin flesh, and remembered how mercilessly she had driven them, as she had driven herself, as she had driven the Negroes and the horses, because there was no choice in the matter. They must labor beyond their strength or perish. Sitting there with her arms around them, she felt her heart break in her breast. She had thought it was a silly phrase. It happened to her. It was not that she was incapable of feeling afterward, for in a way she was more emotional, more quick, but griefs never again lasted with her so long as they had before. This day was the beginning of her spoiling her children and being afraid of them. She said to them after a long dazed silence, when they began to grow restless under her arms: "We'll grow fine ribbon cane here. The soil is perfect for it. We'll have all the sugar we want. But we must be patient."

By the time her children began to marry, she was able to give them each a good strip of land and a little money, she was able to help them buy more land in places they preferred by selling her own, tract by tract, and she saw them all begin well, though not all of them ended so. They went about their own affairs, scattering out and seeming to lose all that sense of family unity so precious to the Grandmother. They bore with her infrequent visits and her advice and her tremendous rightness, and they were impatient of her tenderness. When Harry's wife died–she had never approved of Harry's wife, who was delicate and hopelessly inadequate at housekeeping, and who could not even bear children successfully, since she died when her third was born—the Grandmother took the children and began life again, with almost the same zest, and with more indulgence. She had just got them brought up to the point where she felt she could begin to work the faults out of them—faults inherited, she admitted fairly, from both sides of the house—when she died. It happened quite suddenly one afternoon in early October, after a day spent in helping the Mexican gardener of her third daughter-in-law to put the garden to rights. She was on a visit in far-western Texas and enjoying it. The daughter-in-law was exasperated but apparently so docile, the Grandmother, who looked upon her as a child, did not notice her little moods at all. The son had long ago learned not to oppose his mother. She wore him down with patient, just, and reasonable argument. She was careful never to venture to command him in anything. He consoled his wife by saying that everything Mother was doing could be changed back after she was gone. As this change included moving a fifty-foot adobe wall, the wife was not much consoled. The Grandmother came into the house quite flushed and exhilarated, saying how well she felt in the bracing mountain air—and dropped dead over the doorsill.

E. E. CUMMINGS

[1894–]

Edward Estlin Cummings was never given a temperate reception. He was either immoderately praised as a stubbornly original innovator or immoderately condemned as the arrogantly bad boy of American literature. Born October 14, 1894, in Cambridge, Massachusetts, he was educated at Harvard, where his father taught sociology and economics before becoming an eminent Unitarian minister. When the First World War broke out, Cummings did not wait for the United States to join the Allies: he went to France, drove an army ambulance and, later, became a private in the U. S. Army. While in France he was put in a concentration camp, an experience unforgettably recorded in one of the most notable of war books, The Enormous Room. *As a painter he has exhibited his work from time to time—one of his books was entitled* CIOPW, *an abbreviation for Charcoal, Ink, Oil, Pastel, Water-*

color. EIMI, *now in its fourth edition as a paperback, is the diary of his trip to Soviet Russia in 1931.*

Although his poetic manner is unorthodox, Cummings' views on poetry are anything but revolutionary. At fifty-eight, invited to give the annual Charles Eliot Norton lectures at Harvard, he embodied his ideas in a series of talks—he called them "nonlectures." His prose, like his poetry, was striking not because of what Cummings said, but the way he said it. The chief difficulty with his poetry is its typography. Various reasons have been given for Cummings' odd arrangements. It is said that, following the tradition of modern painting, he distorts the shape of the words in order to draw attention to their values, that he jams several words together to get an effect of speed or puts spaces between syllables to achieve a retarded tempo, that he organizes his material to give it the significant form of a word-picture. If the reader will not let himself be bothered by the peculiarity of the look of the poem on the printed page, he will get real enjoyment from the pure feel of it. He will discover a poet who can be witty and passionate in the same line, who can, with a sleight-of-phrase, give a new twist to an old statement, who can rearrange sonnets and lyrics into fresh patterns and turn platitudes into scathing ironies or plangent love poems.

Six hundred poems from ten previously-published volumes were contained in Poems: 1923–1954, *which won a Special Citation from the National Book Awards Committee, and were followed in 1958, when Cummings was sixty-four, by* Ninety-Five Poems. *Though there was much to irritate—a chip-on-the-shoulder toughness, an arrogant self-consciousness, a rhetorical dependence on the oldest and most sentimental stereotypes of verse—only a prejudiced reader could fail to find a genuinely romantic poet underneath the tricks and trappings.*

IF THERE ARE ANY HEAVENS

if there are any heavens my mother will(all by herself)have
one.   It will not be a pansy heaven nor
a fragile heaven of lilies-of-the-valley but
it will be a heaven of blackred roses

my father will be(deep like a rose
tall like a rose)

standing near my

(swaying over her
silent)
with eyes which are really petals and see

nothing with the face of a poet really which
is a flower and not a face with
hands
which whisper
This is my beloved my

(suddenly in sunlight
he will bow,

& the whole garden will bow)

A WIND HAS BLOWN THE RAIN AWAY AND BLOWN

a wind has blown the rain away and blown
the sky away and all the leaves away,
and the trees stand. It think i too have known
autumn too long

(and what have you to say,
wind wind wind—did you love somebody
and have you the petal of somewhere in your heart
pinched from dumb summer?
O crazy daddy
of death dance cruelly for us and start

the last leaf whirling in the final brain
of air!) Let us as we have seen see
doom's integration . . . . a wind has blown the rain

away and the leaves and the sky and the
trees stand:
the trees stand. The trees,
suddenly wait against the moon's face.

ANYONE LIVED IN A PRETTY HOW TOWN

anyone lived in a pretty how town
(with up so floating many bells down)
spring summer autumn winter
he sang his didn't he danced his did.

Women and men(both little and small)
cared for anyone not at all
they sowed their isn't they reaped their same
sun moon stars rain

children guessed(but only a few
and down they forgot as up they grew
autumn winter spring summer)
that noone loved him more by more

when by now and tree by leaf
she laughed his joy she cried his grief
bird by snow and stir by still
anyone's any was all to her

someones married their everyones
laughed their cryings and did their dance
(sleep wake hope and then)they
said their nevers they slept their dream

stars rain sun moon
(and only the snow can begin to explain
how children are apt to forget to remember
with up so floating many bells down)

one day anyone died i guess
(and noone stooped to kiss his face)
busy folk buried them side by side
little by little and was by was

all by all and deep by deep
and more by more they dream their sleep
noone and anyone earth by april
wish by spirit and if by yes.

Women and men(both dong and ding)
summer autumn winter spring
reaped their sowing and went their came
sun moon stars rain

EDMUND WILSON

[1895–   ]

Learned without being academic, *an incisive but never a captious critic, Edmund Wilson added illumination to analysis. He was born May 8, 1895, in Red Bank, New Jersey.* Son of a lawyer and politician, he received his B.A. from Princeton at twenty-one and, immediately after being graduated, became a reporter on the New York Evening Sun. Although he wrote some of the most important literary criticisms he always insisted on calling himself a journalist. After seeing service with the Intelligence Corps during the First World War, he became managing editor of the ultra-smart magazine Vanity Fair and, after a few years, threw in his lot with its very opposite, the liberal-intellectual New Republic. Nearing fifty, he became book-reviewer for The New Yorker and, when he ceased to perform the weekly stint, continued to contribute articles which were condensed and often iconoclastic essays. He was married four times; his second wife was the novelist, Mary McCarthy.

Besides criticism, Wilson wrote poetry, plays, a novel, and short stories like those collected in Memoirs of Hecate County. The pieces in that volume were underestimated because of one erotic story which caused the book to be banned as obscene in New York. However, Wilson was essentially a critic. Such books as Axel's Castle, The Wound and the Bow, The Triple Thinkers, and The Shores of Light are of value not only because of their reappraisals, but because of their constant challenge to the reader. On account of them he was awarded the National Institute of Arts and Letters' Gold Medal for Criticism in 1955.

The piece which follows is an example of Wilson's commentary in 1939 on one of the phenomena of American life and industry rather than on its literature.

IT'S TERRIBLE! IT'S GHASTLY! IT STINKS!

I have laughed a good deal in reading a new book—*The Great Goldwyn* by Alva Johnston—about Sam Goldwyn, the Hollywood producer. It is fun to hear how Mr. Goldwyn, when told that a script was "too caustic," said: "To hell with the cost! We'll make it anyway!"; and how be brought Maeterlinck to Hollywood in a private car and then, after seeing his first script, rushed out of the room screaming: "My God, the hero is a bee!" Alva Johnston, who is an adept at this kind of personal sketch, has handled his subject with deftness. He has turned out a good piece of light reading, through which the Goldwyn gags are sprinkled in such a way as to give the whole story a certain comic sparkle.

And yet this book makes one slightly sick. It has the slave-brand of Hollywood upon it. Instead of being able to present Sam Goldwyn as the rich humorous character he undoubtedly is, with whatever credit for energy and enterprise he deserves, Mr. Johnston seems to feel forced to flatter him. Mr. Johnston does not, to be sure, offer up his homage to Goldwyn with quite the piety of a denizen of the studios. He is used to writing "profiles" for the *New Yorker*, and he makes a point of turning his paeans off with quick winks and light changes of tone. But the flattery is there just the same. One gets very definitely the impression that Mr. Johnston has written his sketch in such a way that Mr. Goldwyn will be able to read it or to have certain selected passages read to him and imagine that he has been apotheosized by Mr. Johnston, while at the same time Mr. Johnston will be let out with his friends in New York by the delicate irony which he has aimed in their direction but which may not be perceptible to Mr. Goldwyn. Or it may be all a special kind of publicity designed to give more serious weight to Mr. Goldwyn by scaling down his colossal vanity and ignorance, and what sounds from Mr. Johnston's account like a lack of ordinary sportsmanship and decency, to the proportions of amusing foibles which only endear him the more to his friends.

I will quote only two examples—the whole book is written in the same way. "It has been said," says Mr. Johnston, "that if Shakespeare were alive today, Goldwyn would have him. It is an interesting notion; some of the bad plays, like *Cymbeline, Troilus and Cressida* and *Pericles*, might have been tightened up into great dramas if the playwright had had a producer over him to tell him, 'It stinks, Wagspeare. It's lousy. It's terrible. It's ghastly. You're ruining me, Wagstaff.'" Very funny about Goldwyn talking to Shakespeare; but what is Mr. Johnston's object in asserting that the defective plays of Shakespeare could have been converted by Mr. Goldwyn into "great dramas"? Mr. Johnston must know as well as anybody that Mr. Goldwyn would not be able to do anything for the least of Shakespeare's plays except turn it into something different and worse. And here is the conclusion of *The Great Goldwyn:* "Last year was Sam's twenty-third in the movie business; his press department at that time spotted him two years and celebrated the completion of his quarter-century in the business. Next year is Sam's real silver jubilee. It is something for everybody to feel patriotic about. The U.S.A. leads the world by a wider margin in pictures than anything else, and one of the chief reasons is the Great Goldwyn."

Well, I for one will be damned if I will feel patriotic about Sam Goldwyn's silver jubilee, which his agents have been unable to restrain themselves from celebrating two years too early. In what sense does the United States lead the world in moving pictures? We make more of them than any other country and are, I suppose, more proficient technically, but have we ever turned out anything that was comparable artistically to the best German or Russian films? I can think of nothing except Charlie Chaplin, who is his own producer and produces simply himself. There was a time—up to, say, 1930—when our pictures seemed to be improving. There were new actors brought in from Europe and from the speaking stage in New York; there was mechanical experimentation and an aesthetic attention to photography; intelligent directors were given their chance.

But then the depression fell; the producers were frightened and forced to retrench; and the whole movie business seemed to harden into something immovably banal. It nailed down its favorite formulas in all their vulgarity and falsity, and almost entirely abandoned any attempt to make the old situations seem lifelike or to point them up with novel direction. The actors who were brought to Hollywood were handled with extreme stupidity, and, if they stayed there, almost invariably ruined. A lot of talent has been fed into the studios, and what have our pictures to show for it? How shall we ever know now, for example, whether Katharine Hepburn—or, for that matter, Greta Garbo—ever really had anything in her? They set the talented Emil Jannings to performing over and over again wretched parodies of his German masterpieces, with everything that had given them reality and made them human and moving bleached out by the insipid Hollywood sun, until he could stand it no longer and departed. Charles Laughton has also escaped and has returned to England and the Old Vic. Marlene Dietrich, who must have had some ability at least as a night club singer, because she has made marvellous phonograph records in German, has been turned into something in the nature of one of those loose-jointed dolls designed to be propped up against the pillows in boudoirs with sateen bedspreads, and has been made to appear in pictures so foolish, so unsightly and of such horrible taste that the most beautiful woman in the world could not play in them without looking ridiculous. But the only mirrors, apparently, in which film actors can look at themselves are the magazines that exploit the glamor of the trade and are edited for adolescent schoolgirls. That able Soviet actress Anna Sten the Great Goldwyn was unable to use at all; and I see that she is now making for another producer pictures with such titles as *Love Me Again*, *Gorgeous* and *Orchid Girl*. Mae West, whose peculiar attraction was that she worked up her own material and created a legendary world of her own, now has to have savorless imitations written for her by Hollywood hacks, who have quickly converted her fantasies into run-of-the-mill goods. The vultures of the Coast get them all. A director like King Vidor who has serious aspirations ends by turning out the worst kind of monstrosity: the bad serious picture. The shimmering polish of Lubitsch ends as a veneer on the awful old formulas. We have actually got to a point where features like Tarzan and Charlie Chan are the most satisfactory things one can go to. They are absurd, they are fairy tales; but they do have a certain independent existence.

The other day, after long abstinence from the movies, the result of having seen nothing but bad films for a year, I went to one for the first time in months. I had assumed that the Marx brothers were indestructible. True, I had been reading the publicity stories about their new picture, *A Day at the Races:* how it had first been taken all over the country in the form of a stage entertainment, with a view to weeding out every gag that could not be immediately appreciated by the audience of the average town of over two or three thousand inhabitants. (This was partly, apparently, the work of Mr. George S. Kaufman, who, years ago, after his first experience of Hollywood, wrote *Once in a Lifetime* as a satire on it but later went back to learn the trade.) But I hadn't foreseen that the result of this would be to deprive the Marx brothers of all their natural vitality and spontaneity. As if even popular comic art, if this is really to capture the public, were not more a matter of putting over on an audience (as Charlie Chaplin and Walt Disney have) something from one's own imagination than of finding an infallible formula to provoke its automatic reactions! The idea of establishing and exploiting the lowest common denominator of audiences has finally killed the movies. They are absolutely sterile and static. And even the Marx brothers are no longer the Marx brothers. Their corporate élan has been deadened by unnatural selection of their dullest gags; and they now fall asunder helpless. It would be amusing if *A Day at the Races*, after all the special trouble taken with it, should turn out to be a total flop.

And the writers. Before the vultures have picked the bones of theatrical talent, the big white worms of the studios have grown fat on the decaying flesh. But the vultures get the worms, too. Have we not all had needy friends who have gone West with a smile on their lips and who have never returned again?—from whom we have ceased to hear and whose names we no longer mention, whom we remember as young people of promise, wondering what they have found to do and never thinking to connect them with the processed stuff we hear croaked out, between kisses and pistol-shots, by the smooth-faced gigantic phantoms, when we are foolish enough to go to the movies? It is true, as Mr. Johnston tells us, that Sam Goldwyn always wants the best writers; and there they are out on the Golden Coast, cooped up in their little cells, like school children in study-hour. Teacher is the supervisor, and one hopes to be teacher's favorite. There they are, blowing in their money on goofy Los Angeles houses and on ostentatious cocktail parties, at which they talk about their salaries and their options and always speak of their superiors with admiration, while they submit to being spied upon and having their correspondence opened. Those who do not care to admit surrender pretend to be uncompromising Leftist, getting together in little groups to give three discreet cheers for Stalin and to shed a tear for Republican Spain. But when the Writers' Guild was organized, it took only one woof from Schulberg to send them running like prairie-dogs—leaving the job to the technicians and the actors. And now the black-listed leaders are creeping back, having become so profoundly habituated to high salaries for low work that, no matter how radical they claim to be, they don't know how to get along without them.

I remember only one American critic who has seemed to me to do full justice to this subject of the Hollywood producers: Mr. George Jean Nathan in the *Smart Set*. Mr. Nathan had the rich and reckless language for it; I am sorry that my own powers are relatively feeble. That was ten years or more ago; but it is plain that today's producers, including the Great Goldwyn and the late lamented Irving Thalberg, are the same megalomaniac cloak-and-suit dealers that their predecessors were. You have only to look at their products. You have only to look at their staffs. From the servant you may know the master. Mr. Johnston can have had only a brief submergence, and look at the book he has written.

JOHN DOS PASSOS

[1896–   ]

"It was the speech that clung to the ears, the link that tingled in the blood," John Dos Passos wrote, and in the finest of his books he transcribed, accurately and with telling effect, the multitude of sounds which had rung in his ears, creating a kind of literary shorthand with which to set on paper the accents he heard and the men who spoke them. "Epic," "panoramic," or "kaleidoscopic," his style influenced a generation of writers who saw in his method a way to portray the restless, vital energy of America.

Son of a New York lawyer, grandson of a Portuguese immigrant, John Roderigo Dos Passos was born on Chicago's Lakeside Drive on January 14, 1896. "I was carted around a good deal as a child," he wrote, "to Mexico, to Belgium, lived in England a little, in Washington, D.C., and on a farm in Westmoreland County, Virginia." From Choate School in Connecticut he went to Harvard, graduating cum laude in 1916. He went to Spain intending to study architecture, but when the United States entered World War I he "got into a couple of ambulance units and finally into the U.S. Medical Corps as a private." From his wartime experiences in France came, in 1920, his first novel, One Man's Initiation–1917, a reflection of his and his contemporaries' reaction to "inflated patriotism." He was marked as a more than promising novelist when he published, less than two years later, Three Soldiers, an unsparing account of men in battle, one of the first of the novels which spoke out against the glorification of the Great War.

Dos Passos worked as a newspaper correspondent and free-lance writer in Spain, Mexico, the Near East, and New York. Writing about the big city—all of it—he found the idiom which was to be so much his own that his imitators would always be known as "Dos Passos writers." Manhattan Transfer portrayed the minutiae of New York as Dos Passos' major work, U.S.A., was to detail the multitude of facets which, together, made up an entire nation. His was an almost fanatic passion for detail. He attempted to produce in the novel the effect of the film editor's montage of close-ups. Often he succeeded, summing up the lives of men or a pageant of events with a few telling strokes. The 42nd Parallel, the first of the three books which make up U.S.A., appeared in 1930, five years after Manhattan Transfer. Nineteen-Nineteen was published two years later, and The Big Money in 1936.

Dos Passos continued to roam the world. He wrote several travel books as unusual as his novels; among them were Oriental Express, for which he did his own illustrations, and Journeys Between Wars. There were plays—The Garbage Man and Airways, Inc.—which, again, employed a film technique. Occasionally he published verse. Always his conscience drove him from his study to take an active part, as well as to write about, the injustices he saw rampant in the world (he was arrested as a picket at the Sacco-Vanzetti trial).

He married a writer, Katherine Smith. When they were not travelling, they lived at Cape Cod, where Dos Passos wrote, sailed, and painted. In 1947 his wife was killed in an automobile accident. Two years later he married again and moved to his father's farm in Virginia.

As a young man Dos Passos had been angry and effective in expressing his anger, citing injustices where he saw them, not satisfied to paint a picture but baldly exposing the flaws in the subject he portrayed. Politically he veered to the left, but he refused to adhere to any one faction—for this he received more criticism than thanks from those who might have been expected to be among his staunchest admirers. As he grew older he moved toward the right. Disillusionment and bitterness colored the novels he wrote after World War II. He felt more keenly, as Arthur Mizener noted, "his hatred of our failure, humanity's failure, to be what it professes—and what it ought to be." Another trilogy, the ambitious and controversial District of Columbia, burdened with this disillusionment, proved narrow, pessimistic, and, though adhering to that style which had made him unique, somehow superficial.

U.S.A. is Dos Passos' master work, constituting, as one critic said, "an unequaled portrait of twentieth century America, . . . peculiarly native and yet fully aware of our plight." The writer's discontent with his country's faults was founded on his love for the energy of its spirit. Here are industrialists and laborers, slick highways, rutted roads, and the rattle of cities held, noisy and brilliant, in Dos Passos' singular prose. "U.S.A. is the slice of a continent . . ." he wrote, "a group of holding companies, some aggregations of trade unions, a set of lawbooks bound in calf, a radio network, a chain of moving picture companies, . . . the world's greatest rivervalley fringed with mountains and hills, . . . the letters at the end of an address when you are away from home. But, mostly, U.S.A. is the speech of the people."

From U. S. A.

Meester Veelson

THE YEAR THAT BUCHANAN was elected president Thomas Woodrow Wilson

was born to a presbyterian minister's daughter

in the manse at Staunton in the valley of Virginia; it was the old Scotch-Irish stock; the father was a presbyterian minister too and a teacher of rhetoric in theological seminaries; the Wilsons lived in a universe of words linked into an incontrovertible firmament by two centuries of calvinist divines,

God was the Word

and the Word was God.

Dr. Wilson was a man of standing who loved his home and his children and good books and his wife and correct syntax and talked to God every day at family prayers;

he brought his sons up

between the bible and the dictionary.

The years of the Civil War

the years of fife and drum and platoonfire and proclamations

the Wilsons lived in Augusta, Georgia; Tommy was a backward child, didn't learn his letters till he was nine, but when he learned to read his favorite reading was Parson Weems'

Life of Washington.

In 1870 Dr. Wilson was called to the Theological Seminary at Columbia, South Carolina; Tommy attended Davidson college,

where he developed a good tenor voice;

then he went to Princeton and became a debater and editor of the *Princetonian.* His first published article in the Nassau Literary Magazine was an appreciation of Bismarck.

Afterwards he studied law at the University of Virginia; young Wilson wanted to be a Great Man, like Gladstone and the eighteenth century English parliamentarians; he wanted to hold the packed benches spellbound in the cause of Truth; but lawpractice irked him; he was more at home in the booky air of libraries, lecturerooms, college chapel, it was a relief to leave his lawpractice at Atlanta and take a Historical Fellowship at Johns Hopkins; there he wrote *Congressional Government.*

At twentynine he married a girl with a taste for painting (while he was courting her he coached her in how to use the broad "a") and got a job at Bryn Mawr teaching the girls History and Political Economy. When he got his Ph.D. from Johns Hopkins he moved to a professorship at Wesleyan, wrote articles, started a History of the United States,

spoke out for Truth Reform Responsible Government Democracy from the lecture platform, climbed all the steps of a brilliant university career; in 1901 the trustees of Princeton offered him the presidency;

he plunged into reforming the university, made violent friends and enemies, set the campus by the ears,

and the American people began to find on the front pages

the name of Woodrow Wilson.

In 1909 he made addresses on Lincoln and Robert E. Lee

and in 1910

the democratic bosses of New Jersey, hardpressed by muckrakers and reformers, got the bright idea of offering the nomination for governor to the stainless college president who attracted such large audiences

by publicly championing Right.

When Mr. Wilson addressed the Trenton convention that nominated him for governor he confessed his belief in the common man, (the smalltown bosses and the wardheelers looked at each other and scratched their heads); he went on, his voice growing firmer:

that is the man by whose judgment I for one wish to be guided, so that as the tasks multiply, and as the days come when all will feel confusion and dismay, we may lift up our eyes to the hills out of these dark valleys where the crags of special privilege overshadow and darken our path, to where the sun gleams through the great passage in the broken cliffs,

the sun of God,

the sun meant to regenerate men,

the sun meant to liberate them from their passion and despair and lift us to those uplands which are the promised land of every man who desires liberty and achievement.

The smalltown bosses and the wardheelers looked at each other and scratched their heads; then they cheered; Wilson fooled the wiseacres and doublecrossed the bosses, was elected by a huge plurality;

so he left Princeton only half reformed to be Governor of New Jersey,

and became reconciled with Bryan

at the Jackson Day dinner: when Bryan remarked, "I of course knew that you were not with me in my position on the currency," Mr. Wilson replied, "All I can say, Mr. Bryan, is that you are a great big man."

He was introduced to Colonel House,

that amateur Merlin of politics who was spinning his webs at the Hotel Gotham

and at the convention in Baltimore the next July the upshot of the puppetshow staged for sweating delegates by Hearst and House behind the scenes, and Bryan booming in the corridors with a handkerchief over his wilted collar, was that Woodrow Wilson was nominated for the presidency.

The bolt of the Progressives in Chicago from Taft to T.R. made his election sure;

so he left the State of New Jersey halfreformed

(pitiless publicity was the slogan of the Shadow Lawn Campaign)

and went to the White House

our twentyeighth president.

While Woodrow Wilson drove up Pennsylvania Avenue beside Taft the great buttertub, who as president had been genially undoing T.R.'s reactionary efforts to put business under the control of the government,

J. Pierpont Morgan sat playing solitaire in his back office on Wall Street, smoking twenty black cigars a day, cursing the follies of democracy.

Wilson flayed the interests and branded privilege refused to recognize Huerta and sent the militia to the Rio Grande

to assume a policy of watchful waiting. He published *The New Freedom* and delivered his messages to Congress in person, like a college president adressing the faculty and students. At Mobile he said:

I wish to take this occasion to say that the United States will never again seek one additional foot of territory by conquest;

and he landed the marines at Vera Cruz.

We are witnessing a renaissance of public spirit, a reawakening of sober public opinion, a revival of the power of the people the beginning of an age of thoughtful reconstruction . . .

but the world had started spinning round Sarajevo.

First is was *neutrality in thought and deed*, then *too proud to fight* when the *Lusitania* sinking and the danger to the Morgan loans and the stories of the British and French propagandists set all the financial centers in the East bawling for war, but the suction of the drumbeat and the guns was too strong; the best people took their fashions from Paris and their broad "a's" from London, and T.R. and the House of Morgan.

Five months after his reelection on the slogan *He kept us out of war*, Wilson pushed the Armed Ship Bill through congress and declared that a state of war existed between the United States and the Central Powers:

Force without stint or limit, force to the utmost.

Wilson became the state (war is the health of the state), Washington his Versailles, manned the socialized government with dollar a year men out of the great corporations and ran the big parade

of men munitions groceries mules and trucks to France. Five million men stood at attention outside of their tarpaper barracks every sundown while they played *The Star Spangled Banner.*

War brought the eight hour day, women's votes, prohibition, compulsory arbitration, high wages, high rates of interest, cost plus contracts and the luxury of being a Gold Star Mother.

If you objected to making the world safe for cost plus democracy you went to jail with Debs.

Almost too soon the show was over, Prince Max of Baden was pleading for the Fourteen Points, Foch was occupying the bridgeheads on the Rhine and the Kaiser out of breath ran for the train down the platform at Potsdam wearing a silk hat and some say false whiskers.

With the help of *Almighty God, Right, Truth, Justice, Freedom, Democracy, the Selfdetermination of Nations, No indemnities no annexations,*

and Cuban sugar and Caucasian manganese and Northwestern wheat and Dixie cotton, the British blockade, General Pershing, the taxicabs of Paris and the seventyfive gun

we won the war.

On December 4th, 1918, Woodrow Wilson, the first president to leave the territory of the United States during his presidency, sailed for France on board the *George Washington,*

the most powerful man in the world.

In Europe they knew what gas smelt like and the sweet sick stench of bodies buried too shallow and the grey look of the skin of starved children; they read in the papers that Meester Veelson was for peace and freedom and canned goods and butter and sugar;

he landed at Brest with his staff of experts and publicists after a rough trip on the *George Washington.*

La France héroïque was there with the speeches, the singing schoolchildren, the mayors in their red sashes. (Did Meester Veelson see the gendarmes at Brest beating back the demonstration of dockyard workers who came to meet him with red flags?)

At the station in Paris he stepped from the train onto a wide red carpet that led him, between rows of potted palms, silk hats, legions of honor, decorated busts of uniforms, frockcoats, rosettes, boutonnières, to a Rolls Royce. (Did Meester Veelson see the women in black, the cripples in their little carts, the pale anxious faces along the streets, did he hear the terrible anguish of the cheers as they hurried him and his new wife to the hôtel de Mûrat, where in rooms full of brocade, gilt clocks, Buhl cabinets and ormolu cupids the presidential suite had been prepared?)

While the experts were organizing the procedure of the peace conference, spreading green baize on the tables, arranging the protocols,

the Wilsons took a tour to see for themselves: the day after Christmas they were entertained at Buckingham Palace; at Newyears they called on the pope and on the microscopic Italian king at the Quirinal. (Did Meester Veelson know that in the peasants' wargrimed houses along the Brenta and the Piave they were burning candles in front of his picture cut out of the illustrated papers?) (Did Meester Veelson know that the people of Europe spelled a challenge to oppression out of the Fourteen Points as centuries before they had spelled a challenge to oppression out of the ninetyfive articles Martin Luther nailed to the churchdoor in Wittenberg?)

January 18, 1919, in the midst of serried uniforms, cocked hats and gold braid, decorations, epaulettes, orders of merit and knighthood, the High Contracting Parties, the allied and associated powers met in the Salon de l'Horloge at the quai d'Orsay to dictate the peace,

but the grand assembly of the peace conference was too public a place to make peace in

so the High Contracting Parties

formed the Council of Ten, went into the Gobelin Room and, surrounded by Rubens's History of Marie de Medici,

began to dictate the peace.

But the Council of Ten was too public a place to make peace in

so they formed the Council of Four.

Orlando went home in a huff

and then there were three:

Clemenceau,

Lloyd George,

Woodrow Wilson.

Three old men shuffling the pack,

dealing out the cards:

the Rhineland, Danzig, the Polish corridor, the Ruhr, self determination of small nations, the Saar, League of Nations, mandates, the Mespot, Freedom of the Seas, Transjordania, Shantung, Fiume and the Island of Yap:

machine gun fire and arson

starvation, lice, cholera, typhus;

oil was trumps.

Woodrow Wilson believed in his father's God

so he told the parishioners in the little Lowther Street Congregational church where his grandfather had preached in Carlisle in Scotland, a day so chilly that the newspaper men sitting in the old pews all had to keep their overcoats on.

On April 7th he ordered the *George Washington* to be held at Brest with steam up ready to take the American delegation home;

but he didn't go.

On April 19 sharper Clemenceau and sharper Lloyd George got him into their little cosy threecardgame they called the Council of Four.

On June 28th the Treaty of Versailles was ready

and Wilson had to go back home to explain to the politicians who'd been ganging up on him meanwhile in the Senate and House and to sober public opinion and to his father's God how he'd let himself be trimmed and how far he'd made the world safe

for democracy and the New Freedom.

From the day he landed in Hoboken he had his back to the wall of the White House, talking to save his faith in words, talking to save his faith in the League of Nations, talking to save his faith in himself, in his father's God.

He strained every nerve of his body and brain, every agency of the government he had under his control; (if anybody disagreed he was a crook or a red; no pardon for Debs).

In Seattle the wobblies whose leaders were in jail, in Seattle the wobblies whose leaders had been lynched, who'd been shot down like dogs, in Seattle the wobblies lined four blocks as Wilson passed, stood silent with their arms folded staring at the great liberal as he hurried past in his car, huddled in his overcoat, haggard with fatigue, one side of his face twitching. The men in overalls, the workingstiffs let him pass in silence after all the other blocks of handclapping and patriotic cheers.

In Pueblo, Colorado, he was a grey man hardly able to stand, one side of his face twitching:

Now that the mists of this great question have cleared away, I believe that men will see the Truth, eye for eye and face to face. There is one thing the American People always rise to and extend their hand to, that is, the truth of justice and of liberty and of peace. We have accepted that truth and we are going to be led by it, and it is going to lead us, and through us the world, out into pastures of quietness and peace such as the world never dreamed of before.

That was his last speech;

on the train to Wichita he had a stroke. He gave up the speaking tour that was to sweep the country for the League of Nations. After that he was a ruined paralysed man barely able to speak;

the day he gave up the presidency to Harding the joint committee of the Senate and House appointed Henry Cabot Lodge, his lifelong enemy, to make the formal call at the executive office in the Capitol and ask the formal question whether the president had any message for the congress assembled in joint session;

Wilson managed to get to his feet, lifting himself painfully by the two arms of the chair. "Senator Lodge, I have no further communication to make, thank you . . . Good morning," he said.

In 1924 on February 3rd he died.

Tin Lizzie

MR. FORD THE AUTOMOBILEER," the featurewriter wrote in 1900,

"*Mr. Ford the automobileer began by giving his steed three or four sharp jerks with the lever at the righthand side of the seat; that is, he pulled the lever up and down sharply in order, as he said, to mix air with gasoline and drive the charge into the exploding cylinder. . . . Mr. Ford slipped a small electric switch handle and there followed a puff, puff, puff. . . . The puffing of the machine assumed a higher key. She was flying along about eight miles an hour. The ruts in the road were deep, but the machine certainly went with a dreamlike smoothness. There was none of the bumping common even to a streetcar. . . . By this time the boulevard had been reached, and the automobileer, letting a lever fall a little, let her out. Whiz! She picked up speed with infinite rapidity. As she ran on there was a clattering behind, the new noise of the automobile.*

For twenty years or more,

ever since he'd left his father's farm when he was sixteen to get a job in a Detroit machineshop, Henry Ford had been nuts about machinery. First it was watches, then he designed a steamtractor, then he built a horseless carriage with an engine adapted from the Otto gasengine he'd read about in *The World of Science*, then a mechanical buggy with a onecylinder fourcycle motor, that would run forward but not back;

at last, in ninetyeight, he felt he was far enough along to risk throwing up his job with the Detroit Edison Company, where he'd worked his way up from night fireman to chief engineer, to put all his time into working on a new gasoline engine,

(in the late eighties he'd met Edison at a meeting of electriclight employees in Atlantic City. He'd gone up to Edison after Edison had delivered an address and asked him if he thought gasoline was practical as a motor fuel. Edison had said yes. If Edison said it, it was true. Edison was the great admiration of Henry Ford's life);

and in driving his mechanical buggy, sitting there at the lever jauntily dressed in a tightbuttoned jacket and a high collar and a derby hat, back and forth over the level illpaved streets of Detroit,

scaring the big brewery horses and the skinny trotting horses and the sleekrumped pacers with the motor's loud explosions,

looking for men scatterbrained enough to invest money in a factory for building automobiles.

He was the eldest son of an Irish immigrant who during the Civil War had married the daughter of a prosperous Pennsylvania Dutch farmer and settled down to farming near Dearborn in Wayne County, Michigan;

like plenty of other Americans, young Henry grew up hating the endless sogging through the mud about the chores, the hauling and pitching manure, the kerosene lamps to clean, the irk and sweat and solitude of the farm.

He was a slender, active youngster, a good skater, clever with his hands; what he liked was to tend the machinery and let the others do the heavy work. His mother had told him not to drink, smoke, gamble or go into debt, and he never did.

When he was in his early twenties his father tried to get him back from Detroit, where he was working as mechanic and repairman for the Drydock Engine Company that built engines for steamboats, by giving him forty acres of land.

Young Henry built himself an uptodate square white dwellinghouse with a false mansard roof and married and settled down on the farm,

but he let the hired men do the farming;

he bought himself a buzzsaw and rented a stationary engine and cut the timber off the woodlots.

He was a thrifty young man who never drank or smoked or gambled or coveted his neighbor's wife, but he couldn't stand living on the farm.

He moved to Detroit, and in the brick barn behind his house tinkered for years in his spare time with a mechanical buggy that would be light enough to run over the clayey wagonroads of Wayne County, Michigan.

By 1900 he had a practicable car to promote.

He was forty years old before the Ford Motor Company was started and production began to move.

Speed was the first thing the early automobile manufacturers went after. Races advertised the makes of cars.

Henry Ford himself hung up several records at the track at Grosse Pointe and on the ice on Lake St. Clair. In his 999 he did the mile in thirty-nine and fourfifths seconds.

But it had always been his custom to hire others to do the heavy work. The speed he was busy with was speed in production, the records records in efficient output. He hired Barney Oldfield, a stunt bicyclerider from Salt Lake City, to do the racing for him.

Henry Ford had ideas about other things than the designing of motors, carburetors, magnetos, jigs and fixtures, punches and dies; he had ideas about sales,

that the big money was in economical quantity production, quick turnover, cheap interchangeable easilyreplaced standardized parts;

it wasn't until 1909, after years of arguing with his partners, that Ford put out the first Model T.

Henry Ford was right.

That season he sold more than ten thousand tin lizzies, ten years later he was selling almost a million a year.

In these years the Taylor Plan was stirring up plantmanagers and manufacturers all over the country. Efficiency was the word. The same ingenuity that went into improving the performance of a machine could go into improving the performance of the workmen producing the machine.

In 1913 they established the assemblyline at Ford's. That season the profits were something like twentyfive million dollars, but they had trouble in keeping the men on the job, machinists didn't seem to like it at Ford's.

Henry Ford had ideas about other things than production.

He was the largest automobile manufacturer in the world; he paid high wages; maybe if the steady workers thought they were getting a cut (a very small cut) in the profits, it would give trained men an inducement to stick to their jobs,

wellpaid workers might save enough money to buy a tin lizzie; the first day Ford's announced that cleancut properlymarried American workers who wanted jobs had a chance to make five bucks a day (of course it

turned out that there were strings to it; always there were strings to it)
such an enormous crowd waited outside the Highland Park plant
all through the zero January night
that there was a riot when the gates were opened; cops broke heads, jobhunters threw bricks; property, Henry Ford's own property, was destoyed. The company dicks had to turn on the firehose to beat back the crowd.

The American Plan; automotive prosperity seeping down from above; it turned out there were strings to it.
But that five dollars a day
paid to good, clean American workmen
who didn't drink or smoke cigarettes or read or think,
and who didn't commit adultery
and whose wives didn't take in boarders,
made America once more the Yukon of the sweated workers of the world;
made all the tin lizzies and the automotive age, and incidentally,
made Henry Ford the automobileer, the admirer of Edison, the birdlover,
the great American of his time.

But Henry Ford had ideas about other things besides assemblylines and the livinghabits of his employees. He was full of ideas. Instead of going to the city to make his fortune, here was a country boy who'd made his fortune by bringing the city out to the farm. The precepts he'd learned out of McGuffey's Reader, his mother's prejudices and preconceptions, he had preserved clean and unworn as freshprinted bills in the safe in a bank.

He wanted people to know about his ideas, so he bought the *Dearborn Independent* and started a campaign against cigarettesmoking.

When war broke out in Europe, he had ideas about that too. (Suspicion of armymen and soldiering were part of the midwest farm tradition, like thrift, stickativeness, temperance and sharp practice in money matters.) Any intelligent American mechanic could see that if the Europeans hadn't been a lot of ignorant underpaid foreigners who drank, smoked, were loose about women and wasteful in their methods of production, the war could never have happened.

When Rosika Schwimmer broke through the stockade of secretaries and servicemen who surrounded Henry Ford and suggested to him that he could stop the war,

he said sure they'd hire a ship and go over and get the boys out of the trenches by Christmas.

He hired a steamboat, the *Oscar II*, and filled it up with pacifists and socialworkers,

to go over to explain to the princelings of Europe

that what they were doing was vicious and silly.

It wasn't his fault that Poor Richard's commonsense no longer rules the world and that most of the pacifists were nuts,

goofy with headlines.

When William Jennings Bryan went over to Hoboken to see him off, somebody handed William Jennings Bryan a squirrel in a cage; William Jennings Bryan made a speech with the squirrel under his arm. Henry Ford threw American Beauty roses to the crowd. The band played *I Didn't Raise My Boy to Be a Soldier*. Practical jokers let loose more squirrels. An eloping couple was married by a platoon of ministers in the saloon, and Mr. Zero, the flophouse humanitarian, who reached the dock too late to sail,

dove into the North River and swam after the boat.

The *Oscar II* was described as a floating Chautauqua; Henry Ford said it felt like a middlewestern village, but by the time they reached Christiansand in Norway, the reporters had kidded him so that he had gotten cold feet and gone to bed. The world was too crazy outside of Wayne County, Michigan. Mrs. Ford and the management sent an Episcopal dean after him who brought him home under wraps,

and the pacifists had to speechify without him.

Two years later Ford's was manufacturing munitions, Eagle boats; Henry Ford was planning oneman tanks, and oneman submarines like the one tried out in the Revolutionary War. He announced to the press that he'd turn over his war profits to the government,

but there's no record that he ever did.

One thing he brought back from his trip

was the Protocols of the Elders of Zion.

He started a campaign to enlighten the world in the *Dearborn Independent;* the Jews were why the world wasn't like Wayne County, Michigan, in the old horse and buggy days;

the Jews had started the war, Bolshevism, Darwinism, Marxism, Nietzsche, short skirts and lipstick. They were behind Wall Street and the international bankers, and the whiteslave traffic and the movies and the Supreme Court and ragtime and the illegal liquor business.

Henry Ford denounced the Jews and ran for senator and sued the *Chicago Tribune* for libel,

and was the laughingstock of the kept metropolitan press;
but when the metropolitan bankers tried to horn in on his business
he thoroughly outsmarted them.

In 1918 he had borrowed on notes to buy out his minority stockholders for the picayune sum of seventyfive million dollars.

In February, 1920, he needed cash to pay off some of these notes that were coming due. A banker is supposed to have called on him and offered him every facility if the bankers' representative could be made a member of the board of directors. Henry Ford handed the banker his hat,

and went about raising the money in his own way;

he shipped every car and part he had in his plant to his dealers and demanded immediate cash payment. Let the other fellow do the borrowing had always been a cardinal principle. He shut down production and canceled all orders from the supplyfirms. Many dealers were ruined, many supplyfirms failed, but when he reopened his plant,

he owned it absolutely,

the way a man owns an unmortgaged farm with the taxes paid up.

In 1922 there started the Ford boom for President (high wages, waterpower, industry scattered to the small towns) that was skillfully pricked behind the scenes

by another crackerbarrel philosopher,

Calvin Coolidge;

but in 1922 Henry Ford sold one million three hundred and thirtytwo thousand two hundred and nine tin lizzies; he was the richest man in the world.

Good roads had followed the narrow ruts made in the mud by the Model T. The great automotive boom was on. At Ford's production was improving all the time; less waste, more spotters, strawbosses, stoolpigeons (fifteen minutes for lunch, three minutes to go to the toilet, the Taylorized speedup everywhere, reach under, adjust washer, screw down bolt, shove in cotterpin, reachunder adjustwasher, screwdown bolt, reachunderadjustscrewdownreachunderadjust until every ounce of life was sucked off into production and at night the workmen went home grey shaking husks).

Ford owned every detail of the process from the ore in the hills until the car rolled off the end of the assemblyline under its own power, the plants were rationalized to the last tenthousandth of an inch as measured by the Johansen scale;

in 1926 the production cycle was reduced to eightyone hours from the ore in the mine to the finished salable car proceeding under its own power,

but the Model T was obsolete.

New Era prosperity and the American Plan
(there were strings to it, always there were strings to it)
had killed Tin Lizzie.
Ford's was just one of many automobile plants.
When the stockmarket bubble burst,
Mr. Ford the crackerbarrel philosopher said jubilantly,
"I told you so.
Serves you right for gambling and getting in debt.
The country is sound."
But when the country on cracked shoes, in frayed trousers, belts tightened over hollow bellies,
idle hands cracked and chapped with the cold of the coldest March day of 1932,
started marching from Detroit to Dearborn, asking for work and the American Plan, all they could think of at Ford's was machineguns.
The country was sound, but they mowed the marchers down.
They shot four of them dead.

Henry Ford as an old man
is a passionate antiquarian,
(lives besieged on his father's farm embedded in an estate of thousands of millionaire acres, protected by an army of servicemen, secretaries, secret agents, dicks under orders of an English exprizefighter,
always afraid of the feet in broken shoes on the roads, afraid the gangs will kidnap his grandchildren,
that a crank will shoot him,
that Change and the idle hands out of work will break through the gates and the high fences;
protected by a private army against
the new America of starved children and hollow bellies and cracked shoes stamping on souplines,
that has swallowed up the old thrifty farmlands
of Wayne County, Michigan,
as if they had never been).

Henry Ford as an old man
is a passionate antiquarian.
He rebuilt his father's farmhouse and put it back exactly in the state he remembered it in as a boy. He built a village of museums for buggies, sleighs, coaches, old plows, waterwheels, obsolete models of motorcars. He scoured the country for fiddlers to play oldfashioned squaredances.

Even old taverns he bought and put back into their original shape, as well as Thomas Edison's early laboratories.

When he bought the Wayside Inn near Sudbury, Massachusetts, he had the new highway where the newmodel cars roared and slithered and hissed oilily past (*the new noise of the automobile*),

moved away from the door,
put back the old bad road,
so that everything might be
the way it used to be,
in the days of horses and buggies.

The Campers at Kitty Hawk

On December seventeenth, nineteen hundred and three, Bishop Wright of the United Brethren onetime editor of the *Religious Telescope* received in his frame house on Hawthorn Street in Dayton, Ohio, a telegram from his boys Wilbur and Orville who'd gotten it into their heads to spend their vacations in a little camp out on the dunes of the North Carolina coast tinkering with a homemade glider they'd knocked together themselves. The telegram read:

SUCCESS FOUR FLIGHTS THURSDAY MORNING ALL AGAINST TWENTYONE MILE WIND STARTED FROM LEVEL WITH ENGINEPOWER ALONE AVERAGE SPEED THROUGH AIR THIRTYONE MILES LONGEST FIFTYSEVEN SECONDS INFORM PRESS HOME CHRISTMAS

The figures were a little wrong because the telegraph operator misread Orville's hasty penciled scrawl

but the fact remains
that a couple of young bicycle mechanics from Dayton, Ohio
had designed constructed and flown
for the first time ever a practical airplane.

After running the motor a few minutes to heat it up I released the wire that held the machine to the track and the machine started forward into the wind. Wilbur ran at the side of the machine holding the wing to balance it on the track. Unlike the start on the 14th made in a calm the machine facing a 27 mile wind started very slowly. . . . Wilbur was able to stay with it until it lifted from the track after a forty-foot run. One of the lifesaving men snapped the camera for us taking a picture just as it reached the end of the track and the machine had risen to a height of about two feet. . . . The course of the flight up and down was extremely erratic, partly due to the irregularities of the air, partly to lack of experience in handling this machine. A sudden dart when a little over a hundred and twenty feet from the point at which it rose in the air ended the flight. . . . This flight lasted only 12 seconds but it was nevertheless the first in the history of the world in which a machine carrying a man had raised itself by its own power into the air in full flight, had sailed forward without reduction of speed and had finally landed at a point as high as that from which it started.

A little later in the day the machine was caught in a gust of wind and turned over and smashed, almost killing the coastguardsman who tried to hold it down;

it was too bad
but the Wright brothers were too happy to care
they'd proved that the damn thing flew.

When these points had been definitely established we at once packed our goods and returned home knowing that the age of the flying machine had come at last.

They were home for Christmas in Dayton, Ohio, where they'd been born in the seventies of a family who had been settled west of the Alleghenies since eighteen fourteen, in Dayton, Ohio, where they'd been to grammarschool and highschool and joined their father's church and played baseball and hockey and worked out on the parallel bars and the flying swing and sold newspapers and built themselves a printingpress out of odds and ends from the junkheap and flown kites and tinkered with mechanical contraptions and gone around town as boys doing odd jobs to turn an honest penny.

The folks claimed it was the bishop's bringing home a helicopter, a fiftycent mechanical toy made of two fans worked by elastic bands that was supposed to hover in the air, that had got his two youngest boys hipped on the subject of flight

so that they stayed home instead of marrying the way the other boys did, and puttered all day about the house picking up a living with jobprinting,

bicyclerepair work,

sitting up late nights reading books on aerodynamics.

Still they were sincere churchmembers, their bicycle business was prosperous, a man could rely on their word. They were popular in Dayton.

In those days flyingmachines were the big laugh of all the crackerbarrel philosophers. Langley's and Chanute's unsuccessful experiments had been jeered down with an I-told-you-so that rang from coast to coast. The Wrights' big problem was to find a place secluded enough to carry on their experiments without being the horselaugh of the countryside. Then they had no money to spend;

they were practical mechanics; when they needed anything they built it themselves.

They hit on Kitty Hawk,

on the great dunes and sandy banks that stretch south towards Hatteras seaward of Albemarle Sound,

a vast stretch of seabeach

empty except for a coastguard station, a few fishermen's shacks and the swarms of mosquitoes and the ticks and chiggers in the crabgrass behind the dunes

and overhead the gull and swooping terns, in the evening fishhawks and cranes flapping across the saltmarshes, occasionally eagles

that the Wright brothers followed soaring with their eyes

as Leonardo watched them centuries before

straining his sharp eyes to apprehend

the laws of flight.

Four miles across the loose sand from the scattering of shacks, the Wright brothers built themselves a camp and a shed for their gliders. It was a long way to pack their groceries, their tools, anything they happened to need; in summer it was hot as blazes, the mosquitoes were hell;

but they were alone there

and they'd figured out that the loose sand was as soft as anything they could find to fall in.

There with a glider made of two planes and a tail in which they lay flat on their bellies and controlled the warp of the planes by shimmying their hips, taking off again and again all day from a big dune named Kill Devil Hill,

they learned to fly.

Once they'd managed to hover for a few seconds

and soar ever so slightly on a rising aircurrent

they decided the time had come

to put a motor in their biplane.

Back in the shop in Dayton, Ohio, they built an airtunnel, which is their first great contribution to the science of flying, and tried out model planes in it.

They couldn't interest any builders of gasoline engines so they had to build their own motor.

It worked; after that Christmas of nineteen three the Wright brothers weren't doing it for fun any more; they gave up their bicycle business, got the use of a big old cowpasture belonging to the local banker for practice flights, spent all the time when they weren't working on their machine in promotion, worrying about patents, infringements, spies, trying to interest government officials, to make sense out of the smooth involved heartbreaking remarks of lawyers.

In two years they had a plane that would cover twentyfour miles at a stretch round and round the cowpasture.

People on the interurban car used to crane their necks out of windows when they passed along the edge of the field, startled by the clattering pop pop of the old Wright motor and the sight of the white biplane like a pair of ironingboards one on top of the other chugging along a good fifty feet in the air. The cows soon got used to it.

As the flights got longer
the Wright brothers got backers,
engaged in lawsuits,
lay in their beds at night sleepless with the whine of phantom millions, worse than the mosquitoes at Kitty Hawk.

In nineteen seven they went to Paris,
allowed themselves to be togged out in dress suits and silk hats,
learned to tip waiters
talked with government experts, got used to gold braid and postponements and vandyke beards and the outspread palms of politicos. For amusement
they played diabolo in the Tuileries gardens.

They gave publicized flights at Fort Myers, where they had their first fatal crackup, St. Petersburg, Paris, Berlin; at Pau they were all the rage,
such an attraction that the hotelkeeper
wouldn't charge them for their room.
Alfonso of Spain shook hands with them and was photographed sitting in the machine,
King Edward watched a flight,
the Crown Prince insisted on being taken up,
the rain of medals began.

They were congratulated by the Czar
and the King of Italy and the amateurs of sport, and society climbers and the papal titles,
and decorated by a society for universal peace.

Aeronautics became the sport of the day.
The Wrights don't seem to have been very much impressed by the upholstery and the braid and the gold medals and the parades of plush horses,
they remained practical mechanics
and insisted on doing all their own work themselves,
even to filling the gasolinetank.

In nineteen eleven they were back on the dunes
at Kitty Hawk with a new glider.
Orville stayed up in the air for nine and a half minutes, which remained a long time the record for motorless flight.
The same year Wilbur died of typhoidfever in Dayton.
In the rush of new names: Farman, Blériot, Curtiss, Ferber, Esnault-Peltrie, Delagrange;
in the snorting impact of bombs and the whine and rattle of shrapnel and the sudden stutter of machineguns after the motor's been shut off overhead,
and we flatten into the mud
and make ourselves small cowering in the corners of ruined walls,
the Wright brothers passed out of the headlines
but not even headlines or the bitter smear of newsprint or the choke of smokescreen and gas or chatter of brokers on the stockmarket or barking of phantom millions or oratory of brasshats laying wreaths on new monuments
can blur the memory
of the chilly December day
two shivering bicycle mechanics from Dayton, Ohio,
first felt their homemade contraption
whittled out of hickory sticks,
gummed together with Arnstein's bicycle cement,
stretched with muslin they'd sewn on their sister's sewingmachine in their own backyard on Hawthorn Street in Dayton, Ohio,
soar into the air
above the dunes and the wide beach
at Kitty Hawk.

WILLIAM FAULKNER

[1897–]

JUST AS THOMAS HARDY made Wessex his own special province, so William Faulkner created a composite terrain, Yoknapatowpha County, and made it completely his own. Faulkner was born September 25, 1897, in New Albany, Mississippi, the oldest of four brothers, the sons of a once wealthy, landowning family which had been ruined by the Civil War. At the time of William's birth his father was a railroad conductor, as well as the owner of a livery stable and treasurer of the University of Mississippi.

Faulkner grew up in the university town, Oxford, dreaming of a colorful past which offered a contrast to the commonplace present. He could not abide routine schooling and never graduated from high school. When the First World War threatened, he enlisted in the British Air Force—flying for the U.S. Army might have meant being bossed by "Yankees."

Back in Oxford he earned a living doing odd jobs as a carpenter, housepainter, and repairman. He tried formal education again, this time at the University of Mississippi, but left before he had completed his second year. He decided he wanted to be a writer—his head was full of stories he had picked up from farmers and sharecroppers—and went to New York in the hope of finding work with a publisher. Instead he sold books in a department store. After six months he was offered a postmastership in Oxford and went home to be, he said, "the world's worst postmaster."

At twenty-seven, moving on to New Orleans, Faulkner came into contact with Sherwood Anderson and other writers. He sold a few short stories, wrote two novels, and, with Sartoris and The Sound and the Fury, began the creation of the large design into which practically all his subsequent work was to fit. Within the confines of Yoknapatowpha County he constructed his picture of the South, the pattern of a sinister and suffering country, a region of lost luxuries, mansions despoiled and estates ruined, of eroded cotton fields, corrupted towns, swamps and gloomy forests. His land was peopled by the families of aristocrats, living in the memories of a former greatness, lost and lingering into decay; by the new generations of wily opportunists who robbed the land of its last life; and by the negroes, moving from slavery to freedom, and with such a strength in their heritage that in a country which moldered and collapsed, they endured. "This whole land, the whole South, is cursed," cries young McCaslin in "The Bear," one of the longest and most difficult of Faulkner's short stories. "And all of us who derive from it, whom it ever suckled, white and black both, lie under the curse."

At thirty-two Faulkner was already something of a portent. People began to talk of his dark magic and the sinister beauty of his haunted landscapes. He married, had a child who failed to survive infancy, and then a daughter in whom he took great paternal pride. Always he was forced to consider the difference between the writing he had to do and the writing he had to do to earn a living. His grim novel, As I Lay Dying, was composed while he was employed shoveling coal in the power plant of the university—he liked to say he wrote most of it on the back of a wheelbarrow. In his mid-thirties he wrote Sanctuary, "deliberately to make money"—for himself and for the publisher who liked his work but felt he couldn't profitably publish it. Sanctuary did make money. The novel was made into a film—the sensational story of an impotent, degenerate killer and a nymphomaniac college girl appeared in a watered-down version as The Story of Temple Drake—and Faulkner was hired by Hollywood. He stayed there sporadically and spent practically all his time amplifying the Yoknapatowpha saga.

Faulkner always considered himself a farmer. At fifty-two, while cultivating his garden or, to be more exact, while he was spreading lime on his fields, he received the news that he had won the Nobel Prize. His speech of acceptance sounded a note of affirmation which readers had rarely heard coming from Faulkner's jungle of despair. "I believe that man will not merely endure; he will prevail. He is immortal, not because he alone among creatures has an inexhaustible voice, but because he has a soul, a spirit capable of compassion and sacrifice and endurance." Ten years later, addressing a session of UNESCO (United Nations Educational, Scientific, and Cultural Organization) he made another of his infrequent affirmative comments. "There will," he said, "always be a handful who decline to be convinced by failure, who believe somehow that human problems can be solved. . . We will fail again, perhaps, but at least we have learned that the failure will not be important either. That failure will not even have laurels to rest on, since out of that failure also rises its handful, still irreconcilable and undismayed."

Faulkner's readers remain irreconcilably divided. "There will always be a set of readers who dismiss Faulkner as an irresponsible thinker, a charlatan, a man who never mastered English, and so on," wrote

Richard Chase in The American Novel and Its Tradition. *"And there have always been readers who felt the same way about Dostoevski." Part of the reader's dissatisfaction arises from the difficulties of Faulkner's mannerisms: his long interior monologues, his vague time sequences, his disruption of the normal order of events, and what has been called his "game of hide-and-seek between author and reader." On the other hand, as Marcel Aymé wrote, "The humid warmth, the mystery, the half-light in which Faulknerian characters move owe nothing whatever to tricks of technique. . . Generally speaking, we owe all that is particularly moving, fine, and worthwhile in Faulkner's work to his creative genius, his power of evocation."*

Circling, observing, reconsidering his own particular county, Faulkner creates ever more complex patterns, but with them, when he is most successful, he is able to expose more clearly than before the particular personalities of his characters and their land. Truly a writer of sagas, he is unafraid of the immensity of the subject he chooses to tackle, unshy of trying to write of heroes. Although he is the chronicler of decay in a disordered world, he communicates not only the suspense and terror of that world but also its primitive force. It is a cruel country which Faulkner depicts, but it is seldom without psychological significance and a wild, if baleful, magnificence.

THAT EVENING SUN

I

MONDAY IS NO DIFFERENT from any other weekday in Jefferson now. The streets are paved now, and the telephone and electric companies are cutting down more and more of the shade trees—the water oaks, the maples and locusts and elms—to make room for iron poles bearing clusters of bloated and ghostly and bloodless grapes, and we have a city laundry which makes the rounds on Monday morning, gathering the bundles of clothes into bright-colored, specially made motorcars: the soiled wearing of a whole week now flees apparitionlike behind alert and irritable electric horns, with a long diminishing noise of rubber and asphalt like tearing silk, and even the Negro women who still take in white people's washing after the old custom, fetch and deliver it in automobiles.

But fifteen years ago, on Monday morning the quiet dusty, shady streets would be full of Negro women with, balanced on their steady, turbaned heads, bundles of clothes tied up in sheets, almost as large as cotton bales, carried so without touch of hand between the kitchen door of the white house and the blackened washpot beside a cabin door in Negro Hollow.

Nancy would set her bundle on the top of her head, then upon the bundle in turn she would set the black straw sailor hat she wore winter and summer. She was tall, with a high, sad face sunken a little where her teeth were missing. Sometimes we would go a part of the way down the lane and across the pasture with her, to watch the balanced bundle and the hat that never bobbed nor wavered, even when she walked down into the ditch and up the other side and stooped through the fence. She would go down on her hands and knees and crawl through the gap, her head rigid, uptilted, the bundle steady as a rock or a balloon, and rise to her feet again and go on.

Sometimes the husbands of the washing women would fetch and deliver the clothes, but Jesus never did that for Nancy, even before Father told him to stay away from our house, even when Dilsey was sick and Nancy would come to cook for us.

And then about half the time we'd have to go down the lane to Nancy's cabin and tell her to come on and cook breakfast. We would stop at the ditch, because Father told us to not have anything to do with Jesus—he was a short black man, with a razor scar down his face—and we would throw rocks at Nancy's house until she came to the door, leaning her head around it without any clothes on.

"What yawl mean, chunking my house?" Nancy said. "What you little devils mean?"

"Father says for you to come on and get breakfast," Caddy said. "Father says it's over a half an hour now, and you've got to come this minute."

"I ain't studying no breakfast," Nancy said. "I going to get my sleep out."

"I bet you're drunk," Jason said. "Father says you're drunk. Are you drunk, Nancy?"

"Who says I is?" Nancy said. "I got to get my sleep out. I ain't studying no breakfast."

So after a while we quit chunking the cabin and went back home. When she finally came, it was too late for me to go to school. So we thought it was whiskey until that day they arrested her again and they were taking her to jail and they passed Mr. Stovall. He was the cashier in the bank and a deacon in the Baptist church, and Nancy began to say:

"When you going to pay me, white man? When you going to pay me, white man? It's been three times now since you paid me a cent—" Mr.

Stovall knocked her down, but she kept on saying, "When you going to pay me, white man? It's been three times now since—" until Mr. Stovall kicked her in the mouth with his heel and the marshal caught Mr. Stovall back, and Nancy lying in the street, laughing. She turned her head and spat out some blood and teeth and said, "It's been three times now since he paid me a cent."

That was how she lost her teeth, and all that day they told about Nancy and Mr. Stovall, and all that night the ones that passed the jail could hear Nancy singing and yelling. They could see her hands holding to the window bars, and a lot of them stopped along the fence, listening to her and to the jailer trying to make her stop. She didn't shut up until almost daylight, when the jailer began to hear a bumping and scraping upstairs and he went up there and found Nancy hanging from the window bar. He said that it was cocaine and not whiskey, because no nigger would try to commit suicide unless he was full of cocaine, because a nigger full of cocaine wasn't a nigger any longer.

The jailer cut her down and revived her; then he beat her, whipped her. She had hung herself with her dress. She had fixed it all right, but when they arrested her she didn't have on anything except a dress and so she didn't have anything to tie her hands with and she couldn't make her hands let go of the window ledge. So the jailer heard the noise and ran up there and found Nancy hanging from the window, stark naked, her belly already swelling out a little, like a little balloon.

When Dilsey was sick in her cabin and Nancy was cooking for us, we could see her apron swelling out; that was before father told Jesus to stay away from the house. Jesus was in the kitchen, sitting behind the stove, with his razor scar on his black face like a piece of dirty string. He said it was a watermelon that Nancy had under her dress.

"It never come off of your vine, though," Nancy said.

"Off of what vine?" Caddy said.

"I can cut down the vine it did come off of," Jesus said.

"What makes you want to talk like that before these chillen?" Nancy said. "Whyn't you go on to work? You done et. You want Mr. Jason to catch you hanging around his kitchen, talking that way before these chillen?"

"Talking what way?" Caddy said. "What vine?"

"I can't hang around white man's kitchen," Jesus said. "But white man can hang around mine. White man can come in my house, but I can't stop him. When white man want to come in my house, I ain't got no house. I can't stop him, but he can't kick me outen it. He can't do that."

Dilsey was still sick in her cabin. Father told Jesus to stay off our place.

Dilsey was still sick. It was a long time. We were in the library after supper.

"Isn't Nancy through in the kitchen yet?" Mother said. "It seems to me that she has had plenty of time to have finished the dishes."

"Let Quentin go and see," Father said. "Go and see if Nancy is through, Quentin. Tell her she can go on home."

I went to the kitchen. Nancy was through. The dishes were put away and the fire was out. Nancy was sitting in a chair, close to the cold stove. She looked at me.

"Mother wants to know if you are through," I said.

"Yes," Nancy said. She looked at me. "I done finished." She looked at me.

"What is it?" I said. "What is it?"

"I ain't nothing but a nigger," Nancy said. "It ain't none of my fault."

She looked at me, sitting in the chair before the cold stove, the sailor hat on her head. I went back to the library. It was the cold stove and all, when you think of a kitchen being warm and busy and cheerful. And with a cold stove and the dishes all put away, and nobody wanting to eat at that hour.

"Is she through?" Mother said.

"Yessum," I said.

"What is she doing?" Mother said.

"She's not doing anything. She's through."

"I'll go and see," Father said.

"Maybe she's waiting for Jesus to come and take her home," Caddy said.

"Jesus is gone," I said. Nancy told us how one morning she woke up and Jesus was gone.

"He quit me," Nancy said. "Done gone to Memphis, I reckon. Dodging them city *po*-lice for a while, I reckon."

"And a good riddance," Father said. "I hope he stays there."

"Nancy's scaired of the dark," Jason said.

"So are you," Caddy said.

"I'm not," Jason said.

"Scairy cat," Caddy said.

"I'm not," Jason said.

"You, Candace!" Mother said. Father came back.

"I am going to walk down the lane with Nancy," he said. "She says that Jesus is back."

"Has she seen him?" Mother said.

"No. Some Negro sent her word that he was back in town. I won't be long."

"You'll leave me alone, to take Nancy home?" Mother said. "Is her safety more precious to you than mine?"

"I won't be long," Father said.

"You'll leave these children unprotected, with that Negro about?"

"I'm going too," Caddy said. "Let me go, Father."

"What would he do with them, if he were unfortunate enough to have them?" Father said.

"I want to go, too," Jason said.

"Jason!" Mother said. She was speaking to Father. You could tell that by the way she said the name. Like she believed that all day Father had been trying to think of doing the thing she wouldn't like the most, and that she knew all the time that after a while he would think of it. I stayed quiet, because Father and I both knew that Mother would want him to make me stay with her if she just thought of it in time. So Father didn't look at me. I was the oldest. I was nine and Caddy was seven and Jason was five.

"Nonsense," Father said. "We won't be long."

Nancy had her hat on. We came to the lane. "Jesus always been good to me," Nancy said. "Whenever he had two dollars, one of them was mine." We walked in the lane. "If I can just get through the lane," Nancy said, "I be all right then."

The lane was always dark. "This is where Jason got scaired on Hallowe'en," Caddy said.

"I didn't," Jason said.

"Can't Aunt Rachel do anything with him?" Father said. Aunt Rachel was old. She lived in a cabin beyond Nancy's, by herself. She had white hair and she smoked a pipe in the door, all day long; she didn't work any more. They said she was Jesus' mother. Sometimes she said she was and sometimes she said she wasn't any kin to Jesus.

"Yes you did," Caddy said. "You were scairder than Frony. You were scairder than T.P. even. Scairder than niggers."

"Can't nobody do nothing with him," Nancy said. "He say I done woke up the devil in him and ain't but one thing going to lay it down again."

"Well, he's gone now," Father said. "There's nothing for you to be afraid of now. And if you'd just let white men alone."

"Let what white men alone?" Caddy said. "How let them alone?"

"He ain't gone nowhere," Nancy said. "I can feel him. I can feel him now, in this lane. He hearing us talk, every word, hid somewhere, waiting. I ain't seen him, and I ain't going to see him again but once more, with that razor in his mouth. That razor on that string down his back, inside his shirt. And then I ain't going to be even surprised."

"I wasn't scaired," Jason said.

"If you'd behave yourself, you'd have kept out of this," Father said. "But it's all right now. He's probably in Saint Louis now. Probably got another wife by now and forgot all about you."

"If he has, I better not find out about it," Nancy said. "I'd stand there right over them, and every time he wropped her, I'd cut that arm off. I'd cut his head off and I'd slit her belly and I'd shove—"

"Hush," Father said.

"Slit whose belly, Nancy?" Caddy said.

"I wasn't scaired," Jason said. "I'd walk right down this lane by myself."

"Yah," Caddy said. "You wouldn't dare to put your foot down in it if we were not here too."

II

Dilsey was still sick, so we took Nancy home every night until Mother said, "How much longer is this going on? I to be left alone in this big house while you take home a frightened Negro?"

We fixed a pallet in the kitchen for Nancy. One night we waked up, hearing the sound. It was not singing and it was not crying, coming up the dark stairs. There was a light in Mother's room and we heard Father going down the hall, down the back stairs, and Caddy and I went into the hall. The floor was cold. Our toes curled away from it while we listened to the sound. It was like singing and it wasn't like singing, like the sounds that Negroes make.

Then it stopped and we heard Father going down the back stairs, and we went to the head of the stairs. Then the sound began again, in the stairway, not loud, and we could see Nancy's eyes halfway up the stairs, against the wall. They looked like cat's eyes do, like a big cat against the wall, watching us. When we came down the steps to where she was, she quit making the sound again, and we stood there until Father came back up from the kitchen, with his pistol in his hand. He went back down with Nancy and they came back with Nancy's pallet.

We spread the pallet in our room. After the light in Mother's room went off, we could see Nancy's eyes again. "Nancy," Caddy whispered, "are you asleep Nancy?"

Nancy whispered something. It was oh or no, I don't know which. Like nobody had made it, like it came from nowhere and went nowhere, until it was like Nancy was not there at all; that I had looked so hard at her eyes on the stairs that they had got printed on my eyeballs, like the sun does when you have closed your eyes and there is no sun. "Jesus," Nancy whispered. "Jesus."

"Was it Jesus?" Caddy said. "Did he try to come into the kitchen?"

"Jesus," Nancy said. Like this: Jeeeeeeeeeeeeeeeesus, until the sound went out, like a match or a candle does.

"It's the other Jesus she means," I said.

"Can you see us, Nancy?" Caddy whispered. "Can you see our eyes too?"

"I ain't nothing but a nigger," Nancy said. "God knows. God knows."

"What did you see down there in the kitchen?" Caddy whispered. "What tried to get in?"

"God knows," Nancy said. We could see her eyes. "God knows."

Dilsey got well. She cooked dinner. "You'd better stay in bed a day or two longer," Father said.

"What for?" Dilsey said. "If I had been a day later, this place would be to rack and ruin. Get on out of here now, and let me get my kitchen straight again."

Dilsey cooked supper too. And that night, just before dark, Nancy came into the kitchen.

"How do you know he's back?" Dilsey said. "You ain't seen him."

"Jesus is a nigger," Jason said.

"I can feel him," Nancy said. "I can feel him laying yonder in the ditch."

"Tonight?" Dilsey said. "Is he there tonight?"

"Dilsey's a nigger too," Jason said.

"You try to eat something," Dilsey said.

"I don't want nothing," Nancy said.

"I ain't a nigger," Jason said.

"Drink some coffee," Dilsey said. She poured a cup of coffee for Nancy. "Do you know he's out there tonight? How come you know it's tonight?"

"I know," Nancy said. "He's there, waiting. I know. I done lived with him too long. I know what he is fixing to do fore he know it himself."

"Drink some coffee," Dilsey said. Nancy held the cup to her mouth and blew into the cup. Her mouth pursed out like a spreading adder's, like a rubber mouth, like she had blown all the color out of her lips with blowing the coffee.

"I ain't a nigger," Jason said. "Are you a nigger, Nancy?"

"I hellborn, child," Nancy said. "I won't be nothing soon. I going back where I come from soon."

III

She began to drink the coffee. While she was drinking, holding the cup in both hands, she began to make the sound again. She made the sound into the cup and the coffee splashed out onto her hands and her dress. Her eyes looked at us and she sat there, her elbows on her knees, holding the cup in both hands, looking at us across the wet cup, making the sound.

"Look at Nancy," Jason said. "Nancy can't cook for us now. Dilsey's got well now."

"You hush up," Dilsey said. Nancy held the cup in both hands, looking at us, making the sound, like there were two of them: one looking at us and the other making the sound. "Whyn't you let Mr. Jason telefoam the marshal?" Dilsey said. Nancy stopped then, holding the cup in her long brown hands. She tried to drink some coffee again, but it sploshed out of the cup, onto her hands and her dress, and she put the cup down. Jason watched her.

"I can't swallow it," Nancy said. "I swallows but it won't go down me."

"You go down to the cabin," Dilsey said. "Frony will fix you a pallet and I'll be there soon."

"Won't no nigger stop him," Nancy said.

"I ain't a nigger," Jason said. "Am I, Dilsey?"

"I reckon not," Dilsey said. She looked at Nancy. "I don't reckon so. What you going to do, then?"

Nancy looked at us. Her eyes went fast, like she was afraid there wasn't time to look, without hardly moving at all. She looked at us, at all three of us at one time. "You member that night I stayed in yawls' room?" she said. She told about how we waked up early the next morning, and played. We had to play quiet, on her pallet, until Father woke up and it was time to get breakfast. "Go and ask your maw to let me stay here tonight," Nancy said. "I won't need no pallet. We can play some more."

Caddy asked Mother. Jason went too. "I can't have Negroes sleeping in the bedrooms," Mother said. Jason cried. He cried until Mother said he couldn't have any dessert for three days if he didn't stop. Then Jason said he would stop if Dilsey would make a chocolate cake. Father was there.

"Why don't you do something about it?" Mother said. "What do we have officers for?"

"Why is Nancy afraid of Jesus?" Caddy said. "Are you afraid of Father, Mother?"

"What could the officers do?" Father said, "If Nancy hasn't seen him, how could the officers find him?"

"Then why is she afraid?" Mother said.

"She says he is there. She says she knows he is there tonight."

"Yet we pay taxes," Mother said. "I must wait here alone in this big house while you take a Negro woman home."

"You know that I am not lying outside with a razor," Father said.

"I'll stop if Dilsey will make a chocolate cake," Jason said. Mother told us to go out and Father said he didn't know if Jason would get a chocolate cake or not, but he knew what Jason was going to get in about a minute. We went back to the kitchen and told Nancy.

"Father said for you to go home and lock the door, and you'll be all right," Caddy said. "All right from what, Nancy? Is Jesus mad at you?" Nancy was holding the coffee cup in her hands again, her elbows on her knees and her hands holding the cup between her knees. She was looking into the cup. "What have you done that made Jesus mad?" Caddy said. Nancy let the cup go. It didn't break on the floor, but the coffee spilled out, and Nancy sat there with her hands still making the shape of the cup. She began to make the sound again, not loud. Not singing and not unsinging. We watched her.

"Here," Dilsey said. "You quit that, now. You get aholt of yourself. You wait here. I going to get Versh to walk home with you." Dilsey went out.

We looked at Nancy. Her shoulders kept shaking, but she quit making the sound. We stood and watched her.

"What's Jesus going to do to you?" Caddy said. "He went away."

Nancy looked at us. "We had fun that night I stayed in yawls' room, didn't we?"

"I didn't," Jason said. "I didn't have any fun."

"You were asleep in Mother's room," Caddy said. "You were not there."

"Let's go down to my house and have some more fun," Nancy said.

"Mother won't let us," I said. "It's too late now."

"Don't bother her," Nancy said. "We can tell her in the morning. She won't mind."

"She wouldn't let us," I said.

"Don't ask her now," Nancy said. "Don't bother her now."

"She didn't say we couldn't go," Caddy said.

"We didn't ask," I said.

"If you go, I'll tell," Jason said.

"We'll have fun," Nancy said. "They won't mind, just to my house. I been working for yawl a long time. They won't mind."

"I'm not afraid to go," Caddy said. "Jason is the one that's afraid. He'll tell."

"I'm not," Jason said.

"Yes, you are," Caddy said. "You'll tell."

"I won't tell," Jason said. "I'm not afraid."

"Jason ain't afraid to go with me," Nancy said. "Is you, Jason?"

"Jason is going to tell," Caddy said. The lane was dark. We passed the pasture gate. "I bet if something was to jump out from behind that gate, Jason would holler."

"I wouldn't," Jason said. We walked down the lane. Nancy was talking loud.

"What are you talking so loud for, Nancy?" Caddy said.

"Who; me?" Nancy said. "Listen at Quentin and Caddy and Jason saying I'm talking loud."

"You talk like there was five of us here," Caddy said. "You talk like Father was here too."

"Who; me talking loud, Mr. Jason?" Nancy said.

"Nancy called Jason 'Mister,' " Caddy said.

"Listen how Caddy and Quentin and Jason talk," Nancy said.

"We're not talking loud," Caddy said. You're the one that's talking like Father—"

"Hush," Nancy said; "hush, Mr. Jason."

"Nancy called Jason 'Mister' aguh—"

"Hush," Nancy said. She was talking loud when we crossed the ditch and stooped through the fence where she used to stoop through with the clothes on her head. Then we came to her house. We were going fast then. She opened the door. The smell of the house was like the lamp and the smell of Nancy was like the wick, like they were waiting for one another to begin to smell. She lit the lamp and closed the door and put the bar up. Then she quit talking loud, looking at us.

"What're we going to do?" Caddy said.

"What do yawl want to do?" Nancy said.

"You said we would have some fun," Caddy said.

There was something about Nancy's house; something you could smell besides Nancy and the house. Jason smelled it, even. "I don't want to stay here," he said. "I want to go home."

"Go home, then," Caddy said.

"I don't want to go by myself," Jason said.

"We're going to have some fun," Nancy said.

"How?" Caddy said.

Nancy stood by the door. She was looking at us, only it was like she had emptied her eyes, like she had quit using them. "What do you want to do?" she said.

"Tell us a story," Caddy said. "Can you tell a story?"

"Yes," Nancy said.

"Tell it," Caddy said. We looked at Nancy. "You don't know any stories."

"Yes," Nancy said. "Yes I do."

She came and sat in a chair before the hearth. There was a little fire there. Nancy built it up, when it was already hot inside. She built a good blaze. She told a story. She talked like her eyes looked, like her eyes watching us and her voice talking to us did not belong to her. Like she was living somewhere else, waiting somewhere else. She was outside the cabin. Her voice was inside and the shape of her, the Nancy that could stoop under a barbed wire fence with a bundle of clothes balanced on her head as though without weight, like a balloon, was there. But that was all. "And so this here queen come walking up to the ditch, where that bad man was hiding. She was walking up to the ditch, and she say, 'If I can just get past this here ditch,' was what she say . . ."

"What ditch?" Caddy said. "A ditch like that one out there? Why did a queen want to go into a ditch?"

"To get to her house," Nancy said. She looked at us. "She had to cross the ditch to get into her house quick and bar the door."

"Why did she want to go home and bar the door?" Caddy said.

IV

Nancy looked at us. She quit talking. She looked at us. Jason's legs stuck straight out of his pants were he sat on Nancy's lap. "I don't think that's a good story," he said. "I want to go home."

"Maybe we had better," Caddy said. She got up from the floor. "I bet they are looking for us right now." She went toward the door.

"No," Nancy said. "Don't open it." She got up quick and passed Caddy. She didn't touch the door, the wooden bar.

"Why not?" Caddy said.

"Come back to the lamp," Nancy said. "We'll have fun. You don't have to go."

"We ought to go," Caddy said. "Unless we have a lot of fun." She and Nancy came back to the fire, the lamp.

"I want to go home," Jason said. "I'm going to tell."

"I know another story," Nancy said. She stood close to the lamp. She looked at Caddy, like when your eyes look up a stick balanced on your nose. She had to look down to see Caddy, but her eyes looked like that, like when you are balancing a stick.

"I won't listen to it," Jason said. "I'll bang on the floor."

"It's a good one," Nancy said. "It's better than the other one."

"What's it about?" Caddy said. Nancy was standing by the lamp. Her hand was on the lamp, against the light, long and brown.

"Your hand is on that hot globe," Caddy said. "Don't it feel hot to your hand?"

Nancy looked at her hand on the lamp chimney. She took her hand away, slow. She stood there, looking at Caddy, wringing her long hand as though it were tied to her wrist with a string.

"Let's do something else," Caddy said.

"I want to go home," Jason said.

"I got some popcorn," Nancy said. She looked at Caddy and then at Jason and then at me and then at Caddy again. "I got some popcorn."

"I don't like popcorn," Jason said. "I'd rather have candy."

Nancy looked at Jason. "You can hold the popper." She was still wringing her hand; it was long and limp and brown.

"All right," Jason said. "I'll stay a while if I can do that. Caddy can't hold it. I'll want to go home again if Caddy holds the popper."

Nancy built up the fire. "Look at Nancy putting her hands in the fire," Caddy said. "What's the matter with you, Nancy?"

"I got popcorn," Nancy said. "I got some." She took the popper from under the bed. It was broken. Jason began to cry.

"Now we can't have any popcorn," he said.

"We ought to go home, anyway," Caddy said. "Come on, Quentin."

"Wait," Nancy said; "wait. I can fix it. Don't you want to help me fix it?"

"I don't think I want any," Caddy said. "It's too late now."

"You help me, Jason," Nancy said. "Don't you want to help me?"

"No," Jason said. "I want to go home."

"Hush," Nancy said; "hush. Watch. Watch me. I can fix it so Jason can hold it and pop the corn." She got a piece of wire and fixed the popper.

"It won't hold good," Caddy said.

"Yes it will," Nancy said. "Yawl watch. Yawl help me shell some corn."

The popcorn was under the bed too. We shelled it into the popper and Nancy helped Jason hold the popper over the fire.

"It's not popping," Jason said. "I want to go home."

"You wait," Nancy said. "It'll begin to pop. We'll have fun then."

She was sitting close to the fire. The lamp was turned up so high it was beginning to smoke. "Why don't you turn it down some?" I said.

"It's all right," Nancy said. "I'll clean it. Yawl wait. The popcorn will start in a minute."

"I don't believe it's going to start," Caddy said. "We ought to start home, anyway. They'll be worried."

"No," Nancy said. "It's going to pop. Dilsey will tell um yawl with me. I been working for yawl long time. They won't mind if yawl at my house. You wait, now. It'll start popping any minute now."

Then Jason got some smoke in his eyes and he began to cry. He dropped the popper into the fire. Nancy got a wet rag and wiped Jason's face, but he didn't stop crying.

"Hush," she said. "Hush." But he didn't hush. Caddy took the popper out of the fire.

"It's burned up," she said. "You'll have to get some more popcorn, Nancy."

"Did you put all of it in?" Nancy said.

"Yes," Caddy said. Nancy looked at Caddy. Then she took the popper and opened it and poured the cinders into her apron and began to sort the grains, her hands long and brown, and we watching her.

"Haven't you got any more?" Caddy said.

"Yes," Nancy said; "yes. Look. This here ain't burnt. All we need to do is—"

"I want to go home," Jason said. "I'm going to tell."

"Hush," Caddy said. We all listened. Nancy's head was already turned toward the barred door, her eyes filled with red lamplight. "Somebody is coming," Caddy said.

Then Nancy began to make that sound again, not loud, sitting there above the fire, her long hands dangling between her knees; all of a sudden water began to come out on her face in big drops, running down her face, carrying in each one a little turning ball of firelight like a spark until it dropped off her chin. "She's not crying," I said.

"I ain't crying," Nancy said. Her eyes were closed. "I ain't crying. Who is it?"

"I don't know," Caddy said. She went to the door and looked out. "We've got to go now," she said. "Here comes Father."

"I'm going to tell," Jason said. "Yawl made me come."

The water still ran down Nancy's face. She turned in her chair. "Listen. Tell him. Tell him we going to have fun. Tell him I take good care of yawl until in the morning. Tell him to let me come home with yawl and sleep on the floor. Tell him I won't need no pallet. We'll have fun. You member last time how we had so much fun?"

"I didn't have fun," Jason said. "You hurt me. You put smoke in my eyes. I'm going to tell."

V

Father came in. He looked at us. Nancy did not get up.

"Tell him," she said.

"Caddy made us come down here," Jason said. "I didn't want to."

Father came to the fire. Nancy looked up at him. "Can't you go to Aunt Rachel's and stay?" he said. Nancy looked up at Father, her hands between her knees. "He's not here," Father said. "I would have seen him. There's not a soul in sight."

"He in the ditch," Nancy said. "He waiting in the ditch yonder."

"Nonsense," Father said. He looked at Nancy. "Do you know he's there?"

"I got the sign," Nancy said.

"What sign?"

"I got it. It was on the table when I come in. It was a hogbone, with blood meat still on it, laying by the lamp. He's out there. When yawl walk out that door, I gone."

"Gone where, Nancy?" Caddy said.

"I'm not a tattletale," Jason said.

"Nonsense," Father said.

"He out there," Nancy said. "He looking through that window this minute, waiting for yawl to go. Then I gone."

"Nonsense," Father said. "Lock up your house and we'll take you on to Aunt Rachel's."

" 'Twon't do no good," Nancy said. She didn't look at Father now, but he looked down at her, at her long, limp, moving hands. "Putting it off won't do no good."

"Then what do you want to do?" Father said.

"I don't know," Nancy said. "I can't do nothing. Just put it off. And that don't do no good. I reckon it belong to me. I reckon what I going to get ain't no more than mine."

"Get what?" Caddy said. "What's yours?"

"Nothing," Father said. "You all must get to bed."

"Caddy made me come," Jason said.

"Go on to Aunt Rachel's," Father said.

"It won't do no good," Nancy said. She sat before the fire, her elbows on her knees, her long hands between her knees. "When even your own kitchen wouldn't do no good. When even if I was sleeping on the floor in the room with your chillen, and the next morning there I am, and blood—"

"Hush," Father said. "Lock the door and put out the lamp and go to bed."

"I scaired of the dark," Nancy said. "I scaired for it to happen in the dark."

"You mean you're going to sit right here with the lamp lighted?" Father said. Then Nancy began to make the sound again, sitting before the fire, her long hands between her knees. "Ah, damnation," Father said. "Come along, chillen. It's past bedtime."

"When yawl go home, I gone," Nancy said. She talked quieter now, and her face looked quiet, like her hands. "Anyway, I got my coffin money saved up with Mr. Lovelady." Mr. Lovelady was a short, dirty man who collected the Negro insurance, coming around to the cabins or the kitchens every Saturday morning, to collect fifteen cents. He and his wife lived at the hotel. One morning his wife committed suicide. They had a child, a little girl. He and the child went away. After a week or two he came back alone. We would see him going along the lanes and the back streets on Saturday mornings.

"Nonsense," Father said. "You'll be the first thing I'll see in the kitchen tomorrow morning."

"You'll see what you'll see, I reckon," Nancy said. "But it will take the Lord to say what that will be."

VI

We left her sitting before the fire.

"Come and put the bar up," Father said. But she didn't move. She didn't look at us again, sitting quietly there between the lamp and the fire. From some distance down the lane we could look back and see her through the open door.

"What, Father?" Caddy said. "What's going to happen?"

"Nothing," Father said. Jason was on Father's back, so Jason was the tallest of all of us. We went down into the ditch. I looked at it, quiet. I couldn't see much where the moonlight and the shadows tangled.

"If Jesus *is* hid here, he can see us, can't he?" Caddy said.

"He's not there," Father said. "He went away a long time ago."

"You made me come," Jason said, high; against the sky it looked like Father had two heads, a little one and a big one. "I didn't want to."

We went up out of the ditch. We could still see Nancy's house and the open door, but we couldn't see Nancy now, sitting before the fire with the door open, because she was tired. "I just done got tired," she said. "I just a nigger. It ain't no fault of mine."

But we could hear her, because she began just after we came up out of the ditch, the sound that was not singing and not unsinging. "Who will do our washing now, Father?" I said.

"I'm not a nigger," Jason said, high and close above Father's head.

"You're worse," Caddy said, "you are a tattletale. If something was to jump out, you'd be scairder than a nigger."

"I wouldn't," Jason said.

"You'd cry," Caddy said.

"Caddy," Father said.

"I wouldn't!" Jason said.

"Scairy cat." Caddy said.

"Candace!" Father said.

A ROSE FOR EMILY

I

WHEN MISS EMILY GRIERSON DIED, our whole town went to her funeral: the men through a sort of respectful affection for a fallen monument, the women mostly out of curiosity to see the inside of her house, which no one save an old manservant—a combined gardener and cook—had seen in at least ten years.

It was a big, squarish frame house that had once been white, decorated with cupolas and spires and scrolled balconies in the heavily lightsome style of the seventies, set on what had once been our most select street. But garages and cotton gins had encroached and obliterated even the august names of that neighborhood; only Miss Emily's house was left, lifting its stubborn and coquettish decay above the cotton wagons and the gasoline pumps—an eyesore among eyesores. And now Miss Emily had gone to join the representatives of those august names where they lay in the cedar-bemused cemetery among the ranked and anonymous graves of Union and Confederate soldiers who fell at the battle of Jefferson.

Alive, Miss Emily had been a tradition, a duty, and a care; a sort of hereditary obligation upon the town, dating from that day in 1894 when Colonel Sartoris, the mayor—he who fathered the edict that no Negro woman should appear on the streets without an apron—remitted her taxes, the dispensation dating from the death of her father on into perpetuity. Not that Miss Emily would have accepted charity. Colonel Sartoris invented an involved tale to the effect that Miss Emily's father had loaned money to the town, which the town, as a matter of business, preferred this way of repaying. Only a man of Colonel Sartoris' generation and thought could have invented it, and only a woman could have believed it.

When the next generation, with its more modern ideas, became mayors and aldermen, this arrangement created some little dissatisfaction. On the first of the year they mailed her a tax notice. February came, and there was no reply. They wrote her a formal letter, asking her to call at the sheriff's office at her convenience. A week later the mayor wrote her himself, offering to call or to send his car for her, and received in reply a note on paper of an archaic shape, in a thin, flowing calligraphy in faded ink, to the effect that she no longer went out at all. The tax notice was also enclosed, without comment.

They called a special meeting of the Board of Aldermen. A deputation waited upon her, knocked at the door through which no visitor had passed since she ceased giving china-painting lessons eight or ten years earlier.

They were admitted by the old Negro into a dim hall from which a stairway mounted into still more shadow. It smelled of dust and disuse—a close, dank smell. The Negro led them into the parlor. It was furnished in heavy, leather-covered furniture. When the Negro opened the blinds of one window, they could see that the leather was cracked; and when they sat down, a faint dust rose sluggishly about their thighs, spinning with slow motes in the single sun-ray. On a tarnished gilt easel before the fireplace stood a crayon portrait of Miss Emily's father.

They rose when she entered—a small, fat woman in black, with a thin gold chain descending to her waist and vanishing into her belt, leaning on an ebony cane with a tarnished gold head. Her skeleton was small and spare; perhaps that was why what would have been merely plumpness in another was obesity in her. She looked bloated, like a body long submerged in motionless water, and of that pallid hue. Her eyes, lost in the fatty ridges of her face, looked like two small pieces of coal pressed into a lump of dough as they moved from one face to another while the visitors stated their errand.

She did not ask them to sit. She just stood in the door and listened quietly until the spokesman came to a stumbling halt. Then they could hear the invisible watch ticking at the end of the gold chain.

Her voice was dry and cold. "I have no taxes in Jefferson. Colonel Sartoris explained it to me. Perhaps one of you can gain access to the city records and satisfy yourselves."

"But we have. We are the city authorities, Miss Emily. Didn't you get a notice from the sheriff, signed by him?"

"I received a paper, yes," Miss Emily said. "Perhaps he considers himself the sheriff . . . I have no taxes in Jefferson."

"But there is nothing on the books to show that, you see. We must go by the—"

"See Colonel Sartoris. I have no taxes in Jefferson."

"But, Miss Emily—"

"See Colonel Sartoris." (Colonel Sartoris had been dead almost ten years.) "I have no taxes in Jefferson. Tobe!" The Negro appeared. "Show these gentlemen out."

II

So she vanquished them, horse and foot, just as she had vanquished their fathers thirty years before about the smell. That was two years after her father's death and a short time after her sweetheart—the one we believed would marry her—had deserted her. After her father's death she went out very little; after her sweetheart went away, people hardly saw her at all. A few of the ladies had the temerity to call, but were not received, and the only sign of life about the place was the Negro man—a young man then—going in and out with a market basket.

"Just as if a man—any man—could keep a kitchen properly," the ladies said; so they were not surprised when the smell developed. It was another link between the gross, teeming world and the high and mighty Griersons.

A neighbor, a woman, complained to the mayor, Judge Stevens, eighty years old.

"But what will you have me do about it, madam?" he said.

"Why, send her word to stop it," the woman said. "Isn't there a law?"

"I'm sure that won't be necessary," Judge Stevens said. "It's probably just a snake or a rat that nigger of hers killed in the yard. I'll speak to him about it."

The next day he received two more complaints, one from a man who came in diffident deprecation. "We really must do something about it, Judge. I'd be the last one in the world to bother Miss Emily, but we've got to do something." That night the Board of Aldermen met—three graybeards and one younger man, a member of the rising generation.

"It's simple enough," he said. "Send her word to have her place cleaned up. Give her a certain time to do it in, and if she don't . . ."

"Dammit, sir," Judge Stevens said, "will you accuse a lady to her face of smelling bad?"

So the next night, after midnight, four men crossed Miss Emily's lawn and slunk about the house like burglars, sniffing along the base of the brickwork and at the cellar openings while one of them performed a regular sowing motion with his hand out of a sack slung from his shoulder. They broke open the cellar door and sprinkled lime there, and in all the outbuildings. As they recrossed the lawn, a window that had been dark was lighted and Miss Emily sat in it, the light behind her, and her upright torso motionless as that of an idol. They crept quietly across the lawn and into the shadow of the locusts that lined the street. After a week or two the smell went away.

That was when people had begun to feel really sorry for her. People in our town, remembering how old lady Wyatt, her great-aunt, had gone completely crazy at last, believed that the Griersons held themselves a little too high for what they really were. None of the young men were quite good enough to Miss Emily and such. We had long thought of them as a tableau; Miss Emily a slender figure in white in the background, her father a spraddled silhouette in the foreground, his back to her and clutching a horsewhip, the two of them framed by the back-flung front door. So when she got to be thirty and was still single, we were not pleased exactly, but vindicated; even with insanity in the family she wouldn't have turned down all of her chances if they had really materialized.

When her father died, it got about that the house was all that was left to her; and in a way, people were glad. At last they could pity Miss Emily. Being left alone, and a pauper, she had become humanized. Now she too would know the old thrill and the old despair of a penny more or less.

The day after his death all the ladies prepared to call at the house and offer condolence and aid, as is our custom. Miss Emily met them at the door, dressed as usual and with no trace of grief on her face. She told them that her father was not dead. She did that for three days, with the ministers calling on her, and the doctors, trying to persuade her to let them dispose of the body. Just as they were about to resort to law and force, she broke down, and they buried her father quickly.

We did not say she was crazy then. We believed she had to do that. We remembered all the young men her father had driven away, and we knew that with nothing left, she would have to cling to that which had robbed her, as people will.

III

She was sick for a long time. When we saw her again, her hair was cut short, making her look like a girl, with a vague resemblance to those angels in colored church windows—sort of tragic and serene.

The town had just let the contracts for paving the sidewalks, and in the summer after her father's death they began the work. The construction company came with niggers and mules and machinery, and a foreman named Homer Barron, a Yankee—a big, dark, ready man, with a big voice and eyes lighter than his face. The little boys would follow in groups to hear him cuss the niggers, and the niggers singing in time to the rise and fall of picks. Pretty soon he knew everybody in town. Whenever you heard a lot of laughing anywhere about the square, Homer Barron would be in the center of the group. Presently we began to see him and Miss Emily on Sunday afternoons driving in the yellow-wheeled buggy and the matched team of bays from the livery stable.

At first we were glad that Miss Emily would have an interest, because the ladies all said, "Of course a Grierson would not think seriously of a Northerner, a day laborer." But there were still others, older people, who said that even grief could not cause a real lady to forget *noblesse oblige*—without calling it *noblesse oblige*. They just said, "Poor Emily. Her kinsfolk should come to her." She had some kin in Alabama; but years ago her father had fallen out with them over the estate of old lady Wyatt, the crazy woman, and there was no communication between the two families. They had not even been represented at the funeral.

And as soon as the old people said, "Poor Emily," the whispering began. "Do you suppose it's really so?" they said to one another. "Of course it is. What else could . . ." This behind their hands; rustling of craned silk and satin behind jalousies closed upon the sun of Sunday afternoon as the thin, swift clop-clop-clop of the matched team passed: "Poor Emily."

She carried her head high enough—even when we believed that she was fallen. It was as if she demanded more than ever the recognition of her dignity as the last Grierson; as if it had wanted that touch of earthiness to reaffirm her imperviousness. Like when she bought the rat poison, the arsenic. That was over a year after they had begun to say "Poor Emily," and while the two female cousins were visiting her.

"I want some poison," she said to the druggist. She was over thirty then, still a slight woman, though thinner than usual, with cold, haughty black eyes in a face the flesh of which was strained across the temples and about the eye-sockets as you imagine a lighthouse-keeper's face ought to look. "I want some poison," she said.

"Yes, Miss Emily. What kind? For rats and such? I'd recom—"

"I want the best you have. I don't care what kind."

The druggist named several. "They'll kill anything up to an elephant. But what you want is—"

"Arsenic," Miss Emily said, "Is that a good one?"

"Is . . . arsenic? Yes, ma'am. But what you want—"

"I want arsenic."

The druggist looked down at her. She looked back at him, erect, her face like a strained flag. "Why, of course," the druggist said. "If that's what you want. But the law requires you to tell what you are going to use it for."

Miss Emily just stared at him, her head tilted back in order to look him eye for eye, until he looked away and went and got the arsenic and wrapped it up. The Negro delivery boy brought her the package; the druggist didn't come back. When she opened the package at home there was written on the box, under the skull and bones: "For rats."

IV

So the next day we all said, "She will kill herself"; and we said it would be the best thing. When she had first begun to be seen with Homer Barron, we had said, "She will marry him." Then we said, "She will persuade him yet," because Homer himself had remarked—he liked men, and it was known that he drank with the younger men in the Elks' Club—that he was not a marrying man. Later we said, "Poor Emily" behind the jalousies as they passed on Sunday afternoon in the glittering buggy, Miss Emily with her head high and Homer Barron with his hat cocked and a cigar in his teeth, reins and whip in a yellow glove.

Then some of the ladies began to say that it was a disgrace to the town and a bad example to the young people. The men did not want to interfere, but at last the ladies forced the Baptist minister—Miss Emily's people were Episcopal—to call upon her. He would never divulge what happened during that interview, but he refused to go back again. The next Sunday they again drove about the streets, and the following day the minister's wife wrote to Miss Emily's relations in Alabama.

So she had blood-kin under her roof again and we sat back to watch developments. At first nothing happened. Then we were sure that they were to be married. We learned that Miss Emily had been to the jeweler's and ordered a man's toilet set in silver, with the letters H. B. on each piece. Two days later we learned that she had bought a complete outfit of men's clothing, including a nightshirt, and we said, "They are married." We were really glad. We were glad because the two female cousins were even more Grierson than Miss Emily had ever been.

So we were not surprised when Homer Barron—the streets had been finished some time since—was gone. We were a little disappointed that there was not a public blowing-off, but we believed that he had gone on to prepare for Miss Emily's coming, or to give her a chance to get rid of the cousins. (By that time it was a cabal, and we were all Miss Emily's allies to help circumvent the cousins.) Sure enough, after another week they departed. And, as we had expected all along, within three days Homer Barron was back in town. A neighbor saw the Negro man admit him at the kitchen door at dusk one evening.

And that was the last we saw of Homer Barron. And of Miss Emily for some time. The Negro man went in and out with the market basket, but the front door remained closed. Now and then we would see her at a window for a moment, as the men did that night when they sprinkled the lime, but for almost six months she did not appear on the streets. Then we knew that this was to be expected too; as if that quality of her father which had thwarted her woman's life so many times had been too virulent and too furious to die.

When we next saw Miss Emily, she had grown fat and her hair was turning gray. During the next few years it grew grayer and grayer until it attained an even pepper-and-salt iron-gray, when it ceased turning. Up to the day of her death at seventy-four it was still that vigorous iron-gray, like the hair of an active man.

From that time on her front door remained closed, save for a period of six or seven years, when she was about forty, during which she gave lessons in china-painting. She fitted up a studio in one of the downstairs rooms, where the daughters and granddaughters of Colonel Sartoris' contemporaries were sent to her with the same regularity and in the same spirit that they were sent to church on Sundays with a twenty-five cent piece for the collection plate. Meanwhile her taxes had been remitted.

Then the newer generation became the backbone and the spirit of the town, and the painting pupils grew up and fell away and did not send their children to her with boxes of color and tedious brushes and pictures cut from the ladies' magazines. The front door closed upon the last one and remained closed for good. When the town got free postal delivery, Miss Emily alone refused to let them fasten the metal numbers above her door and attach a mailbox to it. She would not listen to them.

Daily, monthly, yearly we watched the Negro grow grayer and more stooped, going in and out with the market basket. Each December we sent her a tax notice, which would be returned by the post office a week later, unclaimed. Now and then we would see her in one of the downstairs windows—she had evidently shut up the top floor of the house—like the carven torso of an idol in a niche, looking or not looking at us, we could never tell which. Thus she passed from generation to generation—dear, inescapable, impervious, tranquil, and perverse.

And so she died. Fell ill in the house filled with dust and shadows, with only a doddering Negro man to wait on her. We did not even know she was sick; we had long since given up trying to get any information from the Negro. He talked to no one, probably not even to her, for his voice had grown harsh and rusty, as if from disuse.

She died in one of the downstairs rooms, in a heavy walnut bed with a curtain, her gray head propped on a pillow yellow and moldy with age and lack of sunlight.

V

The Negro met the first of the ladies at the front door and let them in, with their hushed, sibilant voices and their quick, curious glances, and then he disappeared. He walked right through the house and out the back and was not seen again.

The two female cousins came at once. They held the funeral on the second day, with the town coming to look at Miss Emily beneath a mass of bought flowers, with the crayon face of her father musing profoundly above the bier and the ladies sibilant and macabre; and the very old men—some in their brushed Confederate uniforms—on the porch and the lawn, talking of Miss Emily as if she had been a contemporary of theirs, believing that they had danced with her and courted her perhaps, confusing time with its mathematical progression, as the old do, to whom all the past is not a diminishing road but, instead, a huge meadow which no winter ever quite touches, divided from them now by the narrow bottle-neck of the most recent decade of years.

Already we knew that there was one room in that region above stairs which no one had seen in forty years, and which would have to be forced. They waited until Miss Emily was decently in the ground before they opened it.

The violence of breaking down the door seemed to fill this room with pervading dust. A thin, acrid pall as of the tomb seemed to lie everywhere upon this room decked and furnished as for a bridal: upon the valence curtains of faded rose color, upon the rose-shaded lights, upon the dressing table, upon the delicate array of crystal and the man's toilet things backed with tarnished silver, silver so tarnished that the monogram was obscured. Among them lay a collar and tie, as if they had just been removed, which, lifted, left upon the surface a pale crescent in the dust. Upon a chair hung the suit, carefully folded; beneath it the two mute shoes and the discarded socks.

The man himself lay in the bed.

For a long while we just stood there, looking down at the profound and fleshless grin. The body had apparently once lain in the attitude of an embrace, but now the long sleep that outlasts love, that conquers even the grimace of love, had cuckolded him. What was left of him, rotted beneath what was left of the nightshirt, had become inextricable from the bed in which he lay; and upon him and upon the pillow beside him lay that even coating of the patient and biding dust.

Then we noticed that in the second pillow was the indentation of a head. One of us lifted something from it, and leaning forward, that faint and invisible dust dry and acrid in the nostrils, we saw a long strand of iron-gray hair.

STEPHEN VINCENT BENÉT

[1898–1943]

THE BENÉTS WERE an unusually gifted family, and their chief gift was poetry. The brothers William Rose Benét and Stephen Vincent Benét were poets who married poets—William was married to Elinor Wylie and Stephen to Rosemary Carr, with whom he collaborated on A Book of Americans. A sister, Laura Benét, wrote both poetry and prose.

Stephen Vincent Benét was born July 22, 1898, in Bethlehem, Pennsylvania. His father was an army officer, and the family was constantly moving from one post to another; Stephen was educated in California, in Georgia and, like his older brother, at Yale. He was twenty-two when he went to France, and it was while he was a student at the Sorbonne, that he met Rosemary Carr.

By this time the precocious Benét had already published three volumes—his first book, Five Men and Pompey, a set of six dramatic portraits, appeared when he was seventeen. In his twenties Benét made a name for himself with his fiction, but he never stopped writing poetry. At thirty he received the Pulitzer Prize for John Brown's Body, which leaped into instant popularity and which many consider a true American epic. Stephen shared with his brother a talent for ballad-making, but in John Brown's Body he surpassed him in the skill with which he combined ballads, lyrics, elegies, and even prose passages.

With the advent of the Second World War, Benét gave all his time to the war effort. He wrote an historical pamphlet, America, which was translated into a dozen languages, and a moving "Prayer for the United Nations," which was read on an international broadcast by President Roosevelt. He was at work on a companion-poem to John Brown's Body—the uncompleted work was published posthumously as Western Star—when he succumbed to a heart attack in New York City and died in his forty-fifth year, March 13, 1943. Seven years later his brother also died of heart failure.

Quotation can give no idea of the integrated character of John Brown's Body. Instead the editor has chosen one of the short stories from Benét's collection. Thirteen O'Clock. "The Devil and Daniel Webster" is an enlarged and elaborated folk-tale. Immensely popular in its original form, later made into a play, a film and into a grand opera with music by Douglas Moore, it has assumed a permanent place in American literature.

Another segment of Americana by Benét, "Salem, Massachusetts," may be found on page 62.

THE DEVIL AND DANIEL WEBSTER

IT'S A STORY THEY TELL in the border country, where Massachusetts joins Vermont and New Hampshire.

Yes, Dan'l Webster's dead—or, at least, they buried him. But every time there's a thunderstorm around Marshfield, they say you can hear his rolling voice in the hollows of the sky. And they say that if you go to his grave and speak loud and clear, "Dan'l Webster—Dan'l Webster!" the ground'll begin to shiver and the trees begin to shake. And after a while you'll hear a deep voice saying, "Neighbor, how stands the Union?" Then you better answer the Union stands as she stood, rock-bottomed and copper-sheathed, one and indivisible, or he's liable to rear right out of the ground. At least, that's what I was told when I was a youngster.

You see, for a while, he was the biggest man in the country. He never got to be President, but he was the biggest man. There were thousands that trusted in him right next to God Almighty, and they told stories about him and all the things that belonged to him that were like the stories of patriarchs and such. They said, when he stood up to speak, stars and stripes came right out in the sky, and once he spoke against a river and made it sink into the ground. They said, when he walked the woods with his fishing rod, Killall, the trout would jump out of the streams right into his pockets, for they knew it was no use putting up a fight against him; and when he argued a case, he could turn on the harps of the blessed and the shaking of the earth underground. That was the kind of man he was, and his big farm up at Marshfield was suitable to him. The chickens he raised were all white meat down through the drumsticks, the cows were tended like children, and the big ram he called Goliath had horns with a curl like a morning-glory vine and could butt through an iron door. But Dan'l wasn't one of your gentleman farmers; he knew all the ways of the land, and he'd be up by candlelight to see that the chores got done. A man with a mouth like a mastiff, a brow like a mountain, and eyes like burning anthracite—that was Dan'l Webster in his prime. And the biggest case he argued never got written down in the books, for he argued it against the devil, nip and tuck and no holds barred. And this is the way I used to hear it told.

There was a man named Jabez Stone, lived at Cross Corners, New Hampshire. He wasn't a bad man to start with, but he was an unlucky man. If he planted corn, he got borers; if he planted potatoes, he got blight. He had good-enough land, but it didn't prosper him; he had a decent wife and children, but the more children he had, the less there was to feed them. If stones cropped up in his neighbor's field, boulders boiled up in his; if he had a horse with the spavins, he'd trade it for one with the staggers and give something extra. There's some folks bound to be like that, apparently. But one day Jabez Stone got sick of the whole business.

He'd been plowing that morning and he'd just broke the plowshare on a rock that he could have sworn hadn't been there yesterday. And as he stood at the plowshare, the off horse began to cough—that ropy kind of cough that means sickness and horse doctors. There were two children down with the measles, his wife was ailing, and he had a whitlow on his thumb. It was about the last straw for Jabez Stone. "I vow," he said, and he looked around him kind of desperate, "I vow it's enough to make a man want to sell his soul to the devil! And I would, too, for two cents!"

Then he felt a kind of queerness come over him at having said what he'd said; though, naturally, being a New Hampshireman, he wouldn't take it back. But all the same, when it got to be evening and, as far as he could see, no notice had been taken, he felt relieved in his mind, for he was a religious man. But notice is always taken, sooner or later, just like the Good Book says. And, sure enough, next day, about suppertime, a soft-spoken, dark-dressed stranger drove up in a handsome buggy and asked for Jabez Stone.

Well, Jabez told his family it was a lawyer, come to see him about a legacy. But he knew who it was. He didn't like the looks of the stranger, nor the way he smiled with his teeth. They were white teeth, and plentiful—some say they were filed to a point, but I wouldn't vouch for that. And he didn't like it when the dog took one look at the stranger and ran away howling, with his tail between his legs. But having passed the word, more or less, he stuck to it, and they went out behind the barn and made their bargain. Jabez Stone had to prick his finger to sign, and the stranger lent him a silver pin. The wound healed clean, but it left a little white scar.

After that, all of a sudden, things began to pick up and prosper for Jabez Stone. His cows got fat and his horses sleek, his crops were the envy of the neighborhood, and lightning might strike all over the valley, but it wouldn't strike his barn. Pretty soon he was one of the prosperous people of the county; they asked him to stand for selectman, and he stood for it; there began to be talk of running him for state senate. All in all, you might say the Stone family was as happy and contented as cats in a dairy. And so they were, except for Jabez Stone.

He'd been contented enough the first few years. It's a great thing when bad luck turns; it drives most other things out of your head. True, every now and then, especially in rainy weather, the little white scar on his finger would give him a twinge. And once a year, punctual as clockwork, the stranger with the handsome buggy would come driving by. But the sixth year the stranger lighted, and, after that, his peace was over for Jabez Stone.

The stranger came up through the lower field, switching his boots with a cane—they were handsome black boots, but Jabez Stone never liked the look of them, particularly the toes. And, after he'd passed the time of day, he said, "Well, Mr. Stone, you're a hummer! It's a very pretty property you've got here, Mr. Stone."

"Well, some might favor it and others might not," said Jabez Stone, for he was a New Hampshireman.

"Oh, no need to decry your industry!" said the stranger, very easy, showing his teeth in a smile. "After all, we know what's been done, and it's been according to contract and specifications. So when—ahem—the mortgage falls due next year, you shouldn't have any regrets."

"Speaking of that mortgage, mister," said Jabez Stone, and he looked around for help to the earth and the sky, "I'm beginning to have one or two doubts about it."

"Doubts?" said the stranger not quite so pleasantly.

"Why, yes," said Jabez Stone. "This being the U.S.A. and me always having been a religious man." He cleared his throat and got bolder. "Yes sir," he said, "I'm beginning to have considerable doubts as to that mortgage holding in court."

"There's courts and courts," said the stranger, clicking his teeth. "Still, we might as well have a look at the original document." And he hauled out a big black pocketbook, full of papers. "Sherwin, Slater, Stevens, Stone," he muttered. " 'I, Jabez Stone, for a term of seven years—' Oh, it's quite in order, I think."

But Jabez Stone wasn't listening, for he saw something else flutter out of the black pocketbook. It was something that looked like a moth, but it wasn't a moth. And as Jabez Stone stared at it, it seemed to speak to him in a small sort of piping voice, terrible small and thin, but terrible human. "Neighbor Stone!" it squeaked. "Neighbor Stone! Help me! For God's sake, help me!"

But before Jabez Stone could stir hand or foot, the stranger whipped out a big bandanna handkerchief, caught the creature in it, just like a butterfly, and started tying up the ends of the bandanna.

"Sorry for the interruption," he said. "As I was saying—"

But Jabez Stone was shaking all over like a scared horse.

"That's Miser Stevens' voice!" he said in a croak. "And you've got him in your handkerchief!"

The stranger looked a little embarrassed.

"Yes, I really should have transferred him to the collecting box," he said with a simper, "but there were some rather unusual specimens there and I don't want them crowded. Well, well, these little contretemps will occur."

"I don't know what you mean by contertan," said Jabez Stone, "but that was Miser Stevens' voice! And he ain't dead! You can't tell me he is! He was just as spry and mean as a woodchuck Tuesday!"

"In the midst of life . . ." said the stranger, kind of pious. "Listen!" Then a bell began to toll in the valley and Jabez Stone listened, with the sweat running down his face. For he knew it was tolled for Miser Stevens and that he was dead.

"These long-standing accounts," said the stranger with a sigh; "one really hates to close them. But business is business."

He still had the bandanna in his hand, and Jabez Stone felt sick as he saw the cloth struggle and flutter.

"Are they all as small as that?" he asked hoarsely.

"Small?" said the stranger. "Oh, I see what you mean. Why, they vary." He measured Jabez Stone with his eyes, and his teeth showed. "Don't worry, Mr. Stone," he said. "You'll go with a very good grade. I wouldn't trust you outside the collecting box. Now, a man like Dan'l Webster, of course—well, we'd have to build a special box for him, and even at that, I imagine the wing spread would astonish you. He'd certainly be a prize. I wish we could see our way clear to him. But, in your case, as I was saying—"

"Put that handkerchief away!" said Jabez Stone, and he began to beg and to pray. But the best he could get at the end was a three years' extension, with conditions.

But till you make a bargain like that, you've got no idea of how fast four years can run. By the last months of those years Jabez Stone's known all over the state and there's talk of running him for governor—and it's dust and ashes in his mouth. For every day, when he gets up, he thinks, "There's one more night gone," and every night, when he lies down, he thinks of the black pocketbook and the soul of Miser Stevens, and it makes him sick at heart. Till, finally, he can't bear it any longer, and, in the last days of the last year, he hitches up his horse and drives off to seek Dan'l Webster. For Dan'l was born in New Hampshire, only a few miles from Cross Corners, and it's well known that he has a particular soft spot for old neighbors.

It was early in the morning when he got to Marshfield, but Dan'l was up already, talking Latin to the farm hands and wrestling with the ram, Goliath, and trying out a new trotter and working up speeches to make against John C. Calhoun. But when he heard a New Hampshireman had come to see him, he dropped everything else he was doing, for that was Dan'l's way. He gave Jabez Stone a breakfast that five men couldn't eat, went into the living history of every man and woman in Cross Corners, and finally asked him how he could serve him.

Jabez Stone allowed that it was a kind of mortgage case.

"Well, I haven't pleaded a mortgage case in a long time, and I don't generally plead now, except before the Supreme Court," said Dan'l, "but if I can, I'll help you."

"Then I've got hope for the first time in ten years," said Jabez Stone and told him the details.

Dan'l walked up and down as he listened, hands behind his back, now and then asking a question, now and then plunging his eyes at the floor, as if they'd bore through it like gimlets. When Jabez Stone had finished, Dan'l puffed out his cheeks and blew. Then he turned to Jabez Stone and a smile broke over his face like the sunrise over Monadnock.

"You've certainly given yourself the devil's own row to hoe, Neighbor Stone," he said, "but I'll take your case."

"You'll take it?" said Jabez Stone, hardly daring to believe.

"Yes," said Dan'l Webster. "I've got about seventy-five other things to do and the Missouri Compromise to straighten out, but I'll take your case. For if two New Hampshiremen aren't a match for the devil, we might as well give the country back to the Indians."

Then he shook Jabez Stone by the hand and said, "Did you come down here in a hurry?"

"Well, I admit I made time," said Jabez Stone.

"You'll go back faster," said Dan'l Webster, and he told 'em to hitch up Constitution and Constellation to the carriage. They were matched grays with one white forefoot, and they stepped like greased lightning.

Well, I won't describe how excited and pleased the whole Stone family was to have the great Dan'l Webster for a guest, when they finally got there. Jabez Stone had lost his hat on the way, blown off when they overtook a wind, but he didn't take much account of that. But after supper he sent the family off to bed, for he had most particular business with Mr. Webster. Mrs. Stone wanted him to sit in the front parlor, but Dan'l Webster knew front parlors and said he preferred the kitchen. So it was there they sat, waiting for the stranger, with a jug on the table between them and a bright fire on the hearth—the stranger being scheduled to show up on the stroke of midnight, according to specification.

Well, most men wouldn't have asked for better company than Dan'l Webster and a jug. But with every tick of the clock Jabez Stone got sadder and sadder. His eyes roved round, and though he sampled the jug you could see he couldn't taste it. Finally, on the stroke of 11:30 he reached over and grabbed Dan'l Webster by the arm.

"Mr. Webster, Mr. Webster!" he said, and his voice was shaking with fear and desperate courage. "For God's sake, Mr. Webster, harness your horses and get away from this place while you can!"

"You've brought me a long way, neighbor, to tell me you don't like my company," said Dan'l Webster, quite peaceable, pulling at the jug.

"Miserable wretch that I am!" groaned Jabez Stone. "I've brought you a devilish way, and now I see my folly. Let him take me if he will. I don't hanker after it, I must say, but I can stand it. But you're the Union's stay and New Hampshire's pride! He mustn't get you, Mr. Webster! He mustn't get you!"

Dan'l Webster looked at the distracted man, all gray and shaking in the firelight, and laid a hand on his shoulder.

"I'm obliged to you, Neighbor Stone," he said gently. "It's kindly thought of. But there's a jug on the table and a case in hand. And I never left a jug or a case half finished in my life."

And just at that moment there was a sharp rap on the door.

"Ah," said Dan'l Webster very coolly, "I thought your clock was a trifle slow, Neighbor Stone." He stepped to the door and opened it. "Come in!" he said.

The stranger came in—very dark and tall he looked in the firelight. He was carrying a box under his arm—a black japanned box with little air holes in the lid. At the sight of the box Jabez Stone gave a low cry and shrank into a corner of the room.

"Mr. Webster, I presume," said the stranger, very polite, but with his eyes glowing like a fox's deep in the woods.

"Attorney of record for Jabez Stone," said Dan'l Webster, but his eyes were glowing too. "Might I ask your name?"

"I've gone by a good many," said the stranger carelessly. "Perhaps Scratch will do for the evening. I'm often called that in these regions."

Then he sat down at the table and poured himself a drink from the jug. The liquor was cold in the jug, but it came steaming into the glass.

"And now," said the stranger, smiling and showing his teeth, "I shall call upon you, as a law-abiding citizen, to assist me in taking possession of my property."

Well, with that the argument began—and it went hot and heavy. At first Jabez Stone had a flicker of hope, but when he saw Dan'l Webster being forced back at point after point, he just sat scrunched in his corner, with his eyes on that japanned box. For there wasn't any doubt as to the deed or the signature—that was the worst of it. Dan'l Webster twisted and turned and thumped his fist on the table, but he couldn't get away from that. He offered to compromise the case; the stranger wouldn't hear of it. He pointed out the property had increased in value, and state senators ought to be worth more; the stranger stuck to the letter of the law. He was a great lawyer, Dan'l Webster, but we know who's the King of Lawyers, as the Good Book tells us, and it seemed as if, for the first time, Dan'l Webster had met his match.

Finally, the stranger yawned a little. "Your spirited efforts on behalf of your client do you credit, Mr. Webster," he said, "but if you have no more arguments to adduce, I'm rather pressed for time . . ." and Jabez Stone shuddered.

Dan'l Webster's brow looked dark as a thundercloud.

"Pressed or not, you shall not have this man!" he thundered. "Mr. Stone is an American citizen, and no American citizen may be forced into the service of a foreign prince. We fought England for that in '12 and we'll fight all hell for it again!"

"Foreign?" said the stranger. "And who calls me a foreigner?"

"Well, I never yet heard of the dev—of your claiming American citizenship," said Dan'l Webster with surprise.

"And who with better right?" said the stranger with one of his terrible smiles. "When the first wrong was done to the first Indian, I was there. When the first slaver put out for the Congo, I stood on her deck. Am I not in your books and stories and beliefs, from the first settlements on? Am I not spoken of still in every church in New England? 'Tis true the North claims me for a Southerner and the South for a Northerner, but I am neither. I am merely an honest American like yourself—and of the best descent—for, to tell the truth, Mr. Webster, though I don't like to boast of it, my name is older in this country than yours."

"Aha!" said Dan'l Webster with the veins standing out in his forehead. "Then I stand on the Constitution! I demand a trial for my client!"

"The case is hardly one for an ordinary court," said the stranger, his eyes flickering. "And, indeed, the lateness of hour—"

"Let it be any court you choose, so it is an American judge and an American jury!" said Dan'l Webster in his pride. "Let it be the quick or the dead; I'll abide the issue!"

"You have said it," said the stranger, and pointed his finger at the door. And with that, and all of a sudden, there was a rushing of wind outside and a noise of footsteps. They came, clear and distinct, through the night. And yet they were not like the footsteps of living men.

"In God's name, who comes by so late?" cried Jabez Stone in an ague of fear.

"The jury Mr. Webster demands," said the stranger, sipping at his boiling glass. "You must pardon the rough appearance of one or two; they will have come a long way."

And with that the fire burned blue and the door blew open and twelve men entered, one by one.

If Jabez Stone had been sick with terror before, he was blind with terror now. For there was Walter Butler, the loyalist, who spread fire and horror through the Mohawk Valley in the times of the Revolution; and there was Simon Girty, the renegade, who saw white men burned at the stake and whooped with the Indians to see them burn. His eyes were green, like a catamount's, and the stains on his hunting shirt did not come from the blood of the deer. King Philip was there, wild and proud as he had been in life, with the great gash in his head that gave him his death wound, and cruel Governor Dale, who broke men on the wheel. There was Morton of Merry Mount, who so vexed the Plymouth Colony, with his flushed, loose, handsome face and his hate of the godly. There was Teach, the bloody pirate, with his black beard curling on his breast. The Reverend John Smeet, with his strangler's hands and his Geneva gown, walked as daintily as he had to the gallows. The red print of the rope was still around his neck, but he carried a perfumed handkerchief in one hand. One and all, they came into the room with the fires of hell still upon them, and the stranger named their names and their deeds as they came, till the tale of twelve was told. Yet the stranger had told the truth—they had all played a part in America.

"Are you satisfied with the jury, Mr. Webster?" said the stranger mockingly, when they had taken their places.

The sweat stood upon Dan'l Webster's brow, but his voice was clear.

"Quite satisfied," he said. "Though I miss General Arnold from the company."

"Benedict Arnold is engaged upon other business," said the stranger with a glower. "Ah, you asked for a justice, I believe."

He pointed his finger once more, and a tall man, soberly clad in Puritan garb, with the burning gaze of the fanatic, stalked into the room and took his judge's place.

"Justice Hawthorne is a jurist of experience," said the stranger. "He presided at certain witch trials once held in Salem. There were others who repented of the business later, but not he."

"Repent of such notable wonders and undertakings?" said the stern old justice. "Nay, hang them—hang them all!" And he muttered to himself in a way that struck ice into the soul of Jabez Stone.

Then the trial began, and, as you might expect, it didn't look anyways good for the defense. And Jabez Stone didn't make much of a witness in his own behalf. He took one look at Simon Girty and screeched, and they had to put him back in his corner in a kind of swoon.

It didn't halt the trial though; the trial went on, as trials do. Dan'l Webster had faced some hard juries and hanging judges in his time, but this was the hardest he'd ever faced, and he knew it. They sat there with a kind of glitter in their eyes, and the stranger's smooth voice went on and on. Every time he'd raise an objection, it'd be "Objection sustained," but whenever Dan'l objected, it'd be "Objection denied." Well, you couldn't expect fair play from a fellow like this Mr. Scratch.

It got to Dan'l in the end, and he began to heat, like iron in the forge. When he got up to speak he was going to flay that stranger with every trick known to the law, and the judge and jury too. He didn't care if it was contempt of court or what would happen to him for it. He didn't care any more what happened to Jabez Stone. He just got madder and madder, thinking of what he'd say. And yet, curiously enough, the more he thought about it, the less he was able to arrange his speech in his mind.

Till, finally, it was time for him to get up on his feet, and he did so, all ready to bust out with lightnings and denunciations. But before he started he looked over the judge and jury for a moment, such being his custom. And he noticed the glitter in their eyes was twice as strong as before, and they all leaned forward. Like hounds just before they get the fox, they looked, and the blue mist of evil in the room thickened as he watched them. Then he saw what he'd been about to do, and he wiped his forehead, as a man might who's just escaped falling into a pit in the dark.

For it was him they'd come for, not only Jabez Stone. He read it in the glitter of their eyes and in the way the stranger hid his mouth with one hand. And if he fought them with their own weapons, he'd fall into their power; he knew that, though he couldn't have told you how. It was his own anger and horror that burned in their eyes; and he'd have to wipe that out or the case was lost. He stood there for a moment, his black eyes burning like anthracite. And then he began to speak.

He started off in a low voice, though you could hear every word. They say he could call on the harps of the blessed when he chose. And this was just as simple and easy as a man could talk. But he didn't start out by condemning or reviling. He was talking about the things that make a country a country and a man a man.

And he began with the simple things that everybody's known and felt—the freshness of a fine morning when you're young, and the taste of food when you're hungry, and the new day that's every day when you're a child. He took them up and he turned them in his hands. They were good things for any man. But without freedom they sickened. And when he talked of those enslaved, and the sorrows of slavery, his voice got like a big bell. He talked of the early days of America and the men who had made those days. It wasn't a spread-eagle speech, but he made you see it. He admitted all the wrong that had ever been done. But he showed how, out of the wrong and the right, the suffering and the starvations, something new had come. And everybody had played a part in it, even the traitors.

Then he turned to Jabez Stone and showed him as he was—an ordinary man who'd had hard luck and wanted to change it. And, because he'd wanted to change it, now he was going to be punished for all eternity. And yet there was good in Jabez Stone, and he showed that good. He was hard and mean, in some ways, but he was a man. There was sadness in being a man, but it was a proud thing too. And he showed what the pride of it was till you couldn't help feeling it. Yes, even in hell, if a man was a man, you'd know it. And he wasn't pleading for any one person any more, though his voice rang like an organ. He was telling the story and the failures and the endless journey of mankind. They got tricked and trapped and bamboozled, but it was a great journey. And no demon that was ever foaled could know the inwardness of it—it took a man to do that.

The fire began to die on the hearth and the wind before morning to blow. The light was getting gray in the room when Dan'l Webster finished. And his words came back at the end to New Hampshire ground, and the one spot of land that each man loves and clings to. He painted a picture of that, and to each one of that jury he spoke of things long forgotten. For his voice could search the heart, and that was his gift and his strength. And to one his voice was like the forest and its secrecy, and to another like the sea and the storms of the sea; and one heard the cry of his lost nation in it, and another saw a little harmless scene he hadn't remembered for years. But each saw something. And when Dan'l Webster finished he didn't know whether or not he'd saved Jabez Stone. But he knew he'd done a miracle. For the glitter was gone from the eyes of judge and jury, and, for the moment, they were men again, and knew they were men.

"The defense rests," said Dan'l Webster and stood there like a mountain. His ears were still ringing with his speech, and he didn't hear anything else till he heard Judge Hawthorne say, "The jury will retire to consider its verdict."

Walter Butler rose in his place and his face had a dark, gay pride on it.

"The jury has considered its verdict," he said and looked the stranger full in the eye. "We find for the defendant, Jabez Stone."

With that, the smile left the stranger's face, but Walter Butler did not flinch.

"Perhaps 'tis not strictly in accordance with the evidence," he said, "but even the damned may salute the eloquence of Mr. Webster."

With that, the long crow of a rooster split the gray morning sky, and judge and jury were gone from the room like a puff of smoke and as if they had never been there. The stranger returned to Dan'l Webster, smiling wryly.

"Major Butler was always a bold man," he said. "I had not thought him quite so bold. Nevertheless, my congratulations, as between two gentlemen."

"I'll have that paper first, if you please," said Dan'l Webster, and he took it and tore it into four pieces. It was queerly warm to the touch. "And now," he said, "I'll have you!" and his hand came down like a bear trap on the stranger's arm. For he knew that once you bested anybody like Mr. Scratch in fair fight, his power on you was gone. And he could see that Mr. Scratch knew it too.

The stranger twisted and wriggled, but he couldn't get out of that grip. "Come, come, Mr. Webster," he said, smiling palely: "This sort of thing is ridic—ouch!—is ridiculous. If you're worried about the costs of the case, naturally, I'd be glad to pay—"

"And so you shall!" said Dan'l Webster, shaking him till his teeth rattled. "For you'll sit right down at that table and draw up a document, promising never to bother Jabez Stone nor his heirs or assigns nor any other New Hampshireman till doomsday! For any hades we want to raise in this state, we can raise ourselves, without assistance from strangers."

"Ouch!" said the stranger. "Ouch! Well, they never did run very big to the barrel, but—ouch!—I agree!"

So he sat down and drew up the document. But Dan'l Webster kept his hand on his coat collar all the time.

"And now may I go?" said the stranger, quite humble, when Dan'l seen the document was in proper and legal form.

"Go?" said Dan'l, giving him another shake. "I'm still trying to figure out what I'll do with you. For you've settled the costs of the case, but you haven't settled with me. I think I'll take you back to Marshfield," he said, kind of reflective. "I've got a ram there named Goliath that can butt through an iron door. I'd kind of like to turn you loose in his field and see what he'd do."

E. B. WHITE

[1899–]

A TRENCHANT ESSAYIST, an alternately terrifying and teasing writer of fiction, and a creator of tenderly imaginative stories for children, E. (for Elwyn) B. (for Brooks) White has been cherished with never a reservation. He was born July 11, 1899, in Mt. Vernon, New York, and was educated at Cornell University. During the First World War he was a private in the United States Army. He went to Alaska as a reporter for the Seattle Times, then returned to New York, where, in his twenties, he began writing for The New Yorker and contributed a large part of its characteristic "Talk of the Town." At thirty he married The New Yorker's literary editor and, some years later, retired to spend his time in Maine. With his wife he edited A Subtreasury of American Humor (a model of anthologizing) and brought out the best of his sharply personal columns from Harper's Magazine in a volume appropriately entitled One Man's Meat.

Besides being a keen and occasionally an indignant commentator, White, like Thoreau, is both a naturalist by nature and an appraiser of human nature. Everything draws his close observation and his humanitarian sympathy. He understands the countryside without being sentimental about it; he contemplates the follies of urban civilization with tolerance and wistful hope. With James Thurber, his friend and ex-colleague on The New Yorker, he shares a distaste for the mechanics of the age of automation and shrugs a shoulder at the puzzles and predicaments of modern life.

THE SECOND TREE FROM THE CORNER

EVER HAVE any bizarre thoughts?" asked the doctor.

Mr. Trexler failed to catch the word. "What kind?" he said.

"Bizarre," repeated the doctor, his voice steady. He watched his patient for any slight change of expression, any wince. It seemed to Trexler that the doctor was not only watching him closely but was creeping slowly toward him, like a lizard toward a bug. Trexler shoved his chair back an inch and gathered himself for a reply. He was about to say "Yes" when he realized that if he said yes the next question would be unanswerable. Bizarre thoughts, bizarre thoughts? Ever have any bizarre thoughts. What kind of thoughts *except* bizarre had he had since the age of two?

Trexler felt the time passing, the necessity for an answer. These psychiatrists were busy men, overloaded, not to be kept waiting. The next patient was probably already perched out there in the waiting room, lonely, worried, shifting around on the sofa, his mind stuffed with bizarre thoughts and amorphous fears. Poor bastard, thought Trexler. Out there all alone in that misshapen antechamber, staring at the filing cabinet and wondering whether to tell the doctor about that day on the Madison Avenue bus.

Let's see, bizarre thoughts. Trexler dodged back along the dreadful corridor of the years to see what he could find. He felt the doctor's eyes upon him and knew that time was running out. Don't be so conscientious, he said to himself. If a bizarre thought is indicated here, just reach into the bag and pick anything at all. A man as well supplied with bizarre thoughts as you are should have no difficulty producing one for the record. Trexler darted into the bag, hung for a moment before one of his thoughts, as a hummingbird pauses in the delphinium. No, he said, not that one. He darted to another (the one about the rhesus monkey), paused, considered. No, he said, not that.

Trexler knew he must hurry. He had already used up pretty nearly four seconds since the question had been put. But it was an impossible situation—just one more lousy, impossible situation such as he was always getting himself into. When, he asked himself, are you going to quit maneuvering yourself into a pocket? He made one more effort. This time he stopped at the asylum, only the bars were lucite—fluted, retractable. Not here, he said. Not this one.

He looked straight at the doctor. "No," he said quietly. "I never have any bizarre thoughts."

The doctor sucked in on his pipe, blew a plume of smoke toward the rows of medical books. Trexler's gaze followed the smoke. He managed to make out one of the titles, "The Genito-Urinary System." A bright wave of fear swept cleanly over him, and he winced under the first pain of kidney stones. He remembered when he was a child, the first time he ever entered a doctor's office, sneaking a look at the titles of the books—and the flush of fear, the shirt wet under the arms, the book on t.b., the sudden knowledge that he was in the advanced stages of consumption, the quick vision of the hemorrhage. Trexler sighed wearily. Forty years, he thought, and I still get thrown by the title of a medical book. Forty years and I still can't stay on life's little bucky horse. No wonder I'm sitting here in this dreary joint at the end of this woebegone afternoon, lying about my bizarre thoughts to a doctor who looks, come to think of it, rather tired.

The session dragged on. After about twenty minutes, the doctor rose and knocked his pipe out. Trexler got up, knocked the ashes out of his brain, and waited. The doctor smiled warmly and stuck out his hand. "There's nothing the matter with you—you're just scared. Want to know how I know you're scared?"

"How?" asked Trexler.

"Look at the chair you've been sitting in! See how it has moved back away from my desk? You kept inching away from me while I asked you questions. That means you're scared."

"Does it?" said Trexler, faking a grin. "Yeah, I suppose it does."

They finished shaking hands. Trexler turned and walked out uncertainly along the passage, then into the waiting room and out past the next patient, a ruddy pin-striped man who was seated on the sofa twirling his hat nervously and staring straight ahead at the files. Poor, frightened guy, thought Trexler, he's probably read in the *Times* that one American male out of every two is going to die of heart disease by twelve o'clock next Thursday. It says that in the paper almost every morning. And he's also probably thinking about that day on the Madison Avenue bus.

A week later, Trexler was back in the patient's chair. And for several weeks thereafter he continued to visit the doctor, always toward the end of the afternoon, when the vapors hung thick above the pool of the mind and darkened the whole region of the East Seventies. He felt no better as time went on, and he found it impossible to work. He discovered that the visits were becoming routine and that although the routine was one to which he certainly did not look forward, at least he could accept it with cool resignation, as once, years ago, he had accepted a long spell with a dentist who had settled down to a steady fooling with a couple of dead teeth. The visits, moreover, were now assuming a pattern recognizable to the patient.

Each session would begin with a résumé of symptoms—the dizziness in the streets, the constricting pain in the back of the neck, the apprehensions, the tightness of the scalp, the inability to concentrate, the despondency and the melancholy times, the feeling of pressure and tension, the anger at not being able to work, the anxiety over work not done, the gas on the stomach. Dullest set of neurotic symptoms in the world, Trexler would think, as he obediently trudged back over them for the doctor's benefit. And then, having listened attentively to the recital, the doctor would spring his question: "Have you ever found anything that gives you relief?" And Trexler would answer, "Yes. A drink." And the doctor would nod his head knowingly.

As he became familiar with the pattern Trexler found that he increasingly tended to identify himself with the doctor, transferring himself into the doctor's seat—probably (he thought) some rather slick form of escapism. At any rate, it was nothing new for Trexler to identify himself with other people. Whenever he got into a cab, he instantly became the driver, saw everything from the hackman's angle (and the reaching over with the right hand, the nudging of the flag, the pushing it down, all the way down along the side of the meter), saw everything—traffic, fare, everything—through the eyes of Anthony Rocco, or Isidore Freedman, or Matthew Scott. In a barbershop, Trexler was the barber, his fingers curled around the comb, his hand on the tonic. Perfectly natural, then, that Trexler should soon be occupying the doctor's chair, asking the questions, waiting for the answers. He got quite interested in the doctor, in this way. He liked him, and he found him a not too difficult patient.

It was on the fifth visit, about halfway through, that the doctor turned to Trexler and said, suddenly, "What do you want?" He gave the word "want" special emphasis.

"I d'know," replied Trexler uneasily. "I guess nobody knows the answer to that one."

"Sure they do," replied the doctor.

"Do *you* know what *you* want?" asked Trexler narrowly.

"Certainly," said the doctor. Trexler noticed that at this point the doctor's chair slid slightly backward, away from him. Trexler stifled a small, internal smile. Scared as a rabbit, he said to himself. Look at him scoot!

"What *do* you want?" continued Trexler, pressing his advantage, pressing it hard.

The doctor glided back another inch away from his inquisitor. "I want a wing on the small house I own in Westport. I want more money, and more leisure to do the things I want to do."

Trexler was just about to say, "And what are those things you want to do, Doctor?" when he caught himself. Better not go too far, he mused. Better not lose possession of the ball. And besides, he thought, what the hell goes on here, anyway—me paying fifteen bucks a throw for these séances and then doing the work myself, asking the questions, weighing the answers. So he wants a new wing! There's a fine piece of theatrical gauze for you! A new wing.

Trexler settled down again and resumed the role of patient for the rest of the visit. It ended on a kindly, friendly note. The doctor reassured him that his fears were the cause of his sickness, and that his fears were unsubstantial. They shook hands, smiling.

Trexler walked dizzily through the empty waiting room and the doctor followed along to let him out. It was late; the secretary had shut up shop and gone home. Another day over the dam. "Goodbye," said Trexler. He stepped into the street, turned west toward Madison, and thought of the doctor all alone there, after hours, in that desolate hole—a man who worked longer hours than his secretary. Poor, scared, overworked bastard, thought Trexler. And that new wing!

It was an evening of clearing weather, the Park showing green and desirable in the distance, the last daylight applying a high lacquer to the brick and brownstone walls and giving the street scene a luminous and intoxicating splendor. Trexler meditated, as he walked, on what he wanted. "What do you want?" he heard again. Trexler knew what he wanted, and what, in general, all men wanted; and he was glad, in a way, that it was both inexpressible and unattainable, and that it wasn't a wing. He was satisfied to remember that it was deep, formless, enduring, and impossible of fulfillment, and that it made men sick, and that when you sauntered along Third Avenue and looked through the doorways into the dim saloons, you could sometimes pick out from the unregenerate ranks the ones who had not forgotten, gazing steadily into the bottoms of the glasses on the long chance that they could get another little peek at it. Trexler found himself renewed by the remembrance that what he wanted was at once great and microscopic, and that although it borrowed from the nature of large deeds and of youthful love and of old songs and early intimations, it was not any one of these things, and that it had not been isolated or pinned down, and that a man who attempted to define it in the privacy of a doctor's office would fall flat on his face.

Trexler felt invigorated. Suddenly his sickness seemed health, his dizziness stability. A small tree, rising between him and the light, stood there saturated with the evening, each gilt-edged leaf perfectly drunk with excellence and delicacy. Trexler's spine registered an ever so slight tremor as it picked up this natural disturbance in the lovely scene. "I want the second tree from the corner, just as it stands," he said, answering an imaginary question from an imaginary physician. And he felt a slow pride in realizing that what he wanted none could bestow, and that what he had none could take away. He felt content to be sick, unembarrassed at being afraid; and in the jungle of his fear he glimpsed (as he had so often glimpsed them before) the flashy tail feathers of the bird courage.

Then he thought once again of the doctor, and of his being left there all alone, tired, frightened. (The poor, scared guy, thought Trexler.) Trexler began humming "Moonshine Lullaby," his spirit reacting instantly to the hypodermic of Merman's healthy voice. He crossed Madison, boarded a downtown bus, and rode all the way to Fifty-second Street before he had a thought that could rightly have been called bizarre.

ERNEST HEMINGWAY

[1899–   ]

It was a belittling time. It was a time of resentment, when the old standards of conduct no longer seemed valid, when the concern for the common virtues had no more meaning than the cozy platitudes of a wall motto, and responsibility as well as respectability was rather ridiculous. Picturing this time, sharply and without compromise, in the idioms of ordinary speech rather than the locutions of literature, Ernest Hemingway became perhaps the outstanding novelist, and certainly the greatest literary influence of his—and of the next—generation.

Ernest Miller Hemingway, born July 21, 1899, in Oak Park (virtually a suburb of Chicago), was the son of a doctor-sportsman, who gave him a man-sized gun when he was ten years old, and of a musical mother who hoped he would be a cellist. His formal education was brief. At fifteen he ran away from home. He returned, in 1917, to finish high school. Then he went to Kansas City to work as a reporter, but before he was eighteen he had gone to France to join an ambulance unit. He transferred to the Italian infantry and was wounded almost fatally. He came home again, was married, in 1921, to Hadley Richardson, tried journalism in Toronto, and rushed off to the Near East to report the horrors of the Greco-Turkish War.

The writer and the century were in their early twenties when he went to Paris and joined the group of expatriates whose mentors were Gertrude Stein, Ezra Pound, and Sherwood Anderson. From Stein and Anderson he first learned those theories of writing which he was to develop into the unique "Hemingway style." There could be stories, they said, clear and passionate, without plot and idiom, without rhetoric. Hemingway, twenty-four and determined to be a novelist, set out to find and write "the sequence of motion and fact which made the emotion and which would be as valid in a year or ten years or, with luck and if you stated it purely enough, always."

He published a small book, Three Stories and Ten Poems, and, a year later, in our time, a set of epigraphs and post-war impressions which marked the emergence of an original and powerful, but immature, writer, unsure of his art and a little too sure of himself. Except that they are set down to show that there was no real peace in the nostalgic world before the war, the stories of in our time, idyllic, autobiographical tales of adolescence, would seem at variance with the vignettes which picture a world of violence, war, and sudden death. At twenty-five, Hemingway already was fascinated by ferocity, not only by major terrors and tragedies, but by uncaring nature and the casual cruelties of everyday.

The Torrents of Spring continued the theme of random malevolence. A tribute to—and parody of—Sherwood Anderson, the book was a failure even as a burlesque. Then came The Sun Also Rises, repudiating Anderson and his sexual-social mysticism and establishing Hemingway as unquestionably the novelist-spokesman of his time. "He made his Paris and his Pamplona," Carlos Baker suggests, "into microcosms which relentlessly embodied a considerable part of the social history of the Nineteen-Twenties, both American and foreign." The Sun Also Rises is the undeniable and definitive book (or Bible) of the so-called "lost generation," a generation which saw the First World War as a universal deception, a nightmare of broken promises, a failure of all the idealisms in the name of which the war was fought, a colossal and useless sacrifice of millions of useful lives. The result, as Hemingway indicated, was an inevitable disillusion, a revulsion not only from the stereotypes of romanticism but also from a civilization which had betrayed the world.

The men and women of that collapsed world—and especially the maladjusted and mutilated bohemians of Hemingway's novel—turned to one sensation after another. The traditional hero was gone: in his place were bullfighters, athletes, hunters, and primitive men whose virility was presented as an antidote (or overcompensation) for the impotence of twentieth-century culture. Hemingway himself was the ideal protagonist; an athlete among esthetes, he shared their wounds and cynicisms, but surpassed them in his life and way of writing. The language he chose mirrored the image of his hero: straightforward, simple—suspiciously too simple at times—and stripped of all excess ornamentation. In attitude and style Hemingway created a vogue and founded a school. His manner was imitated and his tight understatements started a fashion of hard-boiled fiction. At twenty-seven he had set the keynote for a new kind of literature. His acceptance, stoic but grim, of accidental anguish and his recognition of irresponsible pleasure were echoed in volumes built on the strange blending of sick brutality and warped sentimentality. Half the young writers tried to imitate him, it was said, and the other half tried not to.

He lived in Paris, went to the Tyrol for skiing, and to Spain for the bullfights. He wrote a series of brilliant short stories. In 1927 his first *marriage ended in a divorce. He was married again, to Pauline Pfeiffer, who bore him two sons. He returned to the United States and published another collection of short stories,* Men Without Women. *He moved to Key West, Florida, became an expert fisherman, and, in 1928, finished* A Farewell to Arms. *This generally is considered his finest novel; in the midst of the degradations of a fruitless war Hemingway's characters play out a melancholy but ennobling love tragedy, the counterpoint of doomed love rising above a chorus of defeat.*

The "canon of death," as one critic called it, takes form and becomes a fixed idea in nearly all of Hemingway's subsequent work. Death in the Afternoon *glorifies bullfighting, a ritualistic mortal combat in which each contestant gambles the life he loves to spite his fear of death and so prove himself noble.* Winner Take Nothing *bears the theme of destruction, as does* Green Hills of Africa, *in which the dangers of big-game hunting replace the risks of the bullfight.*

In To Have and Have Not, *published in 1938, the pattern of death assumes a new shape. In the overthrow of the Spanish Republic Hemingway recognized a pervasive social problem. The hero of his book, Harry Morgan, a cheated smuggler, suddenly is turned into a dying champion of solidarity. Morgan's "No man alone now" became Hemingway's theme but, introduced late and without proper motivation, it split the novel into two parts of a broken book.*

The Fifth Column *and the* First Forty-Nine Stories *contained Hemingway's notable play and some of the most famous writing of the period. Here were "*The Snows of Kilimanjaro,*" "*The Short Happy Life of Francis Macomber,*" "*The Killers,*" "*Fifty Grand,*" and "*The Undefeated,*" all of which have more than withstood constant reprinting and rereading. There were, as well, the less dramatic but more searching "*Hills Like White Elephants*" and "*A Clean, Well-Lighted Place.*" The collection was published when Hemingway was thirty-nine. At forty-two he brought out his largest and, in the opinion of many admirers, his most important work,* For Whom the Bell Tolls.

*Hemingway took his title and his theme from one of John Donne's sermons: "*No man is an Iland, *intire of itself; every man is a peece of the* Continent; . . . *any man's* death *diminishes me, because I am involved in* Mankinde; *And therefore never send to know for whom the* bell tolls; *It tolls for* thee.*" Moved by the battle in Spain, by the courage and the comradeship of the patriots, Hemingway could reconcile his old concern with death and a new affirmation of life. As the loss of freedom anywhere meant the loss of freedom everywhere, so freedom's fight gave a purpose to dying and to living. There was a real* brotherhood of man; for the first time Hemingway dealt in positives.

The feeling of fellowship and the joy of sacrifice which characterized For Whom the Bell Tolls died with the defeat of the Spanish Loyalists. Across the River and Into the Trees, published eight years later, has none of such feeling. Instead there is a nightmare jumble of Hemingway stereotypes—as though the writer were parodying himself—and the celebrated style degenerates into a rehash of repetitions.

At fifty-four Hemingway published The Old Man and the Sea. Once again, as in the stories of hunting and bullfighting, he set in fateful combat the courage of a man keenly aware of his mortality against a beast whose courage, strength, and cunning are as great or greater than his own. Once again there was instinctive power in the writing. The imminence of death, Hemingway's constant theme, was colored by the sense of a fearful kinship between the forces of survival and the forces of destruction. The Old Man, a shrunken Captain Ahab, fights a long and lonely duel with a huge marlin, an ineffectual Moby Dick. A short and seemingly simple story, it communicates a greater excitement and creates a more powerful symbolism than all but Hemingway's most extended works. It brought the novelist a Pulitzer Prize. The following year he was awarded the Nobel Prize for the "style-making mastership" exemplified by this small book. Hemingway received the news in Cuba where he lived with his fourth wife, Mary Welsh, a former war correspondent. (He had been divorced in 1940, had married the writer Martha Gellhorn, and had been divorced from her.)

In January, 1954, a radio flash announced his death; the Hemingways had crashed in a small plane which was taking them on safari in Africa. But they had escaped death—twice, for a rescue plane which picked them up also crashed. It was but another story for the Hemingway legend. "My luck—she is still running good," is what he said himself when he emerged from the forest, carrying, it was said, the last of a bottle of gin and a bunch of bananas.

"Criticism," as Dr. Johnson said of his contemporaries' attempts to analyze Swift, "was lost in wonder." Faced with the Hemingway legend and the impact of his works, the critics argued amongst themselves, trying to explain the magic by which he gave common idioms and familiar phrases a new significance. "His words strike you," the novelist Ford Madox Ford said, "each one, as if they were pebbles fetched from a fresh brook. They live and shine, each in its place." The style is distinctly the man: hard, clipped, clean, persistently masculine.

Harried, then angered by the critics, Hemingway struck ridiculous *poses. His was an intuitive as well as a disciplined intelligence, yet he made it a point to deride intellectuals. Despising weaklings, he refused to be concerned with what conditioned them. He seemed unwilling to examine the motivations for his characters' actions, preferring to glorify simple embodiments of brute strength and blind courage. Stereotyped and submissive, the women he created were no more than complements to his virile and usually violent heroes. The critics objected to the unshakable symbol of death as a mystical union between murderer and murdered, bull and matador, man and marlin; but Hemingway, shrugging off criticism, was not perturbed. He insisted he was not interested in death for death's sake. "Killing," he said, "is the feeling of rebellion against death which comes from its administering."*

The swiftness of Hemingway's prose is irresistible. There is vitality and violence and the evocation of the relentlessness of time. Paradoxically, the writer who made a religion of irresponsibility, who was in love with disaster and obsessed with death, brought fresh life to American writing.

THE UNDEFEATED

MANUEL GARCIA CLIMBED THE STAIRS to Don Miguel Retana's office. He set down his suitcase and knocked on the door. There was no answer. Manuel, standing in the hallway, felt there was someone in the room. He felt it through the door.

"Retana," he said, listening.

There was no answer.

He's there, all right, Manuel thought.

"Retana," he said and banged the door.

"Who's there?" said someone in the office.

"Me, Manolo," Manuel said.

"What do you want?" asked the voice.

"I want to work," Manuel said.

Something in the door clicked several times and it swung open. Manuel went in, carrying his suitcase.

A little man sat behind a desk at the far side of the room. Over his head was a bull's head, stuffed by a Madrid taxidermist; on the walls were framed photographs and bullfight posters.

The little man sat looking at Manuel.

"I thought they'd kill you," he said.

Manuel knocked with his knuckles on the desk. The little man sat looking at him across the desk.

"How many corridas you had this year?" Retana asked.

"One," he answered.

"Just that one?" the little man asked.

"That's all."

"I read about it in the papers," Retana said. He leaned back in the chair and looked at Manuel.

Manuel looked up at the stuffed bull. He had seen it often before. He felt a certain family interest in it. It had killed his brother, the promising one, about nine years ago. Manuel remembered the day. There was a brass plate on the oak shield the bull's head was mounted on. Manuel could not read it, but he imagined it was in memory of his brother. Well, he had been a good kid.

The plate said: "The Bull 'Mariposa' of the Duke of Veragua, which accepted 9 varas for 7 caballos, and caused the death of Antonio Garcia, Novillero, April 27, 1909."

Retana saw him looking at the stuffed bull's head.

"The lot the Duke sent me for Sunday will make a scandal," he said. "They're all bad in the legs. What do they say about them at the Café?"

"I don't know," Manuel said. "I just got in."

"Yes," Retana said. "You still have your bag."

He looked at Manuel, leaning back behind the big desk.

"Sit down," he said. "Take off your cap."

Manuel sat down; his cap off, his face was changed. He looked pale, and his coleta pinned forward on his head, so that it would not show under the cap, gave him a strange look.

"You don't look well," Retana said.

"I just got out of the hospital," Manuel said.

"I heard they'd cut your leg off," Retana said.

"No," said Manuel. "It got all right."

Retana leaned forward across the desk and pushed a wooden box of cigarettes toward Manuel.

"Have a cigarette," he said.

"Thanks."

Manuel lit it.

"Smoke?" he said, offering the match to Retana.

"No," Retana waved his hand, "I never smoke."

Retana watched him smoking.

"Why don't you get a job and go to work?" he said.

"I don't want to work," Manuel said. "I am a bullfighter."

"There aren't any bullfighters any more," Retana said.

"I'm a bullfighter," Manuel said.

"Yes, while you're in there," Retana said.

Manuel laughed.

Retana sat, saying nothing and looking at Manuel.

"I'll put you in a nocturnal if you want," Retana offered.

"When?" Manuel asked.

"Tomorrow night."

"I don't like to substitute for anybody," Manuel said. That was the way they all got killed. That was the way Salvator got killed. He tapped with his knuckles on the table.

"It's all I've got," Retana said.

"Why don't you put me on next week?" Manuel suggested.

"You wouldn't draw," Retana said. "All they want is Litri and Rubito and La Torre. Those kids are good."

"They'd come to see me get it," Manuel said, hopefully.

"No, they wouldn't. They don't know who you are any more."

"I've got a lot of stuff," Manuel said.

"I'm offering to put you on tomorrow night," Retana said. "You can work with young Hernandez and kill two novillos after the Charlots."

"Whose novillos?" Manuel asked.

"I don't know. Whatever stuff they've got in the corrals. What the veterinaries won't pass in the daytime."

"I don't like to substitute," Manuel said.

"You can take it or leave it," Retana said. He leaned forward over the papers. He was no longer interested. The appeal that Manuel had made to him for a moment when he thought of the old days was gone. He would like to get him to substitute for Larita because he could get him cheaply. He could get others cheaply too. He would like to help him though. Still he had given him the chance. It was up to him.

"How much do I get?" Manuel asked. He was still playing with the idea of refusing. But he knew he could not refuse.

"Two hundred and fifty pesetas," Retana said. He had thought of five hundred, but when he opened his mouth it said two hundred and fifty.

"You pay Villalta seven thousand," Manuel said.

"You're not Villalta," Retana said.

"I know it," Manuel said.

"He draws it, Manolo," Retana said in explanation.

"Sure," said Manuel. He stood up. "Give me three hundred, Retana."

"All right," Retana agreed. He reached in the drawer for a paper.

"Can I have fifty now?" Manuel asked.

"Sure," said Retana. He took a fifty-peseta note out of his pocketbook and laid it, spread out flat, on the table.

Manuel picked it up and put it in his pocket.

"What about a cuadrilla?" he asked.

"There's the boys that always work for me nights," Retana said. "They're all right."

"How about picadors?" Manuel asked.

"They're not much," Retana admitted.

" I've got to have one good pic," Manuel said.

"Get him then," Retana said. "Go and get him."

"Not out of this," Manuel said. "I'm not paying for any cuadrilla out of sixty duros."

Retana said nothing but looked at Manuel across the big desk.

"You know I've got to have one good pic," Manuel said.

Retana said nothing but looked at Manuel from a long way off.

"It isn't right," Manuel said.

Retana was still considering him, leaning back in his chair, considering him from a long way away.

"There're the regular pics," he offered.

"I know," Manuel said. "I know your regular pics."

Retana did not smille. Manuel knew it was over.

"All I want is an even break," Manuel said reasoningly. "When I go out there I want to be able to call my shots on the bull. It only takes one good picador."

He was talking to a man who was no longer listening.

"If you want something extra," Retana said, "go and get it. There will be a regular cuadrilla out there. Bring as many of your own pics as you want. The charlotada is over by 10:30."

"All right," Manuel said. "If that's the way you feel about it."

"That's the way," Retana said.

"I'll see you tomorrow night," Manuel said.

"I'll be out there," Retana said.

Manuel picked up his suitcase and went out.

"Shut the door," Retana called.

Manuel looked back. Retana was sitting forward looking at some papers. Manuel pulled the door tight until it clicked.

He went down the stairs and out of the door into the hot brightness of the street. It was very hot in the street and the light on the white buildings was sudden and hard on his eyes. He walked down the shady side of the steep street toward the Puerta del Sol. The shade felt solid and cool as running water. The heat came suddenly as he crossed the intersecting streets. Manuel saw no one he knew in all the people he passed.

Just before the Puerta del Sol he turned into a café.

It was quiet in the café. There were a few men sitting at tables against the wall. At one table four men played cards. Most of the men sat against the wall smoking, empty coffee-cups and liqueur-glasses before them on the tables. Manuel went through the long room to a small room in back. A man sat at a table in the corner asleep. Manuel sat down at one of the tables.

A waiter came in and stood beside Manuel's table.

"Have you seen Zurito?" Manuel asked him.

"He was in before lunch," the waiter answered. "He won't be back before five o'clock."

"Bring me some coffee and milk and a shot of the ordinary," Manuel said.

The waiter came back into the room carrying a tray with a big coffee-glass and a liqueur-glass on it. In his left hand he held a bottle of brandy. He swung these down to the table and a boy who had followed him poured coffee and milk into the glass from two shiny, spouted pots with long handles.

Manuel took off his cap and the waiter noticed his pigtail pinned forward on his head. He winked at the coffee-boy as he poured out the brandy into the little glass beside Manuel's coffee. The coffee-boy looked at Manuel's pale face curiously.

"You fighting here?" asked the waiter, corking up the bottle.

"Yes," Manuel said. "Tomorrow."

The waiter stood there, holding the bottle on one hip.

"You in the Charlie Chaplins?" he asked.

The coffee-boy looked away, embarrassed.

"No. In the ordinary."

"I thought they were going to have Chaves and Hernandez," the waiter said.

"No. Me and another."

"Who? Chaves or Hernandez?"

"Hernandez, I think."

"What's the matter with Chaves?"

"He got hurt."

"Where did you hear that?"

"Retana."

"Hey, Looie," the waiter called to the next room, "Chaves got cogida."

Manuel had taken the wrapper off the lumps of sugar and dropped them into his coffee. He stirred it and drank it down, sweet, hot, and warming in his empty stomach. He drank off the brandy.

"Give me another shot of that," he said to the waiter.

The waiter uncorked the bottle and poured the glass full, slopping another drink into the saucer. Another waiter had come up in front of the table. The coffee-boy was gone.

"Is Chaves hurt bad?" the second waiter asked Manuel.

"I don't know," Manuel said, "Retana didn't say."

"A hell of a lot he cares," the tall waiter said. Manuel had not seen him before. He must have just come up.

"If you stand in with Retana in this town, you're a made man," the tall waiter said. "If you aren't in with him, you might just as well go out and shoot yourself."

"You said it," the other waiter who had come in said. "You said it then."

"You're right I said it," said the tall waiter. "I know what I'm talking about when I talk about that bird."

"Look what he's done for Villalta," the first waiter said.

"And that ain't all," the tall waiter said. "Look what he's done for Marcial Lalanda. Look what he's done for Nacional."

"You said it, kid," agreed the short waiter.

Manuel looked at them, standing talking in front of his table. He had drunk his second brandy. They had forgotten about him. They were not interested in him.

"Look at that bunch of camels," the tall waiter went on. "Did you ever see this Nacional II?"

"I seen him last Sunday, didn't I?" the original waiter said.

"He's a giraffe," the short waiter said.

"What did I tell you?" the tall waiter said. "Those are Retana's boys."

"Say, give me another shot of that," Manuel said. He had poured the brandy the waiter had slopped over in the saucer into his glass and drank it while they were talking.

The original waiter poured his glass full mechanically, and the three of them went out of the room talking.

In the far corner the man was still asleep, snoring slightly on the intaking breath, his head back against the wall.

Manuel drank his brandy. He felt sleepy himself. It was too hot to go out into the town. Besides there was nothing to do. He wanted to see Zurito. He would go to sleep while he waited. He kicked his suitcase under the table to be sure it was there. Perhaps it would be better to put it back under the seat, against the wall. He leaned down and shoved it under. Then he leaned forward on the table and went to sleep.

When he woke there was someone sitting across the table from him. It was a big man with a heavy brown face like an Indian. He had been sitting there some time. He had waved the waiter away and sat reading the paper and occasionally looking down at Manuel, asleep, his head on the table. He read the paper laboriously, forming the words with his lips as he read. When it tired him he looked at Manuel. He sat heavily in the chair, his black Cordoba hat tipped forward.

Manuel sat up and looked at him.

"Hello, Zurito," he said.

"Hello, kid," the big man said.

"I've been asleep." Manuel rubbed his forehead with the back of his fist.

"I thought maybe you were."

"How's everything?"

"Good. How is everything with you?"

"Not so good."

They were both silent. Zurito, the picador, looked at Manuel's white face. Manuel looked down at the picador's enormous hands folding the paper to put away in his pocket.

"I got a favor to ask you, Manos," Manuel said.

Manosduros was Zurito's nickname. He never heard it without thinking of his huge hands. He put them forward on the table self-consciously.

"Let's have a drink," he said.

"Sure," said Manuel.

The waiter came and went and came again. He went out of the room looking back at the two men at the table.

"What's the matter, Manolo?" Zurito set down his glass.

"Would you pic two bulls for me tomorrow night?" Manuel asked, looking up at Zurito across the table.

"No," said Zurito. "I'm not pic-ing."

Manuel looked down at his glass. He had expected that answer; now he had it. Well, he had it.

"I'm sorry, Manolo, but I'm not pic-ing." Zurito looked at his hands.

"That's all right," Manuel said.

"I'm too old," Zurito said.

"I just asked you," Manuel said.

"Is it the nocturnal tomorrow?"

"That's it. I figured if I had just one good pic, I could get away with it."

"How much are you getting?"

"Three hundred pesetas."

"I get more than that for pic-ing."

"I know," said Manuel. "I didn't have any right to ask you."

"What do you keep on doing it for?" Zurito asked. "Why don't you cut off your coleta, Manolo?"

"I don't know," Manuel said.

"You're pretty near as old as I am," Zurito said.

"I don't know," Manuel said. "I got to do it. If I can fix it so that I get an even break, that's all I want. I got to stick with it, Manos."

"No, you don't."

"Yes, I do. I've tried keeping away from it."

"I know how you feel. But it isn't right. You ought to get out and stay out."

"I can't do it. Besides, I've been going good lately."

Zurito looked at his face.

"You've been in the hospital."

"But I was going great when I got hurt."

Zurito said nothing. He tipped the cognac out of his saucer into his glass.

"The papers said they never saw a better faena," Manuel said.

Zurito looked at him.

"You know when I get going I'm good," Manuel said.

"You're too old," the picador said.

"No," said Manuel. "You're ten years older than I am."

"With me it's different."

"I'm not too old," Manuel said.

They sat silent, Manuel watching the picador's face.

"I was going great till I got hurt," Manuel offered.

"You ought to have seen me, Manos," Manuel said, reproachfully.

"I don't want to see you," Zurito said. "It makes me nervous."

"You haven't seen me lately."

"I've seen you plenty."

Zurito looked at Manuel, avoiding his eyes.

"You ought to quit it, Manolo."

"I can't," Manuel said. "I'm going good now, I tell you."

Zurito leaned forward, his hands on the table.

"Listen. I'll pic for you and if you don't go big tomorrow night, you'll quit. See? Will you do that?"

"Sure."

Zurito leaned back, relieved.

"You got to quit," he said. "No monkey business. You got to cut the coleta."

"I won't have to quit," Manuel said. "You watch me. I've got the stuff."

Zurito stood up. He felt tired from arguing.

"You got to quit," he said. "I'll cut your coleta myself."

"No, you won't," Manuel said. "You won't have a chance."

Zurito called the waiter.

"Come on," said Zurito. "Come on up to the house."

Manuel reached under the seat for his suitcase. He was happy. He knew Zurito would pic for him. He was the best picador living. It was all simple now.

"Come on up to the house and we'll eat," Zurito said.

Manuel stood in the patio de caballos waiting for the Charlie Chaplins to be over. Zurito stood beside him. Where they stood it was dark. The high door that led into the bull-ring was shut. Above them they heard a shout, then another shout of laughter. Then there was silence. Manuel liked the smell of the stables about the patio de caballos. It smelled good in the dark. There was another roar from the arena and then applause, prolonged applause, going on and on.

"You ever seen these fellows?" Zurito asked, big and looming beside Manuel in the dark.

"No," Manuel said.

"They're pretty funny," Zurito said. He smiled to himself in the dark.

The high, double, tight-fitting door into the bull-ring swung open and Manuel saw the ring in the hard light of the arc-lights, the plaza, dark all the way around, rising high; around the edge of the ring were running and bowing two men dressed like tramps, followed by a third in the uniform of a hotel bell-boy who stooped and picked up the hats and canes thrown down onto the sand and tossed them back up into the darkness.

The electric light went on in the patio.

"I'll climb onto one of those ponies while you collect the kids," Zurito said.

Behind them came the jingle of the mules, coming out to go into the arena and be hitched onto the dead bull.

The members of the cuadrilla, who had been watching the burlesque from the runway between the barrera and the seats, came walking back and stood in a group talking, under the electric light in the patio. A good-looking lad in a silver-and-orange suit came up to Manuel and smiled.

"I'm Hernandez," he said and put out his hand.

Manuel shook it.

"They're regular elephants we've got tonight," the boy said cheerfully.

"They're big ones with horns," Manuel agreed.

"You drew the worst lot," the boy said.

"That's all right," Manuel said. "The bigger they are, the more meat for the poor."

"Where did you get that one?" Hernandez grinned.

"That's an old one," Manuel said. "You line up your cuadrilla, so I can see what I've got."

"You've got some good kids," Hernandez said. He was very cheerful. He had been on twice before in nocturnals and was beginning to get a following in Madrid. He was happy the fight would start in a few minutes.

"Where are the pics?" Manuel asked.

"They're back in the corrals fighting about who gets the beautiful horses," Hernandez grinned.

The mules came through the gate in a rush, the whips snapping, bells jangling and the young bull ploughing a furrow of sand.

They formed up for the paseo as soon as the bull had gone through.

Manuel and Hernandez stood in front. The youths of the cuadrillas were behind, their heavy capes furled over their arms. In back, the four picadors, mounted, holding their steel-tipped push-poles erect in the half-dark of the corral.

"It's a wonder Retana wouldn't give us enough light to see the horses by," one picador said.

"He knows we'll be happier if we don't get too good a look at these skins," another pic answered.

"This thing I'm on barely keeps me off the ground," the first picador said.

"Well, they're horses."

"Sure, they're horses."

They talked, sitting their gaunt horses in the dark.

Zurito said nothing. He had the only steady horse of the lot. He had tried him, wheeling him in the corrals and he responded to the bit and the spurs. He had taken the bandage off his right eye and cut the strings where they had tied his ears tight shut at the base. He was a good, solid horse, solid on his legs. That was all he needed. He intended to ride him all through the corrida. He had already, since he had mounted, sitting in the half-dark in the big, quilted saddle, waiting for the paseo, pic-ed through the whole corrida in his mind. The other picadors went on talking on both sides of him. He did not hear them.

The two matadors stood together in front of their three peones, their capes furled over their left arms in the same fashion. Manuel was thinking about the three lads in back of him. They were all three Madrilenos, like Hernandez, boys about nineteen. One of them, a gypsy, serious, aloof, and dark-faced, he liked the look of. He turned.

"What's your name, kid?" he asked the gypsy.

"Fuentes," the gypsy said.

"That's a good name," Manuel said.

The gypsy smiled, showing his teeth.

"You take the bull and give him a little run when he comes out," Manuel said.

"All right," the gypsy said. His face was serious. He began to think about just what he would do.

"Here she goes," Manuel said to Hernandez.

"All right. We'll go."

Heads up, swinging with the music, their right arms swinging free, they stepped out, crossing the sanded arena under the arc-lights, the cuadrillas opening out behind, the picadors riding after; behind came the bull-ring servants and the jingling mules. The crowd applauded Hernandez as they marched across the arena. Arrogant, swinging, they looked straight ahead as they marched.

They bowed before the president, and the procession broke up into its component parts. The bullfighters went over to the barrera and changed their heavy mantles for the light fighting capes. The mules went out. The picadors galloped jerkily around the ring, and two rode out the gate they had come in by. The servants swept the sand smooth.

Manuel drank a glass of water poured for him by one of Retana's deputies, who was acting as his manager and sword-handler. Hernandez came over from speaking with his own manager.

"You got a good hand, kid," Manuel complimented him.

"They like me," Hernandez said happily.

"How did the paseo go?" Manuel asked Retana's man.

"Like a wedding," said the handler. "Fine. You came like Joselito and Belmonte."

Zurito rode by, a bulky equestrian statue. He wheeled his horse and faced him toward the toril on the far side of the ring where the bull would come out. It was strange under the arc-light. He pic-ed in the hot afternoon sun for big money. He didn't like this arc-light business. He wished they would get started.

Manuel went up to him.

"Pic him, Manos," he said. "Cut him down to size for me."

"I'll pic him, kid." Zurito spat on the sand. "I'll make him jump out of the ring."

"Lean on him, Manos," Manuel said.

"I'll lean on him," Zurito said. "What's holding it up?"

"He's coming now," Manuel said.

Zurito sat there, his feet in the box-stirrups, his great legs in the buckskin-covered armor gripping the horse, the reins in his left hand, the long pic held in his right hand, his broad hat well down over his eyes to shade them from the lights, watching the distant door of the toril. His horse's ears quivered. Zurito patted him with his left hand.

The red door of the toril swung back and for a moment Zurito looked into the empty passageway far across the arena. Then the bull came out in a rush, skidding on his four legs as he came out under the lights, then charging in a gallop, moving softly in a fast gallop, silent except as he woofed through wide nostrils as he charged, glad to be free after the dark pen.

In the first row of seats, slightly bored, leaning forward to write on the cement wall in front of his knees, the substitute bullfight critic of *El Heraldo* scribbled: "Campagnero, Negro, 42, came out at 90 miles an hour with plenty of gas—"

Manuel, leaning against the barrera, watching the bull, waved his hand and the gypsy ran out, trailing his cape. The bull, in full gallop, pivoted and charged the cape, his head down, his tail rising. The gypsy moved in a zigzag, and as he passed, the bull caught sight of him and abandoned the cape to charge the man. The gyp sprinted and vaulted the red fence of the barrera as the bull struck it with his horns. He tossed into it twice with his horns, banging into the wood blindly.

The critic of *El Heraldo* lit a cigarette and tossed the match at the bull, then wrote in his note-book, "large and with enough horns to satisfy the cash customers, Campagnero showed a tendency to cut into the terrain of the bullfighters."

Manuel stepped out on the hard sand as the bull banged into the fence. Out of the corner of his eye he saw Zurito sitting the white horse close to the barrera, about a quarter of the way around the ring to the left. Manuel held the cape close in front of him, a fold in each hand, and shouted at the bull. "Huh! Huh!" The bull turned, seemed to brace against the fence as he charged in a scramble, driving into the cape as Manuel side-stepped, pivoted on his heels with the charge of the bull, and swung the cape just ahead of the horns. At the end of the swing he was facing the bull again and held the cape in the same position close in front of his body, and pivoted again as the bull recharged. Each time, as he swung, the crowd shouted.

Four times he swung with the bull, lifting the cape so it billowed full, and each time bringing the bull around to charge again. Then, at the end of the fifth swing, he held the cape against his hip and pivoted, so the cape swung out like a ballet dancer's skirt and wound the bull around himself like a belt, to step clear, leaving the bull facing Zurito on the white horse, come up and planted firm, the horse facing the bull, its ears forward, its lips nervous, Zurito, his hat over his eyes, leaning forward, the long pole sticking out before and behind in a sharp angle under his right arm, held half-way down, the triangular iron point facing the bull.

El Heraldo's second-string critic, drawing on his cigarette, his eyes on the bull, wrote: "The veteran Manolo designed a series of acceptable veronicas, ending in a very Belmontistic recorte that earned applause from the regulars, and we entered the tercio of the cavalry."

Zurito sat his horse, measuring the distance between the bull and the end of the pic. As he looked, the bull gathered himself together and charged, his eyes on the horse's chest. As he lowered his head to hook, Zurito sunk the point of the pic in the swelling hump of muscle above the bull's shoulder, leaned all his weight on the shaft, and with his left hand pulled the white horse into the air, front hoofs pawing, and swung him to the right as he pushed the bull under and through so the horns passed safely under the horse's belly and the horse came down, quivering, the bull's tail brushing his chest as he charged the cape Hernandez offered him.

Hernandez ran sideways, taking the bull out and away with the cape, toward the other picador. He fixed him with a swing of the cape, squarely facing the horse and rider, and stepped back. As the bull saw the horse he charged. The picador's lance slid along his back, and as the shock of the charge lifted the horse, the picador was already halfway out of the saddle, lifting his right leg clear as he missed with the lance and falling to the left side to keep the horse between him and the bull. The horse, lifted and gored, crashed over with the bull driving into him, the picador gave a shove with his boots against the horse and lay clear, waiting to be lifted and hauled away and put on his feet.

Manuel let the bull drive into the fallen horse; he was in no hurry, the picador was safe; besides, it did a picador like that good to worry. He'd stay on longer next time. Lousy pics! He looked across the sand at Zurito a little way out from the barrera, his horse rigid, waiting.

"Huh!" he called to the bull, "Tomar!" holding the cape in both hands so it would catch his eye. The bull detached himself from the horse and charged the cape, and Manuel, running sideways and holding the cape spread wide, stopped, swung on his heels, and brought the bull sharply around facing Zurito.

"Campagnero accepted a pair of varas for the death of one rosinante, with Hernandez and Manolo at the quites," *El Heraldo's* critic wrote. "He pressed on the iron and clearly showed he was no horse-lover. The veteran Zurito resurrected some of his old stuff with the pike-pole, notably the suerte—"

"Olé! Olé!" the man sitting beside him shouted. The shout was lost in the roar of the crowd, and he slapped the critic on the back. The critic looked up to see Zurito, directly below him, leaning far out over his horse, the length of the pic rising in a sharp angle under his armpit, holding the pic almost by the point, bearing down with all his weight, holding the bull off, the bull pushing and driving to get at the horse, and Zurito, far out, on top of him, holding him, holding him, and slowly pivoting the horse against the pressure, so that at last he was clear. Zurito felt the moment when the horse was clear and the bull could come past, and relaxed the absolute steel lock of his resistance, and the triangular steel point of the pic ripped in the bull's hump of shoulder muscle as he tore loose to find Hernandez's cape before his muzzle. He charged blindly into the cape and the boy took him out into the open arena.

Zurito sat patting his horse and looking at the bull charging the cape that Hernandez swung for him out under the bright light while the crowd shouted.

"You see that one?" he said to Manuel.

"It was a wonder," Manuel said.

"I got him that time," Zurito said. "Look at him now."

At the conclusion of a closely turned pass of the cape the bull slid to his knees. He was up at once, but far out across the sand Manuel and Zurito saw the shine of the pumping flow of blood, smooth against the black of the bull's shoulder.

"I got him that time," Zurito said.

"He's a good bull," Manuel said.

"If they gave me another shot at him, I'd kill him," Zurito said.

"They'll change the thirds on us," Manuel said.

"Look at him now," Zurito said.

"I got to go over there," Manuel said, and started on a run for the other side of the ring, where the monos were leading a horse out by the bridle toward the bull, whacking him on the legs with rods and all, in a procession, trying to get him toward the bull, who stood, dropping his head, pawing, unable to make up his mind to charge.

Zurito, sitting his horse, walking him toward the scene, not missing any detail, scowled.

Finally the bull charged, the horse leaders ran for the barrera, the picador hit too far back, and the bull got under the horse, lifted him, threw him onto his back.

Zurito watched. The monos, in their red shirts, running out to drag the picador clear. The picador, now on his feet, swearing and flopping his arms. Manuel and Hernandez standing ready with their capes. And the bull, the great, black bull, with a horse on his back, hooves dangling, the bridle caught in the horns. Black bull with a horse on his back, staggering short-legged, then arching his neck and lifting, thrusting, charging to slide the horse off, horse sliding down. Then the bull into a lunging charge at the cape Manuel spread for him.

The bull was slower now, Manuel felt. He was bleeding badly. There was a sheen of blood all down his flank.

Manuel offered him the cape again. There he came, eyes open, ugly, watching the cape. Manuel stepped to the side and raised his arms, tightening the cape ahead of the bull for the veronica.

Now he was facing the bull. Yes, his head was going down a little. He was carrying it lower. That was Zurito.

Manuel flopped the cape; there he comes; he side-stepped and swung in another veronica. He's shooting awfully accurately, he thought. He's had enough fight, so he's watching now. He's hunting now. Got his eye on me. But I always give him the cape.

He shook the cape at the bull; there he comes; he side-stepped. Awful close that time. I don't want to work that close to him.

The edge of the cape was wet with blood where it had swept along the bull's back as he went by.

All right, here's the last one.

Manuel, facing the bull, having turned with him each charge, offered the cape with his two hands. The bull looked at him. Eyes watching, horns straight forward, the bull looked at him, watching.

"Huh!" Manuel said, "Toro!" and leaning back, swung the cape forward. Here he comes. He side-stepped, swung the cape in back of him, and pivoted, so the bull followed a swirl of cape and then was left with nothing, fixed by the pass, dominated by the cape. Manuel swung the cape under his muzzle with one hand, to show the bull was fixed, and walked away.

There was no applause.

Manuel walked across the sand toward the barrera, while Zurito rode out of the ring. The trumpet had blown to change the act to the planting of the banderillos while Manuel had been working with the bull. He had not consciously noticed it. The monos were spreading canvas over the two dead horses and sprinkling sawdust around them.

Manuel came up to the barrera for a drink of water. Retana's man handed him the heavy porous jug.

Fuentes, the tall gypsy, was standing holding a pair of banderillos, holding them together, slim, red sticks, fish-hook points out. He looked at Manuel.

"Go on out there," Manuel said.

The gypsy trotted out. Manuel set down the jug and watched. He wiped his face with his handkerchief.

The critic of *El Heraldo* reached for the bottle of warm champagne that stood between his feet, took a drink, and finished his paragraph.

"–the aged Manolo rated no applause for a vulgar series of lances with the cape and we entered the third of the palings."

Alone in the center of the ring the bull stood, still fixed. Fuentes, tall, flat-backed, walking toward him arrogantly, his arms spread out, the two slim, red sticks, one in each hand, held by the fingers, points straight forward. Fuentes walked forward. Back of him and to one side was a peon with a cape. The bull looked at him and was no longer fixed.

His eyes watched Fuentes, now standing still. Now he leaned back, calling to him. Fuentes twitched the two banderillos and the light on the steel points caught the bull's eye.

His tail went up and he charged.

He came straight, his eyes on the man. Fuentes stood still, leaning back, the banderillos pointing forward. As the bull lowered his head to hook, Fuentes leaned backward, his arms came together and rose, his two hands touching, the banderillos two descending red lines, and leaning forward drove the points into the bull's shoulder, leaning far in over the bull's horns and pivoting on the two upright sticks, his legs tight together, his body curving to one side to let the bull pass.

"Olé!" from the crowd.

The bull was hooking wildly, jumping like a trout, all four feet off the ground. The red shaft of the banderillos tossed as he jumped.

Manuel, standing at the barrera, noticed that he looked always to the right.

"Tell him to drop the next pair on the right," he said to the kid who started to run out to Fuentes with the new banderillos.

A heavy hand fell on his shoulder. It was Zurito.

"How do you feel, kid?" he asked.

Manuel was watching the bull.

Zurito leaned forward on the barrera, leaning the weight of his body on his arms. Manuel turned to him.

"You're going good," Zurito said.

Manuel shook his head. He had nothing to do now until the next third. The gypsy was very good with the banderillos. The bull would come to him in the next third in good shape. He was a good bull. It had all been easy up to now. The final stuff with the sword was all he worried over. He did not really worry. He did not even think about it. But standing there he had a heavy sense of apprehension. He looked out at the bull, planning his faena, his work with the red cloth that was to reduce the bull, to make him manageable.

The gypsy was walking out toward the bull again, walking heel-and-toe, insultingly, like a ballroom dancer, the red shafts of the banderillos twitching with his walk. The bull watched him, not fixed now, hunting him, but waiting to get close enough so he could be sure of getting him, getting the horns into him.

As Fuentes walked forward the bull charged. Fuentes ran across the quarter of a circle as the bull charged and, as he passed running backward, stopped, swung forward, rose on his toes, arm straight out, and sunk the banderillos straight down into the right of the big shoulder muscles as the bull missed him.

The crowd were wild about it.

"That kid won't stay in this night stuff long," Retana's man said to Zurito.

"He's good," Zurito said.

"Watch him now."

They watched.

Fuentes was standing with his back against the barrera. Two of the cuadrilla were back of him, with their capes ready to flop over the fence to distract the bull.

The bull, with his tongue out, his barrel heaving, was watching the gypsy. He thought he had him now. Back against the red planks. Only a short charge away. The bull watched him.

The gypsy bent back, drew back his arms, the banderillos pointing at the bull. He called to the bull, stamped one foot. The bull was suspicious. He wanted the man. No more barbs in the shoulder.

Fuentes walked a little closer to the bull. Bent back. Called again. Somebody in the crowd shouted a warning.

"He's too damn close," Zurito said.

"Watch him," Retana's man said.

Leaning back, inciting the bull with the banderillos, Fuentes jumped, both feet off the ground. As he jumped the bull's tail rose and he charged. Fuentes came down on his toes, arms straight out, whole body arching forward, and drove the shafts straight down as he swung his body clear of the right horn.

The bull crashed into the barrera where the flopping capes had attracted his eye as he lost the man.

The gypsy came running along the barrera toward Manuel, taking the applause of the crowd. His vest was ripped where he had not quite cleared the point of the horn. He was happy about it, showing it to the spectators. He made the tour of the ring. Zurito saw him go by, smiling, pointing at his vest. He smiled.

Somebody else was planting the last pair of banderillos. Nobody was paying any attention.

Retana's man tucked a baton inside the red cloth of a muleta, folded the cloth over it, and handed it over the barrera to Manuel. He reached in the leather sword-case, took out a sword, and holding it by its leather scabbard, reached it over the fence to Manuel. Manuel pulled the blade out by the red hilt and the scabbard fell limp.

He looked at Zurito. The big man saw he was sweating.

"Now you get him, kid," Zurito said.

Manuel nodded.

"He's in good shape," Zurito said.

"Just like you want him," Retana's man assured him.

Manuel nodded.

The trumpeter, up under the roof, blew for the final act, and Manuel walked across the arena toward where, up in the dark boxes, the president must be.

In the front row of seats the substitute bullfight critic of *El Heraldo* took a long drink of the warm champagne. He had decided it was not worth while to write a running story and would write up the corrida back in the office. What the hell was it anyway? Only a nocturnal. If he missed anything he would get it out of the morning papers. He took another drink of the champagne. He had a date at Maxim's at twelve. Who were these bullfighters anyway? Kids and bums. A bunch of bums. He put his pad of paper in his pocket and looked over toward Manuel, standing very much alone in the ring, gesturing with his hat in a salute toward a box he could not see high up in the dark plaza. Out in the ring the bull stood quiet, looking at nothing.

"I dedicate this bull to you, Mr. President, and to the public of Madrid, the most intelligent and generous of the world," was what Manuel was saying. It was a formula. He said it all. It was a little long for nocturnal use.

He bowed at the dark, straightened, tossed his hat over his shoulder, and, carrying the muleta in his left hand and the sword in his right, walked out toward the bull.

Manuel walked toward the bull. The bull looked at him; his eyes were quick. Manuel noticed the way the banderillos hung down on his left shoulder and the steady sheen of blood from Zurito's pic-ing. He noticed the way the bull's feet were. As he walked forward, holding the muleta in his left hand and the sword in his right, he watched the bull's feet. The bull could not charge without gathering his feet together. Now he stood square on them, dully.

Manuel walked toward him, watching his feet. This was all right. He could do this. He must work to get the bull's head down, so he could go in past the horns and kill him. He did not think about the sword, not about killing the bull. He thought about one thing at a time. The coming things oppressed him, though. Walking forward, watching the bull's feet, he saw successively his eyes, his wet muzzle, and the wide, forward-pointing spread of his horns. The bull had light circles about his eyes. His eyes watched Manuel. He felt he was going to get this little one with the white face.

Standing still now and spreading the red cloth of the muleta with the sword, pricking the point into the cloth so that the sword, now held in his left hand, spread the red flannel like the jib of a boat, Manuel noticed the points of the bull's horns. One of them was splintered from banging against the barrera. The other was sharp as a porcupine quill. Manuel noticed while spreading the muleta that the white base of the horn was stained red. While he noticed these things he did not lose sight of the bull's feet. The bull watched Manuel steadily.

He's on the defensive now, Manuel thought. He's reserving himself. I've got to bring him out of that and get his head down. Always get his head down. Zurito had his head down once, but he's come back. He'll bleed when I start him going and that will bring it down.

Holding the muleta, with the sword in his left hand widening it in front of him, he called to the bull.

The bull looked at him.

He leaned back insultingly and shook the wide-spread flannel.

The bull saw the muleta. It was a bright scarlet under the arc-light. The bull's legs tightened.

Here he comes. Whoosh! Manuel turned as the bull came and raised the muleta so that it passed over the bull's horns and swept down his broad back from head to tail. The bull had gone clean up in the air with the charge. Manuel had not moved.

At the end of the pass the bull turned like a cat coming around a corner and faced Manuel.

He was on the offensive again. His heaviness was gone. Manuel noted the fresh blood shining down the black shoulder and dripping down the bull's leg. He drew the sword out of the muleta and held it in his right hand. The muleta held low down in his left hand, leaning toward the left, he called to the bull. The bull's legs tightened, his eyes on the muleta. Here he comes, Manuel thought. Yuh!

He swung with the charge, sweeping the muleta ahead of the bull, his feet firm, the sword following the curve, a point of light under the arcs.

The bull recharged as the pase natural finished and Manuel raised the muleta for a pase de pecho. Firmly planted, the bull came by his chest under the raised muleta. Manuel leaned his head back to avoid the clattering banderillo shafts. The hot, black bull body touched his chest as it passed.

Too damn close, Manuel thought. Zurito, leaning on the barrera, spoke rapidly to the gypsy, who trotted out toward Manuel with a cape. Zurito pulled his hat down low and looked out across the arena at Manuel.

Manuel was facing the bull again, the muleta held low and to the left. The bull's head was down as he watched the muleta.

"If it was Belmonte doing that stuff, they'd go crazy," Retana's man said.

Zurito said nothing. He was watching Manuel out in the center of the arena.

"Where did the boss dig this fellow up?" Retana's man asked.

"Out of the hospital," Zurito said.

"That's where he's going damn quick," Retana's man said.

Zurito turned on him.

"Knock on that," he said, pointing to the barrera.

"I was just kidding, man," Retana's man said.

"Knock on the wood."

Retana's man leaned forward and knocked three times on the barrera.

"Watch the faena," Zurito said.

Out in the center of the ring, under the lights, Manuel was kneeling, facing the bull, and as he raised the muleta in both hands the bull charged, tail up.

Manuel swung his body clear and, as the bull recharged, brought around the muleta in a half-circle that pulled the bull to his knees.

"Why, that one's a great bullfighter," Retana's man said.

"No, he's not," said Zurito.

Manuel stood up and, the muleta in his left hand, the sword in his right, acknowledged the applause from the dark plaza.

The bull had humped himself up from his knees and stood waiting, his head hung low.

Zurito spoke to two of the other lads of the cuadrilla and they ran out to stand back of Manuel with their capes. There were four men back of him now. Hernandez had followed him since he first came out with the muleta. Fuentes stood watching, his cape held against his body, tall, in repose, watching lazy-eyed. Now the two came up. Hernandez motioned them to stand one at each side. Manuel stood alone, facing the bull.

Manuel waved back the men with the capes. Stepping back cautiously, they saw his face was white and sweating.

Didn't they know enough to keep back? Did they want to catch the bull's eye with the capes after he was fixed and ready? He had enough to worry about without that kind of thing.

The bull was standing, his four feet square, looking at the muleta. Manuel furled the muleta in his left hand. The bull's eyes watched it. His body was heavy on his feet. He carried his head low, but not too low.

Manuel lifted the muleta at him. The bull did not move. Only his eyes watched.

He's all lead, Manuel thought. He's all square. He's framed right. He'll take it.

He thought in bullfight terms. Sometimes he had a thought and the particular piece of slang would not come into his mind and he could not realize the thought. His instincts and his knowledge worked automatically, and his brain worked slowly and in words. He knew all about bulls. He did not have to think about them. He just did the right thing. His eyes noted things and his body performed the necessary measures without thought. If he thought about it, he would be gone.

Now, facing the bull, he was conscious of many things at the same time. There were the horns, the one splintered, the other smoothly sharp, the need to profile himself toward the left horn, lance himself short and straight, lower the muleta so the bull would follow it, and, going in over the horns, put the sword all the way into a little spot about as big as a five-peseta piece straight in back of the neck, between the sharp pitch of the bull's shoulders. He must do all this and must then come out from between the horns. He was conscious he must do all this, but his only thought was in words: "Corto y derecho."

"Corto y derecho," he thought, furling the muleta. Short and straight. Corto y derecho, he drew the sword out of the muleta, profiled on the splintered left horn, dropped the muleta across his body, so his right hand with the sword on the level with his eye made the sign of the cross, and, rising on his toes, sighted along the dipping blade of the sword at the spot high up between the bull's shoulders.

Corto y derecho he launched himself on the bull.

There was a shock, and he felt himself go up in the air. He pushed on the sword as he went up and over, and it flew out of his hand. He hit the ground and the bull was on him. Manuel, lying on the ground, kicked at the bull's muzzle with his slippered feet. Kicking, kicking, the bull after him, missing him in his excitement, bumping him with his head, driving the horns into the sand. Kicking like a man keeping a ball in the air, Manuel kept the bull from getting a clean thrust at him.

Manuel felt the wind on his back from the capes flopping at the bull, and then the bull was gone, gone over him in a rush. Dark, as his belly went over. Not even stepped on.

Manuel stood up and picked up the muleta. Fuentes handed him the sword. It was bent where it had struck the shoulder-blade. Manuel straightened it on his knee and ran toward the bull, standing now beside one of the dead horses. As he ran, his jacket flopped where it had been ripped under his arm pit.

"Get him out of there," Manuel shouted to the gypsy. The bull had smelled the blood of the dead horse and ripped into the canvas-cover with his horns. He charged Fuentes's cape, with the canvas hanging from his splintered horn, and the crowd laughed. Out in the ring, he tossed his head to rid himself of the canvas. Hernandez, running up from behind him, grabbed the end of the canvas and neatly lifted it off the horn.

The bull followed it in a half-charge and stopped still. He was on the defensive again. Manuel was walking toward him with the sword and muleta. Manuel swung the muleta before him. The bull would not charge.

Manuel profiled toward the bull, sighting along the dipping blade of the sword. The bull was motionless, seemingly dead on his feet, incapable of another charge.

Manuel rose to his toes, sighting along the steel, and charged.

Again there was the shock and he felt himself being borne back in a rush, to strike hard on the sand. There was no chance of kicking this time. The bull was on top of him. Manuel lay as though dead, his head on his arms, and the bull bumped him. Bumped his back, bumped his face in the sand. He felt the horn go into the sand between his folded arms. The bull hit him in the small of the back. His face drove into the sand. The horn drove through one of his sleeves and the bull ripped it off. Manuel was tossed clear and the bull followed the capes.

Manuel got up, found the sword and muleta, tried the point of the sword with his thumb, and then ran toward the barrera for a new sword.

Retana's man handed him the sword over the edge of the barrera.

"Wipe off your face," he said.

Manuel, running again toward the bull, wiped his bloody face with his handkerchief. He had not seen Zurito. Where was Zurito?

The cuadrilla had stepped away from the bull and waited with their capes. The bull stood, heavy and dull again after the action.

Manuel walked toward him with the muleta. He stopped and shook it. The bull did not respond. He passed it right and left, left and right before the bull's muzzle. The bull's eyes watched it and turned with the swing, but he would not charge. He was waiting for Manuel.

Manuel was worried. There was nothing to do but go in. Corto y derecho. He profiled close to the bull, crossed the muleta in front of his body and charged. As he pushed in the sword, he jerked his body to the left to clear the horn. The bull passed him and the sword shot up in the air, twinkling under the arc-lights, to fall red-hilted on the sand.

Manuel ran over and picked it up. It was bent and he straightened it over his knee.

As he came running toward the bull, fixed again now, he passed Hernandez standing with his cape.

"He's all bone," the boy said encouragingly.

Manuel nodded, wiping his face. He put the bloody handkerchief in his pocket.

There was the bull. He was close to the barrera now. Damn him. Maybe he was all bone. Maybe there was not any place for the sword to go in. The hell there wasn't! He'd show them.

He tried a pass with the muleta and the bull did not move. Manuel chopped the muleta back and forth in front of the bull. Nothing doing.

He furled the muleta, drew the sword out, profiled and drove in on the bull. He felt the sword buckle as he shoved it in, leaning his weight on it, and then it shot high in the air, end-over-ending into the crowd. Manuel had jerked clear as the sword jumped.

The first cushions thrown down out of the dark missed him. Then one hit him in the face, his bloody face looking toward the crowd. They were coming down fast. Spotting the sand. Somebody threw an empty champagne-bottle from close range. It hit Manuel on the foot. He stood there watching the dark, where the things were coming from. Then something whished through the air and struck by him. Manuel leaned over and picked it up. It was his sword. He straightened it over his knee and gestured with it to the crowd.

"Thank you," he said. "Thank you."

Oh, the dirty bastards! Dirty bastards! Oh, the lousy, dirty bastards! He kicked into a cushion as he ran.

There was the bull. The same as ever. All right, you dirty, lousy bastard!

Manuel passed the muleta in front of the bull's black muzzle.

Nothing doing.

You won't! All right. He stepped close and jammed the sharp peak of the muleta into the bull's damp muzzle.

The bull was on him as he jumped back and as he tripped on a cushion he felt the horn go into him, into his side. He grabbed the horn with his two hands and rode backward, holding tight onto the place. The bull tossed him and he was clear. He lay still. It was all right. The bull was gone.

He got up coughing and feeling broken and gone. The dirty bastards!

"Give me the sword," he shouted. "Give me the stuff."

Fuentes came up with the muleta and the sword.

Hernandez put his arm around him.

"Go on to the infirmary, man," he said. "Don't be a damn fool."

"Get away from me," Manuel said. "Get to hell away from me."

He twisted free. Hernandez shrugged his shoulders. Manuel ran toward the bull.

There was the bull standing, heavy, firmly planted.

All right, you bastard! Manuel drew the sword out of the muleta, sighted with the same movement, and flung himself onto the bull. He felt the sword go in all the way. Right up to the guard. Four fingers and his thumb into the bull. The blood was hot on his knuckles, and he was on top of the bull.

The bull lurched with him as he lay on, and seemed to sink; then he was standing clear. He looked at the bull going down slowly over on his side, then suddenly four feet in the air.

Then he gestured at the crowd, his hand warm from the bull blood.

All right, you bastards! He wanted to say something, but he started to cough. It was hot and choking. He looked down for the muleta. He must go over and salute the president. President, hell! He was sitting down looking at something. It was the bull. His four feet up. Thick tongue out. Things crawling around on his belly and under his legs. Crawling where the hair was thin. Dead bull. To hell with the bull! To hell with them all! He started to get to his feet and commenced to cough. He sat down again, coughing. Somebody came and pushed him up.

They carried him across the ring to the infirmary, running with him across the sand, standing blocked at the gate as the mules came in, then around under the dark passageway, men grunting as they took him up the stairway, and then laid him down.

The doctor and two men in white were waiting for him. They laid him out on the table. They were cutting away his shirt. Manuel felt tired. His whole chest felt scalding inside. He started to cough and they held something to his mouth. Everybody was very busy.

There was an electric light in his eyes. He shut his eyes.

He heard someone coming very heavily up the stairs. Then he did not hear it. Then he heard a noise far off. That was the crowd. Well, somebody would have to kill his other bull. They had cut away all his shirt. The doctor smiled at him. There was Retana.

"Hello, Retana!" Manuel said. He could not hear his voice.

Retana smiled at him and said something. Manuel could not hear it.

Zurito stood beside the table, bending over where the doctor was working. He was in his picador clothes, without his hat.

Zurito said something to him. Manuel could not hear it.

Zurito was speaking to Retana. One of the men in white smiled and handed Retana a pair of scissors. Retana gave them to Zurito. Zurito said something to Manuel. He could not hear it.

To hell with this operating-table. He'd been on plenty of operating-tables before. He was not going to die. There would be a priest if he was going to die.

Zurito was saying something to him. Holding up the scissors.

That was it. They were going to cut off his coleta. They were going to cut off his pigtail.

Manuel sat up on the operating-table. The doctor stepped back, angry. Someone grabbed him and held him.

"You couldn't do a thing like that, Manos," he said.

He heard suddenly, clearly, Zurito's voice.

"That's all right," Zurito said. "I won't do it. I was joking."

"I was going good," Manuel said. "I didn't have any luck. That was all."

Manuel lay back. They had put something over his face. It was all familiar. He inhaled deeply. He felt very tired. He was very, very tired. They took the thing away from his face.

"I was going good," Manuel said weakly. "I was going great."

Retana looked at Zurito and started for the door.

"I'll stay here with him," Zurito said.

Retana shrugged his shoulders.

Manuel opened his eyes and looked at Zurito.

"Wasn't I going good, Manos?" he asked, for confirmation.

"Sure," said Zurito. "You were going great."

The doctor's assistant put the cone over Manuel's face and he inhaled deeply. Zurito stood awkwardly, watching.

THOMAS WOLFE

[1900–1938]

THE WRITING OF NO AMERICAN except Whitman ever vibrated with so exuberant and desperate a craving for life—all of life, experienced simultaneously and on every level—as the four novels of Thomas Wolfe, who died before he had lived thirty-eight years.

Thomas Clayton Wolfe was born in Asheville, North Carolina, on October 3, 1900. Though his father's delight in reciting verse aloud filled his ears with the sound of oratorical poetry, it filled neither his pockets nor his stomach; Wolfe's was a miserable childhood spent doing odd jobs in an endless scrabble for pennies. When he was fifteen his family managed to send him to the University of North Carolina, where he edited the college newspaper and magazine. He wrote several one-act plays and, in 1920, entered the drama workshop at Harvard which O'Neill had attended a few years before. Receiving his M.A., he became an instructor at the Washington Square College of New York University, an undedicated teacher who was determined to be a playwright.

His plays were praised but not produced. He was already thinking of a novel when, after six years of teaching, he went to Europe. In London he began writing, "about things I had known," he said, "the immediate life and experience that had been familiar to me in my childhood." He returned to New York and to teaching. Writing came easily to him, often too easily. Words flowed from him freely, inexhaustibly, furiously. Two and a half years' work produced a mammoth book: 350,000 words. During the writing he had been sustained by the stage designer Aline Bernstein; as he attempted to shape his material for publication he was aided by the editor of Scribner's, Maxwell Perkins. These were the two close friends whom he extolled, hurt, loved, and finally—to save his half-arrogant, half-guilty conscience—cast off.

Look Homeward, Angel was published a few days before Wolfe's twenty-ninth birthday. Wolfe, a six-foot-six, black-haired giant, was desperately afraid of criticism, but his novel was received with surprised superlatives except in Asheville, where the citizens, recognizing their town in Wolfe's book, were outraged.

Wolfe went to Paris, where his homesickness brought an onrushing of memories in a "torrential and ungovernable flood" which produced a structureless, uplifted, endless rhapsody, Of Time and the River. It took six years and Perkins' tireless editing and pruning to complete the book which was to catch "all the flicks and darts and haunting lights that flash across the mind." Wolfe had returned to America in 1931, but as the publication date neared, fearful of the critics who could say the second novel failed to match the first, fled to Paris. Again his work was highly praised.

The four novels (the two which appeared during Wolfe's lifetime plus The Web and the Rock and You Can't Go Home Again, published posthumously) are one towering autobiography. In the later two books he changed the name and description of the central figure to evade the identifiable autobiographical elements, but always he wrote about himself.

Wolfe died suddenly, of complications which followed an attack of pneumonia. It was September 15, 1938, before he had passed his thirty-eighth birthday.

Wolfe's faults are a part of his excess—the exuberant egocentrism, the eloquence that slides into verbosity, the rhetoric on the verge of rant. However, properly balanced, the defects are minor blemishes when weighed against the writer's major accomplishments, the grandeur of his aim and the affirmation of his vision. A poet who happened to use the medium of prose, he was the victim of his own gigantism. "Wolfe made the best failure," William Faulkner, his fellow-Southerner, said, "because he tried the hardest to say the most."

CREDO

From *You Can't Go Home Again*

I HAVE NEVER BEFORE MADE a statement of belief [George wrote in his conclusion to Fox],[1] although I have believed in many things and said that I believed in them. But I have never stated my belief in concrete terms because almost every element of my nature has been opposed to the hard framework, the finality, of formulation.

Just as you are the rock of life, I am the web; just as you are Time's granite, so, I think, am I Time's plant. My life, more than that of anyone I know, has taken on the form of growth. No man that I have known was ever more deeply rooted in the soil of Time and Memory, the weather of his individual universe, than was I. You followed me through the course of that whole herculean conflict. For four years, as I lived and worked and explored the jungle depths of Brooklyn—jungle depths coincident with those of my own soul—you were beside me, you followed, and you stuck.

You never had a doubt that I would finish—make an end—round out the cycle—come to the whole of it. The only doubt was mine, enhanced, tormented by my own fatigue and desperation, and by the clacking of the feeble and malicious little tongues which, knowing nothing, whispered that I would never make an end again because I could not begin. We both knew how grotesquely false this was—so false and so grotesque that it was some-

[1] In *You Can't Go Home Again* George Webber is a slightly disguised Thomas Wolfe; Foxhall Edwards is an even less disguised friend, his editor Maxwell Perkins.

times the subject of an anguished and exasperated laugh. The truth was so far different that my own fears were just the opposite: that I might never make an end to anything again because I could never get through telling what I knew, what I felt and thought and *had* to say about it.

That was a giant web in which I was caught, the product of my huge inheritance—the torrential recollectiveness, derived out of my mother's stock, which became a living, million-fibered integument that bound me to the past, not only of my own life, but of the very earth from which I came, so that nothing in the end escaped from its inrooted and all-feeling explorativeness. The way the sunlight came and went upon a certain day, the way grass felt between bare toes, the immediacy of noon, the slamming of an iron gate, the halting skreak upon the corner of a street car, the liquid sound of shoe leather on the pavements as men came home to lunch, the smell of turnip greens, the clang of ice tongs, and the clucking of a hen—and then Time fading like a dream, Time melting to oblivion, when I was two years old. Not only this, but all lost sounds and voices, forgotten memories exhumed with a constant pulsing of the brain's great ventricle, until I lived them in my dreams, carrying the stupendous and unceasing burden of them through the unresting passages of sleep. Nothing that had ever been was lost. It all came back in an endless flow, even the blisters of the paint upon the mantelpiece in my father's house, the smell of the old leather sofa with my father's print upon it, the smell of dusty bottles and of cobwebs in the cellar, the casual stomping of a slow, gaunt hoof upon the pulpy lumber of a livery stable floor, the proud lift and flourish of a whisking tail, and the oaty droppings. I lived again through all times and weathers I had known—through the fag-ends of wintry desolation in the month of March and the cold, bleak miseries of ragged red at sunset, the magic of young green in April, the blind horror and suffocation of concrete places in midsummer sun where no limits were, and October with the smell of fallen leaves and wood smoke in the air. The forgotten moments and unnumbered hours came back to me with all the enormous cargo of my memory, together with lost voices in the mountains long ago, the voices of the kinsmen dead and never seen, and the houses they had built and died in, and the rutted roads they trod upon, and every unrecorded moment that Aunt Maw had told me of the lost and obscure lives they led long, long ago. So did it all revive in the ceaseless pulsings of the giant ventricle, so did the plant go back, stem by stem, root by root, and filament by filament, until it was complete and whole, compacted of the very earth that had produced it, and of which it was itself the last and living part.

You stayed beside me like the rock you are until I unearthed the plant, followed it back through every fiber of its pattern to its last and tiniest enrootment in the blind, dumb earth. And now that it is finished, and the circle come full swing—we, too, are finished, and I have a thing to say:

I believe that we are lost here in America, but I believe we shall be found. And this belief, which mounts now to the catharsis of knowledge and conviction, is for me—and I think for all of us—not only our own hope, but America's everlasting, living dream. I think the life which we have fashioned in America, and which has fashioned us—the forms we made, the cells that grew, the honeycomb that was created—was self-destructive in its nature, and must be destroyed. I think these forms are dying, and must die, just as I know that America and the people in it are deathless, undiscovered, and immortal, and must live.

I think the true discovery of America is before us. I think the true fulfillment of our spirit, of our people, of our mighty and immortal land, is yet to come. I think the true discovery of our own democracy is still before us. And I think that all these things are certain as the morning, as inevitable as noon. I think I speak for most men living when I say that our America is Here, is Now, and beckons on before us, and that this glorious assurance is not only our living hope, but our dream to be accomplished.

I think the enemy is here before us, too. But I think we know the forms and faces of the enemy, and in the knowledge that we know him, and shall meet him, and eventually must conquer him is also our living hope. I think the enemy is here before us with a thousand faces, but I think we know that all his faces wear one mask. I think the enemy is single selfishness and compulsive greed. I think the enemy is blind, but has the brutal power of his blind grab. I do not think the enemy was born yesterday, or that he grew to manhood forty years ago, or that he suffered sickness and collapse in 1929, or that we began without the enemy, and that our vision faltered, that we lost the way, and suddenly were in his camp. I think the enemy is old as Time, and evil as Hell, and that he has been here with us from the beginning. I think he stole our earth from us, destroyed our wealth, and ravaged and despoiled our land. I think he took our people and enslaved them, that he polluted the fountains of our life, took unto himself the rarest treasures of our own possession, took our bread and left us with a crust, and, not content, for the nature of the enemy is insatiate—tried finally to take from us the crust.

I think the enemy comes to us with the face of innocence and says to us: "I am your friend."

I think the enemy deceives us with false words and lying phrases, saying:

"See, I am one of you—I am one of your children, your son, your brother, and your friend. Behold how sleek and fat I have become—and all because I am just one of you, and your friend. Behold how rich and powerful I am—and all because I am one of you—shaped in your way of life, of thinking, of accomplishment. What I am, I am because I am one of you, your humble brother and your friend. Behold," cries Enemy, "the man I am, the man I have become, the thing I have accomplished—and reflect. Will you destroy this thing? I assure you that it is the most precious thing you have. It is yourselves, the projection of each of you, the triumph of your individual lives, the thing that is rooted in your blood, and native to your stock, and inherent in the traditions of America. It is the thing that all of you may hope to be," says Enemy, "for—" humbly—"am I not just one of you? Am I not just your brother and your son? Am I not the living image of what each of you may hope to be, would wish to be, would desire for his own son? Would you destroy this glorious incarnation of your own heroic self? If you do, then," says Enemy, "you destroy yourselves—you kill the thing that is most gloriously American, and in so killing, kill yourselves."

He lies! And now we know he lies! He is not gloriously, or in any other way, ourselves. He is not our friend, our son, our brother. And he is not American! For, although he has a thousand familiar and convenient faces, his own true face is old as Hell.

Look about you and see what he has done.

Dear Fox, old friend, thus we have come to the end of the road that we were to go together. My tale is finished—and so farewell.

But before I go, I have just one more thing to tell you:

Something has spoken to me in the night, burning the tapers of the waning year; something has spoken in the night, and told me I shall die, I know not where. Saying:

"To lose the earth you know, for greater knowing; to lose the life you have, for greater life; to leave the friends you loved, for greater loving; to find a land more kind than home, more large than earth——

"—Whereon the pillars of this earth are founded, toward which the conscience of the world is tending—a wind is rising, and the rivers flow."

OGDEN NASH

[1902–]

Hard Lines, Free Wheeling, Good Intentions, The Bad Parent's Garden of Verse, I'm a Stranger Here Myself, *and* Versus *are some of the titles of Ogden Nash's books, which contain mad rhymes with good reasons. Nash was born August 19, 1902, in Rye, New York, but most of his forebears seem to be Southerners. His great-grandfather was Revolutionary Governor of North Carolina, and this ancestor's brother gave his name to Nashville, Tennessee. Nash's education was haphazard. He spent a term at St. George's School in Newport, Rhode Island where, he says, he ruined his entire nervous system carving lamb for a table of fourteen-year-old monsters. He was a student at Harvard but declined to remain there after a year.*

Coming to New York he intended to be a bond salesman; in two years, he confessed, he sold one bond—to his godmother. He entered literature by way of a couple of publishing houses and The New Yorker; *married and had two daughters, who became writers and artists; moved for a while to Hollywood; wrote the libretto for a musical comedy,* One Touch of Venus, *with S. J. Perelman; and was frequently heard on the lecture platform, on radio, and on television.*

Nash's manner is deceptively casual. His seemingly inconsequential quirks are not those of a clown but of a social critic, a sly recorder of men's—and, more particularly, of women's—foibles. His rhymes are as dexterous as they are astonishing. He is the master of rhymes that miss being perfect but which are livelier than any conventionally matching pair. He joins words which rhyme reluctantly, and even resentfully—words which never before had any relations with each other and which will never be on rhyming terms again. For example:

What would you do if you were up a dark alley with Caesar Borgia
And he was coming torgia . . .

Another example of his weird way with rhymes is his reply to Dorothy Parker's quip, "Men never make passes at girls who wear glasses:"

A girl who is bespectacled
She may not get her necktacled;
But safety pins and bassinets
Await the girl who fassinets.

Nash's style is unlike that of any other humorist; he combines common sense and uncommon nonsense in the most original light verse ever written in America.

FOUR SPECIMENS FROM OGDEN'S MENASHERIE

THE TERMITE

Some primal termite knocked on wood
And tasted it, and found it good,
And that is why your Cousin May
Fell through the parlor floor today.

THE TURKEY

There is nothing more perky
Than a masculine turkey.
When he struts he struts
With no ifs or buts.

When his face is apoplectic
His harem grows hectic,
And when he gobbles
Their universe wobbles.

THE DUCK

Behold the duck.
It does not cluck.
A cluck it lacks.
It quacks.

It is specially fond
Of a puddle or pond.
When it dines or sups,
It bottoms ups.

THE CANARY

The song of canaries
Never varies,
And when they're moulting
They're pretty revolting.

DON'T CRY, DARLING, IT'S BLOOD ALL RIGHT

Whenever poets want to give you the idea that something is particularly meek and mild,
They compare it to a child,
Thereby proving that though poets with poetry may be rife
They don't know the facts of life.
If of compassion you desire either a tittle or a jot,
Don't try to get it from a tot.
Hard-boiled, sophisticated adults like me and you
May enjoy ourselves thoroughly with *Little Women* and *Winnie-the-Pooh*,
But innocent infants these titles from their reading course eliminate
As soon as they discover that it was honey and nuts and mashed potatoes instead of human flesh that Winnie-the-Pooh and Little Women ate.
Innocent infants have no use for fables about rabbits or donkeys or tortoises or porpoises,
What they want is something with plenty of well-mutilated corpoises.
Not on legends of how the rose came to be a rose instead of a petunia is their fancy fed,
But on the inside story of how somebody's bones got ground up to make somebody else's bread.
They'll go to sleep listening to the story of the little beggar-maid who got to be queen by being kind to the bees and the birds,
But they're all eyes and ears the minute they suspect a wolf or a giant is going to tear some poor woodcutter into quarters or thirds.
It really doesn't take much to fill their cup;
All they want is for somebody to be eaten up.
Therefore I say unto you, all you poets who are so crazy about meek and mild little children and their angelic air,
If you are sincere and really want to please them, why just go out and get yourselves devoured by a bear.

THE SEVEN SPIRITUAL AGES OF MRS. MARMADUKE MOORE

Mrs. Marmaduke Moore, at the age of ten
(Her name was Jemina Jevons then),
Was the quaintest of little country maids.
Her pigtails slapped on her shoulderblades;
She fed the chickens, and told the truth
And could spit like a boy through a broken tooth.
She could climb a tree to the topmost perch,
And she used to pray in the Methodist church.

At the age of twenty her heart was pure,
And she caught the fancy of Mr. Moore.
He broke his troth (to a girl named Alice),
And carried her off to his city palace,
Where she soon forgot her childhood piety
And joined in the orgies of high society.
Her voice grew English, or, say, Australian,
And she studied to be an Episcopalian.

At thirty our lives are still before us,
But Mr. Moore had a friend in the chorus.
Connubial bliss was overthrown
And Mrs. Moore now slumbered alone.
Hers was a nature that craved affection;
She gave herself up to introspection;
Then, finding theosophy rather dry,
Found peace in the sweet Bahai and Bahai.

Forty! and still an abandoned wife.
She felt old urges stirring to life.
She dipped her locks in a bowl of henna
And booked a passage through to Vienna.
She paid a professor a huge emolument
To demonstrate what his ponderous volume meant.
Returning, she preached to the unemployed
The gospel according to St. Freud.

Fifty! she haunted museums and galleries,
And pleased young men by augmenting their salaries.
Oh, it shouldn't occur, but it does occur,
That poets are made by fools like her.
Her salon was full of frangipani,
Roumanian, Russian and Hindustani,
And she conquered par as well as bogey
By reading a book and going Yogi.

Sixty! and time was on her hands—
Maybe remorse and maybe glands.
She felt a need for a free confession
To publish each youthful indiscretion,
And before she was gathered to her mothers,
To compare her sinlets with those of others,
Mrs. Moore gave a joyous whoop,
And immersed herself in the Oxford group.

That is the story of Mrs. Moore,
As far as it goes. But of this I'm sure—
When seventy stares her in the face
She'll have found some other state of grace.
Mohammed may be her Lord and master,
Or Zeus, or Mithros or Zoroaster.
For when a lady is badly sexed
God knows what God is coming next.

WOLCOTT GIBBS

[1902–1958]

DISMISSED BY Who's Who *merely as "writer, critic," Wolcott Gibbs was one of the mainstays of* The New Yorker *and a generally invaluable ironist. He was born March 15, 1902, in New York City, and became a reporter for various newspapers before he joined* The New Yorker *as copyreader, editorial writer, and drama critic. At fifty-two he was co-founder and editor of* The Fire Islander *but was too ill to continue his labors on this local magazine or other enterprises. He died August 16, 1958, at his home on Fire Island, New York.*

Gibbs's book of short stories, punningly entitled A Bed of Neuroses, *appeared when he was thirty-five; at forty-four he published* Season in the Sun, *which four years later was turned into a successful satirical comedy. Whether Gibbs indulged in childhood reminiscences or presented pictures of the bizarre and slightly alcoholic society in which he often moved, his touch was light, mettlesome, and as acute as it was brisk.*

RING OUT, WILD BELLS

WHEN I FINALLY got around to seeing Max Reinhardt's cinema version of "A Midsummer-Night's Dream," and saw a child called Mickey Rooney playing Puck, I remembered suddenly that long ago I had taken the same part.

Our production was given on the open-air stage at the Riverdale County School, shortly before the war. The scenery was only the natural scenery of that suburban dell, and the cast was exclusively male, ranging in age from eleven to perhaps seventeen. While we had thus preserved the pure, Elizabethan note of the original, it must be admitted that our version had its drawbacks. The costumes were probably the worst things we had to bear, and even Penrod, tragically arrayed as Launcelot in his sister's stockings and his father's drawers, might have been embarrassed for us. Like Penrod, we were costumed by our parents, and like the Schofields, they seemed on the whole a little weak historically. Half of the ladies were inclined to favor the Elizabethan, and they had constructed rather bunchy ruffs and farthingales for their offspring; others, who had read as far as the stage directions and learned that the action took place in an Athenian wood, had produced something vaguely Athenian, usually beginning with a sheet. Only the fairies had a certain uniformity. For some reason their parents had all decided on cheesecloth, with here and there a little ill-advised trimming with tinsel.

My own costume was mysterious, but spectacular. As nearly as I have ever been able to figure things out, my mother found her inspiration for it in a Maxfield Parrish picture of a court jester. Beginning at the top, there was a cap with three stuffed horns; then, for the main part, a pair of tights that covered me to my wrists and ankles; and finally slippers with stuffed toes that curled up at the ends. The whole thing was made out of silk in alternate green and red stripes, and (unquestionably my poor mother's most demented stroke) it was covered from head to foot with a thousand tiny bells. Because all our costumes were obviously perishable, we never wore them in rehearsal, and naturally nobody knew that I was invested with these peculiar sound effects until I made my entrance at the beginning of the second act.

Our director was a man who had strong opinions about how Shakespeare should be played, and Puck was one of his favorite characters. It was his theory that Puck, being "the incarnation of mischief," never ought to be still a minute, so I had been coached to bound onto the stage, and once there to dance up and down, cocking my head and waving my arms.

"I want you to be a little whirlwind," this man said.

Even as I prepared to bound onto the stage, I had my own misgivings about those dangerously abundant gestures, and their probable effect on my bells. It was too late, however, to invent another technique for playing Puck, even if there had been room for anything but horror in my mind. I bounded onto the stage.

The effect, in its way, must have been superb. With every leap I rang like a thousand children's sleighs, my melodies foretelling God knows what worlds of merriment to the enchanted spectators. It was even worse when I came to the middle of the stage and went into my gestures. The other ringing had been loud but sporadic. This was persistent, varying only slightly in volume and pitch with the vehemence of my gestures. To a blind man, it must have sounded as though I had recklessly decided to accompany myself on a xylophone. A maturer actor would probably have made up his mind that an emergency existed, and abandoned his gestures as impracticable under the circumstances. I was thirteen, and incapable of innovations. I had been told by responsible authorities that gestures went with this part, and I continued to make them. I also continued to ring—a silvery music, festive and horrible.

If the bells were hard on my nerves, they were even worse for the rest of the cast, who were totally unprepared for my new interpretation. Puck's first remark is addressed to one of the fairies, and it is mercifully brief.

I said, "How now, spirit! Whither wander you?"

This unhappy child, already embarrassed by a public appearance in cheesecloth and tinsel, was also burdened with an opening speech of sixteen lines in verse. He began bravely:

"Over hill, over dale,
  Through brush, through brier,
Over park, over pale,
  Through flood, through fire . . ."

At the word "fire," my instructions were to bring my hands up from the ground in a long, wavery sweep, intended to represent fire. The bells pealed. To my startled ears, it sounded more as if they exploded. The fairy stopped in his lines and looked at me sharply. The jingling, however, had diminished; it was no more than as if a faint wind stirred my bells, and he went on:

"I do wander everywhere,
Swifter than the moone's sphere . . ."

Here again I had another cue, for a sort of swoop and dip indicating the swiftness of the moone's sphere. Again the bells rang out, and again the performance stopped in its tracks. The fairy was clearly troubled by these interruptions. He had, however, a child's strange acceptance of the inscrutable, and was even able to regard my bells as a last-minute adult addition to the program, nerve-racking but not to be questioned. I'm sure it was only this that got him through that first speech.

My turn, when it came, was even worse. By this time the audience had succumbed to a helpless gaiety. Every time my bells rang, laughter swept the spectators, and this mounted and mingled with the bells until everything else was practically inaudible. I began my speech, another long one, and full of incomprehensible references to Titania's changeling.

"Louder!" said somebody in the wings. "You'll have to talk louder."

It was the director, and he seemed to be in a dangerous state.

"And for heaven's sake, stop that jingling!" he said.

I talked louder, and I tried to stop the jingling, but it was no use. By the time I got to the end of my speech, I was shouting and so was the audience. It appeared that I had very little control over the bells, which continued to jingle in spite of my passionate efforts to keep them quiet.

All this had a very bad effect on the fairy, who by this time had many symptoms of a complete nervous collapse. However, he began his next speech:

> "Either I mistake your shape and making quite,
> Or else you are that shrewd and knavish sprite
> Called Robin Goodfellow: are you not he
> That . . ."

At this point I forgot that the rules had been changed and I was supposed to leave out the gestures. There was a furious jingling, and the fairy gulped.

> "Are you not he that, that . . ."

He looked miserably at the wings, and the director supplied the next line, but the tumult was too much for him. The unhappy child simply shook his head.

"Say anything!" shouted the director desperately. "Anything at all!"

The fairy only shut his eyes and shuddered.

"All right!" shouted the director. "All right, Puck. *You* begin *your* next speech."

By some miracle, I actually did remember my next lines, and had opened my mouth to begin on them when suddenly the fairy spoke. His voice was a high, thin monotone, and there seemed to be madness in it, but it was perfectly clear.

"Fourscore and seven years ago," he began, "our fathers brought forth on this continent a new nation, conceived . . ."

He said it right through to the end, and it was certainly the most successful speech ever made on that stage, and probably one of the most successful speeches ever made on any stage. I don't remember, if I ever knew, how the rest of us ever picked up the dull, normal thread of the play after that extraordinary performance, but we must have, because I know it went on. I only remember that in the next intermission the director cut off my bells with his penknife, and after that things quieted down and got dull.

JOHN STEINBECK

[1902–]

JOHN STEINBECK WAS painfully conscious of the problems which beset simple people in a hugely complicated, seemingly alien world. He wrote about the odd, forlorn, and displaced—migrant laborers, itinerant fruit-pickers, the misfits and castoffs of society—with compassion, a hatred of cruelty, and a heartfelt love of humanity. He was born February 27, 1902, in Salinas, California, and the best of his writing has the state of his birth as its setting. His father, a county treasurer, was of German descent; his mother, a teacher, came from a Northern Ireland family. Steinbeck attended Stanford University though he didn't take a degree. The courses which interested him most were not literature but marine biology—his Sea of Cortez *is an account of a biological expedition to the Galapagos Islands.*

It took a long time and several books before Steinbeck emerged from obscurity and poverty. He tried reporting but was dismissed because he skimped facts in favor of a personal philosophy. He wrote three novels which few people read and which went almost unnoticed until they were rediscovered more than a decade later. To save himself from starving he carried bricks, painted houses, worked as a caretaker of an estate, and picked fruit like the Joads he portrayed unforgettably in Grapes of Wrath.

Grapes of Wrath *established Steinbeck as one of the most deeply troubled and passionate novelists of his day. It was attacked as "brutally realistic," a "pernicious" representation of a system which the author considered worse than feudalism, and a vicious piece of special pleading. Nevertheless, it won the Pulitzer award, and a film prize when it was made into a motion picture. An almost equally forceful though less moving novel,* East of Eden, *was also turned into a popular film play.* Of Mice and Men, In Dubious Battle, *and some of the stories in* The Long Valley *were similiarly sociological and dramatic.*

Another and almost opposite side of Steinbeck is apparent in The Pearl, *a delicate version of a Mexican legend, and in* Tortilla Flat, Cannery Row, *and* Sweet Thursday, *a series of tales concerning drifters and outcasts—amoral but winning Mexican* paisanos, *hoboes, and others whom life had cast up on the California coast. Steinbeck treated his half-shrewd, half-innocent pagans in the carefree manner of the great naturalists. Because of the humorous frankness of his short stories, he was sometimes compared to Villon, but he disclaimed any relationship to the vagabond poet. He saw the* Tortilla Flat *series as a modern* Gesta Romanorum, *"those outrageous tales with monkish morals appended," but whose main purpose was "to present a little known and to me delightful people—people of laughter and kindness, of honest lust and direct eyes, of courtesy beyond politeness." Whether he writes bitterly or tenderly or broadly, Steinbeck never writes without penetration and sympathetic understanding.*

THE LEADER OF THE PEOPLE

On Saturday afternoon Billy Buck, the ranch-hand, raked together the last of the old year's haystack and pitched small forkfuls over the wire fence to a few mildly interested cattle. High in the air small clouds like puffs of cannon smoke were driven eastward by the March wind. The wind could be heard whishing in the brush on the ridge crests, but no breath of it penetrated down into the ranch-cup.

The little boy, Jody, emerged from the house eating a thick piece of buttered bread. He saw Billy working on the last of the haystack. Jody tramped down scuffing his shoes in a way he had been told was destructive to good shoe-leather. A flock of white pigeons flew out of the black cypress tree as Jody passed, and circled the tree and landed again. A half-grown tortoise-shell cat leaped from the bunkhouse porch, galloped on stiff legs across the road, whirled and galloped back again. Jody picked up a stone to help the game along, but he was too late, for the cat was under the porch before the stone could be discharged. He threw the stone into the cypress tree and started the white pigeons on another whirling flight.

Arriving at the used-up haystack, the boy leaned against the barbed wire fence. "Will that be all of it, do you think?" he asked.

The middle-aged ranch-hand stopped his careful raking and stuck his fork into the ground. He took off his black hat and smoothed down his hair. "Nothing left of it that isn't soggy from ground moisture," he said. He replaced his hat and rubbed his dry leathery hands together.

"Ought to be plenty mice," Jody suggested.

"Lousy with them," said Billy. "Just crawling with mice."

"Well, maybe, when you get all through, I could call the dogs and hunt the mice."

"Sure, I guess you could," said Billy Buck. He lifted a forkful of the damp ground-hay and threw it into the air. Instantly three mice leaped out and burrowed frantically under the hay again.

Jody sighed with satisfaction. Those plump, sleek, arrogant mice were doomed. For eight months they had lived and multiplied in the haystack. They had been immune from cats, from traps, from poison and from Jody. They had grown smug in their security, overbearing and fat. Now the time of disaster had come; they would not survive another day.

Billy looked up at the top of the hills that surrounded the ranch. "Maybe you better ask your father before you do it," he suggested.

"Well, where is he? I'll ask him now."

"He rode up to the ridge ranch after dinner. He'll be back pretty soon."

Jody slumped against the fence post. "I don't think he'd care."

As Billy went back to his work he said ominously, "You'd better ask him anyway. You know how he is."

Jody did know. His father, Carl Tiflin, insisted upon giving permission for anything that was done on the ranch, whether it was important or not. Jody sagged farther against the post until he was sitting on the ground. He looked up at the little puffs of wind-driven cloud. "Is it like to rain, Billy?"

"It might. The wind's good for it, but not strong enough."

"Well, I hope it don't rain until after I kill those damn mice." He looked over his shoulder to see whether Billy had noticed the mature profanity. Billy worked on without comment.

Jody turned back and looked at the side-hill where the road from the outside world came down. The hill was washed with lean March sunshine. Silver thistles, blue lupins and a few poppies bloomed among the sage bushes. Halfway up the hill Jody could see Doubletree Mutt, the black dog, digging in a squirrel hole. He paddled for a while and then paused to kick bursts of dirt out between his hind legs, and he dug with an earnestness which belied the knowledge he must have had that no dog had ever caught a squirrel by digging in a hole.

Suddenly, while Jody watched, the black dog stiffened, and backed out of the hole and looked up the hill toward the cleft in the ridge where the road came through. Jody looked up too. For a moment Carl Tiflin on horseback stood out against the pale sky and then he moved down the road toward the house. He carried something white in his hand.

The boy started to his feet. "He's got a letter," Jody cried. He trotted away toward the ranch house, for the letter would probably be read aloud and he wanted to be there. He reached the house before his father did, and ran in. He heard Carl dismount from his creaking saddle and slap the horse on the side to send it to the barn where Billy would unsaddle it and turn it out.

Jody ran into the kitchen. "We got a letter!" he cried.

His mother looked up from a pan of beans. "Who has?"

"Father has. I saw it in his hand."

Carl strode into the kitchen then, and Jody's mother asked, "Who's the letter from, Carl?"

He frowned quickly. "How did you know there was a letter?"

She nodded her head in the boy's direction. "Big-Britches Jody told me."

Jody was embarrassed.

His father looked down at him contemptuously. "He is getting to be a Big-Britches," Carl said. "He's minding everybody's business but his own. Got his big nose into everything."

Mrs. Tiflin relented a little. "Well, he hasn't enough to keep him busy. Who's the letter from?"

Carl still frowned on Jody. "I'll keep him busy if he isn't careful." He held out a sealed letter. "I guess it's from your father."

Mrs. Tiflin took a hairpin from her head and slit open the flap. Her lips pursed judiciously. Jody saw her eyes snap back and forth over the lines. "He says," she translated, "he says he's going to drive out Saturday to stay for a little while. Why, this is Saturday. The letter must have been delayed." She looked at the postmark. "This was mailed day before yesterday. It should have been here yesterday." She looked up questioningly at her husband, and then her face darkened angrily. "Now what have you got that look on you for? He doesn't come often."

Carl turned his eyes away from her anger. He could be stern with her most of the time, but when occasionally her temper arose, he could not combat it.

"What's the matter with you?" she demanded again.

In his explanation there was a tone of apology Jody himself might have used. "It's just that he talks," Carl said lamely. "Just talks."

"Well, what of it? You talk yourself."

"Sure I do. But your father only talks about one thing."

"Indians!" Jody broke in excitedly. "Indians and crossing the plains!"

Carl turned fiercely on him. "You get out, Mr. Big-Britches! Go on, now! Get out!"

Jody went miserably out the back door and closed the screen with elaborate quietness. Under the kitchen window his shamed, downcast eyes fell upon a curiously shaped stone, a stone of such fascination that he squatted down and picked it up and turned it over in his hands.

The voices came clearly to him through the open kitchen window. "Jody's damn well right," he heard his father say. "Just Indians and crossing the plains. I've heard that story about how the horses got driven off about a thousand times. He just goes on and on, and he never changes a word in the things he tells."

When Mrs. Tiflin answered her tone was so changed that Jody, outside the window, looked up from his study of the stone. Her voice had become soft and explanatory. Jody knew how her face would have changed to match the tone. She said quietly. "Look at it this way, Carl. That was the big thing in my father's life. He led a wagon train clear across the plains to the coast, and when it was finished, his life was done. It was a big thing to do, but it didn't last long enough. Look!" she continued, "it's as though he was born to do that, and after he finished it, there wasn't anything more for him to do but think about it and talk about it. If there'd been any farther west to go, he'd have gone. He's told me so himself. But at last there was the ocean. He lives right by the ocean where he had to stop."

She had caught Carl, caught him and entangled him in her soft tone.

"I've seen him," he agreed quietly. "He goes down and stares off west over the ocean." His voice sharpened a little. "And then he goes up to the Horseshoe Club in Pacific Grove, and he tells people how the Indians drove off the horses."

She tried to catch him again. "Well, it's everything to him. You might be patient with him and pretend to listen."

Carl turned impatiently away. "Well, if it gets too bad, I can always go down to the bunkhouse and sit with Billy," he said irritably. He walked through the house and slammed the front door after him.

Jody ran to his chores. He dumped the grain to the chickens without chasing any of them. He gathered the eggs from the nests. He trotted into the house with the wood and interlaced it so carefully in the wood-box that two armloads seemed to fill it to overflowing.

His mother had finished the beans by now. She stirred up the fire and brushed off the stove-top with a turkey wing. Jody peered cautiously at her to see whether any rancor toward him remained. "Is he coming today?" Jody asked.

"That's what his letter said."

"Maybe I better walk up the road to meet him."

Mrs. Tiflin clanged the stove-lid shut. "That would be nice," she said. "He'd probably like to be met."

"I guess I'll just do it then."

Outside, Jody whistled shrilly to the dogs. "Come on up the hill," he commanded. The two dogs waved their tails and ran ahead. Along the roadside the sage had tender new tips. Jody tore off some pieces and rubbed them on his hands until the air was filled with the sharp wild smell. With a rush the dogs leaped from the road and yapped into the brush after a rabbit. That was the last Jody saw of them, for when they failed to catch the rabbit, they went back home.

Jody plodded on up the hill toward the ridge top. When he reached the little cleft where the road came through, the afternoon wind struck him and blew up his hair and ruffled his shirt. He looked down on the little hills and ridges below and then out at the huge green Salinas Valley. He could see the white town of Salinas far out in the flat and the flash of its windows under the waning sun. Directly below him, in an oak tree, a crow congress had convened.The tree was black with crows all cawing at once.

Then Jody's eyes followed the wagon road down from the ridge where he stood, and lost it behind a hill, and picked it up again on the other side. On that distant stretch he saw a cart slowly pulled by a bay horse. It disappeared behind the hill. Jody sat down on the ground and watched the place where the cart would reappear again. The wind sang on the hilltops and the puff-ball clouds hurried eastward.

Then the cart came into sight and stopped. A man dressed in black dismounted from the seat and walked to the horse's head. Although it was so far away, Jody knew he had unhooked the check-rein, for the horse's head dropped forward. The horse moved on, and the man walked slowly up the hill beside it. Jody gave a glad cry and ran down the road toward them. The squirrels bumped along off the road, and a road-runner flirted its tail and raced over the edge of the hill and sailed out like a glider.

Jody tried to leap into the middle of his shadow at every step. A stone rolled under his foot and he went down. Around a little bend he raced, and there, a short distance ahead, were his grandfather and the cart. The boy dropped from his unseemly running and approached at a dignified walk.

The horse plodded stumble-footedly up the hill and the old man walked beside it. In the lowering sun their giant shadows flickered darkly behind them. The grandfather was dressed in a black broadcloth suit and he wore kid congress gaiters and a black tie on a short, hard collar. He carried his black slouch hat in his hand. His white beard was cropped close and his white eyebrows overhung his eyes like moustaches. The blue eyes were sternly merry. About the whole face and figure there was a granite dignity, so that every motion seemed an impossible thing. Once at rest, it seemed the old man would be stone, would never move again. His steps were slow and certain. Once made, no step could ever be retraced; once headed in a direction, the path would never bend nor the pace increase nor slow.

When Jody appeared around the bend, Grandfather waved his hat slowly in welcome, and he called, "Why, Jody! Come down to meet me, have you?"

Jody sidled near and turned and matched his step to the old man's step and stiffened his body and dragged his heels a little. "Yes, sir," he said. "We got your letter only today."

"Should have been here yesterday," said Grandfather. "It certainly should. How are all the folks?"

"They're fine, sir." He hesitated and then suggested shyly, "Would you like to come on a mouse hunt tomorrow, sir?"

"Mouse hunt, Jody?" Grandfather chuckled. "Have the people of this generation come down to hunting mice? They aren't very strong, the new people, but I hardly thought mice would be game for them."

"No, sir. It's just play. The haystack's gone. I'm going to drive out the mice to the dogs. And you can watch, or even beat the hay a little."

The stern, merry eyes turned down on him. "I see. You don't eat them, then. You haven't come to that yet."

Jody explained, "The dogs eat them, sir. It wouldn't be much like hunting Indians, I guess."

"No, not much—but then later, when the troops were hunting Indians and shooting children and burning teepees, it wasn't much different from your mouse hunt."

They topped the rise and started down into the ranch cup, and they lost the sun from their shoulders. "You've grown," Grandfather said. "Nearly an inch, I should say."

"More," Jody boasted. "Where they mark me on the door, I'm up more than an inch since Thanksgiving even."

Grandfather's rich throaty voice said, "Maybe you're getting too much water and turning to pith and stalk. Wait until you head out, and then we'll see."

Jody looked quickly into the old man's face to see whether his feelings should be hurt, but there was no will to injure, no punishing nor putting-in-your-place light in the keen blue eyes. "We might kill a pig," Jody suggested.

"Oh, no! I couldn't let you do that. You're just humoring me. It isn't the time and you know it."

"You know Riley, the big boar, sir?"

"Yes, I remember Riley well."

"Well, Riley ate a hole into that same haystack, and it fell down on him and smothered him."

"Pigs do that when they can," said Grandfather.

"Riley was a nice pig, for a boar, sir. I rode him sometimes, and he didn't mind."

A door slammed at the house below them, and they saw Jody's mother standing on the porch waving her apron in welcome. And they saw Carl Tiflin walking up from the barn to be at the house for the arrival.

The sun had disappeared from the hills by now. The blue smoke from the house chimney hung in flat layers in the purpling ranch-cup. The puff-ball clouds, dropped by the falling wind, hung listlessly in the sky.

Billy Buck came out of the bunkhouse and flung a wash basin of soapy water on the ground. He had been shaving in mid-week, for Billy held Grandfather in reverence, and Grandfather said that Billy was one of the few men of the new generation who had not gone soft. Although Billy was in middle age, Grandfather considered him a boy. Now Billy was hurrying toward the house too.

When Jody and Grandfather arrived, the three were waiting for them in front of the yard gate.

Carl said, "Hello, sir. We've been looking for you."

Mrs. Tiflin kissed Grandfather on the side of his beard, and stood still while his big hand patted her shoulder. Billy shook hands solemnly, grinning under his straw moustache. "I'll put up your horse," said Billy, and he led the rig away.

Grandfather watched him go, and then, turning back to the group, he said as he had said a hundred times before, "There's a good boy. I knew his father, old Mule-tail Buck. I never knew why they called him Mule-tail except he packed mules."

Mrs. Tiflin turned and led the way into the house. "How long are you going to stay, Father? Your letter didn't say."

"Well, I don't know. I thought I'd stay about two weeks. But I never stay as long as I think I'm going to."

In a short while they were sitting at the white oilcloth table eating their supper. The lamp with the tin reflector hung over the table. Outside the dining-room windows the big moths battered softly against the glass.

Grandfather cut his steak into tiny pieces and chewed slowly. "I'm hungry," he said. "Driving out here got my appetite up. It's like when we were crossing. We all got so hungry every night we could hardly wait to let the meat get done. I could eat about five pounds of buffalo meat every night."

"It's moving around does it," said Billy. "My father was a government packer. I helped him when I was a kid. Just the two of us could about clean up a deer's ham."

"I knew your father, Billy," said Grandfather. "A fine man he was. They called him Mule-tail Buck. I don't know why except he packed mules."

"That was it," Billy agreed. "He packed mules."

Grandfather put down his knife and fork and looked around the table. "I remember one time we ran out of meat—" His voice dropped to a curious low sing-song, dropped into a tonal groove the story had worn for itself. "There was no buffalo, no antelope, not even rabbits. The hunters couldn't even shoot a coyote. That was the time for the leader to be on the watch. I was the leader, and I kept my eyes open. Know why? Well, just the minute the people began to get hungry they'd start slaughtering the team oxen. Do you believe that? I've heard of parties that just ate up their draft cattle. Started from the middle and worked toward the ends. Finally they'd eat the lead pair, and then the wheelers. The leader of a party had to keep them from doing that."

In some manner a big moth got into the room and circled the hanging kerosene lamp. Billy got up and tried to clap it between his hands. Carl struck with a cupped palm and caught the moth and broke it. He walked to the window and dropped it out.

"As I was saying," Grandfather began again, but Carl interrupted him. "You'd better eat some more meat. All the rest of us are ready for our pudding."

Jody saw a flash of anger in his mother's eyes. Grandfather picked up his knife and fork. "I'm pretty hungry, all right," he said. "I'll tell you about that later."

When supper was over, when the family and Billy Buck sat in front of the fireplace in the other room, Jody anxiously watched Grandfather. He saw the signs he knew. The bearded head leaned forward; the eyes lost their sternness and looked wonderingly into the fire; the big lean fingers laced themselves on the black knees. "I wonder," he began, "I just wonder whether I ever told you how those thieving Piutes drove off thirty-five of our horses."

"I think you did," Carl interrupted. "Wasn't it just before you went up into the Tahoe country?"

Grandfather turned quickly toward his son-in-law. "That's right. I guess I must have told you that story."

"Lots of times," Carl said cruelly, and he avoided his wife's eyes. But he felt the angry eyes on him, and he said, " 'Course I'd like to hear it again."

Grandfather looked back at the fire. His fingers unlaced and laced again. Jody knew how he felt, how his insides were collapsed and empty. Hadn't Jody been called a Big-Britches that very afternoon? He arose to heroism and opened himself to the term Big-Britches again. "Tell about Indians," he said softly.

Grandfather's eyes grew stern again. "Boys always want to hear about Indians. It was a job for men, but boys want to hear about it. Well, let's see. Did I ever tell you how I wanted each wagon to carry a long iron plate?"

Everyone but Jody remained silent. Jody said, "No. You didn't."

"Well, when the Indians attacked, we always put the wagons in a circle and fought from between the wheels. I thought that if every wagon carried a long plate with rifle holes, the men could stand the plates on the outside of the wheels when the wagons were in the circle and they would be protected. It would save lives and that would make up for the extra weight of the iron. But of course the party wouldn't do it. No party had done it before and they couldn't see why they should go to the expense. They lived to regret it, too."

Jody looked at his mother, and knew from her expression that she was not listening at all. Carl picked at a callus on his thumb and Billy Buck watched a spider crawling up the wall.

Grandfather's tone dropped into its narrative groove again. Jody knew in advance exactly what words would fall. The story droned on, speeded up for the attack, grew sad over the wounds, struck a dirge at the burials on the great plains. Jody sat quietly watching Grandfather. The stern blue eyes were detached. He looked as though he were not very interested in the story himself.

When it was finished, when the pause had been politely respected as the frontier of the story, Billy Buck stood up and stretched and hitched his trousers. "I guess I'll turn in," he said. Then he faced Grandfather. "I've got an old powder horn and a cap and ball pistol down to the bunkhouse. Did I ever show them to you?"

Grandfather nodded slowly. "Yes, I think you did, Billy. Reminds me of a pistol I had when I was leading the people across." Billy stood politely until the little story was done, and then he said, "Good night," and went out of the house.

Carl Tiflin tried to turn the conversation then. "How's the country between here and Monterey? I've heard it's pretty dry."

"It is dry," said Grandfather. "There's not a drop of water in the Laguna

Seca. But it's a long pull from '87. The whole country was powder then, and in '61 I believe all the coyotes starved to death. We had fifteen inches of rain this year."

"Yes, but it all came too early. We could do with some now." Carl's eye fell on Jody. "Hadn't you better be getting to bed?"

Jody stood up obediently. "Can I kill the mice in the old haystack, sir?"

"Mice? Oh! Sure, kill them all off. Billy said there isn't any good hay left."

Jody exchanged a secret and satisfying look with Grandfather. "I'll kill every one tomorrow," he promised.

Jody lay in his bed and thought of the impossible world of Indians and buffaloes, a world that had ceased to be forever. He wished he could have been living in the heroic time, but he knew he was not of heroic timber. No one living now, save possibly Billy Buck, was worthy to do the things that had been done. A race of giants had lived then, fearless men, men of a staunchness unknown in this day. Jody thought of the wide plains and of the wagons moving across like centipedes. He thought of Grandfather on a huge white horse, marshaling the people. Across his mind marched the great phantoms, and they marched off the earth and they were gone.

He came back to the ranch for a moment, then. He heard the dull rushing sound that space and silence make. He heard one of the dogs, out in the doghouse, scratching a flea and bumping his elbow against the floor with every stroke. Then the wind arose again and the black cypress groaned and Jody went to sleep.

He was up half an hour before the triangle sounded for breakfast. His mother was rattling the stove to make the flames roar when Jody went through the kitchen. "You're up early," she said. "Where are you going?"

"Out to get a good stick. We're going to kill the mice today."

"Who is 'we'?"

"Why, Grandfather and I."

"So you've got him in it. You always like to have someone in with you in case there's blame to share."

"I'll be right back," said Jody. "I just want to have a good stick ready for after breakfast."

He closed the screen door after him and went out into the cool blue morning. The birds were noisy in the dawn and the ranch cats came down from the hill like blunt snakes. They had been hunting gophers in the dark, and although the four cats were full of gopher meat, they sat in a semi-circle at the back door and mewed piteously for milk. Doubletree Mutt and Smasher moved sniffing along the edge of the brush, performing the duty with rigid ceremony, but when Jody whistled, their heads jerked up and their tails waved. They plunged down to him, wriggling their skins and yawning. Jody patted their heads seriously, and moved on to the weathered scrap pile. He selected an old broom handle and a short piece of inch-square scrap wood. From his pocket he took a shoelace and tied the ends of the sticks loosely together to make a flail. He whistled his new weapon through the air and struck the ground experimentally, while the dogs leaped aside and whined with apprehension.

Jody turned and started down past the house toward the old haystack ground to look over the field of slaughter, but Billy Buck, sitting patiently on the back steps, called to him, "You better come back. It's only a couple of minutes till breakfast."

Jody changed his course and moved toward the house. He leaned his flail against the steps. "That's to drive the mice out," he said. "I'll bet they're fat. I'll bet they don't know what's going to happen to them today."

"No, nor you either," Billy remarked philosophically, "nor me, nor anyone."

Jody was staggered by this thought. He knew it was true. His imagination twitched away from the mouse hunt. Then his mother came out on the back porch and struck the triangle, and all thoughts fell in a heap.

Grandfather hadn't appeared at the table when they sat down. Billy nodded at his empty chair. "He's all right? He isn't sick?"

"He takes a long time to dress," said Mrs. Tiflin. "He combs his whiskers and rubs up his shoes and brushes his clothes."

Carl scattered sugar on his mush. "A man that's led a wagon train across the plains has got to be pretty careful how he dresses."

Mrs. Tiflin turned on him. "Don't do that, Carl! Please don't!" There was more of threat than of request in her tone. And the threat irritated Carl.

"Well, how many times do I have to listen to the story of the iron plates, and the thirty-five horses? That time's done. Why can't he forget it, now it's done?" He grew angrier while he talked, and his voice rose. "Why does he have to tell them over and over? He came across the plains. All right! Now it's finished. Nobody wants to hear about it over and over."

The door into the kitchen closed softly. The four at the table sat frozen. Carl laid his mush spoon on the table and touched his chin with his fingers.

Then the kitchen door opened and Grandfather walked in. His mouth smiled tightly and his eyes were squinted. "Good morning," he said, and he sat down and looked at his mush dish.

Carl could not leave it there. "Did—did you hear what I said?"

Grandfather jerked a little nod.

"I don't know what got into me, sir. I didn't mean it. I was just being funny."

Jody glanced in shame at his mother, and he saw that she was looking at Carl, and that she wasn't breathing. It was an awful thing that he was doing. He was tearing himself to pieces to talk like that. It was a terrible thing to him to retract a word, but to retract it in shame was infinitely worse.

Grandfather looked sidewise. "I'm trying to get right side up," he said gently. "I'm not being mad. I don't mind what you said, but it might be true, and I would mind that."

"It isn't true," said Carl. "I'm not feeling well this morning. I'm sorry I said it."

"Don't be sorry, Carl. An old man doesn't see things sometimes. Maybe you're right. The crossing is finished. Maybe it should be forgotten, now it's done."

Carl got up from the table. "I've had enough to eat. I'm going to work. Take your time, Billy!" He walked quickly out of the dining-room. Billy gulped the rest of his food and followed soon after. But Jody could not leave his chair.

"Won't you tell any more stories?" Jody asked.

"Why, sure I'll tell them, but only when—I'm sure people want to hear them."

"I like to hear them, sir."

"Oh! Of course you do, but you're a little boy. It was a job for men, but only little boys like to hear about it."

Jody got up from his place. "I'll wait outside for you, sir. I've got a good stick for those mice."

He waited by the gate until the old man came out on the porch. "Let's go down and kill the mice now," Jody called.

"I think I'll just sit in the sun, Jody. You go kill the mice."

"You can use my stick if you like."

"No, I'll just sit here a while."

Jody turned disconsolately away, and walked down toward the old haystack. He tried to whip up his enthusiasm with thoughts of the fat juicy mice. He beat the ground with his flail. The dogs coaxed and whined about him, but he could not go. Back at the house he could see Grandfather sitting on the porch, looking small and thin and black.

Jody gave up and went to sit on the steps at the old man's feet.

"Back already? Did you kill the mice?"

"No, sir. I'll kill them some other day."

The morning flies buzzed close to the ground and the ants dashed about in front of the steps. The heavy smell of sage slipped down the hill. The porch boards grew warm in the sunshine.

Jody hardly knew when Grandfather started to talk. "I shouldn't stay here, feeling the way I do." He examined his strong old hands. "I feel as though the crossing wasn't worth doing." His eyes moved up the side-hill and stopped on a motionless hawk perched on a dead limb. "I tell those old stories, but they're not what I want to tell. I only know how I want people to feel when I tell them.

"It wasn't Indians that were important, nor adventures, nor even getting out here. It was a whole bunch of people made into one big crawling beast. And I was the head. It was westering and westering. Every man wanted something for himself, but the big beast that was all of them wanted only westering. I was the leader, but if I hadn't been there, someone else would have been the head. The thing had to have a head.

"Under the little bushes the shadows were black at white noonday. When we saw the mountains at last, we cried—all of us. But it wasn't getting here that mattered, it was movement and westering.

"We carried life out here and set it down the way those ants carry eggs. And I was the leader. The westering was as big as God, and the slow steps that made the movement piled up and piled up until the continent was crossed.

"Then we came down to the sea, and it was done." He stopped and wiped his eyes until the rims were red. "That's what I should be telling instead of stories."

When Jody spoke, Grandfather started and looked down at him. "Maybe I could lead the people some day," Jody said.

The old man smiled. "There's no place to go. There's the ocean to stop you. There's a line of old men along the shore hating the ocean because it stopped them."

"In boats I might, sir."

"No place to go, Jody. Every place is taken. But that's not the worst—no, not the worst. Westering has died out of the people. Westering isn't a hunger any more. It's all done. Your father is right. It is finished." He laced his fingers on his knee and looked at them.

Jody felt very sad. "If you'd like a glass of lemonade I could make it for you."

Grandfather was about to refuse, and then he saw Jody's face. "That would be nice," he said. "Yes, it would be nice to drink a lemonade."

Jody ran into the kitchen where his mother was wiping the last of the breakfast dishes. "Can I have a lemon to make a lemonade for Grandfather?"

His mother mimicked—"And another lemon to make a lemonade for you."

"No, ma'am. I don't want one."

"Jody! You're sick!" Then she stopped suddenly. "Take a lemon out of the cooler," she said softly. "Here, I'll reach the squeezer down to you."

ERSKINE CALDWELL

[1903–]

Cruelty and coarse humor, *bawdy skylarking and bitter protests were curiously but effectively combined by Erskine Preston Caldwell. He was born December 17, 1903, in Coweta County, Georgia, in a spot remote from any railroad, without a post office, so small a cluster of houses that it had no name. "The nearest landmark," he remembered, "was a church several miles away. It was called White Oak. . . . From the day of my birth until I reached the age of twenty years I rarely lived longer than six months in the same place. My home was the entire South." His father, a Presbyterian minister and secretary of his denomination, "was required to visit and reside several months at each church"; he took his family with him when he moved.*

Caldwell's education was necessarily peripatetic: a primary school in Virginia, a grammar school in Tennessee, a high school in Georgia, a small college in South Carolina, and the University of Virginia. During intervals he worked as a cotton-picker, stage-hand in a burlesque theatre, professional football player, and cub reporter on the Atlanta Journal. *He married Helen Lannigan, had three children, and wrote about a hundred short stories, all of which were rejected by the magazines.*

He was twenty-nine when he finished Tobacco Road, *which was favorably reviewed but sold poorly. Two years later it was made into a play and achieved a record run of over three thousand continuous performances. Its success stimulated not only the sale of* Tobacco Road *but all Caldwell's subsequent books. In one form or another the aggregate sale of* Tobacco Road, God's Little Acre, Tragic Ground, Jackpot, Journeyman, This Very Earth, Kneel to the Rising Sun, *and other collections of stories short and long mounted into astronomical figures; the paperback editions alone sold more than thirty million copies. Some of the books, excoriated as immoral and obscene, were censored, taken into court, and banned, but all were eventually restored to the book-racks. After a divorce from his first wife, Caldwell married Margaret Bourke-White, the photographer, in 1937. Five years later they were divorced and he married June Johnson, by whom he had a son.*

Like Steinbeck, Caldwell seems to have two sides: he is a serious reformer, a champion of ignorant victims devoted to a wasteland which they themselves laid waste; and he is also a detached observer who derives pleasure from the results of man's earthy naturalness and his unflagging appetites in the face of every hardship. Actually the two sides are not only joined but integrated in Caldwell's chronicles of the underprivileged and underfed. His literary status still perplexes the critics; he cannot be tagged as a grim comedian, a raw satirist, or an indicter of a civilization which permits unspeakable indecencies, for he is inseparably all of these. It is, however, incontrovertible that Caldwell's depiction of a primitive society in the midst of twentieth-century culture assures him an estimable as well as a popular place in American literature.

KNEEL TO THE RISING SUN

A SHIVER went through Lonnie. He drew his hand away from his sharp chin, remembering what Clem had said. It made him feel now as if he were committing a crime by standing in Arch Gunnard's presence and allowing his face to be seen.

He and Clem had been walking up the road together that afternoon on their way to the filling station when he told Clem how much he needed rations. Clem stopped a moment to kick a rock out of the road, and said that if you worked for Arch Gunnard long enough, your face would be sharp enough to split the boards for your own coffin.

As Lonnie turned away to sit down on an empty box beside the gasoline pump, he could not help wishing that he could be as unafraid of Arch Gunnard as Clem was. Even if Clem was a Negro, he never hesitated to ask for rations when he needed something to eat; and when he and his family did not get enough, Clem came right out and told Arch so. Arch stood for that, but he swore that he was going to run Clem out of the country the first chance he got.

Lonnie knew without turning around that Clem was standing at the corner of the filling station with two or three other Negroes and looking at him, but for some reason he was unable to meet Clem's eyes.

Arch Gunnard was sitting in the sun, honing his jack-knife blade on his boot top. He glanced once or twice at Lonnie's hound, Nancy, who was lying in the middle of the road waiting for Lonnie to go home.

"That your dog, Lonnie?"

Jumping with fear, Lonnie's hand went to his chin to hide the lean face that would accuse Arch of short-rationing.

Arch snapped his fingers and the hound stood up, wagging her tail. She waited to be called.

"Mr. Arch, I—"

Arch called the dog. She began crawling towards them on her belly, wagging her tail a little faster each time Arch's fingers snapped. When she was several feet away, she turned over on her back and lay on the ground with her four paws in the air.

Dudley Smith and Jim Weaver, who were lounging around the filling station, laughed. They had been leaning against the side of the building, but they straightened up to see what Arch was up to.

Arch spat some more tobacco juice on his boot top and whetted the jack-knife blade some more.

"What kind of a hound dog is that, anyway, Lonnie?" Arch said. "Looks like to me it might be a ketch hound."

Lonnie could feel Clem Henry's eyes boring into the back of his head. He wondered what Clem would do if it had been his dog Arch Gunnard was snapping his fingers at and calling like that.

"His tail's way too long for a coon hound or a bird dog, ain't it, Arch?" somebody behind Lonnie said, laughing out loud.

Everybody laughed then, including Arch. They looked at Lonnie, waiting to hear what he was going to say to Arch.

"Is he a ketch hound, Lonnie?" Arch said, snapping his finger again.

"Mr. Arch, I—"

"Don't be ashamed of him, Lonnie, if he don't show signs of turning out to be a bird dog or a fox hound. Everybody needs a hound around the house that can go out and catch pigs and rabbits when you are in a hurry for them. A ketch hound is a mighty respectable animal. I've known the time when I was mighty proud to own one."

Everybody laughed.

Arch Gunnard was getting ready to grab Nancy by the tail. Lonnie sat up, twisting his neck until he caught a glimpse of Clem Henry at the other corner of the filling station. Clem was staring at him with unmistakable meaning, with the same look in his eyes he had had that afternoon when he said that nobody who worked for Arch Gunnard ought to stand for short-rationing. Lonnie lowered his eyes. He could not figure out how a Negro could be braver than he was. There were a lot of times like that when he would have given anything he had to be able to jump into Clem's shoes and change places with him.

"The trouble with this hound of yours, Lonnie, is that he's too heavy on his feet. Don't you reckon it would be a pretty slick little trick to lighten the load some, being as how he's a ketch hound to begin with?"

Lonnie remembered then what Clem Henry had said he would do if Arch Gunnard ever tried to cut off his dog's tail. Lonnie knew, and Clem knew, and everybody else knew, that that would give Arch the chance he was waiting for. All Arch asked, he had said, was for Clem Henry to overstep his place just one little half-inch, or to talk back to him with just one little short word, and he would do the rest. Everybody knew what Arch meant by that, especially if Clem did not turn and run. And Clem had not been known to run from anybody, after fifteen years in the country.

Arch reached down and grabbed Nancy's tail while Lonnie was wondering about Clem. Nancy acted as if she thought Arch were playing some kind of a game with her. She turned her head around until she could reach Arch's hand to lick it. He cracked her on the bridge of the nose with the end of the jackknife.

"He's a mighty playful dog, Lonnie," Arch said, catching up a shorter grip on the tail, "but his wagpole is way too long for a dog his size, especially when he wants to be a ketch hound."

Lonnie swallowed hard.

"Mr. Arch, she's a mighty fine rabbit tracker. I—"

"Shucks, Lonnie," Arch said, whetting the knife blade on the dog's tail, "I aint never seen a hound in all my life that needed a tail that long to hunt rabbits with. It's way too long for just a common, ordinary, everyday ketch hound."

Lonnie looked up hopefully at Dudley Smith and the others. None of them offered any help. It was useless for him to try to stop Arch, because Arch Gunnard would let nothing stand in his way when once he had set his head on what he wished to do. Lonnie knew that if he should let himself show any anger or resentment, Arch would drive him off the farm before sundown that night. Clem Henry was the only person there who would help him, but Clem . . .

The white men and the Negroes at both corners of the filling station waited to see what Lonnie was going to do about it. All of them hoped he would put up a fight for his hound. If anyone ever had the nerve to stop Arch Gunnard from cutting off a dog's tail, it might put an end to it. It was plain, though, that Lonnie, who was one of Arch's share-croppers, was afraid to speak up. Clem Henry might; Clem was the only one who might try to stop Arch, even if it meant trouble. All of them knew that Arch would insist on running Clem out of the country, or filling him full of lead.

"I reckon it's all right with you, aint it, Lonnie?" Arch said. "I don't seem to hear no objections."

Clem Henry stepped forward several paces, and stopped.

Arch laughed, watching Lonnie's face, and jerked Nancy to her feet. The hound cried out in pain and surprise, but Arch made her be quiet by kicking her in the belly.

Lonnie winced. He could hardly bear to see anybody kick his dog like that.

"Mr. Arch, I . . ."

A contraction in his throat almost choked him for several moments, and he had to open his mouth wide and fight for breath. The other white men around him were silent. Nobody liked to see a dog kicked in the belly like that.

Lonnie could see the other end of the filling station from the corner of his eye. He saw a couple of Negroes go up behind Clem and grasp his overalls. Clem spat on the ground, between outspread feet, but he did not try to break away from them.

"Being as how I don't hear no objections, I reckon it's all right to go ahead and cut it off," Arch said, spitting.

Lonnie's head went forward and all he could see of Nancy was her hind feet. He had come to ask for a slab of sowbelly and some molasses, or something. Now he did not know if he could ever bring himself to ask for rations, no matter how much hungrier they became at home.

"I always make it a habit of asking a man first," Arch said. "I wouldn't want to go ahead and cut off a tail if a man had any objections. That wouldn't be right. No, sir, it just wouldn't be fair and square."

Arch caught a shorter grip on the hound's tail and placed the knife blade on it two or three inches from the rump. It looked to those who were watching as if his mouth were watering, because tobacco juice began to trickle down the corners of his lips. He brought up the back of his hand and wiped his mouth.

A noisy automobile came plowing down the road through the deep red dust. Everyone looked up as it passed in order to see who was in it.

Lonnie glanced at it, but he could not keep his eyes raised. His head fell downward once more until he could feel his sharp chin cutting into his chest. He wondered then if Arch had noticed how lean his face was.

"I keep two or three ketch hounds around my place," Arch said, holding the blade on the tail of the dog as if it were a razor strop until his actions brought smiles to the faces of the men grouped around him, "but I never could see the sense of a ketch hound having a long tail. It only gets in their way when I send them out to catch a pig or a rabbit for my supper."

Pulling with his left hand and pushing with his right, Arch Gunnard docked the hound's tail as quickly and as easily as if he were cutting a willow switch in the pasture to drive the cows home with. The dog sprang forward with the release of her tail until she was far beyond Arch's reach, and began howling so loud she could be heard half a mile away. Nancy stopped once and looked back at Arch, and then she sprang to the middle of the road and began leaping and twisting in circles. All that time she was yelping and biting at the bleeding stub of her tail.

Arch leaned backward and twirled the severed tail in one hand while he wiped the jack-knife blade on his boot sole. He watched Lonnie's dog chasing herself around in circles in the red dust.

Nobody had anything to say then. Lonnie tried not to watch his dog's agony, and he forced himself to keep from looking at Clem Henry. Then, with his eyes shut, he wondered why he had remained on Arch Gunnard's plantation all those past years, share-cropping for a mere living on short-rations, and becoming leaner and leaner all the time. He knew then how true it was what Clem had said about Arch's share-croppers' faces becoming sharp enough to hew their own coffins. His hands went to his chin before he knew what he was doing. His hand dropped when he had felt the bones of jaw and the exposed tendons of his cheeks.

As hungry as he was, he knew that even if Arch did give him some rations then, there would not be nearly enough for them to eat for the following week. Hatty, his wife, was already broken down from hunger and work in the fields, and his father, Mark Newsome, stone-deaf for the past twenty years, was always asking him why there was never enough food in the house for them to have a solid meal. Lonnie's head fell forward a little more, and he could feel his eyes becoming damp.

The pressure of his sharp chin against his chest made him so uncomfortable that he had to raise his head at last in order to ease the pain of it.

The first thing he saw when he looked up was Arch Gunnard twirling Nancy's tail in his left hand. Arch Gunnard had a trunk full of dogs' tails at home. He had been cutting off tails ever since anyone could remember, and during all those years he had accumulated a collection of which he was so proud that he kept the trunk locked and the key tied around his neck on a string. On Sunday afternoons when the preacher came to visit, or when a crowd was there to loll on the front porch and swap stories, Arch showed them off, naming each tail from memory just as well as if he had had a tag on it.

Clem Henry had left the filling station and was walking alone down the road towards the plantation. Clem Henry's house was in a cluster of Negro cabins below Arch's big house, and he had to pass Lonnie's house to get there. Lonnie was on the verge of getting up and leaving when he saw Arch looking at him. He did not know whether Arch was looking at his lean face, or whether he was watching to see if he were going to get up and go down the road with Clem.

The thought of leaving reminded him of his reason for being there. He had to have some rations before suppertime that night, no matter how short they were.

"Mr. Arch, I . . ."

Arch stared at him for a moment, appearing as if had turned to listen to some strange sound unheard of before that moment.

Lonnie bit his lips, wondering if Arch was going to say anything about how lean and hungry he looked. But Arch was thinking about something else. He slapped his hand on his leg and laughed out loud.

"I sometimes wish niggers had tails," Arch said, coiling Nancy's tail into a ball and putting it into his pocket. "I'd a heap rather cut off nigger tails than dog tails. There'd be more to cut, for one thing."

Dudley Smith and somebody else behind them laughed for a brief moment. The laughter died out almost as suddenly as it had risen.

The Negroes who had heard Arch shuffled their feet in the dust and moved backwards. It was only a few minutes until not one was left at the filling station. They went up the road behind the red wooden building until they were out of sight.

Arch got up and stretched. The sun was getting low, and it was no longer comfortable in the October air. "Well, I reckon I'll be getting on home to get me some supper," he said.

He walked slowly to the middle of the road and stopped to look at Nancy retreating along the ditch.

"Nobody going my way?" he asked. "What's wrong with you, Lonnie? Going home to supper, aint you?"

"Mr. Arch, I . . ."

Lonnie found himself jumping to his feet. His first thought was to ask for the sowbelly and molasses, and maybe some corn meal; but when he opened his mouth, the words refused to come out. He took several steps forward and shook his head. He did not know what Arch might say or do if he said "no."

"Hatty'll be looking for you," Arch said, turning his back and walking off.

He reached into his hip pocket and took out Nancy's tail. He began twirling it as he walked down the road towards the big house in the distance.

Dudley Smith went inside the filling station, and the others walked away.

After Arch had gone several hundred yards, Lonnie sat down heavily on the box beside the gas pump from which he had got up when Arch spoke to him. He sat down heavily, his shoulders drooping, his arms falling between his outspread legs.

Lonnie did not know how long his eyes had been closed, but when he opened them, he saw Nancy lying between his feet, licking the docked tail. While he watched her, he felt the sharp point of his chin cutting into his chest again. Presently the door behind him was slammed shut, and a minute later he could hear Dudley Smith walking away from the filling station on his way home.

II

Lonnie had been sleeping fitfully for several hours when he suddenly found himself wide awake. Hatty shook him again. He raised himself on his elbow and tried to see into the darkness of the room. Without knowing what time it was, he was able to determine that it was still nearly two hours until sunrise.

"Lonnie," Hatty said again, trembling in the cold night air, "Lonnie, your pa aint in the house."

Lonnie sat upright in bed.

"How do you know he aint?" he said.

"I've been lying here wide awake ever since I got in bed, and I heard him when he went out. He's been gone all that time."

"Maybe he just stepped out for a while," Lonnie said, turning and trying to see through the bedroom window.

"I know what I'm saying, Lonnie," Hatty insisted. "Your pa's been gone a heap too long."

Both of them sat without a sound for several minutes while they listened for Mark Newsome.

Lonnie got up and lit a lamp. He shivered while he was putting on his shirt, overalls, and shoes. He tied his shoelaces in hard knots because he couldn't see in the faint light. Outside the window it was almost pitch-dark, and Lonnie could feel the damp October air blowing against his face.

"I'll go help look," Hatty said, throwing the covers off and starting to get up.

Lonnie went to the bed and drew the covers back over her and pushed her back into place.

"You try to get some sleep, Hatty," he said; "you can't stay awake the whole night. I'll go bring Pa back."

He left Hatty, blowing out the lamp, and stumbled through the dark hall, feeling his way to the front porch by touching the wall with his hands. When he got to the porch, he could still barely see any distance ahead, but his eyes were becoming more accustomed to the darkness. He waited a minute, listening.

Feeling his way down the steps into the yard, he walked around the corner of the house and stopped to listen again before calling his father.

"Oh, Pa!" he said loudly. "Oh, Pa!"

He stopped under the bedroom window when he realized what he had been doing.

"Now that's a fool thing for me to be out here doing," he said, scolding himself. "Pa couldn't hear it thunder."

He heard a rustling of the bed.

"He's been gone long enough to get clear to the crossroads, or more," Hatty said, calling through the window.

"Now you lay down and try to get a little sleep, Hatty," Lonnie told her. "I'll bring him back in no time."

He could hear Nancy scratching fleas under the house, but he knew she was in no condition to help look for Mark. It would be several days before she recovered from the shock of losing her tail.

"He's been gone a long time," Hatty said, unable to keep still.

"That don't make no difference," Lonnie said. "I'll find him sooner or later. Now you go on to sleep like I told you, Hatty."

Lonnie walked towards the barn, listening for some sound. Over at the big house he could hear the hogs grunting and squealing, and he wished they would be quiet so he could hear other sounds. Arch Gunnard's dogs were howling occasionally, but they were not making any more noise than they usually did at night, and he was accustomed to their howling.

Lonnie went to the barn, looking inside and out. After walking around the barn, he went into the field as far as the cotton shed. He knew it was useless, but he could not keep from calling his father time after time.

"Oh, Pa!" he said, trying to penetrate the darkness.

He went further into the field.

"Now, what in the world could have become of Pa?" he said, stopping and wondering where to look next.

After he had gone back to the front yard, he began to feel uneasy for the first time. Mark had not acted any more strangely during the past week then he ordinarily did, but Lonnie knew he was upset over the way Arch Gunnard was giving out short-rations. Mark had even said that, at the rate they were being fed, all of them would starve to death inside another three months.

Lonnie left the yard and went down the road towards the Negro cabins. When he got to Clem's house, he turned in and walked up the path to the door. He knocked several times and waited. There was no answer, and he rapped louder.

"Who's that?" he heard Clem say from bed.

"It's me," Lonnie said. "I've got to see you a minute, Clem. I'm out in the front yard."

He sat down and waited for Clem to dress and come outside. While he waited, he strained his ears to catch any sound that might be in the air. Over the fields towards the big house he could hear the fattening hogs grunt and squeal.

Clem came out and shut the door. He stood on the doorsill a moment speaking to his wife in bed, telling her he would be back and not to worry.

"Who's that?" Clem said, coming down into the yard.

Lonnie got up and met Clem half-way.

"What's the trouble?" Clem asked then, buttoning up his overall jumper.

"Pa's not in his bed," Lonnie said, "and Hatty says he's been gone from the house most all night. I went out in the field, and all around the barn, but I couldn't find a trace of him anywhere."

Clem then finished buttoning his jumper and began rolling a cigarette. He walked slowly down the path to the road. It was still dark, and it would be at least an hour before dawn made it any lighter.

"Maybe he was too hungry to stay in bed any longer," Clem said. "When I saw him yesterday, he said he was so shrunk up and weak he didn't know if he could last much longer. He looked like his skin and bones couldn't shrivel much more."

"I asked Arch last night after suppertime for some rations—just a little piece of sowbelly and some molasses. He said he'd get around to letting me have some the first thing this morning."

"Why don't you tell him to give you full rations or none?" Clem said. "If you knew you wasn't going to get none at all, you could move away and find a better man to share-crop for, couldn't you?"

"I've been loyal to Arch Gunnard for a long time now," Lonnie said. "I'd hate to haul off and leave him like that."

Clem looked at Lonnie, but he did not say anything more just then. They turned up the road towards the driveway that led up to the big house. The fattening hogs were still grunting and squealing in the pen, and one of Arch's hounds came down a cotton row beside the driveway to smell their shoes.

"Them fattening hogs always get enough to eat," Clem said. "There's not a one of them that don't weigh seven hundred pounds right now, and they're getting bigger every day. Besides taking all that's thrown to them, they make a lot of meals off the chickens that get in there to peck around."

Lonnie listened to the grunting of the hogs as they walked up the driveway towards the big house.

"Reckon we'd better get Arch up to help look for Pa?" Lonnie said. "I'd hate to wake him up, but I'm scared Pa might stray off into the swamp and get lost for good. He couldn't hear it thunder, even. I never could find him back there in all that tangle if he got into it."

Clem said something under his breath and went on towards the barn and hog pen. He reached the pen before Lonnie got there.

"You'd better come here quick," Clem said, turning around to see where Lonnie was.

Lonnie ran to the hog pen. He stopped and climbed half-way up the wooden-and-wire sides of the fence. At first he could see nothing, but gradually he was able to see the moving mass of black fattening hogs on the other side of the pen. They were biting and snarling at each other like a pack of hungry hounds turned loose on a dead rabbit.

Lonnie scrambled to the top of the fence, but Clem caught him and pulled him back.

"Don't go in that hog pen that way," he said. "Them hogs will tear you to pieces, they're that wild. They're fighting over something."

Both of them ran around the corner of the pen and got to the side where the hogs were. Down under their feet on the ground Lonnie caught a glimpse of a dark mass splotched with white. He was able to see it for a moment only, because one of the hogs trampled over it.

Clem opened and closed his mouth several times before he was able to say anything at all. He clutched at Lonnie's arm, shaking him.

"That looks like it might be your pa," he said. "I swear before goodness, Lonnie, it does look like it."

Lonnie still could not believe it. He climbed to the top of the fence and began kicking his feet at the hogs, trying to drive them away. They paid no attention to him.

While Lonnie was perched there, Clem had gone to the wagon shed, and he ran back with two singletrees he had somehow managed to find there in the dark. He handed one to Lonnie, poking it at him until Lonnie's attention was drawn from the hogs long enough to take it.

Clem leaned over the fence and began swinging the singletree at the hogs. Lonnie slid down beside him, yelling at them. One hog turned on Lonnie and snapped at him, and Clem struck it over the back of the neck with enough force to drive it off momentarily.

By then Lonnie was able to realize what had happened. He ran to the mass of hogs, kicking them with his heavy stiff shoes and striking them on their heads with the iron-tipped singletree. Once he felt a stinging sensation, and looked down to see one of the hogs biting the calf of his leg. He had just enough time to hit the hog and drive it away before his leg was torn. He knew most of his overall leg had been ripped away, because he could feel the night air on his bare wet calf.

Clem had gone ahead and had driven the hogs back. There was no other way to do anything. They were in a snarling circle around them, and both of them had to keep the singletrees swinging back and forth all the time to keep the hogs off. Finally Lonnie reached down and got a grip on Mark's leg. With Clem helping, Lonnie carried his father to the fence and lifted him over to the other side.

They were too much out of breath for a while to say anything, or to do anything else. The snarling fattening hogs were at the fence, biting the wood and wire, and making more noise than ever.

While Lonnie was searching in his pockets for a match, Clem struck one. He held the flame close to Mark Newsome's head.

They both stared unbelievingly, and then Clem blew out the match. There was nothing said as they stared at each other in the darkness.

Clem walked several steps away, and turned and came back beside Lonnie.

"It's him, though," Clem said, sitting down on the ground. "It's him, all right."

"I reckon so," Lonnie said. He could think of nothing else to say then.

They sat on the ground, one on each side of Mark, looking at the body. There had been no sign of life in the body beside them since they had first touched it. The face, throat, and stomach had been completely devoured.

"You'd better go wake up Arch Gunnard," Clem said after a while.

"What for?" Lonnie said. "He can't help none now. It's too late for help."

"Makes no difference," Clem insisted. "You'd better go wake him up and let him see what there is to see. If you wait till morning, he might take it into his head to say the hogs didn't do it. Right now is the time to get him up so he can see what his hogs did."

Clem turned around and looked at the big house. The dark outline against the dark sky made him hesitate.

"A man who short-rations tenants ought to have to sit and look at that till it's buried."

Lonnie looked at Clem fearfully. He knew Clem was right, but he was scared to hear a Negro say anything like that about a white man.

"You oughtn't talk like that about Arch," Lonnie said. "He's in bed asleep. He didn't have a thing to do with it. He didn't have no more to do with it than I did."

Clem laughed a little, and threw the singletree on the ground between his feet. After letting it lie there a little while, he picked it up and began beating the ground with it.

Lonnie got to his feet slowly. He had never seen Clem act like that before, and he did not know what to think about it. He left without saying anything and walked stiffly to the house in the darkness to wake up Arch Gunnard.

III

Arch was hard to wake up. And even after he was awake, he was in no hurry to get up. Lonnie was standing outside the bedroom window, and Arch was lying in bed six or eight feet away. Lonnie could hear him toss and grumble.

"Who told you to come and wake me up in the middle of the night? Arch said.

"Well, Clem Henry's out here, and he said maybe you'd like to know about it."

Arch tossed around on the bed, flailing the pillow with his fists.

"You tell Clem Henry I said that one of these days he's going to find himself turned inside out, like a coat-sleeve."

Lonnie waited doggedly. He knew Clem was right in insisting that Arch ought to wake up and come out there to see what had happened. Lonnie was afraid to go back to the barnyard and tell Clem that Arch was not coming. He did not know, but he had a feeling that Clem might go into the bedroom and drag Arch out of bed. He did not like to think of anything like that taking place.

"Are you still out there, Lonnie?" Arch shouted.

"I'm right here, Mr. Arch. I—"

"If I wasn't so sleepy, I'd come out there and take a stick and—I don't know what I wouldn't do!"

Lonnie met Arch at the back step. On the way out to the hog pen Arch did not speak to him. Arch walked heavily ahead, not even waiting to see if Lonnie was coming. The lantern that Arch was carrying cast long flat beams of yellow light over the ground; and when they got to where Clem was waiting beside Mark's body, the Negro's face shone in the night like a highly polished plowshare.

"What was Mark doing in my hog pen at night, anyway?" Arch said, shouting at them both.

Neither Clem nor Lonnie replied. Arch glared at them for not answering. But no matter how many times he looked at them, his eyes returned each time to stare at the torn body of Mark Newsome on the ground at his feet.

"There's nothing to be done now," Arch said finally. "We'll just have to wait till daylight and send for the undertaker." He walked a few steps away. "Looks like you could have waited till morning in the first place. There wasn't no sense in getting me up."

He turned his back and looked sideways at Clem. Clem stood up and looked him straight in the eyes.

"What do you want, Clem Henry?" he said. "Who told you to be coming around my house in the middle of the night? I don't want niggers coming here except when I send for them."

"I couldn't stand to see anybody eaten up by the hogs, and not do anything about it," Clem said.

"You mind your own business," Arch told him. "And when you talk to me, take off your hat, or you'll be sorry for it. It wouldn't take much to make me do you up the way you belong."

Lonnie backed away. There was a feeling of uneasiness around them. That was how trouble between Clem and Arch always began. He had seen it start that way dozens of times before. As long as Clem turned and went away, nothing happened, but sometimes he stayed right where he was and talked up to Arch just as if he had been a white man, too.

Lonnie hoped it would not happen this time. Arch was already mad enough about being waked up in the middle of the night, and Lonnie knew there was no limit to what Arch would do when he got good and mad at a Negro. Nobody had ever seen him kill a Negro, but he had said he had, and he told people that he was not scared to do it again.

"I reckon you know how he came to get eaten up by the hogs like that," Clem said, looking straight at Arch.

Arch whirled around.

"Are you talking to me . . . ?"

"I asked you that," Clem stated.

"God damn you, yellow-blooded . . ." Arch yelled.

He swung the lantern at Clem's head. Clem dodged, but the bottom of it hit his shoulder, and it was smashed to pieces. The oil splattered on the ground, igniting in the air from the flaming wick. Clem was lucky not to have it splash on his face and overalls.

"Now, look here . . ." Clem said.

"You yellow-blooded nigger," Arch said, rushing at him. "I'll teach you to talk back to me. You've got too big for your place for the last time. I've been taking too much from you, but I aint doing it no more."

"Mr. Arch, I . . ." Lonnie said, stepping forward partly between them. No one heard him.

Arch stood back and watched the kerosene flicker out on the ground.

"You know good and well why he got eaten up by the fattening hogs," Clem said, standing his ground. "He was so hungry he had to get up out of bed in the middle of the night and come up here in the dark trying to find something to eat. Maybe he was trying to find the smokehouse. It makes no difference, either way. He's been on short-rations like everybody else working on your place, and he was so old he didn't know where to look for food except in your smokehouse. You know good and well that's how he got lost up here in the dark and fell in the hog pen."

The kerosene had died out completely. In the last faint flare, Arch had reached down and grabbed up the singletree that had been lying on the ground where Lonnie had dropped it.

Arch raised the singletree over his head and struck with all his might at Clem. Clem dodged, but Arch drew back again quickly and landed a blow on his arm just above the elbow before Clem could dodge it. Clem's arm dropped to his side, dangling lifelessly.

"You Goddamn yellow-blooded nigger!" Arch shouted. "Now's your time, you black bastard. I've been waiting for the chance to teach you your lesson. And this's going to be one you won't never forget."

Clem felt the ground with his feet until he had located the other singletree. He stooped down and got it. Raising it, he did not try to hit Arch, but held it in front of him so he could ward off Arch's blows at his head. He continued to stand his ground, not giving Arch an inch.

"Drop that singletree," Arch said.

"I won't stand here and let you beat me like that," Clem protested.

"By God, that's all I want to hear," Arch said, his mouth curling. "Nigger, your time has come, by God!"

He swung once more at Clem, but Clem turned and ran towards the barn. Arch went after him a few steps and stopped. He threw aside the singletree and turned and ran back to the house.

Lonnie went to the fence and tried to think what was best for him to do. He knew he could not take sides with a Negro, in the open, even if Clem had helped him, and especially after Clem had talked to Arch in the way he wished he could himself. He was a white man, and to save his life he could not stand to think of turning against Arch, no matter what happened.

Presently a light burst through one of the windows of the house, and he heard Arch shouting at his wife to wake her up.

When he saw Arch's wife go to the telephone, Lonnie realized what was going to happen. She was calling up the neighbors and Arch's friends. They would not mind getting up in the night when they found out what was going to take place.

Out behind the barn he could hear Clem calling him. Leaving the yard, Lonnie felt his way out there in the dark.

"What's the trouble, Clem?" he said.

"I reckon my time has come," Clem said. "Arch Gunnard talks that way when he's good and mad. He talked just like he did that time he carried Jim Moffin off to the swamp—and Jim never came back."

"Arch wouldn't do anything like that to you, Clem," Lonnie said excitedly, but he knew better.

Clem said nothing.

"Maybe you'd better strike out for the swamps till he changes his mind and cools off some," Lonnie said. "You might be right, Clem."

Lonnie could feel Clem's eyes burning into him.

"Wouldn't be no sense in that, if you'd help me," Clem said. "Wouldn't you stand by me?"

Lonnie trembled as the meaning of Clem's suggestion became clear to him. His back was to the side of the barn, and he leaned against it while sheets of black and white passed before his eyes.

"Wouldn't you stand by me?" Clem asked again.

"I don't know what Arch would say to that," Lonnie told him haltingly.

Clem walked away several paces. He stood with his back to Lonnie while he looked across the field towards the quarter where his home was.

"I could go in that little patch of woods out there and stay till they get tired of looking for me," Clem said, turning around to see Lonnie.

"You'd better go somewhere," Lonnie said uneasily. "I know Arch Gunnard. He's hard to handle when he makes up his mind to do something he wants to do. I couldn't stop him an inch. Maybe you'd better get clear out of the country, Clem."

"I couldn't do that, and leave my family down there across the field," Clem said.

"He's going to get you if you don't."

"If you'd only sort of help me out a little, he wouldn't. I would only have to go and hide out in that little patch of woods over there a while. Looks like you could do that for me, being as how I helped you find your pa when he was in the hog pen."

Lonnie nodded, listening for sounds from the big house. He continued to nod at Clem while Clem was waiting to be assured.

"If you're going to stand up for me," Clem said, "I can just go over there in the woods and wait till they get it off their minds. You won't be telling them where I'm at, and you could say I struck out for the swamp. They wouldn't ever find me without bloodhounds."

"That's right," Lonnie said, listening for sounds of Arch's coming out of the house. He did not wish to be found back there behind the barn where Arch could accuse him of talking to Clem.

The moment Lonnie replied, Clem turned and ran off into the night. Lonnie went after him a few steps, as if he had suddenly changed his mind about helping him, but Clem was lost in the darkness by then.

Lonnie waited for a few minutes, listening to Clem crashing through the underbrush in the patch of woods a quarter of a mile away. When he could hear Clem no longer, he went around the barn to meet Arch.

Arch came out of the house carrying his double-barreled shotgun and the lantern he had picked up in the house. His pockets were bulging with shells.

"Where is that damn nigger, Lonnie?" Arch asked him. "Where'd he go to?"

Lonnie opened his mouth, but no words came out.

"You know which way he went, don't you?"

Lonnie again tried to say something, but there were no sounds. He jumped when he found himself nodding his head to Arch.

"Mr. Arch, I—"

"That's all right, then," Arch said. "That's all I need to know now. Dudley Smith and Tom Hawkins and Frank and Dave Howard and the rest will be here in a minute, and you can stay right here so you can show us where he's hiding out."

Frantically Lonnie tried to say something. Then he reached for Arch's sleeve to stop him, but Arch had gone.

Arch ran around the house to the front yard. Soon a car came racing down the road, its headlights lighting up the whole place, hog pen and all. Lonnie knew it was probably Dudley Smith, because his was the first house in that direction, only half a mile away. While he was turning into the driveway, several other automobiles came into sight, both up the road and down it.

Lonnie trembled. He was afraid Arch was going to tell him to point out where Clem had gone to hide. Then he knew Arch would tell him. He had promised Clem he would not do that. But try as he might, he could not make himself believe that Arch Gunnard would do anything more than whip Clem.

Clem had not done anything that called for lynching. He had not raped a white woman, he had not shot at a white man; he had only talked back to Arch, with his hat on. But Arch was mad enough to do anything; he was mad enough at Clem not to stop at anything short of lynching.

The whole crowd of men was swarming around him before he realized it. And there was Arch clutching his arm and shouting into his face.

"Mr. Arch, I . . ."

Lonnie recognized every man in the feeble dawn. They were excited, and they looked like men on the last lap of an all-night foxhunting party. Their shotguns and pistols were held at their waists, ready for the kill.

"What's the matter with you, Lonnie?" Arch said, shouting into his ear. "Wake up and say where Clem Henry went to hide out. We're ready to go get him."

Lonnie remembered looking up and seeing Frank Howard dropping yellow twelve-gauge shells into the breech of his gun. Frank bent forward so he could hear Lonnie tell Arch where Clem was hiding.

"You aint going to kill Clem this time, are you, Mr. Arch?" Lonnie asked.

"Kill him?" Dudley Smith repeated. "What do you reckon I've been waiting all this time for if it wasn't for a chance to get Clem. That nigger has had it coming to him ever since he came to this county. He's a bad nigger, and it's coming to him."

"It wasn't exactly Clem's fault," Lonnie said. "If Pa hadn't come up here and fell in the hog pen, Clem wouldn't have had a thing to do with it. He was helping me, that's all."

"Shut up, Lonnie," somebody shouted at him. "You're so excited you don't know what you're saying. You're taking up for a nigger when you talk like that."

People were crowding around him so tightly he felt as if he were being squeezed to death. He had to get some air, get his breath, get out of the crowd.

"That's right," Lonnie said.

He heard himself speak, but he did not know what he was saying.

"But Clem helped me find Pa when he got lost looking around for something to eat."

"Shut up, Lonnie," somebody said again. "You damn fool, shut up!"

Arch grabbed his shoulder and shook him until his teeth rattled. Then Lonnie realized what he had been saying.

"Now, look here, Lonnie," Arch shouted. "You must be out of your head, because you know good and well you wouldn't talk like a nigger-lover in your right mind."

"That's right," Lonnie said, trembling all over. "I sure wouldn't want to talk like that."

He could still feel the grip on his shoulder where Arch's strong fingers had hurt him.

"Did Clem go to the swamp, Lonnie?" Dudley Smith said. "Is that right, Lonnie?"

Lonnie tried to shake his head; he tried to nod his head. Then Arch's fingers squeezed his thin neck. Lonnie looked at the men wild-eyed.

"Where's Clem hiding, Lonnie?" Arch demanded, squeezing.

Lonnie went three or four steps towards the barn. When he stopped, the men behind him pushed forward again. He found himself being rushed behind the barn and beyond it.

"All right, Lonnie," Arch said. "Now which way?"

Lonnie pointed towards the patch of woods where the creek was. The swamp was in the other direction.

"He said he was going to hide out in that little patch of woods along the creek over there, Mr. Arch," Lonnie said. "I reckon he's over there now."

Lonnie felt himself being swept forward, and he stumbled over the rough ground trying to keep from being knocked down and trampled upon. Nobody was talking, and everyone seemed to be walking on tiptoes. The gray light of early dawn was increasing enough both to hide them and to show the way ahead.

Just before they reached the fringe of the woods the men separated, and Lonnie found himself a part of the circle that was closing in on Clem.

Lonnie was alone, and there was nobody to stop him, but he was unable to move forward or backward. It began to be clear to him what he had done.

Clem was probably up a tree somewhere in the woods ahead, but by that time he had been surrounded on all sides. If he should attempt to break and run, he would be shot down like a rabbit.

Lonnie sat down on a log and tried to think what to do. The sun would be up in a few more minutes, and as soon as it came up, the men would close in on the creek and Clem. He would have no chance at all among all these shotguns and pistols.

Once or twice he saw the flare of a match through the underbrush where some of the men were lying in wait. A whiff of cigarette smoke struck his nostrils, and he found himself wondering if Clem could smell it wherever he was in the woods.

There was still no sound anywhere around him, and he knew that Arch Gunnard and the rest of the men were waiting for the sun, which would in a few minutes come up behind him in the east.

It was light enough by that time to see plainly the rough ground and the tangled underbrush and the curling bark on the pine trees.

The men had already begun to creep forward, guns raised as if stalking a deer. The woods were not large, and the circle of men would be able to cover it in a few minutes at the rate they were going forward. There was still a chance that Clem had slipped through the circle before dawn broke, but Lonnie felt that he was still there, He began to feel then that Clem was there because he himself had placed him there for the men to find more easily.

Lonnie found himself moving forward, drawn into the narrowing circle. Presently he could see the men all around him in dim outline. Their eyes were searching the heavy green pine tops as they went forward from tree to tree.

"Oh, Pa!" he said in a hoarse whisper. "Oh, Pa!"

He went forward a few steps, looking into the bushes and up into the tree tops. When he saw the other men again, he realized that it was not Mark Newsome being sought. He did not know what had made him forget like that.

The creeping forward began to work into the movement of Lonnie's body. He found himself springing forward on his toes, and his body was leaning in that direction. It was like creeping up on a rabbit when you did not have a gun to hunt with.

He forgot again what he was doing there. The springing motion in his legs seemed to be growing stronger with each step. He bent forward so far he could almost touch the ground with his fingertips. He could not stop now. He was keeping up with the circle of men.

The fifteen men were drawing closer and closer together. The dawn had broken enough to show the time on the face of a watch. The sun was beginning to color the sky above.

Lonnie was far in advance of anyone else by then. He could not hold himself back. The strength in his legs was more than he could hold in check.

He had for so long been unable to buy shells for his gun that he had forgotten how much he liked to hunt.

The sound of the men's steady creeping had become a rhythm in his ears.

"Here's the bastard!" somebody shouted, and there was a concerted crashing through the dry underbrush. Lonnie dashed forward, reaching the tree almost as quickly as anyone else.

He could see everybody with guns raised, and far into the sky above the sharply outlined face of Clem Henry gleamed in the rising sun. His body was hugging the slender top of the pine.

Lonnie did not know who was the first to fire, but the rest of the men did not hesitate. There was a deafening roar as the shotguns and revolvers flared and smoked around the trunk of the tree.

He closed his eyes; he was afraid to look again at the face above. The firing continued without break. Clem hugged the tree with all his might, and then, with the far-away sound of splintering wood, the top of the tree and Clem came crashing through the lower limbs to the ground. The body, sprawling and torn, landed on the ground with a thud that stopped Lonnie's heart for a moment.

He turned, clutching for the support of a tree, as the firing began once more. The crumpled body was tossed time after time, like a sackful of kittens being killed with an automatic shotgun, as charges of lead were fired into it from all sides. A cloud of dust rose from the ground and drifted overhead with the choking odor of burned powder.

Lonnie did not remember how long the shooting lasted. He found himself running from tree to tree, clutching at the rough pine bark, stumbling wildly towards the cleared ground. The sky had turned from gray to red when he emerged in the open, and as he ran, falling over the hard clods in the plowed field, he tried to keep his eyes on the house ahead.

Once he fell and found it almost impossible to rise again to his feet. He struggled to his knees, facing the round red sun. The warmth gave him the strength to rise to his feet, and he muttered unintelligibly to himself. He tried to say things he had never thought to say before.

When he got home, Hatty was waiting for him in the yard. She had heard the shots in the woods, and she had seen him stumbling over the hard clods in the field, and she had seen him kneeling there looking straight into the face of the sun. Hatty was trembling as she ran to Lonnie to find out what the matter was.

Once in his own yard, Lonnie turned and looked for a second over his shoulder. He saw the men climbing over the fence at Arch Gunnard's. Arch's wife was standing on the back porch, and she was speaking to them.

"Where's your pa, Lonnie?" Hatty said. "And what in the world was all that shooting in the woods for?" Lonnie stumbled forward until he had reached the front porch. He fell upon the steps.

"Lonnie, Lonnie!" Hatty was saying. "Wake up and tell me what in the world is the matter. I've never seen the like of all that's going on."

"Nothing," Lonnie said. "Nothing."

"Well, if there's nothing the matter, can't you go up to the big house and ask for a little piece of streak-of-lean? We ain't got a thing to cook for breakfast. Your pa's going to be hungrier than ever after being up walking around all night."

"What?" Lonnie said, his voice rising to a shout as he jumped to his feet.

"Why, I only said go up to the big house and get a little piece of streak-of-lean, Lonnie. That's all I said."

He grabbed his wife about the shoulders.

"Meat?" he yelled, shaking her roughly.

"Yes," she said, pulling away from him in surprise. "Couldn't you go ask Arch Gunnard for a little bit of streak-of-lean?"

Lonnie slumped down again on the steps, his hands falling between his outspread legs and his chin falling on his chest.

"No," he said almost inaudibly. "No. I aint hungry."

S. J. PERELMAN

[1904–]

"I AM A *thirty-five year old Spartan boy," S. J. Perelman confided in 1939. Though reticent about his personal life, later he expanded this brief autobiography into a* Time*-style note: "Button-cute, rapier-keen, waferthin, and pauper-poor is S. J. Perelman, whose tall, stooping figure is better known to the twilit half-world of five continents than to Publishers' Row. That he possesses the power to become invisible to finance companies; that his laboratory is tooled up to manufacture Frankenstein monsters on an incredible scale; and that he owns one of*

the rare mouths in which butter has never melted are legends treasured by every schoolboy."

Born in New York in 1904, Sidney Joseph Perelman attended Brown University, which, he says, "fulfils the three most important ideals of a college: it is situated on a steep grade, most of the buildings are covered with ivy, and it is included on the itinerary of the Brooks Brothers salesman." Among his college friends was Nathaniel West, whose sister, Laure, became Mrs. Perelman. Setting out to write, he was most influenced, he says, by Ring Lardner, Robert Benchley, Stephen Leacock, George Ade, and James Joyce, whom he considers "the greatest comic writer of our time."

The quiet, bespectacled young man worked his way through College Humor magazine, the old Life, Broun's Nutmeg, and The New Yorker. He became the master of a kind of dead-pan parody which drove writing to the verge of irresponsibility and clear across the borders of insanity. "It was just a matter of time," Benchley said, "before Perelman took over the dementia praecox field." His is the humor of applying logic to the illogical. His prose, seemingly capricious, is coldly critical. His surrealism has the careful lunacy of Dali; it is not merely a set of free associations but a series of satires on over-exuberant advertising copy, the movies, the super-salesman, and himself as the bedevilled traveler or fatigued bon-vivant.

Perelman's works display a prodigious vocabulary and a genius for garbled non-sequiturs. Dawn Ginsbergh's Revenge, a frantic burlesque, appeared in 1929. Perelman went West to write films, "an occupation which, like herding swine, makes the vocabulary pungent but contributes little to one's prose style." He was, however, a natural "gag-man" for the Marx brothers. Some years, several books, and a couple of plays later he did an award-winning script for Jules Verne's Around the World in Eighty Days. It was rather different from his own world travels, riotously chronicled in Westward Ha! and The Swiss Family Perelman.

Perelman's eye for the illogical penultimate and the ballooning cliché waiting to be punctured never dimmed. Parlor, Bedlam and Bath was followed by Strictly From Hunger, Look Who's Talking, Crazy Like a Fox, and a series, "Cloudland Revisited," which concerned itself with early movies and sensational novels.

Recondite and strikingly learned, Perelman also can write of these annoying idiocies which plague everyone. No parent who has faced the appalling jumble of a do-it-yourself kit ("So easy a child can do it!") will fail to recognize the frustration of "Insert Flap 'A.' . ."

Perelman blithely (and mendaciously) reports that he has "retired to peaceful Erwinna, Pa. . . . Those who know hint that the light burning late in his laboratory may result in a breathtaking electric bill. Queried, he shrugs with the fatalism of your true Oriental. 'Mektoub,' he observes curtly, 'It is written.'"

"Mr. Perelman stands alone in this day of humorists," Dorothy Parker wrote. "Robert Benchley, who was nearest to Perelman, and Ring Lardner, who was nearest to nobody, are gone, and so Mr. Perelman stands by himself. Lonely he may be—but there he is."

INSERT FLAP "A" AND THROW AWAY

One stifling summer afternoon last August, in the attic of a tiny stone house in Pennsylvania, I made a most interesting discovery: the shortest, cheapest method of inducing a nervous breakdown ever perfected. In this technique (eventually adopted by the psychology department of Duke University, which will adopt anything), the subject is placed in a sharply sloping attic heated to 340°F. and given a mothproof closet known as the Jiffy-Cloz to assemble. The Jiffy-Cloz, procurable at any department store or neighborhood insane asylum, consists of half a dozen gigantic sheets of red cardboard, two plywood doors, a clothes rack, and a packet of staples. With these is included a set of instructions mimeographed in pale-violet ink, fruity with phrases like "Pass Section F through Slot AA, taking care not to fold tabs behind washers (see Fig 9)." The cardboard is so processed that as the subject struggles convulsively to force the staple through, it suddenly buckles, plunging the staple deep into his thumb. He thereupon springs up with a dolorous cry and smites his knob (Section K) on the rafters (RR). As a final demonic touch, the Jiffy-Cloz people cunningly omit four of the staples necessary to finish the job, so that after indescribable purgatory, the best the subject can possibly achieve is a sleazy, capricious structure which would reduce any self-respecting moth to helpless laughter. The cumulative frustration, the tropical heat, and the soft, ghostly chuckling of the moths are calculated to unseat the strongest mentality.

In a period of rapid technological change, however, it was inevitable that a method as cumbersome as the Jiffy-Cloz would be superseded. It was superseded at exactly nine-thirty Christmas morning by a device called the Self-Running 10-Inch Scale-Model Delivery-Truck Kit Powered by Magic Motor, costing twenty-nine cents. About nine on that particular morning, I was spread-eagled on my bed, indulging in my favorite sport of mouth-breathing, when a cork fired from a child's air gun mysteriously lodged in my throat. The pellet proved awkward for a while, but I finally ejected it by flailing the little marksman (and his sister, for good measure) until their welkins rang, and sauntered in to breakfast. Before I could choke down a healing fruit juice, my consort, a tall, regal creature indistinguishable from Cornelia, the Mother of the Gracchi, except that her foot was entangled in a roller skate, swept in. She extended a large, unmistakable box covered with diagrams.

"Now don't start making excuses," she whined. "It's just a simple cardboard toy. The directions are on the back—"

"Look, dear," I interrupted, rising hurriedly and pulling on my overcoat, "it clean slipped my mind. I'm supposed to take a lesson in crosshatching at Zim's School of Cartooning today."

"On Christmas?" she asked suspiciously.

"Yes, it's the only time they could fit me in," I countered glibly. "This is the big week for crosshatching, you know, between Christmas and New Year's."

"Do you think you ought to go in your pajamas?" she asked.

"Oh, that's O.K.," I smiled. "We often work in our pajamas up at Zim's. Well, goodbye now. If I'm not home by Thursday, you'll find a cold snack in the safe-deposit box." My subterfuge, unluckily, went for naught, and in a trice I was sprawled on the nursery floor, surrounded by two lambkins and ninety-eight segments of the Self-Running 10-Inch Scale-Model Delivery-Truck Construction Kit.

The theory of the kit was simplicity itself, easily intelligible to Kettering of General Motors, Professor Millikan, or any first-rate physicist. Taking as my starting point the only sentence I could comprehend, "Fold down on all lines marked 'fold down'; fold up on all lines marked 'fold up,'" I set the children to work and myself folded up with an album of views of Chili Williams. In a few moments, my skin was suffused with a delightful tingling sensation and I was ready for the second phase, lightly referred to in the directions as "Preparing the Spring Motor Unit." As nearly as I could determine after twenty minutes of mumbling, the Magic Motor ("No Electricity—No Batteries—Nothing to Wind—Motor Never Wears Out") was an accordion-pleated affair operating by torsion, attached to the axles. "It is necessary," said the text, "to cut a slight notch in each of the axles with a knife (see Fig. C). To find the exact place to cut this notch, lay one of the axles over diagram at bottom of page."

"Well, *now we*'re getting someplace!" I boomed, with a false gusto that deceived nobody. "Here, Buster, run in and get Daddy a knife."

"I dowanna," quavered the boy, backing away. "You always cut yourself at this stage." I gave the wee fellow an indulgent pat on the head that flattened it slightly, to teach him civility, and commandeered a long, serrated bread knife from the kitchen. "Now watch me closely, children," I ordered. "We place the axle on the diagram as in Fig. C, applying a strong downward pressure on the knife handle at all times." The axle must have been a factory second, because an instant later I was in the bathroom grinding my teeth in agony and attempting to stanch the flow of blood. Ultimately, I succeeded in contriving a rough bandage and slipped back into the nursery without awakening the children's suspicions. An agreeable surprise awaited me. Displaying a mechanical aptitude clearly inherited from their sire, the rascals had put together the chassis of the delivery truck.

"Very good indeed," I complimented (naturally, one has to exaggerate praise to develop a child's self-confidence). "Let's see—what's the next step? Ah, yes. 'Lock into box shape by inserting tabs C, D, E, F, G, H, J, K, and L into slots C, D, E, F, G, H, J, K, and L. Ends of front axles should be pushed through holes A and B.' " While marshaling the indicated parts in their proper order, I emphasized to my rapt listeners the necessity of patience and perseverance. "Haste makes waste, you know," I reminded them. "Rome wasn't built in a day. Remember, your daddy isn't always going to be here to show you."

"Where *are* you going to be?" they demanded.

"In the movies, if I can arrange it," I snarled. Poising tabs C, D, E, F, G, H, J, K, and L in one hand and the corresponding slots in the other, I essayed a union of the two, but in vain. The moment I made one set fast and tackled another, tab and slot would part company, thumbing their noses at me. Although the children were too immature to understand, I saw in a flash where the trouble lay. Some idiotic employee at the factory had punched out the wrong design, probably out of sheer spite. So that was his game, eh? I set my lips in a grim line and, throwing one hundred and fifty-seven pounds of fighting fat into the effort, pounded the component parts into a homogeneous mass.

"There," I said with a gasp, "that's close enough. Now then, who wants candy? One, two, three—everybody off to the candy store!"

"We wanna finish the delivery truck!" they wailed. "Mummy, he won't let us finish the delivery truck!" Threats, cajolery, bribes were of no avail. In their jungle code, a twenty-nine-cent gewgaw bulked larger than a parent's love. Realizing that I was dealing with a pair of monomaniacs, I determined to show them who was master and wildly began locking the cardboard units helter-skelter, without any regard for the directions. When sections refused to fit, I gouged them with my nails and forced them together, cackling shrilly. The side panels collapsed; with a bestial oath, I drove a safety pin through them and lashed them to the roof. I used paper clips, bobby pins, anything I could lay my hands on. My fingers fairly flew and my breath whistled in my throat. "You want a delivery truck, do you?" I panted. "All right, I'll show you!" As merciful blackness closed in, I was on my hands and knees, bunting the infernal thing along with my nose and whinnying, "Roll, confound you, roll!"

"Absolute quiet," a carefully modulated voice was saying, "and fifteen of the white tablets every four hours." I opened my eyes carefully in the darkened room. Dimly I picked out a knifelike character actor in pince-nez lenses and a morning coat folding a stethoscope into his bag. "Yes," he added thoughtfully, "if we play our cards right, this ought to be a long, expensive recovery." From far away, I could hear my wife's voice bravely trying to control her anxiety.

"What if he becomes restless, Doctor?"

"Get him a detective story," returned the leech, "Or better still, a nice, soothing picture puzzle–something he can do with his hands."

WILLIAM SAROYAN

[1908–]

WILLIAM SAROYAN SAYS that in the year he began writing the San Joaquin Valley, in which he lived, had its first snow since 1856; he thinks it may have been a portent. In any case, he has, ever since, been dropping words onto pages and into theaters with the random capriciousness of snow flurries which form unusual patterns of seemingly accidental beauty or humor and sometimes, when the excitement of the storm is over, turn slushy.

"Sirak Goryan" (a pseudonym) was born in 1933 in Hairenik, an American-Armenian magazine. William Saroyan, "Sirak's" other self, was born August 31, 1908, in Fresno, a California city. His parents were Armenian. Following the death of his father he spent five years in an orphanage. At nine he came home. He completed the second year of

junior high school, working part-time as a newsboy, then took a full-time job as a telegraph messenger. By thirteen he had decided to be a writer and had, he said, already "read every book in the public library." A succession of jobs finally took him to San Francisco where he became the local manager of the Postal Telegraph office. His first story (that is, "Sirak's" first story) was published in 1933 and reprinted in the 1934 Best Short Stories. Then "The Daring Young Man on the Flying Trapeze" appeared in Story magazine. It served as the title-story for the volume which, in 1934, made the name Saroyan famous. ("Sirak" had been retired.) A successful writer, he went to Hollywood to work off some old debts. This done, he returned to San Francisco.

In 1939 Saroyan suddenly became a playwright. My Heart's In the Highlands, which he directed himself, was as unusual as his works which, for lack of a more specific classification, people called stories. In 1940 he won (and refused to accept) the Pulitzer Prize for his hit play The Time of Your Life, an almost plotless modern reverie in a saloon filled with characters whom Saroyan—and his audiences—loved. The ancient, tall-talking cowpoke who "fell in love with a midget" turned up among them. Filmed, televised, and often revived, the play retains that humanizing magic which is Saroyan at his best.

Saroyan returned to Hollywood in 1942 to write and direct The Human Comedy, whose title might appropriately be given to all his works. He retired from the movies when his studio refused to let him continue directing the film he had written.

In 1943 he married Carol Marcus, by whom he had two children; the marriage ended in a divorce six years later. He wrote some half-dozen plays, among them the popular one-act, "Hello Out There." The Assyrian and Other Stories appeared in 1950, and Tracy's Tiger in 1951. He wrote a thoroughly "Saroyanesque" autobiography, Bicycle Rider in Beverly Hills.

A new Broadway play, The Cave Dwellers, was a success, though not an overwhelming one. Here was Saroyan still in love with the world and infatuated by the theater. The play's defects were ones which critics had noted in his other works: those who felt there was too much sweetness in his milk of human kindness said that his pathos frequently turned into bathos. An eccentric writer, sometimes overwhelmed by the thought of his own genius and his mission ("to write the best stories ever written" and "to change the world"), he wrote by instinct, and when the instinct was good so was his work. His best stories seem fabulously improvised rather than thought out and written down. They come complete with ringing, attention-getting titles: "Love,

Here is My Hat," "Ever Fall in Love With a Midget?," "Comedy is Where You Die," and "They Don't Bury You Because You Still Can Walk." They are written with great verve (some said with nerve) and originality, blending the naïve and the noble, the ridiculous and the profound, the spontaneously simple and the elaborately sentimental.

EVER FALL IN LOVE WITH A MIDGET?

I DON'T SUPPOSE you ever fell in love with a midget weighing thirty-nine pounds, did you?

No, I said, but have another beer.

Down in Gallup, he said, twenty years ago. Fellow by the name of Rufus Jenkins came to town with six white horses and two black ones. Said he wanted a man to break the horses for him because his left leg was wood and he couldn't do it. Had a meeting at Parker's Mercantile Store and finally came to blows, me and Henry Walpal. Bashed his head with a brass cuspidor and ran away to Mexico, but he didn't die.

Couldn't speak a word. Took up with a cattle-breeder named Diego, educated in California. Spoke the language better than you and me. Said, Your job, Murph, is to feed them prize bulls. I said, Fine; what'll I feed them? He said, Hay, lettuce, salt, and beer. I said, Fine; they're your bulls.

Came to blows two days later over an accordion he claimed I stole. I borrowed it and during the fight busted it over his head; ruined one of the finest accordions I ever saw. Grabbed a horse and rode back across the border. Texas. Got to talking with a fellow who looked honest. Turned out to be a Ranger who was looking for me.

Yeah, I said. You were saying, a thirty-nine pound midget.

Will I ever forget that lady? he said. Will I ever get over that amazon of small proportions?

Will you? I said.

If I live to be sixty, he said.

Sixty? I said. You look more than sixty now.

That's trouble showing in my face. Trouble and complications. I was fifty-six three months ago.

Oh.

Told the Texas Ranger my name was Rothstein, mining engineer from

Pennsylvania, looking for something worth while. Mentioned two places in Houston. Nearly lost an eye early one morning, going down the stairs. Ran into a six-footer with an iron-claw where his right hand was supposed to be. Said, You broke up my home. Told him I was a stranger in Houston. The girls gathered at the top of the stairs to see a fight. Seven of them. Six feet and an iron claw. That's bad on the nerves. Kicked him in the mouth when he swung for my head with the claw. Would have lost an eye except for quick thinking. Rolled into the gutter and pulled a gun. Fired seven times, but I was back upstairs. Left the place an hour later, dressed in silk and feathers, with a hat swung around over my face. Saw him standing on the corner, waiting. Said, Care for a wiggle? Said he didn't. Went on down the street, left town.

I don't suppose you ever had to put on a dress to save your skin, did you?

No, I said, and I never fell in love with a midget weighing thirty-nine pounds. Have another beer.

Thanks. Ever try to herd cattle on a bicycle?

No, I said.

Left Houston with sixty cents in my pocket, gift of a girl named Lucinda. Walked fourteen miles in fourteen hours. Big house with barb-wire all around, and big dogs. One thing I never could get around. Walked past the gate, anyway, from hunger and thirst. Dogs jumped up and came for me. Walked right into them, growing older every second. Went up to the door and knocked. Big negress opened the door, closed it quick. Said, On your way, white trash.

Knocked again. Said, On you way. Again. On your way. Again. This time the old man himself opened the door, ninety if he was a day. Sawed-off shotgun too.

Said, I ain't looking for trouble, Father. I'm hungry and thirsty, name's Cavanaugh.

Took me in and made mint juleps for the two of us.

Said, Living here alone, Father?

Said, Drink and ask no questions; maybe I am and maybe I ain't. You saw the negress. Draw your own conclusions.

I'd heard of that, but didn't wink out of tact.

Called out, Elvira, bring this gentleman sandwiches.

Young enough for a man of seventy, probably no more than forty, and big.

Said, Any good at cards? Said, No.

Said, Fine, Cavanaugh, take a hand of poker.

Played all night.

If I told you that old Southern gentleman was my grandfather, you wouldn't believe me, would you?

No.

Well, it so happens he wasn't, although it would have been remarkable if he had been.

Where did you herd cattle on a bicycle?

Toledo, Ohio, 1918.

Toledo, Ohio? I said. They don't herd cattle up there.

They don't any more. They did in 1918. One fellow did, leastways. Bookkeeper named Sam Gold. Only Jewish cowboy I ever saw. Straight from the Eastside New York. Sombrero, lariats, Bull Durham, two head of cattle, and two bicycles. Called his place Gold Bar Ranch, two acres, just outside the city limits.

That was the year of the War, you'll remember.

Yeah, I said.

Remember a picture called *Shoulder Arms?*

Sure. Saw it five times.

Remember when Charlie Chaplin thought he was washing *his* foot, and the foot turned out to be another man's?

Sure.

You may not believe me, but I was the man whose foot was washed by Chaplin in that picture.

It's possible, I said, but how about herding them two cows on a bicycle? How'd you do it?

Easiest thing in the world. Rode no hands. Had to, otherwise couldn't lasso the cows. Worked for Sam Gold till the cows ran away. Bicycles scared them. They went into Toledo and we never saw hide or hair of them again. Advertised in every paper, but never got them back. Broke his heart. Sold both bikes and returned to New York.

Took four aces from a deck of red cards and walked to town. Poker. Fellow in the game named Chuck Collins, liked to gamble. Told him with a smile I didn't suppose he'd care to bet a hundred dollars I wouldn't hold four aces the next hand. Called it. My cards were red on the blank side. The other cards were blue. Plumb forgot all about it. Showed him four aces. Ace of spades, ace of clubs, ace of diamonds, ace of hearts. I'll remember them four cards if I live to be sixty. Would have been killed on the spot except for the hurricane that year.

Hurricane?

You haven't forgotten the Toledo hurricane of 1918, have you?

No, I said. There was no hurricane in Toledo, in 1918, or any other year.

For the love of God, then, what do you suppose that commotion was?

And how come I came to in Chicago? Dream-walking down State Street?

I guess they scared you.

No, that wasn't it. You go back to the papers of November, 1918, and I think you'll find there was a hurricane in Toledo. I remember sitting on the roof of a two-story house, floating northwest.

Northwest?

Sure.

Okay, have another beer.

Thaaaaanks. Thanks, he said.

I don't suppose *you* ever fell in love with a midget weighing thirty-nine pounds, did you? I said.

Who? he said.

You? I said.

No, he said, can't say I have.

Well, I said, let *me* tell *you* about it.

THE GENIUS

UP AT IZZY'S one night a young genius in corduroy pants came up to me and said, I hear you're a writer. I've got a story that'll make a great movie, only I need somebody with experience to write it for me. I'd write it myself, only I've got to make a living working and when I get through working I'm too tired to write.

I was a little drunk, but I'm never too drunk and never too busy to listen to a fellow-artist, and I said, Go ahead, tell me the story. If it's good I'll write it and we'll get Metro-Goldwyn-Mayer to make a movie out of it. What happens?

If you've ever had a story printed in a national magazine and been around at all you've met all kinds of people with stories that will make great movies. The world is full of people with movie stories, all unwritten, but it seems the people who manufacture movies never meet these people, or if they do, never let them tell their stories, consequently the average movie is lousy, even in technicolor, even starring Clark Gable, John Barrymore, Norma Shearer, or anybody else. The people who manufacture movies just simply don't care to manufacture good movies.

Up at Izzy's as many as eighty-seven good movies are related in one night, but not one of them is ever filmed.

I told the boy to go ahead and tell me the story.

Shall I begin at the beginning? he said.

Not necessarily, I said. Begin anywhere. Begin at the end and work backward to the beginning. You might even sit down if you like.

Thanks, he said, I'd rather stand.

Take all the time you need, I said.

There ain't much to say, he said. The idea is this. Says, I'll do something. I won't be a clerk all my life. Ships out on a boat to Shanghai.

Who? I said.

The fellow, said the boy. Clark Gable.

Oh, I said. Clark Gable. Says he'll do something. Do what?

Coming up on deck he bumps into the girl.

The girl? I said.

Joan Crawford.

Ah, Joan, I said. What's it come to?

They fall in love.

So the boy does something?

Not right away. That's at the end.

I know, I said. Anything special?

He marries the girl.

How about the money? I said. Who's got the money?

She has. That's where the trouble comes in.

Oh, I said, the trouble.

Yeah, the boy ain't a gigolo, so he won't marry the girl when he finds out she's rich.

Why? I said.

He figures he can't marry a rich girl, even if he is in love with her, so they quarrel.

Just in fun, of course, I said. Nothing serious.

Plenty serious. The girl's got to marry somebody before the boat reaches Shanghai or she won't inherit the eighteen million dollars.

The how many million? I said.

Eighteen.

Do you think that's enough? I said. For all practical purposes?

It's a tidy sum.

A trifle, I said. How does it turn out?

Well, the man who is engaged to the girl is a middle-aged banker. He ain't very good-looking. She don't want to marry him. That's where she gets a chance to do some acting.

Boy, I said.

After the boy and the girl fight, the girl says she's going to marry the banker, just to make the boy jealous.

That's another spot for some fancy acting, I said.

Yeah, so the Captain makes plans for a ship wedding. This is where it gets exciting. One thing after another happens, in quick succession. Chinese pirates take over the ship, and a Chinaman decides to marry the girl himself, without the formality of a wedding of course. The banker doesn't care, because he's scared, but the boy hates the Chinaman. He's a young educated Chinaman and speaks better English than anybody else on board the ship.

So? I said.

The Chinaman gets the girl in her cabin and starts chasing her around.

That's bad, I said.

The Chinaman is chasing the girl around the room, when the boy breaks the door down. The Chinaman and the boy have a fight. The Chinaman gets the boy flat on his back and gets out his dagger and is about to stick it in the boy.

Where? I said.

Right in the heart. The girl hits the Chinaman over the head with a chair.

That's love for you, I said.

In the meantime, a cablegram is received by the ship, asking the Captain to put the banker in chains for grand larceny and bigamy.

Just two little misdemeanors? I said.

And possible murder. The picture ends with the boy kissing the girl.

Boy, what an ending, I said.

How is it? he said.

It's fine, I said.

Is it exciting enough?

It's breath-taking, I said, especially where the Chinaman chases her.

I thought you'd like it, he said. First I think you ought to make a book out of it, and then sell it to the movies.

By God, I said, I'd do that little thing, only I gave up writing day before yesterday.

What for? he said.

I got bored, I said. Same old stuff over and over again.

This is different, he said. Think of the Chinaman. East against West.

Even so, I said. I gave up writing day before yesterday. *You* write it.

Do you think they'll print the book? he said.

They'd be fools not to, I said.

What style should I use? he said.

Oh, I said, don't worry about style. Just put it down on paper the way it comes to you after work and you'll find it'll be full of style. There'll be enough left over for two more movies.

My grammar ain't so hot, he said.

Neither is mine, I said. You don't need to worry about that. That'll be part of your style, part of your originality. Unless I'm badly mistaken, you're a genius.

No, he said, I just get these ideas for books and movies, that's all. I've forgotten enough ideas for books and movies to make a dozen books and a dozen movies.

Write them down, I said. Don't let them get away. You're losing money every minute.

Got a pencil? he said.

I'm afraid not, I said. I gave up writing day before yesterday.

What the hell for? he said.

My stuff's no good for movies, I said. I sell a story for thirty or forty dollars every now and then. I don't get movie ideas. I thought I would after a while, but I didn't, so I gave it up.

That's tough, he said. I get movie ideas left and right.

I know it, I said. All you got to do is get them down on paper and I know you'll be famous and rich in no time.

I'll tell you another idea I got for a movie, he said.

Joe, I said.

Joe came over to the table.

Joe, I said, here's a dime. Go get me a pencil.

Joe went over to Izzy and Izzy looked around and found a pencil. A little tiny one. Joe brought the pencil over to me. I handed it to the boy.

Listen, George, I said, you got no time to lose. Here's a pencil, all sharpened and everything. You take this pencil and go home and write them ideas down on paper. Any old kind of paper. Lincoln wrote his famous speech on the back of an envelope.

He took the pencil, but didn't start to go.

I thought I'd take it easy tonight and start writing tomorrow, he said.

No, I said, that ain't right. You go right home and go to work while the ideas are still fresh in your mind.

All right, he said.

He put the pencil in his inside coat pocket, pulled his hat down over his eyes, and went down the stairs.

Joe, I said, bring me three beers.

LEO C. ROSTEN

[1908–   ]

Although Leo Calvin Rosten engaged in many serious works as doctor of philosophy, night school teacher, researcher on administrative management, deputy director of the Office of War Information, concocter of editorial projects for Look magazine, adviser to various bureaus and corporations, and author of a Guide to the Religions of America, he is best known as "Leonard Q. Ross," creator of the irrepressible, slightly ridiculous, but always triumphant H*y*m*a*n K*a*p*l*a*n. (Under a similar pen-name, Leonard Ross, he wrote more than a dozen melodramas at the rate of approximately one a year.) He was born April 11, 1908, in Lodz, Poland. When he was three years old he was brought to Chicago, where he says he spent his grammar school days "reading Frank Merriwell and François Rabelais." He received a Phi Beta Kappa key from the University of Chicago, studied at the London School of Economics and Political Science, prepared treatises, lectured, and married Priscilla Ann Mead, sister of the anthropologist Margaret Mead.

"Leonard Q. Ross" was born when Rosten was in his late twenties—"to pay my debts I began to write humorous sketches for The New Yorker." The sketches centered about a struggler with the English language, the scourge and terror of the beginner's grade of the American Night Preparatory School for Adults. He was H*y*m*a*n K*a*p*l*a*n—he insisted on the stars—and he pronounced Madison (the fourth President) "Medicine;" he spoke of George Washington as "Judge Vashington," shortened Alexander Hamilton to "L. X. Hamilton," changed Thomas Jefferson to "Tom S. Jefferson," believed that the opposite of "spic" was "span," and contended that, if the plural of "mouse" was "mice," the plural of "blouse" should logically be "blice."

The first collection of the sayings and doings of Mr. Parkhill's (pronounced "Pockheel's") class, The Education of H*y*m*a*n K*a*p*l*a*n appeared in 1937. Twenty-two years later The Return of H*y*m*a*n K*a*p*l*a*n again brought together the disparate students: the hesitant ("always right but never victorious") Miss Mitnick; the floundering Mrs. Moskowitz; the plodding Mr. Bloom; Miss Caravello, who felt that everything good and beautiful must be Latin in origin; Plonsky, the sworn enemy; and Pinsky, the dedicated friend.

Their creator won the reader not only because of the comic misunderstandings and absurd malapropisms but because of his people's warm and sympathetic qualities. They ceased to be stock figures or cleverly manipulated comic characters, and became recognizable human beings.

The wholly serious work of Leo Rosten was well received. The Washington Correspondents *was a revealing "behind the scenes" study, and* Hollywood: The Movie Colony: The Movie Makers *had enthusiastic reviews. But, after two decades Rosten finally resigned himself to being a much-appreciated humorist. "Humor," he acknowledged by way of a happy definition, "is the affectionate communication of insight."*

THE RATHER DIFFICULT CASE OF MR. K★A★P★L★A★N

IN THE THIRD WEEK of the new term, Mr. Parkhill was forced to the conclusion that Mr. Kaplan's case was rather difficult. Mr. Kaplan first came to his special attention, out of the thirty-odd adults in the beginners' grade of the American Night Preparatory School for Adults ("English–Americanization–Civics–Preparation for Naturalization"), through an exercise the class had submitted. The exercise was entitled "Fifteen Common Nouns and Their Plural Forms." Mr. Parkhill came to one paper which included the following:

house	makes..................	houses
dog	"	..................dogies
libary	"	..................Public libary
cat	"	..................Katz

Mr. Parkhill read this over several times, very thoughtfully. He decided that here was a student who might, unchecked, develop into a "problem case." It was clearly a case that called for special attention. He turned the page over and read the name. It was printed in large, firm letters with red crayon. Each letter was outlined in blue. Between every two letters was a star, carefully drawn, in green. The multi-colored whole spelled, unmistakably, H★Y★M★A★N K★A★P★L★A★N.

This Mr. Kaplan was in his forties, a plump, red-faced gentleman, with wavy blond hair, *two* fountain pens in his outer pocket, and a perpetual smile. It was a strange smile, Mr. Parkhill remarked: vague, bland, and consistent in its monotony. The thing that emphasized it for Mr. Parkhill was that it never seemed to leave the face of Mr. Kaplan, even during Recitation and Speech period. This disturbed Mr. Parkhill considerably, because Mr. Kaplan was particularly bad in Recitation and Speech.

Mr. Parkhill decided he had not applied himself as conscientiously as he might to Mr. Kaplan's case. That very night he called on Mr. Kaplan first.

"Won't *you* take advantage of Recitation and Speech practice, Mr. Kaplan?" he asked, with an encouraging smile.

Mr. Kaplan smiled back and answered promptly, "Vell, I'll tell abot Prazidents United States. Fife Prazidents United States is Abram Lincohen, he vas freeink de neegers; Hodding, Coolitch, Judge Vashington, an' Banjamin Frenklin."

Further encouragement revealed that in Mr. Kaplan's literary Valhalla the "most famous tree American wriders" were Jeck Laundon, Valt Viterman, and the author of "Hawk L. Barry-Feen," one Mocktvain. Mr. Kaplan took pains to point out that he did not mention Relfvaldo Amerson because "He is a poyet, an' I'm talkink abot wriders."

Mr. Parkhill diagnosed the case as one of "inability to distinguish between 'a' and 'e.'" He concluded that Mr. Kaplan *would* need special attention. He was, frankly, a little disturbed.

Mr. Kaplan's English showed no improvement during the next hard weeks. The originality of his spelling and pronunciation, however, flourished—like a sturdy flower in the good, rich earth. A man to whom "Katz" is the plural of "cat" soon soars into higher and more ambitious endeavor. As a one-paragraph "Exercise in Composition," Mr. Kaplan submitted:

When people is meating on the boulvard, on going away one is saying, "I am glad I mat you," and the other is giving answer, "Mutual."

Mr. Parkhill felt that perhaps Mr. Kaplan had overreached himself, and should be confined to the simpler exercises.

Mr. Kaplan was an earnest student. He worked hard, knit his brows regularly (albeit with that smile), did all his homework, and never missed a class. Only once did Mr. Parkhill feel that Mr. Kaplan might, perhaps, be a little more *serious* about his work. That was when he asked Mr. Kaplan to "give a noun."

"Door," said Mr. Kaplan, smiling.

It seemed to Mr. Parkhill that "door" had been given only a moment earlier, by Miss Mitnick.

"Y-es," said Mr. Parkhill. "Er—and another noun?"

"Another door," Mr. Kaplan replied promptly.

Mr. Parkhill put him down as a doubtful "C." Everything pointed to the fact that Mr. Kaplan might have to be kept on an extra three months before he was ready for promotion to Composition, Grammar, and Civics, with Miss Higby.

One night Mrs. Moskowitz read a sentence, from "English for Beginners," in which "the vast deserts of America" were referred to. Mr. Parkhill soon discovered that poor Mrs. Moskowitz did not know the meaning of "vast." "Who can tell us the meaning of 'vast'?" asked Mr. Parkhill lightly.

Mr. Kaplan's hand shot up, volunteering wisdom. He was all proud grins. Mr. Parkhill, in the rashness of the moment, nodded to him.

Mr. Kaplan rose, radiant with joy. "'Vast!' It's commink fromm *diraction*. Ve have four diractions: de naut, de sot, de heast, and de vast."

Mr. Parkhill shook his head. "Er—that is 'west,' Mr. Kaplan." He wrote "VAST" and "WEST" on the blackboard. To the class he added, tolerantly, that Mr. Kaplan was apparently thinking of "west," whereas it was "vast" which was under discussion.

This seemed to bring a great light into Mr. Kaplan's inner world. "So is 'vast' vat you eskink?"

Mr. Parkhill admitted that it was "vast" for which he was asking.

"Aha!" cried Mr. Kaplan. "You minn '*vast*,' not"—with scorn—"'vast.'"

"Yes," said Mr. Parkhill, faintly.

"Hau Kay!" said Mr. Kaplan, essaying the vernacular. "Ven I'm buyink a suit clothes, I'm gattink de cawt, de pents, an' de vast!"

Stunned, Mr. Parkhill shook his head, very sadly. "I'm afraid that you've used still another word, Mr. Kaplan."

Oddly enough, this seemed to give Mr. Kaplan great pleasure.

Several nights later Mr. Kaplan took advantage of Open Questions period. This ten-minute period was Mr. Parkhill's special innovation in the American Night Preparatory School for Adults. It was devoted to answering any questions which the students might care to raise about any difficulties which they might have encountered during the course of their adventures with the language. Mr. Parkhill enjoyed Open Questions. He liked to clear up *practical* problems. He felt he was being ever so much more constructive that way. Miss Higby had once told him that he was a born Open Questions teacher.

"Plizz, Mr. Pockheel," asked Mr. Kaplan as soon as the period opened. "Vat's de minnink fromm—" It sounded, in Mr. Kaplan's rendition, like "a big department."

" 'A big department,' Mr. Kaplan?" asked Mr. Parkhill, to make sure.

"Yassir!" Mr. Kaplan's smile was beauteous to behold. "In de stritt, ven I'm valkink, I'm hearink like 'I big de pottment.' "

It was definitely a pedagogical opportunity.

"Well, class," Mr. Parkhill began. "I'm sure that you have all—"

He told them that they had all probably done some shopping in the large downtown stores. (Mr. Kaplan nodded.) In these large stores, he said, if they wanted to buy a pair of shoes, for example, they went to a special *part* of the store, where only shoes were sold—a *shoe* department. (Mr. Kaplan nodded.) If they wanted a table, they went to a different *part* of the store, where *tables* were sold. (Mr. Kaplan nodded.) If they wanted to buy, say, a goldfish, they went to still another part of the store, where goldfish . . . (Mr. Kaplan frowned; it was clear that Mr. Kaplan had never bought a goldfish.)

"Well, then," Mr. Parkhill summed up hastily, "each article is sold in a different *place*. These different and special places are called *departments*." He printed "D-E-P-A-R-T-M-E-N-T" on the board in large, clear capitals. "And a *big* department, Mr. Kaplan, is merely such a department which is large—*big!*"

He put the chalk down and wiped his fingers.

"Is that clear now, class?" he asked, with a little smile. (It was rather an ingenious explanation, he thought; it might be worth repeating to Miss Higby during the recess.)

It *was* clear. There were thirty nods of approval. But Mr. Kaplan looked uncertain. It was obvious that Mr. Kaplan, a man who would not compromise with truth, did *not* find it clear.

"Isn't that clear *now*, Mr. Kaplan?" asked Mr. Parkhill anxiously.

Mr. Kaplan pursed his lips in thought. "It's a *fine* haxplination, Titcher," he said generously, "but I don' unnistand vy I'm hearink de voids de vay I do. Simms to me it's used in annodder minnink."

"There's really only one meaning for 'a big department.' " Mr. Parkhill was definitely worried by this time. "*If* that's the phrase you mean."

Mr. Kaplan nodded gravely. "Oh, dat's de phrase—ufcawss! It sounds like dat—or maybe a leetle more like '*I* big de pottment.' "

Mr. Parkhill took up the chalk. ("*I* big department" was obviously a case of Mr. Kaplan's own curious audition.) He repeated the explanation carefully, this time embellishing the illustrations with a shirt department, a victrola section, and "a separate part of the store where, for example, you buy canaries, or other birds."

Mr. Kaplan sat entranced. He followed it all politely, even the part about "canaries, or other birds." He smiled throughout with consummate reassurance.

Mr. Parkhill was relieved, assuming, in his folly, that Mr. Kaplan's smiles were a testimony to his exposition. But when he had finished, Mr. Kaplan shook his head once more, this time with a new and superior firmness.

"Is the explanation *still* not clear?" Mr. Parkhill was genuinely concerned by this time.

"Is de haxplination clear!" cried Mr. Kaplan with enthusiasm. "Ha! I should live so! Soitinly! Clear like *gold!* So clear! An' netcheral too! But Mr. Pockheel—"

"Go on, Mr. Kaplan," said Mr. Parkhill, studying the white dust on his fingers. There was, after all, nothing more to be done.

"Vell! I tink it's more like '*I* big de pottment.'"

"Go on, Mr. Kaplan, go on." (*Domine, dirige nos.*)

Mr. Kaplan rose. His smile was broad, luminous, transcendent; his manner was regal.

"I'm hearink it in de stritt. Somtimes I'm stendink in de stritt, talkink to a frand, or mine vife, mine brodder—or maybe only stendink. An' somvun is pessink arond me. An' by hexident he's givink me a bump, you know, a *poosh!* Vell, he says, 'Axcuse me!' no? But somtimes, an' *dis* is vat I minn, he's sayink, '*I big de pottment!*'"

Mr. Parkhill studied the picture of "Abram Lincohen" on the back wall, as if reluctant to face reality. He wondered whether he could reconcile it with his conscience if he were to promote Mr. Kaplan to Composition, Grammar, and Civics—at once. Another three months of Recitation and Speech might, after all, be nothing but a waste of Mr. Kaplan's valuable time.

EUDORA WELTY

[1909–]

A DISTINCTIVELY *Southern writer, Eudora Welty was born in Jackson, Mississippi, April 13, 1909. After attending Mississippi State College for Women, she went to the University of Wisconsin, receiving her B.A. there, and came East to Columbia University to study advertising. It did not take her long to become disillusioned with the trick of trying to talk people into things they did not want; she decided to return to her birthplace and become a writer. Her first collection of short stories,* A Curtain of Green, *was published when she was thirty-two;*

her first novel, Delta Wedding, appeared five years later. The Golden Apples, a chronicle of the people who make up a Mississippi town, was published in 1949.

Eudora Welty has been the recipient of several awards, including the Howells Medal given every five years by the American Academy of Arts and Letters for the most distinguished work of American fiction. "Intensity and beauty are qualities that will always come out of man's imagination and out of his passion," said Eudora Welty in an address delivered at the University of Washington in 1947. "It seems to be true that in writing a story, beauty is in greatest accord with sensitivity. . . The two things that cannot be imitated, beauty and sensitivity are or may be kin to each other . . . but it is only one of them we can strive for: sensitivity in ourselves. It is our technique. In the end, our technique is sensitivity, and beauty may be our reward."

The reward is the reader's as well as the writer's, for sensitivity and beauty—and, in the case of "Petrified Man," unforced folk humor—are the qualities in which Eudora Welty excells.

PETRIFIED MAN

REACH IN MY PURSE and git me a cigarette without no powder in it if you kin, Mrs. Fletcher, honey," said Leota to her ten-o'clock shampoo-and-set customer. "I don't like no perfumed cigarettes."

Mrs. Fletcher gladly reached over to the lavender shelf under the lavender-framed mirror, shook a hair net loose from the clasp of the patent-leather bag, and slapped her hand down quickly on a powder puff which burst out when the purse was opened.

"Why, look at the peanuts, Leota!" said Mrs. Fletcher in her marveling voice.

"Honey, them goobers has been in my purse a week if they's been in it a day. Mrs. Pike bought them peanuts."

"Who's Mrs. Pike?" asked Mrs. Fletcher, settling back. Hidden in this den of curling fluid and henna packs, separated by a lavender swing door from the other customers, who were being gratified in other booths, she could give her curiosity its freedom. She looked expectantly at the black part in Leota's yellow curls as she bent to light the cigarette.

"Mrs. Pike is this lady from New Orleans," said Leota, puffing, and pressing into Mrs. Fletcher's scalp with strong red-nailed fingers. "A friend, not a customer. You see, like maybe I told you last time, me and Fred and Sal and Joe all had us a fuss, so Sal and Joe up and moved out, so we didn't do a thing but rent out their room. Se we rented it to Mrs. Pike. And Mr. Pike." She flicked an ash into the basket of dirty towels. "Mrs. Pike is a very decided blonde. *She* bought me the peanuts."

"She must be cute," said Mrs. Fletcher.

"Honey, 'cute' ain't the word for what she is. I'm tellin' you, Mrs. Pike is attractive. She has her a good time. She's got a sharp eye out, Mrs. Pike has."

She dashed the comb through the air, and paused dramatically as a cloud of Mrs. Fletcher's hennaed hair floated out of the lavender teeth like a small storm cloud.

"Hair fallin'."

"Aw, Leota."

"Uh-huh, commencin' to fall out," said Leota, combing again, and letting fall another cloud.

"Is it any dandruff in it?" Mrs. Fletcher was frowning, her hair-line eyebrows diving down toward her nose, and her wrinkled, beady-lashed eyelids batting with concentration.

"Nope." She combed again. "Just fallin' out."

"Bet it was that last perm'nent you gave me that did it," Mrs. Fletcher said cruelly. "Remember you cooked me fourteen minutes."

"You had fourteen minutes comin' to you," said Leota with finality.

"Bound to be somethin'," persisted Mrs. Fletcher. "Dandruff, dandruff. I couldn't of caught a thing like that from Mr. Fletcher, could I?"

"Well," Leota answered at last, "you know what I heard in here yestiddy, one of Thelma's ladies was settin' over yonder in Thelma's booth gittin' a machineless, and I don't mean to insist or insinuate or anything, Mrs. Fletcher, but Thelma's lady just happ'med to throw out—I forgotten what she was talkin' about at the time—that you was p-r-e-g., and lots of times that'll make your hair do awful funny, fall out and God knows what all. It just ain't our fault is the way I look at it."

There was a pause. The women stared at each other in the mirror.

"Who was it?" demanded Mrs. Fletcher.

"Honey, I really couldn't say," said Leota. "Not that you look it."

"Where's Thelma? I'll get it out of her," said Mrs. Fletcher.

"Now, honey, I wouldn't go and git mad over a little thing like that," Leota said, combing hastily, as though to hold Mrs. Fletcher down by the hair. "I'm sure it was somebody didn't mean no harm in the world. How far gone are you?"

"Just wait," said Mrs. Fletcher, and shrieked for Thelma, who came in and took a drag from Leota's cigarette.

"Thelma, honey, throw your mind back to yestiddy if you kin," said Leota, drenching Mrs. Fletcher's hair with a thick fluid and catching the overflow in a cold wet towel at her neck.

"Well, I got my lady half wound for a spiral," said Thelma doubtfully.

"This won't take but a minute," said Leota. "Who is it you got in there, old Horse Face? Just cast your mind back and try to remember who your lady was yestiddy who happ'm to mention that my customer was pregnant, that's all. She's dead to know."

Thelma drooped her blood-red lips and looked over Mrs. Fletcher's head into the mirror. "Why, honey, I ain't got the faintest," she breathed. "I really don't recollect the faintest. But I'm sure she meant no harm. I declare, I forgot my hair finally got combed and thought it was a stranger behind me."

"Was it that Mrs. Hutchinson?" Mrs. Fletcher was tensely polite.

"Mrs. Hutchinson? Oh, Mrs. Hutchinson." Thelma batted her eyes. "Naw, precious, she come on Thursday and didn't ev'm mention your name. I doubt if she ev'm knows you're on the way."

"Thelma!" cried Leota stanchly.

"All I know is, whoever it is'll be sorry someday. Why, I just barely knew it myself!" cried Mrs. Fletcher. "Just let her wait!"

"Why? What're you gonna do to her?"

It was a child's voice, and the women looked down. A little boy was making tents with aluminum wave pinchers on the floor under the sink.

"Billy Boy, hon, mustn't bother nice ladies," Leota smiled. She slapped him brightly and behind her back waved Thelma out of the booth. "Ain't Billy Boy a sight? Only three years old and already just nuts about the beauty-parlor business."

"I never saw him here before," said Mrs. Fletcher, still unmollified.

"He ain't been here before, that's how come," said Leota. "He belongs to Mrs. Pike. She got her a job but it was Fay's Millinery. He oughtn't to try on those ladies' hats, they come down over his eyes like I don't know what. They just git to look ridiculous, that's what, an' of course he's gonna put 'em on: hats. They tole Mrs. Pike they didn't appreciate him hangin' around there. Here, he couldn't hurt a thing."

"Well! I don't like children that much," said Mrs. Fletcher.

"Well!" said Leota moodily.

"Well! I'm almost tempted not to have this one," said Mrs. Fletcher. "That Mrs. Hutchinson! Just looks straight through you when she sees you on the street and then spits at you behind your back."

"Mr. Fletcher would beat you on the head if you didn't have it now," said Leota reasonably. "After going this far."

Mrs. Fletcher sat up straight. "Mr. Fletcher can't do a thing with me."

"He can't!" Leota winked at herself in the mirror.

"No siree, he can't. If he so much as raises his voice against me, he knows good and well I'll have one of my sick headaches, and then I'm just not fit to live with. And if I really look that pregnant already——"

"Well, now, honey, I just want you to know—I habm't told any of my ladies and I ain't goin' to tell 'em—even that you're losin' your hair. You just get you one of those Stork-a-Lure dresses and stop worryin'. What people don't know don't hurt nobody, as Mrs. Pike says."

"Did you tell Mrs. Pike?" asked Mrs. Fletcher sulkily.

"Well, Mrs. Fletcher, look, you ain't ever goin' to lay eyes on Mrs. Pike or her lay eyes on you, so what diffunce does it make in the long run?"

"I knew it!" Mrs. Fletcher deliberately nodded her head so as to destroy a ringlet Leota was working on behind her ear. "Mrs. Pike!"

Leota sighed. "I reckon I might as well tell you. It wasn't any more Thelma's lady tole me you was pregnant than a bat."

"Not Mrs. Hutchinson?"

"Naw, Lord! It was Mrs. Pike."

"Mrs. Pike!" Mrs. Fletcher could only sputter and let curling fluid roll into the ear. "How could Mrs. Pike possibly know I was pregnant or otherwise, when she doesn't even know me? The nerve of some people!"

"Well, here's how it was. Remember Sunday?"

"Yes," said Mrs. Fletcher.

"Sunday, Mrs. Pike an' me was all by ourself. Mr. Pike and Fred had gone over to Eagle Lake, sayin' they was goin' to catch 'em some fish, but they didn't, a course. So we was settin' in Mrs. Pike's car, is a 1939 Dodge ——"

"1939, eh," said Mrs. Fletcher.

"—An' we was gettin' us a Jax beer apiece—that's the beer that Mrs. Pike says is made right in N.O., so she won't drink no other kind. So I seen you drive up to the drugstore an' run in for just a secont, leavin' I reckon Mr. Fletcher in the car, an' come runnin' out with looked like a perscription. So I says to Mrs. Pike, just to be makin' talk, 'Right yonder's Mrs. Fletcher, and I reckon that's Mr. Fletcher—she's one of my regular customers,' I says."

"I had on a figured print," said Mrs. Fletcher tentatively.

"You sure did," agreed Leota. "So Mrs. Pike, she give you a good look —she's very observant, a good judge of character, cute as a minute, you know—and she says, 'I bet you another Jax that lady's three months on the way.' "

"What gall!" said Mrs. Fletcher. "Mrs. Pike!"

"Mrs. Pike ain't goin' to bite you," said Leota. "Mrs. Pike is a lovely girl, you'd be crazy about her, Mrs. Fletcher. But she can't sit still a minute. We went to the travelin' freak show yestiddy after work. I got through early—nine o'clock. In the vacant store next door? What, you ain't been?"

"No, I despise freaks," declared Mrs. Fletcher.

"Aw. Well, honey, talkin' about bein' pregnant an' all, you ought to see those twins in a bottle, you really owe it to yourself."

"What twins?" asked Mrs. Fletcher out of the side of her mouth.

"Well, honey, they got these two twins in a bottle, see? Born joined plumb together—dead a course." Leota dropped her voice into a soft lyrical hum. "They was about this long—pardon—must of been full time, all right, wouldn't you say?—an' they had these two heads an' two faces an' four arms an' four legs, all kind of joined *here*. See, this face looked this-a-way, and the other face looked that-a-way, over their shoulder, see. Kinda pathetic."

"Glah!" said Mrs. Fletcher disapprovingly.

"Well, ugly? Honey, I mean to tell you—their parents was first cousins and all like that. Billy Boy, git me a fresh towel from off Teeny's stack—this 'n's wringin' wet—an' quit ticklin' my ankles with that curler. I declare! He don't miss nothin'."

"Me and Mr. Fletcher aren't one speck of kin, or he could never of had me," said Mrs. Fletcher placidly.

"Of course not!" protested Leota. "Neither is me an' Fred, not that we know of. Well, honey, what Mrs. Pike liked was the pygmies. They've got these pygmies down there, too, an' Mrs. Pike was just wild about 'em. You know, the tee-niest men in the universe? Well, honey, they can rest back on their little bohunkus an' roll around an' you can't hardly tell it they're sittin' or standin'. That'll give you some idea. They're about forty-two years old. Just suppose it was your husband!"

"Well, Mr. Fletcher is five foot nine and one half," said Mrs. Fletcher quickly.

"Fred's five foot ten," said Leota, "but I tell him he's still a shrimp, account of I'm so tall." She made a deep wave over Mrs. Fletcher's other temple with the comb. "Well, these pygmies are a kind of dark brown, Mrs. Fletcher. Not bad-lookin' for what they are, you know."

"I wouldn't care for them," said Mrs. Fletcher. "What does that Mrs. Pike see in them?"

"Aw, I don't know," said Leota. "She's just cute, that's all. But they got this man, this petrified man, that ever'-thing ever since he was nine years old, when it goes through his digestion, see, somehow Mrs. Pike says it goes to his joints and has been turning to stone."

"How awful!" said Mrs. Fletcher.

"He's forty-two, too. That looks like a bad age."

"Who said so, that Mrs. Pike? I bet she's forty-two," said Mrs. Fletcher.

"Naw," said Leota, "Mrs. Pike's thirty-three, born in January, an Aquarian. He could move his head—like this. A course his head and mind ain't a joint, so to speak, and I guess his stomach ain't either—not anyways. But see—his food, he eats it, and goes down, see, and then he digests it"—Leota rose on her toes for an instant—"and it goes out to his joints and before you can say 'Jack Robinson,' it's stone—pure stone. He's turning to stone. How'd you like to be married to a guy like that? All he can do, he can move his head just a quarter of an inch. A course he *looks* just *terrible*."

"I should think he would," said Mrs. Fletcher frostily. "Mr. Fletcher takes bending exercises every night of the world. I make him."

"All Fred does is lay around the house like a rug. I wouldn't be surprised if he woke up someday and couldn't move. The petrified man just sat there moving his quarter of an inch though," said Leota reminiscently.

"Did Mrs. Pike like the petrified man?" asked Mrs. Fletcher.

"Not as much as she did the others," said Leota deprecatingly. "And then she likes a man to be a good dresser, and all that."

"Is Mr. Pike a good dresser?" asked Mrs. Fletcher skeptically.

"Oh, well, yeah," said Leota, "but he's twelve-fourteen years older 'n her. She ast Lady Evangeline about him."

"Who's Lady Evangeline?" asked Mrs. Fletcher.

"Well, it's this mind reader they got in the freak show," said Leota. "Was real good. Lady Evangeline is her name, and if I had another dollar I wouldn't do a thing but have my other palm read. She had what Mrs. Pike said was the 'sixth mind' but she had the worst manicure I ever saw on a living person."

"What did she tell Mrs. Pike?" asked Mrs. Fletcher.

"She told her Mr. Pike was as true to her as he could be and, besides, would come into some money."

"Humph!" said Mrs. Fletcher. "What does he do?"

"I can't tell," said Leota, "because he don't work. Lady Evangeline didn't tell me near enough about my nature or anything. And I would like to go back and find out some more about this boy. Used to go with this boy got married to this girl. Oh, shoot, that was about three and a half years ago, when you was still goin' to the Robert E. Lee Beauty Shop in Jackson. He married her for her money. Another fortuneteller tole me that at the time. So I'm not in love with him any more, anyway, besides being married to Fred, but Mrs. Pike thought, just for the hell of it, see, to ask Lady Evangeline was he happy."

"Does Mrs. Pike know everything about you already?" asked Mrs. Fletcher unbelievingly. "Mercy!"

"Oh yeah, I tole her ever'thing about ever'thing, from now on back to I don't know when—to when I first started goin' out," said Leota. "So I ast Lady Evangeline for one of my questions, was he happily married, and she says, just like she was glad I ask her, 'Honey,' she says, 'naw, he isn't. You write down this day, March 8, 1941,' she says, 'and mock it down three years from today him and her won't be occupyin' the same bed.' There it is, up on the wall with them other dates—see, Mrs. Fletcher? And she says, 'Child, you ought to be glad you didn't git him, because he's so mercenary.' So I'm glad I married Fred. He sure ain't mercenary, money don't mean a thing to him. But I sure would like to go back and have my other palm read."

"Did Mrs. Pike believe in what the fortuneteller said?" asked Mrs. Fletcher in a superior tone of voice.

"Lord, yes, she's from New Orleans. Ever'body in New Orleans believes ever'thing spooky. One of 'em in New Orleans before it was raided says to Mrs. Pike one summer she was goin' to go from state to state and meet some gray-headed men, and, sure enough, she says she went on a beautician convention up to Chicago. . . ."

"Oh!" said Mrs. Fletcher. "Oh, is Mrs. Pike a beautician too?"

"Sure she is," protested Leota. "She's a beautician. I'm goin' to git her in here if I can. Before she married. But it don't leave you. She says sure enough, there was three men who was a very large part of making her trip what it was, and they all three had gray in their hair and they went in six states. Got Christmas cards from 'em. Billy Boy, go see if Thelma's got any dry cotton. Look how Mrs. Fletcher's a-drippin'."

"Where did Mrs. Pike meet Mr. Pike?" asked Mrs. Fletcher primly.

"On another train," said Leota.

"I met Mr. Fletcher, or rather he met me, in a rental library," said Mrs. Fletcher with dignity, as she watched the net come down over her head.

"Honey, me an' Fred, we met in a rumble seat eight months ago and we was practically on what you might call the way to the altar inside of a half an hour," said Leota in a guttural voice, and bit a bobby pin open. "Course it don't last. Mrs. Pike says nothin' like that ever lasts."

"Mr. Fletcher and myself are as much in love as the day we married," said Mrs. Fletcher belligerently as Leota stuffed cotton into her ears.

"Mrs. Pike says it don't last," repeated Leota in a louder voice. "Now go git under the dryer. You can turn yourself on can't you? I'll be back to comb you out. Durin' lunch I promised to give Mrs. Pike a facial. You know–free. Her bein' in the business, so to speak."

"I bet she needs one," said Mrs. Fletcher, letting the swing door fly back against Leota. "Oh, pardon me."

A week later, on time for her appointment, Mrs. Fletcher sank heavily into Leota's chair after first removing a drugstore rental book, called *Life Is Like That*, from the seat. She stared in a discouraged way into the mirror.

"You can tell it when I'm sitting down, all right," she said.

Leota seemed preoccupied and stood shaking out a lavender cloth. She began to pin it around Mrs. Fletcher's neck in silence.

"I said you sure can tell it when I'm sitting straight on and coming at you this way," Mrs. Fletcher said.

"Why, honey, naw you can't," said Leota gloomily. "Why, I'd never know. If somebody was to come up to me on the street and say, 'Mrs. Fletcher is pregnant!' I'd say, 'Heck, she don't look it to me.' "

"If a certain party hadn't found it out and spread it around, it wouldn't be too late even now," said Mrs. Fletcher frostily, but Leota was almost choking her with the cloth, pinning it so tight, and she couldn't speak clearly. She paddled her hands in the air until Leota wearily loosened her.

"Listen, honey, you're just a virgin compared to Mrs. Montjoy," Leota was going on, still absent-minded. She bent Mrs. Fletcher back in the chair and, sighing, tossed liquid from a teacup onto her head and dug both hands into her scalp. "You know Mrs. Montjoy–her husband's that premature-gray-headed fella?"

"She's in the Trojan Garden Club is all I know," said Mrs. Fletcher.

"Well, honey," said Leota, but in a weary voice, "she come in here not the week before and not the day before she had her baby–she come in here the very selfsame day, I mean to tell you. Child, we was all plumb scared to death. There she was! Come for her shampoo an' set. Why, Mrs. Fletcher, in a hour an' twenty minutes she was layin' up there in the Babtist Hospital with a seb'm-pound son. It was that close a shave. I declare, if I hadn't been so tired I would of drank up a bottle of gin that night."

"What gall," said Mrs. Fletcher. "I never knew her at all well."

"See, her husband was waitin' outside in the car, and her bags was all packed an' in the back seat, an' she was all ready, 'cept she wanted her shampoo an' set. An' havin' one pain right after another. Her husband kep' comin' in here, scared-like, but couldn't do nothin' with her a course. She yelled bloody murder, too, but she always yelled her head off when I give her a perm'nent."

"She must of been crazy," said Mrs. Fletcher. "How did she look?"

"Shoot!" said Leota.

"Well, I can guess," said Mrs. Fletcher. "Awful."

"Just wanted to look pretty while she was havin' her baby is all," said Leota airily. "Course, we was glad to give the lady what she was after—that's our motto—but I bet a hour later she wasn't payin' no mind to them little end curls. I bet she wasn't thinkin' about she ought to have on a net. It wouldn't of done her no good if she had."

"No, I don't suppose it would," said Mrs. Fletcher.

"Yeah man! She was a-yellin'. Just like when I give her her perm'nent."

"Her husband ought to could make her behave. Don't it seem that way to you?" asked Mrs. Fletcher. "He ought to put his foot down."

"Ha," said Leota. "A lot he could do. Maybe some women is soft."

"Oh, you mistake me, I don't mean for her to get soft—far from it! Women have to stand up for themselves, or there's just no telling. But now you take me—I ask Mr. Fletcher's advice now and then, and he appreciates it, especially on something important, like is it time for a permanent—not that I've told him about the baby. He says, 'Why, dear, go ahead!' Just ask their *advice*."

"Huh! If I ever ast Fred's advice we'd be floatin' down the Yazoo River on a houseboat or somethin' by this time," said Leota. "I'm sick of Fred. I tole him to go over to Vicksburg."

"Is he going?" demanded Mrs. Fletcher.

"Sure. See, the fortuneteller—I went back and had my other palm read, since we've got to rent the room again—said my lover was goin' to work in Vicksburg, so I don't know who she could mean, unless she meant Fred. And Fred ain't workin' here—that much is so."

"Is he going to work in Vicksburg?" asked Mrs. Fletcher. "And ——"

"Sure, Lady Evangeline said so. Said the future is going to be brighter than the present. He don't want to go, but I ain't gonna put up with nothin' like that. Lays around the house an' bulls—did bull—with that good-for-nothin' Mr. Pike. He says if he goes who'll cook, but I says I never get to eat anyway—not meals. Billy Boy, take Mrs. Grover that *Screen Secrets* and leg it."

Mrs. Fletcher heard stamping feet go out the door.

"Is that that Mrs. Pike's little boy here again?" she asked, sitting up gingerly.

"Yeah, that's still him." Leota stuck out her tongue.

Mrs. Fletcher could hardly believe her eyes. "Well! How's Mrs. Pike, your attractive new friend with the sharp eyes who spreads it around town that perfect strangers are pregnant?" she asked in a sweetened tone.

"Oh, Mizziz Pike." Leota combed Mrs. Fletcher's hair with heavy strokes.

"You act like you're tired," said Mrs. Fletcher.

"Tired? Feel like it's four o'clock in the afternoon already," said Leota. "I ain't told you the awful luck we had, me and Fred? It's the worst thing you ever heard of. Maybe *you* think Mrs. Pike's got sharp eyes. Shoot, there's a limit! Well, you know, we rented out our room to this Mr. and Mrs. Pike from New Orleans when Sal an' Joe Fentress got mad at us 'cause they drank up some homebrew we had in the closet—Sal an' Joe did. So, a week ago Sat'day Mr. and Mrs. Pike moved in. Well, I kinda fixed up the room, you know—put a sofa pillow on the couch and picked some ragged robins and put in a vase, but they never did say they appreciated it. Anyway, then I put some old magazines on the table."

"I think that was lovely," said Mrs. Fletcher.

"Wait. So, come night 'fore last, Fred and this Mr. Pike, who Fred just took up with, was back from they said they was fishin', bein' as neither one of 'em has got a job to his name, and we was all settin' around in their room. So Mrs. Pike was settin' there, readin' a old *Startling G-Man Tales* that was mine, mind you, I'd bought it myself, and all of a sudden she jumps!—into the air—you'd 'a' thought she'd set on a spider—an' says, 'Canfield'—ain't that silly, that's Mr. Pike—'Canfield, my God A'mighty,' she says, 'honey,' she says, 'we're rich, and you won't have to work.' Not that he turned one hand anyway. Well, me and Fred rushes over to her, and Mr. Pike, too, and there she sets, pointin' her finger at a photo in my copy of *Startling G-Man*. 'See that man?' yells Mrs. Pike. 'Remember him, Canfield?' 'Never forget a face,' says Mr. Pike. 'It's Mr. Petrie, that we stayed with him in the apartment next to ours in Toulouse Street in N.O. for six weeks. Mr. Petrie.' 'Well,' says Mrs. Pike, like she can't hold out one secont longer, 'Mr. Petrie is wanted for five hundred dollars cash, for rapin' four women in California, and I know where he is.' "

"Mercy!" said Mrs. Fletcher. "Where was he?"

At some time Leota had washed her hair and now she yanked her up by the back locks and sat her up.

"Know where he was?"

"I certainly don't," Mrs. Fletcher said. Her scalp hurt all over.

Leota flung a towel around the top of her customer's head. "Nowhere else but in that freak show! I saw him just as plain as Mrs. Pike. *He* was the petrified man!"

"Who would ever have thought that!" cried Mrs. Fletcher sympathetically.

"So Mr. Pike says, 'Well, whatta you know about that,' an' he looks real hard at the photo and whistles. And she starts dancin' and singin' about their good luck. She meant our bad luck! I made a point of telling that fortuneteller the next time I saw her. I said, 'Listen, that magazine was layin' around the house for a month, and there was five hundred dollars in it for somebody. An' there was the freak show runnin' night an' day, not two steps away from my own beauty parlor, with Mr. Petrie just settin' there waitin'. An' it had to be Mr. and Mrs. Pike, almost perfect strangers.' "

"What gall," said Mrs. Fletcher. She was only sitting there, wrapped in a turban, but she did not mind.

"Fortunetellers don't care. And Mrs. Pike, she goes around actin' like she thinks she was Mrs. God," said Leota. "So they're goin' to leave tomorrow, Mr. and Mrs. Pike. And in the meantime I got to keep that mean, bad little ole kid here, gettin' under my feet ever' minute of the day an' talkin' back too."

"Have they gotten the five hundred dollars' reward already?" asked Mrs. Fletcher.

"Well," said Leota, "at first Mr. Pike didn't want to do anything about it. Can you feature that? Said he kinda liked that ole bird and said he was real nice to 'em, lent 'em money or somethin'. But Mrs. Pike simply tole him he could just go to hell, and I can see her point. She says, 'You ain't worked a lick in six months, and here I made five hundred dollars in two seconts, and what thanks do I get for it? You go to hell, Canfield,' she says. So," Leota went on in a despondent voice, "they called up the cops and they caught the ole bird, all right, right there in the freak show where I saw him with my own eyes, thinkin' he was petrified. He's the one. Did it under his real name–Mr. Petrie. Four women in California, all in the month of August. So Mrs. Pike gits five hundred dollars. And my magazine, and right next door to my beauty parlor. I cried all night, but Fred said it wasn't a bit of use and to go to sleep, because the whole thing was just sort of coincidence–you know: can't do nothin' about it. He says it put him clean out of the notion of goin' to Vicksburg for a few days till we rent out the room agin–no tellin' who we'll git this time."

"But can you imagine anybody knowing this old man, that's raped four women?" persisted Mrs. Fletcher, and she shuddered audibly. "Did Mrs. Pike *speak* to him when she met him in the freak show?"

Leota had begun to comb Mrs. Fletcher's hair. "I says to her, I says, 'I didn't notice you fallin' on his neck when he was the petrified man—don't tell me you didn't recognize your fine friend?' And she says, 'I didn't recognize him with that white powder all over his face. He just looked familiar,' Mrs. Pike says, 'and lots of people look familiar.' But she says that ole petrified man did put her in mind of somebody. She wondered who it was! Kep' her awake, which man she'd ever knew it reminded her of. So when she seen the photo, it all came to her. Like a flash. Mr. Petrie. The way he'd turn his head and look at her when she took him in his breakfast."

"Took him in his breakfast!" shrieked Mrs. Fletcher. "Listen—don't tell me. I'd 'a' felt something."

"Four women. I guess those women didn't have the faintest notion at the time they'd be worth a hundred an' twenty-five bucks apiece someday to Mrs. Pike. We ast her how old the fella was then, an' she says he musta had one foot in the grave, at least. Can you beat it?"

"Not really petrified at all, of course," said Mrs. Fletcher meditatively. She drew herself up. "I'd 'a' felt something," she said proudly.

"Shoot! I did feel somethin'," said Leota. "I tole Fred when I got home I felt so funny. I said, 'Fred, that ole petrified man sure did leave me with a funny feelin'.' He says, 'Funny-haha or funny-peculiar?' and I says, 'Funny-peculiar.'" She pointed her comb into the air emphatically.

"I'll bet you did," said Mrs. Fletcher.

They both heard a crackling noise.

Leota screamed, "Billy Boy! What you doin' in my purse?"

"Aw, I'm just eatin' these ole stale peanuts up," said Billy Boy.

"You come here to me!" screamed Leota, recklessly flinging down the comb, which scattered a whole ash tray full of bobby pins and knocked down a row of Coca-Cola bottles. "This is the last straw!"

"I caught him! I caught him!" giggled Mrs. Fletcher. "I'll hold him on my lap. You bad, bad boy, you! I guess I better learn how to spank little old bad boys," she said.

Leota's eleven-o'clock customer pushed open the swing door upon Leota paddling him heartily with the brush, while he gave angry but belittling screams which penetrated beyond the booth and filled the whole curious beauty parlor. From everywhere ladies began to gather round to watch the paddling. Billy Boy kicked both Leota and Mrs. Fletcher as hard as he could, Mrs. Fletcher with her new fixed smile.

"There, my little man!" gasped Leota. "You won't be able to set down for a week if I knew what I was doin'."

Billy Boy stomped through the group of wild-haired ladies and went out the door, but flung back the words, "If you're so smart, why ain't you rich?"

JOHN CHEEVER

[1912–]

Some critics were surprised when John Cheever's first novel, The Wapshot Chronicle, *won the 1958 National Book Award, but it was no surprise to the readers who had come to watch for and enjoy his oddly poignant short stories. Over a hundred of the stories preceded the novel and they had established Cheever as one of contemporary America's most published as well as most talented authors of short fiction.*

John Cheever's career began early. Born on May 27, 1912, in Quincy, Massachusetts, he was sent to the Thayer Academy at South Braintree. Expelled from the academy when he was seventeen, he managed to put his expulsion to good use by writing of it in a story which he quickly sold to the New Republic.

He continued writing stories and became one of The New Yorker's *most popular contributors. His first collection was published in 1943; the title,* The Way Some People Live, *aptly describes its author's primary interest: people, urban and suburban, "trying," as one of his readers said, "to make some sense of love, memory, youth, society, and the bank balance."*

Cheever was awarded a Guggenheim Fellowship in 1951 and, in 1956, the $1000 Award in Literature given by the National Institute of Arts and Letters. He did some writing for C.B.S. and, school record notwithstanding, finally went to college, this time as a member of the English Department of Barnard College in New York City. The Wapshot Chronicle *appeared in 1957, but Cheever lost none of his interest in the short story; by 1958 he had written more than enough for another volume,* The Housebreaker of Shady Hill.

Cheever's second collection, published in 1953, had carried the name of his most famous story, "The Enormous Radio," a fantasy of sorts made sharp and ultimately terrifying by its all-too-real details. In a way this tale sums up Cheever's own approach to the modern world about him, for it seems to be his particular job to lay bare the deep anguish underlying the shallow frustration and to find the sad heroes among the men who scurry endlessly from suburb to office and back.

THE ENORMOUS RADIO

JIM AND IRENE WESTCOTT WERE the kind of people who seem to strike that satisfactory average of income, endeavor, and respectability that is reached by the statistical reports in college alumni bulletins. They were the parents of two young children, they had been married nine years, they lived on the twelfth floor of an apartment house in the East Seventies between Fifth and Madison Avenues, they went to the theatre on an average of 10.3 times a year, and they hoped someday to live in Westchester. Irene Westcott was a pleasant, rather plain girl with soft brown hair and a wide, fine forehead upon which nothing at all had been written, and in the cold weather she wore a coat of fitch skins dyed to resemble mink. You could not say that Jim Westcott, at thirty-seven, looked younger than he was, but you could at least say of him that he seemed to feel younger. He wore his graying hair cut very short, he dressed in the kind of clothes his class had worn at Andover, and his manner was earnest, vehement, and intentionally naïve. The Westcotts differed from their friends, their classmates, and their neighbors only in an interest they shared in serious music. They went to a great many concerts—although they seldom mentioned this to anyone—and they spent a good deal of time listening to music on the radio.

Their radio was an old instrument, sensitive, unpredictable, and beyond repair. Neither of them understood the mechanics of radio—or of any of the other appliances that surrounded them—and when the instrument faltered, Jim would strike the side of the cabinet with his hand. This sometimes helped. One Sunday afternoon, in the middle of a Schubert quartet, the music faded away altogether. Jim struck the cabinet repeatedly, but there was no response; the Schubert was lost to them forever. He promised to buy Irene a new radio, and on Monday when he came home from work he told her that he had got one. He refused to describe it, and said it would be a surprise for her when it came.

The radio was delivered at the kitchen door the following afternoon, and with the assistance of her maid and the handyman Irene uncrated it and brought it into the living room. She was struck at once with the physical ugliness of the large gumwood cabinet. Irene was proud of her living room, she had chosen its furnishings and colors as carefully as she chose her clothes, and now it seemed to her that the new radio stood among her intimate possessions like an aggressive intruder. She was confounded by the number of dials and switches on the instrument panel, and she studied them thoroughly before she put the plug into a wall socket and turned the radio on. The dials flooded with a malevolent green light, and in the distance she heard the music of a piano quintet. The quintet was in the distance for only an instant; it bore down upon her with a speed greater than light and filled the apartment with the noise of music amplified so mightily that it knocked a china ornament from a table to the floor. She rushed to the instrument and reduced the volume. The violent forces that were snared in the ugly gumwood cabinet made her uneasy. Her children came home from school then, and she took them to the Park. It was not until later in the afternoon that she was able to return to the radio.

The maid had given the children their suppers and was supervising their baths when Irene turned on the radio, reduced the volume, and sat down to listen to a Mozart quintet that she knew and enjoyed. The music came through clearly. The new instrument had a much purer tone, she thought, than the old one. She decided that tone was most important and that she could conceal the cabinet behind a sofa. But as soon as she had made her peace with the radio, the interference began. A crackling sound like the noise of a burning powder fuse began to accompany the singing of the strings. Beyond the music, there was a rustling that reminded Irene unpleasantly of the sea, and as the quintet progressed, these noises were joined by many others. She tried all the dials and switches but nothing dimmed the interference, and she sat down, disappointed and bewildered, and tried to trace the flight of the melody. The elevator shaft in her building ran beside the living-room wall, and it was the noise of the elevator that gave her a clue to the character of the static. The rattling of the elevator cables and the opening and closing of the elevator doors were reproduced in her loudspeaker, and, realizing that the radio was sensitive to electrical currents of all sorts, she began to discern through the Mozart the ringing of telephone bells, the dialling of phones, and the lamentation of a vacuum cleaner. By listening more carefully, she was able to distinguish doorbells, elevator bells, electric razors, and Waring mixers, whose sounds had been picked up from the apartments that surrounded hers and transmitted through her loudspeaker. The powerful and ugly instrument, with its mistaken sensitivity to discord, was more than she could hope to master, so she turned the thing off and went into the nursery to see her children.

When Jim Westcott came home that night, he went to the radio confidently and worked the controls. He had the same sort of experience Irene had had. A man was speaking on the station Jim had chosen, and his voice swung instantly from the distance into a force so powerful that it shook the apartment. Jim turned the volume control and reduced the voice. Then, a minute or two later, the interference began. The ringing of telephones and doorbells set in, joined by the rasp of the elevator doors and the whir of cooking appliances. The character of the noise had changed since Irene had tried the radio earlier; the last of the electric razors was being unplugged, the vacuum cleaners had all been returned to their closets, and the static reflected that change in pace that overtakes the city after the sun goes down. He fiddled with the knobs but couldn't get rid of the noises, so he turned the radio off and told Irene that in the morning he'd call the people who had sold it to him and give them hell.

The following afternoon, when Irene returned to the apartment from a luncheon date, the maid told her that a man had come and fixed the radio. Irene went into the living room before she took off her hat or her furs and tried the instrument. From the loudspeaker came a recording of the "Missouri Waltz." It reminded her of the thin, scratchy music from an old-fashioned phonograph that she sometimes heard across the lake where she spent her summers. She waited until the waltz had finished, expecting an explanation of the recording, but there was none. The music was followed by silence, and then the plaintive and scratchy record was repeated. She turned the dial and got a satisfactory burst of Caucasian music—the thump of bare feet in the dust and the rattle of coin jewelry—but in the background she could hear the ringing of bells and a confusion of voices. Her children came home from school then, and she turned off the radio and went to the nursery.

When Jim came home that night, he was tired, and he took a bath and changed his clothes. Then he joined Irene in the living room. He had just turned on the radio when the maid announced dinner, so he left it on, and he and Irene went to the table.

Jim was too tired to make even a pretense of sociability, and there was nothing about the dinner to hold Irene's interest, so her attention wandered from the food to the deposits of silver polish on the candlesticks and from there to the music in the other room. She listened for a few moments to a Chopin prelude and then was surprised to hear a man's voice break in. "For Christ's sake, Kathy," he said, "do you always have to play the piano when I get home?" The music stopped abruptly. "It's the only chance I have," a woman said. "I'm at the office all day." "So am I," the man said. He added something obscene about an upright piano, and slammed a door. The passionate and melancholy music began again.

"Did you hear that?" Irene asked.

"What?" Jim was eating his dessert.

"The radio. A man said something while the music was still going on—something dirty."

"It's probably a play."

"I don't think it *is* a play," Irene said.

They left the table and took their coffee into the living room. Irene asked Jim to try another station. He turned the knob. "Have you seen my garters?" a man asked. "Button me up," a woman said. "Have you seen my garters?" the man said again. "Just button me up and I'll find your garters," the woman said. Jim shifted to another station. "I wish you wouldn't leave apple cores in the ashtrays," a man said. "I hate the smell."

"This is strange," Jim said.

"Isn't it?" Irene said.

Jim turned the knob again. " 'On the coast of Coromandel where the early pumpkins blow,' " a woman with a pronounced English accent said, " 'in the middle of the woods lived the Yonghy-Bonghy-Bò. Two old chairs, and half a candle, one old jug without a handle . . .' "

"My God!" Irene cried. "That's the Sweeneys' nurse."

" 'These were all his worldly goods,' " the British voice continued.

"Turn that thing off," Irene said. "Maybe they can hear *us*." Jim switched the radio off. "That was Miss Armstrong, the Sweeneys' nurse," Irene said. "She must be reading to the little girl. They live in 17-B. I've talked with Miss Armstrong in the Park. I know her voice very well. We must be getting other people's apartments."

"That's impossible," Jim said.

"Well, that was the Sweeneys' nurse," Irene said hotly. "I know her voice. I know it very well. I'm wondering if they can hear us."

Jim turned the switch. First from a distance and then nearer, nearer, as if borne on the wind, came the pure accents of the Sweeneys' nurse again: " ' "Lady Jingly! Lady Jingly!" ' " she said, " ' "Sitting where the pumpkins blow, will you come and be my wife," said the Yonghy-Bonghy-Bò . . .' "

Jim went over to the radio and said "Hello" loudly into the speaker.

" ' "I am tired of living singly," ' " the nurse went on, " ' "on this coast so wild and shingly, I'm a-weary of my life; if you'll come and be my wife, quite serene would be my life . . ." ' "

"I guess she can't hear us," Irene said. "Try something else."

Jim turned to another station, and the living room was filled with the uproar of a cocktail party that had overshot its mark. Someone was playing the piano and singing the Whiffenpoof Song, and the voices that surrounded the piano were vehement and happy. "Eat some more sandwiches," a woman shrieked. There were screams of laughter and a dish of some sort crashed to the floor.

"Those must be the Hutchinsons, in 15-B," Irene said. "I knew they were giving a party this afternoon. I saw her in the liquor store. Isn't this too divine? Try something else. See if you can get those people in 18-C."

The Westcotts overheard that evening a monologue on salmon fishing in Canada, a bridge game, running comments on home movies of what had apparently been a fortnight at Sea Island, and a bitter family quarrel about an overdraft at the bank. They turned off their radio at midnight and went to bed, weak with laughter. Sometime in the night, their son began to call for a glass of water and Irene got one and took it to his room. It was very early. All the lights in the neighborhood were extinguished, and from the boy's window she could see the empty street. She went into the living room and tried the radio. There was some faint coughing, a moan, and then a man spoke. "Are you all right, darling?" he asked. "Yes," a woman said wearily. "Yes, I'm all right, I guess," and then she added with great feeling, "But, you know, Charlie, I don't feel like myself any more. Sometimes there are about fifteen or twenty minutes in the week when I feel like myself. I don't like to go to another doctor, because the doctor's bills are so awful already, but I just don't feel like myself, Charlie. I just never feel like myself." They were not young, Irene thought. She guessed from the timbre of their voices that they were middle-aged. The restrained melancholy of the dialogue and the draft from the bedroom window made her shiver, and she went back to bed.

The following morning, Irene cooked breakfast for the family—the maid didn't come up from her room in the basement until ten—braided her daughter's hair, and waited at the door until her children and her husband had been carried away in the elevator. Then she went into the living room and tried the radio. "I don't want to go to school," a child screamed. "I hate school. I won't go to school. I hate school." "You will go to school," an enraged woman said. "We paid eight hundred dollars to get you into that school and you'll go if it kills you." The next number on the dial produced the worn record of the "Missouri Waltz." Irene shifted the control and invaded the privacy of several breakfast tables. She overheard demonstrations of indigestion, carnal love, abysmal vanity, faith, and despair. Irene's life was nearly as simple and sheltered as it appeared to be, and the forthright and sometimes brutal language that came from the loudspeaker that morning astonished and troubled her. She continued to listen until her maid came in. Then she turned off the radio quickly, since this insight, she realized, was a furtive one.

Irene had a luncheon date with a friend that day, and she left her apartment at a little after twelve. There were a number of women in the elevator when it stopped at her floor. She stared at their handsome and impassive faces, their furs, and the cloth flowers in their hats. Which one of them had been to Sea Island, she wondered. Which one had overdrawn her bank account? The elevator stopped at the tenth floor and a woman with a pair of Skye terriers joined them. Her hair was rigged high on her head and she wore a mink cape. She was humming the "Missouri Waltz."

Irene had two Martinis at lunch, and she looked searchingly at her friend and wondered what her secrets were. They had intended to go shopping after lunch, but Irene excused herself and went home. She told the maid that she was not to be disturbed; then she went into the living room, closed the doors, and switched on the radio. She heard, in the course of the afternoon, the halting conversation of a woman entertaining her aunt, the hysterical conclusion of a luncheon party, and a hostess briefing her maid about some cocktail guests. "Don't give the best Scotch to anyone who hasn't white hair," the hostess said. "See if you can get rid of that liver paste before you pass those hot things, and could you lend me five dollars? I want to tip the elevator man."

As the afternoon waned, the conversations increased in intensity. From where Irene sat, she could see the open sky above Central Park. There were hundreds of clouds in the sky, as though the south wind had broken the winter into pieces and were blowing it north, and on her radio she could hear the arrival of cocktail guests and the return of children and businessmen from their schools and offices. "I found a good-sized diamond on the bathroom floor this morning," a woman said. "It must have fallen out of that bracelet Mrs. Dunston was wearing last night." "We'll sell it," a man said. "Take it down to the jeweller on Madison Avenue and sell it. Mrs. Dunston won't know the difference, and we could use a couple of hundred bucks . . ." " 'Oranges and lemons, say the bells of St. Clement's,' " the Sweeneys' nurse sang. " 'Half-pence and farthings, say the bells of St. Martin's. When will you pay me? say the bells at old Bailey . . .' " "It's not a hat," a woman cried, and at her back roared a cocktail party. "It's not a hat, it's a love affair. That's what Walter Florell said. He said it's not a hat, it's a love affair," and then, in a lower voice, the same woman added, "Talk to somebody, for Christ's sake, honey, talk to somebody. If she catches you standing here not talking to anybody, she'll take us off her invitation list, and I love these parties."

The Westcotts were going out for dinner that night, and when Jim came home, Irene was dressing. She seemed sad and vague, and he brought her a drink. They were dining with friends in the neighborhood, and they walked to where they were going. The sky was broad and filled with light. It was one of those splendid spring evenings that excite memory and desire, and the air that touched their hands and faces felt very soft. A Salvation Army band was on the corner playing "Jesus Is Sweeter." Irene drew on her husband's arm and held him there for a minute, to hear the music. "They're really such nice people, aren't they?" she said. "They have such nice faces. Actually they're so much nicer than a lot of the people we know." She took a bill from her purse and walked over and dropped it into the tambourine. There was in her face, when she returned to her husband, a look of radiant melancholy that he was not familiar with. And her conduct at the dinner party that night seemed strange to him, too. She interrupted her hostess rudely and stared at the people across the table from her with an intensity for which she would have punished her children.

It was still mild when they walked home from the party, and Irene looked up at the spring stars. "'How far that little candle throws its beams,'" she exclaimed. "'So shines a good deed in a naughty world.'" She waited that night until Jim had fallen asleep, and then went into the living room and turned on the radio.

Jim came home at about six the next night. Emma, the maid, let him in, and he had taken off his hat and was taking off his coat when Irene ran into the hall. Her face was shining with tears and her hair was disordered. "Go up to 16-C, Jim!" she screamed. "Don't take off your coat. Go up to 16-C. Mr. Osborn's beating his wife. They've been quarrelling since four o'clock, and now he's hitting her. Go up there and stop him."

From the radio in the living room, Jim heard screams, obscenities, and thuds. "You know you don't have to listen to this sort of thing," he said. He strode into the living room and turned the switch. "It's indecent," he said. "It's like looking in windows. You know you don't have to listen to this sort of thing. You can turn it off."

"Oh, it's so horrible, it's so dreadful," Irene was sobbing. "I've been listening all day, and it's so depressing."

"Well, if it's so depressing, why do you listen to it? I bought this damned radio to give you some pleasure," he said. "I paid a great deal of money for it. I thought it might make you happy. I wanted to make you happy."

"Don't, don't, don't, don't quarrel with me," she moaned, and laid her head on his shoulder. "All the others have been quarrelling all day. Everybody's been quarrelling. They're all worried about money. Mrs. Hutchinson's mother is dying of cancer in Florida and they don't have enough money to send her to the Mayo Clinic. At least, Mr. Hutchinson says they don't have enough money. And some woman in this building is having an affair with the superintendent—with that hideous superintendent. It's too disgusting. And Mrs. Melville has heart trouble and Mr. Hendricks is going to lose his job in April and Mrs. Hendricks is horrid about the whole thing and that girl who plays the 'Missouri Waltz' is a whore, a common whore, and the elevator man has tuberculosis and Mr. Osborn has been beating Mrs. Osborn." She wailed, she trembled with grief and checked the stream of tears down her face with the heel of her palm.

"Well, why do you have to listen?" Jim asked again. "Why do you have to listen to this stuff if it makes you so miserable?"

"Oh, don't, don't, don't," she cried. "Life is too terrible, too sordid and awful. But we've never been like that, have we, darling? Have we? I mean we've always been good and decent and loving to one another, haven't we? And we have two children, two beautiful children. Our lives aren't sordid, are they, darling? Are they?" She flung her arms around his neck and drew his face down to hers. "We're happy, aren't we, darling? We are happy, aren't we?"

"Of course we're happy," he said tiredly. He began to surrender his resentment. "Of course we're happy. I'll have that damned radio fixed or taken away tomorrow." He stroked her soft hair. "My poor girl," he said.

"You love me, don't you?" she asked. "And we're not hypercritical or worried about money or dishonest, are we?"

"No, darling," he said.

A man came in the morning and fixed the radio. Irene turned it on cautiously and was happy to hear a California-wine commercial and a recording of Beethoven's Ninth Symphony, including Schiller's "Ode to Joy." She kept the radio on all day and nothing untoward came from the speaker.

A Spanish suite was being played when Jim came home. "Is everything all right?" he asked. His face was pale, she thought. They had some cocktails and went in to dinner to the "Anvil Chorus" from "Il Trovatore." This was followed by Debussy's "La Mer."

"I paid the bill for the radio today," Jim said. "It cost four hundred dollars. I hope you'll get some enjoyment out of it."

"Oh, I'm sure I will," Irene said.

"Four hundred dollars is a good deal more than I can afford," he went on. "I wanted to get something that you'd enjoy. It's the last extravagance we'll be able to indulge in this year. I see that you haven't paid your clothing bills yet. I saw them on your dressing table." He looked directly at her. "Why did you tell me you'd paid them? Why did you lie to me?"

"I just didn't want you to worry, Jim," she said. She drank some water. "I'll be able to pay my bills out of this month's allowance. There were the slipcovers last month, and that party."

"You've got to learn to handle the money I give you a little more intelligently, Irene," he said. "You've got to understand that we won't have as much money this year as we had last. I had a very sobering talk with Mitchell today. No one is buying anything. We're spending all our time promoting new issues, and you know how long that takes. I'm not getting any younger, you know. I'm thirty-seven. My hair will be gray next year. I haven't done as well as I'd hoped to do. And I don't suppose things will get any better."

"Yes, dear," she said.

"We've got to start cutting down," Jim said. "We've got to think of the children. To be perfectly frank with you, I worry about money a great deal. I'm not at all sure of the future. No one is. If anything should happen to me, there's the insurance, but that wouldn't go very far today. I've worked awfully hard to give you and the children a comfortable life," he said bitterly. "I don't like to see all of my energies, all of my youth, wasted in fur coats and radios and slipcovers and—"

"Please, Jim," she said. "Please. They'll hear us."

"*Who'll* hear us? Emma can't hear us."

"The radio."

"Oh, I'm sick!" he shouted. "I'm sick to death of your apprehensiveness. The radio can't hear us. Nobody can hear us. And what if they can hear us? Who cares?"

Irene got up from the table and went into the living room. Jim went to the door and shouted at her from there. "Why are you so Christly all of a sudden? What's turned you overnight into a convent girl? You stole your mother's jewelry before they probated her will. You never gave your sister a cent of that money that was intended for her—not even when she needed it. You made Grace Howland's life miserable, and where was all your piety and your virtue when you went to that abortionist? I'll never forget how cool you were. You packed your bag and went off to have that child murdered as if you were going to Nassau. If you'd had any reasons, if you'd had any good reasons—"

Irene stood for a minute before the hideous cabinet, disgraced and sickened, but she held her hand on the switch before she extinguished the music and the voices, hoping that the instrument might speak to her kindly, that she might hear the Sweeneys' nurse. Jim continued to shout at her from the door. The voice on the radio was suave and noncommittal. "An early-morning railroad disaster in Tokyo," the loudspeaker said, "killed twenty-nine people. A fire in a Catholic hospital near Buffalo for the care of blind children was extinguished early this morning by nuns. The temperature is forty-seven. The humidity is eighty-nine."

IRWIN SHAW

[1913–]

Born in New York City, February 27, 1913, Irwin Shaw started writing radio scripts as soon as he was out of school. During the threadbare Thirties he worked in a department store, a furniture house, and a cosmetics factory; he also wrote theses for students and drove a truck. During the Second World War he served in France, Germany, and Africa, an experience embodied in his first novel, The Young Lions.

Shaw had already been acclaimed for his short stories and plays—particularly for the dramas, Bury The Dead *and* The Gentle People*—and he had supported himself by dramatizing such comic-strips as "Dick Tracy" and "The Gumps," an occupation which he detested and which he tore to shreds in a story entitled "Main Currents of American Thought." He married, lived for a while in Europe, and then returned to the United States where he won awards in the O. Henry Memorial Prize contests.*

Shaw's short stories generate a feeling of participation and power; he paints his portraits with broad strokes and exposes the human drama without histrionics. "The Eighty-Yard Run" is the story of a football hero—Shaw himself was once a football player—and it is typical of Shaw's clean, clear writing as well as his ability to absorb the reader in the unexpected but inevitable development of a personality.

THE EIGHTY-YARD RUN

THE PASS WAS HIGH and wide and he jumped for it, feeling it slap flatly against his hands, as he shook his hips to throw off the halfback who was diving at him. The center floated by, his hands desperately brushing Darling's knee as Darling picked his feet up high and delicately ran over a blocker and an opposing linesman in a jumble on the ground near the scrimmage line. He had ten yards in the clear and picked up speed, breathing easily, feeling his thigh pads rising and falling against his legs, listening to the sound of cleats behind him, pulling away from them, watching the other backs heading him off toward the sideline, the whole picture, the men closing in on him, the blockers fighting for position, the ground he had to cross, all suddenly clear in his head, for the first time in his life not a meaningless confusion of men, sounds, speed. He smiled a little to himself as he ran, holding the ball lightly in front of him with his two hands, his knees pumping high, his hips twisting in the almost-girlish run of a back in a broken field. The first halfback came at him and he fed him his leg, then swung at the last moment, took the shock of the man's shoulder without breaking stride, ran right through him, his cleats biting securely into the turf. There was only the safety man now, coming warily at him, his arms crooked, hands spread. Darling tucked the ball in, spurted at him, driving hard, hurling himself along, his legs pounding, knees high, all two hundred pounds bunched into controlled attack. He was sure he was going to get past the safety man. Without thought, his arms and legs working beautifully together, he headed right for the safety man, stiff-armed him, feeling blood spurt instantaneously from the man's nose onto his hand, seeing his face go awry, head turned, mouth pulled to one side. He pivoted away, keeping the arm locked, dropping the safety man as he ran easily toward the goal line, with the drumming of cleats diminishing behind him.

How long ago? It was autumn then and the ground was getting hard because the nights were cold and leaves from the maples around the stadium blew across the practice fields in gusts of wind and the girls were beginning to put polo coats over their sweaters when they came to watch practice in the afternoons . . . Fifteen years. Darling walked slowly over the same ground in the spring twilight, in his neat shoes, a man of thirty-five dressed in a double-breasted suit, ten pounds heavier in the fifteen years, but not fat, with the years between 1925 and 1940 showing in his face.

The coach was smiling quietly to himself and the assistant coaches were looking at each other with pleasure the way they always did when one of the second stringers suddenly did something fine, bringing credit to them, making their $2,000 a year a tiny bit more secure.

Darling trotted back, smiling, breathing deeply but easily, feeling wonderful, not tired, though this was the tail end of practice and he'd run eighty yards. The sweat poured off his face and soaked his jersey and he liked the feeling, the warm moistness lubricating his skin like oil. Off in a corner of the field some players were punting and the smack of leather against the ball came pleasantly through the afternoon air. The freshmen were running signals on the next field and the quarterback's sharp voice, the pound of the eleven pairs of cleats, the "Dig, now, *dig!*" of the coaches, the laughter of the players all somehow made him feel happy as he trotted back to midfield, listening to the applause and shouts of the students along the sidelines, knowing that after that run the coach would have to start him Saturday against Illinois.

Fifteen years, Darling thought, remembering the shower after the workout, the hot water steaming off his skin and the deep soapsuds and all the young voices singing with the water streaming down and towels going and managers running in and out and the sharp sweet smell of oil of wintergreen and everybody clapping him on the back as he dressed and Packard, the captain, who took being captain very seriously, coming over to him and shaking his hand saying, "Darling, you're going to go places in the next two years."

The assistant manager fussed over him, wiping a cut on his leg with alcohol and iodine, the little sting making him realize suddenly how fresh and whole and solid his body felt. The manager slapped a piece of adhesive tape over the cut and Darling noticed the sharp clean white of the tape against the ruddiness of the skin, fresh from the shower.

He dressed slowly, the softness of his shirt and the soft warmth of his wool socks and his flannel trousers a reward against his skin after the harsh pressure of the shoulder harness and thigh and hip pads. He drank three glasses of cold water, the liquid reaching down coldly inside of him, soothing the harsh dry places in his throat and belly left by the sweat and running and shouting of practice.

Fifteen years.

The sun had gone down and the sky was green behind the stadium and he laughed quietly to himself as he looked at the stadium, rearing above the trees, and knew that on Saturday when the 70,000 voices roared as the team came running out onto the field, part of that enormous salute would be for him. He walked slowly, listening to the gravel crunch satisfactorily under his shoes in the still twilight, feeling his clothes swing lightly against his skin, breathing the thin evening air, feeling the wind move softly in his damp hair, wonderfully cool behind his ears and at the nape of his neck.

Louise was waiting for him at the road, in her car. The top was down and he noticed all over again, as he always did when he saw her, how pretty she was, the rough blonde hair and the large, inquiring eyes and the bright mouth, smiling now.

She threw the door open. "Were you good today?" she asked.

"Pretty good," he said. He climbed in, sank luxuriously into the soft leather, stretched his legs far out. He smiled, thinking of the eighty yards. "Pretty damn good."

She looked at him seriously for a moment, then scrambled around, like a little girl, kneeling on the seat next to him, grabbed him, her hands along his ears, and kissed him as he sprawled, head back, on the seat cushion. She let go of him, but kept her head close to his, over his. Darling reached up slowly and rubbed the back of his hand against her cheek, lit softly by a street lamp a hundred feet away. They looked at each other, smiling.

Louise drove down to the lake and they sat there silently, watching the moon rise behind the hills on the other side. Finally he reached over, pulled her gently to him, kissed her. Her lips grew soft, her body sank into his, tears formed slowly in her eyes. He knew, for the first time, that he could do whatever he wanted with her.

"Tonight," he said. "I'll call for you at seven-thirty. Can you get out?"

She looked at him. She was smiling, but the tears were still full in her eyes. "All right," she said. "I'll get out. How about you? Won't the coach raise hell?"

Darling grinned. "I got the coach in the palm of my hand," he said. "Can you wait till seven-thirty?"

She grinned back at him. "No," she said.

They kissed and she started the car and they went back to town for dinner. He sang on the way home.

Christian Darling, thirty-five years old, sat on the frail spring grass, greener now than it ever would be again on the practice field, looked thoughtfully up at the stadium, a deserted ruin in the twilight. He had started on the first team that Saturday and every Saturday after that for the next two years, but it had never been as satisfactory as it should have been. He never had broken away, the longest run he'd ever made was thirty-five yards, and that in a game that was already won, and then that kid had come up from the third team, Diederich, a blank-faced German kid from Wisconsin, who ran like a bull, ripping lines to pieces Saturday after Saturday, plowing through, never getting hurt, never changing his expression, scoring more points, gaining more ground than all the rest of the team put together, making everybody's All-American, carrying the ball three times out of four, keeping everybody else out of the headlines. Darling was a good blocker and he spent his Saturday afternoons working on the big Swedes and Polacks who played tackle and end for Michigan, Illinois, Purdue, hurling into huge pile-ups, bobbing his head wildly to elude the great raw hands swinging like meat-cleavers at him as he went charging in to open up holes for Diederich coming through like a locomotive behind him. Still, it wasn't so bad. Everybody liked him and he did his job and he was pointed out on the campus and boys always felt important when they introduced their girls to him at their proms, and Louise loved him and watched him faithfully in the games, even in the mud, when your own mother wouldn't know you, and drove him around in her car keeping the top down because she was proud of him and wanted to show everybody that she was Christian Darling's girl. She bought him crazy presents because her father was rich, watches, pipes, humidors, an icebox for beer for his room, curtains, wallets, a fifty-dollar dictionary.

"You'll spend every cent your old man owns," Darling protested once when she showed up at his room with seven different packages in her arms and tossed them onto the couch.

"Kiss me," Louise said, "and shut up."

"Do you want to break your poor old man?"

"I don't mind. I want to buy you presents."

"Why?"

"It makes me feel good. Kiss me. I don't know why. Did you know that you're an important figure?"

"Yes," Darling said gravely.

"When I was waiting for you at the library yesterday two girls saw you coming and one of them said to the other, 'That's Christian Darling. He's an important figure.' "

"You're a liar."

"I'm in love with an important figure."

"Still, why the hell did you have to give me a forty-pound dictionary?"

"I wanted to make sure," Louise said, "that you had a token of my esteem. I want to smother you in tokens of my esteem."

Fifteen years ago.

They'd married when they got out of college. There'd been other women for him, but all casual and secret, more for curiosity's sake, and vanity, women who'd thrown themselves at him and flattered him, a pretty mother at a summer camp for boys, an old girl from his home town who'd suddenly blossomed into a coquette, a friend of Louise's who had dogged him grimly for six months and had taken advantage of the two weeks when Louise went home when her mother died. Perhaps Louise had known, but she'd kept quiet, loving him completely, filling his rooms with presents, religiously watching him battling with the big Swedes and Polacks on the line of scrimmage on Saturday afternoons, making plans for marrying him and living with him in New York and going with him there to the nightclubs, the theatres, the good restaurants, being proud of him in advance, tall, white-teethed, smiling, large, yet moving lightly, with an athlete's grace, dressed in evening clothes, approvingly eyed by magnificently dressed and famous women in theatre lobbies, with Louise adoringly at his side.

Her father, who manufactured inks, set up a New York office for Darling to manage and presented him with three hundred accounts and they lived on Beekman Place with a view of the river with fifteen thousand dollars a year between them, because everybody was buying everything in those days, including ink. They saw all the shows and went to all the speakeasies and spent their fifteen thousand dollars a year and in the afternoons Louise went to the art galleries and the matinees of the more serious plays that Darling didn't like to sit through and Darling slept with a girl who danced in the chorus of *Rosalie* and with the wife of a man who owned three copper mines. Darling played squash three times a week and remained as solid as a stone barn and Louise never took her eyes off him when they were in the same room together, watching him with a secret, miser's smile, with a trick of coming over to him in the middle of a crowded room and saying gravely, in a low voice, "You're the handsomest man I've ever seen in my whole life. Want a drink?"

Nineteen twenty-nine came to Darling and to his wife and father-in-law, the maker of inks, just as it came to everyone else. The father-in-law waited until 1933 and then blew his brains out and when Darling went to Chicago to see what the books of the firm looked like he found out all that was left were debts and three or four gallons of unbought ink.

"Please, Christian," Louise said, sitting in their neat Beekman Place apartment, with a view of the river and prints of paintings by Dufy and Braque and Picasso on the wall, "please, why do you want to start drinking at two o'clock in the afternoon?"

"I have nothing else to do," Darling said, putting down his glass, emptied of its fourth drink. "Please pass the whiskey."

Louise filled his glass. "Come take a walk with me," she said. "We'll walk along the river."

"I don't want to walk along the river," Darling said, squinting intensely at the prints of paintings by Dufy, Braque and Picasso.

"We'll walk along Fifth Avenue."

"I don't want to walk along Fifth Avenue."

"Maybe," Louise said gently, "you'd like to come with me to some art galleries. There's an exhibition by a man named Klee–"

"I don't want to go to any art galleries. I want to sit here and drink Scotch whiskey," Darling said. "Who the hell hung those goddam pictures on the wall?"

"I did," Louise said.

"I hate them."

"I'll take them down," Louise said.

"Leave them there. It gives me something to do in the afternoon. I can hate them." Darling took a long swallow. "Is that the way people paint these days?"

"Yes, Christian. Please don't drink any more."

"Do you like painting like that?"

"Yes, dear."

"Really?"

"Really."

Darling looked carefully at the prints once more. "Little Louise Tucker. The middle-western beauty. I like pictures with horses in them. Why should you like pictures like that?"

"I just happen to have gone to a lot of galleries in the last few years . . ."

"Is that what you do in the afternoon?"

"That's what I do in the afternoon," Louise said.

"I drink in the afternoon."

Louise kissed him lightly on the top of his head as he sat there squinting at the pictures on the wall, the glass of whiskey held firmly in his hand. She put on her coat and went out without saying another word. When she came back in the evening, she had a job on a woman's fashion magazine.

They moved downtown and Louise went out to work every morning and Darling sat home and drank and Louise paid the bills as they came up. She made believe she was going to quit work as soon as Darling found a job, even though she was taking over more responsibility day by day at the magazine, interviewing authors, picking painters for the illustrations and covers, getting actresses to pose for pictures, going out for drinks with the right people, making a thousand new friends whom she loyally introduced to Darling.

"I don't like your hat," Darling said, once, when she came in in the evening and kissed him, her breath rich with Martinis.

"What's the matter with my hat, Baby?" she asked, running her fingers through his hair. "Everybody says it's very smart."

"It's too damned smart," he said. "It's not for you. It's for a rich, sophisticated woman of thirty-five with admirers."

Louise laughed. "I'm practicing to be a rich, sophisticated woman of thirty-five with admirers," she said. He stared soberly at her. "Now, don't look so grim, Baby. It's still the same simple little wife under the hat." She took the hat off, threw it into a corner, sat on his lap. "See? Homebody Number One."

"Your breath could run a train," Darling said, not wanting to be mean, but talking out of boredom, and sudden shock at seeing his wife curiously a stranger in a new hat, with a new expression in her eyes under the little brim, secret, confident, knowing.

Louise tucked her head under his chin so he couldn't smell her breath. "I had to take an author out for cocktails," she said. "He's a boy from the Ozark mountains and he drinks like a fish. He's a Communist."

"What the hell is a Communist from the Ozarks doing writing for a woman's fashion magazine?"

Louise chuckled. "The magazine business is getting all mixed up these days. The publishers want to have a foot in every camp. And anyway, you can't find an author under seventy these days who isn't a Communist."

"I don't think I like you to associate with all those people, Louise," Darling said. "Drinking with them."

"He's a very nice, gentle boy," Louise said. "He reads Ernest Dowson."

"Who's Ernest Dowson?"

Louise patted his arm, stood up, fixed her hair. "He's an English poet."

Darling felt that somehow he had disappointed her. "Am I supposed to know who Ernest Dowson is?"

"No, dear. I'd better go in and take a bath."

After she had gone, Darling went over to the corner where the hat was lying and picked it up. It was nothing, a scrap of straw, a red flower, a veil, meaningless on his big hand, but on his wife's head a signal of something . . . big city, smart and knowing women drinking and dining with men other than their husbands, conversation about things a normal man wouldn't know much about, Frenchmen who painted as though they used their elbows instead of brushes, composers who wrote whole symphonies without a single melody in them, writers who knew all about politics and women who knew all about writers, the movement of the proletariat, Marx, somehow mixed up with five-dollar dinners and the best looking women in America and fairies who made them laugh and half-sentences immediately understood and secretly hilarious and wives who called their husbands "Baby." He put the hat down, a scrap of straw and a red flower, and a little veil. He drank some whiskey straight and went into the bathroom where his wife was lying deep in her bath, singing to herself and smiling from time to time like a little girl, paddling the water gently with her hands, sending up a slight spicy fragrance from the bath-salts she used.

He stood over her, looking down at her. She smiled up at him, her eyes half closed, her body pink and shimmering in the warm, scented water. All over again, with all the old suddenness, he was hit deep inside him with the knowledge of how beautiful she was, how much he needed her.

"I came in here," he said, "to tell you I wish you wouldn't call me 'Baby.'"

She looked up at him from the bath, her eyes quickly full of sorrow, half-understanding what he meant. He knelt and put his arms around her, his sleeves plunged heedlessly in the water, his shirt and jacket soaking wet as he clutched her wordlessly, holding her crazily tight, crushing her breath from her, kissing her desperately, searchingly, regretfully.

He got jobs after that, selling real estate and automobiles, but somehow, although he had a desk with his name on a wooden wedge on it, and he went to the office religiously at nine each morning, he never managed to sell anything and he never made any money.

Louise was made assistant editor and the house was always full of strange men and women who talked fast and got angry on abstract subjects like mural paintings, novelists, labor unions. Negro short-story writers drank Louise's liquor, and a lot of Jews, and big solemn men with scarred faces and knotted hands who talked slowly but clearly about picket lines and battles with guns and leadpipe at mine-shaft-heads and in front of factory gates. And Louise moved among them all, confidently, knowing what they were talking about, with opinions that they listened to and argued about just as though she were a man. She knew everybody, condescended to no one, devoured books that Darling had never heard of, walked along the streets of the city, excited, at home, soaking in all the million tides of New York without fear, with constant wonder.

Her friends liked Darling and sometimes he found a man who wanted to get off in the corner and talk about the new boy who played fullback for Princeton, and the decline of the double wing-back, or even the state of the stock market, but for the most part he sat on the edge of things, solid and quiet in the high storm of words. "The dialectics of the situation

. . . the theatre has been given over to expert jugglers . . . Picasso? What man has a right to paint old bones and collect ten thousand dollars for them? . . . I stand firmly behind Trotsky . . . Poe was the last American critic. When he died they put lilies on the grave of American criticism. I don't say this because they panned my last book, but . . ."

Once in a while he caught Louise looking soberly and consideringly at him through the cigarette smoke and the noise and he avoided her eyes and found an excuse to get up and go into the kitchen for more ice or to open another bottle.

"Come on," Cathal Flaherty was saying, standing at the door with a girl, "you've got to come down and see this. It's down on Fourteenth Street, in the old Civic Repertory, and you can only see it on Sunday nights and I guarantee you'll come out of the theatre singing." Flaherty was a big young Irishman with a broken nose who was the lawyer for a longshoremen's union, and he had been hanging around the house for six months on and off, roaring and shutting everybody else up when he got in an argument. "It's a new play, *Waiting for Lefty*, it's about taxi-drivers."

"Odets," the girl with Flaherty said. "It's by a guy named Odets."

"I never heard of him," Darling said.

"He's a new one," the girl said.

"It's like watching a bombardment," Flaherty said. "I saw it last Sunday night. You've got to see it."

"Come on, Baby," Louise said to Darling, excitement in her eyes already. "We've been sitting in the Sunday *Times* all day, this'll be a great change."

"I see enough taxi-drivers every day," Darling said, not because he meant that, but because he didn't like to be around Flaherty, who said things that made Louise laugh a lot and whose judgment she accepted on almost every subject. "Let's go to the movies."

"You've never seen anything like this before," Flaherty said. "He wrote this play with a baseball bat."

"Come on," Louise coaxed, "I bet it's wonderful."

"He has long hair," the girl with Flaherty said. "Odets. I met him at a party. He's an actor. He didn't say a goddam thing all night."

"I don't feel like going down to Fourteenth Street," Darling said, wishing Flaherty and his girl would get out. "It's gloomy."

"Oh, hell!" Louise said loudly. She looked coolly at Darling, as though she'd just been introduced to him and was making up her mind about him, and not very favorably. He saw her looking at him, knowing there was something new and dangerous in her face and he wanted to say something, but Flaherty was there and his damned girl, and anyway, he didn't know what to say.

"I'm going," Louise said, getting her coat. "I don't think Fourteenth Street is gloomy."

"I'm telling you," Flaherty was saying, helping her on with her coat, "it's the Battle of Gettysburg, in Brooklynese."

"Nobody could get a word out of him," Flaherty's girl was saying as they went through the door. "He just sat there all night."

The door closed. Louise hadn't said good-night to him. Darling walked around the room four times, then sprawled out on the sofa, on top of the Sunday *Times*. He lay there for five minutes looking at the ceiling, thinking of Flaherty walking down the street talking in that booming voice, between the girls, holding their arms.

Louise had looked wonderful. She'd washed her hair in the afternoon and it had been very soft and light and clung close to her head as she stood there angrily putting her coat on. Louise was getting prettier every year, partly because she knew by now how pretty she was, and made the most of it.

"Nuts," Darling said, standing up. "Oh, nuts."

He put on his coat and went down to the nearest bar and had five drinks off by himself in a corner before his money ran out.

The years since then had been foggy and downhill. Louise had been nice to him, and in a way, loving and kind, and they'd fought only once, when he said he was going to vote for Landon. ("Oh, Christ," she said, "doesn't *anything* happen inside your head? Don't you read the papers? The penniless Republican!") She'd been sorry later and apologized for hurting him, but apologized as she might to a child. He'd tried hard, had gone grimly to the art galleries, the concert halls, the book-shops, trying to gain on the trail of his wife, but it was no use. He was bored, and none of what he saw or heard or dutifully read made much sense to him and finally he gave it up. He had thought, many nights as he ate dinner alone, knowing Louise would come home late and drop silently into bed without explanation, of getting a divorce, but he knew the loneliness, the hopelessness, of not seeing her again would be too much to take. So he was good, completely devoted, ready at all times to go anyplace with her, do anything she wanted. He even got a small job, in a broker's office, and paid his own way, bought his own liquor.

Then he'd been offered the job of going from college to college as a tailor's representative. "We want a man," Mr. Rosenberg had said, "who as soon as you look at him, you say 'There's a university man.'" Rosenberg had looked approvingly at Darling's broad shoulders and well-kept waist, at his carefully brushed hair and his honest, wrinkleless face. "Frankly, Mr. Darling, I am willing to make you a proposition. I have inquired about you, you are favorably known on your old campus, I understand you were in the backfield with Alfred Diederich."

Darling nodded. "What happened to him?"

"He is walking around in a cast for seven years now. An iron brace. He played professional football and they broke his neck for him."

Darling smiled. That, at least, had turned out well.

"Our suits are an easy product to sell, Mr. Darling," Rosenberg said. "We have a handsome, custom-made garment. What has Brooks Brothers got that we haven't got? A name. No more."

"I can make fifty, sixty dollars a week," Darling said to Louise that night. "And expenses. I can save some money and then come back to New York and really get started here."

"Yes, Baby," Louise said.

"As it is," Darling said carefully, "I can make it back here once a month, and holidays and the summer. We can see each other often."

"Yes, Baby." He looked at her face, lovelier now at thirty-five than it had ever been before, but fogged over now as it had been for five years with a kind of patient, kindly, remote boredom.

"What do you say?" he asked. "Should I take it?" Deep within him he hoped fiercely, longingly, for her to say, "No, Baby, you stay right here," but she said, as he knew she'd say, "I think you'd better take it."

He nooded. He had to get up and stand with his back to her, looking out the window, because there were things plain on his face that she had never seen in the fifteen years she'd known him. "Fifty dollars is a lot of money," he said. "I never thought I'd ever see fifty dollars again." He laughed. Louise laughed, too.

Christian Darling sat on the frail green grass of the practice field. The shadow of the stadium had reached out and covered him. In the distance the lights of the university shone a little mistily in the light haze of evening. Fifteen years. Flaherty even now was calling for his wife, buying her a drink, filling whatever bar they were in with that voice of his and that easy laugh. Darling half-closed his eyes, almost saw the boy fifteen years ago reach for the pass, slip by the halfback, go skittering lightly down the field, his knees high and fast and graceful, smiling to himself because he knew he was going to get past the safety man. That was the high point, Darling thought, fifteen years ago, on an autumn afternoon, twenty years old and far from death, with the air coming easily into his lungs, and a deep feeling inside him that he could do anything, knock over anybody, outrun whatever had to be outrun. And the shower after and the three glasses of water and the cool night air on his damp head and Louise sitting hatless in the open car with a smile and the first kiss she ever really meant. The high point, an eighty-yard run in the practice and a girl's kiss and everything after that a decline. Darling laughed. He had practiced the wrong thing, perhaps. He hadn't practiced for 1929 and New York City and a girl who would turn into a woman. Somewhere, he thought, there must have been a point where she moved up to me, was even with me for a moment, when I could have held her hand, if I'd known, held tight, gone with her. Well, he'd never known. Here he was on a playing field that was fifteen years away and his wife was in another city having dinner with another and better man, speaking with him a different, new language, a language nobody had ever taught him.

Darling stood up, smiled a little, because if he didn't smile he knew the tears would come. He looked around him. This was the spot. O'Connor's pass had come sliding out just to here . . . the high point. Darling put up his hands, felt all over again the flat slap of the ball. He shook his hips to throw off the halfback, cut back inside the center, picked his knees high as he ran gracefully over two men jumbled on the ground at the line of scrimmage, ran easily, gaining speed, for ten yards, holding the ball lightly in his two hands, swung away from the halfback diving at him, ran, swinging his hips in the almost-girlish manner of a back in a broken field, tore into the safety man, his shoes drumming heavily on the turf, stiff-armed, elbow locked, pivoted, raced lightly and exultantly for the goal line.

It was only after he had sped over the goal line and slowed to a trot that he saw the boy and girl sitting together on the turf, looking at him wonderingly.

He stopped short, dropping his arms. "I . . ." he said, gasping a little though his condition was fine and the run hadn't winded him, "I . . . Once I played here."

The boy and the girl said nothing. Darling laughed embarrassedly, looked hard at them sitting there, close to each other, shrugged, turned and went toward his hotel, the sweat breaking out on his face and running down into his collar.

SHIRLEY JACKSON

[1919–   ]

Her way of turning nonchalantly from hilarity to horror may have made some readers believe that Shirley Jackson sold her soul to achieve the gift of magic, and that her craft was witchcraft. Actually she is a natural writer who is equally at home with fact or fantasy, a placid historian of household comedies and an equally calm recorder of the domain of the terrifying, the macabre, and the abnormal which lies just beyond the borders of ordinary life. She dislikes talking or writing about herself and will give only the barest chronological data. "I was born in San Francisco in 1919," she told the editors of Twentieth Century Authors, "and spent most of my early life in California. I was married in 1940 to Stanley Edgar Hyman, critic and numismatist, and we live in Vermont, comfortably far away from city life. Our major exports are books and children, both of which we produce in abundance."

At forty Shirley Jackson's productions included four children, five novels—the best and most breathless of the latter being Hangsaman, The Sundial, and The Haunting of Hill House—a volume of short stories, and Life Among the Savages, which she calls "a disrespectful memoir of my children," a continually comic account of her relations with her four unpredictable offspring.

"The Lottery," the title story of a volume of the same name, is her most famous single piece of writing; it is also the most concise and compelling. Placed in an average rural setting, told in the most casual manner, the story transforms people of the normal everyday world into creatures obeying an old ritual which is not only blindly demanding but incredibly diabolical.

THE LOTTERY

The morning of June 27th was clear and sunny, with the fresh warmth of a full-summer day; the flowers were blossoming profusely and the grass was richly green. The people of the village began to gather in the square, between the post office and the bank, around ten o'clock; in some towns there were so many people that the lottery took two days and had to be started on June 26th, but in this village, where there were only about three hundred people, the whole lottery took only about two hours, so it could begin at ten o'clock in the morning and still be through in time to allow the villagers to get home for noon dinner.

The children assembled first, of course. School was recently over for the summer, and the feeling of liberty sat uneasily on most of them; they tended to gather together quietly for a while before they broke into boisterous play, and their talk was still of the classroom and the teacher, of books and reprimands. Bobby Martin had already stuffed his pockets full of stones, and the other boys soon followed his example, selecting the smoothest and roundest stones; Bobby and Harry Jones and Dickie Delacroix—the villagers pronounced this name "Dellacroy"—eventually made a great pile of stones in one corner of the square and guarded it against the raids of the other boys. The girls stood aside, talking among themselves, looking over their shoulders at the boys, and the very small children rolled in the dust or clung to the hands of their older brothers or sisters.

Soon the men began to gather, surveying their own children, speaking of planting and rain, tractors and taxes. They stood together, away from the pile of stones in the corner, and their jokes were quiet and they smiled rather than laughed. The women, wearing faded house dresses and sweaters, came shortly after their menfolk. They greeted one another and exchanged bits of gossip as they went to join their husbands. Soon the women, standing by their husbands, began to call to their children, and the children came reluctantly, having to be called four or five times. Bobby Martin ducked under his mother's grasping hand and ran, laughing, back to the pile of stones. His father spoke up sharply, and Bobby came quickly and took his place between his father and his oldest brother.

The lottery was conducted—as were the square dances, the teenage club, the Halloween program—by Mr. Summers, who had time and energy to devote to civic activities. He was a round-faced, jovial man and he ran the coal business, and people were sorry for him, because he had no children and his wife was a scold. When he arrived in the square, carrying the black wooden box, there was a murmur of conversation among the villagers, and he waved and called, "Little late today, folks." The postmaster, Mr. Graves, followed him, carrying a three-legged stool, and the stool was put in the center of the square and Mr. Summers set the black box down on it. The villagers kept their distance, leaving a space between themselves and the stool, and when Mr. Summers said, "Some of you fellows want to give me a hand?," there was a hesitation before two men, Mr. Martin and his oldest son, Baxter, came forward to hold the box steady on the stool while Mr. Summers stirred up the papers inside it.

The original paraphernalia for the lottery had been lost long ago, and the black box now resting on the stool had been put into use even before Old Man Warner, the oldest man in town, was born. Mr. Summers spoke frequently to the villagers about making a new box, but no one liked to upset even as much tradition as was represented by the black box. There was a story that the present box had been made with some pieces of the box that had preceded it, the one that had been constructed when the first people settled down to make a village here. Every year, after the lottery, Mr. Summers began talking again about a new box, but every year the subject was allowed to fade off without anything's being done. The black box grew shabbier each year; by now it was no longer completely black but splintered badly along one side to show the original wood color, and in some places faded or stained.

Mr. Martin and his oldest son, Baxter, held the black box securely on the stool until Mr. Summers had stirred the papers thoroughly with his hand. Because so much of the ritual had been forgotten or discarded, Mr. Summers had been successful in having slips of paper substituted for the chips of wood that had been used for generations. Chips of wood, Mr. Summers had argued, had been all very well when the village was tiny, but now that the population was more than three hundred and likely to keep on growing, it was necessary to use something that would fit more easily into the black box. The night before the lottery, Mr. Summers and Mr. Graves made up the slips of paper and put them into the box, and it was then taken to the safe of Mr. Summers' coal company and locked up until Mr. Summers was ready to take it to the square next morning. The rest of the year, the box was put away, sometimes one place, sometimes another; it had spent one year in Mr. Graves' barn and another year underfoot in the post office, and sometimes it was set on a shelf in the Martin grocery and left there.

There was a great deal of fussing to be done before Mr. Summers declared the lottery open. There were the lists to make up—of heads of families, heads of households in each family, members of each household in each family. There was the proper swearing-in of Mr. Summers by the postmaster, as the official of the lottery; at one time, some people remembered, there had been a recital of some sort, performed by the official of the lottery, a perfunctory, tuneless chant that had been rattled off duly each year; some people believed that the official of the lottery used to stand just so when he said or sang it, others believed that he was supposed to walk among the people, but years and years ago this part of the ritual had been allowed to lapse. There had been, also, a ritual salute, which the official of the lottery had had to use in addressing each person who came up to draw from the box, but this also had changed with time, until now it was felt necessary only for the official to speak to each person approaching. Mr. Summers was very good at all this; in his clean white shirt and blue jeans, with one hand resting carelessly on the black box, he seemed very proper and important as he talked interminably to Mr. Graves and the Martins.

Just as Mr. Summers finally left off talking and turned to the assembled villagers, Mrs. Hutchinson came hurriedly along the path to the square, her sweater thrown over her shoulders, and slid into place in the back of the crowd. "Clean forgot what day it was," she said to Mrs. Delacroix, who stood next to her, and they both laughed softly. "Thought my old man was out back stacking wood," Mrs. Hutchinson went on, "and then I looked out the window and the kids was gone, and then I remembered it was the twenty-seventh and came a-running." She dried her hands on her apron, and Mrs. Delacroix said, "You're in time, though. They're still talking away up there."

Mrs. Hutchinson craned her neck to see through the crowd and found her husband and children standing near the front. She tapped Mrs. Delacroix on the arm as a farewell and began to make her way through the crowd. The people separated good-humoredly to let her through; two or three people said, in voices just loud enough to be heard across the crowd, "Here comes your Mrs., Hutchinson," and "Bill, she made it after all." Mrs. Hutchinson reached her husband, and Mr. Summers, who had been waiting, said cheerfully, "Thought we were going to have to get on without you, Tessie." Mrs. Hutchinson said, grinning, "Wouldn't have me leave m'dishes in the sink, now, would you, Joe?," and soft laughter ran through the crowd as the people stirred back into position after Mrs. Hutchinson's arrival.

"Well, now," Mr. Summers said soberly, "guess we better get started, get this over with, so's we can go back to work. Anybody ain't here?"

"Dunbar," several people said. "Dunbar, Dunbar."

Mr. Summers consulted his list. "Clyde Dunbar," he said. "That's right. He's broke his leg, hasn't he? Who's drawing for him?"

"Me, I guess," a woman said, and Mr. Summers turned to look at her. "Wife draws for her husband," Mr. Summers said. "Don't you have a grown boy to do it for you, Janey?" Although Mr. Summers and everyone else in the village knew the answer perfectly well, it was the business of the official of the lottery to ask such questions formally. Mr.

Summers waited with an expression of polite interest while Mrs. Dunbar answered.

"Horace's not but sixteen yet," Mrs. Dunbar said regretfully. "Guess I gotta fill in for the old man this year."

"Right," Mr. Summers said. He made a note on the list he was holding. Then he asked, "Watson boy drawing this year?"

A tall boy in the crowd raised his hand. "Here," he said. "I'm drawing for m'mother and me." He blinked his eyes nervously and ducked his head as several voices in the crowd said things like "Good fellow, Jack," and "Glad to see your mother's got a man to do it."

"Well," Mr. Summers said, "guess that's everyone. Old Man Warner make it?"

"Here," a voice said, and Mr. Summers nodded.

A sudden hush fell on the crowd as Mr. Summers cleared his throat and looked at the list. "All ready?" he called. "Now, I'll read the names—heads of families first—and the men come up and take a paper out of the box. Keep the paper folded in your hand without looking at it until everyone has had a turn. Everything clear?"

The people had done it so many times that they only half listened to the directions; most of them were quiet, wetting their lips, not looking around. Then Mr. Summers raised one hand high and said, "Adams." A man disengaged himself from the crowd and came forward. "Hi, Steve," Mr. Summers said, and Mr. Adams said, "Hi, Joe." They grinned at one another humorlessly and nervously. Then Mr. Adams reached into the black box and took out a folded paper. He held it firmly by one corner as he turned and went hastily back to his place in the crowd, where he stood a little apart from his family, not looking down at his hand.

"Allen," Mr. Summers said. "Anderson. . . . Bentham."

"Seems like there's no time at all between lotteries any more," Mrs. Delacroix said to Mrs. Graves in the back row. "Seems like we got through with the last one only last week."

"Time sure goes fast," Mrs. Graves said.

"Clark. . . . Delacroix."

"There goes my old man," Mrs. Delacroix said. She held her breath while her husband went forward.

"Dunbar," Mr. Summers said, and Mrs. Dunbar went steadily to the box while one of the women said, "Go on, Janey," and another said, "There she goes."

"We're next," Mrs. Graves said. She watched while Mr. Graves came around from the side of the box, greeted Mr. Summers gravely, and selected a slip of paper from the box. By now, all through the crowd there were men holding the small folded papers in their large hands, turning them over and over nervously. Mrs. Dunbar and her two sons stood together, Mrs. Dunbar holding the slip of paper.

"Harburt. . . . Hutchinson."

"Get up there, Bill," Mrs. Hutchinson said, and the people near her laughed.

"Jones."

"They do say," Mr. Adams said to Old Man Warner, who stood next to him, "that over in the north village they're talking of giving up the lottery."

Old Man Warner snorted. "Pack of crazy fools," he said. "Listening to the young folks, nothing's good enough for *them.* Next thing you know, they'll be wanting to go back to living in caves, nobody work any more, live *that* way for a while. Used to be a saying about 'Lottery in June, corn be heavy soon.' First thing you know, we'd all be eating stewed chickweed and acorns. There's *always* been a lottery," he added petulantly. "Bad enough to see young Joe Summers up there joking with everybody."

"Some places have already quit lotteries," Mr. Adams said.

"Nothing but trouble in *that,*" Old Man Warner said stoutly. "Pack of young fools."

"Martin." And Bobby Martin watched his father go forward. "Overdyke. . . . Percy."

"I wish they'd hurry," Mrs. Dunbar said to her older son. "I wish they'd hurry."

"They're almost through," her son said.

"You get ready to run tell Dad," Mrs. Dunbar said.

Mr. Summers called his own name and then stepped fordward precisely and selected a slip from the box. Then he called, "Warner."

"Seventy-seventh year I been in the lottery," Old Man Warner said as he went through the crowd. "Seventy-seventh time."

"Watson." The tall boy came awkwardly through the crowd. Someone said, "Don't be nervous, Jack," and Mr. Summers said, "Take your time, son."

"Zanini."

After that, there was a long pause, a breathless pause, until Mr. Summers, holding his slip of paper in the air, said, "All right, fellows." For a minute, no one moved, and then all the slips of paper were opened. Suddenly, all the women began to speak at once, saying, "Who is it?," "Who's got it?," "Is it the Dunbars?," "Is it the Watsons?" Then the voices began to say, "It's Hutchinson. It's Bill," "Bill Hutchinson's got it."

"Go tell your father," Mrs. Dunbar said to her older son.

People began to look around to see the Hutchinsons. Bill Hutchinson was standing quiet, staring down at the paper in his hand. Suddenly, Tessie Hutchinson shouted to Mr. Summers, "You didn't give him time enough to take any paper he wanted. I saw you. It wasn't fair!"

"Be a good sport, Tessie," Mrs. Delacroix called, and Mrs. Graves said, "All of us took the same chance."

"Shut up, Tessie," Bill Hutchinson said.

"Well, everyone," Mr. Summers said, "that was done pretty fast, and now we've got to be hurrying a little more to get done in time." He consulted his next list. "Bill," he said, "you draw for the Hutchinson family. You got any other households in the Hutchinsons?"

"There's Don and Eva," Mrs. Hutchinson yelled. "Make *them* take their chance!"

"Daughters draw with their husbands' families, Tessie," Mr. Summers said gently. "You know that as well as anyone else."

"It wasn't *fair*," Tessie said.

"I guess not, Joe," Bill Hutchinson said regretfully. "My daughter draws with her husband's family, that's only fair. And I've got no other family except the kids."

"Then, as far as drawing for families is concerned, it's you," Mr. Summers said in explanation, "and as far as drawing for households is concerned, that's you, too. Right?"

"Right," Bill Hutchinson said.

"How many kids, Bill?" Mr. Summers asked formally.

"Three," Bill Hutchinson said. "There's Bill, Jr., and Nancy, and little Dave. And Tessie and me."

"All right, then," Mr. Summers said. "Harry, you got their tickets back?"

Mr. Graves nodded and held up the slips of paper. "Put them in the box, then," Mr. Summers directed. "Take Bill's and put it in."

"I think we ought to start over," Mrs. Hutchinson said, as quietly as she could. "I tell you it wasn't *fair*. You didn't give him time enough to choose. *Every*body saw that."

Mr. Graves had selected the five slips and put them in the box, and he dropped all the papers but those onto the ground, where the breeze caught them and lifted them off.

"Listen, everybody," Mrs. Hutchinson was saying to the people around her.

"Ready, Bill?" Mr. Summers asked, and Bill Hutchinson, with one quick glance around at his wife and children, nodded.

"Remember," Mr. Summers said, "take the slips and keep them folded until each person has taken one. Harry, you help little Dave." Mr. Graves took the hand of the little boy, who came willingly with him up to the box. "Take a paper out of the box, Davy," Mr. Summers said. Davy put his hand into the box and laughed. "Take just *one* paper," Mr. Summers said. "Harry, you hold it for him." Mr. Graves took the child's hand and removed the folded paper from the tight fist and held it while little Dave stood next to him and looked up at him wonderingly.

"Nancy next," Mr. Summers said. Nancy was twelve, and her school friends breathed heavily as she went forward, switching her skirt, and took a slip daintily from the box. "Bill, Jr.," Mr. Summers said, and Billy, his face red and his feet overlarge, nearly knocked the box over as he got a paper out. "Tessie," Mr. Summers said. She hesitated for a minute, looking around defiantly, and then set her lips and went up to the box. She snatched a paper out and held it behind her.

"Bill," Mr. Summers said, and Bill Hutchinson reached into the box and felt around, bringing his hand out at last with the slip of paper in it.

The crowd was quiet. A girl whispered, "I hope it's not Nancy," and the sound of the whisper reached the edges of the crowd.

"It's not the way it used to be," Old Man Warner said clearly. "People ain't the way they used to be."

"All right," Mr. Summers said. "Open the papers. Harry, you open little Dave's."

Mr. Graves opened the slip of paper and there was a general sigh through the crowd as he held it up and everyone could see that it was blank. Nancy and Bill, Jr., opened theirs at the same time, and both beamed and laughed, turning around to the crowd and holding their slips of paper above their heads.

"Tessie," Mr. Summers said. There was a pause, and then Mr. Summers looked at Bill Hutchinson, and Bill unfolded his paper and showed it. It was blank.

"It's Tessie," Mr. Summers said, and his voice was hushed. "Show us her paper, Bill."

Bill Hutchinson went over to his wife and forced the slip of paper out of her hand. It had a black spot on it, the black spot Mr. Summers had made the night before with the heavy pencil in the coal-company office. Bill Hutchinson held it up, and there was a stir in the crowd.

"All right, folks," Mr. Summers said. "Let's finish quickly."

Although the villagers had forgotten the ritual and lost the original black box, they still remembered to use stones. The pile of stones the boys had made earlier was ready; there were stones on the ground with the blowing scraps of paper that had come out of the box. Mrs. Delacroix selected a stone so large she had to pick it up with both hands and turned to Mrs. Dunbar. "Come on," she said. "Hurry up."

Mrs. Dunbar had small stones in both hands, and she said, gasping for breath, "I can't run at all. You'll have to go ahead and I'll catch up with you."

The children had stones already, and someone gave little Davy Hutchinson a few pebbles.

Tessie Hutchinson was in the center of a cleared space by now, and she held her hands out desperately as the villagers moved in on her. "It isn't fair," she said. A stone hit her on the side of the head.

Old Man Warner was saying, "Come on, come on, everyone." Steve Adams was in the front of the crowd of villagers, with Mrs. Graves beside him.

"It isn't fair, it isn't right," Mrs. Hutchinson screamed, and then they were upon her.

RAY BRADBURY

[1920–]

RAY BRADBURY BELIEVES that his interest in the sociology of the future stems from two sources: the world of fantasy which he found in boyhood when he read Tarzan *and the magazine* Amazing Stories; *and the discovery of the fact that one of his ancestors, Mary Bradbury, had been tried as a witch in Salem. He was born August 22, 1920, in Waukegan, Illinois. His father's ancestors came to America in 1630; his mother was born in Stockholm, Sweden. Although he started writing stories and sending them to the major magazines when he was fifteen, he sold newspapers for three years upon graduating from high school and finally saw his first story published when he was nineteen. After that time everything he wrote—and he wrote hundreds of stories —achieved immediate publication; before he was in his mid-thirties he had appeared in more than sixty anthologies. Married at twenty-seven, he settled in California, made a successful screen play of* Moby Dick, *and started to write his own stories for films.*

The Martian Chronicles, The Illustrated Man, *and* The Golden Apples of the Sun *disclose a man who believes that "science-fiction and fanatasy are the liveliest, freshest approaches to many of our prob-*

lems today." They also reveal a man who, not only a gifted creator ot science-fiction, is also a born lover of liberty and a foe of every kind of suppression, mental as well as physical. Bradbury has a poet's imagination; he delves into the dark territories of the mysterious mind as avidly as he explores the outer galaxies. "The Veldt" is a quietly horrifying, unbelievable, yet plausible tale. It is the kind of story Edgar Allan Poe might have written had he lived in the days of television and faced a future in which nothing would be impossible.

THE VELDT

"George, I wish you'd look at the nursery."

"What's wrong with it?"

"I don't know."

"Well, then."

"I just want you to look at it, is all, or call a psychologist in to look at it."

"What would a psychologist want with a nursery?"

"You know very well what he'd want." His wife paused in the middle of the kitchen and watched the stove busy humming to itself, making supper for four.

"It's just that the nursery is different now than it was."

"All right, let's have a look."

They walked down the hall of their soundproofed, Happylife Home, which had cost them thirty thousand dollars installed, this house which clothed and fed and rocked them to sleep and played and sang and was good to them. Their approach sensitized a switch somewhere and the nursery light flicked on when they came within ten feet of it. Similarly, behind them, in the halls, lights went on and off as they left them behind, with a soft automaticity.

"Well," said George Hadley.

They stood on the thatched floor of the nursery. It was forty feet across by forty feet long and thirty feet high; it had cost half again as much as the rest of the house. "But nothing's too good for our children," George had said.

The nursery was silent. It was empty as a jungle glade at hot high noon. The walls were blank and two dimensional. Now, as George and

Lydia Hadley stood in the center of the room, the walls began to purr and recede into crystalline distance, it seemed, and presently an African veldt appeared, in three dimensions, on all sides, in color, reproduced to the final pebble and bit of straw. The ceiling above them became a deep sky with a hot yellow sun.

George Hadley felt the perspiration start on his brow.

"Let's get out of this sun," he said. "This is a little too real. But I don't see anything wrong."

"Wait a moment, you'll see," said his wife.

Now the odorophonics were beginning to blow a wind of odor at the two people in the middle of the baked veldtland. The hot straw smell of lion grass, the cool green smell of the hidden water hole, the great rusty smell of animals, the smell of dust like a red paprika in the hot air. And now the sounds: the thump of distant antelope feet on grassy sod, the papery rustling of vultures. A shadow passed through the sky. The shadow flickered on George Hadley's upturned, sweating face.

"Filthy creatures," he heard his wife say.

"The vultures."

"You see, there are the lions, far over, that way. Now they're on their way to the water hole. They've just been eating," said Lydia. "I don't know what."

"Some animal." George Hadley put his hand up to shield off the burning light from his squinted eyes. "A zebra or a baby giraffe, maybe."

"Are you sure?" His wife sounded peculiarly tense.

"No, it's a little late to be sure," he said, amused. "Nothing over there I can see but cleaned bone, and the vultures dropping for what's left."

"Did you hear that scream?" she asked.

"No."

"About a minute ago?"

"Sorry, no."

The lions were coming. And again George Hadley was filled with admiration for the mechanical genius who had conceived this room. A miracle of efficiency selling for an absurdly low price. Every home should have one. Oh, occasionally they frightened you with their clinical accuracy, they startled you, gave you a twinge, but most of the time what fun for everyone, not only your own son and daughter, but for yourself when you felt like a quick jaunt to a foreign land, a quick change of scenery. Well, here it was!

And here were the lions now, fifteen feet away, so real, so feverishly and startlingly real that you could feel the prickling fur on your hand, and your mouth was stuffed with the dusty upholstery smell of their heated pelts, and the yellow of them was in your eyes like the yellow of an exquisite French tapestry, the yellows of lions and summer grass, and the sound of the matted lion lungs exhaling on the silent noontide, and the smell of meat from the panting, dripping mouths.

The lions stood looking at George and Lydia Hadley with terrible green-yellow eyes.

"Watch out!" screamed Lydia.

The lions came running at them.

Lydia bolted and ran. Instinctively, George sprang after her. Outside, in the hall, with the door slammed, he was laughing and she was crying, and they both stood appalled at the other's reaction.

"George!"

"Lydia! Oh, my dear poor sweet Lydia!"

"They almost got us!"

"Walls, Lydia, remember; crystal walls, that's all they are. Oh, they look real, I must admit–Africa in your parlor–but it's all dimensional superreactionary, supersensitive color film and mental tape film behind glass screens. It's all odorophonics and sonics, Lydia. Here's my handkerchief."

"I'm afraid." She came to him and put her body against him and cried steadily. "Did you see? Did you feel? It's too real."

"Now, Lydia . . ."

"You've got to tell Wendy and Peter not to read any more on Africa."

"Of course–of course." He patted her.

"Promise?"

"Sure."

"And lock the nursery for a few days until I get my nerves settled."

"You know how difficult Peter is about that. When I punished him a month ago by locking the nursery for even a few hours–the tantrum he threw! And Wendy too. They *live* for the nursery."

"It's got to be locked, that's all there is to it."

"All right." Reluctantly he locked the huge door. "You've been working too hard. You need a rest."

"I don't know–I don't know," she said, blowing her nose, sitting down in a chair that immediately began to rock and comfort her. "Maybe I don't have enough to do. Maybe I have time to think too much. Why don't we shut the whole house off for a few days and take a vacation?"

"You mean you want to fry my eggs for me?"

"Yes," she nodded.

"And darn my socks?"

"Yes." A frantic, watery-eyed nodding.

"And sweep the house?"

"Yes, yes—oh, yes!"

"But I thought that's why we bought this house, so we wouldn't have to do anything?"

"That's just it. I feel like I don't belong here. The house is wife and mother now and nursemaid. Can I compete with an African veldt? Can I give a bath and scrub the children as efficiently or quickly as the automatic scrub bath can? I cannot. And it isn't just me. It's you. You've been awfully nervous lately."

"I suppose I have been smoking too much."

"You look as if you didn't know what to do with yourself in this house, either. You smoke a little more every morning and drink a little more every afternoon and need a little more sedative every night. You're beginning to feel unnecessary too."

"Am I?" He paused and tried to feel into himself to see what was really there.

"Oh, George!" She looked beyond him, at the nursery door. "Those lions can't get out of there, can they?"

He looked at the door and saw it tremble as if something had jumped against it from the other side.

"Of course not," he said.

At dinner they ate alone, for Wendy and Peter were at a special plastic carnival across town and had televised home to say they'd be late, to go ahead eating. So George Hadley, bemused, sat watching the dining-room table produce warm dishes of food from its mechanical interior.

"We forgot the ketchup," he said.

"Sorry," said a small voice within the table, and ketchup appeared.

As for the nursery, thought George Hadley, it won't hurt for the children to be locked out of it awhile. Too much of anything isn't good for anyone. And it was clearly indicated that the children had been spending a little too much time on Africa. That sun. He could feel it on his neck, still, like a hot paw. And the *lions*. And the smell of blood. Remarkable how the nursery caught the telepathic emanations of the children's minds and created life to fill their every desire. The children thought lions, and there were lions. The children thought zebras, and there were zebras. Sun—sun. Giraffes—giraffes. Death and death.

That *last*. He chewed tastelessly on the meat that the table had cut for him. Death thoughts. They were awfully young, Wendy and Peter, for death thoughts. Or, no, you were never too young, really. Long before you knew what death was you were wishing it on someone else. When you were two years old you were shooting people with cap pistols.

But this—the long, hot African veldt—the awful death in the jaws of a lion. And repeated again and again.

"Where are you going?"

He didn't answer Lydia. Preoccupied, he let the lights glow softly on ahead of him, extinguish behind him as he padded to the nursery door. He listened against it. Far away, a lion roared.

He unlocked the door and opened it. Just before he stepped inside, he heard a faraway scream. And then another roar from the lions, which subsided quickly.

He stepped into Africa. How many times in the last year had he opened this door and found Wonderland, Alice, the Mock Turtle, or Aladdin and his Magical Lamp, or Jack Pumpkinhead of Oz, or Dr. Doolittle, or the cow jumping over a very real-appearing moon—all the delightful contraptions of a make-believe world. How often had he seen Pegasus flying in the sky ceiling, or seen fountains of red fireworks, or heard angel voices singing. But now, this yellow hot Africa, this bake oven with murder in the heat. Perhaps Lydia was right. Perhaps they needed a little vacation from the fantasy which was growing a bit too real for ten-year-old children. It was all right to exercise one's mind with gymnastic fantasies, but when the lively child mind settled on one pattern . . . ? It seemed that, at a distance, for the past month, he had heard lions roaring, and smelled their strong odor seeping as far away as his study door. But, being busy, he had paid it no attention.

George Hadley stood on the African grassland alone. The lions looked up from their feeding, watching him. The only flaw to the illusion was the open door through which he could see his wife, far down the dark hall, like a framed picture, eating her dinner abstractedly.

"Go away," he said to the lions.

They did not go.

He knew the principle of the room exactly. You sent out your thoughts. Whatever you thought would appear.

"Let's have Aladdin and his lamp," he snapped.

The veldtland remained; the lions remained.

"Come on, room! I demand Aladdin!" he said.

Nothing happened. The lions mumbled in their baked pelts.

"Aladdin!"

He went back to dinner. "The fool room's out of order," he said. "It won't respond."

"Or—"

"Or what?"

"Or it can't respond," said Lydia, "because the children have thought about Africa and lions and killing so many days that the room's in a rut."

"Could be."

"Or Peter's set it to remain that way."

"Set it?"

"He may have got into the machinery and fixed something."

"Peter doesn't know machinery."

"He's a wise one for ten. That I.Q. of his—"

"Nevertheless—"

"Hello, Mom. Hello, Dad."

The Hadleys turned. Wendy and Peter were coming in the front door, cheeks like peppermint candy, eyes like bright blue agate marbles, a smell of ozone on their jumpers from their trip in the helicopter.

"You're just in time for supper," said both parents.

"We're full of strawberry ice cream and hot dogs," said the children, holding hands. "But we'll sit and watch."

"Yes, come tell us about the nursery," said George Hadley.

The brother and sister blinked at him and then at each other. "Nursery?"

"All about Africa and everything," said the father with false joviality.

"I don't understand," said Peter.

"Your mother and I were just traveling through Africa with rod and reel; Tom Swift and his Electric Lion," said George Hadley.

"There's no Africa in the nursery," said Peter simply.

"Oh, come now, Peter. We know better."

"I don't remember any Africa," said Peter to Wendy. "Do you?"

"No."

"Run see and come tell."

She obeyed.

"Wendy, come back here!" said George Hadley, but she was gone. The house lights followed her like a flock of fireflies. Too late, he realized he had forgotten to lock the nursery door after his last inspection.

"Wendy'll look and come tell us," said Peter.

"She doesn't have to tell *me*. I've seen it."

"I'm sure you're mistaken, Father."

"I'm not, Peter. Come along now."

But Wendy was back. "It's not Africa," she said breathlessly.

"We'll see about this," said George Hadley, and they all walked down the hall together and opened the nursery door.

There was a green, lovely forest, a lovely river, a purple mountain, high voices singing, and Rima, lovely and mysterious, lurking in the trees with colorful flights of butterflies, like animated bouquets, lingering in her long hair. The African veldtland was gone. The lions were gone. Only

Rima was here now, singing a song so beautiful that it brought tears to your eyes.

George Hadley looked in at the changed scene. "Go to bed," he said to the children.

They opened their mouths.

"You heard me," he said.

They went off to the air closet, where a wind sucked them like brown leaves up the flue to their slumber rooms.

George Hadley walked through the singing glade and picked up something that lay in the corner near where the lions had been. He walked slowly back to his wife.

"What is that?" she asked.

"An old wallet of mine," he said.

He showed it to her. The smell of hot grass was on it and the smell of a lion. There were drops of saliva on it, it had been chewed, and there were blood smears on both sides.

He closed the nursery door and locked it, tight.

In the middle of the night he was still awake and he knew his wife was awake. "Do you think Wendy changed it?" she said at last, in the dark room.

"Of course."

"Made it from a veldt into a forest and put Rima there instead of lions?"

"Yes."

"Why?"

"I don't know. But it's staying locked until I find out."

"How did your wallet get there?"

"I don't know anything," he said, "except that I'm beginning to be sorry we bought that room for the children. If children are neurotic at all, a room like that–"

"It's supposed to help them work off their neuroses in a healthful way."

"I'm starting to wonder." He stared at the ceiling.

"We've given the children everything they ever wanted. Is this our reward–secrecy, disobedience?"

"Who was it said, 'Children are carpets, they should be stepped on occasionally'? We've never lifted a hand. They're insufferable–let's admit it. They come and go when they like; they treat us as if we were offspring. They're spoiled and we're spoiled."

"They've been acting funny ever since you forbade them to take the rocket to New York a few months ago."

"They're not old enough to do that alone, I explained."

"Nevertheless, I've noticed they've been decidedly cool toward us since."

"I think I'll have David McClean come tomorrow morning to have a look at Africa."

"But it's not Africa now, it's Green Mansions country and Rima.

"I have a feeling it'll be Africa again before then."

A moment later they heard the screams.

Two screams. Two people screaming from downstairs. And then a roar of lions.

"Wendy and Peter aren't in their rooms," said his wife.

He lay in his bed with his beating heart. "No," he said. "They've broken into the nursery."

"Those screams—they sound familiar."

"Do they?"

"Yes, awfully."

And although their beds tried very hard, the two adults couldn't be rocked to sleep for another hour. A smell of cats was in the night air.

"Father?" said Peter.

"Yes."

Peter looked at his shoes. He never looked at his father any more, nor at his mother. "You aren't going to lock up the nursery for good, are you?"

"That all depends."

"On what?" snapped Peter.

"On you and your sister. If you intersperse this Africa with a little variety—oh, Sweden perhaps, or Denmark or China—"

"I thought we were free to play as we wished."

"You are, within reasonable bounds."

"What's wrong with Africa, Father?"

"Oh, so now you admit you have been conjuring up Africa, do you?"

"I wouldn't want the nursery locked up," said Peter coldly. "Ever."

"Matter of fact, we're thinking of turning the whole house off for about a month. Live sort of a carefree one-for-all existence."

"That sounds dreadful! Would I have to tie my own shoes instead of letting the shoe tier do it? And brush my own teeth and comb my hair and give myself a bath?"

"It would be fun for a change, don't you think?"

"No, it would be horrid. I didn't like it when you took out the picture painter last month."

"That's because I wanted you to learn to paint all by yourself, son."

"I don't want to do anything but look and listen and smell; what else *is* there to do?"

"All right, go play in Africa."

"Will you shut off the house sometime soon?"

"We're considering it."

"I don't think you'd better consider it any more, Father."

"I won't have any threats from my son!"

"Very well." And Peter strolled off to the nursery.

"Am I on time?" said David McClean.

"Breakfast?" asked George Hadley.

"Thanks, had some. What's the trouble?"

"David, you're a psychologist."

"I should hope so."

"Well, then, have a look at our nursery. You saw it a year ago when you dropped by; did you notice anything peculiar about it then?"

"Can't say I did; the usual violences, a tendency toward a slight paranoia here or there, usual in children because they feel persecuted by parents constantly, but, oh, really nothing."

They walked down the hall. "I locked the nursery up," explained the father, "and the children broke back into it during the night. I let them stay so they could form the patterns for you to see."

There was a terrible screaming from the nursery.

"There it is," said George Hadley. "See what you make of it."

They walked in on the children without rapping.

The screams had faded. The lions were feeding.

"Run outside a moment, children," said George Hadley. "No, don't change the mental combination. Leave the walls as they are. Get!"

With the children gone, the two men stood studying the lions clustered at a distance, eating with great relish whatever it was they had caught.

"I wish I knew what it was," said George Hadley. "Sometimes I can almost see. Do you think if I brought high-powered binoculars here and—"

David McClean laughed dryly. "Hardly." He turned to study all four walls. "How long has this been going on?"

"A little over a month."

"It certainly doesn't *feel* good."

"I want facts, not feelings."

"My dear George, a psychologist never saw a fact in his life. He only hears about feelings; vague things. This doesn't feel good, I tell you. Trust my hunches and my instincts. I have a nose for something bad. This is very bad. My advice to you is to have the whole damn room torn down and your children brought to me every day during the next year for treatment."

"Is it that bad?"

"I'm afraid so. One of the original uses of these nurseries was so that we could study the patterns left on the walls by the child's mind, study at our leisure, and help the child. In this case, however, the room has become a channel toward—destructive thoughts, instead of a release away from them."

"Didn't you sense this before?"

"I sensed only that you had spoiled your children more than most. And now you're letting them down in some way. What way?"

"I wouldn't let them go to New York."

"What else?"

"I've taken a few machines from the house and threatened them, a month ago, with closing up the nursery unless they did their homework. I did close it for a few days to show I meant business."

"Ah, ha!"

"Does that mean anything?"

"Everything. Where before they had a Santa Claus now they have a Scrooge. Children prefer Santas. You've let this room and this house replace you and your wife in your children's affections. This room is their mother and father, far more important in their lives than their real parents. And now you come along and want to shut it off. No wonder there's hatred here. You can feel it coming out of the sky. Feel that sun. George, you'll have to change your life. Like too many others, you've built it around creature comforts. Why, you'd starve tomorrow if something went wrong in your kitchen. You wouldn't know how to tap an egg. Nevertheless, turn everything off. Start new. It'll take time. But we'll make good children out of bad in a year, wait and see."

"But won't the shock be too much for the children, shutting the room up abruptly, for good?"

"I don't want them going any deeper into this, that's all."

The lions were finished with their red feast.

The lions were standing on the edge of the clearing watching the two men.

"Now *I'm* feeling persecuted," said McClean. "Let's get out of here. I never have cared for these damned rooms. Make me nervous."

"The lions look real, don't they?" said George Hadley. "I don't suppose there's any way——"

"What?"

"—that they could *become* real?"

"Not that I know."

"Some flaw in the machinery, a tampering or something?"

"No."

They went to the door.

"I don't imagine the room will like being turned off," said the father.

"Nothing ever likes to die—even a room."

"I wonder if it hates me for wanting to switch it off?"

"Paranoia is thick around here today," said David McClean. "You can follow it like a spoor. Hello." He bent and picked up a bloody scarf. "This yours?"

"No," George Hadley's face was rigid. "It belongs to Lydia."

They went to the fuse box together and threw the switch that killed the nursery.

The two children were in hysterics. They screamed and pranced and threw things. They yelled and sobbed and swore and jumped at the furniture.

"You can't do that to the nursery, you can't!"

"Now, children."

The children flung themselves onto a couch, weeping.

"George," said Lydia Hadley, "turn on the nursery, just for a few moments. You can't be so abrupt."

"No."

"You can't be so cruel."

"Lydia, it's off, and it stays off. And the whole damn house dies as of here and now. The more I see of the mess we've put ourselves in, the more it sickens me. We've been contemplating our mechanical, electronic navels for too long. My God, how we need a breath of honest air!"

And he marched about the house turning off the voice clocks, the stoves, the heaters, the shoe shiners, the shoe lacers, the body scrubbers and swabbers and massagers, and every other machine he could put his hand to.

The house was full of dead bodies, it seemed. It felt like a mechanical cemetery. So silent. None of the humming hidden energy of machines waiting to function at the tap of a button.

"Don't let them do it!" wailed Peter at the ceiling, as if he was talking to the house, the nursery. "Don't let Father kill everything." He turned to his father. "Oh, I hate you!"

"Insults won't get you anywhere."

"I wish you were dead!"

"We were, for a long while. Now we're going to really start living. Instead of being handled and massaged, we're going to *live*."

Wendy was still crying and Peter joined her again. "Just a moment, just one moment, just another moment of nursery," they wailed.

"Oh, George," said the wife, "it can't hurt."

"All right—all right, if they'll only just shut up. One minute, mind you, and then off forever."

"Daddy, Daddy, Daddy!" sang the children, smiling with wet faces.

"And then we're going on a vacation. David McClean is coming back in half an hour to help us move out and get to the airport. I'm going to dress. You turn the nursery on for a minute, Lydia, just a minute, mind you."

And the three of them went babbling off while he let himself be vacuumed upstairs through the air flue and set about dressing himself. A minute later Lydia appeared.

"I'll be glad when we get away," she sighed.

"Did you leave them in the nursery?"

"I wanted to dress, too. Oh, that horrid Africa. What can they see in it?"

"Well, in five minutes we'll be on our way to Iowa. Lord, how did we ever get in this house? What prompted us to buy a nightmare?"

"Pride, money, foolishness."

"I think we'd better get downstairs before those kids get engrossed with those damned beasts again."

Just then they heard the children calling, "Daddy, Mommy, come quick—quick!"

They went downstairs in the air flue and ran down the hall. The children were nowhere in sight. "Wendy? Peter!"

They ran into the nursery. The veldtland was empty save for the lions waiting, looking at them. "Peter, Wendy?"

The door slammed.

"Wendy, Peter!"

George Hadley and his wife whirled and ran back to the door.

"Open the door!" cried George Hadley, trying the knob. "Why, they've locked it from the outside! Peter!" He beat at the door. "Open up!"

He heard Peter's voice outside, against the door.

"Don't let them switch off the nursery and the house," he was saying.

Mr. and Mrs. George Hadley beat at the door. "Now, don't be ridiculous, children. It's time to go. Mr. McClean'll be here in a minute and . . ."

And then they heard the sounds.

The lions on three sides of them, in the yellow veldt grass, padding through the dry straw, rumbling and roaring in their throats.

The lions.

Mr. Hadley looked at his wife and they turned and looked back at the beasts edging slowly forward, crouching, tails stiff.

Mr. and Mrs. Hadley screamed.

And suddenly they realized why those other screams had sounded familiar.

"Well, here I am," said David McClean in the nursery doorway. "Oh, hello." He stared at the two children seated in the center of the open glade eating a little picnic lunch. Beyond them was the water hole and the yellow veldtland; above was the hot sun. He began to perspire. "Where are your father and mother?"

The children looked up and smiled. "Oh, they'll be here directly."

"Good, we must get going." At a distance Mr. McClean saw the lions fighting and clawing and then quieting down to feed in silence under the shady trees.

He squinted at the lions with his hand up to his eyes.

Now the lions were done feeding. They moved to the water hole to drink.

A shadow flicked over Mr. McClean's hot face. Many shadows flickered. The vultures were dropping down the blazing sky.

"A cup of tea?" asked Wendy in the silence.

TENDENCIES IN MODERN POETRY

After the first quarter of the twentieth century, poetry, holding the mirror up to nature and reflecting the difficulties of an increasingly complicated world, tended to grow more complex and, to many readers, too difficult. There was little that was simple and carefree and even less that was traditionally tuneful. Expressing the troubled thoughts and anxieties of the day, even the lyrics grew muted and cerebral. In 1959 Karl Shapiro, himself a poet, complained that modern poetry had lost both sensuousness and spontaneity, that it was cold and "impersonal," and that it had been ruined by its efforts to conform to the strictures of contemporary academic criticism. Present-day poetry, he asserted, is "a tangle of subtleties and grotesques . . . The person who can understand modern poetry must first be initiated into the vast and arcane criticism of our day."

As opposed to this view, it was contended that poetry, hospitable to every experiment, had achieved a new range, that it covered a wider gamut, from the reshaping of old myths and the reworking of basic emotions to the abstractions of an autonomous art. There was no denying that, while modern American poetry mirrored the materialism of the age, it also accomplished remarkable effects in craftsmanship, in the alternation of words which were suggestive and precise rather than vaguely "poetic," and in images freed of their overused symbolism and shopworn associations.

If the poetry in the pages which follow is elliptical, full of sliding metaphors and dissolving figures of speech, it is emotionally as well as intellectually provocative. It makes demands upon the kind of reader who regards poetry as an easy anodyne and turns to it only for its lulling sing-song. However, the reader who is willing to listen to it with an alert rather than a nodding mind will be rewarded.

Such poetry does not lack music for sometimes being dissonant, nor strength for being subtle. It is, contrary to its objectors, both sensuous and spontaneous. Even when it is oblique it is not necessarily obscure. Instead of being "impersonal," it is extremely personal, sometimes so personal in its associations that the reader cannot immediately grasp all the references and private allusions. Each of these poems registers a personality, definite and distinctive.

LOUISE BOGAN

[1897–]

CRITIC AS WELL AS POET, *Louise Bogan was born August 11, 1897, in Livermore Falls, Maine. She was educated in country schools in New England and at the Girls' Latin School in Boston. Except for a year abroad and another year in Sante Fé, she made her home in New York, where she became poetry reviewer of* The New Yorker. *Her first book,* Body of This Death, *was published in her mid-twenties and was followed six years later by* Dark Summer; *both volumes were applauded for their lyrical subtleties.* The Sleeping Fury, *published in her fortieth year, showed a greater refinement of her technique, but it was not until* Poems and New Poems *appeared in 1941 that the full measure of her gift could be appraised.*

She was heard in various universities as visiting lecturer, and she held the Chair of Poetry at the Library of Congress in 1945-6. In 1954 she was co-winner with Léonie Adams of the Bollingen Prize and, five years later, she received an award of $5,000 for "distinguished poetic achievement" from the Academy of American Poets.

THE DREAM

O God, in the dream the terrible horse began
To paw at the air, and make for me with his blows.
Fear kept for thirty-five years poured through his mane,
And retribution equally old, or nearly, breathed through his nose.

Coward complete, I lay and wept on the ground
When some strong creature appeared, and leapt for the rein.
Another woman, as I lay half in a swound
Leapt in the air, and clutched at the leather and chain.

Give him, she said, something of yours as a charm.
Throw him, she said, some poor thing you alone claim.
No, no, I cried, he hates me; he's out for harm,
And whether I yield or not, it is all the same.

But, like a lion in a legend, when I flung the glove
Pulled from my sweating, my cold right hand,
The terrible beast, that no one may understand,
Came to my side, and put down his head in love.

LÉONIE ADAMS

[1899–   ]

THE FIFTH *of six children, Léonie Adams was born December 9, 1899, in Brooklyn, New York, of English, Scottish, and Spanish forebears; her mother's ancestors had come to Virginia in the seventeenth century. In childhood she was, due to her father's influence, an agnostic;*

in maturity she became a Roman Catholic. She began writing poetry—or, as she put it more modestly, "composing in metres"—before she was ten; a love of metrical form and a dislike of unshapely free verse remained with her and conditioned her own compositions.

Her first published poems appeared in The New Republic *when she was still an undergraduate at Barnard College; her first volume,* Those Not Elect, *made its appearance when she was twenty-six. She supported herself chiefly by teaching at Bennington College and Columbia University and also by working for a while in the editorial office of the Metropolitan Museum of Art. She married the critic, William Troy, and held the annual appointment as Consultant in Poetry at the Library of Congress in 1948-49.*

In 1954 her Poems: A Selection *was largely responsible for her receiving the Bollingen award, which she divided with Louise Bogan. It disclosed a lyricism which, at first glance, seems almost archaic. The tone was mystical and the music was hushed. Five years later* The Academy of American Poets *presented her with an award of $5000. It was evident that there had been a growing appreciation of Léonie Adams's special quality: a disembodied ecstasy in which the word was more than a word and the meaning was uplifted by pure spirit.*

SUNDOWN

This is the time lean woods shall spend
A steeped-up twilight, and the pale evening drink,
And the perilous roe, the leaper to the west brink,
Trembling and bright, to the caverned cloud descend.

Now shall you see pent oak gone gusty and frantic,
Stooped with dry weeping, ruinously unloosing
The sparse disheveled leaf, or reared and tossing
A dreary scarecrow bough in funeral antic.

Then, tatter you and rend,
Oak heart, to your profession mourning, not obscure
The outcome, not crepuscular, on the deep floor,
Sable and gold match lusters and contend.

And rags of shrouding will not muffle the slain.
This is the immortal extinction, the priceless wound
Not to be staunched; the live gold leaks beyond,
And matter's sanctified, dipped in a gold stain.

HART CRANE

[1899–1932]

Like Stephen Crane, to whom he was not related, Harold Hart Crane had a short and tragic life. Born July 21, 1899, in Garretsville, Ohio, he spent his childhood in Cleveland, where his father owned a large candy company. The boy's relations with his father were never good. His parents were constantly quarreling; he sided with his mother and was afraid of his father. His intense devotion to his mother, and the humiliations which he shared with her, have been considered the source of his later sexual and mental aberrations. In his thirties he wrote, "The slightest disturbance now tends to recall with consummate force all the past and its horrid memories on pretext of the slightest derangement of equilibrium." His parents were eventually divorced, but the grown man never recovered from the shocks of the boy's environment.

Crane refused to share in his father's business; instead he became a riveter in a shipyard, manager of a tearoom, a reporter, a printer, and a writer of advertising copy. Between jobs he lived recklessly, loved indiscriminately, and drank uncontrollably. He published his first volume, White Buildings, when he was twenty-seven; his second, The Bridge, when he was thirty-one. At thirty-two he went to Mexico, where he gave himself up to alcohol and homosexuality. A year later he determined to go back to the United States for a new start. His resolution was never fulfilled. On April 26, 1932, he jumped from a northbound steamer in the Gulf of Mexico; the body was not recovered.

In his poetry Crane pushed impressionism to the limit of communication. His lack of discipline is reflected in his work: a frantic rearrangement of phrases, a collision of ideas, and a compression of images. The images themselves are not only striking but illuminating—Crane wrote by what he called a "logic of metaphors." Parts of his near-epic The Bridge, as well as some of the smaller poems, display the brilliant colors as well as a structural order which Crane was sometimes able to rescue from his inner chaos.

VOYAGES: II

—And yet this great wink of eternity,
Of rimless floods, unfettered leewardings,
Samite sheeted and processioned where
Her undinal vast belly moonward bends,
Laughing the wrapt inflections of our love;

Take this Sea, whose diapason knells
On scrolls of silver snowy sentences,
The sceptered terror of whose sessions rends
As her demeanors motion well or ill,
All but the pieties of lovers' hands.

And onward, as bells off San Salvador
Salute the crocus lusters of the stars,
In these poinsettia meadows of her tides,—
Adagios of islands, O my Prodigal,
Complete the dark confessions her veins spell.

Mark how her turning shoulders wind the hours,
And hasten while her penniless rich palms
Pass superscription of bent foam and wave,—
Hasten, while they are true,—sleep, death, desire,
Close round one instant in one floating flower.

Bind us in time, O seasons clear, and awe.
O minstrel galleons of Carib fire,
Bequeath us to no earthly shore until
Is answered in the vortex of our grave
The seal's wide spindrift gaze toward paradise.

STANLEY KUNITZ

[1905–]

STANLEY JASSPON KUNITZ *was born July 29, 1905, in Worcester, Massachusetts, and lived most of his life in New England and New York. After graduating from Harvard, he spent three years in military service during the Second World War, and on his return divided his time between teaching and writing poetry. His first volume,* Intellectual Things, *was published when he was in his mid-twenties; the title may have been responsible for the general public's lack of interest. Kunitz's acute sensitivity was, however, recognized by his fellow poets —Theodore Roethke spoke of his "bold dramatic imagination that can wrest meanings from bleak and difficult material, turn even the language of science to lyrical purpose with speed and style."*

Kunitz had to wait until he was in his fifties before he received national recognition. He had supported himself not only by teaching but also by editing such reference works as Twentieth Century Authors, *when he received the Pulitzer Prize for his* Selected Poems: 1928-1958. *The volume drew attention to a long neglected poet and he was recognized as one who could translate physical facts and metaphysical ideas into phrases of great clarity and richly illuminated lines.*

THE SCIENCE OF THE NIGHT

I touch you in the night, whose gift was you,
My careless sprawler,
And I touch you cold, unstirring, star-bemused,
That are become the land of your self-strangeness.
What long seduction of the bone has led you
Down the imploring roads I cannot take
Into the arms of ghosts I never knew,
Leaving my manhood on a rumpled field
To guard you where you lie so deep
In absent-mindedness,
Caught in the calcium snows of sleep?

And even should I track you to your birth
Through all the cities of your mortal trial,
As in my jealous thought I try to do,
You would escape me—from the brink of earth
Take off to where the lawless auroras run,
You with your wild and metaphysic heart.
My touch is on you, who are light-years gone.
We are not souls but systems, and we move
In clouds of our unknowing
like great nebulae.
Our very motives swirl and have their start
With father lion and with mother crab.

Dreamer, my own lost rib,
Whose planetary dust is blowing
Past archipelagoes of myth and light,
What far Magellans are you mistress of
To whom you speed the pleasure of your art?
As through a glass that magnifies my loss
I see the lines of your spectrum shifting red,
The universe expanding, thinning out,
Our worlds flying, oh flying, fast apart.
From hooded powers and from abstract flight
I summon you, your person and your pride.
Fall to me now from outer space,
Still fastened desperately to my side;
Through gulfs of streaming air
Bring me the mornings of the milky ways
Down to my threshold in your drowsy eyes;
And by the virtue of your honeyed word
Restore the liquid language of the moon,
That in gold mines of secrecy you delve.
Awake!
                My whirling hands stay at the noon,
Each cell within my body holds a heart
And all my hearts in unison strike twelve.

THEODORE ROETHKE

[1908–]

UNTIL HE BEGAN WINNING one prize after another, Theodore Roethke was regarded as an excellent tennis coach and a widely-esteemed teacher but considered as an important poet only by a few select writers. He was born May 25, 1908, in Saginaw, Michigan, received his M.A. at the University of Michigan, and studied law, although he never really intended to practice it. He began teaching English at Lafayette College when he was twenty-three; later he taught at Pennsylvania State University, Bennington College, and the University of Washington. At thirty-seven he received a Guggenheim Fellowship and, some years later, was a Fulbright lecturer in Italy. The prizes began coming in his fortieth year. He received an award from the

American Academy of Arts and Letters in 1952 and the Pulitzer Prize for poetry in 1953. In 1959, with the publication of his collected verse, Words For the Wind, *he garnered three additional awards, the Bollingen Prize, the Borestone Mountain Award, and the National Book Award.*

Words For the Wind *includes the best of Roethke's preceding volumes along with a group of new poems. It ranges from light pieces, verses for children, and transcripts of the poetry of ordinary life to passages of sheer surrealism. Whatever manner Roethke adopts, it is never without a sense of style, a play of wit, and natural warmth.*

FRAU BAUMAN, FRAU SCHMIDT, AND FRAU SCHWARTZE

Gone the three ancient ladies
Who creaked on the greenhouse ladders,
Reaching up white strings
To wind, to wind
The sweet-pea tendrils, the smilax,
Nasturtiums, the climbing
Roses, to straighten
Carnations, red
Chrysanthemums; the stiff
Stems, jointed like corn,
They tied and tucked,—
These nurses of nobody else.
Quicker than birds, they dipped
Up and sifted the dirt;
They sprinkled and shook;
They stood astride pipes,
Their skirts billowing out wide into tents,
Their hands twinkling with wet;
Like witches they flew along rows
Keeping creation at ease;
With a tendril for needle
They sewed up the air with a stem;
They teased out the seed that the cold kept asleep,—
All the coils, loops, and whorls.
They trellised the sun; they plotted for more than themselves.

I remember how they picked me up, a spindly kid,
Pinching and poking my thin ribs
Till I lay in their laps laughing,
Weak as a whiffet;
Now, when I'm alone and cold in my bed,
They still hover over me,
Those ancient leathery crones,
With their bandannas stiffened with sweat,
And their thorn-bitten wrists,
And their snuff-laden breath blowing lightly over me in my first sleep.

ELIZABETH BISHOP

[1911–]

ELIZABETH BISHOP WAS BORN FEBRUARY 8, *1911, in* Worcester, *Massachusetts. Brought up in New England and Nova Scotia, she graduated from* Vassar College, *traveled widely, and, in her thirty-fifth year, received the Houghton Mifflin Literary Fellowship for her book of poems,* North & South. *She was Consultant in Poetry at the Library of Congress in 1949-50, the recipient of an American Academy of Arts and Letters award in 1951 and, a year later, the Shelley Memorial award.* A Cold Spring, *her second volume, was combined with her first in* Poems, *published in 1955.*

Miss Bishop's fellow poets were quick to praise her. "At last," wrote Marianne Moore, "we have a prize book that has no creditable mannerisms." "Although she frequently writes fantasies," commented Louise Bogan, "she is firmly in touch with the real world and takes a Thoreau-like interest in whatever catches her attention." "In all manner of form: meter, rhythm, diction, timing, shaping, etc." said Robert Lowell, "she is a master."

"The Fish," one of her most quoted pieces, is a small masterwork. A miniature Moby Dick *and a condensed, compassionate complement to Ernest Hemingway's* The Old Man and The Sea, *it is an extraordinary poem which breaks down the line between prose and poetry. It fuses observation and imagination, simple statement and suggestive symbolism.*

THE FISH

I caught a tremendous fish
and held him beside the boat
half out of water, with my hook
fast in a corner of his mouth.
He didn't fight.
He hadn't fought at all.
He hung a grunting weight,
battered and venerable
and homely. Here and there
his brown skin hung in strips
like ancient wall-paper,
and its pattern of darker brown
was like wall-paper:
shapes like full-blown roses
stained and lost through age.
He was speckled with barnacles,
fine rosettes of lime,
and infested
with tiny white sea-lice,
and underneath two or three
rags of green weed hung down.
While his gills were breathing in
the terrible oxygen
—the frightening gills
fresh and crisp with blood,
that can cut so badly—
I thought of the coarse white flesh
packed in like feathers,
the big bones and the little bones,
the dramatic reds and blacks
of his shiny entrails,
and the pink swim-bladder
like a big peony.
I looked into his eyes
which were far larger than mine
but shallower, and yellowed,
the irises backed and packed
with tarnished tinfoil
seen through the lenses
of old scratched isinglass.
They shifted a little, but not
to return my stare.
—It was more like the tipping

of an object toward the light.
I admired his sullen face,
the mechanism of his jaw,
and then I saw
that from his lower lip
—if you could call it a lip—
grim, wet, and weapon-like,
hung five old pieces of fish-line,
or four and a wire leader
with the swivel still attached,
with all their five big hooks
grown firmly in his mouth.
A green line, frayed at the end
where he broke it, two heavier lines,
and a fine black thread
still crimped from the strain and snap
when it broke and he got away.
Like medals with their ribbons
frayed and wavering,
a five-haired beard of wisdom
trailing from his aching jaw.
I stared and stared
and victory filled up
the little rented boat,
from the pool of bilge
where oil had spread a rainbow
around the rusted engine
to the bailer rusted orange,
the sun-cracked thwarts,
the oarlocks on their strings,
the gunnels—until everything
was rainbow, rainbow, rainbow!
And I let the fish go.

KARL SHAPIRO

[1913–]

Karl Jay Shapiro was born November 10, 1913, *in Baltimore, Maryland. He was educated at the University of Virginia and Johns Hopkins University. In the Second World War he was stationed in the*

South Pacific from 1942 to 1945. During that time the poems in his first three books were put together and their publication supervised by his fiancée, Evalyn Katz, whom he married on his return to America and by whom he had three children. The second of his books, V-Letter and Other Poems, was awarded the Pulitzer Prize in 1945; the third, Essay on Rime, is an examination of the confusions in modern poetry, a tour de force, for it was written thousands of miles away from any library. A genuinely critical work, Essay on Rime, is not without its own confusions, full of debatable ideas which, says Shapiro, "aroused the enmity of the literary avant-garde—as it was calculated to do."

At thirty-five he became Consultant in Poetry to the Library of Congress; a year later he joined the faculty of Johns Hopkins. He edited Poetry, A Magazine of Verse for a while, taught at Loyola University and the University of Iowa. A volume of his Collected Poems: 1940–1953 was followed in 1958 by Poems of A Jew.

Although Shapiro seems most at home in the immediate world of war and warring realisms, he delights in fantasies of the imagination. He "thinks with his feelings," wrote Conrad Aiken, and even while Shapiro derides the intellectual element in poetry, his own work is intellectually as well as imaginatively rich.

THE RECOGNITION OF EVE

Whatever it was she had so fiercely fought
Had fled back to the sky, but still she lay
With arms outspread, awaiting its assault,
Staring up through the branches of the tree,
The fig tree. Then she drew a shuddering breath
And turned her head instinctively his way.
She had fought birth as dying men fight death.

Her sigh awakened him. He turned and saw
A body swollen, as though formed of fruits,
White as the flesh of fishes, soft and raw.
He hoped she was another of the brutes
So he crawled over and looked into her eyes,
The human wells that pool all absolutes.
It was like looking into double skies.

And when she spoke the first word (it was *thou*)
He was terror-stricken, but she raised her hand
And touched his wound where it was fading now,
For he must feel the place to understand.
Then he recalled the longing that had torn
His side, and while he watched it whitely mend,
He felt it stab him suddenly like a thorn.

He thought the woman had hurt him. Was it she
Or the same sickness seeking to return;
Or was there any difference, the pain set free
And she who seized him now as hard as iron?
Her fingers bit his body. She looked old
And involuted, like the newly born.
He let her hurt him till she loosed her hold.

Then she forgot him and she wearily stood
And went in search of water through the grove.
Adam could see her wandering through the wood,
Studying her footsteps as her body wove
In light and out of light. She found a pool
And there he followed shyly to observe.
She was already turning beautiful.

MURIEL RUKEYSER

[1913–]

A MODERNIST, MURIEL RUKEYSER *at first seemed limited by the pressures of her time—Stephen Vincent Benét called her "essentially an urban poet." She was born December 1, 1913, in New York City, and was educated at Vassar and Columbia. At nineteen she was a member of committees investigating labor and Negro problems; she was arrested during the second Scottsboro trial in Alabama. She worked her way through a ground-course at Roosevelt Aviation School but, as she was still a minor, was not allowed to fly.*

Her first volume, Theory of Flight, *was published when she was twenty-two years old. In it and in the subsequent* U.S. 1, The Soul and Body of John Brown, *and* The Green Wave, *the poet uses the material of modern life with all its complex emotions, shifting speeds, and changes of mood and action. Her first volume in prose,* Willard Gibbs, *published when she was twenty-nine, came as a surprise to those who didn't believe that a poet could write an imaginative and penetrating study of a scientist.* Body of Waking, *published in 1958, shows a prolonged dramatic intensity and a power of communication sometimes muffled by the very rush of thought, for hers is a spirit which declares itself in impulsive and compelling emotion.*

EFFORT AT SPEECH BETWEEN TWO PEOPLE

Speak to me. Take my hand. What are you now?
I will tell you all. I will conceal nothing.
When I was three, a little child read a story about a rabbit
who died, in the story, and I crawled under a chair:
a pink rabbit: it was my birthday, and a candle
burnt a sore spot on my finger, and I was told to be happy.

Oh, grow to know me. I am not happy. I will be open:
Now I am thinking of white sails against a sky like music,
like glad horns blowing, and birds tilting, and an arm about me.
There was one I loved, who wanted to live, sailing.

Speak to me. Take my hand. What are you now?
When I was nine, I was fruitily sentimental,
fluid: and my widowed aunt played Chopin,
and I bent my head on the painted woodwork, and wept.
I want now to be close to you. I would
link the minutes of my days close, somehow, to your days.

I am not happy. I will be open.
I have liked lamps in evening corners, and quiet poems.
There had been fear in my life. Sometimes I speculate
On what a tragedy his life was, really.

Take my hand. Fist my mind in your hand. What are you now?
When I was fourteen, I had dreams of suicide,
and I stood at a steep window, at sunset, hoping toward death:
if the light had not melted clouds and plains to beauty,
if light had not transformed that day, I would have leapt.
I am unhappy. I am lonely. Speak to me.

I will be open.   I think he never loved me:
he loved the bright beaches, the little lips of foam
that ride small waves, he loved the veer of gulls:
he said with a gay mouth: I love you.   Grow to know me.

What are you now?   If we could touch one another,
if these our separate entities could come to grips,
clenched like a Chinese puzzle . . . yesterday
I stood in a crowded street that was live with people,
and no one spoke a word, and the morning shone.
Everyone silent, moving. . . . Take my hand.   Speak to me.

ROBERT LOWELL

[1917–   ]

BORN MARCH 1, 1917, in Boston, Massachusetts, Robert Traill Spence Lowell came from one of the most eminent New England families. James Russell Lowell was his great-granduncle; Amy Lowell was a distant cousin. He attended Harvard College and, because his chief interest was poetry, changed to Kenyon College, where he studied with John Crowe Ransom. He refused to participate in the Second World War because he considered the indiscriminate bombing of civilians unprincipled mass murder; he went to jail for five months as a conscientious objector. He lectured in poetry at the Salzburg Seminar in American Studies and also in the United States. His first wife was the novelist Jean Stafford, his second, the writer Elizabeth Hardwick.

That Lowell is a Puritan in revolt is apparent in his first book, Land of Unlikeness. *His impatience with the materialism of his times is further stressed in* Lord Weary's Castle, *which, published in his twenty-ninth year, won the Pulitzer Prize. At thirty Lowell became Consultant in Poetry to the Library of Congress, and four years later published* The Mills of The Cavanaughs, *the title poem being a dramatic narrative of some six hundred lines.* Life Studies, *published in 1959, disclosed a mood of autobiographical brooding.*

Much of Lowell's poetry is a reflection of tumult and a Catholic protest against a world which resigns itself to apathy and moral bankruptcy. It is not an easy poetry—its wrenched phrases, sudden transitions, and shifting images recall the baroque metaphysicians of the seventeenth century. But nowhere except in New England and at no other time than the present could this poetry—difficult, intense, and lofty in conception—have been written.

AS A PLANE TREE BY THE WATER

Darkness has called to darkness, and disgrace
Elbows about our windows in this planned
Babel of Boston where our money talks
And multiplies the darkness of a land
Of preparation where the Virgin walks
And roses spiral her enamelled face
Or fall to splinters on unwatered streets.
Our Lady of Babylon, go by, go by,
I was once the apple of your eye;
Flies, flies are on the plane tree, on the streets.

The flies, the flies, the flies of Babylon
Buzz in my ear-drum while the devil's long
Dirge of the people detonates the hour
For floating cities where his golden tongue
Enchants the masons of the Babel Tower
To raise tomorrow's city to the sun
That never sets upon these hell-fire streets
Of Boston, where the sunlight is a sword
Striking at the withholder of the Lord:
Flies, flies are on the plane tree, on the streets.

Flies strike the miraculous waters of the iced
Atlantic and the eyes of Bernadette
Who saw Our Lady standing in the cave
At Massabielle, saw her so squarely that
Her vision put out reason's eyes. The grave
Is open-mouthed and swallowed up in Christ.
O walls of Jericho! And all the streets
To our Atlantic wall are singing: "Sing,
Sing for the resurrection of the King."
Flies, flies are on the plane tree, on the streets.

RICHARD WILBUR

[1921–]

A POET WHO FUSED *the distinctly intellectual and the delicately sensuous, Richard Wilbur won the respect of his fellow poets with his first book,* The Beautiful Changes, *published when he was twenty-six. He was born March 1, 1921, in New York City, moved to New Jersey, and was educated at Amherst College and Harvard University. He served in Italy, France, and Germany during World War II. In 1942, he married Charlotte Ward, by whom he had four children, and became a teacher at Harvard and Wesleyan. In his thirty-third year he was named the winner of the $3,000 Prix de Rome Fellowship of the American Academy of Arts and Letters. His third book,* Things of This World, *received the Pulitzer Prize in 1957.*

Wilbur's outstanding quality is the depth of feeling which is communicated beneath a smoothly organized surface. His work is precise and fastidious—"elegant" is the adjective most often applied to his lines—but there is a sense of reserve in everything he undertakes. In his half-wondering, half-whimsical way he responds to Whitman's vision of the mystery and glory of the commonplace.

AFTER THE LAST BULLETINS

After the last bulletins the windows darken
And the whole city founders easily and deep,
Sliding on all its pillows
To the thronged Atlantis of personal sleep,

And the wind rises. The wind rises and bowls
The day's litter of news in the alleys. Trash
Tears itself on the railings,
Soars and falls with a soft crash,

Tumbles and soars again. In empty lots
Our journals spiral in a fierce noyade
Of all we thought to think,
Or caught in corners cramp and wad

And twist our words. And some from gutters flail
Their tatters at the tired patrolman's feet
Like all that fisted snow
That cried beside his long retreat

Damn you! damn you! to the emperor's horses' heels.
Oh none too soon through the air white and dry
Will the clear announcer's voice
Beat like a dove, and you and I

From the heart's anarch and responsible town
Rise by the subway-mouth to life again,
Bearing the morning papers,
And cross the park where saintlike men,

White and absorbed, with stick and bag remove
The litter of the night, and footsteps rouse
With confident morning sound
The songbirds in the public boughs.

INDEX